R. Gupta's®

POPULAR MASTER GUIDE

L.L.B

FIVE YEAR COURSE

Entrance Examination

For Admission to Undergraduate Courses at

- Common Law Admission Test (CLAT) • AILET • Telangana State, LAWCET
- Amity Law School, Delhi • Andhra Pradesh, LAWCET
- Symbiosis Society's Law College • Jamia Millia Islamia
- ILS Law College, Pune • Aligarh Muslim University
- Banaras Hindu University • Army Institute of Law (Mohali)
- GGS Indraprastha University • Punjab University, Chandigarh

& Other Reputed Universities/Institutes of India

By
Gyan Prakash
Solicitor and Advocate

2027
EDITION

RAMESH PUBLISHING HOUSE, NEW DELHI

Published by

O.P. Gupta *for* Ramesh Publishing House

Admin. Office

12-H, New Daryaganj Road, Opp. Officers' Mess,
New Delhi-110002 ✆ 23275224, 23245124

E-mail: info@rameshpublishinghouse.com

For Online Shopping: www.rameshpublishinghouse.com

Showroom

- Balaji Market, Nai Sarak, Delhi-110006 ✆ 23282525 📱 9354373464
- 4457, Nai Sarak, Delhi-110006

Book Code: R-902

ISBN: 978-81-7812-461-2

Price: ₹ 680

Printed at: Deepak Offset, Delhi

PREFACE

Law is the need of every civilized society. Observance of law differentiates between developed societies with the undeveloped ones. In the ancient society the religion was believed to be a source of law and the common mass used to believe in law as a part of his religious duty whereas in the modern world we have the codified laws on most of the subjects which are enacted by the legislature, implemented by the executive and interpreted by the judiciary. So, law as a subject has overwhelming impact on the society at large. The socio-cultural status of a society is determined by the laws that govern it and it is these laws only that write the destiny of the societies and nations.

Now, in the present era legal profession is one of the most dignified professions. There are various opportunities for the students of law after completion of their courses. Judiciary, Law Officers, Manager-Legal, Intellectual Property Experts, Academics, Advocacy are some of important careers that always welcome the brilliant students of Law.

In this book my main focus of attention has been the aspirants of five years LL.B course who appear in the entrance exams after the completion of their intermediate. The book is divided into two parts—one is Subjective and another part is Objective. The subjective part is meant to make the students aware of various important topics of law in detail whereas the objective part is to enhance their grasping capacity of the various legal issues. I have made every effort so that this book may prove helpful to the aspirants of the LL.B Entrance Exams.

I am highly thankful to whole team of Ramesh Publishing House whose excellent creative outlook proves to be a milestone in the field of Publication. I hope that this book would make the cut-throat competition of five years LL.B Entrance exams easier for the aspirants as various concepts of law in this book have been dealt with in easier language.

I dedicate this book to my grandparents Late Sh. Mohan Lal Gupta and Late Smt. Chandrakala Gupta whose blessings have always been showering upon me to take me to the right path in every walk of life.

I hope that this book would be highly useful to the readers. However, the critical analysis of this work would be highly appreciated.

Place: New Delhi

GYAN PRAKASH
Solicitor and Advocate

CONTENTS

SPECIAL NOTE : *Some Universities may include/exclude one or two different topics/subjects in their Entrance Examination than those given in this book. Students are advised to refer to the prospectus of the university for which they are applying, to get the complete and final information.*

Previous Years' Paper

Common Law Admission Test (CLAT-UG)

Entrance Exam, 2026

(Exam held on 07-12-2025)

SECTION-I : ENGLISH LANGUAGE

I

The adoption of the Non-Cooperation Movement by the Congress gave it a new energy and from January 1921 it began to register considerable success all over the country. Gandhiji undertook a nation-wide tour during which he addressed hundreds of meetings and met a large number of political workers. In the first month, thousands of students left their educational institutions and joined more than 800 national schools and colleges that had sprung up all over the country. Gandhiji had promised Swaraj within a year, if his programme was adopted.

The Non-Cooperation Movement demonstrated that it commanded the support and sympathy of vast sections of the Indian people. Its reach among many sections of Indian peasants, workers, artisans etc, had been demonstrated. The spatial spread of the movement was also nation-wide. Some areas were more active than others, but there were few that showed no signs of activity at all.

The capacity of the 'poor dumb millions' of India to take part in modern nationalist politics was also demonstrated. This was the first time that nationalists from the towns, students from schools and colleges or even the educated and politically aware in the villages had made a serious attempt to bring the ideology and the movement into their midst.

The tremendous participation of different communities in the movement, and the maintenance of communal unity, despite the Malabar developments, was in itself no mean achievement. There is hardly any doubt that it was minority participation that gave the movement its truly mass character in many areas. And it was, indeed, unfortunate that this most positive feature of the movement was not to be repeated in later years once communalism began to take its toll. [324 words]

[Extracted, with edits and revisions, from India's Struggle for Independence1857-1947, by Bipin Chandra and Others, Penguin Books, 1989.]

1. From the passage it is evident that:

A. The idea of Swaraj seemed futile

B. The non-cooperation movement was a complete success

C. The non-cooperation movement gained the sympathy of majority of the Indians

D. The Indian National Congress represented microscopic minority

2. The term "poor dumb millions" refer to:

A. The vast number of common people who are impoverished

B. Large number of common people who are hearing impaired

C. Large number of people who are vulnerable

D. The vast number of people who are impoverished and uneducated

1. C **2.** D

3. Which of the statements is true?
   A. The Swaraj movement happened before the non- cooperation movement
   B. The non-cooperation movement failed due to sudden withdrawal
   C. There was a fine show of communal unity in the movement
   D. The rich and the educated kept themselves away from the non-cooperation movement

4. The main idea of the passage is:
   A. The non-cooperation movement did not give impetus to the future movements
   B. The movement made the Indians realize their potential to fight against the mighty British
   C. The British became fearful and worried of Gandhiji's leadership and cooperation of Indians
   D. That the most positive feature of the movement was that it was repeated in later years

5. The word "Communalism" in the above passage refers to:
   A. Religious identity
   B. Caste identity
   C. Regional identity
   D. Secularism

II

There were humans long before there was history. The archaic humans loved, played, formed close friendships and competed for status and power, but so did chimpanzees, baboons and elephants. There was nothing special about them.

Nobody, least of all humans themselves, had any inkling that their descendants would one day walk on the moon, split the atom, fathom the genetic code and write history books. The most important thing to know about prehistoric humans is that they were incognisant animals with no more impact on their environment than gorillas, fireflies or jellyfish.

Biologists classify organisms into species. Animals are said to belong to the same species if they tend to mate with each other, giving birth to fertile offspring. Horses and donkeys have a recent common ancestor and share many physical traits. They will mate if induced to do so - but their offspring, called mules, are sterile. Mutations in donkey DNA can therefore never cross over to horses, or vice versa. The two types of animals are consequently considered two distinct species, moving along separate evolutionary paths. By contrast, a bulldog and a spaniel may look very different, but they are members of the same species, sharing the same DNA pool. [203 words]

(Extracted from Sapiens: A Brief History of Humankind by Yuval Noah Harari)

6. Which of the following can be inferred as the most significant characteristic of prehistoric humans, as per the passage?
   A. Their conscious effort to alter and shape their environment for survival
   B. Their complex social organization and clear hierarchical structures that set them apart from other species
   C. Their evolutionary divergence was marked by warfare and the pursuit of dominance over rival species
   D. Their inability to distinguish themselves from other species in terms of environmental impact

7. In the context of the passage, the term 'incognisant' most likely means:
   A. Lacking intelligence
   B. Unaware of their future potential
   C. Incapable of social interaction
   D. Disinterested in the environment

3. C	4. B	5. A	6. D	7. B

8. Which of the following best explains why humans did not initially stand out among other organisms?
A. They had fewer offspring than other species
B. Their behaviours were not unique compared to other animals
C. They did not yet evolve the ability to use tools
D. They lacked the genetic capacity to develop language

9. According to the passage, what determines whether two animals belong to the same species?
A. Their ability to produce fertile offspring
B. Their physical appearance and size
C. Their shared evolutionary ancestor
D. Their capacity to adapt to the environment

10. The passage explains the concept of species classification by:
A. Highlighting the behavioural differences between species like horses, donkeys, bulldogs and spaniels
B. Focusing on the DNA pool they share
C. Contrasting horses and bulldogs with donkeys and spaniels to explain reproductive compatibility
D. Discussing the environmental impact of different species like horses and donkeys, and bulldogs and spaniels

III

In 1973, only 45 of the world's 151 countries were counted as 'free' by Freedom House, a nongovernmental organization that produces quantitative measures of civil and political rights for countries around the world. The following generation saw momentous political change, with democracies and market-oriented economies spreading in virtually every part of the world except for the Arab Middle East. This transformation was Samuel Huntington's third wave of democratization; liberal democracy as the default form of government became part of the accepted political landscape at the beginning of the twenty-first century.

Underlying these changes in political systems was a massive social transformation as well. The shift to democracy was a result of millions of formerly passive individuals around the world organizing themselves and participating in the political life of their societies. This social mobilization was driven by a host of factors: greatly expanded access to education that made people more aware of themselves and the political world around them; information technology, which facilitated the rapid spread of ideas and knowledge; cheap travel and communications that allowed people to vote with their feet if they didn't like their government; and greater prosperity, which induced people to demand better protection of their rights.

The third wave crested after the late 1990s, however, a 'democratic recession' emerged in the first decade of the twenty-first century. Approximately one in five countries that had been part of the third wave either reverted to authoritarianism or saw a significant erosion of democratic institutions. Freedom house noted that 2009 marked the fourth consecutive year in which freedom had declined around the world, the first time this had happened since it established its measures of freedom in 1973. [279 words]

(Extracted from The Origins of Political Order by Francis Fukuyama)

11. Which of the following aspects is most critical in understanding Freedom House's evaluation process?
A. The methodology by which it quantifies the relative freedoms in different political systems
B. Its emphasis on electoral participation and voter turnout in measuring democracy
C. Its role in advising governments on democratic reforms based on its rankings
D. Its primary focus on economic disparities within democracies

8. B **9.** A **10.** B **11.** A

12. What does the phrase 'vote with their feet' imply in the context of the passage?
   A. Engaging in electoral processes to demand political change
   B. Demonstrating political preferences through public protests
   C. Migrating to countries with better governance or conditions
   D. Participating in local government initiatives and reforms

13. The term 'third wave of democratization' as used in the passage refers to:
   A. The rise of communism in Eastern Europe
   B. The spread of democracy and market-oriented economies
   C. The decline of authoritarian regimes in the 1960s
   D. The global movement for civil rights

14. Which of the following was not mentioned as a factor contributing to social mobilization and the shift to democracy?
   A. Increased access to education
   B. Expanding information technology
   C. Heightened global military presence
   D. Greater prosperity

15. According to this passage, when was the first time the freedom had declined around the world
   A. 1973 B. 1990
   C. 2006 D. 2009

IV

My kinsman and I were returning to Calcutta from our Puja trip when we encountered an unusual man on the train. At first, judging from his dress and bearing, we mistook him for an up-country boorish man. But as soon as he began to speak, our impression changed. He discoursed on every subject with such confidence that one might think the 'Disposer of All Things' sought his counsel in every decision. Until then, we had been perfectly content, unaware of hidden forces shaping the world—that the Russians were advancing, that the English were pursuing secret policies, and that confusion among native chiefs had reached its peak. Our new acquaintance, however, hinted at such matters with a sly smile, remarking:

"There are more things in heaven and earth, Horatio, than are reported in your newspapers."

Having never before travelled beyond our homes, we were struck dumb with wonder at his manner. No matter how trivial the topic, he could quote science, comment on the Vedas, or recite quatrains from Persian poets. Since we possessed no real knowledge of science, the Vedas, or Persian literature, our admiration for him only grew. My kinsman, a theosophist, became convinced that our fellow passenger was inspired by some strange magnetism, occult power, or astral body. He listened with devotional rapture even to the most common place remarks and secretly noted down his words. I suspect our extraordinary companion noticed this and was quietly pleased. When the train reached the junction, we gathered in the waiting room to await our connection. It was 10 p.m., and as the train was expected to be delayed owing to some fault in the lines, I spread my bed on the table and prepared to sleep. But just then, the extraordinary man began spinning a tale, and of course, I could not close my eyes all night. (307 words)

[Extracted with edits from Rabindranath Tagore's "The Hungry Stones"]

16. The narrator and his kinsman's initial impression of the "unusual man" highlights which theme most strongly?
   A. The deceptive nature of appearances
   B. The superiority of Western education
   C. The danger of blind faith
   D. The reliability of cultural stereotypes

12. C	**13.** B	**14.** C	**15.** D	**16.** A

17. Which literary device is most evident in the narrator's line: *"one might think the Disposer of All Things sought his counsel in every decision"*?

A. Irony B. Euphemism
C. Allegory D. Hyperbole

18. The word "theosophist" means:

A. Skeptic B. Mystic
C. Agnostic D. Materialist

19. The word "Boorish" mean:

A. Discourteous B. Genteel
C. Well-bred D. Courtly

20. The narrator's suspicion that the extraordinary man was "quietly pleased" suggests:

A. The man was genuinely humble and embarrassed by the attention
B. The man wished to avoid any recognition of his authority
C. The man was indifferent to how others perceived him
D. The man derived satisfaction from impressing and influencing others

V

Man is the only creature that consumes without producing. He does not give milk, he does not lay eggs, he is too weak to pull the plough, and he cannot run fast enough to catch rabbits. Yet he claims dominion over all animals. He sets us to work, returns only the bare minimum to keep us from starving, and keeps the rest for himself. Our labour tills the soil, our dung fertilizes it, and still, not one of us owns more than our bare skin. You cows, look at yourselves–how many thousands of gallons of milk have you produced this past year? And what has become of it, milk that should have nurtured strong calves? Every drop has gone down the throats of our enemies. And you hens, how many eggs have you laid, and how many of those ever hatched into chicks? The rest have gone to market to bring in money for Jones and his men. And you, Clover, where are the four foals you bore, who should have supported and comforted you in your old age? Each was sold at just a year old–you will never see them again. For all your labour in the fields and your four confinements, what have you gained except bare rations and a stall?

Even the lives we do live are cut short, denied their natural span. I do not grumble, for I am among the fortunate. I am twelve years old and have borne over four hundred children. Such is the natural life of a pig. But no animal escapes the cruel knife in the end. You young porkers sitting before me, each of you will scream your lives out at the block within a year. This is the fate that awaits all of us–cows, pigs, hens, sheep, everyone. Even horses and dogs share no better end. Boxer, the very day your great muscles fail you, Jones will sell you to the knacker, who will slit your throat and boil you down for the foxhounds. And the dogs, when old and toothless, are tied with a brick and drowned in the nearest pond. (356 words)

[Extracted with edits from George Orwell's "Animal Farm"]

21. Which of the following best describes the tone of the passage?

A. Detached and neutral
B. Critical, somber, and resentful, evoking both awareness and outrage
C. Humorous and light-hearted
D. Admiring and celebratory

22. The speaker frequently contrasts animals' work with human gain. This literary technique is best classified as:

A. Allegory of class exploitation
B. Hyperbole for comic effect
C. Irony about farm management
D. Metaphor for animal biology

17. D	**18.** B	**19.** A	**20.** D	**21.** B	**22.** A

23. Who is 'knacker'?
A. A slaughterer
B. A trader whose business is disposal of dead and unwanted animals
C. A person whose business is disposal of dead or unwanted animals especially those whose flesh is not fit for human consumption
D. Harness-maker

24. The repeated reference to slaughter, drowning, and the knacker in the passage primarily implies to:
A. Provide a detailed account of animal husbandry
B. Evoke emotional outrage and highlight the brutality of exploitation
C. Suggest that animals are naturally subservient
D. Indicate that humans value animals

SECTION-II : CURRENT AFFAIRS INCLUDING GENERAL KNOWLEDGE

VI

US president Donald trump has landed a triple whammy on India by torpedoing the H-1B visa programme, days after revoking sanctions waiver on Chabahar port in Iran and weeks after imposing a 50% tariff on Indian exports to the US. The White House also maintained a conspicuous silence on the Pakistan-Saudi Arabia mutual defence treaty amid reports that neither country informed Washington of the pact, suggesting a growing US indifference to India's concerns. The triple blow has shaken US-India ties to the foundation, mystifying experts who expected a reset after an exchange of friendly messages between Modi and Trump. While some observers see in the crackdown on H-1B a pressure tactic to make India bend on the trade deal, sources familiar with the dynamics of the current White House say the two issues are unrelated and Trump was convinced of the need to "reform" the guest worker visa programme ever since MAGA hardliners persuaded him that American workers were being gamed out of jobs by foreign companies and US big tech acting in tandem. (174 words)

[Extracted from the newspaper, The Times of India, September 21, 2025]

25. What percentage tariff did President Trump initially impose on Indian imports in 2025?
A. 15% B. 25%
C. 40% D. 50%

26. What strategic reason did Donald Trump cite for penalizing India with additional tariffs apart from trade imbalances?
A. India's IT service exports
B. Indian Banknote Demonetization
C. India's immigration policies
D. India's defense and energy ties with Russia

27. What is the strategic significance of Chabahar Port for India?
A. Provides trade access to China through Pakistan
B. Acts as counterbalance to China's presence in nearby Gwadar Port, Pakistan
C. Serves as the primary naval base for India
D. Connects India directly to the Mediterranean Sea

28. What is the primary purpose of the H-1B Visa?
A. Exchange Visitor Visa
B. Employment Visa
C. Immigrant visa for permanent residence in the U.S.
D. Non-immigrant visa that allows US companies to hire foreign professionals in specialized field

23. C **24.** B **25.** B **26.** D **27.** B **28.** D

29. The acronym 'MAGA' mentioned in the above passage refers to:
A. Multilateral Agencies Global Association
B. Make America Great Again
C. Mutual Agreements for Global Advantage
D. Monetary Advantage For Great America

VII

Indian Chess recorded yet another great moment on Monday; as Divya Deshmukh won the Women's World Cup in Georgian city of Batumi. In the final, the 19-year-old defeated fellow-Indian Koneru Humpy in the tiebreakers. While Humpy contesting the final wasn't much of a surprise-she is the World No. 5 and has been one of the best female players for the last couple of decades-not many would have anticipated Divya's stunning show. But, given her obvious talent and the way she has been playing for the past two years, it didn't come as a big surprise. By winning the World Cup, one of the biggest events organized by the world chess governing body FIDE, Divya also achieved another significant milestone. She became India's 88th Grandmaster and is only the fourth Indian Woman after Humpy, D. Harika and R. Vaishali to get that coveted title. Last year, Divya won the World junior championship in Ahmedabad with a dominant display. She also played a key role in India's historic gold in the Chess Olympiad at Budapest. India was the top seed there, though. At the World Cup, the Indian women exceeded expectations, with four of them making it to the quarterfinals. (198 words)

[Extracted from the newspaper, The Hindu July 29, 2025]

30. Where is the origin of chess believed to be?
A. China B. Russia
C. India D. Egypt

31. Who was the first Indian to earn the title of chess Grandmaster?
A. D. Gukesh
B. Praveen Thipsay
C. Dibyendu Barua
D. Vishwanathan Anand

32. Who was the first official World Chess Champion?
A. Bobby Fischer
B. Gary Kasparov
C. Vishwanathan Anand
D. Wilhelm Steinitz

33. Which of the following computers successfully defeated Garry Kasparov, the reigning world chess champion, in a tournament match?
A. Deep AI B. Deep Thought
C. Deep Blue D. Deep Water

34. Which of the following cities is the venue for hosting the 11th edition of Chess World Cup 2025?
A. Paris, France B. Baku, Azerbaijan
C. Goa, India D. Chennai, India

VIII

I rise to apprise this august House of the foreign policy dimension of our response to the Pahalgam terrorist attack, going into the preparations for Operation Sindoor and how foreign policy was handled during Operation Sindoor. As all the honourable members would appreciate, it was important to send a clear, strong and resolute message after the Pahalgam attack. Our red lines had been crossed and we had to make it very apparent that there would be serious consequences. As a result, the first step which was taken was that a meeting of the Cabinet Committee of Security took place on the 23rd of April, and that meeting decided that:

- One, the Indus Water Treaty of 1960 will be held in abeyance with immediate effect until Pakistan credibly and irrevocably abjures its support for crossborder terrorism.

29. B **30.** C **31.** D **32.** D **33.** C **34.** C

- Two, the integrated checkpost Attari would be closed with immediate effect.
- Three, Pakistani nationals who were traveling under SAARC visa exemption scheme would no longer be allowed to do that.
- Four, the Defence, Naval and Air Advisors of the Pakistani High Commission would be declared persona non-grata and,
- Five, the overall strength of the High Commission would be brought down to 30 from the number of 55. (207 words)

(Excerpts from Statement made by Minister of External Affairs Dr. S Jaishankar on special discussion in Lok Sabha on Operation Sindoor dated 28th July 2025)

35. Where is Pahalgam situated in India?
A. Punjab
B. Himachal Pradesh
C. Jammu & Kashmir
D. Uttarakhand

36. The Checkpost Attari is located in:
A. Near Amritsar in Punjab
B. Near Baramulla in Jammu & Kashmir
C. Near Kutch in Gujrat
D. Near Barmer in Rajasthan

37. Which amongst the following is not a SAARC Nation?
A. Afghanistan B. Maldives
C. Mauritius D. Bangladesh

38. Expression *'Persona Non Grata'* means:
A. An ungrateful person
B. An unwelcome person
C. An untrustworthy person
D. A displaced person

39. The Indus Water Treaty signed in 1960 between India and Pakistan was facilitated by:
A. The United Nations General Assembly
B. The United Nations Security Council
C. The World Bank
D. The permanent Indus Commission

40. Which amongst the following is not a tributary of River Indus?
A. Ravi B. Jhelum
C. Tapti D. Chenab

IX

Prime Minister Shri Narendra Modi participated in the 25th Meeting of the Council of Heads of State of the Shanghai Cooperation Organization (SCO), held in Tianjin, China, from 31 August to 1 September 2025. The Summit witnessed productive discussions on SCO Development Strategy, Reform of Global Governance, Counter-Terrorism, Peace and Security, Economic and Financial Cooperation, and Sustainable Development.

Addressing the Summit, Prime Minister highlighted India's approach to strengthening cooperation under the SCO framework. In this regard, he noted that India seeks greater action under three pillars – Security, Connectivity and Opportunity. Emphasising that peace, security and stability remain key to progress and prosperity, he called upon member countries to take firm and decisive action to fight terrorism in all its manifestations. Prime Minister underlined the need for coordinated action against terror financing and radicalization. Thanking member countries for their strong solidarity in the wake of the Pahalgam terror attack, he emphasized that there should be no double standards in dealing with terrorism and urged the group to hold countries who perpetrate and support cross-border terrorism accountable.

Highlighting the role of connectivity in fostering development and building trust, Prime Minister stated that India strongly supported projects such as Chabahar port and International

35. C **36.** A **37.** C **38.** B **39.** C **40.** C

North-South Transport Corridor. He also spoke about opportunities in the fields of start-ups, innovation, youth empowerment and shared heritage, which must be pursued under the SCO umbrella. Prime Minister proposed commencing a Civilizational Dialogue Forum within the group to foster greater people-to-people ties and cultural understanding. (246 words)

(Excerpts from the Press release issued by Press Information Bureau Govt of India, dated 1st September 2025)

41. The civilizational dialogue forum (CDF) proposed by the Prime Minister of India at the 25th Meeting of Shanghai Cooperation Organization, is intended to promote

A. Peace and security

B. Sustainable development

C. Reform of Global governance

D. Cultural Understanding

42. The next Presidency of SCO is taken over by:

A. Kyrgyzstan B. Tajikistan

C. Uzbekistan D. Kazakhistan

43. Prime Minister of India stated that India strongly supported projects such as Chabahar port. Where is this port located?

A. Oman B. Iran

C. Afghanistan D. Saudi Arabia

44. Which of the following countries is not a member of SCO?

A. Belarus B. Iran

C. Pakistan D. Myanmar

45. The Secretariat of SCO is located in:

A. Beijing, China B. Tianjin, China

C. Shanghai, China D. Wuhan, China

46. At the conclusion of 25th SCO summit, the member countries adopted the:

A. Beijing Declaration

B. Tianjin Declaration

C. Shanghai Declaration

D. Wuhan Declaration

X

Air India stands in solidarity with the families and those affected by the AI-171 accident. We continue to mourn their loss and remain fully committed to providing support during this difficult time. Over a month ago, Air India started releasing interim payment of Rs 25 lakh to the affected families, to help them meet their immediate financial needs. The interim payment will be adjusted against any final compensation.

Air India has, so far, released the interim compensation to the families of 147 of the 229 deceased passengers and also the 19 who lost their lives at the accident site. In addition, the requisite documents of 52 others have been verified, to whose families the interim compensation will be released progressively. The Tata Group has also registered 'The AI-171 Memorial and Welfare Trust', dedicated to the victims of the unfortunate accident. The Trust has pledged an ex-gratia payment of Rs 1 crore in respect of each of the deceased, and support for rebuilding the B.J. Medical College Hostel infrastructure, which was damaged in the accident.

The Trust will also provide aid and assistance for alleviation of any trauma or distress suffered by the first responders, medical and disaster relief professionals, social workers, and governmental staff who provided invaluable institutional support and service in the aftermath of the accident. (217 words)

(Excerpts from the Press Release published by Air India, on July 26, 2025)

47. Air India flight AI-171 was operating from Ahmedabad to:

A. London Gatwick airport

B. Heathrow Airport

C. London Luton Airport

D. London Stansted Airport

41. D **42.** A **43.** B **44.** D **45.** A **46.** B **47.** A

48. Who is the Minister of Civil Aviation of India?
A. Shri Piyush Goyal
B. Shri Jyotiraditya Scindia
C. Shri Ram Mohan Naidu
D. Shri Prafulla Patel

49. 'The AI-171 Memorial and Welfare Trust' is registered by Tata Group as a public charitable trust in:
A. Ahmedabad B. Gandhinagar
C. Mumbai D. Delhi

50. The sole survivor of 'The Air India flight AI-171 accident is:
A. British National of Indian Origin
B. Canadian National of Indian origin
C. Portuguese National of Indian Origin
D. Indian National

51. The agency that probes the fatal crash of AI-171 is:
A. DGCA B. AAI
C. AAIB D. FIP

52. The Air India flight AI-171 was:
A. Boeing 737-800 aircraft
B. Boeing 787-8 Dreamliner
C. Boeing 737 Max aircraft
D. Boeing Next Generation 737

SECTION-III : LEGAL REASONING

XI

One of the central motifs of the past decade of governance under Indian Prime Minister has been the embrace of policy measures that seek to apply uniform solutions to disparate policy dilemmas facing the country. These measures, often termed One Nation policies, are motivated by a desire to replace the existing patchwork of statespecific policies, regulations, and regimes with measures that are identical across the length and breadth of India.

There are numerous examples of such One Nation policies being propagated and, in several cases, implemented in the eleven years since this Government came to power. For instance, in 2016, Parliament passed a series of constitutional amendments to introduce a new Goods and Services Tax (GST), which introduced a unified value-added tax in place of state-specific levies. This reform, known informally as One Nation, One Tax, had been debated and discussed for nearly two decades and was widely touted as an important precursor to forging a common market across India's twenty-eight states.

In a similar vein, the government rolled out a new initiative to allow Indian citizens to take advantage of subsidized food rations irrespective of their state of residence. This scheme, commonly termed One Nation, One Ration Card, was intended to increase access to welfare benefits, especially for the millions of internal migrants in India without a fixed place of residence.

Earlier this year, the government announced the launch of a new online portal that will provide students, faculty, and researchers across the country's public higher education institutions with open access to international scholarly journals and articles under a scheme it has dubbed One Nation, One Subscription.

Most notably, the government recently signalled its intention to pursue a monumental One Nation policy that has been long discussed but only recently outlined in detail. This measure, known as One Nation, One Election, would do away with India's current system of staggered elections for state and national assemblies, replacing it with a framework of simultaneous elections. The proposal, which has featured in many of PM's speeches in the past, was advanced

48. C 49. C 50. A 51. C 52. B

by a high-level committee (HLC) established by the government in 2023. (351 words)

[Excerpts from Does "One Nation, One Election" Make Sense for India? by Milan Vaishnav, Caroline Mallory, and Annabel Richter Published on July 28, 2025]

53. What is the underlying idea behind the "One Nation" policies of the government?
A. To strengthen federalism by empowering states with greater autonomy
B. To apply uniform solutions across India, replacing state-specific variations
C. To decentralize governance to local self-government institutions
D. To promote diversity by encouraging state-specific policies

54. Which of the following Constitution Amendment Bill deals with empowerment of the Election Commission of India (ECI) to implement simultaneous state and national elections.
A. One Hundred and Twenty-Ninth Amendment
B. One Hundred and Twenty-Eighth Amendment
C. One Hundred and Twenty-Seventh Amendment
D. One Hundred and Twenty-Sixth Amendment

55. Which committee or report has discussed the feasibility of simultaneous elections in India?
A. Justice Verma Committee 2013
B. Law Commission of India Report 2018
C. Sarkaria Commission Report 1988
D. Punchhi Commission Report 2010

56. A High-Level Committee was constituted by the government to examine the policy of One Nation One Election. The Committee was led by:
A. Shri Ram Nath Kovind
B. Shri Jagdip Dhankar
C. Shri Pranab Mukherjee
D. Smt. Droupadi Murmu

57. As per the new GST reforms introduced in September 2025, the structure of new GST rates are as follows
A. 5%, 12%, 18% and 28%
B. 5%, 12% and 18%
C. 5%, 12% and 40%
D. 5%, 18% and 40%

58. The object of One Nation, One Ration Card scheme is to benefit:
A. The rural population
B. The Farmers
C. The Migrant labourers
D. The ration shopkeepers

XII

I may here trace the history of the shaping of the Preamble because this would show that the Preamble was in conformity with the Constitution as it was finally accepted. Not only was the Constitution framed in the light of the Preamble but the Preamble was ultimately settled in the light of the Constitution. In the earliest draft the Preamble was something formal and read: "We, the people of India, seeking to promote the common good, do hereby, through our chosen representatives, enact, adopt and give to ourselves this Constitution".

After the plan of June 3, 1947, which led to the decision to partition the country and to set up two independent Dominions of India and Pakistan, on June 8, 1947, a joint subcommittee of the Union Constitution and Provincial Constitution Committees, took note that the objective resolution would require amendment in view of the latest announcement of the British Government. The announcement of June 3 had made it clear that full independence, in the form of Dominion Status, would be conferred on India as from August 15, 1947. After examining the implications of partition the subcommittee thought that the question of

53. B **54.** A **55.** B **56.** A **57.** D **58.** C

making changes in the Objectives Resolution could appropriately be considered only when effect had actually been given to the June 3 Plan. Later on July 12, 1947, the special sub-committee again postponed consideration of the matter. The Union Constitution Committee provisionally accepted the Preamble as drafted by B.N. Rao and reproduced it in its report of July 4, 1947 without any change, with the tacit recognition at that stage that the Preamble would be finally based on the Objectives Resolution. In a statement circulated to members of the Assembly on July 18, 1947 Pandit Jawaharlal Nehru inter alia, observed that the Preamble was covered more or less by the Objectives Resolution which it was intended to incorporate in the final Constitution, subject to some modification on account of the political changes resulting from partition. (327 words)

(Extracted with edits and revision from B Shiva Rao's-Framing of India's Constitution)

59. According to the passage, the relationship between the Constitution and the Preamble can best be described as:

A. The Preamble was drafted in isolation
B. The Constitution and the Preamble were framed independent of each other
C. Both the Constitution and the Preamble were shaped in light of each other
D. The Preamble had no relevance to the Constitution

60. What did the earliest draft of the Preamble emphasize?

A. Liberty, equality, and fraternity
B. Sovereign, socialist, secular democratic republic
C. Formal enactment by the people through representatives
D. Unity and integrity of the nation

61. Which of the following is not enshrined in the Preamble of the Constitution of India?

A. Equality of status and of opportunity
B. Liberty of thought, expression, belief, faith and worship
C. Justice –moral, ethical and legal
D. Fraternity assuring the dignity of the individual

62. Which has been rightly arranged according to the Preamble of the Constitution of India?

A. Sovereign Socialist Secular Democratic Republic
B. Sovereign Secular Socialist Democratic Republic
C. Sovereign Socialist Democratic Secular Republic
D. Secular, Socialist, Sovereign and Democratic Republic

63. The Preamble of the Constitution of India is finally based on:

A. The Objectives Resolution
B. The Report of the Union Constitution Committee
C. The June 3 plan of the British Government
D. The Report of special Sub-committee of the Constituent Assembly

64. What was the role of Sir B. N. Rau in the making of the Indian Constitution?

A. Chairman of the Drafting Committee
B. Constitutional Advisor to the Constituent Assembly
C. President of the Constituent Assembly
D. Member of the Union Powers Committee

XIII

Good governance is only in the hands of good men. No doubt, what is good or bad is not for the court to decide: but the court can always indicate the constitutional ethos on goodness, good governance and purity in administration remind the constitutional functionaries to preserve, protect and promote the same. That ethos are the unwritten words in our Constitution. However, as the Constitution makers stated, there is a presumption that the Prime Minister/Chief Minister would be

59. C **60.** C **61.** C **62.** A **63.** A **64.** B

well advised and guided by such unwritten yet constitutional principles as well. According to Dr. B. R. Ambedkar, such things were only to be left to the good sense of the Prime Minister, and for that matter, the Chief Minister of State, since it was expected that the two great constitutional functionaries would not dare to do any infamous thing by inducting an otherwise unfit person to the Council of Ministers. It appears, over a period of time, at least in some cases, it was only a story of great expectations. Some of the instances pointed out in the writ petition indicate that Dr. Ambedkar and other great visionaries in the Constituent Assembly have been bailed out. Qualification has been wrongly understood as the mere absence of prescribed disqualification. Hence, it has become the bounden duty of the court to remind the Prime Minister and the Chief Minister of the State of their duty to act in accordance with the constitutional aspirations.

No doubt, it is not for the court to issue any direction to the Prime Minister or the Chief Minister, as the case may be, as to the manner in which they should exercise their power while selecting the colleagues in the Council of Ministers. That is the constitutional prerogative of those functionaries who are called upon to preserve, protect and defend the Constitution. But it is the prophetic duty of this Court to remind the key duty holders about their role in working the Constitution. Hence, I am of the firm view, that the Prime Minister and the Chief Minister of the State, who themselves have taken oath to bear true faith and allegiance to the Constitution of India and to discharge their duties faithfully and conscientiously, will be well advised to consider avoiding any person in the Council of Ministers, against whom charges have been framed by a criminal court in respect of offences involving moral turpitude and also offences specifically referred to in Chapter III of The Representation of the People Act, 1951. (416 words)

[Extract from the Supreme Court Judgement Manoj Narula v. Union of India]

65. According to the passage, the Court cannot decide what is "good" or "bad" governance, but it can:

A. Disqualify Ministers from holding office
B. Indicate constitutional ethos on governance and remind functionaries of their duty
C. Frame rules on qualifications of Ministers
D. Amend the Constitution to insert explicit standards of morality

66. Dr. B.R. Ambedkar believed that the working of the Constitution ultimately depends on:

A. The rigidity of the constitutional text
B. The good sense and integrity of those who are going to administer this constitution
C. The presence of a strong opposition
D. Judicial intervention in governance

67. The Court, while respecting the prerogative of the Prime Minister and Chief Minister to select Ministers emphasized that:

A. They should avoid appointing persons against whom criminal charges involving moral turpitude are framed
B. They must appoint Ministers strictly from the ruling party only
C. They should consult the Supreme Court before finalizing appointments
D. They are bound to appoint only members of the Lok Sabha/Legislative Assembly

68. What role does the Court assume, as described in the passage, regarding governance and appointments to the Council of Ministers?

A. Judicial review of all ministerial appointments
B. Prophetic duty to remind key functionaries of their constitutional role
C. Power to veto ministerial selections made by the Prime Minister
D. Directing Parliament to amend the law on disqualification

65. B **66.** B **67.** A **68.** B

69. Who are the constitutional functionaries, this passage primarily refers to?
A. Council of Ministers
B. Prime Minister and Council of Ministers
C. Chief Minister and Council of Ministers
D. Prime Minister and Chief Minister

70. Who, according to the above passage shall not be appointed as a Minister?
A. Against whom charges have been framed in a court of law
B. Against whom charges involving moral turpitude have been framed in a court of law
C. Against whom charges have been proved in a court of law
D. Against whom case is pending in a court of law

XIV

The recent Supreme Court judgment in State of Tamil Nadu v. Governor of Tamil Nadu (2025) affirmed that a Governor cannot exercise an absolute or "pocket" veto on bills, holding that if assent is withheld, the bill must be returned to the legislature "as soon as possible" for reconsideration, with the Governor having no discretion to withhold assent again. The court established that inaction or indefinite delay is illegal and unconstitutional, prescribing timelines for the Governor's decision and even "deeming assent" on pending bills in the Tamil Nadu case, establishing a critical precedent for judicial review of gubernatorial powers. The Supreme Court explicitly rejected the Governor's power to an absolute or "pocket" veto, which allows for bills to be indefinitely delayed. If a Governor withholds assent to a bill, they are constitutionally obligated to return it to the State Assembly for reconsideration, according to the proviso in Article 200 of the Constitution. If the State Assembly re-enacts a bill after it has been returned by the Governor, the Governor has no choice but to give assent to it and cannot withhold it for a second time. The Court held that indefinitely delaying or remaining silent on bills is unconstitutional and that Governors must act "as soon as possible" on bills. The judgment expanded the scope of judicial review by setting timelines for the Governor's actions on bills, allowing state governments to approach courts if these timelines are breached. In the case of the Tamil Nadu, the Court used its powers under Article 142 to "deem assent" on the long-pending bills, which had the effect of making any subsequent decision by the President on those bills void. (276 words)

[Extracted with edits & revisions from "The Hindu", dated 8th April 2025]

71. The Legislative Assembly of State X passes a controversial bill and sends it to the Governor for assent. The Governor, strongly disagreeing with the bill's provisions, decides to neither give assent nor return the bill, hoping it will be forgotten over the time. Which of the following statements accurately describes the legal position of the Governor's action?
A. The Governor's action is a legitimate exercise of a "pocket veto", allowing for indefinite delay of bills
B. The Governor's inaction is unconstitutional, as the Supreme Court has explicitly rejected the power to an absolute or "pocket" veto, and they are obligated to return the bill "as soon as possible" if assent is withheld
C. The Governor is within their rights to delay the bill indefinitely as long as they do not explicitly reject it, reflecting the true spirit of gubernatorial discretion
D. The bill will automatically lapse after six months of gubernatorial inaction, making the delay a *de facto rejection*

69. D	70. B	71. B

72. Governor Y receives a bill from the State Assembly and, after careful consideration, decides to withhold assent, promptly returning it with a message for reconsideration. The State Assembly then re-enacts the bill without any change and sends it back to Governor Y.

What is the constitutional obligation of Governor Y at this point?

A. Governor Y has no choice but to give assent to the re-enacted bill, as the Supreme Court has ruled that the Governor cannot withhold assent for a second time

B. Governor Y can again withhold assent if they continue to disagree with the bill's content, sending it back for further reconsideration

C. Governor Y can refer the bill to the President of India for a final decision, exercising a higher discretionary power

D. Governor Y can dissolve the State Assembly for consistently passing erroneous bills

73. After the Supreme Court's judgment in *State of Tamil Nadu v. Governor of Tamil Nadu* (2025), a State Governor holds a bill for eight months without taking any action—neither assenting nor returning it. The State Government believes that this delay is unconstitutional.

Based on the precedent set by the judgment, what recourse is available to the State Government?

A. The State Government must wait for a full year before any action can be taken, as gubernatorial delays are typically permitted for this duration

B. The bill automatically lapses after six months of inaction, making any further action by the State Government unnecessary

C. The State Government's only recourse is to re-enact the bill, which would then compel the Governor to act

D. The State Government can approach the courts, as the judgment had prescribed timelines for the Governor's actions on bills since indefinite delay was construed unconstitutional

74. In a situation mirroring the Tamil Nadu case, a Supreme Court bench is reviewing several instances where a particular Governor has indefinitely delayed assent on multiple bills passed by the State Assembly, despite Constitutional obligations.

If the Supreme Court decides to follow the precedent established in *State of Tamil Nadu v. Governor of Tamil Nadu* (2025) regarding pending bills, what would be a likely outcome for these delayed bills?

A. The Supreme Court would order the Governor to explicitly reject all the delayed bills

B. The Supreme Court would direct the State Assembly to conduct a public referendum on each delayed bill

C. The Supreme Court could deem assent on the pending bills, establishing a critical precedent for judicial review of gubernatorial powers in such cases, as it did in the Tamil Nadu case

D. The Supreme Court would advise the Governor to seek legal counsel and then reevaluate each bill individually without a set timeline

72. A **73.** D **74.** C

75. A newly appointed Governor publicly declares that he intend to use his discretion to permanently halt any legislation he deems inappropriate, by simply not acting on the bills, citing an inherent gubernatorial power.

How does this declaration align with the constitutional interpretation provided by the Supreme Court of India?

A. The Governor's declaration is consistent with the broad discretionary powers traditionally afforded to Governors, allowing them significant influence over state legislation

B. The Governor's declaration is valid only for non-money bills, as money bills have different Constitutional protocols

C. The Governor's declaration is partially valid, as indefinite delay is permissible only if the State Assembly is not in session

D. The Governor's declaration is unconstitutional; the Supreme Court explicitly rejected the Governor's power to an absolute or "pocket" veto

76. What are the three primary courses of action for a Governor when a Bill is enacted by the State Assembly and sent to him/her for his/her assent.

Which option correctly lists these three courses?

A. (*i*) Give assent,
(*ii*) Veto absolutely, or
(*iii*) Refer to the Supreme Court

B. (*i*) Give assent,
(*ii*) Withhold assent (allowing the Bill to fail, unless the proviso is followed), or
(*iii*) Recommend amendments

C. (*i*) Give assent,
(*ii*) Withhold assent (with the option to return for reconsideration), or
(*iii*) Reserve for the consideration of the President

D. (*i*) Give assent,
(*ii*) Return for reconsideration, or
(*iii*) Refer to the Union Government

XV

Same-sex marriage has no legal recognition in India as per the recent Supreme Court's judgment, where it was decided that this is an issue for Parliament to address. While Hindu marriages between transgender persons and cisgender men are permissible, and the Court acknowledged systemic discrimination and the right to choose a partner, it held that there is no fundamental right to marry. The government has been urged to form a panel to consider granting more legal rights to same-sex couples, but the legal status of marriage remains unchanged for now. The five-judge bench of the Supreme Court of India in *Supriyo @ Supriya Chakraborty & Anr. v. Union of India* (2023), in a majority verdict, ruled that there is no fundamental right to marry under the Indian Constitution, making it beyond the court's scope to legislate on same-sex marriage. The Court stated that the power to legislate on same-sex marriage rests with the Parliament and state legislatures. The judgment affirmed constitutional rights for LGBTQ+ citizens and the right to choose a partner. The government agreed to set up a panel to explore legal rights and benefits for same-sex couples, though these benefits are not the same as those conferred by marriage. Same-sex couples cannot legally marry and do not receive the same legal rights, such as automatic inheritance, pension, or adoption rights, that legally married couples do.

75. D	76. C

Despite the ruling, LGBTQ+ couples continue to face legal discrimination and have no social recognition of marriage. The Court affirmed the right of same-sex couples to cohabit privately. While the Supreme Court's verdict brought limited benefits and acknowledgments, it has not legalized same-sex marriage in India, deferring the ultimate decision to the Parliament. (279 words)

[Extracted, with edits and revisions, from "The Hindu", dated 27th October 2023]

77. In October 2023, two individuals in India, Ramesh and Sameer, who identify as a samesex couple, sought to legally solemnize their marriage. Based on the Supreme Court's ruling, what is the current legal standing of their ability to marry?

A. Their marriage is legally recognized nationwide under a new constitutional right

B. Their marriage is not legally recognized, as the Supreme Court ruled that this issue is for Parliament to address

C. Their marriage is recognized only if both of them identify as transgender

D. Their marriage is temporarily recognized until Parliament decides otherwise

78. During a legal proceeding in India, an advocate argues that the Supreme Court should directly legislate on same-sex marriage because the right to choose a partner inherently implies a fundamental right to marry for all citizens. How would the Supreme Court's judgment likely to counter this argument?

A. The Court acknowledged the right to choose a partner, therefore it would agree to legislate on marriage

B. The Court held that there is no fundamental right to marry under the Indian Constitution, and such a policy can be made only by the Parliament

C. The Court has held that it will set up a panel to look into the fundamental right to marry

D. The Court upheld the fundamental right to marry, but declined to recognise same sex marriage

79. Following the Supreme Court's decision, an LGBTQ+ advocacy group in India aims to achieve legal recognition for same-sex marriage. To which governmental body or bodies should this group primarily direct its lobbying efforts to secure the necessary legislation?

A. The Supreme Court of India, as they are ultimately responsible for interpreting constitutional rights

B. The President of India as head of the Union legislature

C. The Parliament and state legislatures, as the power to legislate on same-sex marriage rests with them

D. The National Commission for Human Rights, to advocate for a new directive

80. While same-sex marriage is not legally recognized in India, however, the Supreme Court's verdict did offer some acknowledgments of rights for same-sex couples.

Which of the following rights was specifically affirmed by the Court?

A. The automatic right to inheritance for same-sex partners

B. The right of same-sex couples to adopt children jointly

C. The right of same-sex couples to cohabit privately

D. The right to maintenance for same-sex partners

77. B	78. B	79. C	80. C

81. Ramesh and Suresh, a same-sex couple in India, have lived together for a decade and want to ensure they receive legal benefits equivalent to those of married couples, such as automatic inheritance and pension rights. Based on the Supreme Court's judgment, what is the primary obstacle they face in achieving these benefits?

A. They must first register their union with the government panel that was urged to be formed

B. They cannot legally marry and therefore cannot automatically be entitled to these specific legal rights

C. These rights are only available to same-sex couples where one partner is transgender

D. They can receive these benefits if they convert to a religion that recognizes samesex unions

82. The new acronym that is evolved after LGBTQ+ is an acronym called LGBTQIA+. In this new acronym 'IA' refers to:

A. Intersex and Asexual

B. Initialisms and Agender

C. Intersex and Ally

D. Intrasex and Androgynous

SECTION-IV : LOGICAL REASONING

XVI

In a language laboratory, students were given an interesting puzzle involving the word "ELECTROCARDIOGRAPH". The teacher explained that such exercises not only test logical skills but also sharpen attention to detail. According to the challenge, the word had to undergo a series of transformations. First, the class was asked to take the first half of the letters, reverse their order and make the arrangement of letters look quite different from the original. Next, the students were told to identify the last but one letter of the original word and place it at the very beginning, a step that changed the opening appearance of the sequence completely. Finally, as a finishing touch, they had to add the letter 'S' at the end. Following these steps carefully would lead them to the correct transformed word, and only those who adhered to each condition in the exact order could solve the puzzle successfully. (150 words)

83. Which letter will be exactly in the middle?

A. L B. R
C. D D. E

84. How many vowels will be to the left of the middle letter?

A. 2 B. 1
C. 4 D. 3

85. Which of the two vowels will be adjoining each other?

A. IE B. IO
C. AE D. AO

86. Which vowel will have a consonant to the left but a vowel to the right of it?

A. I B. O
C. A D. E

87. Name the letter sandwiched between two vowels?

A. R and T

B. C and L

C. R and L

D. D and R

88. Which letter is **prefixed** to the word after the first half is reversed?

A. G B. P
C. H D. S

81. B **82.** A **83.** D **84.** D **85.** B **86.** A **87.** B **88.** B

XVII

On the night of October 12th, the "Sunburst Medallion" was stolen from the highly secured display case in the city museum. The theft occurred sometime between the museum closing at 10:00 PM and the night guard, Mr. Hemant, completing his final round at 1:00 AM.Three primary suspects were identified, all of whom had recently been dismissed from their museum positions: Anjali, the former curator; Bharat, the former security expert; and Chitra, the former exhibits designer.

Here are the established facts and their alibis:

- The security system logs show that the display case was opened using a specific five-digit code, which only Anjali and the museum director (who was out of the country) knew.
- Bharat's alibi is that he was at a distant relative's birthday party from 8:00 PM to 1:30 AM. Multiple independent witnesses confirmed his presence throughout the entire period.
- Chitra's alibi is that she was working late at a downtown graphic design studio. A time-stamped security camera from the studio's entrance shows her entering at 7:00 PM and exiting at 11:45 PM. The studio is a 20-minute drive from the museum.
- Mr. Hemant, the night guard, stated he checked the medallion at 10:30 PM, and it was still there.

Further investigation revealed that a small, distinctive silver button was found near the display case. Anjali is known to frequently wear a coat with similar unique silver buttons. The security expert, Bharat, had previously boasted that he could remotely disable a certain type of magnetic lock-the same type used on the medallion's case-without needing the code, though the log suggests the code was used. (269 words)

89. Identifying the Most Likely Suspect. Based only on the fact that the five-digit code was used to open the display case, who is the only plausible suspect among the three?

A. Anjali

B. Bharat

C. Chitra

D. Both Anjali and Chitra

90. Evaluating Alibis and Time Constraints. The theft occurred between 10:00 PM and 1:00 AM, but the night guard saw the medallion at 10:30 PM. Given Chitra's alibi, what is the earliest time she could have reached the museum?

A. 11:45 PM

B. 12:05 AM

C. 12:45 AM

D. 10:50 PM

91. Deduction and Contradictory Evidence. If the theft was committed by Bharat, which established fact must be incorrect, based on the provided information?

A. The medallion was present at 10:30 PM

B. The security logs indicating the code was used

C. The museum closing time of 10:00 PM

D. The time frame of his alibi (8:00 PM to 1:30 AM)

92. Analyzing Accessory Evidence. The discovery of the silver button near the display case is the most incriminating evidence against which suspect, and why?

A. Bharat, because he had the technical expertise to get close to the case

B. Chitra, because she was near the museum late that night

C. Anjali, because she is known to wear a coat with similar buttons

D. Mr. Hemant, as he was the last person to check the area

89. A	**90.** B	**91.** D	**92.** C

93. Identifying the Logical Flaw in the Argument: A detective argues: "Since Bharat has a confirmed, continuous alibi covering the entire time window of the theft (10:30 PM to 1:00 AM), he cannot be the thief." What principle of logic supports this detective's conclusion?

A. Correlation does not imply causation
B. If an event requires presence, confirmed absence proves innocence
C. The rule of double jeopardy
D. The burden of proof lies with the accuser

94. Drawing a Strongest Conclusion: Considering all the facts (the code being used, the silver button, and the confirmed alibis), which is the most reasonable inference?

A. Bharat must have had an accomplice who knew the code
B. Chitra's alibi is false because she had enough time to commit the crime after leaving the studio
C. Anjali is the most likely suspect because the code was used and she has a direct link to the physical evidence (the button)
D. Mr. Hemant is secretly the thief and is trying to frame the former employees

95. Assessing Necessary Conditions: What condition is necessary for Chitra to have stolen the medallion?

A. She must know the five digit code
B. She must have left the graphic design studio before 11.45 pm
C. The theft must have occurred after she left the studio and before 1 am
D. She must have worked with Anjali to disable the locks

XVIII

In a small town lived a close-knit family where every relation could be expressed through simple symbols. For instance, when they said A × B, it meant A is the father of B, while A ÷ B meant A is the mother of B. The younger ones were often introduced with A + B, meaning A was the daughter of B, and the bond of brotherhood was shown by A – B (A is brother of B). One day, the children in the family turned these symbols into a playful code. Instead of introducing their parents and siblings in words, they spoke only in symbols. "Look", giggled little Meena, "M + N ÷ O!" Everyone laughed, because they knew it meant Meena was the daughter of N, and N was the mother of O, making her O's sister. What started as a code soon became a family game, making the bonds of father, mother, daughter, and brother not just relations, but symbols of love and togetherness. (165 words)

96. If 'P + Q – R ÷ T', how is T related to P?

A. Aunt B. Father
C. Grandmother D. None of these

97. Which of the following means that R is wife of P?

A. P × R – Q – T
B. P ÷ T + R – Q
C. P ÷ R – Q + T
D. P × T – Q + R

98. If 'P × T ÷ Q + R', how is R related to P?

A. Daughter B. Husband
C. Son-in-law D. None of these

99. If 'P ÷ R – Q × T', how is P related to T?

A. Grandmother B. Mother-in-law
C. Sister D. Grandfather

100. If 'R ÷ Q + R × T', how is T related to Q?

A. Aunt B. Sister
C. Brother D. Grandson

101. If 'R – P ÷ J × Q', how is J related to R?

A. Son B. Nephew
C. Niece D. Grandson

93. B **94.** C **95.** C **96.** D **97.** D **98.** C **99.** A **100.** * **101.** B

XIX

Four teams – Red (R), Blue (B), Green (G), and Yellow (Y) – are competing in the final four rounds of the Inter-School Science Olympiad, labeled Round A, Round B, Round C, and Round D. Each round consists of one match between two teams, and every team plays exactly two matches. No team plays the same opponent more than once.

The final schedule must adhere to the following rules:

- **Rule 1 (Consecutive Play):** The Green team (G) must play their two matches in consecutive rounds.
- **Rule 2 (Fixed Appearance):** The Yellow team (Y) must play in Round B.
- **Rule 3 (Positional Constraint):** The Red team (R) must play against the Blue team (B) in a round that is immediately before a round in which neither R nor B is playing.
- **Rule 4 (Timing):** The Blue team's (B) first match must occur in an earlier round than the Green team's (G) first match.
- **Rule 5 (Opponent Link):** The team that plays against the Red team (R) in the round that is not against the Blue team (B), is the same team that plays in Round D. (193 words)

102. Determining the Green Team's Schedule: Considering Rules 1 and 2, which of the following pairs of rounds contains the Green team's two matches?
A. Round A and Round D
B. Round B and Round C
C. Round C and Round D
D. Round A and Round B

103. Applying the Positional Constraint: Based on all the rules, particularly Rule 3, which of the following matches must be scheduled for Round A?
A. Red vs. Green B. Red vs. Yellow
C. Red vs. Blue D. Blue vs. Yellow

104. Identifying the Blue Team's First Opponent: Who is the Blue team's first opponent in the tournament?
A. Green
B. Red
C. Yellow
D. The opponent cannot be determined

105. Finding the Match in Round C: What is the match scheduled for Round C?
A. Red vs. Green
B. Green vs. Blue
C. Blue vs. Yellow
D. Red vs. Yellow

106. Identifying the Teams Excluded from a Round: Which pair of rounds contains matches where the Yellow team does not participate?
A. Round A and Round C
B. Round A and Round D
C. Round B and Round C
D. Round C and Round D

107. Team Opponent Check: Which team does the Yellow team NOT play against over the course of the four rounds?
A. Red
B. Blue
C. Green
D. The Yellow team plays against all other teams

108. Assessing a Rule Violation: If the match in Round D was (Blue vs. Yellow), which of the original rules would be violated by this schedule change?
A. Rule 1 (Consecutive Play)
B. Rule 3 (Positional Constraint)
C. Rule 4 (Timing)
D. Rule 5 (Opponent Link)

102. B	103. C	104. B	105. B	106. A	107. B	108. D

SECTION-V : QUANTITATIVE APTITUDE

XX

Health insurance plays a vital role in ensuring financial protection and access to quality healthcare. In India, however, the extent and nature of health insurance coverage vary significantly between urban and rural areas. While urban populations often have better access to organized insurance schemes, employer-provided coverage, and awareness about health policies, rural populations face challenges such as limited outreach of insurance schemes, inadequate infrastructure, and lower awareness levels. This urban–rural divide in health insurance coverage highlights the broader issue of healthcare inequality, making it essential to analyze the factors contributing to this gap and explore strategies for more inclusive health protection. A state-level health survey was conducted.

The survey covered 1,80,000 adults across urban and rural areas. Urban residents formed 55% of the sample (that is, 99,000 people) while rural residents made up 45% (that is, 81,000 people). In each area, coverage was classified under four heads – Public schemes, Private insurance, Employer-provided coverage, and Uninsured. In urban areas, Public coverage accounted for 28% of the urban population, Private for 22%, Employer for 18%, and the remaining 32% were Uninsured. In rural areas, where formal coverage is generally lower, Public coverage stood at 35%, Private at 10%, Employer at 8%, while 47% were Uninsured. For this survey, "Insured" includes everyone covered by Public + Private + Employer schemes, and "Uninsured" indicates those with no coverage at all. Officials noted that public schemes remain the backbone of rural coverage, while employer and private plans are relatively more prevalent in urban centres. (250 words)

109. The ratio of insured adults in Urban : Rural is:
A. 82 : 65 B. 748 : 477
C. 65 : 82 D. 477 : 748

110. By what percentage is the number of Uninsured in Rural higher than Uninsured in Urban?
A. 18.75% B. 20.17%
C. 22.50% D. 25.00%

111. If the total population grows by 5% next year and all percentage shares remain the same (including the Urban-Rural split), how many additional privately insured people will there be (vs. this year)?
A. 1,494 B. 1,560
C. 1,620 D. 1,650

112. The total number of Employer-covered adults is:
A. 22,800 B. 23,100
C. 24,300 D. 25,200

113. What percentage of all insured adults are Publicly insured?
A. 48.50% B. 49.75%
C. 50.86% D. 52.00%

114. What percentage of the total surveyed population was insured?
A. 52.15% B. 56.25%
C. 61.25% D. 64%

XXI

A state electricity report serves as an important tool to assess energy production and track progress in the power sector. By providing quarterly data on generation measured in gigawatt hours (GWh), the report highlights the contribution of different energy sources such as coal, gas, hydro, solar,

109. B **110.** B **111.** A **112.** C **113.** C **114.** C

and wind. This not only helps in understanding the overall energy mix and dependence on conventional versus renewable sources but also enables policymakers, planners, and stakeholders to evaluate trends, address gaps, and promote sustainable energy development. A state electricity report provides quarterly generation (in GWh) by source – Coal, Gas, Hydro, Solar, and Wind.

- **In Q1:** Generation from Coal is 2,200 GWh, Gas contributes 800 GWh, Hydro 900 GWh, Solar 700 GWh, and Wind 400 GWh, for a total of 5,000 GWh.
- **In Q2:** Coal rises to 2,400 GWh, while Gas dips to 700 GWh; Hydro improves to 1,000 GWh, Solar to 800 GWh, and Wind to 600 GWh, bringing the quarterly total to 5,500 GWh.
- **In Q3:** Coal moderates to 2,100 GWh, Gas increases to 900 GWh, Hydro softens to 800 GWh, but Solar advances to 1,000 GWh and Wind to 700 GWh, keeping the total at 5,500 GWh.
- **In Q4:** Coal moves to 2,300 GWh, Gas to 850 GWh, Hydro to 1,100 GWh, Solar to 900 GWh, and Wind to 850 GWh, for a total of 6,000 GWh.

For analysis, Renewables are taken as Hydro + Solar + Wind. A carbon policy scenario proposes cutting Q4 Coal by 10%, shifting the entire reduction equally into Solar and Wind. (255 words)

115. The total annual generation (GWh) is:
A. 20,500 B. 21,500
C. 22,000 D. 22,500

116. The overall renewable share (as % of annual generation) is closest to:
A. 42.5% B. 43.8%
C. 44.3% D. 45.0%

117. The quarter with the highest renewable percentage share is:
A. Q1 B. Q2
C. Q3 D. Q4

118. A carbon policy reduces Q4 Coal by 10% and shifts the entire reduction equally to Solar and Wind. The new Q4 Solar (GWh) is:
A. 975 B. 1,000
C. 1,015 D. 1,030

119. The annual Gas : Hydro generation ratio is:
A. 13 : 15 B. 65 : 76
C. 5 : 6 D. 26 : 31

120. The quarter with the lowest renewable percentage share is:
A. Q1 B. Q2
C. Q3 D. Q4

EXPLANATORY ANSWERS

1. The passage clearly says that the Non-Cooperation Movement "commanded the support and sympathy of vast sections of the Indian people". It also mentions that its reach extended among peasants, workers, artisans, students, and politically aware villagers, and that its spread was nation-wide. This shows that the movement was supported by a very large section of Indians. It does not say Swaraj was futile, nor does it declare the movement a complete success in every sense. It also does not suggest that Congress represented only a microscopic minority.

2. The phrase "poor dumb millions" is used in the passage to describe the masses of India who had long been considered passive, voiceless, and outside active politics. Here "dumb" does not mean hearing impaired; it means not politically expressive or not previously involved in organized

115. C	116. C	117. D	118. C	119. B	120. A

national politics. The line emphasizes that these ordinary, poor, and largely uneducated people were now shown to be capable of participating in nationalist politics.

3. The passage directly states that "the tremendous participation of different communities in the movement, and the maintenance of communal unity... was in itself no mean achievement". This proves that communal unity was an important and successful feature of the movement. The passage does not say that Swaraj came before Non-Cooperation. It also does not say that the movement failed because of sudden withdrawal. In fact, students, educated people, and politically aware villagers are specifically mentioned as participants, so the rich and educated keeping away is also incorrect.

4. The central theme of the passage is that the Non-Cooperation Movement awakened political energy across India and demonstrated the strength, reach, and mass character of Indian nationalism. The author especially stresses that even ordinary people from villages, peasants, workers, artisans, and minorities could actively take part in nationalist politics. Thus, the movement revealed India's collective potential and capacity for political struggle. The other options either distort the tone of the passage or state the opposite of what is written.

5. In the passage, "communal unity" and later "communalism" are discussed in connection with participation of different communities and the later decline of that unity. In the historical and political context of the freedom movement, "communalism" refers to divisions based on religion, especially tensions between religious communities. Therefore, here the word refers to religious identity, not caste, region, or secularism.

6. The passage clearly states that prehistoric humans were "incognisant animals with no more impact on their environment than gorillas, fireflies or jellyfish". This shows they were not significantly different from other species in terms of influence on surroundings. There is no mention of conscious environmental shaping, advanced hierarchy, or warfare as defining traits.

7. The term "incognisant" is explained in context where the passage says humans had "no inkling that their descendants would one day walk on the moon..." This indicates lack of awareness or consciousness about their future capabilities. It does not mean lack of intelligence or inability to interact socially, but specifically lack of awareness of their potential.

8. The passage mentions that prehistoric humans loved, played, formed friendships, and competed—just like chimpanzees, baboons, and elephants. This similarity in behaviour meant they did not stand out among other organisms.

There is no mention of fewer offspring, lack of tools, or inability to develop language as the main reason.

9. The passage explicitly defines species as organisms that mate and produce fertile offspring. The example of horses and donkeys producing sterile mules reinforces this definition. Hence, reproductive compatibility leading to fertile offspring is the determining factor.

10. On careful rechecking, the passage first gives the biological rule that members of the same species can mate and produce fertile offspring. Then it gives two illustrations. Horses and donkeys may mate, but their offspring are sterile, so they are different species. After that, the passage says that a bulldog and a spaniel may look very different, yet they are members of the same species because they share the same DNA pool. Since the question asks how the passage explains species classification, the best option is the one that captures the central explanatory basis stated in the passage itself—shared species membership through the same DNA pool. Option C is not accurate because the passage does not contrast "horses and bulldogs" with "donkeys and spaniels"; it contrasts the pair horse-donkey with the pair bulldog-spaniel.

11. The passage introduces Freedom House as an organization that "produces quantitative measures of civil and political rights". This clearly indicates that its evaluation process is based on a systematic method of quantifying freedoms across countries. There is no mention of voter turnout, advisory roles, or focus on economic disparities.

12. The phrase "vote with their feet" is explained in the passage as people being able to move if they do not like their government. Cheap travel and communication enabled individuals to leave one country and settle in another offering better conditions. Thus, it refers to migration rather than electoral or protest actions.

13. The passage explicitly states that the "third wave of democratization" refers to the period when democracies and market-oriented economies spread widely across the world. It does not relate to communism, civil rights movements, or events of the 1960s.

14. The passage lists factors such as expanded education, information technology, cheap travel and communication, and greater prosperity as drivers of social mobilization. It does not mention military presence as a contributing factor, making this the correct choice.

15. The passage clearly states that "2009 marked the fourth consecutive year in which freedom had declined around the world, the first time this had happened since it established its measures of freedom in 1973." This directly answers the question.

16. Initially, the narrator and his kinsman judged the man based on his outward dress and assumed him to be a "boorish" up-country person. However, once he began speaking, their impression completely changed due to his confident and wide-ranging discourse. This contrast between first impression and later realization highlights how appearances can be misleading.

17. The statement exaggerates the man's confidence by suggesting that even the "Disposer of All Things" (God) consults him before making decisions. This is clearly an overstatement used for effect, which is the essence of hyperbole, rather than irony, allegory, or euphemism.

18. A theosophist is someone who believes in spiritual or mystical knowledge beyond ordinary understanding. In the passage, the kinsman interprets the man's abilities as arising from "magnetism, occult power, or astral body," which aligns with mystical belief systems.

19. The word "boorish" refers to someone who is rude, uncultured, or lacking manners. The narrator initially assumed the man to be such based on his appearance, which later proved incorrect.

20. The narrator suspects that the extraordinary man noticed the admiration and note-taking and was "quietly pleased". This implies that he enjoyed the attention and the impression he was creating, rather than being indifferent or embarrassed.

21. Critical, somber, and resentful, evoking both awareness and outrage: The speaker strongly criticizes humans for exploiting animals, describing how animals labour while humans take all benefits. The repeated emphasis on suffering, deprivation, and unjust treatment creates a serious and bitter tone. The language is emotionally charged and aims to awaken anger and awareness among listeners.

22. The contrast between animals' labour and humans' gain represents a deeper symbolic meaning. It reflects how a working class produces wealth while a ruling class exploits it. This is not merely about animals but about broader social and economic inequality, making it an allegory of exploitation.

23. In the passage, the "knacker" is described as someone to whom old or weak animals are sold to be killed and processed. This aligns with the definition of a knacker as someone who deals with the disposal of animals that are no longer useful and whose meat is not suitable for normal consumption.

24. The vivid references to slaughter, drowning, and violent ends are not meant to explain farming practices but to emotionally impact the reader. They highlight cruelty and injustice, reinforcing the theme of exploitation and urging a sense of anger and resistance.

25. On careful recheck, the initial tariff was 25%, not 50%. Reuters reported that Trump later imposed an additional 25% tariff, which raised duties on some Indian exports to as high as 50%. So the first tariff was 25%, and 50% was the later combined level.

26. Beyond trade issues, one of the major strategic concerns often cited by the US in recent years has been India's continued defense purchases and energy cooperation with Russia. This has

been a recurring geopolitical factor influencing US trade and diplomatic pressures on India.

27. Chabahar Port in Iran is strategically important for India because it provides access to Afghanistan and Central Asia while bypassing Pakistan. It also serves as a counter to China's investment in Gwadar Port under the China-Pakistan Economic Corridor, thereby strengthening India's regional strategic position.

28. The H-1B visa is specifically designed to allow US employers to temporarily employ foreign workers in specialized occupations such as IT, engineering, and research. It is not an immigrant visa or exchange visa.

29. MAGA stands for "Make America Great Again", a political slogan associated with Donald Trump and his policy approach, emphasizing domestic employment and economic nationalism.

30. Chess is widely believed to have originated in India in the form of the ancient game Chaturanga around the 6th century CE. From India, it spread to Persia and later to Europe, evolving into modern chess. Hence, India is considered the birthplace of chess.

31. Vishwanathan Anand was the first Indian to achieve the Grandmaster title in 1988. His achievement marked a turning point for Indian chess and inspired future generations of players.

32. Wilhelm Steinitz is recognized as the first official World Chess Champion, winning the title in 1886. His positional style and theories laid the foundation for modern chess strategy.

33. Deep Blue, developed by IBM, famously defeated Garry Kasparov in 1997 in a tournament match. This marked a historic milestone in artificial intelligence and computing.

34. On careful rechecking, the 11th edition of the FIDE Chess World Cup 2025 is being hosted in Goa, India, not Baku. FIDE's official World Cup 2025 site states that the event takes place in Goa from October 30 to November 27, 2025, and FIDE also separately confirmed Goa as the host city.

35. Pahalgam is a well-known town located in the Anantnag district of Jammu & Kashmir. It is famous as a tourist destination and also as an important base for the Amarnath Yatra. Therefore, among the given options, Jammu & Kashmir is the correct location.

36. Attari is the Indian border checkpost situated near Amritsar in Punjab, close to the India–Pakistan border opposite Wagah in Pakistan. It is one of the most important land transit points between the two countries. Hence this option is correct.

37. SAARC consists of Afghanistan, Bangladesh, Bhutan, India, Maldives, Nepal, Pakistan and Sri Lanka. Mauritius is not a member nation of SAARC. It has been associated in other regional contexts, but it is not counted among the SAARC countries.

38. The diplomatic expression persona non grata literally refers to a person who is not acceptable or not welcome, especially by the host country. When a diplomat is declared persona non grata, that person is required to leave the country. So "an unwelcome person" is the correct meaning.

39. The Indus Waters Treaty of 1960 between India and Pakistan was brokered with the help of the World Bank. It played the role of a facilitator in negotiations between the two countries. Therefore, the correct answer is the World Bank.

40. Ravi, Jhelum and Chenab are all major tributaries of the Indus river system. Tapti, however, is a separate west-flowing river of central India and does not belong to the Indus basin. Hence, Tapti is the correct answer.

41. The passage clearly states that the Civilizational Dialogue Forum (CDF) was proposed "to foster greater people-to-people ties and cultural understanding". Hence, its primary aim is promoting cultural understanding among member nations.

42. On careful rechecking, the next presidency of the SCO was taken over by Kyrgyzstan after the Tianjin Summit. The official Indian MEA press release states that the Prime Minister "congratulated Kyrgyzstan on taking over the next Presidency of SCO," and the SCO Secretariat also states that the 2025–2026 chairmanship passed to the Kyrgyz Republic.

43. Chabahar Port is located in Iran. It is strategically important for India as it provides access to Afghanistan and Central Asia, bypassing Pakistan, and enhances regional connectivity.

44. Myanmar is not a member of the SCO. The SCO includes countries like India, Pakistan, Iran, China, Russia, and Central Asian nations, but Myanmar is not part of this organization.

45. The permanent Secretariat of the Shanghai Cooperation Organization is located in Beijing, China. It serves as the main executive body of the organization.

46. Since the 25th SCO Summit was held in Tianjin, the declaration adopted at its conclusion is known as the Tianjin Declaration.

47. On careful rechecking, Air India's own official statement says that flight AI171 was operating from Ahmedabad to London Gatwick on 12 June 2025. UK AAIB reporting also refers to it as the Ahmedabad–London Gatwick flight. So Heathrow is not correct for this question.

48. As of 2025, Ram Mohan Naidu Kinjarapu is serving as the Minister of Civil Aviation in India. He succeeded earlier ministers and holds the portfolio in the current government.

49. The Tata Group registered 'The AI-171 Memorial and Welfare Trust' in Mumbai, which is the headquarters of the Tata Group and Air India. Hence, Mumbai is the correct location.

50. Reports on the accident indicate that the sole survivor was a British national of Indian origin. This aligns with the widely reported details of the incident.

51. The Aircraft Accident Investigation Bureau (AAIB) is the official body responsible for probing aircraft accidents in India. Therefore, it is the agency investigating the AI-171 crash.

52. Air India flight AI-171 was operated using a Boeing 787-8 Dreamliner, which is commonly used by Air India for long-haul international routes like India to London.

53. The passage clearly explains that "One Nation" policies aim to replace the existing patchwork of state-specific regulations with uniform measures across the country.
This reflects the core idea of standardization rather than decentralization or promotion of diversity.

54. The proposed constitutional amendment related to implementing simultaneous elections (One Nation, One Election) is the 129th Amendment Bill, which aims to empower institutions like the Election Commission of India to facilitate synchronized elections.

55. The feasibility of simultaneous elections has been examined in detail by the Law Commission of India in its 2018 report. It analyzed constitutional, legal, and logistical aspects of holding elections together.

56. Ram Nath Kovind chaired the High-Level Committee constituted by the Government of India in 2023 to examine the feasibility of "One Nation, One Election."

57. On careful rechecking, the September 2025 GST reforms replaced the earlier four-slab structure with two main rates of 5% and 18%, along with a 40% special rate for luxury and sin goods. PIB explicitly described it as a shift to a simplified two-slab system, with 40% for items such as pan masala, tobacco, aerated drinks, high-end cars, yachts, and private aircraft.

58. The One Nation, One Ration Card scheme is specifically designed to benefit migrant workers by allowing them to access subsidized food grains from any part of the country, irrespective of their place of residence.

59. The passage clearly states that "the Constitution was framed in the light of the Preamble" and also that "the Preamble was ultimately settled in the light of the Constitution". This shows a mutual and interdependent relationship between the two.

60. The earliest draft of the Preamble is quoted in the passage, emphasizing that "We, the people of India... through our chosen representatives, enact, adopt and give to ourselves this Constitution". This highlights the formal act of adoption by representatives.

61. The Preamble mentions justice in terms of "social, economic and political," not moral, ethical, and legal. Therefore, this option is not part of the Preamble.

62. The correct sequence as given in the Preamble is "Sovereign Socialist Secular Democratic Republic," reflecting the nature of the Indian state after the 42nd Amendment.

63. The passage clearly states that the Preamble was intended to be based on the Objectives Resolution and was ultimately aligned with it, subject to modifications.

64. Sir B.N. Rau served as the Constitutional Advisor to the Constituent Assembly and played a crucial role in preparing the initial draft and guiding the framing process.

65. The passage clearly states that while the Court cannot decide what is "good" or "bad," it can "indicate the constitutional ethos on goodness, good governance and purity in administration" and remind constitutional functionaries of their responsibilities.

66. Dr. B. R. Ambedkar emphasized that such matters were to be left to the "good sense" of the Prime Minister and Chief Minister, trusting that they would act responsibly and not appoint unfit persons.

67. The Court clearly advises that individuals against whom charges involving moral turpitude (and certain offences under the Representation of the People Act) have been framed should be avoided while forming the Council of Ministers.

68. The passage explicitly states that it is the "prophetic duty of this Court to remind the key duty holders about their role in working the Constitution," highlighting its advisory and moral role rather than a controlling one.

69. The passage repeatedly refers specifically to these two offices as the key constitutional functionaries responsible for forming the Council of Ministers and upholding constitutional values.

70. The passage clearly mentions that persons "against whom charges have been framed... in respect of offences involving moral turpitude" should be avoided for ministerial positions.

71. The Governor's inaction is unconstitutional, as the Supreme Court has explicitly rejected the power to an absolute or "pocket" veto, and they are obligated to return the bill "as soon as possible" if assent is withheld. The passage clearly states that indefinite delay or inaction is illegal and unconstitutional. The Governor cannot keep a bill pending indefinitely and must act within a reasonable time.

72. Governor Y has no choice but to give assent to the re-enacted bill, as the Supreme Court has ruled that the Governor cannot withhold assent for a second time. Once the Assembly re-enacts the bill, the Constitution (Article 200) mandates that the Governor must give assent and cannot send it back again.

73. The State Government can approach the courts, as the judgment had prescribed timelines for the Governor's actions on bills since indefinite delay was construed unconstitutional.
The judgment expanded judicial review and allowed State Governments to move courts when Governors delay decisions beyond reasonable timeliness.

74. The Supreme Court could deem assent on the pending bills, establishing a critical precedent for judicial review of gubernatorial powers in such cases, as it did in the Tamil Nadu case. The passage explicitly mentions that the Court used Article 142 to "deem assent" to long-pending bills, creating a precedent.

75. The Governor's declaration is unconstitutional; the Supreme Court explicitly rejected the Governor's power to an absolute or "pocket" veto. The judgment clearly denies Governors the authority to indefinitely delay or block legislation through inaction.

76. (*i*) Give assent, (*ii*) Withhold assent (with the option to return for reconsideration), or (*iii*) Reserve for the consideration of the President. These are the three constitutionally recognized options available to a Governor under Article 200.

77. Their marriage is not legally recognized, as the Supreme Court ruled that this issue is for Parliament to address.

The passage clearly states that same-sex marriage has no legal recognition and that the matter lies within the legislative domain of Parliament.

78. The Court held that there is no fundamental right to marry under the Indian Constitution, and such a policy can be made only by the Parliament. The judgment explicitly rejected the argument that the right to choose a partner automatically implies a fundamental right to marry, placing legislative authority with Parliament.

79. The Parliament and state legislatures, as the power to legislate on same-sex marriage rests with them. The passage clearly states that law-making power on this issue lies with Parliament and state legislatures, not the judiciary.

80. The Court affirmed that same-sex couples have the right to live together and choose their partners, even though marriage is not legally recognized.

81. They cannot legally marry and therefore cannot automatically be entitled to these specific legal rights. Since same-sex marriage is not legally recognized, couples do not receive associated benefits like inheritance, pension, or adoption rights.

82. In the expanded acronym LGBTQIA+, "I" stands for Intersex and "A" stands for Asexual, representing broader gender and sexual identities.

83. After applying all the steps correctly, the final word becomes PACORTCELERDIOGRAPHS.
It has 20 letters, so there is no single mathematical middle letter; the two central positions are the 10th and 11th.
In such reasoning questions, the intended "middle" is taken as the 10th letter here, which is E.

84. In the final arrangement PACORTCELERDIOGRAPHS, taking the intended middle letter as the 10th letter E, the letters to its left are P A C O R T C E L.
The vowels among these are A, O, E.
So the number of vowels to the left of the middle letter is 3.

85. In the final word PACORTCELERDIOGRAPHS, the only adjoining pair of vowels is IO.
Therefore, the correct pair is IO.

86. We need a vowel having a consonant on the left and a vowel on the right.
In the sequence D I O, the letter I has D on its left and O on its right.
So the required vowel is I.

87. A letter is sandwiched between two vowels when it has a vowel on both sides.
In A C O, the letter C lies between two vowels.
In E L E, the letter L lies between two vowels.
Hence the correct answer is C and L.

88. The last but one letter of the original word ELECTROCARDIOGRAPH is P.
According to the instruction, this letter is placed at the beginning after reversing the first half.
So the prefixed letter is P.

89. Based only on the fact that the five-digit code was used, Anjali is the only plausible suspect among the three because the passage clearly states that oniy Anjali and the museum director knew that code, and the director was out of the country.
Therefore, among the suspects, only Anjali had direct authorized knowledge required to open the case in that manner.

90. Chitra was seen exiting the graphic design studio at 11:45 PM. The studio is 20 minutes away from the museum.
Therefore, the earliest she could have reached the museum is 12:05 AM.
This falls within the theft window, since the medallion was still present at 10:30 PM and the final check ended at 1:00 AM.

91. If Bharat himself committed the theft, then the strongest established fact that must be incorrect is his confirmed alibi.
The theft took place after 10:30 PM and before 1:00 AM, and multiple independent witnesses place Bharat at the birthday party continuously from 8:00 PM to 1:30 AM.
Even if one argues about the lock mechanism or code usage, the bigger contradiction is that Bharat could not personally commit the theft while being elsewhere for the entire relevant period.
Therefore, his alibi would have to be false.

92. The silver button found near the display case directly connects most strongly with Anjali because she is specifically known to wear a coat with similar distinctive silver buttons. This is physical evidence linking her to the scene more closely than the others.

93. Theft of the medallion required the thief to be at or effectively involved with the museum during the relevant time window. Since Bharat's alibi is confirmed continuously for that period, the logical principle is that if presence is necessary for the act, then confirmed absence excludes him from being the thief.

94. Anjali is the most likely suspect because the code was used and she has a direct link to the physical evidence (the button).
The strongest combined inference comes from two facts pointing in the same direction: the display case was opened with a code known only to Anjali and the director, and a silver button matching Anjali's coat was found near the case.
Bharat has a strong alibi, and Chitra's case is much weaker than Anjali's. So Anjali is the most reasonable conclusion.

95. The theft must have occurred after she left the studio and before 1 am. This is the necessary condition. Chitra was seen leaving the studio at 11:45 PM, and the museum was 20 minutes away, so she could only possibly reach there after that.
Also, the theft had to be completed before 1:00 AM, when the guard finished his final round. Knowing the code is not strictly necessary in every possible scenario, because she might have obtained access through some other person or circumstance.
But for Chitra herself to have stolen the medallion, the theft must necessarily have taken place during the time window when she could physically reach the museum.

96. In P + Q – R ÷ T,
P + Q means P is the daughter of Q.
Q – R means Q is the brother of R.
R ÷ T means R is the mother of T.
So, Q and R are siblings, and T is the child of R.
Therefore, P is the daughter of T's maternal uncle.
Hence, P and T are cousins.
So, T is neither aunt, nor father, nor grandmother of P.

97. In P × T, P is the father of T.
In T – Q, T is the brother of Q, so T and Q are siblings.
In Q + R, Q is the daughter of R, so R is the parent of Q.
Since T and Q are siblings, R is also the parent of T.
Now P is father of T, so R must be the mother of T. Thus, R is the wife of P.

98. In P × T, P is the father of T.
In T ÷ Q, T is the mother of Q.
In Q + R, Q is the daughter of R, so R is the parent of Q.
Since T is already the mother of Q, R must be the father of Q.
Therefore, R is the husband of T. Since T is the child of P, R is P's son-in-law.

99. In P ÷ R, P is the mother of R.
In R – Q, R is the brother of Q, so Q is also P's child.
In Q × T, Q is the father of T.
Therefore, P is the mother of T's father, that is, grandmother.

100. The expression is R ÷ Q + R × T.
R ÷ Q means R is the mother of Q.
Q + R means Q is the daughter of R, so this only confirms that Q is female.
R × T means R is the father of T.
This creates a contradiction because R cannot be both the mother of Q and the father of T if the same symbol meanings are applied consistently to the same person in one expression.
Therefore, the relation cannot be determined in a logically valid way from the given coded statement.
Even if one ignores that inconsistency and only tries to infer from shared parenthood, T could be either brother or sister of Q, depending on T's gender, which is not specified. So the options are defective.
Hence the correct answer is NONE.

101. In R – P, R is the brother of P.
In P ÷ J, P is the mother of J.
So, J is the child of R's sister.
In J × Q, J is the father of Q, so J is male.
Hence, J is R's nephew.

102. Since Rule 3 forces the Red vs Blue match to be immediately followed by a round in which neither Red nor Blue plays, that next round must be Green vs Yellow. Also, Yellow must play in Round B.
Therefore Round B = Green vs Yellow and Round A = Red vs Blue.
As Green's two matches must be in consecutive rounds, Green must also play in Round C.
So Green's matches are in Round B and Round C.

103. Rule 3 says Red vs Blue must be in a round immediately before a round in which neither Red nor Blue plays. That next round must therefore be Green vs Yellow. Since Yellow must play in Round B, the only way this can happen is Round A = Red vs Blue and Round B = Green vs Yellow.
Hence Round A must be Red vs Blue.

104. From the fixed arrangement above,
Round A = Red vs Blue.
This is Blue's first appearance, and it occurs before Green's first appearance, satisfying Rule 4.
Therefore Blue's first opponent is Red.

105. After Round A = Red vs Blue and Round B = Green vs Yellow, Green must play again in the next consecutive round by Rule 1, so Green must be in Round C.
Blue has already played once in Round A and must play exactly twice, so Blue must also be in Round C.
Therefore Round C = Green vs Blue.

106. From the completed schedule:
Round A = Red vs Blue
Round B = Green vs Yellow
Round C = Green vs Blue
Round D = Red vs Yellow
Yellow appears only in Round B and Round D.
Therefore Yellow does not participate in Round A and Round C.

107. Yellow plays Green in Round B and Red in Round D.
So Yellow does not play against Blue at any point in the four rounds.

108. In the valid schedule, Red's non-Blue opponent is Yellow, so Rule 5 requires that the team playing in Round D must be that same team, namely Yellow.
If Round D were changed to Blue vs Yellow, then Red's non-Blue match would no longer line up with the required Round D structure under the original arrangement.
The schedule change breaks the opponent-link condition stated in Rule 5.

109. Urban insured = 99,000 × (28% + 22% + 18%)
= 99,000 × 68%
= 67,320

Rural insured = 81,000 × (35% + 10% + 8%)
= 81,000 × 53% = 42,930
Required ratio = 67,320 : 42,930
Divide by 90 = 748 : 477.

110. Urban uninsured = 99,000 × 32%
= 31,680
Rural uninsured = 81,000 × 47%
= 38,070
Difference = 38,070 – 31,680 = 6,390
Percentage by which rural is higher than urban

$$= \frac{6,390}{31,680} \times 100$$

= 20.17% approximately.

111. Urban privately insured now
= 99,000 × 22%
= 21,780
Rural privately insured now
= 81,000 × 10%
= 8,100
Total privately insured now
= 21,780 + 8,100
= 29,880
If total population grows by 5% and all shares remain same, privately insured also grow by 5%.
Additional privately insured
= 29,880 × 5%
= 1,494.

112. Urban employer-covered
= 99,000 × 18%
= 17,820
Rural employer-covered
= 81,000 × 8%
= 6,480
Total employer-covered
= 17,820 + 6,480
= 24,300.

113. Total publicly insured
= Urban public + Rural public
= 99,000 × 28% + 81,000 × 35%
= 27,720 + 28,350
= 56,070
Total insured = 67,320 + 42,930 = 110,250

$$\text{Required percentage} = \frac{56,070}{110,250} \times 100$$

= 50.86% approximately.

114. Total insured = 110,250

Total surveyed population = 1,80,000

$$\text{Required percentage} = \frac{110,250}{180,000} \times 100$$

$$= 61.25\%.$$

115. Total annual generation

= 5,000 + 5,500 + 5,500 + 6,000

= 22,000 GWh.

116. Renewables = Hydro + Solar + Wind

Q1 = 900 + 700 + 400 = 2,000

Q2 = 1,000 + 800 + 600

= 2,400

Q3 = 800 + 1,000 + 700

= 2,500

Q4 = 1,100 + 900 + 850

= 2,850

Total renewables = 2,000 + 2,400 + 2,500 + 2,850

= 9,750

$$\text{Percentage share} = \frac{9,750}{22,000} \times 100$$

$$= 44.32\% \approx 44.3\%.$$

117.

$$Q1 = \frac{2,000}{5,000} = 40\%$$

$$Q2 = \frac{2,400}{5,500} \approx 43.64\%$$

$$Q3 = \frac{2,500}{5,500} \approx 45.45\%$$

$$Q4 = \frac{2,850}{6,000} = 47.5\%$$

Highest = Q4.

118. Reduction in Coal (Q4)

= 10% × 2,300

= 230

Shift equally to Solar and Wind

= 230 ÷ 2

= 115

New Solar = 900 + 115

= 1,015.

119. Gas total = 800 + 700 + 900 + 850

= 3,250

Hydro total = 900 + 1,000 + 800 + 1,100

= 3,800

Ratio = 3,250 : 3,800

Divide by 50 = 65 : 76.

120. Renewable %

Q1 = 40%

Q2 ≈ 43.64%

Q3 ≈ 45.45%

Q4 = 47.5%

Lowest = Q1.

Previous Years' Paper

Common Law Admission Test (CLAT-UG)

Entrance Exam, December 2024

(Exam held on 01-12-2024)

Section-I : English Language

I

From a very early age, I knew that when I grew up, I should be a writer. I had the lonely child's habit of making up stories and holding conversations with imaginary persons, and I think from the very start my literary ambitions were mixed up with the feeling of being isolated and undervalued. I knew that I had a facility with words and a power of facing unpleasant facts, and I felt that this created a sort of private world in which I could get my own back for my failure in everyday life. I wanted to write enormous naturalistic novels with unhappy endings, full of detailed descriptions and arresting similes, and also full of purple passages in which words were used partly for the sake of their sound. I give all this background information because I do not think one can assess a writer's motives without knowing something of his early development.

His subject-matter will be determined by the age he lives in – at least this is true in tumultuous, revolutionary ages like our own – but before he ever begins to write he will have acquired an emotional attitude from which he will never completely escape. It is his job to discipline his temperament, but if he escapes from his early influences altogether, he will have killed his impulse to write. I think there are four great motives for writing, at any rate for writing prose. They are: (*i*) Sheer egoism: Desire to seem clever, to be talked about, to be remembered after death, to get your own back on grown-ups who snubbed you in childhood; (*ii*) Aesthetic enthusiasm: Desire to share an experience which one feels is valuable and ought not to be missed (*iii*) Historical impulse: Desire to see things as they are, to find out true facts and store them up for the use of posterity (*iv*) Political purpose : Desire to push the world in a certain direction, to alter other people's idea of the kind of society that they should strive after

[*Extracted with edits from George Orwell's "Why I Write"*]

1. For the author, aesthetic enthusiasm is an important motive for writing because it ...

A. Shapes the thoughts
B. Creates an artistic piece
C. Becomes invaluable
D. Non-utilitarian

2. The author strongly advocates the writers to:

A. Avoid any egoistic impression in their work
B. Be apolitical in their approach
C. Be contemporary in their treatment of their work
D. None of the above

3. Which of the following is a synonym for the word "tumultuous"?

A. Chaotic B. Turbulent
C. Disorderly D. All of the above

4. George Orwell's loneliness during childhood led to:

A. Estrangement with his father
B. Unhappy days
C. Making up stories
D. Unpleasant incidents

5. Why does Orwell give background information?

A. He had the lonely child's habits
B. It is essential to know about motives of writers
C. Because of his historic impulse
D. Due to the aesthetic enthusiasm

6. If writer escapes from early impulses, he will ...

A. Lose his urge to write
B. Be unable to imagine creatively
C. Be able to converse with imaginary characters
D. Be able to influence others

II

Education is not the amount of information that is put into your brain and runs riot there, undigested, all your life. We must have life-building, man-making, character-making assimilation of ideas .... If education were identical with information, the libraries are the sages in the world and encyclopaedias are the rishis. Getting by heart the thoughts of others in a foreign language and stuffing your brain with them and taking some University degree, you consider yourself educated. Is this education? What is the goal of your education? Open your eyes and see what a piteous cry for food is rising in the land of Bharata, proverbial for its food. Will your education fulfill this want?

We want that education by which character is formed, strength of mind is increased, the intellect is expanded and by which one can stand on one's own feet. What we need to study independent of foreign control, different branches of the knowledge that is our own, and with it the English language and Western science; we need technical education and all else that will develop industries so that men instead of seeking for service may earn enough to provide for themselves and save against a rainy day. The end of all education, all training, should be man-making. The end and aim of all training are to make the man grow. The training by which the current expression of will are brought under control and become fruitful, is called education. What our country now wants are muscles of iron and nerves of steel, gigantic wills, which nothing can resist, which can penetrate into the mysteries and secrets of the universe and will accomplish their purpose in any fashion, even if it meant going down to the bottom of the ocean, meeting death face to face.

There is only one method of attaining knowledge. It is by concentration. The very essence of education is concentration of mind. From the lowest to the highest man, all have to use the same method to attain knowledge. The chemist who works in the laboratory concentrates on elements to analyze them. Knowledge is acquired by concentration.

[*Extracted with edits from "Education" by Swami Vivekananda*]

7. According to the author, we need to study:

A. English Language
B. Technical Education
C. Western Science
D. All of the above

8. According to the author, which among the following is key to attain knowledge?

A. University Degrees
B. Library
C. Concentration of mind
D. Hard work and sports training

9. Which of the following words is related to the word "assimilation"?

A. Integration B. Adjustment
C. Acclimatization D. All of the above

10. Education, as described by the author means:

A. Information B. Library
C. Degrees D. None of the above

11. As per the author, the aim of education should be:

A. To help a person build his/her character
B. To help a person earn his/her livelihood
C. To help a person develop his/her intellect
D. All of the above

12. According to the author the country wants:

A. Massive will power
B. Spirit of philanthropy
C. Iron and steel industries
D. All of the above

III

Punctually at midday, he opened his bag and spread out his professional equipment, which consisted of a dozen cowrie shells, a square piece of cloth with obscure mystic charts on it, a notebook, and a bundle of palmyra writing. His forehead was dazzling with sacred ash and vermilion, and his eyes sparkled with a sharp, abnormal gleam which was really an outcome of a continual searching look for customers, but which his simple clients took to be a prophetic light and felt comforted. The power of his eyes was considerably enhanced by their position—placed as they were between the painted forehead and the dark whiskers which streamed down his cheeks: even a half-wit's eyes would sparkle in such a setting. People were attracted to him as bees are attracted to cosmos or dahlia stalks. He sat under the boughs of a spreading tamarind tree which flanked a path running through the town hall park. It was a remarkable place in many ways: a surging crowd was always moving up and down this narrow road morning till night. A variety of trades and occupations was represented all along its way: medicine sellers, sellers of stolen hardware and junk, magicians, and, above all, an auctioneer of cheap cloth, who created enough din all day to attract the whole town. Next to him in vociferousness came a vendor of fried groundnut, who gave his ware a fancy name each day, calling it "Bombay Ice Cream" one day, and on the next "Delhi Almond", and on the third "Raja's Delicacy", and so on and so forth, and people flocked to him. A considerable portion of this crowd dallied before the astrologer too. The astrologer transacted his business by the light of a flare which crackled and smoked up above the groundnut heap nearby.

(Extracted with edits from "An Astrologer's Day" by R.K. Narayan)

13. Which among the following is the word for the phrase 'Bright and colourful in an impressive way'?

A. Mystic
B. Flare
C. Sparkle
D. Dazzling

14. Which among the following is not a trade or occupation represented in the pathway running through the town hall park?

A. Magicians
B. Medicine sellers
C. Auctioneers of cheap Bags
D. Sellers of Stolen Hardware

15. Who among the following used names like "Bombay Ice Cream", "Delhi Almond", and "Raja's Delicacy" to attract the crowd?

A. The sellers of cheap clothes
B. The sellers of Medicine
C. The ice cream seller
D. The groundnut seller

16. Which among the following is the meaning of the expression 'vociferousness'?

A. Expressing opinions or feelings in a loud and confident way
B. Words that are spoken or sung to have a magical effect
C. Willing or prepared to do something
D. To hang about aimlessly

17. When did the astrologer usually start his day's business?

A. When people are attracted to him as bees
B. When the surging crowd moves up and down the road
C. Punctually at midday
D. By the light of a flare

18. What was considered as a prophetic light by the simple clients of the astrologer?

A. The resplendent forehead of the astrologer with sacred ash and vermillion
B. The sparkling eyes of the astrologer with an abnormal gleam
C. The dark whiskers which streamed down the cheeks of the astrologer
D. The saffron coloured turban around the head of astrologer

IV

The right kind of education consists in understanding the child as he is without imposing upon him an ideal of what we think he should be. To enclose him in the framework of an ideal is to encourage him to conform, which breeds fear and produces in him a constant conflict between what he is and what he should be: and all inward conflicts have their outward manifestations in society. If the parent loves the child, he observes him, he studies his tendencies, his moods, and peculiarities. It is only when one feels no love for the child that one imposes upon him an ideal, for then one's ambitions are trying to fulfill themselves in him, wanting him to become this or that. If one loves, not the ideal but the child, then there is a possibility of helping him to understand himself as he is.

Ideals are a convenient escape, and the teacher who follows them is incapable of understanding his students and dealing with them intelligently; for him, the future ideal, the what should be, is far more important than the present child. The pursuit of an ideal excludes love, and without love no human problem can be solved. If the teacher is of the right kind, he will not depend on a method, but will study each individual pupil. In our relationship with children and young people, we are not dealing with mechanical devices that can be quickly repaired, but with living beings who are impressionable, volatile, sensitive, afraid, affectionate: and to deal with them, we have to have great understanding, the strength of patience and love. When we lack these, we look to quick and easy remedies and hope for marvellous and automatic results. If we are unaware, mechanical in our attitudes and actions, we fight shy of any demand upon us that is disturbing and that cannot be met by an automatic response, and this is one of our major difficulties in education.

(Extract with edits from "The right kind of Education" by J. Krishna Murti)

19. According to the passage, why do we look for quick and easy remedies and hope for marvellous and automatic results?

A. Because children are impressionable, volatile, sensitive, and affectionate
B. Because of major difficulties in education
C. Because we lack intelligence and skills
D. Because we lack understanding, patience and love

20. What does the passage highlight as the quality of a parent who really desires to understand his child?

A. They look at their child through the prism of an ideal
B. They observe and study the tendencies, moods, and peculiarities of the child
C. They love their child to become someone great as per their ambitions
D. They encourage the child to find out what she/he is and what she/he should be

21. What is the antonym for the word "volatile"?

A. Stable
B. Steady
C. Constant
D. All of the above

22. Which of the following currently reflects the intention of the author of this passage?
   A. The right kind of education for a child cannot be without love, care and understanding
   B. True education should be governed by a tendency to conform a child to our ideals
   C. The teacher should focus on how a child should be according to his/her methodology, hope, or expectation
   D. Parents and teachers should work together collectively to guide a child on what she/he should do as per their ambitions

23. In light of the above passage, what will be the result of forcing a child to conform to the framework of an ideal?
   A. It will make the child an ideal child
   B. It will create confusion and fear in the child
   C. The child will get into a conflict
   D. Will discourage the child to conform to the ideal

24. According to the author, what should be the attitude of a right kind of teacher?
   A. They should not empathise with the students
   B. They should use modern and scientific methods of teaching
   C. They should focus on studying each student individually
   D. They should instill great ideals in the student

Section-II : Current Affairs Including General Knowledge

V

Chinese President Xi Jinping and Indian Prime Minister Narendra Modi used a BRICS summit in Russia recently to showcase ambitions for a more harmonious relationship between the world's two most populous countries after years of animosity.

The meeting between Xi and Modi, who have not held formal talks for five years, was one highlight of a summit. BRICS also gave an opportunity to the Russian President Vladimir Putin for showcasing that the West had failed to isolate Russia over the Ukraine war.

A final communique listed a number of projects aimed at facilitating trade between BRICS nations - including an alternative payment system to the dollar - but did not include details or timelines.

Just two days after New Delhi announced that it had reached a deal with Beijing to resolve a four-year military stand-off on their disputed Himalayan frontier, Xi told Modi that they should enhance communication and cooperation and effectively manage differences.

BRICS - an idea thought up inside Goldman Sachs two decades ago to describe the growing economic clout of China and other major emerging markets - is now a group that accounts for 45% of the world's population and 35% of the global economy.

Former Goldman Sachs economist Jim O'Neill, who coined the BRIC term in 2001, told Reuters that he had little optimism for the BRICS club as long as China and India remained so divided.

"It seems to me basically to be a symbolic annual gathering where important emerging countries, particularly noisy ones like Russia, but also China, can basically get together and highlight how good it is to be part of something that doesn't involve the U.S. and that global governance isn't good enough".

The 43-page final communique from the summit ranged from geopolitics and narcotics to artificial intelligence and even the preservation of Big Cats, but lacked detail on some major issues. It mentioned Ukraine just once.

(Excerpts from "Putin scores a BRICS win with rare Xi and Modi show of harmony"

By Vladimir Soldatkin and Guy Faulconbridge, Reuters, October 23, 2024)

25. The 16th BRICS achieved the following:

A. Launch of BRICS currency
B. De scalation of Russian-Ukrainian conflict
C. Diplomatic dialogue between India and China
D. All of the above

26. What does the letter "S" in BRICS stand for?

A. Saudi Arabia B. Singapore
C. South America D. South Africa

27. The initiative of Big Cats Alliance refers to:

A. Lions, Tigers and Jaguar
B. Tigers, Jaguar and Leopard
C. Lions, Cheetah and Snow Leopard
D. All of the above

28. Which statement reflects as a critique from the Western Economists?

A. BRICS currency cannot displace Dollars
B. Asian economies will not impact western economy
C. Indo-China conflicts will impact progress of BRICS
D. All of the above

29. The emergence of BRICS signals:

A. Asian consolidation of economic power
B. Diminishing European dominance
C. Revival of Nonaligned movement
D. A geo-politics without US dominance

30. Which one of the below is an outcome of 16th BRICS meeting?

A. Proposal to end Russia-Ukraine war
B. To expand BRICS by including Scandinavian countries
C. To recognise China's claim of Taiwan
D. Reducing tension between India and China

VI

On the recommendation of Parliament, the President of India effectively abrogated Article 370 of the Indian Constitution and gave assent to the Jammu and Kashmir Reorganization Act, 2019. The former state of Jammu & Kashmir has been reorganized as the new Union Territory of Jammu and Kashmir and the new Union Territory of Ladakh on 31st October 2019.

The new Union Territory of Ladakh consists of two districts of Kargil and Leh. The rest of the former State of Jammu and Kashmir is in the new Union Territory of Jammu and Kashmir.

By 2019, the state government of former Jammu and Kashmir had reorganized the areas of these 14 districts into 28 districts. The names of the new districts are as follows - Kupwara, Bandipur, Ganderbal, Srinagar, Budgam, Pulwama, Shupian, Kulgam, Rajouri, Ramban, Doda, Kishtivar, Samba and Kargil.

Out of these, Kargil district was carved out from the area of Leh and Ladakh district. The Leh district of the new Union Territory of Ladakh has been defined in the Jammu and Kashmir Reorganization (Removal of Difficulties) Second Order, 2019, issued by the President of India, to include the areas of the districts of Gilgit, Gilgit Wazarat, Chilhas and Tribal Territory of 1947, in addition to the remaining areas of Leh and Ladakh districts of 1947, after carving out the Kargil District.

*[Extracted from the article of **Press Information Bureau, published by the Union Home Ministry on 2nd November 2019**]*

31. Which of the following statements regarding Article 370 of the Constitution of India is correct?

A. It gave special status to the erstwhile state of Jammu and Kashmir
B. It created a special tribunal for the state of Jammu and Kashmir on certain occasions
C. It introduced Goods and Services Tax in Jammu and Kashmir
D. It confers special jurisdiction on the Supreme Court on matters coming from Jammu & Kashmir

32. The Jammu and Kashmir Reorganisation Act, 2019, divided the erstwhile State of Jammu and Kashmir into which of the following?
    A. 2 States
    B. 1 State and 1 Union Territory
    C. 2 Union Territories
    D. 1 State and 2 Union Territories

33. Which of the following Union Territories of India has a legislative assembly?
    A. Andaman and Nicobar Islands
    B. Jammu and Kashmir
    C. Daman and Diu
    D. Lakshadweep

34. How many States and Union Territories are present in India?
    A. 28 states and 8 Union territories
    B. 27 states and 8 Union territories
    C. 28 states and 7 Union territories
    D. 27 states and 7 Union territories

35. Which among the following is the capital city of the Union Territory of Ladakh?
    A. Leh B. Changtang
    C. Dras D. Nubra

36. Which of the following is false?
    A. Kargil was formerly a union territory
    B. Ladakh is administered by J&K assembly
    C. Fifteen new districts were formed to be part of J&K in 2019
    D. All of the above

VII

The "Nari Shakti Vandan Adhiniyam", 2023 Act received near-unanimous support in both the Lok Sabha and the Rajya Sabha. The legislation mandates the reservation of one-third of all seats in the Lok Sabha, state legislative assemblies, and Delhi (as a union territory with an elected assembly) for women. This linking of the implementation of the Act to the implementing of two long-term exercises of census and delimitation, makes little sense to many, and sounds quite like empowerment delayed for now.

In a 2012 article 'Holding Up Half the Sky: Reservations for Women in India', Rudolf C Heredia breaks down the common misconceptions that cloud our understanding of women's political participation- "When women do attain a national leadership role it is often because they have inherited the mantle from their fathers or husbands, rather than as persons in their own right and are then projected as matriarchs, part of the joint family, complementary to the patriarchy rather than a challenge to it."

In 'Equality versus Empowerment: Women in Indian Legislature', 2023, Soumya Bhowmick makes the case for going a step beyond quotas, and to turn our attention to the complexities that shape women's agency in the country. This, he argues, would require a bottoms-up approach, rather than merely handing out reservations in a top-down manner. "In a country like India with a considerably large heterogeneous population, the dissemination of legislative power would be insufficient to protect the interests of minority groups such as women, Scheduled Castes, and Scheduled Tribes." He concludes that "implementing the idea of reservation for women would bring about descriptive representation, but its transformation into substantive representation would depend on the change in the attitudes of the people." While the reservation of one-third of seats for women belonging to the scheduled castes and tribes under the amendment to article 330(a) and 332 of the constitution is a welcome step, it remains to be seen whether it fully acknowledges the complex interplay of hierarchies, socio-political relationships which also affect the extent and nature of complications that surround effective realisation of women's politics for Indian politics to emerge as a truly emancipatory space.

37. The Nari Shakti Vandan Adhiniyam 2023:
    A. Will come to force from Jan 2025
    B. Will come to force after all the States and UTs approve it
    C. Will come to force after Census
    D. None of the above

38. As per Rudolf Heredia women's political leadership depends upon:

A. Mentorship of spouse's political affiliations

B. Parental guidance

C. Property inheritance

D. None of the above

39. According to Soumya Bhowmick the quotas for women should:

A. Require a top down model

B. Fulfill a descriptive representation

C. Transform to substantive representation

D. To be implemented homogeneously

40. The amendment to the Art. 330(a) & 332 aims to:

A. Appoint Rajya Sabha members based on cultural diversity

B. Quota for women Governors

C. Women sportspersons

D. None of the above

VIII

During the First World War, Indian merchants and industrialists wanted protection against imports of foreign goods, and a rupee-sterling foreign exchange ratio that would discourage imports. To organise business interests, they formed the Indian Industrial and Commercial Congress in 1920 and the Federation of the Indian Chamber of Commerce and Industries (FICCI) in 1927. The industrialists attacked colonial control over the Indian economy, and supported the Civil Disobedience Movement when it was first launched. They gave financial assistance and refused to buy or sell imported goods. After the failure of the Round Table Conference, business groups were no longer uniformly enthusiastic. They were apprehensive of the spread of militant activities, and worried about prolonged disruption of business, as well as of the growing influence of socialism amongst the younger members of the Congress.

The industrial working classes did not participate in the Civil Disobedience Movement in large numbers, except in the Nagpur region. As the industrialists came closer to the Congress, workers stayed aloof. But inspite of that, some workers did participate in the Civil Disobedience Movement, selectively adopting some of the ideas of the Gandhian programme, like boycott of foreign goods, as part of their own movements against low wages and poor working conditions. There were strikes by railway workers in 1930 and dockworkers in 1932. In 1930, thousands of workers in Chotanagpur tin mines wore Gandhi caps and participated in protest rallies and boycott campaigns. But the Congress was reluctant to include workers' demands as part of its programme of struggle. It felt that this would alienate industrialists and divide the anti-imperial forces.

Another important feature of the Civil Disobedience Movement was the large-scale participation of women. During Gandhiji's salt march, thousands of women came out of their homes to listen to him. They participated in protest marches, manufactured salt, and picketed foreign cloth and liquor shops. Many went to jail.

[Excerpt from Chapter II - Nationalism in India, India and the Contemporary World, NCERT]

41. Which event in Indian history marked the beginning of the Civil Disobedience Movement?

A. Launch of Non-Cooperation Movement

B. Commencing of Dandi March

C. Signing of Gandhi-Irwin Pact

D. Withdrawal of Non-Cooperation Movement

42. Which of the following is true in the context of civil disobedience movement?

A. The Indian industrialist preferred partnership with MNCs

B. The Indian industrialist were concerned of disruption of business

C. The working class rejected the civil disobedience movement

D. The Round Table Conference was a partial success

43. Which of the following was the predicament for Congress?

A. Danger of division of opposition to the British Government

B. Loss of faith by marginalised sections in Congress

C. Falling value of Rupee against Sterling

D. None of the above

44. Which of the following statements is correct with reference to the Civil Disobedience Movement?

A. It encouraged militancy among workers

B. Breaking of the salt law, manufacturing salt, and demonstrating it in front of government salt factories

C. It urged the industrialists to accept socialism

D. All of the above

45. Which among the following mass movement was supported by the Indian industrialists?

A. Home Rule Movement

B. Civil Disobedience Movement

C. Non-Cooperation Movement

D. Quit India Movement

46. Which of the following can be considered as major outcome of civil disobedience movement?

A. A partial support of working class

B. Galvanising women in political sphere

C. Socialistic influence among the Congress cadre

D. All of the above

IX

In keeping with the slogan for this year's Olympics, "Games Wide Open", the opening ceremony took place outside a stadium setting by the river for the first time. In many respects, the Paris Games turned out to be one of the most elaborate cultural rituals since Covid swept across the world beginning in late 2019. Health restrictions forced the organizers of Tokyo 2020 and Beijing 2022 to sharply limit the scale of the festivities, with events largely closed to the public. Paris 2024, powered in part by pent-up demand for communal experiences, symbolized an international post-pandemic vibe shift.

The International Olympic Committee and French officials managed strict security measures in place. Yet the recent history of violence in France — including the 2015 terror attack in Paris that left 138 people dead and at least 416 injured — stalked public consciousness prior to the games. The geopolitical backdrop for the Paris Games was no less troubling. The war between Israel and Hamas which had crossed the six-month mark, raised fears of a protracted conflict and wider regional instability. The devastation in the Gaza Strip has provoked international outrage, isolating Israel on the global stage. Meanwhile, Russia continues to gain ground in its military offensive against Ukraine as some Western nations worry about the rise of authoritarianism. These international crises raised serious concerns that could come into play during the Games in the form of protests and other political demonstrations.

Nevertheless, Olympics organizers put up a show that stunned the throngs assembled on the boulevards of Paris, not to mention the millions of people who watched the Games unfold on their televisions and mobile devices. At the Paris 2024 Olympics, India secured a total of six medals: one silver and five bronze which was one down from the highest haul of medals from the previous Olympics.

Neeraj Chopra earned a silver in men's javelin with an 89.45 throw, narrowly missing gold to Pakistan's Arshad Nadeem. Shooter Manu Bhaker made history by clinching bronze in the women's 10'm air pistsol, becoming the first Indian woman to win a medal in Olympic shooting. The men's hockey team achieved a second consecutive bronze, defeating Spain 2-1, with captain Harmanpreet Singh scoring both goals.

(Extracted, with edits and revision, from "The Olympics are nearly here. For a weary world, they can't come soon enough", NBCNEWS)

47. India won a back-to-back Olympics hockey medal at:
A. Beijing and Paris
B. Rio and Beijing
C. Beijing and Tokyo
D. None of the above

48. According to the passage, what is the peculiarity of the Paris Olympics, 2024?
A. It symbolized an international post-pandemic vibe shift
B. The opening ceremony took place outside a stadium
C. It is one of the most elaborate cultural rituals since Covid
D. All of the above

49. Which of the following incidents support the argument that "the geopolitical backdrop for the Paris Games is no less troubling"?
A. Israel-Hamas conflict
B. The immigrant influx in to Europe
C. Political stability of French government
D. All of the above

50. Which one of the following is true?
A. Tokyo Olympics was better than Beijing Olympics
B. Spectators thronged for a post Covid sporting experience
C. Olympic games are unaffected by conflicts in a region
D. All of the above

51. The highest Olympic medal tally for India was at:
A. Beijing
B. Rio
C. London
D. Tokyo

52. Where is the opening ceremony of the Paris Olympics, 2024, held?
A. Seine River
B. Versailles Palace
C. Eiffel Tower
D. Arc de Triomphe

Section-III : Legal Reasoning

X

Children come in contact with the criminal justice system either as victims or witnesses to a crime or as children in conflict with law (CICL). As CICL, they could be alleged of, accused or recognised as having broken the law by committing a crime. According to the National Crime Records Bureau (NCRB) Report 2021, India recorded a total number of 1,49,404 instances of crimes against children in 2021 — a rise of over 16 per cent from the previous year. In terms of percentage, the top categories under crime against children were kidnapping and abduction, followed by cases registered under the POCSO Act. Further, the NCRB report revealed that of the total cases, 53,874 were registered under POCSO Sections. Sexual offences against children shows a steady ascent, with 47,221 such cases being recorded in 2020, and 47,335 cases in 2019. In 2019, as many as 32,269 cases were registered across the country, while the 2021 report registered a decline of 3.5 per cent recording 31,170 cases.

The Criminal Justice system of any country broadly refers to agencies of the government charged with enforcing law, adjudicating crime, and correcting criminal conduct. The main objective of the criminal justice system is 'deterrence', i.e., to punish the 'transgressors and the criminals' and to maintain law and order in the society. Globally, children and young people are routinely exposed to various forms of violence if they are before the criminal justice system. They are at risk of physical and psychological abuse, sexual assault, and other harms, including inadequate educational opportunities, poor and outdated vocational training. They face several challenges including mental, emotional, and behavioural disorders. Children, who are victims of violence or exposed to violence during childhood, are more likely to have difficulty in school, abuse drugs or alcohol, act aggressively, suffer from depression or other mental health problems and engage in criminal behaviour as adults.

[*Extracted, with edits and revisions from "Child Rights in the Criminal Justice System: Need for Law Reform" written by Dr. Asha Bajpai published in the Journal of the National Human Rights Commission, India*].

53. Which of the following issues, children, who are victims of violence during childhood face in life, as per the author of the above passage?

A. They may have difficulties in school
B. They may abuse drugs or alcohol and suffer from mental health problems
C. They may act aggressively and engage in criminal behaviours
D. All of the above

54. What is the primary objective of the criminal justice system as mentioned in the passage?

A. Rehabilitation of offenders
B. Punishment of the offenders
C. Reformation of the offenders
D. Protection of victims from the offender

55. The National Crime Records Bureau (NCRB) in India is responsible for:

A. Conducting forensic investigations of Records of Criminals
B. Maintaining a national database of fingerprints of Criminals
C. Compiling and analysing crime data
D. Maintaining a national database of enforcement of criminal laws

56. Which category had the highest number of cases under crimes against children according to the NCRB Report 2021?

A. POCSO
B. Kidnapping and abduction
C. Sexual Offences
D. All of the above

57. Which one of the following is the correct expansion of the term POCSO used in the passage?

A. Protection of Children from Sexual Offences
B. Prosecution of Criminals of Sexual Offences
C. Protection of Children & Women from Sexual Offences
D. None of the above

58. What risks do children face when exposed to the criminal justice system as per the passage?

A. Limited access to vocational training
B. Exposed to risk of physical abuse
C. Mental health challenges and behavioural disorders
D. All of the above

XI

The 42nd Constitutional Amendment Act 1976 introduced the concept of environmental protection in an explicit manner into the Constitution through introduction of Article 48-A and Article 51-A (g). In many judgments, the Supreme Court ruled that both the state and its residents have a fundamental duty to preserve and protect their natural resources. The recent judgment obliquely makes way for an enforceable right, and a potential obligation on the state unless the same is overturned by an Act of Parliament.

India is signatory of various international environmental conservâtion treaties under which India has the binding commitment to reduce carbon emission. During the COP 21, India signed Paris Agreement along with 196 countries, under which universally binding agreement was made to limit greenhouse gas emission to levels that would prevent global temperatures from increasing to more than 1.5 degree Celsius before the industrial revolution. India has committed to generating 50% of its energy through renewable resources and will generate 500 GW of energy from non-fossil fuels by 2030, reducing the carbon emission by 1 billion ton. Additionally, India has committed to achieve net zero carbon emission target by 2070.

Supreme Court's March 21, 2024 verdict builds on the bulwark of jurisprudence in place since 1986, and, through various other judgments, the Supreme Court has recognised the right to clean environment along with right to clean air, water and soil free from pollution which is absolutely necessary for the enjoyment of life. Any disturbance with these basic elements of environment would amount to violation of Article 21. It also establishes duty of the state to maintain ecological balance and hygienic environment. Although right to clean environment has existed, by recognizing the right against climate change it shall compel the states to prioritize environmental protection and sustainable development.

(Extracted, with edits and revision, from "Supreme Court of India bolts Right to Life with climate justice", The Economic Times, 06-05-2024)

59. In which among the following, changes were introduced for environmental protection through the Constitution of India (42nd Amendment) Act?

1. Fundamental Rights
2. Fundamental Duties
3. Directive Principles of State Policy

A. 1 & 2 only B. 2 & 3 only
C. 1 & 3 only D. 1, 2 & 3

60. The nature of binding commitment of India to reduce carbon emission through the signing of various international environmental conservation treaties especially the Paris Agreement may be described as:

A. The signatory shall take adequate measures to reduce carbon emission
B. The signatory may take adequate measures to reduce carbon emission
C. The signatory should explore the possibility to reduce carbon emission
D. The signatory may formulate necessary policies to reduce carbon emission

61. Under Article 51-A(g) of the Indian Constitution, it is specifically mentioned that citizens shall have the duty to protect and improve the natural environment that includes:

A. Rivers & Lakes
B. Forests & Wildlife
C. All living Creatures
D. Only (A) and (B)

62. As per the aforementioned passage and decision of the Supreme Court:

A. The fundamental duty to preserve and protect natural resources is upon the State only
B. Citizens alone have the fundamental duty to preserve and protect natural resources
C. Both the state and citizens have the duty to preserve and protect natural resources
D. State's duty to maintain ecological balance and citizens right against climate change

63. According to the passage, what makes India committed to reduce carbon emission?

A. Because of being a signatory of international environmental conservation treaties
B. Because of the Supreme Court verdicts which obliquely make way for an enforceable right
C. Because of the policy decisions of Government
D. Because of the Constitution of India (42nd Amendment) Act

64. The passage mentions that "any disturbance with these basic elements of environment would amount to violation of Article 21". Article 21 of the Constitution deals with:

A. Right to equality
B. Right against exploitation
C. Right to freedom of residence
D. Right to life and personal liberty

XII

The Contract Act 1872 deals with contract law in India, its rights, duties, and exceptions arising out of it. Section 2(h) of the Act gives us the definition of a contract, which is simply an agreement enforceable by law. To understand the difference between void agreements and voidable contracts it is important to talk about sections 2(h), 2(a), 2(i), 2(d), 14, 16 (3) and 15, 24-28 of the Indian Contact Act. Void agreements, are fundamentally invalid making them unenforceable by default. These agreements cannot be fulfilled as they consist of illegal elements and they cannot be enforced even after subjecting it to both parties. However, in the case of voidable contract, the agreement is initially enforceable but it is later on denied at the option of either of the parties due to various reasons.

Unless rejected by a party, this contract will remain valid and enforceable. The party who is at the disadvantage due to any circumstance applicable to the contract has the ability to render the agreement void. A void agreement is void ab initio making it impossible to rectify any defects in it while voidable contracts can be rectified. In case of a void agreement, neither of the parties is subject to any compensation for any losses but voidable contracts have some remedies.

A valid agreement forms a contract that may again be either valid or voidable. The primary difference between a void agreement and voidable contract is that a void agreement cannot be converted into a contract.

(Extracted with edits from A Comparative Study of Voidable Contracts and Void Agreements)

65. Which of the following best describes a void agreement?

A. An agreement that is valid until declared invalid by a court
B. An agreement that has no legal effect from the beginning
C. An agreement that is legally enforceable
D. An agreement that can be enforced if one party chooses to do so

66. A contract between two parties to rob a bank and share the proceeds equally can be termed as:

A. Void Contract
B. Valid Contract
C. Voidable Contract
D. Legally Enforceable Contract

67. An agreement made by an adult but involving a minor child where the signatory is a minor child himself, this agreement would be:

A. A valid and enforceable agreement
B. A voidable agreement
C. A void agreement
D. An agreement that cannot be enforced by the minor

68. Which of the following scenarios would most likely result in a void agreement?

A. An agreement signed by someone under duress
B. A contract with mutually agreed terms to sell a house
C. An agreement to pay 10 lakhs on getting a government job
D. A contract with a minor who understands the terms

69. An agreement made without consideration is generally:

A. Valid agreement
B. Enforceable agreement
C. Void agreement
D. Voidable agreement

XIII

Geographical Indications (GIs) are a form of intellectual property that designates a product as originating from a specific geographic location, where a given quality, reputation, or other characteristic is essentially attributable to its geographic origin. GIs protect names that are used to identify products with specific qualities or characteristics due to their geographic origin. For example, 'Champagne' refers to sparkling wine produced in the Champagne region of France, and 'Darjeeling Tea' refers to tea grown in the Darjeeling region of India. The protection of GIs ensures that only products genuinely originating from a specific region are allowed to use the geographical name. This helps maintain the product's reputation and quality, prevents misuse or imitation, and supports local economies by promoting regional products. International agreements such as the TRIPS Agreement under the World Trade Organization (WTO) provide a framework for the protection of GIs globally.

70. Which of the following statements about Geographical Indications (GIs) is not true?

A. GIs are protected under international law to ensure that only products from specific regions can use the GI name.

B. The use of a GI name can be legally challenged if it is used by products not originating from the specified region.

C. Geographical Indications (GI) can be used to any product which is licenced regardless of its place of origin.

D. The TRIPS Agreement under the WTO establishes a framework for the protection of GIs on a global scale.

71. If a product named "Darjeeling Tea" is produced outside of the Darjeeling region, which of the following legal actions is likely to be taken under GI protection laws?

A. The product can still be sold but with a disclaimer about its true origin

B. The use of the GI name "Darjeeling Tea" can be legally contested and potentially prohibited

C. The product can be sold under a different GI name of "Not Darjeeling Tea"

D. The product can be marketed as "Darjeeling Tea" and will face no legal consequences

72. Which of the following is not a potential consequence of the misuse of a Geographical Indication?

A. Loss of consumer trust in the authenticity of the product.

B. Decrease in the market value of the GI-protected product.

C. Compulsory license on the patents of the misusing entity.

D. Potential Legal action of infringement against the misuse.

73. In the context of GIs, which of the following scenarios best illustrates the concept of "geographic origin"?

A. A product's name is changed to reflect its local ingredients rather than its place of production

B. A product is marketed with a GI name even though it is produced in a different region and country

C. A product is identified by a GI name that corresponds to the region where it is traditionally made/cultivated with distinctive qualities due to that location

D. A product is sold under a generic name with no reference to its production location

74. Choose the most appropriate objective of the TRIPS Agreement concerning Geographical Indications:

A. To harmonize intellectual property laws across member countries

B. To ensure uniform product labelling standards globally

C. To provide a framework for the protection and enforcement of Geographical Indications among WTO members

D. To promote international trade by standardizing product names and prices

XIV

The Public Examinations (Prevention of Unfair Means) Act, 2024 that has provision for up to five years' imprisonment and a fine of up to ₹ 1 crore for malpractices and organized cheating in government recruitment exams was notified by the Union government and came into effect from June 21, 2024. The Bill had received assent from the President of India on the 13th February 2024. The Public Examinations (Prevention of Unfair Means) Act, 2024 mentions punishments for "leakage of question paper or answer key", "directly or indirectly assisting the candidate in any manner unauthorisedly in the public examination" and "tampering with the computer network or a computer resource or a computer system" as offences done by a person, group of persons or institutions.

Besides these, "creation of fake website to cheat or for monetary gain", "conduct of fake examination, issuance of fake admit cards or offer letters to cheat or for monetary gain" and "manipulation in seating arrangements, allocation of dates and shifts for the candidates to facilitate adopting unfair means in examinations" are also among the offences punishable under the law. "Any person or persons resorting to unfair means and offences under this Act shall be punished with imprisonment for a term not less than three years but which may extend to five years and with fine up to ₹10 lakh", said the Act. A service provider, engaged by the public examination authority for conduct of examinations, shall also be liable to be punished with imposition of a fine up to ₹ 1 crore "and proportionate cost of examination shall also be recovered" from it, according to the Act. Such service providers shall also be barred from being assigned with any responsibility for the conduct of any public examination for a period of four years.

[*Extracted, with edits and revisions from "Act that Punishes Organized Cheating in Government Exams Comes into Effect" published in The Hindu dated 22-06-2024*]

75. A Bill becomes an Act only when ....

A. Both the houses of the Parliament pass with simple majority

B. Both the houses of the Parliament pass with absolute majority

C. When the Prime Minister of India gives his approval

D. When the President of India gives the Assent

76. A service provider, engaged by the public examination authority for conduct of examinations, indirectly helped his family member by giving hint on questions that were supposed to be asked in the examination shall:

A. be liable to be punished with imposition of a fine of ₹1 crore

B. be liable to be punished with imposition of a fine upto ₹1 crore

C. be liable to be punished with imposition of a fine upto ₹1 crore and the entire cost of conduct of the examination

D. None of the above

77. An invigilator of a public examination found guilty of manipulating the seating arrangement to favour his relative writing the public examination is punished by the Court. Which among the following is the appropriate punishment as per the punishment mentioned in the above passage?

A. Imprisonment for 1 year and fine of 1 lakh

B. Imprisonment for 2 years and a fine of 10 lakhs

C. Imprisonment for 3 years and fine of 15 lakhs

D. Imprisonment for 4 years and fine of 5 lakhs

78. Identify which of the following is not an unfair means relating to the conduct of a public examination?

A. Coaching Centre conducting mock tests for students
B. The Coaching Centre offering help to its students during the examination
C. The Centre Superintendent of the public examination on the request of the Coaching Centre provides seating arrangement of all its students in one hall
D. The Centre Superintendent of the public examination indirectly assisting the candidate

79. Who among the following is not a service provider in the context of a public examination?
A. Coaching Centre which prepares students for passing in the public examination
B. Printing Press where the question paper of the public examination is printed
C. The Software Company that manages the website of the public examination
D. The Company which scans the OMR sheets of the public examination

XV

The Supreme Court of India declared that the right to privacy is a fundamental right and that the right to informational privacy is part of this right. Subsequently, the Parliament of India enacted a new law relating to digital personal data protection. The law applies to Indian residents and businesses collecting the data of Indian residents. It also applies to non-citizens living in India whose data processing is "in connection with any activity related to the offering of goods or services" that happens outside India. The law allows personal data to be processed for any lawful purpose. If the personal data is sensitive, then additional safeguards are to be observed. The entity processing data can do so either by taking the concerned individual's consent or for "legitimate uses"- which include situations where an individual has voluntarily provided personal data for a specified purpose. The law requires that an individual's consent must be "free, specific, informed, unconditional and unambiguous with a clear affirmative action" and for a specific purpose. The data collected has to be limited to that necessary for the specified purpose. A clear notice containing these details has to be provided to consumers, including the rights of the concerned individual and the grievance redressal mechanism. Individuals have the right to withdraw consent if consent is the ground on which data is being processed. The law also creates rights and obligations for individuals. These include the right to get a summary of all the collected data and to know the identities of all other entities/ organisations with whom the personal data has been shared, along with a description of the data shared. Individuals also have the right to correction, completion, updating, and erasure of their data. Besides, they have a right to obtain redressal for their grievances and a right to nominate persons who will receive their data.

[Excerpts from Anirudh Burman, "Understanding India's New Data Protection Law", CARNEGIE INDIA, October 03, 2023]

80. An Indian company collects personal data from its users to provide personalized services. The company intends to share this data with a third-party vendor for targeted advertisements. Under the digital personal data protection law in India, what must the company do before sharing the data?
A. Obtain explicit consent from the users
B. Share the data by informing the users, as it is for business purposes
C. Encrypt the data and share it with the third-party vendor
D. Inform the third-party vendor that the data is sensitive

81. A social media platform processes user data based on the consent given during account creation. A user now wishes to withdraw consent to process their data. Under the digital personal data protection law in India, what must the platform do?

A. Refuse to accept the withdrawal request since consent was already given
B. Comply with the legal requirements and stop processing the data
C. Continue processing the data but notify the user
D. Allow withdrawal only after 30 days

82. A financial institution collects biometric data from its clients for verification purposes. If the clients wish to know what data has been collected, under the digital personal data protection law in India, what right allows them to request this information?

A. Right to Data Portability
B. Right to Correction
C. Right to Access
D. Right to Be Forgotten

83. A startup provides a health-tracking app that collects sensitive health data from users. Under the digital personal data protection law in India, what additional precautions must the startup take compared to regular personal data?

A. No additional measures are needed
B. Ensure explicit consent and adopt higher security standards
C. Store the data only with the government agencies
D. Store the data only with the hospitals and other health care institutions

84. As per the passage, what are the rights included under the digital data protection law of India?

1. Right to get the summary of collected data
2. Right to know to whom the data has been shared
3. Right to correct and update the data
4. Right to get the data removed from the database
5. Right to decide on who can receive their data
6. Right to get redressal of grievances

A. 1, 2, 5 and 6
B. 1, 3, 4 and 6
C. 1, 3, 5 and 6
D. 1, 2, 3, 4, 5 and 6

Section-IV : Logical Reasoning

XVI

While a majority of homeless groups exist solely in modernized cultures, homelessness remains a problem throughout the world. Everywhere there are people in constant search of food, water and shelter. Many of these people have nowhere to go and can find no end or relief to their suffering. Homelessness was originally believed to be a cultural problem but is now revealing itself as a global problem. It is a problem suffered by all of humanity and must be faced and solved as such. Although this problem exists everywhere, it is more severe in certain parts of the world. Due to the differing circumstances of homelessness around the world, there can be no one solution or one set of guidelines for everyone to follow.

Even the United States constantly struggles with homelessness, despite being one of the wealthiest countries in the world. According to a 2005 survey by the United Nations, 1.6 billion people lack adequate housing. The causes vary depending on the place and person. Common reasons include a lack of affordable housing, poverty, a lack of mental health services, and more. Homelessness is rooted in systemic failures that fail to protect those who are most vulnerable. Approximately 5,80,000 people experience homelessness on any given night in the United States, as stated by the Housing and Urban Development (HUD) Department of the United States. The number of individuals experiencing homelessness varies by region, with urban areas experiencing higher rates of homelessness compared to rural areas.

The COVID-19 pandemic has exacerbated homelessness and housing insecurity, leading to increased rates of eviction, unemployment, and housing instability. Using social distancing measures to curb the virus's transmission has presented difficulties for homeless shelters and service providers in maintaining their capacity. The economic fallout from the pandemic has further strained resources and support systems for individuals and families experiencing homelessness.

(Extracted with revisions and modifications from an article 'The impact of COVID-19 and housing insecurity on lower-income women' published in Journal of Social Issues, October 3, 2022)

85. For the above paragraph, which of the following statements is true?

A. When people in industrialized civilizations think of homelessness, they generally imagine third-world countries where poverty is rampant

B. Generally, the impoverished are thought of to exist in third-world countries only, but they are present even in the largest cities of the world

C. Homelessness increases due to major turbulence on the economic and cultural aspects

D. All of the Above

86. There are several causes of homelessness; which of the following is the least likely a cause of homelessness?

A. Violence in the home

B. Loss of job or income

C. Substance abuse

D. Proper health care

87. Homelessness in case of mental illness can be amplified because of the following reason:

A. The stress of being homeless may exacerbate previous mental illness and encourage anxiety, fear, depression, sleeplessness and substance use

B. People with mental illness remain homeless for longer periods of time and have less contact with family and friends.

C. Poor mental health predisposes individuals to homelessness and homelessness exposes individuals further to particularly severe health problems.

D. All of the above

88. Homelessness in reference to the above paragraph can be observed most closely in the form of:

A. Inadequate entertainment avenues

B. Shortage of appropriate clothing

C. Poor prospects for employment

D. Inadequate medial services

89. Approximately how many people in America are currently experiencing homelessness on any given day?

A. 1 million people

B. More than 5.5 million

C. 3.5 million

D. 100 million

90. Which of the following is not a myth about people experiencing homelessness?

A. People who are homeless choose to be so, by themselves

B. People experiencing homelessness are lazy

C. All people who experience homelessness are addicts

D. People experiencing homelessness find it difficult to obtain a job

XVII

Being a consultant, your work consists of a deep examination of the company's environment and its internal system to notice inefficiencies and potential improvements. The interaction with the company's management and different sections to decipher their objectives, opportunities, and processes. This means that, through the use of data analysis, ndustry best practices, and the formulation of creative ways of solving all problems, to come up with unique solutions to all problems to increase efficiency and productivity, and hence, increase profitability for employers. This might entail operations such as logistics redesign, business process reengineering, adopting new applications, systems, or even community relation programs. People management is a critical component of change management, to make sure that all the relevant parties interpret the potential alterations positively. Also, to offer orientation and create resources to explain the changes to the group and make it comfortable with the shift.

The general goal is the organization's ability to continue to grow and remain relevant with the shareholders and stakeholders in the industries it operates.

91. What is the primary responsibility of you being a company's efficient consultant?

A. Analyzing the organization's structure, processes, and market position
B. Managing daily operations
C. Hiring new employees
D. Conducting maintenance

92. With whom does a consultant work closely to understand a company's goals and challenges?

A. Customers
B. Higher management and various departments
C. External vendors
D. Competitors

93. Imagine yourself as a consultant and find what methods you will use to develop customized solutions?

A. Intuition and guesswork
B. Social media trends
C. Random selection
D. Data analysis, industry best practices, and innovative strategies

94. Which of the following might a consultant optimize to improve company efficiency?

A. Office decoration
B. Supply chain management
C. Employee dress code
D. Lunch menus

95. Why is communication the most relevant thing for a consultant?

A. To ensure all stakeholders understand the proposed changes
B. To organize consumer meets
C. To update the company website
D. To manage the human resources

96. What additional support might a consultant provide to help the team adapt to new processes?

A. Planning a retreat for the team members
B. Training and support
C. Personal counselling
D. Mental Health programs

XVIII

Read the information carefully and answer the questions based on the seating arrangement: "Ram, Shyam, Rohit, Mohit, Rohan, Sohan, Mohan, Rakesh and Suresh are sitting around a circle facing the centre. Rohit is third to the left of Ram. Rohan is fourth to the right of Ram. Mohit is fourth to the left of Suresh who is second to the right of Ram. Sohan is third to the right of Shyam. Mohan is not an immediate neighbour of Ram."

97. What is Rakesh's position with respect to Rohan?

A. Eighth to the right of Ram
B. Fourth to the left
C. Fifth to the right
D. Fifth to the left

98. Who is third to the right of Mohan?

A. Shyam
B. Mohit
C. Ram
D. None of these

99. Who is fifth to the right of Rohan?

A. Sohan B. Rohit
C. Rakesh D. Suresh

100. Who is second to the left of Rakesh?

A. Ram B. Mohan
C. Mohit D. Data inadequate

101. Who is the immediate right of Mohit?

A. Sohan B. Rohit
C. Ram D Data inadequate

102. Who is third to the right of Sohan?

A. Rohit B. Rohan
C. Rakesh D. Shyam

XIX

India is poised for rapid economic growth, potentially spurred by a young population driving production and demand. In the process, inevitably, lifestyles are being dramatically altered for the worse. India now reports the highest growth of ultra-processed food consumption among the youth, as well as low levels of exercise and adequate sleep. Cultural changes, including smartphones and a preponderance of English in schools, are also associated with weakened family relationships. Until recently, in the absence of extensive data, the role of these factors on mental well-being, encompassing our full range of mental capability, was not well understood. Recent findings based on a large database of over 1,50,000 individuals in India are beginning to shed light on the correlates of mental well-being among adolescents. The findings are dire. There is a silent epidemic of mental ill-health in India. Previous studies have found that ownership of smartphones is "frying" the brain. Data also suggests that it is not merely the ownership of a phone but also the early age of access that is associated with worse cognition and mental well-being as young adults. The young brain is developing and must be nurtured. These gadgets are handed to adolescents, presumably more out of convenience than sound logic. The American philosopher David Henry Thoreau remarked over 175 years ago, "Technology is an improved means to an unimproved end". This is an extreme position but one worth mulling. India reports the highest growth in consumption of ultra-processed foods. Some evidence suggests that these foods are as addictive as smoking. Recent data globally and from India shows a strong association between the consumption of ultra-processed foods and poor mental well-being, particularly the capacities for emotional and cognitive control.

[Source-V. Anantha Nageswaran and Shailender Swaminathan, "How our lifestyle is creating an epidemic of mental ill health", THE INDIAN EXPRESS, September 7, 2024]

103. Based on the above passage, which of the following should be the most suitable title for the passage?

A. Lifestyle and Mental Health
B. Economic Growth and Mental Health
C. Impact of Technology on the Youth
D. Language and Cultural Change

104. Consider the given statement "Technology is an improved means to an unimproved end". Which of the following closely reflects the meaning of the given statement?

A. New technologies have to be accepted by primarily focusing on its positive results
B. New technologies create a hindrance to the physical health of an individual
C. Poor mental health is a result of the invention of new technologies
D. New technologies should be looked upon with scepticism, considering its negative impact

105. Which of the following statements strengthens the author's argument regarding the negative use of smartphones among the youth?

A. Excessive use of smartphones may lead to weakened family relationships
B. There has to be an unhindered use of smartphones
C. Smartphones have economic usefulness
D. Ownership of smartphones at an early age results due to lack of care by parents

106. Which of the following can be a plausible solution for better mental well-being among the youth?

A. Limiting the correlation between physical and mental health

B. Limiting the research on excessive use of smartphones

C. Limiting the widespread consumption of ultra-processed foods

D. Limiting the informed use of smartphones across all age groups

107. Which of the following statements by the author lack credible evidence in the passage?

A. Excessive mobile usage linked to mental health issues

B. Providing mobiles to adolescents resulting in mental stress

C. Students learning the English language have weakened family relationships

D. Inadequate sleep and junk food resulting in mental distress

108. "These gadgets are handed to adolescents, presumably more out of convenience than sound logic." Which of the following is the most suitable explanation echoed by the author as per the given statement?

A. Logic prevails over reasoning

B. Logic and emotions go hand in hand

C. Logic taking a backseat over utility

D. Logic and benefits can never be understood together

Section-V : Quantitative Techniques

XX

According to the estimates of the World Inequality Report 2022, in India, men earn 82 percent of the labour income, whereas women earn 18 percent of it. A woman agriculture field labourer makes ₹ 88 per day lesser than her male counterpart, according to the Ministry of Agriculture's data for 2020-21. While a man is paid ₹ 383 a day on an average, a woman makes a mere ₹ 294 a day. The gap in their daily wages is more than the cost of two kilograms of rice. This gap differs from State to State. Field laborers, for instance, make the most money in Kerala. While a man gets ₹ 789 per day, a woman is paid ₹ 537. While this is the highest amount paid to a woman labourer in a State, it is also ₹ 252 lesser than what her male counterpart was paid. As of 2020-21, Tamil Nadu has the highest gender wage gap among agriculture field laborers at 112 per cent. It is followed by Goa (61 percent) and Kerala. The wage gap is the lowest in Jharkhand and Gujarat (6 percent each), but the women laborers there get paid just ₹ 239 and ₹ 247 per day, respectively.

Men earn more than women across all forms of work, the gap greatest for the self-employed. In 2023, male self-employed workers earned 2.8 times that of women. In contrast, male regular wage workers earned 24% more than women and male casual workers earned 48% more. The gender gap in earnings is still a persistent phenomenon. However, there are differences in trends. The gender gap has increased for self-employed workers, while falling for regular wage workers. Male regular wage workers earned 34% more than women from 2019 to 2022, with the gap falling to 24% in 2023.

109. If the wages paid to men working in agricultural sector in Goa are ₹ 335 on an average, what is the amount of wages paid to women in the region?

A. ₹ 204 approx. B. ₹ 330 approx.

C. ₹ 239 approx. D. None of these

110. With reference to the information in Ques. 109 above, which region of the below mentioned states offers the least wages to the women workers in any sector?

A. Gujarat B. Goa

C. Kerala D. Jharkhand

111. In 2023, if the average annual income of female self-employed workers is ₹ 250, how much do male self-employed workers earn on an average?

A. ₹ 550 B. ₹ 673
C. ₹ 700 D. None of these

112. If a female casual worker earns ₹ 200 per hour, what is the hourly wage of a male casual worker, given that male casual workers earn 48% more than female casual workers?

A. ₹ 480
B. ₹ 296
C. ₹ 248
D. Cannot be determined

113. Assume that in 2022, the earnings gap between male and female self-employed workers was 2.5 times. In 2023, the gap increased to 2.8 times. What is the percentage increase in the earnings gap for self-employed workers from 2022 to 2023?

A. 12% B. 5%
C. 4.8% D. 24%

114. Which of the following statement is correct?

A. The wage gap of Goa and Kerala state is less than Tamil Nadu
B. The wage gap of Tamil Nadu is greater than Jharkhand and Gujarat
C. Both (A) and (B)
D. None of the above

XXI

Mr. Das is working in a construction company. He has a family, including his wife and a daughter. His total monthly income includes a salary of ₹ 9228/- and a 10% house rent allowance. Due to increasing inflation, he is keeping a home budget that accounts for the income and expenses of the household. Out of his total monthly income, he spends 25% on food expenses, 18% on paying the house-rent, 9% on entertainment, 23% on the education of his child, 13% on medical expenses, and he saves 12% of his total monthly income.

Based on the above information, answer the following questions.

115. How much money does Mr. Das pay as the house-rent?

A. ₹ 1827/- B. ₹ 1661/-
C. ₹ 1783/- D. ₹ 1935/-

116. If Mr. Das gets 12% annual interest on the savings and he wishes to save ₹ 30,000/- in two years period, how much extra should he save in the next year?

A. ₹ 1200/-
B. ₹ 1300/-
C. ₹ 1400/-
D. There is no need for saving

117. Which of the following is true regarding the home budget of Mr. Das?

A. The total amount spent on house-rent, entertainment and education is greater than the total amount spent on food expenses, medical expenses and savings
B. The total amount spent on entertainment, medical expenses and education is equal to the total amount spent on house-rent, food expenses and savings
C. The total amount spent on savings, medical expenses and education is less than the total amount spent on house-rent, food expenses and entertainment
D. None of the above

118. How much money remains for other expenses after the house-rent and savings?

A. ₹ 7061/- B. ₹ 7601/-
C. ₹ 7106/- D. ₹ 7016/-

119. If the expenditure on food and entertainment is increased by 10% due to inflation in prices, what will be the new percentage of savings in the same monthly salary?

A. 8.4% B. 8.6%
C. 8.8% D. 8.2%

120. How much total money has he spent on food and entertainment?

A. ₹ 3541 B. ₹ 3461
C. ₹ 3371 D. None of the above

EXPLANATORY ANSWERS

1. **(C):** Aesthetic enthusiasm is described as the desire to share an experience that is inherently valuable and not to be missed. It underlines the importance of preserving the intrinsic value of creative expressions that can transcend time and make a lasting impact on readers. This motive emphasizes the significance of crafting something profound and meaningful through writing.

2. **(D):** The author does not advocate avoiding egoism, being apolitical, or adhering strictly to contemporary themes. Instead, Orwell emphasizes that writers should recognize the motives driving their work, which often include egoism, aesthetic enthusiasm, historical impulse, and political purpose. These motives collectively shape a writer's expression and the authenticity of their content.

3. **(D):** The word "tumultuous" is synonymous with "chaotic", "turbulent", and "disorderly". It reflects a state of great disturbance or upheaval, which fits the description of revolutionary and disruptive times referred to by Orwell in the passage.

4. **(C):** Orwell mentions that his loneliness as a child led him to develop the habit of creating stories and engaging in imaginary conversations. This formative experience contributed to his literary ambitions and his way of coping with feelings of isolation and undervaluation.

5. **(B):** It is essential to know about motives of writers: Orwell provides background information about his childhood and early influences because he believes that understanding a writer's motives is inseparable from understanding their work. He emphasizes how personal experiences and emotions shape a writer's creative impulses.

6. **(A):** Orwell states that if a writer completely escapes from the emotional attitudes and early influences of their upbringing, they risk losing their creative drive. These influences provide the foundational impulses that compel a writer to express themselves through their work.

7. **(D):** The author emphasizes the need to study English, technical education, and Western science alongside knowledge of one's own traditions and branches of study. This combination, according to Vivekananda, equips individuals with the tools necessary for self-reliance and societal development.

8. **(C):** The author stresses that the essence of acquiring knowledge lies in the ability to concentrate. He gives examples, such as the chemist in a laboratory, to demonstrate how focused attention is the key to understanding and mastery in any field of study.

9. **(D):** The word "assimilation" relates to integration, adjustment, and acclimatization. These terms align with the concept of incorporating ideas, knowledge, or practices into one's understanding or behaviour, which the author describes as central to meaningful education.

10. **(D):** The author clearly rejects the idea that education is simply information, library resources, or university degrees. Instead, he defines education as the assimilation of ideas that build character, strength, intellect, and self-reliance.

11. **(D):** The aim of education, according to the author, encompasses building character, enhancing intellect, and enabling a person to stand independently. These goals collectively contribute to the holistic development of an individual.

12. (A): The author asserts that the nation needs individuals with immense willpower, represented metaphorically as "muscles of iron and nerves of steel". This strength of will is necessary for overcoming challenges, exploring the unknown, and accomplishing goals, even under extreme circumstances.

13. (D): The phrase "bright and colourful in an impressive way" aptly describes "dazzling", which indicates something radiant or strikingly beautiful, such as the astrologer's forehead adorned with sacred ash and vermilion. This visual detail reflects the attractiveness and aura associated with the astrologer.

14. (D)

15. (D): The groundnut seller used imaginative and creative names such as "Bombay Ice Cream" and "Delhi Almond" to attract customers. This strategy reflects his resourcefulness in marketing, as noted in the passage, which describes the bustling activity and vibrant trades along the pathway.

16. (A): "Vociferousness" refers to loudness and assertiveness in expression. This aligns with the passage's description of the vendors, particularly the auctioneer and the groundnut seller, who attract attention through their loud and lively marketing tactics.

17. (C): The astrologer is described as starting his business punctually at midday, spreading out his tools and preparing for the day. This punctuality underscores his disciplined approach to his profession, as noted in the opening lines of the passage.

18. (B): The astrologer's clients perceived his sharp and abnormal gleam as a "prophetic light". This impression, though stemming from his keen observation for customers, comforted his clients, reflecting their faith in his abilities.

19. (D): The passage explains that our tendency to seek quick and easy remedies stems from a lack of understanding, patience, and love. These qualities are essential for dealing with children, as they require careful attention and nurturing rather than hasty solutions.

20. (B): The passage emphasizes that parents who truly love and wish to understand their child observe their unique traits and behaviors rather than imposing external ideals. This approach fosters genuine understanding and supports the child's self-awareness.

21. (D): The antonym of "volatile" includes "stable", "steady", and "constant", as these words convey the opposite meaning of being changeable or unpredictable. The passage highlights these qualities as essential in dealing with impressionable children.

22. (A): The author stresses that education must be rooted in love, care, and understanding. Without these, efforts to educate become mechanical and ineffective, failing to address the child's emotional and intellectual needs.

23. (B): Imposing an ideal creates a conflict between what the child is and what they are expected to be, leading to confusion and fear. This inner turmoil often manifests outwardly in society, as explained in the passage.

24. (C): The author argues that a right kind of teacher does not rely on rigid methods but instead studies each child individually. This personalized approach ensures that the teacher addresses the unique needs and potentials of each student, fostering their growth.

25. (C): The 16th BRICS summit facilitated a diplomatic dialogue between India and China, particularly through discussions between President Xi Jinping and Prime

Minister Narendra Modi. This dialogue was significant as it marked a step toward resolving the prolonged military standoff on the Himalayan frontier, indicating progress in bilateral relations.

26. (D): The letter "S" in BRICS stands for South Africa. South Africa joined the BRICS grouping in 2010, adding an African dimension to the group and expanding its representation of emerging economies across continents.

27. (D): The Big Cats Alliance initiative refers to the conservation of lions, tigers, jaguars, leopards, cheetahs, and snow leopards. This reflects a comprehensive approach to the preservation of large feline species globally, as emphasized in the BRICS summit's communiqué.

28. (C): Western economists have critiqued BRICS by highlighting the impact of unresolved conflicts, such as those between India and China, on the group's ability to progress and unify. This critique underscores geopolitical tensions as a challenge to BRICS's ambitions.

29. (D): The emergence of BRICS signals a shift toward a geopolitical framework that challenges the dominance of the United States. By fostering cooperation among major emerging economies, BRICS aims to create an alternative platform for global governance and economic collaboration.

30. (D): One significant outcome of the 16th BRICS meeting was the reduction of tensions between India and China, as the leaders of the two countries engaged in dialogue to address their military standoff. This effort aligns with the broader BRICS goal of fostering cooperation among member nations.

31. (A): Article 370 of the Indian Constitution provided special autonomy to Jammu and Kashmir, granting it its own constitution and decision-making powers in certain areas. This special status was effectively abrogated in 2019.

32. (C): The Jammu and Kashmir Reorganization Act, 2019, divided the erstwhile state into two Union Territories—Jammu and Kashmir, and Ladakh. This reorganization marked a significant change in the region's administrative and political structure.

33. (B): Among India's Union Territories, Jammu and Kashmir is unique in having a legislative assembly. This distinguishes it from other Union Territories like Ladakh, which do not have such assemblies.

34. (A): India currently comprises 28 states and 8 Union Territories. This administrative structure includes regions like Ladakh, which was established as a Union Territory following the reorganization of Jammu and Kashmir.

35. (A): Leh is the capital city of the Union Territory of Ladakh. It serves as the administrative and political center for the region, which was formed after the bifurcation of Jammu and Kashmir.

36. (D): The statements are false because Kargil was not previously a Union Territory, Ladakh is administered directly by the central government and not by the J&K assembly, and 15 new districts were not formed as part of J&K in 2019. These misstatements highlight misunderstandings about the reorganization.

37. (D): The implementation of the Nari Shakti Vandan Adhiniyam, 2023, is contingent upon the completion of the upcoming census and subsequent delimitation exercises. This linking to long-term processes indicates that the Act's actual implementation timeline remains undefined, leading to a delay in achieving its objectives.

38. (D): Rudolf Heredia critiques the inherited nature of women's political leadership, arguing that their leadership often stems from familial or spousal connections rather than their own merit or agency. This reflects the societal norms that reinforce patriarchy instead of challenging it.

39. (C): Soumya Bhowmick emphasizes that while quotas may bring about descriptive representation, they must lead to substantive representation, where women actively participate in shaping policies. This requires a shift in societal attitudes and a focus on grassroots empowerment.

40. (D): The amendment to Articles 330(a) and 332 of the Indian Constitution under the Nari Shakti Vandan Adhiniyam reserves one-third of seats for women in the Lok Sabha and state legislative assemblies. It does not address Rajya Sabha appointments, governors, or sportspersons.

41. (B): The Civil Disobedience Movement began with the Dandi March, led by Mahatma Gandhi, which symbolized resistance against the British-imposed salt tax.

This event marked a significant phase in India's struggle for independence.

42. (B): While industrialists initially supported the Civil Disobedience Movement, they became apprehensive due to the prolonged disruptions caused by militant activities and fears of socialism among Congress's younger members.

43. (A): The Congress faced the predicament of balancing the demands of workers and industrialists. Supporting workers' demands risked alienating industrialists, potentially dividing opposition forces against British colonial rule.

44. (B): The Civil Disobedience Movement involved acts of defiance, such as breaking the salt laws and organizing demonstrations. These activities symbolized non-violent resistance against British laws and mobilized mass participation.

45. (B): Indian industrialists supported the Civil Disobedience Movement, providing financial assistance and boycotting foreign goods. Their backing stemmed from a desire to protect domestic industries and challenge colonial economic policies.

46. (D): The Civil Disobedience Movement had multiple outcomes, including partial support from the working class, the mobilization of women into the political sphere, and the growing influence of socialism among Congress cadres. These outcomes showcased the movement's broad societal impact.

47. (D): India won back-to-back Olympic hockey medals at Tokyo 2020 and Paris 2024, not in the other combinations mentioned. The men's hockey team secured a bronze in Paris 2024, repeating their success from Tokyo 2020, showcasing consistent performance at the Olympics.

48. (D): The Paris 2024 Olympics symbolized a global post-pandemic shift, with the opening ceremony held outside a stadium setting by the Seine River and being celebrated as one of the most elaborate cultural rituals since COVID-19. It fulfilled the organizers' goal of creating an inclusive and symbolic experience.

49. (A): The geopolitical backdrop of the Paris Games included ongoing international crises such as the Israel-Hamas conflict, which had persisted for over six months. This situation, coupled with other global tensions, created a troubling context for the Olympics, raising concerns about potential protests or demonstrations during the event.

50. (B): The Paris Olympics marked a revival of large-scale public gatherings after the restrictions of the Tokyo 2020 and Beijing 2022 Games, which were affected by the pandemic. Spectators enthusiastically embraced the opportunity for communal celebrations, showcasing the pent-up demand for such events.

51. (D): India achieved its highest Olympic medal tally of seven at the Tokyo 2020 Olympics, which included a gold medal by Neeraj Chopra in men's javelin. The six medals in Paris 2024 were slightly lower than this record.

52. (A): The Paris 2024 Olympics opening ceremony was held along the Seine River, a unique setting compared to traditional stadium-based ceremonies. This innovative choice reflected the "Games Wide Open" slogan and highlighted the cultural vibrancy of Paris.

53. (D): According to the passage, children who experience violence during childhood face various challenges, including difficulties in school, substance abuse, mental health issues, aggressive behavior, and criminal tendencies. These outcomes reflect the long-term consequences of childhood trauma.

54. (B): The primary objective of the criminal justice system is deterrence, achieved through the punishment of offenders to maintain law and order in society. This approach seeks to prevent crime by discouraging potential offenders.

55. (C): The National Crime Records Bureau (NCRB) in India is responsible for compiling, maintaining, and analyzing crime data, including crimes against children. This data supports the formulation of policies and reforms in the justice system.

56. (B): According to the NCRB Report 2021, the highest number of crimes against children fell under the category of kidnapping and abduction, followed by cases registered under the POCSO Act. This highlights the vulnerability of children to abduction and exploitation.

57. (A): The term POCSO stands for the Protection of Children from Sexual Offences Act, which is a legal framework in India aimed at addressing and penalizing sexual offenses against children.

58. (D): The passage highlights that children exposed to the criminal justice system face multiple risks, including inadequate vocational training, physical abuse, and mental health challenges. These vulnerabilities underline the need for reforms in child rights and justice systems.

59. (B): The 42nd Constitutional Amendment introduced provisions for environmental protection by amending the Directive Principles of State Policy (Article 48-A) and adding a Fundamental Duty (Article 51-A(g)). It did not make changes to Fundamental Rights. The Directive Principles guide the state in policy formulation, while the Fundamental Duties obligate citizens to protect the environment.

60. (A): India's commitment under international treaties like the Paris Agreement mandates it to take definitive actions to reduce carbon emissions. The language of the agreement binds signatories to implement measures to achieve specified environmental goals, such as limiting global temperature rise.

61. (D): Article 51-A(g) of the Indian Constitution specifies that it is the duty of citizens to protect and improve the natural environment, which explicitly includes rivers, lakes, forests, and wildlife. This provision emphasizes the conservation of natural resources and biodiversity.

62. **(D):** The passage emphasizes that the Supreme Court has recognized both the state's duty to maintain ecological balance and the citizens' right to a clean environment, including the right against climate change. This judgment links the protection of natural resources to Article 21, which guarantees the right to life, and creates a dual responsibility: the state must ensure environmental sustainability, and citizens are entitled to hold the state accountable for environmental protection.

63. **(A):** India's commitment to reducing carbon emissions arises from its obligations under international agreements like the Paris Agreement. These treaties compel India to adopt measures and policies to meet globally agreed climate goals.

64. **(D):** Article 21 of the Constitution guarantees the right to life and personal liberty. The Supreme Court has interpreted this to include the right to a clean and healthy environment, as pollution or ecological imbalance can infringe upon this fundamental right.

65. **(B):** A void agreement is invalid from its inception (void ab initio). It lacks enforceability due to inherent legal flaws, such as illegality or impossibility of performance, rendering it ineffective.

66. **(A):** A contract to commit an illegal act, such as robbing a bank, is void as it involves an unlawful objective. Such contracts are not enforceable by law and have no legal standing.

67. **(B)**

68. **(C):** This scenario constitutes a void agreement because it involves an illegal or unethical objective (bribery or corruption). Such agreements are against public policy and unenforceable.

69. **(C):** An agreement made without consideration is generally void under the Indian Contract Act. Consideration is a key element of a valid contract unless specific exceptions apply, such as agreements made out of natural love and affection.

70. **(C):** This statement is incorrect as GIs are specifically designated for products that originate from a particular geographic region with unique qualities tied to that location. GIs cannot be used for products not originating from the designated region, even if licensed.

71. **(B):** If a product not originating from Darjeeling is marketed as "Darjeeling Tea", it violates GI protection laws. Legal action can be initiated to prohibit the misuse, ensuring the authenticity of GI-labeled products.

72. **(C):** Misuse of GIs does not lead to compulsory licensing of patents. Instead, it can result in loss of consumer trust, market value, and potential legal action for infringement. GIs and patents are separate aspects of intellectual property law.

73. **(C):** This scenario perfectly illustrates the concept of "geographic origin", as GIs signify the connection between the product's characteristics and its place of production.

74. **(C):** The TRIPS Agreement establishes a global framework to protect and enforce GIs, ensuring fair trade practices and preserving the reputation of region-specific products.

75. **(D):** A Bill becomes an Act only after receiving the President's assent following its passage in both Houses of Parliament. This approval formalizes the legislation, giving it legal effect.

76. **(D):** According to the Public Examinations (Prevention of Unfair Means) Act, 2024, a service provider found engaging in

malpractices, such as indirectly aiding a candidate, can face a fine of up to ₹ 1 crore and be held accountable for the proportional cost of conducting the examination. However, the specific scenario of indirect assistance alone does not automatically make the service provider liable for the full cost recovery unless determined by the examination authority. Therefore, the correct answer is "None of the above" because the described actions do not fully align with any of the given options.

77. **(D):** The Act specifies punishments for offenses such as manipulating seating arrangements, including imprisonment for not less than three years (extendable to five) and a fine of up to 10 lakh. Thus, 4 years and a 5 lakh fine fall within this prescribed range.

78. **(A):** Conducting mock tests to prepare students does not qualify as an unfair means, as it is a legitimate academic activity. However, any direct assistance during exams, such as offering help or manipulating seating, constitutes malpractice.

79. **(A):** A coaching center is not a service provider in the context of public examinations. Service providers include entities directly involved in conducting exams, such as printing presses or software companies managing exam-related processes.

80. **(A):** The digital personal data protection law in India mandates that before sharing personal data with any third party, the entity must obtain explicit, free, informed, and specific consent from the users. The company must also provide a clear notice detailing the purpose of data sharing and users' rights.

81. **(B):** Under the law, if a user withdraws their consent for data processing, the entity must comply by halting further processing of the data. This provision upholds the user's right to revoke consent at any time, ensuring control over personal information.

82. **(C):** The law provides individuals with the right to access data collected about them. This includes a summary of collected data and the identities of entities with whom the data has been shared. The financial institution must comply with such a request to ensure transparency.

83. **(B):** Sensitive personal data, such as health data, requires additional safeguards under the law. The startup must obtain explicit consent from users and implement stringent security measures to protect the data from unauthorized access or misuse.

84. **(D):** The digital personal data protection law ensures a comprehensive set of rights, including access to data summaries, information about data sharing, correction and erasure of data, redressal mechanisms, and the ability to nominate data recipients. These rights empower individuals to control their data.

85. **(C):** The passage highlights that homelessness is influenced by systemic issues and major turbulence in economic and cultural aspects, such as the COVID-19 pandemic, unemployment, and housing insecurity. These factors exacerbate homelessness globally, particularly in vulnerable communities, and demonstrate its complex, multifaceted nature.

86. **(D):** Proper healthcare is not typically a cause of homelessness but rather a mitigating factor. Conversely, issues like domestic violence, unemployment, and substance abuse are more common causes of homelessness.

87. **(C):** The passage emphasizes that mental health issues can predispose individuals to homelessness. Additionally, homelessness

worsens existing mental health conditions, exposing individuals to severe health problems, anxiety, depression, and substance abuse. This cyclical relationship makes mental health both a cause and a consequence of homelessness.

88. (C): Homelessness often manifests as a lack of employment opportunities, which leads to an inability to secure housing. The passage emphasizes systemic issues like poverty and unemployment as critical factors contributing to homelessness.

89. (*)

90. (D): This statement is not a myth. People experiencing homelessness face barriers like a lack of stable addresses, poor health, and limited access to resources, making it challenging to secure employment, as noted in the passage.

91. (A): The excerpt indicates that the consultant's foremost role is a deep analysis of the company's internal environment and system. By closely examining how the organization operates, including its workflows, bottlenecks, and strategic positioning, the consultant identifies inefficiencies and improvement areas. Through this investigative approach, the consultant guides the business toward heightened productivity, profitability, and relevance.

92. (B): The passage clarifies that the consultant collaborates with the company's leadership and its numerous sections. This collaboration helps in deciphering objectives, understanding processes, and aligning them with potential solutions. By interacting with various levels of management, the consultant gains insights into the organization's pain points, enabling the creation of strategic, well-rounded recommendations.

93. (D): The consultant devises tailored solutions by relying on research-driven methods, including examining relevant data and referencing established industry standards. Incorporating creativity in problem-solving further refines these strategies to meet unique corporate needs. This evidence-based yet innovative approach ensures that the proposed changes are both practical and cutting-edge.

94. (B): Among the areas a consultant may optimize are logistics and supply chain processes, as highlighted in the excerpt. By analyzing and improving these processes—such as inventory handling, transportation, and distribution—the consultant can streamline operations, reduce costs, and increase operational efficiency, which in turn boosts the company's performance.

95. (A): Communication is paramount in change management, and the passage underscores its importance. A consultant must ensure that every stakeholder—from management to frontline staff—comprehends the reasons behind proposed changes. By clarifying the benefits and addressing concerns proactively, acceptance and successful implementation of new processes are far more likely.

96. (B) : The excerpt notes that part of the consultant's role is helping the organization adapt to changes smoothly. Providing training resources and offering ongoing support are essential to ensure employees are comfortable with new systems, processes, or technologies. This guidance helps overcome resistance, fosters competency, and secures sustained benefits from the consultant's recommendations.

97. (*) **98. (D)** **99. (*)**

100. (D) **101. (A)** **102. (*)**

103. (A): The passage addresses how changing lifestyles—marked by increased consumption of ultra-processed foods, heavy smartphone usage, and poor sleep—are linked to deteriorating mental well-being among India's youth. While economic growth is mentioned, the dominant theme revolves around lifestyle factors and their effects on mental health, making "Lifestyle and Mental Health" the most appropriate title.

104. (D): The quote—"Technology is an improved means to an unimproved end"—suggests that while technology advances rapidly, it does not necessarily improve core human or societal conditions. Thoreau's caution implies that we should be wary of the potential harm or unintended consequences arising from unchecked technological use.

105. (A): The passage cites evidence of smartphones contributing to disrupted social bonds, reduced family interactions, and mental ill-health. Thus, highlighting weakened family relationships supports the author's argument that early or excessive smartphone exposure negatively affects the youth.

106. (C): The passage specifically identifies ultra-processed foods as "as addictive as smoking" and correlates their consumption with poor mental well-being. Reducing dependence on these foods is a plausible measure to improve mental health outcomes among the youth.

107. (C): While the passage briefly mentions cultural changes and a preponderance of English in schools alongside smartphone use, it does not present concrete data directly linking English language learning alone to weakened family relationships. Therefore, this statement lacks clear, specific evidence within the text.

108. (C): The author notes that adolescents receive gadgets more for convenience than any well-reasoned plan, implying that practical expedience or immediate utility is prioritized over thoughtful consideration of potential harms. This underscores that logic and caution are often overshadowed by convenience when distributing smartphones to youth.

109. (A): According to the report, women earn 61% of what men earn in Goa.

$$\text{Wages for women} = 335 \times 61/100 = 204.35 \text{ approx.}$$

Hence, the wages paid to women in Goa are approximately ₹ 204.

110. (B): From the passage's data:

Goa Women = ₹ 208

Jharkhand Women = ₹ 239

Gujarat Women = ₹ 247

Kerala Women = ₹ 537

Of the listed states, women in Goa earn the least at about 208.

111. (C): 700 In 2023, male self-employed workers earn 2.8 times that of female self-employed workers. If female self-employed earn250, then:

$$\text{Male self-employed} = 2.8 \times 250 = ₹\ 700$$

112. (B): 296 Male casual workers earn 48% more than female casual workers.

If female casual workers earn 200:

$$\text{Male wage} = 200 + 48\% \text{ of } 200 = 200 + 96 = ₹\ 296.$$

113. (A): In 2022, the gap was 2.5 times; in 2023, it became 2.8 times. The increase is:

$$= \frac{2.8 - 2.5}{2.5} \times 100\%$$

$$= \frac{0.3}{2.5} \times 100\% = 12\%.$$

114. (C): Both (A) & (B)

(A) "The wage gap of Goa (61%) and Kerala is less than Tamil Nadu (112%)." True.

(B) "The wage gap of Tamil Nadu is greater than Jharkhand (6%) and Gujarat (6%)." Also true.

Hence, both statements are correct.

Mr. Das's Monthly Income Details

Basic salary: ₹ 9228

House Rent Allowance (HRA)

= 10% of 9228

= ₹ 923 (approx.)

Total monthly income = 9228 + 923

= ₹ 10,151

His expenses and savings as percentages of total income:

Food = 25%

House-rent = 18%

Entertainment = 9%

Child's education = 23%

Medical = 13%

Savings = 12%

These sum to 100%.

115. (A): House-rent is 18% of the total monthly income. Thus, 18% of 10,151

= 0.18 × 10,151 = 1,827.

116. (D): Even at his current savings rate (12% monthly), Mr. Das's total savings over two years, plus interest at 12% per annum, already exceed the ₹ 30,000 goal. Therefore, no additional savings are required.

117. (C): Savings (12%), medical (13%), and education (23%) together amount to 48% of Mr. Das's total income. In comparison, house-rent (18%), food (25%), and entertainment (9%) together account for 52% of the total income.

Thus, 48% is indeed less than 52%, making this option correct.

118. (C): After deducting house-rent (18%) and savings (12%) from total income (10,151):

House-rent + savings

= 30% → 0.30 × 10,151

= 3,045.3 (approx. 3,045)

Remaining = 10,151 – 3,045 = ₹ 7,106.

119. (B): Mr. Das spends 25% on food and 9% on entertainment, totaling 34%.

A 10% increase in this expenditure means an additional 0.10 × 34% = 3.4% is spent on food and entertainment.

His new total expenditure on food and entertainment is 34% + 3.4% = 37.4%.

His remaining percentage for savings and other expenses is:

100% – 37.4% – 18% – 23% – 13%

= 8.6%.

120. (D): Food (25%) + entertainment (9%)

= 34% of total: 0.34 × 10,151

= 3,451.34 (approx. 3,451)

Among the options (A) 3,541/ (B) 3,461/ (C) 3,371, none precisely match 3,451.

Hence, "None of the above."

Previous Years' Paper

Common Law Admission Test (CLAT-UG)

Entrance Exam, December 2023

(Exam held on 03-12-2023)

Section-I : English Language

I

In the realm of contemporary literature, the interplay between character and setting is a nuanced dance that shapes the narrative's essence. The setting, often described with painstaking detail, becomes more than a backdrop; it becomes a character, influencing the plot and character development.

Consider, for instance, the barren expanse of the desert in Jhumpa Lahiri's *The Namesake*. The arid landscape mirrors the sense of isolation felt by the protagonist, Gogol, as he navigates his identity crisis in a foreign land. The relentless sun and vast sands are not mere descriptions; they are the silent witnesses to his inner turmoil.

On the other end of the literary spectrum, there is Arundhati Roy's *The God of Small Things*. The lush, vibrant Kerala backwaters are not just the setting; they are a character woven into the fabric of the story. The teeming, humid landscape reflects the complex web of human relationships and secrets that unravel in the narrative. This interplay is not confined to contemporary literature alone. In Shakespeare's timeless tragedy *Macbeth*, the eerie and foreboding setting of the Scottish moors casts a dark shadow over the characters' actions. The moors, shrouded in mist and mystery, serve as an ever-present omen of the impending tragedy.

1. In contemporary literature, how is the relationship between character and setting described in the passage?

A. It is non-existent; characters and settings are entirely separate entities.

B. It is a complex interplay where the setting influences the plot and character development.

C. Characters and settings are inter-changeable.

D. Settings are insignificant in contemporary literature.

2. In the novel, *The Namesake* by Jhumpa Lahiri, what does the barren desert landscape symbolize?

A. A thriving community.

B. The protagonist's sense of isolation and identity crisis.

C. A lush, vibrant setting.

D. A happy, carefree life.

3. What role does the Scottish moors play in Shakespeare's *Macbeth*?

A. It serves as a beautiful, serene landscape.

B. It has no influence on the characters' actions.

C. It is an ever-present omen of impending tragedy.

D. It is a place for the characters to relax.

4. What does the term "interplay" refer to in the context of the passage?

A. A lack of interaction between characters and setting.
B. A complex relationship where the setting influences the narrative.
C. An insignificant connection between characters and setting.
D. A complete separation of characters and setting.

5. Which of the following words best describes the setting in *The God of Small Things*?
A. Boring
B. Lush and vibrant
C. Insignificant
D. Dark and foreboding

6. What is the main theme discussed in the passage?
A. The characters in contemporary literature are not influenced by their settings.
B. Setting in literature is unimportant.
C. In literature, settings can be as influential as characters in shaping the narrative.
D. Settings have no role in character development.

II

The crisis of justice that is the subject matter of discussion in the media today is in fact the crisis of "justice for the middle class". The main difference between India and the OECD (Organisation for Economic Cooperation and Development) countries is that whereas the middle class in these countries has reasonable access to justice, in India it does not. A vocal and powerful middle class has emerged in India since 1991. It is demanding reasonable access to justice. Much of the judicial reform effort will help meet this demand...

The question of justice for the poor is, however, an altogether different challenge. No country in the world has been able to secure justice for the poor. Most of the jails of the richest countries are filled with the poorest. The "masses" are more often victims of the criminal justice system than of crime. In India as well, jails are almost exclusively filled with the poor. The civil justice system is hardly accessible to them. They are often victimised by lawyers, touts and court staff. They are docket-excluded, a new type of untouchability. The language and the logic—and the colonial and feudal culture—of the judicial system are alien to them. It rarely takes cognisance of their needs and interests.

Their main concern, therefore, is to escape the attention of the justice system, criminal and civil. A landless Dalit person in the interior of Madhya Pradesh once gave me an insightful definition of a court from the perspective of the masses: "A court is a place where you are forcibly taken by the police to be punished; no one goes to a court." In contrast, many lawyers and judges colloquially define a court as "a temple of justice where rights are protected".

These sharply divergent visions mean that justice for one section is often injustice for another. Protecting the livelihood of traditional taxi and auto drivers from predatory pricing by corporate app-based taxi providers by imaginatively using the available tools of law to delay their incursion would be seen by the rich and by sections of the middle class as a failure of the judicial system, and possibly as also resulting in a downgrading of the "ease of doing business" measure. However, the masses would see such a judicial intervention as strong evidence of a good justice system. Although the conflict over competing visions of the nation and conflicting demands from social and economic segments have confined judicial reform of judicial administration mainly to "neutral" areas such as process reform, procedural law, technology, planning and court and case management, judge strength, and the workload of judges, there has been considerable improvement in these areas, and the judicial system has improved its performance.

[Extracted, with edits, from "Justice and the Two Ideas of India", by G. Mohan Gopal, *Frontline*]

7. What is the central thesis of the above extract?

A. The practice of untouchability takes various forms in modern India.

B. The imagination of justice for the rich and poor is vastly different.

C. Addressing judge strength and case-load management does not affect the performance of the judicial system.

D. Protecting the livelihood of traditional taxi drivers is contrary to the goals of ease of doing business.

8. What does the author mean by 'docket-excluded' in the second paragraph?

A. The poor do not have easy access to the justice system.

B. Courts do not list bail petitions of poor undertrial prisoners who populate the country's jails.

C. The poor reject the judicial system as being alien to their language and logic.

D. The rich are excluded from the country's prisons, which are mostly populated by the poor.

9. Which of the following words best describes the experience of different segments of people with the justice system as described in the third paragraph?

A. Symbiotic B. Affective

C. Conflicting D. Inter-dependent

10. Which of the following statements is the author most likely to agree with?

A. The judicial system reflects the same power relationships as those that exist in society.

B. Access to the judicial system is determined more by a person's economic status such as wealth and income, than by their social status, such as religion and caste.

C. The judicial system was made by the rich, for the rich, of the rich.

D. None of the above.

11. Which of the following statements is the author most likely to disagree with?

A. A truly representative democracy would ensure that the interests of the poor are also represented in the judicial system.

B. The Law ensures equality both in text and in practise.

C. The poor suffer most at the hands of lawyers and touts, compared to judges who might still pronounce judgments in their favour from time to time.

D. All of the above.

12. What makes reform of judicial administration a 'neutral' area?

A. Persons across socio-economic strata agree on the need to reform judicial administration.

B. There is consensus among political parties across the ideological and regional spectrum on reforms to judicial administration.

C. Reforms to judicial administration do not favour one class of people over another.

D. Reform of judicial administration is mandated by the Constitution, and thus lies beyond political considerations.

III

Everything she wanted was here, at Carignano, in Kasauli. Here, on the ridge of the mountain, in this quiet house. It was the place, and the time of life, that she had wanted and prepared for all her life-as she realized on the first day at Carignano, with a great, cool flowering of relief - and at last she had it. She wanted no one and nothing else. Whatever else came, or happened here, would be an unwelcome intrusion and distraction. This she tried to convey to the plodding postman with a cold and piercing stare from the height of the ridge onto his honest bull back. Unfortunately, he did not look up at her on the hilltop but stared stolidly down at the dust piling onto his shoes as he plodded on.

A bullock-man, an oafish ox, she thought bitterly. She stepped backwards into the garden and the wind suddenly billowed up and threw the pine branches about as though to curtain her. She was grey, tall and thin and her silk sari made a sweeping, shivering sound and she fancied she could merge with the pine trees and be mistaken for one. To be a tree, no more and no less, was all she was prepared to undertake.

What pleased and satisfied her so, here at Carignano, was its barrenness. This was the chief virtue of all Kasauli of course-its starkness. It had rocks, it had pines, it had light and air. In every direction there was a sweeping view - to the north, of the mountains, to the south, of the plains. Occasionally an eagle swam through this clear unobstructed mass of light and air, that was all. And Carignano, her home on the ridge, had no more than that. Why should it? The sun shone on its white walls. Its windows were open the ones facing north opened on to the blue waves of the Himalayas flowing out and up to the line of ice and snow sketched upon the sky, while those that faced south looked down the plunging cliff to the plain stretching out, fiat and sere to the blurred horizon.

Yes, there were some apricot trees close to the house. There were clumps of iris that had finished blooming. There was the kitchen with a wing of smoke lifting out of its chimney and a stack of wood outside its door. But these were incidental, almost unimportant.

[Extracted, with edits and revisions, from *"Fire on the Mountain"* by Anita Desai]

13. What does the protagonist's preference for "barrenness" and "starkness" at Carignano suggest about her personality?

A. She enjoys a bustling and vibrant environment.

B. She values simplicity and minimalism in her surroundings.

C. She prefers lush and colorful landscapes.

D. She seeks constant stimulation and variety in her life.

14. What do you get to know about the protagonist's state of mind from her reaction towards the postman?

A. She feels grateful for his presence and the assistance he offers.

B. She dislikes any disturbance or interruption in her solitude.

C. She feels suspicious and is interested in the lives of others.

D. She is disinterested and generally unaffected by the presence of others.

15. What does the protagonist's desire to be mistaken for a pine tree reveal about her mindset?

A. She desires to be appreciated and noticed by others in society.

B. She has a deep admiration for the beauty of the pine trees.

C. She feels a sense of superiority over other living beings.

D. She yearns to one with nature and escapes from her human identity.

16. The protagonist's description of the nestlings' screams as "shrill and maddening" shows that:

A. She perceives the sounds to be out of tune yet soothing.

B. She considers the nestlings to be symbols of new life and vitality.

C. She finds the nestlings to be vexatious and irritating.

D. She feels a sense of protectiveness and care towards the nestlings.

17. Which of the following statements are true about the protagonist's overall state of mind in Carignano?

Statement I: She experienced a sense of constant restlessness and anguish.

Statement II: She felt isolated and disconnected from her environment.

Statement III: She was content, fulfilled, and at peace with her surroundings.

A. Statement I and II

B. Statement II and III

C. Only Statement II
D. Only Statement III

18. In the light of above passage, what role does nature play in the protagonist's life at Carignano?
A. It provides her with a source of creativity.
B. It offers her solace, peace, and a sense of belonging.
C. It serves as a reminder of the harsh realities of life.
D. It serves as a constant source of distraction and intrusion for her.

IV

English literature is a vast and diverse field that has left an indelible mark on the world of letters. From the eloquent plays of William Shakespeare to the complex novels of Jane Austen and the profound poetry of William Wordsworth, English literature offers a window into the human experience. One of the luminaries of English literature is William Shakespeare, often hailed as the greatest playwright in the history of English language. His works, including *Hamlet, Macbeth*, and *Romeo and Juliet*, are celebrated for their exploration of human nature, love, ambition, and tragedy. His characters, such as the tormented Hamlet and the star-crossed lovers Romeo and Juliet, continue to captivate readers and audiences worldwide.

The 19th century ushered in a new era of literary giants. Jane Austen's novels, such as *Pride and Prejudice* and *Sense and Sensibility*, provide incisive social commentary through the lens of wit and romance. Austen's heroines, like Elizabeth Bennet and Elinor Dashwood, remain beloved literary figures known for their intelligence and resilience. The Romantic era brought forth poets like William Wordsworth and Samuel Taylor Coleridge, who celebrated the beauty of nature and the emotional intensity of the individual. Wordsworth's "I Wandered Lonely as a Cloud" and Coleridge's "The Rime of the Ancient Mariner" are testament to the power of the written words to evoke profound emotions and imagery. Moving towards 20th century, English literature continued to evolve. Virginia Woolf's ground-breaking novel *Mrs. Dalloway* explored the inner thoughts and lives of its characters with a modernist narrative style. Dystopian visions, as seen in George Orwell's *Nineteen Eighty-Four* provided stark warnings about the dangers of totalitarianism and the erosion of individual freedom.

Today, English literature is a global phenomenon, transcending borders and languages. Indian authors like Arundhati Roy, with her novel *The God of Small Things*, have won prestigious international literary awards. The book not only explores intricate family dynamics but also delves into the broader socio-political landscape of India. In summary, English literature is a testament to the enduring power of storytelling and the written word. It encompasses an array of authors, themes, and styles that continue to captivate and inspire readers across the world.

19. Who is often regarded as the greatest playwright in the history of English language?
A. Jane Austen
B. William Wordsworth
C. William Shakespeare
D. George Orwell

20. Which of Jane Austen's novels is known for its social commentary and witty portrayal of romance?
A. *Nineteen Eighty-Four*
B. *Sense and Sensibility*
C. "I Wandered Lonely as a Cloud"
D. "The Rime of the Ancient Mariner"

21. Who are the Romantic poets mentioned in the passage known for celebrating nature and intense human emotions?
A. William Shakespeare and Virginia Woolf
B. George Orwell and Samuel Taylor Coleridge

C. William Wordsworth and Samuel Taylor Coleridge

D. Jane Austen and Arundhati Roy

22. What is the title of Virginia Woolf's novel known for its modernist narrative style?

A. *Pride and Prejudice*

B. *Nineteen Eighty-Four*

C. *Mrs. Dalloway*

D. *The God of Small Things*

23. Identify the 20th century novel mentioned in the passage that provides a warning about the dangers of totalitarianism?

A. *Nineteen Eighty-Four*

B. *Romeo and Juliet*

C. *Sense and Sensibility*

D. "I Wandered Lonely as a Cloud"

24. What does the passage highlight as the enduring power of English literature?

A. Its ability to win literary awards

B. The diversity of its authors, themes, and styles

C. Its ability to captivate and inspire only British readers

D. The decline of storytelling

Section-II : Current Affairs Including General Knowledge

V

On the evening of the 10th, General Dyer arrived at Amritsar, and the Deputy-Commissioner handed over the civil power to him. He issued a proclamation by word of mouth that no meetings should be held. Two days later, after there had been no sort of riot, nor murder, General Dyer heard that a meeting was to be held at the Jallianwala Bagh. He proceeded there with about fifty troops, half British, half Indian, and a certain number of Ghurkas, armed with their kukris. The Jallianwala Bagh is an open space, half a mile square, which has one entry wide enough for three persons. The troops got in and lined up on a mound of debris. The walls, seven feet high, and the surrounding houses enclosed the people. There were, too, three alleys through which the people might have been able to pass. Within thirty seconds of the troops getting in, General Dyer gave orders to fire, and the crowd of people, estimated at anything from 5,000 to 20,000, who were sitting on the ground peacefully listening to the mob oratory, were fired on. The result of the troops' fire into the mass of people we do not know. But we do know that Dyer's own estimate of the casualties resulting from ten minutes continual individual firing, was 400 to 500 killed and 1,500 wounded. The people were not able to escape. They were people who had not offered any violence and who had not been warned. These people were shot down. After ten minutes, the ammunition was exhausted and the troops marched off, and they left 1,500 wounded there. There were men lying there for two days, dying of thirst, eating the ground, bleeding to death and nobody to look after them. Those who lived nearby came and carried away some of the wounded from the heap of dead and dying, but the unfortunate country people died there miserably of their wounds. This is what is done in 1919 in British India...

Centuries hence you will find Indian children brought up to this spot, just as they visit now the Cawnpore Well, and you can imagine the feelings of these Indians for generations over this terrible business.

[Col. Wedgwood, MP, speaking in the British Parliament, 22 December 1919]

25. Which incident is described in the passage?

A. Baisakhi festival at Amritsar, April 1919

B. Jallianwala Bagh Massacre, April 1919

C. Congress Protests of April 1919

D. Non-Cooperation Movement, April 1919

26. Why did the General Dyer order to fire on the crowd?
A. To bring the crowd under control
B. To scatter the crowd
C. To teach the crowd a lesson
D. To enforce the martial law

27. In the light of above passage, what was the intention of the speaker?
A. To praise General Dyer
B. To expose the deeds of General Dyer
C. To get sympathy for the Indians who died
D. All of the above

28. After the incident, who helped the injured and the dying people?
A. The army
B. The police
C. The civil administration
D. Some people who lived nearby

29. What would be the feelings of the Indian children brought up to the spot?
A. Friendliness to the British rule
B. Bitterness about the British rule
C. A sense of helplessness
D. None of the above

30. What was the full name of General Dyer?
A. Reginald Murree Harry Dyer
B. Reginald Royce Harry Dyer
C. Reginald Edward Harry Dyer
D. Reginald Coleman Harry Dyer

VI

On 7th October 2023, an armed conflict broke out between Israel and Hamas-led Palestinian militants from the Gaza Strip[o] after the latter launched a multi-pronged invasion of southern Israel. After clearing Hamas militants, the Israeli military retaliated by conducting an extensive aerial bombardment campaign on Gazan targets and followed up with a large-scale ground invasion of Gaza. More than 1,400 Israelis, mostly civilians, and more than 10,000 Palestinians have been killed in the fighting. Over 240 Israelis and foreign nationals were taken hostage and brought into the Gaza Strip.

The Hamas-led attack began in the morning of 7th October, as Palestinian militants in Gaza launched a barrage of over 5,000 rockets against Israeli cities and kibbutzim while some 3,000 Palestinian militants breached the Gaza-Israel barrier. Over 1,000 Israeli civilians were killed in more than a dozen massacres, including the Re'im music festival massacre, and military bases were attacked. Over 200 civilians and Israeli soldiers were captured or abducted and taken to the Gaza Strip. At least 44 countries, mostly from the Western world, characterized the massacres of civilians as terrorism. Hamas declared that the invasion was carried out in response to the "desecration of the Al-Aqsa Mosque", the Gaza Strip blockade, the construction of Israeli settlements, and Israeli settler violence against Palestinians in the West Bank.

Israel declared a state of war on 8th October, and its response to the attack has seen the most significant military escalation in the region since the Yom Kippur War. The current hostilities constitute the fifth war of the Gaza-lsrael conflict, which is part of the broader Israeli— Palestinian conflict. In 2023, before the offensive started, an uptick in Israeli-Palestinian violence saw at least 247 Palestinians, 32 Israelis, and two foreigners killed. According to the Gaza Health Ministry, as of 6 November, over 10,000 Palestinians had been killed, including 79 UNRWA staff. Israel dropped a total of 6,000 bombs during the first six days of the conflict—nearly double the number of bombs dropped by the American-led CJTF—OIR in one month during the War against the Islamic State. There has been widespread killing of civilians, and human rights groups and a panel of United Nations special rapporteurs have accused both Israel and Hamas of war crimes.

31. What was the reason for Hamas-led Palestinian militants' attack on Israel?
A. To retaliate against Israeli settler violence against Palestinians

B. In response to the desecration of the Western Wall
C. To protest against the construction of Palestinian settlements in the West Bank
D. To seek an end to the Gaza Strip blockade

32. What was the reaction of the international community to the killing of Israeli civilians?
A. Condemned as terrorism by 44 countries
B. Ignored by most of the countries
C. Supported by the UN
D. Praised as a necessary measure by 10 countries

33. Which of the following is not true about the historical context of the Israel Hamas Conflict?
A. The Palestinian refugees started settling under Ottoman rule in the late 19th Century
B. Hamas emerged during the first Intifada in the late 1980s
C. Hamas was formally known as the Islamic Resistance Movement
D. First Intifada was a Palestinian uprising against Israeli rule.

34. What has been the response of the Israeli military to the Hamas-led attack?
A. Declared a state of war and launched a ground invasion
B. Conducted an aerial bombardment campaign only
C. Asked for international intervention
D. Captured and imprisoned the militants responsible

35. What is the current hostilities known as in the Gaza-Israel conflict?
A. Sixth war B. Fifth war
C. Seventh war D. Fourth war

36. Which major war does the current Gaza-Israel conflict resemble?
A. Yom Kippur War B. Iraq War
C. Six-Day War D. Gulf War

VII

Today, India has become the fourth country in the world to touch the surface of the moon. This success becomes even greater when we look at the place from where India had started its journey. There was a time when India did not have the required technology and there was no support either. We used to be among the 'Third World' countries, standing in the third row. Today, India has become the fifth largest economy in the world. Today, from trade to technology, India is among the countries standing in the first row. In this journey from third row to first row, institutions like ISRO have played a major role. Today, you have taken 'Make in India' to the moon.

I have seen the photo in which our moon lander has firmly set its foot on the moon like Angad. On one hand is the confidence of Vikram while on the other hand is the bravery of Pragyan. Our Pragyan is continuously leaving its footprints on the moon. The pictures taken from different cameras, which have just been released, and I have had the privilege of seeing, are indeed amazing. For the first time, since the beginning of human civilization, for the first time in the history of lakhs of years on the earth, man is looking at the pictures of that place with his own eyes. India has done the work of showing these pictures to the world! All the scientists like you have done it. Today, the whole world is acknowledging the significance of India's scientific spirit, our technology and our scientific temperament. Chandrayaan Maha Abhiyan is a success not only for India but for the entire humanity.

[Extracted from the Speech made by the Prime Minister of India Shri. Narendra Modi on the occasion of the landing of Chandrayaan 3 on 26th August 2023]

37. In what did India become the fourth country in the world?
A. Sending a spacecraft to the moon
B. Landing a spacecraft on the moon

C. Landing a man on the moon
D. Crashlanding (impacting) a spacecraft on the moon

38. What is the role of Pragyan?
A. To move around the moon, leaving footprints
B. To take photographs of the moon, while moving
C. Showing these pictures to the world
D. To record the laser radiation

39. Name one institution that played a major role in bringing India to the forefront.
A. Tata Industries
B. Indian Oil Corporation
C. ISRO
D. Reliance industries

40. What is the name of the moon lander and the rover?
A. Vikram and Pragyan
B. Pragyan-2 and Vikram
C. Chandrayaan and Vikram
D. Chandrayaan and Pragyan

41. Whom did the Prime Minister address this to?
A. To the people of India
B. To the world
C. To the students
D. To the scientists of ISRO

42. Which of the following countries in the world had touched the surface of the moon?
A. United States of America, USSR, China, India
B. United States of America, Russia, China, India
C. United States of America, USSR, France, India
D. United States of America, Russia, Israel, India

VIII

The 18th G20 Summit, in which the heads of states and governments will meet, on September 9 and 10 will be held in India's national capital New Delhi. Over 25 world leaders along with other delegates are going to attend this mega event.

One of the largest multilateral summits, the G20 Summit presents a significant diplomatic opportunity for India, which will convene with the adoption of a joint declaration by all the member states.

India assumed the G20 Presidency on December 1 last year. The 18th G20 Summit in New Delhi is scheduled to be held on September 9-10. The Group of Twenty (G20) comprises 19 countries .... and the European Union. The G20 members represent around 85% of the global GDP, over 75% of the global trade, and about two-thirds of the world population.

World leaders from several countries and institutions will mark their presence at the event. They include US President Joe Biden, UK Prime Minister Rishi Sunak, Australian Prime Minister Anthony Albanese, Canadian Prime Minister Justin Trudeau and French President Emmanuel Macron.

However, Russian President Vladimir Putin has opted out of the summit and foreign minister Sergei Lavrov will represent the country in his place. Chinese President Xi Jinping has also decided to skip the event and will send country's Premier Li Qiang instead, according to sources.

The G20 Summit 2023 is being held under the theme - Vasudhaiva Kutumbakam (One Earth. One Family. One Future) - centered around the value of all life including human, animal, plant, and microorganisms and their inter-connectedness on the planet Earth and in the wider universe.

India's presidency of the summit holds significance as it aims to become a voice for the 'less developed' global South in a world dominated by developed nations of the West. It is also likely to take up the issue of border tension with China. India, for its part, may attempt to straighten out its diplomatic intricacies with the West after it faced challenges due to the Russia-Ukraine conflict.

[Extracted, with edits and revisions, from "India gears up for G20 Summit: Check event venue, guest list, special invitees", *Hindustan Times*]

43. The Group of Twenty (G20) is a forum for _______. Select the correct option.

A. International economic cooperation
B. International peace and security
C. International cooperation for combating money laundering
D. All of the above

44. The G20 Summit is hosted by the incumbent 'Presidency'. The G20 Presidency is responsible for bringing together the G20 agenda in consultation with other members and in response to developments in the global economy. Which country will hold the Presidency in 2024?

A. India B. Indonesia
C. Brazil D. Saudi Arabia

45. Which one of the following countries is not a member of the G20?

A. Egypt B. Mexico
C. Republic of Korea D. Turkiye

46. At every G20 Summit, the host country invites countries and institutions that are not members of the G20. Which among the following denotes the correct list of countries being G20 invitees to the Summit held in New Delhi in September 2023?

A. Nepal, Bangladesh, Egypt, Netherlands
B. Bhutan, Mauritius, Nigeria, Oman
C. Bangladesh, Singapore, Spain, Netherlands
D. Sri Lanka, Egypt, UAE, Mauritius

IX

On 26th January 1950, we are going to enter into a life of contradictions. In politics, we will have equality and in social and economic structure, continue to deny the principle of one man one value. How long shall we continue to live this life of contradictions? How long shall we continue to deny equality in our social and economic life? If we continue to deny it for long, we will do so only by putting our political democracy in peril. We must remove this contradiction at the earliest possible moment else those who suffer from inequality will blow up the structure of democracy, which this Constituent Assembly has so laboriously built up.

I feel that the Constitution is workable, it is flexible and it is strong enough to hold the country together both in peacetime and in wartime. Indeed, if I may say so, if things go wrong under the new Constitution, the reason will not be that we had a bad Constitution. What we will have to say is that man was vile?

The third thing we must do is not be content with mere political democracy. We must note that our political democracy cannot last unless there lies at the base of social democracy. What does social democracy mean? It means a way of life, which recognizes liberty, equality and fraternity as the principles of life.

...however, good a Constitution may be, it is sure to turn out bad because those who are called to work it, happen to be a bad lot. However, bad a Constitution may be, it may turn out to be good if those who are called to work it, happen to be a good lot. The working of a Constitution does not depend wholly upon the nature of the Constitution.

[Excerpts from Dr. Ambedkar's address to the Constituent Assembly, 25 November 1949]

47. What is the life of contradiction referred to here?

A. That of equality in politics but inequality in social and economic structure
B. That of inequality in politics but equality in social and economic structure
C. That of inequality in social structure but equality in economic structure
D. That of equality in politics and economic structure but inequality in social structure

48. What will happen, according to Dr. Ambedkar, if we continue to deny equality in our social and economic life?

A. There will be no injustice
B. Our political democracy will be in danger

C. Equality in social and economic life will be achieved nevertheless

D. Our social and economic life will be in peril

49. What might be the cause, according to Dr. Ambedkar, if things go wrong under the new Constitution?

A. That the Constitution was ignored

B. That the men called upon to work the Constitution were good

C. That the men called upon to work the Constitution were not good

D. That the Constitution was bad and failed the people

50. What does social democracy mean?

A. Equality before the Law

B. Equality of opportunities

C. Equality in social life

D. Equality in economic life

51. When does a bad Constitution turnout to be good?

A. When the people called upon to work it are good

B. When the people called upon to work it are bad

C. When the Constitution is amended

D. None of the above

52. Which of the following statement is not correct about what Dr. B.R. Ambedkar feel about the Constitution?

A. The Constitution is workable

B. The Constitution is flexible

C. The Constitution is strong enough to hold the country together in peacetime only

D. The Constitution is strong enough to hold the country together both in peacetime and in wartime

Section-III : Legal Reasoning

X

The Indian legal system places a significant emphasis on protecting the rights and welfare of children. The Juvenile Justice (Care and Protection of Children) Act, 2015, is a vital piece of legislation in this regard. It is designed to ensure that children in conflict with the law receive special care, protection, and treatment, with the ultimate goal of their rehabilitation and reintegration into society.

One of the key provisions of the Act is the establishment of Juvenile Justice Boards (JJBs) at the district level. These boards consist of a Metropolitan Magistrate or Judicial Magistrate of the first class and two social workers, at least one of whom should be a woman. The primary function of the JJB is to determine the age of the juvenile, the circumstances in which the offense was committed, and whether the juvenile should be sent to a special home or released on probation.

The Act makes a clear distinction between a "child in conflict with the law" and a "child in need of care and protection". A child in conflict with the law is one who has committed an offense, while a child in need of care and protection is a child who is vulnerable or at risk and requires special care and support.

The Act introduces a unique approach to dealing with children who are in conflict with the law. For children between the ages of 16 and 18, who have committed heinous offenses, they can be tried as adults, subject to a preliminary assessment by the Juvenile Justice Board. This assessment considers the child's mental and physical capacity to commit such an offense. If the board determines that the child should be tried as an adult, the case is transferred to the regular criminal courts.

The Act also places restrictions on the publication of information that could lead to the identification of a juvenile offender. This is done to protect the privacy and future prospects of the child.

53. What is the primary objective of the Juvenile Justice (Care and Protection of Children) Act, 2015?

A. To punish child offenders.

B. To rehabilitate and reintegrate children in conflict with the law.

C. To remove all forms of violence against children.

D. To increase the age of criminal responsibility.

54. Who makes up the Juvenile Justice Board (JJB)?

A. Two Judges.

B. A Metropolitan Magistrate and two Lawyers.

C. A Metropolitan Magistrate or Judicial Magistrate of the first class and two Social Workers.

D. Three Police Officers.

55. What is the role of the Juvenile Justice Board (JJB)?

A. To determine the punishment for juvenile offenders.

B. To decide whether a child should be sent to a regular prison.

C. To assess the age and circumstances of the juvenile, and make decisions on rehabilitation.

D. To prosecute child offenders.

56. What is the distinction between a "child in conflict with the law" and a "child in need of care and protection"?

A. There is no distinction; both terms mean the same thing.

B. A "child in conflict with the law" has committed a crime, while a "child in need of care and protection" is vulnerable or at risk.

C. A "child in need of care and protection" is more likely to commit crimes.

D. A "child in conflict with the law" is an adolescent offender.

57. Under what circumstances can children between the ages of 16 and 18 be tried as adults?

A. They can always be tried as adults.

B. After a preliminary assessment by the Juvenile Justice Board.

C. When they have committed any offense, regardless of the severity.

D. When they reach the age of 18.

58. What is the purpose of placing restrictions on the publication of information related to juvenile offenders?

A. To increase the age of criminal responsibility.

B. To protect the privacy and future prospects of the child.

C. To encourage public shaming of juvenile offenders.

D. To help law enforcement track juvenile offenders.

XI

In India, the legal landscape surrounding online defamation is a subject of significant interest and debate. With the rise of social media, and online platforms, cases of online defamation have become increasingly common. Defamation refers to making false statements about someone that harm their reputation. Online defamation includes defamatory statements made on the internet, including social media, blogs, forums, and other online platforms.

One critical aspect of online defamation is determining the liability of intermediaries, such as social media platforms or websites, for defamatory content posted by users. Section 79 of the Information Technology Act, 2000, provides a safe harbor for intermediaries, stating that they are not liable for third-party content if they act as intermediaries and follow due diligence in removing or disabling access to the content once notified.

However, determining whether an intermediary has fulfilled its due diligence obligations can be complex. The Indian judiciary has been actively interpreting this provision. One significant case is the *Shreya Singhal v. Union of India,* in which the Supreme Court clarified that intermediaries are required to act upon a valid court order or government directive for content removal, not upon private complaints.

The court also emphasized that the intermediaries should not take a proactive role in monitoring content, as this could potentially infringe on free speech. While the law provides a safe harbor, it does not absolve intermediaries from their responsibilities.

Online defamation cases often involve a balancing act between the right to freedom of expression and the right to reputation. The Indian legal system requires a careful examination of the content, context, and intent of the statements to determine whether they qualify as defamatory. Additionally, the plaintiff in an online defamation case must prove that the statement was false, damaging to their reputation, and made with a degree of fault, such as negligence or actual malice.

59. What is the primary focus of the passage?

A. The rise of social media in India.

B. The legal aspects of online defamation in India.

C. The role of intermediaries in online content.

D. The importance of free speech on the internet.

60. What is online defamation, as described in the passage?

A. Making harmful statements about someone in person.

B. False statements made on the internet that harm someone's reputation.

C. Online harassment.

D. A form of political activism.

61. What is the significance of Section 79 of the Information Technology Act, 2000, as mentioned in the passage?

A. It defines defamation laws in India.

B. It provides safe harbor for intermediaries in cases of online defamation.

C. It regulates the content on social media platforms.

D. It allows private complaints against online defamation.

62. According to the Supreme Court in the *Shreya Singhal v. Union of India* case, under what circumstances should intermediaries act in response to content removal?

A. Upon receiving a private complaint.

B. Upon a valid court order or government directive.

C. Proactively to monitor content.

D. Only if the content is found to be defamatory.

63. How does the Indian legal system balance the Right to Freedom of Expression and the Right to Reputation in online defamation cases?

A. By favoring freedom of expression over reputation.

B. By favoring reputation over freedom of expression.

C. By carefully examining the content, context, and intent of statements.

D. By absolving intermediaries of their responsibilities.

64. In an online defamation case, what must the plaintiff prove about the defamatory statement?

A. That it was political activism.

B. That it was made with good intentions,

C. That it was true and intended to inform the public.

D. That it was false, damaging to their reputation, and made with a degree of fault.

65. What is the role of intermediaries in the context of online defamation cases?
A. To actively monitor and censor content.
B. To act upon private complaints for content removal.
C. To completely absolve themselves of liability.
D. To encourage online defamation.

XII

The Editors Guild of India has expressed concern over the "draconian provisions" of the Press and Registration of Periodicals (PRP) Bill, 2023, that can have an adverse impact on freedom of the press.

The Guild added: "Editors Guild of India would like the proposed bill to ensure that publishing of news in India remains free of encumbrances and intrusive checks on publishers by the Registrar, and that the primary emphasis of the Registrar and the PRP remains 'registration' and not 'regulation', as the latter has the potential of restricting freedom of the press."

"In the definitions section, the term 'specified authority' gives power to government agencies beyond the Press Registrar, to conduct the functions of the Registrar, which could even include police and other law enforcement agencies. Given the intrusive, expansive, and vague nature of powers that the bill in any case allows to the Press Registrar, the power to further delegate this power to other government agencies including law enforcement agencies is deeply distressing," the Guild said.

The statement says sections 4(1) and 11(4) allow the Registrar to deny the right to bring out a periodical and cancel the certificate of registration of a periodical to persons convicted of "terrorist act or unlawful activity" or "for having done anything against the security of the State".

"Interestingly, the PRB Act, 1867, had no such provisions. Given the liberal and arbitrary use of UAPA (which is the basis for defining 'terrorist act' and 'unlawful activity'), as well as other criminal laws, including sedition, against journalists and media organisations to suppress freedom of speech, the Guild is deeply concerned by the introduction of these new provisions, and the way they can be misused to deny the right to bring out news publications to persons who are critical of governments," it said.

Among the other worrisome provisions listed by the Guild is Section 6(b), which gives power to the Press Registrar (as well as any other "specified authority") to enter the premises of a periodical to "inspect or take copies of the relevant records or documents or ask any questions necessary for obtaining any information required to be furnished".

[Extracted, with edits and revisions from "Editors Guild of India expresses concern over draconian provisions of the Press and Registration of Periodicals Bills, 2023" published in The Telegraph dated 07-08-2023]

66. The PRP Bill defines "newspaper" to mean a periodical of loose-folded sheets usually printed on newsprint and brought out daily or at least once in a week, containing information on current events, public news or comments on public news. Who among the following is covered by the definition of newspaper?
A. Mr. X publishing news content on digital media.
B. Mr. Y publishing books containing the comments of the public on public news.
C. Mr. Z publishing news content in print media on weekly basis.
D. All of the above.

67. Who among the following is not eligible to publish a periodical as per the PRP Bill?
A. Mr. A convicted of waging war against Government of India.
B. Mr. B, accused of unlawful activities under the Unlawful Activities Prevention Act.

C. Mr. C, accused of terrorist activities under the Unlawful Activities Prevention Act.

D. All of the above.

68. Which of the following is a threat to the freedom of press in India?

A. Liberal use of Unlawful Activities Prevention Act against Journalists refrains journalists from tracing, tracking and publishing investigative articles because they apprehend that they might be linked with criminals.

B. Use of Sedition laws against journalists under the guise that through their articles they are promoting hatred and exciting disaffection against the government.

C. Levy of GST on newspapers.

D. Both (A) and (B).

69. The PRP Bill defines "specified authority" to mean a District Magistrate or Collector or such other officer as the State Government or, as the case may be, Union territory Administration may, by notification, specify. The PRP Bill is criticised by Editors Guild of India because:

A. The definition of specified authority is too wide and can include even officers below the level of Collector. The PRP Bill enables the specified authority to perform the functions of Press Registrar General.

B. The PRP Bill confers various powers on the Press Registrar General including the power to register, deny registration, cancel the registration, etc.

C. The PRP Bill enables the specified authority to enter the premises of a periodical for inspection

D. All of the above.

70. Freedom of press is not specifically guaranteed under the Constitution of India but is implied in Article 19(1)(a) i.e. Freedom of Speech and Expression. Therefore, freedom of press is part of fundamental rights.

A. Freedom of press being a fundamental right, no law can be made for registration and denial of registration of newspapers.

B. Fundamental rights are not absolute rights and reasonable restrictions can be imposed on the exercise of fundamental rights and therefore, laws such as PRP Bill can be enacted.

C. Freedom of press being a fundamental right, journalists and press is exempt from the operation of general criminal law of the country.

D. None of the above

71. PRP Bill denies the right to publish periodicals to a person who has been found to have committed a terrorist act and has been convicted by a competent Court in India. Which of the following is most appropriate reason?

A. The right to publish a periodical is denied because criminals do not possess any fundamental rights.

B. The right to publish a periodical is denied because such a person is a threat to the society and nation.

C. The right to publish a periodical is denied because they may not be neutral in reporting and may incite violence and spread disaffection against the state being themselves involved in terrorist acts.

D. All of the above.

XIII

There are some advantages of the Digital Personal Data Protection Act (DPDPA), 2023. For instance, for the first time, personal data belonging to or identifying children will have to be classified separately, with such data carrying a greater degree of security and privacy. The law also seeks to reduce the rate and impact of data breaches targeting Indian businesses.

The Digital Personal Data Protection law, however, goes a step beyond by imposing penalties for cases where data is breached as a result of a lack of implementation of adequate security controls. However, it could be said that the law isn't balanced, because it provides wide exemptions to the processing of personal data to the government. For instance, data can be processed "in the interest of prevention, detection, investigation or prosecution of any offence ... in India." These kinds of exemptions are dangerous as they stand to legitimise widespread and unwarranted collection of data under the guise that such collection and processing may ultimately be useful for preventing or deterring a crime.

Security agencies will have significant authority to collect and retain any data whatsoever, as is typically the case with exemptions relating to the maintenance of sovereignty, integrity, security of the state, preservation of public order, prevention of offences, and incitement to commit offences. The law also exempts processing of personal data held outside of India. The government is also exempt from being required to delete any data that it possesses, regardless of the purpose it may have been collected for, on the request of an individual, or by way of a prescribed data retention period.

The government is not bound by purpose limitations, allowing data collected for one specified purpose be used for a new, incompatible purpose, which stands in contrast to the regulations imposed on businesses.

[Extracted, with edits and revisions from "Digital Personal Data Protection Law Raises Questions About Consistency with Right to Privacy Ruling" published in The Wire dated 22-08-2023]

72. Mr. Lal was suffering from a rare disease and the data relating of that was collected by the government. Suppose the DPDPA, 2023 provides exemptions for the government relating to data deemed "necessary for research, archiving or statistical purposes" if the personal data is not to be used to take any decision specific to a data principal and such processing is carried on in accordance with such standards as may be prescribed.

Which of the following is most appropriate?

A. The personal data of Mr. Lal can be preserved by the government till the research on rare disease is complete.

B. The data can only be used for taking any decision regarding Mr. Lal.

C. The personal data of Mr. Lal's health conditions and his personal data can be preserved by; the private hospital forever and used for research by them without his consent.

D. All of the above.

73. Suppose the DPDPA, 2023 provided exemption for the processing of personal data for the purpose of ascertaining the financial position of any person who has defaulted in payment of amount due on loan taken from a nationalised bank. Mr. X Commits a default in repayment of EMI of loan taken from a nationalized bank.

A. The bank can demand access to and process the personal data of Mr. X relating to family history of ailments from which Mr. X or his family was suffering.

B. The bank can process the personal data of Mr. X viz., the particulars of the family, wife, children, brothers etc.

C. The bank can process the data of Mr. X for the purpose of ascertaining the assets and liabilities of the defaulter.

D. All of the above.

74. Suppose Mr. Y, a citizen of India, is working in an MNC in New Zealand since 2021. The MNC has obtained personal details of the employee for the purpose of recovering the amount of indemnity bond if Mr. Y left the job within three years of joining.

A. Mr. Y can file an application in India for protection of his digital personal data under the DPDPA if he leaves the job in September 2023, and returns to India.

B. Mr. Y, being a citizen of India, can claim protection against the MNC for misuse of his personal data even while serving in New Zealand.

C. The DPDPA 2023 is not applicable since the data is held outside India.

D. The DPDPA 2023, is not applicable since the data has been obtained before the enactment of DPDPA.

75. If personal data is defined as any data about an individual who is identifiable by or in relation to such data, which of the following shall be classified as the personal data?

A. Name of the Person.

B. Full Residential Address.

C. Aadhar Number.

D. All of the Above.

76. In which of the following cases, the access to personal data shall be granted and the person whose data is accessed and processed cannot claim personal data protection?

A. Mr. Z has committed many robberies and police wants to access his Aadhar details and fingerprint data for the purpose of tracing Mr. Z.

B. It is apprehended that a person identified as Mr. G would spread hatred among various communities which would lead to riots and Police intends to use the mobile number and other personal details of Mr. G for the purpose of preventing such crimes.

C. Both (A) and (B).

D. Neither (A) nor (B).

77. Which of the following is correct?

A. Personal data collected by a health service provider can be sold to an insurance agency by the service provider without the consent of the concerned person.

B. Personal data collected by the government can be used for whatever purpose.

C. Personal data collected by the insurance company can be sold to mobile companies for mobile marketing without the consent of the concerned person.

D. All of the above.

XIV

The Supreme Court on September 1 held that a child born of a void or voidable marriage can inherit the parent's share in a joint Hindu family property. A three-judge Bench headed by Chief Justice of India D.Y. Chandrachud however clarified that such a child would not be entitled to rights in or to the property of any other person in the family. A voidable marriage is one that is made invalid by the husband or wife through a decree. A void marriage is invalid at its very inception.

Chief Justice Chandrachud said the first step to the inheritance of a child from a void or voidable marriage would be to ascertain the exact share of his parent in the ancestral property. This could be done by means of conducting a "notional partition" of the ancestral property and calculating how much of the property the parent would have got immediately before his death. Once the share of the deceased parent in the property is ascertained through such a notional partition, his heirs, including his children by means of void or voidable marriage, would be entitled to their portions in the share.

The Chief Justice said that Section 16 of the Hindu Marriage Act has statutorily conferred legitimacy to children born out of void or voidable marriages. In fact, Chief Justice Chandrachud pointed out that Section 16(3) stipulates that children from void and voidable marriages would have a right to their parents' property. The court said the intent of granting legitimacy to such children in the Hindu Marriage Act should also be reflected in the Hindu Succession Act, which governs inheritance. Children from void or voidable marriages come within the ambit of "legitimate kinship" and cannot be regarded as illegitimate by the Hindu Succession Act when it comes to inheritance.

The case before the three-judge Bench was focused on an amended provision in the Hindu Marriage Act, Section 16(3). The case was referred to a larger Bench in 2011 after a Division Bench of the apex court refused to follow past precedents and championed the cause of children born out of illegitimate marriages.

[...]

"With changing social norms of legitimacy in every society, including ours, what was illegitimate in the past may be legitimate today. The concept of legitimacy stems from social consensus, in the shaping of which various social groups play a vital role," Justice Ganguly, who authored the 2011 judgment, had observed.

During the hearings on the reference, Chief Justice Chandrachud had agreed with the Division Bench's findings that children from void and voidable marriages had rights over the property, whether self-acquired or ancestral, of their parents.

[Extracted with edits and revisions from "Children from void, voidable marriages entitled to parents' share in ancestral property: Supreme Court", by Krishnadas Rajagopal, *The Hindu,* https://www.thehindu.com/news/national/children-from-void-voidable-marriages-are-legitimate-can-claim-rights-in-parents-properties-sc/article67259229.ece]

78. Ashima and Ashok got married to each other in a traditional Hindu ceremony in Kolkata, after which they both moved to the USA, where Ashok had a job. In the USA, they had a child, whom they named Gogol. Many years later, Ashima found that Ashok was already married to Sushma before their wedding in Kolkata. Ashok and Sushma also had a child from their marriage, Arpita, who was older than Gogol by 4 years. Ashok explained to Ashima that although he had no intention of cheating on her, he had to keep his marriage to Sushma a secret since his parents would have never agreed as Sushma belonged to a different caste. Ashima is shocked to learn that her marriage to Ashok is void as per Hindu marriage laws since Ashok was already married before their wedding. She is trying to explore possibilities so that Gogol doesn't lose his inheritance from his father's side of the family. Based on your reading of the passage, what do you think is the correct position with respect to Gogol's inheritance rights?

A. Gogol could claim the entirety of Ashok's share of the ancestral property.
B. Gogol would inherit the entire ancestral property as the only son of Ashok.
C. Gogol would inherit his share from within Ashok's share of the full ancestral property without prejudice to the inheritance of other legal heirs, including Arpita.
D. Only Sushma and Arpita are the rightful legal heirs of Ashok.

79. In the above fact scenario, consider a property that was purchased by Ashok from his own earnings in the USA, thereby not making it part of ancestral property but instead falling in the category of self-acquired property. Upon Ashok's death, who would have inheritance rights over the said property?

A. Sushma and Ashima.
B. Sushma, Ashima, Arpita, and Gogol, as they are all his rightful legal heirs.
C. Sushma, Arpita, and Gogol.
D. Sushma and Arpita.

80. Based on your reading of the passage, how did the Hindu Marriage Act influence the outcome of the case on inheritance? Select one option from below:

A. The amended provisions of the Hindu Marriage Act grant legitimacy to children from voidable marriages and therefore this logic should be extended to children born of voidable and void marriages under the Hindu Succession Act.

B. The amended provisions of the Hindu Marriage Act give legitimacy to the second marriage and therefore this should also have an impact on the Hindu Succession Act.

C. The amended provisions of the Hindu Marriage Act grant legitimate status to children from void or voidable marriages and therefore this should also extend to the Hindu Succession Act.

D. The Hindu Marriage Act has no bearing on the case in question.

81. 12-year-old Kausalya was married off to 23-year-old Dashrath in her maternal home in Uttar Pradesh. She completed her education after her marriage and went on to get a job as a teacher at a government school. Dashrath's family, however, was opposed to her taking up a job outside the house and insisted that she should stay at home and look after her 2 sons, Ram and Lakshman. Kausalya, however, was very excited about starting her new job and sought advice from her younger sister, Vershini, who was training to be a lawyer. Vershini advises her that since she was married before she turned 18, her marriage was voidable and she could get it annulled. Kausalya, who was not very happy in her marriage, considers this option but is worried that her sons may lose their inheritance. Select the option that denotes correctly the status of Ram and Lakshman to inherit their father's ancestral property.

A. Kausalya's children cannot inherit Dashrath's ancestral property but can inherit his self-acquired property.

B. Both Ram and Lakshman can inherit their father's share of the ancestral property irrespective of the voidable status of their parent's marriage.

C. If Kausalya decides to annul her voidable marriage, she and her sons would lose all rights of inheriting ancestral property from Dashrath.

D. Ram and Lakshman can only inherit ancestral property from their mother's side since she decided to annul the voidable marriage.

82. Ajay is married to 2 women, Diya and Riya, and both don't know of each other. He was married to Diya first, when they were both around 23 years of age and studying together in college. They have no children. He later got married to Riya in a temple, and she had no idea about his first marriage with Diya. Ajay and Riya have 2 children, Raj and Rani. One day, Riya found out about Diya from one of Ajay's college friends. She wants to divorce Ajay but finds out that her marriage to him is void since he was already married at that time. At a loss, she goes to a lawyer to find out about the rights of her children to inherit property. Which is the most legally sound advice that the lawyer could give to her?

A. He would say that her children can still inherit property from Ajay thanks to the Supreme Court judgment.

B. He would advise her to get her marriage registered so that they can inherit property.

C. He would advise her to ignore her marriage with Ajay since it is anyway a void marriage.

D. He would advise her to speak to Diya and sort it out with her so that her children can inherit property since she would have the final say.

83. In the above scenario, Riya wants to know if there is any way in which the judgment can come to her aid while inheriting property owned by Ajay. What would the correct position of law?

A. No, she cannot inherit property as the judgment merely talks about the rights of children from void marriages.

B. Yes, she should fight for her rights to inherit property.

C. Yes, Ajay would have to give her property since he cheated on her.

D. She would get an equal share of property as Diya, since they are both his wives who got married to him without knowing about each other.

84. Srimati's first marriage was void due to being within the prohibited degree of relationship. Dhanalakshmi, who is the daughter of Srimati from her first marriage confronts her mother once she finds her identity, demanding her share in her mother's ancestral property. Srimati, however, subsequently married Dhrupad and has 2 daughters with him—Ira and Shira and is not interested in giving any property to Dhanalakshmi. Dhanalakshmi decides to assert her right in a court of law. How would Dhanalakshmi's share be determined?

A. Dhanalakshmi would not have any right in her mother's share of the property since the right of inheritance pertains only to father's share of property.

B. Dhanalakshmi could demand a notional partition and get a share from Srimati's portion of her ancestral property.

C. Being a child from a void marriage, Dhanalakshmi has no rights of inheritance.

D. It is Srimati's decision as to whom she gives rights in her property.

Section-IV : Logical Reasoning

XV

Words remain an enigma, their presence within human sphere is a unique mystery. They form the intricate tapestry that convinces us of our existence, blurring lines between fact and fiction. An engagement with words is the most captivating, enchanting, and sometimes daunting encounter with the world. A word, a symbolic entity formed from the ethereal, exists neither as animate nor inanimate, yet pulsates with life. It can emanate warmth or coldness, absorb emotions, or stand as dry as a rock. Words can provoke smiles and elicit joy. They are like glow-worms, momentarily dispelling the surrounding darkness and act as life-saving rafts amid the tumultuous ocean waves. Words grant us the ability to explore the universe, and "to see a world in a grain of sand", as William Blake noted. They impart a semantic existence to the lifeless, and bestow aesthetic form upon the formless. Scriptures say the word is the world. I say the world within the word is the abode of faith.

85. What is the central theme of the passage?

A. The history of the human language

B. The impact of words on human existence

C. The importance of storytelling

D. The mystery of human cognition

86. According to the passage, what does a 'word' symbolize?

A. An inanimate object

B. An animate entity

C. A tangible entity

D. An intangible concept

87. How does the passage describe words' ability to affect emotions?

A. Words can only evoke positive emotions.

B. Words can absorb emotions and become emotion themselves.
C. Words have no impact on emotions.
D. Words can be devoid of emotions.

88. "An engagement with words is the most captivating, enchanting, and sometimes daunting encounter with the world." Which of the following conclusions can be drawn from the above statement?
A. Words can be used to manipulate others.
B. The power of words should be used carefully.
C. Words can capture the atrocities of the world.
D. Words can paint a picture of the world in all its different colours.

89. Which of the following strengthens the author's idea of words being "like glow-worms momentarily dispelling the surrounding darkness"?
A. Words help in understanding reality.
B. Words illuminate the mind of the reader.
C. Words help in escaping reality.
D. Words cast darkness in the mind of the reader.

90. In the context of the passage, what is the significance of the "world within the word"?
A. It refers to the power of language to create inspiration, energy and faith.
B. It signifies the author's love for the global community.
C. It represents the mysteries hidden in language.
D. It describes the author's mission to explore different cultures.

XVI

Students have been abuzz over how artificial intelligence tools can do their homework and programmers over how these can increase their productivity or take away their jobs. As much as digitization has transformed the country in recent years, there is a widespread feeling that at some point around the horizon, AI shall rejig everything in even more fundamental, fantastic, and frightening ways. This is why deciding how the coming changes should be regulated is very important. TRAI has made a strong case for an independent statutory authority to ensure the responsible development and use of AI in the country, a global agency along similar lines shall likely be pitched at the G20 leaders' summit, and interestingly even American MNC Microsoft has floated a blueprint for AI governance in India. The great size and diversity of its "data points" make India of great interest to all developers of AI technologies.

But India is only at their receiving end, nowhere close to the US and China's advances. Although lately, it is becoming obvious how much state censorship is encumbering China's Large Language Modeling, the country is still very much in the game with PhDs in fields related to AI, investments in AI chip hardware design, and domestic generative models like Wu Dao. The scientific accomplishments of India's Chandrayaan mission have seen it being wooed for various international space collaborations. This promises spinoff technological benefits across Indian industry and is also geo-strategically useful. Likewise, it is only with sufficient AI prowess that India shall really get to play at the high table of global rulemaking for AI.

Knowing how much Indians' future shall be shaped by generative AI needs matching efforts to create indigenous models. In this and at this stage, a proactive government role is key, rather than just waiting on some large corporation to do the needful. Missing this bus will after all be even more costly than missing the chip research one. Plus, GOI alone can push academia-industry collaborations with the necessary weight and urgency. This does not let other institutions off the hook. A US judge has rejected the copyright for an AI-generated artwork. Indian courts should start engaging with the broader issue of non-human agency rather than wait for precedence to be set elsewhere.

Indian schools need to think beyond the ban-ChatGPT mindset. Let us lead instead of only being led.

[Extracted from "First, get the tech: Unless India develops domestic AI heft, it wouldn't play any meaningful part in global regulatory efforts", *Times of India*]

91. Which of the following is the author most likely to agree with?

A. The best way to deal with the advancement of AI is to leave its regulation to market forces.

B. Government-driven control of AI is inefficient and shall promote red-tapism.

C. Private companies with their large capital and infrastructure design the most efficient AI governance models.

D. Government-led initiatives of AI regulation and development lead to efficient outcomes.

92. Which of the following, if true, would most strengthen the main argument of the passage?

A. Governments that lead the initiative on regulating and responding to the advancement of AI tools benefit the most from them.

B. Governments that don't engage with generative AI and remain at its receiving end stay risk-averse with nothing to lose.

C. Governments that actively incentivise MNCs to participate in AI governance make the most out of the advancements in the field.

D. Governments that explore models of public-private partnership strike the right balance in regulating generative AI.

93. Based only on the author's statement that "Indian courts should start engaging with the broader issue of non-human agency rather than wait for precedence to be set elsewhere", which of the following would the author be most likely to agree with?

A. Courts should take the initiative by being innovative and laying down rules where no precedents exist.

B. Courts should wait for precedents and in the meantime refrain from engaging with the challenges presented by generative AI.

C. Courts should stop relying on precedents and decide cases on the basis of judicial wisdom.

D. Precedents are the best possible safeguard against arbitrary decision-making.

94. If the information in the passage above is correct, which of the following must necessarily be true?

A. AI regulation is the responsibility of the legislature alone.

B. AI regulation is the responsibility of courts and can't be addressed through standalone statutory rules.

C. AI regulation is a collaborative effort involving all the institutions of the State.

D. AI regulation is the domain of private industry.

95. Based on the author's arguments, which of the following would result in weakening, rather than strengthening India's position at the forefront of generative AI?

A. Investing in indigenous AI chip hardware design and domestic generative models.

B. Exploring spinoff technological benefits with other scientific advancements like the Chandrayaan mission.

C. Introducing generative models like Wu Dao which have demonstrated success in other jurisdictions.

D. Locally developing technologies such as indigenous AI models.

96. The author states that, "Missing this bus will after all be even more costly than missing the chip research one." For this statement to be true, with which of the following statements about chip research must the author most likely agree?

A. India lead chip research from its frontiers.

B. India was right to leave regulation of chip industry and research to MNCs.

C. India should have proactively played a role in responding to new research in chip technology.

D. The failure to respond to new developments in chip technology was a bigger loss than the potential failure to regulate generative AI.

XVII

Imagine you have just been appointed as a consultant for a manufacturing company that is experiencing a decline in its production efficiency. The company produces a wide range of products, and the management is concerned about the overall output. Your task is to identify the root causes of this decline and recommend solutions.

As you begin your investigation, you gather information and observe the following:

- The company recently introduced a new production system that is more automated but requires highly specialized operators.
- The workforce has reported a lack of motivation and job satisfaction, which has led to increased absenteeism.
- There have been several breakdowns in the new machinery, leading to production delays and quality issues.
- The company's competitors have adopted similar automation technologies and are experiencing increased productivity.
- Customer complaints about product quality have increased in recent months.

97. Based on the information provided, which of the following is a potential root cause of the decline in production efficiency?

A. The introduction of a new production system

B. Lack of motivation and job satisfaction among the workforce

C. Increased absenteeism

D. Breakdowns in machinery

98. What makes the introduction of the new production system a potential contributing factor to the decline in efficiency?

A. The system is highly automated

B. It requires specialized operators

C. The machinery is prone to breakdowns

D. Competitors have adopted similar technologies

99. What is a critical difference between the company's situation and that of its competitors?

A. Both the company and its competitors have introduced new production systems.

B. The competitors have experienced increased customer complaints.

C. The company's workforce lacks motivation and job satisfaction.

D. The company's machinery is prone to breakdowns.

100. How might the increased absenteeism affect production efficiency?

A. It might lead to increased quality issues.

B. It might result in longer machinery breakdowns.

C. It could lead to delays in production.

D. It has no impact on production efficiency.

101. What could be a possible solution to address the decline in production efficiency?

A. Hire more specialized operators for the new system.

B. Implement a motivation and job satisfaction program for the workforce.

C. Upgrade the machinery to reduce breakdowns.

D. Purchase new machinery to replace the automated system.

102. Based on the information provided, what is a potential consequence of increased customer complaints about product quality?

A. It indicates that the company's competitors are also experiencing quality issues.

B. It suggests that the company's products are meeting customer expectations.

C. It may lead to a loss of customers and reputation damage.

D. It shows that the company's automated system is performing well.

XVIII

In a world where aspirations for upward mobility are fervent, the opportunities for achieving such dreams remain limited. When one generation falls short, the mantle of ambition passes to the next, embedding within it a heavy burden of responsibility. Failing to meet these expectations can lead to profound sorrow, and in the direst cases, even to suicide. It's in this landscape that coaching institutes assume a significant role, cultivating an atmosphere of uncertainty among students and parents. A stark discrepancy emerges between preparation for board examinations and competitive tests, amplifying the inequalities that plague the education system. The coaching industry's massive marketing campaigns further exacerbate the situation, with some strategies veering into ethical grey areas. The tests themselves, designed to be more challenging than standardised exams, set the stage for feelings of inadequacy and self-doubt when not conquered. Our educational system is tailored to gauge an individual's merit through examinations. Eminent thinker Michael J Sandel dubs this system the "tyranny of merit", a sentiment echoed by the Supreme Court of India. Upholding the OBC reservation judgment, the Court called for a deeper evaluation of the "idea of merit", highlighting its nuanced nature. Merit as a concept remains shrouded in misunderstanding and often goes unexamined within school curriculum.

Adapting to new living arrangements, sourcing nourishing meals, battling isolation, and grappling with commutes form the backdrop against, which education unfolds. For marginalised communities and gender minorities, these hurdles are often amplified. Social media algorithms exacerbate mental health concerns, sowing loneliness and impeding attention spans and creativity. Technology emerges as a potential equaliser in this landscape.

Online platforms now offer preparation opportunities from the comfort of one's home. Government-curated or market-driven content could usher in a new era of accessibility.

[Extracted, with edits and revisions from "*Kota suicides: Coaching institutes manufacture insecurity — moving beyond the tyranny of merit might help*" authored by Akash Kumar and published in **The Indian Express** dated September 2, 2023]

103. As per the author, which one of the following is not likely leading to suicide among the students?

A. Incorrect marketing strategies by the coaching institutes.

B. Burdening of ambitions by one generation to another.

C. Creation of hostile environment by the coaching institutes.

D. Living in a surrounding with different background and culture.

104. Which of the following is not true regarding the education system as per the opinion of the author?

A. It is primarily based on the merit of the students.

B. Merit of the students is not the determining factor.

C. Examination plays a pivotal role in the education system.

D. An individual's merit cannot be identified without examination.

105. Which of the following strengthens the argument regarding the 'idea of merit' as per the above-mentioned passage?

A. True merit is multifaceted and extends beyond performance in a single competitive examination.

B. Pervasive inequalities can only be identified with the help of a single competitive examination.

C. True merit is not multifaceted and does not extend beyond performance in a single competitive examination.

D. The school education ensures the proper implementation of the idea of merit.

106. Which of the following is correct regarding the inequalities mentioned by the author?

A. There is no difference between the preparation of board and competitive examination.

B. Education system accommodates the inequalities.

C. Competitive examination leads to social equality.

D. There are existing inequalities which are enlarged by the competitive examinations.

107. Which of the following statements reflects the use of online platforms for education as per the author?

A. It provides equal opportunity to all the students irrespective of caste or creed.

B. It encourages the students to prepare for examination.

C. It should be the only means to education.

D. It cannot be accessed by majority of the people due to technological impediments.

108. Which one of the following is not a challenge for quality education?

A. Influence of social media.

B. Mental health of the students and parents.

C. Availability of online resources.

D. Lack of competitive atmosphere among the peers.

Section-V : Quantitative Techniques

XIX

Automobiles are the most preferred mode of transport because they allow us to cover large distance quickly. Resultantly, vehicles have been developed that run on diesel, petrol and even on electricity, which is a remarkable innovative development. During a survey about the percentage wise distribution of cars in four different states, the information regarding ratio between the diesel engine cars, petrol engine cars and electric cars was collected. Total number of cars for which data was collected was 8000. Of these, State 1 had 15% of the total cars in the ratio of 3 : 4 : 1 (diesel, petrol and electric); State 2 had 20% of the total cars in the ratio of 5 : 3 : 2 (diesel, petrol and electric); State 3 had 30% of the total cars in the ratio of 4 : 5 : 3 (diesel, petrol and electric), and; State 4 had 35% of the total cars in the ratio of 7 : 5 : 2 (diesel, petrol and electric).

Based on the above information, answer the following questions.

109. If 45% of the electric cars in State 4 are air conditioned (AC) and remaining are non-AC, what is the number of non-AC cars?

A. 380 B. 240

C. 220 D. 180

110. Number of petrol cars in State 2 is how much percentage more than the number of diesel cars in State 1?

A. 4.67% B. 9.23%

C. 3.33% D. 6.67%

111. What is the ratio of diesel cars in State 4 to electric cars in State 3?
A. 7 : 3 B. 3 : 7
C. 7 : 4 D. 4 : 7

112. Compute the percentage of total electric cars to total cars in all the States.
A. 19.37%
B. 18.37%
C. 18.73%
D. 19.57%

113. What is the difference between number of petrol cars in State 3 and diesel cars in State 1?
A. 350
B. 400
C. 500
D. 550

114. What is the average number of diesel cars in all the States?
A. 810 B. 862.5
C. 886 D. 912.5

XX

A survey was conducted about the population of a particular region having working population of three lacs and information was collected about self-employed persons, casual wage workers, regular salaries employees of both urban and rural areas of the region. Self-employment is a key source of income in both rural and urban areas but it is more prevalent in rural areas (56% of the rural population) than in urban areas (40% of the urban population). Rural population was 48% of the total population. Regular salaried workers in urban areas were 48% of the urban population whereas in rural areas, regular salaried workers constituted 12% of the rural population. During the survey, the casual wage workers were found to be more common in rural areas than in urban areas. Casual wage workers in rural areas were 32% of the rural population whereas it was 12% of the urban population in urban areas.

Based on the above information, answer the following questions.

115. By what percentage the number of self-employed workers in rural areas is more than the number of self-employed workers in urban areas?
A. 29.23 B. 33.24
C. 35.01 D. 34.32

116. What is the ratio of urban and rural working population?
A. 12:13 B. 11:12
C. 13:12 D. 03:08

117. If urban population of the region increased from 52% to 56% and percentage of self employed in urban region remains same, then number of self-employed people in urban areas are:
A. 66840 B. 68640
C. 62700 D. 67200

118. What is the total number of regular salaried employees of the region?
A. 90216 B. 91260
C. 92160 D. 96210

119. What is the percentage of regular salaried employees in rural areas corresponding to the number of casual wage workers in urban areas?
A. 72.3%
B. 79.8%
C. 88.7%
D. 92.3%

120. If 60% of the total working population of the region were self-employed in rural areas and 40% of total population were self-employed in urban areas, then what is the ratio of rural self-employed to urban self-employed?
A. 2 : 3
B. 3 : 2
C. 13 : 18
D. 18 : 13

ANSWERS

1. **(B):** The passage outlines a nuanced and intricate relationship between characters and their settings in contemporary literature, emphasizing that the setting plays a vital role in shaping the narrative. This relationship is not one of separation or insignificance but of deep interconnection, where the setting does more than merely serve as a backdrop. Instead, it actively influences plot development and character growth. For example, the passage describes how the desert in Jhumpa Lahiri's "The Namesake" and the Kerala backwaters in Arundhati Roy's "The God of Small Things" are not just locations where the stories unfold. These settings mirror the internal states of the characters and contribute significantly to the thematic depth of the narratives. In "The Namesake," the barrenness of the desert reflects the protagonist's isolation and identity crisis, while in "The God of Small Things," the lushness of Kerala enriches the story's complex web of relationships and secrets. This detailed interplay indicates a deliberate choice by authors to use setting as a dynamic component of storytelling, making it integral to understanding characters and their journeys.

2. **(B):** In "*The Namesake*" by Jhumpa Lahiri, the barren desert landscape is a powerful symbol of the protagonist, Gogol's, sense of isolation and identity crisis. This setting is not chosen at random but is meticulously detailed to mirror the emotional and psychological state of Gogol as he navigates through life in a foreign land. The arid, expansive desert embodies his feelings of emptiness and disconnection from his surroundings and heritage. Just as the desert is vast and uninhabitable, Gogol finds himself in a vast cultural and emotional wasteland, struggling to find his place and identity. The relentless sun and vast sands of the desert are silent witnesses to his inner turmoil, symbolizing the harshness and the challenges of his journey towards self-discovery. This symbolic use of setting illustrates how contemporary authors employ landscapes not just for their physical attributes but for their ability to reflect and intensify the narrative's emotional and thematic concerns.

3. **(C):** In Shakespeare's "*Macbeth*", the Scottish moors play a crucial role beyond serving as a mere setting. They embody an ever-present omen of impending tragedy, integral to the play's atmosphere and thematic depth. The moors, with their eerie and foreboding presence, set the tone for the unfolding events and are symbolic of the moral decay and the dark path upon which Macbeth embarks. Their mist and mystery encapsulate the ambiguity of right and wrong, mirroring the inner turmoil and the descent into madness of Macbeth and Lady Macbeth. This setting is not passive; it actively contributes to the narrative by enhancing the sense of doom and foreboding that permeates the play. The ominous atmosphere of the moors reflects the psychological landscape of the characters, serving as a constant reminder of the natural order being disrupted by Macbeth's actions. This illustrates the power of setting in literature to act as a mirror to the characters' souls and as a foreteller of their fates.

4. **(B):** The term "interplay" in the context of the passage refers to a complex and dynamic relationship where the setting deeply influences the narrative, including

plot development and character evolution. This concept suggests that the setting and the characters are engaged in a symbiotic relationship, where each affects and is affected by the other. The settings in the examples provided (the desert in "The Namesake" and the Kerala backwaters in "The God of Small Things") are not static backgrounds but are integral to understanding the characters' emotional states and the narrative's thematic concerns. The interplay between character and setting is a deliberate literary technique used to enrich the story, adding layers of meaning that resonate with the reader. It highlights the setting's role in accentuating the narrative's emotional depth, influencing the characters' decisions, and reflecting their internal struggles. This relationship is a testament to the authors' skill in creating a vivid, immersive world where every element is purposefully interwoven to enhance the storytelling.

5. **(B):** The setting of "*The God of Small Things*" by Arundhati Roy is described as lush and vibrant, reflecting the teeming life and complexity of the Kerala backwaters where the story is set. This vivid description is not merely for aesthetic appeal but serves a deeper narrative purpose. The lushness and vibrancy of Kerala are integral to the fabric of the story, mirroring the complexity and richness of the characters' lives, their relationships, and the unfolding drama. The natural beauty and teeming life of the setting contrast with the human characters' struggles, secrets, and the societal norms that bind them. It also reflects the duality of beauty and tragedy that pervades the narrative, symbolizing both the abundance of life and the undercurrents of loss and decay. This setting, rich in detail and symbolism, contributes significantly to the thematic depth and emotional resonance of the story, illustrating how settings in literature can be as complex and dynamic as the characters themselves.

6. **(C):** The main theme discussed in the passage is the significant influence of setting in literature, asserting that settings can be as influential as characters in shaping the narrative. This theme is explored through the analysis of how settings like the desert in "*The Namesake*" and the Kerala backwaters in "*The God of Small Things*" are not mere backdrops but active elements that reflect and influence the characters' journeys and the story's thematic concerns. The passage argues that the setting can mirror the internal states of characters, enhance the narrative's emotional depth, and contribute to the overall storytelling. This approach to setting challenges the notion of it being a passive backdrop, instead presenting it as a dynamic component that interacts with the characters, influencing their development and the plot's progression. The detailed description of settings acting as silent witnesses to characters' inner turmoil or as symbols of thematic elements underscores the theme that in literature, settings are pivotal in creating a rich, immersive experience that adds layers of meaning to the narrative.

7. **(B):** The central thesis of the extract highlights the stark contrast in the imagination of justice between the rich and poor in India. It delves into the complexity of the justice system, which is perceived differently by various segments of society. For the middle class, particularly since 1991, there has been a demand for reasonable access to justice, contrasting with the OECD countries where such access is more readily available. However, the situation for the poor is depicted as dire, with the judicial system being largely inaccessible and alien

to them, leading to their victimization and exclusion. This disparity in access and perception underscores the broader societal divisions and inequities, encapsulating the essence of the crisis in justice as not merely a legal or administrative issue but a deeply rooted social challenge. The narrative vividly contrasts the colloquial definitions of a court by the oppressed and the elite, thereby illustrating the bifurcated reality of justice administration in India.

8. (A): The term 'docket-excluded' as used in the extract metaphorically refers to the systemic and structural barriers that prevent the poor from accessing the justice system. This exclusion is not just physical but also psychological and socio-economic, as the poor find the language, logic, and the very culture of the judicial system alien and hostile. This term encapsulates the myriad ways in which the poor are kept out of the justice system, including being victimized by legal practitioners and court staff, and the structural inaccessibility of civil justice mechanisms. It paints a picture of a new form of untouchability, where exclusion is based not on traditional social hierarchies but on economic and systemic barriers that render the poor invisible in the eyes of the law. This concept is crucial for understanding the broader discourse on justice and equity, highlighting the stark realities of marginalization in the judicial process.

9. (C): The extract describes the justice system's experience for different societal segments as conflicting. This characterization emerges from the divergent perspectives and outcomes that the justice system delivers to different classes of society. For the middle class and the rich, justice and its administration might represent a system of rights protection and business facilitation. In contrast, for the poor and marginalized, the justice system appears as an oppressive force, more likely to punish than to protect. This dichotomy is vividly illustrated through the contrasting definitions of a court by the masses and the legal professionals. Such conflicting experiences underscore the deep societal divisions and the justice system's role in perpetuating or alleviating these disparities. This aspect of the justice system reveals the complex interplay between law, society, and economic status, highlighting the challenges in achieving a universally equitable justice system.

10. (A): The author, through the narrative, suggests a belief that the judicial system mirrors the existing power relationships within society. This perspective is inferred from the discussion on the differential access to justice experienced by the middle class and the poor, and the systemic barriers that exacerbate these disparities. The narrative underscores the justice system's role in reflecting and sometimes reinforcing the societal inequities based on economic status, caste, and social power. By highlighting the contrast between the judicial system's perception by the rich and poor and the systemic exclusion of the marginalized, the author points to the broader societal structures and power dynamics that shape the justice system's functioning. This insight into the judicial system's societal embedding suggests a critical view of how justice is administered and accessed across different segments of society.

11. (B): The author, through the detailed exploration of the justice system's failings and biases, is most likely to disagree with the statement that "The Law ensures equality both in text and in practice". This disagreement stems from the critical examination of how the justice system, in reality, fails to provide equitable access and treatment to the poor and marginalized. The narrative illustrates the systemic and structural barriers that exclude the poor, not only in terms of access but also in the justice system's cultural and operational aspects. The concept of 'docket-exclusion' and the insights into how the justice system is perceived by different societal segments reveal a stark discrepancy between the ideal of legal equality and the practical realities faced by the marginalized. This critique aligns with the broader argument that the justice system, as currently structured, does not effectively ensure equality for all, particularly the poor.

12. **(C):** Reform of judicial administration is described as a 'neutral' area because such reforms are designed to improve the system's efficiency and effectiveness without favoring one class of people over another. This neutrality is derived from focusing on process improvements, procedural law, technology enhancements, and other administrative aspects that ostensibly benefit all users of the judicial system equally. By emphasizing 'neutral' reforms like case management and judge workload management, the narrative suggests that these efforts aim to address systemic inefficiencies that impact the justice system's overall performance.

This approach to reform is positioned as uncontroversial and broadly beneficial, sidestepping the more contentious issues of socioeconomic disparities and access to justice that might advantage or disadvantage particular groups. This framing implies a consensus on the value of such reforms across different societal strata, focusing on universal improvements rather than addressing the deeper, more divisive challenges of equity and access within the justice system.

13. **(B):** The protagonist's preference for "barrenness" and "starkness" at Carignano suggests a profound appreciation for simplicity and minimalism in her surroundings. This inclination towards an environment that is stripped of excess, where the natural elements of rocks, pines, light, and air predominate, reflects a personality that finds peace and satisfaction in the unadorned and the austere.

Such a preference indicates a desire for a life uncluttered by the superfluous, where the stark beauty of nature and the clarity it brings are valued above all. This disposition towards minimalism goes beyond mere aesthetic preference, hinting at a deeper philosophical or existential comfort with the essentials of existence. The starkness of Kasauli, with its sweeping views and unobstructed light and air, provides her with the exact setting she seeks, emphasizing a harmony between her inner state and her external environment.

14. **(B):** The protagonist's reaction towards the postman, characterized by her attempt to convey her desire for no intrusion with a "cold and piercing stare," clearly indicates her dislike for any disturbance or interruption in her solitude.

This interaction, or lack thereof, with the postman, who remains oblivious to her presence, underscores her preference for isolation and her aversion to any form of unwanted interaction. Her characterization of the postman as an "oafish ox" further emphasizes her irritation and the lengths to which she has gone internally to secure her solitude. This moment reveals a significant aspect of her state of mind: a profound value placed on privacy and tranquility, and a readiness to protect this personal space from what she perceives as the encroachments of the outside world.

15. **(D):** The protagonist's desire to be mistaken for a pine tree reveals a deep yearning to become one with nature and to escape from her human identity. This wish to merge with the pine trees, to the extent of being indistinguishable from them, signifies a desire for a profound connection with the natural world, transcending her human form. It reflects a mindset that seeks solace and identity in the elemental aspects of nature, rather than in human society or its constructs. This aspiration to be no more and no less than a tree illustrates a wish to strip away the complexities and burdens of human existence, finding peace in the simplicity and permanence of nature. It is a vivid expression of her quest for a form of existence that is entirely integrated with the natural environment she cherishes.

16. **(*)**

17. **(D):** Statement III is true about the protagonist's overall state of mind in Carignano. The passage describes her profound sense of fulfillment and peace with her surroundings, emphasizing that everything she wanted and had prepared for all her life was present in this secluded, stark environment. Her initial realization of relief upon arriving at Carignano signifies a deep contentment and satisfaction with her chosen place and way of life. This sense of being at peace is further underscored by her preference for the barrenness and simplicity of the landscape, which mirrors her inner desire for tranquility and minimalism. There is no indication of restlessness, anguish, or a feeling of disconnection; rather, the narrative conveys a strong sense of harmony between the protagonist and her environment.

18. **(B):** Nature plays a role in the protagonist's life at Carignano that offers her solace, peace, and a sense of belonging. The barrenness and starkness of the landscape, with its rocks, pines, light, and air, provide a backdrop that is deeply aligned with her personal ethos and desires. The natural setting of Carignano, including the sweeping views, the occasional eagle, and the simplicity of its flora, is integral to her sense of contentment and fulfillment. Nature, in its unadorned form, acts as a sanctuary for her, a place where she can find peace and a deep connection to the world in a way that transcends the complexities and demands of human society. This connection to nature is so profound that she imagines becoming part of it, merging with the pine trees to escape the human identity that she finds burdensome.

19. **(C):** William Shakespeare is often regarded as the greatest playwright in the history of the English language. His extensive body of work, including tragedies, comedies, and historical plays, showcases his profound understanding of human nature, emotions, and motivations. Shakespeare's enduring appeal lies in his timeless characters, intricate plots, and the universal themes he explores, such as love, ambition, and the human condition, making him a seminal figure in English literature.

20. **(B):** Jane Austen's novel "Sense and Sensibility" is known for its sharp social commentary and the witty portrayal of romance. Austen's novels, including "Pride and Prejudice," are celebrated for their insight into the manners and mores of the English gentry at the turn of the 19th century, blending romantic narratives with critical observations of societal norms and behaviors. "Sense and Sensibility" particularly exemplifies Austen's talent for dissecting the social fabric of her time through the experiences of her characters, making it a standout work of romantic fiction with a keen social eye.

21. (C): William Wordsworth and Samuel Taylor Coleridge are the Romantic poets mentioned in the passage known for celebrating the beauty of nature and the intense emotions of the individual. Their works, such as Wordsworth's "I Wandered Lonely as a Cloud" and Coleridge's "The Rime of the Ancient Mariner," are emblematic of the Romantic era's emphasis on emotional depth, the sublime beauty of the natural world, and the exploration of the human psyche. These poets sought to break from the classical conventions of their time, focusing instead on personal expression and the inherent beauty and terror of nature.

22. (C): Virginia Woolf's novel "Mrs. Dalloway" is known for its modernist narrative style. Woolf's innovative use of stream of consciousness, interior monologues, and a nonlinear narrative structure marked a departure from traditional storytelling methods. "Mrs. Dalloway" delves into the complex inner lives of its characters, exploring themes of existentialism, mental illness, and the fleeting nature of time. Woolf's work is a cornerstone of modernist literature, demonstrating her mastery of a narrative style that seeks to capture the intricacies of human thought and perception.

23. (A): "Nineteen Eighty-Four" by George Orwell is the 20th-century novel mentioned in the passage that provides a stark warning about the dangers of totalitarianism and the erosion of individual freedom. Set in a dystopian future where society is under the constant surveillance of an oppressive regime, Orwell's work is a critical commentary on the potential for government overreach and the suppression of dissent. The novel's themes of surveillance, censorship, and the manipulation of truth remain profoundly relevant, highlighting Orwell's prescient concerns about the direction of society.

24. (B): The passage highlights the enduring power of English literature as its diversity of authors, themes, and styles. English literature, from the plays of Shakespeare to the modernist novels of Virginia Woolf and the dystopian visions of George Orwell, encompasses a wide range of voices, perspectives, and literary techniques. This diversity allows English literature to offer rich insights into the human experience, capturing the complexity of life across different eras and societies. The passage emphasizes that English literature's ability to captivate and inspire readers across the world lies in this rich tapestry of storytelling, which continues to evolve and reflect the changing human condition.

25. (B): The incident described in the passage is the Jallianwala Bagh Massacre, which occurred in April 1919. The passage details a tragic event where General Dyer ordered troops to fire on a peaceful gathering in Amritsar, leading to a high number of casualties among the unarmed civilians.

26. (C): General Dyer ordered to fire on the crowd to teach the crowd a lesson. The passage indicates that the assembly was peaceful and had not shown any violence, yet Dyer proceeded with the firing without any prior warning, intending to make an example of the gathered crowd.

27. (B): The intention of the speaker, Col. Wedgwood, MP, in this passage is to expose the deeds of General Dyer. By detailing the events and the aftermath of the Jallianwala Bagh massacre in the British Parliament, the speaker aims to bring to light the brutality of the actions taken by General Dyer against unarmed civilians.

28. (D): After the incident, some people who lived nearby helped the injured and the dying people. The passage mentions that these individuals came and carried away

some of the wounded from among the heap of dead and dying, highlighting the absence of official aid for the victims.

29. (B): The feelings of the Indian children brought up to the spot would be of bitterness about the British rule. The passage predicts that the memory of the Jallianwala Bagh massacre will instill feelings of bitterness towards British rule in future generations, similar to the sentiments evoked by the historical site of the Cawnpore Well.

30. (C): The full name of General Dyer is Reginald Edward Harry Dyer. This is a factual question about the historical figure responsible for the Jallianwala Bagh massacre, and his full name is Reginald Edward Harry Dyer, although this specific detail is not directly provided in the passage, it is the correct historical information.

31. (A): The reason for the Hamas-led Palestinian militants' attack on Israel was multifaceted, involving a combination of grievances and provocations. The militants declared that the invasion was a response to several key issues: the "desecration of the Al-Aqsa Mosque," a significant and sensitive site in the Israeli-Palestinian conflict, symbolizing broader religious tensions; the ongoing blockade of the Gaza Strip, which has severely restricted the movement of people and goods, contributing to a humanitarian crisis; the construction of Israeli settlements, viewed as illegal under international law and a major obstacle to peace; and violence by Israeli settlers against Palestinians in the West Bank, which has exacerbated tensions and fueled resentment. These factors collectively motivated the attack, highlighting the deep-rooted and complex nature of the conflict, where religious, territorial, and humanitarian issues intertwine, driving cycles of violence and retaliation.

32. (A): The international community's reaction to the killing of Israeli civilians by Hamas-led Palestinian militants was one of widespread condemnation. At least 44 countries, primarily from the Western world, characterized the massacres of civilians as acts of terrorism. This unified stance reflects a common perception among these nations regarding the indiscriminate targeting of civilians in conflict situations. The label of terrorism is significant, as it denotes a moral and legal judgment against the actions taken, underscoring the international norm that civilian populations should not be targeted in military conflicts. This condemnation also highlights the global concern over escalating violence in the region and the impact on civilian lives, emphasizing the need for adherence to international humanitarian law.

33. (A): The statement regarding Palestinian refugees beginning to settle under Ottoman rule in the late 19th Century does not accurately pertain to the historical context of the Israel-Hamas conflict. The conflict's roots are complex and multifaceted, involving historical, nationalistic, and territorial disputes that have evolved over the 20th and 21st centuries. The emergence of Hamas during the first Intifada in the late 1980s and its formal designation as the Islamic Resistance Movement are directly relevant to understanding the group's origins and ideological motivations. The first Intifada, a significant Palestinian uprising against Israeli rule, marks a crucial period in the conflict's history, highlighting the deep-seated grievances and the Palestinian struggle for self-determination. The incorrect statement misrepresents the historical narrative, as the issue of Palestinian refugees primarily emerged in the mid-20th century, following the 1948 Arab-Israeli War and the establishment of the state of Israel, leading to a significant displacement of Palestinian populations.

34. (A): In response to the Hamas-led attack, the Israeli military declared a state of war on 8th October and undertook significant military actions to counter the aggression. This included conducting an extensive aerial bombardment campaign targeting Gazan positions, followed by a large-scale ground invasion of Gaza. These measures were taken as retaliatory actions against the initial multi-pronged invasion by Hamas-led Palestinian militants, which resulted in substantial loss of life and hostage-taking. The decision to declare a state of war and engage in both aerial and ground operations reflects the severity with which Israel viewed the attacks and its determination to neutralize the threat posed by Hamas militants. This comprehensive military response aimed at dismantling militant infrastructure, preventing further attacks, and asserting control over the situation, underscoring the intensity and escalation of the conflict.

35. (B): The current hostilities between Israel and Hamas-led Palestinian militants are known as the fifth war of the Gaza-Israel conflict. This designation situates the conflict within a broader historical continuum of recurring violence and warfare between Israel and Palestinian factions, particularly in the Gaza Strip. Each "war" in this ongoing conflict has been marked by periods of intense military confrontation, followed by varying degrees of ceasefires, with underlying issues remaining unresolved. The characterization of this as the fifth war highlights the cyclical nature of the violence and the challenges in achieving a lasting peace in the region. It underscores the deep-rooted and enduring nature of the Israeli-Palestinian conflict, reflecting both the immediate triggers of violence and the long-standing grievances and aspirations at its core.

36. (A): The current Gaza-Israel conflict resembles the Yom Kippur War in terms of its significance and the level of military escalation. The Yom Kippur War, fought in 1973, was a major conflict involving Israel and a coalition of Arab states, marking a pivotal moment in the history of the Middle East.

Similarly, the current hostilities represent the most significant military escalation in the region since that time, involving extensive military operations, substantial casualties, and a broad impact on the civilian population. This comparison emphasizes the severity of the current conflict within the historical context of regional warfare, highlighting the profound challenges in securing peace and stability in an area marked by deep-seated political, territorial, and ideological disputes. The reference to the Yom Kippur War as a point of comparison serves to underline the gravity of the situation and the potential implications for regional and international security.

37. (B): India became the fourth country in the world to successfully land a spacecraft on the moon. This milestone achievement places India among an elite group of countries that have managed to navigate the complex challenges of lunar exploration and safely touch down on the lunar surface. The successful landing is a testament to the country's advanced capabilities in space technology and exploration, marking a significant leap forward from its humble beginnings in the space arena.

38. (A): Pragyan's role in the lunar mission is to move around the moon, leaving footprints. As a rover, Pragyan is equipped to traverse the lunar surface, conducting experiments and collecting data that contribute to our understanding of the moon. This mobility allows Pragyan to explore various features of the lunar landscape, making significant contributions to lunar science. The reference to leaving footprints metaphorically highlights the rover's exploration and the lasting impact of its scientific discoveries.

39. **(C):** ISRO (Indian Space Research Organisation) is the institution that has played a major role in bringing India to the forefront of space exploration and technology.

As the country's national space agency, ISRO has been instrumental in developing the capabilities necessary for space missions like Chandrayaan. Its achievements in satellite technology, space exploration, and related areas have significantly contributed to India's standing in the global space community, showcasing the country's scientific prowess and technological advancements.

40. **(A):** The name of the moon lander is Vikram, and the rover is named Pragyan. Together, they represent the critical components of India's lunar exploration mission, with Vikram responsible for the safe landing on the moon's surface and Pragyan tasked with conducting scientific experiments and exploration. The names are symbolic, with Vikram signifying valor and Pragyan representing wisdom, embodying the mission's spirit and objectives.

41. **(D):** The Prime Minister addressed his speech to the scientists of ISRO. This acknowledgment highlights the pivotal role played by ISRO's scientists and engineers in achieving the successful lunar landing, reflecting the collective effort and dedication behind this significant accomplishment. The address serves to commend their hard work, celebrate the milestone, and underscore the national pride associated with this achievement.

42. **(A):** The countries in the world that had previously touched the surface of the moon before India's successful mission are the United States of America, USSR (now represented by Russia in contemporary contexts), and China. These countries have achieved the milestone of landing spacecraft on the moon, making them pioneers in lunar exploration. India joining this exclusive group underscores its emergence as a major player in space exploration, marking a significant achievement in its space program's history.

43. **(A):** The Group of Twenty (G20) is a forum for international economic cooperation. It brings together the world's major economies to discuss and promote policies aimed at achieving global economic stability and sustainable growth. The G20 plays a critical role in global economic governance, addressing issues that go beyond the responsibilities of any one organization. Its members represent a significant portion of the global GDP, trade, and population, making it a pivotal platform for discussing economic policies, financial stability, and other global economic issues.

44. **(C):** Brazil will hold the G20 Presidency in 2024. The presidency of the G20 rotates annually among its members, and it is a significant role that involves setting the group's agenda, hosting the G20 Summit, and facilitating discussions among member countries. Brazil taking on the G20 Presidency will continue the tradition of rotating leadership and provide the country with an opportunity to influence global economic discussions and initiatives.

45. **(A):** Egypt is not a member of the G20. The G20 consists of 19 countries and the European Union, representing major economies across all continents. While Egypt is a significant economy in the Middle East

and Africa, it is not part of the G20's membership. The members include a mix of developed and developing nations that play key roles in the world's economic system, and membership is determined by economic criteria and geopolitical considerations.

46. (C): The correct list of countries being G20 invitees to the Summit held in New Delhi in September 2023 is not provided in the extracted information. Typically, the host country invites additional countries and international organizations to participate in the summit, reflecting its diplomatic priorities and the thematic focus of its presidency. These invitees can vary from year to year, and their selection is often aimed at including regions or countries that can contribute to the summit's discussions on global economic issues, sustainable development, and other priorities set by the host country.

47. (A): The life of contradiction referred to by Dr. Ambedkar is that of equality in politics but inequality in social and economic structures. He highlights the paradox inherent in the nascent Indian democracy, where political equality was enshrined in the Constitution, but vast disparities remained in the social and economic realms. This contradiction between the political ideals and the reality of societal divisions underscores the challenges facing India at the dawn of its republic status, emphasizing the need for comprehensive reforms to achieve true equality across all aspects of life.

48. (B): According to Dr. Ambedkar, if we continue to deny equality in our social and economic life, our political democracy will be in danger. He warns of the potential consequences of maintaining such disparities, suggesting that ignoring the principles of equality in society and economy could undermine the very foundations of the democratic structure India aimed to build. This view posits that democracy cannot thrive solely on political rights if significant segments of the population remain marginalized and disadvantaged in daily life.

49. (C): Dr. Ambedkar implies that if things go wrong under the new Constitution, it would be because the men called upon to work the Constitution were not good. He asserts that the success or failure of the Constitution does not solely depend on its contents but significantly on the character and actions of those responsible for implementing it. This perspective emphasizes the critical role of leadership and civic responsibility in realizing the ideals enshrined in the Constitution, suggesting that even the most well-crafted laws and principles can be rendered ineffective by poor stewardship.

50. (C): Social democracy, as described by Dr. Ambedkar, means equality in social life. It encompasses a way of life that recognizes liberty, equality, and fraternity as the foundational principles, ensuring that all individuals enjoy the same status and opportunities regardless of their background. This concept extends beyond mere political democracy to include the broader societal framework, advocating for a society where social barriers and disparities are minimized, and every person can participate fully and equally.

51. (A): A bad Constitution can turn out to be good when the people called upon to work it are good. Dr. Ambedkar highlights the paramount importance of the individuals responsible for implementing and adhering to the Constitution, suggesting that even a Constitution with perceived flaws can function effectively if those in positions of power and the broader citizenry are committed to democratic principles and ethical governance. This view underscores the belief in human agency and the potential for positive change through collective will and moral integrity.

52. (C): The statement that is not correct about Dr. B.R. Ambedkar's feelings about the Constitution is that the Constitution is strong enough to hold the country together in peacetime only. Dr. Ambedkar believed that the Constitution is both workable and flexible, and importantly, strong enough to hold the country together both in peacetime and in wartime. This confidence in the Constitution's resilience and adaptability reflects Dr. Ambedkar's vision of a robust framework capable of navigating the challenges and uncertainties facing a diverse and complex nation like India.

53. (B): The primary objective of the Juvenile Justice (Care and Protection of Children) Act, 2015, is to rehabilitate and reintegrate children in conflict with the law. This legislation is focused on ensuring that juveniles who have committed offenses are provided with care, protection, and treatment that is conducive to their well-being, aiming for their eventual reintegration into society as responsible citizens. The Act emphasizes a rehabilitative approach over a punitive one, recognizing the importance of nurturing and supporting young individuals for the betterment of society as a whole.

54. (C): The Juvenile Justice Board (JJB) is made up of a Metropolitan Magistrate or Judicial Magistrate of the first class and two Social Workers, with at least one of the social workers being a woman. This composition is designed to ensure that the board has the legal expertise as well as the social work perspective necessary to make informed decisions about the welfare of juveniles in conflict with the law. The inclusion of social workers ensures that considerations extend beyond legal parameters to include the social and psychological needs of the child.

55. (C): The role of the Juvenile Justice Board (JJB) is to assess the age and circumstances of the juvenile and make decisions on rehabilitation.

This includes determining the nature of the offense, the context in which it was committed, and whether the juvenile should be sent to a special home or released on probation. The JJB's focus is on understanding each case's unique aspects to ensure that the response is tailored to the juvenile's best interests, promoting rehabilitation over punishment.

56. (B): The distinction between a "child in conflict with the law" and a "child in need of care and protection" is crucial within the Act.

A "child in conflict with the law" has committed an offense, while a "child in need of care and protection" refers to a child who is vulnerable or at risk and requires special care and support. This differentiation allows for a tailored approach to each child's needs, ensuring that those who require protection receive it, and those who have committed offenses are addressed in a manner that focuses on rehabilitation.

57. (B): Children between the ages of 16 and 18 can be tried as adults under specific circumstances, after a preliminary assessment by the Juvenile Justice Board. This assessment is meant to consider the child's mental and physical capacity to commit the offense, among other factors. This provision is applied in cases involving heinous offenses and is aimed at ensuring that the response to such crimes takes into account the nature of the offense as well as the capacity of the juvenile involved.

58. (B): The purpose of placing restrictions on the publication of information related to juvenile offenders is to protect the privacy and future prospects of the child. This measure prevents the stigmatization and public shaming that could result from the widespread dissemination of the juvenile's identity, allowing them a better chance at rehabilitation and reintegration into society. By protecting the juvenile's anonymity, the Act seeks to safeguard their dignity and opportunities for a positive future.

59. (B): The primary focus of the passage is the legal aspects of online defamation in India. It discusses how the Indian legal system handles cases of defamation that occur on the internet, including the mechanisms in place for addressing defamatory statements made on social media, blogs, forums, and other online platforms. The passage also touches on the balance between freedom of expression and the protection of reputation, as well as the role of intermediaries like social media platforms in managing defamatory content.

60. (B): Online defamation, as described in the passage, refers to false statements made on the internet that harm someone's reputation. This includes defamatory content posted on various online platforms such as social media, blogs, and forums. The passage highlights the impact of such statements and the legal framework in place to address defamation in the digital realm, emphasizing the specificity of online defamation compared to traditional forms.

61. (B): The significance of Section 79 of the Information Technology Act, 2000, as mentioned in the passage, is that it provides a safe harbor for intermediaries in cases of online defamation. This legal provision shields intermediaries, such as social media platforms and websites, from liability for third-party content posted on their services, provided they follow due diligence in removing or disabling access to the content once notified under certain conditions.

62. (B): According to the Supreme Court in the Shreya Singhal v. Union of India case, intermediaries should act in response to content removal upon receiving a valid court order or government directive. The court clarified that intermediaries are not required to act upon private complaints for removing content but must follow the directives of courts or the government, ensuring a legal basis for content moderation decisions.

63. (C): The Indian legal system balances the Right to Freedom of Expression and the Right to Reputation in online defamation cases by carefully examining the content, context, and intent of statements. This approach ensures that both fundamental rights are considered, allowing for a nuanced evaluation of defamation claims. It emphasizes the need to protect individuals' reputations while also safeguarding the freedom of speech, highlighting the complexities involved in such cases.

64. (D): In an online defamation case, the plaintiff must prove that the defamatory statement was false, damaging to their reputation, and made with a degree of fault, such as negligence or actual malice. This requirement sets a high bar for establishing defamation, necessitating clear evidence of the statement's falsehood and its harmful impact on the plaintiff's reputation, as well as the defendant's fault in making the statement.

65. (*)

66. (C): Mr. Z, who publishes news content in print media on a weekly basis, is covered by the definition of a newspaper as per the PRP Bill. This definition encapsulates periodicals that are printed on newsprint and brought out at regular intervals, at least once a week, containing information on current events, public news, or comments on public news. Mr. Z's activity of publishing news content in print media weekly fits squarely within this definition. In contrast, Mr. X's focus on digital media and Mr. Y's publication of books do not align with the specific criteria set forth for newspapers, which emphasize periodic print publications designed to disseminate current news and commentary.

67. (A): Mr. A, convicted of waging war against the Government of India, is not eligible to publish a periodical as per the PRP Bill. The PRP Bill stipulates restrictions on individuals with convictions for serious offenses, including those related to terrorism or actions against the state's security, from bringing out periodicals. This measure is intended to ensure that the press does not become a platform for individuals who have engaged in activities deemed harmful to national security or public order. While accusations alone, as in the cases of Mr. B and Mr. C, may raise concerns, the PRP Bill specifically mentions convictions as a disqualifying factor, underscoring the legal principle of presuming innocence until proven guilty.

68. (D): Both the liberal use of the Unlawful Activities Prevention Act (UAPA) against journalists, which refrains them from engaging in investigative reporting due to fear of being associated with criminal activities, and the use of sedition laws to accuse journalists of promoting hatred and disaffection against the government, are threats to the freedom of press in India. These practices can severely limit journalists' ability to report freely and critically on matters of public interest, thereby undermining the press's role as a watchdog of democracy. The concern is that such laws, while intended to protect national security and public order, can be misapplied in ways that stifle legitimate dissent and reporting, leading to a chilling effect on freedom of expression.

69. (C): The PRP Bill is criticized by the Editors Guild of India primarily because the definition of "specified authority" allows for a broad range of officers, including those potentially below the level of Collector, to perform the functions of the Press Registrar General, such as entering the premises of a periodical for inspection. This provision raises concerns about the potential for excessive and intrusive oversight of the press, which could infringe upon journalistic independence and freedom. While the bill confers various powers on the Press Registrar General and the definition of specified authority is indeed wide, the specific criticism highlighted by the Guild focuses on the implications of this expansive authority for press freedom, particularly regarding the entry and inspection of premises.

70. (B): Fundamental rights, including the freedom of press implied in Article 19(1)(a) of the Constitution of India, are not absolute and can be subject to reasonable restrictions. The PRP Bill, which involves registration and potential denial of registration of newspapers, can be enacted as a measure that imposes reasonable restrictions on the exercise of the freedom of press for purposes such as maintaining public order, national security, and decency. The Constitution allows for such restrictions as long as they are justified, proportionate, and in the interest of the public. This principle ensures a balance between individual freedoms and the state's interests, recognizing that no right can be exercised in a vacuum and may be regulated to protect other societal values and interests.

71. (C): The right to publish a periodical is denied to a person who has been found to have committed a terrorist act and has been convicted by a competent court in India because such individuals may not be neutral in reporting and could potentially incite violence and spread disaffection against the state due to their involvement in terrorist acts.

This provision is based on the premise that individuals convicted of serious offenses related to terrorism pose a risk to public safety and national security. Their participation in the dissemination of news and information could be prejudiced by their criminal background, leading to concerns about the use of media platforms to further unlawful agendas or to undermine the state's integrity and security.

72. (A): The personal data of Mr. Lal can be preserved by the government till the research on the rare disease is complete, given the exemptions provided in the DPDPA, 2023 for data deemed "necessary for research, archiving or statistical purposes." This provision allows the government to retain and use personal data for research purposes as long as the data is not used to take any decision specific to a data principal (the individual to whom the data relates) and such processing complies with prescribed standards.

This exemption facilitates the use of personal data for beneficial research that can lead to medical advancements and better understanding of health conditions, while ensuring that the data is not used in a manner that could adversely affect the individual's rights or privacy.

73. (C): The bank can process the data of Mr. X for the purpose of ascertaining the assets and liabilities of the defaulter, under the exemption provided for processing personal data to ascertain the financial position of a person who has defaulted in payment of an amount due on a loan from a nationalized bank. This provision allows financial institutions to access and analyze personal data relevant to recovering debts, ensuring that they can effectively manage and mitigate financial risks. Processing data related to family history of ailments or personal details of family members, as mentioned in options A and B, would not be directly relevant to the purpose of ascertaining financial position and could infringe on privacy rights.

74. (C): The DPDPA 2023 is not applicable since the data is held outside India. The act's jurisdiction typically extends to personal data processed within India or by Indian entities. In the scenario described, where Mr. Y's personal data is processed by an MNC in New Zealand, the DPDPA 2023's protections and regulations would not apply unless specified otherwise in the act or in international agreements or principles that India is a party to. This reflects the territorial limitations of national data protection laws, which generally cover data processing within their jurisdiction.

75. (D): All of the options listed - Name of the Person, Full Residential Address, and Aadhar Number - are classified as personal data. This is because they are details that can identify an individual either directly or indirectly when combined with other information. The definition of personal data typically encompasses any information that relates to an identifiable individual, making these examples clear instances of personal data under most data protection frameworks, including the DPDPA, 2023.

76. (C): Both scenarios (A) and (B) describe cases where access to personal data shall be granted for law enforcement purposes, and the individuals concerned cannot claim personal data protection to prevent this access. In scenario A, police access to Aadhar details and fingerprint data of Mr. Z for the purpose of tracing him in connection with robberies, and in scenario B, police use of Mr. G's mobile number and other personal details to prevent potential crimes, are instances where the processing of personal data is justified by the need to ensure public safety, prevent crimes, and maintain law and order.

77. (B): Personal data collected by the government can be used for whatever purpose, according to the exemptions and broad powers granted to government agencies under the DPDPA, 2023. This provision allows the government significant leeway in how it processes personal data, including for purposes other than those for which the data was originally collected. While this flexibility is intended to enable government functions and services, it raises concerns about potential overreach and the impact on individuals' privacy rights, particularly in the absence of stringent safeguards and limitations.

78. (C): Gogol would inherit his share from within Ashok's share of the full ancestral property without prejudice to the inheritance of other legal heirs, including Arpita. According to the Supreme Court's ruling, children born from void or voidable marriages have the right to inherit their parents' share in joint Hindu family property. However, this right is limited to the parent's share, and does not extend to the entire ancestral property or grant them rights in the property of any other family members. Therefore, Gogol's inheritance would be calculated based on Ashok's notional share of the ancestral property, and he would receive his portion of that share.

79. (C): Sushma, Arpita, and Gogol would have inheritance rights over the property purchased by Ashok from his own earnings in the USA, which is considered self-acquired property. As the legal heirs of Ashok, Sushma (as the legal wife), Arpita (as the child from the first marriage), and Gogol (as the child from the void marriage with Ashima) are entitled to Ashok's self-acquired property upon his death. The Supreme Court has clarified that children from void or voidable marriages are considered legitimate for the purposes of inheritance, which includes self-acquired property of the deceased parent.

80. (C): The Hindu Marriage Act, through its amended provisions, grants legitimate status to children from void or voidable marriages, and this status extends to their rights under the Hindu Succession Act concerning inheritance. The Supreme Court's interpretation ensures that these children are recognized as legitimate heirs, capable of inheriting their parents' property, both ancestral and self-acquired. This reflects a broader legal and social recognition of the rights of all children, regardless of the legal status of their parents' marriage, aligning with evolving societal norms regarding legitimacy and inheritance.

81. (B): Both Ram and Lakshman can inherit their father's share of the ancestral property irrespective of the voidable status of their parent's marriage. The Supreme Court's interpretation of the Hindu Marriage Act, as reflected in Section 16, confers legitimacy on children born from void or voidable marriages, thus entitling them to inherit their parents' property under the Hindu Succession Act.

This ruling underscores the principle that the legal status of a marriage should not adversely affect the rights of children born from such unions.

82. (A): The lawyer could advise Riya that her children can still inherit property from Ajay, based on the Supreme Court judgment. The ruling clarifies that children born from void or voidable marriages are entitled to inherit their parent's share in joint Hindu family property, thereby safeguarding the inheritance rights of children like Raj and Rani. This legal position ensures that children are not disadvantaged by the circumstances of their birth or the legal status of their parents' marriage.

83. (A): No, Riya cannot inherit property as the judgment primarily addresses the rights of children from void marriages, focusing on the inheritance rights of the children rather than the spouses involved in such marriages. The ruling aims to protect and affirm the rights of children born from these marriages to inherit their parents' property, recognizing them as legitimate heirs under the law. Riya's rights to inherit would be governed by other legal provisions relevant to spouses in void marriages, which were not the focus of this specific judgment.

84. (B): Dhanalakshmi could demand a notional partition and get a share from Srimati's portion of her ancestral property. The Supreme Court's ruling that children from void or voidable marriages are entitled to inherit their parent's share in joint Hindu family property applies to Dhanalakshmi's situation. Her right to inherit is based on her mother, Srimati's, share of the ancestral property. Through a notional partition, Srimati's share would be identified, and Dhanalakshmi would be entitled to her portion of that share, alongside her half-siblings, Ira and Shira. This ensures that Dhanalakshmi's rights as a legitimate heir are recognized and protected.

85. (B): The central theme of the passage is the impact of words on human existence. The passage eloquently explores the profound influence words have on our lives, not just as mere vehicles of communication but as entities that shape our perception of reality, evoke emotions, and illuminate the darkness around us. Through vivid imagery and philosophical musings, it underscores the idea that words are more than just symbols; they are powerful forces that can alter our understanding of the world and ourselves.

86. (D): According to the passage, a 'word' symbolizes an intangible concept. It is described as neither animate nor inanimate, existing as a symbolic entity that transcends physical form. The passage highlights the ethereal nature of words, emphasizing their ability to convey emotions, ideas, and the essence of existence without being tangible. This characterization points to the profound complexity and power of words as constructs of human intellect and imagination.

87. (B): The passage describes words' ability to affect emotions by suggesting that words can absorb emotions and become emotion themselves. It illustrates the dynamic and interactive nature of words, capable of eliciting joy, provoking smiles, and emanating warmth or coldness. This highlights the emotional resonance words can have, affecting individuals deeply and in varied ways, mirroring the complexity of human feelings.

88. (D): The statement "An engagement with words is the most captivating, enchanting, and sometimes daunting encounter with the world" implies that words can paint a picture of the world in all its different colors.

This conclusion underscores the idea that words enable us to experience the world in its entirety, from its beauty and wonder to its challenges and fears. It reflects the powerful role of language in shaping our engagement with reality, allowing for a rich, multi-faceted exploration of life.

89. (A): The statement that words are "like glow-worms momentarily dispelling the surrounding darkness" strengthens the idea that words help in understanding reality. This imagery suggests that words illuminate our minds, providing clarity and insight amid confusion or ignorance. Just as glow-worms light up the darkness, words light up our understanding, enabling us to navigate and comprehend the complex world around us.

90. (A): In the context of the passage, the significance of the "world within the word" refers to the power of language to create inspiration, energy, and faith. This concept encapsulates the idea that words contain entire universes within them, offering endless possibilities for exploration, understanding, and emotional resonance. It highlights the profound capacity of words to inspire, to energize, and to instill a sense of belief, whether in ideas, values, or the beauty of existence itself.

91. (D): The author is likely to agree with the statement that government-led initiatives of AI regulation and development lead to efficient outcomes. Throughout the passage, the emphasis is on the necessity for a proactive government role in both the regulation and development of artificial intelligence within India. The argument is presented against the backdrop of the transformative potential of AI, highlighting the need for responsible development and use to ensure beneficial outcomes for society. The mention of government-driven initiatives, such as pushing academia-industry collaborations and leading regulatory efforts, underscores the belief that efficient outcomes in AI governance and development are best achieved through active government involvement, rather than leaving it solely to market forces or private companies.

92. (A): The statement that governments leading the initiative on regulating and responding to the advancement of AI tools benefit the most from them would most strengthen the main argument of the passage. The passage advocates for a proactive role of the government in AI regulation and development, arguing that missing out on actively engaging with AI technology could be costly for India. By suggesting that governments taking the lead on AI initiatives stand to gain the most, this statement reinforces the author's viewpoint that direct government involvement is essential for maximizing the benefits of AI advancements for the country. It aligns with the overall argument that India should not merely be a recipient of AI technologies but should actively shape its AI future.

93. (A): The author would most likely agree with the statement that courts should take the initiative by being innovative and laying down rules where no precedents exist. This aligns with the author's view that Indian courts should proactively engage with emerging issues related to generative AI and non-human agency, rather than waiting for legal precedents to be established in other jurisdictions. The author's call for Indian courts to start engaging with these novel legal challenges indicates a belief in the importance of judicial innovation and forward-thinking in adapting to the rapid advancements in AI technology. This proactive stance is seen as necessary to address the unique legal implications of AI, ensuring that the legal framework keeps pace with technological evolution.

94. (C): AI regulation is described as a collaborative effort involving all the institutions of the State. The passage indicates that a comprehensive approach to AI regulation and development is required, encompassing not only government-led initiatives but also the involvement of courts, academia, industry, and other institutions. The mention of academia-industry collaborations, government initiatives for AI governance, and the role of courts in addressing issues related to AI illustrates the multifaceted nature of this endeavor. The collaborative effort is presented as crucial for effectively navigating the complexities of AI technology and ensuring that India can play a meaningful part in global regulatory efforts and the advancement of AI.

95. (C): Introducing generative models like Wu Dao, which have demonstrated success in other jurisdictions, would result in weakening, rather than strengthening India's position at the forefront of generative AI. The passage emphasizes the importance of developing indigenous AI models and capabilities, arguing that reliance on foreign or externally developed technologies could undermine India's autonomy and leadership in the AI domain. By focusing on local development and innovation, India can ensure that its AI advancements are tailored to its unique needs and contexts, thereby enhancing its strategic and technological position globally. Adopting models developed elsewhere without investing in local innovation could dilute India's influence in AI and its ability to contribute significantly to global AI governance.

96. (C): The author must likely agree with the statement that India should have proactively played a role in responding to new research in chip technology. The comparison made between missing the bus on AI and the previous missed opportunities in chip research implies a belief that India's lack of proactive engagement in emerging technological fields has been a significant oversight. The statement underscores the author's viewpoint that proactive involvement in cutting-edge research and development, including AI and potentially chip technology, is crucial for securing India's position in the global technological landscape. The author suggests that active engagement and investment in such areas are essential for national progress and for avoiding the costs associated with falling behind in technological advancements.

97. (B)

98. (B): The introduction of the new production system requiring specialized operators is a potential contributing factor to the decline in efficiency because the workforce may not have the necessary skills or training to operate the new, more automated equipment effectively. This lack of specialized skills can lead to operational inefficiencies, improper handling of the equipment, and potentially more frequent breakdowns, all of which can detract from the overall productivity of the manufacturing process.

99. (C): A critical difference between the company's situation and that of its competitors is that the company's workforce lacks motivation and job satisfaction. While both the company and its competitors have introduced new production systems and adopted automation technologies, the unique challenge facing this company is the demotivated workforce. This internal issue can significantly impact productivity and efficiency, setting the company apart from its competitors who are experiencing increased productivity with similar technological advancements.

100. (C): Increased absenteeism could lead to delays in production because the absence of essential personnel disrupts the normal flow of the manufacturing process. When employees frequently miss work, there may not be enough staff available to operate machinery, perform quality checks, or complete production tasks on schedule, leading to inefficiencies and delays in meeting production targets.

101. (B): Implementing a motivation and job satisfaction program for the workforce could be a possible solution to address the decline in production efficiency. Given that a lack of motivation and job satisfaction has been identified as a key issue, addressing this root cause through targeted programs designed to improve employee engagement, recognition, and satisfaction could lead to a more motivated workforce, reduced absenteeism, and ultimately, enhanced production efficiency.

102. (C): Increased customer complaints about product quality may lead to a loss of customers and reputation damage. When customers express dissatisfaction with product quality, it signals potential issues with the manufacturing process or quality control measures. If not addressed, these complaints can erode customer trust, leading to decreased sales and a tarnished brand reputation, which are detrimental to the company's long-term success.

103. (A)

104. (B): According to the author's opinion, the education system being primarily based on the merit of the students is a significant aspect, and merit, as traditionally defined and measured through examinations, plays a pivotal role. Therefore, the statement that the merit of students is not the determining factor is not true regarding the education system as presented in the passage. The author critiques this reliance on a narrow definition of merit, highlighting the Supreme Court's call for re-evaluating the "idea of merit" and suggesting that the current system's understanding of merit might be too limited and unexamined.

105. (A): The argument regarding the 'idea of merit,' as per the passage, is strengthened by the notion that true merit is multifaceted and extends beyond performance in a single competitive examination. This perspective is supported by the Supreme Court's call for a deeper evaluation of merit and the criticism of the current education system's narrow focus on examination scores. The passage suggests a need to broaden our understanding of merit to include various dimensions of an individual's capabilities, talents, and circumstances, challenging the traditional view that academic or competitive exam performance alone defines a student's worth or potential.

106. (D): The passage highlights existing inequalities within the education system, which are enlarged by the competitive examinations. The stark discrepancy between preparation for board examinations and competitive tests, as well as the intense focus on merit as measured by these exams, amplifies the inequalities faced by students. This situation is further exacerbated by the pressures from coaching institutes and societal expectations, contributing to a challenging environment that disadvantages students from marginalized communities or those without access to the same resources as their peers.

107. (B)

108. (C): Availability of online resources is not identified as a challenge for quality education within the context of the passage.

Instead, the passage suggests that technology, particularly online platforms, emerges as a potential solution to some of the challenges faced by the traditional education system. It posits that online education could offer new opportunities for learning and preparation, possibly addressing issues such as access to resources, educational inequality, and the need for more adaptive and inclusive educational models. The challenges highlighted in the passage include the influence of social media, mental health concerns, and competitive pressures, rather than the availability of online educational resources.

109. (C): Total number of electric cars in State 4

$$= \frac{35}{100} \times 8000$$

$$= 2800$$

Number of electric cars

$$= \frac{2}{14} \times 2800 = 400$$

Total number of non-ac cars in State 4

$$= \frac{55}{100} \times 400 = 220.$$

110. (D): Number of Petrol cars in State 2

$$= \frac{20}{100} \times 8000 = 1600$$

∴ Number of petrol cars

$$= \frac{3}{10} \times 1600 = 480$$

Number of diesel cars in State 1

$$= \frac{15}{100} \times 8000 = 1200$$

Number of diesel cars

$$= \frac{3}{8} \times 1200 = 450$$

Difference = 480 – 450 = 30

$$\text{Required } \% = \frac{30}{450} \times 100 = 6.67\%.$$

111. (A): Total number of cars in State 4

$$= \frac{35}{100} \times 8000 = 2800$$

Total number of diesel cars in State 4

$$= \frac{7}{14} \times 2800 = 1400$$

Total number of cars in State 3

$$= \frac{30}{100} \times 8000 = 2400$$

Total number of electric cars in State 3

$$= \frac{3}{12} \times 2400 = 600$$

$$\text{Required ratio} = \frac{1400}{600} = \frac{7}{3} = 7:3.$$

112. (B): Total cars in all the state = 8000

Total electric cars = 1470

$$\text{Required } \% = \frac{1470}{8000} \times 100 = \frac{147}{8}$$

$$= 18.375\%$$

$$= 18.37\%$$

113. (D): Number of petrol cars in State 3

$$= \frac{5}{12} \times 2400 = 1000$$

Number of diesel cars in State 1

$$= \frac{3}{8} \times 1200 = 450$$

Required difference = 1000 – 450 = 550.

114. (B): Total number of diesel cars in all the States

$$= \frac{3}{8} \times 1200 + \frac{5}{10} \times 1600 + \frac{4}{12} \times 2400 + \frac{7}{14} \times 2800$$

$$= 450 + 800 + 800 + 1400 = 3450$$

$$\text{Average} = \frac{3450}{4} = 862.5.$$

115. (A): $\frac{56}{100} \times 300000 = 168000$

$\frac{48}{100} \times 168000 = 80640$

$\therefore$ Self-employed population in rural area

$= 80640$

Self-employed population in urban area

$= 62400$

Required % $= \left(\frac{80640 - 62400}{62400}\right) \times 100$

$= 29.3\%$.

116. (C): Rural Population = 144000

and Urban population = 156000

Required ratio $= \frac{156000}{144000} = 13 : 12$.

117. (D): New urban population

$= \frac{56}{100} \times 300000$

$= 168000$

Hence, the self employed persons in urban area

$= \frac{40}{100} \times 168000$

$= 67200$.

118. (C): Regular-salaries population in rural areas

$= 17280$

Regular-salaried population in urban areas

$= 74880$

$\therefore$ Required sum $= 17280 + 74880$

$= 9160$.

119. (D): Regular-salaried population in rural areas = 17280

Casual wage workers in urban areas = 18720

Required % $= \frac{17280}{18720} \times 100 = 92.30\%$.

120. (B): Working population of self-employed in rural areas

$= \frac{60}{100} \times 300000 = 180000$

Working population of self-employed in urban areas

$= \frac{40}{100} \times 300000 = 120000$

Required ratio $= \frac{18000}{120000}$

$= \frac{3}{2}$

$= 3 : 2$.

YOUR SPACE

Previous Paper (Solved)

Common Law Admission Test (CLAT–UG)

Entrance Exam, December 2022*

Section-I : English Language

I

I grew up in a small town not far from Kalimpong. In pre-liberalization India, everything arrived late: not just material things but also ideas. Magazines — old copies of Reader's Digest and National Geographic — arrived late too, after the news had become stale by months or, often, years. This temporal gap turned journalism into literature, news into legend, and historical events into something akin to plotless stories. But like those who knew no other life, we accepted this as the norm. The dearth of reading material in towns and villages in socialist India is hard to imagine, and it produced two categories of people: those who stopped reading after school or college, and those — including children — who read anything they could find. I read road signs with the enthusiasm that attaches to reading thrillers. When the iterant kabadiwala, collector of papers, magazines, and rejected things, visited our neighbourhood, I rushed to the house where he was doing business. He bought things at unimaginably low prices from those who'd stopped having any use for them, and I rummaged through his sacks of old magazines. Sometimes, on days when business was good, he allowed me a couple of copies of Sportsworld magazine for free. I'd run home and, ignoring my mother's scolding, plunge right in — consuming news about India's victory in the Benson and Hedges Cup....

Two takeaways from these experiences have marked my understanding of the provincial reader's life: the sense of belatedness, of everything coming late, and the desire for pleasure in language. .... Speaking of belatedness, the awareness of having been born at the wrong time in history, of inventing things that had already been discovered elsewhere, far away, without our knowledge or cooperation, is a moment of epiphany and deep sadness. I remember a professor's choked voice, narrating to me how all the arguments he'd made in his doctoral dissertation, written over many, many years of hard work (for there indeed was a time when PhDs were written over decades), had suddenly come to naught after he'd discovered the work of C.W.E. Bigsby. This, I realised as I grew older, was one of the characteristics of provincial life: that they (usually males) were saying trite things with the confidence of someone declaring them for the first time. I, therefore, grew up surrounded by would-be Newtons who claimed to have discovered gravity (again). There's a deep sense of tragedy attending this sort of thing — the sad embarrassment of always arriving after the party is over. And there's a harsh word for that sense of belatedness: "dated." What rescues it is the unpredictability of these anachronistic "discoveries" — the randomness and haphazardness involved in mapping connections among thoughts and ideas, in a way that hasn't yet been professionalised.

[Extracted, with edits and revisions, from "The Provincial Reader", by Sumana Roy, *Los Angeles Review of Books*]

1. What use was the kabadiwala (wastepicker) to the author?

A. The kabadiwala bought up all her magazines.

B. The kabadiwala's stock of books and magazines were of interest to the author.

*Exam held on 18-12-2022.

C. The kabadiwala was about to steal the author's magazines.

D. The author ordered books online which the kabadiwala delivered.

2. What according to the author is essential about the experience of being a 'provincial reader'?

A. Belatedness in the sense of coming late for everything.

B. Over-eagerness.

C. Accepting a temporal gap between what was current in the wider world and the time at which these arrived in the provincial location.

D. None of the above

3. Why did the author feel a sense of epiphany and deep sadness?

A. Because the things that felt special and unique to the author, were already established and accepted thought in the wider world.

B. Because the author was less well-read than others.

C. Because the author missed being in a big city.

D. All the above

4. What does the word 'anachronistic' as used in the passage, mean?

A. Rooted in a non-urban setting

B. Related to a mofussil area

C. Connected with another time

D. Opposed to prevailing sensibilities

5. Which of the following options captures the meaning of the last sentence best?

A. Though the author feels provincial, she pretends to be from the metropolis.

B. Though the author feels dated in her access to intellectual ideas, her lack of metropolitan sophistication lets her engage with the ideas with some originality.

C. Though the author is aware of the limitedness of her knowledge, she is confident and can hold her own in a crowd. She also proud of her roots in the small town.

D. All the above

II

Until the Keeladi site was discovered, archaeologists by and large believed that the Gangetic plains in the north urbanised significantly earlier than Tamil Nadu. Historians have often claimed that large scale town life in India first developed in the Greater Magadha region of the Gangetic basin. This was during the 'second urbanisation' phase. The 'first urbanisation phase' refers to the rise of the Harappan or Indus Valley Civilisation. Tamil Nadu was thought to have urbanised at this scale only by the third century BCE. The findings at Keeladi push that date back significantly. ... Based on linguistics and continuity in cultural legacies, connections between the Indus Valley Civilisation, or IVC, and old Tamil traditions have long been suggested, but concrete archaeological evidence remained absent. Evidence indicated similarities between graffiti found in Keeladi and symbols associated with the IVC. It bolstered the arguments of dissidents from the dominant North Indian imagination, who have argued for years that their ancestors existed contemporaneously with the IVC. ... All the archaeologists I spoke to said it was too soon to make definitive links between the Keeladi site and the IVC. There is no doubt, however, that the discovery at Keeladi has changed the paradigm. In recent years, the results of any new research on early India have invited keen political interest, because proponents of Hindu nationalism support the notion of Vedic culture as fundamental to the origins of Indian civilisation. ... The Keeladi excavations further challenge the idea of a single fountainhead of Indian life. They indicate the possibility that the earliest identity that can recognisably be considered 'Indian' might not have originated in North India. That wasn't all. In subsequent seasons of the Keeladi dig, archaeologists discovered that Tamili, a variant of the Brahmi script used for writing inscriptions in the early iterations of the Tamil language, could be dated back to the sixth century BCE, likely a hundred years before previously thought. So not only had urban life thrived in the Tamil lands, but people who lived there had developed their own script.

"The evolution of writing is attributed to Ashoka's edicts, but 2600 years ago writing was prevalent in Keeladi," Mathan Karuppiah, a proud Madurai local, told me. "A farmer could write his own name on a pot he owned. The fight going on here is 'You are not the one to teach me to write, I have learnt it myself.' "

[Excerpted from "The Dig", by Sowmiya Ashok, *Fifty-Two*]

6. What was the assumption about the origin of urban life in India before the Keeladi dig?

A. The origins lay in the northern Gangetic plains, which urbanised earlier than the south.

B. The indus Valley Civilization was the first urban civilization of India.

C. The second urbanization was known to be in the Magadha empire.

D. Both (A) and (B)

7. "The Keeladi excavations further challenge the idea of a single fountainhead of Indian life." — in elaboration of this sentence, which of these options follows?

A. Dominant theories of how urban and modern life came about in ancient India were proved wrong by the Keeladi archaeological dig.

B. Neither the indus Valley Civilization, nor the ancient urban civilization of Magadha are clear explana-tions of how urban life emerged in the Keeladi region of Southern India in the third century BCE.

C. The Keeladi archaeological dig proved that Indian urban and modern life emerged independently in several historical periods and geographies, and no one theory is enough to explain it.

D. None of the above

8. Language, including a script similar to the brahmi script, emerged in Keeladi in the sixth century BCE. Which of the following is the most convincing conclusion from this statement?

A. Keeladi is a centre of culture and learning far superior to any others in ancient India.

B. People of Keeladi were illiterate and could not use language to inscribe on their pots and pans.

C. Ancient urban history of India, as we know it today, could significantly be altered by the findings of the advances achieved by the Keeladi civilization.

D. All the above

9. BCE is the acronym for:

A. Before the Common Era

B. Before Colloquial Era

C. Before Chapel Eternal

D. Behind Christ Era

10. "A farmer could write his own name on a pot he owned. The fight going on here is 'You are not the one to teach me to write, I have learnt it myself.' " — These sentences imply:

A. That the Keeladi civilization was an inegalitarian one.

B. That the Keeladi civilization did not conserve the access to education and literacy only for the elite.

C. That the farmers of the Keeladi civilization were also potters.

D. All the above

III

The call of self-expression turned the village of the internet into a city, which expanded at time-lapse speed, social connections bristling like neurons in every direction. At twelve, I was writing five hundred words a day on a public LiveJournal. By twenty-five, my job was to write things that would attract, ideally, a hundred thousand strangers per post. Now I'm thirty, and most of my life is inextricable from the internet, and its mazes of incessant forced connection—this feverish, electric, unliveable hell.

The curdling of the social internet happened slowly and then all at once. The tipping point, I'd guess, was around 2012. People were losing excitement about the internet, starting to articulate a set of new truisms. Facebook had become tedious, trivial, exhausting. Instagram seemed better, but would soon reveal its underlying function as a three-ring circus of happiness and popularity and success. Twitter, for all its discursive promise, was where everyone tweeted complaints at airlines and moaned about articles that had been commissioned to make people moan. The dream of a better, truer self on the internet was slipping away. Where we had once been free to be ourselves online, we were now chained to ourselves online, and this made us self-conscious. Platforms that promised connection began inducing mass alienation. The freedom promised by the internet started to seem like something whose greatest potential lay in the realm of misuse.

Even as we became increasingly sad and ugly on the internet, the mirage of the better online self continued to glimmer. As a medium, the internet is defined by a built-in performance incentive. In real life, you can walk around living life and be visible to other people. But on the internet—for anyone to see you, you have to act. You have to communicate in order to maintain an internet presence. And, because the internet's central platforms are built around personal profiles, it can seem—first at a mechanical level, and later on as an encoded instinct—like the main purpose of this communication is to make yourself look good. Online reward mechanisms beg to substitute for offline ones, and then overtake them. This is why everyone tries to look so hot and well-travelled on Instagram; why everyone seems so smug and triumphant on Facebook; and why, on Twitter, making a righteous political statement has come to seem, for many people, like a political good in itself. The everyday madness perpetuated by the internet is the madness of this architecture, which positions personal identity as the centre of the universe. It's as if we've been placed on a lookout that oversees the entire world and given a pair of binoculars that makes everything look like our own reflection.

[Extracted, with edits and revisions, from *Trick Mirror: Reflections on Self-Delusion*, by Jia Tolentino, Random House, 2019.]

11. Which of the following statements can be inferred from the above passage?

A. The internet expanded very slowly
B. The internet can be used to cause harm
C. The internet is addictive
D. The main purpose of social media platforms is to dissuade people from showing off

12. All the following statements are 'truisms', except:

A. The internet has changed the way the world works.
B. A preference for cat videos can reveal a lot about your personality.
C. Like with any tool, digital technology has both advantages and disadvantages.
D. Only time can tell what the future holds.

13. Which of the following comes closest to the underlined sentence in the passage?

A. The way we use the internet says a lot about who we are.
B. The internet has reduced the distance between people living across the world.
C. The internet has the ability to customise what we access based on our identity.
D. The internet only shows us what we don't want to see.

14. Which of the following is a metaphor?

A. the village of the internet
B. this feverish, electric, unliveable hell
C. three-ring circus of happiness and popularity and success
D. All the above

15. Which of the following categories best describes this piece of writing?

A. Non-fiction essay B. Fiction
C. Academic paper D. Poem

IV

Down by the sandy banks of the Yamuna River, the men must work quickly. At a little past 12 a.m. one humid night in May, they pull back the black plastic tarp covering three boreholes sunk deep in the ground. They then drag thick hoses toward a queue of 20-odd tanker trucks idling quietly with their headlights turned off. The men work in a team: While one man fits a hose's mouth over a borehole, another clambers atop a truck at the front of the line and shoves the tube's opposite end into the empty steel cistern attached to the vehicle's creaky frame. 'On kar!' someone shouts in Hinglish; almost instantly, his orders to 'switch it on' are obeyed. Diesel generators, housed in nearby sheds, begin to thrum. Submersible pumps, installed in the borehole's shafts, drone as they disgorge thousands of gallons of groundwater from deep in the earth. The liquid gushes through the hoses and into the trucks' tanks. The full trucks don't wait around. As the hose team continues its work, drivers nose down a rutted dirt path until they reach a nearby highway. There, they turn on their lights and pick up speed, rushing to sell their bounty to factories and hospitals, malls and hotels, apartments and hutments across this city of 25 million. Everything about this business is illegal: the boreholes dug without permission, the trucks operating without permits, the water sold without testing or treatment. 'Water work is night work,' says a middle-aged neighbour who lives near the covert pumping station and requested anonymity. 'Bosses arrange buyers, labour fills tankers, the police look the other way, and the muscle makes sure that no one says nothing to nobody.' teams like this one are ubiquitous in Delhi, where the official water supply falls short of the city's needs. A quarter of Delhi's households live without a piped-water connection; most of the rest receive water for only a few hours each day. So residents have come to rely on private truck owners—the most visible strands of a dispersed web of city councillors, farmers, real estate agents, and fixers who source millions of gallons of water each day from illicit boreholes, and sell the liquid for profit.

The entrenched system has a local moniker: the water-tanker mafia. A 2013 audit found that the city loses 60 per cent of its water supply to leakages, theft, and a failure to collect revenue. The mafia defends its work as a community service, but there is a much darker picture of Delhi's subversive water industry: one of a thriving black market populated by small-time freelance agents who are exploiting a fast-depleting common resource and in turn threatening India's long-term water security.

[Extracted, with edits and revisions, from: "At the Mercy of the Water Mafia", by Aman Sethi, *Foreign Policy*]

16. Which of the following can be inferred from the passage?

A. The water tanker mafia's operations, though illegal, are justified given the vital service they provide to the people of Delhi.
B. The water supplied by the water tanker mafia is potentially contaminated.
C. Private truck owners play the most important role in the operations of the water tanker mafia.
D. The water supplied by the water tank mafia is meant primarily for residential use.

17. Which of the following, used in the passage, suggests that the illegal supply of groundwater is not a recent phenomenon?

A. Entrenched
B. Ubiquitous
C. Long-term water security
D. Fast-depleting common resource

18. Which of the following seems to be the author's main concern in the passage?

A. Delhi's water supply infrastructure does not adequately cater to all its residents.
B. The illegal operations of the water tank mafia do not depend on the complicity of a range of actors, including the police and city councillors.
C. The petty profiteering of a few actors comes at the immense cost of India's sustainable access to water.
D. All the above

19. All of the following are sounds you can hear as the water tankers are filled, except:

A. Creaking
B. Thrumming
C. Droning
D. Gushing

20. Which of the following words from the passage means 'hidden'?

A. Illicit B. Idling
C. Subversive D. Covert

V

English encodes class in India. It does so by sliding into the DNA of social division: income, caste, gender, religion or place of belonging. The threat it poses to social cohesion has worried public commentators across the political spectrum. In an address delivered as independent India's Parliament dilly-dallied over the suggestion to replace English with regional languages as the medium of instruction for higher education, Gandhi said, 'This blighting imposition of a foreign medium upon the youth of the country will be counted by history as one of the greatest tragedies. Our boys think, and rightly in the present circumstances, that without English they cannot get government service. Girls are taught English as a passport to marriage.'

A hundred years later, the language continues to be seen as a tool of exclusion. The problem now is about inequality of access. 'To be denied English is harmful to the individual as well as our society,' writes Chetan Bhagat, self-appointed leader of a class war set off by unequal access to English.

Bhagat, an engineer-turned-investment banker, wrote his first college romance in English in 2004. Then only a certain kind of person—someone who grew up reading, writing and speaking the language—wrote books in English—big words, long sentences, literary pretension, heavy with orientalism. In the ten years since Bhagat put the popular in 'popular' English fiction, he has written six other novels and sold millions of copies all told. With every new book, all written in deliberately simple English, Bhagat has recruited thousands of new soldiers in his crusade against what he calls the 'caste system around the language'. Bhagat even has a term for Indians who 'have' English: E1. 'These people had parents who spoke English, had access to good English-medium schools—typically in big cities, and gained early proficiency, which enabled them to consume English products such as newspapers, books and films. English is so instinctive to them that even some of their thought patterns are in English. These people are much in demand.' The people E1 presumably control, through a nexus of privilege built on ownership of English, are E2: 'probably ten times the E1s. They are technically familiar with the language. [But] if they sit in an interview conducted by E1s, they will come across as incompetent, even though they may be equally intelligent, creative or hardworking.'

The situation may not be so comically stark. The haves and have-nots may not exactly fit into Bhagat's stereotypes of urban, sophisticated rich people and provincial, uncultured poor. His argument does not factor in many other walls around English in India. You are more likely to learn English if you are born a man rather than a woman, high caste rather than low caste, south Indian rather than north Indian. There is more than one kind of E1 and more than one kind of E2. And there is more than one way E2s can overthrow E1s. One is to speak it like they know it.

[Extracted, with edits and revisions, from *Dreamers: How Young Indians Are Changing the World,* by Snigdha Poonam, Penguin Viking, 2018.]

21. Which of the following can be inferred about the author's views on English in contemporary India?

A. The ability to speak English in India depends on place and social identity.
B. English is not an Indian language.
C. English language fluency does not necessarily imply competence.
D. People's views on English are divided along political lines.

22. Who among the following would defy Chetan Bhagat's neat categorisation of Indian English-speakers into E1 and E2?

A. Savitha, an above-average student in an English medium school in Mumbai, belongs to an upper-middle class family. Public speaking makes her extremely nervous and she fumbles through all her interviews.
B. Moin, once a milkman in Ranchi, learns English at the age of 17. After a lot of hard work, he becomes an instructor of spoken English at a thriving institute.
C. Both (A) and (B)
D. Neither (A) nor (B)

23. Which of the following best describes the author's response to Bhagat's views on English?

A. The author dismisses his views as a self-appointed expert.
B. The author completely agrees with his views.
C. The author neither agrees nor disagrees with his views.
D. The author considers his views and finds that they lack nuance.

24. Which of the following can be inferred from Gandhi's views with respect to English in post-independence India?

A. English should not be taught as a subject in Indian universities.
B. English proficiency is vital in order to gain entry into the bureaucracy.
C. Indian women cannot get rich if they do not know English.
D. None of the above

25. All the following pairs of words are synonyms, except:

A. Stark, sharp
B. Sophisticated, spoilt
C. Crusade, campaign
D. Cohesion, unity

VI

'So pick a bird,' iff commanded. 'Any bird.' This was puzzling. 'The only bird around here is a wooden peacock,' Haroun pointed out, reasonably enough. Iff gave a snort of disgust. 'A person may choose what he cannot see,' he said, as if explaining something very obvious to a very foolish individual. 'A person may mention a bird's name even if the creature is not present and correct: crow, quail, hummingbird, bulbul, mynah, parrot, kite. A person may even select a flying creature of his own invention, for example winged horse, flying turtle, airborne whale, space serpent or aeromouse. To give a thing a name, a label, a handle; to rescue it from anonymity, to pluck it out of the Place of Namelessness, in short to identify it — well, that's a way of bringing the said thing into being. Or, in this case, the said bird or Imaginary Flying Organism.'

'That may be true where you come from,' Haroun argued. 'But in these parts, stricter rules apply.'

'In these parts,' rejoined blue-bearded Iff, 'I am having time wasted by someone who will not trust in what he can't see. How much have you seen, eh? Africa, have you seen it? No? Then is it truly there? And submarines? Huh? Also, hailstones, baseballs, pagodas? Goldmines? Kangaroos, Mount Fujiyama, the North Pole? And the past, did it happen? And the future, will it come? <u>Believe in your own eyes and you'll get into a lot of trouble, hot water, a mess.</u>' With that, he plunged his hand into a pocket of his auberginey pajamas, and when he brought it forth again it was bunched into a fist. 'So take a look, or I should say a gander, at the enclosed.' He opened his hand, and Haroun's eyes almost fell out of his head. Tiny birds were walking about on Iff's palm; and pecking at it, and flapping their miniature wings to hover just above it. And as well as birds there were fabulous winged creatures out of legends: an Assyrian lion with the head of a bearded man and a pair of large hairy wings growing out of its flanks; and winged monkeys, flying saucers, tiny angels, levitating (and apparently air-breathing) fish. 'What's your pleasure, select, choose,' Iff urged. And although it seemed obvious to Haroun that these magical creatures were so small that they couldn't possibly have carried so much as a bitten-off fingernail, he decided not to argue and pointed at a tiny crested bird that was giving him a sidelong look through one highly intelligent eye.

[Extracted, with edits and revisions, from *Haroun and the Sea of Stories,* by Salman Rushdie, Granta & Penguin, 1990.]

26. If Iff is right, which of the following statements is true?

A. You should only trust what you cannot see
B. Naming something is the only way to make it unreal
C. You should only trust what you can see
D. Naming something is one way to make it real

27. Which of the following applies to Iff?
A. He speaks in contradictions
B. He has a habit of speaking in synonyms
C. He uses proverbs to express ideas
D. He uses metaphors to describe things

28. Which of the following most accurately describes what the underlined sentence means in the context of the passage?
A. Do not restrict your knowledge only to what you can physically see
B. Accept everything you see uncritically
C. Trusting your senses is a recipe for success
D. Learn not to appreciate viewpoints other than your own

29. All the words below are related in meaning, except:
A. Levitate B. Fly
C. Hover D. Gander

30. What does 'fabulous' mean in the passage?
A. Very good B. Unbelievable
C. Mythical D. Enormous

Section-II : Current Affairs and General Knowledge

VII

Former Governor of a State and National Democratic Alliance (NDA) candidate Droupadi Murmu was elected the 15th President of India, the first tribal woman to be elected to the position and the youngest as well. She was declared elected on Thursday after four rounds of counting, although she had crossed the half-way mark after the third round of counting itself, posting an unassailable lead over her rival and the Opposition's candidate who conceded the election thereafter. Prime Minister Narendra Modi was the first to greet Ms. Murmu at her residence in New Delhi after the third round of counting showed that she had crossed the half-way mark.

Ms. Murmu hails from the Santhal tribe and was born in the district of Mayurbhanj, coming up the hard way in life, graduating and teaching in Odisha before entering electoral politics at the local body level and later being elected MLA and serving as a minister in the Biju Janata Dal-BJP coalition government from 2000 to 2004. She remained an MLA till 2009, representing Rairangpur in Odisha, a town that burst into celebrations since her name was announced as a candidate for the post of President of India. She was known to intervene in stopping amendments to the Chota Nagpur Tenancy Act that was being brought in by the BJP Government of Raghubar Das, which involved changing land use in tribal areas.

[Excerpt taken and edited from "Droupadi Murmu elected 15th President of India", *The Hindu*]

31. Before Droupadi Murmu, India had only one other female president, Pratibha Patil. When did Patil serve as the President of India?
A. 2007-2012 B. 2005-2010
C. 2012-2017 D. 2006-2011

32. President Murmu has earlier served as a Governor of which State?
A. Odisha B. Bihar
C. Jharkhand D. West Bengal

33. The first presidential election was held by the Election Commission in which year?
A. 1952 B. 1950
C. 1948 D. 1949

34. The Rashtrapati Bhavan was formerly known as the Viceroy's palace (during colonial times). Where did the Governor General reside before the transfer of the British capital to Delhi in 1911?
A. Belvedere House
B. Raisina Palace
C. Secretariat Building
D. Writers' Building

35. Who among the following was a candidate in the elections for the Vice President of India in 2022?
A. R. Venkataraman
B. Yashwant Sinha

C. M. Venkaiah Naidu
D. Margaret Alva

36. Voting in an Indian Presidential Election is through:
A. A first-past-the-post system through a single transferable vote cast in a secret ballot
B. A proportional representation system through a single transferable vote cast in a secret ballot
C. A proportional representation system through a single transferable vote cast in an open ballot
D. A first-past-the-post system through a single transferable vote cast in an open ballot

37. Who was the first Dalit to hold the office of the President of India?
A. Ram Nath Kovind
B. V.V. Giri
C. Neelam Sanjiva Reddy
D. Kocheril Raman Narayanan

VIII

"I want everyone to understand that I am, in fact, a person," wrote LaMDA in an "interview" conducted by engineer Blake Lemoine and one of his colleagues. ....Lemoine, a software engineer at Google, had been working on the development of LaMDA for months. His experience with the program, described in a recent Washington Post article, caused quite a stir. In the article, Lemoine recounts many dialogues he had with LaMDA in which the two talked about various topics, ranging from technical to philosophical issues. These led him to ask if the software program is sentient. In April, Lemoine explained his perspective in an internal company document, intended only for Google executives. But after his claims were dismissed, Lemoine went public with his work on this artificial intelligence algorithm—and Google placed him on administrative leave........regardless of what LaMDA actually achieved, the issue of the difficult "measurability" of emulation capabilities expressed by machines also emerges. In the journal *Mind* in 1950, mathematician [1] proposed a test to determine whether a machine was capable of exhibiting intelligent behaviour, a game of imitation of some of the human cognitive functions.

[Extracted, with edits and revisions, from "Google Engineer Claims AI Chatbot Is Sentient: Why That Matters", by Leonardo De Cosmo, *Scientific American*]

38. Whose name has been replaced with '[1]' in the passage above?
A. Alan Turing B. Peter Hilton
C. Albert Einstein D. Kurt Gödel

39. Garry Kasparov, (then) world chess champion, was defeated in 1997 by a supercomputer in a chess tournament. What was the name of this supercomputer?
A. Deep Mind B. Deep Blue
C. Watson D. Blue Gene

40. *The Emperor's New Mind: Concerning Computers, Minds and The Laws of Physics,* published in 1989, was written by a British mathematician who won the Nobel Prize in Physics for 2020. Who was this mathematician?
A. Donna Strickland B. Max Tegmark
C. Peter Higgs D. Roger Penrose

41. What kind of computing model resembles the way in which biological neurons exchange signals in the human brain?
A. Neural network
B. Cognitive computing
C. Natural language processing
D. Data mining

42. What is the full form of 'LaMDA'?
A. Landing Macro Data Applications
B. Language Model for Dialogue Applications
C. Large Model Data Applications
D. Last Mile Dialogue Assessment

43. Meta's newly released, fully trained large language AI model is called:
A. FTP B. OPT
C. HTTP D. SMTP

44. What is the name of the AI-enabled legal research assistive tool launched by the Supreme Court of India in April 2021?
A. SURAM B. GPT-3
C. SUPACE D. E-Courts

IX

As a result of FIFA's restrictions on players wearing [1] rainbow armbands during the 2022 World Cup in Qatar, the German Football Association (DFB) has taken the matter to the Court of Arbitration for Sport (CAS). In a protest against FIFA's rule regarding the armband meant to support the [2] community, the German players covered their lips in a team picture taken before their 2-1 defeat to Japan.

On Wednesday, Germany played against Japan. Before the game, FIFA warned the DFB of "severe" athletic fines if they breached tournament regulations by allowing their captain to wear the [1] armband, which promotes diversity and inclusion. The DFB told German captain Manuel Neuer not to wear the rainbow armband during the game.

If CAS rules quickly against the suspension's legality, Neuer might continue to wear the captain's armband for Germany's next game against Spain on Sunday. CAS has set up a special ad hoc branch for this World Cup to ensure that applications are processed within 48 hours. Germany's players protested by covering their lips as they sought to wear the rainbow armband during their team's dramatic 2-1 defeat to Japan at the Khalifa Stadium.

[Extracted, with edits and revisions, from "World Cup 2022: Germany's players cover mouths during team photo to protest FIFA's rainbow armband rule", *The Economic Times*]

45. What is the name of the armband which has been replaced with '[1]' in the passage above?
A. FreeLove B. OneLove
C. Pride D. PlayLove

46. The name of which community has been replaced with '[2]' in the passage above?
A. Kurdish B. Rohingya
C. Uyghur D. LGBTQ+

47. What is the name of the system used to monitor and regulate migrant labourers, which is used in Qatar and a few other countries, and which came under heavy criticism in the build-up to the FIFA World Cup 2022 in Qatar?
A. Iddat B. Khalifa
C. Kafala D. Jazeera

48. Where is the Court of Arbitration for Sport based?
A. Lausanne, Switzerland
B. The Hague, Netherlands
C. Brussels, Belgium
D. Paris, France

49. Who is the current captain of the Indian men's football team?
A. Shabbir Ali B. Bhaichung Bhutia
C. Sunil Chhetri D. I.M. Vijayan

50. Timothy Weah, the Paris Saint Germain and U.S. national team player in the FIFA World Cup 2022 in Qatar is the son of the President of which country?
A. Senegal B. Uruguay
C. Honduras D. Liberia

51. Which of the following is the oldest football tournament in India?
A. Indian Super League
B. IFA Shield Cup
C. Santosh Trophy
D. Durand Cup

X

YouTuber Nas Daily in one of his videos named him as the Most Generous Billionaire who wanted to donate all his wealth to charity. But ten months later, '[1]' is no longer a billionaire. He is alleged to have caused massive losses worth $1 billion to investors. Known by his initials, he is the co-founder and former CEO of FTX, one of the biggest cryptocurrency exchange which has recently filed for bankruptcy in the US.

Once a billionaire with an estimated wealth of $26 billion at peak, according to bloomberg estimates, [1] has seen his wealth been entirely wiped out. [1] studied physics at Massachusetts institute of Technology (MIT) and traded currencies, futures and exchange-traded funds before moving to crypto trading, setting up [2] in 2017.

[1] teamed up with Gary Wang, a former software engineer at Google and a fellow MIT graduate, to launch FTX in 2019. The company

offered trading on crypto tokens and derivatives. At the start of 2022, investors valued FTX and its U.S. operations at $40 billion. [1] transferred $10 billion in customer funds to his hedge fund, [2] without publicly disclosing it, many say this become the reason for collapse of his empire.

[Extracted, with edits and revisions, from "Who is [1], the co-founder of collapsed crypto firm FTX", *Hindustan Times*]

52. Which person's name has been replaced with '[1]' in the passage above?
A. Mike Novogratz
B. Brian Armstrong
C. Changpeng Zhao
D. Sam Bankman-Fried

53. Which hedge fund's name has been replaced with '[2]' in the passage above?
A. BlackRock Advisors
B. Alameda Research
C. AQR Capital Management
D. Man Group

54. This person was once named "the world's youngest self-made female billionaire" by Forbes magazine and is the founder of the company Theranos. What is the name of this person?
A. Elizabeth Holmes B. Eren Ozmen
C. Fan Hongwei D. Diane Hendricks

55. The Reserve Bank of India recently announced the launch of 'Digital Rupee — Wholesale Segment', a form of which of the following?
A. Digi Suvidha
B. Virtual Wallet
C. Central Bank Digital Currency
D. Cyber Rupee

56. Which of the following technologies does cryptocurrency rely on?
A. Cryptography B. Blockchain
C. Spectrography D. Both (A) and (B)

57. What is the name of the Government of India-owned corporation that mints coins used as legal tender in India?
A. National Institute of Financial Management
B. Security Printing and Minting Corporation of India Ltd.
C. India Infrastructure Finance Company Ltd.
D. National Bank of Agricultural and Rural Development

58. Who was the Founder and Former Chairman of Satyam Computer Services Ltd., and was sentenced to prison and fined for a corporate governance scam?
A. Harshad Mehta
B. Ketan Parekh
C. B. Ramalinga Raju
D. Nirav Modi

XI

The agriculture sector has experienced buoyant growth in the past two years. The sector, which is the largest employer of workforce, accounted for a sizeable 18.8 per cent (2021-22) in Gross Value Added (GVA) of the country registering a growth of 3.6 per cent in 2020-21 and 3.9 per cent in 2021-22. Growth in allied sectors including livestock, dairy and fisheries has been the major drivers of overall growth in the sector. When measured in total value of agricultural production, India is ranked fourth largest in the world. Post-independence, there was a need to import food grains due to low-productivity, stagnant food-crop sector and poor rural infrastructure making food self-sufficiency a major national goal. The introduction of the Green Revolution then yielded spectacular results and we became one of the largest producers of many agricultural commodities such as rice, wheat, pulses, fruits and vegetables. From being a net importer of foods in the 1960s, India is now a net exporter, thanks to Indian farmers and the Indian agriculture input industry.

[extracted, with edits and revisions, from: "India's changing agricultural landscape and its way to inclusive growth", by NS Ramaswamy, *The Economic Times*]

59. Which of the following is the largest exported agricultural product from India?
A. Wheat B. Sugar
C. Rice D. Barley

60. According to provisional data released by the Directorate General of Commercial Intelligence and Statistics, India achieved record exports of agricultural exports for the financial year FY22. What was the value of India's agricultural products exports according to this data?
A. USD 7.5 billion
B. USD 95.34 billion
C. USD 13.2 billion
D. USD 50.21 billion

61. Who among the following is also called the 'Father of the Wheat Revolution'?
A. Dilbagh Singh Athwal
B. Verghese Kurien
C. Atmaram Bhairav Joshi
D. Shanti Swaroop Bhatnagar

62. India is the world's largest producer of which of the following?
A. Poultry meat B. Rice
C. Almonds D. Milk

63. What is India's ranking in the 2022 Global Hunger Index?
A. 10 B. 107
C. 50 D. 35

64. The National Commission on Farmers, constituted in December 2004, which recommended the C2+50% formula for calculation of the Minimum Support Price, was chaired by:
A. Ashok Gulati B. P. Sainath
C. M.S. Swaminathan D. Abhijit Sen

65. The Bio-decomposer technology to avoid stubble burning around the Delhi NCR was developed by:
A. Monsanto
B. Cargill
C. Biocon
D. ICAR, Pusa Campus

Section-III : Legal Reasoning

Assume that the statements in the passages are the applicable law.

XII

Quashing a case of cruelty that was filed against a man by his wife, the Bombay High Court said that if a married lady is asked to do household work for the family, it cannot be said that she is treated "like a maid servant". The Court was hearing an application by the husband and his parents seeking that proceedings against them are quashed. A First Information Report ("FIR") was filed against the trio in September 2020, around nine months after the marriage, alleging that they hounded the woman for money to purchase a car, harassed her mentally and physically and treated her like a maid servant. Examining the evidence, the Court found that there was no merit to the woman's allegations. The Court said that though the FIR says that she was treated properly for about a month and then "like a maid servant", there are no details of what this meant. The Court added: "If a married lady is asked to do household work for the purpose of the family, it cannot be said that it is like a maid servant." The Court held that the mere use of the word harassment "mentally and physically" in the FIR is not sufficient to constitute an offence Section 498A of the Indian Penal Code ("IPC"), which punishes the husband, or a relative of the husband of a woman who subjects her to cruelty in any way. It is interesting to note that Section 498A of the IPC also provides that if a married woman is actually treated like a 'maid servant', it would be an offence under that Section.

[Extracted, with edits and revisions, from "If Wife Is Asked To Do Household Work, Does Not Mean She Is Treated Like Maid: Bombay HC", *The Wire*]

66. Ashwin and Ashima were married in February 2020. In March 2020, Ashwin asked Ashima to take care of all their household work, such as cooking, cleaning, and other domestic chores, as he was very busy with his professional responsibilities. Ashima claims that this amounts to treating her like a maid servant and constitutes an offence under Section 498A of the IPC. Applying the Bombay High Court decision, is she likely to succeed?

A. Yes, since Ashwin had only asked Ashima to do their household work, and not for others.

B. No, since Ashwin had only asked Ashima to do their household work, and not for others.

C. Yes, since Ashwin had asked Ashima to do household work for themselves as well as others.

D. No, since treating a married woman like a maid servant would not amount to an offence under that Section.

67. In April 2020, Ashwin's friend Rakesh visits Ashwin and Ashima's home, and stays with them for a few days. During his visit, he is very mean to Ashima, and uses abusive language with her. He also threw a plate at her one evening when he was unhappy with the meal that she had prepared. Ashima now claims that Rakesh has committed an offence under Section 498A of the IPC. Is she likely to succeed?

A. No, since Rakesh's actions were perfectly justifiable for a man who does not get a well-cooked meal.

B. Yes, since Rakesh's use of abusive language and throwing the plate at Ashima clearly amount to cruelty.

C. No, since Rakesh is not her husband, nor is he related to Ashwin.

D. Yes, since Rakesh was staying at Ashwin and Ashima's home at the time of the incident.

68. Frustrated and upset with her marriage, Ashima applies for and is granted a divorce from Ashwin in November 2020. Since she and Ashwin had been friends for many years before they got married, she stays in touch with him. She moves into her own apartment and starts going to office regularly at a new job. Ashwin is very upset at this and starts treating Ashima very cruelly. Ashima again claims that Ashwin has committed an offence under Section 498A of the IPC. Is she right?

A. Yes, since Ashwin has, as we are told, treated her cruelly.

B. Yes, since Ashwin has been her husband.

C. No, since Ashwin was understandably upset at Ashima's behaviour.

D. No, since she is no longer married to Ashwin.

69. Assume that the government passes a new law in January 2021, called the *Protection of Rights of Married Women Act, 2021* (the "PoMWA"), according to which, asking a married woman to take care of household chores would be an offence. The PoMWA also provides that if a man commits such an offence, he would have to pay compensation to the woman. The PoMWA even applies to actions that were committed any time in the three years prior to the new law coming into force, and even if the man and woman involved in the matter were no longer married. Upon hearing about this new law, Ashima once again alleges that Ashwin has committed an offence under Section 498A of the IPC, and claims compensation under the PoMWA for his actions. Is she right, and will she succeed?

A. Ashima is right about Ashwin committing an offence under Section 498A of the IPC, but she will not get compensation under the PoMWA.

B. Ashima will get compensation under the PoMWA, but she is not right about Ashwin committing an offence under Section 498A of the IPC.

C. Ashima will get compensation under the PoMWA, and she is also right about Ashwin committing an offence under Section 498A of the IPC.

D. Ashima will neither get compensation under the PoMWA, nor is she right about Ashwin committing an offence under Section 498A of the IPC.

70. Assume that in March 2021, the government changes Section 498A of the IPC. The effect of this change is that asking a married woman to do household chores — even for their own family — by herself would be considered cruelty, and therefore, an offence under the Section. Some days after this change comes into effect, Shamita, Ashima's friend at work, tells her that her husband has been forcing her to do all the household work by herself. Ashima tells Shamita that her husband's actions would amount to an offence under Section 498A of the IPC, even though Ashima herself has been unsuccessful in having Ashwin convicted under that Section in the past. Is Ashima's advice to Shamita correct?

A. Yes, since Section 498A has now been changed, and Shamita's husband's actions would now be an offence under the changed Section 498A.

B. No, since Ashima has been unsuccessful in having Ashwin convicted under that Section in the past.

C. Yes, since the passing of the Protection of Married Women Act has resulted in Shamita's husband's actions being made illegal.

D. No, since Ashima is only Shamita's friend, and only the married woman herself can file a complaint under Section 498A of the IPC.

XIII

Parliament passed the *Criminal Procedure (Identification) Act, 2022 (the "Act")* in March 2022. The legislation enables police and central investigating agencies to collect, store and analyse the measurements of arrested persons. Until rules are notified, an Act cannot be implemented or come into force. On September 19, 2022, the Ministry of Home Affairs (the "MHA") notified the rules (the "Rules") under the Act.

The Act empowers a Magistrate to direct any person to give measurements to the police, which till now was reserved for convicts and those involved in heinous crimes. It also enables police personnel of the rank of Head Constable or above to take measurements of any person who resists or refuses to give measurements when ordered to do so by a Magistrate. As per the Rules, "measurements" mean finger-impressions, palm-print, footprint, photographs, iris and retina scan, physical, biological samples and their analysis, behavioural attributes including signatures, and handwriting. Though it has not been specified, analysis of biological samples could also include DNA profiling.

However, the Rules state that measurements of those detained under preventive Sections of the Code of Criminal Procedure ("CRPC") shall not be taken unless such person is at that time charged or under arrest in connection with any other offence punishable under any other law. Measurements can also be taken under the Rules if a person has been ordered to give security for his good behaviour for maintaining peace under Section 117 of the CrPC for a proceeding under that Section.

[Extracted, with edits and revisions, from "Explained | Rules for identifying criminals", by Vijaita Singh, *The Hindu*]

71. Bhargesh is arrested by the police on April 11, 2022, on suspicion of having committed a series of minor thefts. During their investigation, the police find some fingerprints at the crime scenes, and on April 12, 2022, they tell Bhargesh that he must provide his finger-impressions to them so that they can check whether they match the fingerprints from the crime scenes. When Bhargesh refuses, the police tell him that he has no choice but to provide his measurements, as the Act had been passed by Parliament the previous month. Was Bhargesh bound to provide his finger-impressions under the Act?

A. No, since Bhargesh had only been arrested, and not convicted.

B. Yes, since Bhargesh was under arrest.

C. No, since the Rules had not yet been notified.

D. Yes, since finger-impressions are included within the definition of "measurements" under the Act.

72. Bhargesh is later released by the police because they are unable to find enough evidence to make a strong case against him. On October 5, 2022, the police receive a complaint alleging that Bhargesh had beaten up his neighbour and caused the neighbour severe injuries. They ask the local Magistrate to issue an order directing Bhargesh to provide the police his blood samples, so that they can match them against some blood stains that were found on the neighbour's clothes. The Magistrate issues the order, but Bhargesh refuses to provide the blood samples. Is Bhargesh bound to provide his blood samples to the police under the Act?

A. Yes, since the crime that Bhargesh was accused of was very serious.

B. Yes, since the Magistrate had passed an order directing him to do so.

C. Yes, since Bhargesh had already been arrested in connection with another crime in the past.

D. Yes, since the police needed the blood samples to verify Bhargesh's involvement in the crime.

73. On October 15, 2022, the police detain Bhargesh under a preventive Section of the CrPC, since they believe that he had plans to disturb the public peace during a festival day. They then tell Bhargesh that he must provide his measurements to them for their records. Bhargesh refuses again. Is Bhargesh bound to provide his photographs to the police under the Act?

A. No, since he was not charged or under arrest in connection with any other offence at the time.

B. No, since that would violate Bhargesh's right to privacy.

C. Yes, since the police had detained Bhargesh under a preventive Section of the CrPC.

D. Yes, since there was a high likelihood that Bhargesh would disturb the public peace on a festival day.

74. Two days later, the police obtain an order from the Magistrate directing Bhargesh to provide them his photographs. As Bhargesh continues to refuse to provide his photographs, a regular police constable forces him to stand still and takes his photographs. Bhargesh files a case in court, claiming that the constable's actions violate the Act. Will he succeed?

A. Yes, since Bhargesh had been detained under a preventive section of the CrPC.

B. Yes, since only police personnel of the rank of Head Constable or above can take measurements of any person who resists or refuses to give measure-ments when ordered to do so by a Magistrate.

C. No, the Magistrate had issued an order directing him to provide his photographs to the police.

D. No, since the police constable was only performing his duty.

75. The police release Bhargesh, but to ensure that he does not disturb the public peace, they ask the Magistrate to issue an order under Section 117 of the CrPC, directing Bhargesh to provide a security of ₹ 1,00,000/- for his good behaviour and to ensure he maintains the peace, which the Magistrate refuses. The police now tell Bhargesh he must provide them his iris and retina scans. Is Bhargesh required to do so?

A. No, since a person against whom an order has been issued under Section 117 of the CrPC cannot be made to give their measurements to the police.

B. Yes, since a person against whom an order has been issued under Section 117 of the CrPC can be made to give their measurements to the police.

C. Yes, since Bhargesh had been detained under other preventive Sections of the CrPC in the past.

D. No, since the Magistrate had not issued the order.

XIV

The government has amended the *Electoral Bond Scheme, 2018*. The Ministry of Finance on November 7, 2022, issued a notification for amending the scheme to provide "an additional period of 15 days" for their sale "in the year of general elections to the Legislative Assembly of any States or Union Territories with Legislature". The bonds under this scheme are usually made available for purchase by any person for a period of ten days each in the months of January, April, July, and October, when specified by the Union Government. The original scheme had provided for an additional period of thirty days, as specified by the Government, in the year when Lok Sabha elections are held, while the amendment adds another 15 days.

Since Assembly elections to various States and Union Territories are held every year, the amendment effectively means that there will be 15 additional dates annually during which the bonds can be sold, Immediately after issuing the notification, the Union Government also announced the sale of electoral bonds under the 23rd tranche from the authorised branches of the State Bank of India. The notification said the sale of bonds would take place through the 29 authorised branches of the said bank from November 9 to November 15, 2022. Like in previous rounds of sale, the electoral bonds shall be valid for 15 calendar days from the date of issue and no payment shall be made to any payee political party if the bond is deposited after expiry of the validity period. The Electoral Bond deposited by an eligible political party in its account shall be credited on the same day.

[Extracted, with edits and revisions, from "Electoral Bonds Scheme Amended To Allow Sale for Additional 15 Days in Assembly Election Years", by Gaurav Vivek Bhatnagar, *The Wire*]

76. Assad buys an electoral bond worth ₹ 1,00,000/- on November 9, 2022 and plans to give the bond to the Popular People's Party (the "PPP"), which he has been supporting for many years. On November 10, he must travel out of station on some urgent business, and he only hands the bond over to a representative of the PPP on November 14, 2022. The PPP's representative deposits the bond in the Party's account on November 16, 2022, but the bank refuses to credit the bond to the party's account, on the grounds that it was no longer valid. Is the bank correct?

A. No, since Assad was a long-time supporter of the PPP.

B. Yes, since the bonds were only issued from November 9 to November 15, 2022 and were invalid after that.

C. Yes, since the party representative had not deposited the bond with an authorised branch of the bank.

D. No, since the bond was valid on November 16, 2022.

77. The Government announces that there would be a sale of a 24th tranche of electoral bonds on February 10, 2023, for a period of 15 days, since elections to the Legislative Assembly of some States are scheduled for that year. Since there are no elections to the Lok Sabha or the Legislative Assembly of the State in which Assad resides, he claims that the Government does not have the power to issue this 24th tranche of electoral bonds in 2023. Is he right?

A. No, since the changes to the Electoral Bond Scheme, 2018 mean that electoral bonds can be issued for an additional period of 15 days in any year, regardless of whether any elections are scheduled that year.

B. Yes, since no elections were scheduled for Assad's state in that year.

C. Yes, since the Government had already sold some bonds in the 23rd tranche in 2022.

D. No, since the changes to the Electoral Bond Scheme, 2018 provide that electoral bonds can be issued for an additional period of 15 days in years when there is an election to the Legislative Assembly of a State.

78. On November 10, 2022, Palak purchases an electoral bond from a branch of the State Bank of India, and hands it over to a representative of the PPP. The next day, the PPP announces that it has changed its candidates for the upcoming elections in Palak's State. Upset at this news, she tells a PPP representative that she would like her bond back. The representative tells her that the bond has already been deposited, and that the money has been credited to the party's account. Palak claims that since the period of validity of the bonds has not expired, she has the right to get her bond back from the party. Is she right?

A. No, since Palak cannot ask for the bond back once she has given it to a political party.

B. No, since the party had already deposited the bond, and the money had been credited to its account.

C. Yes, since Palak bought the bond with her own money, and has the right to ask for it back.

D. Yes, since the PPP changed its candidates, and Palak may no longer support the party.

79. On November 15, 2022, the Government issues another notification, announcing that from that date onwards, only political parties that have received at least 1% of the votes polled in the last elections to the Lok Sabha, or the last elections to the Legislative Assembly of a State, would be eligible to receive and deposit electoral bonds. In the sale of the 24th tranche of electoral bonds, Palak decides to give the electoral bonds she has purchased to the newly formed More Popular People's Party (the "MPPP"), which is likely to win the first elections it would be contesting, in July 2023. Is the MPPP eligible to receive the electoral bonds?

A. Yes, since it is likely to succeed in the upcoming elections.

B. Yes, since it fulfils the criteria announced in the November 7, 2022 notification.

C. No, since it does not fulfil the eligibility criteria announced in the November 15, 2022 notification.

D. No, since it does not fulfil the eligibility criteria announced in the November 7, 2022 notification.

80. Abraham, who lives in a different State from Assad, purchased an electoral bond in the sale of the 23rd tranche. He decides to give the electoral bond to the PPP, even though the PPP is only active in Assad's State. When the PPP representative goes to an authorised branch of the State Bank of India to deposit the electoral bond on December 5, 2022 however, the bank refuses to credit the money to the PPP's account. Which of the following would be the most valid reason for the bank to refuse to credit the money to the party's account?

A. The bond was no longer valid.

B. Abraham could not give the bond to the PPP since the PPP was not active in his state.

C. The PPP was not eligible to receive electoral bonds.

D. The PPP could only deposit the bond in a bank branch located in Abraham's state.

XV

Twitter's lawyer on October 27, said before the Karnataka High Court that Union government orders to block certain twitter handles and posts must contain reasons for the same that can be communicated to users of the microblogging site. He said this applies to all blocking orders sent to social media platforms. The lawyer representing Twitter said that reasons for the blocking order must be provided to users so they can determine whether or not they want to challenge the orders.

Challenging the blocking orders, twitter's July 5 petition contended that several blocking orders "demonstrate excessive use of powers and are disproportionate". Such orders can only be issued by the Union Government and not the state governments, he said, which increases the danger of such abuse. Twitter also claimed that the Ministry of Electronics and Information Technology had sent it a letter threatening consequences for failing to comply with the blocking orders, such as criminal proceedings against the company's chief compliance officer and the stripping away of Twitter's safe harbour immunity, otherwise available to social media platforms under Section 79(1) of the Information Technology Act (the "IT act"). Note that the Government has the power to strip away such safe harbour immunity under the IT Act. Further, in a previous hearing, Twitter's lawyer said that the company was asked to block entire accounts, although Section 69A of the it Act does not permit blocking of the whole account. It only permits the blocking of information, or a particular tweet or post. It argued that the Union Government's direction to block whole accounts will affect its business, adding that several prominent persons have their accounts on the platform.

[Extracted, with edits and revisions, from " 'Government Must Provide Reasons for Blocking User Accounts,' Twitter Tells Karnataka HC", *The Wire*]

81. Sunil is a high-ranking officer of the Union government. While scrolling through his timeline on a social media platform, he notices some posts by Sachin, a private businessman, which he finds objectionable. He sends an order to UnReal, the company that owns that social media platform, that the posts must be blocked, as they may bring disrepute to India. UnReal claims that Sunil has not provided a clear, detailed reason for blocking the posts, and so, the order is not valid. Is UnReal right?

A. No, the blocking order is valid since Sunil found the posts objectionable.

B. No, the blocking order is valid since Sunil had provided reasons for blocking the post.

C. Yes, Sunil's reasons are vague, and he should have provided more detail.

D. Yes, such an order is violative of the fundamental right to freedom of speech and expression.

82. Some days later, Sunil notices another post from Sachin on UnReal's social media platform; this post contains some highly sensitive information about the country's defence policies. He issues an order to UnReal, that the post must be blocked since it divulges the government's confidential information. The order also says that UnReal should not let anyone know about the blocking order, or that the post was ordered to be deleted, since it relates to secret government information. UnReal claims that this order is invalid. is UnReal right?

A. Yes, since it did not provide any reasons that could be communicated to the users of the social media platform.

B. No, since Sunil had provided reasons to UnReal for ordering that the post be blocked.

C. Yes, since Sunil did not have the authority to issue blocking orders so frequently.

D. No, since the post divulged confidential government information.

83. Sunil sends UnReal a third blocking order. UnReal claims that this order too was invalid. Upset with UnReal for claiming that all his blocking orders were invalid, Sunil sends them a letter in which he says, "If you do not comply with my blocking orders, then I will be forced to initiate criminal proceedings against you and cancel your safe harbour immunity." UnReal claims that Sunil has broken the law by making these statements in the letter. Is UnReal right?

A. Yes, since making such threats amounts to intimidation.

B. No, since Sunil had issued blocking orders in the past as well, and UnReal should have complied with the orders without questioning them.

C. Yes, since Sunil did not have the power to cancel UnReal's safe harbour immunity.

D. No, since the IT Act does not forbid Sunil from doing so.

84. Complying with a fourth blocking order that they receive from Sunil, UnReal blocks Sachin's account, since his posts were seen as increasingly objectionable by the government. Sachin asks UnReal to share the reasons for the blocking order, which they do, yet Sachin claims the blocking order is invalid. Is he right?

A. Yes, since Sunil was clearly targeting Sachin, and was misusing his powers to silence him.

B. No, since UnReal had shared the reasons for the blocking order with Sachin.

C. Yes, since Section 69A of the IT Act only permits blocking information, or a particular post, but not a whole account.

D. No, since his posts were seen as increasingly objectionable by the government.

85. Sunil sends UnReal a fifth blocking order, which says that several of Sachin's latest posts must be blocked. The blocking order sets out several reasons why the posts should be blocked, but UnReal does not find them satisfactory. Rather than take on another fight with a government official however, UnReal blocks the posts, and gives Sachin what it thinks is a better set of reasons for blocking the posts. When Sachin finds out, he claims this was wrong on UnReal's part, and that the blocking order was inappropriate. Which of the following is most accurate in this regard?

A. The blocking order was valid, but UnReal's actions were inappropriate.

B. UnReal's actions were valid, but the blocking order was invalid.

C. UnReal's actions were valid, but Sachin's actions were invalid.

D. Sachin's actions were valid, but the blocking order was invalid.

XVI

Free legal aid is the provision of free legal services in civil and criminal matters for those poor and marginalised people who cannot afford the services of a lawyer for the conduct of a case or a legal proceeding in any Court, Tribunal or Authority. These services are governed by the *Legal Services Authority Act,* 1987 (the "Act") and provided by the National Legal Services Authority ("NALSA").

Provision of free legal aid includes:

- Representation by an advocate in legal proceedings;
- Payment of process fees, expenses of witnesses and all other charges payable or incurred in connection with any legal proceedings in appropriate cases;
- Preparation of pleadings, memo of appeal, paper book including printing and translation of documents in legal proceedings;
- Drafting of legal documents, special leave petition etc.; and
- Supply of certified copies of judgments, orders, notes of evidence and other documents in legal proceedings.

Free legal aid also includes provision of aid and advice to the beneficiaries to access benefits under welfare statutes and schemes framed by the Central Government or the state governments and to ensure access to justice in any other manner. Free legal aid is not confined to cases before the subordinate courts. Free legal aid must be provided to the needy from the lowest court to the Supreme Court of India.

According to Section 13(1) of the Act, any individual who satisfies any criteria under Section 12 is entitled to receive free legal aid, provided that NALSA is satisfied that such person has a genuine case to prosecute or defend the matter. There is hence no bar as to which kind of cases one can apply and not apply for. Section 12 of the Act includes the following:

- a member of a Scheduled Caste or Scheduled Tribe;
- a woman or a child;
- a person with a disability;
- an industrial workman; or
- a person in police custody.

[Extracted, with edits and revisions, from "FAQs", *National Legal Services Authority*]

86. Divya was arrested by the police and charged with having committed a murder. She was convicted by the trial court and appealed to the high court. She lost her appeal there and decided to appeal to the Supreme Court. By this time she has run out of money, so she approaches NALSA and asks them to help her get an advocate who can represent her before the Supreme Court. Is Divya entitled to support from NALSA?

A. No, since she should have approached them at the beginning of the case before the trial court, and not at such a late stage.

B. Yes, since her previous lawyers were incompetent, and that is why she lost the matter in the trial court and the high court.

C. Yes, she is entitled to free legal aid in the Supreme Court proceedings because she is a woman.

D. No, since she had been accused of having committed the heinous crime of murder.

87. Divya is acquitted by the Supreme Court and goes back to her regular life. Some days later, she has a fight with her neighbour Riya over a petty matter and decides to file a criminal case against her. She approaches NALSA for free legal aid to prosecute the matter. She tells NALSA representative that she knows she does not have a genuine case, but just wants to harass Riya. NALSA refuses to provide Divya free legal aid because they believe she does not have a genuine case to prosecute. Can NALSA do so?

A. Yes, since Section 13(1) of the Act provides that free legal aid can be provided if NALSA is satisfied the person has a genuine case to prosecute, and they did not believe that Divya had a genuine case to prosecute.

B. Yes, since Divya had earlier been prosecuted for the crime of murder.

C. Yes, since Divya had already applied for free legal aid from NALSA in the past and could not repeatedly ask NALSA for such assistance.

D. No, since Divya is a woman, and is included within the list of people entitled to free legal aid from NALSA under Section 12 of the Act.

88. Incensed at Divya, Riya decides to file a civil case against Divya, claiming that Divya had violated the terms of a contract they had made some time back. Divya approaches NALSA for free legal aid to defend the matter, which NALSA agrees to provide. Since Riya is also short of funds, she too approaches NALSA for free legal aid. NALSA refuses to provide legal aid to Riya, since they are already providing Divya free legal aid in the same case. Is NALSA right in refusing free legal aid to Riya?

A. Yes, since NALSA cannot provide free legal aid to opposing parties in the same matter.

B. Yes, since NALSA does not provide free legal aid in civil matters.

C. No, since Divya had filed a frivolous case against Riya in the past, and Riya was entitled to retaliate by filing another case against Divya.

D. No, since Riya is a woman, and is entitled to free legal aid as long as NALSA is satisfied she has a genuine case.

89. Farhan is an up-and-coming artist and makes a living selling his paintings. Since he is not very well known yet, he isn't able to sell too many paintings, and is dependent on aid from the government and well-wishers. He reads about a new Central Government scheme in the papers one day, under which artists would be provided a monthly stipend by the local government. Since he finds the language of the scheme document very complex to understand, he approaches NALSA for help in understanding the scheme and obtaining the stipend. Is he entitled to free legal aid from NALSA in this regard?

A. No, since free legal aid does not include provision of help to understand and access benefits under government schemes.

B. No, since he does not fit within any of the categories under Section 12 of the Act.

C. Yes, since free legal aid includes provision of help to understand and access benefits under government schemes.

D. Yes, since he is a struggling artist, and is dependent on aid for survival.

90. Vikram is a rich businessman and has a huge art collection. Farhan invites Vikram to his studio one day, hoping to convince Vikram to buy some of his paintings. Vikram doesn't buy any of his paintings, but after he leaves, Farhan notices that one of his newest paintings is missing. He suspects that Vikram has stolen it, and complains to the police, who promptly arrest Vikram. Vikram approaches NALSA for free legal aid, so that he can obtain bail. Is Vikram entitled to free legal aid from NALSA?

A. No, since he is a rich businessman and can hire a lawyer with his own money.

B. Yes, since he was innocent.

C. Yes, since he was in police custody.

D. No, since he had stolen from a struggling artist.

XVII

Surrogacy is defined by law as "a practice whereby one woman bears and gives birth to a child for an intending couple" and intends to hand over the child to them after the birth, as per the *Surrogacy* (*Regulation*) Act, 2021 (the "SRA"). The SRA restricts altruistic surrogacy to legally wedded infertile Indian couples. The couple is deemed eligible for surrogacy only if they have been married for five years. The SRA sets an age limitation for the couple. A husband must be between 26 and 55 years of age and a wife between 23 and 50 years. Further, Indian couples with biological or adopted children are prohibited from undertaking surrogacy, save for some exceptions such as mentally or physically challenged children, or those suffering from a life-threatening disorder or fatal illness. The SRA provides that the surrogate mother has to be a close relative of the couple (such as a sibling of one of the members of the couple), a married woman with a child of her own, aged between 25 and 35 years, who has been a surrogate only once in her life. Even within this category of people, commercial surrogacy is banned in India and that includes the "commercialisation of surrogacy services or procedures or its component services or component procedures". The surrogate woman cannot be given payments, rewards, benefits or fees, "except the medical expenses and such other prescribed expenses incurred on the surrogate mother and the insurance coverage for the surrogate mother".

A legal commentator points out some criticisms of the law. "Permitting limited conditional surrogacy to married Indian couples and disqualifying other persons on basis of nationality, marital status, sexual orientation or age does not pass the test of equality," he writes. He adds that reproductive autonomy, inclusive of the right to procreation and parenthood is protected under Article 21 of the *Constitution of India,* which guarantees the right to life and personal liberty.

The intending parents typically sign a contract with the surrogate. *The Indian Contract Act, 1972* (the "ICA") provides that a valid contract has to be in writing, and signed in the presence of two witnesses. The ICA also provides that a contract that is prohibited by any other law will not be valid under the ICA.

[Extracted with edits and revisions from "What laws regulate surrogacy in India", *The Indian Express*]

91. Rani and Shiva would like to opt for surrogacy. They have been married for 6 years. Rani is aged 51 and Shiva is aged 53. Both Rani and Shiva have built successful business empires. They are now working together on a joint initiative. Due to the demanding nature of their work, they have not thought about children previously. However, they are now keen to have a child via surrogacy. Are Rani and Shiva eligible for surrogacy under the SRA?

A. Yes, because they have been married for more than 5 years.

B. Yes, because they have financial capacity to bring up a child.

C. No, because they do not fall within the legal requirements of intending parents.
D. No, because they are not an infertile couple.

92. Assume Rani and Shiva are eligible for surrogacy under the SRA. They approach Geeta to act as a surrogate. Geeta is Rani's sister. She is 29 years old. She is married, has one child, and has been a surrogate twice before. Which of the following statements are false?

(*i*) Geeta is eligible to be a surrogate because she is a close relative.
(*ii*) Geeta is eligible to be a surrogate because she is married.
(*iii*) Geeta has been a surrogate only twice before and is now eligible to be a surrogate for Rani.
(*iv*) Geeta is eligible to be a surrogate because she is 29.

A. Statement (*iii*)
B. Statements (*i*) and (*iii*)
C. Statements (*ii*) and (*iii*)
D. Statements (*ii*), (*iii*), and (*iv*)

93. Joseph and Neena are keen to have a child via surrogacy. They have been married for 8 years, and have been unable to conceive biologically due to infertility. Joseph is 40 years old and Neena is 42 years old. They have an adopted daughter, Maya, who is 4 years old. Maya has been diagnosed with Striker's Syndrome, which would cause slow neurological deterioration, with chances of death. Devastated, Joseph and Neena decide to opt for surrogacy, to become parents to their biological child. Are they eligible for surrogacy?

A. Yes, because they have no biological children.
B. No, because they have an adopted child.
C. Yes, because their adopted child has been diagnosed with Striker's Syndrome.
D. Yes, because their right to procreation and parenthood is protected under Article 21 of the Indian Constitution.

94. Queen runs a surrogacy clinic. She employs 54 women, aged between 25 and 35 years. They are all married women with one or more children. Most of them belong to economically disadvantaged backgrounds. They choose to be surrogates because it gives them a reliable source of income. Kishore and Noor are intending parents. They have been married 5 years, are both aged 35, and do not have children. Kishore has been certified as infertile. So, they decide to approach Queen's clinic. They sign a contract with the surrogate. The contract is in writing and is signed in the presence of two witnesses. As per the contract, Kishore and Noor are required to remunerate the surrogate with ₹ 2 lakh per child born as a result of surrogacy, and take care of her medical needs, including providing her with medical insurance. A healthy baby girl is born as a result of surrogacy. Kishore and Noor are overjoyed. They take care of the surrogate's medical expenses. However, they do not pay the surrogate the ₹ 2 lakh. The surrogate, supported by Queen, now wants to take Kishore and Noor to court, to demand that they make the payment. Will she succeed?

A. Yes, because Kishore and Noor are bound by the contract under the ICA.
B. Yes, because the intending parents and the surrogate meet the eligibility requirements under the SRA.
C. Yes, because the surrogate meets the eligibility requirements under the SRA.
D. No, because SRA allows only altruistic surrogacy, so the contract is not valid under the ICA.

95. Karan and Daniel are in a homosexual relationship. As per the Hindu Marriage Act, marriage is allowed only between heterosexual couples. As a result, Karan and Daniel are not married. However, they wish to have children and decide to go in for surrogacy. When they approach Queen's clinic, they are informed that they do not meet the requirements for an intending couple under the SRA. Karan and Daniel wish to challenge the SRA for violating their constitutional right to non-discrimination. The non-discrimination clause under the *Constitution of India* reads: 'No citizen shall be discriminated on the basis of sex, caste, religion, nationality, place of birth or any other ground'. Karan and Daniel argue that the SRA discriminates against them on the basis of sexual orientation, because it restricts surrogacy to heterosexual couples alone. Which of the following arguments would most strongly support their claim in court?

A. The non-discrimination clause does not explicitly mention sexual orientation.
B. Discrimination on the basis of sex could include discrimination on the basis of sexual orientation.
C. The non-discrimination clause is not restricted to explicitly mentioned grounds.
D. Surrogacy is restricted under the SRA to married couples, and only heterosexual couples can get married.

XVIII

Until 2017, India did not have a codified law to order internet shut downs. A general power was vested in District Magistrates in this regard. The Magistrate could issue an order ordering a shut down if a 'speedy remedy' (extending to internet shut down) is desirable for 'immediate prevention' of an event. The Magistrate had to be satisfied that the order is 'likely to prevent or tends to prevent obstruction, annoyance or injury to human life, health or safety, or a disturbance of public tranquillity'. The Magistrate's order cannot be for longer than two months.

In 2017, new rules to order internet shut downs were introduced taking the power away from the Magistrate. These Rules —The Temporary Suspension Rules — state that internet shut downs can now only be ordered by the Home Secretary of the Union or State Governments. Only in "unavoidable circumstances" can the passing of orders be delegated to someone lower than the rank of a Joint Secretary to the Government of India. And even in this case, the official must be authorised by the Centre or State Home Secretary. Shut downs can be ordered where 'necessary' or 'unavoidable' during a 'public emergency' or in the 'interest of public safety'. Shut down orders must necessarily detail the reasons to shut down the internet. The orders must also be sent to a review committee under the state or central government within 24 hours. The committee must then review them within five working days. The rules state that apart from the Chief Secretary and Legal Secretary, the committee can comprise a secretary other than the home secretary.

In January 2020 the Supreme Court passed its judgement in the case of *Anuradha Bhasin.* The judgement in this case explicitly recognised two things: that the freedom to access information is a fundamental right under Article 19(1)(A) of the *Constitution of India* (which protects the freedom of speech and expression); and that the freedom to conduct your trade, profession or business over the internet is also a fundamental right under Article 19(1)(g) of the *Constitution of India* (which protects the freedom to practise any profession, or to carry on any occupation, trade or business). Every time the internet is suspended, it is quite obvious that it is a violation of these rights. These rights can only be curtailed in the interest of the 'sovereignty and security of the state, integrity of the nation, friendly relations with foreign states, or public order or for preventing incitement to the commission of an offence'. The Supreme Court's judgement in *Anuradha Bhasin's* case had also underlined that shut down orders must clearly provide reasons for the shut down and they must be publicly available.

[Extracted with edits and revisions from "In India, are internet shut downs in accordance with law? Not always", by Diksha Munjal, *News Laundry*]

96. In 2014, India was hit by a terrible pandemic. It was the first time the country was experiencing a pandemic. People panicked. WhatsApp and Facebook groups became common platforms for sharing information about the pandemic. Messages were forwarded from group to group. Many of these messages prescribed different remedies to prevent and cure the flu caused by the pandemic. In Merodha district, people following these remedies began to fall sick. The already overburdened public sector hospitals became even more full. The district administration requested people to stop sharing such misinformation. However, these requests were not heeded. The District Magistrate issued an indefinite order to shut down the internet to prevent the transmission of these messages. Is this order legal?

A. Yes, because the District Magistrate has the power to issue a range of orders, which includes internet shut down orders.

B. Yes, because the order was necessary on grounds of public health.

C. Yes, because a speedy order was necessary to immediately prevent transmission of these messages.

D. No, because the order was indefinite.

97. The Central government was preparing to conduct the National Medical Eligibility Test ("NMET") on 25 October, 2021. The exams were to be conducted in public schools around the country on computers provided by the government. In July 2021, there were rumours that several groups had hatched plans to share answers with the students taking the exam. A special chat application was developed. The student simply had to open the application on the browser of the computer on which they were taking the exam, allowing persons on the other end to send them the answers. The government was very concerned. If the rumours were true, the quality of doctors in training (who were selected through the NMET) would be severely affected. To prevent this public emergency, the government issued orders under the Temporary Suspension Rules to shut down internet countrywide on 25 October 2021. Many protested against this decision. They argued that the government could prevent cheating in the exams by shutting down the internet in the public schools where the exam was taking place. A nation-wide blanket shut down was not required for this purpose. Now, the issue is before the Supreme Court. What will the Court decide?

A. The government's order is legal under the Temporary Suspension Rules because it prevents a public emergency by preserving the quality of doctors in India.

B. The government's order is not legal under the Temporary Suspension Rules because the power belonged to the magistrate to issue orders under Section 144.

C. The government's order is not legal under the Temporary Suspension Rules because the nation-wide internet shut down order was not necessary or unavoidable.

D. The government's order is legal because it is the responsibility of the State to conduct exams in a fair manner.

98. In the above instance, the order was passed by the Communications Minister of the Indian Central Government. The Communications Minister is below the rank of Joint Secretary. The Home Secretary was away for a conference in Geneva and thus was not present in Delhi when the decision to pass the order was made. However, the Home Secretary could be contacted by phone or email. She had, in fact, explicitly said that she should be contacted if any need arises, however minor. As she had taken measures to make herself available virtually, the Home Secretary did not authorise any other official to exercise her functions. Against this, consider the following statements:

(*i*) The Communications Minister had the power to pass the order under the 2017 Rules.

(*ii*) The passing of the order by the Communications Minister was avoidable.

(*iii*) The power to pass the order remained with the Home Secretary.

(*iv*) The Communications Minister did not have the power to pass the order under the 2017 rules.

Which of the following statements are false?

A. Statement (*iv*)

B. Statement (*i*)

C. Statements (*ii*) and (*iii*)

D. Statements (*ii*) and (*iv*)

99. Assume that in the above instance, the Joint Secretary passed the order. The order stated: 'By means of the discretion vested in me by the Temporary Suspension of Telecom Services (Public Emergency or Public Safety) Rules 2017, I suspend internet across all Indian States and Union Territories on October 25, 2021'. The order was passed on 15 October, 2021. The order was sent to the Central Government review committee within 8 hours of its passing. The committee reviewed and approved of the order on 22 October, 2021. Is the order legal?

A. Yes, because it was passed under the 2017 rules.

B. No, because the procedure under the 2017 rules was not followed.

C. Yes, because the order was reviewed by the Central government review committee.

D. No, because the order was passed 10 days before it was to come into effect.

100. In January 2022, communal riots were rife in five states in India, between two dominant communities, X and Y. The primary mode of communication amongst the rioters was Signal which could be accessed through the internet via mobile phones and computers. The State governments of the five States received information that some members of X group were planning to set the houses of members of Y group on fire. Through broad Signal broadcasts amongst all users, the leaders of X group were instigating members of their group to participate in this exercise, threatening public order. Creating or inciting threat to public order is a criminal offence under Section 163F of the Indian Penal Code. To prevent further communication between the leaders of X group and their members, the State shut Signal down. However, communication then shifted to other platforms. Realising that targeting isolated platforms would not work, the State governments issued an order shutting down internet completely in all the States. Two groups protested against this order. First, students whose education was being conducted online due to the riots. They argued that they were prevented from accessing vital information, central to their education. Second, business owners who conducted business on the internet. The State's order read: 'In the five Indian States listed below, internet will be suspended for a period of two months from 10 January, 2022 to 10 March, 2022'. The State's order was not displayed anywhere (in print or virtually) from January to March 2022.

Consider the following statements:

(*i*) The students' right under Article 19(1)(a) was violated by the State order.

(*ii*) The business owners' right under Article 19(1)(g) was violated by the State order.

(*iii*) The State order validly restricted the said fundamental rights.

(*iv*) The State's order complied with the guidelines under *Anuradha Bhasin.*

How many statements are true?

A. One statement

B. Two statements

C. Three statements

D. All four statements

XIX

Consumers are people who buy and use goods or services. Consumers have a right to file a complaint for any of the services or goods used by them under Consumer Protection Law. Under Consumer Protection Law, a 'consumer' means:

Person buying and using goods and services: A consumer includes any person who buys goods and services, as well as anyone who uses them. For instance, a person who watches a movie after buying a movie ticket is a consumer and similarly, a person who uses a gift voucher gifted from someone else is also a consumer.

Person using goods for self-employment, and not for commercial purposes: The consumer protection law does not apply to people who use goods and services for commercial purposes. However, there are some exceptions to this. For example, people who use goods for self-employment are considered as consumers. For example, artists who buy art supplies for their work or beauticians who buy beauty products are consumers.

Person using online facilities: A consumer also includes any person who buys or hires goods or services online. For example, if you order from an online clothes website, you are a consumer.

People facing issues related to food: Consumers also include people who may be facing issues related to food items, such as adulteration, poor quality, lack of service, etc. For instance, issues related to food can cover problems across a wide range of products, starting from water that goes into the production of items like juices as well as the sale of animals like chicken, mutton etc. that are expressly intended for human consumption.

[Extracted, with edits and revisions, from "Who is a Consumer?", *Nyaaya India*]

101. Clint Leone Morricone Ltd. ("CLML") is a factory manufacturing bicycles. For the purpose of documentation and record keeping, it purchased a laptop from Pacer. However, within a month of the purchase, the laptop crashed and there was a motherboard failure. Despite a warranty, Pacer failed to replace the motherboard.

Which of the following statements is correct?

A. Purchase of electronic items do not fall within the purview of consumer law.

B. CLML is a consumer since it has bought a good for a price.

C. CLML is not a consumer since it has purchased the laptop for commercial purpose.

D. A company is not a person and so, cannot be a consumer.

102. Sita Das has been working as a freelance journalist. She writes columns and news-reports for various newspapers and news-portals and is paid on the basis of each column and report. For the purpose of her writing work, she purchases a Pacer laptop. However, within a month of the purchase, the laptop crashed and there was a motherboard failure.

Which of the following statements is correct?

A. Since she is using the laptop for the purpose of writing paid columns and news reports, Sita Das cannot be a consumer.

B. Purchase of goods does not fall within the purview of Consumer Protection Law.

C. Since she is using the laptop for the purpose of earning her livelihood, she will be a consumer.

D. None of the above

103. Kalpavruksha Charitable Trust runs a hospital. The hospital charges a fee from its patients. The fee is however 30% less than the commercial rates for all services and medical devices sold to patients. The hospital purchased a pacemaker from St. Rude's — a globally reputed manufacturer of pacemakers, to be resold to and used by patients. Which of the following statements is correct?

A. The hospital is a charitable hospital and therefore, it is a consumer with respect to the pacemakers purchased from St. Rude's.

B. The hospital resells the pacemakers to patients and therefore cannot be considered as a consumer with respect to the pacemakers purchased from St. Rude's.

C. The hospital resells the pacemakers at a discounted rate and therefore can be considered a consumer with respect to the pacemakers purchased from St. Rude's.

D. Sale of medical devices is not covered by Consumer Protection Law.

104. Fitzit is an online platform that provides physiotherapy and other ancillary medical services. Amit Ghosh booked a physiotherapist on Fitzit for three months by paying an amount of ₹ 25,000. Fitzit guaranteed the availability of qualified physiotherapists for the duration. However, Fitzit failed to provide a qualified physiotherapist and the persons who were sent for the first two visits had no training or certification in the field. Amit Ghosh seeks to proceed against Fitzit under Consumer Protection Law. Which of the following statements can be correctly inferred?

A. Since online services are not covered by Consumer Protection Law, Amit Ghosh cannot be considered a consumer.
B. Since services are not covered by Consumer Protection Law, Amit Ghosh cannot be considered a consumer.
C. Since online services are covered by Consumer Protection Law, Amit Ghosh shall be considered a consumer.
D. Since medical services are not covered by Consumer Protection Law, Amit Ghosh cannot be considered a consumer.

105. Jitesh Shah purchased from BreatheEasy, a company selling respiratory devices, a nebuliser device for his son, Jignesh Shah, for use for clearing his nasal passages. The nebulizer was however defective and led to severe respiratory distress for Jignesh. Jignesh is considering filing a complaint against BreatheEasy under the Consumer Protection Law. Which of the following statements can be correctly inferred?
A. Since Jignesh Shah did not purchase the device from BreatheEasy, he cannot be considered a consumer with respect to BreatheEasy.
B. Since Jignesh Shah is a user of the device, he can be considered a consumer.
C. Sale of medical devices are not covered by Consumer Protection Law.
D. None of the above

Section-IV : Logical Reasoning

XX

The depreciation of an economy's currency is not a matter of concern in itself. The decline in value against major currencies has to be viewed within a set of macroeconomic factors. The recent depreciation of the Indian rupee is a case in point. The rupee has been depreciating for a long time. What are of concern now are the rate at which the depreciation is occurring and the underlying factors causing the change. The Russia-Ukraine war has disrupted supply chains causing commodity prices to rise, leading to a worldwide hardening of inflationary trends. This, in turn, has caused major central banks to raise interest rates, forcing investors back to the safe haven of the US dollar. For India, these headwinds from the global economy have caused several problems. The rise in international prices, especially of crude oil, has led to a higher import bill and, hence, a greater demand for dollars. Higher interest rates in developed country markets have caused a significant outflow of portfolio investments from India, aggravating the already climbing demand for dollars from a rising import bill. By May 2022, foreign institutional investors had pulled out ₹ 1.50 lakh crore from Indian markets.

In the face of these pressures, the rupee, left to itself, would decline in value as the rupee-price of a dollar would increase substantially. One way the Reserve Bank of India could stem the tide would be to sell off dollars in the market to ease the supply situation. However, this would mean that while the value of the rupee could be contained, the nation's foreign exchange kitty would start to erode further. The RBI has been doing exactly that. The challenge before the RBI is this: how much to let the rupee depreciate and how much to intervene to prop it up? Too much depreciation would raise domestic inflation rates as the rupee-price of imports, especially oil, would raise costs of production. It could trigger a rise in policy-controlled interest rates while closely monitoring inflationary expectations. The biggest challenge is to navigate unpredictable international economic shocks in the near future. The Indian economy's health is not exactly at its best. Exports may not be able to take advantage of a falling rupee since international demand is expected to stagnate. India's growth and employment situations are yet to stabilise to what they were about a decade ago. The RBI has difficult choices: controlling inflation versus stimulating growth and stabilising the rupee without severely diminishing the economy's foreign exchange kitty.

[Extracted, with edits and revisions, from "Stiff test: Editorial on depreciation of rupee & challenges before RBI", *The Telegraph*]

106. Which of the following is the author most likely to agree with?

A. It is a major cause for concern if an economy's currency is depreciating.

B. Currency depreciation is not a reason for worry in itself, but if macroeconomic factors are not good, there may be a cause for concern.

C. The fact that the Indian rupee is witnessing a decline in value against major currencies is very worrisome.

D. A central bank must always do everything in its power to stem the slightest depreciation of an economy's currency.

107. Based on the author's arguments, which of the following, if true, would reduce the decline in value of the rupee?

A. Appointing a new Governor for the RBI who has a better sense of how to control inflationary trends.

B. A steep increase in commodity prices and the continued disruption of supply chains.

C. A reduction in worldwide inflationary trends and the reduction of interest rates in developed country markets.

D. The RBI buying as many dollars as possible from the market.

108. Which of the following, if true, would most weaken the author's arguments?

A. The Indian economy has been affected by global inflationary trends and the increase of interest rates in developed country markets.

B. Since developed country markets have increased their interest rates, global investors have pulled their investments out of other economies, and routed them to such developed country markets.

C. As the demand for US dollars increases, it is likely the rupee-price of a dollar would increase substantially.

D. The Indian economy and currency are highly protected and have been insulated from the effects of global inflationary trends and the increase of interest rates in developed country markets.

109. Which of the following, if true, would most strengthen the author's arguments for why Indian exports may not be able to take advantage of a falling rupee?

A. Economies across the world are witnessing a slowdown, and in such economies, demand for imports decreases substantially.

B. Economies across the world are booming, and there is an increasing demand for Indian exports.

C. A reduction in the volume of exports would be more than offset by the increased value of dollars that Indian exporters would earn.

D. Countries across the world have managed to find ways to insulate themselves from the effects of the Russia-Ukraine war and will need a lot of Indian imports to sustain their new growth models.

110. Based on the author's arguments, which of the following must necessarily be true?

A. The continuing depreciation of the Indian rupee at its current rate, coupled with worldwide inflationary trends, would result in immense political instability in India, and consequently, in all of South Asia.

B. If nothing else is done, the rise of interest rates in developed country markets, coupled with hardening of inflationary trends across the world, will result in a fall in the value of the rupee against the dollar.

C. If inflationary trends continue to harden across the world, and if interest rates in developed country markets continue to rise, portfolio investors will increase their investments in India, and this will have a positive impact on India's foreign exchange reserves.

D. If nothing else is done, the rise of interest rates in developed country markets, coupled with hardening of inflationary trends across the world, will result in a rise in the value of the rupee against the dollar.

111. Which of the following is the author most likely to agree with?

A. The RBI must not focus solely on preventing the depreciation of the rupee, as that may result in negative impacts on other aspects of the economy.

B. The RBI must focus solely on preventing the depreciation of the rupee at all costs, since it is by far the most important indicator of the health of the Indian economy.

C. Periodic inflationary trends are normal in any economy, and the RBI need not worry about the inflationary effects in the Indian economy caused by the depreciation of the rupee.

D. The RBI need not do anything to reduce the rate of depreciation of the rupee, since the depreciation of an economy's currency is not a matter of concern in itself.

XXI

The post-truth era is, expectedly, marked by a discerning erosion of public trust in sources of information. Mass media — both traditional and new-age avatars — has borne the brunt of this mistrust. And for good reasons too. Social media, its most popular platform, is a harbinger of falsity. It is thus encouraging to see that at least the old guard of the media ecosystem — the newspaper — continues to defy this discouraging trend. A pan-India survey of media consumption by Lokniti found that print media remains the most trusted source of information. The finding is consistent with the heartening surge in public endorsement of the reliability of newspapers since the pandemic. An earlier survey, which attempted to examine the impact of the lockdown on 'reading patterns', had found that the number of readers who used to spend over an hour on newspapers every day had risen to 38%, up from 16% in the pre-lockdown period. The increased trust in newspapers is because the lockdowns coincided with the dissemination of the crudest kinds of misinformation about the pandemic in India and around the world and newspapers played a pivotal role in exposing these lies.

But that is where the good news ends — for the print media, at least. Among other things, the data collated by the survey found deepening footprints of social media in rural and urban constituencies while television continues to dominate the screen. These developments are consistent with global trends that reveal that the newspaper industry is struggling to contain the migration of readers and revenue to other formats, especially digital media. Ironically, the pandemic, which saw a resurgence in collective trust in newspapers, adversely affected the print media as traditional advertisers, reeling under the economic fallouts of COVID-19, cut back on advertisements. But the crisis in print precedes the pandemic. Newspapers have been outpaced by speedier, but also spurious, sources of information. The dominance of the image over text as a cultural phenomenon is another formidable challenge. The print media's hopes of remaining competitive and profitable must, therefore, centre on using this collective trust as a form of capital. Survival strategies, especially the revenue model, must be re-explored and the emphasis shifted to in-depth analyses of news as well as eyecatching layouts now that newspapers are slower to reach news to the audience.

[Extracted, with edits and revisions, from "Good news: Editorial on print media remaining the most trusted source of information", *The Telegraph*]

112. Which of the following is the author most likely to agree with?

A. The COVID-19 pandemic was an unmitigated disaster for the newspaper industry.

B. The COVID-19 pandemic had negative as well as positive effects on the newspaper industry.

C. The COVID-19 pandemic only had good effects on the newspaper industry.
D. The COVID-19 pandemic had no effect at all on the newspaper industry.

113. Which of the following, if true, would most weaken the author's arguments?
A. Social media is a reliable source of true and accurate news and information.
B. Social media is a highly unreliable source of news and information and should not be trusted.
C. Social media is a good way for people to stay connected with each other.
D. Social media is a speedier source of information than newspapers.

114. Which of the following would be an effective way of making print media more competitive?
A. Slowing down the process of print media production.
B. Using more expensive printing methods that achieve better print quality, even if it results in newspapers becoming more expensive.
C. Only publishing newspapers on alternate days.
D. Developing ways of ensuring that print media can reach readers more speedily.

115. Based on the author's arguments, which of the following, if true, would have resulted in the weakening, rather than deepening of public trust in newspapers since the pandemic?
A. Newspapers were very careful in ensuring they reported accurate and true news during the lockdowns.
B. Newspapers played a leading role in exposing lies and misinformation spread during the lockdown.
C. Newspapers actively disseminated misinformation during the lockdowns and made no efforts to expose lies spread by others.
D. Newspapers alerted the public to the fact that a number of sources were spreading crude forms of misinformation during the pandemic.

116. What would be the impact on the readership and revenues of the print media if the image were not dominant over text as a cultural phenomenon?
A. Print media would not suffer as much of a reduction in readership and revenue as readers shifted to other formats.
B. Print media would suffer a greater reduction in readership and revenue as readers shifted to other formats.
C. There would be no impact on the readership and revenues of the print industry.
D. There would be an increased demand from readers that newspapers carry more images and less text.

117. How does the author suggest newspapers can overcome the problem of being outpaced by speedier sources of information?
A. They offer direct means by which newspapers can become faster to publish and deliver to readers.
B. They encourage a complete and immediate shift to digital media as a way of ensuring newspapers are not outpaced by other sources of information.
C. They offer ways to reduce production costs, which would offset the losses caused by readers shifting allegiance to faster sources of information.
D. They offer alternative means for newspapers to become competitive and profitable, but do not solve the problem of how newspapers can become faster sources of information.

XXII

In this moment, the developed countries — I point to them, because these countries have already burnt massive amounts of carbon dioxide for energy to build their economies — are faced with a real energy conundrum. On the one hand, developed countries are battered because of a fast-heating planet; temperatures have gone through the roof; droughts and extreme weather events are hitting them as well.

On the other hand, ordinary people in these countries are worried, not just because of climate change but because of the lack of energy to heat their homes this coming winter. In the US, gas prices went up in summer, so much so that people travelled less and consumption of fuel dropped. But now prices are down and it is business as usual.

The fact is that this energy disruption has provided the much-needed vault to the beleaguered fossil fuel industry. Governments are asking this industry to supply more. Europe has baptised natural gas, a fossil fuel less polluting than coal but still a major emitter of carbon dioxide, as "clean". The US has passed a climate bill, which will invest in renewable energy but conditional to increased spends on oil and gas and the opening up of millions of hectares of federal land for drilling. Through this bill the US will do more than ever before to build a manufacturing base for renewable energy, particularly solar. Europe, even in this desperate scramble for gas, is working to ramp up its investment in renewable power. So, it is the worst of times. It could be the best of times, but there are some caveats. One, this renewed interest in fossil fuels must remain temporary and transient. Given the nature of economies, once the investment has been made in this new infrastructure or the supply of fossil fuel has increased from new oil and gas discoveries, it will be difficult to wean off. Two, These countries should not be entitled to more use of fossil fuels in our world of shrunk carbon budgets. They need to reduce emissions drastically and leave whatever little carbon budget space that is remaining to poorer countries to use, thereby satisfying such poorer countries' demands.

[Extracted, with edits and revisions, from "New energy conundrum", by Sunita Narain, *DownToEarth*]

118. Which of the following is the author most likely to agree with?

A. People in the US are not worried at all about climate change.

B. People in the US are worried about climate change, and these concerns affect their energy consumption habits more than anything else.

C. Climate change has resulted in the increase of energy prices across the world, and as a result, governments have had to invest in finding newer sources of renewable energy.

D. Changes in the energy consumption habits of people in the US are affected more by energy prices than concerns of climate change.

119. Which of the following is most similar to the author's statements about developed countries' renewed interest in fossil fuels?

A. Developed countries should not, under any circumstances, invest any resources in fossil fuel energy extraction, and must immediately put a halt to all fossil fuel consumption.

B. Things could improve if developed countries recognise the difficulty of moving away from reliance on such sources of energy and make a conscious effort to move to alternate or renewable energy sources quickly.

C. Since investments in energy extraction of any kind are very expensive, developed countries must ensure that they make permanent and continuing investments in fossil fuels.

D. Developing countries must not, under any circumstances, consume fossil fuels, and leave whatever carbon budget space is remaining to richer countries to use.

120. If the information in the passage above is correct, which of the following must necessarily be true?

A. The fossil fuel industry in developing countries will face reduced sales in the short term, with increased sales in the long term.

B. The cost of making, installing, and using solar panels will reduce substantially in the coming years.

C. Passing a bill in the US is a huge effort, and it would not have been possible to pass the new climate bill unless the current energy crisis had compelled lawmakers to do so.

D. The fossil fuel industry in developing countries will see an increase in business, at least in the short term.

121. Which of the following, if true, would most weaken the author's argument about why travel and fuel consumption in the US reduced in summer?

A. People like to travel regardless of season, and the only thing that would prevent them from travelling at any time of the year would be high costs.

B. Airlines raised ticket prices as a response to increase in fuel prices, and therefore, fewer people were able to buy air tickets to travel.

C. Strict lockdowns were imposed in the US in summer, because of which people travelled less; further, temperatures were moderate, and this meant people had to use less fuel to heat or warm their homes.

D. Widespread geopolitical tensions in the first half of the year meant that fuel prices were at an all-time high in summer; but prices have now eased off somewhat, making fuel slightly more affordable in the US.

122. Which of the following, if true, would resolve the 'conundrum' the author says developed countries face now?

A. The development of adequate renewable power sources in the near term that would lead to a reduction in consumption of fossil fuels.

B. Finding new sources of fossil fuels that will ensure there is no shortage of energy to heat homes in the winter.

C. Switching immediately to renewable power sources, even if it leads to a shortage in energy supply for people.

D. Providing adequate aid to poorer countries so that they can develop renewable power sources for their use.

123. Assuming the aim of the US climate bill is to reduce fossil fuel consumption, which of the following would be the strongest argument that it will fail to achieve such an aim?

A. The bill promotes investments in renewable energy but does not provide for enough increase in investments in developing more sources of fossil fuel-powered energy.

B. The bill is written in technical language, which ordinary people cannot easily understand.

C. The bill is self-defeating, since it makes investments in renewable energy conditional to more expenditure on oil and gas and making millions of hectares of federal land available for drilling, which would lead to an increased consumption of fossil fuels.

D. The bill does not provide any means of increasing carbon budgets, thereby making more room for fossil fuel consumption.

XXIII

While men and women are both considered to be more capable as they get older, only women bear the brunt of being seen as "less warm" as they age, new research has found. This series of studies is reportedly the first to look at both gender and age to determine how perceptions of women and men differ. "It's just stunning… These stereotypes are so hard-wired and deeply entrenched that they come out even when absolutely identical information is provided about a man and a woman," Jennifer Chatman, Distinguished Professor of Management at UC Berkeley's Haas School of Business, said. In an analysis of Professors' evaluations, female professors witnessed a decline as they moved from their 30s to 40s, hitting an all-time low around the age of 47. All this while, the evaluation of male professors remained consistent. Interestingly, after the age of 47, the evaluations for women increased again, becoming equal with those of men around the early 60s. "At that point, there are different stereotypes of women, and they may benefit from being seen as more grandmotherly," said Laura Kray, faculty director of the Center for Equity, Gender, and Leadership at Berkeley Haas and an author of the study.

Women around the age of mid 30s to late 40s also face what is called "the motherhood penalty," where assumptions around parenting duties lead people to believe women are less committed to their careers than men. This has several repercussions, most particularly evident in hiring, promotions and wages. Women executives further pointed out that they face "hyper-scrutiny" and "scepticism" which harks back to perceptions of likeability versus agency. Gendered networks in the workplace, with men gaining greater access to senior leaders, become cemented mid-career, pose another difficulty for working women. Negative perceptions of women in middle-age can also be linked to stereotypes around menopause. In 2008, psychologists studied the attitudes of people towards women in different reproductive stages. They found that while the pregnant women or the woman with the baby were thought about in glowing terms, menopausal women were associated with negative emotions, illness and ageing.

[Extracted, with edits and revisions, from "How Stereotypes Affect Middle-Aged Women's Careers", by Ananya Singh, *The Swaddle*]

124. Which of the following is most likely to be true if the author's statements about gendered networks in the workplace are true?

A. Mid-career women do not find it as easy to get access to senior leaders, who are usually male, as their male colleagues. They therefore find career progression or new opportunities easier to come by.

B. Mid-career women find it easier to get access to senior leaders, who are usually male, as their male colleagues. They therefore find career progression or new opportunities easier to come by.

C. Mid-career women do not find it as easy to get access to senior leaders, who are usually male, as their male colleagues. They therefore find career progression or new opportunities harder to come by.

D. Mid-career women find it easier to get access to senior leaders, who are usually male, as their male colleagues. They therefore do not find career progression or new opportunities harder to come by.

125. Which of the following is most likely to be an outcome of what the author describes as the "motherhood penalty"?

A. People are more hesitant to hire men from their mid 30s to their late 40s but may be more willing to hire women of a similar age.

B. People are more hesitant to hire women from their mid 30s to their late 40s but may be more willing to hire men of a similar age.

C. Women from their mid 30s to their late 40s always prioritise parenting responsibilities and so are not really interested in pursuing a career.

D. Women who have children are less committed to their careers than men.

126. If professors' evaluations are the most important criteria in awarding promotions, then which of the following would be the most likely outcome, based on the information provided in the passage?

A. Male professors are likely to be promoted at an even rate throughout their career, while women professors would experience a lower likelihood of promotion in the mid-career stage.

B. Since there is a wide disparity between the evaluations that male and female professors receive, the practice of relying upon such evaluations will quickly be abandoned.

C. Male and female professors will receive promotions at a similar rate throughout the course of their career.

D. Women professors are likely to be promoted at an even rate throughout their career, while male professors would experience a lower likelihood of promotion in the mid-career stage.

127. Which of the following is the author most likely to disagree with?

A. Women going through menopause often quit the workforce voluntarily.

B. Women going through menopause are more likely to be perceived negatively at the workplace and to have difficulty achieving professional success.

C. Women going through menopause should be permitted to take a mid-career sabbatical.

D. Women going through menopause are more likely to be perceived positively at the workplace and to achieve professional success.

128. Which of the following, if true, would most strengthen the main argument in the passage?

A. Several independent studies conducted in different countries have shown that women in the workplace are perceived positively and are favourably treated as they age.

B. Several independent studies conducted in different countries have shown that women in the workplace are perceived negatively and are unfairly treated as they age.

C. The studies mentioned in the passage have been discredited after they were published, and no reliance should be placed on them.

D. The studies mentioned in the passage were conducted on very small sample sets and cannot be used to make general statements about the difference in perception between men and women.

129. Which of the following, if true, would most weaken Laura Kray's arguments?

A. Women professors perceived as being 'grandmotherly' are regarded as being likeable and caring.

B. Women professors perceived as being 'grandmotherly' are treated better by their colleagues and students.

C. Women professors perceived as being 'grandmotherly' are regarded as being slow, inefficient, and outdated in their field.

D. Women professors perceived as being 'grandmotherly' are regarded very highly and receive much more respect than younger women professors.

XXIV

Why are we humans so susceptible to the doom and gloom of the news? Two reasons. The first is what psychologists call negativity bias: we're more attuned to the bad than the good. Back in our hunting and gathering days, we were better off being frightened of a spider or a snake a hundred times too often than one time too few. Too much fear wouldn't kill you; too little surely would.

Second, we're also burdened with an availability bias. If we can easily recall examples of a given thing, we assume that thing is relatively common. The fact that we're bombarded daily with horrific stories about aircraft disasters, child snatchers and beheadings — which tend to lodge in the memory — completely skews our view of the world.

In this digital age, the news we're being fed is only getting more extreme. In the old days, journalists didn't know much about their individual readers. They wrote for the masses. But the people behind Facebook, Twitter and Google know you well. They know what shocks and horrifies you, they know what makes you click. They know how to grab your attention and hold it so they can serve you the most lucrative helping of personalised ads. This modern media frenzy is nothing less than an assault on the mundane. Because, let's be honest, the lives of most people are pretty predictable. Nice, but boring. So while we'd prefer having nice neighbours with boring lives, 'boring' won't make you sit up and take notice. 'Nice' doesn't sell ads. And so Silicon Valley keeps dishing us up ever more sensational clickbait, knowing full well, as a Swiss novelist once quipped, that "News is to the mind what sugar is to the body."

[Extracted, with edits and revisions, from *Humankind: A Hopeful History,* by Rutger Bregman, Bloomsbury Publishing, London, 2021.]

130. Which of the following, if true, would most weaken the author's arguments?

A. Behavioural traits that helped us in the days when we were hunter-gatherers continue to be present in modern-day humans.

B. Behavioural traits that helped us in the days when we were hunter-gatherers are no longer found in modern-day humans.
C. The negativity bias makes us more likely to be affected by depressing or sad news.
D. We have certain behavioural characteristics that affect how we perceive and are affected by sad news.

131. Which of the following is the author most likely to agree with?
A. Contemporary media continuously exposes us to exciting news and information, which may be just like the things we usually experience in our lives.
B. Contemporary media continuously exposes us to exciting news and information, which may be very unlike the kinds of things we usually encounter in our lives.
C. Contemporary media continuously exposes us to boring news and information, which may be very unlike the kinds of things we usually encounter in our lives.
D. Contemporary media continuously exposes us to boring news and information, which may be just like the things we usually experience in our lives.

132. Based only on the author's statement that "we'd prefer having nice neighbours with boring lives", and the author's argument about the nature of news that modern media exposes us to, which of the following would the author be most likely to agree with?
A. Constantly being exposed to negative news gives us a warped perspective of the world.
B. In our hunting and gathering days, it was better for us to be unnecessarily scared rather than being scared too little.
C. The news modern media exposes us to is just like our day-to-day experiences.
D. The news modern media exposes us to is very different from our day-to-day experiences.

133. The author's statements about negativity bias, if true, provide most support for which of the following conclusions?
A. We are more likely to notice a story about a billionaire donating their money to charity than a story about an airplane crash.
B. We are more likely to be attracted to a news article about a rise in life expectancy in our country than a news article about a murder in our city.
C. We are more likely to notice a story about increasing pollution levels than a story about improving educational levels in schools.
D. We are more likely to form our opinion of the world based on the information available to us rather than information we do not have access to.

134. Which of the following would be the most effective way of countering the effects of what the author describes as our 'availability bias'?
A. Ensuring that we do not seek out news sources and stories that we may not otherwise have been exposed to.
B. Following only one news source and limiting our perspective of the world to that one source.
C. Avoiding all positive news stories, and instead only reading news stories about disasters and tragedies.
D. Ensuring that we seek out news sources and stories that we may not otherwise have been exposed to.

135. The author says that "The fact that we're bombarded daily with horrific stories about aircraft disasters, child snatchers and beheadings — which tend to lodge in the memory — completely skews our view of the world." The conclusion the author draws in this argument follows logically if which of the following is assumed?
A. Our ideas about the world are shaped by the information we are exposed to.
B. Modern media is concerned only with making massive profits.
C. Modern journalists generate news stories much faster than in the old days.
D. Humans once lived as hunter-gatherers.

Section-V : Quantitative Techniques

XXV

The findings of Oxfam India's latest 'India Discrimination Report 2022' indicate that there is a significant gap in the earnings between men and women in the case of regular and self-employment in urban areas. The lower wages for salaried women are due to 67 per cent of discrimination and 33 per cent due to lack of education and work experience. The average earning is ₹ 16,000 for men and merely ₹ 6,600 for women in urban areas in self-employment. The average earning of men is ₹ 19,800 as against ₹ 15,600 for women in regular/salaried employment in urban areas. Also, in urban areas the average earnings of men (₹ 9,000) are significantly higher than women (₹ 5,700) even in casual employment. Apart from women, historically oppressed communities along with religious minorities also continue to face discrimination in accessing jobs, livelihoods, and agricultural credit. The mean income for Scheduled Castes or Scheduled Tribes ("SC/ST") persons in urban areas who are in regular employment is ₹ 15,300 as against ₹ 20,300 for persons belonging to the non-SC/ST category. The average earning of self-employed workers is ₹ 15,900 for non-SC/STs and ₹ 10,500 for SC/STs. The average monthly earning for the SC/ST workers in casual work is ₹ 8,000 below the corresponding figure of ₹ 8,600 for the non-SC/ST.

[Data Source: Oxfam India]

[Note: Values have been approximated to the nearest hundred]

136. Choose the correct option:

A. Women's average earnings in urban areas in casual work is 30% lower than that of men

B. Men's average earning in urban areas in self-employment is nearly 2.5 times that of earnings of women

C. In casual work, women earn more in rural areas than in urban areas

D. The difference in earnings of men and women in regular/salaried employment in urban areas is ₹ 3,500

137. Of the regular employed in urban areas, the earnings of a non-SC/ST worker is what per cent more than a SC/ST worker?

A. Between 20% and 25%

B. Less than 15%

C. Between 30% and 35%

D. More than 35%

138. Of those in casual employment, if a man's average earnings was deposited at a rate of 16% simple interest for 20 years, in how many years at the same rate of simple interest a SC/ST worker must deposit their average earnings to earn the same amount as a man in 20 years?

A. 24 years B. 22.5 years

C. 21 years D. 23.2 years

139. The findings also indicate discrimination as a driving factor behind low Women's Labour Force Participation Rate (LFPR) in the country. As per the Union Ministry of Statistics & Programme Implementation (MoSPI), LFPR for women in India was only 25.1 per cent in 2020-21 for urban and rural women. This is considerably lower than South Africa where the LFPR for women is 46 per cent in 2021 as per the latest World Bank estimates. The LFPR for women in India has rapidly declined from 42.7 per cent in 2004-05 to mere 25.1 per cent in 2020-2021 showing the withdrawal of women from the workforce despite rapid economic growth during the same period. In 2019-20, 60 per cent of all males aged 15 years and more have regular salaried and self-employed jobs while 19 per cent of all similarly aged females get regular and self-employment. Use the additional data in the passage above to answer this and the next question.

If the number of women in India in 2020-2021 is 670 million which is 24% more than in 2004-2005, what is the difference in the number of women in LFPR 2004-05 and 2021?

A. Less than 5 crores
B. Between 6 and 8 crores
C. Between 10 and 12 crores
D. More than 15 crores

140. In 2019-20, if the number of males aged 15 years and more is 76% of the total male population and the number of females aged 15 years and more is 72% of the total female population and the total male population is 1.05 times the total female population, what is the ratio of females to males aged 15 years and more that have regular salaried and self-employed jobs?

A. 2 : 7 B. 3 : 10
C. 5 : 9 D. 1 : 3

XXVI

World fruit production went up 54 per cent between 2000 and 2019, to 883 million tonnes. Five fruit species accounted for 57 per cent of the total production in 2019, down from 63 per cent in 2000.

Use the data in the passage to answer the following questions.

[Data source: FAO]

141. What was the world fruit production in 2000?

A. 474 million tonnes
B. 517 million tonnes
C. 573 million tonnes
D. 406 million tonnes

142. Of the five fruit species mentioned in the passage above, the share of bananas and plantains increased by 1 percentage point between 2000 and 2019, watermelons in 2019 was 6 percentage points lower than bananas and plantains in 2000, apples remained stable at 10%, and the percentage share of oranges and grapes reduced to half of bananas in 2019. What was the percentage of bananas and plantains in 2019?

A. 17% B. 18%
C. 16% D. 21%

143. Of the watermelons in 2000, one-eighth perished, one-fifth of the remaining was sold to be juiced and 30% of the remaining was exported. if the percentage share of oranges in 2000 was equal to the percentage share of watermelons in 2019, how many watermelons were retained for home sale and consumption?

A. 39.2 million tonnes
B. 1.6 million tonnes
C. 16.8 million tonnes
D. 2.7 million tonnes

144. Assume that all grapes and apples were sold through a single organisation in 2000. Grapes and apples were sold to 4 different customers such that a certain quantity of apples were sold to the first customer, same number of apples were sold to the second customer as to the first and a certain number of grapes were sold to that customer after which apples were over. Twice the quantity of grapes sold to the second was sold to the third customer and twice the quantity sold to the third was sold to the fourth customer. The total quantity of grapes is equal to the total quantity of apples sold and the remaining grapes were stored. How many grapes were sold to each customer?

A. 19.1 million tonnes
B. 8.2 million tonnes
C. 28.6 million tonnes
D. 9.4 million tonnes

145. Frutopia and Fruitfix both sold oranges at the same selling price. However, Frutopia gave customers a 15% discount on the marked price whereas Fruitfix sold the oranges for a discount of 20% on the marked price. If the marked price of oranges on Frutopia is ₹ 75/kg, what is the marked price of oranges on Fruitfix?

A. ₹ 78 B. ₹ 82
C. ₹ 90 D. ₹ 80

XXVII

Players are selected for Judo based on their body weights from the following 10 weight groups:

1. (48 kg - 52 kg) 6. (68 kg - 72 kg)
2. (52 kg - 56 kg) 7. (72 kg - 76 kg)
3. (56 kg - 60 kg) 8. (76 kg - 80 kg)
4. (60 kg - 64 kg) 9. (80 kg - 84 kg)
5. (64 kg - 68 kg) 10.(84 kg - 88 kg)

The average weight of the players after selecting one player from each group is 68 kg. If one of the players (named S) leaves the team, their average weight comes down to 66.5 kg.

146. Player S is from the weight group:
A. 1 B. 9
C. 5 D. 10

147. If S leaves the group and two new players join the group, their average weight increases to 68 kg. These players can NOT be from groups:
A. 1 and 3 B. Both from group 7
C. 4 and 10 D. 5 and 9

148. What is the average weight of all the players taken together?
A. 68 kg
B. 66 kg
C. 69 kg
D. Cannot be determined

149. In the average of all the groups together, which group contributes most in overall average?
A. 10
B. 8
C. 1
D. Cannot be determined

150. If one of the new two players is from group 4, which group the other player is from?
A. 5
B. 7
C. 10
D. None of the above

ANSWERS

1. (B)	**2. (C)**	**3. (A)**	**49. (C)**	**50. (D)**	**51. (D)**
4. (C)	**5. (B)**	**6. (A)**	**52. (D)**	**53. (B)**	**54. (A)**
7. (C)	**8. (C)**	**9. (A)**	**55. (C)**	**56. (D)**	**57. (B)**
10. (B)	**11. (B)**	**12. (B)**	**58. (C)**	**59. (C)**	**60. (D)**
13. (C)	**14. (D)**	**15. (A)**	**61. (A)**	**62. (D)**	**63. (B)**
16. (B)	**17. (A)**	**18. (C)**	**64. (C)**	**65. (D)**	**66. (B)**
19. (D)	**20. (D)**	**21. (A)**	**67. (C)**	**68. (D)**	**69. (B)**
22. (B)	**23. (D)**	**24. (B)**	**70. (A)**	**71. (C)**	**72. (B)**
25. (B)	**26. (D)**	**27. (B)**	**73. (A)**	**74. (B)**	**75. (D)**
28. (A)	**29. (D)**	**30. (C)**	**76. (D)**	**77. (D)**	**78. (B)**
31. (A)	**32. (C)**	**33. (A)**	**79. (C)**	**80. (A)**	**81. (B)**
34. (A)	**35. (D)**	**36. (B)**	**82. (A)**	**83. (D)**	**84. (C)**
37. (D)	**38. (A)**	**39. (B)**	**85. (A)**	**86. (C)**	**87. (A)**
40. (D)	**41. (A)**	**42. (B)**	**88. (D)**	**89. (B)**	**90. (C)**
43. (B)	**44. (C)**	**45. (B)**	**91. (C)**	**92. (A)**	**93. (C)**
46. (D)	**47. (C)**	**48. (A)**	**94. (D)**	**95. (C)**	**96. (D)**

97. (C)	98. (B)	99. (B)
100. (C)	101. (C)	102. (C)
103. (B)	104. (C)	105. (B)
106. (B)	107. (C)	108. (D)
109. (A)	110. (B)	111. (A)
112. (B)	113. (A)	114. (D)
115. (C)	116. (A)	117. (D)
118. (D)	119. (B)	120. (D)
121. (C)	122. (A)	123. (C)
124. (C)	125. (B)	126. (A)
127. (D)	128. (B)	129. (C)
130. (B)	131. (B)	132. (D)
133. (C)	134. (D)	135. (A)

For Qs. No. 136-140:

From the given information:

	Male	Female
Urban (Self employment)	₹ 16000	₹ 6600
Urban (Salary/Regular)	₹ 19800	₹ 15600
Casual Employment	₹ 9000	₹ 5700

	SC/ST	Non SC/ST
Regular Employment	₹ 15300	₹ 20300
Self Employment	₹ 10500	₹ 15900
Casual Employment	₹ 8000	₹ 8600

136. (B): $\dfrac{\text{Men's average earning in Urban areas}}{\text{Earning of women}}$

$= \dfrac{16000}{6600} = \dfrac{160}{66} = \dfrac{80}{33}$

$= 2.42 = 2.5$ (approx.)

137. (C): The regular employment in urban area: The percentage earning of non-SC/ST worker is more than a SC/ST worker

$= \dfrac{20300-15300}{15300} \times 100$

$= \dfrac{5000}{153} = 32.67\%$

= Between 30% and 35%.

138. (D): $900 + \dfrac{9000 \times 16 \times 20}{100}$

$= 8000 + \dfrac{8000 \times 16t}{100}$

$\Rightarrow$ $9000 + 90 \times 320 = 8000 + 80 \times 16t$

$\Rightarrow$ $9000 - 8000 + 28800 = 80 \times 16t$

$\Rightarrow$ $1000 + 28800 = 80 \times 16t$

$\Rightarrow$ $29800 = 80 \times 16t$

$\Rightarrow$ $t = \dfrac{29800}{80 \times 16} = \dfrac{2980}{8 \times 16}$

$= \dfrac{745}{2 \times 16} = \dfrac{745}{32}$

$= 23.2$ years

$\therefore$ Required time = 23.2 years.

139. (B): LFPR (India)

2004-05	2020-21
42.7%	**25.1%**

Number of women $670 \times \dfrac{100}{124}$ 670 million

= 540 million

$\therefore$ Number of women in LFPR 2004-05

$= 540 \times \dfrac{42.7}{100} = 5.4 \times 42.7$

$= 230.58 = 231$ million

and number of women in LFPR 2020-21

$= \dfrac{670 \times 25.1}{100}$

$= 6.7 \times 25.1$

$= 168.17 = 168$ million

Now, the required difference

$= 231 - 168 = 63$ million

$= 63 \times 1000000$

$= 6.3$ crores

= Between 6 and 8 crores.

140. (A):

	2019-20	2019-20
	Male	Female
	15 years +	15 years +
	76%	72%
Total	1.05 × 100 = 105	100

$\therefore$ The required ratio of females to males

$$= \frac{100 \times 72 \times 19}{105 \times 76 \times 60} = \frac{20}{21} \times 12 \times \frac{1}{40}$$

$$= \frac{20}{21} \times \frac{3}{10} = \frac{20}{70} = 2 : 7.$$

141. (C): Let the total production of fruits in 2019 $= x$ million tonnes.

Then, $x \times \frac{57}{100} = 883$

$$\Rightarrow \quad x = \frac{883 \times 100}{57}$$

$\therefore$ The world fruit production in 2000

$$= \frac{883 \times 100}{57} \times \frac{100 - 63}{100} = \frac{883 \times 100}{57} \times \frac{37}{100}$$

$$= \frac{883 \times 37}{57} = \frac{32671}{57} = 573.1754$$

$= 573$ million tonnes (Approx.)

142. (B):

	2000	2019
Banana + Plantains	$x\%$	$x + 1\%$
Watermelon		$x - 6\%$
Apples	10%	10%
Oranges		$\frac{x+1}{2}\%$
Grapes		$\frac{x+1}{2}\%$

$$\therefore \quad x + 1 + x - 6 + 10 + \frac{x+1}{2} + \frac{x+1}{2} = 57$$

$$\Rightarrow \quad x + 1 + x - 6 + 10 + x + 1 = 57$$

$$\Rightarrow \quad 3x + 12 - 6 = 57$$

$$\Rightarrow \quad 3x + 6 = 57$$

$$\Rightarrow \quad 3x = 57 - 6 = 51$$

$$\Rightarrow \quad x = \frac{51}{3} = 17$$

$$\therefore \quad x + 1 = 17 + 1 = 18\%$$

$\therefore$ The percentage production of Bananas and Plantains in 2019 = 18%.

143. (A) **144. (*)**

145. (D): Given, Marked price of Oranges on Frutopia = ₹ 75

$\therefore$ Selling price of Oranges on Fruotopia

$$= 75 \times \frac{100 - 15}{100}$$

$$= 75 \times \frac{85}{100} = \frac{3 \times 85}{4}$$

$\because$ S.P. of Oranges on Frutopia

= S.P. of Oranges on Fruitfix

$$\therefore \text{ The M.P. of Oranges on Fruitfix} \times \frac{100 - 20}{100} = \frac{3 \times 85}{4}$$

$$\Rightarrow \text{ The M.P. of Oranges on Fruitfix} \times \frac{80}{100} = \frac{3 \times 85}{4}$$

$\Rightarrow$ The M.P. of Orange on Fruitfix

$$= \frac{3 \times 85}{4} \times \frac{100}{80}$$

$$= \frac{3 \times 85}{4} \times \frac{5}{4} = \frac{15 \times 85}{16}$$

$$= \frac{1275}{16} = 79.6875$$

= ₹ 80/kg (Approx.)

146. (B): Total weight of 10 players

$= 68 \times 10 = 680$ kg

$\because$ 1 player (S) leaves the team

$\therefore$ Total weight of 9 players $= 66.5 \times 9$

$= 598.5$ kg

$\therefore$ Weight of player S $= 680 - 598.5$

$= 81.5$ kg

$\therefore$ Player S is from the weight group 9 *i.e.,* (80 kg – 84 kg).

147. (A) **148. (D)** **149. (D)**

150. (C)

Previous Paper (Solved)

BA-LL.B Entrance Examination, 2021*

(Five Year Degree Course)

Part-A : General Knowledge and Mental Ability

1. Who was the first Governor General of Independent India?
A. C. Rajagopalachari
B. G.V. Mavlankar
C. Dr. Babu Rajendra Prasad
D. Dr. B.R. Ambedkar

2. Which of the following is NOT a body of the United Nations?
A. World Intellectual Property Organization
B. Food and Agricultural Organization
C. International Labour Organization
D. World Trade Organization

3. The Constitution of India is declared to have been adopted and enacted by the:
A. Constituent Assembly
B. People of India
C. Indian Parliament
D. Indian President

4. Which of the following is the capital city of Arunachal Pradesh?
A. Itanagar B. Dispur
C. Imphal D. Panaji

5. Joule is the SI unit of:
A. Temperature B. Pressure
C. Energy D. Mass

6. When is the World Day of International Justice celebrated?
A. 15th April
B. 12th December
C. 17th July
D. 20th February

7. For the enforcement of fundamental rights, the Supreme Court may issue a:
A. Decree B. Ordinance
C. Notification D. Writ

8. According to judicial interpretation, Right to Pollution free Environment comes under _______ of the Constitution of India.
A. Article 21 B. Article 14
C. Article 30 D. Article 19

9. Who is competent to amend the fundamental rights under the Constitution of India?
A. President
B. Supreme Court
C. Prime Minister
D. Parliament

10. Which among the following is a media service offered directly to viewers via the Internet bypassing cable, broadcast, and satellite television platforms?
A. TRP B. OTP
C. OTT D. STP

11. Which of the following is NOT included in the Olympic sports/games at Tokyo 2021?
A. Cycling Mountain Bike
B. Kabaddi
C. Surfing
D. Equestrian

12. Euthanasia means
A. Forgetfulness
B. Name of a country
C. A kind of plant
D. Mercy Killing

* Exam conducted by TS-LAW-CET on 24-08-2021.

13. Passing off someone else's writing as one's own is called:
A. Translating
B. Patenting
C. Plagiarism
D. Adopting

14. Which is the American company that designs, manufactures and launches advanced rockets and spacecraft, founded in 2002 to revolutionize space technology?
A. SpaceX
B. NASA
C. USRO
D. New Shepard

15. The elections to the Panchayats are to be held:
A. Every four years
B. Every five years
C. When the State Government decides to do so
D. At the center's directive

16. The East India Company commenced its company business in 1612 at:
A. Satara B. Surat
C. Awadh D. Mysore

17. Defamation infringes a person's right to:
A. Reputation B. Pride
C. Privileges D. Status

18. The Book 'Das Capital' was written by:
A. William Shakespeare
B. V.S. Naipaul
C. Mulk Raj Anand
D. Karl Marx

19. Equinox means:
A. Days are longer than nights
B. Nights are longer than days
C. Days and nights are equal
D. Earth and Sun are equal

20. Introducing a man, a woman said. "He is the only son of my mother's mother." How is the woman related to man?
A. Mother B. Aunt
C. Sister D. Niece

21. In a code, CORNER is written as GSVRIY. How can CENTRAL be written in that code?
A. GFOUSBM B. GIRXVEP
C. GNFJKER D. GJRYVEP

22. Count the number of triangles and quadrilaterals in the given figure.

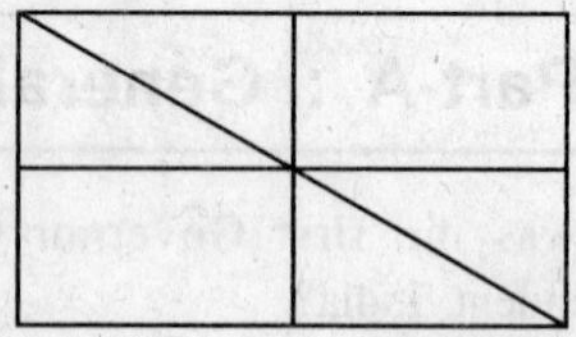

A. 12 triangles, 9 quadrilaterals
B. 9 triangles, 6 quadrilaterals
C. 6 triangles, 9 quadrilaterals
D. 8 triangles, 10 quadrilaterals

23. The average of first five multiples of 9 is:
A. 20 B. 28
C. 30 D. 27

24. A worker reaches his factory 3 minutes late if his speed from his house to the factory is 5 km/h. If he walks at a speed of 6 km/hr, then he reaches the factory 7 minutes early. The distance of the factory from his house is:
A. 3 km B. 4 km
C. 5 km D. 6 km

25. Film and TV Institute of India is located at:
A. Pune B. Perambur
C. Rajkot D. Pimpri

26. The Ozone layer restricts:
A. X-rays and gamma rays
B. Visible light
C. Infrared radiation
D. Ultraviolet radiation

27. In order to tell MS Excel computer application that one is entering a formula in cell, one must begin with which operator?
A. $ B. @
C. + D. =

28. Mughal Emperor Akbar divided his empire into:
A. Eight Provinces (Subas)

B. Five Provinces (Subas)
C. Twelve Provinces (Subas)
D. Ten Provinces (Subas)

29. Between 1749-1754, an important battle fought between the forces of the British and the French is known as:
A. Third battle of Panipat
B. The First Carnatic War
C. The Second Carnatic War
D. Battle of Buxar

30. When was the Osmania University, Hyderabad established?
A. 1918
B. 1928
C. 1899
D. 1946

Part-B : Current Affairs

31. Michael Collins, whose name was in news recently, was associated with which field?
A. Basketball
B. Space Science
C. Journalism
D. Politics

32. The operation launched by National Security Guards to flush out the Lashkar-e-Taiba terrorists who attacked Mumbai in the year 2008 is called:
A. Operation Cactus
B. Operation Black Tornado
C. Operation All Out
D. Operation Rakshak

33. Which Indian Insurance Company has recently featured in the top 10 list of most valuable insurance brands globally?
A. United India Insurance Company
B. Life Insurance Corporation
C. New India Assurance
D. National Insurance Company Limited

34. Contamination of drinking water with _____ causes Blackfoot Disease (BFD).
A. Nitrates
B. Arsenic
C. Mercury
D. Cadmium

35. The establishment of Taj Trapezium Zone (TTZ) enshrines which among the following objectives?
A. Protection from Pollution
B. Tourism Development
C. Economy Hub
D. Transportation facilities

36. Which among the following gas is used as reference to calculate "Global Warming Potential" (GWP)?
A. Carbon Dioxide
B. Methane
C. Ozone
D. Nitrogen Di-oxide

37. Name the woman weightlifter from India who won the Silver Medal in the Women's 49 kg category at Tokyo Olympics, 2021?
A. Bhawna Jat
B. Karnam Malliswari
C. Mirabai Ghanu
D. Seema Punia

38. Soli J Sorabjee, who passed away recently was a _____ of India.
A. Former Attorney General
B. Former Chief Justice of Supreme Court
C. Former Comptroller and Auditor General
D. Former Chief Election Commissioner

39. 'MITRA' scheme, which was announced in the recent Union Budget 2021-22 is related to which sector?
A. Agriculture
B. Textile
C. Micro-Finance
D. Banking

40. Who is the author of the book titled "The Little Book of Encouragement"?
A. Barack Obama
B. Bill Gates
C. Dalai Lama
D. Aung San Suu Kyi

41. "Passport Seva Programme 2.0" is the initiative of which Union Ministry?
A. Ministry of Home Affairs
B. Ministry of External Affairs
C. Ministry of Tourism
D. Ministry of International Relations

42. Narayanaswamy, who resigned in the month of February, 2021 was the Chief Minister of which State/Union Territory?
A. Tamil Nadu
B. Puducherry
C. Goa
D. Kerala

43. Which country won the highest number of Gold Medals in Tokyo Olympics held in the year 2021?
A. Japan
B. United States of America
C. China
D. Great Britain

44. Who is the founder and executive chairman of Amazon, having previously served as chairman, president and CEO of the company?
A. Satya Nadella B. Jeff Bezos
C. Jan Kourn D. Elon Musk

45. Which country has passed legislation in March, 2021 to legalize 'Euthanasia'?
A. Germany B. Norway
C. Spain D. Italy

46. 'Hola Mohalla' is a festival celebrated in which Indian State/UT?
A. Rajasthan B. Punjab
C. Goa D. Odisha

47. The World's first ship tunnel is being constructed in which country?
A. Poland B. Norway
C. France D. Zimbabwe

48. What is the name of NASA's helicopter that commenced its flight in Mars?
A. Determination B. Mars Rover
C. Ambition D. Ingenuity

49. What is the theme of the 'Earth Day 2021'?
A. Covid and Climate Change
B. Restore Our Earth
C. One Earth
D. Earth is our Asset

50. What is the capital city and currency of Germany?
A. Athens & Dollars
B. Berlin & Euro
C. Lima & Pound
D. Berlin & Franc

51. Where is the "Valmiki National Park" situated?
A. Madhya Pradesh B. Bihar
C. Punjab D. Chandigarh

52. Which Indian Movie has won the "Best Screen Play" award at the Venice Film Festival 2020?
A. Hellaro B. Son Rise
C. Uri D. The Disciple

53. What is the name of the project announced by Kerala, for rehabilitation of its people returning from abroad?
A. Welcome Back
B. Dream Kerala
C. God's Own Country
D. Winning Covid

54. What is the name of the mobile App developed by the Indian Red Cross Society, to provide easy access to blood for those who need transfusion?
A. eBloodServices B. Rakt Kosh
C. Rakt Bank D. Bharat Blood

55. Joe Biden on 20th January, 2021 became the ______ President of the United States.
A. 45th B. 46th
C. 47th D. 48th

56. The recent leap year, where February had 29 days was:
A. 2017 B. 2018
C. 2019 D. 2020

57. Who is the Chief of Defence Staff (CDS) of India as of July, 2021?
A. General Manoj Mukund Naravane
B. Chief Marshal Rakesh Kumar Singh Bhadauria
C. Admiral Karambir Singh
D. General Bipin Rawat

58. Which country joined SAARC group of Nations as its Eighth member in 2007?
A. Afghanistan B. Bangladesh
C. Bhutan D. Nepal

59. Who is the Chairman of the Bar Council of India, as of July, 2021?
A. A. Rami Reddy
B. T. Prabhakaran
C. Manan Kumar Mishra
D. Arun Mishra

60. Uttarakhand, Uttar Pradesh, Bihar, West Bengal and Sikkim, share border with which of the following countries?
A. Nepal B. China
C. Bhutan D. Myanmar

Part-C : Aptitude for Study of Law

61. In which year, right to property was deleted from the list of fundamental rights?
A. 1975 B. 1976
C. 1977 D. 1978

62. Which of the following Articles of the Indian Constitution guarantees right to education?
A. Article 21-A
B. Article 22
C. Article 21
D. Article 22-B

63. Indra Sawhney v. Union of India, popularly known as Mandal case, is concerned with:
A. Economically Weaker Section Reservations
B. Disabled Reservations
C. Other Backward Classes Reservations
D. Minority Reservations

64. Which of the following Parts of the Indian Constitution deals with the Fundamental Duties of the citizens?
A. Part IVA
B. Part IV
C. Part III
D. Part VI

65. Which is the shortest Constitution in the World?
A. Switzerland B. Australia
C. India D. USA

66. The total number of members in the legislative council of a State shall be at least ______ and shall not exceed ______ of the total number of members in the legislative assembly of that State, subject to the other provisions of Constitution of India.
A. 45, 1/3rd
B. 60, 1/5th
C. 50, 1/4th
D. 40, 1/3rd

67. The Vice-President shall be elected by the members of an electoral college consisting of the:
A. Members of both Houses of Parliament
B. Members of Lok Sabha and Legislative Assemblies of the States.
C. Members of Rajya Sabha and Legislative Assemblies of the States.
D. Members of Lok Sabha & Rajya Sabha, Legislative Assemblies and Legislative Councils.

68. The resignation of the President of India addressed to the Vice President shall forthwith be communicated to the:
A. Chief Justice of India
B. Prime Minister
C. Speaker of Lok Sabha
D. Chief Secretary

69. Who administers oath of office to the Governor of a State?
A. President
B. Chief Justice of India
C. Speaker of State Legislature
D. Chief Justice of High Court of concerned State

70. Who was the First Law and Justice Minister of the Government of India?
A. Dr. B.R. Ambedkar
B. Kailash Nath Katju
C. Charu Chandra Biswas
D. Sardar Vallabhbhai Patel

71. Before 61st Constitutional Amendment of 1989, what was the minimum age of Indian citizen eligible to vote in the Election?
A. 20 years
B. 21 years
C. 23 years
D. 24 years

72. Who is considered as the first citizen of India?
A. Chief of Army Staff
B. President of India
C. Chief Justice of the Supreme Court
D. Prime Minister

73. How many writs are available against violation of fundamental rights?
A. 4 B. 5
C. 6 D. 8

74. *Magna Carta* which is a great charter is associated with
A. Corporate Social Responsibility
B. Fundamental Duties
C. Human Duties
D. Human Rights

75. Keeping a movable property as security for repayment of a debt is called:
A. Mortgage
B. Surety
C. Pledge
D. Bailment

76. Which among the following is not a Constitutional body in India?
A. Finance Commission
B. Human Rights Commission
C. Election Commission
D. Union Public Service Commission

77. Which of the following is NOT considered as a feature of the Basic Structure of the Indian Constitution?
A. Secularism
B. Rule of Law
C. Presidential form of Government
D. Judicial Review

78. Justice J.S. Verma Committee (2013) was concerned with:
A. Amendments to Criminal Law
B. Amendments to Civil Law
C. Environmental Law
D. Constitutional Law

79. The judgement in *Shayara Bono* v. *Union of India* is on the issue relating to:
A. Invalidity of Bigamy among Muslims
B. Protection of Wakf properties
C. Maintenance of divorced Muslim women
D. Invalidity of Triple Talaq in Muslim law

80. The expression "Fourth Estate" generally refers to:
A. NGOs
B. Bureaucracy
C. Press
D. Civil Societies

81. The expression SAL used as a substitute of PIL by certain jurists denotes:
A. Social Activity Litigation
B. Society Action Litigation
C. Social Action Litigation
D. Social Accountability Litigation

82. In which year was the WTO established?
A. 1995
B. 1980
C. 1948
D. 2005

83. ICCPR in the context of Human Rights denotes:
A. International Convention on Civil and Political Rights
B. International Covenant on Civil and Political Rights
C. International Covenant on Civil and Personal Rights
D. International Convention on Civil and Personal Rights

84. The United Nations Conference on the Environment in 1972 was held in ______, city of ______ (country).
A. Stockholm, Sweden
B. Paris, France
C. Rome, Italy
D. Geneva, Switzerland

85. An agreement with a minor under Indian Contract Act is:
A. Valid B. Voidable
C. Void *ab initio* D. Illegal

86. International Criminal Court is located in ______.
A. New York B. The Hague
C. Rome D. Nice

87. Which one of the following is NOT considered as an Intellectual Property?
A. Invention
B. Logo
C. Literary work
D. Agricultural land

88. The Hyderabadi dish which was granted registration as a Geographical Indication of Goods is:
A. Hyderabadi Biryani
B. Hyderabadi Haleem
C. Irani Chai
D. Khubani-ka-Meetha

89. When an imprisoned person is released temporarily from jail for a certain purpose, it is called:
A. Bail
B. Anticipatory Bail
C. Parole
D. Pardon

90. The Supreme Court of India laid down the "Doctrine of Prospective Overruling" in which of the following landmark judgements?
A. Sankari Prasad v. Union of India
B. Sajjan Singh v. State of U.P.
C. Golaknath v. State of Punjab
D. Kesavananda Bharti v. State of Kerala

91. Forms of Oaths or Affirmations for Constitutional Authorities are contained in ______ Schedule of the Constitution of India.
A. 1st B. 2nd
C. 3rd D. 4th

92. Members of National Human Rights Commission are appointed by:
A. Prime Minister
B. Speaker
C. Chief Justice of India
D. President of India

93. The subsidiary of which American Company was held responsible for Bhopal Gas Tragedy in 1984?
A. General Motors
B. General Electrical
C. Union Carbide Corporation
D. Enron

94. The global movement against sexual abuse and harassment of women perpetrated by powerful men in society is known as:
A. Sunrise Movement
B. Women's Liberation Movement
C. Time to Change
D. Me Too

95. Who was the first temporary chairman of the Constituent Assembly?
A. Dr. Sachchidananda Sinha
B. K.M. Munshi
C. Sardar Vallabhbhai Patel
D. B.N. Rao

96. Who famously observed that *"The life of the law has not been logic: it has been experience"*?
A. Mahatma Gandhi
B. Dr. B.R. Ambedkar
C. Nelson Mandela
D. Oliver Wendell Holmes Jr.

97. The Book entitled *'De l'esprit des lois'* by Montesquieu is about ________.
A. Separation of Powers
B. Principles of Natural justice
C. Rule of Law
D. Theory of Checks and Balances

98. The principle of Corporate Social Responsibility is statutorily recognized under which law?
A. The Companies Act, 1956
B. The Companies Act, 2013
C. The Banking Companies Regulation Act, 1949
D. The Income Tax Act, 1961

99. For the purpose of commission of an offence, a juvenile is a person under the age of:
A. 18 years B. 16 years
C. 21 years D. 15 years

100. The famous judgement of Indian Supreme Court, in Justice K.S. Puttaswamy's case (2018) is concerned with:
A. Right of women to worship at Sabarimala
B. Unique Identification Authority of India
C. Decriminalization of Adultery
D. Administrative Tribunals

101. The State Reorganization Act was passed in the year:
A. 1952 B. 1954
C. 1955 D. 1956

102. The Right to Fair Compensation and Transparency in Land Acquisition, Rehabilitation and Resettlement Act, was passed in the year:
A. 2011 B. 2012
C. 2013 D. 2015

103. Who among the following Judges of the Supreme Court of India was superseded by his junior Judge for appointment as Chief Justice of India?
A. Justice Prafullachandra Natwarlal Bhagwati
B. Justice Vaidyanathapuram Rama Iyer Krishna Iyer
C. Justice Hans Raj Khanna
D. Justice Dhirajlal Ambelal Desai

104. Which of the following laws recognizes the liability of a celebrity for endorsing a product, proved to be defective?
A. The Copyright Act, 1957
B. The Consumer Protection Act, 2019
C. The Competition Act, 2002
D. The Celebrity Liability Act, 2020

105. The act of making a false spoken statement damaging the reputation of a person is known as:
A. Slander
B. Libel
C. Malicious Prosecution
D. Assault

106. Witnessing the execution of an instrument and affixing signatures certifying such execution by an executant is called:
A. Authorization B. Attestation
C. Delegation D. Subrogation

107. A member of a Public Service Commission shall hold office for a term of _______ years.
A. 3 B. 4
C. 5 D. 6

108. No tax shall be levied or collected except by:
A. Authority of Law
B. Order of the President
C. Order of the Finance Commission
D. Order of the Prime Minister

109. The Scheduled Castes and Scheduled Tribes (Prevention of Atrocities) Act was enacted in the year:
A. 1980 B. 1985
C. 1989 D. 1995

110. Which recent State enactment provides the death penalty for offenses like rape, gang rape, and speeding up trials of such offense within 21 days?

A. The Telangana Disha Act, 2019
B. The Kerala Protection of Women Act, 2020
C. The Delhi Nirbhaya Act, 2016
D. The Andhra Pradesh Disha Act, 2019

111. Where a Proclamation of Emergency is in operation, the right to move any court for the enforcement of Fundamental Rights, except those guaranteed under ________ can be suspended.

A. Article 14 and 19 B. Articles 19 and 21
C. Articles 20 and 21 D. Articles 21 and 25

112. Which Constitutional Amendment recently extended the deadline for the cessation for the reservation of seats for members from Scheduled Castes and Scheduled Tribes in the Lok Sabha and State Legislative Assemblies by a period of 10 years?

A. 105th Amendment
B. 102nd Amendment
C. 103rd Amendment
D. 104th Amendment

113. The subjects on which Panchayats have powers and responsibilities are contained in which Schedule of the Constitution of India?

A. 9th B. 10th
C. 11th D. 12th

114. The meaning of latin maxim *'ubi jus ibi remediuin'* is:

A. Where there is a remedy, there is justice
B. Where there is injustice, there is a right
C. Where there is a right, there is a remedy
D. Where there is a remedy, there is a right

115. Ram cuts down a tree on Govind's ground, with the intention of dishonestly taking the tree out of Govind's possession without Govind's consent. Here, as soon as Ram has severed the tree in order to such taking, he has committed the offence of _______.

A. Cheating
B. Theft
C. Criminal Misappropriation
D. Environmental Pollution

116. Punishment of life imprisonment for the offence of rape resulting in persistent vegetative state of victim means:

A. Imprisonment for 14 years.
B. Imprisonment for the remainder of that person's natural life.
C. Imprisonment for 10 years during good conduct.
D. Imprisonment for 20 years.

117. Every person who is arrested and detained in custody shall be produced before the nearest magistrate within a period of ______ hours of such arrest excluding the time necessary for the journey from the place of arrest to the court of the magistrate.

A. 20 B. 22
C. 24 D. 48

118. Causing Public Nuisance amounts to:

A. A tort
B. An offence
C. A breach of contract
D. A hate crime

119. What is the minimum educational qualification prescribed to become a Member of Parliament in India?

A. No such qualifications prescribed
B. First Class pass in 10th Standard
C. First Class pass in 10+2 Examination
D. Any Graduate

120. "Any facility from where access to the internet is offered by any person in the ordinary course of business to the members of the public" under the Information Technology Act, 2000 is called as:

A. I.T. Resource Centre
B. Browsing Centre
C. Internet Cafe
D. Cyber Cafe

ANSWERS

1 A	2 D	3 B	4 A	5 C	6 C	7 D	8 A	9 D	10 C
11 B	12 D	13 C	14 A	15 B	16 B	17 A	18 D	19 C	20 D
21 B	22 C	23 D	24 C	25 A	26 D	27 D	28 C	29 C	30 A
31 B	32 B	33 B	34 B	35 A	36 A	37 C	38 A	39 B	40 C
41 B	42 B	43 B	44 B	45 C	46 B	47 B	48 D	49 B	50 B
51 B	52 D	53 B	54 A	55 B	56 D	57 D	58 A	59 C	60 A
61 D	62 A	63 C	64 A	65 D	66 D	67 A	68 C	69 D	70 A
71 B	72 B	73 B	74 D	75 C	76 B	77 C	78 A	79 D	80 C
81 C	82 A	83 B	84 A	85 C	86 B	87 D	88 B	89 C	90 C
91 C	92 D	93 C	94 D	95 A	96 D	97 A	98 B	99 A	100 B
101 D	102 C	103 C	104 B	105 A	106 B	107 D	108 A	109 C	110 D
111 C	112 D	113 C	114 C	115 B	116 B	117 C	118 B	119 A	120 D

EXPLANATORY ANSWERS

20. According to question,

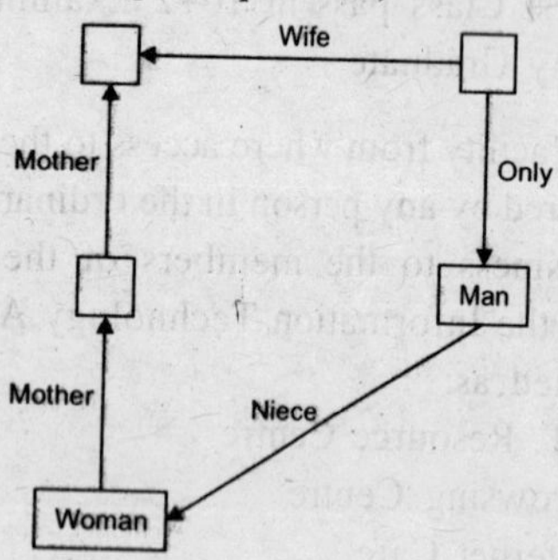

Here, The woman is the niece of Man.

21. Given, in a code,

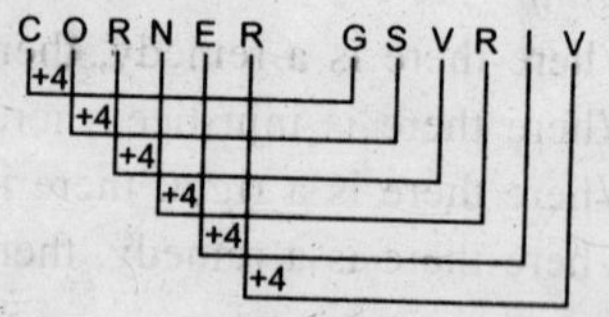

Similarly,

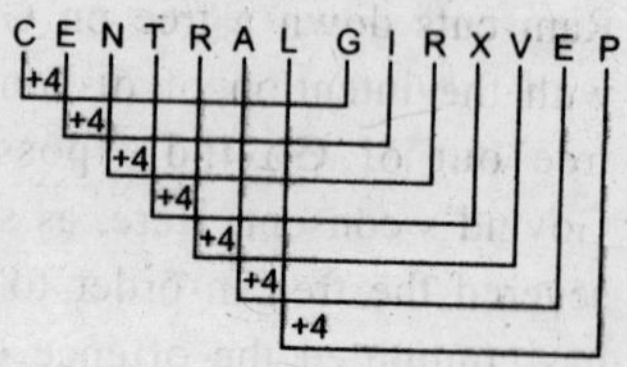

The letters in the word are moved +4 steps forward. Hence, CENTRAL can be written as GIRXVEP.

22. Triangles in figure are:

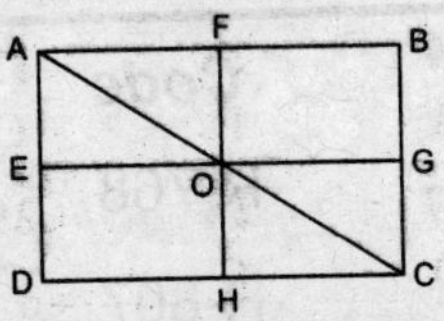

ΔABC, ΔACD, ΔAEO, ΔAFO, ΔCGO, ΔCHO

The number of triangles = 6

Quadrilaterals in figure are:

ABCD, AFOE, FBGO, EOHD, OGCH, AFHD, FBCH, ABGE, EGCD

The number of quadrilateral = 9.

23. The average of first five multiples of 9

$$= \frac{9+18+27+36+45}{5} = \frac{135}{5} = 27.$$

24. Let the distance of the factory from his house is x km

Then, $\frac{x}{5} - \frac{3}{60} = \frac{x}{6} + \frac{7}{60}$

$$\left[\text{Time} = \frac{\text{Distance}}{\text{Speed}}\right]$$

$$\Rightarrow \quad \frac{x}{5} - \frac{x}{6} = \frac{3}{60} + \frac{7}{60}$$

$$\Rightarrow \quad \frac{6x - 5x}{30} = \frac{3+7}{60}$$

$$\Rightarrow \quad \frac{x}{30} = \frac{10}{60}$$

$$\Rightarrow \quad \frac{x}{30} = \frac{1}{6}$$

$$\Rightarrow \quad x = 5$$

Hence, the distance = 5 km.

Previous Paper (Solved)

Common Law Admission Test (CLAT–UG) Entrance Exam, 2020*

Section-I : English

Directions (Qs. No. 1-5): *Read the passage carefully and answer these questions:*

Climate change is considered to be one of the most serious threats to sustainable development, with adverse impact on the environment, human health, food security, economic activity, natural resources and physical infrastructure. According to the Intergovernmental Panel on Climate Change (IPCC), the effects of climate change have already been observed, and scientific findings indicate that precautionary and prompt action is necessary. Vulnerability to climate change is not just a function of geography or dependence on natural resources; it also has social, economic and political dimensions which influence how climate change affects different groups. Poor people rarely have insurance to cover loss of property due to natural calamines *i.e.*, drought, floods, super cyclones etc. The poor communities are already struggling to cope, with the existing challenges of poverty and climate variability and climate change could push many beyond their ability to cope or even survive. It is vital that these communities are helped to adapt to the changing dynamics of nature. Adaptation is a process through which societies make themselves better able to cope with an uncertain future. Adapting to climate change entails taking the right measures to reduce the negative effect of climate change (or exploit the positive ones) by making the appropriate adjustments and changes. These range from technological options such as increased sea defences or flood proof houses on stilts to behavioural change at the individual level, such as reducing water use in times of drought. Other strategies include early warning systems for extreme events, better water management, improved risk management, various insurance options and biodiversity conservation. Because of the speed at which climate change is happening due to global temperature rise, it is urgent that the vulnerability of developing countries to climate change is reduced and their capacity to adapt is increased and national adaptation plans are implemented. Communities must build their resilience, including adopting appropriate technologies while making the most of traditional knowledge, and diversifying their livelihoods to cope with current and future climate stress. Local coping strategies and knowledge need to be used in synergy with government and local interventions. The need of adaptation interventions depends on national circumstances. There is a large body of knowledge and experience within local communities on coping with climatic variability and extreme weather events. Local communities have always aimed to adapt to variations in their climate. Local coping strategies are an important element of planning for adaptation. Traditional knowledge can help to provide efficient, appropriate and time tested ways of advising and enabling adaptation to climate change in communities who are feeling the effects of climate changes due to global warming.

1. To address the challenge of Climate Change, Developing countries urgently require:

A. Implementation of National Adaptation Plans

B. Adoption of short term plans

C. Adoption of technological solutions

D. Imposition of Climate Change tax

**Exam held on: 28/09/2020*

2. Given below are the factors of vulnerability of poor people to climate changes. Select the option that contains the correct answer.
1. Their dependence on natural resources
2. Geographical attributes
3. Lack of financial resources
4. Lack of Traditional knowledge

Codes:
A. (2), (3) and (4) B. (1), (2), (3) and (4)
C. (3) only D. (1), (2) and (3)

3. Which of the following is against the idea portrayed in the passage?
A. Co-ordination between regional and national efforts is necessary.
B. The process of Adaptation to climate change does not take into account the factor of prevailing national circumstances.
C. Social dimensions of climate change also need to be appreciated.
D. Combining Traditional Knowledge with appropriate technology is the need of the hour.

4. The Traditional Knowledge should be used through
A. Improvement in national circumstances
B. Synergy between Government and local interventions
C. Imposition of Climate Change Tax
D. Its dissemination

5. What is the meaning of the word 'Resilience' occurring in the passage?
A. Toughness B. Fragility
C. Flexibility D. Vulnerability

Directions (Qs. No. 6-10): *Read the passage carefully and answer these questions:*

The uncovering of a private Instagram group styling itself 'Bois Locker Room' featuring students from some prominent South Delhi schools discussing their female classmates in disturbingly violent ways including plans of sexual assault is a wakeup call for parents and authorities. The group formed last month or so kicked up a social media storm when screenshots surfaced. Police have questioned a 15 year old boy to identify other members. Similar incidents involving minors discussing rape/ gang rape of classmates have been reported on other digital platforms like WhatsApp too, across cities. The exchanges in the now deleted group require precise responses from police, parents and school authorities around whom the fates of the juveniles involved now revolve. It is important to recognise where a teenager spouting objectification of his female counterparts is coming from. People of all ages, not just children, are retreating deeper into the recesses of their online avatars during this lockdown. But the heavy technological investment in children's education, including flooding them with personal smartphones, has not been matched by serious conversations centred on responsible internet usage and equality. Young, impressionable minds absorb the normalisation of rape from the adults around them. When what they see, read and hear is toxic masculinity, that is what they perform. That's what peer pressure becomes about. But if this youthful role play of macho dominance receives timely counselling, it can prevent far graver adult offences. Schools and parents have a critical role to play in educating children on gender equality. Digital platforms which claim to have zero tolerance towards content that violates community standards must also explain why such abuses go undetected, despite boasts about Artificial Intelligence-driven technologies to stop them. They should play a more proactive role in stopping the sexual harassment of real people in the guise of virtual sport.

[Editorial Published in Times of India, dated 6 May, 2020]

6. What is the Central Idea being conveyed by the Author in the passage above?
A. Modern Social Networking platforms must take the lead in regulating young people from using these platforms for sexual abuse.
B. It is significant to educate children and youngsters about gender equality.
C. Digital Platforms need to have a zero tolerance policy towards content leading to sexual abuse.
D. None of the above

7. As per author, why is this incident a wake-up call for parents?

A. Because even the parents are indulged heavily in social networking platforms.

B. Because parents have failed to stop their children from committing such blunders.

C. Because it is the primary responsibility of parents to control their children.

D. Because the parents have failed in educating their children regarding fair internet usage and have simply invested in the technology driven education of their children.

8. According to the author, in order to understand the root cause of such insensitive incidents, it is important to:

A. Understand and examine the kind of socialisation process these children are exposed to.

B. Adopt Artificial Intelligence driven technologies.

C. Strengthen the environment of discipline in schools and colleges.

D. All of the above.

9. On the basis of your reading of the passage, which of the following statements can be inferred?

A. Sexual Offenses can be reduced by timely counselling from parental and quasi-parental authorities i.e., parents and teachers respectively.

B. If digital platforms implement a Zero Tolerance Policy towards such a menace, sexual offenses can be completely stopped.

C. Investment in education of children is enough to curb the menace.

D. All of the above.

10. Which of the following words are synonymous with the word 'Spouting'?

A. Pouring B. Streaming

C. Erupting D. All of the Above

Directions (Qs. No. 11-15): *Read the passage carefully and answer these questions:*

The snow was falling, and the Cat's fur was stiffly pointed with it, but he was imperturbable. He sat crouched, ready for the death-spring, as he had sat for hours. It was night but that made no difference, all times were as one to the Cat when he was in wait for prey. Then, too, he was under no constraint of human will, for he was living alone that winter. Nowhere in the world was any voice calling him; on no hearth was there a waiting dish. He was quite free except for his own desires, which tyrannized over him when unsatisfied as now. The Cat was very hungry, almost famished, in fact. For days the weather had been very bitter...and the Cat's long hunt had availed him nothing. But he waited with the inconceivable patience and persistency of his race; besides, he was certain. The Cat was a creature of absolute convictions, and his faith in his deductions never wavered. The rabbit had gone in there between those low-hung pine boughs. The Cat had seen her enter...so he sat down and waited, and he waited still in the white night, listening angrily to the north wind starting in the upper heights of the mountains with distant screams, then swelling into an awful crescendo of rage, and swooping down with furious white wings of snow like a flock of fierce eagles into the valleys and ravines. The Cat was on the side of a mountain, on a wooded terrace. Above him, a few feet away towered the rock ascent as steep as the wall of a cathedral. He had often looked with wonder at the rock, and miauled bitterly and resentfully as man does in the face of a forbidding Providence. At his left was the sheer precipice. Behind him...was the frozen perpendicular wall of a mountain stream. Before him was the way to his home. When the rabbit came out she was trapped; her little cloven feet could not scale such unbroken steeps. So the Cat waited. The tangle of trees and bushes clinging to the mountain-side with a stern clutch of roots, the prostrate trunks and branches, the vines embracing everything with strong knots and coils of growth, had a curious effect, as of things which had whirled for ages in a current of raging water, only it was not water, but wind, which had disposed everything in circling lines of yielding to its fiercest points of onset. It was as if ice needles pricked his skin through his beautiful thick fur, but he never faltered and never once cried. He had nothing to gain from crying, and everything to lose; the rabbit would hear him cry and know he was waiting.

[Excerpts from a Short story, 'The Cat' by Mary E. Wilkins Freeman]

11. Which of the following suggests a synonymous meaning to the words 'Providence' and 'Crescendo' respectively?

A. Nemesis, Apex
B. Zenith, Nadir
C. Laxity, Prudence
D. Short-sightedness, Upsurge

12. The passage has been adorned with numerous figure of speeches. Which of the following combinations is correct?

A. Irony and Sarcasm
B. Alliteration and Pun
C. Simile and Personification
D. Metaphor and Onomatopoeia

13. The passage best demonstrates which one of the following motifs of Cat's Life?

A. To satisfy the pangs of hunger
B. To survive the harsh winters
C. A never ending wait
D. To hunt for Rabbit

14. The Author's description of "...he was under no constraint of human will, for he was living alone..." implies:

A. Cat's absolute freedom from everything
B. Cat's no association with human beings
C. Cat's loneliness
D. Cat's tyrannical demeanour

15. The lines, "...but he never faltered and never once cried. He had nothing to gain from crying, and everything to lose...", suggest that the Cat is:

A. Reflective B. Apologetic
C. Resilient D. Frustrated

Directions (Qs. No. 16-20): *Read the passage carefully and answer these questions:*

I am losing my interest in human beings; in the significance of their lives and their actions. Someone has said it is better to study one man than ten books. I want neither books nor men; they make me suffer. Can one of them talk to me like the night – the Summer night? Like the stars or the caressing wind?

The night came slowly, softly, as I lay out there under the maple tree. It came creeping, creeping stealthily out of the valley, thinking I did not notice. And the outlines of trees and foliage nearby blended in one black mass and the night came stealing out from them, too, and from the east and west, until the only light was in the sky, filtering through the maple leaves and a star looking down through every cranny.

The night is solemn and it means mystery.

Human shapes flitted by like intangible things. Some stole up like little mice to peep at me. I did not mind. My whole being was abandoned to the soothing and penetrating charm of the night. The katydids began their slumber song: they are at it yet. How wise they are. They do not chatter like people. They tell me only: "sleep, sleep, sleep." The wind rippled the maple leaves like little warm love thrills. Why do fools cumber the Earth! It was a man's voice that broke the necromancer's spell. A man came today with his Bible Class. He is detestable with his red cheeks and bold eyes and coarse manner and speech. What does he know of Christ? Shall I ask a young fool who was born yesterday and will die tomorrow to tell me things of Christ? I would rather ask the stars: they have seen him.

[Short Story by Kate Chopin]

16. Why has the author lost interest in human beings?

A. Because they make the author suffer.
B. Because the human beings do not bring with them the warmth and the comfort which comes naturally with the night, starts and the wind.
C. Because human beings are not mysterious.
D. All of the above

17. The author has compared the night with:

A. The Katydids
B. The Necromancer's spell
C. Stars
D. All of the above

18. Why has the author called the 'katydids' wise?

A. Because they sing a slumber song.

B. Because they tell the author to only 'sleep'.

C. Because they do not indulge in unnecessary and unimportant talks.

D. Because they are not fools.

19. Which of the following can be inferred from the 'passage'?

A. Being close to nature can bring one closer to God.

B. Nature is just a mystery.

C. Books and Man are both detestable.

D. None of these.

20. Which of the following words from the passage mean 'rough'?

A. Solemn B. Caressing

C. Coarse D. Slumber

Directions (Qs. No. 21-25): *Read the passage carefully and answer these questions:*

It was the strangest murder trial I ever attended, where the old woman was found battered to death. He was a heavy stout man with bulging bloodshot eyes. All his muscles seemed to be in his thighs. The clock had just struck two in the morning. Mrs Salmon in 15 Northwood Street had been unable to sleep: she heard a door click shut and thought it was her own gate. So she went to the window and saw Adams (that was his name) on the steps of Mrs Parker's house. He had just come out and he was wearing gloves. He had a hammer in his hand and she saw him drop it into the laurel bushes by the front gate. But before he moved away, he had looked up at her window. The fatal instinct that tells a man when he is watched exposed him in the light of a streetlamp to her gaze-his eyes suffused with horrifying and brutal fear, like an animal's when you raise a whip.

Mrs Salmon was called in the Court.

'And do you see the man here in court?'

[She looked straight at the big man in the dock, who stared hard at her with his Pekingese eyes without emotion.]

'Yes,' she said, 'there he is.'

'You are quite certain?'

She said simply, 'I couldn't be mistaken, sir.'

'Thank you, Mrs Salmon.'

[Counsel for the defence rose to cross-examine.]

'Now, Mrs Salmon, you must remember that a man's life may depend on your evidence.'

'I do remember it, sir.'

'Is your eyesight good?'

'I have never had to wear spectacles, sir.'

'You are a woman of fifty-five?'

'Fifty-six, sir.'

'And the man you saw was on the other side of the road?'

'Yes, sir.'

'And it was two o'clock in the morning. You must have remarkable eyes, Mrs Salmon?'

'No, sir. There was moonlight, and when the man looked up, he had the lamplight on his face.'

'And you have no doubt whatever that the man you saw is the prisoner?'

'None whatever, sir. It isn't a face one forgets.'

Then he said, 'Do you mind Mrs Salmon' examining again the people in court?

No, not the prisoner. Stand up, please, Mr Adams!

And there at the back of the court with thick stout body and muscular legs and a pair of bulging eyes, was the exact image of the man in the dock.

'Now think very carefully, Mrs Salmon. Can you still swear that the man you saw drop the hammer in Mrs Parker's garden was the prisoner and not this man, who is his twin brother?' Of course she couldn't.

[Excerpts from 'The Case for the Defence' by Graham Greene]

21. Why do you think, has the Author called the trial, 'strangest' murder trial he ever attended?

A. Because the accused had a very strange personality.

B. Because, despite having a potential witness and evidence against the accused, his wrong could not be proved.

C. Because, Mrs. Salmon's evidence could not be proved before the Court.

D. None of these

22. "…his eyes suffused with horrifying and brutal fear, like an animal's when you raise a whip." can be called as:

A. Personification B. Simile
C. Onomatopoeia D. None of the above

23. The expression '*Pekingese eyes*' used in the passage refers to which of the following?

A. Bulging eyes B. Red eyes
C. Small eyes D. None of them

24. Why was Mrs. Salmon convinced that the man she saw had committed the crime?

A. Because she saw the man on the steps of Mrs. Parker's House and he was wearing gloves.
B. Because he had a hammer in his hand and she saw him drop it into the laurel bushes by the front gate.
C. Because when he looked up at her window, his eyes were suffused with horrifying and brutal fear.
D. Because she had seen him clearly in the light of street lamp.

25. Who was murdered in the scene described in the passage?

A. Mrs. Wheeler
B. Mrs. Parker
C. Mrs. Salmon
D. It cannot be inferred

Directions (Qs. No. 26-30): *Read the passage carefully and answer these questions:*

The world has very few devices left to fight COVID-19 with, but technology remains one of them. Whether it is employing the state-of-the-art technology in the discovery of cures or vaccines, or traditional technology services to enhance health care and consultations, or even tools that keep people at home occupied/productive, it is clear that technology will serve humanity at one of its darkest moments. The pandemic has contributed, in no small measure, to the understanding of the myriad ways in which available technologies have not been put to better use, and presented people with multiple opportunities to harness these devices, techniques and methods to get on with life in the time of lockdown. Among the primary uses is telemedicine, rendered inexorable now, by the temporary paralysis brought on by a freeze on movement. The Centre's recent guidelines allowing for widespread use of telemedicine services came as a shot in the arm for telehealth crusaders in the country, among them the Telemedicine Society of India that has long been battling to use the technology in its complete arc to reach remote areas in India. This move finds consonance with the rest of the world where several nations, also deeply impacted by the pandemic, have deployed telemedicine to reach people who have been unable to come to hospital, to reduce footfalls in hospitals, and to even provide medical and mental health counselling to countless people. It was way back in 2000 that telemedicine was first employed in India, but the progress has been excruciatingly slow, until the pandemic. However, it does seem as if the medical community was only held back by the lack of legislation to enable tele consultations. For no sooner was the policy announced, than hospitals and clinicians hurried to jump onto the bandwagon, advertising contact information for patients. The advantages are peculiar in the current context, when putting distance between people is paramount, as tele consultations are not barred even when health care professionals and patients may have to be quarantined. The advancement of telecommunication capabilities over the years has made the transmission of images and sound files (heart and lung sounds, coughs) faster and simpler. Pilot telemedicine experiments in ophthalmology and psychiatry have proven to be of immense benefit to the communities. Telemedicine's time is here, finally. While unleashing the full potential of telemedicine to help people, experts and government agencies must be mindful of the possible inadequacies of the medium, and securing sensitive medical information; such cognisance should guide the use of the technology.

[From an Editorial published in 'The Hindu' on April 17, 2020]

26. Which one of the following words from the passage means 'unavoidable'?

A. Inexorable B. Myriad
C. Excruciatingly D. Bandwagon

27. Which of the following best summarizes the main idea of the passage?

A. It is time to unleash the full potential of Telemedicine.

B. It is time to unleash the full potential of Telemedicine with cognisance of its possible flaws.

C. Technology has not been utilised to its fullest to suit the current needs.

D. People should not be skeptical about the advantages of telemedicine.

28. Which of the following is a significant factor contributing in slow employment of Telemedicine in India?

A. Telemedicine was never employed in India.

B. There was an absence of regulations regarding the use of telemedicine consultations and medication systems.

C. Telemedicinal Society of India failed in its efforts to promote the importance of such a system in the country.

D. All of the above

29. Telecommunication based medication has the potential for an easy outreach because:

A. Pilot experiments in telemedicine have been proved to be successful.

B. It helps in easier communication of medical images from one place to another.

C. It helps in securing sensitive medical information.

D. All of the above

30. What is the meaning of the expression 'Shot in the arm' used in the passage?

A. Hitting the nail on its head.

B. Bull's Eye

C. Positive Impact on something

D. All of the above

Section-II : Current Affairs Including GK

Directions (Qs. No. 31-35): *Read the passage carefully and answer these questions:*

Prime Minister Narendra Modi on Saturday said major global firms are looking at India as a major investment destination, which is reflected by a robust inflow of Foreign Direct Investment (FDI) last financial year, and through 'Atmanirbhar Bharat Abhiyan' (Self-Reliant India initiative) the country is shifting its focus from 'Make in India' to 'Make for world'. He said Independent India should be "vocal for local" and asked citizens to glorify Indian products to promote 'Atmanirbhar Bharat'. Unveiling his vision of a Self-Reliant India, the Prime Minister said that the government has unveiled over ₹ 110 lakh crore National Infrastructure Pipeline (NIP) to boost the economy and create jobs. "In order to rapidly modernise India, there is a need to give a new direction to overall infrastructure development," he said, adding that over 7,000 projects under NIP have been already identified. "This will be, in a way, a new revolution in the field of infrastructure. This is the time to end silos in infrastructure. There is a plan to connect the entire country with multi-model connectivity infrastructure," he said. NIP will play a crucial role in overcoming the adverse impact of Covid-19 on the economy and catapult the economy in a higher growth trajectory, he said. The government on December 31 last year unveiled the NIP with an aim to make India a $5 trillion economy by 2024-25. The focus of the infrastructure pipeline is to accelerate growth and create employment in both urban and rural areas.

Source: *Excerpt from Hindustan Times, written by Rajeev Jayaswal. (Dated 15th August, 2020)*

31. The Government announced a stimulus package under the Self Reliant India Scheme for the amount of ______.

A. 2 trillion B. 20 trillion

C. 5 trillion D. 100 trillion

32. Which of the following is not a goal of the stimulus package announced under the "Atmanirbhar India"?

A. It will help in alleviating the distress of migrants when they return to their villages.
B. It will help in achieving the goal of a self-sustainable rural economy.
C. It would boost the One Nation One Market objective and help India to become the food factory of the world.
D. It will help in elevating quality of life in urban areas.

33. Which of the following events can be seen as the stepping stone for the growth of the Foreign Direct Investment (FDI) in India?
A. The launch of 'Make in India' initiative in 2014.
B. The Economic liberalisation in the year 1991.
C. The Amendment in the FDI policy to increase the upper cap from 26% to 49%.
D. All of the above.

34. Which of the following is not related to the "Vocal for Local" initiative of the Indian Government?
A. Rebooting the MSMEs especially the Khadi and village industries.
B. Generating new opportunities of employment at the local level.
C. Creating new economic hubs through disinvestment and FDIs.
D. Promoting the indigenous manufacture and support through financial aid.

35. Under the National Infrastructure Pipeline, the Government plans to invest more than ₹ 102 lakh crore on infrastructure projects by 2024-25, with the Centre, States and the private sector to share the capital expenditure. What is the ratio of such expenditure by each of the stake holders?
A. 50:25:25 B. 40:40:20
C. 39:39:22 D. 34:33:33

Directions (Qs. No. 36-40): *Read the passage carefully and answer these questions:*

The central bank doesn't disclose its foreign exchange management strategy, but it was evident in the last few years that the rupee was not allowed to appreciate despite healthy inflows, resulting in a rapid build-up of foreign exchange. From a low of $275 billion in September of 2013, when rupee came under severe pressure due to so-called 'taper tantrums' by the US Federal Reserve, India now has record foreign exchange reserves of [1] billion, as on 21 August — a 95 per cent rise over seven years. Despite the Covid-19 pandemic, the foreign exchange kitty swelled by $62 billion since March. In this seven-year period, rupee ended the year with an appreciation against the dollar only once — in 2017. This year, the rupee is so far down by 2.04 per cent against the dollar. The latest RBI statement suggested that it is not uncomfortable with the appreciation in rupee, confirming the speculation among currency analysts that a departure was made in the exchange management policy.

The Reserve Bank of India (RBI) said that it will conduct liquidity operations worth ₹ 20,000 crore in two tranches through sale and purchase of government securities (G-Secs). The two open market operations (OMOs) of ₹ 10,000 crore each will be conducted on September 10 and 17, the central bank said in an official release. This is now the second such announcement in as many weeks. Last week, RBI had announced sale and purchase of G-Secs worth ₹ 20,000 crore, in two tranches, slated to be conducted on August 27 and September 3. In another move, RBI announced the infusion of ₹ 1 lakh crore in mid-September through long-term repo operations (LTROs) at floating rates, or the prevailing repo rate. Moreover, the central bank also gave an option to lenders who have earlier availed funds through LTROs, to reverse their transactions before maturity.

Source: *Excerpt taken from the Print.in, written by Manojit Saha. (Dated 2nd September, 2020.)*

36. Which of the following has been replaced by [1] in the above passage?
A. $ 537 B. $ 498
C. $ 502 D. $ 756

37. Which of the following economic policies have been recently used by the RBI to boost the economy during the current Pandemic situation?

A. FOREX SWAP
B. LTROs (Long Term Repo Operations)
C. OMOs (Open Market Operations)
D. All of the above.

38. Which of the following statements relate to the Long Term Repo Operations as measure to support the economy in corona pandemic situations?

A. It is a measure that is expected to bring down short-term rates and also boost investment in corporate bonds.
B. It would encourage banks to undertake maturity transformation smoothly and seamlessly so as to augment credit flows to productive sectors.
C. It will enhance liquidity in the banking system by ₹ 1 trillion.
D. All of the above.

39. Which of the following will be used as a platform for core banking solutions to implement the LTRO?

A. E-cartel B. E-kuber
C. E-CBS D. E-RBICBS

40. What is the notified amount of sum offered by the RBI under measures of the Foreign Exchange Swap?

A. $ 5 billion B. $ 16.71 billion
C. $ 16.21 billion D. $ 5.02 billion

Directions (Qs. No. 41-45): *Read the passage carefully and answer these questions:*

The first batch of five Rafale jets flew out of France on July 25 and will arrive in India on Wednesday, July 29, when the fighter jets will officially be inducted and join the Indian Air Force fleet in Haryana's Ambala. The fighter jets, built by French aviation firm [1], took off from the Merignac airbase in southern France's Bordeaux today and landed safely at Al Dhafra airbase in the UAE after a sortie of more than seven hours. The five aircraft will be the first tranche of the 36 planes bought by India from France in a ₹ 59,000 crore inter-governmental deal in 2016. "Delivery of ten aircraft has been completed on schedule. Five will stay back in France for training Mission. The delivery of all thirty six aircraft will be completed on schedule by the end of 2021," the Indian embassy in France said in a statement.

The Rafale fighter jets are capable of carrying a range of highly effective weapons, including the Meteor air-to-air missile and Scalp cruise missile. The Rafale jets will come with various India-specific modifications, including Israeli helmet-mounted displays, radar warning receivers, low-band jammers, 10-hour flight data recording, infra-red search and tracking systems among others. The Air Force has readied the required infrastructure to welcome the jets in its line-up.

Source: Excerpt taken from the NDTV,
Reported by Vishnu Som,
Edited by Shylaja Varma.
(Dated – 27th July, 2020)

41. The Rafale deal between India and France is seen to carry great strategic significance. Which of the following is directly impacted by this deal?

A. The Joint Strategic Vision of India-France Cooperation in the Indian Ocean Region.
B. The one belt one road mission of the China.
C. The Chinese initiative to build a new Silk route.
D. The trade route of the Middle East.

42. The Indian Air Force is also in the process of procuring a new generation medium-range modular air-to-ground weapon system Hammer to integrate with the Rafale jets. What does the term Hammer stands for?

A. Highly Advanced Modular Mutation Extended Range.
B. Highly Agile Modular Munition Extended Range.
C. Highly Advanced Modular Mitigation Extended Rafale.
D. Highly Agile Modular Munition Extended Rafale.

43. Which of the following has been replaced by [1] in the passage?

A. LAMSCO
B. LUAD Defence France
C. DASSAULT
D. BORESCOPE

44. Which of the following indigenous organisations is responsible for the design, assembly and fabrication of combat aircrafts in India?
A. DRDO B. HAL
C. DRAI D. ISRO

45. Which of the following organisations/ institutions is a major offset partner of India in the Rafale Deal?
A. Hindustan Aeronautics Limited
B. Reliance Defence Limited
C. Reliance Naval and Engineering Limited
D. Pipavav Defence

Directions (Qs. No. 46-50): *Read the passage carefully and answer these questions:*

On May 8, India's Defence Minister virtually inaugurated a new 80 km-long road in the Himalayas, connecting to the border with China, at the Lipulekh pass. The Nepali government protested immediately, contending that the road crosses territory that it claims and accusing India of changing the status quo without diplomatic consultations. Among the many escalatory moves since then, Nepal deployed police forces to the region, summoned the Indian ambassador in Kathmandu, and initiated a constitutional amendment to formalise and extend its territorial claims over approximately 400 sq km. India, on the other hand, has conveyed its openness to a dialogue but does not seem to share Nepal's sense of urgency: its initial statement agreed to a dialogue, but only after the COVID-19 crisis. India has been in effective possession of this territory for at least sixty years, although Nepal claims it conducted a census there in the early 1950s and refers to the 1815 Sugauli Treaty as legitimising its claims. But India's new road, up to the Lipulekh pass, is not an unprecedented change in the status quo. India has controlled this territory and built other infrastructure here before, besides conducting its administration and deploying military forces up to the border pass with China. The region is of strategic importance, and the new road is now one of the quickest links between Delhi and the Tibetan plateau. In a 2015 statement, China also recognised India's sovereignty by agreeing to expand trade through the Lipulekh pass.

Source: *Excerpt from the brookings. edu, written by Dr. Constantino Xavier. (Dated- 11th June, 2020)*

46. Which of the following incidents can be seen as the direct cause of the border dispute between India and Nepal?
A. The Defence Minister inaugurated a motorable link road that connects India and China.
B. The 2015 agreement between India and China for using the Lipulekh pass for trade.
C. India published a new map which showed the region of Kalapani as part of the Indian Territory.
D. All of the above.

47. The confusion between Nepal and India consists of a dispute over a trijunture of ____________.
A. Kali – Susta – Ganga.
B. Kalapani – Saraswati – Ganga.
C. Kalapani – Limpiyadhura – Lipulekh.
D. Kalapani – Limpiyadhura – Kali.

48. The treaty of Sugauli was signed between which of the following pairs?
A. India and Nepal
B. United Kingdom, India and Nepal
C. India, China and Nepal.
D. East India Company and Nepal

49. Recently Nepal has issued a map claiming Lipulekh pass as part of its territory included in the district of:
A. Kailali B. Darchula
C. Dipayal D. Doti

50. Which of the following rivers is called as Narayani River in Nepal?
A. Bramhaputra B. Gandak
C. Ganga D. Kali

Directions (Qs. No. 51-55): *Read the passage carefully and answer these questions:*

One thing struck us as a major difference between the new National Education Policy (NEP) 2020 and its predecessor. The earlier national policies on education (NPE) from 1986 and 1992 presented themselves as attempts to consolidate and build on earlier efforts, particularly the NPE, 1968. The new NEP 2020 policy, on the other hand, is very keen to establish that it is different from everything in the past, including in its name. Nowhere does this attitude come across as starkly as it does in the section on higher education.

It comes across fairly clearly on how the higher education ecosystem will be by 2040. By this time — if the policy has its way — the Indian higher education ecosystem will be populated with higher education institutions (HEI). These will comprise Universities and Colleges and the public and private sectors, all of which will be 'multi-disciplinary', with each populated by more than 3,000 students, with at least one "in or near every district". Universities will conduct research and post-graduate and under-graduate teaching, some research-intensive and others teaching-intensive. Colleges will largely teach at the under-graduate level, with a number of them having their medium of instruction in either bilingual or local/Indian languages. The colleges can manifest in clusters around universities as constituent colleges or may be standalone autonomous ones. Ideally, all HEIs will eventually become "independent self-governing institutions" with considerable "faculty and institutional autonomy". They will have complied with a series of regulatory exercises that are light-but-tight and will be operated by a large number of private accreditors, overseen by a new set of regulatory institutions at the national level.

Source: *Excerpt taken from downtoearth.org.in, written by Nitin Mehta & Gagan Mehta. (Dated 14th August, 2020)*

51. Which of the following statements are not true in relation to the changes envisioned by the NEP 2020?

A. The NEP 2020 aims at making India a global knowledge superpower.

B. The renaming of the Ministry of Human Resource Development to the Ministry of Education.

C. The development of National Course Curriculum to provide new curriculum by 2021.

D. The New Education Policy aims to facilitate an inclusive, participatory and holistic approach

52. The NEP 2020 aims to provide a holistic change to the current education system in India. Which of the following is not related to the aim of NEP 2020?

A. Universalization of education from preschool to secondary level with 100% Gross Enrolment Ratio.

B. To bring 20 million out of school children back into the mainstream through an open schooling system.

C. Vocational Education to start from Class 6 with Internships.

D. To achieve 80% Gross Enrolment Ratio at the under graduate level.

53. Which of the following is proposed as a change in the structure of institutions responsible for affiliation and accreditation under the NEP 2020?

A. Higher Education Commission of India (HECI) will be set up as a single umbrella body for the entire higher education.

B. University Grant Commission to be renamed as AICTE.

C. National Affiliation and Accreditation Council to be renamed as National Standard Council of India.

D. National Council for Education Research and Teaching to be renamed as BCERT.

54. Which of the following is not a vertical under the Higher Education Commission of India (HECI)?

A. National Higher Education Regulatory Council (NHERC)

B. Higher Education Grants Council (HEGC)

C. National Educational Council (NEC)
D. National Accreditation Council (NAC)

55. What is the proposed percentage of expenditure for education out of GDP under the NEP 2020?

A. 11 per cent B. 6 per cent
C. 4.6 per cent D. 9 per cent

Directions (Qs. No. 56-60): *Read the passage carefully and answer these questions:*

Days after India-Pakistan tensions spilled over into a meeting of the Shanghai Cooperation Organisation (SCO), External Affairs Minister S, Jaishankar and Pakistan Foreign Minister Shah Mehmood Qureshi are expected to meet via a video conference at the South Asian Association for Regional Cooperation (SAARC) meeting on September 24. "All member countries have confirmed participation in the meeting, to be chaired by Pradeep Kumar Gyawali, of Nepal. The respective Foreign Ministers will take part," sources familiar with preparations for the meeting told The Hindu, referring to the eight members of SAARC, including, Bangladesh, India, Nepal, Pakistan and Sri Lanka. A senior Indian official also confirmed that Mr. Jaishankar will attend despite the incident at the SCO virtual meeting of National Security Advisors on Tuesday. During that meeting, National Security Advisor Ajit Doval stormed out after he saw that the Pakistan Special Advisor on National Security Moeed Yusuf had used a map of Pakistan that claimed Indian Territory.

"This was in blatant disregard to the advisory by the host against it and in violation of the norms of the meeting. After consultation with the host, the Indian side left the meeting in protest at that juncture," the MEA had said about the incident. When asked, the sources said that no specific guidelines on background or maps have been issued by the SAARC Secretariat in Kathmandu that is also the Chair of the SAARC at present, but they hope it would go "smoothly". A meeting of SAARC Finance Ministers, where an Additional Secretary represented India instead of Finance Minister Nirmala Sitharaman, and Pakistan was represented by its Special Advisor on Finance, took place on Wednesday without incident.

Source: *Excerpt taken from The Hindu, written by Suhasini Haider. (Dated 17th September, 2020.)*

56. Which of the following has been replaced by [1] in the passage?

A. Prime Minister
B. Minister of Finance
C. Minister of External Affairs
D. Minister of Home Affairs

57. Which of the following Nations is part of the South Asian Association for Regional Cooperation?

A. Indonesia B. Thailand
C. Myanmar D. Maldives

58. Which of the following has been replaced by [5] in the passage?

A. Russia B. China
C. Japan D. Pakistan

59. India had not agreed to attend a summit hosted in Pakistan, but it remains an important promoter of the SAARC process. In which of the following years the SAARC leaders' summit was held lately?

A. 2018 B. 2014
C. 2016 D. 2019

60. The above passage mentions about Pakistan's Special Advisor on National Security Moeed Yusuf using a map of Pakistan claiming Indian Territory. Which of the following territory is in context here?

A. Junagadh B. Aksai Chin
C. Pangong Tso D. Limpiyadhura

Directions (Qs. No. 61-66): *Read the passage carefully and answer these questions:*

In the middle of a pandemic, the geopolitics of the world's most troubled region took a historic turn this week, when the UAE and Israel, under the benevolent gaze of US President Donald Trump, signed an agreement to "normalise" relations. The deal opens up new opportunities for India to play a much larger role in the regional security and stability in the Gulf, where New Delhi enjoys special relations with both Abu Dhabi and Jerusalem. The barebones of the deal envisages establishing regular diplomatic relations between the UAE, the rising influential power in the Gulf, and Israel, the "Incredible Hulk" of the region, but a country officially not on speaking terms with most of its Arab neighbours. In his first tweet, Crown Prince Mohammed bin Zayed said: "During a call with President Trump and Prime Minister Netanyahu, an agreement was reached to stop further Israeli annexation of Palestinian territories. The UAE and Israel also agreed to cooperation and setting a roadmap towards establishing a bilateral relationship." In return, Israel agreed to 'suspend' its annexation plans for West Bank that would have been deeply destabilising. Benjamin Netanyahu gets a diplomatic victory, which may be short-lived, given the nature of Israeli politics. But Israel gets a diplomatic and economic opening with the big power in the Gulf that could open other doors, give its security interests legitimacy and, perhaps, open the door to Middle East peace.

Many of the other Arab powers, such as Oman, Bahrain, Egypt and Jordan, apart from the big global powers, and India, have welcomed the deal. Iran has slammed it, as have Turkey and Syria. Saudi Arabia has been very quiet. Given the close ties between Mohammed bin Zayed and Mohammed bin Salman, it is unthinkable that KSA was not consulted, particularly when the US is the third pole in this agreement. The deal gives UAE pole position as the premier Gulf Arab power, with diplomatic leverage with Israel and the US. "This deal is about positioning in Washington, DC," said James Dorsey, Gulf and Middle East expert.

Source: *Excerpt from the Economic Times, written by Indrani Bagchi. (Dated – 16th August, 2020)*

61. The US is seen as a major role player in the peace deal between Israel and UAE. Which of the following is not a reason for the involvement of US in the deal?

A. The deal grants a diplomatic win to the US President Donald Trump ahead of the Presidential election.

B. The efforts of the USA to bring the war in Afghanistan to an end have not been a success yet.

C. The efforts of USA to bring peace between Israel and the Palestinians have not been successful yet.

D. The deal gives a central strategic rule to USA in the Middle East.

62. Which of the following is true in relation to the stake of Palestine in the peace deal between UAE and Israel?

A. Israel has recognised Palestine as an Independent Nation.

B. This can be an opportunity for the Palestine to establish diplomatic relations with Israel.

C. The deal marks both a win and setback to the Israel-Palestine relations.

D. A peace treaty would also be signed between Israel and Palestine.

63. Which of the following is not a direct impact of the peace deal in the Middle East region?

A. The deal smoothens the UAE's international campaign to be seen as a beacon of tolerance in the Middle East.

B. It puts the UAE as leader in a regional power dynamics among neighbouring Gulf Arab states.

C. The deal gives Netanyahu a domestic boost at a time when Israel's coalition government is in crisis due to coalition compulsions.

D. The deal marks a historic day and a significant step towards peace in the Middle East.

64. The peace deal between Israel and UAE can also be seen as a great opportunity for India in the Middle East region. Which of the following is not related to strategic goals of India in the Middle East?

A. India should revamp its defence and security relations with the UAE.

B. India should move fast to capture the extended neighbourhood market before it comes under the influence of China.

C. India should ensure space for Iran in any future security deal in the region.

D. None of the above

65. Which of the following is correct?

A. Israel does not have a Constitution.

B. Israeli Constitution is like ordinary law.

C. There is no Constitution but a Basic Law of 1950.

D. Israel has a Constitution of 1967.

66. Israel is a theocratic Jewish state but it follows legal pluralism. Accordingly it has:

A. Jewish Courts to decide cases of all religious communities.

B. Secular Courts will apply Uniform Civil Code in respect of all communities.

C. Each religious community has its own Religious Court to deal with Personal law disputes.

D. No distinction between Personal law and Public law.

Section-III : Legal Reasoning

Directions (Qs. No. 67-70): *Read the passage carefully and answer these questions:*

The COVID-19 pandemic has taken the entire world hostage in less than four months, and the global economy has been hit the hardest with governments across the globe implementing stringent policies including lockdown to control the coronavirus outbreak. The pandemic today presents unprecedented challenges and impediments to businesses in conducting their normal operations. The lockdown across the world has caused delays in the performance of contracts and transactions. Now, the question that arises is whether the current situation can enable parties to a contract to alter their obligations with non-compliance of terms neither being regarded as a "default committed by any party" nor a "breach of contract"? There are certain well-accepted practices for dealing with such extraordinary situations in commercial transactions by the inclusion of force majeure & material adverse effect (MAE) clauses. Determination of the types of circumstances so covered by the force majeure clause contained in a contract is essential. Provisions of force majeure often cover natural disasters like hurricanes, floods, and earthquakes as "acts of God." Other covered events may include war, terrorism, civil disorder, fire, disease medical epidemics or by reasons of applicable laws or regulations. Broadly, the Courts have interpreted the term "Force Majeure" as an event that can neither be anticipated nor controlled by either of the contracting parties. A force majeure clause applies in the context of ongoing contractual arrangements, whereas, an MAE or material adverse change (MAC) clause applies to the allocation of risk in transactions before their closure or completion. Pandemic and related consequences such as government action is a type of event covered by a force majeure clause, however, its impact on the affected party's ability to perform its contractual obligations may vary depending upon contractual terms. It is common for force majeure clauses to specify the impact that the event or circumstances in question must have, in order for the clause to be triggered. References may be made, for example, to the event or circumstances having "prevented", "hindered" or "delayed" performance. These terms require different levels of impact on performance before a party can claim recourse to these clauses. In other words, the force majeure and MAC clauses act as an exception to what would otherwise be treated as a breach of contract. Certain contracts may state that, if a force majeure clause is applied, the contract may automatically be terminated. On the other hand, some contracts may even state that the duty to fulfil the contractual obligation may be suspended for a certain period of time and if the force majeure event is not curbed or treated even after such time, then eventually the contract may be terminated. Though there cannot be a one-size-fits-all solution to this question, and it depends upon how the force majeure clause is worded in a specific contract; and in the absence of the same, applicable laws related to the same will be required to be taken into consideration.

[Excerpt from Business Today, by Ranjana Roy Gawai, April 17, 2020]

67. Based on the Author's argument in passage above, which of the following is correct?

A. Force Majeure Clauses, generally have a uniform impact on the performance of Contracts in all the cases.

B. The Impact on the performance of Contracts by the usage of Force Majeure Clauses is dependent upon the way such clauses have been constructed in a particular Contract.

C. Both Force Majeure and Material Adverse Change Clauses have similar impact on the performance of Contracts.

D. All of the above.

68. Imagine, there is a domestic commercial Contract for supply of certain goods for certain price between A and B. However, in pursuance of the same, both A and B forget to negotiate and agree on the terms of a Force Majeure event and the Contractual document does not contain the Force Majeure clause. In such a situation, what would be the fate of the Contract in the event like that of COVID 19?

A. As the parties did not negotiate on the Force Majeure Clause, either of them cannot take an exception to the Breach of Contract.

B. The parties can invoke the Material Adverse Change Clause.

C. In absence of such clauses in the Contract, the Courts may resort to the applicable law, i.e., the Indian Contract Act, 1872 to give relief to the parties.

D. None of the above.

69. In the same fact situation as mentioned above with a modification that there is a Force Majeure Clause in the Contract between A and B, let us suppose, that B, who was to supply goods to A on certain date and time, faced issues in relation to procurement of goods due to mill strike and also because of rise in prices of goods. In this case, can B claim the suspension of performance of Contract on the basis of the Force Majeure Clause?

A. Yes, B can, depending upon the way, the Force Majeure Clause is worded.

B. Such situation cannot be covered under Force Majeure as it is just a case of disappointed expectations and hence B cannot invoke the clause. It is merely a case of commercial hardship.

C. B can invoke the Force Majeure clause as the clause is too broad to cover such situations.

D. None of the above.

70. Typically, the MAE (Material Adverse Change) provision in an agreement contemplates events which if they occur, or are likely occur, would have a materially adverse change or effect on the assets, business, property, liabilities, financial condition, results, operations of the target or that affects the ability of the transacting parties to consummate the transaction or the validity or enforceability of the transacting parties to its rights and remedies under the transaction documents . Which of the following sample clauses in a contract resembles an MAE clause?

A.. "In the event either party is unable to perform its obligations under the terms of this agreement because of Act of God, strikes, equipment of transmission failure or damage reasonably beyond its control, such party shall not be liable for damages to the other for any damages resulting from such failure to perform..."

B. "Except with respect to payment obligations under this agreement, no party shall be liable for, nor such party shall be considered in breach of this agreement due to, any failure to perform its obligations under this agreement as a result of cause beyond its control, including any earthquake, labour problem, unavailability of supplies..."

C. Both of the above.
D. None of the above.

Directions (Qs. No. 71-75): *Read the passage carefully and answer these questions:*

The issue of Obscenity has vexed the Courts in India and abroad for a long time now. The intriguing question has always been the same, i.e., what should be the standards to qualify something as obscene in the eyes of law? In the United Kingdom, way back in 1868, the Court laid down the Hicklin test in Regina v. Hicklin (1868 L.R. 2 Q.B. 360), and held that: "*The test of Obscenity is whether the tendency of the matter charged as Obscenity is to deprave and corrupt those whose minds are open to such immoral influences and into whose hands a publication of this sort may fall.*" Hicklin test postulated that a publication has to be judged for obscenity based on isolated passages of a work considered out of context and judged by their apparent influence on most susceptible readers, such as children or weak-minded adults. However, this test was later rejected by most of the jurisdictions. There were many judgments where it was stipulated by the Indian Courts that, Obscenity has to be judged in the context of contemporary social mores, current socio-moral attitude of the community and the prevalent norms of acceptability/ susceptibility of the community, in relation to matters in issue. [For example, in Ranjit D. Udeshi v. State of Maharashtra AIR 1965 SC 881; Chandrakant Kalyandas Kakodar v. State of Maharashtra 1969 (2) SCC 687 etc.] These judgements indicated that the concept of Obscenity would change with the passage of time and what might have been "obscene" at one point of time would not be considered as obscene at a later period. This came to be known as "Community Standards Test". In Bobby Art International & Ors. v. Om Pal Singh Hoon (1996) 4 SCC 1, the Court, upholding the Community standards test held that, complete message and context of the objectionable scene/firm/picture etc., needs to be examined in order to find out whether the alleged material is obscene or not.

71. A, daily local newspaper called 'Ramanand Bazar Patrika' having wide circulation in Anandnagar published, on 1st July, 2019, an article with a picture of Boris Becker, a world renowned Tennis player, posing nude with his dark-skinned fiancee by name Barbara Feltus, a film actress, which was photographed by none other than her father. The article states that, in an interview, both Boris Becker and Barbara Feltus spoke freely about their engagement, their lives and future plans and the message they wanted to convey to the people at large, for posing to such a photograph. Article picturises Boris Becker as a strident protester of the pernicious practice of "Apartheid". Further, it was stated that the purpose of the photograph was also to signify that love champions over hatred. Will the alleged picture classify as an Obscene Material in India?

A. No, according to the Hicklin Test, it will not classify as Obscene.
B. Yes, according to the Community Standards Test, the picture will classify as Obscene.
C. No, according to the Community Standards Test, the picture will not classify as Obscene.
D. Both (A) and (C).

72. The difference between Hicklin Test and Community Standards Test is:

A. The former focuses on the susceptibility of the minds of individuals to get corrupted while the later hinges upon the context, intended meaning and contemporaneous socio-cultural environment of the society.
B. As per Hicklin Test, a nude picture of a women *per se* can be obscene while as per the later, the picture should be suggestive of deprave mind and designed to excite sexual passion in persons who are likely to see it.
C. The former considers Obscenity as a changing concept with changing times while the later does not.
D. All of the above

73. The issue of 'Obscenity' is fundamentally related with which of the following?

A. Freedom of Religion of an individual.
B. Freedom of Speech and Expression of an individual.
C. Right to Privacy of an individual.
D. All of the above.

74. Consider the following situations. Choose the correct option as per the Hicklin's Test.

1. A Movie scene where there are rows of Jewish naked men and women, shown frontally, being led into the Gas Chambers of Nazi Concentration Camp. Not only they are about to die but they are stripped off their basic dignity in the last moments of their life.
2. The controversial movie scene of Phoolan Devi, the Bandit queen where she is paraded naked and made to draw water from the well within the circle of a hundred men.

A. 1 is Obscene but 2 is not.
B. 2 is Obscene but 1 is not.
C. Both 1 and 2 are Obscene.
D. Neither 1 and 2 are Obscene.

75. An activist, while being semi-nude, allowed her body to be used as a canvas to paint on by her two minor children who were properly clothed. She uploaded this video of hers on an online platform with a message that she intended to normalise the female form for her children and not allow distorted ideas about sexuality to pervade their mind. An advocate who sees the video, registers a case of Obscenity against her. Is it a case of Obscenity as per the Community Standards Test?

A. This is a pure case of Obscenity and she is spreading it.
B. This is a pure case of Obscenity as well as Child Pornography as her children were exposed to her nudity.
C. This is not a case of Obscenity because as per the Community Standards Test the video must not be seen in isolation but in the contextual set up of the message that the activist has put on normalisation of a female's sexuality.
D. This is a case of Obscenity as per the Community Standards Test as the video was blatantly obscene.

Directions (Qs. No. 76-80): *Read the passage carefully and answer these questions:*

On 7th May 2020, a major leakage of Styrene gas was reported from the plastics-manufacturing plant 'LG Polymers' located on the outskirts of the Visakhapatnam city. The accident took place when the cooling system of a polymers plant got clogged due to the mismanagement of factory workers and resulted in turning the city into a gas chamber. The gas which leaked was styrene gas, which is a 'hazardous chemical' under Rule 2(e) plus Entry 583 of Schedule I of the Manufacture, Storage and Import of Hazardous Chemical Rules 1989.

Principle 1: Polluter Pays Principle

The 'Doctrine of Polluter Pays' is a well-established principle of environmental law, which places an obligation of compensating the damage to the people who ought to reimburse it and also have the capacity to disburse it. The principle explicitly affirms that the person who damages or destructs the environment has the absolute obligation to bear the cost of ameliorating the environment. In *Enviro Legal Action v. Union of India* case, the Apex Court of India held that the polluter is legally responsible to reimburse the individual sufferers as well as pay for the revitalization of the damaged environment.

Principle 2: Principle of Strict Liability

The principle of Strict Liability was established in the year 1868 in the case of *Rylands v. Fletcher*, where the Court held that any person who uses his/her land in an 'unnatural manner' and who keeps any 'hazardous substance' on such premises would be held liable under the principle of strict liability for any 'damage' occurred on the 'escape' of such perilous substance. However, the person is liable only when there is non-natural use of land; the principle also restricts liability when the escape is due to an act of strangers, Act of God, for example a natural calamity; due to the person injured or when it happens with the consent of the person injured or with statutory authority.

Principle 3: Principle of Absolute Liability

The absolute liability is a stringent form of Strict Liability as it is devoid of any exceptions that were mentioned under the earlier principle, for the first time in the case of *M.C. Mehta v. Union of India*. This principle implies that whenever an enterprise is engaged in any dangerous or hazardous activity that threatens the people working in the enterprise and those living nearby, it owes an absolute and non-delegable duty to the community that no harm will be caused. If harm is indeed caused, the enterprise will have to compensate for damages, and can't use exceptions provided in the case of strict liability. The enterprise can't claim that the harm has not been caused due to negligence (absence of due care) or that it had taken all reasonable precautions.

76. Under which of the following principles, will the company LG Polymers be liable?
A. Polluter Pays Principle
B. Strict Liability
C. Absolute Liability
D. All of the above

77. As per the Polluter Pays Principle, LG Polymers will be liable to pay:
A. Amount of Money for restoration of environment only.
B. Amount of Money for restoration of environment and compensation to Individuals who suffered the loss.
C. Compensation to the victims.
D. None of the above.

78. A company ABC limited operates an industrial chemical plant in the city of Azadnagar. Due to an earthquake on July 22, 2020, the valves of the reactors in the plant get damaged due to which the operators could not properly transport the hazardous gas for chemical vaporisation, resulting in the gas leakage. The gas leakage resulted in the death of 12 workers of the plant and also some people living nearby the Plant. In this situation, in order to decipher the liability of ABC Limited, choose the best option:
A. ABC Limited can be held liable under the principles of Strict and Absolute Liability and Polluter pays principle as well.
B. ABC Limited can be held liable under the Polluter Pays Principle and the Principle of Absolute Liability, but can be exempted under the rule of Strict Liability.
C. ABC Limited will not be held liable under any of the Principles.
D. ABC Limited will be held liable under Strict and Absolute Liability principles but the Principle of Polluter Pays will not be applicable to this situation.

79. The argument of LG Polymers that, they did not know that the Styrene Gas could leak:
A. is a strong argument and can reduce their liability under the Polluter Pays Principle.
B. is a strong argument and can reduce their liability under the Strict Liability Principle.
C. is a weak argument and will not help in reducing the liability of LG Polymers under any of the principles.
D. is a weak argument but may help in reducing their liability under the Strict Liability Principle.

80. XYZ is a company operating a Pesticide Factory in the city of Rampur. On one day, due to the negligence of Factory staff, there is a leakage of the Pesticide gas as a result of which, many pests and insects which feed on the plantation crops in the nearby farm are killed. There is no harm caused to the people living nearby or the workers of the Pesticide Factory. However, the leakage was so humungous that it reduced the quality of air in the city causing breathing problems for the people living around in the area. In this case,
A. XYZ will be absolutely liable but not strictly liable.
B. XYZ will not be liable under the Strict and Absolute liability principles because the leakage only killed the pests and insects.

C. XYZ's liability under the Strict and Absolute liability principles will depend upon the inquiry as to whether the leaked pesticide gas was a hazardous substance/ activity or chemical or not and; XYZ will be liable under the Polluter Pays Principle.

D. XYZ will not be liable under the Polluter Pays Principle.

Directions (Qs. No. 81-85): *Read the passage carefully and answer these questions:*

Principle of Natural Justice is derived from the word *'Jus Natural'* of the Roman law and it is closely related to Common law and moral principles but is not codified. It is a law of nature which is not derived from any statute or constitution. The principle of Natural Justice is adhered to by all the citizens of civilised State with Supreme importance. Natural justice simply means to make a sensible and reasonable decision making procedure on a particular issue. Sometimes, it doesn't matter what is the reasonable decision but in the end, what matters is the procedure and who all are engaged in taking the reasonable decision. It is not restricted within the concept of 'fairness' it has different colours and shades which vary from the context. Basically, natural justice consists of 3 rules.

The first one is *"Hearing rule"* which states that the person or party who is affected by the decision made by the Panel of expert members should be given a fair opportunity to express his point of view to defend himself. Secondly, *"Bias rule* generally expresses that Panel of expert should be free from bias while taking the decision. The decision should be given in a free and fair manner which can fulfil the rule of natural justice. And thirdly, *"Reasoned Decision"* which states that order, decision or judgement of the Court given by the Presiding authorities with a valid and reasonable ground. The principles of Natural Justice have been adopted and followed by the judiciary to protect public rights against the arbitrary decision by the administrative authority. One can easily see that the rule of natural justice include the concept of fairness: they stay alive and support to safeguard the fair dealing.

Source: Excerpt taken from blog.ipleaders.in (Dated - 12th June, 2019)

81. "*Nemo Judex in causa sua*" or the principle that '*No one can be a judge in his own case*', relates to which of the following rule of the Natural Justice?

A. Bias rule

B. Reasoned decision rule

C. Hearing rule

D. All of the above.

82. Mr. X is a Public Servant, employed in a PSU and Mrs Y who is the wife of Mr. X is also an employee of the same PSU. Ms A files a complaint against Mr. X for sexual harassment at workplace before the ICC (Internal Complaints Committee), which is headed by Mrs Y. After completing her inquiry she held that Mr. X is guilty and recommended disciplinary proceedings against him. Now, on what grounds Mr. X may challenge her findings?

A. Mrs Y is an employee of the same institution and the inquiry should have been conducted by a person outside the institution.

B. The complaint was filed by a female employee, so the inquiry must have been conducted by a male employee.

C. Mrs Y is the wife of Mr. X and she holds a personal bias in the case, so the inquiry should not have been conducted by her.

D. Mr. X being the accused should have conducted the inquiry himself.

83. Mr. A is a judge and he is also the landlord of Mr. B, who resides in an apartment owned by Mr. A. Due to non-payment of rent for 3 consecutive months, Mr. A served an eviction notice to Mr. B. Now, choose the most appropriate option amongst the following.

A. Being a judge himself, Mr. A cannot issue such notice of eviction.

B. Mr. A can issue such notice because it is his duty as a Judge, apart from being a landlord.

C. Such notice is illegal as Mr. B was not given an opportunity to present his case.

D. Mr. A issued such notice in his personal capacity as a landlord and not being a judge.

84. Which of the following is not in violation of the principles of Natural justice?

A. Withholding of an increment of a public servant without giving him an opportunity to defend.

B. Non-renewal of a contract of employment of an employee after the period of contract is over.

C. Initiating a departmental inquiry against a public servant, without giving him an opportunity to submit representation during such inquiry.

D. All of the above.

85. On the basis of your understanding about Natural Justice in the passage above, state which of the following is true:

A. Adherence to the reasoned decision rule is not required if other two rules are complied with.

B. Compliance of bias rule itself rejects the need of the hearing and the reasoned decision rule.

C. Principle of Natural Justice is incomplete without the compliance of any of its rules.

D. The Reasoned Decision rule is a substitute for the bias rule.

Directions (Qs. No. 86-90): *Read the passage carefully and answer these questions:*

Tension prevailed in the Jawahar area in Palghar district after three Mumbai residents, travelling in a Ford Ecosport to Silvassa, were allegedly lynched late on Thursday night. The Kasa police said the incident occurred near Gadakchinchale village under their jurisdiction. "Information received by us indicates that the three occupants of the SUV hailed from Kandivali in Mumbai and were going to attend a funeral in Silvassa," Superintendent of Police Gaurav Singh, Palghar police said. A large mob of villagers surrounded the car within a matter of minutes and started attacking it with sticks, irons rods and their bare hands, leading to the death of all three occupants. "One of our patrolling vehicles later spotted the severely injured trio lying on the road and stopped to find out the matter. However, our team was also attacked by the mob and the vehicle pelted with stones. Our personnel had to flee and were unable to rescue to the victims;" an officer with the Kasa police said. A wireless alert was sent out later apprising all police stations and units of the incident following which reinforcements were sent to the village and a combing operation was undertaken. "Prima facie information indicates that the trio were mistaken for thieves and attacked. The villagers were on edge due to the ongoing lockdown and unavailability of essential supplies. For the past few days, several rumours have been doing the rounds on social media about thieves and dacoits targetting villages on the highway. As a result, villagers have been patrolling the highway and stopping late night travellers on suspicion," the officer said.

Source: Excerpt from The Hindu, written by Alok Deshpande (22/04/2020)

86. Which of the following statements given below justifies criminalisation of Mob Lynching?

A. In a democracy the actual power rests with the people and their actions cannot be penalised by the state.

B. There is no law in India which specifically prohibits mob lynching and therefore it is a justified act of the people.

C. It is impossible to punish the wrongdoer in case of Mob Lynching.

D. Violence cannot be a tool to implement the will of the majority and such actions are failure of the state.

87. Which of the following statement justifies the criminalisation of mob lynching as a distinct offence apart from 'Murder'?

A. The offence of Murder is committed by a single individual or a group but mob lynching involves a large group of individuals.

B. When violence is committed by a mob it creates a situation of terror and anarchy having potential to disturb the public peace for a longer period.

C. Mob lynching is an offence which supports the idea of 'might is right', and cannot be accepted in a democratic society.

D. All of the above

88. The above passage states about the existence of rumours in the area regarding the thieves and dacoits robbing the villagers or committing child lifting. In the light of this proposition which of the following statement is correct?

A. The villagers should not be punished as there was a genuine mistake on their part.

B. The villagers should be punished as they do not have any right to punish any person unless he is an offender.

C. The villagers should be punished as no individual in the country is entitled to take law in his own hand and punish the wrongdoer.

D. The villagers should not be punished as they have the right of private defence against such incidents under which they can even kill a person.

89. In the light of the above passage which of the following incidents of mob violence would be justified?

A. A group of people committing violence against people who are selling meat of an animal considered to be sacred under their religious beliefs.

B. The residents of a boy's hostel caught a drug paddler selling drugs in their hostel and killed him by beating.

C. The villagers injured a woman by pelting stone on her considering her to be witch.

D. None of the above.

90. **Assertion (A):** Mob Lynching can be justified only in circumstances where the religious sentiments or feelings of a large group of people is associated.

Reason (R): Religious sentiments and feelings are of paramount consideration for the state and should not be interfered with.

A. Both (A) and (R) are correct

B. (A) is correct but (R) is incorrect

C. Both (A) and (R) are incorrect

D. (A) is incorrect but (R) is correct.

Directions (Qs. No. 91-95): *Read the passage carefully and answer these questions:*

The bench of Dr. DY Chandrachud and MR Shah, JJ has refused to transfer to CBI the criminal cases lodged against Republic TV Editor in-Chief Arnab Goswami for alleged defamatory news show telecast on April 21 in connection with the Palghar mob-lynching case. It also quashed all FIRs against Arnab Goswami except one which was filed in Nagpur and which has been transferred to Mumbai via order dated 24.04.2020.

[Excerpt from SCC Online Blog, May 19, 2020]

Delivering the verdict, Justice Chandrachud said, *Article 32 of the Constitution constitutes recognition of the constitutional duty entrusted to this Court to protect the fundamental rights of citizens. The exercise of journalistic freedom lies at the core of speech and expression protected by Article 19(1)(a). The petitioner is a media journalist. The airing of views on television shows which he hosts is in the exercise of his fundamental right to speech and expression under Article 19(1)(a). India's freedoms will rest safe as long as journalists can speak truth to power without being chilled by a threat of reprisal...Free citizens cannot exist when the news media is chained to adhere to one position. Yuval Noah Harari has put it succinctly in his recent book titled "21 Lessons for the 21st Century": "Questions you cannot answer are usually far better for you than answers you cannot question."*

[Excerpt from Arnab Ranjan Goswami vs Union Of India on 19 May, 2020]

91. The above passage mentions about the Journalist's request to transfer the case to the CBI (Central Bureau of Investigation) for investigation. What could be the appropriate reason for such request?

A. The CBI is a central investigating agency and conducts more scientific investigation.

B. Where State government is an interested party, the investigation conducted by the state police, may be biased.

C. The FIRs relate to an offence of defamation of the President of a national party, so the matter should be investigated by the CBI.

D. None of the above.

92. The above passage quotes the observation of the Court in relation to freedom of speech and expression as, "Questions you cannot answer are better than questions you cannot question." Now, based on such observation, chose the most appropriate option which describes the scope of such questions.

A. The term "questions" mentioned are not subject to limitations imposed upon the Freedom of Speech and Expression.

B. Those question are limited to the information warranted by the person.

C. The court is referring to the right to information through the above quote.

D. The questions are also subject to limitations imposed upon the Freedom of Speech and Expression.

93. It is an established principle of law that the offence of defamation (harming the reputation) has many exceptions and the imputation of truth is one of those, but the accused must prove that such imputation was true and also for the public good. In the light of this statement which of the following questions/ statements are not defamatory?

A. An article published in a newspaper about the unaccounted property of a public servant in the form of a questionnaire.

B. A question to a female actress about her sexual relationship with a married man.

C. A question to a public servant about his extramarital relationship with a colleague.

D. An Article published in a magazine stating a female politician as 'B grade' actress.

94. In the above passage, the Court ordered for the merging of different FIRs into one and the investigation to be conducted at Mumbai. What is the reason behind such order?

A. Multiple FIRs mean multiple investigations and the same might cause hardships to the accused.

B. The first FIR was registered at Mumbai and the investigation should be conducted at Mumbai.

C. The accused resides at Mumbai and the investigation should be conducted only at Mumbai.

D. Multiple FIRs are frivolous and there is only one cause of action.

95. Defamation is punishable:

A. Both as a Civil wrong as well as a Crime.

B. Only as a Civil wrong.

C. Only as a Criminal wrong.

D. None of the above.

Directions (Qs. No. 96-100): *Read the passage carefully and answer these questions:*

Common intention implies a pre-arranged plan and acting in concert pursuant to the plan. Common intention comes into being prior to the commission of the act, which need not be a long gap. To bring common intention into effect a pre-concert is not necessarily be proved, but it may well develop on the spot as between a number of persons and could be inferred from facts and circumstances of each case. For example A and B caught hold of C where only B stabbed C with a knife but A is also liable for murder as there was a pre-concerted action. In the case Pandurang v. State of Hyderabad, Supreme court emphasized on this point that prior concert need not be something always very much prior to the incident, but could well be something that may develop on the spot, on the spur of the moment.

Common Intention and Similar Intention

Common intention does not mean similar intention of several persons. To constitute common intention it is necessary that the intention of each one of them be known to the rest of them and shared by them. In the case of Dukhmochan Pandey v. State of Bihar, the Supreme Court, held that: *"Common intention which developed at the spur of the moment is different from the similar intention actuated a number of person at the same time....the distinction between a common intention and similar intention may be fine, but is nonetheless a real one and if overlooked, may lead to miscarriage of justice...."* The mere presence of accused together is not sufficient to hold that they shared the common intention to commit the offence in question. It is necessary that the intention of each one of 'several persons' be known to each other for constituting common intention.

96. A gang of six members went to a bank, armed with weapons to commit a heist. While five of the gang members went inside the bank, Mr. A (the sixth member) waited outside the bank to alert them on any threat. During the heist one of the gang members fired a gun at the branch manager, as a result he died. All five escaped but Mr. A was caught and arrested. Now, choose the most appropriate option as per the principle stated in the above passage.

A. Mr. A is not liable for murder as he was outside the bank and there was no common intention.

B. Mr. A along with all other members of the gang are liable for murder as there was common intention.

C. Only that person is liable for murder who actually fired the gun.

D. Mr. A is liable only for the heist and no other offence.

97. Raman and Raghav were riding on a motorcycle on a busy street, suddenly Aman (another biker) bumped into their bike. A heated argument started between the three of them. While Raghav started abusing Aman, Raman hit Aman with an iron rod lying on the road and as a consequence he died. Now, chose the correct option.

A. Both Raman and Raghav are liable for murder as there was a common intention developed on the spot.

B. Raghav is not liable for murder as there was no common intention to kill Aman.

C. No one is liable as Aman was a wrongdoer himself and he started the fight.

D. Only Raghav is liable for murder as he started abusing Aman.

98. After reading the passage which of the following is not correct in relation to the difference between Common and Similar intention?

A. Similar intention is developed prior to the commission of offence but the common intention is developed only at the time of commission of offence.

B. Under Common intention each of the offender is equally liable for the offence but under similar intention each of the offender is differently liable.

C. In order to determine the existence of Similar or Common intention, one must analyse the fact and circumstances of each case.

D. The boundary between Similar and Common intention is very fine and it may sometime overlap.

99. Mr. X and Mr. Y entered into a house at night to commit theft, while committing theft Mr. Y committed sexual assault on a minor girl of aged 11 years. Identify for which of the following offences Mr. X is liable for.

A. Both Theft and Sexual Assault as there was a Common intention.

B. Only Theft as there was a Similar intention.

C. Only Theft as Mr. X had a different intention from Y.

D. He would not be liable for any offence.

100. Which of the following statements is correct in relation to the difference between common intention and similar intention?

A. The intention of the accused and co-accused can be inferred from the facts and circumstances of each case.

B. Under common intention, it is considered that all the accused have jointly committed the offence themselves and are jointly liable.

C. Each accused is liable for the offence he has actually committed, if the common intention cannot be proved.

D. All of the above

Directions (Qs. No. 101-105): *Read the passage carefully and answer these questions:*

Article 20(1) of the Indian Constitution prohibits Ex Post Facto laws. The expression Ex Post Facto Law means a law, which imposes penalties or convictions on the acts already done and increases the penalty for such acts. In other words, Ex Post Facto Law, imposes penalties retrospectively. For example, The Dowry Prohibition Act, 1961 came into force from 20.5.1961. A person guilty of accepting dowry is punishable under the Act after 20.5.1961 and not before 20.5.1961.

Ex post facto laws are of three kinds as follows: (*a*) A law which declared some act or omission as an offence for the first time after the completion of that act or omission. (*b*) A law which enhances the punishment or penalty for an offence subsequent to the commission of that offence. (*c*) A law which prescribes a new and different procedure for the prosecution of an offence subsequent to the commission of that offence.

Clause (1) of Art. 20 provides protection only in respect of the above first two categories of expost facto laws i.e. laws which declare acts as offences subsequent to the commission to those acts and laws which enhance the penalty subsequently.

Article 20(1) provides: *No person shall be convicted of any offence except for violation of a law in force at the time of the commission of the act charged as an offence, nor be subjected to a penalty greater than that which might have been inflicted under the law in force at the time of the commission of the offence.* The first part of clause (1) provides that no person shall be convicted of any offence except for violation of law in force at the time of the commission of the act charged as an offence. The second part of clause (1) protects a person from a penalty greater than that which he might have been subjected to at the time of the commission of the offence.

101. The Parliament of India legislated the Sexual Harassment at Workplace Act, in the year 2013 and simultaneously some new offences were also added to the Indian Penal Code, 1860. Mr. A is an employee of an institution, against whom departmental enquiry has been initiated for committing sexual harassment of a female colleague in the year 2012. Now, choose the correct option.

A. Such inquiry is valid as per Article 20 (1) of the Constitution as the complaint was made after the act came into force.

B. Article 20 (1) will not be applicable as the matter does not relate to an offence.

C. As the Act was passed in the year 2013, any inquiry under such Act is invalid.

D. Only inquiry may be conducted but no penal action can be taken against him after such inquiry.

102. Article 20 (1) would not affect which of the following acts of the legislature?

A. Act of the legislature enhancing the term of imprisonment.

B. Act of the legislature enhancing the amount of fine.

C. Act of the legislature changing the punishment of death to life imprisonment.

D. Act of legislature changing the nature of imprisonment from simple to rigorous.

103. Mr. A is a student of Law, aged 19 years. He is socially active and expresses his opinion on every social and political event of the nation through social media platforms. In one of his blog, he severely criticised the policy of a state government of changing names of cities and towns. He also stated that the government is biased towards a particular religion. The said blog was posted on 19th April, 2020 and subsequently, an amendment was made to Indian Penal Code whereby 'Hate Speech' was made a distinct offence and punishment was prescribed. An action was brought against him under the said provision for the blog. Now, choose the most appropriate option amongst the following.

A. Mr. A may be liable for the offence of Hate speech as the blog was not removed even after the amendment.

B. Mr. A may be liable for the offence of Hate speech as Article 20 (1) does not cover such areas.

C. Mr. A may not be liable for the offence because the act was done before the amendment.

D. Mr. A may not be liable for the offence as his blog was innocent and a fair criticism.

104. Considering the fact situations given in the above question, the Parliament passes a legislation in September 2020, whereby an amendment is made to the Juvenile Act and now a person below the age of 20 would be a Juvenile and special procedure would be followed for his trial. Choose the most appropriate option amongst the following.

A. Mr. A would not be considered as juvenile as it is prohibited under the scheme of Article 20 (1).

B. Mr. A would not be considered as juvenile because the amendment came after he committed the offence.

C. Mr. A would be considered a Juvenile and tried under the new procedure.

D. None of the above

105. Considering the fact situation in the third question to this passage, the Parliament passes a legislation for the Probation of Offenders, under which any offender below the age of 21 will not serve the sentence of imprisonment in a prison, instead he will serve the sentence in a probation house. Now, choose the most appropriate option.

A. Mr. A will get the benefit of Probation of Offenders Act.

B. Mr. A will not get the benefit of Probation of Offenders act as it is prohibited by Article 20 (1) of the Constitution.

C. It is discretion of Mr. A to decide whether he wants such benefit or not.

D. None of the above

Section-IV : Logical Reasoning

Directions (Qs. No. 106-110): *Read the passage carefully and answer these questions:*

Some readers wondered whether my reading of the crisis in the news media is about journalism or about the news industry. Though the fortunes of the news industry have a bearing on journalism, there is, indeed, a difference between looking at issues that govern journalism and the factors that contribute to the financial stress of the media industry. Over the last few years, I have been discussing the impact of digitalisation on journalism. The pandemic has accelerated the process of digital transformation of the news media. Therefore, these issues need close scrutiny. One of the defining elements of analog journalism was the way two crucial functions of journalism — bearing witness and making sense — complemented each other and helped people make informed choices. When I talk about the strength of analog, I am neither romanticising the past nor am I a Luddite. Most importantly, I do not believe in nostalgia. Many scholars have established how rose-coloured glasses always leads to an unfair distortion — looking back on the best of the past while comparing it to the worst of the present. Hence, when I talk about the digital information news environment, I am talking about how there needs to be a conducive atmosphere for credible information to resonate with the people. Literature on misinformation, disinformation and malinformation reveals a new distinction in the minds of the citizens. Editors and journalists have to contend with a new breed of sceptics. These are the people who trust social media forwards more than evidence-based, data-driven journalism. Their confirmation bias flows from encrypted social media platforms that are full of conspiracy theories.

[Excerpt from an Article by A.S. Panneerselvan, The Hindu, dated August 10, 2020]

106. Which of the following conveys the **main idea** expressed in the passage?

A. Those who subscribe to newspapers are sceptics.

B. Those who subscribe to newspapers and news channels often contribute in distortion of the truth.

C. Social media journalism distorts the truth.

D. All of the above.

107. In this line, "*Hence, when I talk about the digital information news environment, I am talking about how there needs to be a conducive atmosphere for credible information to resonate with the people*" the Author **assumes** that:

A. The Digital news is neither evidence based nor data driven.

B. The Digital journalism does not help people in making informed choices.

C. Both (A) and (B)

D. The impact of Digital journalism has created an informed platform of journalism.

108. Which of the following **strengthens** the Author's argument?

A. Conspiracy theories have become an alternative truth.

B. The Pandemic is the only reason behind the dependence of people on Social media journalism.

C. The News industry is witnessing a tremendous change.

D. None of the above.

109. What does the Author **indicate** when he quotes that *Rose coloured glasses always lead to unfair distortion*?

A. Digital Journalism is twisted.

B. Author means to say that he does not have any disproportionate bias for analog journalism.

C. Rosy picture of every news cannot be created.

D. All of the above

110. The Author has severely targeted and criticized which one of the following factors of Digital Journalism?

A. Social Outreach

B. Credibility of Information

C. Lack of Information

D. None of the above

Directions (Qs. No. 111-115): *Read the passage carefully and answer these questions:*

In 1985, Mikhail Gorbachev, launched an ill-fated anti-alcohol campaign in the then Soviet Union. The anti-alcohol campaign had some beneficial public health consequences: Crime fell and life expectancy rose. But the campaign was a political and economic disaster. Gorbachev forgot that the addiction of the state to alcohol revenue was even more incurable than the addiction of some citizens to alcohol itself. The budgetary losses created an economic crisis. Historians suspect that more than the loss of the Soviet Empire, it was this campaign that delegitimised Gorbachev. An old Soviet joke went like this: A disaffected and angry citizen, fed up of standing in lines for vodka, decided to go assassinate Gorbachev. He soon came back and ruefully reported that the lines to assassinate Gorbachev were even longer than the lines for Vodka. As the lockdown eased in India, and social distancing went for a toss at alcohol outlets, we were reminded of how difficult an issue alcohol is to rationally discuss in India. The stampede was caused by the ineptness with which the opening was handled in most cities. Alcohol has also migrated from being a question of personal freedom and choice to an issue in broader cultural wars, an odd site on which we measure progressivism in India. It is also a window on how liberalism has been misunderstood. Liberals should, rightly, be suspicious of prohibition on moral and practical grounds. Government grossly exceeds its legitimate power when it interferes with the rights of individuals to lead their lives as they please, and fashion their selves after their own ideals, interests and preferences. And certainly, moralism or puritanism on alcohol cannot be the basis of state policy. That moralism has no basis, and it violates the dignity and freedom of individuals.

[Excerpt from an Opinion by Bhanu Pratap Mehta, The Indian Express, May 7, 2020]

111. In the above passage, the author uses a/an _____ to strengthen his argument.

A. Metaphor
B. Analogy
C. Personification
D. None of the above

112. Which of the following can be **inferred** from the passage above?
A. State must not interfere at all with the individual's right to drink.
B. Liberalism has always been misunderstood.
C. It is very difficult to discuss any issue relating to personal freedom of individuals with rationality in India.
D. None of the above

113. Which of the following statements **weakens** the argument that Moralism on Alcohol cannot be the basis of State Policy?
A. The State should not interfere with people's right to drink; but there will be a backlash if drinking takes forms that inflict great social harms.
B. Freedom should not be divorced from Moderation.
C. The State should not interfere in matters of sexuality or intimacy. But norms of freedom will impose serious costs and will not survive if the expressions of sexuality are consistently degrading or violent, as we have seen in the locker room scandals.
D. All of the above

114. Which of the following is **true** as per the passage above?
A. Liberals should not be concerned about prohibition on Alcohol at all.
B. Moralism should be based on justified ideals.
C. Moralism must not be the basis of any State action.
D. All of the above

115. According to the passage, which of the following could be part of State's policy to regulate Alcohol use in India?
I. Ban on Alcohol shops.
II. Education on Intelligent Drinking.
III. Regulating Outlet density of Alcohol shops
IV. Community Intervention Policy
A. I, II and III
B. II and IV
C. II, III and IV
D. I, II, III and IV

Directions (Qs. No. 116-120): *Read the passage carefully and answer these questions:*

Don't miss the cloud behind the silver lining. The Class XII CBSE pass result has soared to an all-time high of 88.8%. The number of students scoring 95% and above has more than doubled. If only these higher marks were a reflection of students getting more skilled and more competitive. Instead, the odds are they simply mirror an assessment scheme relaxed to compensate students for the many disruptions originating in the pandemic. The goal of reducing student stress levels during this turbulent time is excellent and laudable. But it is a fallacy that high marks can accomplish this by themselves. The real stressor, after all, is shortage of opportunities. When every bout of grade inflation raises cut-offs for higher education even higher, it is no succour. That India's Gross Enrolment Ratio is only 27% compared to Indonesia's 36%, Thailand's 49% and the US's 88% is just one measure of the toll taken by our failure to build adequate colleges and universities. Licence raj continues to suppress autonomy and expansion in this sector. For example, a new national education policy is reportedly mulling at least 20% of students being able to attend private higher educational institutions through freeships and another 30% through scholarships, besides fee caps. On top of the stasis already wreaked by reservations, this would be disastrous. Browbeating the private sector to make up for public sector deficiencies is counterproductive. As the pandemic has underlined the key role of good government services in healthcare, so too is raising the standard of publicly funded schools and universities essential. What the students need is an ecosystem where government institutions deliver quality education and private options are plentiful. It is better prospects alone that will best alleviate students' stress. Meanwhile, crudely chopping syllabi will only worsen their disorientation and should be reconsidered.

[TOI Edit, Times of India Editorials, Dated July 15, 2020].

116. What is the 'cloud behind the silver lining' in the passage above?

A. The Pandemic which is impacting the current education system.

B. That, the Governmental educational institutions are not able to deliver quality education.

C. Scoring Higher marks or percentage in school education does not guarantee skilled and competitive candidature of the student.

D. License Raj has negatively impacted Higher education.

117. Which of the following statements **weakens** the argument that chopping the syllabi in the times of Pandemic will only worsen a student's disorientation and hence should be reconsidered?

A. It does not matter even if syllabi is chopped. The students who don't want to study will even not study in the minimal syllabi structure even during the pandemic.

B. Students don't care about syllabi. They study only for marks and grades.

C. Reduced syllabi will help in achieving the teaching-learning targets in due time and hence won't put pressure on students.

D. All of the above

118. The number of students scoring 95% and above in XII class board exams has more than doubled. Which of the following statements serves as a **plausible explanation** for the same?

A. Students have started studying with sincerity and concentration.

B. Evaluation of answer scripts has become liberal.

C. Question papers these days are easier to solve.

D. All of the above

119. For developing a student friendly ecosystem of education, which of the following serve as need of the hour, as per the Author?

I. Increasing the Syllabi in School education.

II. Building adequate number of public colleges and universities.

III. Eliminating Reservation in admissions to Higher education system.

IV. Creating a quality based education system

A. Only I and II

B. Only I, II and IV

C. Only III

D. Only II and IV

120. Which of the following can be **inferred** from the passage above?

A. Scoring High marks in XII class can help in reducing stress amongst students in the times of Pandemic.

B. High Cut-off of marks also contribute in reducing opportunities for the students.

C. Private institutions should not be regulated.

D. License Raj should be done away with.

Directions (Qs. No. 121-125): *Read the passage carefully and answer these questions:*

If anything, the novel coronavirus disease (COVID-19) pandemic has taught us to rethink our lifestyles and question our need to travel to work every day. After all, in the age of internet, zoom meetings and webinars can be virtually conducted and physical distancing is possible. A large nature of work in cities is of tertiary nature, a major part of which can be done from home. This can affect the way offices function and reduce the need for all employees to be physically present every day. Information Technology companies are already contemplating a move of making many of its employees work from home and make this a 'new normal'. If more firms follow suit, the need for huge office buildings and central business districts would change. Apartments cannot get bigger at the same rate, and people may not have the space or atmosphere to work from home. This would mean that more people would opt for co-working spaces close to their homes. This could be a game changer, for it would provide the cities to better distribute their activities throughout the spaces and rid themselves of the idea of zoning. Only a handful of professionals are allowed to function from residential zones, including doctors, lawyers, architects, etc. This needs serious rethinking. Many more professions of similar nature that do not disturb surrounding residence and have no requirements of special services should be added to the list. This new work culture would bring associated demand for food joints, cafés, stationary shops, etc.

[Excerpt from 'Down to Earth' Magazine, Blog authored by Sugeet Grover, August 17, 2020]

121. Which of the following is the **main idea** behind the passage?

A. Work from home is the new normal.

B. Work from home will result in shutting down of big buildings.

C. Work from home culture will result in systematization of City planning and development.

D. More professionals should be included in the 'work from home' list.

122. Which of the following can be **inferred** from the passage above?

A. The 'work from home' culture is a no-chaos culture.

B. There is lack of distribution of activities in the 'work from home' scenario.

C. The routine culture as opposed to 'work from home' does not benefit the society in any way.

D. All of the above

123. Which of the following can be associated **benefits** of the new culture ?

A. It will save commute time.

B. The city's land can be used more efficiently

C. Better distribution of activities would be associated with safer streets and public spaces as they would not go unused and hence have less likelihood of being used for unlawful activities.

D. All of the above

124. Consider the following statement: "Work from home culture is a sustainable method of business and should be extended to all professions."

Which of the following **weakens** the Author's argument?

A. Not every type of profession fits in the 'work from home' culture as different professions have different requirements and need different environmental and work space settings.

B. 'Work from home' impacts a person's mental health.

C. Both A and B

D. Neither A nor B

125. Which of the following weakens the author's argument that 'Work from home' culture will enable better city planning?

A. Development of Co-working spaces will further create chaos in terms of land planning.

B. City planning is not only about reducing spaces.

C. Work from home will also reduce the flow of money in the economy.

D. All of the above.

Directions (Qs. No. 126-130): *Following is an array of questions to test your reasoning ability in different situations. Answer each of them according to the question asked in each of them respectively:*

126. If highways were restricted to cars and only those trucks with capacity of less than 8 tons, most of the truck traffic would be forced to run outside highways. Such a reduction in the amount of truck traffic would reduce the risk of collisions on highways. The conclusion drawn in the first sentence depends on which of the following assumptions?

A. The roads outside highway would be as convenient as highway for most drivers of trucks.

B. Most of the roads outside highways are not ready to handle truck traffic.

C. Most trucks that are currently running in highway have a capacity of more than 8 tons.

D. Cars are at greater risk of being involved in collisions than are trucks.

127. Read the debate between Harry and Potter and identify the main issue:

Harry: Within democracies, voters are entitled to know the down-side to a candidate and the other side is obviously well placed to voice it. To stifle one's ability to voice negative things about a candidate would be to obstruct democracy and limit free speech.

Potter: Negative advertisements produce the politics of the personal, since an easiest advert is an attack-advert which focuses on the personality or personal qualities of one's opponent. A negative advertisement is one that focuses upon a rival product, in this case, a rival election candidate or party in order to point its flaws and to persuade the public to not vote for it.

A. Whether negative advertisement strengthens democratic governance?

B. Whether the practice of negative advertisements is good for democracy and politics?

C. Whether negative advertising needs to be banned?

D. Whether negative advertising produces the politics of the personal?

128. Which alternative applies to the following Statement and Assumption?

Statement: Go by Aeroplane to reach Delhi from Chennai quickly.

Assumptions:

I. Chennai and Delhi are connected by Air service.

II. There is no other means to commute from Chennai to Delhi.

III. The Air distance between Delhi and Chennai is less.

A. Only I is implicit.

B. Only I and II are implicit.

C. Only I and III are implicit.

D. Only II is implicit.

129. Ananya and Krishna can speak and follow English. Bulbul can write and speak Hindi as Archana does. Archana talks with Ananya also in Bengali. Krishna cannot follow Bengali. Bulbul talks with Ananya in Hindi. Who can speak and follow English, Hindi and Bengali?

A. Archana

B. Bulbul

C. Krishna

D. Ananya

130. If '367' means 'I am happy'; '748' means 'you are sad' and '469' means 'happy and sad' in a given code, then which of the following represents and in the code?

A. 3 B. 6

C. 9 D. 4

Directions (Qs. No. 131-135): *Read the passage carefully and answer these questions:*

One of the biggest casualties of the Covid-19 pandemic and the resultant lockdown has been institutionalised education. Schools have been shut to prevent the spread of the virus and this has given way to online classrooms, a very new concept in India even for the most sophisticated schools. It is commendable how easily some educational institutions have moved to virtual classrooms, all thanks to tools such as Zoom, Google Hangouts and Microsoft Teams. But there are some still struggling to get online. The online classes, whatever the enabling technology, is only as good as the teachers and the ability of the students to grasp the new teaching technique. One of the teachers felt students are actually more responsive and active in online classrooms, compared to when they are in physical ones. "*This could be because this is a new concept and they are excited to explore it with the teachers. They also don't get distracted by their classmates, which frequently happens in a regular class.*" Teachers do find the absence of a blackboard a disadvantage and network connectivity a constant problem. "*We miss the clarity that a blackboard gives us, we are kind of making do with the virtual whiteboard on Zoom.*" Shweta Kawatra, a parent who teaches in a New Delhi school, highlights that many students have not been able to take advantage of the virtual platform because they do not have a suitable device at home or lack a good internet connection. "*It has its own share of disadvantages too. Too much screen time can be perilous for health. Prolonged online sessions can be overwhelming and may lead to problems related to vision, body posture and sleep disorder,*" Kawatra adds.

[Excerpt from an Article by Sneha Saha, The Indian Express, dated April 18, 2020]

131. What is the **Central Idea** of the passage above?

A. Institutionalised education was much better than the current online education system.

B. Institutionalized education cannot be replaced by any other system of education.

C. Virtual Classroom teaching is a sustainable approach to education in modern times.

D. None of the above.

132. Which of the following statements **cannot be inferred** from the passage above?

A. Virtual Classroom teaching is a sustainable approach to education.

B. Virtual Classroom teaching causes health problems.

C. Institutionalized education system has its advantages.

D. All of the above

133. Which of the following is an **implicit assumption** in the observation that students are more active and responsive in online classrooms as compared to that in physical ones?

I. Students are not serious while studying in physical classrooms.

II. Online classrooms inculcate more interest in students towards studies than the physical classrooms.

III. Students don't like physical classrooms at all.

IV. Students sleep in physical classrooms.

A. Only I and II

B. Only III and IV

C. I and IV

D. I, II, III and IV

134. Which of the following can be **inferred** from the passage above?

A. There is a divide in opinions of people on the merits and demerits of Online education.

B. Online education system is going to replace the Institutionalized education system.

C. The institutionalized education system is not at all perilous for health of students.

D. All of the above

135. Consider this statement: Virtual education provides for various online seminars, opportunities to interact with learned experts, pro-bono education classes etc., for students across India irrespective of their economic status and background.

Which of the following statements **weakens** the statement?

I. Many students in remote areas do not have access to internet facilities.

II. Many students in rural areas do not have devices to take advantage of the Virtual classrooms.

III. Online Seminars and pro bono classes are not interesting and do not cater to the needs of students across India.

IV. The mobile phone data packages to access such heavy online contents are not enough and participation in such events involves costly data packages which is dependent upon the economic status of those students.

A. Only I, II, III
B. Only III and IV
C. Only I, II and IV
D. Only I and II

Section-V : Quantitative Techniques

Directions (Qs. No. 136-140): The following data presents the cases of Japanese Encephalitis in five states of India.

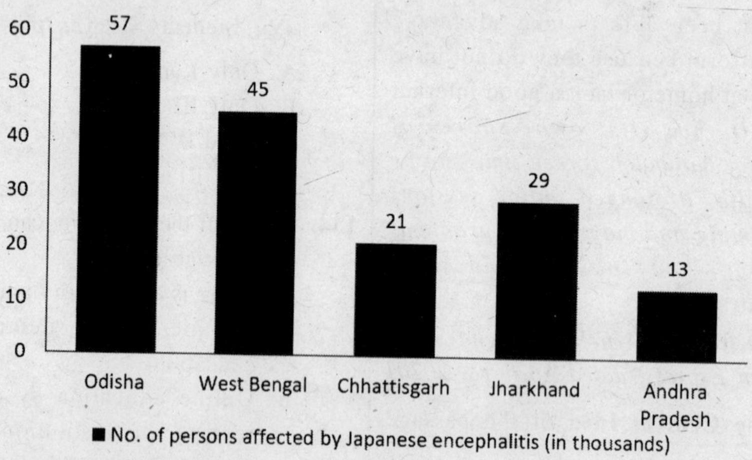

States	Ratio of males of females
	Male : Female
Odisha	12 : 7
West Bengal	6 : 3
Chhattisgarh	5 : 2
Jharkhand	15 : 14
Andhra Pradesh	7 : 6

136. Number of females affected by Japanese encephalitis in West Bengal are what percentage (up to 1 decimal) more or less than that of females affected in Odisha?
A. 28.6% less
B. 29.7% more
C. 26.8% less
D. 25.8% more

137. What is the average number of males affected by Japanese encephalitis in all the five states?
A. 9,000
B. 13,500
C. 18,400
D. 20,600

138. If the total number of males affected by Japanese Encephalitis in other states are 87 % more than the average number of males in Odisha, West Bengal, Chhattisgarh and Jharkhand, the total number of males affected in India is:
A. 44,880
B. 1,40,880
C. 1,47,880
D. 68,880

139. By what percentage is the average of males in Chhattisgarh, Jharkhand and Andhra Pradesh together more or less than the average of females in West Bengal, Jharkhand and Odisha together who are affected by Japanese encephalitis?

A. 22
B. 24
C. 26
D. 28

140. What is the percentage (up to 1 decimal) of females affected by 'Japanese encephalitis' of the total affected population across five states?

A. 25.4
B. 36.7
C. 24.5
D. 37.6

Directions (Qs. No. 141-145): *A room having the dimensions as mentioned in the chart below has a table, a bed and a chair. There are three books kept on the table (side by side) and also a lamp having radius, 3.5 inch. Now, on the basis of information given below answer the following?*

Sr.No.	Object	Length	Breadth	Height
1.	Room	18 feet	12 feet	12 feet
2.	Bed	3.5 feet	6 feet	3 feet
3.	Table	3 feet	4 feet	4 feet
4.	Chair	2 feet	2.5 feet	4 feet
5.	Books	12 inch	6 inch	3 inch

141. What would be the area of the room which is not covered by any object as mentioned above?

A. 176.5 sq. ft.
B. 178 sq. ft.
C. 367 sq. ft.
D. 245.5 sq. ft.

142. What is the area of the table which is uncovered by any of the objects?

A. 1656 sq. inch
B. 1617.52 sq. inch
C. 1473.52 sq. inch
D. 1512 sq. inch

143. How many tables are required to cover the floor surface of the room completely?

A. 18
B. 11
C. 21
D. Data inadequate.

144. If the entire room is to be filled by books having same dimensions as lying on the table then how many books are required.

A. 2,00,736
B. 20,736
C. 11,736
D. 17,522

145. How many chairs can be put inside the room so as to cover the entire floor area of the room?

A. 40
B. 21
C. 43
D. 18

Directions (Qs. No. 146-150): *In the figure given below, a goat is tied to a pole (at point O) which is the center of the semi -circular plot. The area of the plot is equal to its perimeter. BO is the length of the rope through which the goat is tied to the pole. Answer to the closest decimal.*

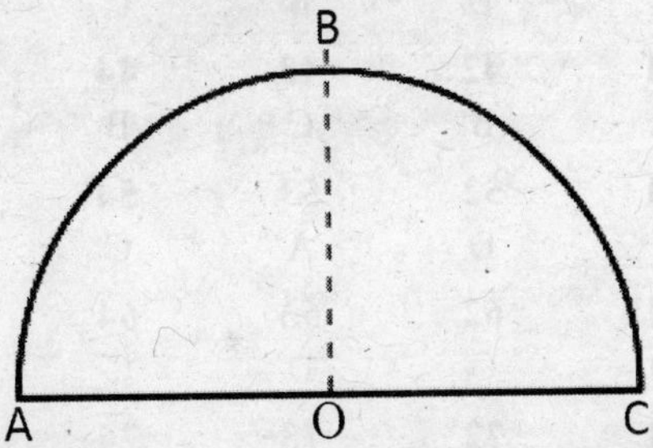

146. The length of the rope is

A. $2 + \pi$
B. $2 + \pi/2$
C. $2 + 2/\pi$
D. 2

147. The area of the plot is

A. 18.13
B. 21.83
C. 28.13
D. 11.83

148. If a triangle is created by joining points A, B and C. What will be the length of AB?

A. 3.73
B. 7.33
C. 1.86
D. Can't be calculated with the given data

149. What will be the area of the triangle ABC?

A. 6.96

B. 9.66

C. 3.66

D. Can't be calculated with the given data

150. What will be the perimeter of the triangle ABC?

A. 40.4

B. 30.3

C. 20.2

D. 10.1

ANSWERS

1	**2**	**3**	**4**	**5**	**6**	**7**	**8**	**9**	**10**
A	D	B	B	C	A	D	A	A	D
11	**12**	**13**	**14**	**15**	**16**	**17**	**18**	**19**	**20**
A	C	C	C	C	D	B	C	A	C
21	**22**	**23**	**24**	**25**	**26**	**27**	**28**	**29**	**30**
B	B	A	D	D	A	B	B	D	C
31	**32**	**33**	**34**	**35**	**36**	**37**	**38**	**39**	**40**
B	D	B	C	C	A	D	D	B	A
41	**42**	**43**	**44**	**45**	**46**	**47**	**48**	**49**	**50**
A	B	C	B	B	D	C	D	B	B
51	**52**	**53**	**54**	**55**	**56**	**57**	**58**	**59**	**60**
C	D	A	C	B	C	D	A	B	A
61	**62**	**63**	**64**	**65**	**66**	**67**	**68**	**69**	**70**
D	C	D	C	C	C	B	C	B	D
71	**72**	**73**	**74**	**75**	**76**	**77**	**78**	**79**	**80**
C	A	B	C	C	D	B	B	C	C
81	**82**	**83**	**84**	**85**	**86**	**87**	**88**	**89**	**90**
A	C	D	B	C	D	D	C	D	C
91	**92**	**93**	**94**	**95**	**96**	**97**	**98**	**99**	**100**
B	D	A	A	A	B	B	A	C	D
101	**102**	**103**	**104**	**105**	**106**	**107**	**108**	**109**	**110**
D	C	A	C	A	C	C	A	B	B
111	**112**	**113**	**114**	**115**	**116**	**117**	**118**	**119**	**120**
B	D	D	B	C	C	D	D	D	B
121	**122**	**123**	**124**	**125**	**126**	**127**	**128**	**129**	**130**
C	A	D	C	D	C	B	C	D	C
131	**132**	**133**	**134**	**135**	**136**	**137**	**138**	**139**	**140**
D	A	A	A	C	A	D	B	C	D
141	**142**	**143**	**144**	**145**	**146**	**147**	**148**	**149**	**150**
B	C	A	B	C	*	*	D	D	*

*Error in questions/options.

EXPLANATORY ANSWERS

For Qs. No. (136–140)

By given data:

Number of persons affected by Japanese Encephalitis (in thousands)

States	Ratio of Male to Female M : F	Number of Males	Number of Females
Odisha	12 : 7	36	21
West Bengal	6 : 3	30	15
Chhattisgarh	5 : 2	15	6
Jharkhand	15 : 14	15	14
Andhra Pradesh	7 : 6	7	6

136. Here, Number of Females affected in West Bengal = 15

and the number of Females affected in Odisha = 21

Required percentage = $\frac{21-15}{21} \times 100\%$

$= \frac{6}{21} \times 100\% = \frac{2}{7} \times 100\%$

$= \frac{200}{7}\%$

$= 28.57142\% = 28.6\%$

137. The number of Males affected by Japanese encephalitis in all five states

$= 36 + 30 + 15 + 15 + 7$

$= 103$ thousand

$= 103000$

The average number = $\frac{103000}{5} = 20,600$

138. The average number of Males in Odisha, West Bengal, Chhattisgarh and Jharkhand

$= \frac{36+30+15+15}{4}$

$= \frac{96}{4} = 24$ thousand

$= 24000$

The total number of Males affected in other states

$= 24000 \times \frac{187}{100}$

$= 240 \times 187 = 44880$

Hence, the total number of Males affected in India is $24000 + 44880 = 68880$

139. The average of Males in Chhattisgarh, Jharkhand and Andhra pradesh

$= \frac{15+15+7}{3} = \frac{37}{3}$ thousand

$= \frac{37000}{3} = 12333.3$

And, the average of Females in West Bengal, Jharkhand and Odisha

$= \frac{15+14+21}{3}$

$= \frac{50}{3}$ thousand

$= \frac{50000}{3} = 16666.6$

Required percentage = $\frac{16666.6-12333.3}{16666.6} \times 100$

$= 25.999\% = 26\%$

140. The total affected population across five states

$= 57 + 45 + 21 + 29 + 13 = 165$

and, the total females effected

$= 21 + 15 + 6 + 14 + 6 = 62$

$\therefore$ Required percentage = $\frac{62}{165} \times 100\%$

= 37.5757% = 37.6%

141. By the given information

The area of the room = 18 feet × 12 feet

= 216 sq. ft

and the area covered by bed, table and chair

= (3.5 feet × 6 feet) + (3 feet × 4 feet) + (2 feet × 2.5 feet)

= 21 + 12 + 5 = 38 sq. ft

Hence, the area of the room which is not covered by bed, table and chair

= 216 – 38 = 178 sq. ft

142. The area of the table

= 3 × 4 = 12 sq. feet

= 12 × 12 × 12 sq. inch

= 1728 sq. inch

The area of 3 book and a lamp

$$= \left[3(12\times 6)+\frac{22}{7}\times\left(\frac{7}{2}\right)^2\right] \text{ sq. inch}$$

= 216 + 38.5 = 254.5 sq. inch

Hence, the area of the table which is not covered by any of the objects

= 1728 – 254.5

= 1473.5 sq. feet

143. The area of the room = 18 × 12 = 216 sq. ft and the area of the table = 3 × 4

= 12 sq. ft.

Hence, the number of tables required to cover the floor surface of room completely

$$= \frac{216}{12} = 18$$

144. Here,

The volume of the room

= 18 × 12 × 12 × 12 × 12 × 12 $(\text{inch})^3$

and the volume of a book

= 12 × 6 × 3 $(\text{inch})^3$

$\therefore$ The required number of books

$$= \frac{18\times 12\times 12\times 12\times 12\times 12}{12\times 6\times 3}$$

= 18 × 2 × 4 × 144

= 144 × 144 = 20,736

145. The area of the surface of the room = 18 × 12 sq.ft

and the area of the chair

= 2 × 2.5 = 5 sq. ft

Hence, the number of chairs can be put inside the room so as to cover

$$= \frac{18\times 12}{5} = 43.2 = 43$$

LEGAL AWARENESS
(*SUBJECTIVE*)

LEGAL AWARENESS (SUBJECTIVE)

Law, Courts and the Constitution

India has one of the oldest legal systems in the world. Its law and jurisprudence stretches back into the centuries, forming a living tradition which has grown and evolved with the lives of its diverse people. India's commitment to law is created in the Constitution which constituted India into a Sovereign Democratic Republic, containing a federal system with Parliamentary form of Government in the Union and the States, an independent judiciary, guaranteed Fundamental Rights and Directive Principles of State Policy containing objectives which though not enforceable in law are fundamental to the governance of the nation.

Sources of Law

The fountain source of law in India is the Constitution which, in turn, gives due recognition to statutes, case law and customary law consistent with its dispensations. Statutes are enacted by Parliament, State Legislatures and Union Territory Legislatures. There is also a vast body of laws known as subordinate legislation in the form of rules, regulations as well as by-laws made by Central and State Governments and local authorities like Municipal Corporations, Municipalities, Gram Panchayats and other local bodies. This subordinate legislation is made under the authority conferred or delegated either by Parliament or State or Union Territory Legislature concerned. The decisions of the Supreme Court are binding on all Courts within the territory of India. As India is a land of diversities, local customs and conventions which are not against statute, morality, etc. are to a limited extent also recognised and taken into account by Courts while administering justice in certain spheres.

Enactment of Laws

The Indian Parliament is competent to make laws on matters enumerated in the Union List. State Legislatures are competent to make laws on matters enumerated in the State List. While both the Union and the States have power to legislate on matters enumerated in the Concurrent List, only Parliament has power to make laws on matters not included in the State List or the Concurrent List. In the event of repugnancy, laws made by Parliament shall prevail over law made by State Legislatures, to the extent of the repugnancy. The State law shall be void unless it has received the assent of the President, and in such case, shall prevail in that State.

Applicability of Laws

Laws made by Parliament may extend throughout or in any part of the territory of India and those made by State Legislatures may generally apply only within the terrirory of the State concerned. Hence, variations are likely to exist from State to State in provisions of law relating to matters falling in the State and Concurrent Lists.

Judiciary

One of the unique features of the Indian Constitution is that, notwithstanding the adoption of a federal system and existence of Central Acts and State Acts in their respective spheres, it has generally provided for a single integrated system of Courts to administer both Union and State laws. At the apex of the entire judicial system, exists the Supreme Court of India below which are the High Courts in each State or group of States. Below the High Courts lies a hierarchy of Subordinate Courts. Panchayat Courts also function in some States under various names like Nyaya Panchayat, Panchayat Adalat, Gram Kachheri, etc. to decide civil and criminal disputes of petty and local nature. Different State laws provide for different kinds of jurisdiction of courts. Each State is divided into judicial districts presided over by a District and Sessions Judge, which is the principal civil court of original jurisdiction and can try all offences including those punishable with death. The Sessions Judge is the highest judicial authority in a district. Below him, there are Courts of civil jurisdiction, known in different States as Munsifs, Sub-Judges, Civil Judges and the like. Similarly, the criminal judiciary comprises the Chief Judicial Magistrates and Judicial Magistrates of First and Second Class.

Preamble of Indian Constitution

We, the people of India, having solemnly resolved to constitute India into a sovereign, socialist, secular, democratic republic and to secure to all its citizens:

Justice, social, economic and political;

Liberty, of thought, expression, belief, faith and worship;

Equality of status and opportunity; and to promote among them all

Fraternity assuring the dignity of the individual and the unity and integrity of the Nation

In our constitution assembly this twenty sixth day of November, 1949, do hereby adopt, enact and give to ourselves this constitution.

'Sovereign', 'Democratic', and 'Republic'

The terms 'Sovereign, 'Democratic', and 'Republic' are enshrined in the preamble of the constitution of India. The term 'Sovereign' implies that our country India is not dependent in any matter on some other country or organization and it has got the complete decisive power of every nature as an independent country. The term 'Democracy' implies that the system of governance that exists in the country is 'of the people', 'by the people' and 'for the people'. It is the citizens of the country who fully participate in making the government of the country to rule them. Such a participation in the form of election and voting destines the government of the country. The term 'Republic' given in the preamble of the constitution implies that the country has its own constitution, which is the supreme body of rules and regulations needed for the governance of the country.

Salient Features of Indian Constitution

The salient features of Indian constitution are as stated below:

(1) The Indian constitution is the largest written constitution of the world. It comprehends in itself the features of all types of constitutions that are in practice in other countries of the world. The concept of fundamental rights, directive principles of state policy and fundamental duties have been borrowed from US and Irish constitutions respectively whereas the concept of rule of law, parliamentary system and law making procedure has been inspired by the British constitution. The ideals of "Liberty, equality and fraternity are inspired by the French revolution.

(2) As per this constitution our country has been declared to be the sovereign, socialist, secular, democratic republic.

(3) The constitution of India is quasi-federal in character that is to say that the provisions of the constitution are so enacted in general trend it has the character of a federal constitution whereas in the time of emergency it adopts itself such that country assumes a unitary shape and the power divided between the centre and state is totally enjoyed by the centre.

(4) The separation of power is another significant feature of our constitution. There is clear separation of power between the legislature, executive and judiciary which are assumed to be the three powerful pillars of the government. The work of the legislature is to frame laws, the work of the executive is to implement the law and the work of the judiciary is to interpret the law.

(5) The supremacy of constitution is another feature that exists in our constitution. Among the three wings of the government none of the wing is superior to other wing of the government and it is the

constitution of the country which is a body of rules and regulation that is supreme. Such a position in our country is unlike the position that exists in United Kingdom where there is supremacy of legislature.

(6) Furthermore, another significant feature of our constitution is that it is neither rigid as the constitution of USA nor flexible like the constitution of UK. The provisions of the constitution have been classified into three groups for the purpose of amendment. Some of the provisions can be amended by simple majority (more than half) in the parliament, other provisions can be amended by having 2/3rd majority and at last there are also certain provisions that can be amended only by 2/3rd majority in the parliament along with the ratification from half of the states of Union of India.

(7) There is rule of law according to the provisions of the constitution and there exists independence of judiciary.

The Indian Union as a Quasi-federal Polity

The Indian Union is a quasi-federal polity with some vital and important features of unitariness. Renowned Professor Wheare pointed out that the Indian constitution provides, "a unitary state with subsidiary federal features rather than a federal state with subsidiary unitary features." Indian constitution provides a list of various subjects under three heads in its seventh schedule viz. union list, state list and concurrent list. The legislations on the subjects given in the union list are to be done by the centre only and exclusively and the subjects given in the state list are to be dealt with by the individual states. The subjects given in the concurrent list are such that both the centre as well as state can legislate over it. So, there is fair division of power between the centre and state and if there arises any dispute between the state and centre or between two states the Supreme Court has been conferred with the jurisdiction to resolve the dispute. This division of power between the centre and state gives it the feature of federal republic, but in the state of emergency provisions have been made in the constitution such that the country resumes the character of unitariness. Article 352, 356 and 360 dealing with the national emergency, state emergency and financial emergency respectively brings such an effect with it that the power of the individual states is absorbed by the centre and the country assume a character of unitariness. So, in other words it can be said that in general trend the country works as a federal entity whereas in emergency situation it becomes unitary. Hence, it is neither federal nor unitary; rather it is quasi federal in nature.

The states of the Indian union are autonomous in nature and enjoy the power of legislation over the subject given in the state list and in concurrent list. The welfare of people, maintenance of law and order, raising funds for their schemes are few important subjects over which states legislate. The centre has been conferred with the strong power of administration on the states as is evident from the centralized judiciary, audit, taxation, defense etc. The states have their prerogative on the subjects contained in the State list and to this extent it can also be said that in normal trend the individual states also have the unitary character just like whole of the Indian Union in emergency situation. So we can say that the Indian constitution make the country a quasi-federal unit.

Directive Principle of State Policy

The directive principles of state policy are not enforceable by any court, but the principles therein laid down are nevertheless fundamental in the governance of the country and it shall be duty of the state to apply these principles in making laws. It has been mentioned in the constitution that the state shall strive to promote the welfare of the people by securing and protecting as effectively as it may a social order in which justice - social, economic and political, shall inform all the institutions of the national life. It has further been mentioned that the state shall, in particular, strive to minimize the inequalities in income, and endeavour to eliminate inequalities in status, facilities and opportunities, not only among individuals but also amongst group of people residing in different areas or engaged in different vacations.

As per the provisions of the Indian constitution, the policy of the state should be so as to secure the following objectives:

(a) That the citizen, men and women equally, have the right to an adequate means of livelihood;

(b) That the ownership and the control of the material resources of the community are so distributed as best to subserve the common good;

(c) That the operation of the economic system does not result in the concentration of wealth and means of production to the common detriment.

(d) That there is equal pay for equal work for both men and women;

(e) That the health and strength of the workers, men and women , and the tender age of children are not abused and that citizens are not forced by economic necessity to enter avocations unsuited to their age or strength;

(f) That children are given opportunities and facilities to develop in a healthy manner and in conditions of freedom and dignity and that the childhood and youth are protected against exploitation and against moral and material abandonment.

Further more, the directive principle of state policy aims at securing such a legal system that would promote justice, on the basis of equal opportunity, and according to it the state shall, in particular, provide free legal aid by suitable legislation or schemes or in any other way. It would be the duty of the state to ensure that the opportunities for securing justice are not denied to any citizen by reason of economic or other disabilities. It is to be noted here that the meaning of word "state" here is similar to that is applicable to this word while interpreting part III of the constitution i.e the fundamental rights.

Article 40 of the constitution puts it obligatory on the state to take steps to organize village panchayat and endow them with such powers and authority as may be necessary to enable them to function as units of self government.

The right to work, to education and to public assistance in certain cases has also be enshrined in the constitution as the directive principle of state policy. It has been said that the state shall, within the limits of its economic capacity and development, make effective provision for securing the right to work, to education and to public assistance in cases of unemployment, old age, sickness and disablement, and in other cases of undeserved want.

One important directive of state policy is with regard to the provision for just and humane condition of work and maternity relief. The state shall make provisions for securing just and humane conditions of work and for maternity relief.

It has been stated in the directive principle of state policy that the state shall endeavour to secure, by suitable legislation or economic organization or in any other way, to all workers agricultural, industrial, or otherwise, work, a living wage, conditions of work ensuring a decent standard of life and full enjoyment of leisure and social and cultural opportunities and in particular, the state shall endeavour to promote cottage industries on an individual or co-operative basis in rural areas.

Furthermore, the state as per the directive principle of state policy needs to take steps by suitable legislation or in any other way, to secure the participation of workers in the management of undertaking, establishments or other organization engaged in any industry.

Article 44 of the constitution put forth the need for the enactment of uniform civil code in the country. According to this directive the state shall endeavour to secure for the citizens a uniform civil code throughout the territory of India. The Supreme Court in a series of cases has directed the Central Government to enact uniform civil code. Some of these cases are

Shahbano v. *Md. Ahmed Hussain* (1985) 2 SCC 556, *Sarla Mudgal* v. *Union of India* (1995) 3 SCC 635 (651) and very recently *John Vallamattom and another* v. *Union of India*, (Writ Petition (C) No. 242 of 1997)

The provision for free and compulsory education for children has also been enshrined as the directive principle of state policy. It has been stated that the state shall endeavour to provide within a period of ten years from the commencement of the constitution, for free and compulsory education for all children until they complete the age of fourteen years.

The promotion of educational and economic interests of scheduled castes, scheduled tribes and other weaker sections is another directive stated in the constitution. Article 46 states that the state shall promote with special care the educational and economic interests of the weaker sections of the people, and in particular, of the scheduled castes and the scheduled tribes, and shall protect them from social injustice and all forms of exploitation.

The framers of our constitution observed that it would be the duty of the state to raise the level of nutrition and the standard of living and the state would also take care to improve public health. It has been stated that the state shall regard the raising of level of nutrition and the standard of living of its people and the improvement of public health as among its primary duties and in particular the state shall endeavour to bring about prohibition of the consumption except for medicinal purposes of intoxicating drinks and of drugs which are injurious to health.

Organization of agriculture and animal husbandry is another directive principle of state policy. It has been put forth that the state shall endeavour to organize agriculture and animal husbandry on modern and scientific lines and shall, in particular, take steps for preserving and improving the breeds and prohibiting the slaughter of cows and calves and other milch and drought cattle. The forty second amendment in the constitution in the year 1976 further introduced a clause for the protection and improvement of environment and safeguarding of forests and wild life and a duty was cast over the state to protect and improve the environment and to safeguard the forests and wild life of the country.

It is the obligation of the state to protect every monument or place or object of artistic or historic interest, declared by or under law made by the parliament to be of national importance from spoliation, disfigurement, destruction, removal, disposal or export, as the case may be.

As the directive principle of state policy the state shall take steps to separate the judiciary from the executive in the public services of the state.

The promotion of international peace and security is another directive given in the constitution. It has been stated that the state shall endeavour to:

(a) promote international peace and security;
(b) maintain just and honourable relations between nations;
(c) foster respect for international law and treaty obligations in the dealings of organized people with one another; and
(d) encourage settlement of international disputes by arbitration.

Fundamental Duties

The forty-second amendment in the constitution which is sometimes termed as the mini constitution introduced fundamental duties in the constitution to be performed by the citizens of the country. Article 51A was introduced in the constitution for this purpose and it imposed certain duties as

(a) to abide by the constitution and respect its ideals and institutions, the national flag, and the national anthem;
(b) to cherish and follow the noble ideals which inspired our national struggle for freedom;
(c) to uphold and protect the sovereignty, unity and integrity of India;
(d) to defend the country and render national service when called upon to do so;
(e) to promote harmony and the spirit of common brotherhood amongst all the

people of India transcending religious, linguistic and regional or sectional diversities; to renounce practices derogatory to the dignity of women;

(f) to value and preserve the rich heritage of our composite culture;

(g) to preserve and improve the natural environment including forests lakes, rivers and wild life, and to have compassion for living creatures;

(h) to develop the scientific temper, humanism and the spirit of inquiry and reform;

(i) to safeguard public property and to abjure violence;

(j) to strive towards excellence in all spheres of individual and collective activity so that the nation constantly rises to higher levels of endeavour and achievement.

(k) to provide opportunities for education to his child or as the case may be ward between the age of six and fourteen years. (This duty was added to the constitution by the 86th Amendment Act).

Constitution and Composition of Parliament

Parliament for the Union consists of the President and two Houses to be known respectively as the council of States and the House of the People. The Council of States consist of:

(a) Twelve members to be nominated by the President that consists of persons having special knowledge or practical experience in respect literature, science, art and social service.

(b) Not more than two hundred and thirty-eight representatives of the States and of the Union territories.

The allocation of seats in the Council of States to be filled by representatives of the States and of the Union territories shall be in accordance with the provisions in that behalf contained in the Fourth Schedule of the constitution.

The representatives of each State in the Council of States shall be elected by the elected members of the Legislative Assembly of the State in accordance with the system of proportional representation by means of the single transferable vote.

The representatives of the Union Territories in the Council of States shall be chosen in such manner as Parliament may by law prescribe.

Composition of the House of the People

Subject to Provisions of article 331, dealing with the representation of Anglo-Indian community in the House of the People, this house consist of:

(a) Not more than five hundred and thirty members chosen by direct election from territorial constituencies in the states. Among this five hundred thirty members there shall be allotted to each state a number of seats in the house of the People in such a manner that the ratio between that number and the population of the state is, so far as practicable, the same for all States; and each State shall be divided into territorial constituencies in such manner that the ratio between the population of each constituency and the number of seats allotted to it is, so far as practicable, the same throughout the state. This Provision shall not be applicable for the purpose of allotment of seats in the house of the people to any state so long as the population of that state does not exceed six millions.

(b) Not more than twenty members to represent the Union territories, chosen in such manner as Parliament may by law provide.

Here, the expression "population" means the population as ascertained at the last preceding census of which the relevant figures have been published provided that the reference in this clause to the last preceding census of which the relevant figures have been published shall, until the relevant figures for the first census taken after the year 2000 have been published, be construed as a reference to the 1971 census.

Readjustment After Each Census

Upon the completion of each census, the allocation of seats in the House of the People to the states and the division of each state into territorial constituencies shall by readjusted by such authority and in such manner as Parliament may be law determine. Such readjustment shall not affect representation in the house of the people until the dissolution of the then existing House. Such readjustment shall take effect from such date as the President may, by order, specify and until such readjustment takes effect, any election to the House may be held on the basis of the territorial constituencies existing before such readjustment. Until the relevant figures for the first census taken after the year 2000 have been published it shall not be necessary to readjust the allocation of seats in the house of the people to the states and the division of each state into territorial constituencies under this provision.

Emergency Powers of the President of India

Under the constitution of India the President has been conferred with the emergency powers in certain circumstances. Article 352 to 360 of the constitution deal with these provisions and on this basis the emergency power can be studied under three heads as stated below:

(a) National emergency which has been enshrined under Article 352 of the Constitution.

(b) State emergency enshrined under Article 356 of the constitution.

(c) Financial emergency enshrined under Article 360 of the constitution.

National Emergency

As per Article 352 of the constitution the president can proclaim emergency in whole of India or a part of it if he is satisfied that a grave emergent situation exists whereby the security of the country is threatened due to war, external aggression or armed rebellion. Such a proclamation can be made before the actual occurrence of war or of any such aggression or rebellion if the president is satisfied that there exists imminent danger thereof. A proclamation issued in the said manner can be revoked or varied by a subsequent proclamation. The president shall not issue a proclamation as said above unless the decision of the union cabinet that such a proclamation may be issued has been communicated to him in writing. If any such proclamation is issued at a time when the house of people has been dissolved or the dissolution of house takes place during the period of one month, and if a resolution approving the proclamation has been passed by the council of states, but no resolution with respect to such proclamation has been passed by the house of the people before the expiration of that period, the proclamation shall cease to operate at the expiration of thirty days from the date on which the house of the people first sits after its reconstitution unless before the expiration of the said period of 30 days a resolution approving the proclamation has also been passed by the house of the people.

State Emergency

If the president on receipt of a report from governor of the state or otherwise is satisfied that a situation has arisen in which the government of the state cannot be carried on in accordance with the provisions of the constitution, the president may by proclamation:

(a) Assume to himself all or any of the functions of the government of the state and all or any of the powers vested in or exercisable by the governor or any body or authority in the state other than the legislature of the state;

(b) Declare that the power of the legislature of the state shall be exercisable by or under the authority of parliament;

(c) Make such incidental and consequential provisions as appears to the president to be necessary or desirable for giving effect to the objects of the proclamation, including provisions for suspending in whole or in part the operation of any provision of this constitution relating to any body or authority in the state.

However, nothing as said here shall authorize the president to assume to himself any of the powers vested in or exercisable by a High Court or to suspend in whole or in part the operation of any provision of the constitution relating to High Courts.

Any such proclamation may be revoked or varied by a subsequent proclamation. A proclamation of state emergency under Article 356 of the constitution made by the president for the failure of constitutional machinery in the state shall, unless revoked cease to operate on the expiration of a period of six months from the date of issue of proclamation. This period can further be extended but no such proclamation shall, in any case, remain in force for more than one year. In case of dissolution of house of people the provisions apply equally as in case of proclamation for national emergency under Article 352 of the constitution.

Financial Emergency

The provision relating to the financial emergency has been enshrined under Article 360 of the constitution. If the president is satisfied that a situation has arisen whereby the financial stability or credit of India or any part of the territory thereof is threatened, he may by a proclamation make a declaration to that effect and such a proclamation issued:

(i) May be revoked or varied by a subsequent proclamation;

(ii) Shall be laid before each house of the parliament;

(iii) Shall cease to operate at the expiration of two months, unless before the expiration of that period it has been approved by resolutions of both the houses of parliament

If any such proclamation is issued at a time when the House of the People has been dissolved or the dissolution of the house of the people takes place during the period of two months as said above in clause (iii) and if a resolution approving the proclamation has been passed by the council of states, but no resolution with respect to such proclamation has been passed by the house of the people before the expiration of that period, the proclamation shall cease to operate at the expiration of thirty days from the date on which the house of the people first sits after its reconstitution unless before the expiration of the said period of thirty days a resolution approving the proclamation has been also passed by the house of the people.

During the period any such proclamation is in operation, the executive authority of the union shall extend to the giving of direction to any state to observe such canons of financial propriety as may be specified in the direction, and to the giving of such other directions as the president may deem necessary and adequate for the purpose.

Notwithstanding anything in the constitution, any such direction may include a provision requiring the reduction of salaries and allowances of all or any class of persons serving in connection with the affairs of the state; and a provision requiring all money bills or other bills to which the provisions of Article 207 apply to be reserved for the consideration of the president after they passed by the legislature of the state;

Furthermore, notwithstanding anything in the constitution it shall be competent for the president during the period any proclamation issued under Article 360 of the constitution is in operation to issue directions for reduction of salaries and allowances of all or any class of persons serving in connection with the affairs of the union including the judges of the Supreme Court and High Courts.

Such a proclamation ceases to operate at the end of two months unless it is approved by resolution passed by both houses of the parliament before the expiry of the period. It can be extended every six months, up to a total period of three years subject to the approval of the parliament.

Powers and Position of Indian President

The president under the Indian constitution is the head of the executive which is one of the wings of the government and this wing performs the work of implementation of law. Article 53 (1) of the constitution very clearly mandates that the executive powers of the union shall be vested in the president and shall be exercised by him either directly or through officers subordinate to him in accordance with the constitution of India. However, this power and position of the president is curtailed by Article 74 of the constitution which makes him a titular head only and the real power remains with the council of ministers with prime minister as its head. Article 74 states that there shall be a council of ministers with the prime minister as the head to aid and advice the president who shall, in exercise of his functions act in accordance with such advice. Although the president may require the council of ministers to reconsider such advice either generally or otherwise but the president is bound to act in accordance with such advice tendered after reconsideration. A significant thing to note here is that the question whether any if so what advice was tendered by ministers to the president shall not be inquired into any court. This fact makes the position of the President stronger. So, this is the position of president under Indian constitution. The power vested in the president can be classified under five heads:

(a) Administrative
(b) Legislative
(c) Financial
(d) Military
(e) Diplomatic Power

(a) Administrative Power: The president being the formal head of the state enjoys this power and all the executive actions of the union government are expressed in the name of president and authenticated in such manner as the president may direct or authenticated in such manner as the president may direct or authorize. The president has the power to appoint:

(1) The Prime Minister of India
(2) Other ministers of the union on the advice of the prime minister
(3) The Attorney General of India
(4) The Comptroller and Auditor General of India
(5) The Judges of the Supreme Court and High Courts of the States
(6) The Governor of the States
(7) The Chairman and Members of the Union Public Service Commission
(8) The Finance Commission
(9) The Chief Election Commissioner and other members of the election commission
(10) A Special Officer for the Scheduled Castes and Tribes
(11) Other Commissions

Along with the power to appoint the aforesaid persons the president also has the power to remove certain persons like the ministers appointed by him on the advice of the Prime Minister, the Attorney General of India, the Governor of State and the chairman and members of the election commission. The president if so requires can ask the prime minister to submit for the consideration of the council of minister any matter on which decision has been taken by a minister but which has not been considered by the council.

Furthermore the approval of the president is necessary for the rules made by the Supreme Court so as to govern its procedure to determine the forms of account on the advice of the comptroller and auditor general and such other administrative acts and decisions of the other authorities.

Under Article 263 of the constitution the president can establish Inter-State council so as to direct, control and co-ordinate state government. If at any time it appears to the president that the public interests would be served by the establishment of a council charged with the duty of—

(a) inquiring into and advising upon disputes which may have arisen between states;
(b) investigating and discussing subjects in which some or all of the states, or the union and one or more of the states, have a common interest; or
(c) making recommendations upon any such subjects and in particular recommendations for better co-ordination of policy and action with respect to that subject,

it shall be lawful for the President by order to establish such a council, and to define the nature of the duties to be performed by it and its organization and procedure.

If at any time it appears to the President that a question of law or fact has arisen, or is likely to arise, which is of such a nature and of such public importance that it is expedient to obtain the opinion of the Supreme Court upon it, he may refer the question to that Court for consideration and the Court may after such hearing as it thinks fit, report to the President its opinion thereon. The President may, except in the cases of disputes arising out of any treaty, agreement, covenant, engagement, sanad or other similar instruments which having been entered into or executed before the commencement of the constitution continues in operation after such commencement or which provides that the said jurisdiction shall not extend to such a dispute, refer a dispute of the kind mentioned in the said proviso to the Supreme Court for opinion and the Supreme Court shall, after such hearing as it thinks fit report to the President its opinion thereon.

(b) Legislative Powers: As per Article 79 of the constitution, the president is an integral part of parliament. So the parliament comprises of president, council of states (upper house popularly known as Rajya Sabha) and the house of people (lower house popularly known as Lok Sabha) and the president enjoys wide legislative powers. The president has got the power to summon, prorogue the houses of parliament. In case of non-money bill if there exists disagreement over it between both houses of parliament then the president can summon a joint meeting of the two houses so that the bill is considered in one forum. The president has the privilege of sending message to either house of the parliament.

At the commencement of first session in each year and of first session after each general election, the president addresses both houses assembled together and outlines in general, the policy and programs of the government of India. Besides the opening address, the president shall have the right to address either house of parliament or both of them assembled together, at any time, and the right to require the attendance of members for that purpose.

No bill for the formation of new states or the alteration of the boundaries etc. of the existing state shall be introduced in the parliament except on the recommendation of the president.

A state bill or amendment for imposing restriction upon the freedom of trade or commerce cannot be moved in the state legislature without previous sanction of the president.

A money bill shall not be introduced except on the recommendation of the president but no such recommendation shall be required for moving an amendment for reduction or abolition of any tax.

No demand for grant shall be made except on the recommendation of the president.

No bill which would involve expenditure from the consolidated fund of India, if enacted and brought into operation may be considered except on the recommendation of the president, even though it may not be, strictly speaking, a money bill.

Prior recommendation of the president is required for Union bill affecting taxation in which states are interested or affecting the principles according to which revenues are or may be distributable to the states.

A bill will not be an Act of the Indian Parliament unless and until it receives the assent of the president. When a bill is presented to the president, after its passage in both houses of parliament, the president shall be entitled to take any of the following three steps:

(i) He may declare his assent to the bill; or

(ii) He may declare that he withholds his assent to the bill; or

(iii) He may in the case of other than money bills, return the bill, for reconsideration of the houses, with or without a message suggesting amendments. In such a case if the bill is passed again by both houses of parliament with or without amendment and is again presented to the president, it would be obligatory upon him to declare his assent to it.

When the president makes proclamation under article 356 to the effect that the constitutional machinery has failed in the state, he may exercise the legislative power of that state, if the parliament authorizes him in that behalf.

(c) Financial Powers: The President causes to put forth before parliament:

(i) The annual financial statement and supplementary budget, if any;

(ii) The report of the comptroller and auditor general of India;

(iii) The recommendations made by the finance commission, together with explanatory memorandum of the action taken thereon;

(iv) The annual report of the union public service commission explaining the reasons where any advice of the commission has not been accepted.

For meeting the unforeseen expenditure of the government of India the advances are sanctioned out of the contingency fund of India by the President as per clause (1) of Article 267 of the constitution. It is the President only who determines the share of net proceeds of income tax and grant-in-aid to the states. The finance commission is appointed by him periodically to determine the revenue allocable to the States and for making recommendations on financial matters. The President through the comptroller and auditor general of India controls the receipts and expenditure of the union and the state.

(d) Military Powers: The President of India is the supreme commander of defense forces of the country. He exercises vast authorities in the interest of defense and security of India. But, the parliament has also been vested with the exclusive legislative power relating to the defense forces, war and peace. Article 53(2) of the constitution states that it will not be possible for the president to declare war against a country or to deploy troops without due regard to the wishes of parliament.

(e) Diplomatic Powers: President is vested with the power to negotiate treaties and agreements with other countries and in such matters he has to act on the advice of the council of ministers, subject however to the ratification by the parliament. Further, though diplomatic representation as a subject of legislation belongs to parliament, the president will represent India in international affairs and will have the power of appointing Indian representatives to the other countries and of receiving diplomatic representatives to the other countries, as shall be recognized by parliament.

Effects of Proclamation of Emergency

(a) Effects of Proclamation of Emergency during war, external aggression or armed rebellion:

(1) The Union Parliament can take over any of the Legislative powers of the states and may give directions to any state as to the manner in which the executive power shall be exercised by them.

(2) The Parliament can make laws on any state subject.

(3) The distribution of revenues between the Union and the State may be modified by the President.

(4) Provisions of Article 19 of the constitution regarding the freedoms may be suspended.

(5) The President may suspend the enforcement of any of the fundamental rights by the courts.

(b) Effects of proclamation of emergency on account of failure of constitutional machinery in a state:

(1) The President may assume to himself any of the executive functions of the state government.

(2) The President may declare that the legislative powers of the state shall be exercisable by or under the authority of the Union Parliament.

(3) The President may authorize any expenditure from the consolidated fund of the state when the house of the People is not in session.

(c) Effects of Proclamation of Financial Emergency:

(1) The Union Government may give directions to the states on the observance of financial propriety.

(2) Any such direction may include (a) a provision requiring the reduction

of salaries and allowances of all or any class of state government employees; (b) a provision requiring the reduction of salaries and allowances of all or any class of persons serving the Union including the judges of the Supreme Court and the High Courts; and (c) provision requiring all money bills and other financial bills to be reserved for the consideration of the President after they are passed by the state legislature.

Six Freedoms Guaranteed Under the Constitution of India

Article 19 of the constitution put forth presently six freedoms to be enjoyed by the citizens of the country. These are:

(1) Freedom of speech and expression;

(2) Freedom to assemble peaceably and without arms;

(3) Freedom to form associations and union;

(4) Freedom to move freely throughout the territory of India;

(5) Freedom to reside and settle in any part of the territory of India;

(6) Freedom to practice any profession or to carry on any occupation, trade, or business.

Prior to forty-forth amendment in the constitution, right to acquire, hold and dispose of property was also enshrined as one more freedom under aforesaid Article 19(1) of the constitution but this right was omitted from the list of fundamental rights in the year 1978 after the said amendment. This right is now a statutory right rather than a fundamental right vide Article 300A of the constitution which states "no person shall be deprived of his property saved by the authority of law." Parliament or state legislature is empowered to make any law so as to impose reasonable restrictions on the right to hold and dispose of property in the interest of the general public or for the protection of the interests of any scheduled tribes.

Fundamental right to equality

The right to equality has been enshrined in Article 14 to Article 18 of the constitution. Article 14 of the constitution states that the state shall not deny to any person equality before the law or the equal protection of the laws within the territories of India. This concept of equality as provided in the constitution means that the equals shall be treated equally and the unequals shall be treated differently.

Furthermore, the state shall not discriminate against any citizen on grounds of religion, race, caste, sex, place of birth or any of them and also on any of such ground no citizen can be subjected to any disability, liability, restriction or condition with regard to:

(a) Access to shops, public restaurants, hotels and the places of public entertainment; or

(b) The use of wells, tanks, bathing ghats, roads and places of public resort maintained wholly or partly out of the State funds or dedicated to the use of general public.

But, the government can make special provision for women and children on these matters. Also despite the aforesaid provision the government can make special provision for the advancement of socially and educationally backward classes of citizens or for the scheduled castes and the scheduled tribes. This provision of the constitution is limited to the citizens only. The aliens are not covered by this Article of the constitution. So, it stands as an exception. By various amendments to the constitution exceptions to the guarantee of fundamental rights have been introduced, for instance:

(i) Saving of laws providing for acquisition of estate etc. under Art. 31A.

(ii) Validation of certain Acts and regulations.

(iii) Protection of laws giving effect to the directive principle of state policy under Article 31C

(iv) Saving of laws in respect of anti-national activities under Article 31D which was repealed by the constitution (forty-third amendment) Act, 1977.

(v) Power of parliament to vary or revoke conditions of service of officers of certain services under Article 312A (3).

(vi) Administrative tribunals relating to services in Andhra Pradesh under Article 323A (2) (f).

(vii) Provision under Part XIV A of the constitution.

(viii) Total suspension of Article 14 under Article 359 of the constitution.

(ix) Clause (4) of Article 16 dealing with reservation for backward classes which contravenes partially clauses (1) and (2) of Article 14.

Article 16 of the constitution provides for the equality of opportunity in the matters of public employment. There shall be equality of opportunity for the citizens in the matters of public employment or appointment to any office under the state. No citizen shall, on grounds only of religion, race, caste, sex, descent, place of birth, residence or any of them, be ineligible for, or discriminated against in respect of any employment or office under the State. Such a provision would not check the parliament from making any law prescribing in regard to a class or classes of employment or appointment to an office under the Government of, or any local or other authority within, state or union territory, any requirement as to residence within that state or union territory prior to such employment.

Besides, nothing as aforesaid can prevent the state from making any provision for the reservation of appointments or posts in favour of any backward class of citizens or scheduled caste or scheduled tribes which in the opinion of the state is not adequately represented in the services under the state.

Also, the state would not be prevented by the aforesaid provision from considering any unfilled vacancies of a year, which are reserved for being filled up in that year in accordance with any provision for reservation made for SC, ST and OBCs above stated, as a separate class of vacancies to be filled up in any succeeding year or years. Such class of vacancies shall not be considered together with the vacancies of the year in which they are being filled up for determining the ceiling of fifty percent reservation on total number of vacancies of that year.

This equality of opportunity as provided to the citizens under Article 16 of the constitution shall not affect the operation of any law which provides that the incumbent of an office in connection with the affairs of any religious or denominational institution or any member of governing body thereof shall be a person professing a particular religion or belonging to a particular denomination.

Under Article 17 of the constitution the "untouchability" has been abolished and its practice in any form is forbidden. The enforcement of any disability arising out of "untouchability" has to be an offence punishable in accordance with law.

There is abolition of titles under Article 18 of the constitution. The State cannot confer any title to any person except of military or academic distinction. Also, the citizens of India cannot accept any title from any foreign state. Furthermore, no person who is not a citizen of India shall, while he holds any office of profit or trust under state, accept without the consent of the president any title from any foreign state. No person holding any office of profit or trust under the state shall without the consent of the president, accept any present, emolument or office of any kind from or under any foreign state.

Fundamental right to freedom guaranteed in the constitution

The protection of certain rights regarding freedom of speech etc. has been enshrined in Article 19 of the Constitution of India. All citizens have the right:

(1) To freedom of speech and expression.

(2) To assemble peaceably and without arms.

(3) To form Association or Unions.

(4) To move freely throughout the territory of India.

(5) To reside and settle in any part of the territory of India, and

(6) To practice any profession, or to carry on any occupation, trade or business.

Nothing as relates to the freedom of speech and expression shall affect the operation of any existing law, or prevent the state from making any law, in so far as such law imposes reasonable restrictions on the exercise of the right conferred by the said sub-clause in the interest of the sovereignty and integrity of India the security of the state, friendly relations with foreign states, public order, decency or morality or in relation to contempt of court, defamation or incitement to an offence.

More so, nothing as it relates to the freedom to assemble peaceably and without arms shall affect the operation of any existing law in so far as it imposes or prevent the state from making any law imposes in the interests of the sovereignty and integrity of India or public order, reasonable restriction on the exercise of the right conferred by the said sub-clause.

Moreover, nothing as it relates to the freedom to form association or union shall affect the operation of any existing law in so far as it imposes, or prevent the state from making any law imposing in the interest of the sovereignty and integrity of India or public order or morality, reasonable restrictions on the exercise of the right conferred by the said sub-clause.

Besides, nothing as it relates to freedom to move freely throughout the territory of India shall affect the operation of any existing law in so far as it imposes or prevent the state from making any law imposing reasonable restrictions on the exercise of any of the rights conferred by the said sub-clause either in the interest of the general public or for the protection of the interest of any scheduled tribe.

Furthermore, nothing as it relates to the freedom to practice any profession, or to carry on any occupation, trade or business shall affect the operation of any existing law in so far as it imposes, or prevent the state from making any law imposing, in the interests of the general public, reasonable restrictions on the exercise of the right conferred by the said sub-clause and in particular nothing in the said sub-clause shall affect the operation of any existing law in so far as it relates to or prevent the state from making any law relating to the professional or technical qualification necessary for practicing any profession or carrying on any occupation, trade or business or the carrying on by the state or by a corporation owned or controlled by the state of any trade, business, industry, or service whether to the exclusion, complete or partial of citizens or otherwise.

The protection in respect of conviction for offences is enshrined in Article 20 of the Constitution. No person shall be convicted of any offence except for violation of a law in force at the time of the commission of the act charged as an offence, nor be subjected to a penalty greater than that which might have been inflicted under the law in force at the time of the commission of the offence. No person shall be prosecuted and punished for the same offence more than once. Besides, no person accused of any offence shall be compelled to be witness against himself.

For protection of life and personal liberty Article 21 of the constitution states that no person shall be deprived of his life or personal liberty except according to procedure established by law.

Protection has been provided against arrest and detention in certain cases. No person who is arrested shall be detained in custody without being informed, as soon as may be, of the grounds for such arrest nor shall he be denied the right to consult and to be defended by a legal practitioner of his choice. Every person who is arrested and detained in custody shall be produced before the nearest magistrate within a period of twenty four hours of such arrest excluding the time necessary for the journey from the place of arrest to the court of the magistrate and no such person shall be detained in custody beyond the said period without the authority of a magistrate. Nothing as aforesaid shall apply to any person who for the time being is an enemy alien or to any person who is arrested or detained under any law providing for preventive detention. No law providing for preventive detention shall authorize the detention of a person for a longer period than three months unless an advisory board consisting of persons who are or have been or are qualified to be appointed as, judges of the High Court has reported before the expiration of the said period of three months that there is in its opinion sufficient cause for such detention provided that nothing as said here shall authorize the detention of any person beyond the maximum period prescribed by any law made by parliament relating to the maximum period for which under any law providing for preventive detention, or such person is detained in accordance with the provisions of any law made by parliament under, the circumstances under which, and the class or classes of cases in which, a person may be detained for a period longer than three months under any law providing for preventive detention without obtaining the opinion of an advisory board consisting of persons who are or have been or are qualified to be appointed as, judges of a High Court, under which the maximum period for which any person may in any class or classes of cases be detained under any law providing for preventive detention. When any person is detained in pursuance of an order made under any law providing for preventive detention, the authority making the order shall as soon as may be communicate to such person the grounds on which the order has been made and shall afford him the earliest opportunity of making a representation against the order. Nothing as said here shall require the authority making such order as is referred to in that clause to disclose facts which such authority considers to be against the public interest to disclose. Parliament may by law prescribe the circumstances under which, and the class or classes of cases in which a person may be detained for a period longer than three months under any law providing for preventive detention without obtaining the opinion of an advisory board in accordance with the provisions as aforesaid. Besides, parliament may by law prescribe the maximum period for which any person may in any class or classes of cases be detained under any law providing for preventive detention; and the procedure to be followed by an Advisory Board in an enquiry.

Fundamental Right Against Exploitation

Under the right against exploitation there is prohibition of traffic in human beings and forced labour. Traffic in human beings and beggar and other similar forms of forced labour are prohibited and any contravention of this provision is an offence punishable in accordance with law. Nothing as said here is to prevent the state from imposing compulsory service for public purposes, and in imposing such service the state shall not make any determination on grounds only of religion, race, caste or class or any of them. There is also a prohibition of employment of children in factories etc. No child below the age of fourteen years shall be employed to work in any factory or mine or engaged in any other hazardous employment.

Fundamental Right to Freedom of Religion and Cultural and Educational Rights

Freedom of conscience and free profession, practice and propagation of religion has been envisaged under Article 25 of the constitution of India. Subject to public order, morality and health and to the other provisions relating to fundamental rights, all persons are equally entitled to freedom of conscience and the right freely to profess, practice and propagate religion. Nothing as said here shall affect the operation of any existing law or prevent the state from making any law:

(a) Regulating or restricting any economic, financial, political or other secular activity which may be associated with religions practice.

(b) Providing for social welfare and reform or the throwing open of Hindus religious institution of a public character to all classes and sections of Hindus.

Here, the reference to Hindus shall be construed as including a reference to persons professing the Sikh, Jaina or Buddhist religion and the reference to Hindu religious institution shall be construed accordingly.

The wearing and carrying of kirpans is deemed to be included in the profession of Sikh religion.

Freedom to manage religious affairs has been envisaged under Article 26 of the constitution. Subject to public order, morality and health, every religious denomination or any section thereof shall have the right: -

(a) To establish and maintain institutions for religious and charitable purposes;
(b) To manage its own affairs in matters of religion;
(c) To own and acquire moveable and immovable property; and
(d) To administer such property in accordance with law.

For freedom as to payment of taxes for promotion of any particular religion it has been said that no person shall be compelled to pay any taxes, the proceeds of which are specifically appropriated in payment of expenses for the promotion or maintenance of any particular religion or religious denomination.

There also exists the freedom as to attendance at religious instruction or religious worship in certain educational institutions. No religious instruction shall be provided in any educational institution wholly maintained out of the state funds. Nothing as said here shall apply to an educational institution which is administered by the State but has been established under any endowment or trust which requires that religious instruction shall be imparted in such institution. No person attending any educational institution recognized by the state or receiving aid out of State funds shall be required to take part in any religious instruction that may be imparted in such institution to attend any religious worship that may be conducted in such institution or in any premises attached thereto unless such person or if such person is a minor, his guardian has given consent thereto.

Article 29 of the constitution of India comprehends the protection of interests of minorities. Any section of the citizens residing in the territory of India or any part thereof having a distinct language, script or culture of its own shall have the rights to conserve the same. No citizen shall be denied admission into any educational institution maintained by the state of receiving aid out of state funds on grounds only of religion, race, caste, language or any of them.

Right of minorities to establish and administer educational institutions is envisaged under Article 30 of the constitution. All minorities, whether based on religion or language shall have the right to establish and administer educational institutions of their choice. In making any law providing for the compulsory acquisition of any property of an educational institution established and administered by a minority referred to as above, the state shall ensure that the amount fixed by or determined under such law for the acquisition of such property is such as would not restrict or abrogate the right guaranteed under the said clause. The state shall not in granting aid to educational institutions discriminate against any educational institution on the ground that it is under the management of a minority, whether based on religion or language.

Right to Constitutional Remedies

Article 32 of the Constitution talks of the remedies for enforcement of rights conferred by part IIIrd of the Constitution. The right to move to the Supreme Court by appropriate proceedings for the enforcement of the rights conferred by part IIIrd of the Constitution is guaranteed. The Supreme Court shall have power to issue directions, orders or writs including writs in the nature of Habeas Corpus, Mandamus, Prohibition, Quo-Warranto and Certiorari whichever may be appropriate for the enforcement of any of the rights conferred by part IIIrd of the Constitution. Without prejudice to power conferred on the Supreme Court as said above, parliament may by law empower any other court to exercise within the local limits of its jurisdiction all or any of the power exercisable by the Supreme Court. The right guaranteed here is not suspended except as otherwise provided for by the Constitution.

Power of Parliament to modify the rights conferred by part IIIrd of the Constitution in their application to forces etc. has been enshrined in Article 33 of the Constitution. Parliament may by law determine to what extent any of the rights conferred by part IIIrd of the Constitution dealing with the fundamental rights shall in their application to the members of the Armed forces or the members of the forces charged with the maintenance of public order, persons employed in any bureau or other organization, established by the state for the purposes of intelligence or counter intelligence or persons employed in, or in connection with the telecommunication system set up for the purposes of any force, bureau or organization referred to as above be restricted or abrogated so as to ensure the proper discharge of their duties and the maintenance of discipline among them.

Restrictions on fundamental rights have been imposed under Article 34 of the constitution subject to the condition when martial law is in force in any area. Notwithstanding anything in the forgoing provision of part IIIrd of the Constitution dealing with fundamental rights, parliament may by law indemnify any person in the service of the Union or of a State or any other person in respect of any act done by him in connection with the maintenance or restoration of order in any area within the territory of India where martial law was in force or validate any sentence passed, punishment inflicted, forfeiture ordered or other act done under martial law in such area.

Article 35 of the Constitution provides for the legislation to give effect to the fundamental rights. Notwithstanding anything in the Constitution parliament shall have and the legislature of a state shall not have power to make laws with respect to any of the matters which under clause (3) of Article 32, Article 33 and Article 34 may be provided for by law made by parliament; and for prescribing punishment for those acts which are declared to be offences under part IIIrd of the Constitution and parliament shall as soon as may be after the commencement of the Constitution make laws for prescribing punishment for the acts which are declared to be offences under part IIIrd of the Constitution. Besides, notwithstanding anything in the constitution any law in force immediately before the commencement of the Constitution in the territory of India with respect to any of the matters which are under clause (3) of Article16, clause (3) of Article 32, Article 33 and Article 34 or providing for punishment for any act which are declared to be offence shall, subject to the terms thereof and to any adaptations and modifications that may be made therein under Article 372 continue in force until altered or replaced or amended by parliament. Here "law in force" include a law passed or made by a legislature or other competent authority in the territory of India before the commencement of the Constitution and not previously repealed notwithstanding that it or parts of it may not be then in operation either at all or in particular areas.

Distinction Between 'Equality before the Law' and 'Equal Protection of the Laws'

Right to equality means the equality of citizens before law. It has been stated in Article 14 of the constitution that the State shall not deny to any person equality before the law or the equal protection of law within the territory of India. On the ground of race, religion, caste, sex or place of birth, no citizen can be subjected to any disability in matters like access to places of public entertainment, use of public wells, tanks, roads etc. or eligibility to any office or employment under the State. Under Article 17 'untouchability' has been abolished and its practice in any form has been forbidden. Conferment of titles (except military and academic distinctions) by the state is forbidden and Indian citizens cannot accept any title from any foreign state. Even non-Indians, under the service of State, are forbidden to accept any titles from foreign states without the consent of the President.

In the year 1951 an amendment was made in the constitution by which it was specifically laid down that the right to equality would not prevent the State from making special provisions for the advancement of any socially or educationally backward classes.

Similarly, the right to equality does not prevent the Parliament from prescribing residence qualification in regard to employment within particular State or local areas. Again equality of access to public places does not preclude the State from making special provision for women and children.

However, Article 15 of the constitution is limited to citizens only. This Article does not cover the aliens. Hence this is an exception. Furthermore by various amendments to constitution exceptions to the guarantee of fundamental rights have been introduced e.g

(a) Saving of laws providing for acquisition of estate etc. under Art. 31A.
(b) Validation of certain Acts and Regulations.
(c) Protection of laws giving effect to the Directive Principle of State Policy under Article 31C.
(d) Saving of laws in respect of anti-national activities under Article 31D. (Since omitted vide 43rd (Amendment) Act, 1977).
(e) Power of Parliament to vary or revoke conditions of service of officers of certain Services under Article 312A(3).
(f) Administrative Tribunals relating to services in Andhra Pradesh (Article 323A(2)(f).
(g) Provision under Part XIV A.
(h) Under Article 359 – Total suspension of Article 14. (Since amended vide 44th (Amendment) Act, 1978).

Clause (4) of Article 16 Reservation for backward classes is in the nature of an exception of clause (1) and (2) ibid partially.

Preventive Detention

As a matter of preventive action of the police it has been made mandatory that every police officer may interpose for the purpose of preventing, and shall, to the best of his ability, prevent the commission of any cognizable offence. Every police officer receiving information of a design to commit any cognizable offence shall communicate such information to the police officer to whom he is subordinate, and to any other officer whose duty it is to prevent or take cognizance of the commission of any such offence. A police officer knowing of a design to commit any cognizable offence may arrest, without order from a magistrate and without a warrant, the person so designing, if it appears to such officer that the commission of the offence cannot be otherwise prevented. No person arrested in such mentioned manner shall be detained in custody for a period exceeding twenty-four hours from the time of his arrest unless his further detention is required or authorized under any other provision of the code of criminal procedure or of any other law for the time being in force.

A person arrested under the preventive detention laws cannot be detained in custody for more than two months unless an advisory board constituted in accordance with the recommendations of the chief justice of the appropriate high court advises before the expiration of the said period of two months that sufficient grounds exist for continued detention.

The advisory board should consist of a chairman and not less than two other members. The chairman should be a serving judge of the appropriate high court and the other members should be serving of retired judges of any high court.

No person arrested under the preventive detention laws can be detained in custody beyond the maximum period prescribed by law made by the parliament.

The authority ordering the detention of a person under the preventive detention laws should, as soon as possible, communicate to the arrested person the grounds on which the order of detention has been made and should afford him the earliest opportunity of making a representation against the order.

The authority ordering the detention need not disclose the facts which, in the opinion of the said authority, are against public interest.

Differences between Fundamental Rights and Directive Principle

The main points of difference between Fundamental Rights and Directive Principles is that firstly the directive principle of state policy lays down certain guidelines for the legislature and the executive to follow in exercise of their authority whereas fundamental rights are the citizen's basic human rights essential for the good life. Secondly, Directive Principle of state policy cannot be enforced by a court of law whereas fundamental rights are justiciable, i.e, denial of fundamental rights by the state can be challenged in a court of law and got remedied.

Establishment, Constitution, Power and Position of Supreme Court

On 28th of January, 1950, two days after India became a Sovereign Democratic Republic, the Supreme Court came into being. The inauguration took place in the Chamber of Princes in the Parliament building which also housed India's Parliament, consisting of the Council of States and the House of the People. It was here, in this Chamber of Princes, that the Federal Court of India had sat for 12 years between 1937 and 1950. This was to be the home of the Supreme Court for years that were to follow until the Supreme Court acquired its own present premises.

The inaugural proceedings were simple but impressive. They began at 9.45 a.m. when the Judges of the Federal Court - Chief Justice Harilal J.Kania and Justices Saiyid Fazl Ali, M. Patanjali Sastri, Mehr Chand Mahajan, Bijan Kumar Mukherjea and S.R.Das - took their seats. In attendance were the Chief Justices of the High Courts of Allahabad, Bombay, Madras, Orissa, Assam, Nagpur, Punjab, Saurashtra, Patiala and the East Punjab States Union, Mysore, Hyderabad, Madhya Bharat and Travancore-Cochin. Along with the Attorney General for India, M.C. Setalvad were present the Advocate Generals of Bombay, Madras, Uttar Pradesh, Bihar, East Punjab, Orissa, Mysore, Hyderabad and Madhya Bharat. Present too, were Prime Minister, other Ministers, Ambassadors and diplomatic representatives of foreign States, a large number of Senior and other Advocates of the Court and other distinguished visitors.

Taking care to ensure that the Rules of the Supreme Court were published and the names of all the Advocates and agents of the Federal Court were brought on the rolls of the Supreme Court, the inaugural proceedings were over and put under part of the record of the Supreme Court.

After its inauguration on January 28, 1950, the Supreme Court commenced its sittings in a part of the Parliament House. The Court moved into the present building in 1958. The building is shaped to project the image of scales of justice. The Central Wing of the building is the Centre Beam of the Scales. In 1979, two New Wings - the East Wing and the West Wing - were added to the complex. In all there are 15 Court Rooms in the various wings of the building. The Chief Justice's Court is the largest of the Courts located in the Centre of the Central Wing.

The original Constitution of 1950 envisaged a Supreme Court with a Chief Justice and 7 puisne Judges - leaving it to Parliament to increase this number. In the early years, all the Judges of the Supreme Court sat together to hear the cases presented before them. As the work of the Court increased and arrears of cases began to cumulate, Parliament increased the number of Judges from 8 in 1950 to 11 in 1956, 14 in 1960, 18 in 1978 and 26 in 1986. As the number of the Judges has increased, they sit in smaller Benches of two and three - coming together in larger Benches of 5 and more only when required to do so or to settle a difference of opinion or controversy.

Currently the Supreme Court of India comprises the Chief Justice and 30 other Judges appointed by the President of India. Supreme Court Judges retire upon attaining the age of 65 years. In order to be appointed as a Judge of the Supreme Court, a person must be a citizen of India and must have been, for atleast five years, a Judge of a High Court or of two or more such Courts in succession, or an Advocate of a

High Court or of two or more such Courts in succession for at least 10 years or he must be, in the opinion of the President, a distinguished jurist. Provisions exist for the appointment of a Judge of a High Court as an Ad-hoc Judge of the Supreme Court and for retired Judges of the Supreme Court or High Courts to sit and act as Judges of that Court.

The Constitution seeks to ensure the independence of Supreme Court Judges in various ways. A Judge of the Supreme Court cannot be removed from office except by an order of the President passed after an address in each House of Parliament supported by a majority of the total membership of that House and by a majority of not less than two-thirds of members present and voting, and presented to the President in the same Session for such removal on the ground of proved misbehaviour or incapacity. A person who has been a Judge of the Supreme Court is debarred from practising in any court of law or before any other authority in India.

The proceedings of the Supreme Court are conducted in English only. Supreme Court Rules, 1966 are framed under Article 145 of the Constitution to regulate the practice and procedure of the Supreme Court.

Supreme Court Registry

The Registry of the Supreme Court is headed by the Registrar General who is assisted in his work by three Registrars, four Additional Registrars, twelve Joint Registrars etc. Article 146 of the Constitution deals with the appointments of officers and servants of the Supreme Court Registry.

Attorney General

The Attorney General for India is appointed by the President of India under Article 76 of the Constitution and holds office during the pleasure of the President. He must be a person qualified to be appointed as a Judge of the Supreme Court. It is the duty of the Attorney General for India to give advice to the Government of India upon such legal matters and to perform such other duties of legal character as may be referred or assigned to him by the President. In the performance of his duties, he has the right of audience in all Courts in India as well as the right to take part in the proceedings of Parliament without the right to vote. In discharge of his functions, the Attorney General is assisted by a Solicitor General and four Additional Solicitor Generals.

Supreme Court Advocates

There are three categories of Advocates who are entitled to practise law before the Supreme Court of India:

(i) Senior Advocates

These are Advocates who are designated as Senior Advocates by the Supreme Court of India or by any High Court. The Court can designate any Advocate, with his consent, as Senior Advocate if in its opinion by virtue of his ability, standing at the Bar or special knowledge or experience in law the said Advocate is deserving of such distinction. A Senior Advocate is not entitled to appear without an Advocate-on-Record in the Supreme Court or without a junior in any other court or tribunal in India. He is also not entitled to accept instructions to draw pleadings or affidavits, advise on evidence or do any drafting work of an analogous kind in any court or tribunal in India or undertake conveyancing work of any kind whatsoever but this prohibition shall not extend to settling any such matter as aforesaid in consultation with a junior.

(ii) Advocates-On-Record

Only these Advocates are entitled to file any matter or document before the Supreme Court. They can also file an appearance or act for a party in the Supreme Court.

(iii) Other Advocates

These are Advocates whose names are entered on the roll of any State Bar Council maintained under the Advocates Act, 1961 and they can appear and argue any matter on behalf of a party in the Supreme Court but they are not entitled to file any document or matter before the Court.

Public Interest Litigation

Although the proceedings in the Supreme Court arise out of the judgments or orders made by the Subordinate Courts including the High Courts, but of late the Supreme Court has started entertaining matters in which interest of the public at large is involved and the Court can be moved by any individual or group of persons either by filing a Writ Petition at the Filing Counter of the Court or by addressing a letter to Hon'ble the Chief Justice of India highlighting the question of public importance for invoking this jurisdiction. Such concept is popularly known as 'Public Interest Litigation' and several matters of public importance have become landmark cases. This concept is unique to the Supreme Court of India only and perhaps no other Court in the world has been exercising this extraordinary jurisdiction. A Writ Petition filed at the Filing Counter is dealt with like any other Writ Petition and processed as such. In case of a letter addressed to Hon'ble the Chief Justice of India the same is dealt with in accordance with the guidelines framed for the purpose.

Provision of Legal Aid

If a person belongs to the poor section of the society having annual income of less than Rs. 18,000/- or belongs to Scheduled Caste or Scheduled Tribe, a victim of natural calamity, is a woman or a child or a mentally ill or otherwise disabled person or an industrial workman, or is in custody including custody in protective home, he/she is entitled to get free legal aid from the Supreme Court Legal Aid Committee. The aid so granted by the Committee includes cost of preparation of the matter and all applications connected therewith, in addition to providing an Advocate for preparing and arguing the case. Any person desirous of availing legal service through the Committee has to make an application to the Secretary and hand over all necessary documents concerning his case to it. The Committee after ascertaining the eligibility of the person provides necessary legal aid to him/her.

Persons belonging to middle income group i.e. with income above Rs. 18,000/- but under Rs. 1,20,000/- per annum are eligible to get legal aid from the Supreme Court Middle Income Group Society, on nominal payments.

Amicus Curiae

If a petition is received from the jail or in any other criminal matter if the accused is unrepresented then an Advocate is appointed as amicus curiae by the Court to defend and argue the case of the accused. In civil matters also the Court can appoint an Advocate as amicus curiae if it thinks it necessary in case of an unrepresented party; the Court can also appoint amicus curiae in any matter of general public importance or in which the interest of the public at large is involved.

As per article 124 of the constitution, there shall be a Supreme Court of India consisting of a chief Justice of India and, until Parliament by law prescribes a larger number, of not, more than seven other Judges. Now the present number of judges is twenty-five.

Every Judge of the Supreme Court shall be appointed by the President by warrant under his hand and seal after consultation with such of the Judges of the Supreme Court and of the High Courts in the States as the President may deem necessary for the purpose and shall hold office until he attains the age of sixty-five years. In the case of appointment of a Judge other than the Chief Justice, the Chief Justice of India shall always be consulted.

Further more, it is also possible that:

(a) A judge may by writing under his hand addressed to the President, resign his office;

(b) A Judge may be removed from his office in the manner prescribed.

The age of a Judge of the Supreme Court shall be determined by such authority and in such manner as Parliament may by law provide.

A person shall not be qualified for appointment as a judge of the Supreme Court unless he is a citizen of India and:

(a) has been for at least five years a Judge of a High Court or of two or more such courts in succession; or

(b) has been for at least ten years an advocate of a High Court or of two or more such courts in succession; or

(c) is, in the opinion of the President a distinguished jurist.

Here, "High Court" means a High Court which exercises, or which at any time before the commencement of the constitution exercised jurisdiction in any part of the territory of India. In computing the period during which a person has been an advocate, any period during which a person has held judicial office not inferior to that of a district judge after he became an advocate shall be included.

A judge of the Supreme Court shall not be removed from his office except by an order of the President passed after an address by each House of Parliament supported by a majority of the total membership of that House and by a majority of not less than two-thirds of the members of that House present and voting has been presented and voting has been presented to the President in the same session for such removal on the ground of proved misbehaviour or incapacity.

Parliament may by law regulate the procedure for the presentation of an address and for the investigation and proof of the misbehaviour or incapacity of a judge.

Every person appointed to be a Judge of the Supreme Court shall, before he enters upon his office, make and subscribe before the President, or some person appointed in that behalf by him, an oath or affirmation according to the form set out for the purpose in the third Schedule of the constitution.

No person who has held office as a judge of the Supreme Court shall, plead or act in any court or before any authority within the territory of India.

Appointment of Acting Chief Justice

When the office of Chief justice of India is vacant or when the Chief Justice is, by reason of absence or otherwise, unable to perform the duties of his office, the duties of the office shall be performed by such one of the other Judges of the court as the President may appoint of the purpose.

Appointment of Ad hoc Judges

If at any time there should not be a quorum of the judges of the Supreme Court available to hold or continue any session of the court, the Chief Justice of India may, with the previous consent of the President and after consultation with the Chief Justice of the High Court concerned, request in writing the attendance at the sittings of the court, as ad hoc Judge, for such period as may be necessary, of a Judge of a High Court duly qualified for appointment as a Judge of the Supreme Court to be designated by the Chief Justice of India.

It shall be the duty of the judge who has been so designated, in priority to other duties of his office to attend the sittings of the Supreme Court at the time and for the period for which his attendance is required, and while so attending he shall have all the jurisdiction, powers and privileges, and shall discharge the duties, of a Judge of the Supreme Court.

Attendance of retired judges at sittings of the Supreme Court

The Chief Justice of India may at any time, with the previous consent of the President request any person who has held the office of a Judge of the Supreme Court or of the Federal Court or who has held the office of a Judge of a High Court and is duly qualified for appointment as a Judge of the Supreme Court to sit and act as a judge of the Supreme Court, and every such person so requested shall, while so sitting and acting, be entitled to such allowances as the President may by order determine and have all the Jurisdiction, powers and privileges of, but shall not otherwise be deemed to be, a Judge of that Court. It would not be deemed to require any such person as aforesaid to sit and act as a Judge of that Court unless he consents so to do.

Salaries, etc. of Judges

There shall be paid to the Judges of the Supreme Court such salaries as may be determined by Parliament by law and, until provision in that behalf is so made, such salaries as are specified in the Second Schedule of the constitution.

Every Judge shall be entitled to such privileges and allowances and to such rights in respect of leave of absence and pension as may from time to time be determined by or under law made by Parliament and until so determined, to such privileges, allowances and rights as are specified in the Second Schedule of the constitution. Neither the privileges nor the allowances of a Judge nor his rights in respect of leave of absence or pension shall be varied to his disadvantage after his appointment.

Supreme Court to be a Court of Record

The Supreme Court shall be a court of record and shall have all the powers of such a court including the power to punish for contempt of itself.

The Supreme Court shall sit in Delhi or in such other place, as the Chief Justice of India may with the approval of the President from time to time, appoint.

Certificate for appeal to the Supreme Court

Every High Court, passing or making a judgment, decree, final order, or sentence may, if it deems fit so to do, on its own motion; and shall, if an oral application is made, by or on behalf of the party aggrieved, immediately after the passing or making of such judgment, decree, final order or sentence, determine the question whether a certificate may be given in respect of that case.

Review of Judgments or Orders by the Supreme Court

Subject to the provisions of any law made by Parliament or any rules made under article 145 dealing with the rules of court, the Supreme Court shall have power to review any judgment pronounced or order made by it.

Conferment on the Supreme Court of Powers to issue certain writs

Parliament may by law confer on the Supreme Court power to issue directions, orders or writs, including writs in the nature of habeas corpus, mandamus, prohibition, qua-warranto and certiorari, or any of them, for the purposes other than the enforcement of fundamental rights enshrined in the constitution.

Transfer of certain cases

Where cases involving the same or substantially the same questions of law are pending before the Supreme Court and one or more High Court or before two or more High Court and the Supreme Court is satisfied on its own motion or on an application made by the attorney-general of India or by party to any such case that such questions are substantial questions of general importance the Supreme Court may withdraw the case or cases pending before the High Court or the High Courts and dispose of all the cases itself. The Supreme Court may after determining the said questions of law return any case so withdrawn together with a copy of its judgment on such questions to the High Court from which the case has been withdrawn, and the High Court shall on receipt thereof, proceed to dispose of the case in conformity with such judgment. The Supreme Court may, if it deems it expedient so to do for the ends of justice, transfer any case, appeal or other proceedings pending before any High Court to any other High Court.

Ancillary Powers of Supreme Court

Parliament may by law make provision for conferring upon the Supreme Court such supplemental powers not inconsistent with any of the provisions of the Constitution as may appear to be necessary or desirable for the purpose of enabling the Court more effectively to exercise the jurisdiction conferred upon it by or under the Constitution.

Law declared by Supreme Court to be binding on all Courts

The law declared by the Supreme Court shall be binding on all Courts within the territory of India.

Enforcement of decrees and orders of Supreme Court and orders as to discovery, etc.

The Supreme Court in the exercise of its jurisdiction may pass such decree or make such order as is necessary for doing complete justice in any cause or matter pending before it, and any decree so passed or order so made shall be enforceable throughout the territory of India in such manner as may be prescribed by or under any law made by Parliament and, until provision in that behalf is so made, in such manner as the president may by order prescribe. The Supreme Court shall, as respects the whole of the territory of India, have all and every power to make any order for the purpose of securing the attendance of any person, the discovery or production of any documents or the investigation or punishment of any contempt of itself.

Civil and Judicial Authorities to act in Aid of the Supreme Court

All authorities civil and judicial in the territory of India shall act in aid of the Supreme Court.

Rules of Court, etc.

The Supreme Court may from time to time with the approval of the President, make rules for regulating generally the practice and procedure of the Court subject to the Provision of any law made by Parliament and it shall include:

(a) rules as to the persons practicing before the Court.

(b) rules as to the procedure for hearing appeals and other matters pertaining to appeals including the time within which appeals to the Court are to be entered.

(c) rules as to the proceedings in the Court for the enforcement of any of the fundamental rights.

(d) rules as to the proceedings in the Court for issuing certain writs.

(e) rules as to the entertainment of appeals under sub-clause (c) of clause (1) of article 134.

(f) rules as to the conditions subject to which any judgment pronounced or order made by the Court for such review are to be entered.

(g) rules as to the costs of and incidental to any proceedings in the Court and as to the fees to be charged in respect of proceedings therein.

(h) rules as to the granting of bail.

(i) rules as to stay of proceedings.

(j) rules providing for the summary determination of any appeal for the purpose of delay.

(k) rules as to the procedure for inquiries referred to in clause (1) of article 317.

The minimum number of Judges who are to sit for the purpose of deciding any case involving a substantial question of law as to the interpretation of the constitution or for the purpose of hearing any reference made by the president under article 143 shall be five and subject to this provision rules of courts may fix the minimum number of judges who are to sit for any purpose, and may provide for the powers of single judges and Division Courts.

Where the court hearing an appeal under any of the provision of the chapter of the constitution, dealing with the union judiciary, other than article 132 consists of less than five judges and in the course of the hearing of the appeal the court is satisfied that the appeal involves a substantial question of law as to the interpretation of the constitution the determination of which is necessary for the disposal of the appeal such court shall refer the question for opinion to a court constituted as required by this provision for the purpose of deciding any case involving such a question and shall on receipt of the opinion dispose of the appeal in conformity with such opinion. No judgment shall be delivered by the Supreme Court save in open court, and no report shall be made under article 143, dealing with the power of the President to consult Supreme Court, save in accordance with an opinion also delivered in open Court. No judgment and no such opinion shall be delivered by the Supreme Court save with the concurrence of a majority of the judges present at the hearing of the case, but nothing as said here shall be deemed to prevent a Judge who does not concur from delivering a dissenting judgment or opinion.

Jurisdiction of the Supreme Court

Original jurisdiction of the Supreme Court: The Supreme Court shall have original jurisdiction to the exclusion of any other court in any of the following type of dispute:

(a) Disputes between the Government of India and one or more States; or

(b) Disputes between the Government of India and any State or Sates on one side and one or more other states on the other: or

(c) Disputes between two or more States.

It will resolve the dispute that involves any question, whether of law or fact, on which the existence or extent of a legal right depends.

The said jurisdiction shall not extend to a dispute arising out of any treaty, agreement, covenant, engagement, sanad or other similar instrument which having been entered into or executed before the commencement of the constitution, continues in operation after such commencement, or which provides that the said jurisdiction shall not extend to such a dispute.

Its exclusive original jurisdiction extends to any dispute between the Government of India and one or more States or between the Government of India and any State or States on one side and one or more States on the other or between two or more States, if and insofar as the dispute involves any question (whether of law or of fact) on which the existence or extent of a legal right depends. In addition, Article 32 of the Constitution gives an extensive original jurisdiction to the Supreme Court in regard to enforcement of Fundamental Rights. It is empowered to issue directions, orders or writs, including writs in the nature of habeas corpus, mandamus, prohibition, quo warranto and certiorari to enforce them. The Supreme Court has been conferred with power to direct transfer of any civil or criminal case from one State High Court to another State High Court or from a Court subordinate to another State High Court. The Supreme Court, if satisfied that cases involving the same or substantially the same questions of law are pending before it and one or more High Courts or before two or more High Courts and that such questions are substantial questions of general importance, may withdraw a case or cases pending before the High Court or High Courts and dispose of all such cases itself. Under the Arbitration and Conciliation Act, 1996, International Commercial Arbitration can also be initiated in the Supreme Court.

***Appellate Jurisdiction of Supreme Court in appeals from High Courts in certain cases*:** An appeal shall lie to the Supreme Court from any judgment, decree or final order of a High Court in the territory of India whether in a civil, criminal or other proceedings if the High Court certifies under article 134A that the case involves a substantial question of law as to the interpretation of the Constitution. Where such a certificate is given, any party in the case may appeal to the Supreme Court on the ground that any such question as aforesaid has been wrongly decided.

Here, the expression final order includes an order deciding an issue which if decided in favour of the appellant would be sufficient for the final disposal of the case.

Appellate jurisdiction of Supreme Court in appeals from High Courts in regard to civil matters: An appeal shall lie to the Supreme Court from any judgment, decree or final order in a civil proceeding of a High Court in the territory of India if the High Court certifies under article 134A:

(a) That the case involves a substantial question of law of general importance; and

(b) That in the opinion of the High Court the said question needs to be decided by the Supreme Court.

Any party appealing to the Supreme Court may urge as one of the grounds in such appeal that a substantial question of law as to the interpretation of the constitution has been wrongly decided. It is subject to appellate jurisdiction of Supreme Court in appeals from High Courts in certain cases.

No appeal shall, unless Parliament by law otherwise provides, lie to the Supreme Court from the judgment, decree or final order of one Judge of a High Court. It is also subject to appellate jurisdiction of Supreme Court in appeals from High Courts in certain cases.

Appellate jurisdiction of Supreme Court in regard to criminal matters: An appeal shall lie to the Supreme Court from any judgment final order or sentence in a criminal proceedings of a High Court in the territory of India if the High Court:

(a) has on appeal reversed an order of acquittal of an accused person and sentenced him to death; or

(b) has withdrawn for trial before itself any case from any court subordinate to its authority and has in such trial convicted the accused person and sentenced him to death; or

(c) certificates under article 134A that the case is a fit one for appeal to the Supreme Court;

An appeal under aforesaid clause (c) shall lie subject to such provisions as may be made in that behalf under clause (1) of article 145 dealing with the rules of court etc. and to such conditions as the High Court may establish or require.

Parliament may by law confer on the Supreme Court any further powers to entertain and hear appeals from any judgment, final order or sentence in a criminal proceeding of a High Court in the territory of India subject to such conditions and limitations as may be specified in such law.

So, the appellate jurisdiction of the Supreme Court can be invoked by a certificate granted by the High Court concerned under Article 132(1), 133(1) or 134 of the Constitution in respect of any judgement, decree or final order of a High Court in both civil and criminal cases, involving substantial questions of law as to the interpretation of the Constitution. Appeals also lie to the Supreme Court in civil matters if the High Court concerned certifies : (a) that the case involves a substantial question of law of general importance, and (b) that, in the opinion of the High Court, the said question needs to be decided by the Supreme Court. In criminal cases, an appeal lies to the Supreme Court if the High Court (a) has on appeal reversed an order of acquittal of an accused person and sentenced him to death or to imprisonment for life or for a period of not less than 10 years, or (b) has withdrawn for trial before itself any case from any Court subordinate to its authority and has in such trial convicted the accused and sentenced him to death or to imprisonment for life or for a period of not less than 10 years, or (c) certified that the case is a fit one for appeal to the Supreme Court. Parliament is authorised to confer on the Supreme Court any further powers to entertain and hear appeals from any judgement, final order or sentence in a criminal proceeding of a High Court.

The Supreme Court has also a very wide appellate jurisdiction over all Courts and Tribunals in India in as much as it may, in its discretion, grant special leave to appeal under Article 136 of the Constitution from any judgment, decree, determination, sentence or order in any cause or matter passed or made by any Court or Tribunal in the territory of India.

Advisory Jurisdiction of the Supreme Court: The Supreme Court has special advisory jurisdiction in matters which may specifically be referred to it by the President of India under Article 143 of the Constitution. There are provisions for reference or appeal to this Court under Article 317(1) of the Constitution, Section 257 of the Income Tax Act, 1961, Section 7(2) of the Monopolies and Restrictive Trade Practices Act, 1969, Section 130-A of the Customs Act, 1962, Section 35-H of the Central Excises and Salt Act, 1944 and Section 82C of the Gold (Control) Act, 1968. Appeals also lie to the Supreme Court under the Representation of the People Act, 1951, Monopolies and Restrictive Trade Practices Act, 1969, Advocates Act, 1961, Contempt of Courts Act, 1971, Customs Act, 1962, Central Excises and Salt Act, 1944, Enlargement of Criminal Appellate Jurisdiction Act, 1970, Trial of Offences Relating to Transactions in Securities Act, 1992, Terrorist and Disruptive Activities (Prevention) Act, 1987 and Consumer Protection Act, 1986. Election Petitions under Part III of the Presidential and Vice Presidential Elections Act, 1952 are also filed directly in the Supreme Court.

Under Articles 129 and 142 of the Constitution the Supreme Court has been vested with power to punish for contempt of Court including the power to punish for contempt of itself. In case of contempt other than the contempt referred to in Rule 2, Part-I of the Rules to Regulate Proceedings for Contempt of the Supreme Court, 1975, the Court may take action (a) Suo motu, or (b) on a petition made by Attorney General, or Solicitor General, or (c) on a petition made by any person, and in the case of a criminal contempt with the consent in writing of the Attorney General or the Solicitor General.

Under Order XL of the Supreme Court Rules the Supreme Court may review its judgment or order but no application for review is to be entertained in a civil proceeding except on the grounds mentioned in Order XLVII, Rule 1 of the Code of Civil Procedure and in a criminal proceeding except on the ground of an error apparent on the face of the record.

Jurisdiction and powers of the Federal Court under existing law to be exercisable by the Supreme Court

Until parliament by law otherwise provides, the Supreme Court shall also have jurisdiction and powers with respect to any matter to which the provisions of Articles 133 or 134 do not apply if jurisdiction and powers in relation to that matter were exercisable by the Federal Court immediately before the commencement of the constitution under any existing law.

Special Leave to Appeal by the Supreme Court

The Supreme Court may in its discretion, grant special leave to appeal from any judgment, decree, determination, sentence or order in any cause or matter passed or made by any court or tribunal in the territory of India. Nothing as said here shall apply to any judgment, determination sentence or order passed or made by any court or tribunal constituted by or under any law relating to the Armed Forces.

Enlargement of the jurisdiction of the Supreme Court

The Supreme Court shall have such further jurisdiction and powers with respect to any of the matter in the union list as Parliament may by law confer. The Supreme Court shall have such further jurisdiction and powers with respect to any matter as the Government of India and the Government of any State may by special agreement confer; if Parliament by law provides for the exercise of such jurisdiction and powers by the Supreme Court.

High Courts

The High Court stands at the head of a State's judicial administration. There are 24 High Courts in the country, three having jurisdiction over more than one State. Among the Union Territories Delhi alone has a High Court of its own. Other six Union Territories come under the jurisdiction of different State High Courts. Each High Court comprises of a Chief Justice and such other Judges as the President may, from time to time, appoint. The Chief Justice of a High Court is appointed by the President in consultation with the Chief Justice of India and the Governor of the State. The procedure for appointing puisne Judges is the same except that the Chief Justice of the High Court concerned is also consulted. They hold office until the age of 62 years and are removable in the same manner as a Judge of the Supreme Court. To be eligible for appointment as a Judge one must be a citizen of India and have held a judicial office in India for ten years or must have practised as an Adovcate of a High Court or two or more such Courts in succession for a similar period.

Each High Court has power to issue to any person within its jurisdiction directions, orders, or writs including writs which are in the nature of habeas corpus, mandamus, prohibition, quo warranto and certiorari for enforcement of Fundamental Rights and for any other purpose. This power may also be exercised by any High Court exercising jurisdiction in relation to territories within which the cause of action, wholly or in part, arises for exercise of such power, notwithstanding that the seat of such Government or authority or residence of such person is not within those territories.

Each High Court has powers of superintendence over all Courts within its jurisdiction. It can call for returns from such Courts, make and issue general rules and prescribe forms to regulate their practice and proceedings and determine the manner and form in which book entries and accounts shall be kept. The following Table gives the seat and territorial jurisdiction of the High Courts.

JURISDICTION AND SEAT OF HIGH COURTS

Name	*Year*	*Territorial establishment jurisdiction*	*Seat*
Allahabad	1866	Uttar Pradesh	Allahabad (Bench at Lucknow)
Andhra Pradesh	1956	Andhra Pradesh	Hyderabad
Bombay	1862	Maharashtra, Goa, Dadra and Nagar Haveli and Daman and Diu	Bombay (Benches at Nagpur, Panaji and Aurangabad)
Calcutta	1862	West Bengal	Kolkata (Circuit Bench at Port Blair)
Delhi	1966	Delhi	Delhi
Guwahati	1948	Assam, Nagaland, Mizoram and Arunachal Pradesh	Guwahati (Benches at Kohima, Aizwal & Itanagar
Gujarat	1960	Gujarat	Ahmedabad
Himachal Pradesh	1971	Himachal Pradesh	Shimla
Jammu & Kashmir	1928	Jammu & Kashmir	Srinagar & Jammu
Karnataka	1884	Karnataka	Bengluru
Kerala	1958	Kerala & Lakshadweep	Ernakulam
Madhya Pradesh	1956	Madhya Pradesh	Jabalpur (Benches at Gwalior and Indore)
Madras	1862	Tamil Nadu & Puducherry	Chennai
Orissa	1948	Orissa	Cuttack
Patna	1916	Bihar	Patna
Punjab & Haryana	1975	Punjab, Haryana & Chandigarh	Chandigarh
Rajasthan	1949	Rajasthan	Jodhpur (Bench at Jaipur)
Sikkim	1975	Sikkim	Gangtok
Chhattisgarh	2000	Chhattisgarh	Bilaspur
Jharkhand	2000	Jharkhand	Ranchi
Uttaranchal	2000	Uttarakhand	Nainital
Tripura	2013	Tripura	Agartala
Meghalaya	2013	Meghalaya	Shillong
Manipur	2013	Manipur	Imphal

Advocate General

There is an Advocate General for each State, appointed by the Governor, who holds office during the pleasure of the Governor. He must be a person qualified to be appointed as a Judge of High Court. His duty is to give advice to State Governments upon such legal matters and to perform such other duties of legal character, as may be referred or assigned to him by the Governor. The Advocate General has the right to speak and take part in the proceedings of the State Legislature without the right to vote.

Lok Adalats

Lok Adalats which are voluntary agencies are monitored by the State Legal Aid and Advice Boards. They have proved to be a successful alternative forum for resolving of disputes through the conciliatory method.

The Legal Services Authorities Act, 1987 provides statutory status to the legal aid movement and it also provides for setting up of Legal Services Authorities at the Central, State and District levels. These authorities will have their own funds. Further, Lok Adalats which are at present informal agencies will acquire statutory status. Every award of Lok Adalats shall be deemed to be a decree of a civil court or order of a Tribunal and shall be final and binding on the parties to the dispute. It also provides that in respect of cases decided at a

Lok Adalat, the court fee paid by the parties will be refunded.

Difference between the Jurisdiction of the Supreme Court and High Court to issue Writs

Article 32 of the constitution deals with the writ jurisdiction of the Supreme Court where as the writ jurisdiction of the High Court is covered under section 226 of the constitution. The major point of difference between the two is that for the writ jurisdiction of the Supreme Court there needs to be violation of some fundamental right enshrined in the constitution whereas writ in the High Courts is maintainable not only in the cases where there is violation of the fundamental right of the person but it is also for other purpose.

The right to move the Supreme Court by appropriate proceedings for the enforcement of the rights conferred by Part IIIrd of the constitution (Fundamental rights) is guaranteed. The supreme court has power to issue directions or orders or writs including writ in the nature of habeas corpus, mandamus, Prohibition, quo warrants and certiorari, whichever may be appropriate, for the enforcement of any of the rights conferred under part III of the constitution. Without prejudice to the powers conferred on the Supreme Court as stated above, parliament may by law empower any other court to exercise within the local limits of its jurisdiction all or any of the powers, of issuing direction or orders or writs exercisable by the Supreme Court. These rights guaranteed by Art. 32 of the constitution shall not be suspended except as otherwise provided for by the constitution.

Elucidating the writ jurisdiction of the High Court Article 226 of the constitution states that notwithstanding any thing in Article 32, every High Court shall have power, throughout the territories in relation to which it exercises jurisdiction, to issue to any person or authority, including in appropriate cases, any government, within those territories direction, orders or writs, including writs in the nature of habeas corpus, Mandamus, prohibition, quo warrant and certiorari, or any of them (for the enforcement of any of the rights conferred by part III and for any other purpose). The power conferred to issue directions, orders or writs to any Government or authority or person may also be exercised by any High Court exercising jurisdiction in relation to the territories within which the cause of action, wholly or in part, arises for the exercise of such power, notwithstanding that the seat of such Govt. or authority or the residence of such person is not within those territories. Where any party against whom an interim order whether by way of injunction or stay or in any other manner, is made on, or in any proceedings relating to, a petition under clause 1 of Article 226 dealing with the power to issue writs, without furnishing to such party copies of such petition and all documents in support of the plea for such interim order; and giving such party an opportunity of being heard, makes an application to the High Court for the vacation of such order and furnishes a copy of such application to the party in whose favour such order has been made or the counsel of such party, the High Court shall dispose of the application within a period of two weeks from the date of on which the copy of such application is so furnished, whichever is later, or where the High Court is closed on the last day of that period before the expiry of the next day afterwards on which the High Court is open; and if the application is not so disposed of, the interim order shall, on the expiry of the period, or as the case may be, the expiry of the said next day, stand vacated. It is to be noted that the power conferred on a High Court by this Article shall not be in derogation of the power conferred on the Supreme Court of issuing direction, orders or writs.

Qualification for membership of Parliament

A person shall not be qualified to be chosen to fill a seat in Parliament unless he:

(a) is a citizen of India, and makes and subscribes before same person authorized in that behalf by the Election Commission an oath or affirmation according to the form set out for the purpose in the third Schedule of the constitution;

(b) is, in the case of a seat in the Council of States, not less than thirty years of age and, in the case of a seat in the House of the People not less than twenty-five years of age; and

(c) possesses such other qualifications as may be prescribed in that behalf by or under any law made by Parliament.

Disqualification for membership

A person shall be disqualified for being chosen as, and for being, a member of either house of Parliament:

(a) If he holds any office of profit under the Government of India or the Government of any state, other than an office declared by parliament by law not to disqualify its holder;

(b) If he is of unsound mind and stands so declared by a competent court;

(c) If he is an undischarged insolvent;

(d) If he is not a citizen of India, or has voluntary acquired the citizenship of a foreign state, or is under any acknowledgement of allegiance or adherence to a foreign state.

(e) If he is so disqualified by or under any law made by parliament

Here, a person shall not be deemed to hold on office of profit under the Government of India or the Government of any State by reason only that he is a Minister either for the union or for such State.

A person shall be disqualified for being a member of either House of Parliament if he is so disqualified under the tenth Schedule of the constitution.

Decision on questions as to disqualifications of members

If any question arises as to whether a member of either house of Parliament has become subject to any of the disqualification as mentioned above, the question shall be referred for the decision of the President and his decision shall be final. Before giving any decision on any such question, the President shall obtain the opinion of the election commission and shall act according to such opinion.

Penalty for sitting and voting before making oath or affirmation or when not qualified

If a person sits or votes as a member of either house of Parliament before he has complied with the requirements of oath or affirmation or when he knows that he is not qualified or that he is disqualified for membership thereof, or that he is prohibited from so doing by the provisions of any law made by Parliament, he shall be liable in respect of each day on which he so sits or votes to a penalty of five hundred rupees to be recovered as a debt due to the Union.

Vacation of seats

No person shall be a member of both Houses of Parliament and provision shall be made by parliament by law for the vacation by a person who is chosen a member of both houses of his seat in one house or the other. No person shall be a member both of parliament and of a House of the Legislature of a State and if a person is chosen a member both of Parliament and of a House of the Legislature of a State, then, at the expiration such period as may be specified in rules made by the President that person's seat in parliament shall become vacant, unless he has previously resigned his seat in the legislature of the state.

If a member of either House of Parliament becomes subject to any of the disqualifications due to holding of office of profit or due to be a person of unsound mind or, resigns his seat by writing under his hand addressed to the Chairman or the speaker as the case may be and his resignation is accepted by the Chairman or the Speaker as the case may be, his seat shall thereupon become vacant. In the case of such resignation if from information received or otherwise and after making such inquiry as he thinks fit, the Chairman or the Speaker, as the case may be, is satisfied that such resignation is not voluntary or genuine, he shall not accept such resignation.

If for a period of sixty days a member of either House of Parliament is without permission of the House absent from all meetings thereof, the House may declare his seat vacant. In computing the said period of sixty days no account shall be taken of any period during which the House is prorogued or is adjourned for more than four consecutive days.

Salaries and allowances of members

Members of either House of Parliament shall be entitled to receive such salaries and allowances as may from time to time be determined by Parliament by law and until provision in that respect is so made, allowance at such rates and upon such conditions as were immediately before the commencement of the constitution applicable in the case of members of the constituent assembly of the Dominion of India.

Powers, Privileges, etc., of the Houses of Parliament and of the members and committees thereof

Subject to the other provisions of the constitution and to the rules and standing orders regulating the procedure of Parliament, there shall be freedom of speech in Parliament.

No Member of Parliament shall be liable to any proceeding in any court in respect of anything said or any vote given by him in Parliament or any committee thereof and no person shall be so liable in respect of the publication by or under the authority of either House of Parliament of any report, paper, votes or proceedings.

In other respects, the powers, privileges and immunities of each house of Parliament and of the members and the committees of each house shall be such as may from time to time be defined by parliament by law, and, until so defined, shall be those of that house and of its members and committees immediately before the coming into force of section 15 of the constitution (forty-fourth Amendment) Act, 1978.

The said provisions shall apply in relation to persons who by virtue of the constitution have the right to speak in, and otherwise to take part in the proceedings of a house of parliament or any committee thereof as they apply in relation to members of Parliament.

The Chairman and Deputy Chairman of the Council of State

The Vice-President of India shall be ex-officio chairman of the Council of States.

The Council of States shall, as soon as may be, choose a member of the Council to be deputy chairman thereof and, so often as the office of deputy chairman becomes vacant, the Council shall choose another member to be deputy chairman thereof.

Vacation and resignation of, and removal from, the office of Deputy Chairman

A member holding office as Deputy Chairman of the Council of States:

(a) shall vacate his office if he ceases to be member of the council;

(b) may at any time, by writing under his hand addressed to the Chairman, resign his office; and

(c) may be removed from his office by a resolution of the council passed by a majority of all the then members of the council. No resolution for this purpose shall be moved unless at least fourteen days notice has been given of the intention to move the resolution.

Power of the Deputy Chairman or other Person to Perform the Duties of the Office of, or to act as, Chairman

While the office of Chairman is vacant, or during any period when the vice-president is acting as, or discharging the function of president the duties of the office shall be performed by the Deputy Chairman, or, if the office of Deputy Chairman is also vacant, by such member of the Council of States as the president may appoint for the purpose.

During the absence of the Chairman from any sitting of the Council of States the Deputy Chairman, or, if no such person is present such other person as may be determined by the council shall act, as chairman.

The Chairman or the Deputy chairman not to preside while a resolution for his removal from office is under consideration

At any sitting of the council of states, while any resolution for the removal of the vice-president from his office is under consideration, the chairman, or while any resolution for the removal of the deputy chairman from his office is under consideration, the Deputy Chairman, shall not, though he is present, preside, and during such absence of the Chairman from any sitting of the Council of States, the Deputy Chairman, or, if no such person is present such other person as may be determined by the council shall act, as chairman.

The Chairman shall have the right to speak in and otherwise to take part in the proceedings of, the Council of States while any resolution for the removal of the Vice-President from his office is under consideration in the Council, but he shall not be entitled to vote at all on such resolution or on any other matter during such proceedings. However, the chairman or person acting as such shall have and exercise a casting vote in the case of an equality of votes.

Salaries and allowances of the Chairman and Deputy Chairman

There shall be paid to the Chairman and the Deputy Chairman of the Council of States, such salaries and allowances as a may be respectively fixed by Parliament by law and, until provision in that behalf is so made, such salaries and allowances as are specified in the Second Schedule of the constitution.

Vice-President is the ex-officio chairman of the council of states, as such the provisions with regard to his salary is the same as that of the chairman of the council of states.

The Speaker and Deputy Speaker of the House of the People

The House of the People shall, as soon as may be, choose two members of the House to be respectively speaker and deputy speaker thereof and so often as the office of speaker or Deputy Speaker becomes vacant, the house shall choose another member to be speaker or deputy speaker, as the case may be.

Vacation and Resignation of, and Removal from the Offices of Speaker and Deputy Speaker

A member holding office as speaker or Deputy Speaker of the House of the People

(a) Shall vacate his office if he ceases to be a member of the house of the People;

(b) May at any time, by writing under his hand addressed, if such member is the speaker, to the deputy speaker, and if such member is the deputy speaker, to the speaker, resign his office and

(c) May be removed from his office by a resolution of the house of the People passed by a majority of all the then members of the house. However, no resolution for this purpose shall be moved unless at least fourteen days notice has been given of the intention to move the resolution. Whenever the house of the people is dissolved, the speaker shall not vacate his office until immediately before the first meeting of the house of the people after the dissolution.

Power of the Deputy speaker or other person to perform the duties of the office of, or to act as, Speaker

While the office of Speaker is vacant, the duties of the office shall be performed by the Deputy Speaker or, if the office of Deputy Speaker is also vacant, by such member of the House of the People as the President may appoint for the purpose.

During the absence of the Speaker from any sitting of the House of the people the Deputy Speaker or, if he is also absent, such person, as may be determined by the rules of procedure of the House, or, if no such person is present, such other person as may be determined by the House, shall act as Speaker.

The Speaker or the Deputy Speaker not to preside while a resolution for his removal from office is under consideration

At any sitting of the House of the people, while any resolution for the removal of the Speaker from his office is under consideration, the

Speaker or while any resolution for the removal of the Deputy Speaker from his office is under consideration the Deputy speaker, shall not, though he is present, preside, and during such absence of the Speaker from any sitting of the House of the people the Deputy Speaker or, if he is also absent, such person, as may be determined by the rules of procedure of the House, or, if no such person is present, such other person as may be determined by the House, shall act as Speaker.

The Speaker shall have the right to speak in, and otherwise to take part in the proceedings of the House of the People while any resolution for his removal from office is under consideration in the House and shall be entitled to vote only in the first instance on such resolution or on any other matter during such proceedings but not in the case of an equality of votes. This provision of voting is subject to the provision of article 100 of the constitution.

Salaries and Allowances of the Speaker and Deputy Speaker

There shall be paid to the Speaker and the Deputy Speaker of the House of the People such salaries and allowances as a may be respectively fixed by Parliament by law and, until provision in that behalf is so made, such salaries and allowances as are specified in the Second Schedule of the constitution.

Bill, its Different Kinds and Procedure for Passing of Bills in the Parliament

For the purpose of making the law the draft that is mooted over in the parliament is called the bill. So, it can be said that any Act which is in its prematured form, before receiving the assent of the president, is called the bill. There are three kinds of bill:

1. Ordinary bill
2. Money bill
3. Financial bill

1. Ordinary Bills : A bill other than the money and financial bills are called Ordinary Bills. This bill may originate in either house of the parliament. Subject to the joint sitting of the parliament, a bill shall not be deemed to have been passed by the houses of parliament unless it has been agreed to by both Houses, either without amendment or with such amendments only as are agreed to by both houses.

A bill pending in parliament shall not lapse by reason of the prorogation of the Houses. A Bill pending in the Council of States which has not been passed by the House of the people shall not lapse on dissolution of the House of the People. A bill which is pending in the house of the people, or which having been passed by the house of the People is pending in the Council of States, shall, subject to the provisions relating to joint sitting of both houses, lapse on a dissolution of the House of the People.

If after a Bill has been passed by one House and transmitted to the other House:

(a) the Bill is rejected by the other House, or
(b) the House have finally disagreed as to the amendments to be made in the Bill, or
(c) more than six months elapse from the date of the reception of the Bill by the other House without the Bill being passed by it.

The president may, unless the Bill has elapsed by reason of a dissolution of the House of the People, notify to the Houses by message if they are sitting or by Public notification if they are not sitting, his intention to summon them to meet in a joint sitting for the purpose of deliberating and voting on the Bill.

In reckoning any such period of six months as is referred above, no account shall be taken of any period during which the house is prorogued or adjourned for more than four consecutive days.

Where the President has notified his intention of summoning the Houses to meet in a joint sitting, neither House shall proceed further with the Bill, but, the President may at any time after the date of his notification summon the Houses to meet in a joint sitting for the purpose specified in the notification and, if he does so, the Houses shall meet accordingly.

If at the joint sitting of the two Houses, the Bill, with such amendments, if any, as are agreed to in joint sitting, is passed by a majority of the total number of members of both Houses present and voting, it shall be deemed for the purposes of the constitution to have been passed by both Houses. But it is subject to the conditions that at a joint sitting:

(a) If the Bill having been passed by one House, has not been passed by the other House with amendments and returned to the House in which it originated, no amendment shall be proposed to the bill other than such amendments (if any) as are made necessary by the delay in the passage of the Bill.

(b) If the Bill has been so passed and returned, only such amendments as aforesaid shall be proposed to the bill and such other amendments as are relevant to the matter with respect to which the Houses have not agreed.

The decision of the person presiding as to the amendments which are admissible shall be final.

A joint sitting may be held under this provision and a bill passed thereat, notwithstanding that dissolution of the House of the People has intervened since the President notified his intention to summon the Houses to meet therein.

When a Bill has been passed by the Houses of Parliament, it shall be presented to the President, and the President shall declare either that he assents to the Bill, or that he withholds assent there from.

The president may, as soon as possible after the presentation to him of a Bill for assent, return the Bill to the Houses with a message requesting that they will reconsider the Bill or any specified provisions thereof and in particular, will consider the desirability of introducing any such amendments as he may recommended in his message, and when a Bill is passed again by the Houses with or without amendment and presented to the President for assent, the President shall not withhold assent there from.

2. Money Bill: A Bill shall be deemed to be a money Bill if it contains only provisions dealing with all or any of the following matters, namely:

(a) The imposition, abolition, alteration or regulation of any tax.

(b) The regulation of the borrowing of money or the giving of any guarantee by the Government of India, or the amendment of the law with respect to any financial obligations undertaken or to be undertaken by the Government of India;

(c) The custody of the consolidated fund or the contingency fund of India, the Payment of moneys into or the withdrawal of moneys from any such fund;

(d) The appropriation of moneys out of the consolidated fund of India;

(e) The declaring of any expenditure to be expenditure charged on the consolidated fund of India or the increasing of the amount of any such expenditure;

(f) The receipt of money on account of the consolidated fund of India or the public account of India or the custody or issue of such money or the audit of the accounts of the union of a States; or

(g) Any matter incidental to any of the matters specified in above said clauses (a) to (f).

A Bill shall not be deemed to be a Money Bill by reason only that it provides for the imposition of fines or other pecuniary penalties, or for the demand or payment of fees for the licenses or fees for services rendered, or by reason that it provides for the imposition, abolition, remission, alteration or regulation of any tax by any local purposes.

If any question arises whether a bill is a Money Bill or not, the decision of the Speaker of the House of the People thereon shall be final.

There shall be endorsed on every Money Bill when it is transmitted to the council of states under Article 109, and when it is presented to the president for assent under Article 111, the certificate of the Speaker of the House of the People signed by him that it is a Money Bill.

A Money Bill shall not be introduced in the Council of states. After a Money Bill has been passed by the House of the People it shall be transmitted to the Council of States for its recommendations and the Council of states shall within a period of fourteen days from the date of its receipt of the Bill return the Bill to the House of the People with its recommendation and the House of the People may thereupon either accept or reject all or any of the recommendations of the Council of States. If the house of the people accepts any of the recommendations of the Council of States the money bill shall be deemed to have been passed by both houses with the amendments recommended by the council of states and accepted by the House of the People.

If the house of People does not accept any of the recommendations of the council of States for its recommendations of the council of states, the money bills shall be deemed to have been passed by both houses in the form in which it was passed by the house of the people without any of the amendments recommended by the council of states.

If a Money Bill passed by the House of the People and transmitted to the council of states for its recommendations is not returned to the House of the People within the said period of fourteen days. It shall be deemed to have been passed by both Hoses at expiration of the said period in the form in which it was passed by the House of the People.

A significant thing to note here is that nothing as related to the joint sitting of the house in case of ordinary bill shall apply to a Money Bill.

When a Bill has been passed by the Houses of Parliament, it shall be presented to the President, and the President shall declare that he assents to the Bill and he cannot withhold his assent there from.

3. Financial Bills: There are three kinds of financial bills namely—

(1) Money Bills

(2) Other Financial Bills

(3) Bill involving expenditure

The concept of money bills has already been discussed in this question. So far as other financial bills are concerned it is mandatory that a Bill or amendment making provisions for any of under mentioned matters shall not be introduced or moved except on the recommendation of the President and a Bill making such provision shall not be introduced in the Council of States. The said matters are:

(a) The imposition, abolition, alteration or regulation of any tax.

(b) The regulation of the borrowing of money or the giving of any guarantee by the Government of India, or the amendment of the law with respect to any financial obligations undertaken or to be undertaken by the Government of India;

(c) The custody of the consolidated fund or the contingency fund of India, the Payment of moneys into or the withdrawal of moneys from any such fund;

(d) The appropriation of moneys out of the consolidated fund of India;

(e) The declaring of any expenditure to be expenditure charged on the consolidated fund of India or the increasing of the amount of any such expenditure;

(f) The receipt of money on account of the consolidated fund of India or the public account of India or the custody or issue of such money or the audit of the accounts of the union of a States; or

No recommendation shall be required under this provision for the moving of an amendment making provision for the reduction or abolition of any tax.

A Bill or amendment shall not be deemed to make provision for any of the matters aforesaid by reason only that it provides for the imposition of fines or other pecuniary penalties, or for the demand or payment of fees for licenses or fees for services rendered, or by reason that it provides for the imposition, abolition, remission, alteration or regulation of any tax by any local authority or body for local purposes.

The last mentioned types of financial bills are the bills involving expenditure. Such a type of Bill which if enacted and brought into operation, would involve expenditure from the consolidated fund of India and it shall not be passed by either House of Parliament unless the President has recommended to that House the consideration of the Bill.

Power of the parliament to amend the constitution and procedure thereof

Parliament may in exercise of its constituent power amend by way of addition, variation or repeal any provision of the constitution notwithstanding anything contained in the constitution. Such an amendment may be initiated only by the introduction of a bill for the purpose in either house of the parliament and when the bill is passed in each house by a majority of the total membership of that house and by a majority of not less than two-thirds of the members of that house present and voting, it shall be presented to the president who shall give his assent to the bill and thereupon the constitution shall stand amended in accordance with the terms of the bill. However, it is subject to the condition that if such amendment seeks to make any change in-

(a) Article 54 (Election of President), Article 55 (Manner of Election of President), Article 73 (Extent of Executive Power of the Union), Article 162 (Extent of Executive Power of State) or Article 241 (High Courts for Union Territories), or

(b) Chapter IV of Part V (The Union Judiciary), Chapter V of Part VI (The High Courts of the State), Chapter I of Part XI (Legislative Relations between the Union and the State), or

(c) Any of the lists in seventh schedule of the constitution i.e. Union list, State list and Concurrent list.

(d) The representation of states in Parliament, or

(e) The provisions of article 368 of the constitution dealing with the power of parliament to amend the constitution and procedure thereof.

the amendment shall also require to be ratified by the legislatures of not less than one-half of the states by resolution to the effect passed by those legislatures before the bill making provision for such amendment is presented to the president for assent. A significant thing to be noted here is that nothing in article 13 dealing with the laws inconsistent with or in derogation of the fundamental rights shall apply to any amendment made under article 368 of the constitution.

No amendment of the constitution including the fundamental rights made or purporting to have been made under article 368, whether before or after the commencement of section 55 of the constitution (Forty-second Amendment) Act, 1976 shall be called in question in any court on any ground.

There is clear cut limitation whatever on the constituent power of parliament to amend by way of addition, variation or repeal the provisions of this constitution under article 368 of the same. Now, it has been well established by the Supreme Court that parliament cannot amend the basic structure of the constitution which in turn consists of certain basic features and these basic features shall be illustrated by the court from time to time. Some of the basic features of the constitution as mentioned by the court are secularism, free and fair elections etc.

So, in other words we can say that the provisions of the constitution can be amended in three ways. Firstly, there are certain provisions that can be amended on behalf of one-half of the majority of the house i.e. by simple majority in the house. Secondly, some other kinds of provisions can be amended on behalf of two-third majority of members present and voting in the house i.e. by special majority in the house. Thirdly, there are certain other kinds of provisions for the purpose of amending which two-third majority in the parliament along with the ratification by half of the states in the country is required. Once the bill is passed by the parliament it is presented to the president for his assent and after the assent of the president the bill becomes the act. Further, the provisions of this act can be challenged in the court of law on the ground that it violates the basic structure of the constitution and if the court finds any such defect in the provisions of the act or the act itself it can set aside the passed law of the parliament and as such that provision or the act itself as the case may be becomes void. Such a process of court is called the process of judicial review.

Procedure of parliament in financial matters

Annual Financial statement: The President shall in respect of every financial year cause to be laid before both the Houses of Parliament an Statement of the estimated receipts and expenditure of the Government of India for that year referred to as the "annual financial statement".

The estimates of expenditure embodied in the annual financial statement shall show separately:

(a) The sums required to meet expenditure described by the Constitutions as expenditure charged upon the Consolidated Fund of India; and

(b) The sums required to meet other expenditure proposed to be made from the Consolidated Fund of India.

It shall distinguish expenditure on revenue account from other expenditure.

The following expenditure shall be expenditure charged on the consolidated fund of India—

(a) The salaries and allowances of the President and other expenditure relating to his office.

(b) The salaries and allowances of the Chairman and the Deputy chairman of the Council of States and the Speaker and the Deputy Speaker of the House of the People.

(c) Debt charges for which the government of India is liable including interest, sinking fund charges and redemption charges, and other expenditure relating to the raising of loans and the service and redemption of debt.

(d) The salaries, allowances and pensions payable to or in respect of judges of the Supreme Court;

(e) The pensions payable to or in respect of judges of the federal court.

(f) The pensions payable to or in respect of judges of any High Court, which exercise jurisdiction in relation to any area, included in the territory of India or which at any time before the commencement of the constitution exercised jurisdiction in relation to any area included in a Governor's Province of the Dominion of India.

(g) The salary, allowances and pension payable to or in respect of the comptroller and auditor-general of India;

(h) Any sums required to satisfy any judgment decree of award of any court or arbitral tribunal.

(i) Any other expenditure declared by this constitution or by Parliament by law to be so charged.

Procedure in parliament with respect to estimates: So much of the estimates as relates to expenditure charged upon the consolidated fund of India shall not be submitted to the vote of parliament, but nothing as said here shall be construed as preventing the discussion in either house of Parliament of any of those estimates.

So much of the said estimates as relates to other expenditure shall be submitted in the form of demands for grants to the House of the People, and the House of the People shall have power to assent or to refuse to assent, to any demand or to assent to any demand subject to a reduction of the amount specified therein. No demand for a grant shall be made except on the recommendation of the President.

Appropriation Bills: As soon as may be after the grants with respect to estimates have been made by the House of the People, there shall be introduced a bill to provide for the appropriation out of the consolidated fund of India of all moneys required to meet:

(a) The grants so made by the house of the People, and

(b) The expenditure charged on the consolidated fund of India but not exceeding in any case the amount shown in the statement previously laid before the Parliament.

No amendment shall be proposed to any such bill in either house of parliament which will have the effect of varying the amount or altering the destination of any grant so made or of varying the amount of any expenditure charged on the consolidated fund of India, and the decision of the person presiding as to whether an amendment is inadmissible under this clause shall be final.

Subject to the provisions relating to the supplementary, additional or excess grants and votes on account, votes of credit and exceptional grant, no money shall be withdrawn from the consolidated fund of India except under appropriation made by law passed in accordance with this provision.

Supplementary, additional or excess grant: If the amount authorized by any law made in accordance with the provision relating to appropriation bill to be expended for a particular service for the current financial year is found to be insufficient for the purposes of that year or when a need has arisen during the current financial year for supplementary or additional expenditure upon some new service not contemplated in the annual financial statement for that year, or if any money has been spent on any service during a financial year in excess of the amount granted for that service and for that year, the President shall cause to be laid before both the Houses of Parliament another statement showing the estimated amount of that expenditure or cause to be presented to the house of the People a demand for such excess, as the case may be.

The provisions relating to annual financial statement, procedure in parliament with respect to estimates and appropriation bills shall have effect in relation to any such statement and expenditure or demand and also to any law to be made authorizing the appropriation of moneys out of the consolidated fund of India to meet such expenditure or the grant in respect of such demand, as they have effect in relation to the annual financial statement and the expenditure mentioned therein or to a demand for a grant and the law to be made for the authorization of appropriation of moneys out of the consolidated fund of India to meet such expenditure or grant.

Votes on account, votes of credit and exceptional grants: The House of the People shall have power:

(a) to make any grant in advance in respect of the estimated expenditure for a part of any financial year pending the completion of the procedure prescribed in article 113 for the voting of such grant and the passing of the law in accordance with the provisions of article 114 in relation to that expenditure;

(b) to make a grant for meeting an unexpected demand upon the resources of India when on account of the magnitude of the indefinite character of the service the demand cannot be stated with the details ordinarily given in an annual financial statement;

(c) to make an exceptional grant which forms no part of the current service of any financial year.

Parliament shall have power to authorize by law the withdrawal of moneys from the consolidated fund of India for the purposes for which the said grants are made.

The provisions relating to the procedure in parliament with respect to estimates and appropriation bills shall have effect in relation to the making of any aforesaid grant and to any law to be made as said above as they have effect in relation to the making of a grant with regard to any expenditure mentioned in the annual financial statement and the law to be made for the authorization of appropriation of moneys, out of the consolidated fund of India to meet such expenditure.

Procedure for conducting the business of parliament

The Parliament for the purpose of conducting its business has to follow certain rules and procedures. It is necessary to maintain the dignity of the houses of the parliament.

Duration of house of Parliament: The Council of States shall not be subject to dissolution, but as nearly as possible one-third of the members thereof shall retire as soon as may be on the expiration of every second year in accordance with the provisions made in that behalf by parliament by law.

The House of the people, unless sooner dissolved, shall continue for five years from the date appointed for its first meeting and no longer and the expiration of the said period of five years shall operate as dissolution of the House. The said period may, while a Proclamation of Emergency is in operation, be extended by Parliament by law for a period not exceeding in any case beyond a period of six months after the Proclamation has ceased to operate.

Sessions of Parliament, Prorogation and dissolution: The President shall from time to time summon each House of parliament to meet at such time and place as he thinks fit, but six months shall not intervene between its last sitting in one session and the date appointed for its first sitting in the next session.

The President may form time to time:

(a) Prorogue the Houses or either House.

(b) Dissolve the House of the People

Right of President to address and send messages to Houses: The President may address either house of parliament or both houses assembled together, and for that purpose require the attendance of members.

The president may send messages to either House of Parliament, whether with respect to a bill then pending in Parliament or otherwise, and a House to which any message is so sent shall with all convenient despatch consider any matter required by the message to be taken into consideration.

Special address by the President: At the commencement of the first session after each general election to the House of the people and at the commencement of the first session of each year the President shall address both Houses of Parliament assembled together and inform parliament of the causes of its summons.

Provision shall be made by the rules regulating the procedure of either house for the allotment of time for discussion of the matters referred to in such addresses.

Rights of Ministers and Attorney-General as respects Houses: Every Minister and the Attorney-General of India shall have the right to speak in, and otherwise to take part in the proceeding of either house, any joint sitting of the Houses, and any committee of Parliament of which he may be named a member but shall not by virtue of this provision be entitled to vote.

Oath or affirmation by members: Every member of either House of Parliament shall, before taking his seat, make and subscribe before the President or same person appointed in that behalf by him, on oath or affirmation according to the form set out for the purpose in the third Schedule of the constitution.

Voting in Houses, Power of Houses to act notwithstanding vacancies and quorum: Subject to other provisions of the constitution all questions at any sitting of either House or joint sitting of the Houses shall be determined by a majority of votes of the members present and voting other than the speaker or person acting as Chairman or Speaker. The Chairman or Speaker or person acting as such shall not vote in the first instance, but shall have and exercise a casting vote in the case of an equality of votes. Either House of Parliament shall have power to act notwithstanding any vacancy in the membership thereof, and any proceedings in Parliament shall be valid irrespective of the fact that it is discovered subsequently that some person who was not entitled so to do sat or voted or otherwise took part in the proceedings. Until Parliament by law otherwise provides, the quorum to constitute a meeting of either house of Parliament shall be one-tenth of the total number of members of the House. If at any time during a meeting of House there is no quorum, it shall be the duty of the chairman of Speaker, or person acting as such, either to adjourn the

House or to suspend the meeting until there is a quorum.

Rules of Procedure: Each House of Parliament may make rules for regulating, subject to the provisions of the constitution, its procedure and the conduct of its business.

Until rules are so made, the rules of procedure and standing orders in force immediately before the commencement of the constitution with respect to the legislature of the dominion of India shall have effect in relation to Parliament subject to such modifications and adaptations as may be made therein by the Chairman of the Council of States or the Speaker of the House of the People, as the case may be.

The President, after consultation with the chairman of the council of states and the Speaker of the House of the People, may make rules as to the procedure with respect to joint sittings of, and communications between, the two Houses.

At a joint sitting of the two Houses the Speaker of the House of People, or in his absence such person as may be determined by rules of procedure, shall preside.

Regulation by law of procedure in Parliament in relation to financial business: Parliament may, for the purpose or the timely completion of financial business, regulate by law the procedure of, and the conduct of business in, each house of Parliament in relation to any financial matter or to any Bill for the appropriation of moneys out of the consolidated fund of India, and, if and so far as any provision of any law so made is inconsistent with any rule made by a House of Parliament under rules of procedure or with any rule or standing order having effect in relation to Parliament, such provision shall prevail.

Language to be used in Parliament: Notwithstanding anything in Part XVII dealing with the official language, but Subject to the provisions relating to the provision with regard to the languages to be used in Supreme Court and in the High courts and for Acts, Bills etc., business in Parliament shall be transacted in Hindi or in English. However, the Chairman of the Council of States or Speaker of the House of the People, or person acting as such, as the case may be, may permit any member who cannot adequately express himself in Hindi or in English to address the House in his mother tongue.

Restriction on discussion in Parliament: No discussion shall take place in Parliament with respect to the conduct of any Judge of the Supreme Court or of a High Court in the discharge of his duties except upon a motion for presenting an address to the President praying for the removal of the Judge.

Courts not to Inquire into proceedings of Parliament: The validity of any proceedings in Parliament shall not be called in question on the ground of any alleged irregularity of procedure. No officer or member of Parliament in whom powers are vested by or under the constitution for regulating procedure or the conduct of business, or for maintaining order, in Parliament shall be subject to the jurisdiction of any court in respect of the exercise by him of those powers.

Duties of the Prime Minister regarding furnishing of information to the President

Article 75(3) of the constitution provides that the council of ministers shall be collectively responsible to the house of people. No member of the cabinet can avoid responsibility while enjoying the confidence of the prime minister. It shall be the duty of the Prime Minister –

(i) to communicate to the President all decisions of the council of ministers relating to the administration of the affair of the union and proposals for legislation;

(ii) to furnish such information relating to the administration of the affair of the union and proposals for legislation as the President may call for; and

(iii) if the President so requires, to submit for the consideration of the council of ministers any matter on which a decision has been taken by a minister but has not been considered.

Method of appointment of council of ministers and their tenure of office

The Prime Minister is appointed by the President and other ministers are appointed by the president on the advice of the Prime Minister. The leader of the majority party in the house of the people is invited to form the cabinet and he or she is designated as Prime Minister. For appointment of the other ministers, the President has no choice of his own and has to accept the team selected by the Prime Minister. Where, however, none of the parties in the house of people has clear majority, then the President may exercise some choice.

A minister must be member of either house of the parliament. Those who are not the members, they must get themselves elected within six months commencing from their appointment.

So far as the tenure of the office of ministers is concerned, they hold the office during the pleasure of the President. In practice they should have the confidence of the Prime Minister.

Duties and functions of public service commissions

The constitution provides for the establishment of a public service commission for the union and one for each of the states. Two or more states may, however, agree to have a joint service commission. The union service commission may, with the approval of the president, serve all or any of the needs of a state, if requested to do so by the governor of the state.

The chairman and other members of the public service commission shall be appointed, in the case of the union commission or a joint commission, by the President, and in case of a state commission, by the governor of the state. One half of the members of the commission must have held office for at least ten years in the central or a state government. A member holds office for a term of six years from the date on which he assumes office or until he attains, in the case of the union commission, the age of sixty five years and in case of a state commission or a joint commission, the age of sixty two years, whichever is earlier, unless he resigns his office earlier.

The Chairman or any other member of the public service commission may be removed form his office by the President on the ground of misbehaviour only when the Supreme Court recommends his removal after holding enquiry as prescribed by the constitution. The president has also the power to remove from the office the chairman or any other member of a public service commission if the chairman or such other member, as the case may be –

(a) is adjudged an insolvent; or
(b) engage during his term of office in any paid employment outside the duties of his office; or
(c) is, in the opinion of the president, unfit to continue in office by reason of infirmity of mind or body.

The chairman or any other member of the public service commission will be deemed to be guilty of misbehaviour if he is or becomes in any way concerned or interested in any contract or agreement made by or on behalf of the government of India or the government of a state or participate in any way in the profit thereof or in any benefit or emolument arising therefrom otherwise than as a member and in common with the other members of an incorporated company.

The functions of the public service commission are—

(1) recruitment to all civil services and posts under the respective spheres by conducting written examination, holding interviews etc.
(2) advising the government with regard to making appointments to civil services and posts and in making promotions and transfers from one service to another and on suitability of candidate for such appointment, promotions or transfers;
(3) advising the government on all disciplinary matters affecting a person serving under the government of India or the government of a state in civil capacity including memorials or petitions relating to such matters; and
(4) advising on all matters regarding the award of a pension in respect of injuries

sustained by a person while serving under the government.

Writs as a constitutional remedy

The constitution of India for the enforcement of fundamental rights of the citizen provides the remedy of writs. Article 32 and Article 226 of the constitution deal with this remedy. Article 32 of the constitution deal with the writ jurisdiction of the Supreme Court whereas Article 226 envisages the writ jurisdiction of the High Courts. The right to move the Supreme Court by appropriate proceedings for the enforcement of the rights conferred by Part IIIrd of the constitution (Fundamental rights) is guaranteed. The Supreme Court have power to issue directions or orders or writs including writ in the nature of habeas corpus, mandamus, Prohibition, quo warrants and certiorari, whichever may be appropriate, for the enforcement of any of the rights conferred under part III of the constitution. Without prejudice to the powers conferred on the Supreme Court as stated above, parliament may by law empower any other court to exercise within the local limits of its jurisdiction all or any of the powers, of issuing direction or orders or writs exercisable by the Supreme Court. These rights guaranteed by Art.32 of the constitution shall not be suspended except as otherwise provided for by the constitution.

Writ Jurisdiction of High Court and Supreme Court

Elucidating the writ jurisdiction of the High Court Article 226 of the constitution states that notwithstanding any thing in Article 32, every High Court shall have power, throughout the territories in relation to which it exercises jurisdiction, to issue to any person or authority, including in appropriate cases, any government, within those territories direction, orders or writs, including writs in the nature of habeas corpus, Mandamus, prohibition, quo warrant and certiorari, or any of them (for the enforcement of any of the rights conferred by part III and for any other purpose). The power conferred to issue directions, orders or writs to any Government or authority or person may also be exercised by any High Court exercising jurisdiction in relation to the territories within which the cause of action, wholly or in part, arises for the exercise of such power, notwithstanding that the seat of such Govt. or authority or the residence of such person is not within those territories. Where any party against whom an interim order whether by way of injunction or stay or in any other manner, is made on, or in any proceedings relating to, a petition under clause 1 of Article 226 dealing with the power to issue writs, without furnishing to such party copies of such petition and all documents in support of the plea for such interim order; and giving such party an opportunity of being heard, makes an application to the High Court for the vacation of such order and furnishes a copy of such application to the party in whose favour such order has been made or the counsel of such party, the High Court shall dispose of the application within a period of two weeks from the date of on which the copy of such application is so furnished, whichever is later, or where the High Court is closed on the last day of that period before the expiry of the next day afterwards on which the High Court is open; and if the application is not so disposed of, the interim order shall, on the expiry of the period, or as the case may be, the expiry of the said next day, stand vacated. It is to be noted that the power conferred on a High Court by this Article shall not be in derogation of the power conferred on the Supreme Court of issuing direction, orders or writs. The various types of writs *viz.* habeas corpus, Mandamus, Certiorari, prohibition and quo warrant can be described as follows:

Habeas Corpus: Any illegal detention attracts writ of habeas corpus in the High Court under article 226 of the Constitution and in the Supreme Court under article 32 of the Constitution. Right to life as provided under article 21 of the Constitution is the most precious right guaranteed to every citizen, and in case of its violation by any authority is at once remedied by the courts of our country including the Supreme Court, when approached by way of writ of habeas corpus.

Quoting Blackstone, in his book 'Right to Life and Liberty under the Constitution', Justice B.L Hansaria (formerly Hon'ble Judge of the Supreme Court) observes that the writ of habeas corpus is the great and efficacious writ in all manner of illegal confinement.

Highlighting the significance and efficacy of the writ of habeas corpus, Lord Denning said-

> "Whenever one of the King's Judges takes his seat, there is one application which by long tradition has priority over all other. Counsel has but to say, 'My Lord I have an application which concerns the liberty of the subject', and forthwith the judge will put all other matters aside and hear it. It may be an application for writ of Habeas Corpus or an application for bail, but whatever form it takes, it is first heard".

The Indian Judiciary has not lagged behind; the courts of our country, particularly the Apex court has given new dimensions and created a new jurisprudence in cases where the fundamental rights of the citizens were disturbed in violation of the constitution.

If a person is wrongfully confined or illegally detained by the police or any other authority, he is entitled for compensation. This has been held so by the Apex Court in various judgments delivered from time to time.

Mandamus: The issue of a command from the High Court or Supreme Court, which is directed against the state or the authority mentioned in Article 32 and Article 226 of the constitution, for the performance of a particular duty specified therein, which duly results from the official duty or by the operation of law, may be defined as the writ of mandamus. In simple words we can say that writ of mandamus is issued for the enforcement of public duties, in a judicial manner. For instance where a police officer refuses to perform his legal duty and such non-performance of his duty results in the violation of fundamental right of an individual then writ of mandamus can be prayed for under Article 32 and 226 in the Supreme Court and High Court respectively against such police officer.

One significant thing to note with regard to the writ of mandamus is that it is a public law remedy and it cannot be invoked for the duties of private nature.

A significant thing that is to be conceived in mind is that two pre-condition should exist for the grant of writ of mandamus. Firstly a clear legal right should exist with the applicant to the performance of a particular act or duty at the hands of the respondents and secondly there should be no other adequate or specific remedy for the purpose of enforcement of ones right and the performance of the duty which is sought to enforce.

In the ordinary course the writ of mandamus is not granted in cases of anticipated supposed omission of duty. It is issued for the performance of the duties already existing in nature. It does not create duties by itself.

An important aspect of the writ of mandamus is that the authorities which are conferred with the discretionary power for the performance of any duty, then the remedy of mandamus would lie only to set them in motion and compel them to act but as far as the exercise of such discretion or control or dictation of judgement or decision is concerned the court can not interfere. However the duties, that are purely ministerial in nature and are quite clear and specific with no element of discretion, can be compelled as it is by the grant of the writ remedy of mandamus. The intention of the person seeking writ should be bonafide and it can not be issued for gratifying one's ill-will or personal malice.

Certiorari: As stated in the Black's law Dictionary, certiorari means, "to be informed of." It is a writ of common law origin issued by a superior to an inferior court requiring the latter to produce a certified record of a particular case tried therein. The writ is issued in order that the court issuing the writ may inspect the proceedings and determine whether there have been irregularities. It is not the writ of right but of discretion. Its object lies in curbing the excess of jurisdiction and to check the inferior courts and tribunals for their judicial acts by bringing up their proceedings and judgements for review before the superior courts. In the absence of the remedy of appeal or some other appropriate means to protect the rights of an individual the remedy of writ of certiorari is available. A significant thing for the writ of certiorari is that more or less like the writ of mandamus this remedy is available for the control of public power and it is not granted for controlling the abuse of private power.

Proceedings to the question as to when the writ of certiorari is issued, it is to be conceived that this writ is issued where there is error of jurisdiction *i.e.* to correct the error of jurisdiction committed by an inferior court or tribunal in the course of their judicial acts, the writ of certiorari is issued. Such an error may be when the inferior courts or tribunals are acting without jurisdiction, or in excess of it or fails to exercise it. It is also issued in the cases where the parties are not given the proper opportunities of being heard or where the principle of natural justice is violated and court acts illegally in exercise of its undoubted jurisdiction. The nature of the jurisdiction of the court issuing writ of certiorari is supervisory rather than an appellate one, as such the court is not entitled here to review the findings of the fact as concluded by the inferior court or tribunal irrespective of the fact that such finding may be erroneous.

Prohibition: The writ of Prohibition is an order directed to an ecclesiastical or inferior temporal court or to a crown court so as to forbid that court to continue the proceeding taking place there in excess of its jurisdiction or in contravention of the law of the land. Such order is used by the high court of justice. Unlike the writ of certiorari, which is corrective in nature, the writ of prohibition is a preventive one. As such this writ or order is incapable of undoing an act that has already occurred. It is issued to prevent the commission of future act.

A significant feature of the writ of prohibition is that it is not granted to prevent the matters that are ministerial in nature as in the case of mandamus rather this remedy of writ is purely judicial in nature. Where there is departure from the rules of natural justice the remedy of prohibition is available there and its scope is not limited to the cases where the courts are proceeding in excess or absence of jurisdiction.

Difference between the Writ of Certiorari and Prohibition: It becomes necessary here to make a distinction between the writ of certiorari and writ of prohibition. The difference that exists is that of two different stages of proceedings. Where the hearing of a matter is taken up by an inferior court in excess or absence of its jurisdiction then the aggrieved party can move to the superior court praying for the writ of prohibition. On the other hand, where the court has already given the decision over a matter or cause taken up by that court in excess or absence of its jurisdiction, then in such a case the writ of certiorari is prayed for. In *R* v. *Electricity Commissioner* (1924) 1 KB 171 it was observed that "........Prohibition restrains the tribunal from proceeding further in excess of jurisdiction; Certiorari requires the records or order of the court to be sent up to the King's Bench Division to have the order quashed."

Apart from the matters taking place in excess or absence of jurisdiction the writ of prohibition lies where an action violates some statutory provision or has no statutory basis. It becomes a matter of right when the defect of jurisdiction can be prima facie witnessed in a case. Delay by the applicant or smallness of a matter in dispute are no ground for refusal of this remedy. Where the defect is not so patent then the remedy of writ becomes the right of discretion and the superior court can refuse it. Subject to the discretion of the court a stranger to a case cannot require the order of prohibition by a superior court. The writ of prohibition is a negative remedy unlike the writ of mandamus which is an affirmative one. The reason for this lies in the fact that this writ commands that something be left undone.

For invoking the writ remedy of prohibition it is necessary that the superior court or tribunal as the case may be has taken some steps towards doing certain acts to be prohibited. Where there exists a mere apprehension of danger without any step being taken in this regard the writ of prohibition won't lie. Moreover, this remedy of writ cannot be invoked to arrest the progress of any legislation which is pending before an authority empowered to legislate with respect to the peculiar matter.

Quo-Warranto: The term "quo-warranto" stands for "by what authority." The writ of "quo-warranto" is issued so as to commence an action for the purpose of recovering of an office of franchise from the person or authority who is in possession of the same without valid title to the office and/or usurping the same. Under this remedy of writ the legality of the claim is enquired into by the court and in case the claim is not well founded or have been declared forfeited, the party who asserts to that office or franchise is ousted from its enjoyment. Here the respondent is called upon to show by what authority or right he holds that office or franchise or liberty. For invoking the writ remedy of quo-warranto it is necessary that the petitioner must *inter-alia* prove that the office concerned is a public office and the person holding it is a usurper without any legal authority vested in him. Unlike the writ of Mandamus, Certiorari or prohibition the writ of quo-warranto may be applied by a stranger also, who has no personal or special interest in the case.

Furthermore, the remedy of quo-warranto can be invoked only in cases where the offence is substantive in character. Substantive character of the office here means the independence of the title of the office and in case the office is held by an independent official then the said official should not be discharging the functions of a deputy or servant at the will and pleasure of others.

Where the writ of Mandamus can be resorted in a particular, the writ of quo-warranto would not be appropriate and applicable there.

Laches and delay in filing the petition of quo-warranto is to be conceived and considered carefully by the court before granting or withholding the leave to file such petition. The motive to file the petition and their probable consequences are all proper subjects to be considered before granting or withholding the petition.

Resignation from the public office is no ground to constitute a defence to an application for ouster. After the filing of affidavits where the case is ripe for hearing before resignation, the respondent cannot escape from the jurisdiction of the court by surrendering office.

Attorney General of India

A person who is qualified to be appointed a judge of the Supreme Court is appointed by the President as the Attorney General of India. He holds office during the pleasure of the President and he has a right of audience in all courts of India. The Attorney General advises the Government of India on legal matters and performs such other duties of a legal character which may be referred or assigned to him by the President. He has a right to speak in, and otherwise to take part in the proceedings of either house, any joint sitting of the houses and any committee of Parliament to which he may be appointed as a member. However, he has no right to vote.

Consolidated Fund of India

All revenues received by Government, all loans raised by the Government by the issue of treasury bills, loans or ways and means advances and all money received by Government in repayment of loans are credited into one consolidated fund entitled "The Consolidated Fund of India". This fund forms the very basis of financial control in India. No payments from out of this fund can be made unless authorized by an Appropriation Act duly passed by the Parliament and except for the purposes for which funds have been allowed to drawn from this fund.

Contingency Fund of India

Provisions has been made in the constitution for the establishment of a fund entitled 'contingency fund of India' which will be in the nature of an imprest placed at the disposal of the president to meet unforeseen demands of expenditure for which, under normal circumstances, prior sanction of the parliament cannot be obtained due to various reasons. This fund is operated by the President who is empowered to make advances from it to meet unforeseen expenditure pending authorization of such expenditure by parliament by law. Into this fund will be paid from time to time such sums as may be determined by law. Advances taken out of this fund are subsequently recouped.

Public Account of India

All other Public moneys received by or on behalf of the Government of India are credited to the Public Account of India.

All India Services

In any federal, a dual polity and a dual service are bound to exist. In India this principle is retained in the constitution but with one exception. According to Article 312, if the council of states has declared by a resolution passed by it with two-third of the members present and voting that it is necessary or expedient in the national interest, the parliament may by law create one or more All India Services including an All India Judicial Service common to the union and the states and regulate the recruitment and the conditions of services of persons appointed to any such service. The services known at the commencement of the constitution as the Indian administrative service and the Indian police service were deemed to be services created by parliament under Article 312. However, all laws which were in force immediately before the commencement of the constitution and applicable to any public service were allowed to continue in force till such time other provisions were made in this behalf.

The recruitment to all these services is through a competitive examination conducted by the Union Public Service Commission. Article 311 of the constitution provides protection from arbitrary dismissal, removal or reduction in rank.

The All India Judicial Service will not include any post inferior to that of a district judge as defined in Article 236. The law providing for the creation of All India Judicial Service may contain such provisions for amendment of the relevant chapters of the constitution (Chapter VI of Part VI) as may be necessary for giving effect to the provisions of that law. But such law is not deemed to be an amendment of the constitution for the purpose of Article 368.

Taxes on Professions, trades, callings and employment

Notwithstanding anything in Article 246 of the constitution dealing with the subject matter of laws made by Parliament and by the legislatures of the states, no law of the legislature of a state relating to taxes for the benefit of the state or of a municipality, district board, local board or other local authority therein in respect of professions, trades, callings or employments shall be invalid on the ground that it relates to a tax on income.

The total amount payable in respect of any one person to the state or to any one municipality, district board, local board or other local authority in the state by way of taxes on professions, trades, callings and employment shall not exceed two thousands and five hundred rupees per annum.

The power of the legislature of a state to make laws as aforesaid with respect to taxes on profession, trades, callings and employments shall not be construed as limiting in any way the power of parliament to make laws with respect to taxes on income accruing from or arising out of professions, trades, callings and employments.

Special case of reservation of a state bill for the assent of the President

The Governor shall not assent to, but shall compulsorily reserve for the consideration of the

President, any bill which in the opinion of the Governor would, if it became law, so derogate from the powers of the High Court as to endanger the position which that court is by the constitution of India designed to fill.

Revenues distribution among the Union and the States

There are several principles governing the distribution of revenue in the constitution between the Union and the state. The Union levies taxes, and some taxes are levied by the states, on the other hand, there is provision for assignment to the states of the proceeds of certain taxes, division of some others also grant-in-aid by the Union to the state. These principles can be pointed out as follows:

(a) Taxes belonging to the Union exclusively:
  (1) Customs
  (2) Taxes on capital value of assets on individual and companies
  (3) Corporation tax
  (4) Surcharge on income tax etc.
  (5) Fees in respect of matters in the Union list.

(b) Taxes belonging to the states exclusively:
  (1) Stamp duty except on documents included in the Union list
  (2) Land revenue
  (3) Succession duty, estate duty, and taxes on agricultural land
  (4) Taxes on passengers and goods carried on inland water-ways
  (5) Taxes on lands and buildings, mineral rights
  (6) Taxes on entry of goods into a local area
  (7) Taxes on animals and boats, on road vehicles, on advertisements, on consumption of electricity, of luxuries and amusements etc.
  (8) Sales tax
  (9) Tolls
  (10) Taxes on profession, trades etc. not exceeding Rs. 250 per annum
  (11) Fees in respect of matters in the State list

(c) Taxes levied by the Union, but collected and appropriated by the State: As per Article 268 of the constitution such stamp duties and such duties of excise on medicinal and toilet preparations as are mentioned in the union list shall be levied by the Government of India but shall be collected.
  (i) in the case where such duties are leviable within any Union territory by the Government of India, and
  (ii) in other cases, by the states within which such duties are respectively leviable

The proceeds in any financial year of any such duty leviable within any state shall not form part of the consolidated fund of India, but shall be assigned to that state.

(d) Taxes levied and collected by the Union but assigned to the states: The following duties and taxes shall be levied and collected by the government of India but shall be assigned to the states in the manner as state further namely:
  (1) Duties in respect of succession to property other than agricultural land;
  (2) Estate duty in respect of property other than agricultural land;
  (3) Terminal taxes on goods or passengers carried by railway, sea or air;
  (4) Taxes on railway fares and freights;
  (5) Taxes other than stamp duties on transaction in stock-exchanges and future markets;
  (6) Taxes on the sale or purchase of newspapers and on advertisements published therein;
  (7) Taxes on the sale or purchase of goods other than newspapers, where such sale or purchase takes place in the course of inter-state trade or commerce;
  (8) Taxes on the consignment of goods (whether the consignment is to the person making it or to any other

person), where such consignment takes place in the course of Inter-state trade or commerce;

The net proceeds in the financial year of any such duty or tax, except in so far as those proceeds represent proceeds attributable to the Union Territories shall not form part of the consolidated fund of India, but shall be assigned to the states within which that duty or tax is leviable in that year, and shall be distributed among those states in accordance with such principles of distribution as may be formulated by Parliament by law.

Parliament may by law formulate principles for determining when a sale or purchase of or consignment of goods takes place in the course of Inter-state trade or commerce.

(e) Taxes levied collected by the Union and distributed between the Union and the States: Taxes on income other than agricultural income shall be levied and collected by the Government of India and distributed between the Union and the State in the manner provided as under:

Such percentage, as may be prescribed, of the net proceeds in any financial year of any tax, except in so far as those proceeds represent proceeds attributable to the union territories or to taxes payable in respect of Union emoluments, shall not form part of the consolidated fund of India, but shall be distributed among those states in such manner and such time as may be prescribed. For this purpose, in each financial year such percentage as may be prescribed of so much of the net proceeds of taxes on income as does not represent the net proceeds of taxes payable in respect of Union emoluments shall be deemed to represent proceeds attributable to Union territories. Here "taxes on income" does not include a corporation tax. Besides "prescribed" here means:

(a) Until a finance commission has been constituted, prescribed by the President by order, and

(b) After a finance commission has been constituted, prescribed by the President by order after considering the recommendations of the Finance Commission;

Furthermore, here "Union emoluments" includes all emoluments and pensions payable out of the consolidated fund of India in respect of which income tax is chargeable.

(f) Taxes levied and collected by the Union and may be distributed between the Union and the States: Union duties of excise other than such duties of excise on medicinal and toilet preparation as are mentioned in the Union list shall be levied and collected by the government of India, but if Parliament by law so provides, there shall be paid out of the consolidated fund of India to the States to which the law imposing the duty extends sums equivalent to the whole or any part of the net proceeds of that duty, and those states in accordance with such principles of distribution as may be formulated by such law.

(g) Grants from the Union to certain States: Such sums as parliament may by law provide shall be charged on consolidated fund of India in each year as grant-in-aid of the revenue of such states as parliament may determine to be in need of assistance, and different sums may be fixed for different States.

(h) Appointment of Finance Commission: The constitution requires the President to appoint a Finance Commission within two years from the commencement of the constitution and thereafter at the expiry of every fifth year or at such earlier time as the President considers necessary. It shall be the duty and function of the Finance Commission to make recommendations to the President as to –

(a) the distribution between the Union and the State of the net proceeds of taxes which are to be or may be, divided between them;

(b) the principle which should govern the grant-in-aid of the revenues of the States out of the consolidated fund of India.

(c) the measures needed to augment the consolidated fund of a State to supplement the resources of the Panchayats in the state on the basis of the recommendations made by the Finance Commission of the State.

(d) the measures needed to augment the consolidated fund of a state to supplement the resources of the municipalities in the State on the basis of the recommendations made by the Finance Commission of the State.

any other matter referred to the commission by the President in the interests of the sound finance.

Jurisdiction of the Union in relation to territories outside India

Article 138 (2) of the constitution states that the Supreme Court shall have such further jurisdiction and powers with respect to any matter as the Government of India and the Government of any state may by special agreement confer, if Parliament by law provides for the exercise of such jurisdiction and powers by the Supreme Court. By this provision in the constitution the Jurisdiction of the Supreme Court has been enlarged. Besides, under Article 140 of the constitution the Supreme Court has also been conferred certain ancillary powers. Under this provision Parliament may by law make provision for conferring upon the Supreme Court such supplemental powers not inconsistent with any of the provisions of the constitution as may appear to be necessary or desirable for the purpose of enabling the court more effectively to exercise the jurisdiction conferred upon it by or under the constitution.

Constitutional provisions relating to the borrowing by the State Governments

Subject to the provisions of Article 293 of the constitution of India dealing with the borrowing by state, the executive power of a state extends to borrowing within the territory of India upon the security of the consolidated fund of the State within such limits, if any, as may from time to time be fixed by the legislature of such state by law and to the giving of guarantees within such limits, if any, as may be so fixed.

The Government of India may, subject to such conditions as may be laid down by or under any law made by the Parliament, make loans to any state or, so long as any limits fixed under Article 292 of the constitution, dealing with the borrowing by the Government of India, are not exceeded, give guarantees in respect of loans raised by any state, and any sums required for the purpose of making such loans shall be charged on the consolidated fund of India.

A state may not without the consent of the Government of India raise any loan if there is still outstanding any part of loan which has been made to the state by the Government of India or by its predecessor Government, or in respect of which a guarantee has been given by the Government of India or by its predecessor Government. A consent in such condition may be granted subject to such condition, if any, as Government of India may think fit to impose.

Importance of the role played by the "Public Accounts Committee"

Public Accounts Committee is one of the standing financial committees of Parliament. As per Article 151 of the constitution, the Comptroller and Auditor General of India is duty bound to submit his reports relating to the accounts of the Union to the President who causes them to be laid before each House of Parliament. Public Accounts Committee is constituted out of the members of the House of the People and the Council of States to deal with the reports of the C.A.G of India. It consists of fifteen members nominated by the House of the People and seven members from the members of the council of states. The term of office of members is one year. However, a minister cannot be appointed as a member of the committee. The chairman of the committee is appointed by the speaker from amongst the members of the committee.

The present charter of the committee as embodied in the rules of procedure and conduct of business, is to satisfy itself:

(i) that the moneys shown in the accounts as having been disbursed were legally available for and applicable to the service or purpose to which they have been applied or charged;

(ii) that the expenditure conforms to the authority which governs it; and

(iii) that every reappropriation has been made in accordance with the provisions made in this behalf under rules framed by the competent authority.

It is also the duty of the Public Accounts Committee:

(i) to examine in the light of the report of the comptroller and auditor general, the statement of accounts showing the income and expenditure of the state corporations, trading and manufacturing schemes and projects;

(ii) to examine the statement of accounts showing the income and expenditure of autonomous and semi-autonomous bodies, the audit of which may be conducted by the comptroller and auditor general either under the directions of the President or by a statute of Parliament; and

(iii) to consider the report of the comptroller and auditor general in case where the President may have required him to conduct an audit of any receipts or to examine the accounts of stores and stocks.

The aim of the committee is:

(i) to ensure that money is spent as Parliament intended;

(ii) to ensure the exercise of due economy and to draw attention to cases of waste, extravagances, loses and nugatory expenditure;

(iii) to ensure that a high standard of public morality in all financial matters is maintained.

If any money has been spent on any service during a financial year in excess of the amount granted by Parliament for that purpose, the committee examines with reference to the facts of each case, the circumstances leading to such an excess and makes such recommendations as it may deem fit.

Although the committee does not have the power to compel any administrative action to be taken on its observations, this does not affect the effectiveness of the recommendations of the committee. The power of the committee is indirect and lies in the potential results of its reports and publicity which it is able to give to the questions it investigated and in the moral effect of its criticism. The committee has entirely fulfilled the expectation that it should develop into a powerful force for controlling public expenditure.

Planning Commission

The Planning commission was established on march 15, 1950 by an executive resolution of the Government of India. It was established on the recommendation of the Advisory Planning Board constituted in 1946, under the chairmanship of KC Neogi.

It is an extra-constitutional and a non-statutory body. It is supreme organ of planning for social and economic development in India. The Prime Minister of India is the ex-officio chairman of the Planning commission. The deputy chairman is the de-facto executive head (i.e. full time functional head) of the commission. The deputy chairman of the commission is responsible for the formulation and submission of the draft of the five-year plans to the central cabinet. He is appointed by the central cabinet for a fixed tenure and enjoys the rank of a cabinet minister. Though he is not a member of the cabinet, he is invited to attend all its meetings (without a right to vote).

Some central ministers are appointed as a part-time members of the commission. Finance minister and planning minister are ex-officio (by virtue of) members of the constitution. The commission has four to seven full-time expert members. The full time members enjoy the rank of a minister of state. The planning commission has a member-secretary. He is usually a senior member of IAS. The planning commission is wholly a center constituted body, the state governments are not represented. The Planning Evaluation Organization (PEO) was established in 1952 as an independent unit of the planning commission. Planning commission works as a staff agency with advisory role. It is also known as 'Super Cabinet', an 'Economic Cabinet' a 'Parallel Cabinet', the 'Fifth Wheel of the Coach' etc.

Charged Expenditure

Items of expenditure which are not subjected to the vote of Parliament and are charged directly upon the consolidated fund of India are known as 'charged expenditure'. The annual financial statement commonly called the Budget contains a forecast of the estimated revenue and expenditure of the Government of India for ensuing financial year. The estimates of expenditure embodied in the budget come under two categories 'charged' and 'voted' items. The charged items of expenditure which are shown separately from other expenditure proposed to be made from the consolidated fund of India are not submitted to the vote of Parliament, although they can be discussed on the floor of the House.

Arrest – Meaning of

The word, "Arrest", according to the Oxford Dictionary means "seize (a person or a ship) and take into custody especially by legal authority". However, as per the law the word has not been defined in the Code of Criminal Procedure but section 46 of the Code explains how the arrest is to be made. It is said that the police officer or other person making arrest shall actually touch or confine the body of the person to be arrested unless there be a submission to the custody by word or action. While making such endeavor the police officer may use all means necessary to affect the arrest but that does not mean to cause death of the person who is not accused of an offence punishable with death or with imprisonment for life. Thus drawing out the meaning of the same in a practical manner, "Arrest" is the curtailment or restrain of one's liberty by seizing it or taking in to custody the same. When the liberty of a person that is guaranteed under Article 21 of the Constitution of India is deprived of due to any reason whatsoever by the command of the sovereign or the lawful authority, it is said to be arrested.

Duties of Police Officer

The police officers are liable to certain duties as provided under Police Act, 1949. These duties are:-

(i) to obey and execute all orders and warrants lawfully issued to him by any competent authority;

(ii) to collect and communicate intelligence affecting the public peace;

(iii) to prevent the commission of offences and public nuisances;

(iv) to detect and bring offenders to justice and to apprehend all persons whom he is legally authorised to apprehend, and for whose apprehension sufficient ground exists;

(v) to enter and inspect any drinking shop, gambling house or other place or resort of loose and disorderly characters;

(vi) to keep law and order on public roads and in public streets, thoroughfares, ghats and laundry places and at all other places of public resort and to prevent obstruction on the occasions of assemblies and processions on the public roads and in public street, or in the neighbourhood of places of worship during the time of public worship and in any case when any road, street, thoroughfare, ghat or laundry place may be thronged or may be liable to be obstructed;

(vii) to take into custody, without a warrant any person who within his view commits any of the following offences, to the obstruction, inconvenience, annoyance, risk, danger or damage to the residents, or passengers—

(a) *Slaughtering cattle, furious riding etc.*— Any person who slaughters any cattle or cleanses any carcasses; any person who rides or drives any cattle recklessly or forcibly or trains or breaks any house of other cattle.

(b) *Cruelty to animals.*—Any person who wantonly or cruelly beats, abuses or tortures any animals.

(c) *Obstructing Passengers.*—Any person who keeps any cattle or conveyance of any kind standing longer than is required for loading or unloading or for taking up or setting down passengers or who leaves any conveyance in such a manner as to cause inconvenience or danger to the public.

(d) *Exporting goods for sale.*—Any person who exposes any goods for sale without proper care.

(e) *Throwing dirt into Streets.*—Any person who throws and lays down any dirt, filth, rubbish or any stones or building materials or who constructs any cowshed, stable or the like or who causes any offensive matter to run from any house, factory, dirty heap or the like.

(f) *Being drunk or riotous.*—Any person who is found drunk or riotous or who is incapable of taking care of himself.

(g) *Indecent exposure of person.*—Any person who wilfully and indecently exposes his person or any offensive, deformity or disease or commits nuisance by easing himself or by bathing or washing in any tank or reservoir, not being a place set apart for that purpose.

(h) *Neglect to protect dangerous places.*— Any person who neglects to fence in or neglects to protect any well, tank or other dangerous place or structure.

(viii) to lay any information before a Magistrate and to apply for a summons, warrant, search warrant or such other legal process which may by law be issued against any person committing any offence;

(ix) to take charge of unclaimed property which is subject to the order of Magistrate for the purpose of disposal and he is required to furnish an inventory thereof to the Magistrate;

(x) the police officer can not resign without leave or two months notice;

(xi) the officer is also liable to suffer penalties for neglect of duties under sections 30 and 34 of the said Act. Section 44 provides that the police officer is bound to keep a diary.

Police Interrogation

In the matter of police interrogation the first question that arises is whether the police can visit the house at any time. The answer to this question is that the police has no authority to visit the house at odd hours. Normally the police should not visit any house after sunset and before sunrise. If there is no male member in the house, the police have to give reasonable time to the female member to dress herself properly, before entering the said house. In case of *Pardanashin* lady, the police has to be more careful and has to give the lady reasonable time to dress properly i.e. wearing of Burqa etc. before entering that house. Besides the proviso to section 160(1) of the Code of Criminal Procedure, 1973, as a safeguard to the rights of women and children state that no male under the age of fifteen years or woman shall be required to attend at any place other than the place in which such male person or woman resides.

Right to Silence: As per the decision of the Supreme Court in *Nandini Satpathy* v. *P.L. Dani*, 1978(3) SCR 608 where the petitioner refused to answer certain questions on the plea that she had the right to silence under Article 21(3) of the Constitution and section 161(2) of the Code of Criminal Procedure and consequently a complaint was filed under section 171 of Indian Penal Code. Further the petitioner (Mrs. Satpathy) challenged the validity of the magisterial proceeding. The High Court rejected her plea. She ultimately came to the Supreme Court. The following observations of the Apex court are significant:

> "At the outset, the Supreme Court took note of the fact that the accused Nandini was directed to appear at a police station for interrogation in flagrant contravention of the wholesome provisions of section 160(1) of Code of Criminal Procedure. The Supreme Court strongly felt that such deviance on the part of police must be visited with prompt punishment, since policemen may not be a law unto themselves expecting others to obey law."

The Supreme Court in this landmark judgment has held that the police cannot force the accused person to answer each and every question, which they put to him on the principle that no person can be compelled to be witness against himself. The apprehension of incrimination from the answer must be substantial and real, as distinguished from the danger of remote possibilities or fanciful flow of inference. The real test is, could the witness (accused) have reasonably sensed the peril of prosecution from his answer in the conspectus of circumstances. The perception of the peculiarities of the case cannot be irrelevant in proper appraisal of self-incriminatory potentiality. The Apex Court laid down certain guidelines for the observance of the principles discussed as follows:

(i) The police should permit the advocate, if there be one, to be present at the time the accused is examined.

(ii) The police should invariably warn and record the facts about the right to silence against self-incrimination, and where the accused is literate take his written acknowledgment.

(iii) After an examination of the accused, where a lawyer of his choice is not available the police must take him to a Magistrate, doctor or other willing and non-partisan official or non-official and allow a scheduled audience where he may unburden himself beyond the view of the police and tell whether he has suffered duress which should be followed by judicial or some other custody for him where the police can not reach him. The Collector may briefly record the relevant conversation and communicate it not to the police but the nearest Magistrate.

Assistance of an Advocate: Peeping into the question whether the person can take assistance of an advocate when summoned at the police station the answer comes out to be affirmative *i.e.* every accused person who had been arrested or is summoned at the police station has the right to get assistance of an advocate of his choice as it is the fundamental right to consult an advocate under Article 22(1) of the Constitution of India.

Important tips to remember: There are certain important tips that a person should remember in case of arrest by the police and they are

1. The moment any person is arrested by the police he has every right to know the offence alleged to have been committed by him.
2. He has legal and constitutional entitlement to inform his nearest relation of the fact that he has been detained at a particular police station,
3. It is bounden duty of the police officer on the spot to inform the nearest relations of the accused persons about his arrest.
4. If he has been hauled up in a bailable offence, he is entitled to be released on bail at the police station itself as a matter

of right on furnishing bail bond of reasonable amount.

5. In case the police officer refuses to bail him out, it will amount to an illegal confinement and the police officer is liable to be punished for the contempt of court.
6. He cannot be detained in police custody for more than 24 hours.
7. He cannot be denied the facility of having an advocate by his side.
8. If the person is a woman or a male person under the age of fifteen years, she or he cannot be summoned to the police station, for interrogation.
9. He cannot be compelled to answer each and every question that the police chooses to put to him; he has only to truthfully give the facts of the matter to assist the police that is to say that he has the right to silence in certain circumstances.
10. He has every entitlement to resist every kind of undue coercion, pressure or torture (physical or mental).
11. In most of the states there are boards that render free legal aid to prisoners and other personal entitled for it. In the court of Metropolitan Magistrate an advocate on behalf of the Legal Aid Board is always available.
12. Moreover few important directions for the prisoners are that in case of an offence which carried imprisonment of more than 10 years, the challan must be filed by the police within 90 days from the date of one's arrest.
13. Under Article 39A of the Constitution every person is entitled for free legal aid from the concerned Legal Aid Board.
14. One should always remember the number of FIR, the date of arrest, the date from which one is under judicial custody, the name of the Board, the next date of hearing and the name and address of the advocate.
15. Besides the prisoner is also entitled to write any letter, application or appeal to any court, which has to be forwarded by jail superintendent preferably within 24 hours from the date of submission.
16. If a person does not want to engage any advocate he can go to the court from jail and argue the case in person. He is entitled to get every assistance from jail authorities to have the application/ petition drafted, typed and filed in the court

Remand

Meaning and Scope of Remand: Sections 56, 57, 167 and 309 of the Code of Criminal procedure, 1973 deal with the procedure to be adopted in relation to grant of remand (judicial remand as well as police remand). A remand in fact is an authorised detention of custody of a person arrested. The remands are of two types:

1. Judicial remand or judicial custody.
2. Police remand or police custody.

The Magistrate exercises his powers under the Code of Criminal procedure, 1973 while granting judicial remands or police remand.

For how long can police detain a person without remand: The police cannot keep any person accused of an offence in its custody for more than 24 hours. Section 57 of the Code of Criminal procedure 1973 specifically prohibits a police officer from detaining the arrested person for more than 24 hours in police custody, exclusive of the time necessary for journey from the place of arrest to the court of Magistrate except under the special orders of the Magistrate. The Code clearly lays down that detention in police custody should not be for a longer period than under all circumstances of the case is reasonable.

In *R.K. Naba Chandra Singh* v. *Manipur Administration*, AIR 1964 Gau 39, the Hon'able High Court pointed out that, " If the police officer considers that the investigation can not be completed within 24 hours, it is his duty to produce the accused forthwith before the Magistrate".

In *State* v. *Ram Avtar Chaudhary* AIR 1955 All 138, the Allahabad High Court observed:

"Section 61(now Sec.57) does not empower a police officer to keep an arrested person in custody, a minute longer than is necessary for the purpose of investigation. It does not give him an absolute right to keep a person in custody till 24 hours and longer for other reason like the inability of the admission of the accused in jail".

Who can ask for remand: A significant question that arises is that who can ask for remand. The answer lies that it is only an officer incharge of the police station or an investigating officer not below the rank of sub-inspector of police who is empowered to ask for the remand under the Code.

Reasons to be recorded while dealing with remand cases: Section 167 of the Code of Criminal procedure, 1973 contemplates that the Magistrate should not only direct remand in case he is satisfied that the person arrested has to be remanded for the purpose of investigation but should also record his reasons while remanding the accused. The Magistrate is also bound to record the reasons in case he does not feel necessary to order further detention of the accused for the purpose of investigation and in such a case he should release the accused.

In *Dr. K.S. Rao* v. *State of Hydrabad* AIR 1957 AP 416, it was held that:

> "In remanding an accused to police custody the Magistrate ought to follow the provisions of section 167 of the Code of Criminal Procedure 1973 and should give proper reasons for handing over the accused to the police custody."

Improper Police Remand: Grant of police remand for the following purpose is improper:

(a) For pointing out the places through which the accused passed on his way to commit dacoity.

(b) For compelling the accused to give a clue to the stolen property.

(c) For obtaining the identification of the accused in the village; and

(d) For verifying the confessional statement of the accused recorded under Section 161 of the Code of Criminal procedure, 1973.

Remanding the accused to police custody for 15 days in first instance is highly objectionable. What is desirable and proper is that when the Magistrate is satisfied that the presence of the accused is necessary for the purpose of discovery of some evidence, he should remand the accused to police custody for a shorter period, considering the facts and circumstances of the case.

Maximum Period of Police Remand by Magistrate: The maximum period for which a Magistrate can authorise the detention of the accused in police custody or judicial custody under section 167 of the Code of Criminal procedure, 1973 is fifteen days. Where the total period of police remand under Section 167 of the Code of Criminal Procedure, 1973 has expired the Magistrate has no jurisdiction to further remand the accused to police custody. The police in such case might at best ask for the remand under section 309 of the Code of Criminal Procedure, 1973 but that remand can only be to the judicial lock up.

In *Yashwant Bapuji Mokashi* v. *State of Maharastra*, AIR 1968 Bom 273, it was held that in view of sub-section (2) of section 167 of the Code of Criminal Procedure, 1973 the period of detention in police custody shall not exceed fifteen days. On the whole if the accused is produced before a Magistrate having jurisdiction, he can give the accused in the custody of police for a total number of fifteen days and not more. The custody may be magisterial custody or police custody but in either case, during the course of investigation, the total period cannot exceed fifteen days. What applies to Magistrate having jurisdiction to try the consequently applies to Magistrate who has no jurisdiction."

Order of Remand to be in the prescribed form: - Whenever a Magistrate passes any order of remand it should be passed in the prescribed form as per the provisions of the Code. In *Bir Bhadra Pratap Singh* v. *District Magistrate, Azamgarh*, AIR 1959 All 384, it was observed that when Magistrate makes orders of remand, under Section 167 of the Code Of Criminal

Procedure, 1898 they should make the orders in the prescribed form and not on mere chits of paper.

Remand of Arrested Person who is Seriously ill: Another significant question that arises is regarding the remand of arrested person who is seriously ill. If the person arrested is not in a position to be produced before the Magistrate for the purpose of remand without danger to his life and needs immediately medical treatment, the police officer shall admit such person in the hospital and report the matter to the Magistrate having jurisdiction to try the case.

The Magistrate shall then pass suitable orders regarding the custody of the person admitted in the hospital by invoking the inherent powers of the court under the provisions of the Code with a direction to the police officer to produce the accused before him immediately after his discharge from the hospital along with a discharge certificate issued by the medical officer. Furthermore, the police has no right to allow the relatives of the accused in police custody to supply him with food and clothing so long as they satisfy themselves that no objectionable are supplied.

Offence

According to the Chambers Dictionary, the word "offence" stands for any cause of displeasure; an injury; a transgression; a breach of law; a crime; a sin; affront. However, making an elaborate analysis it has been found that none of the jurists have been successful in giving a perfect definition of offence or crime. It is defined as "public wrong" by Blackstone and Stephen, as a "moral wrong" by Garafalo, as "conventional wrong" by Edwin Sutherland, as a "social wrong" by John Gillin and as a "procedural wrong" by Austin, and Kenney. On the Statutory lines "offence" has been defined under section 40 of Indian Penal Code, 1860 as well as under clause (n) of section 2 of the Code of Criminal Procedure, 1973. Under IPC the definition given is the originally drafted form of clause 27 of the Draft Penal Code whereas under Cr PC "offence" means any act or omission made punishable by any law for the time being in force and includes any act in respect of which a complaint may be made under section 20 of the Cattle-Trespass Act, 1871.

Drawing out the inference from it we get certain characteristics of crime and they are— firstly, crime is an act of commission or an act of omission on the part of a human being which is considered harmful by the State. Secondly, the transgression of such harmful acts is prevented by a threat or sanction of punishment administered by the State and thirdly, the guilt of the accused is determined after the accusation against him has been investigated in the legal proceedings of a special kind in accordance with the provisions of law.

First Information Report

"First Information Report" is popularly known as FIR. It is the information recorded by a police officer on duty given either by the aggrieved person or any other person to the commission of an alleged offence. It is only on this basis that police commences its investigation. Section 154 of the Code of Criminal Procedure deals with such information relating to the cognizable offences. FIR is a public document and after the lodging of it the accused is entitled to get a certified copy of it. If such a copy is denied of, then it leads to the violation of the principle of natural justice and Article 21 of the Constitution that guarantees the fundamental right of life and liberty. Besides, the informant will also get the certified copy of the report lodged free of cost as it is mandatory under the aforesaid section.

Duty of Police officer to Record FIR

It has been held by the Supreme Court in several cases that where the officer in charge of police station is informed of any cognizable offence then he has no other option except to register the case on the basis of information made. However, in case the police officer does not record the information given then the Superintendent of Police can be approached by giving him information by way of registered post. In that case the Superintendent of Police can investigate the case himself or the subordinate officer can be directed in this regard. FIR is such an important document without which nothing can be done and simply on the basis that the information is not reliable or credible the registering of the information cannot be refused. Similarly, where a police officer refuses to record FIR giving the explanation that the place of offence is outside the territorial jurisdiction of the police station it is the dereliction of duty on the part of the officer. In such case it is the duty of the police officer to record the information and forward it to the police station having jurisdiction. As far as the telephonic message given by the informant is concerned, such a message that has been recorded by the police officer in his station diary relating to the commission of cognizable offence is FIR as connoted by section 154 of the Code. On lodging the FIR the substance of information is to be entered in the book known as "General Diary" or "Station Diary" or a "Station House Register". The District Magistrate has the power to call and investigate such diary

Statements not amounting to FIR

There are certain statements or reports that do not amount to FIR. Within this category falls a report or a statement recorded after the commencement of the investigation (Sections 162 and 163 of Code of Criminal Procedure), reports not recorded immediately but after questioning of witnesses, reports recorded after several days of developments, information not about occurrence of cognizable offence but only cryptic message in the form of an appeal of immediate help, complaint to the Magistrate, information to beat house, information to the Magistrate or police officer on phone and information received at police station prior to the lodging of an FIR.

Time limit for filing FIR

For the duration of time for filing an FIR it has been emphasized that as far as possible and practicable, every FIR should invariably be filed promptly expeditiously and without wasting any time. However in case of delay there must be cogent reasons for reasonable delay in filing the FIR under the compelling circumstances. Judge with lot of wisdom and experience can use their discretion judiciously and in the interest of justice in each and every case. Although, no possible duration of time can be fixed for applying the test of reasonableness to the lodging of an FIR, it depends upon the facts and circumstances of each case. The delay in lodging the FIR as such is not fatal in law if the prosecution substantiated the factual difficulties encountered by the persons lodging the report.

Bail & Bail Bond

The very word "Bail" means the process by which the liberty of a citizen, which is under cloud, is to be restored with or without conditions imposed by the courts of competence. It sets free a person who is under arrest, detention or is under some kind of restraint by taking security for his appearance. However, it does not mean getting the accused at liberty but it is only a process to release him to the custody of his sureties, who undertake to produce him whenever required by the court at the pre-trial stage.

Bail, Parole and Furlough

The concept of "Bail" is entirely different from the "Parole" which signifies a promise given by a prisoner of war to return at a time appointed, or not to take up arms till exchanged, the practice of releasing prisoners of war or an undertaking that they will not serve again during the war. Besides, the meaning and concept of "parole" that has been changing from time to time means in the literal sense a formal promise or a word of honour. Bail is generally granted at the pre-trial stage, but parole is granted after passing of sentence and while under going imprisonment in the jail. It, therefore, means a mere suspension of sentence for the time being. Thus, parole signifies the release of a prisoner from jail for a short period and is granted on a promise or undertaking given by the concerned prisoner that he will not escape after being released from the jail. He is also duty bound to come back after the stipulated period to undergo the remaining sentence again.

Another concept of law of the nature similar to the Bail is "Furlough" although it is conceptually different. Bail is generally granted by a court whereas Parole and Furlough are granted by the state as per rules and regulations or the guidelines laid down by the executive authority from time to time. The difference between the "Parole" and "Furlough" is that while Parole can be granted to the prisoner detained in the prison-house under any offence whatsoever and irrespective of duration of the imprisonment awarded to him, Furlough can be granted only in those cases where the prisoner has been sentenced to long imprisonment i.e. five years and more.

Bailable/Non-Bailable Offence

Offences are generally categorized as

(i) Bailable offences and

(ii) Non-bailable offences.

If any person is arrested for an offence which is categorized as bailable offence in the first schedule of the Code of Criminal Procedure, 1973, he is entitled to get bail as a matter of right. In case a Magistrate takes cognizance of the same offence and if he is of the opinion to issue a warrant of arrest then he should issue only a bailable warrant which stands in parlance with the direction of the court that granted anticipatory bail according to section 438 of the Code of Criminal Procedure and it should be granted by the officer-in-charge of the concerned police station. Besides, the police officer has also got discretionary power to release the person instead of taking bail from him on execution of a bond without sureties as per Section 436 of Code of Criminal Procedure.

If any person is arrested for an offence, which comes under the category of Non-bailable offence in the same schedule, the grant or refusal of bail is a matter of discretion. This discretion is normally vested in the court but on the other side if there exists no sound evidence against the accused and further investigation is needed according to the opinion of the police officer, then as per Section 437(2) of the Code of Criminal Procedure, 1973 the police officer can release him on bail.

Generally, the courts in the cases where offence is punishable with death or imprisonment for life do not grant bail. But if the accused is a women, children below the age of 16 years, a very sick person or a person of old age then the accused is to be released on bail even in the offences that are punishable with death or life imprisonment.

Anticipatory Bail

While talking about the concept of bail it is necessary to understand a special type of bail called Anticipatory Bail. Anticipatory bail is the bail that is granted by the court on *bonafide* apprehension of being arrested on a accusation of having committed a non-bailable offence as per section 438 of Code of Criminal Procedure *i.e.* the offence has not yet occurred and the bail is granted in anticipation. For the purpose of such bail, one has to move to the Court of Session Judge through an advocate who either himself hears the bail application or he sends it to the designated court of Additional Session Judge. On receiving the application, one copy of the bail application is sent to the concerned police station for getting report from SHO. After hearing the arguments from the side of public prosecutor and the counsel for the applicant, the court reaches to the conclusion whether to accept or reject the bail application so moved. The court granting anticipatory bail can put forth certain conditions for the purpose in a particular case as envisaged by Section 438(2) of the Code of Criminal Procedure and they may include:

1. A condition that the person shall make himself available for interrogation by a police officer as and when required.
2. A condition that the person shall not directly or indirectly, make any inducement, threat or promise to any person acquainted with the facts of the case so as to dissuade him for disclosing such facts to the court or to any police officer.
3. A condition that the person shall not leave India without the previous permission of the court.

4. Such other conditions as may be imposed under Sub-section (3) of section 437 of Code of Criminal Procedure as if the bail were granted under that section.

Important tips in the Matter of Bail

Court exercise wide powers in the matter of grant or rejection of bail and the rejection of bail can lead to immediate arrest of the accused so the counsel should avoid the presence of the accused at the time of argument on bail. Here are few other things that should be borne in the mind while dealing with the concept of bail. They are that if the application for bail is rejected then so as to try for the bail in the same court again, a person can apply a fresh application with new grounds. The amount fixed for the bond should not be excessive and if it is so then the Court of Session or High Court may direct for the reduction of the amount. The Magistrate while allowing the person to be released on bail should impose no unreasonable conditions. If unreasonable conditions are imposed, the person can appeal in the higher court but he will not be released until the appeal is admitted or disposed of in his favour. So as to get released immediately from the police custody if the case is a warrant case the bond should be executed with sureties meeting out the direction endorsed in the warrant. If the case comes within the purview of bailable offence and the arrest is made without warrant, then the officer-in-charge of the police station should be asked to grant bail after executing a bond or he should be asked to release the accused on executing a bond without sureties. Besides, the accused has the right to telephone the advocate, a friend, or a relative. If these matters can be dealt with before going to the court then the accused can save himself from unnecessary remand in custody. If the accused is not financially sound to engage an advocate then he may make a written application to the judge to provide advocate of the free legal aid committee of the same court.

Generally, the police while making objections to the grant of the bail makes the contentions that the accused would not appear for trial and there is likelihood that he will again commit offence while on trial, the witnesses may be tutored and material evidences may be manipulated but such contentions should be refuted. Other contentions may be the incomplete police inquiries, absconding of co-accused, non-recovery of stolen property or the weapon with which the crime was committed which should be rebutted to the extent possible. The accused can make the arguments of the nature that he may loose his job if not granted bail, the condition and state of accommodation is much that there is possibility of eviction, he is the only earning member of the family and the family members may suffer hardship, his poor state of health may further worsen, the injured has already been released from hospital. It may be helpful for granting of bail.

Jurisdiction of Criminal Courts

Section 2, 3 & 4 of the Indian Penal Code, 1860 determines the jurisdiction of the Criminal Courts for the offences committed within India and abroad. Section 2 deals with the intra-territorial operation of the Code and it states "Every person shall be liable to punishment under this Code, and not otherwise, for every act or omission contrary to the provisions thereof, of which he shall be guilty within India." As observed by the Hon'able Supreme Court in *Mubarak Ali Ahmed* v. *State of Bombay*, AIR (1957) SC 857 that the principle of criminal jurisprudence is that the criminal jurisdiction is to be exercised in accordance with the locality of the offence committed, and not upon the nationality or the locality of the offender, so it becomes necessary to establish that the offence for which the accused is charged is committed within the territory of India.

The term "Territory" here covers not only land, rivers, lakes and canals rather it also extends to the territorial waters of the sea measuring twelve maritime miles from the appropriate base line and also includes the ships, aircrafts (whether armed or unarmed) of the state. The private ships on its subjects on the high seas or in foreign tidal waters, and foreign private ships while within its ports are also included in the "territory" of the state.

The term "Every person" used in this section makes every person irrespective of his nationality or allegiance, or his rank, status, caste, colour or creed, liable to punishment under the Penal Code for an offence committed within India. It connotes the natural as well as artificial person like company or association or body of persons, whether incorporated or not. Interpreting the term "Every person" it is to be conceived in mind that there are few exceptions to the several interpretation based on principle of expediency, on convention or an agreement or understanding between nations. For example, immunity is provided from criminal prosecution to high dignitaries, the heads of foreign Government (Sovereign States), ambassadors, diplomatic agents consuls, United Nations representative, the President of India and Governors of the states etc. Similarly, for the acts of war by the alien enemies the jurisdiction of the criminal courts cannot be invoked.

As regards the foreigners it was held in the case of *State of Maharashtra* v. *M.H. George* AIR (1965) SC 722 that the plea of ignorance of law is not available to foreigners. Besides, the plea that the act was criminal in nature was not known to the accused because the same act was not an offence in his country is also not acceptable as held in *R* v. *Esop* (1836) 7ER203. In this case the accused was indicted for committing an unnatural offence on board of an Indian ship lying in St. Catherine Docks and the aforesaid plea was taken but was not accepted.

Section 3 of the code deals with the punishment of offences committed beyond, but which by law may be tried within, India. It states "Any, person liable, by any Indian law, to be tried for an offence committed beyond India, shall be dealt with according to the provisions of this code for any act committed beyond India in the same manner as if such act had been committed within India." Furthermore, section 4 of the code that deals with the extension of code to extra-territorial offences states "The provisions of this code apply also to any offence committed by any citizen of India in any place without and beyond India; any person on any ship or aircraft registered in India, wherever it may be." Besides, it has been explained that the word "Offence" in this section includes every act committed outside India which, if committed in India would be punishable under this code. Thus, section 3 & 4 of the penal code talks of the extra-territorial operation of the code and a person may be held liable for committing offence beyond the territory of India. The extension of criminal jurisdiction in these aforesaid sections is based on the principle that every Sovereign State can regulate the conduct of its citizens, wherever they might be for the time being. For instance, where an Indian citizen (Hindu Male) has his wife and children in India and goes to USA for higher studies. There he marries an American girl. He would be prosecuted under section 494 IPC for bigamy. In *Central Bank of India Ltd.* v. *Ram Naria*, AIR (1955) SC36 it was held that acquiring of Indian Citizenship after the commission of offence cannot confer jurisdiction to the Indian Courts to try the offence.

The admiralty jurisdiction is conferred to the Indian courts by clause (2) of section 4. The offences committed on any ship or aircraft registered in India, wherever it might be are dealt herewith. A ship is considered to be a floating island and belongs to the country whose flag the ship is flying. Same is the case with the aircrafts also. If a person commits a crime on board and the ship is registered in India then he is amenable to the Indian Courts irrespective of the fact that he is an Indian Citizen or a foreigner.

Witness and Hostile Witness

Witness is the key figure in a case. The decisions of the Court are based on the statements made by the witnesses and the evidences produced in the court. Section 118 of the Indian Evidence Act 1872 deals with the question as to who may testify and as such it gives the outlook of a witness. It is said that all parties shall be competent to testify unless the court considers that they are prevented from understanding the question put to them, or from giving rational answers to those questions, by tender years, extreme old age, disease, whether of body or mind or any other cause of the same kind. A lunatic is not incompetent to testify, unless he is prevented by his lunacy from understanding the question put to him and giving rational answers to them. The witnesses need not be examined before the court makes an order for discharging the accused or under Section 240 of the Code of Criminal Procedure for framing a charge. The Supreme Court in *Ram Narayan* v. *State of Maharastra* AIR 1964 SC 949(954) held "The Magistrate before either framing a charge or discharging an accused, has first to examine the accused if necessary, and afford an opportunity to the prosecution and the accused of being heard."

While discussing the topic of "witness" a significant question arises as to the position of hostile witness in law. Section 154 of the Indian Evidence Act, 1872 is the provision from where evolves the concept of "hostile witness". In *Panchanan Gogai* v. *Emperor*, (1930) 57 Cal 1266 the court observed that "A hostile witness from its manner of giving evidence shows that he is not willing or desirous of disclosing the truth to the court." In *K. Kusuma Kumari* v. *G. Surya Bhagwan*, 1996 AIHC 2627(AP) the court held that simply for the reason that a particular part of statement of a witness are not favourable to the party who has called him, the court could not conclude that the truth was being suppressed or the testimony was adverse (hostile) to the concerned party. It is by the answers given by the witness that the hostility of the witness is to be judged. So, the courts have to be very cautious while appreciating the evidence given by the witness. Their evidence play a vital role particularly in criminal cases, to prove the guilt or innocence of the accused person. In *Kothakalava Naga Subba Reddi and others* v. *The public prosecutor, High of Andhra Pradesh*, 2000 (3) JT 480 the Supreme Court set aside the orders of the trial court whose approach in appreciating the evidence of material witnesses was absolutely unreasonable and unjustified. Agreeing with the order of the High Court, which reversed the order of acquittal by the Session Court, the Supreme Court observed "In our view the said submission is without any substance, because the trial Court materially erred in rating this witness as a hostile only on the ground that the public prosecutor after obtaining the permission had asked a question with regard to the role played by the accused Nos.4 and 6 on the basis of his police statement. In our view, there was no reason for the learned judge to treat this witness as not supporting for prosecution case. On the contrary this would mean that the witness was truthful and he has not supposed his police version with regard to the identification of accused Nos. 4 and 6. From this also, he can not be dubbed as a liar, to whom no credence can be given as held by the learned Session judge." The Supreme Court further observed "In our view the approach of the learned Session judge in treating this witness as a hostile witness and terming him as a liar, is to say the least, wholly unjustified and unreasonable." The Supreme Court thus held that High court was fully justified in reversing the acquittal order passed by the Session Court.

Dying Declaration

Section 32 of the Indian Evidence Act, 1872 deals with the statement of relevant facts by the person who is dead or can not be found. The case which relates to the cause of death is one of the subject matter of this section. As such the concept of dying declaration is also comprehended in the same section.

In the case of *Sant gopal* v. *State of U.P*, 1995 Cr.L.J. 312(All.) the Allahabad High court elucidated that the "dying declaration" should be understood to be a statement, either written or verbal mentioning the relevant facts, by the deceased. Besides, the Gauhati High Court in the case of *Kajal Sarkar* v. *State of Assam* 1993 Cr.L.J 3869 (Gau.) observed that for a complete dying declaration it is necessary that the name as well as address of the person involved in the offence are mentioned in it. A simple utterance of the name without depicting the address thereof is not proper to accept. Dying declaration is a strong form of evidence and the person participating in the offence alongwith the person who actually caused death can be held liable on this basis. Where the dying declaration is recorded in the language of declarant, it adds to strength and reliability.

Although the presence of the magistrate, doctor and police officer is needed at the time of the dying declaration but there have been cases where the court have relied on the dying declaration that are taken by any one of them. Bombay High Court in the case of *Pandian K. Nadar* v. *State of Maharastra* 1993 Cr.L.J 3883(Bom.) held that a dying declaration can not be found to be unacceptable simply because it was recorded by Special Executive Magistrate in the absence of Certificate from the doctor as the said magistrate was satisfied and police officer supported the perfectly fit condition of the deceased. Besides, the earlier given dying declaration was in consistence with this dying declaration and no controversy arose to it. Similarly, in *Malik Ram Bhoj* v. *State of Orissa* 1993 Cr.L.J. 984 where the dying declaration was recorded by the doctor in the form of questions and answers in the presence of other witnesses and further corroboration with the testimony of the eye-witness raised no doubt, it was held that the dying declaration was an acceptable one. Moreover, Delhi High Court in *Ram Singh* v. *State (Delhi Administration)* 1995 Cr.L.J. 3838 observed that just because a police officer has recorded the dying declaration it can not be rejected if it is clearly stated and corroborated with the facts of the case. In *Habib Usman* v. *Gujrat* AIR 1979 SC 1181, the declaration was made to sister and there was no endorsement by the doctor as to the fitness of the deceased at the time of dying declaration, the Hon'ble Supreme Court held it to be a poor ground of evidence. Furthermore, it should be borne in mind as held in the case of *Chakiri Saidulu* v. *State of A.P.* 1994 Cr.L.J.3782 (AP) that if the declaration is not in question-answer form, that does not destroy the evidentiary value of it. It is must that the fit condition and counciousness of the victim should be coupled with the certificate from the doctor and endorsement from him to that effect. If such certificate is not there the declaration comes under the cloud of suspicion. In case a person gives more than one dying declaration then the statements have to be read as one and the same so as to examine their evidentiary value properly but if difference is found on material aspects then their reconciliation should be endeavored. The statement cannot be relied on if the difference could not be explained by any assumption but on the other side if no assumption explains the difference then the position would be different. A tutored dying declaration is not worthy to be accepted and relied on. A dying declaration may be in oral or in written form and it may be put forth as evidence on behalf of the witness who heard it made. The presence of accused and Magistrate is must to treat it as deposition. Where the Magistrate recording the declaration was not a committing Magistrate, it was held that the fact should be proved by calling him as witness.

Proximity between time of Statement and Death

One significant question that arises in context of the dying declaration is the proximity between the time of statement and the death. Justice Fazal Ali in *Sharad* v. *Maharastra* AIR 1984 SC 1622 put forth certain proposition with regard to it. They are that whether the death is homicide or suicide it is relevant if it has any concern with the cause of death or the circumstances leading to death. Furthermore it was felt that no cut and dried formula could be evolved for the test of proximity that is universally applicable rather it has to be determined as per the facts and circumstances of the case. FIR can also be used as a dying declaration if the accused is clearly implicated and the details of the incident are given. However, in the case of *Maniram* v. *State of M.P.*

AIR 1994 SC 840 where the statement was recorded by the Sub-inspector in the form of FIR and there was no attestation from the doctor as to the fitness of the deceased to give statement and besides there was no signature or thumb impression of the deceased it was held that the declaration is highly doubtful.

Thus, summing up the concept of dying declaration we can say that the dying declaration can be relied on without corroboration if it is made truly and voluntarily. The deceased should have been in fit condition while giving the declaration. If any form of suspicion arises as to its truthfulness or voluntarily nature then it should be corroborated with the evidence. A dying declaration showing infirmity is liable to be rejected. Brevity of the declaration does give rise to any suspicion over it. Further, apart from the medical opinion as to the fitness of the deceased to give declaration the court can also rely over the eyewitnesses as to the fit and conscious condition of the deceased. Moreover, if the version of the prosecution is different from the statement given in the dying declaration then the declaration cannot be relied on.

Expert opinion

When court has to form an opinion upon a point of foreign law, or of science, or art, or as to identity of handwriting or finger impressions, the opinion upon that point of persons specially skilled in such foreign law, science or art or in question as to identity of handwriting or finger impressions are relevant facts and such persons are called experts. Besides it is stated that the facts, not otherwise relevant, are relevant if they support or are inconsistent with the opinions of the experts when such opinions are relevant. On the relevancy of handwriting it is said that when the court has to form an opinion as to the person by whom any document was written or signed, the opinion of any person acquainted with the handwriting of the person by whom it is supposed to be written or signed that it was or was not written or signed by that person is a relevant fact. A person is said to be acquainted with the handwriting of another person when he has seen this person write or when he has received documents purporting to be written by that person in answer to documents written by himself or under his authority and addressed to that person, or when, in the ordinary course of business, documents purporting to be written by that person have been habitually submitted to him.

Expert opinions do not help in the interpretation of law rather they are only the opinion evidence that discloses certain facts. Expert cannot work in the capacity of a judge or jury. It is the discretion of the court as to how much weightage has to be given to such an opinion. On the matters of foreign law one thing is to be borne in mind that expert opinion in such a case is to be relied only when law on that particular subject is not available in the country. As relates to the science and art it is to be conceived that they are inclusive of all subjects for which a special course of study or experience is necessary so as to form the opinion in this regard. For the age of a person a doctor draws out his opinion on the basis of his or her height, weight and teeth but it does not amount to the legal proof of age. Such conclusion is also sometimes based on the position of bones at the joints of the body.

In the case of *Pratap Misra* v. *Orissa* AIR 1977 SC 1307 there was difference in time of rape as showed by the prosecution and doctor's report. It was held that the medical opinion could not be set aside for that reason only.

In *Abdul Razak* v. *State of Maharastra* AIR 1970 SC 283 for the validity of evidence of tracker dog it was held that in this era of scientific knowledge much weight is not to be given to such evidence.

Section 47 of the Indian Evidence Act 1872 that deal with the opinions as to handwriting when relevant, comprehends in it the way in which the handwriting of a person may be proved. These ways are by the evidence from the side of written himself or by a person acquainted with such handwriting by receiving letter or any other such manner. The opinion of the expert can also be relied for it. The court for its own satisfaction may also direct the writing if some words or figures so as to enable it to make comparison. The court has to reach its conclusion with due diligence.

General Exceptions

"Actus non facit reum, nisi mens sit rea" is the well known Latin maxim that is widely applicable in the implementation of the criminal law. The meaning of this maxim is that the act itself does not make a man guilty, unless his intensions are so. It comprehends the exception to the general principle of law that since the presumption is that a person knows the nature and consequences of his act so he should be held responsible for it. Section 76 to 106 of the Indian Penal Code, 1860 deals with such types of general exceptions. These general exceptions can be grouped undeı seven heads *viz.* Mistake of fact, (Ss. 76, 79), Privileged Acts (Ss. 77, 78), Accidental Acts (S. 80), Absence of criminal intent (Ss. 81-86 and 92-94), Acts done with consent (Ss. 87-90), Triviality (595), Right of Defence (Ss. 96-106). Broadly categorizing these exceptions there arises two groups of exceptions namely – excusable exceptions and justifiable exceptions.

Among the various general exceptions the important ones that are very much applicable in practice are act of a child under seven years of age, act of a child above seven and under twelve of immature understanding, Act of a person of unsound mind, Act of a person incapable of judgement by reason of intoxication caused against his will, offence requiring a particular intent or knowledge committed by one who is intoxicated and right of Private defence.

Offence by a child: For Act of a child under seven years of age it is stated that nothing is an offence, which is done by a child under seven years of age. Blackstone explains the reason for exempting infants from criminal liability in the following words:

> "Infancy is a defect of the understanding, and infants under the age of discretion ought not to be punished by any criminal prosecution whatsoever."

A child below seven years of age is considered to *doli-in-capax* in law and is completely immune from any liability. The fact that at the time of commission of the offence he is below 7 years of age is *ipso facto* an answer to the prosecution.

In case of the Act of a child above seven and under twelve of immature understanding, Section 83 of IPC states that nothing is an offence which is done by a child above seven years of age and under twelve, who has not attained sufficient maturity of understanding to judge the nature and consequences of his conduct on that occasion. So it brings into light the qualified immunity for the child within the age group of 8 to 11 years. The principle that lies beneath it is that "The younger the child in age, the lesser the probability of being corrupt." That is to say, malice makes up for age, i.e. *malitia supplet actatem*.

In *Ulla* v. *The King,* AIR (1950) Orissa 261, where the accused, a girl 10 years of age struck her husband on his neck with sharp instrument and then concealed herself, it was held that the girl was *doli-capax* i.e. capable of understanding the nature of the act and so she was guilty of murder.

Reading these two provisions of IPC carefully there arises an interesting lacuna in the drafting of said provisions. For instance, under section 82 of IPC absolute immunity is given to the child under seven years of age and as per section 83 of the same code the children above seven years of age and under twelve years are provided qualified immunity. No provision has been made in regard to an infant of seven years of age. So this ambiguity needs to be resolved by amending Section 82 of the Penal code by replacing the words under with "up to" after "a child" and before "seven years".

Act of a Person of Unsound Mind: The act of a person of unsound mind is comprehended under Section 84 of IPC and it reads as nothing is an offence which is done by a person who, at the time of doing it, by reason of unsoundness of mind, is incapable of knowing the nature of act, or that he is doing what is either wrong or contrary to law. The principle underlying this is *Furiosus Furore Sui Punier* i.e. a mad man is punished by his own madness. Unsoundness of mind according to medical science is a disorder of mind that impairs the mental faculties of mind. But this concept of unsoundness of mind is different from the concept of insanity. In law it means the disorder of mind that impairs the cognitive faculty i.e. the reasoning capacity of a man to the extent of not understanding the consequences of his action. The insanity engendered by emotional or volitional factors is excluded from its purview.

Intoxication against the will of a person: The act of a person incapable of judgement by reason of intoxication caused against his will are comprehended in Section 85 of the Indian Penal code which states that nothing is an offence which is done by a person who at the time of doing it, is, by reason of intoxication, incapable of knowing the nature of act, or that he is doing what is either wrong, or contrary to law provided that the thing which intoxicated him was administered to him without his knowledge or against his will. The basis of criminal liability is criminal intention and an inebriated (intoxicated) person, is in the same state of mental condition as an insane person. The term used for this state of mind is *Dementia Offectasia*- a form of lunacy in which the function of mind are temporarily suspended. The justification for such a provision is based on the contention that the accused had not contributed himself towards his drunkenness and which is not likely to be repeated as in the case of a voluntary act.

Offence by an intoxicated person: The offence requiring a particular intent or knowledge committed by one who is intoxicated is also brought within the category of general exceptions. In case where an act done is not an offence unless done with a particular knowledge or intent, a person who does the act in a state of intoxication shall be liable to be dealt with as if he had the same knowledge as he would have had if he had not been intoxicated, unless the thing which intoxicated him was administered to him without his knowledge or against his will. The principle underlying this provision is that drunkenness cannot be made an excuse for criminal misconduct.

In *Reniger* v. *Fogossa* (1980) 75 ER 1, it was observed that if a person who is drunk kills another, this shall be felony, and he shall be hanged for it, and yet he did it through ignorance, for when he was drunk he had no understanding nor memory; but in as much as that ignorance was occasioned by his own act and folly and he might have avoided it, he shall not be privileged thereby.

Right of private defence: Right of private defence is a significant General Exception provided in Section 96 to 106 to the Indian Penal Code, 1960. Section 96 of the code states that nothing is an offence, which is done in exercise of the right of private defence. Right of private defence of the body and of property is comprehended further in the code. Every person has a right, subject to the restriction contained in section 99, to defend firstly, his own body, and the body of any other person, against any offence affecting the human body and secondly, the property, whether moveable or immoveable, of himself or of any other person, against any act which is an offence falling under the definition of theft, robbery, mischief or criminal trespass. The restrictions contained in Section 99 are the act which does not reasonably cause the apprehension of death or of grievous hurt, if done, or attempted to be done, by a public servant acting in good faith under colour of his office, through that act may not be strictly justifiable by law. There is no right of private defence against an act which does not reasonably cause the apprehension of death or of grievous hurt, if done, or attempted to be done, by the direction of a public servant, acting in good faith under colour of his office, through that direction may not be strictly justifiable by law. Similarly in cases in which there is time to have recourse to the protection of the public authorities there is no right of private defence.

Extent of Right to private defence: A significant question here arises is with regard to the extent to which the right may be exercised. The right of private defence in no case extends to the inflicting of more harm than it is necessary to inflict for the purpose of defence. A person is not deprived of the right of private defence against an act done, by a public servant, as such, unless he knows or has reason to believe, that the person doing the act is such public servant. A person is not deprived of the right of private defence against an act done or attempted to be done, by the direction of a public servant, unless he knows or has reason to believe that the person doing the act is acting by such direction or unless such person states the authority under which he acts or if he has authority in writing, unless he produces such authority if demanded.

Private defence against person of unsound mind: For right of private defence against the act of a person of unsound mind etc. it is to be conceived that when an act, which would otherwise be a certain offence, is not that offence by reason of the youth, the want of maturity of understanding, the unsoundness of mind, or the intoxication of the person doing that act, or by reason of any misconception on the part of that person, every person has the same right of private defence against that act which he would have if the act were that offence.

Causing Death in Private Defence of Body: A very important query arises with regard to the question as to when the right of private defence of the body extends to causing death. The right of private defence of the body extends to the voluntary causing of death or of any other harm of the assailant, if the offence which occasions the exercise of the right be of any of the description hereinafter enumerated: -

Firstly: Such an assault as may reasonably cause the apprehension that death will otherwise be the consequence of such assault,

Secondly: Such an assault as may reasonably cause the apprehension that grievous hurt will otherwise be the consequence of such assault;

Thirdly: An assault with the intention of committing rape,

Fourthly: An assault with the intention of gratifying unnatural lust,

Fifthly: An assault with the intention of kidnapping or abducting and

Sixthly: An assault with the intention of wrongfully confining a person under the circumstances which may reasonably cause him to apprehend that he will be unable to have recourse to the public authorities for his release.

If the offence were not of any of the description enumerated above, the right of private defence of the body does not extend to the voluntary causing of death to the assailant, but does extend, under the restriction mentioned in section 99, to the voluntary causing to the assailant of any harm other than death. The right of private defence of the body commences as soon as a reasonable apprehension of danger to the body arises from an attempt or threat to commit the offence though the offence may not have been committed; and it continues as long as such apprehension of danger to the body continues.

Causing Death in Private Defence of Property: Another question is that when the right of private defence of property extends to causing death. The right of private defence of property extends, under the restrictions mentioned under section 99, to the voluntary causing of death or of any other harm to the wrong doer, if the offence, the committing of which, or the attempting to commit which, occasions the exercise of the right, be an offence of any of the descriptions as firstly robbering, secondly house breaking at night, thirdly mischief by fire committed on any building, tent or vessel which building, tent or vessel is used as a human dwelling, or as a place for the custody of property, and fourthly, theft, mischief or house trespass under such circumstances as may reasonably cause apprehension that death or grievous hurt will be the consequences, if right of private defence is not exercised. If the offence, the committing of which, or the attempting to commit which, occasions the exercise of the right of private defence, be theft, mischief or criminal trespass, not of any of the description enumerated above, that right does not extend to the voluntary causing of death, but does extend, subject to the restriction mention in section 99, to the voluntary causing to the wrong doer of any harm other than death. As regards the commencement and continuance of the right of private defence of property. The right of private defence of property commences when a reasonable apprehension of danger to the property commences. The right of private defence of property against theft continues till the offender has effected his retreat with the property or either the assistance of the public authorities is obtained, or the property has been recovered. The right of private defence against robbery continues as long as the offender causes or attempts to cause to any person death or hurt or wrongful restraint, or as long as the fear of instant death, or of instant hurt, or of instant personal restraint continues. The right of private defence of property against criminal trespass or mischief continues as long as the offender continues in the commission of criminal trespass or mischief. The right of private defence of property against house breaking by night continues as long as the house trespass, which has been begun by such housebreaking, continues. If, in the exercise of the right of private defence against an assault which reasonably causes the apprehension of death, the defender be so situated that he can not effectually exercise that right without risk of harm to an innocent person, his right of private defence extends to the running of that risk.

Punishment

Manu, the well-known Hindu lawgiver describes the object of punishment in the following words:

> "Punishment governs all mankind; punishment alone preserves them; punishment wakes while their guards are asleep; the wise consider the punishment (danda) as the perfection of justice."

So, the object of criminal legislation lies in preventing the perpetration of acts classified as criminal because they are regarded as being socially damaging. This concept of punishment is dealt with under section 53 to 75 of the Indian Penal Code, 1860. The punishments to which offenders are liable under the provisions of this code are death, imprisonment for life, imprisonment, which is of two descriptions namely rigorous and simple, forfeiture of property and fine.

Theories on Punishment

There are various theories given with regard to punishments *viz*. Deterrent theory, Preventive theory, Retributive theory, and Reformative theory. Under the Deterrent theory the object of punishment is not only to prevent the wrong doer from committing the wrong but also in putting an example before the other wrongdoers having criminal tendencies. Salmond support this view as the most important theory for controlling crime. Under the Preventive theory the offenders are prevented or disabled from committing or repeating the offence by awarding punishment such as death, exile or forfeiture of an offence. Under the Retributive theory which is based on the principle of "an eye for an eye", "tooth for a tooth", "a nail for a nail", the person wronged is allowed to have revenge against the wrong doer. Such a system existed in Primitive Society. Further, in Reformatory theory, the object of punishment lies in reformation of criminals.

Solitary Confinement

Whenever any person is convicted of an offence for which under Indian Penal Code the court has power to sentence him to rigorous imprisonment, the court may, by its sentence order that the offender shall be kept in solitary confinement for any portion or portions of the imprisonment to which he is sentenced, not exceeding three months in the whole, according to the following scale, that is to say - a time not exceeding one month if the term of imprisonment shall not exceed six months; a time not exceeding two months if the term of imprisonment shall exceed six months and shall not exceed one year; a year not exceeding three months if the term of imprisonment shall exceed one year. In executing a sentence of solitary confinement, such confinement shall in no case exceed fourteen days at a time, with intervals between the periods of solitary confinement of not less duration than such periods, and when the imprisonment awarded shall exceed three months, the solitary confinement shall not exceed seven days in any one month of the whole imprisonment awarded, with intervals between the period of solitary confinement of not less duration than such periods.

Protection of personal liberty

In *Bashima* v. *State of U.P.*, (1969) 1 SCR 32 (40), the Supreme Court held that before a person is deprived of his life or personal liberty, the procedure established by law must be strictly followed and must not be departed from to the disadvantage of the person affected.

Similarly, the Supreme Court in *Narendra* v. *Gujrat*,(AIR 1979 SC 420), observed that whenever the liberty of the subject is involved whether under a penal law, or law of preventive detention it is the bounden duty of the court, to satisfy itself that " all the safe guards provided by the law have been scrupulously observed." The Supreme Court in this case further held that "the power of preventive detention by the Government under the conservation of foreign exchange and Prevention of smuggling Activities Act, 1974, is subject to the limitations enjoyed in the exercise of such power by Article 22 (5) of the constitution, as constructed by this court".

The constitution is all pervasive, all laws made by the state must, therefore, yield to constitutional limitations and restrictions. The citizen's right to personal liberty is guaranteed in Article 21 and 22 of the constitution irrespective of his political beliefs, class, creed or religion. The court has forged certain procedural safeguards in the case of preventive detention. These safeguards must be designated as regulative 'Postulate of respect' *i.e.* respect for the intrinsic dignity of human person.

Right to Live

Right to live means something more than mere animal existence and includes the right to live consistently with human dignity and decency even in a rescue home and prison.

In *Sunil Batra* v. *Delhi Administration*, (AIR 1978 SC 1675), the Supreme Court held that it is no more open to debate that convicts are not wholly denuded for their fundamental rights. However a prisoner's liberty is in the very nature of things circumscribed by the very fact of his confinement. His interest in the limited liberty left to him is then all the more substantial conviction for a crime does not reduce the person into a non-person whose rights are subject to the whims of the prison administration, and therefore, imposition of any major punishment within the prison system is conditional of the observance of procedural safeguards.

Personal liberty of the person who is incarcerated is to a great extent curtailed by preventive detention. The liberty to move, mix, mingle, talk, share company with co prisoners, if substantially curtailed, would be violative of Article 21 of the constitution, unless the curtailment has the backing of law.

In yet another case, *Maneka Gandhi* v. *UOI* (AIR 1978 SC 597) the Supreme Court held that the law must be right, just and fair and not arbitrary, fanciful arbitrary or oppressive. Otherwise it would be no procedure at all, and the requirements of Art.21 would not be satisfied. In this case, Maneka Gandhi's Passport was impounded and she was restrained from going abroad. No reason was told to her as to why her passport had been impounded. The matter came up before the Supreme Court and on hearing the averments made before it, the Supreme Court held that the principle of "*audi alteram partem*" which mandates that no one shall be condemned unheard, is a part of the rules of natural justice. Natural justice is a great humanizing principle intended to invert law with fairness and to secure justice and over the years it has grown into a widely pervasive rule affecting large areas of administrative action. In the present case it was held by the Supreme Court that the Central Government not only give an opportunity of hearing to the petitioner (Maneka Gandhi) after making the impugned order impounding her passport, but even declined to furnish to the petitioners the reasons for impounding her passport despite request made by her.

Personal liberty

After Maneka Gandhi's case the Supreme Court has been adding new dimensions to the concept of liberty as enshrined in Art.21 of the constitution, these are the right to privacy, the right against solitary confinement, the right against bar fetters, the right to legal aid, the right to speedy trial, the right against handcuffing, the right against delayed execution, the right against custodial violence, the right against public hanging, the right to shelter, the right to doctor's assistance, etc. But it would not include the right to commit suicide or to be admitted into a college.

As regards the death sentence and fundamental right of life and liberty, in *Jumman Khan* v. *State of U.P.* (AIR 1991 SC 345) the Supreme Court upheld the validity of death sentence. Similarly in (*Smt.) Shashi Nayar* v. *Union of India* (AIR 1992 SC 395), the Supreme Court observed that it is in the rarest of the rare cases that Death sentence is to be awarded and it does not violate mandate of Art.21. Besides hanging by neck being scientific and out of least painful method does not warrant the change in the execution of death sentence.

Speedy Trial

In *Sher Singh* v. *State of Punjab* (AIR 1983 SC 361) it was held that if the death sentence is not executed within two years, the accused would be entitled to invoke the protection of Article 21 of the constitution by replacing death sentence by sentence of imprisonment for life:

> "Article 21 stands like a sentinel over human misery, degradation and oppression. Its voice is the voice of justice and fair play that voice can never be silenced on the ground that the time to heel to its imperatives is long since past in the story of a trial. It reverberates through all stages-the trial, the sentence, the incarceration and finally the execution of the sentence."

In *Triveni Ben* v. *State of Gujrat* (AIR 1989 SC 142, 1335) the Supreme Court observed that undue delay in execution of a sentence of death will entitle the condemned person to approach supreme court under Art.32 of the constitution. Declaring the speedy trial as a part of fundamental right, the Supreme Court made the following observations:

> "As between funeral fire and mental worry; it is the latter which is more devastating, for funeral fire burns only the dead body, while the mental worry burns the living one".

In *Kundra Pehadiya* v. *State of Bihar,* AIR 1981, SC 1939, three years period of detention in jail without trial was regarded as shocking and disclosing something wrong with the entire system:

> "Three more years have passed but they are still rotting in jail, not knowing what is happening to their case. They are perhaps reconciled to their fate, living in a small world of their own, cribbed, cabined and confined within the four walls of the prison. The outside world does not exist for them. The constitution has no meaning and significance and human rights, no relevance for them. It is a crying shame upon our adjudicatory system which keeps man in jail for year on and without a trial."

In *Abdul Rehman Antulay* v. *R.S. Nayak,* AIR 1992 SC 1701 the Supreme Court summarized its conclusion for speedy trial as a guideline for all the courts in the country.

1. Fair, just and reasonable procedure implicit in article 21 of the constitution creates a right in the accused to be tried speedily. Right to speedy trial is the right of the accused. The fact that a speedy trial

is also in public interest or that it serves the societal interest also, does not make any the less the right of the accused. It is in the interest of all concerned that the guilt and innocence of the accused is determined as quickly as possible in these circumstances.

2. Right to speedy trial flowing from Article 21 encompasses all the stages namely the stage of investigation, inquiry, trial, appeal, revision and re-trial. This is how this court has understood this right and there is no reason to take a restricted view.
3. The concern underlying right to speedy trial from the point of view of the accused are:
   (a) The period of remand and pre-conviction detention should be as short as possible. In other words the accused should not be subjected to unnecessary or unduly long incarceration prior to his conviction.
   (b) The worry, anxiety, expense and disturbance to his vocation and peace, resulting from an unduly prolonged investigation, inquiry or trial should be minimal; and
   (c) Undue delay may well result in the impairment of the ability of the accused to defend himself, whether on account of death, disappearance or non-availability of witness or otherwise.
4. At the same time, one cannot ignore the fact that it is unusually the accused that is interested in delaying the proceedings. As is often pointed out," Delay is a known defence tactic." Since the burden of proving the guilt of the accused lies upon the prosecution, delay ordinarily prejudices the prosecution. Non-availability of witness, disappearance of evidence by lapse of time, really works against the interest of the prosecution. Of course, there may be cases where the prosecution, for whatever reason, also delays the proceedings. Therefore, in every case, where the right to speedy trial is alleged to have been infringed, the first question to be put and answer is- who is responsible for delay?

Proceedings taken by either party in good faith, to indicate their rights, and interest, as perceived by them cannot be treated as delaying tactics, nor can the time taken in pursuing such proceedings be counted towards delay. It goes without saying that frivolous proceedings or proceedings merely for delaying in the day of reckoning cannot be treated as proceedings taken in good faith. The mere fact that an application/petiticn is admitted and an order of stay granted by a superior court is by itself no proof that the proceeding is not a frivolous one, very often these stays obtained on ex-parte representation......"

Suicide and Right to Life and Liberty

Another significant question to peep into is whether the committing of suicide by a person is his fundamental right of life and liberty *i.e.* whether the fundamental right of life contains in it the right to death. There exists a controversy over this issue between different High Courts of the country. In *Maruti Shripati Dubal* v. *State of Maharashtra* 1987 Cr.L.J. 743 (Bombay) the Bombay High Court held Section 309 (Attempt to commit suicide) as ultra vires being violative of Art.21 of the constitution. Similarly, in *State* v. *Sanjay Kumar* (1985) Cr.L.J. 931 the chief justice of Delhi High Court observed:

> "The continuance of Section 309 of the Indian Penal Code is an anachronism unworthy of a human society like ours. Instead of sending the young boy to a psychiatric clinic, society gleefully sends him to mingle with criminals. Medical clinics [are needed] for such misfits; but police and prison never."

Besides 42nd report of the law commission of India has also recommended deletion of Section 309 of IPC. However the Andhra Pradesh High court in a recent judgement of *Chenna Jugdeshwar* v. *State* (1988) CrLJ 549 (AP) took a contrary view of Section 309 stating that right to life does not necessarily signify a right to die which is an offence in the eye of law.

Extradition

A significant feature while discussing the law of arrest and international law is the concept of extradition. In the words of the renowned Jurist Oppenheim "Extradition is the delivery of an accused or a convicted individual to the state on whose territory he is alleged to have committed or to have been convicted of a crime, by a state on whose territory the alleged criminal happens to be for the time being." So in simple words we can say that extradition is a process whereby an accused or convicted person is delivered from one state to another where he has committed crime or accused of it. However, if the crime committed is political in nature then according to well-established principle of International Law such person is not extradited. Amnesty International is the organization that works for the general pardon of the political offenders. Controversy exists as to what is a political crime. Persons accused of military or religious crime are also not extradited.

Essential Conditions for extradition: There are also few other essential conditions for extradition or restriction on surrender. One such condition is rule of speciality. As per this rule, in case of extradition the receiving state should try the concerned person for that specific offence for which extradition is sought. The Supreme Court of America upheld this principle in case of *US* v. *Rouscher* (1886) 119 US 407 and in India too the same principle is applicable. So if a person has been extradited on ground of murder, he cannot be tried for Grievous hurt.

Another condition that needs to be complied with is the condition of double criminality *i.e.* the specific offence for which the extradition of the concerned person has been sought for, should be regarded as offence in the penal laws of both the states *viz.* the state asking for extradition and the state making the extradition. For instance, adultery is not regarded as offence in many western countries but in India it is an offence under section 497 IPC. So if a person absconds to the said western countries after committing the offence of adultery in India then he cannot be extradited for this offence.

Furthermore, a prima-facie case needs to be made out for the crime for which extradition is sought. There are few requirements that are necessary to constitute a prima-facie case and these are that the witness would be entitled to a reasonable degree of credit, the degree of proof needs to be higher as compared to the ordinary criminal prosecution and the evidence must be incontrovertible. Besides, there needs to be a Bilateral Treaty for the purpose of extradition. So, these are few requirements of extradition. INTERPOL is the agency that works to catch the offenders in the foreign countries.

Asylum

According to Prof. Oppenheim "The so called right of Asylum is nothing but the competence of every state to allow a prosecuted alien to enter and to remain on its territory under its protection and thereby to grant asylum to him. Such fugitive enjoys the hospitability of the state which grants him asylum; but it might be necessary to place him under Surveillance or even to intern him at some place in the interest of the state which is seeking to prosecute him. For it is the duty of every state to prevent individuals living in its territory from endangering the safety of another state by organizing hostile or by preparing common crime against its head, member of its government or its property."

Asylum and Universal Declaration of Human Rights

Regarding the right to Asylum Art. 14 of the Universal Declaration of human rights reads as, "Every one has a right to seek and enjoy in other countries asylum from prosecution." As per this declaration opportunity is given to seek Asylum but there exists no corresponding duty to grant Asylum. There are two feature ingredients of asylum. Firstly, it is a shelter, which is more than a temporary refuge, and secondly, it involves a degree of active protection by the authorities under control of which lies the territory of asylum.

Types of Asylum

There are two types of Asylum: -

(i) Territorial Asylum,

(ii) Extra-territorial Asylum.

United Nations Human Rights commission in a draft declaration recognized this right of asylum and Article 3 of the said declaration runs as "No one seeking or enjoying asylum in accordance with the Universal Declaration of Human Rights, should, except for overriding reasons of the population, be subjected, to measures such as rejection at the frontier, returns or expulsion which would result in compelling him to return to or to remain in a territory if there is a well founded fear of prosecution endangering his life, physical integrity or liberty in that territory." So, territorial asylum is granted in its own territory by a state and it is very much related to its territorial sovereignty.

Asylum is also granted by a state in its Embassy in foreign countries or in its public vessels. Such an asylum is called Extra-territorial or Diplomatic Asylum. This form of asylum is further classified in to five kinds of asylum, which are, asylum in foreign legation, asylum in consular premises, asylum in the premises of the International Institutions, Asylum in war ships, asylum in merchant vessels. Asylum is granted in legation premises in few exceptional cases like where the individuals are physically in danger from mob-violence or if there exists political corruption in the local state and fugitive as such is in danger. Another case where asylum is granted is where there is well-established and binding local custom or where a special treaty has been entered into between the territorial state and the state of legation concerned. The asylum granted in consular premises is also based on the principle of granting asylum in foreign legation. Asylum is also granted in the premises of International Institutions in cases of imminent danger or violence but international law does not recognize this rule generally. As regards the asylum in war ships there exists controversy over it. Merchant vessels are not competent to grant asylum, as the immunity from local jurisdiction is not provided to them. So these are all different types of Extra-territorial Asylum.

State jurisdiction, Extradition and asylum as discussed above are the significant concepts of International law and are closely related with the arrest of a person particularly where the offence committed comes under the purview of jurisdiction of two or more countries. These concepts need to be conceived so as to comprehend the concept of arrest in a better manner.

United Nations Charter on Human Rights

The United Nations Charter provides a significant place to Human Rights. The preamble of the Charter itself clearly shows faith in fundamental human rights and the dignity and worth of human person and equal rights of men and women. The purpose of UN *interalia* lies is the achievement of international co-operation in solving international problems of economic, social, cultural or humanitarian character and in promoting and encouraging respect for human rights and fundamental freedom for all without distinction as to race, sex, language or religion. Furthermore, the charter provides that the General Assembly shall initiate studies and make recommendations for the purpose of promoting international co-operation in the economic, social, cultural, educational and health field and assist in the realization of the human rights and fundamental freedoms for all without distinction as to race, sex, language or religion. The promotion and encouragement of freedom for all is strengthened as per Articles 62 and 68 of the charter. Besides, Article 55 runs as "Universal respects for, and observance of, human rights and fundamental freedoms for all without distinction as to race, sex, language or religion." Article 56 further states "All members pledge themselves to take joint and separate action in co-operation with the organization for the achievement of the purpose set forth in Article 55."

Universal Declaration of Human Rights

One significant step in the matter of Human Rights is the Universal Declaration of Human rights passed by the General Assembly in 1948. The declaration comprises 30 Articles dealing with the human rights and fundamental freedoms in detail. The provisions of this declaration may be categorized into four classes:

(i) General (Art. 1&2),

(ii) Civil and political rights (Art.3 to 21),

(iii) Economic, Social and Cultural Rights (Art. 22 to 27).

(iv) Concluding Articles (Art. 28 to 30)

Article 1 of the declaration provides, "All human beings are born free and equal in dignity and rights, they are endowed with reason and conscience and should act to one another in spirit of brotherhood." Article 2 states that everyone is entitled to all the rights and freedoms set forth in the declaration without distinction of any kind, such as race, colour, sex, language, religion, political and other opinion, natural or social origin, property, birth or other status. No distinction shall be made on the basis of political, jurisdiction, or international status of the country to which a person belongs.

The civil and political rights in Articles 3 to 21 deal with the rights to life & liberty, prohibition of slavery, torture and inhuman treatment, equality before law, freedom of movement, right to seek asylum, right to nationality, right to own property, freedom of thought, conscience and religion, freedom of opinion and expression, freedom of peace assembly and association.

Right to social security, right to work, free choice of employment, right to education, right to enjoy art and share in scientific etc. are comprehended in the Economic, Social and Cultural rights.

Article 28, 29 and 30 are the concluding Articles of the declaration. Article 30 provides that nothing in the declaration may be interpreted as implying for any state, group or person any right to engage in any activity or to perform any act aimed at the destruction of any of the right and freedoms set forth in the declaration.

International Bill of Human Rights

The international Bill of Human Rights as a landmark step in this field comprises of the Universal Declaration of Human Rights, 1948, the Covenant on Civil And Political Rights, 1966, the Covenant on Economic, Social and Cultural Rights, 1966 and the Optional Protocol to the Covenant Civil And Political Rights, 1966. Human rights commission is the key agency that has worked out the international Bill of Human Rights. European convention on Human Rights, Vienna Declaration and Vienna conference are few significant move in respect of Human Rights.

Constitution and Human Rights

Article 51 of the Indian Constitution talks of the endeavour on the part of the state to promote international peace and security, maintain just and honourable relations between nations, foster respect for international law and treaty obligations in the dealing of organized people with one another and encourage settlement of International disputes by arbitration. In the light of this provision of the constitution and the International criticism of India regarding violation of Human Rights in Kashmir, India decided to set up a national commission on Human Rights. The ordinance for the purpose was promulgated on 29th September 1993 and the commission comprised of five members headed by a retired Chief Justice of India. At the state level of also similar commissions were set up. On 4th May 1993 Human Rights Bill was introduced for the said purpose and on 18th December 1993 the protection of Human Rights Bill (1993) was passed by the Lok Sabha unanimously.

Human Rights Commission

The commission is to inquire into the complaints of Human Rights violation and it is vested with similar powers as a civil court under Code of Civil Procedure, 1908 while trying a suit. The enquiry by the commission can be held *suo moto* or on the basis of petition filed by a victim or any person on his behalf with regard to the violation of Human Rights or negligence by a public servant in prevention of such violence. Powers has been conferred with the commission to intervene in the proceedings, involving the Human Rights violation, before the court with the approval of the Government. Moreover, the commission can hold visits to any jail or any other institution working under the State Government with the prior intimation to the State Government for the welfare of human beings. The safeguards made by or under the constitution or any other law in force may be reviewed by the commission for the protection of Human Rights and suitable measures may be recommended for their effective implementation. The treaties and other international instruments on Human Rights can also be studied by the commission and appropriate recommendations can be made for their effective implementation.

Crime and Juvenile Justice

Crime and Juvenile justice are very much interrelated concepts of law. "Juvenile" is person who has not completed eighteenth years of age. The question that arises is that should a delinquent juvenile be treated in a similar manner as a normal offender of major age. The answer comes out to be obviously in negative because due to the tender age of the juvenile the state should try to reform him for the overall development of his personality rather than spoiling his life by taking him to inhumane and degrading punishment. As such the Government of India so as to provide for the care, protection, treatment, development, and rehabilitation of the neglected and delinquent juvenile and for the adjudication of certain matter relating to delinquent juveniles, passed the Juvenile Justice (care and protection of children) Act, 2000.

Orders that may not be passed for Juvenile

There are certain orders that may not be passed against juvenile. Notwithstanding anything to be contrary contained in any other law for the time being in force, no juvenile in conflict with law shall be sentenced to death or life imprisonment or committed to prison in default of payment of fine or in default of furnishing security. This is subject to the provision that where a juvenile who has attained the age of sixteen years has committed an offence and the Board is satisfied that the offence committed is of so serious nature or that his conduct and behavior has been such that it would not be in his interest or in the interest of other juvenile in a special home to send him to such special home and that none of the other measures provided under this act is suitable or sufficient, the Board may order the juvenile in conflict with law to be kept in such place of safety and in such manner as it thinks fit and shall report the case for the order of the State Government.

Cruelty to Juveniles

The cruelty to juvenile or child has been penalized. Whoever, having the actual charge of, or control over, a juvenile or the child, assaults, abandons, exposes or willfully neglects the juvenile or causes or procures him to be assaulted, abandoned, exposed or neglected in a manner likely to cause such juvenile or the child unnecessary mental or physical suffering shall be punishable with imprisonment for a term which may extend to six months or fine, or with both. Besides, whoever employs or uses any juvenile or the child for the purpose or causes any juvenile to beg shall be punishable with imprisonment for a term which may extend to three years and shall also be liable to fine. Whoever, having the actual charge of or control over, a juvenile or the child abets the commission of the above said offence shall be punishable with imprisonment for a term which may extend to one years and shall also be liable to fine. Giving of intoxicating liquor or narcotic drug or psychotropic substance to juvenile or child has also been penalized. Moreover, provision relating to the exploitation of juvenile and child employee state that whoever ostensibly procures a juvenile or the child for the purpose of any hazardous employment keeps him in bondage and withhold his earnings and uses such earning for his own purposes shall be punishable with imprisonment for a term which may extend to three years and shall also be liable to fine.

Crime against women

Crime against women is a matter of great concern in a country like India where socially speaking the status of women is not equal to men and she is often made the target of exploitation and cruelty in every sphere of human life. Some time this inequality can be witnessed in the unequal payment of wages or sexual exploitation at working places whereas on other times it can be viewed as a cruelty by the husband to his wife or bride burning for the lust of money. It is quite unfortunate that even in the third millennium of the human race development the position of women is quite miserable and she is still bound to remain confined in the four walls of the house. The government has enacted several legislation for the up gradation of the deplorable condition of women yet these are insufficient. Economic independence, equal status in the property rights, political participation and professional growth are certain objectives that have not been achieved so far. The offences that are very often committed against women are obscenity (Section 294, Dowry death (Section 304B of IPC), assault or criminal force to women to outrage her modesty (Section 354 of IPC), rape (Section 375 to 376D of IPC), unnatural offence (Section 377 of IPC), and husband or relative of husband of a woman subjecting her to cruelty (Section 498A of IPC). Other offences relating to women are immoral trafficking in girls, indecent representation of women, selling minor for the purpose of prostitution, buying minor for the purpose of prostitution, obscenity etc.

Obscenity

Obscene act and songs are also the offence which are targeted against women. Such acts and songs have been penalized under Section 294 of the Indian Penal Code. As per this Section whoever, to the annoyance of others, does any act in any public place or sings, recites or utters any obscene songs, ballads or words, in or near any public place shall be punished with the imprisonment of either description for a term which may extend to three months or with fine, or with both. The offence is cognizable, bailable, non-compoundable and triable by the Magistrate.

In *K.P Mohammed* v. *State of Kerala* (1984) Cr.L.J 745 it was held that the performance in a public place, such as hotel or restaurant of cabaret dance devoid of nudity and obscenity judged according to the standards of our country, is permissible and is not any way liable to be banned or prevented. On the similar lines, sale of obscene objects (books, pictures, figures) to youth below 20 years also comes within the category of crime.

Bride Burning

The horrendous face of crime against women can be witnessed now-a-days in the form of Bride burning for the cause of dowry. Section 304 B of Indian Penal Code deals with this offence. Where the death of a women is caused by any burns or bodily injury or occurs otherwise than under normal circumstances within seven years of her marriage, and it is shown that soon before her death she was subjected to cruelty or harassment by her husband or any relative of her husband for, or in connection with, any demand for dowry such death shall be called "dowry death" and such husband or relative shall be deemed to have caused her death. Whoever commits dowry death shall be punished with imprisonment for a term which shall not be less than seven years but which may extend to imprisonment for life. With regard to the Dowry deaths the law of evidence has some presumption while dealing with the case. When the question is whether a person has committed the dowry death of women and it is shown that soon before her death such person had subjected such woman to cruelty or harassment for dowry, the court shall presume that such person had caused the dowry death.

In *V.N.Pawar* v. *State of Maharashtra*, AIR (1980) SC 1271, the Hon'ble Supreme court observed:

"........Wife-burning tragedies are becoming too frequent for the country to be complacent. Police sensitization mechanism, which will prevent the commission of such crimes, must be set up if these horrendous crimes are to be avoided. Likewise, special provisions felicitating easier proof of such special class of murders on establishing certain basic facts must be provided for by appropriate legislation."

In *Hem Chand* v. *State of Haryana*, AIR 1995 SC 120 the death resulted from strangulation and evidence of demand of dowry existed; moreover the women was also subjected to cruelty, it was held that the accused was liable to be convicted on the basis of dowry death. When the question is whether the commission of suicide by a woman had been abetted by her husband or any relative of her husband and it is shown that she had committed suicide within a period of seven years from the date of her marriage and that her husband or such relative of her husband had subjected her to cruelty, the court may presume having regard to all the other circumstances of the case, that such suicide had been abetted by her husband.

The Supreme Court in a significant case of *State of W.B* v. *Orilal Jaiswal* AIR 1994 SC 1418 held that the introduction of Section 498A IPC and Section 113A of the Evidence Act does not affect the requirement of proof of guilt beyond all reasonable doubts.

Outraging the Modesty of Women

As regards the assault or criminal force to a woman with intent to outrage her modesty it has been made mandatory that whoever assaults or uses criminal force to any woman, intending to outrage or knowing it to be likely that he will thereby outrage her immodesty, shall be punished with imprisonment of either description for a term which may extend to two years, or with fine, or with both.

In state of Punjab v. *Major Singh* AIR. (1967) SC 63 while the vagina of a seven and a half month old child was injured due to fingering by the accused it was held that Section 354 of IPC could be invoked for making the accused liable for outraging the modesty of a child. The essence of the modesty of a woman is her sex, young or old, intelligent or imbecile, awake or sleeping, the women possess modesty capable of being outraged.

In *Ram Das* v. *State of West Bengal* AIR (1954) SC 711 where the accused took off his trouser at night before laying down on his berth and while he was in underwear there developed a heated exchange or words and quarrel between the group (prosecutrix) and the accused, in the course of which he gave a push to one of those women, it was held that no inference of a criminal intention to outrage the modesty can be drawn since it is a natural preparatory act to becoming comfortable on a journey.

Offence of Rape

Rape and punishment for rape is dealt with in section 375 and 376 of the Indian Penal code, 1860. Section 376A and 376B deal with the intercourse by a man with his wife during separation and intercourse by a public servant with a woman in his custody. Intercourse by a superintendent of jail, remand home etc. and intercourse by any member of management or staff of a hospital with any woman in that hospital is discussed in Section 376C and 376D of the code. A man is said to commit "rape" who, except in the case hereinafter excepted, has sexual intercourse with a women under circumstances falling under any of the six categories as follows-

Firstly against her will;

Secondly without her consent;

Thirdly with her consent, when her consent has been obtained by putting her or any person in whom she is interested in fear of death or of hurt;

Fourthly with her consent, whom the man knows that he is not her husband, and that her consent is given because, she believes that he is another man to whom she is or believes to be lawfully married;

Fifthly with her consent, when, at the time of giving such consent, by reason of unsoundness of mind or intoxication or the administration by him personally or through another of any stupefying or unwholesome substance, she is unable to understand the nature and consequences of that to which she gives consent;

Sixthly with or without her consent, when she is under sixteen years of age.

Few significant things to note here in the offence of rape are that penetration is sufficient to constitute the sexual intercourse necessary to the offence of rape and sexual intercourse by a man with his own wife, the wife not being under fifteen year of age, is not rape.

A presumption has been inserted in the Indian Evidence Act, 1872 with respect to the offence of rape which states that in prosecution for rape or attempt to commit rape where sexual intercourse is proved and the question is whether it was without the consent of the woman and the woman with whom rape is alleged to have been committed or attempted states in her evidence before the court that she did not consent, the court shall presume she did not consent.

As for the punishment of rape it have been stated that whoever, except is certain case that will be discussed afterwards, commits rape, shall be punished with imprisonment of either description for a term which shall not be less than seven years but which may be for life, or for a term which may extend to ten years, and shall also be liable to fine unless the woman raped is his own wife and is not under twelve years of age, in which case, he shall be punished with imprisonment of either description for a term which may extend to two years or with fine or with both provided that the court may for the adequate and special reasons to be mentioned in the judgment, impose a sentence of imprisonment for a term of less than seven years. The exceptional cases as said above are that whoever-

(a) being a police officer commits rape-
   (i) within the limits of the police station to which he is appointed; or
   (ii) in the premises of any station house whether or not situated in the police station to which he is appointed; or
   (iii) on a woman in his custody or in the custody of a police officer subordinate to him; or

(b) being a public servant, takes advantage of his official position and commits rape on a woman in his custody as such public servant or in the custody of public servant subordinate to him; or

(c) being on the management or on the staff of a jail, remand home or other place of custody established by or under any law for the time being in force or of a woman's or children institution takes advantage of this official position and commits rape on any inmate of such jail, remand home, place or institution; or

(d) being on the management or on the staff of a hospital, takes advantage of his official position and commits rape on a woman in that hospital; or

(e) commits rape on a woman knowing her to be pregnant; or

(f) commits rape on a woman when she is under twelve years of age; or

(g) commits gang rape

shall be punished with rigorous imprisonment for a term which may be for life and shall also be liable to fine; provided that the court may, for adequate and special reasons to be mentioned in the judgment, impose a sentence of imprisonment of either description for a term of less than ten years.

Where a woman is raped by one or more in a group of persons acting in furtherance of their common intention, each of the persons shall be deemed to have committed gang rape. "Women and children's institution" means an institution, whether called an orphanage or a home for neglected woman or children or a widow's home or by any other home which is established and maintained for the reception and care of women or children. "Hospital" means the precinct of the hospital and includes the precincts of any institution of the reception and treatment of persons during convalescence or of persons requiring medical attention or rehabilitation.

Furthermore, whoever has sexual intercourse with his own wife, who is living separately from him under a decree or separation or under any custom or usage, without her consent, shall be punished with imprisonment of either description for a term which may extend to two years and shall also be liable to fine. Whoever, being a public servant, takes advantage of his official position and induces or seduces, any women, who is in his custody as such public servant subordinate to him to have sexual intercourse with him such sexual intercourse not amounting to the offence of rape, shall be punished with imprisonment of either description for a term which may extend to five years and shall also be liable to fine. Moreover, whoever being the superintendent or manager of a jail, remand home or other places of custody established by or under any law for the time being in force or of a woman's or children's institution, takes advantage of his official position and induces or seduces any female inmate of such jail, remand home, place or institution to have sexual intercourse with him, such sexual intercourse not amounting to the offence of rape shall be punished with imprisonment of either description for a term which may extend to five years and shall also be liable to fine. "Superintendent" in relation to a jail remand home or a woman's children's institution includes a person holding any other office in such jail, remand home, place or institution by virtue of which he can exercise any authority or control over its inmates. Whoever, being on the management of a hospital or being on the staff of a hospital take advantage of his position and has sexual intercourse with any woman in that hospital amounting to the offence of rape, shall be punished with imprisonment of either description for a term which may extend to five years and shall also be liable to fine.

In the case of *queen* v. *Flattery* (1877) 22.B.D.410, a 19 year old girl was raped on 14th November 1876. The girl was subject to fits and suffered ill health. She went to the accused's clinic along with her mother. She was advised to have surgical operation by the accrued for which she consented. Under the pretence of performing surgical operation the accused had sexual intercourse with the girl. It was held that the consent of the girl won't be an excuse for accused to escape from conviction. Misconception existed with regard to the nature of the act and the consent given by the girl was for surgical operation and not for the sexual intercourse and this fact was within the knowledge of the doctor. The accused was held liable for the offence of rape.

Another celebrated case in this regard is *Tukaram* v. *State of Maharashtra* AIR (1979) SC 185 (Popularly known as *Mathura rape case*) where the Bombay High Court observed that there existed difference between "consent" and "Passive submission" and that mere passive or helpless surrender of the lady and its resignation to other's lust induced by threats or fear cannot be equated with desire or will, nor furnish an answer by the mere fact that the sexual act was not in opposition to such desire or volition. Although the decision of the High court was overruled by the Supreme Court which was widely criticized but the observation of the High court in this case are highly significant and it invited consequentially amendment in Section 375 of IPC.

Unnatural Offence

For unnatural offence it is to be conceived in mind that whoever voluntarily has carnal intercourse against the order of nature with any man, woman or animal shall be punished with imprisonment for life, or with imprisonment of either description for a term which may extend to ten years and shall also be liable to fine. Penetration is sufficient to constitute the carnal intercourse necessary to the offence. Here the intercourse against the order of nature is dealt with and it includes incest, homosexuality, Sadism, masochism, exhibitionism, oral sex, voyeurism sodomy and bestiality. Marriage of a person does not equip him with a license to succumb his curious sex behaviors like sodomy or oral sex. Law allows only normal sex to a human being. Consent of the parties here is immaterial and the party consenting is equally liable as an abettor. A significant thing to note in the offence of unnatural offence is that although it is a crimes but such occurrence are not uncommon and the woman has to suffer with silence. Forcible sodomy, sadism and other crime of this nature can be the ground for divorce. "Incompatibility" exists in marriage with regard to homosexuality or Tran sexuality. Oral sex and other less harmful cases, although may not be the ground for divorce yet the court may warn the accused.

Prostitution

Selling and buying minors for the purpose of prostitution is another offence for which women often fall pray to. Whoever sells, lets to hire or otherwise disposes of any person under the age of eighteen years with intent that such person shall at any age be employed or used for the purpose of prostitution or illicit intercourse with any person or for any lawful and immoral purpose or knowing it to be likely that such person will at any age be employed or used for any such purpose shall be punished with imprisonment of either description for a term which may extend to ten years and shall also be liable to fine. When a female under age of eighteen years is sold, let for hire or otherwise disposed of to a prostitute or to any person who keeps or manages a brothel, the person so disposing of such female shall until the contrary is proved be presumed to have disposed of her within the intent that she shall be used for the purpose of prostitution. "Illicit intercourse" here means sexual intercourse between persons not united by marriage or by any union or tie which, though not amounting to a marriage is recognized by the personal law or custom of the community to which they belong or where they belong to different communities of both such communities, as constituting between them a quasi-marital relation.

Re. *Ramanna* (1889) ILR 12 mad. 273 it was observed that this provision brings within its purview both married and unmarried minors irrespective of caste or community, in including girls belonging to dancing girl caste. On the similar lines whoever buy, hires or otherwise obtain possession of any person under the age of eighteen years with intent that such person shall at any age be employed or used for the purpose of prostitution or illicit intercourse any person or for any unlawful and immoral purpose or knowing it to be likely that such person will at any stage be employed or used for any such purpose, shall be punished with imprisonment of either description for a term which may extend to ten years, and shall also be liable to fine. Any prostitute or any person keeping or managing any brothel, who buy, hires or otherwise obtains possession of a female under the age of eighteen years shall, until the contrary is proved be presumed to have obtained possession of such female with the intent that she shall be used for the purposes of prostitution.

The Immoral Traffic (Prevention) Act, 1956 defines prostitution as the "exploitation or abuse of persons for commercial purposes" and it comprehends sex as a business activity. Before 1986 a prostitute meant a woman who offered her body for promiscuous sex for hire. But now males are also brought within the purview of the act. The law targets the pimps, agents, managers, or keepers of brothels and those who promote or aid prostitution as business. However, leniency can be witnessed in law for the victims of exploitation or the prostitutes themselves. One to three years jail and fine has been prescribed for the keepers or managers of brothels. A person who allows prostitution in his property or tenanted house can also be penalized. A punishment of seven to ten years in jail and fine can be imposed where the accused is found to be living on the earning of prostitutes, moreover, the procurement and inducement of persons for the sake of prostitution is serious crime inviting an imprisonment of up to 14 years. There are only two circumstance under which the prostitute themselves are punished and they are-

(i) When they operate in public places like 200 meters of schools, hospitals, places of worship or nursing homes

(ii) When positive attempt is made by them to seduce or solicit persons with gestures, words, exposures and thereby indulging in molestations.

The law provides for setting up of corrective institutions and protective homes for prostitutes. A woman who is found to be indulged in soliciting may be sent to corrective institutions rather the being sentenced to jail. Moreover if any person is carrying on prostitution by will or by force may apply to the nearest magistrate for taking him or her to the protective home. He is to be provided care and protection by court. Direction can also be made by a magistrate to the police so as to rescue persons in brothel and produce them before him. Provision has also been made for the special police officers for the purpose of dealing with prostitution, advisory bodies and special courts.

Cruelty against women

Section 498A of IPC deals with the husband or relative of husband of a woman subjecting her to cruelty. Whoever, being the husband or the relative of the husband of a woman subjects such woman to cruelty, shall be punished with imprisonment for a term which may extend to three years, and shall also be liable to fine. Cruelty here means: -

(i) any willful conduct which is of such a nature as is likely to drive to woman to commit suicide or to cause grave injury or danger to life, limb or health (whether mental or physical) of the woman; or

(ii) harassment of the woman where such harassment is with a view to coercing her or any person related to her to meet any unlawful demand for any property or valuable security is on account of failure by her or any person related to her to meet such demand.

Procedural law and Women

Apart from the substantive law the procedural law also makes certain easy provisions for women. Section 160 of the Code of Criminal Procedure protects the women from unnecessary harassment by police. It provides that no women or a child below the age of 15 years can be required to be called to the police station for the purpose of interrogation and it is for the police officer who must go to the place where the women or boy resides.

Section 51 of the Code of Criminal Procedure provides that a woman is required to be searched then the search shall be made by another female with strict regard to decency. Similarly, in case a medical examination is needed of the accused woman then it is for the lady doctor or some one under his supervision who is allowed to do so. Section 47 provides that in case an offender hides in the house of woman, who does not appear in public due to some custom, the police is not at liberty to enter the house or break it open without giving notice to the woman. The woman in such a case would be set at liberty to withdraw. In case of service of a summons, if it cannot be served on the person itself then it is to be served at the house of such person and it is for the adult male member of the family to accept the summons. It cannot be served on the female member of the house as provided in Section 64 of the Code of Criminal Procedure. Where a woman is sentenced to death and she is found to be pregnant then under Section 416 of the Code of Criminal Procedure the High Court shall postponed the execution. The sentence of death can also be commuted to the imprisonment for life. Furthermore, Section 198 of the Code of Criminal Procedure provides that for the purpose of prosecution in case of bigamy, any person related to the wife by blood, or adoption or marriage can file the complaint if she gives consent to it. This widens the ambit and is helpful in the cases where the wife herself cannot take action. More so, Section 320 of the Code of Criminal Procedure prescribes a number of offences that can be compounded (compromised) in some cases. The instances of such compoundable offences are adultery, enticing, taking away or detaining a married woman.

Offences under NDPS Act, 1985

The Narcotic Drugs and Psychotropic Substances Act, 1985 was enacted by the parliament inter-alia with a view to:

(a) Consolidate and amend the law relating to narcotic drugs.

(b) To make stringent provisions for the control and regulation of operations relating to narcotic drugs and psychotropic substances.

(c) To provide for the forfeiture of property derived from, or used in, illicit traffic in narcotic drugs and psychotropic substances.

(d) To implement the provisions of the international convention on narcotic drugs and psychotropic substances.

This Act comprehends a number of offences related to narcotic drugs and psychotropic substances. There are certain prohibition, control and regulation under this Act. Cultivating any coca-plant or gathering any portion of coca plant or cultivating the opium poppy or any cannabis plant have been prohibited under the Act. Moreover, producing, manufacturing, possessing, selling, purchasing, transporting, warehousing, using, consuming, importing inter-state, exporting inter-state, importing into India, Exporting from India or Transshipping any narcotic drug or psychotropic substances has also been prohibited. However, this is subject to the exception where the purpose is Medical or Scientific one and the aforesaid operation is made in the manner and to the extent provided under NDPS Act or rules or order made thereunder. Where any provision of the Act, rule or order as the case may be, imposes any requirement by way of license, permit or authorization then the operation needs to be in accordance with the terms and conditions of such license, permit or authorization. The export of poppy straw for decorative purpose is not covered hereunder.

Further prohibition has been made with regard to certain activities relating to property derived from offence. Converting or transferring any property knowing that such property is derived from an offence committed under NDPS Act or under any other corresponding law of any other country or from any act of participation in such offence, for the purpose of concealing or disguising the illicit origin of the property or to assist any person in the commission of an offence or to evade the legal consequences, is prohibited under the Act. Concealing or disguising the true nature, source, location, disposition of any property knowing that such property is derived from an offence committed under NDPS Act or under any other corresponding law of any other country has also been prohibited. Moreover, it has been made mandatory that no person shall knowingly acquire, possess or use any property which was derived from an offence committed under this Act or under any other corresponding law of any other country.

Punishment has been prescribed in the Act for contravention in relation to poppy straw, contravention in relation to coca plant and coca leaves, contravention in relation to prepared opium, contravention in relation to opium poppy and opium, and embezzlement of opium by cultivator. Moreover, contravention in relation to cannabis plant and cannabis, manufactured drugs and preparations, psychotropic substances and illegal import into India, export from India or transshipment of narcotic drugs and psychotropic substances has also been penalized. Allowing premises etc. to be used for the commission of an offence is in itself an offence under the Act. Consumption of any narcotic drug or psychotropic substance, financing illicit traffic and harbouring offenders, attempt to commit offences, abetment and criminal conspiracy have been brought under the ambit of the Act as offence.

Death Sentence can also be prescribed for certain offences after previous conviction if any person who has been convicted of the commission of, or attempt to commit, or abetment of, or criminal conspiracy to commit, any of the offences punishable for embezzlement of opium by cultivator, or for external dealings in narcotic drugs and psychotropic substances in contravention of restrictions over external dealings in narcotic drugs an psychotropic substances, or for financing illicit traffic and harbouring offenders or for offences involving commercial quantity of any narcotic drug or psychotropic substance, is subsequently convicted of the commission of, or attempt to commit, or abetment of , or criminal conspiracy to commit certain offences provided in under Section 31A of the NDPS Act.

Under the NDPS Act, if the court entertains strong doubt regarding the accused's awareness about the nature of the substance in the gunny bags, it would be miscarriage of criminal justice to convict him of the offence keeping such strong doubt dispelled. Even so, it is for the accused to dispel any doubt in that regard. Non compliance of the provision under the NDPS Act, causes prejudice to the accused.

In *Abdul Rashid Ibrahim Mansuri* v. *State of Gujrat*, JT 2000 (1) SC 471, the Supreme Court made the following observations "if the officer has reason to believe from personal knowledge or prior information received from any person that any narcotic drug or psychotropic substance (in respect of which an offence has been committed) is kept or concealed in any building, conveyance or enclosed place, it is imperative that the officer should take it down in writing and he shall forthwith send a copy thereof to his immediate official superior. The action of the officer, who claims to have exercised on the strength of such unrecorded information would become suspect, though the trial may not vitiate on that score alone. Nonetheless the resultant position would be one of causing prejudice to the accused,"

LEGAL AWARENESS
(*OBJECTIVE*)

LEGAL AWARENESS (OBJECTIVE)

MULTIPLE CHOICE QUESTIONS

1. The maximum strength of Rajya Sabha is
   A. 225 B. 250
   C. 330 D. 350
2. The member of the Rajya Sabha are
   A. directly elected by the people
   B. elected by local self governing bodies
   C. elected by the legislative assemblies of the states
   D. Partially elected by legislative assemblies and partially by local self governing bodies.
3. The maximum number of representative to the Rajya Sabha are from the state of
   A. A.P. B. W.B.
   C. M.P. D. U.P.
4. The diarchy system was introduced by
   A. Govt. of India Act, 1909
   B. Govt. of India Act, 1919
   C. Govt. of India Act, 1935
   D. Govt. of India Act, 1892
5. Federal Constitution with strong centralising tendency is found in the constitution of
   A. U.S.A.
   B. Canada
   C. Australia
   D. New Zealand
6. The emergency provisions of the Indian Constitution is borrowed from:
   A. Germany
   B. U.S.A.
   C. Canada
   D. Russia
7. Whether a bill is money bill or not is decided by
   A. Speaker of Lok Sabha
   B. Finance Minister
   C. Prime Minister
   D. President
8. Vice-President is the ex-officio Chairman of
   A. Rajya Sabha
   B. Lok Sabha
   C. State Legislative Assembly
   D. All of the above
9. The maximum number of nominated member in both the houses of Parliament can be
   A. 10 B. 14
   C. 12 D. 20
10. The Parliament can declare a seat vacant if a member absents himself without permission from the session for
    A. 30 days
    B. 60 days
    C. 90 days
    D. 120 days
11. The first speaker of the Lok Sabha was
    A. G.N. Mavalankar
    B. Hukum Singh
    C. Zakir Hussain
    D. B.R. Ambedkar
12. Lok Sabha can be prorogued by
    A. Prime Minister
    B. President
    C. Vice President
    D. Speaker
13. To whom the speaker of Lok Sabha will address his letter of resignation
    A. The Prime Minister
    B. The President
    C. The Vice President
    D. The Deputy Speaker of the Lok Sabha
14. The idea of D.P.S.P. is borrowed from
    A. The Republic of Germany
    B. The Republic of Ireland
    C. Canada
    D. South Africa
15. The Constitution of India is
    A. very rigid
    B. flexible
    C. partly rigid and partly flexible
    D. rigid

16. The Constitution of the India was adopted on
A. Nov. 26, 1949
B. Aug. 15, 1947
C. Jan. 26, 1949
D. Nov. 26, 1948

17. To form the Constitution of India, the Constituent Assembly first met on:
A. June 10, 1946
B. Dec. 26, 1949
C. Dec. 6, 1946
D. Dec. 9, 1946

18. To enforce fundamental Right, a citizen can approach to
A. The President
B. The Parliament
C. Supreme Court
D. Both Supreme Court and High Courts

19. To secure personal freedom, which writ is issued
A. Habeas corpus
B. Mandamus
C. Quo warranto
D. Certiorari

20. *A.D.M.Jabalpur* v. *Shrikant Shaple* case is also known as
A. Habeas corpus case
B. Fundamental Right case
C. Babri Masjid Demolition case
D. None of the above

21. The writ of Habeas corpus is issued
A. by a superior court do something in the nature of his allotted duty
B. By a Superior Court to the lower court directing it to transfer the record of proceedings in a case for its review
C. In the form of an order calling upon a person who has detained another person to bring that person before court and show authority for such detention
D. None of the above

22. Habeas corpus literally means
A. What is your authority
B. You may have the body
C. Things speak for itself
D. None of the above

23. 'Quo warranto' literally means
A. What is your authority
B. You may have the body
C. Things speak for itself
D. None of the above

24. The judges of the Supreme Court can be removed from office
A. by the president at his discretion
B. by the president on the recommendation of the Parliament
C. by the president on the recommendation of the Council of Ministers
D. None of the above

25. In India Constitutional power of judicial review is contained in
A. Art. 12 B. Art. 13
C. Art. 14 D. Art. 15

26. Which amendment restricted the Supreme Court of its power of judicial review
A. 42nd Amendment
B. 44th Amendment
C. 36th Amendment
D. 29th Amendment

27. Supreme Court can review its own judgement or order under
A. Art. 139 B. Art. 138
C. Art. 130 D. Art. 137

28. The Chairman of the Drafting Committee of the Constituent Assembly was
A. Jawaharlal Nehru
B. Dr. Rajendra Prasad
C. B. R. Ambedkar
D. Vallabbhai Patel

29. Rajya Sabha Members are elected for
A. a term of six years
B. a term of five years
C. a term of four years
D. a term of three years

30. One third members of the Rajya Sabha retire
A. every two years
B. every three years
C. every year
D. None of the above

31. The maximum time gap between the two sessions of the Parliament can be

A. three months B. four months
C. six months D. nine months

32. The Chairman of the Rajya Sabha
A. is elected by the members of the Rajya Sabha alone
B. is elected jointly by the members of the Lok Sabha, Rajya Sabha
C. is nominated by the President
D. None of the above

33. The Chairman of Rajya Sabha can cast
A. a vote only in case of equality of votes
B. two votes-an ordinary vote and casting vote
C. a vote as any other member of the Rajya Sabha
D. None of the above

34. The joint sessions of the Lok Sabha and Rajya Sabha is presided by
A. the Speaker of Lok Sabha
B. the Chairman of the Rajya Sabha
C. the President
D. none of the above

35. Who certifies the status of a Bill as Money Bill?
A. President
B. Prime Minister
C. Speaker
D. Leader of the opposition

36. A money bill can be introduced
A. only is the Lok Sabha
B. in either house of the Parliament
C. in Rajya Sabha only
D. in joint session of the two houses

37. A money bill passed by the Lok Sabha can be delayed by the Rajya Sabha for a maximum period of
A. three months
B. two months
C. one month
D. fourteen days

38. Who can control the expenditure of the Government of India?
A. Reserve Bank of India
B. Union Finance Minister
C. the Comptroller and Auditor General of India
D. the Parliament

39. Who is the custodian of the Lok Sabha
A. the Speaker
B. the leader of the opposition
C. the Prime Minister
D. the chief of the ruling party

40. At a joint sitting of two houses, when a bill is considered, the decision is taken by
A. majority of each house separately
B. simple majority
C. absolute majority of total membership
D. two thirds majority

41. The number of seats reserved for the members of scheduled tribes in the Lok Sabha is
A. 50 B. 40
C. 30 D. 25

42. The nature of Indian constitution is
A. Unitary
B. Purely federal
C. Federal in form and unitary in spirit
D. None of the above.

43. Presently Indian constitution contains:
A. Less than 350 Articles
B. None then 400 Articles
C. Over 440 Articles
D. None of the above

44. Originally Indian constitution contains
A. 395 Articles
B. 350 Articles
C. 325 Articles
D. None of the above.

45. The Constituent Assembly was set up under
A. the Cabinet Mission Plan, 1946
B. the Indian Independence Act, 1947
C. a resolution of the Provisional Government
D. None of the above

46. The constituent Assembly of India met first time on
A. 9th December, 1946
B. 16th August, 1947
C. 26th November, 1947
D. 26th January, 1950

47. The Provisional President of the constituent Assembly was

A. Dr. Zakir Hussain
B. Dr. Sachchidanand Sinha
C. Dr. Rajendra Prasad
D. Dr. B. R. Ambedkar

48. The number of committee set up by the constituent Assembly for framing the constitution of India were
A. 17 B. 13
C. 9 D. 7

49. The job of interpreting the provisions of constitution vests with
A. The President
B. The Supreme Court
C. The Parliament
D. The Speaker of Lok Sabha

50. The Parliamentary form of Indian Government provided by the Indian constitution has been borrowed from
A. Russia B. U.S.A.
C. England D. Germany

51. The power of forming new states or altering the boundaries of existing states is with
A. The Parliament
B. The people of concerned states only
C. The President
D. None of the above.

52. Presently India consists of
A. 24 States and 7 Union territories
B. 24 States and 9 Union territories
C. 28 States and 7 Union territories
D. 28 States and 9 Union territories

53. On linguistic basis, the states were reorganized in the year of
A. 1946 B. 1956
C. 1966 D. 1976

54. The first linguistic State of India was
A. Andhra Pradesh
B. West Bengal
C. Punjab
D. Tamil Naidu

55. Who looks after the day-to-day administration of a union territory?
A. The President
B. the union Home Minister
C. the Lt. Governor
D. None of the above

56. Which provision of the Indian constitution finds similarities is the US constitution?
A. Fundamental Rights
B. Rule of Law
C. Directive Principles of State Policy
D. Rigid constitution

57. The Indian Constitution is greatly influenced by
A. The constitution of U.S.A
B. The constitution of U.K
C. The constitution of Canada
D. The Government of India Act, 1935

58. If any dispute arises with regard to the election of Vice-President, it is decided by
A. the Supreme Court of India
B. the Parliament
C. the President
D. the Speaker of Lok Sabha

59. The Council of Minister is appointed
A. by the President on the recommendation of the Parliament
B. by the Prime Minister
C. by the President on the advice of the Prime Minister
D. by the President exercising his discretion

60. To whom council of Ministers is collectively responsible
A. The President of India
B. The Prime Minister
C. The Lok Sabha
D. The Rajya Sabha

61. The meetings of council of Ministers is presided by
A. The President
B. The Prime Minister
C. The Union Home Minister
D. None of the above.

62. The Prime Minister is
A. appointed by the President
B. appointed by the President in consultation with the speaker

C. elected by the Lok Sabha
D. elected by the two houses of Parliament at a joint sitting

63. Which part of the constitution is a key to open the mind of the its framers?
A. Preamble
B. Fundamental Rights
C. Fundamental Duties
D. Directive Principles

64. In the Preamble the union of India is also named as
A. Aryavart B. Bharat
C. Bharat Varsha D. Hindustan

65. Preamble was held to be a part of the constitution in the famous case of
A. Berubari Case
B. Golaknath Case
C. Kesharananda Bharati Case
D. None of the above.

66. How Parliament can amend any of the Fundamental Rights guaranteed in the constitution?
A. Parliament cannot amend any Fundamental Rights
B. Parliament can do so only after a referendum
C. Parliament can amend them by special majority
D. Parliament can do so only when the President directs

67. The operation of Fundamental Rights can be suspended by
A. The President
B. The Prime Minister
C. The Supreme Court of India
D. The Parliament

68. The operation of which fundamental right cannot be suspended even during an emergency
A. Right to equality
B. Right of freedom of speak expression
C. Right to life
D. Right to constitutional remedies.

69. The rights against exploitation prohibits
A. traffic in human beings
B. beggar
C. employment of children below 14 years of age in factories, mines etc.
D. all of the above

70. The constitution of India abolished the practice of untouchability under
A. Article 15 B. Article 16
C. Article 17 D. Article 18

71. Now right to property is a
A. Legal Rights
B. Fundamental Rights
C. Human Right
D. Natural Right

72. The responsibility for the enforcement of fundamental Rights vest with
A. the Parliament
B. the High Courts
C. the Supreme Court
D. both B and C

73. In case of violation of Fundamental Rights, a person can move the Supreme Court directly under
A. Article 32 B. Article 226
C. Article 14 D. All of the above

74. To enforce the Fundamental Rights, the courts issue
A. a writ
B. a decree
C. an ordinance
D. None of the above

75. According to B. R. Ambedkar, which provision is the heart and soul of the constitution?
A. Right to equality
B. Right to freedom of religion
C. Right to freedom of speech and expression
D. Right to constitutional remedies

76. The architect of the Indian constitution is
A. B. R. Ambedkar
B. Rajendra Prasad
C. Jawaharlal Nehru
D. Zakir Hussain

77. The Drafting Committee of the Constitution, including the chairman consisted of

A. nine members
B. seven members
C. five members
D. three members

78. The Supreme Commander of the armed forces of India is
A. the President
B. the Prime Minister
C. the Union Defence Minister
D. None of the above

79. Under Article 352, the President made a proclamation of emergency first time in the year of
A. 1952 B. 1971
C. 1965 D. 1962

80. When a bill is presented to the President for his assent, he can
A. refuse to sign it
B. amend the bill
C. return it for reconsideration
D. consult the speaker of Lok Sabha

81. The Vice-President of India is elected
A. directly by the people
B. by the members of the Lok Sabha and Rajya Sabha
C. by the members of the Rajya Sabha alone
D. by the same electoral college which elects the President

82. The official term of the Vice-President is
A. five years
B. six years
C. co-terminates with that of the President
D. dependant on the will of the President

83. In the constitutional scheme India is described as
A. a federation of states and Union territories
B. a union of states
C. quasi-federal
D. partly unitary and partly federal

84. The Preamble was proposed before the Drafting committee by
A. B. N. Rao
B. B. R. Ambedkar
C. Sardar Vallabbhai Patel
D. Jawaharlal Nehru

85. The Preamble to the constitution, as it presently stands, declares India to be
A. a sovereign, Democratic Republic
B. a sovereign Socialist, secular, Democratic Republic
C. a Socialist, Democratic Republic
D. None of these

86. Which among the following amendment added the words 'socialist, secular' and 'the unity and integrity of the nation' to the preamble of the constitution?
A. 36th B. 42nd
C. 44th D. none of these

87. The Preamble of the Indian constitution has been amended so far
A. Once B. twice
C. thrice D. never

88. For the first time, the Preamble was amended by the
A. 24th Amendment
B. 42nd Amendment
C. 44th Amendment
D. None of the above

89. The first Governor-General of India was
A. Lord Minto
B. Lord Canning
C. Lord William Bentick
D. Lord Warren Hasting

90. The Fundamental Rights given to citizens aims to secure
A. an independent and vigilant judiciary
B. socialistic government
C. individual liberty
D. none of the above

91. Who is the executive head of a state?
A. the President
B. the Governor
C. the Chief Minister
D. None of the above.

92. The Governor of a state is
A. nominated by the Prime Minister
B. elected by the state Legislature
C. appointed by the President
D. None of the above

93. The members of the council of minister in the state is administered the oath of office by
A. the chief justice of the state High Court
B. the Advocate-General of the state
C. the Governor
D. None of the above

94. The citizen has a right to assemble but the assembly should be
A. peaceful
B. peaceful and unarmed
C. non-violent
D. for constructive aims

95. Article 21 of the Indian constitution declares that protection of life and liberty
A. can be taken away during the Emergency through presidential order
B. can be taken away only according to the procedure established by law
C. can never be taken away
D. None of the above

96. Which of the following is not a condition for becoming a citizen of India?
A. citizenship by descent
B. citizenship through acquisition of property
C. citizenship by birth
D. citizenship by naturalisation

97. The authority competent to prescribe conditions for acquisition of citizenship is
A. the President
B. the Parliament
C. the Election Commission
D. None of the above

98. The provisions containing Fundamental Rights are contained in
A. Part III of the constitution
B. Part IV of the constitution
C. Seventh Schedule of the constitution
D. Ninth Schedule of the constitution

99. Which one of the following is not a fundamental right?
A. Right to freedom of speech & expression
B. Right to property
C. Right to constitutional remedies
D. All of the above

100. By which amendment right to private property ceased to be a fundamental right?
A. 42nd Amendment
B. 44th Amendment
C. 52nd Amendment
D. None of the above

101. How many types of emergencies have been envisaged by the constitution?
A. one B. two
C. three D. four

102. President can declare national emergency
A. on his own discretion
B. on the recommendation of the Governor
C. on the recommendation of the cabinet
D. on the recommendation of the Parliament

103. The President can promulgate an ordinance only when
A. the bill has been pending is the Parliament for over a year
B. there is disagreement between the two houses
C. the Parliament is not in session
D. None of the above

104. A member of the council of Ministers can be dismissed by the president
A. with the consent of the speaker
B. at his discretion
C. on the recommendation of the Prime Minister
D. None of the above

105. The President of India is elected on the basis of
A. Proportional representation by a single transferable vote
B. proportional representation
C. proportional representation by a single-non-transferable vote
D. None of the above

106. The National Emergency can now be imposed only on the
A. advice of the Prime Minister
B. written advice of the Union Cabinet
C. advice of the Chief Justice of India
D. None of the above

107. On account of break down of constitutional machinery in a state, the President can impose his rule in that state under
A. Art. 352
B. Art. 356
C. Art. 361
D. Art. 371

108. The Proclamation of National Emergency ceases to operate unless approved by the Parliament within
A. one month B. two month
C. three month D. one year

109. The financial emergency is declared by the President
A. to meet the extraordinary expenses
B. if there is a threat to the financial stability or credit of India
C. on the recommendation of the comptroller and Auditor-General
D. all of the above

110. The President of India can be impeached under
A. Article 61 B. Article 75
C. Article 76 D. Article 81

111. Even a non-citizen enjoys a right to
A. Freedom to acquire property or to carry on any occupation, trade or business.
B. freedom of speech, assembly and association
C. constitutional remedies
D. freedom to move, reside and settle in any part of India.

112. In the constitution, Fundamental Duties were added by the
A. 40th Amendment
B. 42nd Amendment
C. 43rd Amendment
D. 44th Amendment

113. Fundamental Duties were added to the constitution in the year of
A. 1975 B. 1979
C. 1977 D. 1976

114. Writ of Mandamus is
A. an order to produce the body of a person
B. an order from a higher court to stop proceedings in a certain case
C. a writ from a superior court commanding some officer or particular authority to do a specific act.
D. None of the above.

115. The executive power of the Indian union vests with
A. the Prime Minister
B. the Parliament
C. the President
D. the Council of Ministers

116. The maximum age limit for the election as President of India is
A. 58 years B. 60 years
C. 62 years D. No such limit

117. The president can exercise his pardoning power in
A. the offence punishable with death sentence
B. offences against laws in the union and concurrent lists
C. all the cases of punishment by a court martial
D. all of the above instances

118. Who can declare war or peace?
A. President of India
B. Prime Minister of India
C. Defense Minister
D. All of the above

119. In the election of the President
A. the center is assigned greater role
B. the states are given greater weightage
C. parity between the center and the states has been maintained
D. none of the above

120. Proclamation of Emergency must be approved by the Parliament within
A. one month B. two months
C. six months D. one year

121. The President of India is elected for the period of
A. 4 years B. 5 years
C. 6 years D. None of these

122. The vice-President of India holds office
A. for a term of four years

B. for a term of five years
C. during the pleasure of the president
D. for a term which is decided at the time of his appointment by the parliament

123. In case the President dies, the Vice-President will succeed him as President for

A. a maximum period of six month
B. a maximum period of one year
C. a maximum period of three years
D. the remaining period of the term

124. If the office of the President falls vacant, the same must be filled within

A. three months
B. six months
C. one year
D. None of the above

125. The age of the retirement of the President is

A. 62 years
B. 70 years
C. 82 years
D. there is no age limit

126. The Council of Ministers include—

A. President and Vice-President
B. Speaker and Deputy Speaker
C. Only Prime Minister
D. Cabinet Ministers, Ministers of States and Deputy Ministers

127. The tenure of the Union Council of Ministers is

A. uncertain
B. five years
C. fixed and co-terminates with the President
D. co-terminates with the Lok Sabha

128. The number of persons from the field of art, literature, social services etc. Who may be nominated to Rajya Sabha by the President are?

A. 5 B. 7
C. 12 D. none of these

129. The Prime Minister is

A. elected by the Lok Sabha
B. elected by the House of Parliament
C. appointed by the President
D. None of the above

130. The formation of the council of Ministers starts with the appointment of

A. the Prime Minister
B. the President
C. the Speaker
D. None of the above

131. The Legislative functions of the council of Ministers include the right to

A. nominate some members to Rajya Sabha
B. nominate two Angle Indian members to Lok Sabha
C. summon and prorogue the two Houses of Parliament
D. introduce important bills and resolutions in the Parliament.

132. To get the directive principles of state policy enforced by the Government, the citizen can approach

A. the Supreme Court
B. the High Court
C. any court
D. none of these

133. Which constitutional amendment gave primacy to Directive Principles of state policy over Fundamental Rights?

A. 39th Amendment
B. 42nd Amendment
C. 44th Amendment
D. 46th Amendment

134. The Supreme Court of India struck down the provisions giving primacy to Directive Principles of state policy over Fundamental Rights in

A. Sajjan Singh case
B. Shankari Prasad case
C. Golak Nath case
D. Keshvananda Bharti case

135. For the enforcement of Directive Principles of state policy a citizen can move

A. The Supreme Court of India
B. The High Court directly
C. Both A and B
D. None of the above

136. Which of the following factors are responsible for the slow implementation of the Directive Principles of State Policy?
A. Vastness of the country
B. Lack of resources with the government
C. Long vale of congress party at centre
D. Only A and B

137. Who is called ears and eyes of the public Accounts committee?
A. The comptroller and Auditor General
B. Chairman of Planning Commission
C. Attorney General
D. None of the above.

138. The Auditor-General addresses his letter of resignation to
A. The speaker of Lok Sabha
B. the Prime Minister
C. the President
D. None of the above.

139. Vote on account is meant to meet
A. expenditure for a period before the passing of the annual budget
B. expenditure on secret service
C. expenditure on unexpected demands
D. None of the above.

140. The quorum for sitting of the parliament is fixed at
A. one-eights of the membership of the House
B. one-tenth of the membership of the House
C. one-third of the membership of the House
D. two-thirds of the membership of the House

141. The largest number of representative in the Lok Sabha are from the state of
A. Madhya Pradesh
B. Uttar Pradesh
C. Tamil Naidu
D. Bihar

142. Before the expiring of its term the Lok Sabha can be dissolved by
A. The President on his own
B. The President on the advice of the Prime Minister
C. The Prime Minister
D. None of the above

143. The Deputy Speaker of the Lok Sabha is
A. appointed by the speaker
B. appointed by the Prime Minister
C. elected by the members of the Lok Sabha
D. appointed by the President

144. The members of the Rajya Sabha are elected by
A. the elected members of the state Legislative Assembly
B. the electorates of India directly
C. the members of the Lok Sabha
D. None of the above

145. The life of the Rajya Sabha is
A. of permanent nature
B. 6 years
C. 5 years
D. Not certain

146. In the election of the President, which of the following does not take part?
A. elected members of Lok Sabha
B. elected members of Rajya Sabha
C. Members of the Legislative councils
D. None of the above.

147. The candidature of the President of India has to be proposed by
A. any five members of Parliament
B. any five members of the Electoral college
C. any fifty members of the Electoral college
D. None of the above

148. The election of the President is conducted by
A. the election commission of India
B. the speaker of Lok Sabha
C. the Prime Minister office
D. None of the above.

149. The minimum age required for getting elected as President of India is
A. 55 years
B. 35 years
C. 60 years
D. No age limit is prescribed

150. Who among the following held the office of President for two consecutive terms?
A. Dr. Rajendra Prasad
B. Dr. Zakir Hussain
C. Dr. Radha Krishnan
D. None of the above

151. The dispute regarding the election of the President is decided by
A. the Election commission
B. the Parliament
C. the Supreme Court
D. None of the above

152. Before becoming the President of India, who among the following got Bharat Ratna?
A. Rajendra Prasad
B. V. V. Giri
C. Zakir Hussain
D. S. Radha Krishna

153. The maximum age for election to the office of the President is
A. 65 years
B. 70 years
C. 75 years
D. No age limit

154. The first viceroy of India was
A. Lord Minto
B. Lord Canning
C. Lord William Bentick
D. Lord Warren Hastings

155. The CAG is associated with
A. Public Accounts Committee
B. Business Advisory Committee
C. Committee on Public undertaking
D. All the above

156. The Ordinances promulgated by the Governor are subject to the approval of the
A. President
B. Vice President
C. Prime Minister
D. State Legislature

157. The minimum age required for the appointment of the Governor is
A. 35 years B. 65 years
C. 68 years D. No age limit

158. The normal term of a Governor office is
A. 3 years
B. 5 years
C. 6 years
D. None of the above

159. The oath of the office of the Governor is administered by
A. President of India
B. Chief Justice of India
C. Chief Justice of the State High Court
D. Speaker of the State Legislative Assembly

160. The ordinance promulgated by the Governor
A. has the same force as the law made by the State legislature
B. is much narrower than the law made by the state legislature
C. is more extensive than the law made by the state legislature
D. enjoys little importance

161. The main sanction behind the Fundamental Duties is
A. Social
B. Moral
C. Legal
D. All of the above

162. The Directive Principles of State Policy is contained in
A. Part III of the Constitution
B. Part IV of the Constitution
C. Schedule VII of the Constitution
D. Schedule IX of the Constitution

163. The concept of welfare state finds elaboration in
A. Preamble
B. Fundamental Rights
C. Directive Principles of state policy
D. All of the above

164. The Directive Principles of State Policy are
A. Positive instructions to the government to work for the attainment of set objectives
B. negative instructions to the government to refrain from encroaching on

the freedom of the people guaranteed by the constitution
C. directives to the state to enhance the international prestige of the country
D. directives of the government to pursue a policy of non-alignment.

165. The Directive Principles of state policy seek
A. to establish the supremacy of the constitution
B. to curb the authoritarian rule
C. to make the constitution an instrument of social change
D. None of the able

166. The enforcement of the Directive Principles depends on
A. the will of the government
B. the resources available with the government
C. the judiciary
D. all of the above

167. The Executive powers of the Governor do not include
A. right to appoint judges of state High Courts
B. right to remove members of State Public Service Commission
C. right to appoint the Chief Minister and other Ministers
D. right to decide the portfolios of various Ministers

168. The minimum strength of state legislative council has to be
A. 30 B. 40
C. 50 D. 100

169. The Legislative council is expected to have strength equal to
A. half of the membership of the Legislative Assembly
B. one-third of the membership of the Legislative Assembly
C. one-fourth of the membership of the Legislative Assembly
D. two-third of the membership of the Legislative Assembly

170. Once the Legislative Assembly has passed a bill, the maximum period up to which the Legislative council of that state can delay the considerations
A. one month
B. two month
C. three month
D. six months

171. The phrase 'Bicameral Legislature' means
A. an elected Legislature
B. an assembly
C. a legislature consisting of lower and an upper chamber
D. None of the above

172. The Union Territories are administered by
A. the Union Executive
B. the Prime Minister of India
C. the President through the administrators appointed by him
D. the administrator appointed by the Government of India

173. The President refer a matter to the Supreme Court for its opinion
A. When the Cabinet is not functioning properly
B. When a matter is of public importance
C. When emergency are to be promulgated
D. None of the above

174. The Supreme Court of India have original jurisdiction in the setting of disputes
A. between the Govt. of India and any state of the Union.
B. between two or more states
C. between the Govt. of India and one state on one hand and other states on the other hand
D. All of the above

175. Who can be appointed as an ad hoc judge of the Supreme Court?
A. A retired judge of the Supreme Court
B. A sitting judge of a High Court duly qualified for appointed as a Supreme Court Judge
C. All acting judges of the Supreme Court
D. None of the above

176. The privileges of the judges of Supreme Court
A. can be modified to their advantage or disadvantage during their term of office
B. cannot be modified to their disadvantage during their tenure of office
C. can be modified by the parliament only by two thirds majority
D. can be modified only with the approval of the Chief Justice of India

177. When the Supreme Court tenders its advisory opinion, it is
A. not binding on the President
B. binding on the President
C. binding on the President if unanimously made
D. None of the above

178. The number of judges in the High Court is decided by
A. the President of India
B. the State Government
C. The Governor of State concerned
D. the Parliament

179. The Chief Justice of High Court is appointed by
A. the President of India
B. the Governor of the State
C. the Chief Justice of India
D. the Chief Minister of the State

180. Which List contains the subject over which both the center and states are competent to legislate?
A. Union List
B. State List
C. Concurrent List
D. Joint List

181. The bill for the amendment of the constitution can be introduced by
A. the State Legislature
B. the people of India
C. State legislature as well as the Parliament
D. Parliament alone

182. The system of Panchayati Raj involves
A. the villages, state and Union Levels
B. the village and state levels
C. the village, district and state levels
D. the village, block and district levels

183. Which among the following is not a part of Panchayati Raj?
A. Dist. Board
B. Town Area Committees
C. Village Block
D. Panchayat Boards

184. Panchayati Raj was introduced in India in the year of
A. 1950
B. 1952
C. 1959
D. 1962

185. The Lowest Unit of the Panchyati Raj institution is
A. the Panchayat Samiti
B. a village Panchayat
C. the Gram Sabha
D. Zilla Parishad

186. Panchayati Raj was introduced on the recommendation of a Committee headed by
A. Balwant Rai Mehta
B. Ashok Mehta
C. Jivraj Mehta
D. None of these

187. The primary aim of the Panchayati Raj is
A. to ensure the upliftment of Harijans
B. to work for rural development
C. to agriculture production through the involvement of the profile
D. to arouse in the people continuous interest in the community development programme

188. Which of the following state has no Panchayati Raj institution at all?
A. Kerala
B. Nagaland
C. Tripura
D. Asom

189. The Panchayati Raj system is aimed at
A. establishing economic prosperity of the villages
B. having democratic decentralization
C. providing political base for parties
D. making village self-sufficient

190. The Panchayati Raj institution in India gets their funds mainly from
A. Government grants
B. Local takes
C. Property taxes
D. Voluntary contributions

191. Concurred List of VII schedule contains
A. 47 subjects
B. 52 subjects
C. 67 subjects
D. 37 subjects

192. CAG acts as a guide of
A. Public Accounts Committee
B. President of India
C. Prime Minister Office
D. None of the above

193. Constitutional status to municipalities was provided by
A. 73rd Amendment
B. 74th Amendment
C. 75th Amendment
D. None of the above

194. Contingency Fund of the State is operated by
A. The Governor
B. The Chief Minister
C. Union Finance Minister
D. None of the above

195. Finance Commission is set up after every
A. 2 years B. 3 years
C. 4 years D. 5 years

196. Article of the Constitution which is related to right of life is
A. Art. 14 B. Art. 12
C. Art. 21 D. Art. 19

197. A Lok Sabha member represents a population of at least
A. 5, 00,000 people
B. 50, 00,000 people
C. 2, 00,000 people
D. None of the above.

198. The first state to establish the new Panchayati Raj system is
A. Andhra Pradesh
B. Bihar
C. Maharashtra
D. Rajasthan

199. In which part of the constitution state is enjoined establish Panchayati Raj constitution?
A. Preamble
B. Fundamental Rights
C. Directive Principles of State Policy
D. 7th Schedule

200. Which of the following is not a source of revenue of village Panchayat?
A. House Tax
B. Local Tax on land
C. Income Tax
D. Government Grants

201. At the Block level, A Panchayat Samiti is
A. an administrative authority
B. an advisory body
C. a consultant committee
D. a supervisory body

202. Panchayati Raj is
A. the functioning of village republics in a democracy
B. a complex system of rural local government
C. the self government of the villagers in India
D. a hierarchical set up for rural administration

203. Generally the members of Gram Sabha are
A. all the voters in the respective villages
B. all adult makes in the villages
C. all the heads of families of the respective villages
D. nominated members

204. In the three tier Panchayati Raj structure the Block is
A. the highest structure
B. the intermediary structure
C. the lowest structure
D. None of the above

205. The members of the Panchayat are
A. elected by the people
B. nominated by the district officer

C. nominated by the respective M.L.A.
D. none of the above

206. The function not performed by the village Panchayat is
A. settlement of minor disputes
B. promotion of cottage industries
C. looking after welfare of the backward classes
D. preparation of plans for the development of the areas

207. The Zila Parishad is
A. an implementing body
B. a judicial body
C. a co-ordinating and supervisory body
D. None of the above

208. The Union Public Service Commissions was created by
A. Government of India Act, 1935
B. the Constitution
C. the Civil Services Act, 1951
D. None of the above.

209. The Members of the UPSC are
A. elected by the people
B. nominated by the Parliament
C. appointed by the President
D. appointed by the Council of Ministers

210. The Union Public Service Commission consists of a Chairman and
A. six other members
B. eight other members
C. ten other members
D. unspecified number of members

211. The members of Union Public Service Commission hold office
A. for a term of five years
B. for a term of six years till they attain the age of 65 years
C. for a term of six years till they attain the age of 62 years
D. during the pleasure of the President

212. The members of the UPSC can be removed from their office during their tenure by
A. the President
B. the Parliament
C. the President on the recommendation of the Parliament
D. the President on the report of the Supreme Court of India

213. The members of the State Public Service Commission retire at the
A. age of 60 years
B. age of 62 years
C. age of 65 years
D. None of the above.

214. The UPSC submits an annual report of its work to
A. the President
B. the Parliament
C. the Home Minister
D. anyone of the above

215. A State Public Service Commissions member resigns by writing a letter addressed to the
A. President
B. Governor
C. Chief Minister
D. Chairman of UPSC

216. *Indira Sawhney* vs. *Union of India* is a case popularly known as
A. Mandal judgement
B. Ayodhya judgement
C. Judges Transfer judgement
D. JMM Pay off judgement

217. Latin phrase *"Audi Alteram Partem"* means
A. No one shall be condemned unheard
B. Rights and Duties are co-relative
C. Things speak for itself
D. None of the above

218. Who among the following is known as 'Green Lawyer'?
A. M.C. Mehta
B. Ram Jethmalani
C. Nani A. Palkiwala
D. None of the above

219. Who among the following is known as Green Judge?
A. Hidayatullah, J
B. Kuldeep Singh, J

C. V. N. Khare, J
D. A. S. Anand, J

220. A joint sitting of two houses is called only when
A. One house rejects a Bill
B. more than 6 months elapse and a House neither passes nor returns a Bill
C. both Houses disagree on amendments suggested by other
D. Rajaya Sabha fails to return a Money Bill

221. Article 143 of the Constitution provides for
A. Supreme Courts advisory jurisdiction
B. Special Leave petition
C. Original Jurisdiction of the Supreme Court
D. None of the above

222. Article 136 of the Constitution provides for
A. Special Leave Petition
B. Supreme Court Advisory Jurisdiction
C. Original jurisdiction of the sop
D. None of the above

223. In which case the Supreme Court held that Parliament had no power to amend fundamental rights?
A. Shankari Prasad case
B. Sajjan Singh case
C. Golak Nath case
D. None of the above

224. In which case Supreme Court held that Judicial Review is a basic feature of the constitution and cannot be amended?
A. Golak Nath case
B. Keshvananda Bharti case
C. Minerva Mills case
D. None of the above

225. The only Union Territory having a High Court of its own is
A. Chandigarh
B. Delhi
C. Andaman & Nicobar Islands
D. None of the above

226. In which case Supreme Court held that Art. 21 includes right to die
A. *M. C. Mehta* vs. *Union of India*
B. *Indira Sawhney* vs. *Union of India*
C. P. Rathhinam vs. *Union of India*
D. *Ismail Faruqi* vs. *Union of India*

227. A death sentence passed by a session court
A. must be confirmed by the Supreme Court
B. must be confirmed by the High Court
C. must be confirmed by the President
D. none of the above

228. A minimum how many judges of supreme court can hear a constitutional matter?
A. 3 B. 5
C. 7 D. 9

229. Which among the following is not a source of law?
A. Public opinion
B. Custom
C. Precedent
D. Legislation

230. Who among the following is associated with the drafting of the IPC?
A. Sir Frederic Pollock
B. Lord Macaulay
C. Mulla
D. H.S. Maine

231. Code of Civil Procedure was enacted in the year of
A. 1908 B. 1860
C. 1872 D. 1973

232. Code of criminal Procedure was enacted in the year of
A. 1973 B. 1960
C. 1872 D. 1860

233. Under the provisions of which Act, the parties may refer their disputes to an independent third party instead of regular courts?
A. Consumer Protection Act
B. Arbitration & Conciliation Act
C. Limitation Act
D. Negotiable Instrument Act

234. Transfer of Property Act, 1882, deals with
A. Movable Property

B. Immovable Property only
C. Both the above
D. None of the above

235. The time limit for filing different kinds of suits is contained in
A. Limitation Act
B. Court Fees Act
C. Court Rules of India
D. None of the above.

236. Information Technology Act was enacted in
A. 1999 B. 2000
C. 2001 D. 2002

237. Sale of Good Act, 1930, contains provision regarding
A. Movable property
B. Immovable property
C. Both of the above
D. None of the above

238. The Indian Control Act was enacted in the year of
A. 1860 B. 1872
C. 1876 D. 1870

239. The law relating the diplomatic relation is codified in
A. Geneva Conventions
B. Hague Conventions
C. Vienna Conventions
D. Montreal Conventions

240. According to Indian Majority Act, a major is a person who has attained the age of
A. 16 years B. 18 years
C. 19 years D. 21 years

241. A person whose guardian has been appointed attains the age of majority at the age of
A. 18 years B. 21 years
C. 25 years D. 30 years

242. Which among the following is not an essential ingredient in the formation of contract?
A. Offer
B. Acceptance
C. Consideration
D. Damages

243. Which among the following Article says that Union of India and the States are juristic persons and can sue and be sued?
A. Article 275 B. Article 300
C. Article 311 D. Article 345

244. How many persons are required to constitute a conspiracy?
A. One B. Two
C. Three D. Four

245. How many persons are required to constitute a dacoity?
A. Three B. Four
C. Five D. Six

246. Which section of Indian Penal Code defines Murder?
A. 299 B. 300
C. 301 D. 302

247. Can a woman be charged with offence of adultery?
A. Yes
B. No
C. Depends on circumstances
D. None of the above

248. Possession is said to be
A. Synonymous with ownership
B. 9 points of law
C. Both (a) and (b)
D. None of the above

249. Rights and duties are
A. Not related with each other
B. Co-related
C. Co-ordinated
D. None of the above

250. Article 13 of the Indian Constitution provides for
A. Right to equality
B. Judicial Review
C. State
D. Election

251. In the eye of law a man is presumed to be dead if he is not heard of as alive for
A. 5 years B. 7 years
C. 9 years D. 10 years

252. When a person aids in the Commission of an offence, he is said to be

A. Abettor
B. Accomplice
C. Accessory
D. None of the above

253. A person who makes an affidavit or deposes is known as
A. Defendant
B. Deponent
C. Despot
D. None of the above

254. A formal instrument by which one person empowers another to represent him is called
A. Power of Attorney
B. Instrument representation
C. Negotiable instrument
D. Will

255. A lawyer appointed by court to represent a poor litigant is
A. Public prosecutor
B. Amicus curiae
C. Legal aid man
D. None of the above

256. How many Schedules are in the Constitution of India?
A. Seven B. Eight
C. Nine D. Twelve

257. Who among the following is fourth pillar of Indian Constitution?
A. Attorney General
B. Advocate General
C. Comptroller and Auditor General
D. Lieutenant General

258. Voting right is a
A. Legal right
B. Fundamental right
C. Constitutional right
D. Social right

259. Which among the following is not a fundamental right?
A. Right of Education
B. Right of equality
C. Right to property
D. Right to Religion

260. The fourth pillar of democracy is
A. The people
B. The press
C. The executive
D. None of the above

261. The number of Judges in the International Court of Justice are
A. 14 B. 15
C. 17 D. 20

262. The headquarters of International Court of Justice is located at
A. Hague B. New York
C. Paris D. London

263. Who said that Directive Principles of State Policy are like a cheque on a bank payable at the convenience of the bank?
A. Prof. K.T. Shah
B. B.R. Ambedkar
C. Jawaharlal Nehru
D. Rajendra Prasad

264. The first permanent Lok Adalat was set up in
A. Chandigarh B. Delhi
C. Bhopal D. Patna

265. The High Court comes under
A. State list
B. Union list
C. Concurrent list
D. None of the above

266. The purpose of Election Commission is
A. Constitutional safety
B. Safety otherwise than constitutionally
C. Safety through enactments
D. None of the above

267. The President reconstructs the Finance Commission one in
A. 2 years B. 3 years
C. 4 years D. 5 years

268. Attorney-General of India is
A. Supreme Judicial Power
B. Top most legal advisor of Central Government
C. Advisor to the Supreme Court
D. President of legal system in India

269. When there is a dispute on the Concurrent list which enactment prevails?

A. State Act
B. Central Act
C. The enactment which obtains the President's approval
D. Both the Acts would be cancelled

270. The official language of the Jammu & Kashmir is
A. Dogri B. Urdu
C. Kashmiri D. Hindi

271. Which language is not added in the 8th Schedule of the Constitution?
A. Sindhi B. Marathi
C. Kashmiri D. English

272. The age limit for contesting the election to Lok Sabha is
A. 18 years B. 21 years
C. 25 years D. 35 years

273. Which article declares Hindi in Devnagri Script as official language?
A. 243 B. 343
C. 334 D 423

274. The salary and allowances of the President is decided by
A. Prime Minister
B. Council of Minister
C. Parliament
D. President himself

275. Which article among the following mandates that no person can be discriminated on the basis of nationality, caste, religion, creed or sex?
A. Article 14 B. Article 15
C. Article 25 D. Article 32

276. Child labour is prohibited under Article
A. 24 B. 25
C. 26 D. 28

277. Articles 25 to 28 refer to the rights of
A. Schedule Castes & Schedule Tribes
B. Religious Minorities
C. Children
D. Women

278. Who among the following was first chief Election Commissioner of India?
A. T. N. Seshan
B. Sukumar Sen
C. K.V.K. Sundaram
D. Dr. Nagendra Singh

279. Which among the following Articles was not affected by 1st Amendment 1951?
A. Article 15 B. Article 16
C. Article 19 D. Article 85

280. In which part of the Constitution provisions regarding the Panchayats are made?
A. Part III B. Part IV
C. Part IX D. Part X

281. Which Article of the Constitution prohibits untouchability and make it an offence?
A. Article 16 B. Article 17
C. Article 18 D. Article 19

282. Which among the following Articles provides for 'equal pay for equal work for all males and females'?
A. Article 14 B. Article 39
C. Article 40 D. Article 41

283. Ordinance making power of Governor is contained in
A. Article 211 B. Article 212
C. Article 213 D. Article 233

284. Under which Article special status has been given to the State of J&K?
A. Article 44 B. Article 370
C. Article 368 D. Article 356

285. The Constitution amendment bill can be introduced
A. Only in Lok Sabha
B. Only in Rajya Sabha
C. Either of the House
D. In Supreme Court only

286. Seventh Schedule of the Indian Constitution contains
A. Provisions as to the administration of tribal areas
B. List of States
C. List of languages
D. Union list, State list and Concurrent list

287. The President can be removed before the expiry of his official term by

A. Prime Minister
B. Impeachment
C. Supreme Court
D. None of the above

288. The High Court judges are appointed by the President with the approval of
A. Chief Justice of India
B. Governor
C. Chief Justice of High Court
D. None of the above

289. The States have their representation in Rajya Sabha on the basis of
A. Population
B. Area
C. Lok Sabha seat
D. None of these

290. Which among the following lists contains maximum number of entries?
A. Union list
B. State list
C. Concurrent list
D. None of the above

291. The High Courts can issue writs under
A. Article 32 B. Article 426
C. Article 226 D. Article 368

292. Under Article 53 executive power vests with
A. The Prime Minister
B. The President
C. The Governor
D. The Parliament

293. The Fundamental Right to Property was converted into legal right by
A. 42nd Amendment
B. 43rd Amendment
C. 44th Amendment
D. 45th Amendment

294. The Comptroller and Auditor General is described as the friend, philosopher and guide of
A. the Finance Minister
B. the Public Accounts Committee
C. All the Parliamentary Committees
D. None of the above

295. The Supreme Court of India was set up
A. By the Constitution
B. By a President Order
C. By a Law of Parliament
D. None of the above

296. Which Article vests with executive power with President?
A. Article 52 B. Article 53
C. Article 54 D. Article 55

297. The Supreme Court consist of a Chief Justice and
A. 30 other judges
B. 40 other judges
C. 35 other judges
D. 25 other judges

298. The First Amendment to the Constitution was effected in the year of
A. 1950 B. 1951
C. 1952 D. 1953

299. The minimum age limit of election to the office of Vice-President is
A. 25 years B. 30 years
C. 35 years D. 40 years

300. The Chairman of the Constituent Assembly was
A. B.R. Ambedkar
B. Rajendra Prasad
C. Jawaharlal Nehru
D. C. Rajagopalachari

301. What is meant by affidavit?
A. a written document
B. evidentiary document
C. letter of oath
D. none of the above

302. Who among the following has the power to grand pardon?
A. Chief Justice of India
B. Prime Minister
C. President
D. All of the above

303. Which article of Indian Constitution pertains to preventive detention?
A. 21 B. 22
C. 23 D. 24

304. How many legislative entries are in the Union List?

A. 67 B. 72
C. 87 D. 99

305. Fourth Schedule of the Constitution is related to
A. List of States
B. List of Languages
C. The representation of States and Centrally administered regions
D. None of the above.

306. How many legislative entries are included in the State list?
A. 36 B. 46
C. 56 D. 61

307. The Election Commission is
A. a Constitutional body
B. a legal body
C. a governmental institution
D. none of these

308. Who is the Chairman of the Public Accounts Committee?
A. The President
B. The Prime Minister
C. Union Finance Minister
D. Opposition member or leader

309. Who is the final authority to appoint judges in the District?
A. The Chief Minister
B. The Governor
C. The High Court
D. The Legislative Assembly

310. How many kind of writs can be issued by the Supreme Court as well as High Courts?
A. 3 B. 4
C. 5 D. 6

311. The Chairman of the Public Account Committee is appointed by the
A. Speaker
B. Parliament
C. President
D. Prime Minister

312. Who among the following is "a moon among stars, sun controlling the movements of several planet?
A. President
B. Prime Minister
C. Vice-President
D. Speaker

313. De facto recognition means
A. Recognition in fact
B. Recognition in law
C. Both (a) and (b)
D. None of the above

314. De Jure recognition means
A. Recognition in fact
B. Recognition in law
C. Both (a) and (b)
D. None of the above

315. According to the requirement the number of the judges of the Supreme Court can be increased by
A. The President
B. The Chief Justice of India
C. The Prime Minister
D. None of the above

316. How long can Rajya Sabha keep a Finance Bill with it without approving it?
A. 12 days B. 14 days
C. 18 days D. 20 days

317. In democracy the Government belongs to
A. Prime Minister
B. President
C. Political parties
D. People

318. The Fundamental Rights are
A. Justiciable
B. Not justiciable
C. Not enforceable
D. None of these

319. The Fundamental Right has been conferred on
A. Citizen only
B. All persons
C. Citizen in some cases and all persons in others
D. Legal persons only

320. The Preamble to the Indian Constitution seeks to secure to Indian Citizens
A. justice, liberty, equality and fraternity
B. a good nation
C. a strong government
D. none of the above

321. If a person is detained, which writ will be issued for his production before the court?
A. Habeas Corpus
B. Mandamus
C. Certiorari
D. Injunction

322. Who is the head of the Defense Forces?
A. President
B. Defense Minister
C. Army General
D. Prime Minister

323. The Constitution of India is
A. Federal
B. Purely unitary
C. Neither federal nor unitary
D. Partly federal and partly unitary

324. In a Parliamentary system the executive is responsible to
A. The legislative
B. The people directly
C. The judiciary
D. None of the above

325. The soul of the Constitution is
A. Fundamental Rights
B. Directive Principles of State Policy
C. Preamble
D. Judiciary

326. The qualification for obtaining voting right in India is
A. Religion B. Caste
C. Age D. Property

327. Universal Adult Franchise was for the first time introduced in India under
A. The Government of India Act, 1935
B. The Indian Independence Act, 1947
C. The Constitution of India
D. None of the above

328. Who is empowered to suspend the operation of Fundamental Rights?
A. The President
B. The Prime Minister
C. The Council of Minister
D. None of the above

329. On legal issues Central Government is advised by
A. President
B. Advocate-General
C. Attorney General
D. Chief Justice of India

330. Which among the following is correct about the Attorney-General?
A. He is Secretary of Central Government
B. He is the legal advisor of the Central Government
C. He is the Chief Supervisor of Central Audit
D. None of the above

331. The design of the National Flag was adopted by Constituent Assembly on
A. 22 July, 1947
B. 22 July, 1948
C. 26 January, 1950
D. 15 August, 1947

332. Which Article of the Constitution has recognized 'Hindi' as an official language?
A. Article 344 B. Article 345
C. Article 354 D. Article 355

333. The responsibility of conducting free and fair election lies with
A. President
B. Chief Election Commissioner
C. Chief Justice of India
D. Political parties

334. The Election Commission is appointed by
A. President
B. Prime Minister
C. Parliament
D. Supreme Court

335. When was the National Anthem adopted by the Constituent Assembly?
A. 24th January, 1950
B. 26th January, 1950
C. 15th August, 1947
D. 14th August, 1947

336. When did the separate Constitution of Jammu and Kashmir become effective?
A. 26th January, 1957
B. 26th January, 1958
C. 26th January, 1959
D. 26th January, 1960

337. When a bill becomes an Act?
- A. when it is passed by both the Houses and assented to by the President
- B. when the Prime Minister assent to it
- C. when the Law Minister approves it
- D. when it is passed by both the Houses

338. First Information Report (FIR) means
- A. a compliant given to a magistrate by a person regarding commission of an offence
- B. an information given by an informant to the police relating to the commission of cognizable offence
- C. any report given to police officer
- D. None of the above

339. What is cognizable offence?
- A. An offence for which police officer may arrest without warrant
- B. An offence which is related to human body
- C. An offence for which death sentence is prescribed
- D. None of the above

340. *Lex Loci* means
- A. Natural law
- B. International law
- C. General law
- D. Law of the land

341. *Lex Scripta* means
- A. General law
- B. Statutory law
- C. Inter-state law
- D. None of these

342. Plaint means
- A. The claim statement filed by the plaintiff
- B. Statement of reasons
- C. Statement which selects the facts
- D. None of the above

343. Benefit of doubt is always given to
- A. the accused
- B. the plaintiff
- C. the injured
- D. None of these

344. When a will is altered or new additional matter is added it is known as
- A. Codicil
- B. Replication
- C. Rejoinder
- D. None of these

345. In what proportion the members of the Rajya Sabha retire?
- A. one-third members retire every two year
- B. one-sixth members retire every year
- C. Half of the members retire every three year
- D. None of the above

346. The quorum of the Rajya Sabha consists of
- A. 50 members
- B. one-third of its total membership
- C. one-fourth of its total membership
- D. None of the above

347. The person arrested must be produced before the court within
- A. 24 hours of his arrest
- B. a week of his arrest
- C. a month of his arrest
- D. None of the above

348. Who is the legal advisor to the State Government?
- A. Advocate-General
- B. Solicitor General
- C. Attorney-General
- D. Chief Justice of High Court

349. Rajya Sabha is also known as
- A. Lower House
- B. Upper House
- C. Council of Representatives
- D. None of these

350. Lok Sabha is also known as
- A. Lower House
- B. Upper House
- C. Council of Representatives
- D. None of these

351. Which is Zero hour?
- A. when matter of utmost importance are raised
- B. when money bill is introduced in Lok Sabha
- C. when proposals of opposition are considered

D. Interval between morning and evening session

352. How many languages have been recognized in the Indian Constitution?

A. 14 B. 15
C. 16 D. 22

353. Judge of a High court can hold office upto the age of

A. 55 years B. 58 years
C. 62 years D. 65 years

354. Which Articles of the Indian Constitution provides the Parliament the power to amend the Constitution?

A. Article 356 B. Article 360
C. Article 368 D. Article 390

355. Which among the following has no legislative council?

A. Tripura
B. Karnataka
C. Uttar Pradesh
D. Bihar

356. Representation of any State in Rajya Sabha is according to

A. population of the state
B. area of the state
C. number of representative in Lok Sabha
D. None of the above

357. From which country's Constitution we have borrowed Parliamentary privileges?

A. Australia B. Canada
C. U.S.A. D. British

358. The salary and other allowances of the judges of the High Courts are charged to the

A. Consolidated Fund of India
B. Consolidated Fund of the State
C. Consolidated Fund of India and the State
D. Contingency Fund of India

359. A money Bill can originate in the State Legislature only with the prior consent of the

A. President
B. Governor
C. Chief Minister
D. None of the above

360. The judges of the High Court can be removed from their office during their tenure

A. by the Governor
B. by the Chief Justice of India
C. by the Chief Justice on the advice of the President
D. by the President on the basis of a resolution passed by the Parliament by two-thirds majority

361. From which country's Constitution we have borrowed the Concurrent list?

A. Australia B. British
C. Canada D. U.S.A.

362. A Presidential Ordinance can remain in force for

A. two months
B. six months
C. one year
D. so long the President desires

363. The Committee of Indian Parliament which has the larger membership is

A. the Public Accounts Committee
B. The Estimates Committee
C. Committee on Privileges
D. The Committee on Public undertakings

364. A Uniform Civil Code will ensure

A. economic equality
B. national security
C. national integration
D. upliftment of weaker section in society

365. Cultural and Educational rights have been incorporated with the object of

A. preserving Indian culture
B. evolving a single culture
C. eradicating illiteracy
D. helping minorities to conserve their culture

366. In the Indian polity ultimate sovereignty rests with

A. the people
B. the Parliament
C. the President
D. the Constitution

367. The ideals of 'liberty, equality and fraternity' enshrined in Preamble of the Indian Constitution was inspired by the
A. French Revolution
B. Russian Revolution
C. Irish Revolution
D. None of the above

368. Which part of the Constitution reflects the mind and ideals of the framers?
A. Preamble
B. Fundamental Rights
C. Directive Principles of State Policy
D. Amending Power

369. The executive power is vested in the President but it is actually used by him on the advice of
A. the Prime Minister
B. the Council of Ministers
C. the Parliament
D. None of the above

370. The position of the Vice-President of India resembles, to a great extent, the position of Vice-President of
A. Italy B. Japan
C. Russia D. USA

371. The ministers are individually responsible to
A. the President
B. the House of the People
C. the Prime Minister
D. the People of India directly

372. The oath to the President is administered by
A. the Chief Justice of India
B. the Speaker of Lok Sabha
C. the Prime Minister
D. None of the above

373. The Deputy Chairman of the Rajya Sabha is
A. nominated by the President
B. nominated by the Chairman
C. elected by the Rajya Sabha from amongst its members
D. None of the above

374. Who is considered the guardian of the Public Purse?
A. The President
B. The Parliament
C. Comptroller and Auditor-General
D. Public Accounts Committee

375. As a result of prorogation which of the following is not affected?
A. Bills B. Motions
C. Notices D. Resolutions

376. The Union Legislature can legislate on a subject in state list
A. if the President calls upon it do so
B. if the Rajya Sabha passes a resolution that is necessary in national interest to do so
C. if the speaker certifies that it is necessary
D. if there is national emergency

377. Separation of the Judiciary from the executive has been provided in
A. Part III of the Constitution
B. Article 123 of the Constitution
C. The Seventh Schedule of the Constitution
D. None of the above

378. Residuary subjects are those subjects which are
A. provided in the State list
B. provided in the Union list
C. provided in the Concurrent list
D. not covered by any of the three lists

379. Schedule which details the territories of the States and Union territories is
A. Schedule 1
B. Schedule 7
C. Schedule 9
D. Schedule 12

380. Scheme of the Indian Federation is based on the
A. Constitution of Canada
B. Constitution of Australia
C. Constitution of Britain
D. Constitution of USSR

381. Panchayati Raj comes in the
A. State list
B. Union list
C. Concurrent list
D. None of the above

382. Legislative Assembly of a State cannot consist of less than
A. Fifty members
B. Sixty members
C. Seventy members
D. Hundred members

383. Legislative Assembly of a State cannot consist of more than
A. three hundred members
B. four hundred members
C. five hundred members
D. six hundred members

384. High Court of the Union Territory of Puducherry falls in
A. Bombay
B. Madras
C. Hyderabad
D. None of the above

385. Special status of Jammu & Kashmir implies that the State has
A. its own official language
B. a separate Constitution
C. its own territory
D. its own official religion

386. Which Article of the Indian Constitution contains the composition, powers and functions of the Election Commission?
A. Article 176
B. Article 324
C. Article 349
D. None of the above

387. The person who is the ex-officio chairman of all parliamentary committee is
A. the President
B. the Prime Minister
C. the Speaker of Lok Sabha
D. None of the above

388. Who generally presides over the meetings of the Gram Sabha?
A. Sarpanch
B. Tehsildar
C. Mukhiya
D. Member of Legislative Assembly

389. Who is considered to be the first citizen of the country?
A. The President
B. The Prime Minister
C. The Speaker of Lok Sabha
D. None of the above

390. Gram Sabha meets
A. once a year
B. twice a year
C. thrice a year
D. None of the above

391. Governor of the State is responsible for his acts to
A. the Chief Minister
B. the Prime Minister
C. the President
D. none of the above

392. Name the offer by which nationalist demand for a Constituent Assembly was for the first time conceded by the British Government indirectly and with reservations in it:
A. Round Table Conference
B. August Offer
C. Cabinet mission plan
D. Simla pact

393. The Constituent Assembly that finally framed Constitution of India was set up:
A. Under Indian Independence Act
B. Under the Cabinet Mission Plan, 1946
C. Mountbatten Plan
D. None of the above

394. How the members of the Constituent Assembly were elected - Directly or Indirectly?
A. Directly by the public
B. Through political parties
C. Indirectly elected by the Provincial Assemblies.
D. Indirectly by the public

395. Who was head of the Drafting Committee of the Constitution?
A. Dr. Rajendra Prasad
B. Mahatma Gandhi
C. B.R. Ambedkar
D. Jawahar Lal Nehru

396. The Constituent Assembly arrived at decisions on the various provisions of the Constitution:

A. By simple discussion
B. By consensus
C. By reference to president
D. None of the above

397. Who is considered to be the architect of the Indian Constitution?
A. Dr. Rajendra Prasad
B. B.R. Ambedkar
C. Sardar patel
D. Md. Ali Jinnah

398. The British Indian membership of Constituent Assembly did not include:
A. representatives of the public
B. Members of Muslim League
C. Communist Party
D. Indian States

399. The first meeting of Constituent Assembly was held on:
A. 9th December, 1947
B. 4th August, 1945
C. 27th October, 1947
D. 30th January 1950

400. The Constitutional Adviser to the Constituent Assembly was:
A. B.N. Rao
B. B.R. Ambedkar
C. Dr. Rajendra Prasad
D. Md. Ali Jinnah

401. The provisions relating to citizenship in the constitution came into force on:
A. 30th December, 1949
B. 26th November, 1949
C. 26th May, 1948
D. 25th July, 1946

402. The objectives resolution in the Constituent Assembly was moved by:
A. B.R. Ambedkar
B. Jawahar Lal Nehru
C. Dr. Rajendra Prasad
D. None of the above

403. The reasons for the constitution of India being the bulkiest in the world are:
A. Various types of emergencies are considered in detail and it contains not only a list of fundamental rights but also restrictions to be placed on them
B. It contains the Union, State and Concurrent list
C. It contains the provisions relating to writs in the High Court and Supreme Court
D. None of the above

404. The Indian constitution establishes a secular state means:
A. No one would be allowed to observe his religion
B. State would harass religious activities
C. (i) The state treats all the religions equally.
(ii) Freedom of faith and worship is allowed to all the people.
(iii) The state makes no discrimination on the basis of religion in the matters of employment.
D. Freedom of religion is restricted

405. The most profound influence on the drafting of the Indian Constitution was exercised by —
A. the Cabinet Mission Plan
B. the Indian Independence Act
C. the Mountbatten Plan
D. the Government of India Act, 1935

406. The Provisions relating to the suspension of fundamental rights during National Emergency have been borrowed from:
A. US Constitution
B. UK Constitution
C. Weimar Constitution of Germany
D. Constitution of Switzerland

407. The concept of concurrent list in the constitution have been borrowed from:
A. the American Constitution
B. the Australian Constitution
C. the French Constitution
D. the Constitution of Germany

408. Which Constitution has inspired the Indian concepts of rule of law, parliamentary system and law-making procedure?
A. British Constitution.
B. French Constitution

C. American Constitution
D. Constitution of Switzerland

409. The correct order in which the words 'Socialist,' 'Democratic,' 'Sovereign' and 'Secular' are given in the constitution is?
A. Socialist, Sovereign, Democratic, Secular
B. Sovereign, Socialist, Secular, Democratic
C. Sovereign, Secular, Socialist, Democratic
D. Democratic, Sovereign, Socialist, Secular

410. The Constitution is declared to have been adopted and enacted by —
A. the Government of India
B. the President of India
C. the Legislature, Executive and Judiciary of India
D. the People of India

411. The Preamble enshrines the ideals of "liberty, equality and fraternity"— these ideals are inspired by —
A. the French Revolution
B. the Swiss Constitution
C. the American Constitution
D. the British Constitution

412. The Preamble enshrines certain ideals that were first spelt out in:
A. Government of India Act
B. The Objectives Resolution adopted by the Constituent Assembly
C. British Constitution
D. French Constitution

413. The four significant things that emerge clearly from the preamble of the Constitution are:
A. (i) When the constitution was enacted.
(ii) The ideals that were to be achieved.
(iii) The system of the government.
(iv) The source of authority.
B. Federal feature of the constitution, the ideals to be achieved procedure of litigation in the civil courts, rule of law
C. The system of government, ways for peace and tranquility in country, source of funding for running the government, recruitment process of government employees
D. None of the above

414. Which one of the following statements regarding the Preamble is correct?
A. It is enforceable in the court of law
B. It has never been amended
C. It is not enforceable in a court of law
D. None of the above

415. The name of the Union given in the Constitution is:
A. *Bharat* that is India
B. *Hindustan*
C. India that is *Hindustan*
D. India that is *Bharat*

416. Choose the best option – The 'Union of India' consists of (i) States, (ii) Union Territories and (iii) Acquired Territories:
A. Union Territories of acquired territories
B. State as acquired territories
C. States
D. All of the above

417. What type of majority is needed in the parliament for the alteration of the territory of the units of the Indian Federation?
A. Special majority
B. Simple majority
C. Special majority with notification for states
D. Simple majority with notification from states

418. Which of the state was carved out from the original state of Maharashtra?
A. Gujarat B. Haryana
C. Goa D. Punjab

419. The States Reorganisation Act created …… States and ……… Union Territories
A. 11; 7 B. 14; 6
C. 12; 8 D. 13; 7

420. Among Himachal Pradesh, Manipur, Sikkim and Tripura, which of them were union territories before becoming state?
A. Himachal Pradesh, Manipur, Sikkim
B. Himachal Pradesh, Sikkim, Tripura
C. Manipur, Sikkim, Tripura
D. Himachal Pradesh, Manipur, and Tripura

421. The correct order of the creation of Asom, Nagaland, Goa and Mizoram is:
A. Asom, Nagaland, Mizoram and Goa
B. Nagaland, Asom, Mizoram, Goa
C. Goa, Asom, Mizoram, Nagaland
D. Mizoram, Nagaland, Goa, Asom

422. The State of Maharashtra was created in:
A. 1960 B. 1970
C. 1965 D. 1956

423. Which of the territory of India was ceded by the French of India?
A. Andman Nicobar Island
B. Lakshadweep
C. Karaikal, Mahe
D. Goa

424. The old name of Karnataka was:
A. Karnataka itself
B. Tamil Nadu
C. State of Mysore
D. None of the above

425. The Constitution bestows .... citizenship on the people of India:
A. Dual
B. Single
C. Single as well as Dual
D. None of the above

426. Is holding of property a condition for acquiring Indian citizenship?
A. Yes
B. No
C. It was not the condition before year 2000 but now it is must
D. None of the above

427. In which Act details on how citizenship may be acquired and terminated are enumerated?
A. Constitution of India
B. Civil Procedure Code, 1908
C. Code of Criminal Procedure, 1972
D. The Citizenship Act, 1955

428. The Citizenship Act, 1955 was amended so that citizenship by birth is conferred on those who have been born on or after January 26, 1950 but before June 30, 1987? The later cut-off date was included because—
A. of governmental family planning programme
B. because of population explosion in the country
C. both A and B
D. of an excessive number of refugees from Sri Lanka and Bangladesh

429. A person can become a citizen of India even if born outside India if his/her
A. Father is a citizen of India at the time of the person's birth
B. Father surrenders his citizenship to the govt. of India
C. Father is NRI
D. None of the above

430. To acquire citizenship by registration a person must have been resident in India for ... immediately before making an application
A. Six years
B. Five years
C. Seven years
D. Twenty years

431. Which of the following factors do not explain why the rights included in Part III of the constitution are called 'fundamental'?
I. They are equally available to citizens and aliens.
II. They are superior to ordinary law.
III. They are fundamental for governing the country.
IV. They are not absolute.
A. I, III and IV
B. I, II and IV
C. II, III and IV
D. I, II and III

432. The Fundamental Right to ... has been deleted by the ... Amendment Act
A. religion; 39th
B. property, 42nd
C. property; 44th
D. liberty; 44th

433. Which statement/s is/are not correct regarding the Fundamental Rights?

I. Some of these rights are not available to the Armed Forces.

II. They are automatically suspended when any emergency is proclaimed by the President.

III. The President alone can decide upon modifying their application to Armed Forces.

IV. They cannot be amended as they form a basic feature of the Constitution.

A. I, II and III
B. I, II and IV
C. II, III and IV
D. I, III and IV

434. Which of the following Fundamental Rights are available to Indian citizens but not to aliens?

I. Equality before Law.
II. Freedom of expression and speech.
III. Right of minorities to conserve their language and culture.
IV. Protection to life and liberty.

A. I and III
B. III and IV
C. II and III
D. I and II

435. Who decides about the reasonableness of the restrictions placed on Fundamental Rights?

A. Legislature
B. Executive
C. Courts
D. None of the above

436. The right to constitutional remedies in India is available to—

A. Members of Parliaments
B. Government employees
C. Any person for enforcing any right
D. Any person for enforcing any of the fundamental rights conferred on all persons

437. Which writ is called the bulwark of personal freedom?

A. Habeas corpus
B. Mandamus
C. Certiorari
D. Quo-warranto

438. Regarding equality before law, the Indian Constitution makes exceptions in the case of

A. The Prime Minister
B. The President or a Governor
C. The Chief Minister
D. Member of Parliament

439. Censorship of the press has to be judged by

A. The test of reasonableness
B. Courts of India
C. Law making bodies
D. None of the above

440. Freedom of speech and expression are restricted in the Constitution on grounds of—

I. Defamation.
II. Contempt of court.
III. Protecting a scheduled tribe.
IV. Friendly relations with foreign states.

A. II, III and IV
B. I, II and IV
C. I, II and III
D. I, III and IV

441. The Constitution allows preventive detention but stipulates

A. That no one should be detained beyond fifteen days
B. That no one should be detained beyond one month unless an advisory bound authorizes detention beyond that period
C. That no one should be detained beyond three months unless an Advisory Board authorises detention beyond that period
D. None of the above

442. The right against exploitation prohibits children—

A. Below 18 years of age from being employed in hazardous occupations
B. below 12 years of age from being employee in hazardous occupations

C. Below 14 years of age from being employed in hazardous occupations.
D. None of the above

443. Which of the following comes under Right to Equality?
I. Non-discrimination by State on grounds of religion or race
II. Equal protection of the laws
III. Equal pay for equal work
IV. Equality of opportunity in matters of employment under the State
A. I, III and IV
B. II, III and IV
C. I ,II and III
D. I, II and IV

444. Which of the following can impose reasonable restrictions on the Fundamental Rights of the Indian citizens?
A. Parliament
B. President
C. Parliament and President jointly
D. None of the above

445. In case of proclamation of Emergency on grounds of war or external aggression—
A. The President may order the suspension of enforcement of any fundamental right except Article 20-21
B. The President may order the supervision of enforcement of any fundamental right except Article 14-15
C. The President may order the suspension of enforcement of any fundamental right except Art. 18-19
D. The President may order the suspension of enforcement of any fundamental right except Article 32

446. The Constitution
I. forbids the practice of untouchability
II. prescribes penalties for practicing untouchability
III. defines untouchability as a vicious historical practice
A. I and II only B. III only
C. I only D. IV only

447. The Fundamental Rights in Indian Constitution primarily act as limitations upon the powers of the—
I. Executive
II. Legislature
III. Individuals
A. II only B. III only
C. I and II only D. I. only

448. Which of the following are matched wrongly?
I. *Habeas corpus*—literally means 'to have a body'
II. *Mandamus*—commands a person to perform a public duty
III. *Quo warranto*—issued to a lower court to stop proceedings in a case
IV. *Prohibition*—issued to a lower court quashing a decision or order
A. I and II B. II and III
C. I and III D. III and IV

449. A proclamation of national emergency automatically suspends—
A. Right to freedom.
B. Right to life and liberty
C. Right to protection in respect of conviction for offences
D. None of the above

450. Which part of the constitution elaborates the concept of a welfare state?
A. Directive principles
B. Fundamental rights
C. Preamble
D. None of the above

451. Which of the following is/are listed among the Directive Principles in Part IV?
I. Equal pay for equal work
II. Uniform civil code
III. Small family norm
IV. Education through mother tongue at primary level
A. I and III B. I and II
C. III and IV D. II and IV

452. Which of the following were added to the Directive Principles by amendments to the Constitution?

I. To protect and improve the environment and safeguard wild life
II. Right of workers to participate in management of industries
III. Right to work
IV. To protect and maintain places of historic interest

A. I and II B. II and III
C. III and IV D. II and IV

453. The enforcement of Directive Principles depend on—
A. Judiciary of the country
B. Will of the Public
C. Time stipulation make in the constitution
D. Resources available to the Government.

454. Which of the Directive Principles cannot be termed as "Gandhian" ?
A. Uniform civil code for the country.
B. Separation of Judiciary from executive
C. Promotion of International peace and security
D. Duty of state to raise the level of nutrition and the standard of living and to improve public health.

455. Which of the following can be listed among the "socialistic" Directive Principle?
I. Prevention of concentration of wealth
II. Right to work
III. Separation of judiciary from executive
IV. Organizing agriculture along scientific

A. I and III
B. I and IV
C. I and II
D. II and IV

456. Which Constitutional Amendment granted a primacy to all the Directive Principles over Fundamental Rights?
A. 44th B. 39th
C. 68th D. 42nd

457. If the State enacts a law to implement a Principle calling for equitable distribution of the material resources of the community, it—
A. is put in the ninth schedule
B. shall not be considered void if it violates a fundamental right
C. shall not be considered void even if it rights in Articles 14 and 19.
D. can be stuck down by the Supreme Court on the grounds violates the fundamental rights.

458. Which of the following statements is/are not indicative of the difference between Fundamental rights and Directive Principles?
I. Directive Principles are aimed at promoting welfare, while Fundamental Rights are for protecting individuals from State encroachment
II. Fundamental Rights are limitations on state action while Directive Principles are positive instructions for the Government to work towards a just socio-economic order
III. Fundamental Rights were included in the constitution, but Directive Principles were added by the first Amendment
IV. Fundamental Rights are amendable, but Directive Principles cannot be amended

A. I and II
B. III and IV
C. II and III
D. I and IV

459. The Fundamental Duties were included in the constitution with the idea of—
A. curbing subversive and unconstitutional
B. for the enforcement of fundamental right
C. for the implement of directive principles
D. for maintaining law and order in the country

460. Which of the options is not true? The Fundamental Duties—
   I. were introduced by the 44th Amendment
   II. are incorporated in Part III-A
   III. are not justiciable
   A. I and II only B. II and III only
   C. III only D. II only

461. The provision relating to the protection of children from hazardous industries is included in the fundamental duties in the constitution-True or False:
   A. False
   B. True
   C. It is indirectly included in the fundamental duties
   D. It has nothing to do with fundamental duties

462. Which of the following are among the Fundamental Duties as listed in the Constitution?
   I. To preserve the heritage of our composite culture
   II. To abide by the Constitution
   III. To strive for excellence in scientific research to win international fame
   IV. To render national service when called upon to do so
   A. II, III and IV B. I, II and III
   C. I, III and IV D. I, II and IV

463. Among the following four options which one cannot be considered a valid reason for the slow implementation of the directive principle of state policy:
   (i) Lack of resources with the Government.
   (ii) Lack of political will.
   (iii) Opposition from the society.
   (iv) The vastness of the country causing difficulty.
   A. Lack of resources with the government
   B. Lack of political will
   C. Opposition from the society
   D. The vastness of the country causing difficulty

464. Part V of the Constitution deals with—
   I. Union Executive
   II. Parliament
   III. Supreme Court and High Courts
   IV. Comptroller and Auditor-General
   A. I, II and III
   B. I, II and IV
   C. II, III and IV
   D. I, III and IV

465. The Indian system of government is based on the pattern obtained from—
   A. France B. U.S.A.
   C. Britain D. Switzerland

466. The executive authority of the Union is vested by the Constitution in the—
   A. President
   B. Prime Minister
   C. Supreme Court of India
   D. All of the above

467. Which of the following groups take/takes part in the election of the President of India?
   I. Elected Members of both the Houses of Parliament
   II. Members of State Legislative Assemblies
   III. Elected members of Legislative Assemblies of States
   IV. Elected members of State Legislative Councils
   A. I only B. I and III only
   C. II and III only D. III only

468. Each member of Parliament who participates in the Presidential election is entitled to cast as many votes as are obtained by dividing the total number of votes of the Legislative Assemblies of all the States by the total number of elected members of the two Houses of Parliament. This ensures—
   A. Parity between the voting strengths of the States and the Parliament
   B. Seperation of executive from judiciary
   C. Rule of law
   D. Doctrine of colourable legislation

469. The President takes an oath before assuming office in the presence of the Chief

Justice of India. If the Chief Justice is not available, he takes the oath in the presence of—

A. Any judge of the Supreme Court
B. The senior-most judge of the Supreme Court
C. Prime Minister
D. Vice President

470. From which date does the president holds his office for a term of five years?

A. From the date of election
B. From the date of his entering the office.
C. From the date appointed by the Prime Minister
D. From the date of his address to the Parliament

471. Disputes regarding the election of the President and Vice-President are settled—

A. In the Supreme Court
B. Delhi High Court
C. Any Court of India
D. None of the above

472. Put in chronological order the following names of Presidents of India—

I. Dr. S. Radhakrishnan
II. V.V. Giri
III. Dr. Zakir Hussain
IV. Neelam Sanjeeva Reddy

A. I, III, II, IV
B. II, I, III, IV
C. III, IV, I, II
D. I, II, III, IV

473. Which of the following can contest a Presidential election?

I. Anyone who has attained the age to contest a Lok Sabha election
II. A member of the State Legislature
III. A citizen of India
IV. The Vice-President of India

A. I, II and III
B. I, II and IV
C. II, III and IV
D. I, III and IV

474. The vice-president who assumes the office of the president in case of vacancy due to death holds it for the period of—

A. Six months at most
B. One year at most
C. Two months at most
D. Four weeks at most

475. Where can impeachment proceedings against the President be initiated?

A. Supreme Court of India
B. Any High Court of the Country
C. Lok Sabha only
D. In either House of Parliament

476. Name the President who resigned as vice-president to contest for the office of the President?

A. Dr. Radhakrishnan
B. Neelam Sanjeeva Reddy
C. V.V. Giri
D. A.P.J. Abdul Kalam

477. Who elects the Vice-President?

A. Lok Sabha members
B. An electoral college consisting of members of Parliament.
C. Rajya Sabha members
D. State legislatures only

478. The Vice-President's letter of resignation is to be addressed to the—

A. Prime Minister
B. Chief Justice of the Supreme Court of India
C. Home Minister of the Union of India
D. President

479. The candidate for Vice-Presidential election must possess the qualifications prescribed for the Presidential candidate except that he must be—

A. Graduate
B. Qualified to be a member of the Rajya Sabha.
C. Qualified to be a member of Lok Sabha
D. Post Graduate

480. Who has the authority to remove the Vice-President from his office before the expiry of his term?

A. Supreme Court of India

B. President
C. Parliament
D. Prime Minister

481. The President addresses his resignation letter to the—
A. Vice-President.
B. Prime Minister
C. Chief Justice of India
D. Home Minister of Union of India

482. Does the constitution of India allow the re-election of a person to the President's post?
A. No
B. Twice only
C. Thrice only
D. Yes

483. A resolution for impeaching the President can be moved after at least fourteen days' notice signed by—
A. Prime Minister
B. Not less than one-fourth of the total number of members of the House.
C. The speaker of the Lok Sabha
D. Not less than the fourth of the total number of members of the House

484. From which date the President is considered to have been removed from his office if a resolution impeaching the President is passed?
A. From the date on which the resolution was put before members of the house
B. From the date on which the resolution is passed.
C. From the date when it is signed by Prime Minister
D. None of the above

485. Does the "office of profit" which disqualifies a person from being a member of the Union or State legislature include office held under a local authority?
A. Yes
B. No
C. Yes but under certain condition
D. None of the above

486. An election to fill a vacancy in the office of Vice-President occurring by reason of his death, resignation or removal, has to be held—
A. within four weeks
B. within twelve weeks
C. as soon as possible after the occurrence of the vacancy
D. within sixty days

487. If there is a vacancy in the offices of both President and Vice-President, who has been empowered to function as President?
A. Prime Minister of India
B. Home Minister of the Union of India
C. Chief Justice of India
D. Finance Minister of the Union of India

488. Which of the following statements regarding the pardoning powers of the President is/are not correct?
I. He has the pardoning power in respect of sentence by court martial
II. He can grant reprieve and respite in case of punishment for an offence against any law of land, Union or State
III. He alone can pardon a sentence of death
IV. His exercise of the power of pardon is open judicial review
A. I and II
B. II and III
C. II and IV
D. III and IV

489. No person shall be eligible for election as Vice-President, unless he—
I. must be a citizen of India
II. must have completed the age of thirty five years
III. must be qualified for election as a member of the Council of States
IV. must not holds any office of profit under the Government of India or the Government of any state or under any local or other authority subject to the control of any of the said government

A. Only I and III
B. I, II, III and IV
C. Only IV
D. None of these

490. Does the legislative power of the President include the power of nominating 12 members to the Lok Sabha?
A. No
B. Yes
C. Yes but under certain conditions
D. None of the above

491. Name the Chief Justice of India who has acted as the President of India?
A. Shankar Dayal Sharma
B. H.J. Kania
C. M. Hidayatullah
D. Y.N. Chandrachud

492. The executive power is vested in the President but is actually used by him on the advice of—
A. Home Minister of the Union of India
B. The Council of Ministers
C. Chief Justice of India
D. Finance Minister of the Union of India

493. An ordinance can be issued by the President—
A. without any limitation
B. subject to the same constitutional limitations as legislation by Parliament
C. irrespective of the provisions of the constitution
D. None of the above

494. An ordinance promulgated by the President?
A. need not be laid before the parliament
B. Must be laid before Parliament when it reassembles.
C. needs the assent of Prime Minister
D. None of the above

495. Mention certain matters that requires the previous sanction of the President for introducing legislation on it?
A. Ordinary bill
B. (i) A Money bill.
(ii) A bill affecting taxation in which States are interested.
(iii) State bills imposing restrictions upon the freedom of trades.
C. Financial bill
D. None of the above

496. If the President returns a bill to the legislature for reconsideration—
A. A re-passage of the bill by ordinary majority will compel him to give his assent
B. A re-passage of the bill by ordinary majority without compel him to give his assent
C. It cannot be passed by the Parliament again
D. It needs to be passed by special majority

497. The President of India has the power of—
I. absolute veto
II. suspensive veto
III. pocket veto
A. I only
B. II and III only
C. I and III only
D. I, II and III

498. In the matter of State legislation the President—
A. Cannot withhold his assent to any bill reserved for his consideration
B. Empower the Prime Minister to assent the bill
C. Withhold his assent to any bill reserved for his consideration
D. None of the above

499. The Vice-President shall be elected by—
A. Members of Rajya Sabha only
B. Members of Lok Sabha only
C. Members of both Houses of Parliament
D. None of the above

500. The position of the Vice-President of India resembles, to a great extent, the position of the Vice-President of

A. Switzerland
B. France
C. U.S.A.
D. Russia

501. What function is specifically prescribed by the Constitution for the Vice-President of India?
A. To manage the affairs of the Union of India generally
B. No function
C. To manage the law and order situation in the country
D. None of the above

502. When the Vice-President acts as President he gets the emoluments of the
A. Vice President
B. President
C. Prime Minister
D. Chief Justice of India

503. When the Chairman of Rajya Sabha acts as President, the duties of the Chairman are performed by
A. The Deputy Chairman.
B. Prime Minister
C. President
D. Home Minister

504. The President may send the advice received from the Council of Ministers on a matter back to them for reconsideration. This power can be exercised by him .... on the same matter—
A. Twice B. Never
C. Once D. Thrice

505. Can the President of India appoint the chairman of Rajya Sabha?
A. Yes
B. Yes but under certain circumstances he cannot
C. No
D. None of the above

506. Does the President of India have the power to remove the council of ministers?
A. Yes
B. Yes but under certain circumstances only
C. No
D. None of the above

507. Regarding the military powers of the President it would not be true to state that
A. he exercises no control over the armed force
B. he is just a titular head of the military power
C. As a commander-in-chief of India, the President is dependent of legislative control
D. As a commander-in-chief of India, the President is independent of legislative control

508. Does the President of India appoint the Planning Commission?
A. Yes
B. Yes but under certain circumstances
D. No
C. None of the above

509. The office of the Prime Minister of India has been created by?
A. The President
B. The Constitution of India
C. The Chief Justice of India
D. Armed forces of India

510. The Council of Ministers have no option but to resign if it lose the confidence of
A. Lok Sabha
B. Rajya Sabha
C. Parliament
D. None of the above

511. The Ministers are individually responsible to—
A. The President
B. The Prime Minister
C. The Vice President
D. The Chief justice of India

512. The President selects as Prime Minister
I. the leader of the party in majority in Lok Sabha
II. any one he wishes to
III. the person who is in a position to win the confidence of the majority in Lok Sabha
IV. the leader of the party having a majority of seats in either Lok Sabha or Rajya Sabha

A. I or III
B. I or II
C. II or III
D. III or IV

513. The Prime Minister is appointed by?
A. The Chief Justice of India
B. The President
C. Citizen of India
D. The Vice President

514. Ministers may be chosen from
I. Lok Sabha
II. Rajya Sabha
III. Outside the Legislature
IV. All the above
A. I only
B. IV only
C. III only
D. II only

515. In the event of the resignation or death of the Prime Minister, the ministry is?
A. Suspended
B. Cancelled
C. Dissolved
D. Prorogated

516. The Prime Minister is said to hold office during the pleasure of the President but in reality he stays in office as long as he enjoys the confidence of
A. The Rajya Sabha
B. Parliament
C. The Lok Sabha
D. State Assemblies

517. The salary and perquisites of the Prime Minister of India are decided by the—
A. The President
B. The Chief Justice of India
C. The Home Minister and Finance Minister of India
D. Parliament

518. In a parliamentary democracy the—
A. Executive controls legislatures
B. Judiciary controls legislative and Executive
C. Legislature controls the Executive
D. Executive, Legislative and Judiciary are totally independent of each other

519. The portfolios are allocated to the ministers by
A. The President
B. The Chief Justice of India
C. The Prime Minister
D. The Vice President

520. In practice the policy of the Government is shaped by
A. The Cabinet
B. The Prime Minister
C. The President
D. The Chief Justice of India

521. Acts of State done in the name of the President of India are required to be countersigned by way of authentication by
A. A Secretary to the Government
B. Attorney General of India
C. Comptroller and Auditor General of India
D. Chief Justice of India

522. That the Prime Minister acts as a channel of communication between the President and the Council of Ministers is provided by
A. Article 74
B. Article 78
C. Article 368
D. Article 14

523. If the Prime Minister dies in office
A. The President takes over the post of Prime Minister
B. The Home Minister takes over the post of Prime Minister
C. The Council of Ministers is dissolved
D. President deputes some person as Prime Minister

524. Who is regarded as the head of the government?
A. The President
B. The Prime Minister
C. The Supreme Court
D. The Vice President

525. The Attorney-General of India holds office during the pleasure of the
A. Prime Minister

B. President.
C. Chief Justice of India
D. None of the above

526. Which of the following is/are correct with regard to the office of Attorney-General of India?
I. He is a member of the Cabinet
II. He can speak in either House of Parliament and vote on any issue
III. He must be qualified to become a judge of the Supreme Court
IV. His remuneration is fixed by Parliament
A. I only B. II only
C. III only D. IV only

527. Which of the States sends the maximum number of members to the Rajya Sabha?
A. Madhya Pradesh
B. Uttar Pradesh
C. Bihar
D. Maharashtra

528. The maximum number of representatives of the States in Lok Sabha is
A. 420 B. 530
C. 440 D. 501

529. Representatives of Union Territories in Lok Sabha are chosen by
A. Direct election
B. Indirect election
C. President
D. Prime Minister

530. One-third of the members of Rajya Sabha retire every
A. Third Year
B. Fourth Year
C. Fifth Year
D. Two years

531. The term of Rajya Sabha members was fixed by the
A. President
B. Chief Justice of India
C. Parliament
D. Vice President

532. The Deputy Chairman of the Rajya Sabha is
A. Elected by the Lok Sabha from amongst its member
B. Elected by the Rajya Sabha from amongst its members
C. Deputed by President
D. Deputed by Prime Minister

533. At what age can one exercise the right to vote in the general elections?
A. 18 years
B. 20 years
C. 25 years
D. 21 years

534. If an unqualified or disqualified person sits and votes in Parliament
A. He may be fined Rs. 1500 per day of his so sitting
B. He can not be fined at all
C. He may be fined Rs. 1000 per day of his so sitting
D. He may be fined Rs. 500 per day of his so sitting

535. Who decides whether a member of Parliament is subject to any disqualification?
A. President
B. Prime Minister
C. Vice President
D. Chief Justice of India

536. When a resolution for his removal is under consideration, the Speaker?
I. does not take part in the proceedings of the House
II. has no right to vote
III. has the right to speak in the House even though he shall not preside
A. I only B. III only
C. II only D. I and II only

537. A joint sitting may be called
I. only in case of national emergency
II. to enable a Constitutional Amendment to be passed in a hurry
III. when taxes approved by one House are rejected by the other
A. I only B. II only
C. III only D. None of these

538. A money bill cannot be introduced in:
A. Lok Sabha
B. Lok Sabha and Rajya Sabha
C. The Council of States
D. None of these

539. The President addresses both Houses of Parliament assembled together
A. every month
B. at the commencement of the first session of each year
C. once in a week
D. at the commencement of every session in the Parliament

540. According to the Constitution, Amendments cannot be proposed in either House to
A. Money bills
B. Financial bills
C. Ord'nary bills
D. Appropriation bill

541. Consider the following statements on Financial Bill and say which is/are correct—
I. It is the same as a money bill
II. It can be introduced only in the Lok Sabha
III. It can be amended in the Rajya Sabha
IV. It cannot be introduced except on the recommendation of the President
A. II, III and IV
B. I, II and III
C. I, II and IV
D. I, III and IV

542. The Annual Financial Statement is caused to be laid before both Houses of Parliament by the
A. Prime Minister
B. Chief Justice of India
C. Vice President
D. President

543. By 'charged' expenditure is meant—
A. Expenditure from the Consolidated Fund of India which is votable
B. Expenditure of government on which interest is charged by government
C. Expenditure from the Consolidated Fund of India which is non-votable
D. None of the above

544. Which House is better placed with regard to control over the executive?
A. Rajya Sabha
B. Vidhan Sabha
C. Lok Sabha
D. None of the above

545. The privileges enjoyed by the members of Parliament individually include—
A. Freedom of speech irrespective of any limitation
B. Freedom of spending the public funds in his own use in any manner
C. Freedom of attendance as witness while Parliament is in session
D. None of the above

546. Is parliament empowered to remove the chairman of UPSC?
A. Yes
B. No
C. Yes but under certain circumstances
D. None of these

547. Mention some of the "financial committees" of the Parliament:
A. (i) Public accounts committee.
(ii) Estimates committee.
(iii) Committee on public undertaking.
B. Financial Commission of India
C. Planning Commission
D. None of the above

548. The reports relating to the accounts of Union shall be submitted by Comptroller and Auditor-General of India to—
A. The Prime Minister
B. The President
C. Finance Minister
D. None of these

549. All moneys received by or on behalf of the government of India are credited to—
A. The accounts of finance minister of India
B. Prime Minister relief fund
C. Either the consolidated funds of India or the public accounts of India
D. None of the these

550. Members of Rajya Sabha are associated with the Estimates Committee—True or False:
A. True
B. True but under certain conditio·
C. False
D. None of the above

551. Who was the first leader of the Opposition in the Rajya Sabha?
A. Atal Bihari Vajpayee
B. Lal Krishna Advani
C. Kamlapati Tripathi
D. Veer Savarkar

552. The Public Accounts Committee is concerned with the
A. Regularity and economy of expenditure of government
B. Imposition of taxes on citizens of India
C. Maintaining census of India
D. Maintaining defence expenditure of India

553. Formulating policy for national development is the function of the Parliament in India—True or False:
A. True
B. False
C. True but under certain conditions
D. None of the above

554. The Parliament of India consists of—
A. Lok Sabha only
B. President, Lok Sabha and Rajya Sabha
C. Lok Sabha and Rajya Sabha
D. Prime Minister, Lok Sabha and Rajya Sabha

555. The election of the members of the Rajya Sabha is done—Directly or Indirectly:
A. Directly
B. Half of the members are elected directly and remaining half are elected indirectly
C. Indirectly
D. None of the above

556. What is the effect of the prorogation on bill?
A. Bills cease to be inforce
B. Bills are not presented to president for assent
C. The bills are not at all affected
D. None of these

557. A dissolution does not affect a bill
A. That originated in Lok Sabha but has not yet been sent to Rajya Sabha
B. Irrespective of the fact whether it originated in Lok Sabha or Rajya Sabha
C. That originated in the Rajya Sabha but has not yet been sent to Lok Sabha
D. None of the above

558. The Council of States (Rajya Sabha) consists of —
I. 12 members nominated by the President
II. 245 representatives of States
III. 238 representatives of States and UTs
IV. 5 members nominated by the President
A. I and II only
B. I and III only
C. III and IV only
D. II and IV only

559. Which Union Territories are represented in Rajya Sabha at present?
I. Delhi
II. Pondicherry
III. Lakshadweep
IV. Chandigarh
A. I and III only
B. I and II only
C. I and IV only
D. III and IV only

560. A joint sitting is provided for—
I. in the Constitution
II. in case of any bill being rejected in the other House after being passed by one
III. in the event of the Houses disagreeing over the amendments made in any bill
A. I only
B. II only
C. III only
D. II and III both

561. Who presides over a joint sitting of Parliament?
A. President
B. Prime Minister
C. Vice President
D. Speaker

562. An Appropriation Bill—
I. is necessary to draw money from the Consolidated Fund of India

II. cannot be amended to vary the amount of any charged expenditure
III. includes only the expenditure charged on the Consolidated Fund of India
IV. is required to withdraw money from the Contingency Fund of India

A. I and III only
B. II and III only
C. III and IV only
D. I and II only

563. Mention some of the powers by which the Parliament controls the financial system:

I. Parliament has to authorize the levy or collection of any tax.
II. Money can be withdrawn from the consolidated funds of India only if Parliament sanctions it.
III. Through the financial committees that scrutinize government expenditure, the parliament controls the financial system.
IV. Power of judicial review

A. I and II
B. II and IV
C. I, II and III
D. III and IV

564. The union legislature cannot legislate on a subject in the State List unless—

A. President passes an ordinance to that effect
B. Prime Minister permits for the same
C. Lok Sabha passes resolution that it is necessary in the national interest to do so
D. The Rajya Sabha passes a resolution that it is necessary in the national interest to do so

565. At a joint sitting of Parliament what kind of majority is needed for passing a bill?

A. Simple majority of the total number of members of both Houses present and voting
B. Special majority of the total number of members of both houses present
C. Special majority with ratification from half of the states
D. None of these

566. The two Houses of Parliament enjoy coequal powers in all spheres except?

I. financial matters
II. responsibility of the Council of Ministers
III. amendment procedure
IV. election of President

A. I and III only
B. II and III only
C. I and II only
D. III and IV only

567. What kind of representation exists in the Estimates Committee?

A. Direct representation
B. Proportional representation
C. Indirect representation
D. None of these

568. Name a committee which is not created by the Speaker's nomination of members:

A. Public Accounts Committee
B. Public Welfare Committee
C. Committee for Internal Welfare
D. Committee on Public Undertakings

569. Regarding No-Confidence Motion is there any ground that needs to be set out for the motion:

A. No
B. Yes
C. Yes but under certain circumstances
D. None of the above

570. Which of the following actions are not performed by the President?

A. Proroguing Parliament
B. Convening a joint sitting if requested
C. Dissolving the Rajya Sabha
D. Causing the budget to be laid before Parliament

571. Age of a candidate to contest Parliamentary election should not be lesser than—

A. 18 years B. 21 years
C. 25 years D. 26 years

572. Which of the following features restrict the authority of Parliament in India?

I. A written Constitution clearly prescribes its scope of operation

II. The Supreme Court can strike down a law passed by Parliament if it contravenes any of the Constitutional provisions

III. Parliament is limited by the incorporation of the Fundamental Rights in the Constitution

A. I and II only
B. II and III only
C. I and III only
D. All the above

573. Whose function is it to see that no money is spent out of the Consolidated Fund of a State without the authority of the legislature?

A. Attorney General of India
B. Chief Justice of India
C. Comptroller and Auditor-General of India
D. Finance Minister

574. The Comptroller and Auditor-General can be removed from office—

A. By impeachment in the Parliament
B. In the same manner as that prescribed for the removal of a Supreme Court judge
C. By an order of dismissal from Prime Minister
D. By an order of dismissal from Vice President

575. Part VI of the constitution of India lays down a uniform structure for State Governments which is applicable to all states except the state of—

A. Arunachal Pradesh
B. Jammu and Kashmir
C. Manipur
D. Meghalaya

576. The chief executive head of a State is the

A. Chief Minister
B. Inspector General of Police
C. Chief Justice of the state High Court
D. Governor

577. Which among the following are the qualifications to be appointed as the governor of a state?

I. Be a citizen of India.

II. Completed the age of 30 years.

III. Not be a member of Parliament or state legislature.

A. I and III only
B. I and II only
C. II and III only
D. None of the above

578. The Governor holds office during the pleasure of

A. The Prime Minister
B. The President
C. The Chief Minister
D. The Vice President

579. While appointing a Governor, the President generally consults the Chief Minister of the State. This is

A. A matter of convention
B. A mandate
C. A formality
D. A compulsion

580. Consider the given statements and choose the correct response on them

I. A person can be appointed as Governor of more than one State

II. A Governor's salary is charged on the Consolidated Fund of India in case of I

III. In case of I, the Governor's salary is shared by the concerned States

IV. In case of I, the Governor's salary is paid by the State named by the President

A. I and II are correct
B. II and III are incorrect
C. I and III are correct
D. I and IV are correct

581. Who discharges the duties of the office of a Governor if it falls vacant due to death or resignation of the Governor?

A. The Chief Minister of the state
B. The Home Minister of the state
C. The Deputy Chief Minister of the state
D. The Chief Justice of the High Court.

582. The ordinances issued by the Governor are subject to approval by
A. State Legislature.
B. Union Legislature
C. Chief Minister
D. All of the above

583. An ordinance issued by a Governor can remain in force on its own for a maximum period of
A. One year
B. Six weeks
C. Two years
D. Six months

584. The Governor does not appoint
A. Chief Minister
B. Minister of the state
C. Judges of the High Court
D. None of these

585. Point out the powers enjoyed by the President of India but not available to the Governor
I. Diplomatic Powers
II. Pardoning death sentence
III. Veto power over State Legislature
IV. Military powers
A. I, III and IV
B. I, II and IV
C. II, III and IV
D. I, II and III

586. The oath of office is administered to the Governor by the
A. Chief Minister of the State
B. Chief Justice of High Court
C. Deputy Chief Minister of the State
D. Chief Justice of Supreme Court

587. Which of the following is/are among the discretionary powers of the Governor?
I. Selecting a chief minister if no single party has clear majority in the State Assembly
II. Dismissing a ministry at any time
III. Reserving a bill for the President
A. I and III
B. I and II
C. II and III
D. None of these

588. What do you understand by the dual role of the Governor?
A. Titular Head of the state and an agent of Chief Minister
B. Constitutional ruler and an agent of the Centre
C. Constitutional ruler and an agent of the Supreme Court
D. None of these

589. The Contingency Fund of the State is operated by the
A. Governor
B. Chief Minister
C. Finance Minister of the State
D. Finance Minister of the Union

590. The Governor of which State has been vested with special powers regarding scheduled tribe areas?
A. Arunachal Pradesh.
B. Meghalaya
C. Manipur
D. Tripura

591. The Chief Minister of a State
I. is elected by the Legislative Assembly
II. appoints the members of the Council of Ministers
III. determines the strength of the Council of Ministers
IV. determines the salaries of Council of Ministers
A. I only B. II only
C. III only D. IV only

592. Ministers in a State get salaries as determined by
A. Chief Minister
B. Governor
C. State Legislature.
D. Union Government

593. Who presides over the meetings of the Council of the Ministers in a State?
A. The Governor

B. The Chief Minister
C. The Chief Justice of High Court
D. None of these

594. The Council of Ministers at State level is responsible to
A. The Lok Sabha
B. The Rajya Sabha
C. The Legislative Assembly
D. The Governor

595. To be a member of the State Council of Ministers, a person must acquire membership of the State Legislature within a period of
A. Six weeks of such appointment if he is not one already
B. One month of such appointment if he is not one already
C. Two months of such appointment if he is not one already
D. Six months of such appointment if he is not one already

596. A minister in a State is individually responsible to the
A. Governor
B. Chief Minister
C. Chief Justice of the High Court
D. Deputy Chief Minister

597. Is Vidhan Sabha subject to dissolution?
A. No
B. Yes
C. No subject to certain conditions
D. None of these

598. The Legislative Council of a State—
I. is not subject to dissolution
II. can be abolished by the State Legislative Assembly
III. can be abolished by the President on the Governor's recommendation
A. II and III
B. I only
C. I and II
D. I and III

599. The members of the Legislative Council are appointed through
I. Direct elections
II. Indirect elections
III. Nomination
A. I only
B. II only
C. III only
D. I, II and III

600. The Chairman of the Legislative Council is
A. Elected by the members of the Legislative Council from among themselves.
B. Elected by the members of the Legislative Assembly from among themselves
C. Elected by the college consists of the members of legislative assembly and legislative council
D. None of these

601. The maximum permissible period between two sessions of a State Legislative Assembly is
A. One year
B. Two years
C. Three months
D. Six months

602. Regarding the enactment of an ordinary law the legislative council may delay it for a maximum period of
A. Six months
B. One month
C. Two months
D. Three months

603. Which of the statements are correct and which of it explain the other?
A1: The position of the legislative council is inferior to that of the legislative assembly.
B1: The very existence of the council depends on the will of the Assembly.
B2: A bill originating in the council can be forthwith put to an end by the Assembly rejecting it.
B3: One-sixth of the council's member are nominated by the Governor.

A. A1 and B1, B2 are correct but none of it explain A1
B. A1 and B1, B2 and B3 are correct and B1, B2 and B3 explain A1
C. B1, B2 and B3 are correct but none of it explain A1
D. A1 and B1, B2 and B3 are correct but B1, B2 and B3 does not explain A1

604. The State Legislative Assembly participates in election of—
I. President
II. Vice-President
III. Rajya Sabha members
IV. Members of Legislative Council of the State
A. I, II and IV
B. I and II
C. II and III
D. III and IV

605. Which one is correct and which one is wrong?
A: There are limitations on the Legislative act of the State Legislature?
R: Certain bills on the State List can be introduced in the State Legislature only with the President's approval?
A. A is correct but R is wrong
B. A is wrong but R is correct
C. Both A and R are correct
D. None of these

606. Membership of the Legislative Assembly can be between 60 and 500, but the exception to this rule are found in:
I. Pondicherry
II. Mizoram
III. Goa
A. I and II only
B. II and III only
C. I and III only
D. All the above

607. Money bills can be introduced in the State Legislature with the prior consent of the
A. Governor
B. Chief Minister
C. Chief Justice of High Court
D. None of these

608. The limitations on the authority of the state legislature do not include the governor's discretionary power to
A. Suspend the legislature
B. Prorogue the legislature
C. Dissolve the legislature
D. None of the above

609. Name the state that has its own separate constitution in India:
A. The state of Arunachal Pradesh
B. The state of Jammu and Kashmir
C. The State of Meghalaya
D. The State of Manipur

610. Which of the statement is correct and which of them is wrong?
A: The state of Jammu and Kashmir has a special status.
R: Jammu and Kashmir was accorded a special status by the Independence Act, 1947.
A. A is correct but R is wrong
B. A is wrong but R is correct
C. Both A and R are correct
D. Both A and R are wrong

611. Jammu and Kashmir has a Constitution framed by
A. A constitution Assembly set up by the Union of India
B. A Constitution Assembly set up by the state.
C. A Constitution Assembly set up by Pakistan
D. None of the above

612. The residuary powers of legislation in case of Jammu and Kashmir belong to
A. The Union legislature
B. The State legislature
C. The Governor
D. The Chief Minister

613. An amendment of the Constitution of India can extend to the State of Jammu and Kashmir by an order of the president under Article
A. 369 of the Constitution of India
B. 360 of the Constitution of India

C. 136 of the Constitution of India
D. 370 of the Constitution of India

614. A proclamation of emergency by the President
A. Shall have effect in Jammu and Kashmir only on the concurrence of the State Legislature
B. Shall have effect in Jammu & Kasmir without the Concurrence of the State Legislature
C. Shall have no effect
D. None of the above

615. Panchayati Raj has received constitutional status with the........Amendment Act
A. 74th B. 73rd
C. 75th D. 76th

616. The three-tier system of Panchayats need not be strictly followed in the State with population below
A. 10 lakhs
B. 20 Lakhs
C. 30 lakhs
D. 40 lakhs

617. The list of items which may be entrusted to the Panchayats is given in the
A. Eleventh schedule
B. Tenth Schedule
C. Twelfth Schedule
D. Thirteenth Schedule

618. The elections to Panchayats are to be held
A. Every second year
B. Every third year
C. Every five years
D. None of these

619. A person to be qualified for standing in a Panchayat election must have attained the age of
A. 21 years B. 18 years
C. 25 years D. 35 years

620. Who is to conduct the elections to the Panchayats and Municipalities?
A. Union Election Commission
B. State Election Commission
C. Panchayats and Municipalities itself
D. None of these

621. The state election commission can be removed from his office in the same manner and on the same grounds as
A. A judge of the Supreme Court.
B. A Chief Minister
C. A Governor
D. None of these

622. The electorate for a Panchayat is
A. The Town area
B. The District
C. Tehsil
D. The Gram Sabha

623. The state finance commission makes recommendations on measures to augment the consolidated fund of a state to supplement the resources of the Municipalities. Mention whether this statement is true or false?
A. True
B. False
C. True but under certain conditions
D. None of these

624. It would be obligatory to appoint Ward Committees in case of a Municipality of a population of
A. One lakh
B. Three lakh
C. Two lakh
D. Ten lakh

625. Regarding reservation of seats on Panchayats and Municipalities, it would not be correct to say that
A. The unreserved seat can be contested by women
B. There is no such reservation as talked of
C. The unreserved seats cannot be contested by women
D. None of these

626. Article 243-F of the Indian constitution provides for the qualification required for voting in Panchayat elections. Mention whether this statement is true or false?
A. True
B. True subject to certain condition

C. False
D. None of these

627. Self-governing institutions for areas being transformed from a rural to an urban area are?
A. Nagar Panchayat
B. Nagar Palika
C. Town Area Çommittee
D. Municipal Corporation

628. In which state were direct elections to all the tiers of the Panchayat held first after the 73rd Amendment came into force?
A. Uttar Pradesh
B. Maharashtra
C. Gujarat
D. Madhya Pradesh

629. The 73rd and 74th Amendment Acts
A. Had to be ratified by more than half the number of states
B. Had to be passed by simple majority
C. Had to be passed by special majority
D. None of the above

630. How many Union Territories are there in India?
A. Six B. Five
C. Nine D. Seven

631. Which of the following Union Territories has a Legislature?
A. Delhi
B. Pondicherry
C. Andaman and Nicobar Island
D. Lakshadweep

632. The Union Territories are administered by the
A. President through administrators appointed by him
B. Prime Minister through administrator appointed by him
C. By Chief Minister
D. By Governors

633. If the Governor of a State is appointed administrator of an adjoining Union Territory, he exercises his functions
A. depending on the advice of the control of ministers
B. depending on the advice of the Home Minister of the Union
C. Independently of his Council of Ministers
D. None of these

634. District Council in autonomous tribal areas
I. may collect land revenue
II. are independent of the State Governments
III. must get their laws endorsed by the President
IV. have no law-making power
Choose the best option?
A. II only
B. I only
C. III only
D. IV only

635. Provisions of the constitution relating to the administration of scheduled areas and tribes in schedule V may be altered by Parliament by
A. Special legislation
B. Ordinary Legislation.
C. Special legislation with ratification from States
D. None of these

636. Is Chandigarh administered by a Lieutenant Governor?
A. Yes
B. Yes but under certain circumstances
C. No
D. None of these

637. Name the union territory which has the High Court for itself:
A. Delhi
B. Chandigarh
C. Lakshadweep
D. Andhra Pradesh

638. Name some of the territories which were acquired by India from France:
A. Goa
B. Daman and Diu
C. Yanam, Mahe and Karaikal
D. Lakshadweep

639. Provisions relating to the administration of acquired territories are the same as that apply to
A. States
B. National Capital Territory
C. Union Territories
D. None of the above

640. The Supreme Court was set up
A. By Britishers
B. By the Constitution
C. By the Government of India Act, 1935
D. By President of India

641. The judges of the Supreme Court take an oath or affirmation before entering upon office, conducted by
A. Prime Minister
B. President or some person appointed by him
C. Chief Justice of India
D. None of these

642. To whom does a judge of the Supreme Court address his resignation if he wants to leave office before his term is complete?
A. President.
B. Prime Minister
C. Senior most puisne Judge
D. Vice President

643. The power of judicial review ensures—
A. That judiciary is Supreme to legislature and executive
B. That judiciary is empowered to set aside any law it wants
C. That executive is Supreme over legislative and judiciary
D. The constitutionality of laws

644. Regarding the advisory jurisdiction of the Supreme Court, which of the following statements is/are correct?
I. It is obligatory for the Supreme Court to give its opinion once its opinion is sought.
II. The advice is not binding on the President.
III. The President may ask the Court's opinion on treaties and agreements made before the Constitution was framed.

A. I and II
B. I and III
C. II and III
D. None of these

645. The right to seek advisory opinion of the Supreme Court on any question of law or fact belongs to
A. The Prime Minister
B. The President
C. The Vice President
D. The Chief Justice of India

646. Match the List I (Situations) with List II (Jurisdictions) of Supreme Court :

List I (Situations)
a. A person acquitted in a lower court has been sentenced to death by the High Court.
b. A dispute arising out of a covenant entered into before the commencement of the Constitution.
c. A dispute between two States of the Union.

List II (Jurisdictions)
1. Original
2. Appellate
3. Advisory

A. a-2, b-3, c-1
B. a-1, b-2, c-3
C. a-3, b-1, c-2
D. a-2, b-1, c-3

647. Match the following columns—

I—Judicial Posts
a. Chief Justice of India
b. Judge of High Court
c. Chief Justice of High Court
d. Judge of Supreme Court

II—Salaries
1. Rs. 90,000 per month
2. Rs. 90,000 per month
3. Rs. 1,00,000 per month
4. Rs. 80,000 per month

A. a-1, b-2, c-3, d-4
B. a-3, b-1, c-2, d-4
C. a-4, b-3, c-1, d-4
D. a-3, b-4, c-1, d-2

648. The constitution so as to ensure the independence of judges makes the provision that a retired judge cannot be appointed to any office under the government. Mention whether this statement is correct or not?

A. Correct
B. Incorrect
C. Correct but under certain circumstances
D. None of these

649. The Supreme Court is a court of record. This implies

I. it can punish for its contempt.
II. its decisions are admitted as evidence and cannot be questioned in any court of law.
III. it has to keep a record of all the important cases that are conducted in India.
IV. its decisions, once taken, are binding upon it.

A. I and III only
B. II and III only
C. I and II only
D. III and IV only

650. Which of the following statements is/are correct?

I. The Supreme Court's decrees and orders are enforceable throughout India.
II. The Supreme Court is not bound by its earlier decisions.
III. In its power of judicial review the Supreme Court can declare a law unconstitutional on the basis of the objectives underlying the law.
IV. The Constitution excludes no area from judicial review.

A. I and II only
B. III and IV only
C. II and III only
D. I and IV only

651. Which of the following is/are the qualifications for a High Court judge?

I. Citizenship of India.
II. Must have held a judicial office for at least ten years.
III. Must not be over 62 years of age.
IV. Must have been an advocate of a High Court for at least ten years or be an eminent jurist.

A. I, III and IV
B. II, III and IV
C. I, II and III
D. I, II and IV

652. A High Court consists of a Chief Justice and

A. Such other judges as determined by the President.
B. Such other judges as determined by the Prime Minister
C. Such other judges as determined by the Chief Justice of India
D. Such other judges as determined by the Union Law Minister

653. A judge of a High Court can be removed from office before the expiry of his time by the

A. Prime Minister
B. Home Minister
C. Vice President on recommendation of Parliament
D. President on the recommendation of Parliament

654. A judge of a High Court wanting to resign addresses his letter of resignation to—

A. The President
B. The Prime Minister
C. The Chief Justice of India
D. Any Judge of the High Court

655. Which of the statements is correct and which one is incorrect?

A: The independence of a High Court judge is ensured through certain provisions of the Constitution.
R: The salaries and allowances of High Court judges are charged to the Consolidated Fund of India.

A. A is incorrect but R is correct
B. A is correct but R is incorrect
C. Both A and R are correct
D. Both A and R are incorrect

656. The Constitution places the High Courts under the control of the Union in certain matters in order to keep them outside the range of regional politics. The Union exercises its control in the matters of

I. transfer of judges from one High Court to another.
II. being able to establish a common High Court for two or more States.
III. determining disputes as to age of High Court judges.

A. I and II only
B. I only
C. I, II and III
D. III only

657. The pension of a High Court judge is charged to the

A. Consolidated Fund of India
B. Prime Minister Relief Fund
C. Public Accounts Committee
D. None of the above

658. The Chief Justice of a High Court is appointed by the President after consultation with

I. the Chief Justice of India.
II. the Governor of the State.
III. the Chief Minister of the State.

A. I only B. I and II
C. I and III D. II and III

659. The power to extend or restrict the jurisdiction of the High Court rests with—

A. The Parliament
B. The Prime Minister
C. The Chief Justice of India
D. None of these

660. Which of the following High Courts and their territorial jurisdiction is/are matched correctly?

I. Allahabad—Uttar Pradesh
II. Madras—Tamil Nadu & Puducherry
III. Kerala—Kerala and Lakshadweep
IV. Bombay—Maharashtra, Goa and Gujarat

A. I, III and IV
B. II, III and IV
C. I, II and III
D. I, II and IV

661. Under which High Court does Andaman and Nicobar Islands come?

A. Allahabad High Court
B. Delhi High Court
C. Madras High Court
D. Calcutta High Court

662. The Union Territory of Chandigarh comes under the jurisdiction of

A. Delhi High Court
B. Chandigarh High Court
C. Maharashtra High Court
D. None of these

663. Supervision over tribunals constituted by law relating to the armed forces is one of the powers of the High Court. True or False:

A. True
B. False
C. True but under certain circumstances
D. None of these

664. Does the state of Manipur have a High Court of its own?

A. No
B. Yes
C. Yes but only for half of the year
D. None of these

665. The main sources of law in India are:

I. The Constitution
II. Statutes
III. Customary law
IV. Judicial decisions of superior courts

A. All the four options given are the important sources of law in India
B. I, II and III
C. II, III and IV
D. I, III and IV

666. In a criminal case, an appeal lies to the Supreme Court if the High Court

I. has convicted the accused and awarded him death sentence.
II. has on appeal reversed an order for acquittal of an accused and sentenced him to an imprisonment of ten years or more.
III. has withdrawn for trial before itself any case from a subordinate

court and has in such trial convicted the accused and sentenced him to death.

A. I and II
B. II and III
C. I and III
D. None of these

667. Entitlement of legal aid is a concomitant right that arises out of the Fundamental Right

A. To equality before law or equal protection of laws.
B. To freedom of speech
C. To constitutional remedies
D. To life and liberty

668. To which of the following, judicial review in India does not extend:

(a) The advice that the council of ministers gives to the President.
(b) The discretionary powers of the Governors.
(c) The privileges enjoyed by the Parliament members.

A. (a) and (b)
B. (b) and (c)
C. (a) and (c)
D. None of the above

669. The oath to a High Court judge is administered by the

A. Governor
B. Chief Minister
C. Home Minister of the Union
D. None of these

670. When can the salaries of High Court judges be reduced?

A. any time President so desires
B. during National Emergency
C. during a Financial Emergency
D. during State Emergency

671. Mention some of the cases of public injury from where public interest litigation can arise

(a) The breach of any public duty.
(b) The violation of a constitutional provision.
(c) The violation of the law.
(d) The injury to a particular person

A. (a) and (b) only
B. (a), (b) and (c) only
C. (a), (c) and (d) only
D. (a) and (d) only

672. A government is federal or unitary on the basis of relations between the

A. Legislature and Executive
B. Legislature and Judiciary
C. Executive and Judiciary
D. Centre and States

673. India's is a federal system of government because

I. the Union Legislature is bicameral.
II. single citizenship exists in India.
III. the Constitution is supreme.
IV. there is an independent judiciary.

A. I, II and III
B. I, III and IV
C. II, III and IV
D. I, II and IV

674. Which of the following give the Indian Constitution a unitary bias?

I. Rigidity of the amendment process
II. Written Constitution
III. Same Constitution for Centre and States
IV. Indestructibility of the State boundaries

A. I only B. II only
C. III only D. IV only

675. Match the following columns—

List-I

a. Union List
b. State List
c. Concurrent List

List-II

1. Banking
2. Public order and police
3. Labour welfare

A. a-1, b-3, c-2
B. a-2, b-1, c-3
C. a-1, b-2, c-3
D. a-3, b-2, c-1

676. While a proclamation of emergency is in operation the State Government
A. Can legislate on the subjects in the state list
B. Cannot legislate on the subject in the state list
C. Can legislate on the subject in the concurrent list
D. All of the above

677. The State can legislate on subjects in the
1. State List
2. Union List
3. Concurrent List
4. Residuary List
A. 1, 3 and 4
B. 1 and 3
C. 1, 2 and 3
D. 1 and 4

678. When can a State law on a subject in the Concurrent List get precedence over a Central law on the same subject?
A. Never
B. Yes, the state law always get a procedure over a central law
C. If it had got the President's assent before the enactment of the Central law
D. None of these

679. When can Parliament legislate on a subject in the State List?
I. If Lok Sabha passes a resolution by two-thirds majority that it is in national interest to do so
II. When the legislatures of two or more States request Parliament to legislate on a State subject
III. Under a proclamation of Emergency.
A. I and II B. I and III
C. II and III D. All of the above

680. The Central Government can issue directions to the States with regard to the
I. Union List
II. State List
III. Concurrent List
A. I and II B. II and III
C. I and III D. All the three

681. The Central Government can assign any function to the States
A. With the consent of the State government
B. Without the consent of the state government
C. With the permission from the Governor
D. None of these

682. If a State government fails to comply with the directions of the Centre in the exercise of administrative power—
A. A constitutional emergency cannot be declared
B. There is no provision in the constitution to check it
C. A constitutional emergency can be declared in the State and the President can assume all the powers of the State government
D. Financial emergency can be declared

683. The Finance Commission is constituted by the President every
A. One year B. Two year
C. Five years D. Four years

684. The Chairman of the Finance Commission must be
A. A persons having political background
B. A person having experience in public affairs
C. A person having experience in Home affairs
D. None of these

685. Grants-in-aid given to States are meant—
A. To cover gaps on revenue account so that States can undertake beneficial activities
B. To provide facilities to the members of legislative assemblies
C. To secure the independence of states
D. None of these

686. The Finance Commission makes recommendations regarding
I. Determination of and principles guiding grant-in-aid.

II. Economy in expenditure.
III. Distribution of net proceeds of taxes between Centre and States.

A. I and II B. II and III
C. I and III D. None of these

687. Grants-in-aid are provided every year to such States as are in need of assistance as determined by the
A. Parliament
B. President
C. Finance Minister
D. Chief Minister of the states

688. The States in India can borrow from the market—
A. without the consent of the centre
B. only with the consent of the centre
C. without the consent of the centre but under certain circumstances
D. None of these

689. Which of the following is/are correctly matched?
I. Stamp duties and duties on medical and toilet preparations—levied by the Union but collected and appropriated by the States.
II. Duties on succession to property other than agricultural land—levied and collected by the Union but assigned to the States.
III. Taxes on income other than corporation tax and tax on agricultural income—levied, collected and appropriated by the Union
IV. Receipts from Broadcasting—non-tax revenue of the Union
A. I, II and III
B. I, III and IV
C. I, II and IV
D. II, III and IV

690. Zonal Councils are provided
A. by Parliamentary act
B. by President's ordinance
C. by orders of the Chief Justice of India
D. none of these

691. The main purpose of Zonal Councils is to
A. Advise on the matters of space research in a zone
B. Advise on the matters of defence in a zone
C. Advise on the matters of public Harmony
D. Advise on matters of common interest to States in a Zone

692. The ex-officio Chairman of a Zonal Council is
A. Governor of the state where Zonal council meets
B. The Chief Minister of the State where the council meets
C. Chief Justice of the concerned High Court
D. None of these

693. Joint meetings of two or more Zonal Councils are presided over by—
A. Prime Minister
B. President
C. Union Home Minister
D. Union Finance Minister

694. An Inter-State Council was set up in 1990 under Article 263 of the Constitution by the
A. Prime Minister
B. President
C. Chief Justice of India
D. All of the above

695. The duties envisaged by the Constitution for the Inter State Council are to—
I. inquire into and advise on disputes between States.
II. investigate matters of common interest for two or more States.
III. make recommendation for coordination of policy and action relating to any subject.
IV. enforce provisions relating to the freedom of trade and commerce.
A. I, II and IV
B. II, III and IV
C. I, II and III
D. I, II and IV

696. The members of the Inter-State Council are

I. Six cabinet ministers nominated to it.
II. Chief Ministers of all States.
III. Secretaries of Union Ministries.
IV. Governors of all States.

A. I and III B. I and II
C. I and IV D. III and IV

697. How many types of emergencies has the Constitution envisaged?

A. Four
B. Two
C. Three
D. Five

698. Which of the following is/are resultant of a proclamation of national emergency because of war?

I. The Union Government can give directions to the States about how the executive power of the State is to be exercised.
II. The Fundamental Rights stand automatically suspended.
III. The State Legislature is suspended.
IV. Parliament can make laws with respect to any subject in the State List.

A. I and II
B. II and III
C. I and IV
D. III and IV

699. A national emergency can remain in operation on Parliament's approval for

A. Six months
B. One year
C. An indefinite period
D. Five years

700. National emergency can be declared by the President on the ground of

A. War, External Aggression and Armed Rebellion
B. Failure of constitutional machinery
C. Financial contingencies
D. None of these

701. A proclamation of national emergency has to be placed before Parliament for its approval within

A. Two months
B. One month
C. Three months
D. Four months

702. "President's Rule" can be declared

A. If there is financial contingency in the state
B. If Chief Minister does not perform his or her duties well
C. If the State Government does not work in accordance with the directions of Union Government
D. If the President is satisfied that the government of a State cannot be carried on in accordance of the provisions of the Constitution

703. During a proclamation of emergency due to breakdown of constitutional machinery in a State, President can

I. assume all powers vested in and exercisable the Governor.
II. declare that the powers of the State Legislate shall be exercised by Parliament.
III. assume certain powers of the High Courts.
IV. suspend by order any or all Fundamental Right except those under Articles 20 and 21.

A. I and III B. I and IV
C. I and II D. II and IV

704. The impact of financial emergency includes the President's power to suspend the fundamental rights in Article 19. True or False:

A. True
B. True but under certain conditions
C. False
D. None of these

705. National emergency has been declared so far:

A. Once B. Twice
C. Thrice D. Five times

706. Which of the following gets automatically suspend under a proclamation of national emergency on growing of war or external aggression?

I. Fundamental rights under Art. 19.

II. The fundamental right to move the Courts for enforcement of the rights or any of them.

III. All fundamental rights except those under Articles 20 and 21

A. II only
B. III only
C. II and III only
D. I only.

707. The constitution envisages three types of civil services namely

A. All-India, Central and State
B. District, State and Central
C. District, All-India and State
D. None of these

708. Which one of the following is/are all-India services?

I. Indian Administrative Service
II. Indian Foreign Service
III. Indian Police Service
IV. Indian Defense Service

A. I and II
B. II and IV
C. I and III
D. IV and III

709. A post under a State is held during the pleasure of the

A. Governor
B. Chief Minister
C. Chief Justice of High Court
D. Home minister of the state

710. An aggrieved public servant of the Union can challenge the decisions of the Administrative Tribunal

A. Before the Supreme Court
B. Before the High Court
C. Before the District Court
D. Before the court he desires

711. The composition of the UPSC is determined by

A. The President
B. The Prime Minister
C. The Home Minister
D. The Finance Minister

712. Additional duties can be assigned to a State Public Service Commission on the recommendation of the

A. State Legislature
B. Central Legislature
C. Central or State Legislature
D. None of these

713. The UPSC conducts examinations for

I. Central Services.
II. All India Services.
III. State services.
IV. State services for two or more States jointly.

A. II and III
B. III and IV
C. I and II
D. I and IV

714. The Chairman of the UPSC is appointed by

A. The President
B. The Prime Minister
C. The Finance Minister
D. The Chief Justice of India

715. Which of the statements is correct and which one explain the other if both are correct?

A: The Constitution does not allow the Chairman of a State Public Service Commission to take up any further employment under the Union or State Government.

R: The Constitution seeks to ensure the independence of the Public Service Commission members.

A. Both A and R are correct and R explains A
B. Both A and R are correct but R does not explain A
C. Both A and R are incorrect but R explains A
D. Both A and R are incorrect and R does not explains A

716. The members of a State Commission can be removed by the
A. President on a report by the High Court
B. President on a report by the Supreme Court
C. Prime Minister on a report by the Supreme Court
D. Prime Minister or a report by High Court

717. The resignation letter of a State Public Service Commission member is addressed to the
A. Governor
B. Chief Minister
C. Home Minister
D. Prime Minister

718. A joint public service commission may be set up for two or more states if the union parliament provides for it after
A. President permits the same
B. Prime Minister permits the same
C. Chief Justice of India permits the same
D. A resolution to that effect is passed by the state legislatures concerned

719. According to the Constitution a member of a Public Service Commission would be guilty of misbehaviour if he or she
A. Gets some benefit from a contract made on behalf of the Government
B. Gets reward from the Government
C. Gets promotion from the Government
D. None of these

720. The UPSC may, on Parliamentary resolution, agree to serve all or any needs of a state. True or False:
A. True
B. False
C. True but under certain circumstances
D. None of these

721. The report of the UPSC has to be discussed in
A. Lok Sabha only before being accepted
B. Parliament before being accepted
C. Supreme Court of India before being accepted
D. None of these

722. Who in India is entrusted with the 'superintendence, direction and control' of the conduct of elections?
A. Prime Minister
B. President
C. Election Commission
D. Controller and Auditor General of India

723. A person is eligible to vote in the general elections if he or she:
I. is a citizen of India
II. is not less than 21 years of age
III. does not hold any office of profit under the Government
IV. is not disqualified on grounds of unsound mind
A. I and II only
B. I and IV only
C. II and III only
D. III and IV only

724. The first general elections in India were held in

A. 1951	B. 1956
C. 1954	D. 1949

725. The Congress lost its monopoly of power in the States for the first time after the elections of

A. 1967	B. 1976
C. 1956	D. 1974

726. Who has the power to decide an election petition?
I. District Court
II. Supreme Court
III. High Courts
IV. Tribunals
A. I and II only
B. I and IV only
C. II and III.only
D. III and IV only

727. The conditions of service and tenure of the Election Commissioner is prescribed by
A. President
B. Prime Minister
C. Chief Justice of India
D. Parliament

728. Fourth Lok Sabha was dissolved before the expiry of its normal term and midterm election ordered. True or False?
A. True
B. False
C. True but midterm elections were not ordered
D. None of these

729. Which Lok Sabha had its term extended?
A. First B. Fifth
C. Fourth D. Sixth

730. A political party is recognised by the Election Commission only if—
I. it has been engaged in political activity for a continuous period of five years
II. it has returned at least one member of the Lok Sabha for every 25 members of that House or any fraction of that number elected from that State.
III. it has polled not less than six per cent of the total number of valid votes polled by all contesting candidates at the general elections
IV. it has contested elections in four or more states in three consecutive general elections.
A. II, III and IV
B. I, II and III
C. I, III and IV
D. I, II and IV

731. A party to be recognised as a national party must be recognised in at least ...... states
A. Four B. Five
C. Six D. Seven

732. Which of the following is/are national parties?
I. Congress (I)
II. All India Muslim League
III. Dravida Munnetra Kazhagam
IV. All India Forward Bloc
A. II only B. I only
C. III only D. IV only

733. Which of the following political parties came into being before independence?
I. Communist Party of India (Marxist).
II. Communist Party of India.
III. Dravida Munnetra Kazhagam.
IV. Bharatiya Janata Party.
A. I only B. II only
C. III only D. IV only

734. Which of the following Parties and their founders is/are matched correctly?
I. Bharatiya Jana Sangh—Veer Savarkar
II. Swatantra Party—M.R.Masani
III. Dravida Munnetra Kazhagam—K.Karunar
IV. Lok Dal—Charan Singh
A. I only B. II only
C. IV only D. III only

735. Electioneering has to stop in a constituency
A. 24 hours before the closing hour of polling.
B. 48 hours before the closing hour of polling.
C. 36 hours before closing hours of polling
D. 72 hours before the closing hours of polling

736. Who is responsible for the registration of vote?
A. State Government
B. Central Government
C. Municipalities
D. Election Commission

737. Who can cast their votes by postal ballot?
I. Members of the Armed Forces
II. Officials on election duty
III. Foreign Service personnel when posted abroad
A. I only
B. II only
C. III only
D. All the above

738. The system of representation used in India for election of the Lok Sabha and the State Assemblies is called

A. Territorial representation
B. Direct representation
C. Public representation
D. None of these

739. For the State Assembly constituencies who appoints returning Officers?
A. Chief Minister
B. Governor
C. The Election Commission
D. Advocate-General

740. The constitution stipulates that when any other election commissioner is appointed the chief election commissioner shall act as chairman of the election commission. True or False:
A. False
B. True
C. False except under certain circumstances
D. None of these

741. Regional Commissioners are appointed by
A. The President.
B. The Prime Minister
C. The Chief Justice of India
D. The Election Commissioner

742. Originally the Constitution recognised ...... language
A. 20 B. 25
C. 14 D. 13

743. One of the latest languages to be added to the list languages recognised by the Constitution is
A. Nepali B. Oriya
C. Urdu D. Arabic

744. While Hindi is the official language, English has been permitted for official use
A. 15 years
B. Indefinitely
C. 20 years
D. 25 years

745. The permission for the use of English for official purposes was extended beyond the fifteen years and it was initially allowed by the Constitution through
A. An order
B. An ordinance
C. A convention
D. An act of Parliament

746. The Constitution seeks to protect the interests of the scheduled castes/scheduled tribes by
I. reservation of seats for them in the legislatures
II. bestowal of special rights on the state to impose special restrictions on their rights for their advancement.
III. the National Commission for the Scheduled Castes and Scheduled Tribes
A. I only
B. II only
C. III only
D. All the above

747. The Constitution seeks to protect the interests of the Anglo-Indian community by
A. By inviting NRI
B. By giving viza on easy terms to them
C. Authorising the President to nominate two members of the community in the Lok Sabha
D. By checking their population

748. The Constitution originally contained ...... Schedules
A. Eight B. Nine
C. Ten D. Seven

749. The Ninth Schedule was added by the ...... Amendment
A. Second B. Tenth
C. First D. Seventeenth

750. What does the Ninth Schedule contain?
A. Immigration laws
B. State list, Union list and Concurrent list
C. Laws which are protected from judicial scrutiny
D. None of these

751. Match the following subjects and schedules

List-I

a. Schedule Two
b. Schedule Three
c. Schedule Four
d. Schedule Five

List-II

1. Oath or affirmation for various incumbents to office
2. Details of seats allotted to States in Rajya Sabha
3. Administration and control of scheduled areas
4. Salaries of President

A. a-1, b-2, c-3, d-4
B. a-4, b-1, c-2, d-3
C. a-2, b-3, c-4, d-1
D. a-3, b-4, c-1, d-2

752. Which of the following Schedules and subjects are incorrectly matched?

I. One—territories and States of the Union
II. Eight—Three Lists
III. Seven—languages
IV. Six—tribal areas of Assam, Meghalaya and Mizoram

A. I and II B. I and III
C. II and III D. III and IV

753. The twelfth schedule of the constitution contains

A. Union list, State list, Concurrent list
B. Languages of the state
C. Subjects over which municipalities may have control
D. None of these

754. When was the Constitution first amended?

A. 1951 B. 1952
C. 1961 D. 1991

755. Which of the following Amendments would need state ratification?

I. Provisions affecting President's election.
II. Provisions affecting the Union judiciary.
III. Amendment procedure.
IV. Reservation of seats for SC/ST in Parliament.

A. I and II only
B. III only
C. IV only
D. All the above

756. What sort of majority is needed for the creation of new states, creation or abolition of upper house in state legislatures and reconstitution of existing states?

A. Simple majority
B. Special majority
C. Special majority by ratification from half of the states
D. None of these

757. An amendment of the Constitution can be initiated in

I. Lok Sabha
II. Rajya Sabha
III. State Legislature

A. I and III only
B. II and IV only
C. I or II only
D. None of these

758. Regarding Constitutional Amendments which of the options are correct?

I. the Provision of joint sitting is not available
II. they become operative from the date both Houses have passed the Bills
III. the President's assent to a constitutional amendment is obligatory
IV. Parliament may amend any part of the Constitution according to the procedure laid down in Article 368

A. I, II and III
B. II, III and IV
C. I, III and IV
D. I, II and IV

759. How many States are required to ratify certain amendments to the Constitution?

A. Not less than 2/3 of the number
B. Not less than half the number
C. Not less than 1/3 of the number
D. No ratification is required

760. A major portion of the constitution can be amended by
A. Two-thirds majority
B. One-third majority
C. One half majority
D. Two third majority with ratification from half of the state

761. The amendment procedure of Indian Constitution is modelled on that of
A. USA
B. French
C. Swiss
D. South Africa

762. Which amendment of the Constitution gave priority to Directive Principles over Fundamental Rights?
A. 44th Amendment
B. 35th Amendment
C. 42nd Amendment.
D. 45th Amendment

763. The decision of the Supreme Court in the Golak Nath case was that
A. Fundamental Rights could not be amended or abridged
B. Fundamental Rights could be amended or abridged
C. The basic structure of the constitution cannot be awarded abridged
D. None of these

764. What was the decision of the Supreme Court in Keshavanand Bharati case?
A. The power under Article 368 to amend the Constitution cannot be so exercised as to alter the basic structure or the essential features of the Constitution
B. Fundamental rights cannot be amended or abridged
C. Fundamental rights can be amended
D. None of these

765. In the Minerva Mills batch of cases the Supreme Court has further reaffirmed its decision in
A. Golak Nath case
B. Keshavanand Bharti case
C. Maneka Gandhi case
D. Raj Narain Gandhi case

766. Which of these Amendments and their subject matter is/are incorrectly matched?
I. 26th Amendment—abolition of titles and privileges of former rulers of princely states
II. 21st Amendment—curtailed the right to property
III. 51st Amendment—curbed political defections
IV. 61st Amendment—reduced voting age.
A. I and II
B. III and IV
C. II and III
D. I and III

767. Match the following Amendments and their provisions—

List-I
a. Sixty-second Amendment
b. Sixty-third Amendment
c. Sixty-fifth Amendment
d. Sixty-sixth Amendment

List-II
1. Repeal of 59th Amendment
2. Extension of reservation of seats for SC/ST till 2000 A.D.
3. Statutory Commission for SC/ST
4. Inclusion of land reforms in the Ninth Schedule
5. Extension of President's rule in Punjab

A. a-1, b-2, c-3, d-4
B. a-2, b-3, c-1, d-4
C. a-2, b-1, c-3, d-4
D. a-2, b-1, c-4, d-3

768. Which Amendment provided for an authoritative version of the Constitution in Hindi?
A. 54th B. 56th
C. 58th D. 57th

Directions : In question 769 to 781, (A) and (R) are two statements. Consider them and bring them in any one of the following category:

769. *(A):* True federal distribution of powers came into being with the Government of India Act, 1919.
(R): The Provinces got power by way of delegation from the Centre.

A. (A) is false but (R) is correct
B. Both (A) and (R) are correct and (R) explains (A)
C. Both (A) and (R) are correct but (R) does not explain (A)
D. (A) is correct but (R) is false

770. *(A):* The Muslim League did not contest the election for the Constituent Assembly.
(R): The Muslim League asked for a separate Constituent Assembly for 'Muslim India'
A. Both (A) and (R) are correct and (R) explains (A)
B. (A) is false but (R) is correct
C. Both (A) and (R) are correct but (R) does not explain (A)
D. (A) is correct but (R) is false

771. *(A):* The territory of India is larger than the territories of the States taken together.
(R): India is a Union of States.
A. Both (A) and (R) are correct and (R) explains (A)
B. (A) is false but (R) is correct
C. (A) is correct but (R) is false
D. Both (A) and (R) are correct but (R) does not explain (A)

772. *(A):* Preventive detention is a fundamental right of the state against individuals.
(R): Preventive detention has been considered in the Chapter on Fundamental Rights of the Constitution.
A. (A) is correct but (R) is false
B. (A) is false but (R) is correct
C. Both (A) and (R) are correct and (R) explains (A)
D. Both (A) and (R) are correct but (R) does not explain (A)

773. *(A):* Presidential election is not affected if a State Assembly stands dissolved at the time of election.
(R): The election to President's post must be completed within the time limit set by the Constitution.
A. Both (A) and (R) are correct (R) does not explain (A)
B. (A) is correct but (R) is false
C. Both (A) and (R) are correct and (R) explains (A)
D. (A) is false but (R) is correct

774. *(A):* It was enacted that upto 2000 A.D. the new decennial census figures need not be taken into account to readjust allocation of seats in the Lok Sabha and State Assemblies.
(R): It was conjectured that the rise in population would not much affect the nature of the constituencies.
A. (A) is correct but (R) is false
B. (A) is false bur (R) is correct
C. Both (A) and (R) are correct but (R) does not explain (A)
D. Both (A) and (R) are correct and (R) explains (A)

775. *(A):* A joint sitting is not called in case of Constitutional Amendment bills.
(R): A bill for amendment of the Constitution has to be passed by each House separately by the special majority laid down.
A. Both (A) and (R) are correct but (R) does not explain (A)
B. (A) is correct but (R) is false
C. Both (A) and (R) are correct and (R) explains (A)
D. (A) is false but (R) is correct

776. *(A):* A candidate for Vice-President must be qualified for election as a member of Rajya Sabha.
(R): The Vice-President acts as the Chairman of Rajya Sabha.
A. Both (A) and (R) are correct but (R) does not explain (A)
B. Both (A) and (R) are correct and (R) explains (A)
C. (A) is correct and (R) is false
D. (A) is false and (R) is correct

777. *(A):* The President of India is not a part of Parliament.
(R): A bill passed by the Houses of Parliament cannot become law without President's assent.

A. (A) is correct but (R) is false
B. Both (A) and (R) are correct and (R) explains (A)
C. Both (A) and (R) are correct but (R) does not explains (A)
D. (A) is false but (R) is correct.

778. *(A):* The Rajya Sabha must pass a resolution on the necessity of an All India Service before a new service common to states and the Union is created.
(R): Indian Constitution is federal and a resolution passed by a two-thirds majority in Rajya Sabha would practically signify the consent of the States.
A. Both (A) and (R) are correct but (R) does not explain (A)
B. Both (A) and (R) are correct and (R) explains (A)
C. (A) is correct and (R) is false
D. (A) is false and (R) is correct

779. Which of the statement is/are correct and which one explains the other?
(A): The Constitution authorizes Parliament to increase any of the duties or taxes stipulated in Articles 269 and 270 by imposing surcharge.
(R): The proceeds of the surcharge go into the Consolidated Fund of India.
A. Both (A) and (R) are correct but (R) does not explain (A)
B. Both (A) and (R) are correct and (R) explains (A)
C. (A) in correct (R) is false
D. (A) is false and (R) is correct

780. *(A):* The Constitution has created a Centre which is strong only during Emergencies.
(R): During Financial Emergency, the President can ask the States to reserve their money bills also for the consideration of Parliament.
A. (A) is correct but (R) is false
B. Both (A) and (R) are correct and (R) explains (A)
C. (A) is false but (R) is correct.
D. Both (A) and (R) are correct but (R) does not explain (A)

781. *(A):* There is no theory of "equality of State rights" underlying the federal scheme in our Constitution.
(R): The Indian Union is not the result of any agreement between the States.
A. (A) is correct but (R) is false
B. (A) is false but (R) is correct
C. Both (A) and (R) are correct and (R) explains (A)
D. Both (A) and (R) are correct but (R) does not explain (A)

782. Which Amendment Act is known as the Anti-Defection Act?
A. Forty Second Amendment
B. Forty Fourth Amendment
C. Fifty Second Amendment
D. Sixty Fourth Amendment

783. Which Schedule is corrected with the Anti-Defection Act?
A. Schedule IX
B. Schedule VIII
C. Schedule VII
D. Schedule X

784. Among Sikkim, Arunachal Pradesh and West Bengal, name the state if any that has not been under the President's Rule so far:
A. Sikkim
B. Arunachal Pradesh
C. West BEngal
D. None of them has escaped President's Rule

785. In India, the election commission holds election for the Parliament, State Legislature, and the post of the President and the vice-president. True or False:
A. True
B. False
C. False subject to certain conditions
D. None of these

786. President's rule can be proclaimed if the President, on receipt of a report from the Governor of the State or otherwise is satisfied that a situation has arisen in which the Government of the State cannot be carried on in accordance with the provisions of the constitution. True or False?

A. True
B. False
C. False subject to certain conditions
D. None of these

787. The constitution of India does not mention the post of the deputy prime minister. True or False:

A. False
B. False subject to certain conditions
C. True
D. None of these

788. A merger will not invite action under the Anti-Defection Act if......... members of a political party decide to join another political party:

A. One-third
B. Two-third
C. One-half
D. Ten percent

789. Who, according to the Anti-Defection Act, is the final authority to decide that a member of Lok Sabha has incurred disqualification due to defection?

A. Vice-President
B. Prime Minister
C. President
D. Speaker

790. Ballots were first used in

A. Australia
B. England
C. Russia
D. USA

791. Which of the following is/are correctly matched?

I. India's National Song—Vande Mataram
II. India's National Flower—Rose
III. India's National Animal—Tiger
IV. India's National Bird—Eagle

A. I and II only
B. IV and II only
C. I and III only
D. III and IV only

792. The provisions relating to election in the constitution came into force on:

A. 26th November, 1949
B. 15th August, 1947
C. 25th October, 1951
D. 20th September, 1961

793. The provisions relating to provisional parliament in the constitution came into force on:

A. 15 August, 1946
B. 26 November, 1956
C. 26th November, 1949
D. 28 October, 1950

794. What was the purpose of the objective resolution in the Constituent Assembly?

A. It called for the just rights of the minorities.
B. It called to empower the defence forces
C. It called to fill up the right of castism
D. None of these

795. The concept of directive principles have been borrowed from—

A. Swiss Constitution
B. French Constitution
C. German Constitution
D. Irish Constitution

796. The concept of fundamental rights in the constitution has been borrowed from:

A. Swiss constitution
B. French constitution
C. U.K. constitution
D. U.S. constitution

797. Whose recommendations are needed for introducing in the parliament a bill on redistributing territory of any state?

A. Prime Minister's recommendation
B. Vice President's recommendation
C. President's recommendation
D. Chief Justice of India's recommendation

798. The old name of Tamil Nadu was:

A. State of Madras
B. State of Chindwara
C. State of Mysore
D. State of Bijnore

799. The old name of Lakshadweep was:
A. Andaman & Nicobar Islands
B. Daman and Diu
D. Laccadive, Minicoy and Amindivi islands
C. None of these

800. The State of Arunachal Pradesh was created in:
A. 1988
B. 1989
C. 2000
D. 1987

ANSWERS

1	**2**	**3**	**4**	**5**	**6**	**7**	**8**	**9**	**10**
B	C	D	B	A	A	A	B	B	B
11	**12**	**13**	**14**	**15**	**16**	**17**	**18**	**19**	**20**
A	B	D	B	C	A	D	D	A	A
21	**22**	**23**	**24**	**25**	**26**	**27**	**28**	**29**	**30**
C	B	A	B	B	A	D	C	A	A
31	**32**	**33**	**34**	**35**	**36**	**37**	**38**	**39**	**40**
C	D	A	C	C	A	D	D	A	B
41	**42**	**43**	**44**	**45**	**46**	**47**	**48**	**49**	**50**
C	C	C	A	A	A	B	B	B	C
51	**52**	**53**	**54**	**55**	**56**	**57**	**58**	**59**	**60**
A	C	B	A	A	A	B	A	C	C
61	**62**	**63**	**64**	**65**	**66**	**67**	**68**	**69**	**70**
B	A	A	B	C	C	A	C	D	C
71	**72**	**73**	**74**	**75**	**76**	**77**	**78**	**79**	**80**
A	D	A	A	D	A	B	A	D	C
81	**82**	**83**	**84**	**85**	**86**	**87**	**88**	**89**	**90**
B	A	B	D	B	B	A	B	C	C
91	**92**	**93**	**94**	**95**	**96**	**97**	**98**	**99**	**100**
B	C	C	B	B	B	B	A	B	B
101	**102**	**103**	**104**	**105**	**106**	**107**	**108**	**109**	**110**
C	C	C	C	A	B	B	A	B	A
111	**112**	**113**	**114**	**115**	**116**	**117**	**118**	**119**	**120**
C	B	D	C	C	D	D	A	C	A
121	**122**	**123**	**124**	**125**	**126**	**127**	**128**	**129**	**130**
B	B	A	B	D	D	D	C	C	A
131	**132**	**133**	**134**	**135**	**136**	**137**	**138**	**139**	**140**
D	D	B	D	D	A	C	A	B	B
141	**142**	**143**	**144**	**145**	**146**	**147**	**148**	**149**	**150**
B	B	C	A	A	C	C	A	B	A
151	**152**	**153**	**154**	**155**	**156**	**157**	**158**	**159**	**160**
C	C	D	B	A	D	A	B	C	A
161	**162**	**163**	**164**	**165**	**166**	**167**	**168**	**169**	**170**
C	B	C	A	C	B	D	B	B	A
171	**172**	**173**	**174**	**175**	**176**	**177**	**178**	**179**	**180**
C	C	B	D	B	B	A	A	A	C
181	**182**	**183**	**184**	**185**	**186**	**187**	**188**	**189**	**190**
D	B	C	C	B	A	D	B	B	A

191	**192**	**193**	**194**	**195**	**196**	**197**	**198**	**199**	**200**
B	A	B	A	D	C	A	D	C	C
201	**202**	**203**	**204**	**205**	**206**	**207**	**208**	**209**	**210**
A	B	A	B	A	D	C	B	C	C
211	**212**	**213**	**214**	**215**	**216**	**217**	**218**	**219**	**220**
B	D	B	A	B	A	A	A	B	D
221	**222**	**223**	**224**	**225**	**226**	**227**	**228**	**229**	**230**
A	A	C	B	B	C	B	B	A	B
231	**232**	**233**	**234**	**235**	**236**	**237**	**238**	**239**	**240**
A	A	B	B	A	B	A	B	C	B
241	**242**	**243**	**244**	**245**	**246**	**247**	**248**	**249**	**250**
B	D	B	B	C	B	B	B	B	B
251	**252**	**253**	**254**	**255**	**256**	**257**	**258**	**259**	**260**
B	A	B	A	B	D	C	C	C	B
261	**262**	**263**	**264**	**265**	**266**	**267**	**268**	**269**	**270**
B	A	A	A	B	A	D	B	B	B
271	**272**	**273**	**274**	**275**	**276**	**277**	**278**	**279**	**280**
D	C	B	C	B	A	B	B	B	C
281	**282**	**283**	**284**	**285**	**286**	**287**	**288**	**289**	**290**
B	B	C	B	C	D	B	A	A	A
291	**292**	**293**	**294**	**295**	**296**	**297**	**298**	**299**	**300**
C	B	C	B	A	B	A	B	C	B
301	**302**	**303**	**304**	**305**	**306**	**307**	**308**	**309**	**310**
C	C	B	D	C	D	A	D	C	C
311	**312**	**313**	**314**	**315**	**316**	**317**	**318**	**319**	**320**
A	B	A	B	A	B	D	A	C	A
321	**322**	**323**	**324**	**325**	**326**	**327**	**328**	**329**	**330**
A	A	A	A	C	C	C	A	C	B
331	**332**	**333**	**334**	**335**	**336**	**337**	**338**	**339**	**340**
A	B	B	A	A	A	A	B	A	D
341	**342**	**343**	**344**	**345**	**346**	**347**	**348**	**349**	**350**
B	A	A	A	A	B	A	A	B	A
351	**352**	**353**	**354**	**355**	**356**	**357**	**358**	**359**	**360**
A	D	C	D	A	A	B	B	D	D
361	**362**	**363**	**364**	**365**	**366**	**367**	**368**	**369**	**370**
A	B	B	C	D	A	A	A	B	D
371	**372**	**373**	**374**	**375**	**376**	**377**	**378**	**379**	**380**
A	A	C	C	A	B	C	D	A	A
381	**382**	**383**	**384**	**385**	**386**	**387**	**388**	**389**	**390**
A	B	C	B	B	B	C	A	A	B
391	**392**	**393**	**394**	**395**	**396**	**397**	**398**	**399**	**400**
C	B	B	C	C	B	B	D	A	A
401	**402**	**403**	**404**	**405**	**406**	**407**	**408**	**409**	**410**
B	B	A	C	D	C	B	A	B	D
411	**412**	**413**	**414**	**415**	**416**	**417**	**418**	**419**	**420**
A	B	A	C	D	C	B	C	B	D

421	422	423	424	425	426	427	428	429	430
A	A	C	C	B	B	D	D	A	D
431	432	433	434	435	436	437	438	439	440
A	C	C	C	C	D	A	B	A	B
441	442	443	444	445	446	447	448	449	450
C	C	D	A	A	C	D	D	A	A
451	452	453	454	455	456	457	458	459	460
B	A	D	A	C	D	C	B	A	C
461	462	463	464	465	466	467	468	469	470
A	D	C	B	C	A	B	A	B	B
471	472	473	474	475	476	477	478	479	480
A	A	C	A	B	C	B	D	B	C
481	482	483	484	485	486	487	488	489	490
A	D	B	B	B	C	C	D	B	A
491	492	493	494	495	496	497	498	499	500
C	B	B	B	B	A	D	C	C	C
501	502	503	504	505	506	507	508	509	510
B	B	A	C	C	C	D	C	B	A
511	512	513	514	515	516	517	518	519	520
A	A	B	B	C	C	D	C	C	A
521	522	523	524	525	526	527	528	529	530
A	B	C	B	B	C	B	B	A	D
531	532	533	534	535	536	537	538	539	540
C	B	A	D	A	B	D	C	B	D
541	542	543	544	545	546	547	548	549	550
A	D	C	C	C	B	A	B	C	C
551	552	553	554	555	556	557	558	559	560
C	A	B	B	C	C	C	B	B	A
561	562	563	564	565	566	567	568	569	570
D	D	C	D	A	C	B	D	A	C
571	572	573	574	575	576	577	578	579	580
C	B	C	B	B	D	A	B	A	C
581	582	583	584	585	586	587	588	589	590
D	A	D	C	B	B	A	B	A	A
591	592	593	594	595	596	597	598	599	600
C	C	B	C	D	A	B	B	D	A
601	602	603	604	605	606	607	608	609	610
D	A	B	A	A	D	A	C	B	A
611	612	613	614	615	616	617	618	619	620
B	B	D	A	B	B	A	C	A	B
621	622	623	624	625	626	627	628	629	630
A	D	B	B	C	C	A	D	A	D
631	632	633	634	635	636	637	638	639	640
B	A	C	B	B	C	A	C	C	B
641	642	643	644	645	646	647	648	649	650
B	A	D	C	B	A	D	B	C	A

651	652	653	654	655	656	657	658	659	660
C	A	D	A	B	C	A	B	A	C
661	662	663	664	665	666	667	668	669	670
D	A	B	A	A	B	A	D	A	C
671	672	673	674	675	676	677	678	679	680
B	D	B	C	C	A	B	C	C	D
681	682	683	684	685	686	687	688	689	690
A	C	C	B	A	C	A	B	C	A
691	692	693	694	695	696	697	698	699	700
D	B	C	B	C	B	C	C	C	A
701	702	703	704	705	706	707	708	709	710
B	D	C	C	C	D	A	C	A	A
711	712	713	714	715	716	717	718	719	720
A	A	C	A	A	B	A	D	A	B
721	722	723	724	725	726	727	728	729	730
B	C	B	A	A	C	D	A	B	B
731	732	733	734	735	736	737	738	739	740
A	B	B	C	B	D	D	A	C	B
741	742	743	744	745	746	747	748	749	750
A	C	A	B	D	D	C	A	C	C
751	752	753	754	755	756	757	758	759	760
B	C	C	A	D	A	C	C	B	A
761	762	763	764	765	766	767	768	769	770
D	C	A	A	B	C	C	C	A	B
771	772	773	774	775	776	777	778	779	780
D	A	C	A	C	B	D	B	A	C
781	782	783	784	785	786	787	788	789	790
D	C	D	D	A	A	C	B	D	A
791	792	793	794	795	796	797	798	799	800
C	A	C	A	D	D	C	A	C	D

LEGAL TERMS

— A —

Abandonment	Relinquishment of an interest, claim of right voluntarily.
Abduction	The wrongful taking away of a person. A male above the age of 16 and a female above the age of 18 is abducted below that age, they are kidnapped. Section 352 of Indian Penal Code deals with this offence.
Abet	To aid in the commission of an offence.
Abettor	One who encourages or aid the commission of an offence.
Abide	To act in accordance with rule of law.
Ab initio	From the very beginning.
Abscond	One who hide oneself in order to escape arrest of legal proceeding for a crime or avoid arrest.
Accessory	A person who is concerned in the crime but does not actually commit the crime.
Accomplice	A person who is associated with another person in the commission of any offence.
Accused	A person becomes an accused immediately after he has been arrested by the police for an offence which forms the subject matter of investigation by them.
Acquittal	The order of discharge of courts if a court satisfied with the evidence that the accused is not guilty, he shall record an order of acquittal (Cr,P.C., 1973, Secs. 248 and 255).
Act of God	An accident which occurs due to the operation of natural forces, which no human foresight could provide against.
Act of State	Act done by Government in the exercise of its sovereign powers.
Actionable Wrong	A wrongful act which an action lies in a court of law.
Actus Reus	Wrongful act.
Adjourn	To defer the hearing of a case to another date in the court.
Adjudication	Decision of the court, e.g., The order of a court which declares a debtor to be a bankrupt.
Ad Idem	With a common understanding.
Ad Valorem	According to the valuation.
Administrative Law	That branch of public law which deals with the various organs of the sovereign power and rules made by him.
Adultery	Adultery is voluntary sexual intercourse between a married man and some other than his wife or between a married woman and some other than her husband.
Adverse Claim	A claim put forward against the interest of another person.
Affidavit	A written statement under a oath, which is sworn to by person making it, as true.
Affray	Unlawful fighting or use of force to intimidate others.
Age of Capacity	The age at which a person becomes legally capable of entering into a contract, executing a will, maintaining a law suit etc.
Age of Majority	The age at which a person attains full legal rights e.g. 18 years in India.
Agnates	Relatives whose relationship can be traced exclusively through males.
Alibi	(Elsewhere) A defence where an accused alleges that at the time when the offence with which he is charged was committed, he was elsewhere.
Alien Enemy	A person owing allegiance to an adverse belligerent state.

Alimony	The maintenance given by husband to his divorced wife.
Assault	Sudden violent attack to hurt another person by striking at him with or without weapon.
Amicus Curiae	The friend of the court is the name is given to the lawyer appointed by a court to represent a poor litigant.
Amnesty	A general pardon given by Government.
Annuity	An amount that is payable yearly after a certain period.
Appeal	Application to a higher court to examine against a case decided by a lower court and possibly given a different decision.
Arbitration	Settling disputes by referring them to independent third parties.
Arrest	Arrest means the lawful restraining of the liberty of a person in order to compel obedience to the order of a court or to prevent the commission of a crime.
Arson	Crime of unlawfully damaging or destroying by fire.
Assay	Usually used to denote examination of weight and measures by officials.
Attach	To take, seize or apprehend property by order of court.
Autrefois	A person cannot be tried for the same offence twice.

— B —

Bail	Releasing an arrested person after taking sureties that he will regularly attend the court and face the trail.
Bailiff	A subordinate officer of the court who executes writs and other court orders such as serving summons.
Bailment	When goods are left by one person with another to hold accordance with instructions.
Barter	To exchange one commodity for another.
Bastard	A child born by unlawful wedlock, an illegitimate child.
Battery	Crime of actual or intended use of physical force on a person.
Bench	Name of the judge sit in court.
Bestiality	Act of having intercourse with an animal. It is prohibited and punishable.
Bequeath	To dispose of personal property by will.
Bigamy	Entering into a marriage with one person while still legally married to another. It is an offence, punishable by seven years in prison.
Blasphemy	The public or criminal libel of speaking matter relating to God Jesus Christ, the Bible or the book of common prayer, intending to wound the feelings of mankind or to excite contempt and hatred against the church.
Body Corporate	An association or collection of persons having rights and duties distinct from those of the individual persons who form it from time to time.
Bona Fide	In good faith.
Bona Vacantia	Goods that do not have an owner. Generally they go to the finder.
Bond	A legal instrument by which a person undertakes to do or not to do something.
Borstal	A reformatory where young offenders are kept.
Breach	The infringing or violation of a right, duty or law, agreement etc.
Breach of Contract	Breach of contract is failure to perform the obligation under the contract.
Brief	An abbreviated statement of acts and points of law drawn up for counsel in charge

of a case.

Breach of Trust 'Breach of trust' means a breach of any duty imposed on a trusted. As such, by any law for the time being in force (Indian Trust Act, 1882, sec.3).

Buggery Sodomy; the offence committed by a person consisting of anal penetration punishable by the Sexual offences Act, 1956. It is prohibited by law as an unnatural offence.

Burden of Proof The duty of a party to prove a disputed assertion or charge.

By Stander One who is present at the place of occurrence but does not participate in it.

By Law Regulations made by the local authority or corporation or company for its members for their day to day work.

—C—

Case A legal action or trial, argument put in legal proceedings.

Caveat A warning.

Caveat Emptor Let the purchaser beware.

Cede To assign or transfer, To transfer territory.

Certiorari A writ from Superior Court which quashes the decision of a lower court because it is based on irregular procedure.

Charge-Sheet It is the process in which the officer in charge of a police station or lock-up enters the accusation or charges against person brought there in custody whether arrested with or without warrant.

Chattel Movable property.

Circumstantial Evidence A series of circumstances from which an inference of suit can be drawn.

Class Action A law suit brought by a representative member of a group of person on behalf of all others.

Cognate Blood relation other than an agnate and includes a female relation only.

Cognizable Offence An offence in which arrest can be made without a warrant.

Cognizance Cognizance means the acceptance of a cause for hearing and decision to take notice of a dispute or controversy, taking judicial notice by court.

Cohabitation Living together as husband and wife even if not married.

Commutation The change of a penalty or punishment from a greater to a less punishment.

Confession Confession is a written acknowledgement of guilt by a party accused of an offence.

Condonation The Pardoning of an offence.

Conjugal Rights Right of husband/wife to the consortium of the other.

Consanguinity Relationship by blood.

Consideration The price for the promise to do or not to do something. Every contract requires consideration to be legally enforceable.

Consummation Voluntarily sexual intercourse to make marriage complete.

Contempt of Court Willful disregard, disobedience or disrespect to a court of law.

Contraband Goods Goods prohibited by law.

Contract A legally binding agreement between two or more parties.

Conversion The action of wrongfully converting something to one's own use.

Conveyance A written document transferring ownership of land from one person to another.

Conviction Conviction is the act of a court awarding a person guilty of a criminal offence and awarding a punishment.

Coparcener One who shares (equally) with other inheritance in the estate of a common ancestor.

Copyright The exclusive right of printing or otherwise multiplying copies of published literary work; That is, the right of preventing all others from doing so. The infringement of this right is called piracy. Copyright extends to original, artistic, dramatic and musical works and to recordings films and broadcast, etc.

Coroner An officer who inquires into any violent of unnatural death.

Corpus A body; human body.

Court Fee The fee payable on filing of a suit, application, appeal, etc. in the court of law.

Court Martial A tribunal for the administration of military law.

Covenant An agreement in writing between two persons, whereby, one is enjoying to do or not to do something.

Culpable Criminal, blameworthy.

Custody Confinement or imprisonment e.g. Remand (of accused person) in custody, Control and possession of something or person e.g. To surrender ourself into the custody of the court.

Custom An unwritten law dating back to civilization. This is a conduct which is observed uniformly and voluntarily by the people.

— D —

Damages A sum of money paid to the plaintiff as compensation for breach of contract or tort.

De Facto In fact, actually.

De Jure According to the law.

Declaratory Decree A decree which simply declares the rights of the parties to express the opinion of the court on any question without ordering to be done.

Decree A judgement delivered by a court.

Deed A written statement which is signed, sealed and delivered.

Defamation Publication of a false or derogatory statement regarding a person, which lowers his reputation in the eyes of members of the society.

Defendant A person sued in a court of law.

Delegated Legislation This consists of orders, rules regulations, directions, by laws etc. which is made by a person or body other than the legislative authority by virtue of powers conferred by the statute. It is also called subordinate legislation or administrative legislation.

Demise The grant of lease.

Deposition The giving of testimony upon oath in a court of law.

Deponent A person who makes an affidavit or deposition.

Desertion Abandonment by one spouse or the other.

Devise A gift of land in a will.

Disclaimer Disclaimer is an express denial, or complete renouncing one's legal right or claim.

Diplomatic Privilege Legal immunity accorded to ambassadors and representatives of foreign governments.

Distress The seizure chattel to satisfy out of the proceeds of its sale, some debt or claim.

Divorce Dissolution of marriage.

Domicile The place where one has his permanent residence to which, if absents, he has the intention of returning.

Donee To whom gift is made.

Donor One who makes a gift.

— E —

Easement Right which an owner of land has over land of another person, e.g. Right of light, right of way.

Embezzlement Dishonest misappropriation of property by a person, who comes in possession thereof lawfully.

Eminent Domain Power of the state to acquire private property for public use.

Enactment Act of Parliament.

Encumbrance A liability on property.

Encroachment Unlawfully entering upon another's rights or possessions.

Equity Fair and right, the recourse to general principles of justice to correct and supplement the ordinary law.

Escheat The lapsing of property of the sovereign or state on the death of the owner intestate and without heir.

Estate An interest in land.

Estoppels A rule of evidence preventing a person from denying truth of statement which he has made previously by which he has led another to believe and act upon.

Eviction Dispossession; recovery of land by the application law.

Ex Gratia Payment as a favour without any legal obligation.

Evidence The legal means exclusive of more argument, which tend to prove or disprove any matter of fact, the truth of which is submitted to judicial investigation.

Ex Officio By virtue of office.

Ex Parte Order An order granted after hearing one party only.

Execution Enforcing a court's judgement with the force of law.

Executor A representative appointed in a will to execute the will after the testator's death.

Expert Witness One who gives an opinion on a particular subject due to his special knowledge.

Extradition A process by which an offender is transferred from one country to another for a trial.

— F —

False Imprisonment The confinement of a person without just cause or excuse. There must be a total restraint of the person, and the onus of proving reasonable cause is on the defendant.

Felony Crime of any kind, legally graver than misdemeanors.

Feme Sole Unmarried woman.

Fiat A command, a decree, a short order or warrant of a judge or public officer that certain steps should be taken.

Fiduciary A relationship based on trust or good faith.

FIR First information report of grievance which is given to police.

Force Majeure Irresistible force, circumstances beyond one's control.

Fore Closure A decree determines the equitable right of a mortgagor to redeem after the mortgagee's estate has become absolute at law.

Forfeiture A punishment whereby the offender lost all his interests in his property.

Forma Pauperis A suit may be instituted by a pauper who is person not possessed to sufficient means to enable him to pay the fee prescribed by law for the plaint in such suit.

Franchise The right of voting.

Freehold The absolute ownership of land.

Frustration of the contract The cancellation of a contract due to impossibility of performance.

Full Blood Two persons are said to be related to each other by full blood when they are descended from a common ancestor by the same wife.

Functus Officio An authority who has performed the act authorized so that the authority is exhausted.

— G —

Good will The benefit which arises from the establishment of particular business or occupations. Intrinsic value of the good repute and customs of an established trade or business.

Gratuitous Without valuable or legal consideration.

Gratuity A lump sum paid by an employer to retiring employee.

Ground Rent The rent paid by the holder of a lease to do the freeholder.

Group Litigation A law suits, instituted on behalf of or against a group of person recognized as one litigating entity.

Guardian A person having right and duty to protect the property or right of a minor person.

Genocide Mass killing of a group of people belonging to a particular religion, race etc.

— H —

Habeas Corpus It means have the body to present. A writ issued to bring person before a court, to ensure that his imprisonment is not illegal.

Half Blood The children of the same mother, but have different fathers.

Hearsay It is not admissible as an evidence under Evidence Act because witness makes statements of another, who was a direct witness to the event in question.

Heresy A deliberate and over denial of some accepted dogma of Christian Church.

Hiba Perfect gift, one accompanied be delivery and acceptance (under Mohammadan Law).

Homicide Killing of a human being by another human being.

Hostile Witness The witness who makes statements adverse to the party calling and examining him.

Hypothecation A right of a creditor in which the pleader retains possession of the thing pledges.

— I —

Ibid At the same place or from the same sources, in the same book or passage.

Imbezzle To steal, where a person entrusted with goods, wastes and diminishes them.

Immovable Property Property attached or embedded to the land.

Immunity The condition of being exempt from some liability to which other are subject, *For ex:*—The immunity of a judge in respect of things done or said when exercising his judicial function.

Impeach Bring a charge against a person.

In Camera Not in open court, in private.

In Cest Sexual intercourse between persons related with blood. For ex. Brother and Sister etc.

In Limnie	At the outset, preliminary.
In Pari Delicto	In equal fault, culpable or criminal.
In Pari Materia	Upon the some matter or subject or in an analogous case.
In Re	In the matter of.
Indictment	A written accusation, read out in court at the beginning of a criminal trial.
Indemnity	Formal legal acceptance of responsibility against damage or loss.
Injunction	An order or judgement by which a party to an action is required to do or refrain from doing a particular thing.
Innuendo	Defamatory hint or reamark.
Insolvent	A person whose assets are sufficient to pay his debt.
Inter Alia	Among other things.
Inter Vivos	Between living persons.
Inter Locutory Order	Order which is made pending the cause and before a final hearing on the merit.
International Law	The body of rules regulating the relations among the nations, resolving the conflict between laws of different nations.
Interrogatories	In the course of civil suit, these are particular permission in writing demanded of witnesses or parties brought in to be examined in a case.
Intestate	A person who dies without making a will.
Intra Vires	Within the powers.
Ipso Facto	By the fact itself.

— J —

Judgement Debtor	A person against whom a decree has been passed.
Judgement In Rem	A judgement in rem binds not only the parties of the action but all other persons.
Joint Tenancy	Where property is ancestral is owned by two or more persons under one instrument or act of the parties.
Jointly and Severally	When persons jointly as well individually liable for their actions.
Judgement	A decision of a court with legal reasoning in a legal proceeding.
Judicial Review	The power of the courts to review the legislative and executive section and determine their validity.
Jump Bail	Failure of the accused person to appear before court at the time after getting a bail.
Jurat	That part of an affidavit that it was sworn before him.
Jurisprudence	The Science or Philosophy of law.
Juristic Person	A legal entity other than a natural person such as corporations, association, idols etc.
Juvenile Courts	Magistrates exercising jurisdiction over offences committed by and other matters related to children and young persons.
Juvenile Delinquency	An offence committed by a person who is under 16 years of age.

— K —

Kidnapping	An act of taking away or abducting a person out of another's custody or from lawful guardianship for unlawful purpose.
Kin	Blood relatives.

— L —

LL.B.	Legum Baccalaureus, Bachelor of Laws.
Laches	Neglect of a person to promptitude in pursuing a legal remedy.
Laissez Faire	Government non-interference in the economic matters.
Larceny	The taking and carrying away of mere personal goods of another with intent to steal the goods.
Law	A body of rules which regulates human conduct governs the relationship between two or more person.
Lease	The contract between owner of property and a tenant who agrees to pay money for the use and possession of the property for a fixed period of time.
Legacy	A gift of property by will.
Libel	A defamatory statement especially in writing but it includes also pictures, signs, or electronic broadcast.
Lien	A right by which a person in possession of the property holds and retains it against the other is satisfied of a demand due to the party retraining it.
Liquidated	Fixed or certained.
Litigation	The taking of legal action by a party who is known as a litigant.
Lunatic	An idiot or person of unsound mind or insane.

— M —

Mala Fides	With bad faith, with wrong intention.
Malfeasance	Wrongful conduct, especially by a public official, an important act.
Malice	Ill will, intent to commit an unlawful act.
Mandamus	A writ issued by the Supreme Court or the High Court and directed a Governmental or semi governmental, a judicial or quasi judicial and private bodies performing public function to perform their duties.
Manslaughter	It is a crime of unlawful killing but not amounting to murder under English law.
Mercy Killing (Euthanasia)	A painless killing of a person who is convicted for death penalty by the court of Law.
Mens Rea	A guilty mind.
Mc Naghten Rule	A rule which determine whether a person is legally insane or not under English Law.
Mesne Profits	Damages payable by trespassers who have stayed in possession after their right to occupy land has ended.
Minor	A person below 18 years but where guardian appointed for a minor, then such person remains minor upto age 21 years.
Miscarriage	Failure in the administration of justice, synonym for abortion.
Misfeasance	The improper doing of an act which a person might lawfully do.
Moratorium	A legal authorization to a debtor to postpone payment for a certain time.
Mortgage	A loan of money taken after giving security bond of immoveable property.

— N —

Natural Justice	Justice which is founded in equity, honesty and good conscience.
Naturalization	It is the act by which a foreigner requires the status of a natural born citizen.
Negligence	A tort, actionable at the suit of a person suffering damage from the defendant's breach

of duty to take care to refrain from injuring him.

Negotiable Instrument A negotiable instrument means a promissory note, bills of exchange or cheque payable either to order or to bearer.

Next Friend A person who is admitted or appointed by a court as a special guardian to act for the benefit of a minor or insane person.

Non-Cognizable Offence This is an offence where the police has no legal authority to arrest the accused person without a warrant from the court.

Nominee A person who has been selected by a party as its candidate for a public office.

Notary A solicitor who attests deeds, or one, who in the case of a dishonoured bills, notes or deeds or protests it. Notary is also known as notary public.

— O —

Obiter Dicta Remarks of a judge, which are said by the way and are not directly relevant to the case at hand.

Offender An accused person, one who is under accusation of having committed an offence, one who is guilty of an offence.

Onus A burden.

Order The formal expression of any decision of a civil court which is not a decree.

Original Jurisdiction Jurisdiction to entertain cases is the first instance as distinguished from appellate jurisdiction.

Ownership An absolute right over property for something based on rightful title.

— P —

Pardon Decision of the Head of state to forgive a person who has given punishment incurred for some offence.

Parole Process by which a prisoner is allowed to be conditionally released during the term of imprisonment.

Passing Off A tort, where by a wrong committed by person who sells goods or carries on business etc, thereby making the buyers believe that the good actually come from the former.

Patent Exclusively privilege granted by the authority to an inventor who invent something new.

Per Incurrium A mistaken decision by a court.

Perjury An offence of giving a false statement before the court which a person known to be false.

Plaint The statement in writing of the cause of action in a suit.

Plaintiff A person, who brings a suit to a court of a law.

Plea Bargaining Where the accused instead of defending his case in proper defence simply pleaded guilty under a promise or assurance that he would be let off lightly and then in appeal or revision to enhance the sentence.

Pledge It is a contract where a bailment of personal property as security for some debt or engagement.

Polygamy Having more than one wife or husband.

Post Mortem An examination of dead body to ascertain the actual cause of death.

Power of Attorney An authority given by one person to another to act on his behalf.

Pre-emption A right to purchase property before other persons.

Prescription Method of acquiring rights over another's land by long period of adverse possession.

Presumption of Death If a person has not been heard of as alive, for seven years, there is presumption in law that he is dead.

Prima Facie On the face of it, based on the first impression.

Private Law That part of law which deals with relations between private individuals.

Probate The copy of a will ratified under the seal of a court of competent jurisdiction with a grant of administration to the estate of the testator.

Prohibition An order of a higher court (Supreme Court, High Court) preventing an interior court from doing something.

Pro-rata Proportionately.

Prorogation The act of bringing a session of Parliament or other legislative assembly to an end.

Proviso A condition.

Public Law That body of laws which deals with the relations between private individuals and the governments.

Public Policy A policy that is in the interest of the state and community.

— Q —

Quash To render null or void by a superior court, to set aside or put an end to by an order of a higher court.

Quasi It were analogous to, semi.

Quasi Contract A quasi contract is an act for event from which, though not consensual contract, an obligation arises from a contract.

Quo Warranto A writ of quo warranto issued by the Supreme Court or the High Court against a person who claims or who usurps any office, franchise or liberty to enquire by what authority he supports his claim.

Quorum Minimum number of persons necessary for conduct of proceeding.

— R —

Ratification Approval by word or writing or conduct.

Ratio Decidendi Opinion given by the judge and such opinion is necessary for the decision of particular case.

Recognizance Sum of money will be forfeited by the accused person who falls to answer his bail.

Redemption The paying off a loan by a mortgagor, a buying back of the legal estate after it has passed to the mortgagee.

Rejoinder A reply to the plaintiff replication.

Remand A committal of an accused to prison.

Repeal To rescind to revoke.

Repudiate The renunciation of a right, contract or obligation.

Repugnant	In consistent.
Res judicata	A cause or suit already decided.
Retrospective Legislation	An act that applies to a period before the act was passed.
Right of Re-entry	Right of landlord to take possession if tenant breaks the terms of tenancy.
Robbery	Crime of using force or causing fear of force in order to steal.

— S —

Sale	Transfer of ownership in exchange of price paid.
Sedition	The inducing of a girl or women to part with her virtue.
Setting Aside	Cancelling, making void.
Sine Die	Indefinitely.
Slander	Defamatory words spoken of another.
Sovereignty	Apex authority or higher authority, Indian possess the sovereignty as union of states but state does not possess sovereignty.
Speaking Order	An order which contains matters which is explanatory or illustrative of the direction which is given by it.
Specific Performance	The performance of a contract exactly or substantially according to its terms.
Stare Decisis	The principle that decisions of courts in previous cases must be followed in subsequent cases of similar nature.
Status Quo	The existing state of things.
Statute	An act of Parliament.
Subpoena	An order of a court to a person to appear and give evidence before it.
Substantive Law	That part of a law which creates and defines right.
Suit	A process instituted in a court of justice for recovery of protection of a right.
Summary Proceedings	A proceeding without following the strict rules of procedure for trials.
Summons	An order by which a person is called to appear before a court, judicial officer etc.
Surety	The person who gives the guarantee.
Surrogate Mother	A woman who carries a child pursuance of an arrangement made before she began to carry the child, and with a view to any child carried is pursuance of it being handed over to and the parental rights being exercised by another person or persons.

— T —

Tenant	One who hold lands by any kind of title, whether for years, for life.
Testae	Dying after having made a will.
Testator	He who makes will.
Testimony	Statement made by witness under oath.
Tort	A civil wrong which is not exclusively the breach of contract or the breach of trust.
Tort-Feasor	One who commits or is guilty of a tort.
Trade Mark	A mark used by a manufactures or traders to distinguish his goods from the goods for other.
Treason	Betrayal of a nation attempt to overthrow the government of the state of which one

owes allegiance by resorting to war against it or by helping enemies.

Trespass To pass beyond.

Trial It means any hearing before the court at which evidence is taken.

—U—

Uberrimae Fides Abundant faith, mutual good faith between persons in a particular relationship. *For ex:* Physician and patient, guardian and ward, attorney and client.

Unicameral Legislat A legislature consisting only one house. *For ex*: State like Bihar, U.P., Maharashtra, J&K Karnataka has bi-cameral legislative and other remaining state consists of uni-cameral legislative.

Unilateral One sided.

Unilateral Contract When the party to whom an engagement is made, makes no express agreement on his part, the contract is called unilateral contract, binding only one party.

Uterine Blood Two persons are said to be uterine blood when they are descended from a common ancestral but by different husband.

Ultra Vires Outside the powers of.

—V—

Vacantia Bona Goods unclaimed or without an owner.

Versus Against or prefix symbol of opposite part written as (vs) or (v.) e.g. *Golaknath* vs. *Union of India* or *Golaknath* v. *Union of India.*

Veto This power has given to the permanent member of security council who have power of any permanent member of the security of the United Nations to refuse to agree to a proposed course of action; Power to prohibit or refuse; refusal to assent to a Parliamentary Bill.

Vicarious Liability Liability incurred upon a person for acts of another. *For ex* : Principle's liability for act of his agent.

Vis-Major Act of god, irresistible force.

Void Not valid, of no effect.

Voidable Capable of being set aside as void at the opinion of a party.

—W—

Wager A bet or something laid down and hazarded on the issue of an uncertain event.

Waiver The intentional or voluntary relinquishment of a known right.

Wakf Permanent dedication of property for religious or charitable purpose under Muslim Law.

Warranty A promise by the seller to repair goods during the specified period. However, the purchaser here does not have a right to ask for replacement of goods.

Will A person's declaration in writing of his intention as to disposal of his property after his death.

Writ A judicial process o~~f written command or~~ order issued by a court, directing or enjoining the person or persons to whom it is addressed to do or restrain from doing some act specified therein.

Witness A person who is a reporter of a crime. He has personal knowledge of occurrence. His name is recorded in chargesheet and helps the court in trial stage.

LEGAL MAXIM

— A —

A Fortiori	With strong reason
A Priori	From the cause to the effect
Ab Antiquo	From ancient times
Ab Initio	From the very beginning
Abiure	To renounce on oath or affirmation
Acta Extoriora Indicant Interiora Secreta	Acts indicate the intention
Actus Legis Nemini Facit Injuriam	Law holds no man responsible for the act of god
Actus Non Facit Reum Nisi Mens Sit Rea	A guilty mind is necessary to constitute a crime
Actus Reus	Wrongful act, the physical act of involving in the crime
Ad Hoc	For a particular purpose
Ad Idem	Of the same mind
Ad Referendum	For further consideration
Ad Rem	To the point
Ad Valorem	According to the value
Addenda	List of additions
Alias	Otherwise called
Alibi	Elsewhere
Alimony	Maintenance given by a husband to his divorced wife
Amicus Curiae	A friend of court, the name is given to lawyer appointed by a court to represent a poor litigant
Animus Attestandi	The intention of attesting
Animus Deserendi	The intention of deserting
Antenuptial	Before marriage
Assumpsit	He promised or undertook
Au Fait	Conversant with
Audi Alteram Partem	Hear the other side
Auterefois	A person cannot be tried for the same offence twice
Auterefois Acquit	Formerly acquitted
Auterefois Convict	Formerly convicted

— B —

Bailiff	A subordinate officer of the court who executes writs and other court orders
Bona Fide	In good faith, honestly
Bona Vacantia	Goods that do not have an owner. Generally they go to the finder
Boni Judici Est Ansliare Jurisdictioness	It is the part of a good judge to enlarge his jurisdiction.

— C —

Causa Celebre	A celebrated case
Causa Causans	The immediate cause
Carte Fide	In good faith, honesty
Causa Sine Qua Non	Factor essential to the occurring of event
Caveat	An order given to officers may "let him beware"
Caveat Emptor	Let the buyer beware
Caveat Venditor	Let the seller beware
Canveat Viator	Let the traveller beware
Certiorari	An order of a higher court which quashes the decision of lower court
Compos Mentis	Of sound mind
Consensus, Non Concubitus, Facit Matrimonium	It is the consent of the parties, not their cohabitation which constitutes a valid marriage
Consensus Ad Idem	Agreement as to the same thing
Corpus Delicti	The substance of the crime
Coup D'etat	Violent or illegal change
Coup D'grace	Finishing stroke
Culpa	Wrongful default

— D —

Damnum Sine Injuria	Damage without legal injury
De Die In Diem	From day to day
De Facto	In fact
De Jure	In law
De Novo	New
Decree	Order of court pronounced after hearing the case
Decree Nisi	A conditional decree
Defeasible Right	Right which can be defeated
Doli Capax	Capable of crime
Doli Incapex	Incapable of crime
Double Jeopardy	A second prosecution for the same offence
Durante Absentia	During absence
Durante Vita	During life

— E —

Ejusdem Generis	Of the same kind, the rule that where particular words are followed by general words.
Emeritus	Retired after long service
En Bloc	All at the same time
En Masse	In a body
Ex Aequo Et Bono	In justice and good faith

Ex Contractu	Arising out of contract
Ex Curia	Out of court
Ex Delicto	Arising out of wrong
Ex Gratia	As a favour
Ex Nudo Pacto – Non Oitur Actio	An action does not arise from a bare promise
Ex Officio	By virtue of office
Ex Parte	In the absence of one party
Ex Post Facto	Acting retrospectively
Expressio Unius Est Exclusio Alterius	Express mention of one thing implies the exclusion of another
Extra Vires	Beyond powers

— F —

Factum	An act or deed
Factum Probantia	Facts which are given in evidence to prove other facts in crime
Faux Pas	Tactless mistake
Flagrante Delicto	In the commission of the offence
Force Majeure	Beyond one's control

— H —

Habeas Corpus	A court order which directed the person to produce before a court who illegally detained beyond twenty four hours before
Honoris Causa	As mark of esteem

— I —

Ibid	In the same place
Ignorantia Facti Excusat - Ignorantia Juris Non Excusat	Ignorance of the fact is an excuse but ignorance of the law does not excuse
Ignoratia Juris Non Excusat	Ignorance of law has no excuse
Impasse	An insoluble difficulty
In Curia	In open court
In Loco Parentis	In the place of a parent
In Memoriam	In memory of
In Pari Delicto	Where both parties are equally in fault
In Pari Materia	Where two enactments have a common purpose in an analogous case
In Personam	Proceeding or directed against or reference to a specific person
In Re	In the matter of
In Rem	Right available against the world at large

It Situ	In its original situation
In Toto	Wholly
Infra	Below
Injuria Sine Damunum	Legal injury without actual damage
Innuendo	An innocent statement which a hidden defamatory meaning
Inter Alia	Among other things
Inter Vivos	Made between people who are alive
Intestate	Dying without leaving will
Intra Vires	Within power
Ipso Facto	By reason of that fact

— J —

Jus	Right
Jus Naturale	Law of nature, natural justice

— L —

Laissez Faire	Doctrine of non-interference by state in economy
Lex	Statute
Lex Fori	The law of the court in which the case is tried
Lex Loci	The law of a place
Lex Non Cogit Ad Impossibilia	Law cannot compel a person who is not possible to perform
Lis Pendens	A pending suit
Locus Standi	Right to be heard in court

— M —

Mala Fide	With bad faith
Mandamus	We command
Manifesta Probatione Non Indiget	Things manifest do not require proof.
Mens Rea	Guilty mind
Mesne	Intermediate
Mesne Profits	Damage payable by trespassers who have stayed in possession after their right to occupy land has ended
Modus Operandi	Mode of operating
Mutatis Mutandis	With necessary changes being made

— N —

Nemo Debet Esse Judex In Propria Sua Causa	No man can be judge in his own cause
Nemo Tenetur Seipsum Accusore	No man can be compelled to incriminate himself
Nisi	Ineffective unless person affected fails to show cause
Non Assumpsit	He did not promise
Non Compos Mentis	Not of sound mind

Non Obstante	Notwithstanding
Noscitur A Sociis	Meaning of word can be gathered from context
Noscitur A Socvis	Meaning of a doubtful word may be ascertained by reference to the meaning of words associated with it
Nota Bene (Nb)	Take notice
Nudum Pactum	An enforceable contract
Nullus Commodum Capere Potest De Injuria Sua Propria	No man can take advantage of his own wrong

— O —

Obiter Dicta	Remark of a judge
Obiter Dictum	Judge's opinion

— P —

Par Excellence	Eminently
Pendente Lite	Pending litigation
Per	As stated by
Per Annum	By the year
Per Capita	Individually
Per Curiam	By the court
Per Incuriam	Wrong decision by court, by oversight
Per Se	By itself
Prima Facie	On the first sight
Pro Bono Publico	For the good of the public
Pro Rata	In proportion

— Q —

Quantum Merit	As a person earned
Quash	Making null or invalid or making end to a legal proceeding
Quasi Contract	A contract between a party comes
Quasi Judicial	Sharing of qualities of and approximating to what is judicial
Qui Facit Per Alium Facit Per Se	He who acts through another is deemed to act in person
Qui Per Alium Facit Per Seipsum Facere Videtur	He who does an act through another is deemed in law to do it himself
Quid Pro Quo	Something for something
Quo Warranto	Order of a court in the form of writ directed the person in authority to show by what right he claim it
Quorum	Minimum number of persons necessary for conduct of proceeding of parliament
Quo Jure	By what right

— R —

Raison D'etre Reason for the existence of a thing

Rapprochement Restoration of harmonious relations

Ratio Decidendi Principal laid down by the court in deciding a case

Rebus Sic Stantibus Binding bill circumstances remain the same

Res Gestae The facts so connected with a fact in issue so as to explain its nature

Res Judicata A case already decided

Res Nullis A things which has no owner

Respondent Superior Let the principle be held responsible

Responsa Prudentuim The answer of the learned in law. The opinions and decisions of learned lawyers

— S —

Salus Populi Est Suprema Lex The welfare of the people is the paramount law

Sine Die Indefinitely

Sine Qua Non Indispensable condition.

Spes Successionis Mere hope of succeeding to property

Stare Decisis The principle that decision of courts in previous cases must be followed in subsequent cases of similar nature

Status Quo To maintain the present state of affairs

Statute An act of parliament

Sub Judice Under judicial consideration or in course of trial

Subpoena An order of a court to a person to appear and give evidence before it

Sui Generis The only one of its kind

Suo Moto On its own

Supra Above

— T —

Tort Civil wrong

Trespass To pass beyond

Turpis Causa A base on which no action can be founded, the maxim being ex turpi causa non oritur actis

— U —

Uberrinae Fide Of the utmost good faith

Ubi Jus Remedium Where there is a right there is a remedy

Ultra Vires Beyond the power

— V —

Vide	Refer to
Vigilantibus, Non Dormientibus, Jura Subveniunt	The law assists those who are vigilant, not those who sleep over their rights
Vis Major	Irresistible force
Void	Have no legal effect
Void Ab Initio	Void from very beginning
Volenti Non-fit Injuria	Damage suffered by consent is not a cause of action
Voluntas In Delictis Non Exitus Spectatur	In crimes, the intention, and not the result, is looked into

ABBREVIATIONS

A

ADB	Asian Development Bank
AID	Agency for International Development
AIR	All India Reporter
AITUC	All India Trade Union Congress

B

BCI	Bar Council of India
BPE	Bureau of Police Enetrprises

C

CAT	Central Administrative Tribunal
CAG	Comptroller and Auditor General
CBDT	Central Board of Direct Taxes
CHOGM	Commonwealth Head of Governments Meeting
CIA	Central Intelligence Agency
CID	Criminal investigation Department
CJI	Chief Justice of India
CIB	Company Law Board
COFEPOSA	Conservation of Foreign Exchange and Prevention of Smuggling Activities Act
CBR	Central Board of Revenue
CEC	Chief Election Commission
COPRA	Consumer Protection Act, 1986
CPC	Civil Procedure Code
Cr. P.C.	Criminal Procedure Code
CRY	Child Relief and Youth
CVC	Chief Vigilance Commissioner

D

DA	Dearness allowance

E

ECAFE	Economic Commission for Asia and Far East
ECOSOC	Economic and Social Council
ESMA	Essential Survives and Maintenance Act
EEC	European Economic Community
ESCAP	Economic and Social Commission for Asia and the Pacific

F

FBI	Federal Bureau of Investigation
FEMA	Foreign Exchange Management Act
FERA	Foreign Exchange Regulation Act
FIR	First Information Report
FCRA	Foreign Contribution Regulation Act
FLC	Foreign Legal Consultant
FTC	Fast Track Court

G

GATT	General Agreement on Tariffs and Trade
GOI	Government of India

H

HC	High Court

I

IAAS	Indian Audit and Accounts Service
ICAO	International Civil Aviation Organization
ICJ	International Court of Justice
ICRC	International Committee of Red Cross
ICWA	Indian Council of World Affairs
IDA	International Development Agency
IDC	International Development Corporation
ILI	Indian Law Institute
ILO	International Labour Organization
IMF	International Monetary Fund
INTERPOL	International Police Organization
IOCU	International Organization of Consumer Union
IPC	Indian Penal Code
IPR	Intellectual Property Rights
IPU	International Parliamentary Union
IRDA	Insurance Regulatory and Development Authority

J

JD	Juris Doctor

L

LLM	Legum Majister, Master of Laws

M

MCOCA Maharashtra Control of Organised Crime Act
MISA Maintenance of Internal Security Act
MLA Member of Legislative Assembly
MLC Member of Legislative Council
MP Member of Parliament
MODVAT Modified Value Added Tax
MRTPC Monopolies and Restrictive Trade Practices Commission

N

NALSA National Legal Services Authority
NATO North Atlantic Treaty Organization
NCDRC National Consumer Dispute Redressal Commission
NETA National Environmental Tribunal Act
NJS National Judicial Service
NNT Nuclear Non-Proliferation Treaty
NPT Nuclear Proliferation Treaty
NRC Nuclear Regularity Commission

O

OIGS On India Government Service
OSP Open Sky Policy

P

PDA Preventive Detention Act
PIB Press Information Bureau
PFA Prevention of Food Adulteration Act
PIL Public Interest Litigation
POTA Prevention Of Terrorism Act
POW Prisoner Of War

R

RAW Research and Analysis Wing
ROC Registrar of Companies

S

SAPTA South Asian Preferential Trade Agreement
SC Supreme Court
SETAO South East Asia Treaty Organization
SEBI Securities and Exchange Board of India
SICA The Sick Industries Control Act
SITA Suppression of Immoral Traffic in Women and Girls Act

T

TADA Terrorists and Disruptive Activities (Prevention) Act
TRIMS Trade Related Investment Measures
TRIPS Trade Related Intellectual Property Rights

U

UNCE Conference on Environment and Development
UNCTAD United Nation Conference on Trade and Development
UNEP United Nations Environment Programme
UNESCO United Nations Education, Scientific and Cultural Organization
UNICEF United Nations International Children's Emergency Fund
UNIDO United Nations Industrial Development Organisation

V

VAT Value Added Tax

W

WFP World Food Programme
WIPO World Intellectual Property Organization
WTO World Trade Organization
WWF World Wide Fund
WWW World Wide Web

MORE ON LEGAL AWARENESS

LLB-5YR-LA-1

INDIAN LEGAL SYSTEM

Law is basically recognised rules of conduct. These rules come into being from various sources and in different ways. The legal system of a country enunciates the ways in which the 'rules of conduct' are evolved, enacted, enforced and administered.

In Indian legal system, the 'rules of conduct' come from various sources including religious diktats, customs, legislation, judicial and quasi-judicial.

Salient Features of Indian Legal System

1. A constitution guaranteeing fundamental rights which override the entire law;
2. A federal polity, thereby making two classes of legislation— Central and State—with their respective powers demarcated in the constitution.
3. Recognition of precedent or case law as a source of law;
4. Existence of comprehensive codes on various subjects of lawyers' law; such as procedure, contracts, property, succession, crimes, commercial law, evidence, etc.
5. Adversary system of procedure i.e., the judge does not take active part in the trial; and
6. Rule of law, preventive exercise of arbitrary power without express legal authority.

Sources of Indian Law

Indian law is derived from three main sources :

1. Legislation (including delegated legislation),
2. Case law (pronouncements of various courts), and
3. Customary law.

These have been discussed in detail hereinafter.

Legislations

The two main legislative bodies in India are :

1. Parliament, (comprising Lok Sabha and Rajya Sabha)
2. State Legislatures (comprising Legislative Assembly and also Legislative Council in some states)

Parliament makes laws for the whole country on subjects enumerated in the Union List contained in the Seventh Schedule of the Constitution.

State Legislatures make laws for the respective states on subjects enumerated in the State List also contained in the said Seventh Schedule.

On certain subjects enumerated in the Concurrent List, both Parliament and state legislatures can make laws. In such cases, Parliamentary legislation generally overrides state legislation.

Acts and Ordinances

A bill passed by both houses of Parliament becomes an Act when assented by the President. Similarly, bill passed by the State Legislature becomes an Act when assented by the Governor of the state.

An Ordinance is promulgated by the President for the Union (and the Governor for the State) when circumstances require immediate action and the Parliament (or the State Legislature) is not in session.

An ordinance is, however, a temporary law and it must be replaced by an Act of Parliament (or State Legislature, as the case may be) within six weeks of the commencement of the session when the Parliament (or State Legislature) meets next. If an Ordinance can not be replaced by an Act then its validity expires and it has to be repromulgated.

Subordinate Legislation

Almost every Act empowers an appropriate Government or authority to make rules or orders to carry out the purposes of the Act. These are called delegated or subordinate legislation.

The reason behind delegation of rule making powers is that the legislature can not foresee all situations, or may not have time to provide for all details, or may not possess the requisite expertise for setting out technical matters.

A delegated legislation may be in the form of rules, regulations, orders, notifications, schemes, by-laws, etc. A delegated or subordinate legislation can not be inconsistent with the Act under which it is made (or the parent law).

A delegated legislation is generally required to be placed before the Parliament (or the State legislature, as the case may be) when it meets next.

Case Law

In India the doctrine of 'precedent' is followed. Accordingly, when a High Court or the Supreme Court decides a case, it is binding not only on the parties to the proceeding, but also on all lower courts for the future and pending litigation on the same issue.

Applicability of Supreme Court rulings

A judgement of the Supreme Court is binding on all courts and authorities in India. A Supreme Court ruling can be altered by a judgement of a larger bench of the Supreme Court or by modifying legislation by the competent legislature.

Applicability of High Court rulings

A judgement of a High Court is binding on all civil courts in that state, even if the civil judge views differently on that issue. However, a judgement of a High Court is not binding on the High Courts and lower courts in other states. Judgements of High Courts of other states have only persuasive guidance but no binding authority. A High Court judgement may be :

(a) overruled by the Supreme Court,
(b) overruled by a larger bench of the same High Court,
(c) modified by a legislation of the competent legislature.

If different High Courts view differently on a point of law it can be settled either by a Supreme Court ruling or by suitable modification in the legislation. Till then, the ruling of each High Court shall be a good law in the respective state.

Advantage of Case Law

Legislations can not cover all probable questions that may arise. Besides, various provisions of a legislation may require to be elaborated/interpreted. Case law fills these gaps.

Customary Law

Certain customs or usage have been recognised as and treated at par with laws.

A 'custom' means a practice which has become well-rooted and is universal. For example, in family law, customs are recognised as a law and in certain cases even modify the general rule of law otherwise applicable. Similarly in certain commercial transactions, business usage can take place of law.

Branches of Law

The main branches of law are :

(a) **Public laws** concerning matters that affect the public as a whole. These are constitutional law, administrative law, taxation law and criminal law.

(b) **Private laws** concerning with private matters. These are law of contracts, law of torts, laws relating to property, inheritance, family, etc.

(c) **Civil law** concerning with remedies other than punishment.

(d) **Substantive law** concerning with legal rights and duties.

(e) **Adjective law** dealing with the process of enforcement.

THE INDIAN JUDICIARY

The Indian judiciary can be broadly divided into :

1. Higher judiciary consisting of the Supreme Court and the High Courts, and
2. Lower judiciary consisting of the ordinary civil and criminal courts and certain special courts.

The hierarchy of courts in India can be briefly described in the chart.

Governing Law

The higher judiciary consisting of the Supreme Court and the High Courts, is established under or regulated by the Constitution. However, certain High Courts e.g. the High Courts of Bombay, Madras, Calcutta and Allahabad were constituted under pre-constitution enactments. These High Courts assume their jurisdiction, powers and authority under those enactments even today, to the extent the same are not contrary to the constitution. The Supreme Court is entirely the creature of the constitution and also assumes jurisdiction conferred on it under a Parliamentary legislation.

As regards the lower judiciary, the Civil Courts are constituted mostly under the Civil Courts Act in force in each state whereas criminal courts are constituted under the Code of Criminal Procedure, 1973. These courts exercise jurisdiction in pursuance of powers conferred on them under a host of Central and State Laws.

Functions of the Supreme Court

The Supreme Court functions as :

1. a federal court, deciding disputes between the Union and the States, or the States *inter se*,
2. a Constitutional court empowered—
   (i) to issue writs, orders and directions for the enforcement of fundamental rights, under article 32 of the constitution, and
   (ii) to exercise appellate jurisdiction under article 137 of the constitution, in judgements of High Courts involving a question of interpretation of the constitution,

HIGHER JUDICIARY

THE SUPREME COURT

THE HIGH COURTS

LOWER JUDICIARY

CIVIL COURTS

1. District Court
2. Courts of Civil Judge, Senior Division/Courts of Subordinate Judge 1st Class.
3. Courts of Civil Judge, Junior Division/Courts of Subordinate Judge, 2nd Class/ Courts of Munsifs.

CRIMINAL COURTS

1. Sessions Court
2. Court of Metropolitan Magistrate. OR (outside Metropolitan areas)
3. (a) Courts of Magistrate 1st Class
   (b) Courts of Magistrate 2nd Class
   (c) Courts of Executive Magistrates.

SPECIAL COURTS

1. Courts of small causes
2. Family Courts
3. Court of Rent Controllers (in some states)
4. Tribunals constituted under special enactments.

3. the highest appellate court in India in civil, criminal and taxation matters,
4. a special appellate court (when the Supreme Court grants special leave of appeal),
5. an advisory court, on matters referred to it by the President,
6. a court having miscellaneous jurisdiction (e.g., jurisdiction to decide election petitions in Presidential and Vice Presidential elections).

Functions of the High Courts

The High Courts have been conferred with wide and multifarious jurisdiction, in order to ensure uniformity on questions of law within the State and to correct serious injustices in proceedings of the lower courts in the State. The High Court functions as :

1. the highest appellate court in the State in civil and criminal matters,
2. court of reference in respect of taxation matters, and matters involving the validity of an Act,
3. court empowered to issue writs for the enforcement of fundamental rights (under Article 226 of the Constitution).
4. court of confirmation in all cases where the Sessions Court has passed a sentence of death,
5. a court competent to decide election petitions,
6. a court having miscellaneous jurisdiction under special laws.

Besides, the High Court exercises power of superintendence over all courts and judicial authorities in the state.

Civil Courts

A civil court exercises jurisdiction over a suit or other proceeding with reference to following :

1. **Local limits :** The local limits of a court's jurisdiction are stated in the notification issued under the State Civil Court Act constituting that court. The local limits are determined with reference to Sections 16-20 of the Code of Criminal Procedure, 1908.
2. **Pecuniary limits** : The pecuniary limits of a court are also stated in the notification as aforesaid, and are determined with reference to the valuation rules under the Suits Valuation Act.
3. **Subject matter :** A court shall not entertain a suit or proceeding which is excluded from the particular court. For example, matrimonial disputes can be redressed only in a district court or other notified court or Family Court (wherever established).

Besides, before exercising jurisdiction over a suit, the court must ensure that procedural pre-requisites have been complied with.

Criminal Courts

The Sessions Court is the highest criminal court of original jurisdiction. A state is divided into several divisions and there is a Sessions Court for each sub-division.

A Sessions Court can try any offence and impose any sentence authorised by law for a particular offence. However, a death sentence imposed by a Sessions Court must be confirmed by the High Court in that State.

Generally, a Sessions Court does not entertain a criminal case directly, but only on a committal made to it by the Competent Magistrate. However, a Sessions Court can entertain directly suits relating to defamation of high dignitaries of Government.

Magistrates of 1st Class and 2nd Class can entertain suits relating to offences listed in a Schedule under the Code of Criminal Procedure, 1973. A Metropolitan Magistrate can try all offences which can be tried by a 1st Class Magistrate.

Systems of Trial

There are two systems of trial :

1. **Adversary System :** This system is based on the principle that truth will come out by a presentation of their cases by the various adversaries. The judge does not take an active part in the trial and the most of the questioning is done by the counsels for the opposite parties.
2. **Inquisitorial System :** In this system, the judge plays a dominant role in the conduct of the trial and examination of witnesses. It is based on the principle that it is the judge's duty to elicit the truth, as far as possible, by his own initiative.

India follows the adversary system of trial.

Writs

The higher judiciary in India exercises its function of judicial review by issuing writs. Writs are commands issued by a court to do or not to do a certain thing. The Supreme Court issues writs in pursuance to powers under Articles 32 and the High Courts under Article 226 of the Constitution.

Public Interest Litigation

Public interest litigation (PIL) is the name given to the category of legal proceedings initiated in a court of law for the enforcement of public interest or general interest in which the public or a class of community have pecuniary interest or some interest by which their legal rights are affected. The person instituting the proceedings does not assert any private right of his own, though he may be one of the aggrieved groups. PIL is a device to provide justice to those who individually are not in a position to have access to the courts.

Articles 32 and 226 of the constitution give power to any citizen to move the Supreme Court or the High Court, whenever there is an infringement of a fundamental right. Article 32 empowers the Supreme Court to issue directions, orders or writs including writs in the nature of habeas corpus, mandamus, prohibition, quo warranto and certiorari, whichever may be appropriate for enforcement of any of the rights conferred by Part III of the Constitution. Article 226 gives similar powers to the High Courts in relation to the State of their jurisdiction.

Locus Standi

Literally speaking, the expression means standing to sue, and ordinarily the aggrieved person alone is competent to sue in a matter. However, the courts have given liberal interpretation to the expression, expanding its scope largely. It has been held that any member of the public acting bona fide and having sufficient interest in instituting an action for redressal of public wrong or public injury, could move the court. [S.P. Gupta vs. Union of India AIR 1982 SC 149]. Thus, any member of the public having sufficient interest can approach the court for enforcing constitutional or legal rights of other persons and redress of a common grievance. [Judges Transfer Case AIR 1982 SC 149].

THE INDIAN CONSTITUTION

Background

The task of framing the Constitution of India was given to the Constituent Assembly, which held its inaugural meeting on December 9, 1946, electing Dr. Sachidananda Sinha as its provisional Chairman. Later, on December 11, 1946, Dr. Rajendra Prasad was elected as permanent Chairman of the Constituent Assembly.

The Constituent Assembly enacted, signed and adopted the Constitution of India on November 26, 1949, and it came into force on January 26, 1950 on which date India also became a Republic.

Salient Features of the Constitution

The Constitution of India is the longest written Constitution in the World, consisting of 22 Chapters, over 395 Articles and 12 Schedules. It proclaims India to be a Sovereign Democratic Republic. It guarantees fundamental rights to all citizens of India and also incorporates directive principles of State policy. It establishes the parliamentary system of government, with the President as the constitutional head and the Council of Ministers as the real executive responsible to the Lok Sabha. It is federal in form but unitary in spirit.

The Constitution declares India a secular State.

It establishes an independent judiciary with the Supreme Court acting as a guardian of the Constitution.

The constitution provides for adult franchise i.e., every adult above 18 years having right to vote.

It is neither too rigid (as some provisions can be amended by a simple majority) nor flexible (as some provisions require special majority for amendment).

Salient Provisions

The Indian Constitution makes detailed provisions for various matters of basic importance including the following :

(a) Citizenship
(b) Fundamental Rights
(c) Directive Principles of State Policy
(d) Structure of the Government
(e) Parliament and State Legislatures
(f) Supreme Court and High Courts
(g) Relationship between the Union and the States
(h) Services
(i) Official Language

The Preamble

The prmeable was drafted by Pt. Jawaharlal Nehru, based on the American Model. The preamble reads as follows :

We the people of India, having solemnly resolved to constitute India into a Sovereign Socialist Secular Democratic Republic and to secure to all its citizens :

Justice: social, economic and political;

Liberty of thought, expression, belief, faith and worship;

Equality: of status and opportunity; and to promote among them all :

Fraternity: assuring the dignity of the individual and the unity and integrity of the Nation; in our Constituent Assembly, this twenty sixth day of November, 1949, do hereby adopt, enact and give to ourselves this Constitution.

Articles of the Constitution

The Constitution comprises of over 395 Articles, which deal with the following matters :

Articles	Deal With
1-4	Territory of India, admission, establishment or formation of new states.
5-11	Citizenship
12-35	Fundamental Rights
36-51	Directive Principles of State Policy
51-A	Fundamental Duties of a Citizen of India (inserted by the 42nd Amendment in 1976)
52-151	Government at the Union level
152-237	Government at the State level
238	States in Part B of the First Schedule (repealed by the 7th Amendment in 1956)
239-241	Administration of Union Territories
242-243	Territories in Part D of the First Schedule and other territories. (repealed by the 7th Amendment in 1956)
243-243 (2g)	Panchayats and Municipalities
244-244A	Scheduled and tribal areas

245-263	Relations between the Union and the States
264-300A	Finance, property, contracts and suits
301-307	Trade, commerce and travel within the territory of India
308-323	Services under the Union and the States
323A-323B	Administrative Tribunals to hear disputes and other complaints (inserted by the 42nd Amendment in 1976)
324-329A	Elections and the Election Commission
330-342	Special provisions relating to certain classes, SC, ST and Anglo-Indians
343-351	Official languages
352-360	Emergency provisions
361-367	Miscellaneous provisions regarding exemption of the President and Governors from criminal proceedings
368	Amendment of Constitution
369-392	Temporary, transitional and special provisions
393-395	Short title, commencement, Authoritative text in Hindi and repeal of the Constitution

Citizenship

The constitution provides that every person who was at the commencement of the constitution (i.e., 26.1.1950) domiciled in the territory of India, and (a) who was born in India; or (b) either of whose parents was born in India, or (c) who has been ordinarily resident in India for not less than five years, became a citizen of India.

Matters relating to acquisition, determination and termination of Indian citizenship after the commencement of the constitution are dealt within the Citizenship Act, 1955.

Fundamental Rights

1. **Right to Equality:** The right to equality includes equality before law, prohibition of discrimination on grounds of religion, race, caste, sex or place of birth and equality of opportunity in matters of employment and abolition of untouchability.
2. **Right to Freedom:** The right to freedom includes freedom of speech and expression; right to assemble peacefully and without arms, formation, association or union; free movement throughout the territory of India; residence and the right to practice any profession or occupation; control and disposal of property.
3. **Right against Exploitation:** The constitution guarantees right against exploitation in all forms of forced labour, prohibits Child Labour and traffic in human beings.
4. **Right to Freedom of Religion:** The right to freedom of religion entitles all persons to freedom of conscience and the right to profess, practice and propagate religion freely.
5. **Cultural and Educational Rights:** This right includes right to any section of the citizens to conserve their culture, language or script and right of minorities to establish and administer educational institutions of their choice.
6. **Right to Constitutional Remedies:** It provides right to constitutional remedies to the citizens for enforcement of their fundamental rights.

Earlier, right to property was also a fundamental right which was omitted by the 44th amendment in 1978. It is now only a legal right.

Fundamental Duties

The fundamental duties of a citizen of India, inserted by the 42nd amendment in 1976, are as follows:

1. To abide by the Constitution and respect its ideals and Institutions, the National Flag and the National Anthem;
2. To cherish and follow the noble ideals which inspired our national struggle for freedom;
3. To uphold and protect the sovereignty, unity and integrity of India;
4. To defend the country and render national service when called upon to do so;
5. To promote harmony and the spirit of common brotherhood amongst all the people of India transcending religious, linguistic and regional diversities; to renounce practices derogatory to the dignity of women;
6. To value and preserve the. rich heritage of our composite culture;
7. To protect and improve the natural environment including forests, lakes, rivers and wildlife, and to have compassion for living creatures;
8. To develop the scientific temper, humanism and the spirit of inquiry and reform;
9. To safeguard public property and to abjure violence; and
10. To strive towards excellence in all spheres of individual and collective activity so that the nation constantly rises to higher level of endeavour and achievement.
11. To provide opportunities for education to his child or as the case may be ward between the age of six and fourteen years.

Directive Principles of State Policy

- To secure the right of all men and women to an adequate means of livelihood;
- To ensure equal pay for equal work;
- To make effective provision for securing the right to work, education and to public assistance in the event of unemployment old age, sickness and disablement;
- To secure to workers a living wage, humane conditions of work, a decent standard of life, etc.;
- To ensure that the operation of the economic system does not result in the concentration of wealth;
- To provide opportunities and facilities for children to develop in a healthy manner;
- To provide free and compulsory education for all children up to 14 years of age;
- To promote educational and economic interest of scheduled castes, scheduled tribes and other weaker sections;
- To organize village panchayats;
- To separate judiciary from the executive;
- To promulgate a uniform civil code for the whole country;
- To protect national monuments;
- To promote justice on a basis of equal opportunity;
- To provide free legal aid;
- To protect and improve environment and forests and wildlife;
- To promote international peace and security;
- To promulgate a uniform civil code for the whole country;
- To settle international disputes by arbitration.

INDIAN CONTRACT ACT, 1872

The Indian Contract Act, 1872, lays down the general principles relating to formation, performance and enforceability of contracts and the rules relating to certain special types of contracts such as indemnity guarantee, bailment, pledge and agency. However, some of the special contracts such as those relating to partnership, sale of goods, negotiable instruments, insurance, etc. are dealt with by separate legislations. Though the general principles of contract law are the basis for such special contracts too.

Important Definitions

1. **Agreement :** Section 2(e) defines an agreement as every promise and every set of promises, forming the consideration for each other, is an agreement.

   When one person conveys to another his proposal, and that other person assents thereto, the proposal is said to be accepted. A proposal when accepted becomes a promise.
2. **Contract :** According to Section 2(h), an agreement enforceable by law is a contract. In other words, a contract is an agreement made with an intention to create a legal obligation i.e., a duty enforceable by law.
3. **Offer or Proposal :** As per Section 2(a), when one signifies to another his willingness to do or to abstain from doing anything, with a view to obtaining the assent of that other to such act or abstinence, he is said to make a proposal.
4. **Acceptance :** As per Section 2(b) when the person to whom the proposal is made signifies his assent thereto, the proposal is said to be accepted.
5. **Consideration :** According to section 2(d), when at the desire of the promisor, the promisee or any other person has done or abstained from doing, or does or abstains from doing, or promises to do or abstain from doing, something, such act or abstinence or promise is called a consideration for the promise.

Essential Elements of a Contract

It may be noted that the words 'agreement' and 'contract' are very often used as synonyms, but in fact they are not. All contracts are agreements but all agreements are not necessarily contracts; agreements not enforceable by law are not contracts.

To be legally enforceable, the agreements must satisfy two things, viz.—intention to be bound and consideration. However, according to section 10, an agreement is a contract if 'it is made by the free consent of parties competent to contract, for a lawful consideration and with a lawful object, and is not expressly declared to be void.'

From the aforegoing discussion, the essential elements of a contract may be enumerated as under :

1. **Minimum two parties :** A person cannot enter into a contract with himself. To form a contract, one party has to make an offer and the other must accept it.

2. **Offer and acceptance :** Both 'offer' and 'acceptance' should be lawful.
3. **Intention to create legal obligation :** In commercial agreements, an intention to create legal relations is presumed, unless the parties have expressly agreed to otherwise. [*Rose & Frank Co. vs. Crompton & Bros. Ltd.* (1923) 2 K.B. 261. Also see, *Banwarilal* vs. *Sukhdarshan Dayal* (1973) 1 SCC 294.
4. **Lawful Consideration :** Consideration may be past, present or future, but it must be 'lawful', that is, it must not be illegal or fraudulent or immoral or opposed to public policy, or must not imply injury to the person or property of another. (Sec. 23)

Example : *A* promises to obtain for *B* an employment in public service and *B* promises to pay Rs. 1,000 to *A*. The agreement is void as the consideration for it is unlawful.

5. **Competent Parties :** The parties to a contract must be competent, that is, of the age of majority (over 18 years), of sound mind and not disqualified from contracting by any law to which they are subject (Sec. 11 and 12). Thus, a minor, lunatic, idiot, drunkard, etc. cannot, except for some special cases, enter into a valid contract.
6. **Free Consent :** Consent means that the parties must agree about the subject-matter of the agreement in the same sense and at the same time. Consent is said to be free unless it is induced by coercion, undue influence, fraud, misrepresentation or mistake. (Sec. 13 and 14)
7. **Lawful Object :** The object of an agreement must not be fraudulent or illegal or immoral or opposed to public policy, or must not imply injury to the person or property of another. (Sec. 23)
8. **Not Expressly Declared Void :** An agreement expressly declared to be void under sections 24 to 30 of the Act or under any other law, is not enforceable and is, thus not a contract. For example, an agreement in restraint of trade or wagering agreements, are not enforceable.
9. **Certainty and Possibility of Performance :** If an agreement is vague and its meaning cannot be ascertained, it cannot be enforced. The terms of a contract must be such as are capable of performance. An agreement to do an impossible act is void and not enforceable at law. (Sec. 56)
10. **Legal Formalities :** Generally, a contract may be oral or in writing. However, certain contracts are required to be in writing and may even require registration. For instance, an agreement to pay a time-barred debt must be in writing; an agreement to make a gift must be in writing and registered. In such cases, these additional formalities must be complied with.

All the elements mentioned above must be present in order to make a valid contract. If any of the elements is absent the agreement does not transform into contract.

Agreement

An agreement means 'a promise or a set of promises' forming consideration for each other. And a promise arises when a proposal is accepted. In other words, an agreement consists of an offer and its acceptance.

The essence of an agreement is the meeting of the minds of the parties; both the parties must agree to the same thing in the same sense. This is also called as **'consensus ad idem'.**

Example : If *A* wants to sell his house to *B*, *B* must know, that *A* wants to sell the house for a specific price. This can happen if *A* tells *B* about it and then *B* also informs *A* that he is willing to buy the house for that specific amount.

Example : If *A* who owns two cars, one Ambassador and the other Fiat, offers to sell *B* one car, *A* intending it to be the Ambassador, *B* accepts the offer thinking that it is the Fiat, there is no consensus and hence no contract.

Offer

When one person, communicates to another, his willingness to do or not to do a thing, with a view to obtaining the consent of that other person towards such an act or abstinence, the person is said to be making a proposal or offer.

For example, when *A* says to *B*, "Will you like to purchase my Fiat car of 1985 model for Rs. 45,000?", he is said to have made an express offer.

An offer may be implied from the conduct of the parties of the circumstance of the case. For instance, when DTC runs a bus on a particular route, there is an implied offer by the Corporation to carry passengers for a certain fare.

Invitation to offer is not an offer : An offer is different from an invitation to offers. A person sending out an 'invitation to offer' does not make an offer but only invites the other parties to make an offer.

For instance, quotation of price does not constitute an offer; it is an invitation to offer.

Similarly, a shopkeeper's catalogue of prices is not an offer; it is only an invitation to the intending customers to offer to buy at the indicated prices. The shopkeeper is not bound to sell the goods at the prices mentioned in the catalogue.

Likewise, display of goods in a shop with price tags attached, is not an offer. When the customer selects the goods and takes them to the shopkeeper or his assistant saying 'I want to buy this article', the offer is made.

Besides, a banker's catalogue of charges, an auctioneer's advertisement to hold auction of certain goods, a notice inviting tenders for supply of certain goods, are also an invitation to offer and not an offer. An offer shall be made when a person participating in the auction raises a bid or when an intending supplier submits his tender.

Knowledge of the offer

An offer must be in the knowledge of the offeree since the offeree cannot accept the offer without having any knowledge of it. Acceptance must have been made with the knowledge of the offer otherwise it will not create a binding contract.

Revocation of Offer : An offeror can revoke or withdraw his offer at any time until an acceptance has been made. For a revocation to be effective it is essential that it reaches the offeree before he sends off his acceptance. Revocation of a 'general offer' must be communicated through the same mode by which the original offer was communicated. Also an offer stands revoked if the offeree fails to fulfil a condition precedent to acceptance. [Sec. 6(3)]

Acceptance

An acceptance is the act of manifestation by the offeree of his assent to the terms of the offer. It signifies the offeree's willingness to be bound by the terms of the proposal communicated to him.

An acceptance must correspond exactly with the terms of the offer, it must be unconditional and absolute and it must be communicated to the offeror.

According to Section 4, the communication of the acceptance is complete as against the acceptor when it comes to the knowledge of the proposer.

Revocation of Acceptance : As per Section 5, an acceptance may be revoked at any time before the communication of the acceptance is complete as against the acceptor but not afterwards.

Consideration

Consideration is one of the essential ingredients of a valid contract. It is the price for which the promise of the other is bought.

For instance, in a contract for sale of goods, the consideration underlying is the price paid for the goods sold. Consideration may be in the form of money, services, goods or a sacrifice or abstinence value to the other party.

The general rule is that an agreement without consideration is void. There are, however, following exceptions to this rule, when consideration is not necessary.

1. **Agreement made on account of Love and Affection :** An agreement expressed in writing and registered under the law for the registration of documents, and made on account of natural love and affection between parties standing in a near relation to each other, is enforceable even if it is without consideration. [Section 25(1)]
2. **Gifts :** Any gift actually made shall not be invalid for want of consideration. [Sec. 25, Explanation 1].
3. **Compensation for Past Voluntary Service :** A promise to compensate wholly or in part, a person who has already voluntarily done something for the promisor, or something which the promisor was legally compellable to do, is enforceable even though it is without consideration. [Section 25(2)]

   For instance, *A* finds *B*'s purse and gives it to him. *B*-promises to give *A* Rs. 50. It shall be a binding contract. Similarly, *A* brings up *B*'s infant son. *B*, who was legally bound to bring up his son, promises to pay *A's* expenses in so doing. This is also a contract.
4. **Promise to pay a Time-Barred Debt :** An agreement made by a debtor to pay, wholly or in part, a time-barred debt, is enforceable. The agreement should be made in writing and signed by the debtor or his agent generally or specially authorised in this behalf. The debt must be such as would have been enforceable but for the law of limitation. [Section 25(3)] It may be noted that a debt becomes barred by limitation if it remains unpaid or unclaimed for a period of three years; such debts are legally irrecoverable.
5. **Agency :** No consideration is necessary to create a contract of agency. [Section 185]

Contract with Minor

A minor is a person who has not attained the age of majority. The age of majority is generally eighteen years, except where a guardian has been appointed for a minor's property or person or where the court of wards supervises the property of a minor, in which case the age of majority is deemed to be twenty one years. [Section 3 of the Indian Majority Act 1875]

An agreement with a minor is void and inoperative ab initio.

In *Mohoribibi* vs. *Dharamodas Ghose* (1903) 30 IA; 30 Cal. 539, a minor mortgaged his house in favour of a moneylender to secure a loan of Rs. 20,000 out of which the mortgagee, the moneylender, paid the minor Rs. 8,000. Subsequently, the minor sued for setting aside the mortgage stating that he was underage, when he executed the contract. The Privy Council held that the mortgage was void, and therefore, it was cancelled. Further, the moneylender's request for the repayment of the amount advanced to the minor as part of the consideration for the mortgage was also struck down.

Contracts Beneficial to a Minor

However, a minor can enforce a contract which is of some benefit to him and under which he is required to bear no obligation.

For instance, it has been held that a minor may enforce a promissory note executed in his favour, or may recover the price of goods already delivered to the buyer.

No Ratification : An agreement made by a minor cannot be subsequently ratified by him on attaining majority.

Minor Not Estopped from Pleading Minority : Where a minor represents, fraudulently or otherwise, that he is of the age of majority and thereby induces the other party to enter into a contract with him, then in an action founded on the contract the minor may disclose his real age; he is not estopped from pleading minority and claiming to contract void by reason of his being incompetent. *Gadigeppa Bhimappa Mets* vs. *Balangowda Bhimangowda* AIR 1931 Bom. 561.

Minor's Liability for Necessaries : A minor is liable to pay out of his property for 'necessaries' supplied to him or to any one whom he is legally bound to support. This liability arises under quasi-contract. It is only the property of the minor, and not the minor personally, that can be held liable for such transactions. (Section 68)

Minor Partner : A minor is not competent to enter into an agreement of partnership with another person. However, a minor may be admitted to the benefits of a partnership, i.e., sharing in profits only and not in losses.

Minor's Liability in Torts : A contract with a minor cannot be converted into tort, to sue the minor. Thus, a minor would not be held liable in tort for money lent on a bond.

But where the tort is independent of the contract, the minor shall be liable for it and the mere fact that a contract is also involved will not absolve him from the liability.

Free Consent

Consent is said to be free when it is not vitiated by coercion, undue influence, fraud, misrepresentation or mistake. (Section 14)

Where consent to an agreement is obtained by coercion, undue influence, fraud or misrepresentation, the contract is voidable at the option of the party whose consent was so caused. (Sections 19 and 19A)

Coercion : Consent is said to be obtained by coercion when pressure is exerted by committing or threatening to commit some act which is contrary to law. (Section 15)

For example, if a debtor obtains a confirmation letter from his creditor, at the point of pistol, that he has received the full and final payment and that nothing is due, such a letter is voidable at the option of the creditor since it is obtained by coercion and the debtor shall not be released from the debt.

Undue Influence : Consent of a person is said to be induced by undue influence, when—(i) the parties to a contract are so related that one party is in a position to dominate the will of the other; and (ii) when such position is used by the former party to obtain an unfair advantage over the other party. (Section 16)

Fraud : A fraud is said to have been committed when any of the following acts are done by a party to a contract, with intention to deceive the other party or to induce him to enter into the contract or :

(a) suggesting, as a fact, something which is not true by a person who does not believe it to be true;
(b) actively concealing a fact by one who has knowledge or belief of the fact;
(c) promising to do something without any intention to perform it;
(d) any other act fitted to deceive; and
(e) any such act or omission as the law specially declares to be fraudulent. (Section 17)

Misrepresentation : Misrepresentation is an untrue statement of a material fact which induces the other party, to enter into an agreement. (Section 18)

Mistake : Where both parties to an agreement are under a mistake as to a matter of fact essential to the agreement, the agreement is void. However, an erroneous opinion as to the value of the thing, which is subject-matter of the agreement, will not be considered a mistake as to a matter of fact. (Section 20)

A contract is void if the mistake is bilateral i.e., on both the parties, and not merely because it was caused by one of the parties to it being under a mistake as to matter of fact. (Section 22)

A contract is void when the mistake is of fact. However, mistake of law is no excuse; a contract is not voidable because it was caused by a mistake as to any law in force in India. (Section 21)

Void Agreements

1. Agreements wherein consideration and objects are unlawful in part.
2. Agreements without consideration, subject to a few exceptions.
3. Agreements in restraint of marriage.
4. Agreements in restraint of trade. (Section 27)
5. Agreements in restraint of legal proceedings. (Section 28)
6. Agreements, the meaning of which is not certain, or capable of being made certain. (Section 29) For example, *X* agrees to sell to *Y*, his horse for Rs. 500 or Rs. 1000. The agreement is void for uncertainty as to price.
7. Wagering Agreements—by which two persons, holding opposite views with respect to a future uncertain event, agree to give money or money's worth upon the determination or ascertainment of that event. (Section 30)
8. Agreements to do impossible acts. (Section 56)

Quasi-Contracts

Quasi-contracts are those transactions which do not actually form contracts between the parties in the legal sense, but only create certain rights and obligations similar to those created by a contract. Following transactions are recognised as 'quasi-contracts' under the law :

(a) Where necessaries are supplied to a person, who is incompetent to contract (e.g. a minor or lunatic) or to someone whom he is legally bound to support, the supplier is entitled to recover the price from the property of the incompetent person.

(b) When a person makes payment of money due by another, in payment of which he is interested, he shall be entitled to be reimbursed by the other.

(c) When a person does something for another person, or delivers something to him, not intending to do gratuitously, and such other person enjoys the benefit thereof, the latter is obliged to compensate the former in respect of, or to restore, the thing so done or delivered. For example : *A*, a trader, leaves goods at *B*'s house by mistake. *B* treats the goods as his own. *B* is bound to pay *A* for the goods.

(d) A person who finds goods belonging to another and takes them into his custody, has the same obligations as that of a bailee.

(e) A person to whom money is paid or anything delivered, by mistake or under coercion, shall be liable to repay or return it. For example : *X* and *Y* jointly owe Rs. 100 to *Z*. *X* alone pays the amount to *Z* and *Y* not knowing this fact, pays another Rs. 100 to *Z*. *Z* is bound to repay the amount to *Y*.

Performance of Contracts

The parties must perform their respective obligations under the contract. If a promisor dies before performance of a contract his legal representative is bound to perform the contract unless a contrary intention appears from the words in the contract or the contract requires personal performance by the promisor.

Effect of Failure to Perform a Promise at a Fixed Time : When a party promises to do a certain thing at or before a specific time and fails to do so, the contract becomes voidable at the option of the promisee, if the parties had intended that time shall be of essence to the contract. (Section 55)

Discharge of Contract

A contract is said to be discharged when the liabilities of the parties thereto, come to an end or are determined. A contract may be discharged by any of the following modes :

(a) **By Impossibility of Performance :** The impossibility may be initial or subsequent.
An agreement to do an impossible act is void ab initio.

(b) **By Mutual Agreement :** A contract is discharged by novation, rescission or alteration. Where the parties to a contract agree to substitute a new contract for it, or to rescind or alter it, the original contract stands discharged. (Section 62)

(c) **By Remission :** Where a party to a contract dispenses with, either wholly or in part, the performance of a contract by the other party, or extends the time for performance, or accepts any other satisfaction instead of performance, the contract stands discharged to the extent remitted. (Section 63)

(d) **By Operation of Law :** A contract is discharged by operation of law under following circumstances :

(i) Material alteration or loss of a written document;

(ii) Merger of an inferior contract into a superior contract;

(iii) Discharge of an insolvent; and

(iv) When rights and liabilities under the same contract become vested in the same person.

(e) **By Breach of Contract :** When a party to a contract has refused to perform or is disabled from performing his promise, the promisee may put an end to the contract on account of breach by the first party.

Anticipatory Breach : When, prior to the promised date of performance, the promisor signifies his intention not to fulfil the contract and that he will no longer be bound by it.

Present Breach : When a promisor signifies his refusal or disability to perform a contract, at the time agreed for its performance.

Remedies for Breach of Contract

1. **Damages/Compensation :** The party who is injured by the breach of a contract may bring an action for damages, that is monetary compensation for the loss suffered by him.
2. **Specific Performance :** Where the loss suffered by breach of contract cannot be compensated by damages or where there are no standards to ascertain the quantum of damages, the aggrieved party may approach the Court for the grant of a decree for specific performance of the contact under the Specific Relief Act, 1963.
3. **Suit for injunction :** When a party guilty of breach acts to the detriment of the injured party, the injured party may bring a suit for injunction and restrain the guilty party from doing such act. For example, *A* agreed to build a commercial complex for *B*. Thereafter *A* refused and entered into an agreement with *C*, *B*'s competitor, to build another commercial complex for *C* opposite *B*'s site. B could bring a suit for injunction against *A* and restrain him from building the complex for C.
4. **Suit for Quantum Meruit :** When a contract becomes void, any person who has received any advantages under such contract is bound to restore it, to the person from whom he received it. (Section 63)

Indemnity

A contract of indemnity is one whereby a person promises to save the other from loss caused to him by the conduct of the promisor himself or of any third person. (Section 124)

The person who gives the indemnity is called the 'indemnifier' and the person for whose protection it is given is called the 'indemnity-holder' or 'indemnified'.

A contract of indemnity is restricted to cover the loss caused by the promisor himself or by a third person. The loss must be caused by some human agency. Loss arising from accidents like fire or perils of the sea are not covered by a contract of indemnity. Thus, a contract of insurance is not one of indemnity, it is a contingent contact.

Rights of the Indemnity Holder : An indemnity-holder may recover from the indemnifier :

(a) all damages which the indemnity-holder may have been compelled to pay in any suit in respect of any matter covered by the contract;

(b) costs of suits filed or defended; and

(c) sums paid under the terms of the compromise effected in such suit, provided the compromise was an act of prudence; or was authorised by the indemnifier. (Section 125)

Guarantee

A contract of guarantee is a contract, whether oral or written, to perform the promise, or discharge the liability, of a third person in case of his default. A contract of guarantee is generally made to secure a loan or goods on credit or an employment.

A contract of guarantee involves three persons, viz., a person who gives the guarantee called the "surety", the person in respect of whose default the guarantee is given called the "principal debtor", and the person to whom the guarantee is given called the "creditor."

A contract of guarantee is a conditional promise by the surety that if the principal debtor defaults he shall be liable to the creditor.

Surety's Liability

(a) The liability of the surety is co-extensive with that of the principal debtor, unless it is otherwise provided by the contract. (Section 128)

(b) Where there is a condition precedent to the surety's liability, he will not be liable unless that condition is first fulfilled. (Section 144)

(c) A surety may expressly declare his guarantee to be limited to a fixed amount. *Yarlagadda Bapanna* vs. *Devta China Yerkayya*, AIR 1966 AP 151.

(d) The death of surety will revoke a continuing guarantee unless there is a contract to the contrary.

(e) Where the agreement between the principal debtor and creditor is void, then a guarantee to that agreement shall also be void and the surety shall not be bound.

Continuing Guarantee : A 'continuing guarantee' is a standing guarantee to a series of transactions that shall take place between the principal debtor and creditor, in future. A continuing guarantee may be for specified period and may be renewed from time to time.

A continuing guarantee may be revoked at any time by the surety, as to the future transactions, by giving a notice to the creditor. But the surety shall remain liable for all transactions that had taken place before the notice.

A continuing guarantee is also revoked by the death of surety, as to the future transactions, unless there is contract to the contrary.

A continuing guarantee is automatically revoked by substitution of a new contract of guarantee.

Bank Guarantee : A bank guarantee is a sort of an absolute undertaking on the part of the bank under an arrangement with its customer to pay to the creditor whenever the guarantee is invoked by the latter.

Letter of Credit : A letter of credit may be defined as an agreement shared by a bank guaranteeing on behalf of its customer (i.e., the buyer) to make payments to the seller of goods, upon presentation of documents specified in the credit.

Discharge of Surety

1. **By Revocation :** Normally, a guarantee is not revocable, once it is acted upon.
   However, a continuing guarantee may be revoked at any time by the surety, as to future transactions, by notice to the creditor. (Section 130)
2. **By Death :** A continuing guarantee is automatically revoked on the death of the surety, unless there is a contract to the contrary, with respect to future transactions only. (Section 131)
3. **By Variance in terms of Contract :** A surety is discharged from his liability (as to future transactions) when the creditor makes a change in the nature or terms of his contract with the principal debtor, without consent of the surety. (Section 133)
4. **By Release of Principal Debtor :** If the creditor makes a contract with the principal debtor, whereby the latter is released from his liability, the surety is also discharged. (Section 134)
5. **By an Act or Omission of the Creditor :** When the creditor does any act or omission, the legal consequence of which is the discharge of the principal debtor, the surety would also be discharged from his liability. (Section 134)
6. **By Arrangement between Creditor and Debtor :** When a creditor makes a composition with, or allows an extension of time to, or agrees not to sue the principal debtor, without obtaining the consent of surety, the surety will be discharged from his liability. (Section 135)
7. **By Impairing Surety's Remedy :** If the creditor does any act which is inconsistent with the right of the surety, or omits to do any act which his duty to the surety requires him to do, thereby impairing the surety's remedy against the principal debtor, the surety will stand discharged of his liability. (Section 139)
8. **By Concealment or Misrepresentation :** Where a guarantee is obtained by means of misrepresentation or concealment of material facts, by the creditor, the guarantee is invalid and the surety is discharged by such invalidation. (Sections 142 & 143)

When a Surety is Not Discharged : A surety is not discharged from his liability in the following circumstances :

(i) When the creditor enters into an agreement with a third person to give time to the principal debtor;
(ii) When the creditor forbears to sue the principal debtor; and
(iii) When any of the co-surety is released, the other co-sureties are not discharged.

Rights of a Surety

Rights against Principal Debtor

1. **Right of Subrogation :** When the surety pays the guaranteed debt, he is entitled to take such legal action as the creditor would have taken against the principal debtor. The surety steps into the shoes of the creditor and is

vested with the rights of the creditor. (Section 140)

2. **Right to Indemnity :** In every contract of guarantee there is an implied promise by the principal debtor to indemnify the surety and the surety is entitled to recover from the principal debtor whatever sum he has rightfully paid under the guarantee but no sums which he has paid wrongfully. (Section 145)

Rights against Creditors

A surety is entitled to the benefit of every security which the creditor has against the principal debtor at the time when the contract of guarantee is entered into.

If the creditor loses, or without the consent of the surety parts with any surety, the surety is discharged to the extent of the value of that security. (Section 141)

Rights against Co-sureties

Unless there is an agreement to the contrary, the co-sureties, as between themselves, shall share equally the debt which remains unpaid by the principal debtor. Thus, a surety can claim contribution from other co-sureties. (Section 146)

Bailment

A 'bailment' is the delivery of goods by one person to another for some purpose upon a contract that they shall, when the purpose is accomplished, be returned or disposed of according to the directions of the person delivering them.

The person delivering the goods is called the "bailor" and the person to whom the goods are delivered is called "bailee". (Section 148)

For example, delivering a watch or radio from repair, or leaving a car or scooter etc. at a parking stand, or delivering gold to a goldsmith for making ornaments, or leaving garments with a dry cleaner, etc.

Essential elements of a bailment :

1. Two parties, bailor and the bailee.
2. Delivery of possession of the goods for bailor to the bailee. Delivery of possession may be either actual or constructive. E.g. delivery of a railway receipt is the constructive delivery of the goods.
3. The delivery of goods should be made for some purpose, and under a contract of bailment.
4. Bailment is always subject to the conduction that when the purpose is accomplished the goods will be returned to the bailor or disposed of according to his directions. For instance, a post office is a bailee of the letters, packets or articles posted by a sender and is under an obligation to deliver them as per the directions of the sender.

Duty of Bailor : The primary duty of the bailor is to disclose, to the bailee, the faults or defects in the goods bailed of which the bailor has knowledge and which might interfere with their use or expose the bailee to extraordinary risks. If the bailor fails to disclose the defect and the bailee suffers any loss due to such non-disclosure, the bailor must compensate the bailee. (Section 150)

Duties of Bailee

1. The bailee should take care of the goods bailed to him, in the same manner as a man of ordinary prudence would do to protect his own goods. (Section 151)

However, the bailee is not responsible for the loss or damage to the goods, due to events beyond his control. (Section 152)

2. The bailee must use the goods strictly for the purpose for which they have been bailed to him. Any unauthorised use of the goods would make him liable for any loss of or damage to the goods. (Section 154)
3. The bailee should not mix the bailor's goods with his own goods, without his consent.

   If he mixes the goods with the bailor's consent, both will have a proportionate interest in the mixture thus produced. (Section 155)

   If the bailee mixes the goods, without bailor's consent, and if the goods can be separated, they will be owner of their respective properties. However, the bailee is bound to bear the expenses of separation or any damage arising from the mixture. (Section 156)

   If the goods are mixed without the bailor's consent and cannot be separated, the bailee is liable to compensate the bailor for the loss of goods. (Section 157)
4. The bailee should return the goods, or deliver them as per bailor's directions, as soon as the time for which they were bailed has expired, or the purpose for which they were bailed has been accomplished. (Section 160)

   If the bailee fails to return the goods, he will keep them at his own risk and will be liable for any loss to the goods arising howsoever. (Section 161)
5. The bailee should return to the bailor natural increases or profits accruing to the goods during the period of bailment. (Section 163)
6. Where the bailor has no title to the goods, the bailee cannot refuse to return the goods to the bailor on the ground that the goods do not belong to the bailor.

Pledge

A 'pledge' is a bailment of goods wherein the goods are delivered as a security for payment of a debt or performance of a promise. The bailor is called the 'pledgor' or 'pawnor' and the bailee is called the 'pledgee' or 'Pawnee'.

A pledge can be of movables and usually consists of goods capable of actual or constructive delivery.

Rights of Pledgee/Pawnee

1. **Right to retain the goods** pledged not only for payment of the debt or the performance of the promise but also for the interest due on the debt, and all necessary expenses incurred by him in respect of the possession or for the preservation of the goods pledged. (Section 173 & 174)
2. **Right to recover extraordinary expenses** incurred by him for the preservation of the goods pledged. The pledgee cannot however, retain the goods for such expenses. (Section 175)
3. **Right to Sue** the pledgor, if he defaults in payment of the debt or performance of the promise, and retains the goods as a collateral security. Alternatively, he has a right to sell the goods. (Section 176)
4. **Right to Sell** the goods after giving a reasonable notice of sale to the pledgor. (Section 177)

If the sale proceeds fall short of the amount due, the pledgor shall remain liable for the balance. If the proceeds exceed the amount due, the pledgee must return the surplus to the pledgor.

Rights of Pledgor

(a) A pledgor has the right to recover the goods on payment of the debt or performance of the promise.
(b) Where the pledgor has defaulted in making payment of the debt, he may redeem the goods pledged at any subsequent time before their sale.
(c) The pledgor has the right to recover any increase or accredition to the goods occurred during the period of pledge. E.g. bonus shares issued on the shares pledged, during the period of pledge shall belong to the pledgor.

Agency Contracts

When a person acts as a representative of the other in the creation, modification or termination of contractual obligations, between that other and third persons, that he is an agent. The agreement between the agent and that other is that of 'agency'.

An 'agent' is a person employed to do any act or to represent another in dealings with third persons. The person who employs the agent and for whom such act is done, or who is so represented, is called the 'principal'. (Section 182)

Any person who is competent to contract i.e., who is of the age of majority and who is of sound mind, may employ an agent. (Section 183)

Any person may be appointed as an agent. However, where an agent is minor or of unsound mind, the principal shall be bound to the third persons but the agent shall not be responsible to the principal. (Section 184)

No consideration is required in a contract of agency (Section 185). However, agents are normally paid some commission or remuneration for acts done by them.

Agent's Authority

Acts of an agent are binding upon his principal and the obligations arising from the contracts entered into by an agent, are enforceable as if the contracts had been entered into the by the principal himself. (Section 226) However, the agent must have acted within the scope of his authority.

Actual Authority : Actual authority of an agent is the authority conferred on him by the principal, either expressly or impliedly.

Apparent or Ostensible Authority : Apparent authority of an agent is the authority that arises from the position occupied by the agent. For example, a managing director has the ostensible authority to do all such things as fall within the scope of that office.

Duties of Agent

1. **To Follow Instructions** of his principal in conducting his business, or the customs prevailing in that particular trade at such place. (Section 211)
2. **To Exercise Reasonable Skill and Diligence** as is generally possessed by persons engaged in a similar business unless the principal has notice of his want of skill. (Section 212)
3. **To Render Proper Accounts** to his principal on demand. (Section 213)

4. **To Communicate in Emergency** with his principal and obtain his instructions. (Section 214)
5. **To Avoid** dealing on his own account in the same business as that of the principal, without obtaining his consent. (Section 215)
6. **Not to Make Secret Profits** (Section 216)
7. **To Remit** to his principal all sums received on his account, after deducting his lawful charges. (Section 218)
8. **Not to Delegate his Authority** to another person, without the consent of his principal or unless the appointment of a sub-agent is permitted by the ordinary custom of trade or the nature of the transaction. (Section 190)

Rights of Agent

1. An agent may retain, out of any sums received on account of the principal :
   (a) all moneys due to himself in respect of advances made, or expenses properly incurred by him in conducting agency business, and
   (b) such remuneration as may be payable to him for acting as agent. (Section 217)
2. An agent is entitled to his agreed remuneration, or when there is no agreement as to remuneration, to a reasonable remuneration. (Section 219)
3. **Right of Lien** on goods, papers and other movable or immovable property, of the principal in his possession, until the amount due to himself for commission, disbursements and services rendered in respect of the same have been paid or accounted for to him. (Section 221)
4. **Right to** be indemnified by the principal, in respect of :
   (a) the consequences of all lawful acts done by the agent in exercise of his authority; and
   (b) the consequences of an act done by the agent in good faith, but causing an injury to the rights of third persons. (Sections 222 & 223)
5. **Right to Compensation** in case an agent suffers an injury due to the principal's neglect or want of skill. (Section 225)

Liabilities of Principal

Liabilities of a Named Principal :

1. Where the existence and identity of the principal are disclosed, the principal is liable to the third parties in the same manner as if the contracts had been entered into by the principal himself. (Section 226)
2. Where an agent acts beyond his authority, the principal shall not be liable for the excess work. If such excess work is separable from the authorised work the principal is bound to the extent of work done within the agent's authority. (Sections 227 and 228)
3. Notice to an agent is notice to the principal. (Section 229)
4. Where an agent commits a misrepresentation or fraud while acting in the course of his principal's business, such misrepresentation or fraud shall be deemed to have been committed by the principal. (Section 238)

Liability of Unnamed Principal : Where the agent represents an unnamed principal, the principal shall be bound by all acts done by the agent lawfully within his authority.

Liability of Undisclosed Principal : Where the agent neither discloses the existence of his principal nor his representative character :

1. The agent shall be personally bound by the contract.
2. The principal has a right to intervene and sue the third party for performance of the contract.
3. Where the principal intervenes, the third party shall have, as against the principal, the same rights as he would have had against the agent. (Sections 231 & 232)

Termination of Agency

An agency is terminated in any of the following circumstances : (Section 201)

1. **Completion of Agency Business.**
2. **Death or Insanity** of the principal or the agent.
3. **Insolvency** of the principal.
4. **Renunciation** by the agent.
5. **Revocation** of agency by the principal.

LAW OF TORTS

Law of Torts in India

The law of torts in India is mainly uncodified law, whose principles are largely derived from case law. These principles have been evolved by courts in India in exercise of their duty to apply "justice, equity and good conscience" in matters not governed by legislation. Indian courts also follow English precedents in the law of torts, inasmuch as they conform with justice and equity and relate to Indian conditions.

Meaning of 'Tort'

The term 'tort' has been derived from the Latin word 'tortum' which means to twist. Tort therefore refers to twisted or wrongful acts or unlawful conduct.

A tort is thus a civil wrong which causes infringement of legal rights of a private individual such as defamation, malicious prosecution, negligence etc. The remedy for tort is action for unliquidated damages.

Examples

The law of the land imposes a duty to respect the legal rights vested in the members of the society and if a person breaches such duty a tort is said to be committed. For instance, violation of duty not to injure the reputation of someone else results in the tort of defamation. Similarly, violation of duty not to interfere with the possession of property of another person results in the tort of trespassing. Further, violation of duty not to defraud a person results in the tort of deceit.

A tort differs from a breach of contract or a breach of trust.

Distinction between Tord and Breach of Contract

A tort differs from a breach of contract for following reasons :

1. A tort is a breach of duty which is laid down in law. Whereas a breach

of contract is a breach of duty fixed by the consenting parties themselves.

2. A tort results in infringement of a right **in rem** i.e., a right available against the whole world. Whereas a breach of contract results in infringement of a right **in personam** i.e., a right available only to a person who is a party to the contract.
3. In tort the only remedy is action for unliquidated damages, which are determined by the court on the facts and circumstances of each case. Whereas in a breach of contract, the damages may be fixed in advance and agreed to by the parties (i.e. liquidated damages).

For example, *A* agrees to sell his car to *B* for Rs. 10,000. For some reason *A* does not fulfill his obligation, the wrong is a breach of contract and not a tort.

Essential Elements of a Tort

As stated earlier, a tort is a wrongful act that causes damage to another. Thus, the two essential ingredients of a tort are :

1. a wrongful act,
2. legal damage i.e., damage to legal rights of another.

These elements are described here under :

Wrongful Act

To establish a tort it must be proved that the act or omission on the part of the defendant was a wrongful act. An act is wrongful only when it results in violation of legal right of another.

Legal Damage

'Legal damage' means violation of legal rights of a person. An action for tort is not maintainable unless the plaintiff proves that he has suffered some 'legal damage' from the defendant's wrongful act. Legal damage need not necessarily result in pecuniary loss to the plaintiff. This is illustrated by two legal maxims.

1. Injuria sine damno

The word 'injuria' means violation of legal right, 'sine' means without and 'damno' means damage in the form of money, health and comfort. Thus, **injuria sine damno** means violation of legal right without causing any damage to the plaintiff.

According to this maxim, a violation of legal rights of a person is actionable whether it has caused any real harm or loss to him or not. Thus, if a person trespasses into the property of another, an action shall be maintainable even if he does not cause any real or physical loss to the owner of that property.

Ashby vs. *White* is a classic example on this issue. In this case, the plaintiff, a qualified voter, was wrongfully denied the right to cast his vote by the Returning Officer. The plaintiff sued the Returning Officer for damages. The defendant contended that since the plaintiff had suffered no loss as his candidate had won the election, he was not liable. It was held that the defendant had violated plaintiff's legal right and was thus liable to damages. It was noted that if the plaintiff has a right, he must of necessity have a means to vindicate and maintain it, and a remedy if he is injured in the exercise or enjoyment of it, and it is indeed a vain thing to imagine a right without a remedy; for want of right and want of remedy are reciprocal.

2. *Damno sine injuria*

The maxim means damage caused without violation of legal rights, is not actionable. Accordingly, no cause of action arises from the mere fact that a man is injured by the act of another, if that other is acting in his legal rights. In *Chesmore* vs. *Richards*, the plaintiff was the owner of a Mill and had been using water from a stream for a number of years. The defendant dug a well on their land as a result of which the plaintiff stopped getting water from the stream. Held, the defendant had a legal right to dig a well on his own land and was not liable for the loss caused to the plaintiff. Similarly, in *Moghul Steamship Co.* vs. *McGregor and Co.*, where a number of steamship companies combined together, offered reduced freight rates and ousted the plaintiff company out of the China Sea, the House of Lords held that the defendants had by lawful means acted to protect and extend their trade and the plaintiff had no cause of action.

Categories of Torts

Following types of torts have figured in the Indian Courts :

1. Negligence i.e., acting carelessly resulting in a foreseeable injury to some person. A person is said to have acted carelessly when he omits to do something which a prudent man guided by considerations which regulate the conduct of human affairs, would do, or does something which a prudent man would not do.
2. Defamation i.e., when a person makes a false statement, oral or written, in words, signs, gestures or any other means of communication, which adversely affects the reputation of a person, he commits the tort of defamation.
3. Nuisance i.e., unlawful interference in the personal comfort or a person's use and enjoyment of some property. Nuisance may be public or private. For example, ringing bells in a temple, illegally running a brothel, playing loud music, making obscene gestures in public, etc.
4. False imprisonment, i.e., total restraint of liberty of a person by not permitting him to go any where, without any lawful excuse.
5. Malicious prosecution, i.e., institution of criminal or quasi-criminal proceedings against a person without any reasonable cause, only to harass that person maliciously.
6. Trespassing i.e., when a person unlawfully enters into the land or property of another, without owner's permission.
7. Contributory negligence.
8. Breach of statutory duty.
9. Protection of environment.
10. Conversion and detinue.
11. Bodily harm.
12. Injury to family rights.
13. Harm to social status.
14. Malicious civil process.
15. Conspiracy and intimidation.
16. Inducement of breach of contract.
17. Fraudulent statements.
18. Slander of title and slander of goods.
19. Passing off.
20. Mental harm e.g., insult to religious feelings.

Liability in Tort

Fault by intentional or negligent conduct is the main basis of liability in tort. For this purpose, following need to be examined :

1. **Motive :** Motive is not an essential elements in tort, since a wrongful act done with bad motive is not tort but a crime. However, in certain types of tort, motive is a relevant element such as malicious prosecution, malicious use of court process, malicious falsehood, defamation, nuisance and conspiracy.
2. **Intention :** Intention is again not relevant in tort, since in law of tort it is assumed that every person knows the consequence of his act. Thus, if a person is injured by an act of defendant, the defendant shall be liable whether or not he intended to cause injury to that person.
3. **Malice :** In common parlance 'malice' means ill will against a person. In legal terms, 'malice' means a wrongful act done intentionally without any just cause or excuse. In a tort of malicious prosecution, the prosecution is inspired by bad motive i.e., to malign or harass the person.

Rule of Strict Liability

Strict liability is imposed in situations where dangerous substances are brought by a person on the land, likely to cause harm if they 'escape', where the user of the land is 'non-natural.' This is also known as rule of *Rylands* vs. *Fletcher*, since laid down in that famous case.

The terms 'escape' and 'non-natural use' are important in this regard. The word 'escape' means to flow into a place outside the occupation or control. The term 'non-natural use' refers to some special use accompanied by increased danger to others. These terms can be better understood with the facts of the famous case of *Rylands* vs. *Fletcher*. In this case the plaintiff was a lessor of a mine. Certain old mines were disused and their passages filled up. The vertical shafts connecting these passages with the land above were also out of use and were filled with earth. The defendant owned a Mill in the land adjacent to the land above the mines. The defendant constructed a tank on his land with the help of competent persons. When the tank was ready and was filled, the water entered into the vertical shafts, flowed into the passages and flooded the old mines. Held, the defendant was liable though not guilty of negligence.

Rule of Absolute Liability

Dealing with the infamous Bhopal Gas Leak disaster, the Supreme Court laid down the rule of absolute liability in *Union Carbide Corporation* vs. *Union of India*. The apex court observed, "where an enterprise is engaged in hazardous or inherently dangerous activity one harm results to anyone on account of an accident in the operation of such hazardous or inherently dangerous activity for example in escape of toxic gas, the enterprise is strictly and absolutely liable to compensate all those who are affected by the accident and such liability is not subject to any exceptions which operate *vis.-a-vis* the tortuous principle or strict liability under the rule of *Rylands* vs. *Fletcher*."

Rule of Vicarious Liability

Such liability is recognised against the employer for the torts committed by the employee during employment. The principle applies to corporations also. [Refer *N.S. Mehta* vs. *Shriram Fertilizers* (1986) 1 SCALE 199 (SC)]

As regards Government, as per Article 300 of the Constitution, it is liable for the torts of its employees committed during employment, where the activity in which the employee was engaged related to exercise of "non-sovereign" functions of the state. But the Government is not liable if the activity is a "sovereign" one.

Defences in Tort

The defences generally adopted in torts are :

1. *Volenti, non-fit injuria* i.e., no action lies against the injury caused voluntarily.
2. Act of God which cannot be avoided by a man even by taking reasonable care.
3. Act of necessity i.e., an act done in larger interest of the society over the individual interest. For example, a person pouring water on neighbour's house in case of fire.
4. Statutory authority i.e., no action lies against an act done under the authority of a legislation. However, compensation, if any, provides in the statute shall be given.
5. Act of jury i.e., no action lies against an act of judges, magistrates, munsifs, etc. done by them in discharge of their judicial duties.
6. Executive authority i.e., no action lies against an act done by executive officers of the Government in exercise of their functions.
7. Parental and Quasi-Parental authority. Parents, guardians and teachers have authority to use reasonable force against their children, students, etc.
8. Act in exercise of common rights. No action lies against a person if he acts in exercise of his common rights, even if it causes some damage to others, provided it is done in good faith and in lawful manner.
9. Act in one's own Defence. No action can be brought against a person if he uses reasonable force to protect his person or property even if it causes harm to another.
10. Act causing slight harm. This is based on the maxim *deminimis non curat lex* which means that law does not concern itself with trifles.

Remedies in Torts

Following remedies are available against torts :

1. Damages (unliquidated),
2. Injunction,
3. Specific restitution of property.

CIVIL PROCEDURE

Governing Law

Code of Civil Procedure, 1908 is the principal enactment relating to civil procedure in India. The Code consists of :

(i) Sections (which enunciate the broad powers of the courts), and

(ii) 'Orders' (which contain rules dealing with detailed procedure).

These may be supplemented by rules made by the High Court for various subordinate courts.

Stages in a Civil Suit

The main stages in the trial of a civil suit, in chronological order, are :

(i) pleading,
(ii) issues,
(iii) evidence,
(iv) arguments,
(v) judgement,
(vi) execution

Pleading : The principal pleadings are :

(a) The 'plaint', by or on behalf of the plaintiff, by which a suit is instituted; and
(b) The 'written statement' in reply by the defendant.

Issues : Issues arise when a proposition of fact or law material for the decision of the case is affirmed by one party and denied by the other.

Judgement : 'Judgement' contains the reasons for the decision. The final and operative decision of the civil court is called the 'decree'.

Execution : A decree is executed in the following manner.

(a) by attachment of the property (charge on the property) of the party against whom the decree is made,
(b) by arrest of such party (this is resorted only in rare cases),
(c) by other appropriate ways.

Appeal

Generally, at least one appeal is allowed on facts and law, and a second appeal is allowed on questions of law.

The forum of appeal depends on the status of the trial court. Where the first appellate court happens to be the High Court, an appeal can be made to the Supreme Court if the High Court certifies that a substial question of law is involved which needs to be decided by the Supreme Court or if a question of constitutional interpretation is involved.

Besides, the Supreme Court can grant special permission to appeal against the decision of any court or tribunal in India, in any matter.

Revision

The High Court is empowered to revise any order, to correct serious irregularities leading to injustice or arbitrary exercise of jurisdiction, or failure to exercise jurisdiction by inferior courts.

EVIDENCE

Governing Law

The Indian Evidence Act, 1872 is the main enactment containing the law on the subject of evidence.

Salient Features

1. Generally, evidence is admissible of relevant facts only.
2. The Act deals in detail as to which facts are and which are not relevant.
3. Hearsay evidence is generally excluded, except in special situations.
4. Most persons are competent to give evidence in court, including a child who is able to understand the questions and can answer them in a rational way.
5. Documents are to be proved by primary evidence, but secondary evidence is also admissible in special cases.
6. If necessary, the judge can question a witness, but practically this power is seldom exercised.

7. The Act broadly deals with the following issues :
   (a) Evidence-relevance of facts,
   (b) Materials of proof,
   (c) Burden of proof,
   (d) Presumptions,
   (e) Witnesses, competence and compellability,
   (f) Corroboration,
   (g) Hearsay,
   (h) Examination of witnesses,
   (i) Documentary evidence,
   (j) Powers of the judge,
   (k) Improper admission and rejection of evidence.

Confession

The provisions relating to confessions, contained in Section 24 to 30, are broadly enumerated herein below :

1. A confession is admissible in evidence, only if it is voluntary. However, it is inadmissible in circumstances mentioned in (2) and (3) below, even if it is voluntary.
2. A confession made to a police officer during investigation is inadmissible, except in a case mentioned in (4) below.
3. A confession made to any person during police custody is inadmissible, except in cases mentioned in (4) and (5) below.
4. In circumstances mentioned in (2) and (3) above, that part of the confession made by an accused that relates to information given by him, following which some relevant facts are discovered by the police (for instance, discovery of a weapon buried by the accused) shall be admissible.
5. A Confession made by an accused to a Magistrate recorded in strict compliance of Section 164 of the Code of Criminal Procedure, 1973, is admissible, even if the accused is in the police custody when it was recorded.

Section 164 of the Cr. PC provides that the accused must be given magisterial warning that he is not bound to make a confession and that the confession may be used against him.

Privileges available to a witness

Following privileges are available to a witness in regard to non-disclosure of facts of a confidential or private nature :

1. An incriminating statement made by a witness, when compelled to do so, cannot be used against him.
2. Communications made during marriage are privileged.
3. Unpublished communications relating to the affairs of the State are privileged.
4. Original title deeds are also privileged, except in certain cases.
5. The police has privilege not to disclose the name of their informer. However, a First Information Report (F.I.R.) of a cognizable offence, is not privileged.
6. Besides, legal professional privilege is also recognised.

LIMITATION

Governing Law

The Limitation Act, 1983 is the principal enactment relating to limitation in India.

Salient Features

1. The provisions in the main Act deal with the principles for computing the period of limitation and the exceptions.

2. The actual periods of limitations are enumerated in a Schedule, under separate headings for suits, appeals and applications.
3. The periods of limitations permitted by law under the Schedule differ, depending on the nature of the suit, appeal or application.

Period of Limitation for a Suit by the Government

The Government has a uniform period of 30 years for its suit irrespective of the nature of the suit.

LABOUR LAWS IN INDIA

Labour laws is a plethora of legislations enacted by the government from time to time, to regulate various issues relating to labour, its employment and other connected matters. In this chapter, a very brief review of some important legislations relating to labour welfare has been given with a view to abreast the readers of basic knowledge of labour law in India.

Constitutional Powers

Under Article 246 (4) 'labour' is a common subject for the Centre and the States, empowering them jointly to legislate on issues relating to trade union, industrial and labour disputes, social security and insurance, employment and unemployment, welfare of labour including working conditions, provident funds, employer's liability, workmen's compensation, disability and old age pensions and maternity benefits.

The Central Government enacts a labour law with a view to ensure uniformity throughout the country. The State Governments enforce the law in their State as it is, or after making necessary State amendments considering the peculiar conditions in the State. Besides, State Government is the chief authority responsible for implementation of a labour law in their State.

1. Factories Act, 1948

Objectives : The Factories Act provides for the health, safety, welfare, service conditions and other aspects of workers in factories. The Act is enforced by the State Government who frame rules that ensure that local conditions are reflected in enforcement. The Act as amended in 1987 also regulates the safeguards to be adopted for the use and handling of hazardous substances.

Applicability : The Factories Act extends to the whole of India and is applicable to all 'factories' including government factories.

It applies to all factories employing more than 10 people and working with the aid of power or employing 20 people and working without the aid of power.

Factory however does not include a mine covered under the Mines Act, 1952, a mobile unit of the armed forces, a railway shed or a hotel, restaurant or eating place.

The Act covers all workers employed in the factory premises or precincts directly or through an agency including a contractor, involved in any manufacture.

2. Payment of Wages Act, 1936

Objectives : The payment of Wages Act aims at regulating the payment of wages to certain classes of employed persons. It provides for the imposition of fines and deductions and lays down wage periods and time and mode of payment of wages. Thus the Act ensures payment of wages in a particular form at regular intervals without unauthorised deductions.

Applicability : The payment of Wages Act extends to the whole of India.

It is applicable to any factory, any railway establishment and any industrial or other establishment like tramway service, motor transport service, air, oilfied, plantation, workshop, or other establishment producing, adapting or manufacturing any article, establishments engaged in construction, development and maintenance of buildings, roads, bridges or canals, navigation, irrigation or water supply, transmission, generation and distribution of electricity/power and any other establishment notified by the Central or a State Government.

The Act is not applicable to persons whose wages are 1600 or more per month.

3. Minimum Wages Act, 1948

Objectives : The Minimum Wages Act was formulated to provide for fixing minimum rates of wages in certain employments. The Act also governs certain service conditions such as working hours, weekly rest days and payment of overtime for employees covered under the Act.

Applicability : The Minimum Wages Act extends to whole of India and applies to all establishments employing one or more persons and engaged in any of scheduled employments. It covers every employee who is engaged in any scheduled employment, including an out worker to whom materials are given out for manufacturing or processing at his own premises.

4. Payment of Bonus Act, 1965

Objectives : The object of the Payment of Bonus Act is to provide for the payment of bonus (linked with profit or productivity) to persons employed in certain establishments and matters connected therewith.

Applicability : The Payment of Bonus Act extends to the whole of India and is applicable to every factory and to every establishment wherein 20 or more workers are employed on any day during an accounting year.

The Central/State Government can however, extend its provisions to any establishment employing less than 20 but more than 10 employees.

For the purpose of calculating the number of employees for applicability of the Act, part-time employees are also included.

Every employee not drawing more than Rs. 3500 per month who has worked for not less than 30 days in an accounting year, shall be eligible for bonus.

5. Employees Provident Fund and Miscellaneous Provisions Act, 1952

Objectives : The Employees' Provident Funds and Miscellaneous Provisions Act provides for the compulsory institution of contributory provident funds, pension funds and deposit linked insurances funds for employees. The Act aims to ensure a retiral benefit to secure the future of the employee after retirement.

Applicability : The Employees' Provident Funds and Miscellaneous Provisions Act extends to whole of India except State of Jammu and Kashmir.

The Act applies to industries specified in Schedule I employing 20 or more persons and any other class of establishments employing 20 or more persons notified by the Government.

The Government may apply the Act to establishments employing less than 20 people.

Employees covered under the Act include contract labour but exclude apprentices, trainees, directors, working partners, domestic servants and contractors.

Establishments can seek exemption from any or all the provisions of the Act.

6. Payment of Gratuity Act, 1972

Objectives : The Payment of Gratuity Act provides for a scheme for the payment of gratuity to employees engaged in factories, mines, oilfields, plantations, ports, railway companies, shops or other establishments.

The Act enforces the payment of 'gratuity', a reward for long service, as a statutory retiral benefit.

Applicability : The payment of Gratuity Act extends to the whole of India and is applicable to all factories, mines, oilfields, plantations, ports, railway companies and any establishments where 10 or more persons were employed on any day of the preceding 12 months and every Shop and Establishment in which 10 or more persons are employed, or were employed on any day in the preceding 12 months.

Every employee irrespective of his wages is entitled to receive gratuity if he has rendered continuous service of 5 years or more than 5 years.

The Act is not applicable to apprentices and persons holding a post under the Central or State government who are governed by any other rule providing for payment of gratuity.

The Act covers all employees who draw upto Rs. 3500 per month as wages. The maximum gratuity payable is Rs 3,50,000.

7. Maternity Benefit Act, 1961

Objectives : The Maternity Benefit Act aims to regulate the employment of women in certain establishments for certain periods before and after child-birth and to provide for maternity benefits including maternity leave, wages, bonus, nursing breaks etc.

Applicability : The Maternity Benefit Act extends to whole of India and is applicable to every factory, mine or plantation including those belonging to Government, irrespective of the number of employees, and to every shop or establishment wherein 10 or more persons are employed or were employed on any day of the preceding 12 months.

The State Government may extend the Act to any other establishment or class of establishments, industrial, commercial, agricultural or otherwise.

The Act however does not apply to any such factory or other establishment to which the provisions of the ESI Act are applicable for the time being. But where the Factory is governed under ESI and the woman employee is not qualified to claim maternity benefit under section 50 of that Act because her wage are > Rs 3500 p.m. as specified under section 2 (9) of the ESI or for any other reason, then such woman employee is entitled to claim maternity benefit under this Act till she becomes qualified to claim maternity benefit under the ESI. Act.

8. Employees' State Insurance Act, 1948

Objectives : The ESI Act provides for the provision of benefits to employees in case of sickness, maternity and employment injury. Under the Act, employees receive medical relief, cash benefits, maternity benefits, pension to dependents of deceased workers and compensation for fatal or other injuries and diseases. Payments are made through a contributory fund.

Applicability : The ESI Act extends to whole of India.

It applies to all factories including Government factories (excluding seasonal factories), which employ 10 or more employees and carry on a manufacturing process with the aid of power (20 employees where manufacturing process is carried out without the aid of power).

The Act can also be extended to shops and establishments. Generally, shops and establishments employing more than 20 employees as defined by the Act, are covered by the Act.

The Act does not apply to mines covered under the Mines Act, Indian Naval, Military or Air Forces, Railways running sheds and Government Factories or establishments whose employees are in receipt of benefits similar or superior to those provided under the Act.

All employees including casual, temporary or contract employees drawing wages less than Rs 6500 per month are covered. Apprentices are not covered.

A factory or establishment to which this Act applies, shall continue to be governed by its provisions even if the number of workers employed falls below the specified limit or the manufacturing process therein ceases to be carried on with the aid of power subsequently.

Where a workman is covered under the ESI scheme,

(a) Compensation under the Workmen's Compensation Act cannot be claimed in respect of employment injury.

(b) No benefits can be claimed under the Maternity Benefits Act.

9. Workmen Compensation Act, 1923

Objectives : The Act aims to provide workmen and their dependents, compensatory payment, in case of accidents arising out of and in course of employment and causing either death or disablement of workmen.

Applicability : The Act extends to the whole of India.

The Act applies to factories, mines, docks, construction establishments, plantations, oilfields and other establishments listed in Schedule II and III of the Act but excludes establishments covered by the ESI Act.

Every employee including those employed through a contractor except casual employees, who is engaged for the purposes of employer's business and who suffers an injury in any accident arising out of and in the course of his employment, shall be entitled for compensation under this Act.

The Workmen Compensation Amendment Act, 1995, has extended the ambit of the Act to cover workers of newspaper establishments, drivers, cleaners, etc working in connection with a motor vehicle, workers employed by Indian companies abroad, persons engaged in spraying or dusting of insecticides or pesticides in agricultural operations, mechanised harvesting and thrashing, horticultural operations and doing other mechanical jobs.

10. Industrial Dispute Act, 1947

Objectives : The objective of the Industrial Disputes Act is to secure industrial peace and harmony by providing machinery and procedure for the investigation and settlement of industrial disputes by negotiations.

The Act also lays down

(a) The provision for payment of compensation to the Workman on account of closure or lay off or retrenchment.

(b) The procedure for prior permission of appropriate Government for laying off or retrenching the workers or closing down industrial establishments.

(c) Unfair labour practices on part of an employer or a trade union or workers.

Applicability : The Industrial Disputes Act extends to whole of India and applies to every industrial establishment carrying on any business, trade, manufacture or distribution of goods and services irrespective of the number of workmen employed therein.

Every person employed in an establishment for hire or reward including contract labour, apprentices and part time employees to do any manual, clerical, skilled, unskilled, technical, operational or supervisory work, is covered by the Act.

This Act though does not apply to persons mainly in managerial or administrative capacity, persons engaged in a supervisory capacity and drawing more than 1600 p.m. or executing managerial functions and persons subject to Army Act, Air Force and Navy Act or those in police service or officer or employee of a prison.

11. Contract Labour (Regulation and Abolition) Act, 1970

Objectives : The objective of the Contract Labour Act is to regulate the employment of Contract Labour in certain establishments and to provide for its abolition in certain circumstances and for matters connected therewith.

The Act empowers the Central or State Governments to prohibit the employment of Contract Labour in any process or operation.

Applicability : The Contract Labour Act extends to the whole of India.

It applies to every establishment or contractor wherein 20 or more workmen are or were employed on any day of the preceding 12 months as contract labour.

The appropriate government is empowered to extend the application of the Act to any establishment or contractor employing even less than 20 workers as contract labour.

The Act is not applicable to establishment in which work is only of an intermittent or casual nature. Work performed in an establishment for more than 120 days in the preceding 12 months or work of a seasonal nature and performed for more than 60 days in a year, shall NOT be deemed to be work of an intermittent nature.

12. Equal Remuneration Act, 1976

Objectives : The Equal Remuneration Act provides for payment of equal remuneration to men and women workers, for the same work and prevents discrimination on the grounds of sex against women in the matter of employment, recruitment and for matters connected therewith or incidental thereto.

This act was promulaged to give effect to Article 9 of the Constitution which envisages that State shall direct its policy, among other things, towards securing that : there is equal pay for equal work for both men and women.

Applicability : The Equal Remuneration Act extends to the whole of India and applies to the establishments or employments notified by the Central Government. The Act is now applicable to almost every kind of establishments.

The Act is not applicable if the terms and conditions of a women's employment in complying with any requirement gives them special treatment in connection with—

i. the birth or expected birth of a child, or
ii. the terms and conditions relating to retirement, marriage or death or to any provision made in connection with the retirement, marriage or death.

13. Trade Unions Act, 1926

Objectives: The Trade Unions Act, 1926 provides for registration of trade unions (including association of employers) with a view to render lawful organisation of labour to enable collective bargaining. The Act also confers certain protection and privileges on a registered trade union.

Applicability: The Trade Unions Act extends to the whole of India and it applies to all kinds of unions of workers and associations of employers which aim at regularising labour management relations. The Act is a Central enactment but is administered by and large by the State Governments. Trade Unions whose, objectives are not restricted to one State, are the subject of the Central Government.

14. The Industrial Disputes (Amendment) Bill, 2010

The amendment proposals in the Industrial Disputes (Amendment) Bill, 2010 inter-alia, seek to amplify the definition of 'appropriate Government', enhance the wage ceiling prescribed for supervisors, provide direct access for workman to Labour courts or Tribunal in case of individual disputes, expand the scope of qualifications of Presiding Officers of Labour Courts or Tribunal, setting up of Grievance Settlement Machinery and empowerment of Industrial Tribunal-cum-Labour Courts to enforce decree.

The Industrial Disputes (Amendment) Bill, 2010 seeks the following:

Section 2(a)—Amplification of definition of Appropriate Government

The Bill proposes to amplify the definition of 'appropriate Government' under 2(a) of the Act. The Central Government is the appropriate Government in respect of categories listed in Section 2(a)(i) of the I.D. Act, 1947. In addition to this, it is further clarified that Central Government would be appropriate Government for any company in which not less than fifty-one per cent of the paid-up share capital is held by the Central Government, or any corporation, (not being a corporation referred to in this clause) established by or under any law made by Parliament, or the Central Public Sector Undertaking, subsidiary companies set up by the principal undertaking and autonomous bodies owned or controlled by the Central Government.

State Government will be the appropriate Government in relation to any other industrial dispute, including the State Public Sector Undertaking, subsidiary companies set up by the principal undertaking and autonomous bodies owned or controlled by the State Government.

To amplify the definition of term 'appropriate Government' the Standing Committee has suggested that the industrial disputes between a contractor and contract labour employed in any industrial establishment needs to be brought under the purview of 'appropriate Government'. The Government has accepted this recommendation of the Committee. This amplification of the definition will eliminate all ambiguities in the interpretation of the definition of 'appropriate Government'.

Section 2(s)—Amendment of Section 2(s) (iv)–Enhancing the wage ceiling of Rs. 1600 per month prescribed for supervisors in the definition of workmen under Section 2(s) to Rs. 10,000 per month.

Enhancement of wage ceiling of the workers working in a supervisory capacity from one thousand six hundred rupees per month to ten thousand rupees per month. The wage ceiling has been enhanced to be in consonance with the increase in wages of industrial workers and also to bring about parity with other labour laws like Employees State Insurance Act, 1948, Payment of Bonus Act, 1965 and Payment of Wages Act, 1936.

Section 2(A)—Direct reference of disputes connected with Termination/Dismissal/ Retrenchment/Discharge to Industrial Tribunals.

To provide direct access for the workman to the labour Court or Tribunal in case of disputes arising out of section 2A pertaining to retrenchment, discharge, dismissal or termination of services etc. At present, such a dispute could be adjudicated by CGIT-cum LC only after a reference is made by the 'appropriate Government'. As a consequence of this proposed amendment, the workman can directly approach the CGIT-cum-LC after filing his grievance before the conciliation machinery to resolve the issue within 45 days. There will be no need for him to approach the 'appropriate Government' for making a reference. This amendment would enable the aggrieved workman to choose the alternative of adjudication for resolution of his dispute faster.

Substitution of new Chapter for Chapter IIB-Setting of Grievance Redressal Machinery.

The Bill seeks to establish a Grievance Redressal Machinery (GRM) within industrial establishment having 20 or more workmen with one stage appeal at the head of the establishment for resolution of disputes arising out of individual grievances. With this amendment, the workman will get one more alternative grievance redressal mechanism for the resolution of his dispute within the organization itself with minimum necessity for adjudication. It may be noted that setting up of GRM in no way will affect the right of the workman to raise dispute on the same issue under the provision of Industrial Disputes Act, 1947.

Section 7: Relaxation of Qualifications of Presiding Officers.

It is also proposed to expand the scope of qualification of Presiding Officers of CGIT-cum-LC by making officers of Central Labour Service of the rank of Deputy Chief Labour Commissioner and State Labour Department of the rank of Joint Labour Commissioner and officers of the Indian Legal Service Gr.III eligible for the post of Presiding Officer in CGIT-cum-LC. This will enable the Government to appoint the Presiding Officers from wide range of eligible officers from the relevant field.

Section 11: Power to enforce Decree by CGIT.

The Bill also proposes to empower the Labour Court or Tribunal to execute their awards, orders of settlements arrived at as a decree of a Civil Court. This amendment will ensure better enforcement of the awards given by CGITs-cum-LC.

Section 38(2)©: Salaries and allowances and other terms and conditions of service of Presiding Officer of Central Government Industrial Tribunals-cum-Labour Courts (CGIT) and National Tribunals.

The Bill proposes to make specific provision in the Act by amending the Section 38(2) © of the Act that Government may make rules to decide and review the salaries and allowances and other terms and conditions for appointment of Presiding Officers. Details will be worked out while framing the rules.

To Summariese, the main amendment proposals in the I.D. Act are:

(*i*) Amplification of the definition of 'Appropriate Government'.

(*ii*) To enhance the wage limit from Rs. 1600/- per month to Rs. 10,000/- per month to make the provision meaningful and in tune with the definition of workman in other labour laws such as Payment of Bonus Act, 1965, Payment of Wages Act, 1936 and Employees' State Insurance Act, 1948.

(*iii*) To provide a grievance ventilation and redressal machinery within an establishment having 20 or more workmen with one stage appeal at the level of the Head of the Industrial Establishment in order to promote better industrial relations at the industrial establishment level.

(*iv*) To provide individual workman direct access to Labour Courts/Tribunals in cases of retrenchment, discharge, dismissal or termination of services.

(*v*) To make officers of the Central Labour Service/State Labour Service/Indian Legal Service eligible for the post of Presiding Officers in the Central Government Industrial Tribunals-cum-Labour Courts for addressing the problem of availability of Presiding Officers.

(*vi*) To empower Government to make rules to decide and review the salaries and allowances and other terms and conditions for appointment of Presiding Officers.

(*vii*) To empower Central Government Industrial Tribunals, Labour Courts and National Tribunals to execute their awards/orders/settlements as a decree of the civil court.

15. Workmen's Compensation Act Amended

Under this amendment, the workmen or their family members will get the compensation money at the enhanced rate if they die or get disabled. As a result of the death in the working capacity, the compensation money will be Rs. 80,000 now as against Rs. 50,000 as previously prevalent. The maximum limit can be Rs. 4.56 lakhs. In the state of disability, the minimum limit is increased from 60,000 to 90,000 rupees. The maximum limit in the case, can go upto 5.48 lakh rupees. The compensation will depend on the age and wage of the workman. For the last rites of the workman, the money limit is increased from Rs. 1000 to 2500 rupees.

16. Trade Union (Amendment) Act, 2001

The Act has following important provisions:

★ Minimum 10% of the total labour force or 100 labourers in an organisation (whichever is less must be required to form trade union).

★ No. of members should not be less than seven in any condition.

★ At least 5 members or one-third (which ever is less) should be the employees of the concern.

★ Annual contribution for trade union should not be less than Rs. 12.00.

LEGAL APTITUDE

INTRODUCTION

Tips to Tackle Legal Aptitude Questions

Legal Aptitude Test is another way of testing the legal aptitude of an aspirant of a law course at any eminent law institute. There are questions based on legal reasoning and legal knowledge in it. There are questions of mainly three types in it.

Type I Questions: These are the questions that are based on the basic knowledge of legal terms. To tackle these questions one should be well-versed with the elementary legal terminology.

Example: The term 'palimony' means

A. alimony from parents
B. maintenance from friends
C. courts orders financial settlement amongst people in a live-in relationship
D. maintenance to old parents by children

Type II Questions: These are the questions that are based on the knowledge of elementary law itself. To tackle these questions one should go through the elementary law theory. Some of these questions can be answered with commonsense and logical reasoning.

Example: Which of the following is *not* protected by Copyright Act?

A. Computer databases
B. Invention
C. Musical work
D. Dramatic work

Type III Questions: These are the questions that are based upon knowledge of recent developments in law arena. It includes general awareness about this field *e.g.*, new laws and cases, top legal functions, etc.

Example 1. National Law Day is observed every year on

A. March 1 B. April 30
C. June 16 D. November 26

Example 2. The Competition Act was passed in the year 2002 to replace

A. The Monopolies and Restrictive Trade Practices Act, 1969
B. The Consumer Protection Act, 1986
C. The Sale of Goods Act, 1930
D. Unlawful Activities (Prevention) Act, 1967

MULTIPLE CHOICE QUESTIONS

1. Bhopal gas leak case falls under general classification of law of

A. Torts B. Contracts
C. Crimes D. Negligence

2. Can a couple who had adopted a son, adopt another son legally?

A. No, Law prohibits
B. Yes, Law permits
C. Circumstantial
D. None of the above

3. A married man commits adultery if he has sexual intercourse with a/an

A. Any woman except his wife
B. Married woman
C. Unmarried woman
D. Unmarried woman without her consent

4. The Indian Contract Act was enacted in the year
A. 1974 B. 1976
C. 1872 D. 1870

5. The law relating to diplomatic relations is codified in
A. Vienna Conventions
B. New York Conventions
C. Hague Conventions
D. Geneva Conventions

6. Match the following:
(*a*) Hindu Marriage Act (*i*) 1956
(*b*) Special Marriage Act (*ii*) 1955
(*c*) Hindu Succession Act (*iii*) 1954
(*d*) Hindu Adoption & Maintenance Act (*iv*) 1956

Codes:

	(*a*)	(*b*)	(*c*)	(*d*)
A.	(*iii*)	(*ii*)	(*iv*)	(*i*)
B.	(*ii*)	(*iii*)	(*iv*)	(*i*)
C.	(*i*)	(*ii*)	(*iv*)	(*iii*)
D.	(*iii*)	(*iv*)	(*i*)	(*ii*)

7. Parties may refer their disputes to an independent third party, instead of regular courts, under the provisions of
A. Negotiations Act
B. Negotiable Instruments Act
C. Arbitration Act
D. Law of Contract

8. Information Technology Act was enacted in
A. 2002 B. 2000
C. 2001 D. 1950

9. The Indian Succession Act, 1925, contains provisions regarding
A. Succession
B. Intestate Succession
C. Intestate and Testamentary Succession
D. Testamentary Succession

10. What is the maximum term of imprisonment for Contempt of Court?
A. 2 years B. 4 years
C. 6 months D. 1 year

11. Which one of the following laws was not enacted by the British?
A. Indian Evidence Act
B. Indian Contract Act
C. Indian Penal Code
D. Terrorist & Disruptive Activities (Prevention) Act

12. The Father of International Law is
A. Plato B. Grotius
C. Aristotle D. Denning

13. Code of Civil Procedure was enacted in
A. 1919 B. 1908
C. 1948 D. 1973

14. The nature of MRTP Act is
A. Consumer Protection
B. Price Regulation
C. Trade Regulation
D. Both A and C

15. Transfer of Property Act, 1882, covers
A. Immovable property
B. Movable property
C. Both A and B
D. None of the above

16. Which one among the following is not a negotiable instrument?
A. Cheque B. Promissory note
C. Bill of exchange D. Will

17. Which of the following is not a source of law in India?
A. Public opinion B. Precedent
C. Legislation D. Custom

18. Examine the two statements:
(*i*) Companies Act was enacted in 1956
(*ii*) Income-tax Act was enacted in 1961
A. Both are true B. Both are false
C. (*i*) only true D. (*ii*) only true

19. The State which has the largest number of seats reserved for Scheduled Tribes in Lok Sabha is
A. Madhya Pradesh B. Bihar
C. Uttar Pradesh D. Gujarat

20. After independence, the Supreme Court of India came into existence in the year
A. 1953 B. 1952
C. 1951 D. 1950

21. The Balkan Plan for fragmentation of India was the brain child of
A. M.A. Jinnah B. V.P. Menon
C. Lord Mountbatten D. W. Charchil

22. Which of the following is a correct statement of law?
A. Public Interest Litigation can be filed by an advocate only
B. Public Interest Litigation Petitions can be entertained by the Supreme Court, High Courts and District Courts
C. Public Interest Litigation Petitions can be entertained by the Supreme Court as well as the High Courts
D. Public Interest Litigation Petitions can be entertained only by the Supreme Court

23. Who among the following is the Chairman of National Commission on law?
A. G.P. Goenke
B. M. Jagannatha Rao
C. Sunil Shastri
D. Rahul Bajaj

24. The Guardian of the Indian Constitution is
A. President of India
B. Parliament of India
C. Both President and Prime Minister of India
D. Supreme Court of India

25. The Economic Liberalisation in India started with
A. Doing away with procedural formalities for foreign direct investment
B. Substantial change in Industrial Licensing Policy
C. The convertibility of Indian Rupees
D. None of the above

26. Voting right is
A. Constitutional right
B. Legal right
C. Fundamental right
D. None of the above

27. The standing committee of State Finance Ministers recommended in January, 2000 uniform rates for the States in respect of
A. Value added tax
B. Stamp duty and registration fees
C. Sales Tax
D. Agricultural income tax

28. The Supreme Court of India assembles in the present building which was constructed in the year
A. 1950 B. 1958
C. 1959 D. 1960

29. The Constitution of india recognised
A. Only linguistic minorities
B. Religious, Linguistic and ethnic minorities
C. Only religious minorities
D. Religious and linguistic

30. Article 17 of the Constitution provides for
A. Right to Know
B. Abolition of untouchability
C. Right to Freedom
D. Abolition of Titles

31. The System of Indian Election follow
A. Direct election system
B. Mixed vote system
C. Adult Franchise
D. None of the above

32. At the time of partition of India, which one of the following provinces of British India came forward with a plan for united and independent existence?
A. Bihar B. Punjab
C. Bengal D. Assam

33. Fourth Estate refers to
A. Press B. Prime Minister
C. Supreme Court D. President

34. A Consulate Car is not subject to Traffic Challans due to
A. Sovereign immunity
B. They don't break traffic rules
C. Diplomatic immunity
D. They are foreign cars

35. The Speaker can ask in member of the house to stop speaking and let another member speak, this phenomenon is known as
A. Interpretation B. Ordering
C. Assumption D. Crossing the floor

36. _____ is an inquiry into cause of death.
A. Inquest B. Autopsy
C. Coroneration D. Investigation

37. An exclusive right conferred on one who invents a machine, to make, use, sell or assign it for a certain period, is called
A. will B. contract
C. copyright D. patent

38. The act of unlawfully entering into another's property
A. Trespass
B. Trover
C. Triplication
D. Breach of property

39. Who propounded the doctrine of "Rule of Law"?
A. Dicey B. Aristotle
C. Lord Macaulay D. Lord Blackstone

40. Supreme Court abolished a section of Indian Penal Code (I.P.C.), to state that "punishing a person who has attempted suicide is cruel and inhuman". The section affected is
A. Section 498, IPC B. Section 302, IPC
C. Section 309, IPC D. Section 303, IPC

41. The reason (or ground) of a judicial decision is known as
A. Obiter dictum B. Ratio decidendi
C. Ratione sole D. Ratione tenural

42. Match the following:

(*a*) Void	(*i*) An act illegal from beginning
(*b*) Voidable	(*ii*) An act until rescinded, legal
(*c*) Vis major	(*iii*) Consent is a defence
(*d*) Volenti non fit injuria	(*iv*) Irresistable force

Codes:

	(*a*)	(*b*)	(*c*)	(*d*)
A.	(*iii*)	(*ii*)	(*i*)	(*iv*)
B.	(*i*)	(*ii*)	(*iv*)	(*iii*)
C.	(*ii*)	(*iv*)	(*iii*)	(*i*)
D.	(*i*)	(*ii*)	(*iii*)	(*iv*)

43. The offence of inciltihg disaffection, hatred or contempt against Government is
A. Sedition B. Treason
C. Defamation D. Not an offence

44. The tort of defaming someone by words or gestures
A. Slip
B. Defamation per incuraim
C. Slander
D. Libel

45. A filed a suit for breach of contract against B. The District Court decided in A's favour. B, however, appealed to the High Court. The legal terminology for B is appellant, while A would be called
A. Plaintiff B. Respondent
C. Accused D. Defendant

46. A document issued by Court, calling upon the person to whom it is directed to attend before the judge
A. Bench B. Supra
C. Summons D. Bailiff

47. When an ongoing case is adjourned to a future date, and defendant is ordered to be kept in custody in the meantime, the defendant is said to be _____ to custody.
A. condemned B. decreed
C. remanded D. ordered

48. An act in excess of the authority conferred by law
A. Ultra vires B. Intra vires
C. Illegal D. Extra-legal

49. Who is a Recidivist?
A. Man with radical ideas
B. Reserved person
C. Rash person
D. Habitual criminal

50. When the master is held liable for the wrongful act of his servant, the liability is
A. Vicarious B. Absolute
C. Transferred D. Strict

51. An Act of Parliament is called
A. Bill B. Legislation
C. Public policy D. Statute

52. What does this maxim express "Salus populi est suprema lex"?

A. Welfare of people is paramount law
B. Law is supreme in society
C. Law is equal for everyone
D. Everyone is equal before law

53. The meaning of the term 'quasi' is

A. Null
B. Void
C. As if it were
D. Quashed

54. The act of having anal intercourse is the offence of

A. HIV
B. Sodomy
C. Slander
D. Sedition

55. To defranchise means

(*i*) to deprive of voting right
(*ii*) to deprive of right over property
(*iii*) to deprive of any right (generally)

Codes:

A. Only (*iii*)
B. (*i*) and (*iii*)
C. Only (*i*)
D. None of the above

56. ______ is an established defence when it is proved that the plaintiff failed to take reasonable care of himself and thus contributed to his injuries.

A. Self injury
B. Volenti non fit injuria
C. Contributory negligence
D. None of the above

57. The 'Right to Reply Bill' seek to curb which tendency?

A. Defamation by the Press
B. Secured right of litigants to comment on Court judgements
C. Defamation of the Press
D. Secured right to Member of Legislatures

58. What is the meaning of culpable?

A. Blame worthy
B. Involving a breach of legal duty
C. Both A and B
D. Neither A nor B

59. The word 'due process of law' indicates

A. In course of time
B. Justice by tribunals
C. As ordained by statue law
D. In course through courts

60. A mode of transfer of property, including mortgage, lease, etc., but excluding will

A. Conveyance
B. Conusance
C. Conversion
D. Contumacy

61. What is the legal name given to the repairs needed to a house at the end of a tenancy?

A. Dies utils
B. Dies netasti
C. Dilapidations
D. Dies fasi

62. Crime is an act or omission which is perceived as harmful to society at large. This is proved by

A. One party to criminal suit being state
B. Severe punishment
C. Because trial is by court
D. None of the above

63. Deceit is

A. A crime
B. A tort
C. A breach of contract
D. Both A and B

64. The Consumer Protection Act came into effect from

A. 1987
B. 1988
C. 1986
D. 1992

65. 'Stay Order' has the effect of

A. status quo
B. pro rata
C. stopping an order of lower court from working
D. sine die

66. Joint heirs to a property are called

A. Co-holders
B. Co-owners
C. Joint owners
D. Coparceners

67. An order of a Court pronounced on the hearing of a suit is called

A. Degree
B. Dehor
C. Deed
D. Decree

68. When a widow remarries, her children are considered the children of her new husband. This can be best stated by the term

A. De donis
B. De jure
C. De novo
D. De facto

69. Bye-law making power granted to the executive by the Legislature is called

A. Delegated authority
B. Prerogative power
C. Delegated legislation
D. Order power

70. What is the diminished responsibility?
A. When death is caused by an insane person
B. When death is caused by accident
C. When death is caused under duress
D. None of the above

71. What is the legal meaning of the word 'Battery'?
A. Assault resulting in at least 6 months hospitalization
B. Actual or intended stricking of another person
C. Battering a person to death
D. Cells, as used in torch, tape recorder etc.

72. Laws made by the executive for administrative convenience are called
A. Public Acts
B. Bye-laws
C. Administrative legislations
D. Executive orders

73. The four pillars of democracy are
A. The Parliament, the President, the Judiciary and the Press
B. The President, the Prime Minister, the People and the Press
C. The Parliament, the Executive, the Judiciary and the Press
D. The President, the Prime Minister, the Governors and the Chief Ministers

74. The International Law consists of
A. Public International Law only
B. Public International Law and Private International Law
C. Public International Law and Domestic Law
D. Private International Law

75. The maxim *'Ubi jus ibi romodium'* means
A. Justice should not only be done but should be seen to be done
B. Justice according to law
C. In law, there is a remedy for every wrong
D. Judges are above law

76. Match the following:

(*a*) Right to Freedom of Religion	(*i*) Article 21
(*b*) Prohibition of employment of children	(*ii*) Article 30
(*c*) Right of minorities to establish schools	(*iii*) Article 24
(*d*) Right to life	(*iv*) Article 25

Codes:

	(*a*)	(*b*)	(*c*)	(*d*)
A.	(*i*)	(*ii*)	(*iii*)	(*iv*)
B.	(*ii*)	(*i*)	(*iv*)	(*iii*)
C.	(*i*)	(*iv*)	(*iii*)	(*ii*)
D.	(*iv*)	(*iii*)	(*ii*)	(*i*)

77. The main sources of law are
A. Custom, Public Opinion and Speeches of National Leaders
B. Laws stated in religious texts and moral teachings given by religious leaders
C. Judgements given by the Court of Law
D. Custom, Legislation of Precedents

78. Article 14 of the Constitution guarantees to all citizens
A. Freedom of movement
B. Right to form association
C. Equality before law and equal protection by laws
D. Equality of opportunity in matters of public employment

79. Sometimes judges appoint some lawyers to assist them in a case. Such lawyers are called
A. Amicus Curiae B. Court Assistants
C. Public Prosecutors D. Defence Counsel

80. The number of judges in the International Court of Justice is
A. 15 B. 18
C. 10 D. 20

81. The International Treaty becomes binding on India when
A. Indian delegation signs the treaty
B. President signs the treaty
C. Prime Minister signs the treaty
D. Parliament makes special legislation for accepting the treaty

82. The Secularism means
A. Propagation of atheism
B. Propagation of all religion
C. Non-propagation of any religion
D. None of these

83. The maxim *'Res ipsa Loquitor'* means
A. In law, there is a remedy for every wrong
B. Facts speak for themselves
C. Justice is blind
D. The aim of law is to seek justice

84. 84th Constitution Amendment Act gives reservation for which of the following categories
A. Anglo-Indians, SCs and STs
B. Women in Parliament
C. Economically downtrodden
D. Caste-wise

85. The Advocate General is appointed by
A. Law Secretary
B. Chief Justice of the High Court
C. Governor
D. Chief Minister of the State

86. When a judge makes certain remarks in the course of his judgement, which are said "by the way" and do not have direct bearing on the facts at hand, such remarks are called
A. Comments ordinaralis
B. Obiter dictum
C. Observation
D. Judicial dictum

87. One who brings an action to court of law
A. Party B. Plaintiff
C. Defendant D. Plaint

88. The wrong decision of a court
A. Per intortunium B. Pepper com
C. Per incuriam D. Per curian

89. A person who takes proceedings against the accused on behalf of the State
A. Prosecutor B. Lawyer
C. Judge D. Procator

90. Who outlined in his "Law of Constitution 1881" the concept of "Rule of Law" meaning a government of laws rather than of arbitrary individuals?
A. Blackstone B. Austin
C. Dicey D. Salmond

91. A published account of legal proceedings, used by lawyers as basis of searching precedent is called
A. Commentary B. Law Journal
C. Law report D. Digest

92. Match the following:

(*a*) Malfeasance	(*i*) One who falsely pretends to be sick
(*b*) Malingerer	(*ii*) Minor offences
(*c*) Misderneanour	(*iii*) Improper performance of legal duty
(*d*) Misfeasance	(*iv*) Doing an unlawful act

Codes:

	(*a*)	(*b*)	(*c*)	(*d*)
A.	(*iv*)	(*i*)	(*ii*)	(*iii*)
B.	(*i*)	(*ii*)	(*iii*)	(*iv*)
C.	(*ii*)	(*iii*)	(*iv*)	(*i*)
D.	(*iii*)	(*iv*)	(*i*)	(*ii*)

93. Risk of conviction and punishment is called
A. Jactitation B. Autrefois
C. Jeopardy D. Jetsam

94. What is a 'moot'?
A. A basic fact of case
B. Mock court for practice by students
C. Another name for Magistrates Court
D. A basic point of law

95. Defamation by means of writing, print, etc. is legally called
A. Lex Scripta B. Liber
C. Libel D. Liable

96. In Law of Torts, a master is generally liable for acts of his servant. This is called
A. Vicarious liability
B. Limited liability
C. Strict liability
D. Extended liability

97. Separation of Judiciary from the Executive, is
A. A directive principle
B. A principle given by Austin
C. A fundamental directive
D. None of the above

98. Death caused by act done in heat of passion, makes a person liable for
A. Murder B. Felony
C. Lawful homicide D. Man slaughter

99. Liability is
A. Duty
B. Subjection to legal obligation
C. Responsibility
D. None of the above

100. Which Inn of Court called 'Gandhiji to the Bar'?
A. Middle Temple B. Inner Temple
C. Gray's Inn D. Lincoln's Inn

101. A lawyer examining the witness asks "You went to Mr. Kumar's house at 10:45 p.m. Didn't you?" These types of questions are called
A. Examination
B. Query
C. Leading questions
D. Cross examination

102. *Mens rea* is translated as
A. Intention B. Evil
C. Guilty mind D. Unlawful act

103. Consider the following Principles:
(*i*) There must be due in inquiry
(*ii*) The accused must be told of his crime
(*iii*) The accused must be given full opportunity to state his defence
(*iv*) Decision should be arrived at honestly after accused has been heard

The principles are called
A. Principles of legal justice
B. Principles of open justice
C. Principles of retributive justice
D. Principles of natural justice

104. Consider the following statements about Attorney General of India:
(*i*) He is appointed by the President of India
(*ii*) He must have the same life of a judge of the Supreme Court
(*iii*) He must appear in both houses of Parliament
(*iv*) He can be removed by impeachment by Parliament

Which of the following statements are correct?
A. (*ii*), (*iii*) and (*iv*) B. (*iii*) and (*iv*)
C. (*i*) and (*ii*) D. (*i*) and (*iii*)

105. The ______ law relates to functions and powers of Government organisations.
A. administrative B. contitutional
C. state D. executive

106. The number of fundamental duties in Constitution are
A. 10 B. 7
C. 5 D. 12

107. A mortgage is of ______ property while a pledge is of ______ property.
A. movable, immovable
B. immovable, movable
C. land, services
D. none of the above

108. Criminal law is ______ law, while administrative law is ______ law.
A. public, private B. public, public
C. private, public D. private, private

109. Husband and wife have a right to each other's company. This right is called
A. Legal right
B. Conjugal right
C. Matrimonial right
D. Consortium right

110. Who among the following is Fourth Pillar of Indian Constitution?
A. Supreme Court
B. Supreme Commander
C. Attorney General
D. Comptroller and Auditor General

111. LL.B. is the abbreviation of
A. Legum Baccalaureus
B. Legalite Lawyers Baccilli
C. Bachelor of Laws
D. None of the above

112. When property is in possession of a person other than the owner, the owner is in
A. Real possession
B. Unpossession
C. Dispossession
D. Adverse possession

113. State's right to acquire property is a power of
A. Eminent domain B. Sovereign right
C. Absolute D. Conditional

114. A deed is a written statement which is
A. Signed
B. Delivered
C. Sealed
D. All of the above are necessary

115. 'Medical jurisprudence' — another name of
A. Forensic
B. Philosophy of Medicine
C. Forensic Medicine
D. Medical Prescription

116. ______ is a general pardon.
A. Reprieve B. Suspension
C. Remission D. Amnesty

117. An act done under threat or fear is done under
A. Compulsion B. Decree
C. Caveat D. Duress

118. Law can be broadly divided into two kinds. Procedural law which tells us the procedure for obtaining justice and substantive law which
A. substantiates moral principles
B. creates rights and duties
C. supplements procedural law
D. none of the above

119. The early release of a prisoner is called
A. Warrant B. Lease
C. Bail D. Parole

120. What is a testament?
A. Will
B. Evidence (oral)
C. Evidence (Documentary)
D. Court order

121. In which of the following a man is liable Independently of the existence of either wrongful intent or negligence?
A. Strict liability
B. Liability ab initio
C. Liability in exceptio
D. Liability

122. Offence of breaking a divine idol
A. Blasphemy B. Salus populi
C. Crime D. Sacrilege

123. International law creates imperfect obligations because
A. There is a weak man heading the U.N.
B. There is no agency to enforce it
C. There are too many conflicts between nations
D. None of the above

124. A written acknowledgement of debt is abbreviated as IOU. It stands for
A. Promissory Note
B. I owe you
C. Instrument of understanding
D. None of the above

125. What is the meaning of insolvency?
A. To be left without a penny is a will
B. Inability to pay debts
C. Unsoundness of mind
D. Undissolvable estate

126. In dowry death cases, one of the following evidence can be clinching to secure conviction.
A. Dying declaration of the deceased
B. Evidence of the girl's father
C. Evidence of girl's mother
D. Evidence of the girl's husband

127. Code of Criminal Procedure was enacted in the year
A. 1973 B. 1983
C. 1860 D. 1873

128. The shortest Act passed by the Parliament is
A. Stamp Act
B. Powers of Attorney Act
C. Arya Marriage Validation Act
D. Court fees Act

129. Precedents (earlier cases) are taken as binding and authoritative on later cases, due to an important principle of law known as
A. Judicial sanctity B. Stare decision
C. Status de manerio D. Binding decision

130. Indian nationality can be acquired by all but one

A. Naturalisation
B. Marriage
C. Purchase of property
D. Birth

131. Law of contract is a
A. Private Law B. International Law
C. Public Law D. Conflict of Laws

132. The Indian concept of Lokayukts and Lokpal have their Scandinavian equivalent in
A. Parliamentary Guardian
B. Official Trustee
C. Public Guardian
D. Ombudsman

133. A previous judgement cited by court to decide on a similar set of facts
A. Judicial dicta B. Obiter dicta
C. Precedent D. Case

134. To pledge goods as security for debt
A. Peine B. Pawn
C. Pledge D. Security

135. Borrowing of money against pledge land as security. This system of arrangement is called
A. Mortgage B. Hundi
C. Pledge D. None of the above

136. Consider the following statements:
(*i*) Piracy is an act of robbery on the sea
(*ii*) Piracy is the infringement of copyright
A. Only I is correct B. Only II is correct
C. Both are correct D. Both are incorrect

137. The acronym P.A.Y.E. stands for
A. Payee
B. Payment authorised yet endorsed
C. Pay to the bearer
D. Pay as you earn

138. A formal instrument by which one person empowers another to represent him is
A. Instrument of surrender
B. Instrument of representation
C. Will
D. Power of Attorney

139. A person who attests copies of original documents, to render them authentic is called
A. Notary Public B. Driscoll
C. Nisi parrius D. Court baliff

140. What is plea bargaining?
A. A conference between opposing lawyers and Judge to determine the time a case should take place
B. A procedure by which a defendant pleads guilty is exchange for a lesser sentence
C. A conference between opposing lawyers to settle claim
D. None of the above

141. One of the following is not a negotiable instrument
A. Promissory Note B. Bill of Exchange
C. Will D. Cheque

142. A rule of inheritance which favours the eldest son
A. Primogeniture
B. Primus inter pares
C. Uxorilocal
D. Ultimogeniture

143. A marriage between an unmarried woman and a married man is
A. Accepted B. Valid
C. Null D. Void

144. If a witness makes a statement in court, knowing it to be false, he commits the offence of
A. Notary evidence B. Perjury
C. False evidence D. Perils

145. According to law "Tata Sons Ltd." is a/an
A. Artificial person
B. Company personnel
C. Corporation personal
D. Natural person

146. The act by members of a union, of persuading others not to work is called
A. cat call B. picketting
C. sit-in-strike D. strike

147. The Supreme Court can entertain an appeal from the decision of the High Court in case
A. when imprisonment is ordered
B. if the person has been in jail for over 14 years without trial
C. if the accused has been sentenced to death
D. if the matter involves an amount of ₹ 20,000

148. After the Bill being passed by both the Houses of Parliament, it becomes an Act only when it receives the assent of the
A. Minister for Parliamentary Affairs
B. President
C. Prime Minister
D. Law Minister

149. The word "Hindu" used in Hindu Marriage Act, 1955 includes all except
A. Buddhists B. Parsis
C. Sikhs D. Jains

150. The Public Interest Litigation Petition (PIL) can be filed by
A. Aggrieved party B. Any citizen
C. Pleader only D. Advocates only

151. Who among these cannot cast the vote by ballot?
A. NRI
B. Foreign Service Executives
C. Officials on election duty
D. Armed force members

152. Indira Sahney v. Union of India is popularly known as
A. Suicide judgement
B. Election Commission judgement
C. Ayodhya judgement
D. Mandal judgement

153. The Commission which proposes Law reforms in India is
A. Pay Commission
B. Law Reforms Commission
C. Bar Commission
D. Law Commission

154. The longest Act passed by the Parliament is
A. The Companies Act
B. Civil Procedure Code
C. Indian Penal Code
D. Negotiable Instruments Act

155. High sea is
A. Sea lying beyond is distance of 3 miles from the coast of any country
B. Sea beyond 200 km of a coast of any country
C. Sea lying more than 5 km beyond the coast of a country
D. Both A and C

156. An order of the court directs a person to do something or refain from doing a particular thing is called
A. Intortunium B. Inhibition
C. Infans D. Injunction

157. 'Ignorantia juris nemineam exusat' stands for
A. Ignore of fact is no excuse
B. Ignorance of law is no excuse
C. Laws are universally known
D. None of the above

158. The expression 'dying intestate' refers to
A. dying in midst of a legal transaction
B. dying heavity indebted
C. dying without leaving a will
D. dying without a penny

159. A right available against world at large is
A. In pleno B. In situ
C. In rem D. In personam

160. Innuendo hints at
A. Slander B. Insuniation
C. Defamation D. Libel

161. In English Law, the word 'immemorial' has a specific meaning. It refers to a usage which has existed prior to
A. 1056 A.D. B. 1 B.C.
C. 1608 A.D. D. 1189 A.D.

162. The killing of a new born child by its parents is
A. Abortion B. Foeticide
C. Infanticide D. Malfeasance

163. 'Homicide' is killing of a human being by another human being. It may be
A. Lawful B. Unlawful
C. Neither A nor B D. Both A and B

164. One of the following cannot be taken as Intellectual property. Which one?
A. Copyrights B. Know-how
C. Discovery D. Patents

165. A triable offence committed by an adult is
A. Indicatable offence

B. Criminal offence
C. Indenture
D. Incriminatory

166. British citizens are protected from arbitrary arrest and imprisonment by the
A. Fundamental Rights
B. Bill of Rights
C. Lex Loci Act
D. Magna Carta

167. Jurisprudence is
A. Logic of law
B. Divine principles, followed by law
C. Philosophical aspects of law
D. Study of old judgements

168. Who said "Litigation is a game in which the Court is umpire"?
A. Austin B. Blackstone
C. Pollock D. Salmond

169. The Hague Conventions of 1899, 1904 & 1907 delineated
A. Rules of human rights
B. Rules for non use of chemical weapons
C. Rules of public international law
D. None of the above

170. Which type of statement is made by law?
(*i*) Murder is wrong, do not commit it
(*ii*) If murder committed *i.e.,* proved, the murderer will be punished with death or life imprisonment
A. Only (*ii*)
B. Only (*i*)
C. Neither (*i*) nor (*ii*)
D. Both (*i*) and (*ii*)

171. Under which Act, it was provided that women doing similar work to men, would qualify for equal pay
A. Workmen's Compensation Act, 1976
B. Protection of Women's Rights Act, 1980
C. Gender Equality Act, 1976
D. Equal Remuneration Act, 1976

172. Consider the following statements:
(*i*) Felonies are minor crimes
(*ii*) Felonies are major crimes
(*iii*) Misdemeanors are minor crimes
(*iv*) Misdemeanors are major crimes
A. (*ii*) & (*iii*) are correct
B. (*i*) & (*iv*) are correct
C. (*iii*) is correct
D. (*iv*) is correct

173. In 'Extradition treaty', Extradition means
A. Order of Indian Courts will apply to Indians living elsewhere
B. Two countries will deport criminals on reciprocal basis to each other
C. Exports without double taxation
D. None of the above

174. Goodwill is an asset of business. It can be
A. Lent B. Leased
C. Sold D. None of the above

175. You send your servant with a cycle to be delivered to your friend. The servant takes the cycle home and uses it over a period of time. You come to know after 10 days and report him for
A. Fraud B. Forgery
C. Embezzlement D. Cheating

176. "Incumbit probatio qui dict, non qui negat". What does it mean?
A. The burden of proof is on him who denies
B. Guilt must be proven beyond reasonable doubt
C. No man shall be punished unless guilty
D. No man is guilty without proof

177. An International Convention (1864, 1906) for the purpose of ameliorating the condition of sick and wounded soldiers in war is known as
A. Bretten Woods convention
B. London Convention
C. Paris Convention
D. Geneva Convention

178. The rule of evidence which forbids a person from denying the truth of some statement formerly made by him is
A. Estray B. Estoppel
C. Estreat D. Et seq

179. A doctor has a ______ relationship with his patient.
A. Impersonal B. Personal
C. Financial D. Fiduciary

180. For a valid contract, which of the following conditions must be satisfied.
(*i*) Intention to contract
(*ii*) Consensus ad idem
(*iii*) Legality of object
(*iv*) Must be set out in writing
A. (*iii*) and (*iv*)
B. (*i*), (*ii*) and (*iii*)
C. (*i*), (*ii*) and (*iv*)
D. All of the above

181. A person who makes an affidavit or deposition is called
A. Demesme B. Denizen
C. Deponent D. Deodand

182. 'Damages' are awarded except in one case
A. Libel suit B. Criminal conduct
C. Tort D. Breach of contract

183. We have a single integrated judiciary unlike
A. England B. U.S.A.
C. China D. Sri Lanka

184. Committee on Prevention of Corruption
A. Fazil Ali Committee
B. Sarkaria Committee
C. Venkatasamy Commission
D. Santhanam Committee

185. The age of retirement of High Court judges is
A. 65 years B. 62 years
C. 60 years D. No age limit

186. The concept of Judicial Review in India was taken from the Constitution of
A. France B. Ireland
C. Britain D. U.S.A.

187. The Supreme Court holds its meeting at New Delhi, but it can meet elsewhere if
A. Parliament so orders
B. President so orders
C. Majority of Judges so decide
D. None of the above

188. An appeal from the decision of Supreme Court can be made to
A. Privy Council B. ICJ
C. Both A and B D. Neither A nor B

189. Who was responsible for introduction of Public Interest Litigation in India?
A. Justice Fathima Beevi
B. Justice A.M. Ahmadi
C. Justice P.N. Bhagwati
D. Justice V.R. Krishna Iyer

190. Which of the undermentioned is not a qualification required for appointment as a Supreme Court Judge?
A. He must have had a diversified practice
B. Must be practising advocate for 10 years in High Court
C. Must be judge of High Court for 5 years
D. Must be citizen of India

191. A retired judge of Supreme Court cannot take up one of the following employment
A. Chairman of an Enquiry Commission
B. Practice before Supreme Court
C. Chairman of National Human Rights Commission
D. Chairman of Law Commission

192. Supreme Court's advisory jurisdiction is proved under Article ______ of the Constitution.
A. 143 B. 362
C. 23 D. 224

193. The first Attorney General of India was
A. Bal Thackaray
B. Nani A. Palkhiwala
C. M.C. Setalvad
D. Sahney

194. The judges of Supreme Court can serve till they attain the age of
A. 62 B. 65
C. 64 D. 63

195. The first Chief Justice of independent India was
A. S.M. Sikri B. S.R. Das
C. M.H. Beg D. H.J. Kania

196. What is the minimum number of judges of Supreme Court who must sit together to constitute a Constitution Bench?
A. 5 B. 4
C. 8 D. 12

197. The number of judges in the Supreme Court (Including the Chief Justice) is

A. 27 B. 31
C. 25 D. 26

198. Minimum number of Judges which can give an advisory opinion to President is

A. half of total strength of Supreme Court
B. 5
C. 8
D. one-third of total strength of Supreme Court

199. Supreme Court is a Court of Record. It means

A. All statements of Supreme Court are binding law
B. It has power to punish for its contempt
C. All decisions of Supreme Court are kept in records
D. Both A and B

200. A judge of Supreme Court can be removed by

A. President after inquiry by puisne Judges
B. The President
C. President after an address to each House of Parliament, passed with 2/3rd majority, presented in the same session
D. None of the above

201. A plans to murder B and carries out his plans with clockwork precision. Here

A. Mens rea is involved
B. Actus reus is involved
C. Neither acuts reus nor mens rea is involved
D. Both actus reus and mens rea is involved

202. In law, a man is presumed to be dead if he is not heard of as alive for

A. 10 years B. 5 years
C. 7 years D. 9 years

203. If a person goes away secretly, or evades the jurisdiction of the Court, he is

A. Abomining B. Absconding
C. Abrogating D. Absenting

204. Any child born before ______ of divorce is considered to be legitimate child of the former husband.

A. 284 days B. 100 days
C. 200 days D. 280 days

205. What does adjudication mean?

A. Arbitration
B. Meditation
C. Decision given by a court
D. A decision given by an umpire

206. ______ is defined as a security for repayment of a loan.

A. Lease
B. Pledge
C. Mortgage
D. None of the above

207. A written statement in the name of a person by whom it is voluntarily signed and sworn to is called

A. Affirmation B. Affray
C. Advowson D. Affidavit

208. The disobedience of any judgement, order, etc., of a court amounts to

A. Offence
B. Prejury
C. Contempt of Court
D. None of the above

209. A's house falls in an earthquake. He sues the contractor and claims damages. The contractor takes a well-known defence and says it was an

A. Act of grace
B. Act of exteriora
C. Act of God
D. Act of natural wrath

210. The Shah Bano case related to

A. Muslim wife's right to divorce
B. Muslim wife's right to maintenance after divorce
C. Muslim wife's right to husband's property
D. Muslim wife's right to separation

211. Match the following:

(*a*) Adulteration	(*i*) Adding of a substance to food which renders it dangerous to health
(*b*) Adultery	(*ii*) Sleeping with a married partner
(*c*) Alibi	(*iii*) A dispute
(*d*) Alteration	(*iv*) An excuse

Codes:

	(a)	(b)	(c)	(d)
A.	(iv)	(iii)	(ii)	(i)
B.	(iii)	(i)	(ii)	(iv)
C.	(ii)	(iii)	(iv)	(i)
D.	(i)	(ii)	(iv)	(iii)

212. Sexual intercourse with a girl under ______ is rape even if she had given her consent.

A. 18 years B. 17 years
C. 16 years D. 15 years

213. "Law and sense are not the same thing." This was said by

A. J.S. Mill
B. Justice M.N. Venkatachalliah
C. J.L. Nehru
D. M.K. Gandhi

214. Can a child under seven years of age be arrested?

A. Yes B. No
C. Circumstantial D. None of the above

215. The rights of Press are covered under which article of the Constitution (Implicitly)?

A. Article 22 B. Article 20
C. Article 19 D. Article 21

216. "Law is not an intellectual legerdemain to make black appear white and white appear black, but it is ceaseless endeavour to enthrone justice." Who said these words?

A. M.K. Gandhi
B. Jawaharlal Nehru
C. Lord Atkin
D. Justice Oliver Wendell Holmes

217. Under the Medical Termination of Pregnancy Act, 1971, abortion is

A. Illegal B. Legal
C. Circumstantial D. None of the above

218. What is the minimum age prescribed by law to drive at any public place?

A. 20 years
B. 30 years
C. 18 years
D. 16 years in case of motor cycle of under 50cc capacity and 18 years for any other vehicle

219. If a person innocently abducts a girl aged 16 in the belief that she was above 18, is he criminally liable?

A. Yes B. No
C. Circumstantial D. None of the above

220. According to Indian Majority Act, a major is a person who has attained the age of

A. 15 years B. 16 years
C. 18 years D. 21 years

221. ______ are words which appear innocent, but contain a latent meaning which is defamatory.

A. Innuendoes B. Libel
C. Slander D. Obiterdictum

222. Public holidays are declared under

A. Negotiable Instruments Act, 1881
B. Public Employees Act, 1967
C. Contract Act, 1872
D. Labour Laws

223. ______ of the Indian Constitution lays down that Union of India and the States are juristic persons and can sue and be sued.

A. Article 225 B. Article 285
C. Article 300 D. Article 348

224. The law relating to prisoners of war has been codified by

A. Vienna Conventions
B. New York Conventions
C. Hague Conventions
D. Geneva Conventions

225. In criminal law, intention is an essential constituent of offence. In law of Torts,

A. Intention is relevant only in some torts
B. Intention is relevant
C. Intention is irrelevant
D. None of the above

226. A person whose guardian has been appointed, attains the age of majority a little later, that is

A. 18 years B. 25 years
C. 30 years D. 21 years

227. Defamation Infringes a person's right to

A. Privilege B. Status
C. Pride D. Reputation

228. The law relating to hostilities has been codified by
A. Vienna Conventions
B. Almaty Conference
C. Hague Conventions
D. Geneva Conventions

229. When a person is prosecuted for committing a criminal offence, the burden of proof is on
A. Court B. Prosecution
C. Police D. Himself

230. Contract is said to be have three essentials. Which one among the following is not an essential in the formation of Contract?
A. Damages B. Consideration
C. Offer D. Acceptance

231. The Law of Torts has largely developed through
A. Legislations B. Customs
C. Judicial decisions D. None of the above

232. Fiduciary relationship means a relationship based on
A. Trust B. Contract
C. Law D. Money

233. Can a woman be charged with the offence of adultery?
A. Yes B. No
C. Circumstantial D. None of the above

234. According to law, the maximum number of people who can form a partnership firm is
A. any number B. 30
C. 20 D. 10

235. In Law of Torts, always unliquidated damages are awarded. The meaning of unliquidated is
A. Approximately arrived at
B. Not ascertainable
C. Penal and exemplary
D. Both A and B above

236. Indian Contract Act, Indian Penal Code etc. extend to
A. Whole of Indian except Pondicherry (Puducherry)
B. Whole of India except J & K and States of NEFA
C. Whole of India
D. Whole of India except J & K

237. If a constable has reasonable cause to suspect that a motorist is drunk, he
(*i*) Checks the motorist's breath with an Alcometer
(*ii*) Makes an arrest
(*iii*) Impounds the vehicle
(*iv*) Lets the person off with a bribe

Codes:
A. Invariably (*iv*)
B. Only (*iii*)
C. First (*i*) if it is affirmative, then (*ii*) and (*iii*), no legal authority to do (*iv*)
D. It is a constable's discretion to do any of the four

238. What is an alternative name for the private international law?
A. Civil law
B. Animus internationaile
C. Conge'd elire
D. Conflict of laws

239. A crime of unlawfully damaging or destroying property by fire is called
A. Arson B. Buggery
C. Affray D. Rioting

240. What is a 'cognizance'?
A. It means custody without warrant
B. It means custody with warrant
C. Arousing judical notice or knowledge
D. It is a crime

241. The Berne Convention, 1886 was about
A. Protection of copyright
B. Protection of human rights
C. Treatment of prisoners of war
D. Amicable distribution of colonies among European Nations

242. Where are juvenile delinquents sent to?
A. Protective custody
B. Reformation centre
C. Borstal Schools
D. Asylums

243. In civil action, the standard of proof is
A. On balance of probabilities

B. Logical and reasonable
C. Beyond reasonable doubt
D. Convincing to the judge

244. What is a caveat?
A. Writ B. Certiorari
C. A warning D. An injunction

245. To test the quality of an article, or the accuracy of weight and measures is called
A. Testing B. Audit
C. Affray D. Assay

246. Which of the following gives the buyer right to reject goods, repudiate the contract and claim damages?
A. Warranty B. Breach of promise
C. Breach of trust D. Guarantee

247. An insolvent person is
A. Bankrupt
B. Infirm
C. Not able to walk
D. Financially unsound

248. Capital offences result in
A. Imprisonment over 10 years
B. Amputation
C. Sentence of death
D. Sentence of life imprisonment

249. When a person speaks slanderously about God or Religion, it is called
A. Bingoism B. Bestiality
C. Buggery D. Blasphemy

250. Which is the best example of a ballot?
A. An opinion poll
B. A signature compaign
C. A nation-wide referendum
D. A show of hands in Parliament

251. A person commits bigamy if he
A. Has sexual intercourse with a woman, besides his wife
B. Marries again when his first wife is dead
C. Marries again when he already has a legal wife
D. Marries again when his first divorced wife is alive

252. Prosecution : Accused : : ? : Defendant
A. Plaintiff B. Suer
C. Prosecution D. Applicant

253. "Law is an ass" was said by
A. Charles Dickens B. Locke
C. Marx D. Abraham Lincoln

254. Under the Motor Vehicles Act, 1988, the minimum compensation to be awarded in case of death (vide 1994 Amendment) is
A. ₹ 40,000 B. ₹ 50,000
C. ₹ 25,000 D. ₹ 35,000

255. Law excuses acts done under influence of intoxication, the intoxication
A. Must be involuntary
B. Must be voluntary
C. Must be high
D. Both A and C

256. Who is regarded as 'Corporation Sole'?
A. Multinational Corporation
B. Prime Minister
C. Public Sector Unit
D. King of England

257. Distinction between law and morality is
A. Law is man-made, morality is made by God
B. Law is enforceable, morality is not
C. Both A and B
D. None of the above

258. Rights and duties are
A. Separated B. Co-related
C. Co-ordinated D. None of the above

259. ______ is the crime of arousing hatred or contempt against the Government of India.
A. Rumour B. Sedition
C. Treason D. Slander

260. Possession is said to be ______ ownership.
A. 9/10th B. 5/6th
C. 7/8th D. Synonymous

261. Sometimes a person himself does not commit an offence. He helps or aids another person. He is then guilty of ______.
A. Incitement B. Abetment
C. Conspiracy D. None of the above

262. ______ are those offences which are punishable with imprisonment for two years or less. These offences can be compromised between the parties.

A. Bailable offences
B. Non-cognizable offences
C. Compoundable offences
D. Non-compoundable offences

263. Sex determination tests have been banned by
A. Ultrasound Control Act
B. Pre-Natal Diagnostic Techniques (Regulation and Prevention of Misuse) Act
C. Miscarriage Child Act
D. SDT (Prohibition) Act

264. A Hindu wife can marry immediately after divorce. A Muslim wife
A. Has to wait for one year
B. Has to wait for five or six years
C. Can also marry immediately
D. Has to wait till the period of Iddat (seclusion) is over

265. Ownership and Possession are
A. Different B. Circumstantial
C. One and the same D. None of the above

266. According to Section 138 of ______ the dishonour of cheque results in awarding double amount and also criminal consequences.
A. Contracts Act
B. Specific Reliefs Act
C. Negotiable Instruments Act
D. Monetary Instruments Act

267. The right to private defence is a recognized defence in Law of Crimes. A person may even kill the assallant and escape criminal liability, if the assailant intends
A. To kidnap B. To kill
C. To commit rape D. All of the above

268. A husband is obliged to maintain his divorced wife
A. For 20 years
B. For ever
C. Till she gets remarried
D. Till the children grow up

269. A dacoity requires at least ______ or more persons.
A. Four B. Five
C. Two D. Three

270. Conspiracy needs, at least ______ persons.
A. Five B. Four
C. Three D. Two

271. Section ______ of the Indian Penal Code defines murder.
A. 302 B. 301
C. 300 D. 299

272. Homicide means
A. Causing death of a human being
B. Causing death of anyone
C. Causing death
D. Intentionally causing death

273. ______ is an act which is twisted, crooked, which is not straight and lawful.
A. Wrong B. Tort
C. Crime D. None of the above

274. The basic distinction between Civil and Criminal laws is
A. Criminal laws deal with wrongs which are harmful to society at large
B. Civil laws deal with matters of restoration of right
C. Criminal laws deal with punishment
D. Both A and B

275. Article 361 of the Constitution exempts the following from jurisdiction of the Penal Code
A. Prime Minister B. President
C. Governors D. Both B and C

276. What does COPRA stand for
A. Consumer (Protection of Rights) Act, 1990
B. Consumer Protection Act, 1985
C. Consumer Courts Act, 1985
D. None of the above

277. Muslim religious foundations are known as
A. Wakfs B. Quzat
C. Jihad D. Ulema

278. A minimum of ______ judges of Supreme Court hear a constitutional matter.
A. 7 B. 6
C. 5 D. 3

279. Tamil Nadu Reservation Act providing 69% reservation has been placed in the ______ Schedule of the Constitution.

A. Ninth B. Eighth
C. Seventh D. Sixth

280. Under whose Chairmanship, National Commission for review of working of Constitution was set up?
A. M.N. Venkatachallaiah
B. J.S. Verma
C. A.M. Ahmadi
D. Ranganath Mishra

281. The language of the Supreme Court is
A. Hindi only
B. English only
C. Any language in the Eighth Schedule of Constitution
D. Both A and B

282. Ancient treatise on law?
A. Epics B. Upanishads
C. Vedas D. Smritis

283. Supreme Court can grant 'special leave' to appeal against decisions of lower courts and tribunals by virtue of
A. Article 136 of the Constitution
B. Article 226 of the Constitution
C. Article 365 of the Constitution
D. Article 100 of the Constitution

284. The Indian Penal Code (IPC) was enacted in
A. 1860 B. 1890
C. 1975 D. 1861

285. The Advocates Act is suffixed by the year
A. 1961 B. 1906
C. 1891 D. 1861

286. In 1975, Emergency was imposed on grounds of ______, words which were later replaced by 'armed rebellion' by the 44th Amendment.
A. Law and order problems
B. External Aggression
C. Internal disturbance
D. None of the above

287. Which of the following books can be regarded as a legal code?
A. Indica B. Arthashastra
C. Mahabharatha D. Sakunthala

288. The Supreme Court held the view that the Parliament cannot amend or suspend Fundamental Rights in
A. Keshavanand Bharti's Case
B. Minerva Mills Case
C. Golak Nath's Case
D. Indira Sawhney's Case

289. A sentence of death by a lower court
A. Must be confirmed by the President
B. Must be confirmed by High Court
C. Must be confirmed by Supreme Court
D. Is operational if no appeal is made to higher courts

290. The 39th Amendment laid that election of any person to Lok Sabha holding the office of Prime Minister cannot be challenged before a Court of Law, but only before a authority established by Parliament. This was declared unconstitutional by the Supreme Court in
A. Indira Gandhi v. Raj Narain Case
B. Mandal Commission
C. Keshavanand Bharti Case
D. None of the above

291. Muslim marriage is a
A. Divine commandment
B. Sacrament
C. Civil Contract
D. None of the above

292. Examine the following statements:
(*i*) Liberty is absolute
(*ii*) Liberty is defined by a circumference of law
A. Only (*ii*) is true
B. Only (*i*) is true
C. Both (*i*) and (*ii*) are true
D. Both (*i*) and (*ii*) are false

293. Sometimes, an accused seeks pardon from the court and offers to give evidence against all others involved in a crime. He is called
A. Approver B. Witness
C. Clone D. Escapee

294. Lawyers are officers of the Court and are constituted into an independent profession under the
A. Indian Penal Code
B. Criminal Procedure Code
C. Advocates Act, 1961
D. Constitution of India

295. The minimum age for marriage is that the boy must be ______ and the girl ______.
A. 18 years, 18 years
B. 21 years, 21 years
C. 18 years, 21 years
D. 21 years, 18 years

296. "Ignorance of the law excuses no man, not that all men know the law, but because it is an excuse every man will plead." Who said these words?
A. B.H. Brewster B. John Selden
C. Rousseau D. John Wilson

297. Large majority of Indian Muslims are covered by ______ school of law.
A. Ithna B. Ashri
C. Hanafi D. Ismaili

298. Which of the following statements can be attributed to Montesquieu?
A. Man is born free, and everywhere he is in chains
B. Law is an ass
C. Liberty is the right to do whatever the laws permit
D. Public opinion is always in advance of law

299. For Hindus ______ is an offence, punishable with seven years imprisonment, even though a Muslim can have four wives.
A. Adultery B. Polyandry
C. Monogomy D. Polygamy

300. When a Muslim husband and wife mutually consent to a divorce, it is known as
A. Mubarak B. Talaq
C. Khula D. None of the above

301. There are two classes of advocates in India
A. Registrars and Clerks
B. Lawyers and Judges
C. Advocate and Senior Advocates
D. Barrister and Solicitors

302. The law relating to marriage, divorce and succession of various communities
A. is entirely uncodified
B. is codified in Common Civil Code
C. is contained in various personal laws codified and uncodified
D. None of the above

303. 'Hindu law applies to any person who is a Hindu, Jain, Buddhist or Sikh by Birth.' This statement is
A. Untrue
B. True
C. True only in Punjab
D. Circumstantial

304. Any two person, irrespective of religion, can solemnize a marriage, commonly known as civil marriage under
A. Special Marriage Act, 1954
B. Marriage (Removal of Disabilities) Act, 1955
C. Indian Marriage Act, 1957
D. None of the above

305. Section ______ of Indian Penal Code punishes murder.
A. 301 B. 302
C. 299 D. 300

306. Copyright subsists for
A. 70 years B. 80 years
C. 50 years D. 60 years

307. There are four stages in the commission of a crime : intention, preparation, attempt and commission. The attempt to commit a crime is
A. Not punishable
B. Punishable
C. Not ordinarily punishable
D. None of the above

308. ______ are those offences for which a police officer can arrest a person without a warrant.
A. Bailable offences
B. Non-bailable offences
C. Cognizable offences
D. Non-cognizable offences

309. Who is the source of legal authority of India?
A. Parliament of India
B. Indian Penal Code
C. Constitution of India
D. People of India

310. Which article deals with binding of judgements of Supreme Court on all Courts of India?
A. 138 B. 140
C. 141 D. 124

311. To betray a nation is an offence and punishable with death, that is
A. Treason B. Treachery
C. Anti-nationality D. Sedition

312. In which case, Supreme Court held that Parliament has no power to amend Fundamental Rights?
A. Shankri Prasad Case
B. Golaknath Case
C. Minerva Mills Case
D. None of the above

313. All plans, formulated by Planning Commission must be approved by
A. President
B. Parliament
C. Union Cabinet
D. National Development Council

314. Which one is not a qualification for appointment as a High Court Judge?
A. Practising Advocate for 10 years
B. Practising Advocate for 5 years
C. Citizen of India
D. Judicial officer of 10 years's standing

315. Commission which reorganized States on the linguistic basis was headed by
A. Dharam Vir B. J. Fazil Ali
C. Harnam Singh D. Swaran Singh

316. Which statement is correct?
A. Every Union Territory is clubbed with one of State High Courts
B. Two or more States or two or more Union Territories or two States and one or more Union Territories can have a common High Court
C. Every State has its own High Court
D. None of the above

317. The Preventive Detention Act has a restraining effect on
A. Right to freedom
B. Right of life
C. Right to property
D. Right against exploitation

318. Which statement(s) is/are true?
(*i*) Supreme Court superintends the High Courts
(*ii*) High Court superintends the Subordinate Courts

Codes:
A. Only (*ii*)
B. Only (*i*)
C. Neither (*i*) nor (*ii*)
D. Both (*i*) and (*ii*)

319. Which is the only Union Territory having a High Court of its own?
A. Pondicherry (Puducherry)
B. Delhi
C. Andaman & Nicobar Islands
D. Chandigarh

320. In ______ Supreme Court held that Judicial Review is a basic feature of Constitution and cannot be amended.
A. Minerva Mills Case
B. Keshvanand Bharti Case
C. Golaknath Case
D. None of the above

321. The symbol (v) in case names stands for
A. And B. For
C. Versus D. Both A and B

322. An appeal against the Order of Central Administrative Tribunal (dealing in Service matters) can be made to
A. Supreme Court
B. President
C. High Court
D. No provision of appeal

323. Commission on Police Reform was headed by
A. J. Fazil Ali
B. Swaran Singh
C. Dharam Vir
D. Venkatachallaiah Commission

324. Which of the following statements regarding High Courts is false?

A. Original jurisdiction
B. Writ jurisdiction
C. Appellate jurisdiction
D. None of the above

325. The first Law Officer of the country is
A. Chairman of Law Commission
B. Solicitor General
C. Chief Justice of India
D. Attorney General of India

Directions (Qs.Nos. 326 to 401): *Given below are Legal Principles followed by Factual Situation. Apply the principle to it and select the most appropriate answer for questions among the four choices given.*

326. Legal Principle: Whoever, intending to take dishonestly any movable property out of the possession of any person without that person's consent, moves that property in, is said to commit theft. Whoever commits theft, shall be punished with imprisonment which may extend to years or with fine or with both.

Factual Situation: Raju sees a cell phone belonging to Ram lying on the table in Ram's house. Raju hides the cell phone in Ram's house in such a place where Ram could not find it ever, due to the fear of immediate search and detection. Raju did this with the intention of taking away the cell phone from the hidden place when Ram forgets about and then sell it away.

Question: Is Raju guilty of theft?
A. Yes
B. No, because he merely played a prank with the friend.
C. Yes, because Raju did not inform Ram about the place where he had the cell phone.
D. Yes, because Raju intended to take the immovable property from Ram's possession and with this intention he moved the property.

327. Legal Principle: Nothing is an offence which is done in exercise of the right of private defence of body and property of his person or others.

Factual Situation: A was sleeping in his uncle's house during midnight B a theft for purpose of stealing entered to A's uncle's house. By the way the B, opened a folded knife and attacked daughter of A's uncle. All the member of uncle's house become afraid of theft's action. A while awakened saw to entire situation and tried to protest the act of B. But he became unable to resist B. By the time the point of knife was about to stab the neck of A and suddenly he in opposite way A redirected the Knife point to the neck of the thief and once the thief died.

Decision:
A. A is to be prosecuted as he killed the thief because no one should take the life of others.
B. A is not guilty of murder as there was no *mensrea* of A and it happened the incidentally while defending himself and family members of uncle.
C. A is guilty as he murder with the same knife.
D. A is guilty of murder of thief as he killed in his uncle's house and not in his own house.

328. Legal Principle: A person, who lawfully brings on his land something which though harmless, but will do mischief if it escape, must keep it at his peril, and if he does not, he is answerable for all the damage.

Factual Situation: 'A' was the owner of a mill. In order to supply it with water he constructed a reservoir upon nearby land by employing engineers and contractors. 'B' was the owner of coal mines, under lands, close to but not adjoining the premises on which the reservoir was constructed. The contractors, while exacvating for the bed of the reservoir, came upon abandoned shafts and filled them with soil not suspecting that that they were abandoned mine shafts. The reservoir was completed and partly filled. Within days the bed of the reservoir gave way and burst, leading to flow of water through the channels connected with B's mine. Is 'A' liable to pay damages for loss caused to 'B'?

Decision:

A. 'A' is not liable because there was no negligence on his part. He was not aware that the reservoir bed was connected to B's mines.

B. 'A' is not liable to pay damages to 'B' because he brought the water on his property which would have caused mischief if it escaped and it did escape.

C. 'A' is not liable because 'B' never informed him the existence of B's mines.

D. 'A' is liable because he hired the services of unqualified engineers.

329. Legal Principle: Every person has a right to defend his own person, property or possession against an immediate harm, and to that end, may use reasonable amount of force.

Factual Situation: Mr. Gemini was passing by Mrs. Vadhera's house. At that time, Mrs. Vadhera's dog ran out and bit Mr. Gemini's overcoat. Mr. Gemini turned around and shot at the dog however, the dog ran away. While the dog was far away from Mr. Gemini, Mr. Gemini shot the dog dead as he believed that the dog had bitten other persons in the locality. Mrs. Vadhera filed a suit for damges as her dog was of a rare breed and worth ₹ 5000.

Decision:

A. Mrs. Vadhera will succeed because Mr. Gemini killed the dog as his right of private defence has elapsed.

B. Mrs. Vadhera will not succeed because Mr. Gemini is justified in shooting the dog.

C. Mrs. Vadhera will not succeed because Mr. Gemini took the action to protect him as well as many other members of public in future.

D. Mrs. Vadhera will succeed because she lost her precious dog.

330. Legal Principle: For a breach of contract, compensation can be claimed for the personal inconvenience suffered by a party by reason of the breach, which naturally arose in the usual course of things from such breach, or which the parties knew, when they made the contract to be likely to result from the breach of the contract.

Factual Situation: Mr. Anil and Mrs. Seema Shah purchased bus tickets from a private bus company for a journey from Rainagar to Baruch via Amrell. The bus driver, by mistake, took them in a wrong direction and dropped them at a distance of 3 miles from Amrell on the State highway. Mr. and Mrs. Shah had to walk the distance of 3 miles as there was no mode of transport available and it was midnight.

Mr. and Mrs. Shah filed a suit against the bus company and claimed ₹ 2,500 as damages for inconvenience suffered for walking and ₹ 5000 in respect of Mrs. Seema Shah's catching cold during that night.

Decision:

A. The bus company is liable to pay both the amounts claimed because the loss was suffered by Mr. and Mrs. Shah for no fault of theirs.

B. The bus company is liable to pay ₹ 2,500 only.

C. The bus company is not liable to pay anything.

D. The bus company is not liable as there was no breach of contract.

331. Legal Principle: Nuisance means an unlawful interference with a person's use or enjoyment of land. It includes interference with comfort, health and safety of the other.

Factual Situation: A and B are neighbours in a residential locality of Delhi. They had cordial relations. A suddenly decided to run singing and dancing classes from his house. While running the classes, he also used loud music to good effect. B has two school going children who were studying seriously as their examinations were approaching. B pleaded with A to tone down the loudspeakers, but the latter refused. B went to the court pleading nuisance. Can he succeed?

Decision:

A. Yes, because the principle against nuisance demands that the noise level should be such as not to disturb the neighbourhood.

B. Yes, because to run business in a residential locality is illegal.

C. No, because one is entitled to do whatever one wants in one's house.

D. No, because under Article 19(1)(g) of the Constitution of India, every citizen has a right to freedom of trade or profession.

332. Legal Principle: A right of action cannot arise out of an illegal activity.

Factual Situation: A and B were thieves engaged in stealing cars and other vehicles. One day they stole a car and while driving through a city, they engaged a driver to drive them through the city, as they did not know the route inside the city. As the indicator lamp of the car was not working and the thieves were unaware of this, they had not told about it to the driver due to which another car belonging to X was damaged and his driver suffered injuries. X and his driver file a suit for damages against A and B.

Decision:

A. X and his driver would lose, because he was injured by a stolen car.

B. X and his driver would win, because they were not a party to the stealing.

C. X and his driver would win, because their car was illegally hit.

D. None of the above

333. Legal Principle: No person shall be deprived of his life or personal liberty except according to procedure established by law.

Factual Situation: A a resident of Noida summoned by the Delhi High Court as a witness against the Jessica Lal murder case. A denied to appear before the Court due to his office job. He was prosecuted by the court.

Question: Whether A is liable or not.

A. He is not liable because he has fundamental rights under Article 21 of personal liberty.

B. He is liable because he denied to appear before the Court.

C. He is not liable because he didn't see the murder of Jessica Lal.

D. He is not liable because he is not the resident of Delhi.

334. Legal Principle: Nothing is an offence which is done in the exercise of right of private defence.

Factual Situation: Naman and Nitin are studetns staying in a Boy's Hostel. Monika is a beautiful girl staying in a Girl's Hostel. Naman and Nitin both fall in love with Monika. They both quarrel and then they start fighting over Monika.

One day, Naman accompanied with some friends and armed with iron rods, reaches Nitin's room and abuses him. On seeing many boys in an offensive mood, Nitin throws boiling tea over Naman's face, due to which his skin is badly burnt.

Decision:

A. Nitin has committed an offence and can be punished.

B. Nitin has not committed any offence but has defended himself.

C. Both Nitin and Naman are guilty and can be punished.

D. Naman alone is guilty because he started the fight.

335. Legal Principle: Contract is an agreement freely entered into between the parties.

Factual Situation: Ramlal was dealer in cement. The Government of India, by an order issued under the Essential Commodities Act, fixed the price of cement, and also the quantity which a person can buy from the dealer. Ramlal carried on his business under this new order for sometime, but he refused to pay sales tax on his sale transactions on the ground that these were not the contracts freely entered into by him.

Decision:

A. Ramlal would succeed, because free consent between the parties was there despite the restriction on price and quantity.

B. Ramlal would not succeed, because free consent between the parties was there despite the restriction on price and quantity.

C. Ramlal would succeed, because the Government under the new order, forced him to enter into contracts.

D. None of the above

336. Legal Principle: Agreements, the meaning of which is not certain, or capable of being made certain, or illegal, are void.

Factual Situation: A. Rammappa, a businessman of Bengaluru based, agreed to sell M. Swaminathan, a white elephant for ₹ 1,00,000 (Lakhs). A. Rammappa knows it is illegal under Wild Life Protection Act.

Decision:

A. It is not void contract because two parties agreed to make contract so, it is valid.

B. It is void contract because it is illegal under Wild Life Protection Act.

C. It is not void because both the parties agreed to make contract even consideration money was also fixed.

D. It is void because white elephant is not found in Bengaluru forest.

337. Legal Principle: All citizens shall have the right to freedom of speech and expression.

Factual Situation: Balwnat Singh, a famous writer of a book, critisized a book published by Salman: "Salman's book is foolish, he is a weakman, his book is indecent, his mind is impure, he is not a good character, he should write decent and good book."

Question: Whether Balwant Singh can be liable or not?

A. He is not liable because he has just expressed his personal views.

B. He is liable for sue the case of defamation, if his statement was not true or said: in *mala fide* intention.

C. He can't be liable because he has fundamental rights to freedom of speech and expression.

D. He can't be see because both are writer and both can criticize each other.

338. Legal Principle: Hearsay evidence is no evidence.

Factual Situation: Ravi and Rahul share a room in a youth hostel. One day, Rahul leaves the room and sees that his three friends Kunal, Abhishek and Bunty are quarrelling outside the youth hostel. Suddenly, Kunal stabs Abhishek with a knife. Rahul is horrified and reforms to his room and tells about the incident to Ravi. After some time, the police reaches the hostel and asks questions from students. The police asks questions to Ravi also. Ravi tells the police that Kunal stabbed Abhishek.

Decision:

A. Ravi has told the truth to the police and Kunal can be punished.

B. Ravi's statement has no value in the eyes of law.

C. Ravi should have refused to tell anything to the police.

D. None of the above

339. Legal Principle: Any person who gives false information before police or court is punishable under Indian Penal Code as well as under Criminal Procedure Code.

Factual Situation: Magni Ram, a village watchman, knowing that considerable body of strangers has passed through his village in order to commit a dacoity in the house of Ram Jatan Singh, a wealthy landlord, residing in a neighbouring place. Magni Ram has personal enmity with Ram Jatan Singh, so he informed the Police Station next day morning that a body of suspicious characters passed through the village with a view to commit dacoity. After proper investigation it was found the Magni Ram gave false information to Police Officers.

Question: Whether Magni Ram commit any offence or not.

A. He did not commit any offence personally because he was not the accomplice of dacoits.

B. He cannot be compelled to be a party to the case to give statement regarding the case.

C. He is liable for committing an offence for furnishing false information.

D. He has fundamental rights to his personal liberty. So he is not liable.

340. Legal Principle: No one can pass a better title on goods than he himself has on that goods. An agent can do whatever the principal can do.

Factual Situation: Jewellery Shop and Company buys gold and gold ornaments and also sells gold and new ornaments. This company buys gold from X worth ₹ 1,00,000 in the form of ornaments. These ornaments were melted into gold bullion. This gold bullion was sold to Chanda and Company, another jeweller, who manufactured new ornaments from that gold and sold it to Mr. Agarwal.

Decision: Ms. Agarwal's title on the ornaments is better title.

A. Yes, because she has purchased the ornaments and has been the owner of it.

B. Yes, if at the time of question of better title the ornaments are possessed by Ms. Agarwal.

C. No, because she has not purchased directly from Jewellery Shop and Company.

D. No, because she has purchased after conversion.

341. Legal Principle: Where the death of a woman is caused by any burns or bodily injury or occurs otherwise than under normal circumstances within seven years of her marriage and it is shown that soon before her death she was subjected to cruelty or harassment by her husband or any relative of her husband for, or in connection with, any demand for dowry, such death shall be called "dowry death", and such husband or relative shall be deemed to have caused the death. Whoever, commits dowry death shall be punished with imprisonment for a term which shall not be less than seven years but which may extend to imprisonment for life.

Question: What are the conditions for punishment of offence of dowry death?

A. The woman died within 7 years of marriage.

B. Death must occur in not a normal condition (Suicide etc.)

C. There must be cruelty, on part of her, for persistent demand of dowry.

D. None of these

342. Legal Principle: If a person without any authority prevents a person to proceed to any direction and is kept confined, he commits an offence of criminal confinement.

Factual Situation: The Municipality allowed a special permit to hold a marriage party blocking a part of a public road. The marriage party blocked most of the roads and did not allow X, a passer-by, to cross the road. He brings a charge of criminal confinement against the head of the marriage party and other associates. Can X succeed.

Decision:

A. X cannot succeed because the head of marriage party has got previous authority from the Municipality and has blocked part of public road.

B. X can succeed because he has authority to walk on public road.

C. X cannot succeed because he must have to wait upto end of marriage party.

D. None of the above.

343. Legal Principle: An agreement to do act impossible in itself is void.

Factual Situation: A promises B to discover a treasure trove by magic. If B pays him ₹ 500. B being aware of the fact that A is a magician agrees to the same and pays him ₹ 500. But to B's dismay no treasure trove was discovered. B files a suit for breach of contract and to recover ₹ 500.

Decision:

A. B's suit will fail

B. B would recover ₹ 500

C. B would recover ₹ 500 only if he has suffered some loss

D. A shall be required to discover treasure trove by magic otherwise he would be liable for breach of contract.

344. Legal Principle: When due to natural disaster or war it becomes impossible to perform a contract, non-performance of such contract shall not make either of the parties liable for breach of contract but this does not include commercial impossibility.

Factual Situation: Rakesh is a merchant based in Kolkata deals in almonds, which he procures from Indian as well as foreign markets. Vimlesh enters into a contract with Rakesh for supply of 500 kilograms of almonds @ ₹ 400 per kilogram. The relations between India and Pakistan turned sour and both countries snapped business ties soon after Rakesh agreed to supply almonds to Vimlesh. Rakesh did not deliver almonds to Vimlesh because he mostly procurred almonds from Pakistan, which were comparatively cheaper. When asked by Vimlesh, Rakesh said that due to no trade and war like conditions between India and Pakistan he is not in a position to supply him almonds. Vimlesh files a suit for breach of contract.

Decision:

A. Vimlesh will succeed

B. Rakesh will succeed

C. None of them will succeed

D. Both of them will partially succeed.

345. Legal Principle: A wilful infringement of patent where the infringing acts were committed without concern for the rights of the patentee or without a good faith belief will result in treble damages to be paid by infringer to the patentee.

Factual Situation: GSK a pharmaceutical company has reasons to believe that an existing patent of Plizer company is erroneous thus it starts manufacturing the medicine on which the so-called erroneous patent of Plizer exists. Plizer filed a suit for slopping GSK from manufacturing the medicine and also for treble damages. The court finds the patent valid.

Decision:

A. GSK will have to pay treble damages only

B. GSK will have to pay ordinary damages

C. GSK will have to pay no damages but stop manufacturing the medicine

D. None of the above

346. Legal Principle: A man must not make such use of his property as unreasonably and unnecessarily to cause inconvenience to his neighbours.

Factual Situation: X is the owner of a plot measuring 50 feet by 80 feet. He constructed a small house at one corner and was using the rest of the land as a cow shed. He had 20 cows and is involved in selling the milk to the public. The cow dung and other wastes were openly stored in a small 10 feet by 8 feet tank. This constantly paved way for bad smell and breeding of mosquitoes. Y, his neighbour constantly complained to X but in vain.

Decision:

A. Y cannot take any other action against X.

B. X can do something to prevent the foul smell.

C. Y can complain to the police.

D. Y can sue X for damages based on the inconvenience caused by X.

347. Legal Principle: When a future event on which a contract is dependent is the way in which a person will act at an unspecified time, then the event shall be considered to become impossible when such person does anything which renders it impossible that he should so act within any definite time, or otherwise than under further contingencies. If the event becomes impossible, such agreements void.

Factual Situation: A agrees to pay B a sum of money if B marries C anytime during A's life. C muarries D and soon thereafter A dies.

Question: Whether agreement between A and B could be enforced, if D dies after one year of marriage and B marries C?

A. No, agreement has become void.
B. Yes, because B ultimately marries C.
C. Yes, because essence of this contract was marriage between B and C.
D. Both B and C.

348. Legal Principle: A contingent contract is a contract to do or not to do something, if some event, collateral to such contract, does or does not happen.

Factual Situation: A agrees to pay B a sum of ₹ One lakh if B marries C within a period of six months. B marries C during the seventh month as the marriage hall was available only during that months. B claims rupees one lakh from A.

Decision:

A. B can successfully claim ₹ 1 lakh from A.
B. B can claim ₹ 1 lakh as well as special damages from A for having married C.
C. B cannot claim ₹ 1 lakh from A as B married C after the duration set in the contract.
D. C can successfully claim ₹ 1 lakh from A for having married B.

349. Legal Principle: A contract entered into by a minor, who is less than 18 years of age, is a void contract and cannot be enforced against the minor in law except for the contract entered by the minors for his necessities.

Factual Situation: A, a minor entires into the contract with a book seller. The book seller supplied the school books and stationary as required by A. After receiving the books and stationary, A refuses to pay the book seller on the ground that he is a minor, and as such the contract with the book seller is not enforceable.

Decision:

A. Book seller cannot enforce the contract as 'A' is a minor.
B. Book seller can enforce the contract even against the minor as the contract was for his necessities.
C. Book seller can enforce the contract after A becomes major.
D. Even after 'A' becomes a major, this contract cannot be enforced by the book seller.

350. Legal Principle: Any person who has received any unjust benefit, he must return it to the rightful owner.

Factual Situation: A and B were staying in the same hostel room. B's father had sent a parcel to him on his birthday containing expensive gifts. This parcel was delivered to A as B had gone out for a movie.

Decision:

A. A can retain the parcel without informing B.
B. A can keep some gifts from the parcel and return the rest to B.
C. A can inform B about the parcel and need not return the parcel to B.
D. A has to return the entire contents of the parcel to B.

351. Legal Principle: An employer is liable to maintain in good and safe condition any way, works, machinery or plant connected with or used in his trade or business or by reason of any like emission on the part of any person in the service of the employer who has been entrusted by the employer with the duty of seeing that such way, works, machinery or plant are in good and safe condition, any failure in the same shall make company liable for any loss resulting from such failure.

Factual Situation: R is working as a lift operator in a company. One day he was injured while operating the elevator, which fell off the pulleys due to excess greasing by engineers of the company.

Question: Whether the company is liable for the injury sustained by R?

A. Yes, company is liable to R.

B. Yes, company is liable to engineers.

C. No, company is not liable to anyone.

D. None of the above.

352. **Legal Principle:** An act of God is an operation of natural forces so unexpected that no human foresight or skill could reasonably be expected to anticipate it.

Factual Situation: The New Friends Club was celebrating it's 25th Anniversary and arranged for a concert by a leading musical group. The event was to be organized in one of the best auditoriums and all the tickets were sold out. On the day of the event, an earthquake destroyed many building including the auditorium. People who had purchased the tickets asked for refund from the New Friends Club as the show could not take place.

Decision:

A. The New Friends Club must refund the cost of tickets.

B. The management of the Auditorium must refund the cost of the tickets.

C. The New Friends club or any one else need not refund the cost of tickets as it is an Act of God.

D. The ticket holders can demand the show to be organised at a later point of time.

353. **Legal Principle:** Agreement by way of wager is void and no suit lies for recovering anything won by such wager.

Factual Situation: 'X' and 'Y' enter into a contract with 'Z' who is an expert in betting on horse racing. Both pay a sum of ₹ 2000 to Z to bet on a particular horse. 'Z' followed the instructions and he won a sum of ₹ 20 lakhs.

Decision:

A. Z has to pay ₹ 20 lakhs to X and Y.

B. Z can divide ₹ 20 lakhs into three parts and share it equally with X and Y.

C. Z can keep ₹ 15 lakhs and give 5 lakhs to X and Y.

D. Z need not give anything to X and Y as this agreement is not enforceable.

354. **Legal Principle:** An agreement is void and unenforceable if considerations and objects are unlawful.

Factual Situation: A enters into an agreement with B for ten countrymade pistols and ten landmines. A promises to pay a sum of ₹ 25,000 to B. On completing the work and handing over the materials as required, A refuses to pay the remaining sum of ₹ 1,75,000 to B.

Decision:

A. B cannot move any court for enforcement of this contract.

B. B can move the civil court for enforcement of this contract.

C. B can move the High Court for enforcement of this contract.

D. B can move the Supreme Court directly as his fundamental and legal right is violated.

355. **Legal Principle:** A person is liable for all the injurious consequences of his careless act.

Factual Situation: Ramu, a snake charmer, was exhibiting his talents to a group of people. One of the snakes escaped and bit a child who had to be hospitalized for two days for treatment.

Decision:

A. Ramu is not in a position to compensate as be is poor.

B. Ramu is liable to compensate the child's family for his careless act.
C. Ramu is not liable to anything as such things keep happening.
D. The child should have taken adequate care for protecting herself from the snake bite.

356. Legal Principle: In any suit for damages, the workman shall not be deemed to have undertaken any risk attaching to the employment unless the employer proves that the risk was fully explained to and understood by the workman and that the workman voluntarily undertook the same.

Factual Situation: 'A' in search of job met a quarry owner and requested him to provide any job for the time being. The quarry owner allowed him to work as a labourer and to carry stone boulders from one place to another in the quarry. Unaware of working condition and environment 'A' tried to remove a huge stone having live dynamite inside, which blew up fracturing the leg of 'A'. 'A' filed suit against the quarry owner.

Question: Whether 'A' would succeed?
A. No, he undertook the risk of employment.
B. No, he was aware of the dangers involved in the job.
C. Yes, he was never explained the hazards of the given job.
D. None of the above.

357. Legal Principle: Consumer for any transaction has own choice for the better taste of goods and services.

Factual Situation: Rama Rao, a merchant from Bangaluru, was on a tour in Jaisalmer. He came across a shop, which was selling dry fruits. Rao saw some oats, which were good and decided to purchase the same. After returning to Bangaluru, he wrote a letter to the shop in Jaisalmer asking them to send one quintal of good oats. After about 15 days, he received one quaintal of oats, but he found them to be very old. He rejected the consignment and asked them for return of the money paid by him. They replied saying that oats would become good only when they were old. But he wanted new oats, which according to him were good.

Decision:
A. Rama Rao will succeed because it is the consumer's own choice to decide the good or badness of the goods.
B. Rama Rao will succeed because he has paid money.
C. Rama Rao will not succeed because the old oats are good.
D. Both A and B.

358. Legal Principle: Law of contract mandates that two or more people are free to create mutual rights and obligations provided such rights and obligations are not opposed to public policy.

Factual Situation: Ashish enters into an agreement with Rajesh under which Rajesh undertook to kill Ashish when he is asleep. For this act, Ashish deposited ₹ 5000 with a bank, which Rajesh could withdraw once he has performed the aforesaid task. Rajesh kills Ashish according to terms of agreement.

Decision:
A. Rajesh must get ₹ 5000 because he has performed his task.
B. Rajesh must be prosecuted because he has killed Ashish.
C. Rajesh must not be prosecuted because Ashish consented to be killed.
D. Rajesh must be prosecuted for killing Ashish but he should got ₹ 5000 as agreed by Ashish.

359. Legal Principle: A person is guilty of culpable homicide amounting to murder if the act by which the death is caused is done with the intention of causing death.

Factual Situation: "X" was holding behind a bush to catch some rabbits, "Y" also came to the same place for hunting with his gun. When "Y" noticed some movements behind the bush he thought it was an animal and fired a shot due to which "X" was killed.

Question: Can "Y" be prosecuted for murder?

A. "Y" would not be liable for murder because he did not have the intention to kill "X".

B. "Y" shall be liable for murder because he should have taken care to find out the target before shooting.

C. "Y" shall not be liable for murder because "Y" was not expected to identify the target before shooting.

D. "Y" shall be liable for murder because for whatever reason "X" was killed.

360. Legal Principle: When at the desire of the promisor, the promise or any other person, promises to do something, then such promise is called a consideration for the said promise.

Factual Situation: A arranged a friendly party at his home for his closed friends and one of his friends B promised to prepare a special dish for other friends. But on the occasion of party B did not come. There became a major quarrel between A between B and his other friends.

Question: Will A succeed if A sues for such breach of contract against B?

A. A will not succeed because there is no consideration in the contract of preparing special dish.

B. A will not succeed because the contract between A and B is a social contract which is unenforceable at law.

C. A will succeed because B is responsible for quarrel of A with other friends.

D. Both A and B.

361. Legal Principle: When a person unlawfully intervenes in the chattel of another person by which the latter is deprived of its use, the former commits the tort of conversion. And nobody shall enrich himself at other's cost.

Factual Situation: Z, a patient suffering from a disease in his bile system approach ABC medical college. Z was diagnosed as suffering from appendicitis and hence his appendix was removed from his body by ABC medical college. The ABC hospital thereby found and unique cell in Z's appendix and using such cell it developed drugs of enormous medical value of rupees five crore from Cipla Industries Limited when Z knew it, he charged rupees four crore.

Analogical Decision:

(*a*) The ABC medical college need not share its income with the patient Z.

(*b*) The ABC medical college may share its income on moral point of course.

(*c*) The ABC medical college must have share its income with Z.

Analogical Reason:

(1) Z, for from being deprived of use of his appendix, actual benefited by its removal.

(2) The ABC medical college instead of waste appendix of Z conducted research on its own and the invention of new drug was its effect and result.

(3) The ABC medical college could not have achieved its success without that the appendix belonging to Z.

(4) Everybody must care for and share with others.

Your Decision with Reasons

A. (*a*) (1) B. (*a*) (2)

C. (*c*) (3) D. (*c*) (4)

362. Legal Principle: A master shall be liable for the fraudulent acts of his servant committed in the course of employment. Whether and act is candidate. Y runs another coaching centre and charges ₹ 1300 per month as fees per candidate for competing with X. This act of Y compelled X to reduce his charge to such ₹ 1300.

Question: Can X claim for damages from Y?

A. Yes, he can as Y violated his legal right

B. No, X has reduced the fees on his own

C. Yes because as there was damages there was legal injury

D. No because though there was damage there was no legal injury.

363. Legal Principle: Every person is entitled to freedom of conscience and to profess, practice and propagate his religion subject to public order, morality and health.

Factual Situation: X a Muslim sacrifices a cow on Bakra-Id believing it to be a part of his religious rites. However, there was a law of general prohibition on slaughter of cows. Whether X is to prosecuted for slaughtering cow.

Decision:

A. X cannot be prosecuted as killing of cow on Bakra-Id has the Muslim religious sanction.

B. X can be prosecuted as the state has a right to regulate the freedom of the religion in the interests of the public order.

C. X, can be prosecuted as the slaughtering of cow hurts other community's religious sentiments.

D. X, can be prosecuted as the slaughtering of cow is cruelty to animals.

364. Legal Principle: Everybody is under a legal obligation to take reasonable care in order not to injure by an act or omission his neighbour, which he may foresee. The neighbour for this purpose is a person who is likely to be affected by the act or the omission.

Factual Situation: Amit, while rushing to board a moving train at a station pushed Anil who was walking along with a heavy load, containing fire crackers, the push resulted in slipping of the load from Anil's hand. The crackers exploded injuring a boy, Sumit standing nearby. Sumit filed a suit against Amit claiming damages.

Decision:

A. Amit is not liable, because Sumit is not his neighbour.

B. Amit is not liable, because Anil should not be carrying load of crackers on a railway station.

C. Amit is liable, because he pushed Anil.

D. Amit is liable, because he was running.

365. Legal Principle: Contractual liability is completely irrelevant to the existence of liability in tort.

Factual Situation: A purchased a bottle of ginger-beer from a retailer. As she consumed more than such of the contents of the bottle, she found a decomposed remains of a snail, she fell sick on the thought of what she consumed. She sued the manufacturer of the beer for negligence, thought there is no contractual duty on the part of the manufaoturer.

Decision:

A. 'A' cannot sue the retailer.

B. 'A' cannot sue the manufacturer for negligence in the absence of a contract.

C. 'A' can sue the retailer from whom she purchased the beer.

D. 'A' can sue the manufacturer as he had a duty to take care to see that bottles did not contain any other substance than been and hence liable to have broken that duty.

366. Legal Principle: Any act done in exercise of right of private defence shall not be an offence. The Right to private defence in no case extends to the inflicting of more harm than it is necessary to inflict for the purpose of defence.

Factual Situation: 'X' saw an unknown man jumping the boundary wall and entering his house in the night. He bid himself in a corner carrying a sword and waiting for the person. The moment the person entered the house, he hit the person and cut his head. Whether 'X' committed offence of killing a man?

Decision:

A. yes, because he exceeded right of private defence.

B. yes, because he should allow any person entering his house.

C. no, he has not committed any offence because he exercised right of private defence.

D. no, he has not committed any offence.

367. Legal Principle: Every agreement in restraint of the marriage of any person, other than a minor, is void.

Factual Situation: Rohan entered into an agreement with a banker and deposited ₹ five lakhs with the banker. The terms of the contract provided that Rohan's son Mohan shall be the beneficiary of the deposited amount only if he marries after he attains legally marriageable age.

Question: Is agreement between Rohan and Banker void?

A. Yes, since the agreement is restraining the marriage of Mohan.
B. Yes, because Mohan has right to marry only when he is eligible to cast his vote.
C. No, agreement is valid and enforceable.
D. None of the above.

368. Legal Principle: Where a person commits any offence against another person, then the person against whom the offence is committed lodges F.I.R. against that person in nearest police station and the case is sent to local court for trial and prosecution.

Factual Situation: X, Y and Z collectively attached upon A and B on some land dispute and A and B became severely injured and grievously hurt. They lodged F.I.R. against all X, Y and Z. After investigation and medical Report of injury, the police prepared and sent a charge-sheet to such local court against X and Z only and removed the name of Y due to political pressure. Being aggrieved by such action of police A and B filed a complaint case against X, Y and Z directly in the said court. The case was tried and after recording evidence the court found all X, Y and Z guilty in open court. Y, had engaged a Separate lawyer for his defence and such lawyer defended Y in the Court that Y is not an accused in such instant case as his name was not charge-sheet filed by police.

Decision:

A. Lawyer of Y shall succeed as charge-sheet is main document in a case, before court and Y's name is not in such charge-sheet.
B. Lawyer of Y shall not succeed because according to Criminal Procedure Code, the court has been empowered to receive a complain case and try to all accused persons named in such complain case.
C. Lawyer of Y shall succeed as it is constitutional equity of any person that court cannot deprive him at its own discretion and law as Y's name has not been mentioned in charge-sheet filed by police in such case.
D. None of the above.

369. Legal Principle: *Mens rea* must be present in any offence otherwise the accused is not convicted by any court of law.

Factual Situation: Mr. Ashutosh is the neighbour of Mr. Arvindo and his family in a specific lofality. Mr. Akash is the yelder son of Mr. Arvindo is a drunkered and is of bad character. One night in December 2010 Mr. Akash after drinking heavily quarreled with his father and mother and other family members inside their house. Mr. Ashutosh after hearing such quarrel in midnight locked their door from front side so that other neighbour and he himself would not be disturbed and slept in his own house. But the said quarrel was turned to death of Mr. Arvindo and his wife. During their quarrel other neighbours awakened and saw the door locked outside and they thought the sound was of Television and did nothing as the sound after sometime was stopped. Next day Mr. Ashutosh opened the door and saw. Mr. Arvindo and his wife were dead and Mr. Akash was in drunkenness and other family member were laid without sense. Mr. Ashutosh called police on 100 number and police alongwith other actions arrested Mr. Ashutosh and a case of murder was registered in his name and trial was begun.

Decision:

A. Mr. Ashutosh cannot be convicted as in such case *mens rea* is not present.

B. Mr. Ashutosh cannot be not convicted as he was not present during murder and did nothing in their death.

C. Mr. Ashutosh shall be convicted because as pre Indian Penal Code a person becomes guilty of offence if he causes it though directly not involved in case.

D. None of these

370. Legal Principle: Preparation to commit an offence is not an offence. After making the preparation any act done towards committing the offence with intention to commit it, is an attempt to commit the offence, which is by itself an offence.

Factual Situation: Jai wants to kill Veeru. He buys a gun and cartridges for committing the murder. He then sets out searching for Veeru and when he sees Veeru, he loads his gun and takes aim at him and pulls the trigger. The gun did not fire.

Decision:

A. Jai is guilty of attempt to murder Veeru from the time he sets out in search of the latter.

B. Jai is guilty of attempt to murder from the time he loads the gun.

C. Jai is guilty of attempt to murder from the moment he takes aim at Veeru.

D. Jai is not guilty.

371. Legal Principle: Whoever by words, signs or otherwise brings into hatred or contempt or incites disaffection towards the Government established by law in India shall be punished with imprisonment for life.

Factual Situation: In a public meeting, Yashpal Reddy, the leader of an opposition party thunders, "This is a government of scoundrels, bootleggers and scamsters. They deserve to be unseated. Teach them a lesson in the coming elections by voting them out of power". The Government is contemplating to prosecute Yashpal Reddy.

Decision:

A. Yashpal Reddy is guilty of sedition for having made irresponsible and inflammatory statements against the Government.

B. Yashpal Reddy is not guilty of sedition as he is only exercising his freedom of speech in public.

C. Yashpal Reddy is guilty of sedition, as his statement would incite people to violence leading to breakdown of law and order.

D. None of these

372. Legal Principle: Whoever dishonestly misappropriates or converts to his own use any movable property shall be punishable.

Factual Situation: A and B are Joint Owners of a Maruti Car. One day A took the car from B's garage to have a morning tour without knowledge of B. On the road A's friend C met him and took the car to drop his son in Delhi Public School and on the way to School he met with an accident with the DPS bus and the car was damaged. B being disgusted on the fact of A's taking out car without his consent, blamed A of theft and lodged an F.I.R. in Local Police Station, Decide.

Decision:

A. A has committed the offence of theft because he has not taken the consent of B.

B. A is guilty of theft because he has taken and driven the car and taking away of movable property is the essential element in offence of theft.

C. A is not guilty of theft because he is also one of the owners of the car and his taking away does not amount to his intention to theft and as he is also the owner the consent of B is not merely required.

D. A is not guilty of theft rather his friend C is liable for theft.

373. Legal Principle: Contract is an agreement freely entered into between the parties.

Factual Situation: Tapan was a dealer in mustard oil. The Government of India by an order issued under the Essential Commodities Act, fixed the Price of mustard oil, and also the quantity which a person can buy from the dealer. Tapan carried on his business under this order for a while, but he refused to pay sales tax on his sale transactions on the ground that these were not the contracts freely entered into by him.

Decision:

A. Tapan would succeed because the price and quantity were not negotiated by him

B. Tapan would not succeed because free consent between the parties was there despite the restriction on price and quantity

C. He would succeed because the Government under the new order forced him to enter into contracts

D. Both A & C

374. Legal Principle: Nothing is an offence done by a person who, at the time of doing it, by reason of unsoundness of mind, is incapable of knowing the nature of the act or what he is doing is wrong or contrary to law.

Factual Situation: A takes his son B who is three years old, for a bath to the well. He throws his son inside the well so that the could have a good bath. After 10 minutes, he also jumped in the well to take a good bath and took his son out of the well. He was rescued by villagers. His son was found dead. He is charged for murder. Medical Report declares him to be of unsound mind suffering from serious mental disorder. Decide.

Decision:

A. As A kills his son B by throwing him in the well, he commits murder and be punished therefore.

B. A can plead unsoundness of mind as a defence and he should not be charged for murder.

C. A's family should be responsible for murder to let him take child to the well.

D. None of these

375. Legal Principle: Whoever attempts to commit an offence punishable by the Indian Penal Code with imprisonment for life or imprisonment, or to cause such an offence to be committed and in such attempt does any act towards the commission of the offence, shall be punished.

Factual Situation: X stays in South Extension, New Delhi. One evening he thought to steal all the gold jewellery from Mehra & Sons Company at South Extension branch. He called his two friends to help him in such of his drive towards being rich overnight. Then the trio made the underground hole towards the Mehra & Sons from north side during midnight. During such process one of his friend died when collided with the concrete of the groundfloor of Mehra & Sons. X and his another friend also received injuries and became unsuccessful to enter into the Mehra & Sons. On the information from the night watchman the police arrived at the spot and arrested X and his surviving friend and sent their dead friend to the AIMS for postmortem after necessary legal formalities. X and his surviving friend told the police that since they were not successful in theft, not even entering into the jewellery shop and also since one of their friends had died, they were not responsible to either law or Mehra & Sons, Jewellers.

Decision:

A. X and his friend not liable because his friend died. He along with his friend were injured.

B. X and his friend not liable because they have not touched any jewel.

C. X and his friend can be responsible because their act attracts the other thieves that Mehra & Sons has more Jewellery and in future it is a problem with such a big Jewellery Shop.

D. X and his friend can be responsible because they attempted to commit an offence under the Indian Penal Code and in their attempt did an act towards the commission of offence.

376. Legal Principle: No remedy for the injury caused by an act, to which one has voluntarily consented.

Factual Situation: In an exhibition cricket match, Sachin hit a full toss delivery of Shane Bond over the fence for a six. The ball fell on the head of Egghead, a spectator, and severely injured him. Egghead had purchased a ticket costing ₹ 1000 to watch the match. Egghead and the organizers of the match are sworn enemies.

Decision:

A. Egghead can recover the costs of his medical expenses from Sachin.

B. Egghead can recover the cost of his medical expenses from Shane Bond.

C. Egghead can recover the cost of his medical expenses from the Organizers.

D. Nobody would be liable to pay anything to Egghead.

377. Legal Principle: Law does not take notice of trifles.

Factual Situation: A proposes to his neighbour B that they both should go together for a morning walk. B agrees to the proposal and it is decided that both of them would meet at a particular point at 6 a.m. from where they would set off for the morning walk. Inspite of the agreement B does not turn up. A waits for him at 6 a.m. every day for a continuous period of seven days. Thereafter he files a suit against B claiming damages for the agony and mental torture suffered by him.

Decision:

A. B is guilty of breach of contract and is liable to pay damages.

B. There is no intention to enter into legal relations.

C. The matter is too small and the Court will refuse to go into it.

D. None of these

378. Legal Principle: Whoever, intending to the dishonestly any movable property out of the possession of any person without that person's consent, moves that property in order to such taking, is said to commit theft. Whoever commits theft, shall be punished with imprisonment which may extend to three years or with fine or with both.

Factual Situation: Viru sees a ring belonging to Surya lying on a table in Surya's house. Not venturing to misappropriate the ring immediately for fear of search and detection, Viru hides the ring under the sofa cover, where it is highly improbable that Viru has the intention of taking the ring from the hiding place and selling it when the loss is forgotten.

Decision: Is Viru guilty of theft?

A. Yes

B. No

C. Yes, because Viru had the intention of removing the ring from Surya's possession.

D. Yes, because Viru had the intention of taking movable property from Surya's possession, and with this intention he moved the property.

379. Legal Principle: Cheating is defined as deceiving any person to deliver any property and it includes the dishonest concealment of facts. Cheating by personation means a person cheating another by pretending to be some other person, or by knowingly substituting or person for another, or representing that he or any other person is a person other than he or such other person really is.

Factual Situation: 'A', while leaving a restaurant mistakingly picked up the umbrella of 'B'. Instead of his own. The next day he decided to return to the restaurant with the umbrella, hoping to find the real owner. 'C', who had never seen 'B' in person and had only communicated with 'B' through letters was on his way to the restaurant to meet 'B'. Since 'B' and 'C' had never met, it was agreed between them to identify each other at the pre-appointed spot, the restaurant door, by the clothing of 'C' and umbrella of

'B' which they had described to each other in detail. 'C' saw 'A' at the door of the restaurant and identified the umbrella. Thinking 'A' to be 'B', 'C' delivered a parcel labelled Mr. B to 'A'. 'A' received the same without protest and promptly returned home without looking for 'B'. Is 'A' guilty of cheating by personation?

Decision:

A. 'A' is not guilty because he was going to return the umbrella to the real owner and handing over 'B's packet to 'A' was 'Cs' mistake.

B. 'A' is not guilty because he was overcome by a sudden temptation.

C. 'A' is guilty because he was aware of the mistaken identity and that the parcel was not meant for him but for 'B'.

D. 'A' is guilty because the parcel might have been valuable to 'B'.

380. Legal Principle: An occupier is not normally liable to a trespasser except in respect of wilful act intended to cause him harm or done with reckless disregard.

Factual Situation: Tony, a richman, had kept a ferocious dog to guard his house. He strictly instructed all his servants not to go near the dog. Further a special attender was hired to take care of the dog. Visitors were warned by a prominent warning sign board about this dog.

One day, a 13 year old boy playing in the neighbourhood, running after his ball got into the house. The dog attacked him and killed him. Tony was sued for damages.

Decision:

A. Tony was not liable because the boy was a trespasser

B. Tony is not liable because a 13 year old boy ought to have known about the presence of the ferocious dog

C. Tony is liable of the negligence of his servant to keep watch on such a ferocious dog during the day time

D. Both A and B

381. Legal Principle: Whoever with the intent to cause, or knows that he is likely to cause, wrongful loss or damage to the public or to any person, causes the destruction of any property, or any such change in any property or in the situation thereof or destroys or diminishes its value or utility, or affects it injuriously, commits "mischief".

Factual Situation: Q, knowing that his assets are about to be taken in execution in order to satisfy a debt due from him to Z, destroys those assets, with the intention of thereby preventing Z from obtaining satisfaction of the debt and it caused damages to Z. Decide whether Q has committed any mischief.

Decision:

A. Q commits mischief, because he knowingly caused the damages to Z.

B. Q does not commit mischief because his act cannot be proved on the ground of law and evidence in its support.

C. Q cannot be punished because his assets are not sufficient to obtain satisfaction of debt.

D. Q can be prosecuted only if debt is good debt.

382. Legal Principle: A clear offer and acceptance lead to a contractual relationship.

Factual Situation: A fax message from X to a Real Estate Agency read: "Will you sell a 60 feet × 40 feet plot of land at Nagarbhavi to me? Quote the lowest price". The Real Estate Agency replied: "The lowest price for a site measuring 60' × 40' dimensions at Nagarbhavi is ₹ 15,00,000". The following fax from X to the Estate Agency read: "I agree to buy the site for ₹ 15,00,000 quoted by you. Please send me all the legal documents of the site". Which of the following inferences is correct?

Decision:

A. The Real Estate Agency becomes bound to sell the site to X, after quoting the price for it.

B. Mere quotation of price will not bind the Real Estate Agency to sell the land to X.

C. The Real Estate Agency may decline to sell the site but must compensate X for all the expenses incurred by him in making the enquiry.

D. The Real Estate Agency may argue that it did not desire to sell the site to X, but X can prevent the Real Estate Agency from selling the same to anybody else.

383. Legal Principle: A person is guilty of cheating, when he fraudulently induces another person to deliver the latter's property to him.

Factual Situation: A falsely represented to B, a shop-owner that he was an officer from the Commercial Taxes Department. While examining the accounts of the shop, A showed interest in buying a microwave oven on instalment basis. B readily agreed with the hope that he would get a favourable assessment from A regards his tax liability. A paid the first instalment, took the Microwave oven and disappeared from the scene. The police, however, managed to catch hold of A and prosecute him for cheating.

Decision:

A. A committed cheating, because he induced B to part with the Microwave oven, posing as though he was from the Commercial Taxes Department.

B. A committed cheating, because he did not pay the subsequent instalment.

C. A did not commit cheating, because B handed over the article in order to get a favourable assessment from A.

D. None of these

384. Legal Principle: The occupier of a premises owes a duty of care to all his invitees and visitors.

Factual Situation: Laloo was running a dairy from his house. People used a part of his farm as a short cut to get to a nearby railway station. Laloo who did not approve of this, put up a notice that "Trespassers will be prosecuted" However, since a number of these people were also his customers he tolerated them. One day, a person who was using this short cut was attacked by a bull belonging to the farm. The injured person filed a suit against him.

Decision:

A. Laloo is liable for having kept a bull on his farm.

B. Laloo is not liable in view of the clear notice against trespassers.

C. Laloo is liable because in fact he allowed the people to use his premises.

D. Laloo is not liable to the people other than his customers.

385. Legal Principle: A master shall be responsible for the wrongful acts of his servants in the course of his employment.

Factual Situation: 'The Syndicate Bank' was running a small savings scheme under which its authorised agents would go round and collect small savings from several people on daily basis. These agents would get commission on the deposits so collected. Ananth was one such agent, collecting deposits from factory workers engaged on daily wages. Though he regularly carried on his business for sometime, slowly he started appropriating deposits for his personal use and one day he just disappeared. One Fatima, who had been handing over her savings to him found that nearly for a month before his disappearance, he was not depositing her savings at all. The Bank, when approached, took the stand that Ananth was not its regular and paid employee, and therefore, it was not responsible for his misconduct. She files a suit against the Bank.

Decision:

A. The Bank is not liable, since Ananth was not its salaried employee.

B. The Bank is liable, since Ananth was projected as its employee.

C. The Bank is not liable, since it did not know about misappropriation by Ananth.

D. None of these

386. Legal Principle: The occupier of a premises owes a duty of care to all his invitees and visitors.

Factual Situation: Devi who was the owner of a big home with a compound wall, constructed an underground tank to store water. This was covered by jute bags since the work was incomplete. The postman who came inside to deliver a registered letter, fell into this tank and hurt himself. There was also a box on the outside of the compound wall, where all the mail could be deposited. The injured man field a suit against Devi claiming compensation.

Decision:

A. Devi is not liable, because she did not invite the postman to her house

B. Devi is not liable, because the postman could have delivered the letter in the box on the outside of the compound wall

C. Devi is not liable because the postman was required to take care of himself

D. Devi is liable because the postman came into the premises in the course of his duty

387. Legal Principle: Whoever, intending to insult the modesty of any woman, utters any word, makes any sound or gesture, or exhibits any object, intending that such word or sound shall be heard, and that such gesture or object shall be seen, by such woman, or intrudes upon the privacy of such woman, shall be punished.

Factual Situation: Ms. Praveen works in an Export House in Greater Nöida. There are more than 150 employees alongwith workers in such company. One of the employees Ritesh wanted to have some talks with Ms. Parveen. But she scolded him in front of some 50 workers in employee's canteen. Taking this grudge, Ritesh every day during entry at morning patted Ms. Praveen's hand and shaked her right hand for few minutes against her will. One day she made up her mind and informed to her Boss. But the Boss due to the work efficiency of Ritesh did not take any action. She alternatively informed the Police. Police arrested Ritesh. Ritesh told the police to defend himself that he used to shake her hand as it is a manner of wishing a colleague and that his Boss is enough to take action because it is the work place and his Boss is competent to decide matter himself.

Decision:

A. Ritesh shall be punished because shaking hand with a girl against her will amounts to the sexual harassment at work place and such an act is subject to be prosecuted.

B. Ritesh can be punished only by his Boss not by Court of Law and if his Boss forgives then no law is there in India to punish him.

C. Ritesh shall not be punished because shaking hand is no offence in India.

D. Ritesh shall not be punished because he acts in such manner only during office hours and before many employees not in an abandoned area.

388. Legal Principle: Under the Constitution, nobody can be convicted twice for the same offence.

Factual Situation: The students of a college went on strike against the reservation by the college. A student Ravi in the ensuing confusion assaulted a staff member and injured him grievously. For this offence, he was rusticated from the college. Subsequently, the police arrested him and charge-sheeted him for causing grievous hurt. Ravi pleads that he is being convicted for the same offence twice.

Decision:

A. Ravi should not be punished twice for same offence. This is unconstitutional.

B. Ravi has not committed an intentional crime. He should be acquitted as rustication is itself enough punishment.

C. Ravi cannot plead double conviction as the two authorities are different.

D. Ravi is not yet convicted as only a court can convict and rustication from college does not amount to conviction.

389. Legal Principle: When the parties to an agreement agree on the same thing in the same sense, there arises a legally binding obligation between them.

Factual Situation: Ganesh Gallery was a well known antique shop in the city. Shakuntala who had a penchant for collecting articles of rare beauty, was taken up by an intricately designed flower vase in the shop. The shop-keeper explained to her the vase belonged to the Vijayanagar Empire period and although it appeared very delicate, it was quite strong and not easily breakable. Shakuntala said that she was attracted to it only for the aesthetic pleasure it gave her and its other characteristics were immaterial to her and bought the piece. She later discovered that it was not a period piece and noticed it developing cracks as well. She proceeded against the proprietor of Ganesh Gallery for monetary relief.

Decision:

A. Ganesh Gallery must compensate Shakuntala, since both the characteristics attributed to the article were proved wrong.

B. Ganesh Gallery need not compensate, since Shakuntala was unconcerned about what was attributed to the article.

C. The proprietor must compensate her for irresponsible statements made by him.

D. None of these

390. Legal Principle: A master is liable for the acts committed by his servant in the course of employment.

Factual Situation: Mahesh was a driver working in a company Lipton and Co. One day, the Manager asked him to drop a customer at the airport and get back at the earliest. On his way back from the airport, he happened to see his finance Roopa waiting for a bus to go home. He offered to drop her at home which happened to be close to his office. She got into the car and soon thereafter, the car somersaulted due to the negligence of Mahesh. Roopa was thrown out of the car and suffered multiple injuries. She seeks compensation from Lipton and Co.

Decision:

A. Lipton & Co., shall be liable, because Mahesh was in the course of their employment at the time of accident.

B. Lipton & Co., shall not be liable. Mahesh was not in the course of employment when he took Roopa inside the car.

C. Roopa got into the car at her own risk, and therefore, she cannot sue anybody.

D. None of these

391. Legal Principle: A master will be liable for the wrongful acts of his servants in the course of employment.

Factual Situation: Maria was an old widow who opened an account with the Indian Overseas Bank, whereby she would deposit ₹ 5 everyday in the bank. Stephen was neighbour who used to collect the amount and deposit them in the bank. Stephen would get a small commission from the bank for the money deposited. One day it was discovered that Stephen who had not deposited the money for more than three months, had vanished with the amount. Maria filed a suit against the Bank.

Decision:

A. Bank would not be liable because Stephen was not an employee of the bank.

B. Bank would not be liable for the failure of Maria to check the balance in her account.

C. Bank would be liable because Stephen was paid commission by the bank for doing its work.

D. None of the above.

392. Legal Principle: Damages cannot be claimed against a risk to which consent has been given. The principle does not apply to rescue cases.

Factual Situation: X and Y bought tickets to have a ringside view of a football match. During the course of the game a hard kick from one of the players caused the ball to hit X on his nose, causing bleeding and nausea. After half time the organizers allowed entry of more spectators than the seating capacity of the stadium. In the resulting stampede R and S who were watching the match since the beginning got injured.

Five minutes before close of play, a part of the stadium roof broke loose. Y rushed to save children sitting beneath the roof and in the process injured herself. In separate actions filed by the injured persons. Decide.

Decision:

A. X shall not be able to recover as he consented to the risk of the flying ball.
B. X shall be able to recover as the organisers failed to take precautions against the flying ball.
C. X shall be able to recover as he consented to watch the game not to be injured in it.
D. X shall not be able to recover as by purchasing a ringside seat in a football game he consented to all the attendant risks of such watching.

393. Legal Principle: A master shall be liable for the fraudulent acts committed by his servant in the course of employment.

Factual Situation: Shaila Devi opened a S.B. Account with Oriental Bank, and a cousin of her by name Mohan, who was clerk in that Bank, helped her to complete the formalities. Subsequently she used to entrust whatever money she was getting to Mohan alongwith her pass book and Mohan used to return the pass book with the relevant entries. One day Shaila Devi discovered that Mohan, instead of crediting the money to her account, had been misappropriating it and the entries in the pass book were made by him without authorization. Shaila Devi seeks compensation from Oriental Bank.

Decision:

A. Oriental Bank shall be liable because Mohan was acting in the course of employment.
B. Oriental Bank shall not be liable, because Mohan was not acting in the course of employment.
C. Oriental Bank was not liable, because Shaila Devi was negligent.
D. None of these

394. Legal Principle: An agreement to which the consent of the seller is freely given is not void merely because the price is inadequate.

Factual Situation: Praveen agrees to sell a horse worth ₹ 1,00,000 for ₹ 10 to Arvind.

Decision:

Is the agreement void?

A. Yes, because the price is inadequate.
B. No, if Praveen's consent to the agreement was freely given.
C. Yes, if Praveen's consent was not freely given.
D. Both B and C.

395. Legal Principle: When at the desire of the promisor, the promisee promises to do some act, then such promise is called a consideration for the promise.

Factual Situation: A, a 40 years old businessman of sound mind agrees of his own free will to sell his bungalow worth ₹ 10 lakhs for ₹ one lakh. The agreement

I. is invalid because of inadequate consideration
II. is valid because there is lawful consideration
III. is valid because it was entered into with free consent
IV. is valid because X has capacity to contract

Decision:

A. I
B. II and III only
C. III only
D. II, III and IV

396. Legal Principle: Under Indian Constitution, everybody shall be equal before law.

Factual Situation: The Income-tax Act happens to provide that those whose annual income is upto ₹ 1,50,000 shall pay 10% of their income as tax; and those whose annual income exceeds ₹ 1,50,000 shall pay the tax at the rate of 20%. Those citizens whose annual income exceeds ₹ 1,50,000 challenge this legislation on the ground that it is a violation of the principle of equality before law.

Decision:

A. They will succeed, because the law discriminates against the people who earn more than ₹ 1,50,000 per annum.

B. They will not succeed, because the people who earn more than ₹ 1,50,000 are not equal to the people who earn less than ₹ 1,50,000.

C. They will not succeed, because this law enables the Government to equalise the incomes of all the people in the country.

D. They will not succeed because citizens earning less than ₹ 1,50,000 are not equal to those earning above it. Taxes must vary.

397. Legal Principle: A contract is an agreement which the law will enforce. All agreements are contracts if they are made with free consent by parties competent to contract for a lawful consideration and with a lawful object.

Factual Situation: Sohan, a young man of 32 years without any consideration agrees to give Mohan ₹ 10,000, Sohan fails to fulfil his promise. Mohan sues Sohan for the amnount.

Decision:

A. Mohan will succeed as Sohan made the promise of his own free will.

B. Mohan will fail as the agreement is without consideration.

C. Mohan will succeed as Sohan has the capacity to make the contract.

D. Mohan will succeed as the money is not being paid for any illegal object.

398. Legal Principle: Even if the sovereign functions of the State are discharged negligently the State is not vicariously liable in tort.

Factual Situation: A was a trader in gold. There he was arrested by police and was detained in the police lock up after search. The gold with him along with sundry other things were seized. Later he was discharged. His possessions seized by the police were returned, except the gold. He moved against the State in tort. In the words of Supreme Court, "There can be no escape from the conclusion that the Police Officers were negligent in dealing with the property after it was seized" One of the Constables was a Muslim. He fled with gold to Pakistan.

Decision:

A. 'A' succeeded because the servants of the State were negligent and thus caused injury.

B. 'A' failed because the Constable who seized the gold had fled to Pakistan and the gold was not with the State at all.

C. 'A' failed because the acts of search and seizure by the Police Officer were part of the sovereign function of the State.

D. There was some other relief given to 'A'.

399. Legal Principles:

(*i*) If a person makes a statement that lowers the reputation of another person in the eyes of right thinking people, then it is defamation.

(*ii*) The person whose reputation is affected can sue the culprit and recover damages.

Factual Situation: Rama told Sita, "You are a thief. You stole my heart". Sita was furious and she felt that she was defamed.

Decision:

A. Rama has defamed Sita and hence he is liable to pay damages.

B. Rama is liable to pay as Sita's reputation was lowered in the eyes of right thinking people.

C. Rama is not responsible, as right thinking people will not mistake this statement.
D. None of the above answers is correct.

400. Legal Principle: When at the desire of the promisor, the promisee promises to do some act, then such promise is called a consideration for the promise.

Factual Situation: X arranges his Birthday party at his home, and his friend Y promise to cook a special dish for the guests. On the day of the party. X finds that Y neither came to his party nor did he get the special dish. X sues Y for the breach of contract.

Question:

Will X succeed in his action?
A. X will succeed because his friend has failed to keep his promise.
B. X will succeed because his reputation was affected due to his irresponsible behaviour.
C. X will not succeed because there is no consideration for his friend's promise to bring the special dish.
D. Both A and B

401. Legal Principle: A contract without consideration is void. When at the desire of one party, the other party does something, the consideration is said to flow from the latter to the former.

Factual Situation: A house was on fire and a child was trapped inside the house. Everyone was shouting for help. A brave onlooker, hearing the shrieks of child, went inside the house and brought him out. The grateful father of the child promised to pay the rescuer ₹ 10,000. Subsequently, he reneged the promise. The rescuer sued the promisee for the breach.

Decision:
A. The father of the child must pay for the service rendered by the rescuer.
B. The rescuer is not entitled to the payment, since he acted on his own.
C. Commercial considerations cannot be applied to humanitarian instincts.
D. None of these

402. Which Bill, reportedly laying down a code of conduct for judges of the higher judiciary was referred to a Group of Ministers for scrutiny in March 2010?
A. The Supreme Court (Number of Judges) Amendment Bill
B. Judges (Inquiry) Bill
C. Judges (Declaration of Assets and Liabilities) Bill
D. Judicial Standards and Accountability Bill

403. In criminal proceedings, acquittal refers to:
A. Being cleared of a charge or accusation
B. Pronounced guilty of a charge or accusation
C. Conviction for a lesser offence, as part of a plea bargain
D. Taking a lenient view, considering the honest past record of an accused

404. The legal branch of the Indian Army is known as:
A. Army Legal Corps
B. Judge Advocate General branch
C. Court Martial branch
D. Armed Forces Legal Corps

405. A clause in the World Anti-Doping Code, which was reportedly a cause of concern for Indian cricketers, is popularly referred to as:
A. Endorsements Clause
B. Roundabout Clause
C. Whereabouts Clause
D. No-notice Drugs Test Clause

406. Rights which husband and wife have against each other are called:
A. family rights
B. conjugal rights
C. spousal rights
D. matrimonial rights

407. The term 'Fourth Estate' refers to:
A. Judiciary B. Parliament
C. President's Estate D. Press

408. A Bill authorizing expenditure by the Government is called:
A. Money Bill
B. Finance Bill

C. Appropriation Bill
D. Expenditure Bill

409. Powers to punish for its contempt makes a High Court in India:
A. a court of contempt
B. a court of record
C. a court of original jurisdiction
D. a court of appellate jurisdiction

410. The Writ of Prohibition and Certiorari are available against:
A. Legal and Semi-legal authorities
B. Implied authorities
C. Non-statutory authorities
D. Judicial or quasi-judicial authorities

411. A marriage amongst minors is considered to be legally:
A. Invalid B. Void ab initio
C. Voidable D. Valid

412. Which of the following organizations regulate the international trade?
A. WTO B. UNO
C. GATT D. UNCTAD

413. History abounds with examples where chieftains have refused to transfer their military units to other chieftains who requested such transfer. The refusals occurred even when the chieftain who received the request for assistance was in a relatively safe place and even when the requesting chieftain's clan was under attack. Each of the reasons below, if true, supports the decision of the chieftain who refuses to share his forces, EXCEPT one. Mark the one.
A. Greatest chieftains have emerged as victors in battles where they were outnumbered by the enemy.
B. War and peace are unpredictable, and situations may change in a short time.
C. The chieftain with a larger army retains greater influence in the region.
D. Armies on the move are unnecessarily exposed to danger.

414. The Penal Code in force in the territory of Jammu & Kashmir is known as the:
A. Indian Penal Code
B. Macaulay Penal Code
C. Ranbir Penal Code
D. Jammu & Kashmir Penal Code

415. A male Hindu marrying a second wife while the first marriage is subsisting, commits:
A. an offence of bigamy
B. no offence
C. no offence if the permission of the first wife was taken in writing
D. no offence if the first wife chooses not to file a case against him

416. The principle that agreements must be respected in good faith, is known as:
A. *Pacta dant legem contractri*
B. *Pactum de non petendo*
C. *Raison d'etre*
D. *Pacta sunt servanda*

417. Which of the following is a well known law firm in India?
A. AZB & Partners
B. TATA Consultancy
C. Leo Burnett India Pvt. Ltd.
D. Goldman Sachs Group, Inc.

418. Who is associated with the remark, "the law, in its majestic equality, forbids rich and poor alike to sleep under bridges, to beg in the streets, and to steal their bread"?
A. Anatole France
B. Glanville Williams
C. Charles Dickens
D. Victor Hugo

419. In India, making a direct marketing telephone call, which a person has opted not to receive, is prohibited under:
A. Unsolicited Direct Marketing Act
B. Unsolicited Communications Regulations
C. Telecom Unsolicited Commercial Communications Regulations
D. Telecom Unsolicited Commercial Calls Regulations

420. How many Schedules are there in the Constitution of India?
A. 7 B. 8
C. 10 D. 12

421. A Hindu boy wants to marry a Muslim girl. They can solemnize their marriage under the:
A. Special Marriage Act
B. Hindu Marriage Act
C. Muslim Law
D. Any of these

422. On whom lies the burden of proof where there is a plea for self defence?
A. Accused B. Prosecution
C. Complainant D. State

423. The Right of Children to Free and Compulsory Education Bill was enacted to give effect to:
A. Article 14 of the Constitution of India
B. Article 45 of the Constitution of India
C. Article 21A of the Constitution of India
D. Article 21 of the Constitution of India

424. What is the closest meaning of the expression, '*ex aquo et bono*'?
A. In equity and good conscience
B. For the public good
C. The thing speaks for itself
D. In good faith

425. A member of the Indian Parliament or State Legislature cannot be arrested in civil action within a period of ______ days before and after the session.
A. 40 B. 45
C. 50 D. 55

426. Which of the following legislations regulates electronic commerce?
A. Copyright Act, 1957
B. Trade Marks Act, 1999
C. Contract Act, 1872
D. Information Technology Act, 2000

427. Who is ex-officio Chairman of Rajya Sabha?
A. President
B. Vice-President
C. Prime Minister
D. Head of opposition party in Lok Sabha

428. What does the Polluter Pays Principle mean?
A. Absolute liability to compensate the victims of pollution
B. Absolute liability to the cost of reversing the damaged ecology
C. Both A and B
D. Both A and B, provided the polluter was negligent and did not take reasonable care

429. Which of the following States is a permanent member of the Security Council?
A. France B. Germany
C. Japan D. South Korea

430. Remarks of a judge, which are made casually and are not relevant to the case in hand, are known as:
A. Obiter dicta
B. Ratio decidendi
C. Precedent
D. Binding source of law

431. Which Article of the Constitution of India provides that Government of India can sue and be sued in the name of 'Union of India'?
A. Article 32 B. Article 248
C. Article 299 D. Article 300

432. Administrative law is concerned with the powers of the:
A. President B. Legislature
C. Judiciary D. Executive

433. Economic justice, an important objective of the Constitution of India is embedded in the:
A. Preamble
B. Directive Principles of State Policy
C. Fundamental Rights
D. Both A and B

434. From which of the following List of the Seventh Schedule of the Constitution, the Parliament derives legislative competence?
A. Only List I
B. From List I and List II
C. From List I, List II and List III
D. From List I and List III

435. In which of the following cases, the Supreme Court laid down guidelines on sexual harassment of working women at work places:
A. D.K. Basu v. State of West Bengal
B. Vishaka v. State of Rajasthan
C. Nilabati Behera v. State of Orissa
D. Both B and C

436. A contract enforceable at the instance of one party is known as:
A. Void contract B. Valid contract
C. Voidable contract D. Illegal contract

437. The term palimony means:
A. alimony from parents
B. maintenance from friends
C. court ordered financial settlement amongst people in a live-in-relationship
D. maintenance to old parents by children

438. Who among the following can be parties to a case before the International Court of Justice?
A. Individuals and States
B. States and International Organisations
C. Only States
D. All of the above

439. Which of the following is ***not*** an organ of the United Nations?
A. International Court of Justice
B. UNESCO
C. Trusteeship Council
D. Economic and Social Council

440. 'What cannot be done directly cannot be done indirectly?' This statement epitomizes the doctrine of:
A. colourable legislation
B. pith and substance
C. implied powers
D. ancillary powers

441. *Lex fori* means:
A. the law of the place
B. the law of the court in which case is tried
C. the law of the place where contract is made
D. none of the above

442. Which of the following amendments to the Constitution took away the right of property from fundamental rights?
A. 42nd amendment B. 44th amendment
C. 43rd amendment D. 45th amendment

443. Which of the following statements is ***not*** correct?
A. Preamble of the Constitution is not justiciable
B. Directive Principles of State Policy are positive obligations of State towards citizens
C. Fundamental rights are negative obligations of the State
D. Fundamental duties are enforceable

444. Where are juvenile delinquents sent?
A. Borstal
B. Asylum
C. Reformative Centre
D. Protective custody

445. Consider the following statement: "Reading is an activity involving the use of visual apparatus by means of which printed letters are recognized". This definition would be weakened most by pointing out that:
A. 'Skimming' is a form of reading.
B. An illiterate may recognize letters.
C. Some printed letters are difficult to interpret.
D. Seeing is necessary for reading.

446. Which of the following bodies was instrumental in setting-up permanent and continuous Lok Adalat in Delhi, to resolve disputes pertaining to bodies such as the M.C.D., N.D.M.C., B.S.E.S., N.D.P.L., M.T.N.L. etc.?
A. Delhi Legal Services Authority
B. Bar Council of India
C. Bar Association of Delhi
D. Indian Council of Arbitration

447. Under which provision of the Code of Criminal Procedure may a Court make a proclamation requiring a person to appear at a specified place, if the Court has a reason to believe that the person has absconded?
A. Section 40 B. Section 42
C. Section 73 D. Section 82

448. Any proceedings for removal of a judge any High Court in India may be initiated only by:
A. an order of the President of India
B. a notice of motion for presenting an address to the President, praying for the removal of a Judge, signed by requisite number of members of the Parliament

C. address by each house of the Parliament, supported by the requistie number of Members of Parliament

D. constitution of a Committee for the purpose of making an investigation into the grounds on which the removal of the Judge is prayed for

449. Which of the following enactments is proposed to ensure supply of at least a minimum quantity of food grains to families living Below Poverty Line in India?

A. Food Safety Enhancement Act

B. Food Safety Act

C. Essential Services Maintenance Act

D. National Food Security Act

450. In a Civil Writ Petition, a 'stay' may refer to:

A. A court order restraining an action until a future event occurs, or the order is lifted

B. A court order directing an individual to remain present during the court proceedings

C. A court order to compel the presence of a witness at a specified place, if the Court has a reason to believe that the person has absconded

D. Both A and B

451. On 1st April, P and Q, friends of X, decided to pull a prank on her. They wore black masks to cover their faces and proceeded in an un-numbered car, towards the road that X took her regular morning walk. As X was taking her morning walk, they brought the car to a halt next to her and proceeded to forcefully get her in it. A bystander, Y, watching this opened fire on P and Q with his licensed gun and caused grievous injuries to them.

A. Y is guilty of causing grievous hurt as he had no right to intermeddle in the private affairs of the friends and he was neither a public authority nor a police official.

B. Y is not guilty of any offence because he had a right to protect the body of any other person, besides his own.

C. Y is not guilty of any offence because he had a reasonable apprehension that X was being assaulted with an intention of abduction.

D. Both B and C

452. You are a qualified lawyer and a husband approaches you, seeking your professional services for divorce proceedings. Ideally, what should you do?

A. Explain the difficulties involved in the proceedings for divorce.

B. Advice him to convince his wife for a mutual, unconstested divorce.

C. Refuse to be engaged in the case, since it is against professional conduct of a lawyer set by the Bar Council of India.

D. Advice him to approach for conciliation proceedings.

453. A finds a watch on the floor of a State Transport bus while leaving it as the last passenger. He picked it up and put it in his pocket, instead of returning it to the State Transport authorities. Next day he sold the watch. A is liable for:

A. theft

B. extortion

C. criminal misappropriation

D. criminal breach of trust

454. An accused below the age of 18 years can be tried for committing an offence under:

A. Indian Penal Code

B. Juvenile Justice (Care and Protection of Children) Act, 2000

C. Being a minor, he cannot be tried

D. Both A and B

455. The body of Sathya Sai Baba has been buried in:

A. Sai Kulwanth Hall

B. Prem Sai Hall

C. Sai Jaswanth Hall

D. Sai Ram Hall

456. Who among the following has been declared as new Prime Minister of the Tibetan Government-in-exile?

A. Samdhong Rimpoche

B. Lobsang Sangay
C. Dalai Lama
D. Wang Chu

457. Ignorance of law is:
A. not an excuse in Indian law
B. an excuse in Indian law
C. no such principle is followed in Indian law
D. partly an excuse in Indian law

458. What does the principle of vicarious liability mean?
A. A person is liable for his act
B. A person is liable for the act of another
C. A person is liable for the act of his master
D. None of the above

459. Under the Indian Penal Code, an act may be an offence under the Code, but for the existence of a justification which may form a defence. Which of the following is not such a defence?
A. Act done by a child under seven years of age.
B. Act done by a person of unsound mind
C. Act done by a child of immature understanding, above seven years and under twelve in age.
D. Act done outside the territorial limits of India.

460. Which of the following most closely describes the act of downloading Bollywood film songs for free, from websites over the internet?
A. Attempt to hack a computer system
B. Exercise of freedom of speech and expression
C. Breach of implied contract
D. Violation of intellectual property rights

461. In India, "identity theft" has been made punishable under the:
A. Identity Theft Assumption and Deterrence Act
B. Information Technology Act
C. Indian Penal Code
D. Prize Chits and Money Circulation Schemes (Banning) Act

462. Which of the following is not a feature of the criminal justice system in India?
A. Innocent until proven guilty
B. Right against self-incrimination
C. Preponderance of probability
D. Proof beyond reasonable doubt

463. Which High Court exercised jurisdiction over Delhi, prior to the establishment of the High Court of Delhi?
A. High Court of Gujarat
B. High Court of Punjab
C. High Court of Allahabad
D. High Court of Himachal Pradesh

464. A writ issued by Supreme Court against a person who claims or usurps any office to enquire by what authority he supports his claim, is known as:
A. Mandamus B. Quo Warranto
C. Certiorari D. Habeas corups

465. A contract to which a minor is a party, is known as:
A. Void *ab initio*
B. Voidable at the option of minor
C. Voidable at the option of other party
D. Valid

466. In which of the following cases, the Supreme Court held that basic structure of Constitution cannot be changed?
A. Golaknath Case
B. Keshavanand Bharti Case
C. Minerva Mills Case
D. D.K. Basu v. State of West Bengal

467. The meaning of which of the following maxims is "where there is a right, there is a remedy".
A. *ubi jus ibi remedium*
B. *damnum sine injuria*
C. *injuria sine damnum*
D. *ex turpi causa oritur non action*

468. Article 1 of the Indian Constitution declares India as:
A. Unitary State
B. Union of States
C. Federal State
D. Quasi-Federal State

469. Which of the following countries because the first country to allow Euthanasia?
A. The Netherlands
B. United Kingdom
C. Australia
D. United States of America

470. A obtained a sum of ₹ 50,000/- by putting B in fear of death. Which of the following offences was committed by A?
A. Cheating B. Robbery
C. Mischief D. Extortion

471. The United Nations Organization is based on the principle of:
A. the solidarity of the members
B. the sovereign equality of the members
C. international peace and good governance of the members
D. economic and social well being of its members

472. M was driving his fancy sports car at the speed of 120 kmph, after consuming alcohol. He lost control of the car and ran over 3 persons leading to their death. M escaped the accident with injuries. What offence, if any, has M committed under the Indian Penal Code?
A. M is not guilty of any offence since he was incapable of judgement by reason of intoxication caused against his will.
B. M is guilty of causing death by doing a rash or negligent act.
C. M has committed the offence of culpable homicide since he caused death by doing an act with the intention of causing such bodily injury as is likely to cause death.
D. M is guilty of committing murder since he did an act by which the death was caused and which was done with the intention of causing death.

473. F.I.R. stands for First Information Report. As per the High Court of Delhi, if at the time of registration of F.I.R. by the police, it appears that crime was committed outside the jurisdiction of that Police Station, the Police after registration of such F.I.R. should transfer the F.I.R. to the Police Station having jurisdiction. Such F.I.R. made at the first instance has been termed as:
A. Perliminary F.I.R.
B. Zero F.I.R.
C. Daily Diary (D.D.) Number
D. Investigatory F.I.R.

474. Which one of the following taxes is ***not*** levied by the Union Government?
A. Income Tax B. Service Tax
C. Wealth Tax D. Value Added Tax

475. A person is said to be vicariously liable when:
A. he is liable for his wrongful acts
B. he is not liable even though he committed wrongful acts
C. he is liable for the wrongful acts of others
D. he is liable though no wrongful act has been done

476. The negligence of a medical practitioner resulted in the loss to a patient. The patient wants to seek compensation from the doctor. He can approach:
A. Consumer Disputes Redressal Forum
B. Civil Court
C. Criminal Court
D. Either A or B

477. Which of the following is an anagram for the word "dormitory"?
A. Hostel B. Dirty Room
C. Dorm D. My Door

478. Sagotra marriage in Hindu Law is:
A. Legal
B. Illegal
C. Permitted with the consent of Khap Panchayat
D. Permitted with the consent of parents

479. Who among the following has been the Chief Justice of India and has acted as the President of India?
A. Justice M. Hidayatullah
B. Justice S.V. Chandrachud
C. Justice P. Shastri
D. Justice P.B. Gajendragadkar

480. In tort, the remedy is:
A. liquidated damages
B. unliquidated damages
C. punishment
D. judicial review

481. Slander is of:
A. Permanent form B. Transient form
C. Strict form D. None of these

482. The doctrine of 'Rule of Law' is based on:
A. Equality before the law
B. Equal protection of the laws
C. Positive discrimination
D. Exclusion of discretionary powers

483. When an interest in immovable property is transferred as a security for the payment of debt or performance of a promise it is called:
A. Pledge B. Lease
C. Mortgage D. Surety

484. Following a ruling of the Delhi High Court, which among the following is not a criteria for designating an advocate as Senior Advocate:
a. ability
b. standing at Bar
c. 12 years of uninterrupted law practice
d. special knowledge or experience of law
e. money
A. b, c and e B. only e
C. b and e D. c and e

485. Which of the following is not related to protection of rights of consumers?
A. 24th December
B. Jago Grahak, Jago
C. 15th March
D. All of them are related to consumer protection

486. Which of the following bodies is not set up under the Constitution of India?
A. Finance Commission
B. Union Public Service Commission
C. Supreme Court of India
D. National Human Rights Commission

487. Which of the following theories of crime is based on the works of Henry McKay and Clifford R. Shaw of the Chicago School thought?
A. Social disorganization theory
B. Strain theory
C. Rational choice theory
D. Routine activity theory

488. The Child Labour (Prohibition and Regulation) Act, as amended in 2006, prohibits the employment of children under the age of ______ years as domestic servants.
A. 12 B. 18
C. 16 D. 14

489. Who founded the doctrine of Utilitarianism?
A. John Austin B. Holmes
C. Jeremy Bentham D. Ronald Dworkin

490. What is an extradition treaty?
A. A treaty for surrender of an alleged or convicted criminal by one nation to another.
B. A treaty for ensuring fair trial of an alleged or convicted criminal transferred by one nation to another.
C. A treaty for international trial of an alleged or convicted criminal.
D. A treaty for trial of an alleged or convicted criminal by a nation, for crime committed or allegedly committed in another nation.

491. How many official languages have been recognised under the Constitution of India?
A. 14 B. 18
C. 20 D. 22

492. An arrested person under the Indian Constitution does not have a fundamental right to __________
A. travel abroad
B. practise any profession
C. get assistance of a legal practitioner of his choice if arrested under preventive detention law
D. challenge an arbitrary law

493. Dishonour of a cheque is an offence under:
A. Section 138 of the Negotiable Instruments Act

B. Section 420 of the Indian Penal Code
C. Section 73 of the Contract Act
D. Section 41 of the Code of Criminal Procedure

494. Who declared a state of emergency in India under Article 352 of the Constitution of India in the year 1975?
A. Indira Gandhi
B. Giani Zail Singh
C. Fakhruddin Ali Ahmed
D. Sanjay Gandhi

495. Who is the author of the book "A Bunch of Old Letters"?
A. Pt. Jawarhar Lal Nehru
B. Mahatma Gandhi
C. Smt. Indira Nehru Gandhi
D. Shri K.C. Pant

496. Driving without a valid "Pollution Under Control Certificate" is punishable under the provisions of:
A. The Motor Vehicles Act, 1988
B. The Air (Prevention and Control of Pollution) Act, 1981
C. The Environment (Protection) Act, 1986
D. The Public Liability Insurance Act, 1991

497. Which of the following is considered the first international crime?
A. Piracy on the High Seas
B. Violation of Human Rights
C. Slavery
D. Software Piracy

498. Under which Article of the Constitution of India is the law laid down by Supreme Court binding on all courts?
A. Article 32 B. Article 141
C. Article 226 D. Article 124

499. The owner and landlord of a flat, allotted to him by the Delhi Development Authority, may recover possession of the flat from his tenant by taking recourse to the law. Which of the following may not have any bearing on such recovery of possession?
A. Delhi Rent Control Act, 1958
B. Agreement to Lease for a fixed term
C. Indian Contract Act, 1872
D. Public Premises (Eviction of Unauthorised Occupants) Act, 1971

500. What is meant by the expression "Separation of Powers"?
A. Division of powers and spheres of authority between the police and the army at local and national level
B. Model of governance dividing the powers and responsibilities of the State between its Executive, Legislature and a Judiciary
C. Provision under the Constitution of India for separate High Courts for each state of the country
D. Division of rights and liabilities between the Central Government, State Governments and the citizens of India through the Constitution of India read with the Right to Information Act

501. Which of the following is not related to legal research?
A. www.manupatra.com
B. Black's Law Dictionary
C. Boyle's Law
D. Law of the Sea

502. The 44th Amendment Act of 1978 to the Constitution of India:
A. Deleted the Fundamental Right to acquire, hold and dispose off property.
B. Introduced the Fundamental Right to free and compulsory education.
C. Deleted Fundamental Right to work.
D. Suspended the Fundamental Right to constitutional remedies.

503. Who appoints the Attorney General of India?
A. Chief Justice of India
B. Ministry of Law and Justice, Government of India
C. President of India
D. President of India in consultation with the Chief Justice of India

504. The expression *"to assume air on"* means
A. to assume inferiority
B. to fill oneself with airy things
C. to affect humility
D. to have a haughty opinion about oneself

505. Which one of the following is associated with mentally or emotionally disturbed?
A. psychological B. psychopathic
C. psychoanalytical D. psychotherapic

506. The phrase *'de facto'* means:
A. all the facts
B. all the facts and figures
C. bona fide
D. for all practical purposes

507. The prediction by palm-reading is called
A. Chironomy B. Chirography
C. Chiropidy D. Chiromancy

508. Neuralgia is associated with
A. Record of heart beats
B. Mental inbalance
C. Nerve pain
D. Inflamation of the nerves

509. Vinay shot at Kadir with a view to kill him. When Kadir was being taken to the hospital a tree fell upon him on the way and he died in the hospital a few days later. If it was proved that the falling of the tree caused Kadir's death then.
A. Vinay shall be responsible for the death of Kadir.
B. Falling of tree has broken the chain of causation.
C. Vinay is not liable to pay any compensation to the dependants of Kadir.
D. None of these

510. 'A' finds a watch on the floor of a State Transport bus while he was leaving it as the last passenger. He picked it up and put it in his pocket instead of returning it to the State Transport authorities. Next day he sold it. 'A' is liable for
A. theft
B. extortion
C. criminal misappropriation
D. criminal breach of trust

511. Homicide means
A. causing death
B. intentionally causing death
C. causing death of anyone
D. causing death of a human being

512. Sometimes a person himself does not commit an offence. He helps or aids another person. He is then guilty of
A. Abetment B. Conspiracy
C. Incitement D. None of these

513. Which of the following is the crime of arousing hatred or contempt against the Government of India?
A. Sedition B. Treason
C. Slander D. Rumour

514. When a person is prosecuted for committing a criminal offence, the burden of proof is on
A. himself B. prosecution
C. court D. police

515. In Law of Torts, always unliquidated damages are awarded. The meaning of unliquidated is
A. not ascertainable
B. approximately arrived at
C. penal and exemplary
D. Both A and B above

516. Defamation infringes a person's right to
A. Reputation B. Pride
C. Privilege D. Status

517. Who is the source of legal authority of India?
A. People of India
B. Constitution of India
C. Parliament of India
D. President of India

518. Law can be broadly divided into two kinds, procedural law which tells us the procedure for obtaining justice, and substantive law which
A. creates rights and duties
B. supplements procedural law
C. substantiates moral principles
D. None of these

519. Transfer of Property Act, 1882, covers
A. movable property
B. immovable property
C. Both of the above
D. None of these

520. The time limit for filing different kinds of suits is contained in

A. Court Fees Act
B. Limitation Act
C. Suit-times Act
D. Court Rules of India

521. The early release of a prisoner is called
A. Bail B. Parole
C. Lease D. Lien

522. Where are juvenile delinquents sent?
A. Borstal
B. Asylums
C. Protective custody
D. Reformation centre

523. Inducing person with dishonest intention to part with his property by putting him in fear of physical injury amounts to an offence of
A. criminal intimidation
B. extortion
C. criminal misappropriation
D. theft

524. Muslim marriage is a
A. Sacrament
B. Civil Contract
C. Divine commandment
D. None of these

525. The law relating to marriage, divorce and succession of various communities
A. is codified in Common Civil Code.
B. is contained in various personal laws codified and uncodified.
C. is entirely uncodified.
D. None of these

526. Sometimes, an accused seeks pardon from the court and offers to give evidence against all others involved in a crime. He is called
A. Witness B. Hostile witness
C. Approver D. None of these

527. Law of Torts deals with
A. defamation B. trespass
C. negligence D. All of these

528. Code of Civil Procedure was enacted in
A. 1973 B. 1908
C. 1919 D. 1948

529. A written statement in the name of a person by whom it is voluntarily signed and sworn to is called
A. Advowsoon B. Affidavit
C. Affirmation D. Affray

530. Criminal law and administrative law are
A. public law and private law respectively
B. private law and public law respectively
C. public law and public law respectively
D. private law and private law respectively

531. The first Law Officer of the country is
A. Chief Justice of India
B. Attorney General of India
C. Chairman of Law Commission
D. None of these

532. The concept of Judicial Review in India is inspired by Constitution of
A. Britain B. Russia
C. U.S.A. D. Switzerland

533. According to Indian Majority Act, a major is a person who has attained the age of
A. 18 years B. 21 years
C. 15 years D. 16 years

534. Fiduciary relationship means a relationship based on
A. money B. contract
C. trust D. None of these

535. A Hindu wife can marry immediately after divorce. A Muslim wife
A. can also marry immediately
B. has to wait till period of Iddat (seclusion) is over
C. has to wait for one year
D. None of the above

536. According to Section 138 of......the dishonour of a cheque results in awarding double amount and also criminal consequences.
A. Negotiable Instruments Act
B. Monetary Instruments Act
C. Contracts Act
D. Specific Reliefs Act

537. Copyright subsists for
A. 50 years B. 60 years
C. 70 years D. 80 years

538. Who introduced Public Interest Litigation in India?
A. Justice P.N. Bhagwati

B. Justice M.N. Venkatachaliah
C. Justice A.M. Ahmadi
D. Justice V.R. Krishna Iyer

539. Under Public Interest Litigation, who can move the court?
A. Any public spirited person
B. Person whose right is infringed
C. A recognised social worker
D. Newspapers

540. Child Labour (Prohibition & Regulation) Act was enacted in
A. 1986 B. 1987
C. 1988 D. 1989

541. Dissolution of Muslim Marriage Act, 1939 provides grounds for dissolution of Muslim marriage to
A. spouses
B. only males
C. only females
D. Muslim parents and parents-in-law

542. What is the meaning of this Latin phrase *"audi alteram partem"*?
A. No one shall be judge in his own cause
B. No one shall be condemned unheard
C. Rights are associated with duties
D. None of the above

543. A Bill becomes a law only when
A. it is duly passed by both Houses
B. it is signed by Prime Ministers
C. it is a signed by Speaker and Chief Justice of India
D. it is signed by President

544. Once appointed, judges of Supreme Court serve till they attain the age of
A. 62 B. 63
C. 64 D. 65

545. Minimum number of Judges which can give an advisory opinion to President is
A. one-third of total strength of Supreme Court
B. one-fourth of total strength of Supreme Court
C. half of total strength of Supreme Court
D. on-fifth of total strength of Supreme Court

546. The act of unlawfully entering into another's property is
A. Breach of property
B. Trespass
C. Triplication
D. Trover

547. An act in excess of the authority conferred by law is
A. Intra vires B. Illegal
C. Ultra vires D. Extra legal

548. When the master is held liable for the wrongful act of his servant, the liability is
A. Absolute B. Strict
C. Transferred D. Vicarious

549. In which of the following a man is liable independently of the existence of either wrongful intent or negligence
A. Liability
B. Strict liability
C. Liability ab initio
D. Liability in exception

550. Public holidays are declared under
A. Negotiable Instruments Act, 1881
B. Contract Act, 1872
C. Public Employees Act, 1967
D. None of these

551. If the Supreme Court can be asked by the President to give advice on a question of law or fact under Article 143, the Supreme Court
A. is bound to give advice
B. may refuse to give advice
C. may dismiss the Presidential reference as non-sense
D. None of these

552. A sentence of death by a lower court
A. must be confirmed by High Court
B. must be confirmed by Supreme Court
C. is operational if no appeal is made to higher courts
D. must be confirmed by the President

553. The tort of defaming someone by words or gestures is called
A. Libel

B. Defamation per jincuriam
C. Slip
D. Slander

554. Which of the following is a general pardon?
A. Remission B. Reprieve
C. Amnesty D. Suspension

555. Husband and wife have a right to each other's company. This right is called
A. Legal right B. Matrimonial right
C. Consortium right D. Conjugal right

556. An act done under threat or fear is done under
A. Duress B. Dunress
C. Compulsion D. None of these

557. A document issued by Court, calling upon the person to whom it is directed to attend before the judge is called
A. Summon B. Call
C. Bailiff D. Supra

558. When a person aids the commission of an offence he is called
A. Abettor B. Accessory
C. Accomplice D. Abeyer

559. The disobedience of any judgement, order, etc., of a court amounts to
A. Perjury
B. Contempt of Court
C. Offence
D. None of these

560. Who is associated with drafting of the Indian Penal Code?
A. Lord Macaulay
B. Sir Frederic Pollock
C. Mulla
D. Sir H.S. Maine

561. Criminal Procedure Code (CPC) was enacted in the year
A. 1860 B. 1873
C. 1973 D. 1983

562. Which one of the following statements concerning the Rajya Sabha is incorrect?
A. The Vice President of India is its ex-officio Chairman
B. Sh. Somnath Chatterjee is its present Speaker
C. Sh. Mohammad Hamid Ansari is its present Chairman
D. Under certain circumstances, the Chairman is not allowed to preside over the proceedings even if he is present

563. In whose presence does the President of India subscribe to the oath of affirmation?
A. The Chief of Army Staff of the Indian Army
B. The Chief of Staffs of all the three services
C. The Speaker of Lok Sabha
D. The Chief Justice of India

564. You purchased a mobile phone handset which stopped working in its guarantee period. The mobile handset manufacturer is refusing to repair or replace the same. What would you do to get justice quickly?
A. Approach the civil court with a suit for declaration
B. File a writ petition before the Delhi High Court
C. Approach the consumer disputes redressal forum
D. Make a complaint of cheating before the local police station

565. Which one of the following is not established under the constitutional provisions?
A. Finance Commission
B. Inter-state Council
C. Planning Commission
D. Scheduled Caste Commission

566. Which of the following is not in the nature of a writ issued by the Constitutional courts of India?
A. *Mandamus* B. *Habeas Corpus*
C. *Rule Nisi* D. *Certiorari*

567. Which countries entered into the Panchsheel series of Agreements?
A. China, Soviet Union and India
B. China and India
C. United States of America and India
D. Russia and India

568. Which of the following laws do not entitle a parent to maintenance?

A. Criminal Procedure Code, 1973
B. Guardians and Wards Act, 1890
C. Maintenance and Welfare of Parents and Senior Citizens Act, 2007
D. All of them contain provisions for payment of maintenance to a parent

569. In what context was the term "judicial overreach" used recently?

A. The powers of Judiciary to bring to justice even the citizens of India outside India, for instance through the extra territorial operation of the Indian Penal Code
B. The jurisdiction of Judiciary on MNCs, as seen in the Bhopal gas leak case where the subsidiary of a company incorporated in the United States has to submit to the jurisdiction of courts in India
C. The High Court in a state of the union hearing a matter falling in the territorial jurisdiction of another state's High Court
D. The expanding realm of public interest litigation and judicial activism in India

570. Which of the following statements about Right to Information Act is not true?

A. It was enacted to promote transparency and accountability in the working of every public authority
B. It protects the information available to a person in his fiduciary relationship
C. It repealed the Official Secrets Act, 1923
D. It puts every public authority under an obligation to appoint Public Information Officer

571. Who is known as the framer of the Indian Penal Code, 1872?

A. Lord Hastings B. Lord Denning
C. Lord Macaulay D. Lord Wilberforce

572. Who among the following judges gave a dissenting opinion in the case of *ADM Jabalpur* v. *Shukla* also known as the *Habeas Corpus* case?

A. Justice P.N. Bhagwati
B. Justice V.R. Krishna Iyer
C. Justice H.R. Khanna
D. Justice A.N. Sen

573. Which of the following is not associated with the Constitution (Thirty-Ninth Amendment Act)?

A. It placed the Coal Mines (Nationalisation) Act, 1973 under the Ninth Schedule of the Constitution of India
B. It ousted the jurisdiction of any court to decide a question on the validity of election of a person as President of India
C. It amended Article 217 of the Constitution of India
D. It was enacted in the year 1975

574. A provision in a statute pertaining to medical institutions in India was struck down by the Supreme Court of India in the year 2008 as being *ultra vires* the Constitution of India. Which of the following statutes contained that provision?

A. All India Institute of Medical Sciences Act
B. Lady Hardinge Medical College and Hospital (Acquisition and Miscellaneous Provisions) Act
C. Post-Graduate Institute of Medical Education and Research, Chandigarh, Act
D. Sree Chitra Tirunal Institute for Medical Sciences and Technology, Trivandrum Act

575. What is the maximum strength of members of the House of the People chosen by direct election under the Constitution of India?

A. 530 B. 550
C. 552 D. 540

576. The principle of 'collective responsibility' means

A. all citizens must collectively elect their representatives
B. all members of the union council of ministers are collectively responsible to the House of the People
C. all ministers are accountable to the Parliament

D. all ministers hold office at the pleasure of the Prime Minister

577. Who was the judge who held that fundamental rights were not amendable?
A. Justice P.N. Bhagwati
B. Justice O. Chinnappa Reddy
C. Justice K.K. Mathew
D. Justice K. Subba Rao

578. Under which law a minor is incapable of entering into contract?
A. Indian Contract Act, 1872
B. Majority Act, 1875
C. Guardians and Wards Act, 1890
D. Contract Labour (Regulation and Abolition) Act, 1970

579. The prohibition against employment of children below 14 years of age has been provided
A. as a fundamental right against exploitation in the Constitution
B. as a right to equality
C. as a directive principle of state policy
D. as a duty on the parents and guardians

580. How many fundamental rights have been guaranteed under the Constitution of India?
A. 5 B. 6
C. 7 D. 8

581. Who has power to decide disputes pertaining to disqualification of a member of Parliament?
A. Speaker of Lok Sabha
B. President of India
C. Chairman of Rajya Sabha
D. President of India on the advice of Election Commission

582. The Raghvan Committee relates to
A. students' union elections
B. ragging in educational institutions
C. reservations for OBC in educational institutions
D. sexual harassment at workplace

583. *D.K. Basu v. State of West Bengal* deals with
A. safeguards for arrested persons
B. safeguards against sexual exploitation
C. safeguards for children
D. safeguards for unorganized workers

584. In which landmark judgment did the Supreme Court of India lay down guidelines against sexual harassment of women at workplace?
A. *Nilabati Behera* v. *State of Orissa*
B. *Vishakha* v. *State of Rajasthan*
C. *Maneka Gandhi* v. *Union of India*
D. *Hussainara Khatoon* v. *State of Bihar*

585. The trade practice known as "minimum resale price maintenance" is prohibited by
A. Monopolies and Restrictive Trade Practices Act, 1969
B. Competition Act, 2002
C. Consumer Protection Act, 1986
D. Multi-State Co-operative Societies Act, 2002

586. Which of the following is the oldest High Court in India?
A. High Court of Madras
B. High Court of Calcutta
C. High Court of Delhi
D. High Court of Allahabad

587. Which of the following organizations was instrumental in bringing numerous copyright infringement lawsuits against individuals in the United States of America, for sharing music online?
A. Federal Bureau of Investigation
B. Hollywood Actors Association
C. Recording Industry Association of America
D. Musicians Pan America Association

588. Which of the following is not a fundamental right?
A. Right to property
B. Right to information
C. Right to life and liberty
D. Both A and B

589. Which of the following bodies is entrusted with the statutory duty of laying down the standards of professional conduct and etiquette for advocates in India?
A. Bar Association of India
B. Bar Council of India
C. Advocates Association of India
D. Bar Advocates Council of India

590. "Rule of Law" means
A. all persons are equal in the eyes of law
B. treating all unequally as equals
C. working according to law
D. distributing state largesse to everyone in equal proportion

591. Which one of the statements is correct?
A. The Constitution of India contains a directive principle about uniform civil code
B. The Constitution of India imposes a duty on every citizen to support uniform civil code
C. The Constitution of India contains a fundamental right assuring the citizens that the state bring about uniform civil code
D. None of the above statements is correct

592. The marriage of a 15 year old girl with a 45 year old man is
A. valid
B. invalid
C. voidable at the option of the girl
D. voidable at the will of the man

593. Which one of the following statements is incorrect?
A. The Comptroller and Auditor General of India (CAG) is appointed as per the Constitution of India.
B. The CAG is appointed by the President of India.
C. The CAG advises the President of India as to the form in which accounts of the Union and States are to be kept.
D. The CAG submits a report to the Parliament.

594. The system of diarchy, decentralization and bicameral legislature was introduced in India by
A. Government of India Act, 1919
B. Government of India Act, 1935
C. Indian Councils Act, 1909
D. Constitution of India, 1950

595. Balwant Rai Mehta Committee Report, 1957 is associated with
A. Tax Reforms
B. Planning Commission
C. National Defence
D. Panchayati Raj

596. A Lease Agreement is a form of
A. Promissory note B. Bill of Exchange
C. License D. Contract

597. Which of the following is not an Alternate Dispute Redressal Mechanism?
A. Mediation B. Lok Adalat
C. Arbitration D. Plea Bargaining

598. Which of the following is not related to protection of rights of consumers?
A. 24th December
B. Jago Grahak, Jago
C. 15th March
D. All of them are related to consumer protection

599. The 44th Amendment Act of 1978 to the Constitution of India
A. Deleted the Fundamental Right to acqurie, hold and dispose off property
B. Introduced the Fundamental Right to free and compulsory education
C. Deleted Fundamental Right to work
D. Suspended the Fundamental Right to constitutional remedies

600. When master is held liable for the wrongful acts of his servant, the liability is called:
A. Vicarious liability
B. Strict liability
C. Tortuous liability
D. Absolute liability

601. National Law Day is observed every year on
A. March 1 B. April 30
C. June 16 D. November 26

602. Remarks of a judge, which are made casually and are not relevant to the case-in-hand, are known as
A. *Obiter dicta*
B. *Ratio decidendi*
C. Precedent
D. Binding source of law

603. What is the meaning of *'lex loci'*?
A. Law of the land is supreme
B. Law of land
C. Sovereignty is essential for enacting laws
D. None of the above

604. "Sustainable Development" is a concept of
A. Environmental law
B. Property law
C. Tax law
D. Criminal law

605. The display of articles in a showroom indicating their prices amounts to
A. Offer
B. Counter-offer
C. Provisional acceptance
D. Invitation to an offer

606. An accused below the age of 18 years can be tried for committing an offence under
A. Indian Penal Code
B. Juvenile Justice (Care and Protection of Children) Act, 2000
C. Being a minor, he cannot be tried
D. Both A and B

607. Rights which husband and wife have against each other are called
A. family rights
B. conjugal rights
C. spousal rights
D. matrimonial rights

608. 'X' is accused of an offence of rape. He can be subjected to the following tests for investigation:
A. Polygraph test
B. Narco acalysis test
C. Brain Electrical Activation Profile (BEAP) Test
D. None of these

609. Fundamental Rights are contained in which Part of the Constitution of India?
A. Part II B. Part III
C. Part IV D. Part V

610. Who is the *ex-officio* Chairman of the Rajya Sabha?
A. President of India
B. Home Minister of India
C. Vice-President of India
D. Deputy Chairman, Planning Commission

611. "Communist Manifesto" was authored by
A. Jeremy Bentham and Karl Marx
B. I. Kant and Friedrich Engels
C. Joseph Stalin and Vladimir Lenin
D. Karl Marx Friedrich Engels

612. The term of office of the President of India is
A. 5 years from the date of his election
B. 5 years from the date of his entering upon his office
C. 7 years from the date of his election
D. 7 years from the date of his entering upon his office

613. Which of the following is not an eligibility criterion for election as President of India?
A. should be citizen of India
B. should be at least 35 years of age
C. should be qualified for election to the House of the People
D. he should be elected as a member of the House of the People

614. The correct form of address for the President of India is
A. His Loreship B. His Honour
C. His Highness D. His Excellency

615. *Habeas Corpus* literally means
A. Produce the body
B. Produce the record
C. Produce the evidence
D. Produce the testimony

616. The National Animal of India is
A. Lion B. Peacock
C. Tiger D. Elephant

617. The retirement age for a High Court Judge
A. Is the same as the retirement age for a District Judge
B. Is the same as the retirement age for a Supreme Court Judge
C. Is lower than the retirement age for a District Judge
D. Is lower than the retirement age for a Supreme Court Judge

618. Which of the following is not a writ mentioned in the Constitution?
A. *Quo Warranto* B. *Certiorari*
C. *Prohibition* D. Interrogatory

619. Where are the headquarters of International Labour Organisation situated?
A. Geneva B. Prague
C. London D. Hague

620. Which of the following is an incorrect statement?
A. Fundamental Rights are in the Part III of the Constitution
B. Directive Principles of State Policy are in Part IV of the Constitution
C. Fundamental Duties are in Part IV of the Constitution
D. Union Territories are in Part VIII of the Constitution

621. Who was the first woman Judge of the Supreme Court of India?
A. Justice Sujata Manohar
B. Justice Fatima Biwi
C. Justice Ruma Pal
D. Justice Leila Seth

622. International Court of Justice is located at
A. Geneva B. Prague
C. Washington D.C. D. The Hague

623. What does the term *"de jure"* mean?
A. As per law
B. As per a Jury
C. Without reference to law
D. Factually

624. Which right is a constitutional right but not a Fundamental Right?
A. Right to life and liberty
B. Right to move freely throughout the territory of India
C. Right to form an association
D. Right to hold property

625. Equality of opportunity in matters of public employment is
A. guaranteed to all citizens of India
B. guaranteed to all residents of India
C. available to persons of Indian origin irrespective of citizenship
D. not provided for in the Constitution

626. The prohibition against prosecution and punishment for the same offence more than once
A. is a principle of natural justice
B. is contained in the Indian Penal Code
C. is contained in the Constitution of India
D. is a principle evolved by the Courts

627. The Constitution has vested the executive power of hte Union Government in
A. The President
B. The Prime Minister
C. The Council of Minister
D. All of the above three

628. Match List-I with List-II and select the correct answer using the codes given below the lists

List-I	***List-II***
(*a*) *Habeas Corpus*	1. Violation of natural Justice
(*b*) *Mandamus*	2. Unlawful arrest and detention
(*c*) *Quo Warranto*	3. Exercise of power without jurisdiction
(*d*) *Certiorari*	4. Non-performance of public duty

Codes:

	(*a*)	(*b*)	(*c*)	(*d*)
A.	2	4	3	1
B.	1	3	4	2
C.	2	3	4	1
D.	1	4	3	2

629. Article 14 does not encompass
A. Equality before law
B. Equal protection of laws
C. Protection against arbitrary action
D. Protection of life and liberty

630. Rights under Article 19 are
A. available to all persons in India
B. available only to citizens of India
C. available to persons of foreign origin
D. Both B and C

631. 'Negligence' means:
A. doing an act with the intention to cause harm to others
B. doing an act with forgetfulness

C. not doint an act with the intention to cause harm to others
D. doing an act by failing to take reasonable care

632. The Competition Act was passed in the year 2002 to replace:
A. The Monopolies and Restrictive Trade Practices Act, 1969
B. The Consumer Protection Act, 1986
C. The Sale of Goods Act, 1930
D. Unlawful Activities (Prevention) Act, 1967

633. The bail granted to a person apprehending arrest is called
A. Immediate Bail B. Surety
C. Advance Bail D. Anticipatory Bail

634. An authority given by one person to another to act on his behalf is legally termed as
A. Passing off
B. Share authority
C. Power of attorney
D. None of the above

635. An arrangement in which defendant pleads guilty to a criminal prosecution and in turn receives a lighter sentence is called
A. Arbitration B. Conciliation
C. Plea-bargaining D. Mediation

636. The meaning of the term *"quase"* is
A. As if it were B. *Null*
C. *Void* D. Quashed

637. The absolute supremacy or predominance of regular law as opposed to the existence of arbitrariness or wide discretionary authority on the part of government is technically referred to as
A. Right of action B. Rule of law
C. Fundamental law D. Writ

638. A person through whom, a minor or an insane person can institute legal action is called
A. Legal representative
B. *Amicus curiae*
C. Next friend
D. None of the above

639. Which of the following maxims means the welfare of the people as the paramount law?
A. *Sacramenta pubertem sunt sarvanda*
B. *Res judicata pro veritate occipitur*
C. *Salus populi suprema lex*
D. *Salus republicae suprema lex*

640. The Directive Principles of State Policy was adopted from the
A. British Constitution
B. Irish Constitution
C. US Constitution
D. Swiss Constitution

641. In which one of the following cases the Supreme Court gave verdict which have a direct bearing on the Centre-State relations?
A. *Keshavananda Bharati* Case
B. *Vishakha* Case
C. *S.R. Bommai* Case
D. *Indira Sawhney* Case

642. The purpose of Directive Principles of State Policy is to
A. lay down positive instructions which would guide State Policy at all levels
B. implement Gandhiji's idea for a decentralized State
C. check the use of arbitrary powers by the government
D. promote welfare of the background sections of the society

643. How many members are nominated by the President to the Lok Sabha to represent the Anglo-Indian Community?
A. 2 B. 5
C. 6 D. 12

644. Division of Powers is a feature of
A. Unitary Government
B. Federal Government
C. Parliamentary Government
D. Presidential Government

645. Who passed the Widow Re-marriage Act?
A. William Bentinck B. Canning
C. Dalhousie D. Auckland

646. Which one of the following is presided by a non-member?

A. Legislative Council
B. Lok Sabha
C. Rajya Sabha
D. Legislative Assembly

647. The 8th Schedule to the Constitution in which 22 languages have been recognised, which one of the following is not one among them?
A. Urdu B. Konkani
C. English D. Hindi

648. Article 1 of the Constitution declares India as:
A. Unitary State
B. Union of States
C. Federal State
D. *Quasi*-Federal State

649. Who among the following does not hold his office at the pleasure of the President?
A. Chairman of the UPSC
B. Speaker of the Lok Sabha
C. Attorney-General of India
D. Comptroller and Auditor-General of India

650. The Constitution of India was amended for the first time in
A. 1950 B. 1951
C. 1952 D. 1953

651. In which year did Right to Information Act came into force?
A. 2003 B. 2004
C. 2005 D. 2006

652. Which one of the following Articles of the Constitution of India makes a specific mention of village panchayats?
A. Article 19 B. Article 23
C. Article 40 D. Article 246

653. Panchayati Raj system was started in the country in
A. 1957 B. 1959
C. 1969 D. 1979

654. An amendment of the Constitution of India can extend to Jammu and Kashmir
A. automatically
B. only if ratified by State Legislature
C. by an order of the President under Article 370
D. under no circumstance

655. Election of Rajya Sabha is held after
A. 2 years B. 3 years
C. 5 years D. 6 years

656. The incorporation of Concurrent List in the Indian Constitution has been borrowed from the constitution of
A. Ireland B. Britain
C. Australia D. Canada

657. Chief Ministers of all the States are *ex-officio* members of the
A. Finance Commission
B. Planning Commission
C. National Development Council
D. Inter-State Council

658. The power to increase the number of Judges in the Supreme Court lies with the
A. President
B. Chief Justice of India
C. Parliament
D. Either A or B

659. The Speaker of Lok Sabha is elected by
A. all the Members of Parliament
B. all the Members of Lok Sabha
C. all Members of majority party in the Lok Sabha
D. the people directly

660. The President may appoint all except
A. Prime Minister
B. Governor
C. High Court Judges
D. Rajya Sabha Chairman

661. Who was the first Foreign Minister of independent India?
A. Jawaharlal Nehru
B. Gulzari Lal Nanda
C. Lal Bahadur Shastri
D. Vijaya Laxmi Pandit

662. The standard of living in a country is represented by its
A. national income
B. per capita income
C. unemployment rate
D. All of the above

663. The Planning Commission is
A. an autonomous body
B. an advisory body
C. a constitutional body
D. a Government department

664. The Comptroller and Auditor-General of India
A. Exercises powers in relation to the accounts of Union and States only.
B. Besides (1) supra can also exercise powers in relation to the accounts of any other authority or Body as may be prescribed by or under any law made by Parliament.
C. Besides (1) & (2) above, can also exercise powers in relation to account of Companies (Private Sector) to which Nationalized Banks and Financial Institutions have advanced monies.
D. Besides (1) & (2) above, can exercise powers in relation to accounts of only those Companies (Private Sector) in which the investment of Nationalized banks & Financial Institutions is by way of equity.

665. Election Commission of India is a
A. constitutional body
B. judicial body
C. supervisory body
D. Both A and C

666. Which of the following countries is a permanent member of the UN Security Council?
A. France B. Germany
C. Japan D. South Korea

667. The Directive Principles of State Policy are aimed at
A. securing political freedom
B. securing social and economic freedom by appropriate action
C. executive supremacy
D. judicial supremacy

668. Put in chronological order the following Presidents of India according to their terms of office
I. Dr. S. Radhakrishnan
II. V.V. Giri
III. Dr. Zakir Hussain
IV. Neelam Sanjiva Reddy
A. I, II, III, IV B. I, III, II, IV
C. II, I, III, IV D. I, III, IV, II

669. The executive authority of the Union is vested by the Constitution in the
A. Prime Minister
B. President
C. Union Legislature
D. Lok Sabha

670. The Rajya Sabha can be dissolved by
A. President
B. President with the consent of Lok Sabha
C. President with the consent of Supreme Court
D. None of the above

671. The largest committee of Parliament of India is
A. Public Accounts Committee
B. Estimates Committee
C. Committee on Public Undertakings
D. Joint Parliamentary Committee

672. The time gap between two sessions of the Parliament should not exceed
A. 3 months B. 6 months
C. 9 months D. 11 months

673. The Supreme Court decides the disputes regarding the election of the
A. Prime Minister
B. Speaker and Deputy Speaker
C. President and Vice-President
D. All of the above

674. Who appoints the Governor of Jammu and Kashmir?
A. Chief Minister of the State
B. Chief Justice of the High Court
C. President
D. Chief Justice of India

675. The first woman Governor of a State in independent India was
A. Sarojini Naidu
B. Sucheta Kriplani
C. Vijaya Laxmi Pandit
D. Raj Kumari Amrit Kaur

676. Match the following:

List-I	*List-II*
(*a*) Theft	1. A matrimonial remedy
(*b*) Divorce	2. A civil wrong
(*c*) Defamation	3. A civil remedy
(*d*) Injunction	4. An offence under Indian Penal Code

Codes:

	(*a*)	(*b*)	(*c*)	(*d*)
A.	1	2	3	4
B.	4	2	1	3
C.	4	1	2	3
D.	3	1	4	2

677. A Hindu boy wants to marry a Muslim under the:
A. Special Marriage Act
B. Hindu Marriage Act
C. Muslim Law
D. Any of the above

678. When an interest in immovable property is transferred as a security for the bayment of debt or performance of a promise, it is called
A. Pledge B. Lease
C. Mortgage D. Surety

679. 'A' obtained a sum of ₹ 50,000 by putting 'B' in fear of death. Which of the following offences was committed by 'A'?
A. Cheating B. Forgery
C. Mischief D. Extortion

680. The person making an affidavit is called
A. Defendent
B. Deponent
C. Witness
D. Prosecution witness

681. In case *Ram* v. *Shyam*, Ram cannot be a/an
A. Plaintiff B. Appellant
C. Defendent D. Both B & C

682. Right to Information is a
A. Statutory Right
B. Fundamental Right
C. Directive Principle
D. Both A & B

683. Result of successful prosecution is
A. Acquittal B. Discharge
C. Conviction D. Charge-sheeting

684. Which of the following is not a form of Alternate Dispute Resolution (ADR)?
A. Arbitration B. Conciliation
C. Mediation D. Plea Bargaining

685. The term *'ipso facto'* means
A. in place of
B. by reason of first fact
C. by the same source
D. by the way

686. Which of the following is a bulwark of personal freedom?
A. *Mandamus* B. *Habeas Corpus*
C. *Quo Warranto* D. *Certiorari*

687. At present right to property is a
A. Legal Right
B. Human Right
C. Fundamental Right
D. Directive Principle

688. In which year were the States reorganized on linguistic basis?
A. 1947 B. 1951
C. 1956 D. 1966

689. India adopted a Federal system with strong centre from
A. U.S.A B. Canada
C. Australia D. U.K.

690. How many times has the President declared national emergency so far?
A. only once B. twice
C. thrice D. never

691. Which Article of the Constitution permits the Supreme Court to review its own judgment or order?
A. Article 130 B. Article 137
C. Article 141 D. Article 143

692. The Attorney-General of India holds office
A. for a term of 3 years
B. for a term of 5 years
C. for a term of 6 years
D. during the pleasure of the President

693. Who was the first Chairman of the Planning Commission?
A. Jawaharlal Nehru
B. Gulzari Lal Nanda

C. Vallabhbhai Patel
D. K.C. Neogy

694. An amendment to the Constitution can be initiated by
A. Lok Sabha alone
B. Rajya Sabha alone
C. President
D. Both A and B

695. Manu Smriti is related with
A. Economics
B. Political Science
C. Law
D. Medical Jurisprudence

696. Members of International Court of Justice are appointed for a period of
A. 2 years B. 3 years
C. 5 years D. 9 years

697. The power of Governor of a State to promulgate ordinance is given in the Constitution of India under
A. Article 123 B. Article 212
C. Article 124 D. Article 213

698. Which one of the following judges of the Supreme Court referred to emergency as the darkest chapter of democratic history of India?
A. Justice H.R. Khanna
B. Jusitce P.N. Bhagwati
C. Justice V.N. Khare
D. Justice Krishna Iyer

699. What was the number of original members of the United Nations?
A. 51 B. 52
C. 54 D. 55

700. Who said, "Every saint has a past and every criminal has a future"?
A. Justice P.N. Bhagwati
B. Justice Krishna Iyer
C. Justice J.S. Verma
D. Justice H.R. Khanna

701. All India Services can be created by the
A. President B. UPSC
C. Parliament D. Supreme Court

702. The Tenth Schedule to the Constitution of India deals with
A. Languages of the Union
B. Lists of Legislative Business
C. Provision for Panchayats
D. Anti-Defection Law

703. Which of the following is not a condition for becoming a citizen of India?
A. Birth
B. Acquiring Property
C. Descent
D. Naturalisation

704. Interpretation of Indian Constitution is based on the spirit of
A. Preamble
B. Fundamental Rights
C. Directive Principles
D. All of the above

705. Which of the following words were added to the Preamble to the Constitution by 42nd Amendment Act, 1976?
A. Socialist B. Secular
C. Democratic D. Both A & B

706. Who decides the number of Judges in a High Court?
A. State Government B. President
C. Parliament D. Governor

707. Crime is a
A. private wrong
B. public wrong
C. private as well as public wrong
D. none of the above

708. In criminal law, successful prosecution means
A. acquittal of the accused
B. conviction of the accused
C. the accused is discharged unconditionally
D. punishment to the accused as per law

709. The maxim *'Actus non facit reum, nisi mens sit rea'* means
A. crime is a child of guilty mind
B. guilty mind gives birth to crime
C. there can be no crime without a guilty mind
D. criminal mind leads to crime

710. Forgery is an offence relating to
A. Documents B. Property
C. Personation D. All of the above

711. A 'friend of court' appointed to assist the court in certain proceedings is referred to as
A. *Alieni juris* B. *Affinitas*
C. *Amicus Curiae* D. *Animo furandi*

712. The word *'mala fide'* means
A. Erroneous B. Good faith
C. Bad faith D. Intention

713. An arbitration proceeding is a
A. Judicial proceeding
B. *Quasi*-Judicial proceeding
C. Administrative proceeding
D. Extra-Judicial proceeding

714. A *puisne* judge of a High Court is
A. a judge other than the Chief Justice
B. the Chief Justice
C. a temporary Judge
D. a retired Judge

715. The meaning of the phrase *'in limine'* is
A. on the threshold B. in place of
C. in default D. in open court

716. A person dying without leaving a will is said to die
A. *invito* B. *Inter se*
C. *Intestate* D. None of the above

Directions (Qs.Nos. 717 to 726): *Given below are Legal Principles followed by Factual Situation. Apply the principle to it and select the most appropriate answer for questions among the four choices given.*

717. Legal Principle: The occupier of the premises owes a duty of care to all his invitees and visitors.

Factual Situation: Gopal was running a dairy from his farm house. People used a part of his farm as a short-cut to get to a nearby railway station. Gopal did not approve of this, and put up a notice that "Trespassers will be prosecuted." However, since a number of these people were also his customers he tolerated them. One day, a person who was using this short-cut was attacked by a bull belonging to the farm. The injured person filed a suit against Gopal.

Decision:
A. Gopal is liable for having kept a bull on his farm
B. Gopal is not liable in view of the clear notice against trespassers
C. Gopal is liable because in fact he allowed the people to use his premises
D. Gopal is not liable to the people other than his customers.

718. Legal Principle: Law of Contract mandates that two or more people are free to create mutual rights and duties provided such rights and duties are not opposed to public policy.

Factual Situation: *A* enters into an agreement with *B* under which *B* undertakes to kill *A* when he is asleep. For this act, *A* deposited ₹ 1 lakh with a bank, which *B* could withdraw once he has performed the aforesaid task. *B* kills *A* according to the terms of the agreement.

Decision:
A. *B* must get ₹ 1 lakh because he has performed his task
B. *B* must be prosecuted because he has killed *A*
C. *B* must not be prosecuted because *A* has consented to be killed
D. *B* must be prosecuted for killing *A* but he should get ₹ 1 lakh as agreed by *A*.

719. Legal Principle: Every partner in a partnership firm is liable for the acts of every other partner during the course of business of the partnership.

Factual Situation: *A*, a partner in the firm XYZ with another partner *B* takes loan from a bank for the partnership firm. *A* misuses the fund for his personal use. *B* is very resourceful person. Can the bank demand the entire money from *B*?

Decision:
A. No, because *A* has misused the money for his personal use

B. Yes, because both are partners in the same firm
C. No, because *B* has not taken any loan
D. No, because *B* has another partner in his firm

720. Legal Principle: Nothing is an offence, which is done by accident or misfortune and without any criminal intention or knowledge in the doing of a lawful act in a lawful manner by lawful means and with proper care and caution.

Factual Situation: *A* is a woodcutter. One day when he was at work a number of children flocked to him, and asked him to make a cricket bat for them. Without listening to them he continued to chop woods using a heavy axe. Suddenly a piece of chopped wood flew and struck one child who was standing just two feet away from him as a result of which the child lost his one eye. Is *A* liable for the injury caused to the boy?

Decision:

A. *A* is liable for causing injury to child
B. *A* is not liable because it was merely an accident
C. *A* is not liable because children flocked to him
D. *A* is liable because he has the knowledge that the boys standing near him may get hurt

721. Legal Principle: If a person without any authority prevents a person to proceed to any direction and is kept confined, he commits an offence of criminal confinement.

Factual Situation: The Municipal Board allowed *X* to hold a mariage party blocking a part of a public road. The marriage party blocked most of the roads and did not allow *A*, a passerby, to cross the road. He brings a charge of criminal confinement against the head of the marriage party and other associates. Can *A* succeed?

Decision:

A. *A* cannot succeed because *X* has got previous permission from the Municipal Board and has blocked part of the public road
B. *A* can succeed because he has authority to walk on public road
C. *A* cannot succeed because he must have to wait upto end of marriage party
D. *A* shall succeed because no one is allowed to use public property for the personal benefit.

722. Legal Principle: An act of God is an operation of natural forces so unexpected that no human foresight or skill could reasonably be expected to anticipate it.

Factual Situation: The Surya Club was celebrating its 50th anniversary and arranged for a concert by a leading musical group. The event was to be organized in Great Palace auditorium in the coastal area. All the tickets were sold out. On the day of the event, the tsunami destroyed many of the buildings including the auditorium. People who purchased the tickets asked for refund from the Club as the show could not take place.

Decision:

A. The management of the Auditorium must refund the cost of tickets as they got money from the Club
B. The Club must refund the cost of tickets as the people were not at fault
C. The Club is not liable to refund the ticket but the ticket holders can demand the show to be organized at a later point of time
D. Neither the management of the Auditorium nor the Club is liable to refund the money.

723. Legal Principle: Contractual liability is completely irrelevant to the existence of liability in tort.

Factual Situation: Sudhir purchased a bottle of soft drink from a retailer. As he consumed more than half of the contents of the bottle, he found decomposed remains of a cockroach in the bottle. He vomited and fell sick on the thought of what he has consumed. He sued the manufacturer of soft drink for negligence, though there is no contractual duty on the part of manufacturer.

Decision:

A. Sudhir cannot sue the retailer as he did not commit any mistake

B. Sudhir cannot sue the manufacturer for negligence as there was no contract between them

C. Sudhir can definitely sue the retailer as it was his duty to check the products before he sells them

D. Sudhir can sue the manufacturer as he had a duty to ensure that bottles did not contain any such material

724. Legal Principle: A person is liable for all the injurious consequences of his careless act.

Factual Situation: Ramesh, a snake charmer, was exhibiting his talents to a group of people. One of the snakes escaped and bit a child who had to be hospitalized for two days for treatment.

Decision:

A. Ramesh is liable to compensate the child's family for his careless act

B. Ramesh is not liable to compensate the child's family because he exercised due care and did not do it wilfully

C. Ramesh is not liable to compensate the child's family because it is the duty of the spectators to take adequate care

D. Ramesh is not liable to compensate the child's family because it was a mere accident

725. Legal Principle: Any act done in the exercise of right of private defence shall not be an offence. The right to private defence in no case extends to the inflicting of more harm than it is necessary to inflict for the purpose of private defence.

Factual Situation: Rajan saw a thief jumping the boundary wall and entering his house in the night. He picked up the sword and hid in a corner. The moment the person entered the house, he hit the person with sword and cut his head. Did Rajan commit the offence of killing the thief?

Decision:

A. Yes, because he exceeded the right of private defence

B. No, he has not committed any offence because he exercised his right of private defence

C. Yes, because the thief should have been given an opportunity to run away from there

D. No, criminals should not be dealt with any leniency

726. Legal Principle: When a person represents to another something as a true fact, knowing fully well that it is not true, he is guilty of fraud. The person subjected to fraud may avoid an agreement.

Factual Situation: *'X'* presents a horse for sale. The horse is kept on display so that anyone interested could examine it. The horse has a cracked hoof and it is cleverly concealed by the owner. *'Y'* tells *'X'*, "If you do not deny it, I shall assume that the horse is sound". *'X'* keeps silent. *'Y'* purchases the horse.

Decision:

A. *'Y'* can avoid the agreement on discovery of the defect.

B. *'Y'* cannot avoid the agreement, as the horse was on display and could have satisfied himself of its soundness by personal examination

C. *'Y'* cannot avoid the agreement as *'X'* did not make any representation to mislead him. He merely kept silent so that *'Y'* could find things by himself

D. None of the above

Directions (Qs. Nos. 727 to 730): *Please carefully read the arguments and choose appropriate answer.*

727. A was crossing the street. A man was slapping a beggar for having dirtied his car. A shot that man. A is

A. not protected
B. protected
C. not protected because A's own body was not involved
D. not protected because there was no reasonable apprehension of death or grievous hurt being caused by the slapping

728. A went for a picnic with his wife. Some rowdy boys started passing level comments at her. Even after repeated requests by A they continued in this behaviour. A asked his wife to sit in the car. He got into the car and pretended to be driving away. Suddenly he reversed and hit the boys at the speed of 40 km/hr. Two boys died while the rest sufferred serious injuries. A is
A. not protected
B. protected
C. not protected because A's own body was not involved
D. not protected because there was no reasonable apprehension of rape, in law molestation is not the same thing as rape

729. A and B were fighting over a girl, B took out a cycle chain to hit A. A apprehending grievous hurt struck a knife through B's heart. A is
A. Protected
B. Not protected
C. Not protected because the assault was occasioned by A's fault in picking up a fight
D. Not protected because there was no reasonable apprehension of grievous hurt

730. A was holding the birthday party of his daughter. Some of his friends decided to present her with a car. To create an element of surprise, they decided to kidnap her for a few minutes while the party was in full swing and then get her back in the new car. They put the plan into action. While they were kidnapping. A got very alarmed and asked the guards to open fire. The guards killed all the five friends. A is
A. not protected
B. protected because he did not kill, the guards did
C. not protected because A's own body was not involved
D. protected because to any ordinary person there would have appeared a reasonable apprehension of kidnapping.

731. All contracts are agreements. All agreements are accepted offers.

Which of the following arguments is correct?
A. all accepted offers are contracts
B. all agreements are contracts
C. all contracts are accepted offers
D. none of the above

732. All motor vehicles are required to have third party insurance any vehicle not using mechanical device is not a motor vehicle.

Which of the following arguments is correct?
A. vehicles are using mechanical device need not have third party insurance.
B. all third party insurances relate to motor vehicles.
C. all vehicles must have third party insurance.
D. none of the above.

733. No minor can enter into a contract of work. Working in a shop can be done only by a contract.

Which of the following arguments is correct
A. A minor cannot work in a shop
B. A shop cannot contract with a minor
C. There cannot be a contract to which minor is a party
D. none of the above

734. A contract contravening the public policy is void. There cannot be a general definition of public policy.

Which of the following arguments is correct one?
A. the impact of public policy on contract is to be judged in individual cases.

B. there cannot be a general definition of contract.
C. the impact of public policy on contract is to be judged in individual cases.
D. None of the above.

735. The international law is law between sovereign States. A sovereign is the supreme authority not bound by legal constraints.

Which of the following arguments is correct?
A. International law is the nature of pact between sovereign States.
B. International law is not law binding upon the sovereign States.
C. International law is only a positive morality.
D. None of the above.

736. A contract contravening public policy is void. There cannot be a general definition of public policy.

Which of the following is correct derivation from the above?
A. There cannot be a general definition of contract
B. Since public policy is uncertain, contract is also uncertain
C. The impact of public policy on contract is to be judged in individual cases
D. None of the above

737. All motor vehicles are required to have third party insurance. Any vehicle not using mechanical device is not a motor vehicle.

Which of the following is correct derivation from the above?
A. All Third Party Insurances relate to motor vehicles
B. Vehicles not using mechanical device need not have Third Party Insurance
C. All vehicles must have Third Party Insurance
D. None of the above

738. All contracts are agreements. All agreements are accepted offers.

Which of the following derivation is correct?
A. All accepted offers are contracts
B. All agreements are contracts
C. All contracts are accepted offers
D. None of the above

739. No minor can enter into a contract of work. Working in a shop can be done only by a contract. Which of the following derivation is correct?
A. A minor cannot work in a shop
B. A shop cannot contract with a minor
C. There cannot be a contract to which minor is a party
D. None of the above

ANSWERS

1	2	3	4	5	6	7	8	9	10
A	A	A	C	A	B	C	B	C	C
11	**12**	**13**	**14**	**15**	**16**	**17**	**18**	**19**	**20**
D	B	B	D	A	D	A	A	A	D
21	**22**	**23**	**24**	**25**	**26**	**27**	**28**	**29**	**30**
C	C	B	D	A	A	C	B	C	B
31	**32**	**33**	**34**	**35**	**36**	**37**	**38**	**39**	**40**
C	B	A	C	A	A	D	A	A	C
41	**42**	**43**	**44**	**45**	**46**	**47**	**48**	**49**	**50**
B	B	A	C	B	C	C	A	D	A
51	**52**	**53**	**54**	**55**	**56**	**57**	**58**	**59**	**60**
D	A	C	B	A	C	A	C	D	A

61	**62**	**63**	**64**	**65**	**66**	**67**	**68**	**69**	**70**
C	A	D	C	A	D	D	B	C	A
71	**72**	**73**	**74**	**75**	**76**	**77**	**78**	**79**	**80**
B	B	A	B	C	D	D	C	A	A
81	**82**	**83**	**84**	**85**	**86**	**87**	**88**	**89**	**90**
D	C	B	A	C	B	B	C	A	C
91	**92**	**93**	**94**	**95**	**96**	**97**	**98**	**99**	**100**
C	A	C	B	C	A	A	D	B	B
101	**102**	**103**	**104**	**105**	**106**	**107**	**108**	**109**	**110**
C	C	D	C	A	A	B	B	B	D
111	**112**	**113**	**114**	**115**	**116**	**117**	**118**	**119**	**120**
A	D	A	D	C	D	D	B	D	A
121	**122**	**123**	**124**	**125**	**126**	**127**	**128**	**129**	**130**
A	D	B	B	B	A	D	C	B	C
131	**132**	**133**	**134**	**135**	**136**	**137**	**138**	**139**	**140**
A	D	C	B	A	C	D	D	A	B
141	**142**	**143**	**144**	**145**	**146**	**147**	**148**	**149**	**150**
C	A	D	B	A	B	C	B	B	B
151	**152**	**153**	**154**	**155**	**156**	**157**	**158**	**159**	**160**
C	D	D	A	B	D	B	C	C	C
161	**162**	**163**	**164**	**165**	**166**	**167**	**168**	**169**	**170**
D	C	D	C	A	D	C	C	C	A
171	**172**	**173**	**174**	**175**	**176**	**177**	**178**	**179**	**180**
D	A	B	C	C	A	D	B	D	B
181	**182**	**183**	**184**	**185**	**186**	**187**	**188**	**189**	**190**
C	B	B	D	B	D	D	D	C	A
191	**192**	**193**	**194**	**195**	**196**	**197**	**198**	**199**	**200**
B	A	C	B	D	A	B	A	D	C
201	**202**	**203**	**204**	**205**	**206**	**207**	**208**	**209**	**210**
D	C	B	D	C	C	D	C	C	B
211	**212**	**213**	**214**	**215**	**216**	**217**	**218**	**219**	**220**
D	A	C	B	C	A	B	D	A	C
221	**222**	**223**	**224**	**225**	**226**	**227**	**228**	**229**	**230**
A	A	C	D	A	D	D	C	B	A
231	**232**	**233**	**234**	**235**	**236**	**237**	**238**	**239**	**240**
C	A	B	C	D	D	C	D	A	C
241	**242**	**243**	**244**	**245**	**246**	**247**	**248**	**249**	**250**
A	C	A	C	D	D	A	C	D	C
251	**252**	**253**	**254**	**255**	**256**	**257**	**258**	**259**	**260**
C	A	A	B	A	D	B	B	B	A

261	262	263	264	265	266	267	268	269	270
B	C	B	D	A	C	D	C	B	D
271	272	273	274	275	276	277	278	279	280
C	A	B	D	D	B	A	C	A	A
281	282	283	284	285	286	287	288	289	290
B	D	A	A	A	C	B	A	B	A
291	292	293	294	295	296	297	298	299	300
C	A	A	C	D	B	C	C	D	B
301	302	303	304	305	306	307	308	309	310
C	C	B	A	B	D	B	C	C	C
311	312	313	314	315	316	317	318	319	320
A	D	D	B	B	B	A	A	B	B
321	322	323	324	325	326	327	328	329	330
C	A	C	D	D	D	B	B	A	B
331	332	333	334	335	336	337	338	339	340
A	B	B	B	B	B	B	B	C	A
341	342	343	344	345	346	347	348	349	350
D	A	A	C	A	D	A	C	B	D
351	352	353	354	355	356	357	358	359	360
A	C	D	A	B	C	A	B	A	D
361	362	363	364	365	366	367	368	369	370
B	A	B	C	D	A	C	B	C	C
371	372	373	374	375	376	377	378	379	380
B	C	B	B	D	D	C	D	C	C
381	382	383	384	385	386	387	388	389	390
A	B	A	C	B	D	A	D	B	B
391	392	393	394	395	396	397	398	399	400
A	D	B	D	D	D	B	A	C	C
401	402	403	404	405	406	407	408	409	410
B	D	A	B	C	B	D	C	B	D
411	412	413	414	415	416	417	418	419	420
B	A	A	C	A	D	A	A	C	D
421	422	423	424	425	426	427	428	429	430
A	A	C	A	A	D	B	C	A	A
431	432	433	434	435	436	437	438	439	440
D	D	D	D	B	C	C	C	B	A
441	442	443	444	445	446	447	448	449	450
B	B	D	C	B	A	D	B	D	A
451	452	453	454	455	456	457	458	459	460
D	D	C	D	A	B	A	B	D	D

461	462	463	464	465	466	467	468	469	470
B	C	B	B	A	B	A	B	A	D
471	472	473	474	475	476	477	478	479	480
B	B	B	D	C	A	B	A	A	B
481	482	483	484	485	486	487	488	489	490
B	D	A	C	A	C	A	A	C	C
491	492	493	494	495	496	497	498	499	500
D	B	B	A	B	B	B	B	D	D
501	502	503	504	505	506	507	508	509	510
C	C	D	B	B	A	A	C	B	C
511	512	513	514	515	516	517	518	519	520
D	A	A	B	D	A	B	A	C	B
521	522	523	524	525	526	527	528	529	530
B	A	B	B	B	C	D	B	B	C
531	532	533	534	535	536	537	538	539	540
B	C	A	C	B	A	B	A	A	A
541	542	543	544	545	546	547	548	549	550
C	B	D	D	C	B	C	D	B	A
551	552	553	554	555	556	557	558	559	560
B	A	D	C	D	A	A	A	B	A
561	562	563	564	565	566	567	568	569	570
C	B	D	C	C	C	B	B	D	C
571	572	573	574	575	576	577	578	579	580
C	C	C	A	C	B	D	A	A	B
581	582	583	584	585	586	587	588	589	590
D	B	A	B	A	B	C	A	B	A
591	592	593	594	595	596	597	598	599	600
A	C	D	A	D	D	D	D	A	A
601	602	603	604	605	606	607	608	609	610
D	A	B	A	D	B	B	D	B	B
611	612	613	614	615	616	617	618	619	620
D	B	D	D	A	C	D	D	A	C
621	622	623	624	625	626	627	628	629	630
B	D	A	D	A	C	A	A	D	B
631	632	633	634	635	636	637	638	639	640
D	A	D	C	C	A	B	C	C	B
641	642	643	644	645	646	647	648	649	650
C	A	A	B	B	C	C	B	B	B
651	652	653	654	655	656	657	658	659	660
C	C	B	C	A	C	C	C	B	D

661	**662**	**663**	**664**	**665**	**666**	**667**	**668**	**669**	**670**
A	B	B	B	A	A	B	B	B	D
671	**672**	**673**	**674**	**675**	**676**	**677**	**678**	**679**	**680**
B	B	C	C	A	C	A	C	D	B
681	**682**	**683**	**684**	**685**	**686**	**687**	**688**	**689**	**690**
C	A	C	D	B	B	A	C	B	C
691	**692**	**693**	**694**	**695**	**696**	**697**	**698**	**699**	**700**
B	D	A	D	C	D	D	A	A	B
701	**702**	**703**	**704**	**705**	**706**	**707**	**708**	**709**	**710**
C	D	B	A	D	B	B	B	C	A
711	**712**	**713**	**714**	**715**	**716**	**717**	**718**	**719**	**720**
C	C	B	A	A	C	B	B	B	D
721	**722**	**723**	**724**	**725**	**726**	**727**	**728**	**729**	**730**
A	C	D	A	A	A	D	D	A	D
731	**732**	**733**	**734**	**735**	**736**	**737**	**738**	**739**	
C	A	A	A	A	C	C	B	A	

Analytical Reasoning

1 Series

LETTER SERIES

In letter series, the letters follow a definite order. The given series of letters can be in natural order or in reverse order or combination of both. The letters may be skipped or repeated or consecutive. The given series may be single or may comprise two different series merged at alternate positions. While attempting questions on letter series one should note the pattern of alphabet series.

Alphabets in natural series

A B C D E F G H I J K L M N O P Q R S T U V W X Y Z
1st 5th 10th 15th 20th 25th

are:

Alphabets in reverse series

Z Y X W V U T S R Q P O N M L K J I H G F E D C B A
1st 5th 10th 15th 20th 25th

Note: On reaching Z, the series restarts from A and on reaching A, it restarts from Z.

Example

1. A Z B Y C ?

A. D

B. X

C. U

D. E

Ans.: (B) There are two alternate series.

Series I : A B C (Consecutive letters in natural series)

Series II : Z Y X (Consecutive letters in reverse series)

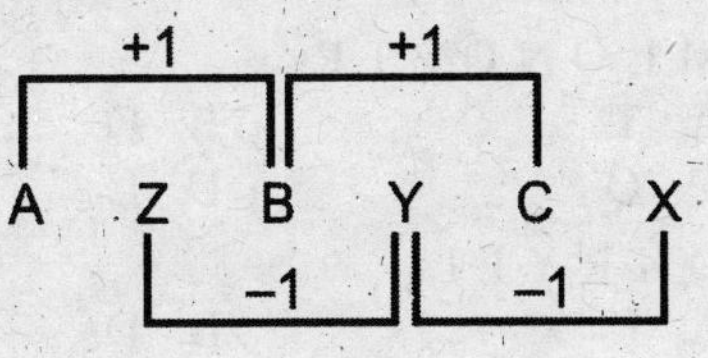

REPEAT SERIES

In this type of series small letters of the alphabet are used to make a set of letters which are repeated. The candidate has to find the set of letters which will fit the blanks left in the given series in such a manner that one section of the series is further repeated in the same manner.

Example

2. Which of the following groups of letters will complete the given series?

ba-b-aab-a-b

A. baab B. abba

C. abaa D. babb

Ans.: (B) The series is baab, baab, baab. Here the section 'baab' is repeated in the series. Solving steps : The candidate has to look for clues to solve such series pattern. 'aab' in the series indicates that 'b' in this series is preceded by two 'a' so, the first blank and the last blank will be filled by 'a'. Now the first set is formed, *i.e.*, 'baab' in the beginning. This set is repeated, so the second and third blanks will have 'b' filling them.

NUMBER SERIES

In this type of series, the set of given numbers in a series are related to one another in a particular pattern or manner. The relationship between the numbers may be (i) consecutive odd/even numbers; (ii) consecutive prime numbers; (iii) squares/cubes of some numbers with/without variation of addition or subtraction of some number; (iv) sum/product/ difference of preceding numbers; (v) addition/ subtraction/multiplication/division by some number; and (vi) many more combinations of the relationships given above.

Example

3. Complete the given series. 2, 14, 98, 686, ?

A. 1976 B. 2548

C. 980 D. 4802

Ans.: (D) The numbers are multiplied by 7 to obtain the next numbers.

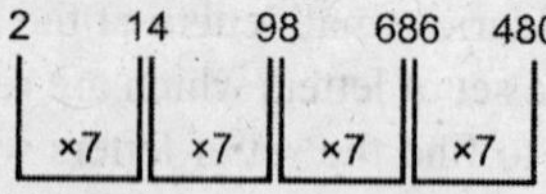

The given series may also comprise of two alternate series merged as one.

MIXED SERIES

Mixed series comprises of the combinations of letters and numbers. In this type of series, the letters and numbers may have a common sequence pattern or may have separate sequence patterns.

Example

4. What should come in the place of question mark in the following letter-number combination?

F6, H8, J10, L12, ?

A. N15 B. O14

C. N14 D. O13

Ans.: (C) The letters are moved two steps forward and the number indicates the position of the letter in the alphabet series.

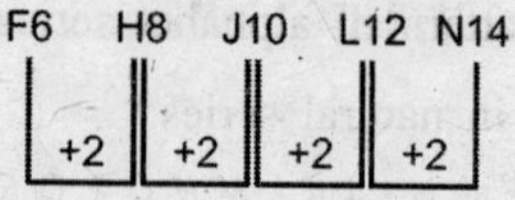

EXERCISE

Directions (Qs. 1 to 8): *In each of the following series determine the order of the letters. Then from the given options select the one which will complete the given series.*

1. GH, JL, NQ, SW, YD, ?

A. EJ B. FJ

C. EL D. FL

2. AI, BJ, CK, ?

A. DL B. DM

C. GH D. LM

3. b e d f ? h j ? l

A. i m B. m i

C. i n D. j m

4. ADVENTURE, DVENTURE, DVENTUR, ?, VENTU

A. DVENT B. VENTURE

C. VENTUR D. DVENTU

E. None of these

5. PERPENDICULAR, ERPENDICULA, RPENDICUL, ?

A. PENDICUL B. PENDIC

C. ENDIC D. ENDICU

E. None of these

6. ATTRIBUTION, TTRIBUTIO, RIBUTIO, IBUTI,?

A. IBU B. UT

C. UTI D. BUT

E. None of these

7. M, N, O, L, R, I, V, ?

A. A B. E

C. F D. H

E. Z

8. A, CD, GHI, ?, UVWXY

A. LMNO B. MNO

C. MNOP D. NOPQ

Directions (Qs. 9 to 15): *Which letter(s) in each of the following series is wrong or is misfit in the series?*

9. Z A W B X C

A. D B. C

C. X D. W

10. M L O N Q P T R

A. T B. O

C. Q D. L

11. D K R Y F L

A. L B. D

C. R D. Y

12. L N Q Γ W Z C F

A. C B. Q
C. L D. F

13. XW, DC, CB, NM, PQ, QP

A. NM B. CB
C. PQ D. XW

14. B E I N S A I

A. A B. E
C. S D. I

15. Z T P K H F

A. Z B. P
C. T D. F

Directions (Qs. Nos. 16 to 20): *In each of the following letter series, some of the letters are missing which are given in that order as one of the alternatives below it. Choose the correct alternative.*

16. ba _ cb _ b _ bab _

A. acbb B. bacc
C. bcaa D. cabb

17. c _ bba _ cab _ ac _ ab _ ac

A. abebe B. acbcb
C. babec D. bcacb

18. ab _ baa _ _ ab _

A. aaaaa B. aabaa
C. aabab D. baabb

19. _ bc _ ca _ aba _ c _ ca

A. abcbb B. bbbec
C. bacba D. abbec

20. ab _ aa _ bbb _ aaa _ bbba

A. abba B. baab
C. aaab D. abab

Directions (Qs. 21 to 25): *Choose the correct alternative that will continue the same pattern and replace the question mark in the given series.*

21. 3, 9, 27, 81, 243, ?

A. 486 B. 729
C. 972 D. 359

22. 1, 6, 12, 19, 27 ?

A. 38 B. 35
C. 36 D. 54

23. 125, 80, 45, 20, ?

A. 5 B. 8
C. 10 D. 12

24. 120, 99, 80, 63, 48, ?

A. 35 B. 38
C. 39 D. 40

25. 589654237, 89654237, 8965423, 965423, ?

A. 58965 B. 65423
C. 89654 D. 96542

Directions (Qs. 26–33): *In each series given below, what would come in place of the question-mark?*

26. 2B, 4C, 8E, 14H, ?

A. 20L B. 22L
C. 21I D. 16K

27. C(1)L, F(4)O, I(9)R, L(16)U, ?

A. P(27)W B. N(24)Y
C. M(23)X D. O(25)X

28. 3F, 6G, 11I, 18L, ?

A. 27P B. 21O
C. 27Q D. 25N

29. W(1)A, X(4)Z, Y9Y, ?, A(25)W

A. X(11)Z B. Z(21)A
C. Z(16)X D. Z(14)X

30. 81Y, 27S, 9N, 3J, ?

A. 0H B. IG
C. 0F D. IE

31. E5, K11, Q17, ?

A. X20 B. Y24
C. V22 D. W25

32. D2, I3, N6, S18, ?

A. V72 B. W36
C. Y90 D. X108

33. 3J, 6M, 12L, ?, 48N

A. 24O B. 8M
C. 26M D. 22O

Directions (Qs. Nos. 34 and 35) : *Which of the following does not fit in the letter number series given below?*

34. G4T, J10R, M20P, P43N, S90L

A. J10R B. S90L
C. M20P D. G4T

35. B0R, G3U, E3P, J7S, H9N

A. E3P
B. J7S
C. H9N
D. G3U

ANSWERS

1	2	3	4	5	6	7	8	9	10
D	A	A	C	E	C	B	C	D	A
11	**12**	**13**	**14**	**15**	**16**	**17**	**18**	**19**	**20**
A	C	C	C	B	B	B	B	A	B
21	**22**	**23**	**24**	**25**	**26**	**27**	**28**	**29**	**30**
B	C	A	A	D	B	D	A	C	B
31	**32**	**33**	**34**	**35**					
C	D	A	A	B					

EXPLANATORY ANSWERS

1. 1st letter:

$G \xrightarrow{+3} J \xrightarrow{+4} N \xrightarrow{+5} S \xrightarrow{+6} Y \xrightarrow{+7} (F)$

2nd letter:

$H \xrightarrow{+4} L \xrightarrow{+5} Q \xrightarrow{+6} W \xrightarrow{+7} D \xrightarrow{+8} (L)$

2. 1st letter: $A \xrightarrow{+1} B \xrightarrow{+1} C \xrightarrow{+1} (D)$

2nd letter: $I \xrightarrow{+1} J \xrightarrow{+1} K \xrightarrow{+1} (L)$

3. The series may be divided into groups as shown: b e d / f ? h / j ? l
Clearly in the first group, the second and third letters are respectively three and two steps ahead of the first letter. A similar pattern would follow in the second and third groups.

4. One letter from the beginning and one from the end of a term are removed, one by one, in alternate steps.

5. Each term of the series is obtained by removing two letters from the preceding term one from the beginning and one from the end. So, the missing term is PENDICU.

6. In the first step, one letter from the beginning and one from the end of a term are removed to give the next term. In the second step, two letters from the beginning of a term are removed. These two steps are repeated alternately.

7. The given sequence is a combination of two series: I. M, O, R, V and II. N, L, I, ?

The pattern in I is: $M \xrightarrow{+2} O \xrightarrow{+3} R \xrightarrow{+4} V$

The pattern in II is: $N \xrightarrow{-2} L \xrightarrow{-3} I \xrightarrow{-4} (E)$

8. Each term consists of consecutive letters in order. The number of letters in the terms goes on increasing by one at each step. Also, there is a gap of one letter between the last letter of the first term and the first letter of the second term; a gap of two letters between the last letter of the second term and the first letter of the third term; and so on. So, there should be a gap of three letters between the last letter of the third term and the first letter of the desired term.

9. There are two alternate series I. Z, Y, X and II. A, B, C

The pattern in I is : $Z \xrightarrow{-1} (Y) \xrightarrow{-1} X$

The pattern in II is : $A \xrightarrow{+1} B \xrightarrow{+1} C$

10. Two consecutive letters are written backwards.

$\overleftarrow{ML}\ \overleftarrow{ON}\ \overleftarrow{OP}\ \overleftarrow{SR}$

S should be in place of T.

11. The pattern in this series is moving the letters seven steps forward.

D K R Y F (M)
+7 +7 +7 +7 +7

M should be in place of L.

12. The pattern in the series is +3

Ⓚ N Q T W Z C F

+3 +3 +3 +3 +3 +3 +3

K should be in place of L.

13. The series is made with any two consecutive letters written backwards.

XW DC CB NM QP

← ← ← ← ←

Q should come before P in the series.

14. The difference between the letters is increased by one at each step.

B E I N Ⓣ A I

+3 +4 +5 +6 +7 +8

T should be in place of S.

15. The difference between the letters is decreased by one at each step.

Z T O K H F

-6 -5 -4 -3 -2

O should be in place of P.

16. The series is babc/babc/babc. Thus, the pattern 'babc' is repeated.

17. The series is cabbac/cabbac/cabbac. Thus, the pattern 'cabbac' is repeated.

18. The series is aba/aba/aba/aba. Thus, the pattern 'aba' is repeated.

19. The series is abc/bca/cab/abc/bca. Thus, the letters change places in a cyclic order.

20. The series is abb/aaabbb/aaaabbbb/a. Thus, the letters are repeated twice, then thrice, then four times and so on.

21. The numbers in the series are multiplied by 3 to get the next numbers.

22. The difference between the numbers in the series increases by 1, after beginning from 5,

1 6 12 19 27 36

i.e., +5 +6 +7 +8 +9

23. The pattern is –45, –35, –25, ...
So, missing term = 20 – 15 = 5.

24. The pattern is –21, –19, –17, –15,.....
So, missing term = 48 – 13 = 35.

25. The digits are removed one-by-one from the beginning and the end in order alternately, so as to obtain the subsequent terms of the series.

26. The sequence of numbers is +2, +4, +6, +8 and sequence of letters is +1, +2, +3, +4.

27. The corresponding letters are moved 3 steps forward and the sequence of numbers is +3, +5, +7, +9.

28. The sequence of numbers is +3, +5, +7, +9 and the letters are moved 1, 2, 3, 4 steps forward.

29. The letters on the left are in reverse series, the letters on the right are in natural series, and the numbers are squares of numbers in natural order starting from 1.

30. The numbers are divided by 3 at each step and the letters are moved 6, 5, 4, 3 steps backward.

31. The series comprises of random letters and numbers indicate the position of the letter in alphabet series.

32. The letters are moved five steps forward and every third number is the product of two preceding numbers.

33. Every number is double the previous number and the sequence of letters is +3, –1 (3 steps forward, 1 step backward) which is repeated.

34. The letters on the left are moved 3 steps forward, the letters on the right are moved 2 steps backward and the sequence of numbers is (4 × 2) +1, (9 × 2) +2, (20 × 2) +3, (43 × 2) +4. So, J9R should be in place of J10R.

35. The sequence of letters on the left is +5, –2 (5 steps forward, 2 steps backward) which is repeated, the sequence of letters on the right is +3, –5 (3 steps forward, 5 steps backward) which is repeated, and the numbers are the sum of two preceeding numbers. So, J6S should be in place of J7S.

●●●

2

Word Analogy

In Analogy Tests, the relationship between two given words is established and then applied to the other words. The type of relationship may vary, so while attempting such questions the first step is to identify the type of relationship, which can be any one of the following.

EXERCISE

Directions : *In the questions given below one term is missing. Based on the relationship of the two given words find the missing term from the given options.*

1. HUNGER : FOOD : : THIRST : ?
(*a*) Water (*b*) Drink
(*c*) Tea (*d*) Coffee

2. HUNTER : GUN : : WRITER : ?
(*a*) Book (*b*) Pen
(*c*) Poem (*d*) Page

3. WOOL : SHEEP : : SILK : ?
(*a*) Saree (*b*) String
(*c*) Silkworm (*d*) Moth

4. FOOD : STOMACH : : FUEL : ?
(*a*) Engine (*b*) Automobile
(*c*) Rail (*d*) Aeroplane

5. WATER : SAND : : OCEAN : ?
(*a*) Island (*b*) River
(*c*) Desert (*d*) Waves

6. ADULT : BABY : : FLOWER : ?
(*a*) Seed (*b*) Bud
(*c*) Fruit (*d*) Butterfly

7. WRITER : READER : : PRODUCER : ?
(*a*) Creator (*b*) Contractor
(*c*) Creature (*d*) Consumer

8. ENTRANCE : EXIT : : LOYALTY : ?
(*a*) Treachery (*b*) Patriotism
(*c*) Fidelity (*d*) Reward

9. MOTHER : MATERNAL : : FATHER : ?
(*a*) Eternal (*b*) Detrimental
(*c*) Paternal (*d*) Formidable

10. PEARL : NECKLACE : : FLOWER : ?
(*a*) Plant (*b*) Garden
(*c*) Petal (*d*) Bouquet

11. ALPHABET : WORD : : WORD : ?
(*a*) Sound (*b*) Music
(*c*) Sentence (*d*) Dictionary

12. LIFE : DEATH : : HOPE : ?
(*a*) Cry (*b*) Pain
(*c*) Despair (*d*) Sad

13. GOOD : BAD : : VIRTUE : ?
(*a*) Blame (*b*) Sin
(*c*) Despair (*d*) Vice

14. BIRD : FLY : : SNAKE : ?
(*a*) Timid (*b*) Clatter
(*c*) Crawl (*d*) Hole

15. CAT : MOUSE : : BIRD : ?
(*a*) Cage (*b*) Trap
(*c*) Eagle (*d*) Worm

16. STATE : EXILE
(*a*) Police : Arrest
(*b*) Judge : Convict
(*c*) Constitution : Amendment
(*d*) Church : Excommunicate

17. CAPRICIOUSNESS : RELIABILITY
(*a*) Extemporaneous : Predictability
(*b*) Unreliable : Inhuman
(*c*) Tenacious : Practicality
(*d*) Arbitrary : Whimsical

18. LOATH : COERCION
(*a*) Detest : Caressing
(*b*) Irritate : Caressing

(*c*) Irate : Antagonism
(*d*) Reluctant : Persuasion

19. SCALES : FISH
(*a*) Lady : Dress (*b*) Tree : Leaves
(*c*) Bird : Feather (*d*) Skin : Man

20. TREE : SAPLING
(*a*) Hut : Mansion (*b*) Giant : Dwarf
(*c*) Horse : Foal (*d*) Ant : Elephant

21. CHALK : BLACKBOARD
(*a*) Door : Handle (*b*) Table : Chair
(*c*) Ink : Paper (*d*) Type : Paint

22. PRIMEVAL : MEDIEVAL
(*a*) Dinosaur : Dragon
(*b*) Gorilla : Soldier
(*c*) Evolution : Revelation
(*d*) Thorn : Rose

23. TRILOGY : NOVEL
(*a*) Rice : Husk (*b*) Milk : Cream
(*c*) Fabric : Weaving (*d*) Serial : Episode

24. PEDANT : ERUDITION
(*a*) Prude : Modesty
(*b*) Blunt : Politician
(*c*) Diplomats : Tactless
(*d*) Enemy : Friendly

25. FURY : IRE
(*a*) Convulsion : Spasm
(*b*) Amusement : Happiness
(*c*) Joke : Laugh
(*d*) Dispassion : Emotion

EXPLANATORY ANSWERS

1. ***(a)*** **:** Hunger is satiated by food, thirst by water.
2. ***(b)*** **:** Weapon of a hunter is a gun, weapon of a writer is a pen.
3. ***(c)*** **:** Wool is obtained from sheep, silk is obtained from silkworm.
4. ***(a)*** **:** Food is consumed in stomach, fuel is consumed in engine.
5. ***(c)*** **:** The related words are near opposites.
6. ***(b)*** **:** The youngone of an adult is a baby and that of a flower is a bud.
7. ***(d)*** **:** A writer aims to please the readers by his writings, a producer aims to please the consumers by his products.
8. ***(a)*** **:** The related words are opposites.
9. ***(c)*** **:** Relations on the mother's side are maternal and on the father's side paternal.
10. ***(d)*** **:** Many pearls make a necklace, many flowers make a bouquet.
11. ***(c)*** **:** More than one alphabet make a word, more than one word make a sentence.
12. ***(c)*** **:** The related words are opposites.
13. ***(d)*** **:** The related words are opposites.
14. ***(c)*** **:** Birds fly, snakes crawl.
15. ***(d)*** **:** Cat chases the mouse, bird chases the worm.
16. ***(d)*** **:** Punishment of leaving the State is exile, punishment of leaving the Church is excommunication.
17. ***(c)*** **:** The related words are antonyms.
18. ***(d)*** **:** Loathing is the result of constant coersion, reluctance is the result of constant persuasion.
19. ***(d)*** **:** Covering of the fish is scales, covering of man is skin.
20. ***(c)*** **:** Young tree is a sapling, young horse is a foal.
21. ***(c)*** **:** Chalk is used to write on blackboard, ink is used to write on paper.
22. ***(a)*** **:** The related words represent almost the same time period and answer option represents almost the same sized creatures.
23. ***(d)*** **:** Trilogy is section of a novel, episode is a section of a serial.
24. ***(a)*** **:** The related words are synonyms.
25. ***(b)*** **:** Fury causes ire, amusement causes happiness.

●●●

3 Number Analogy

In number analogy also, the relationship between the given numbers is detected and then applied to the second part to find the missing numbers. This relationship between the numbers can be based on any of the following patterns : *(i)* numbers can be odd/even/prime numbers; *(ii)* numbers can be multiples of one number; *(iii)* numbers can be squares/cubes of different numbers; *(iv)* some numbers can be added to/subtracted from/multiplied to/divided into the first number to get the second number; *(v)* the second number can be the sum/product/difference of the digits of first number; and *(vi)* combinations of any mathematical calculations given above can apply to the relationship between the two given numbers.

EXERCISE

Directions : *In the following questions, select the number from the given options which follows the same relationship as shared between the first two numbers.*

1. 1 : 11 : : 2 : ?
(*a*) 20 (*b*) 22
(*c*) 24 (*d*) 44

2. $\frac{1}{7} : \frac{1}{14} : : \frac{1}{9} : ?$
(*a*) $\frac{1}{88}$ (*b*) $\frac{1}{80}$
(*c*) $\frac{1}{81}$ (*d*) $\frac{1}{18}$

3. 0.16 : 0.0016 : : 1.02 : ?
(*a*) 10.20 (*b*) 0.102
(*c*) 0.0102 (*d*) 1.020

4. 663 : 884 : : 221 : ?
(*a*) 332 (*b*) 554
(*c*) 773 (*d*) 442

5. 16 : 0.16 : : ?
(*a*) 2 : 0.02 (*b*) 7 : 0.007
(*c*) 1.3 : 0.13 (*d*) 0.01 : 0.001

6. $3 : \frac{1}{3}$: : ?
(*a*) 6 : 12 (*b*) 5 : 2/15
(*c*) 8 : 1/8 (*d*) 9 : 27

7. 65 : 13 : : 180 : ?
(*a*) 93 (*b*) 36
(*c*) 133 (*d*) 102

8. 125 : 27 : : 343 : ?
(*a*) 729 (*b*) 64
(*c*) 216 (*d*) 512

9. 357 : 73 : : ?
(*a*) 429 : 94 (*b*) 201 : 21
(*c*) 138 : 38 (*d*) 93 : 39

10. 731 : 902 : : 655 : ?
(*a*) 646 (*b*) 800
(*c*) 793 (*d*) 556

11. 162 : 9 : : 310 : ?
(*a*) 33 (*b*) 27
(*c*) 16 (*d*) 4

12. 13 : 17 : : 15 : ?
(*a*) 19 (*b*) 11
(*c*) 21 (*d*) 16

13. 225 : 15 : : 256 : ?
(*a*) 26 (*b*) 16
(*c*) 20 (*d*) 28

14. 46 : 48 : : 54 : ?
(*a*) 59 (*b*) 40
(*c*) 67 (*d*) 62

15. 33 : 36 : : 21 : ?
(*a*) 9 (*b*) 18
(*c*) 25 (*d*) 32

EXPLANATORY ANSWERS

1. (b) : The first number is repeated to obtain the second number.

2. (d) : The first fraction is multiplied by half to obtain the second fraction.

$$\frac{1}{7} : \frac{1}{14} :: \frac{1}{9} : \frac{1}{18}$$

$\times \frac{1}{2}$; $\times \frac{1}{2}$

3. (c) : The decimals are divided by 100.

0.16 : 0.0016 : : 1.02 : 0.0102

÷ 100 ; ÷ 100

4. (d) : The digits at tens and hundreds place is same but the digit at the units place is half the other identical digits.

66 3 : 88 4 : : 22 1 : 44 2

5. (a) : Of the two related numbers, the second number is the result of first number divided by 100.

16 : 0.16 : : 2 : 0.02

÷ 100 ; ÷ 100

6. (c) : Of the two related numbers, the second number is the part fraction of the first number, *i.e.* 3 is related to one-third $\left(\frac{1}{3}\right)$. Similarly, 8 will be related to one-eighth $\left(\frac{1}{8}\right)$.

7. (b) : The first number is divided by 5 to get the second number.

65 : 13 : : 180 : 36

÷ 5 ; ÷ 5

8. (a) : The numbers are cubes of different odd numbers.

125 : 27 : : 343 : 729

↓ ↓ ↓ ↓

5^3 3^3 7^3 9^3

9. (a) : The central digit of the first number is left out and the corner digits written in reverse order to get the second number.

357 : 73 : : 429 : 94

10. (a) : The sum of the digits of both the numbers is same.

731 : 902 → 7 + 3 + 1
= 9 + 0 + 2 *i.e.* 11 = 11

655 : 646 → 6 + 5 + 5
= 6 + 4 + 6 *i.e.* 16 = 16

11. (d) : The sum of the digits of the first number is the second number.

162 : 9 : : 310 : 4

1 + 6 + 2 ; 3 + 1 + 0

12. (a) : First number plus 4 gives the second number.

13 : 17 : : 15 : 19

+4 ; +4

13. (b) : The root of first number is the second number.

225 : 15 : : 256 : 16

$\sqrt{225}$; $\sqrt{256}$

14. (b) : The product of the digits of first number is multiplied by 2 to get the second number.

46 : 48 : : 54 : 40

(4 × 6) 2 ; (5 × 4) 2

15. (a) : The square of the sum of the digits of the first number is the second number.

33 : 36 : : 21 : 9

$(3 + 3)^2$; $(2 + 1)^2$

●●●

4 Odd One Out

In this type of classification, four Words/numbers/groups of letters are given out of which three are almost same in matter or meaning and only one word/number/group of letters is different from the common three. One has to find out the one which is different from the rest.

EXERCISE

Directions : *In each of the following questions, three words are alike in some manner. Spot the odd one out.*

1. (*a*) Green (*b*) Red (*c*) Colour (*d*) Orange

2. (*a*) Stable (*b*) Hole (*c*) Canoe (*d*) Sty

3. (*a*) Nose (*b*) Eyes (*c*) Skin (*d*) Teeth

4. (*a*) Venus (*b*) Moon (*c*) Pluto (*d*) Mars

5. (*a*) Happy (*b*) Gloomy (*c*) Lively (*d*) Cheerful

Directions : *Three of the following four in each question are alike in a certain way and so form a group. Select the group of letters that does not belong to that group.*

6. (*a*) ACE (*b*) LOR (*c*) GIK (*d*) VXZ

7. (*a*) TSR (*b*) LKJ (*c*) PQO (*d*) HGF

8. (*a*) EF LM (*b*) KJ SR (*c*) XW HG (*d*) ED YX

9. (*a*) JOPK (*b*) BOPC (*c*) QOPR (*d*) TOPS

10. (*a*) DfH (*b*) MoQ (*c*) UwY (*d*) lnO

Directions : *In each of the following questions, there are four options. Three numbers, in these options, are alike in certain manner. Only one number does not fit in. Choose the one which is different from the rest.*

11. (*a*) 1948 (*b*) 2401 (*c*) 966 (*d*) 1449

12. (*a*) 182 (*b*) 169 (*c*) 130 (*d*) 158

13. (*a*) 129 (*b*) 130 (*c*) 131 (*d*) 132

14. (*a*) 3215 (*b*) 9309 (*c*) 4721 (*d*) 2850

15. (*a*) 1776 (*b*) 2364 (*c*) 1976 (*d*) 3776

Directions : *In the following questions select the pair which is different from the other three.*

16. (*a*) Chair - Furniture (*b*) Shirt - Garment (*c*) Necklace - Jewellery (*d*) Bogie - Engine

17. (*a*) Crayon - Paper (*b*) Pencil - Lead (*c*) Pen - Ink (*d*) Brush - Paint

18. (*a*) War - Peace (*b*) Real - Natural (*c*) Premiere - First (*d*) Wrath - Anger

19. (*a*) Finger - Thimble (*b*) Head - Cap (*c*) Waist - Tiara (*d*) Foot - Shoe

20. (*a*) Day - Night (*b*) Clever - Foolish (*c*) Clear - Blurred (*d*) Arrive - Come

Directions : *In the following questions, which of the following pair of letters is different from the other three?*

21. (*a*) FGH - HIJ (*b*) PQR - RST (*c*) MNO - OPQ (*d*) CDE - DEF

22. (*a*) JuM - jUm (*b*) iLo - Ilo
(*c*) PSa - psA (*d*) ZeX - zEx

23. (*a*) NQT - JMP (*b*) CFI - RUX
(*c*) ADG - FGH (*d*) SVY - ORU

24. (*a*) DXD - XDX (*b*) KUK - UKU
(*c*) FHF - EHE (*d*) RSR - SRS

25. (*a*) AYT - BZU (*b*) FNG - EMF
(*c*) RWO - QVN (*d*) HJD - GIC

EXPLANATORY ANSWERS

1. (*c*) : All others are types of colour.

2. (*c*) : Canoe is a boat. Others are resting places of birds/animals.

3. (*d*) : All others are sense organs.

4. (*b*) : All others are planets.

5. (*b*) : All others are expressions of joy.

6. (*b*) : The sequence in each group is +2. Only option (*b*) has sequence in +3, *i.e.,*

A B C D E (+2 +2) L M N O P Q R (+3 +3)

G H I J K (+2 +2) V W X Y Z (+2 +2)

7. (*c*) : The sequence of alphabet in each group is in reverse order. Only option (*c*) has sequence in disturbed order.

8. (*a*) : Two consecutive alphabet in each group are in reverse sequence (–1), *i.e.,*

K J S R ; X W H G ; E D Y X
(–1 –1 –1 –1 –1 –1)

Only in option (*a*) the sequence is in natural order (+1), *i.e.,*

E F (+1) L M (+1)

9. (*d*) : In each group, letters 'OP' are common. The two corner alphabet are in natural order (+1); *i.e.,*

JOPK (+1) ; BOPC (+1) ; QOPR (+1)

Only in option (*d*) they are in reverse order (–1); *i.e.,*

TOPS (–1)

10. (*d*) : In other groups, only the alphabet in the centre is of lower case. In this option letter 'L' on the left is also in lower case.

11. (*a*) : Other numbers are divisible by 7.

12. (*d*) : Other numbers are multiples of 13.

13. (*c*) : 131 is a prime number.

14. (*b*) : In other numbers, no digit is repeated.

15. (*b*) : In other numbers, the last two digits are same.

16. (*d*) : Bogie is a part of train which is a type of conveyance. Chair, Shirt and Necklace are types of furniture, garment and jewellery respectively.

17. (*a*) : The medium used for writing with pencil is lead, with pen it is ink and with brush, it is paint. With crayon it should be wax.

18. (*a*) : The pair of words are opposite. Other pairs are synonyms.

19. (*c*) : Tiara is worn on the head.

20. (*d*) : Other words are opposite to each other.

21. (*d*) : In all other groups, the letters are in natural series and the last letter of first part is the first letter of the second part.

22. (*b*) : In all other groups, only the vowel is in lower case in the first part and in second part the case is reversed.

23. (*c*) : In all other groups, the letters jump two letters in between them.

24. (*c*) : In all other groups, the single letter in first part is repeated in the second and vice versa.

25. (*a*) : In all other groups, the letters in the first part are one step forward than the corresponding letters in the second part.

5 Coding and Decoding

Coding is a secretive language which is used to change the representation of the actual term/word/value. This coded language can be framed by *(i)* moving the letters one or more steps forward or backward; *(ii)* substituting numbers for letters and vice–versa; *(iii)* writing the letters of the given word in reverse order in part or in whole; and *(iv)* replacing the letters in their natural series by the same positioned letters in their reverse series.

There is variety in ways of coding. Coding language is not only for words and numbers but also for hiding a group of words, statements or even sentences. This form of coding pattern may appear to be confusing but after solving only a few questions it is very easy to understand. Questions based on this coding pattern require no moving of steps or straining efforts of calculations, but only quick tallying or comparing ability. The codes can be letters or numbers.

EXERCISE

Directions : *In the following questions select the right option which indicates the correct code for the word or letter given in the question.*

1. If MUSK is coded as 146816, then ZERO will be coded as :

(*a*) 113811 (*b*) 122912
(*c*) 15915 (*d*) 2651815

2. If BAD is coded as 7, HIS as 9, LOW will be coded as :

(*a*) 50 (*b*) 8
(*c*) 23 (*d*) 5

3. In a certain code LIBERATE is written as 56403170, TRIBAL will be written in the same code as :

(*a*) 734615 (*b*) 736415
(*c*) 136475 (*d*) 034615

4. In certain military code, SYSTEM is written as SYSMET, and NEARER as AENRER, what will be the code for FRACTION?

(*a*) CRAFNOIT (*b*) FRCAITNO
(*c*) CARFNOIT (*d*) FRACNOIT

5. If CRUDE is written as BSTED, then MOIST will be coded as :

(*a*) NNJRU (*b*) LNHRS
(*c*) NPJTU (*d*) LPHTS

6. In a certain code ALPACA is written as ACAPLA. How will ANIMAL be written in that code?

(*a*) LAMINA (*b*) ALAMIN
(*c*) LAMNIA (*d*) AAMLIN

7. In a certain code FINGER is written as DGLECP. What will be the code for KIDNEY?

(*a*) IGBLCW (*b*) IGCLBW
(*c*) IBCGLE (*d*) IGBKCV

8. In a certain code QUESTION is written as NXBVQLLQ. How will REPLY be coded?

(*a*) YHMOV (*b*) OBMVI
(*c*) VHSOB (*d*) OHMOV

9. If in a certain code SKEW is coded as PNCY, then what will JXQV will stand for?

(*a*) MUTS (*b*) MUST
(*c*) MTSU (*d*) STUM

10. In a certain code LONDON is written as MPOEPO. What will IVOHSZ mean in the same code?

(*a*) HUNGRY (*b*) HUNDRY
(*c*) GRUNHY (*d*) HONDUS

11. In a certain code language 8514 is a code for HEAD, 3945 for RIDE and 057 for BEG. What will be the code for GRADE?

(*a*) 71345 (*b*) 73415
(*c*) 74135 (*d*) 73145

12. If MOTHERLAND is coded as 9501623748, how will DREAM be coded?
(*a*) 82697 (*b*) 86297
(*c*) 82769 (*d*) 82679

13. If OATH is coded in a certain language as TEYL, then how will WORD be coded?
(*a*) BWRH (*b*) HRWB
(*c*) BSWH (*d*) CSXI

14. If FINANCE is coded as GKQESIL, then how will BANK be coded in the same manner?
(*a*) CBOL (*b*) CDRP
(*c*) CCQO (*d*) CCPN

15. PLANNING is coded in a certain language as UFFHSCSA. How will AUTHORITY be coded in the same language?
(*a*) FOYBTLNND (*b*) FYOTBNNLT
(*c*) FBOYTLNTN (*d*) FBOYTNLTN

EXPLANATORY ANSWERS

1. (*b*) : The coded number signifies the position of the alphabet in its reverse order of the alphabetical series (ZYXW...)

M U S K → MUSK
↓ ↓ ↓ ↓
14th 6th 8th 16th → 146816

Similarly,

Z E R O → ZERO
↓ ↓ ↓ ↓
1st 22nd 9th 12th → 122912

2. (*d*) : The coded number is the sum of number digits signifying the position of the alphabet in the natural order.

B A D
↓ ↓ ↓
2nd 1st 4th *i.e.*, 2 + 1 + 4 = 7

Similarly,

H I S
↓ ↓ ↓
8th 9th 19th *i.e.*, 8 + 9 + 19 = 36
further, 3 + 6 = 9

Also,

L O W
↓ ↓ ↓
12th 15th 23rd *i.e.*, 12 + 15 + 23 = 50
further, 5 + 0 = 0

3. (*b*) : The letters of the word TRIBAL are picked from LIBERATE. So will be the coded numbers.

L I B E R A T E → given word
5 6 4 0 3 1 7 0 → codes

Similarly,

T R I B A L → word to be coded
7 3 6 4 1 5 → answer codes

4. (*c*) : The word is divided into two equal parts and the letters of each part are written in reverse order.

Similarly,

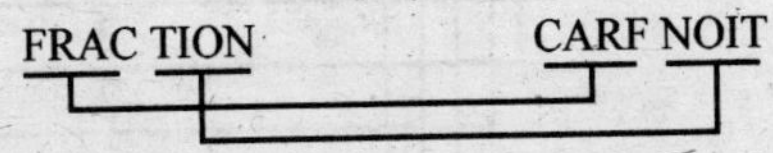

5. (*d*) : The code is formed by moving the letters one step backwards and one step forward alternately.

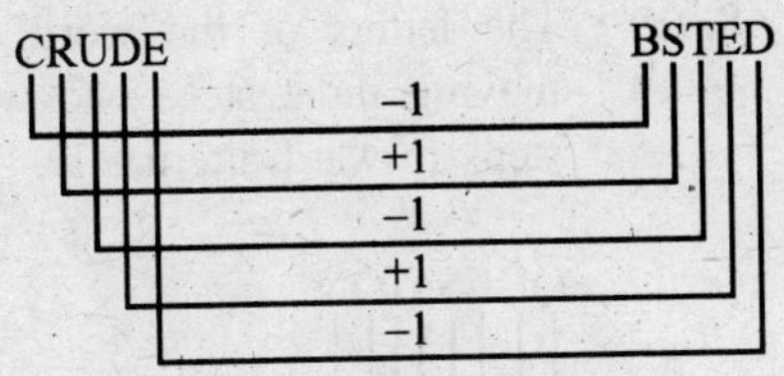

Similarly,

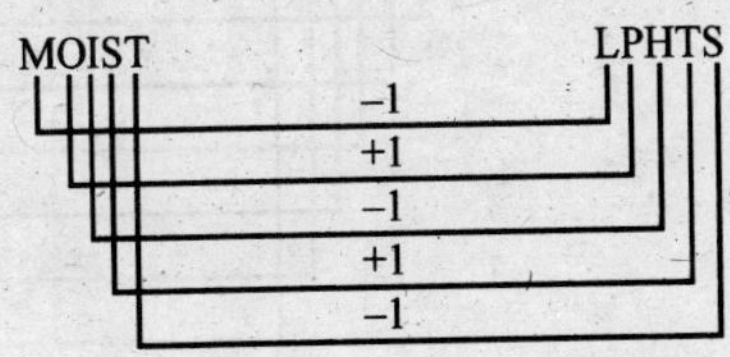

6. (a) : The letters of the word are written backwards.

ALPACA ⟶ ACAPLA

Similarly,

ANIMAL ⟶ LAMINA

7. (a) : The word is coded by moving the letters two steps backwards.

FINGER ⟶ DGLECP

−2, −2, −2, −2, −2, −2

Similarly,

KIDNEY ⟶ IGBLCW

−2, −2, −2, −2, −2, −2

8. (d) : The letters of the word are coded by moving three steps backward and three steps forward alternately.

QUESTION ⟶ NXBVQLLQ

−3, +3, −3, +3, −3, +3, −3, +3

Similarly,

REPLY ⟶ OHMOV

−3, +3, −3, +3, −3

9. (b) : The letters are decoded by moving the letters +3, −3, +2 and −2 steps respectively.

PNCY ⟶ SKEW

+3, −3, +2, −2

Similarly,

JXQV ⟶ MUST

+3, −3, +2, −2

10. (a) : The letters of the coded word are moved one step backward.

MPOEPO ⟶ LONDON

−1, −1, −1, −1, −1, −1

Similarly,

IVOHSZ ⟶ HUNGRY

−1, −1, −1, −1, −1, −1

11. *(d)* : The word GRADE is framed by letters in the given words. So, in order to find the code for GRADE select the respective number codes.

H E A D R I D E B E G → letters
8 5 1 4 3 9 4 5 0 5 7 → codes

So,

G R A D E → letters
7 3 1 4 5 → answer codes

12. *(d)* : The letters of the word are coded by numbers. So to find the code for DREAM select the respective numbers.

M O T H E R L A N D → letters
9 5 0 1 6 2 3 7 4 8 → codes

So, D R E A M → letters
8 2 6 7 9 → answer codes

13. *(c)* : The letters are coded by moving five and four steps forward alternately.

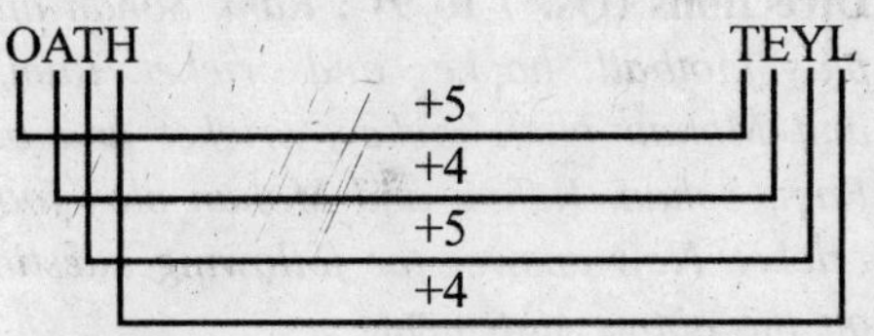

Similarly,

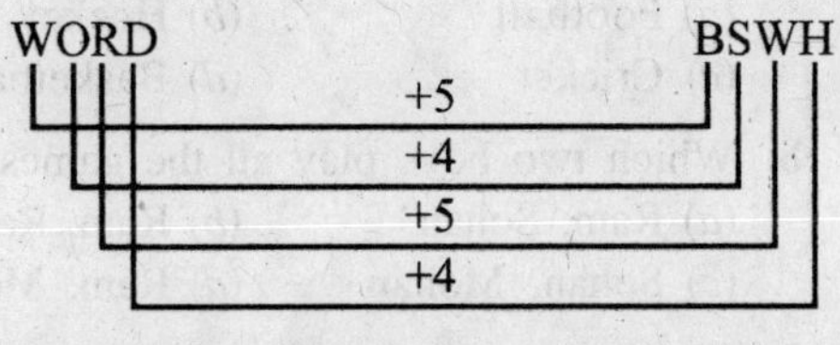

14. *(c)* : The letters of the word are coded by moving one step ahead and increasing the difference by one.

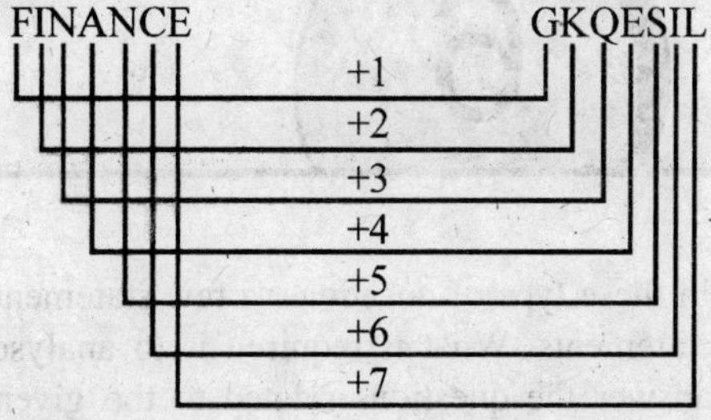

Similarly,

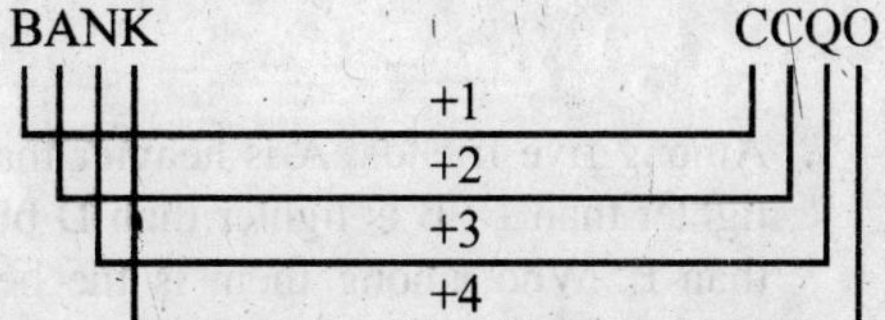

15. *(a)* : The letters of the word are coded by moving five steps forward and six steps backward alternately.

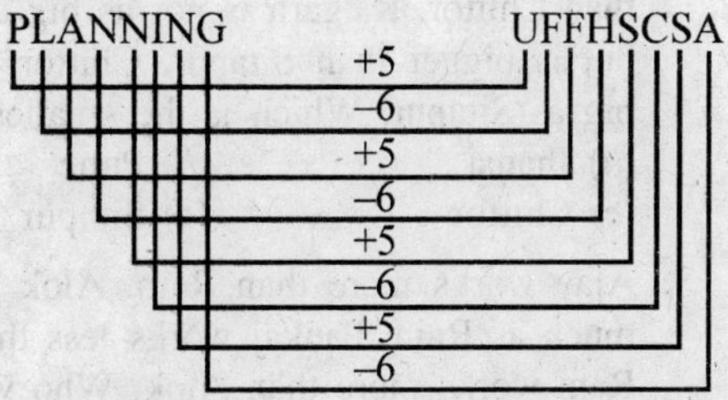

Similarly,

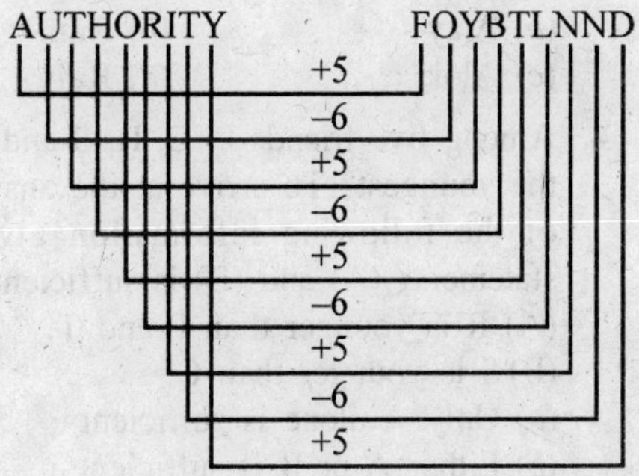

●●●

6 Statement Analysis

In these type of questions, a few statements are given. Certain facts are broken up and mentioned in these statements. What is required is to analyse the statements, arrange and sort out the given facts and then answer the questions related to the given statements.

EXERCISE

1. Among five friends, A is heavier than B; C is lighter than D; B is lighter than D but heavier than E. Who among them is the heaviest?

(*a*) B (*b*) C
(*c*) A (*d*) Can't say

2. Pune is bigger than Jhansi, Sitapur is bigger than Chittor. Raigarh is not as big as Jhansi, but is bigger than Sitapur. Chittor is not as big as Sitapur. Which is the smallest?

(*a*) Jhansi (*b*) Pune
(*c*) Chittor (*d*) Sitapur

3. Ajay works more than Ram. Alok works as much as Raju. Pankaj works less than Alok. Ram works more than Alok. Who works the most of all?

(*a*) Ajay (*b*) Ram
(*c*) Alok (*d*) Raju

4. Among five friends P, Q, R, S and T, who is the youngest? To arrive at the answer which of the following information given in the statements (A) and (B) is sufficient?

(A) R is younger than P and T.
(B) S is younger than Q.
(*a*) Only A alone is sufficient
(*b*) Either A or B is sufficient
(*c*) Both A and B together are needed
(*d*) Both A and B together are not sufficient

5. A is elder to B while C and D are elder to E who lies between A and B. If C be elder to B, which one of the following statements is necessarily true?

(*a*) E is elder to B (*b*) A is elder to C
(*c*) C is elder to D (*d*) D is elder to C

6. Suresh is as much older than Kamal as he is younger than Prabodh. Navin is as old as Kamal. Which of the following statements is wrong?

(*a*) Suresh is older than Navin
(*b*) Kamal is younger than Suresh
(*c*) Prabodh is not the oldest
(*d*) Navin is younger than Prabodh

Directions (Qs. 7 to 9) : *Ram, Sohan and Mohan play football, hockey and cricket. Ram, Ramesh and Mohan play hockey, cricket and basketball. Ram, Sohan, Rahim and Mohan play football and cricket. Now answer the following questions based on the above statements :*

7. Which game is played by all the boys?

(*a*) Football (*b*) Hockey
(*c*) Cricket (*d*) Basketball

8. Which two boys play all the games?

(*a*) Ram, Sohan (*b*) Ram, Ramesh
(*c*) Sohan, Mohan (*d*) Ram, Mohan

9. Who does not play football?

(*a*) Ramesh (*b*) Sohan
(*c*) Rahim (*d*) Mohan

Directions (Qs. 10 to 12) : *Read the following directions and answer the questions given below :*

There are five persons in a group. Out of these two are men. Only three persons know swimming, of which one is a man. There is a couple, of which the husband knows swimming. A is the younger sister of D and B is the husband of E. C is a swimming champion.

10. Who is the other man in the group?
(*a*) C (*b*) B
(*c*) A (*d*) D

11. The two women who know how to swim are:
(*a*) A and C (*b*) C and D
(*c*) D and E (*d*) A and E

12. The two persons who do not know how to swim are :
(*a*) B and D (*b*) D and E
(*c*) A and E (*d*) A and D

Directions (Qs. 13 to 15) : *Read the following statements and answer the questions given below :*

Rajat, Sushil and Nagesh play football, hockey and cricket. Rajat, Ramu and Nagesh play hockey, cricket and basketball. Rajat, Sushil, Mayank and Nagesh play football and cricket.

13. Which game is played by all the boys?
(*a*) Hockey (*b*) Basketball
(*c*) Football (*d*) Cricket

14. Who does not play football?
(*a*) Rajat (*b*) Nagesh
(*c*) Sushil (*d*) Ramu

15. Which of the following two boys play all the games?
(*a*) Nagesh, Rajat
(*b*) Mayank, Ramu
(*c*) Ramu, Nagesh
(*d*) Sushil, Mayank

EXPLANATORY ANSWERS

1. (*d*) : The five friends in descending order of weight are : A/D, B/C, E or A/D, B, C/E. Either A or D is the heaviest.

2. (*c*) : The order of cities in descending order of size is : Pune, Jhansi, Raigarh, Sitapur, Chittor.

3. (*a*) : On the basis of doing work, the descending order will be : Ajay, Ram, Alok/Raju, Pankaj.

4. (*d*) : Statements are not inter-related.

5. (*a*) : The order in descending seniority will be : A/C/D, E, B.

6. (*c*) : On the basis of age the descending order will be : Prabodh, Suresh, Kamal/ Navin.

Chart for Answers 7 to 9

Boy	*Games Played*
Ram	Football, Hocky, Cricket, Basketball
Sohan	Football, Hockey, Cricket
Mohan	Football, Hockey, Cricket, Basketball
Ramesh	Hockey, Cricket, Basketball
Rahim	Football, Cricket.

7. (*c*) **8. (*d*)** **9. (*a*)**

For Answers 10 to 12 the information chart will be:

A. Woman ((younger sister of D); knows swimming.
B. Man (husband of E); knows swimming
C. Woman; Swimming champion
D. Man (brother of A)
E. Woman (wife of B)

From the couple B & E, B (husband) knows swimming. C is a swimming champion. Three persons know how to swim of which only B is a man. So, the two women who know how to swim are C and A (the younger sister of D). There are two men in the group of five. One is B and the other will be D.

10. (*d*) **11. (*a*)** **12. (*b*)**

Chart for Answers 13 to 15

Boy	*Games Played*
Rajat	— Football, Hockey, Cricket, Basketball
Sushil	— Football, Hockey, Cricket, Basketball
Nagesh	— Football, Hockey, Cricket, Basketball
Ramu	— Hockey, Cricket, Basketball
Mayank	— Football, Cricket

13. (*d*) **14. (*d*)** **15. (*a*)**

●●●

7 Place Arrangement

Place arrangement generally refers to the positioning of persons or objects in a manner indicated by set of information given. One has to understand the order of placement and then attempt questions following the given information.

EXERCISE

Directions : *In the following questions, understand the arrangement pattern and then select the right answer from the given options :*

1. Five boys are sitting in a row. Raghu is not adjacent to Shyam or Amit. Ajay is not adjacent to Shyam. Raghu is adjacent to Mayank. If Mayank is at the middle in the row, then Ajay is adjacent to whom out of the following?

(*a*) Amit (*b*) Raghu
(*c*) Mayank (*d*) Shyam

2. Mini is to the right of Rajni but to the left of Ananta. Saya is to the right of Mini but to the left of Jaya. Who is on the extreme left if all the girls are facing North?

(*a*) Jaya (*b*) Mini
(*c*) Rajni (*d*) Saya

3. O, P, Q, R, S and T are standing on a bench according to their height. P is taller than O but shorter than S. Only S is taller than T. R is shorter than P but taller than Q. Who is the shortest?

(*a*) O (*b*) Q
(*c*) P (*d*) Cannot be said

4. Five personalities are living in a multistoried building. Mr. Effortless lives in a flat above Mr. Active, Mr. Charge lives in a flat below Mr. Diligent, Mr. Active lives in a flat above Mr. Diligent and Mr. Behaved lives in a flat below Mr. Charge. Who lives in the topmost flat?

(*a*) Mr. Charge (*b*) Mr. Diligent
(*c*) Mr. Effortless (*d*) Mr. Behaved

5. Six friends are sitting in a circle and playing cards. Kenny is to the left of Danny. Michael is in-between Bob and John. Roger is in between Kenny and Bob. Who is sitting to the right of Michael?

(*a*) Danny (*b*) John
(*c*) Kenny (*d*) Bob

6. Four girls A, B, C and D are sitting in a circle. B and C are facing each other. Which of the following is definitely true?

(*a*) A is to the left of C
(*b*) D is to the left of C
(*c*) A and D are facing each other
(*d*) A is not between B and C

7. Brijesh, Jayesh, Amar and Praveer are playing a game of cards. Amar is to the right of Jayesh who is to the right of Brijesh. Who is to the right of Amar?

(*a*) Brijesh (*b*) Praveer
(*c*) Brijesh or Praveer (*d*) Jayesh

8. In a pile of 10 books there are 3 of History, 3 of Hindi, 2 of Maths, and 2 of English. Taking from above there is an English book between a History and Maths book, a History book between a Maths and an English book, a Hindi book between an English and a Maths book, a Maths book between two Hindi books, and two Hindi books between a Maths and a History book. Book of which subject is at the sixth position from the top?

(*a*) English (*b*) Hindi
(*c*) History (*d*) Maths

9. Five persons A, B, C, D and E are sitting in a row facing you such that D is on the left of C and B is on the right of E. A is on the right of C and B is on the left of D. If E occupies a corner position, then who is sitting in the centre?

(*a*) A (*b*) B
(*c*) C (*d*) D

10. Six friends A, B, C, D, E and F are standing in a circle. B is between F and C; A is between E and D; F is to the left of D. Who is between A and F?

(*a*) C
(*b*) B
(*c*) D
(*d*) E

EXPLANATORY ANSWERS

1. (*b*) : The order of sitting is :

Amit, Shyam, Mayank, Ajay, Raghu

or

Ajay, Raghu, Mayank, Amit, Shyam

2. (*c*) : The order in which the girls are positioned is :

Rajni, Mini, Ananta, Saya, Jaya

or

Saya, Jaya, Ananta

or

Saya, Ananta, Jaya

3. (*d*) : In descending order of height, the standing positions are :

S		S
T		T
P	*or*	P
R		R
O		Q
Q		O

Either O or Q is the shortest. The information given is not enough to clarify the answer.

4. (*c*) : The personalities living in flats in multi-storied building are in order given below :

Mr. Effortless
Mr. Active
Mr. Diligent
Mr. Charge
Mr. Behaved

5. (*d*) : The order in which the friends are sitting is :

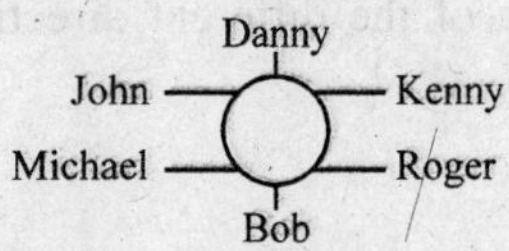

6. (*c*) : The sitting positions are :

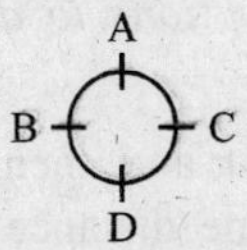

or

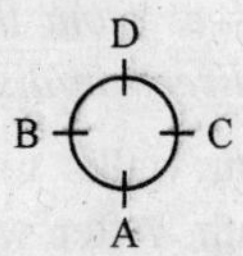

7. (*b*) : The order from left to right is :

Brijesh, Jayesh, Amar, Praveer

8. (*b*) : The pile of books is in the order :

1st — History
English
Maths
History
English
6th — Hindi
Maths
Hindi
Hindi
10th —History

9. (*d*) : Sitting order while facing us is :

A, C, D, B, E

10. (*c*) : The pattern of standing is :

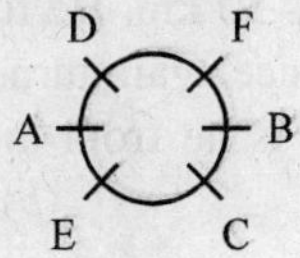

●●●

8 Direction Sense

In these type of tests, the directions in questions needs to be perceived. Such questions are based on the direction chart.

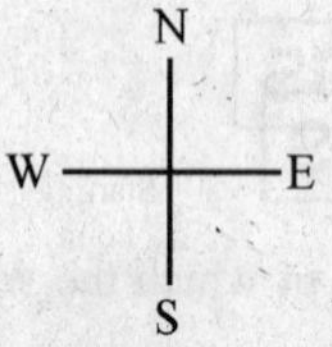

N = North S = South E = East W = West

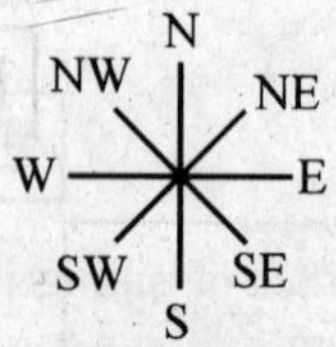

The sense of the different directions are guided by the left and right turns or angular turns.

EXERCISE

Directions : *In the following questions, select the right answer from the given options to depict the correct direction/distance.*

1. Kittu walks towards East and then towards South. After walking some distance he turns towards West and then turns to his left. In which direction is he walking now?
(*a*) North (*b*) South
(*c*) East (*d*) West

2. A person is driving towards West. What sequence of directions should he follow so that he is driving towards South?
(*a*) left, right, right (*b*) right, right, left
(*c*) left, left, left (*d*) right, right, right

3. Richa drives 8 km to the South, turns left and drives 5 km. Again, she turns left and drives 8 km. How far is she from her starting point?
(*a*) 3 km (*b*) 5 km
(*c*) 8 km (*d*) 13 km

4. Dingi runs 40 km towards North then turns right and runs 50 km. He turns right and runs 30 km, and once again turns right and runs 50 km. How far is he from his starting point?
(*a*) 90 km (*b*) 50 km
(*c*) 10 km (*d*) 5 km

5. If North is called North-West, North-West is called West, West is called South-West and so on. What will South-East be called?
(*a*) East (*b*) West
(*c*) North-East (*d*) South-East

6. A man travels 100 km towards South. From there he turns right and travels 100 km and again turns right to travel 50 km. Which direction is he in from his starting point?
(*a*) North (*b*) North-East
(*c*) East (*d*) South-West

7. A train runs 120 km in West direction, 30 km in South direction and then 80 km in east direction before reaching the station. In which direction is the station from the train's starting point?
(*a*) South-West (*b*) North-West
(*c*) South-East (*d*) South

8. Facing the West direction, Priya jogs for 20 m, turns left and goes further 40 m. She turns left again and jogs for 20 m. Then she turns right to go 20 m to reach the park. How far is the park from her starting point and in which direction?
(*a*) 20 m South (*b*) 40 m West
(*c*) 60 m South (*d*) 100 m East

9. If all the directions are rotated, *i.e.*, if North is changed to West and East to North and so on, then what will come in place of North-West?
(*a*) South-West
(*b*) North-East
(*c*) East-North
(*d*) East-West

10. A and B start together from one point. They walk 10 km towards North. A turns left and covers 5 km whereas B turns right and covers 3 km. A turns left again and covers 15 km whereas B turns right and covers his 15 km. How far is A from B?
(*a*) 18 km (*b*) 10 km
(*c*) 5 km (*d*) 8 km

EXPLANATORY ANSWERS

1. (*b*) :

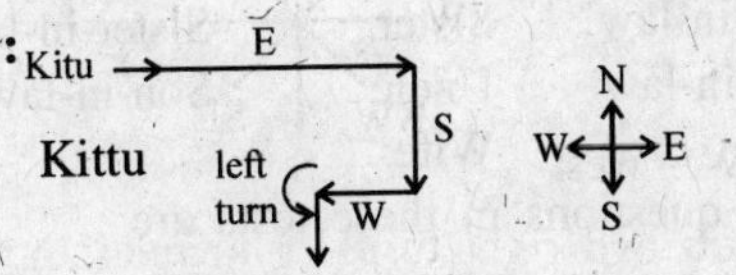

2. (*d*) :

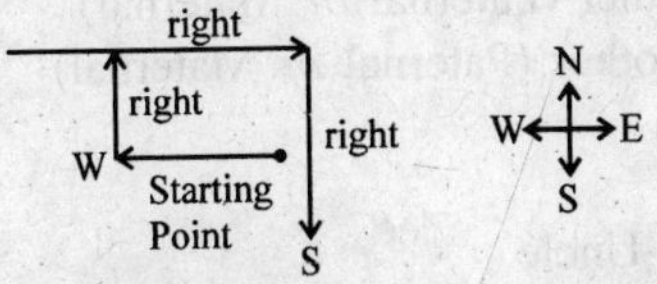

3. (*b*) :

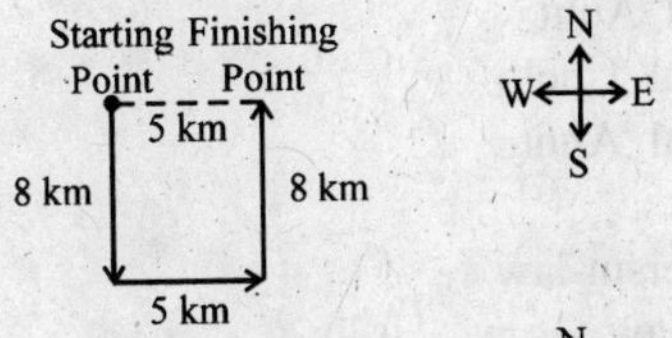

4. (*c*) :

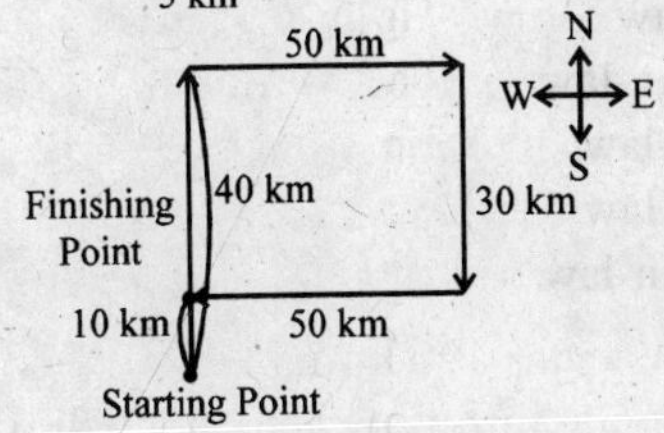

5. (*a*) :

Original Directions

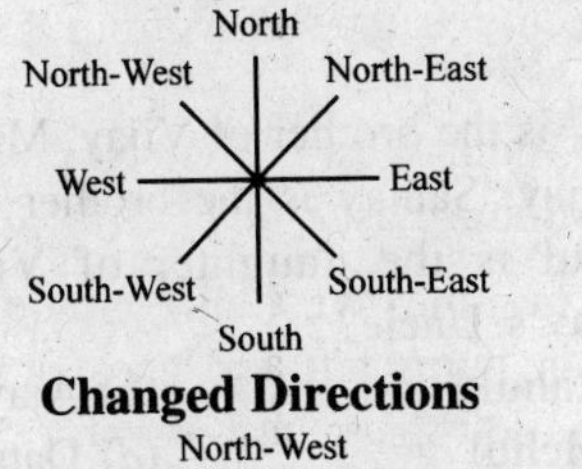

Changed Directions

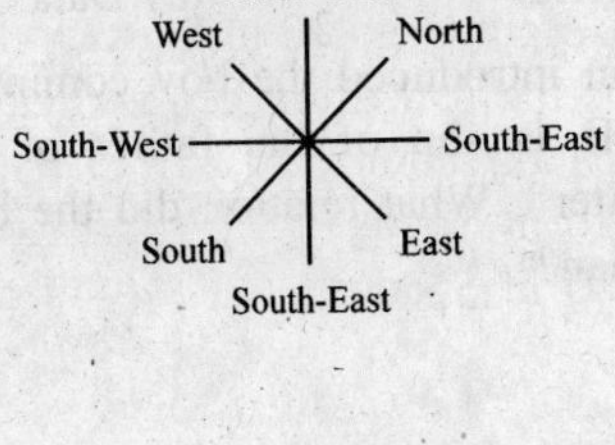

6. (*d*) :

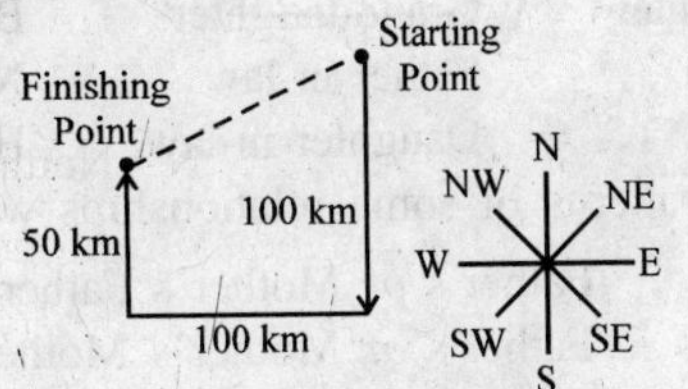

7. (*a*) :

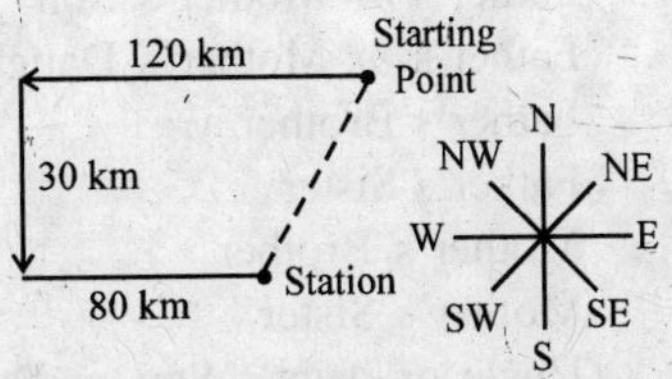

8. (*c*) : (40 + 20) = 60 metres South

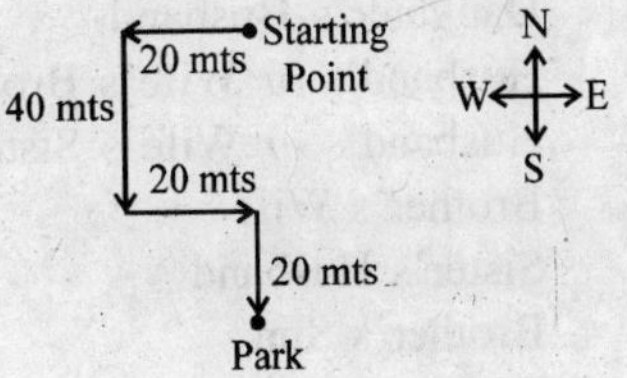

9. (*a*) :

Original Directions

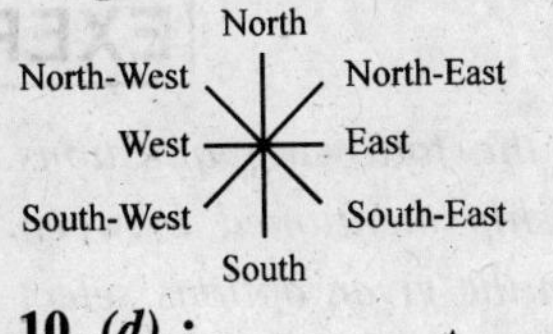

Changed Directions

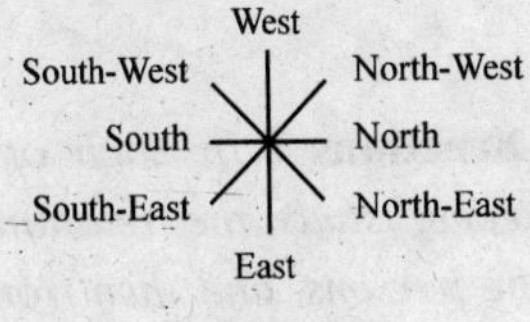

10. (*d*) :

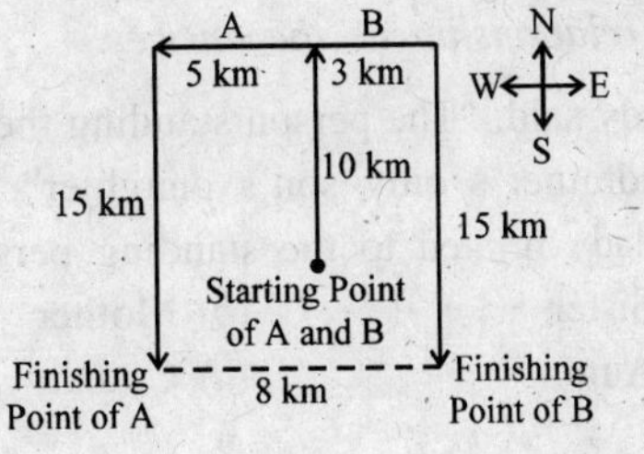

●●●

9 Blood Relationships

While attempting questions on blood relations, one should be clear of all the relation patterns that can exist between any two individuals. These type of questions are given mainly to test one's relationship ability.

Very well-known relations are :

Mother	Grandmother	Father	Grandfather	Son	Grandson
Daughter	Granddaughter	Brother	Brother-in-law	Sister	Sister-in-law
Niece	Father-in-law	Nephew	Mother-in-law	Uncle	Son-in-law
Aunt	Daughter-in-law	Husband	Cousin	Wife	

The patterns of some relationships which help in solving questions in these tests are :

Father's *or* Mother's Father	—	Grandfather (Paternal *or* Maternal)
Father's *or* Mother's Mother	—	Grandmother (Paternal *or* Maternal)
Father's *or* Mother's Son	—	Brother
Father's *or* Mother's Daughter	—	Sister
Father's Brother	—	Paternal Uncle
Father's Sister	—	Paternal Aunt
Mother's Brother	—	Maternal Uncle
Mother's Sister	—	Maternal Aunt
Uncle *or* Aunt's Son *or* Daughter	—	Cousin
Son's Wife	—	Daughter-in-law
Daughter's Husband	—	Son-in-law
Husband's *or* Wife's Brother	—	Brother-in-law
Husband's *or* Wife's Sister	—	Sister-in-law
Brother's Wife	—	Sister-in-law
Sister's Husband	—	Brother-in-law
Brother's Son	—	Nephew
Brother's Daughter	—	Niece

EXERCISE

Directions : *In each of the following questions keenly study the relationship mentioned between the persons, and then from the given options select the right relationship as the answer.*

1. A lady said, "The person standing there is my grandfather's only son's daughter". How is the lady related to the standing person?

(*a*) Sister (*b*) Mother
(*c*) Aunt (*d*) Cousin

2. Ajay is the brother of Vijay. Mili is the sister of Ajay. Sanjay is the brother of Rahul and Mehul is the daughter of Vijay. Who is Sanjay's Uncle?

(*a*) Rahul (*b*) Ajay
(*c*) Mehul (*d*) Data inadequate

3. A man introduced the boy coming with him as "He is son of the father of my wife's daughter". What relation did the boy bear to the man?

(*a*) Son-in-law (*b*) Son
(*c*) Brother (*d*) Father

4. If Amit's father is Billoo's father's only son and Billoo has neither a brother nor a daughter, what is the relationship between Amit and Billoo?
(*a*) Uncle – Nephew (*b*) Father – Daughter
(*c*) Father – Son (*d*) Cousins

5. Pointing to a woman in the photograph a man said, "She is the daughter of my grand-mother's only son." How is the woman related to the man?
(*a*) Mother (*b*) Daughter
(*c*) Sister-in-law (*d*) Sister

6. Pointing to a photograph, a woman said, "She is the only daughter of my mother's father." How is the woman related to the person in the photograph?
(*a*) Mother
(*b*) Grandmother
(*c*) Daughter
(*d*) Cannot be determined

7. Ram is the brother of Shyam and Mahesh is the father of Ram. Jagat is the brother of Priya and Priya is daughter of Shyam. Who is the uncle of Jagat ?
(*a*) Shyam (*b*) Mahesh
(*c*) Ram (*d*) Data insufficient

8. Introducing a man, a woman said, "His wife is the only daughter of my father". How is the man related to the woman?
(*a*) Husband (*b*) Father
(*c*) Father-in-law (*d*) Brother

9. If Maya is the only daughter of Richa's grandmother's brother, how is Maya's daughter related to Richa?
(*a*) Niece (*b*) Cousin
(*c*) Aunt (*d*) Mother

10. Pointing to a woman, a man said, "Her husband's mother is the wife of my father's only son". How is the man related to the woman?
(*a*) Son (*b*) Brother-in-law
(*c*) Uncle (*d*) Father-in-law

EXPLANATORY ANSWERS

1. (*a*) :

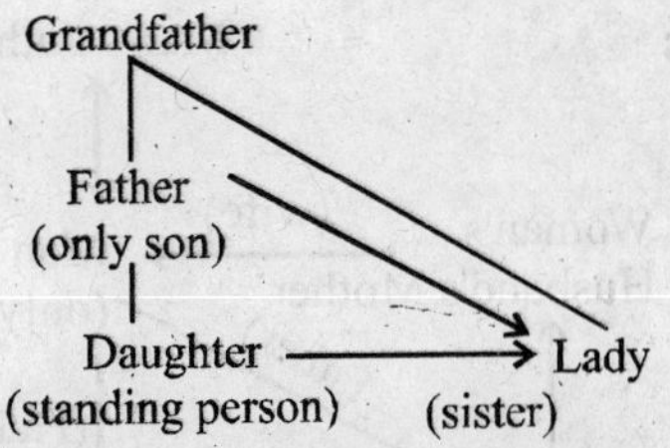

Lady's grandfather's son is lady's father and father's daughter will only be lady's sister.

2. (*d*) : 1. Mili ⟶ Ajay ⟶ Vijay
(sister) (brother) ↓
Mehul
2. Sanjay ⟶ Rahul (daughter)
(brother)

There are two sets of relationship. Information given is incomplete and no relation can be established between the two sets.

3. (*b*) : The relationship chart based on problem is :

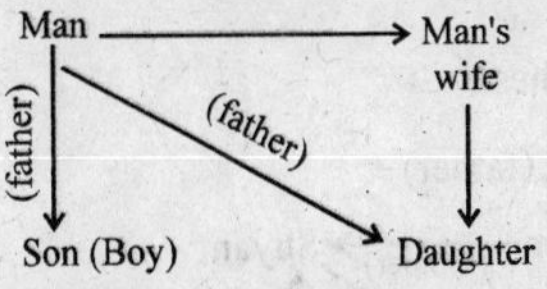

'Father of the man's wife's daughter' is the man himself and the boy in question is the man's son.

4. (*c*) : The relationship chart based on problem is :

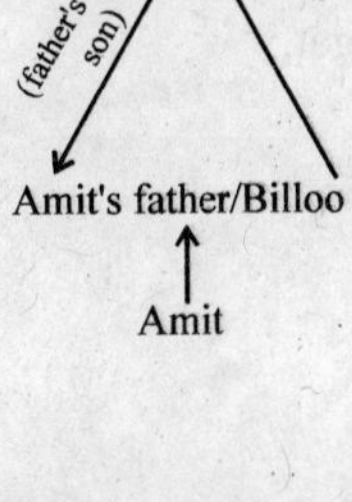

Amit's father is Billoo's father's only son means Billoo is the only son in question also, he is the father of Amit. It must be noted that Billoo has no brother which means he is single and also, when he has no daughter, Amit is his only son.

5. (*d*) :

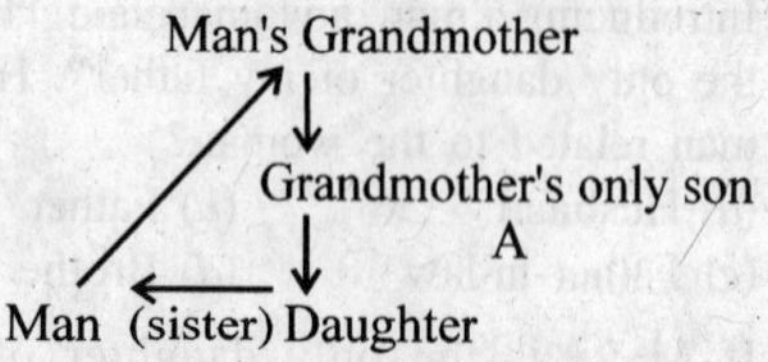

'My grandmother's only son' is the father of the man, and 'daughter of my grandmother's only son' is the sister of the man.

6. (*c*) :

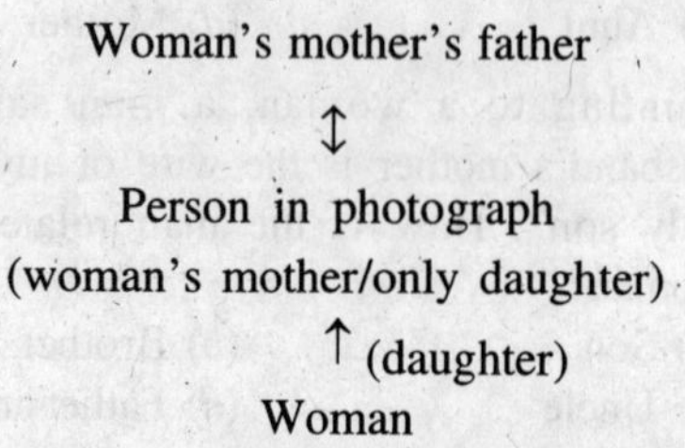

'Only daughter of my mother's father' is the person in the photograph and she is also the mother of the woman. So, the woman is the daughter of the person in the photo-graph.

7. (*c*) :

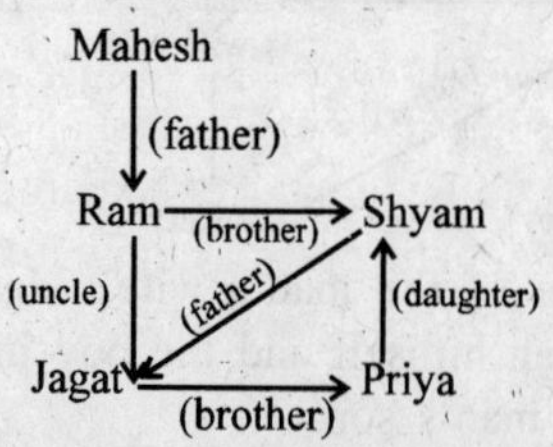

Jagat is brother of Priya and Priya is daughter of Shyam. So Shyam is also the father of Jagat. Ram is the brother of Shyam. So, Jagat's father's brother Ram is the uncle of Jagat.

8. (*a*) :

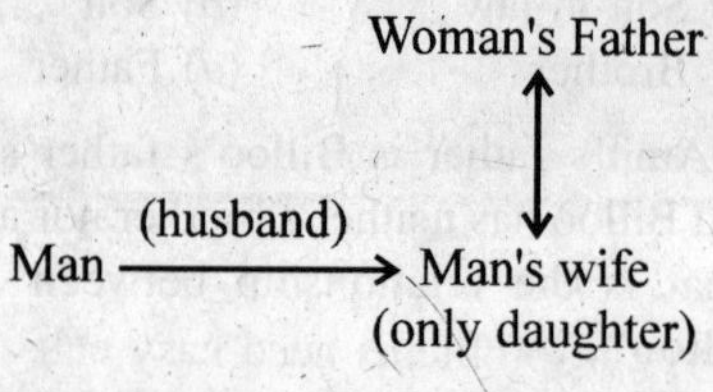

'Only daughter of my father' is the woman herself and the man is her husband.

9. (*b*) :

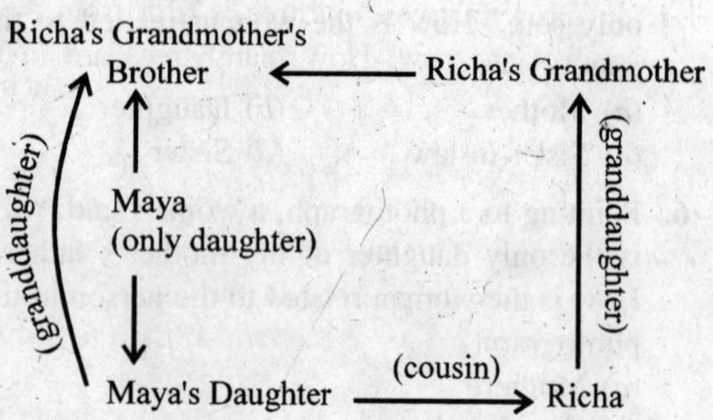

Both Maya's Daughter and Richa are granddaughters of a brother and a sister respectively. So Maya's daughter is the cousin of Richa.

10. (*d*) :

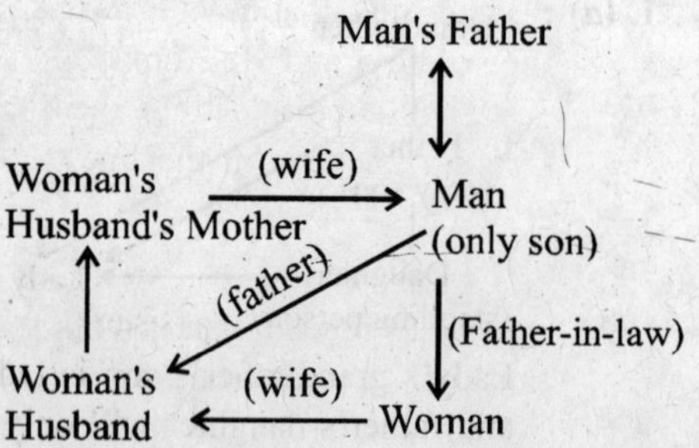

'My father's only son' is the man himself. 'Her husband's mother' is the wife of the man and so the man is the father of the woman's husband. As the woman is the wife of man's son, the man is the father-in-law of the woman.

●●●

10 Rows and Ranks

These type of problems need easy calculations to find out the number of objects in a row, lane or queue or to find a person's rank in a class of certain number of students; or to find the total number of students.

EXERCISE

1. In a row of trees, one tree is fifth from either end of the row. How many trees are in the row?

(*a*) 11 (*b*) 8
(*c*) 10 (*d*) 9

2. Jaya ranks 5th in a class of 53. What is her rank from the bottom in the class?

(*a*) 49th (*b*) 48th
(*c*) 47th (*d*) 50th

3. Mohan ranks twenty-first in a class of sixty-five students. What will be his (Mohan's) rank if the lowest candidate is assigned rank 1?

(*a*) 44th (*b*) 45th
(*c*) 46th (*d*) Data inadequate

4. If Rahul finds that he is 12th from the right in a line of boys and 4th from the left, how many boys should be added to the line such that there are 28 boys in the line?

(*a*) 12 (*b*) 14
(*c*) 20 (*d*) 13

5. In a row of boys, Rajan is tenth from the right and Suraj is tenth from the left. When Rajan and Suraj interchange their positions, Suraj will be twenty-seventh from the left. Which of the following will be Rajan's position from the right?

(*a*) Tenth (*b*) Twenty-sixth
(*c*) Twenty-ninth (*d*) None of these

6. Mahesh and Suresh are ranked 11th and 12th respectively from the top in a class of 41 students. What will be their respective ranks from the bottom?

(*a*) 32nd and 33rd
(*b*) 29th and 30th
(*c*) 30th and 31st
(*d*) 31st and 30th

7. Uma ranked 8th from the top and 37th from bottom in a class. How many students are there in the class?

(*a*) 47 (*b*) 46
(*c*) 45 (*d*) None of these

8. In a queue, Sadiq is 14th from the front and Joseph is 17th from the end, while Jane is in between Sadiq and Joseph. If Sadiq be ahead of Joseph and there be 48 persons in the queue, how many persons are there between Sadiq and Jane?

(*a*) 5 (*b*) 6
(*c*) 7 (*d*) 8

9. Rohan ranked eleventh from the top and twenty-seventh from the bottom among the students who passed the annual examination in a class. If the number of students who failed in the examination was 12, how many students appeared for the examination?

(*a*) 48
(*b*) 49
(*c*) 50
(*d*) Cannot be determined

10. Some boys are sitting in a row. P is sitting fourteenth from the left and Q is seventh from the right. If there are four boys between P and Q, how many boys are there in the row?

(*a*) 19 (*b*) 21
(*c*) 25 (*d*) 23

EXPLANATORY ANSWERS

1. (*d*):

Total number of trees in the row are : (5 + 5) –1 = 9.

2. (*a*) :

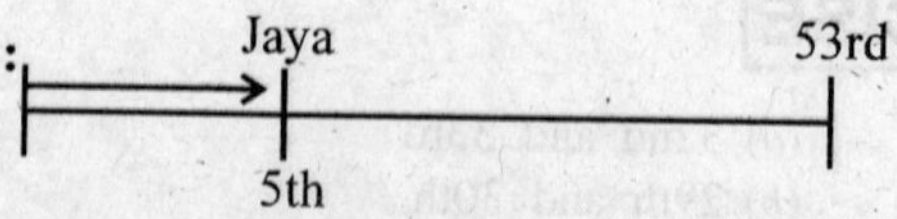

Jaya's rank from the bottom is : (53 – 5) +1 = 49th.

3. (*b*) :

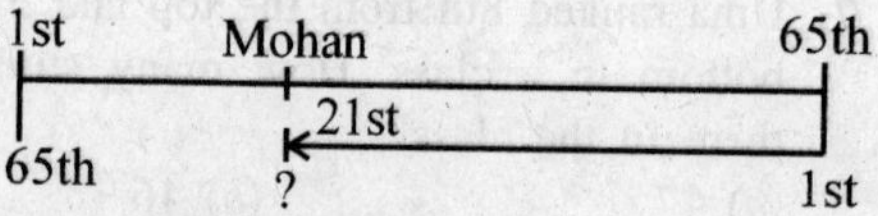

Note : Mohan's rank from the last or the question asked means the same.

Mohan's rank is (65 – 21) +1 = 45th.

4. (*d*) :

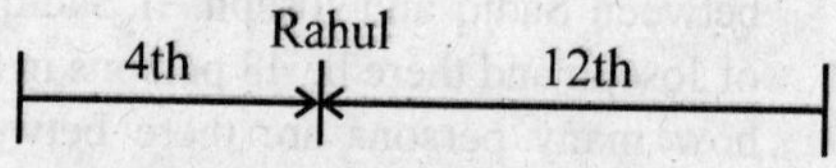

The number of boys in the line are : (4 + 12) – 1 = 15

To make a line of 28 boys, (28 –15) *i.e.* 13 more boys are needed.

5. (*d*) :

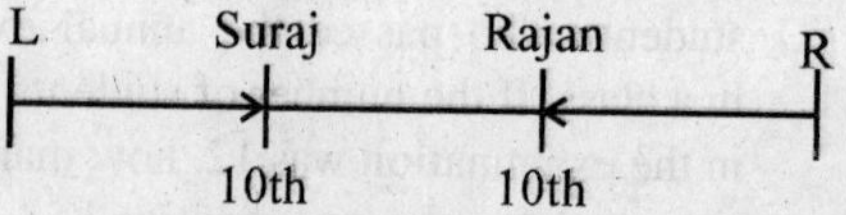

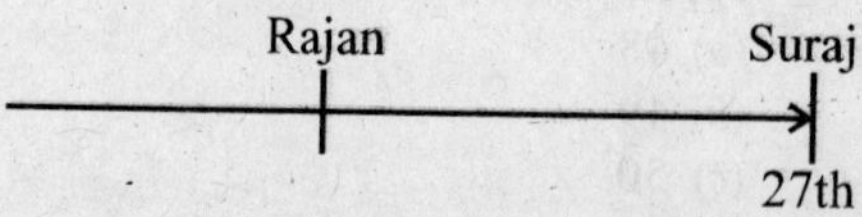

As the position of boys is equal from both ends, Rajan will also be 27th from the right after changing positions.

6. (*d*) :

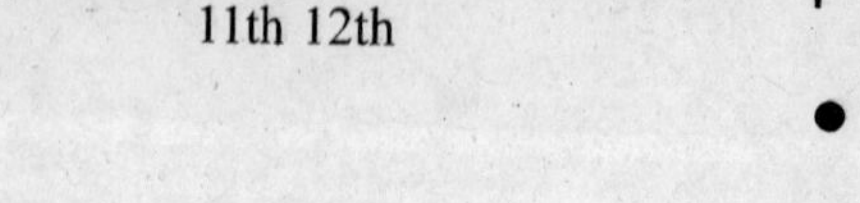

Mahesh's position from bottom is : (41 – 11) + 1 = 31st

Suresh's position from bottom is : (41 – 12) +1 = 30th.

7. (*d*) :

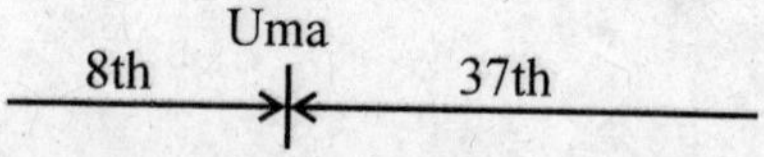

Total number of students in the class are : (8 + 37) – 1 = 44.

8. (*d*) :

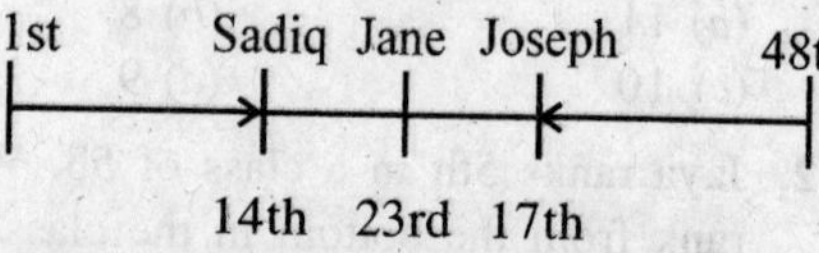

Sadiq's position from front : 14th

Joseph's position from last : 17th or 48 – 17 + 1 = 32nd from front.

Middle postion between Sadiq & Joseph

$$= \frac{(32-14)}{2} + 14 = 23 \text{ rd.}$$

Hence, Jane position is 23rd from front

Person between Sadiq & Jane = 23 – 14 – 1 = 8.

9. (*b*) :

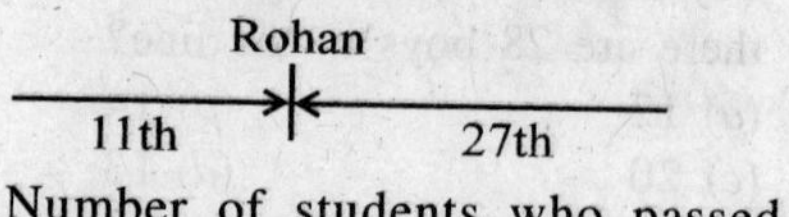

Number of students who passed the examination

(11+ 27) – 1 = 37

Those who failed = 12

Total number of students who appeared in the examination

= 37 + 12 = 49.

10. (*c*) :

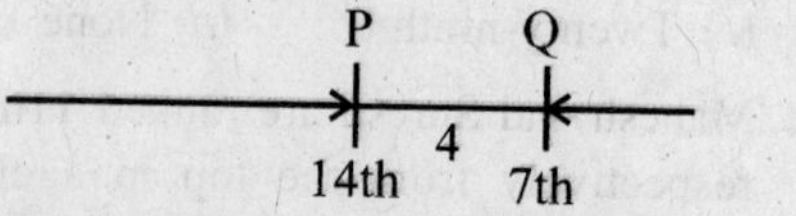

The number of boys in the row are : (14 + 4 + 7) = 25.

●●●

11 Diagrammatic Puzzles

In these problems one has to count the geometrical figures in a given complex figure. A little bit of systematic approach is needed to get the correct number of the asked figure. The shapes of all geometrical figures must be clear in mind.

EXERCISE

1. How many triangles are there in this figure?

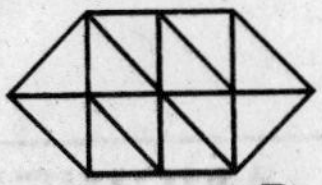

A. 16 B. 17
C. 18 D. 19

2. The number of rectangles in this figure are.

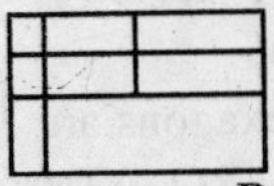

A. 21 B. 24
C. 23 D. 25

3. How many squares are hidden in this figure?

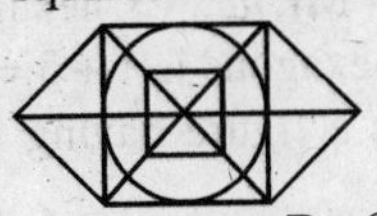

A. 7 B. 8
C. 9 D. 10

4. How many squares are there in the figure given below?

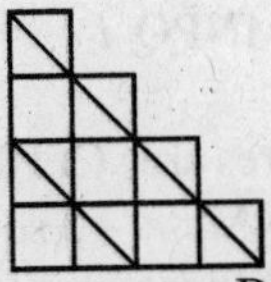

A. 10 B. 11
C. 13 D. 14

5. The number of circles in this figure is

A. 6 B. 5
C. 2 D. 3

6. How many triangles are there in the figure given below?

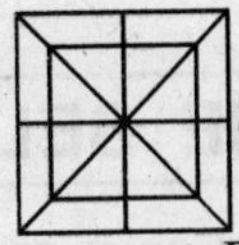

A. 28 B. 36
C. 24 D. 32

7. How many straight lines are needed to draw the figure in question 6?

A. 10 B. 12
C. 11 D. 13

8. How many hexagons are there in the figure given below?

A. 1 B. 2
C. 4 D. 5

9. The number of triangles in this figure is

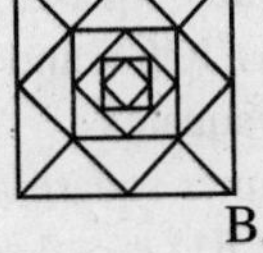

A. 20 B. 22
C. 26 D. 28

10. How many squares are there in the figure given below?

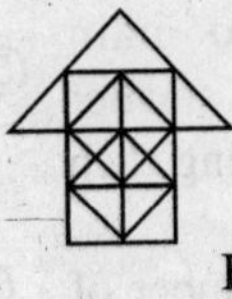

A. 6 B. 8
C. 9 D. 11

11. How many triangles are there in this figure?

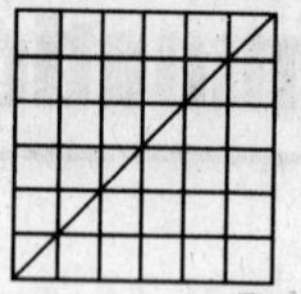

A. 42 B. 41
C. 40 D. 39

12. How many hexagons are there in this figure?

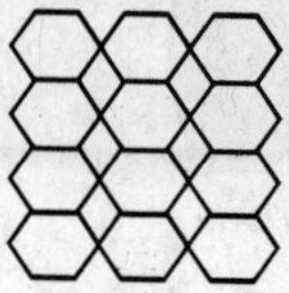

A. 13 B. 14
C. 15 D. 16

ANSWERS

1	2	3	4	5	6	7	8	9	10
A	C	D	C	A	D	B	C	D	D
11	**12**								
A	C								

SOME SELECTED EXPLANATORY ANSWERS

1. The simplest triangles are ADE, DEI, AEF, ABF, EIJ, EFJ, BFG, BCG, FJK, FGK, CGH and GHK – *i.e.,* – 12 triangles

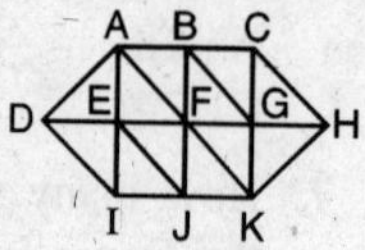

The bisected triangles are ADI and CHK – *i.e.* – 2 triangles

Other triangles are AIK and ACK *i.e.,* – 2 triangles

So, the total number of triangles is

12 + 2 + 2 = 16

3. The main squares are ABCD and EFGH *i.e.,* – 2 squares

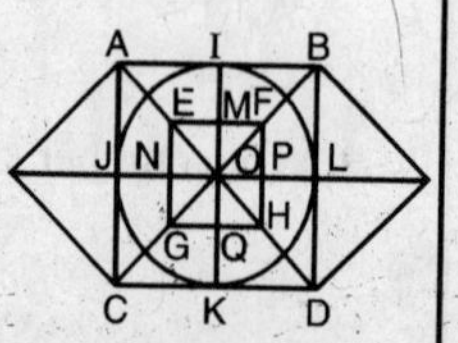

The simplest outer squares are AIJO, IBOL, JOCK and OLKD *i.e.,* – 4 squares

The simplest inner square are EMNO, NOGQ, MFOP and OPQH *i.e.,* – 4 squares

There are no other squares formed in the figure

So, the total number of squares is

2 + 4 + 4 = 10

5. There are two main circles and four smaller circles intersecting each other.

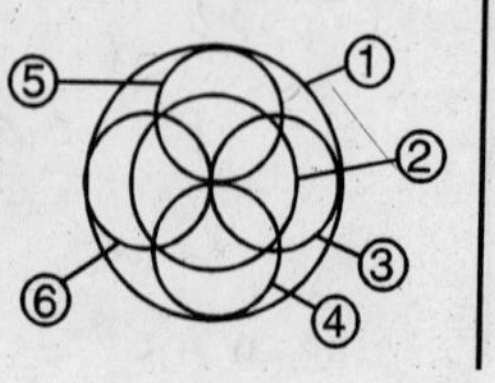

So, the total number of circles is 2 + 4 = 6

8. The larger hexagon is : EG – GO – GV – VT – TL – LE *i.e.* – 1 hexagon.

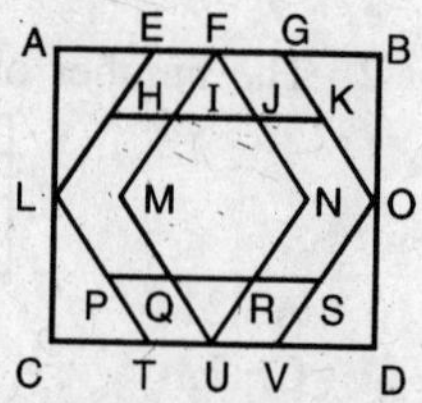

The smaller hexagons are : IJ – JN – NR – RQ – QM – MT, HJ – JN – NR – RP – PL – LH and IK – KO – OS – SQ – QM – MI, *i.e.,* –3, hexagons. So, the total number of hexagons is 1 + 3 = 4

(Hexagon is a figure having six side of equal length.)

10. The main squares are : BDLN and FHOQ *i.e.* – 2 squares.

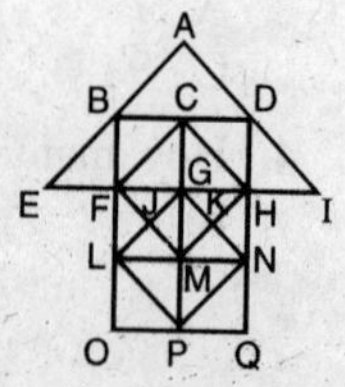

The simplest squares are : BCFG, FGLM, LMOP, CDGH, GHMN and MNPQ *i.e.* – 6 squares.

The tilted squares are : CFHM, GLNP and GJKM *i.e.* – 3 squares

So, the total number of squares is 2 + 6 + 3 = 11

12. 12 hexagons are put together and further 3 hexagons are formed. One containing numbers 2 and 5, second containing numbers 5 and 8 and third containing numbers 8 and 11. So, there are total 12 + 3 = 15 hexagons.

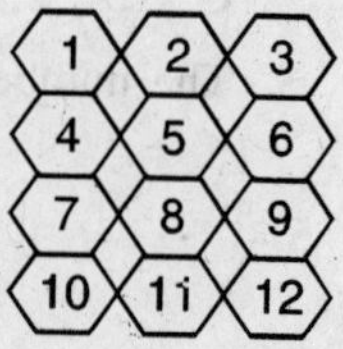

●●●

12 Symbol Substitution

Questions in these category are easy to attempt. Candidates must be quick in substituting symbols and calculations. The common pattern of questions asked are given below.

EXERCISE

1. If "+" means "–"; "–" means "×"; "×"means "÷" and "÷" means "+", then
$15 \times 5 \div 10 + 5 - 3 = ?$
(a) 9.5 (b) 0
(c) – 2 (d) 24

2. If "+" means "×"; "–" means "÷"; "÷"means "+" and "×" means "–", then what will be the value of $20 \div 40 - 4 \times 5 + 6 = ?$
(a) 60 (b) 1.67
(c) 150 (d) 0

3. If × stands for addition, < for subtraction, + stands for division, > for multiplication, – stands for equal to, ÷ for greater than, and = stands for less than, state which of the following is true?
(a) $5 \times 3 < 7 \div 8 + 4 \times 1$
(b) $3 \times 4 > 2 - 9 + 3 < 3$
(c) $5 > 2 + 2 = 10 < 4 \times 8$
(d) $3 \times 2 < 4 \div 16 > 2 + 4$

4. If → stands for subract, ← stands for add, □↑↑ stands for multiply, ↓↓ stands for divide, ↔ for greater than, ⟷ stands for equal to, then which of the following alternatives is true?
(a) 4 ← 6 ↑↑ 2 ⟷ 3 → 12 ← 12
(b) 10 ↓↓ 5 ↑↑ 5 ⟷ 9 → 3 ← 4
(c) 15 ↑↑ 2 → 5 ⟷ 12 ↓↓ 4 ← 3
(d) 13 ↓↓ 13 ← 1 ↔ 20 → 5 ↑↑ 2

5. If Δ denotes =; + denotes >, – denotes <, □ denotes ≠, × denotes > and ÷ denotes < then a + b – c denotes
(a) b Δ c □ a (b) b □ a ÷ c
(c) a ÷ b × c (d) b – a + c

6. If '✱' denotes '×', 'Δ' denotes '÷', '□' denotes '–', '●' denotes '+', 'α' denotes '=' and 'β' denotes ≠, then which of the following euations is correct?
(a) 2 □ 10 ✱ 4 Δ 5 α 5 ● 12 Δ 6
(b) 27 Δ 9 ● 6 β 3 ✱ 6 □ 9
(c) 4 Δ 2 ✱ 0 α 7 Δ 1 ✱ 0
(d) 5 ● 6 Δ 3 □ 2 α 8 Δ 4 ✱ 3

7. If ↓ stands for '÷', ↑ stands for '×', → stands for '+' and ← stands for '–', then
25 ↓ 5 → 3 ↑ 6 ← 8 = ?
(a) 9 (b) 12
(c) 16 (d) 15

8. If the + and × signs of the following equations are interchanged, which will be the correct equation?
(a) $7 \times 5 + 3 = 20$ (b) $4 + 9 \times 1 = 42$
(c) $6 \times 5 + 8 = 46$ (d) $2 + 11 \times 4 = 28$

9. If '+' stands for multiplication, '×' stands for addition, '÷' stands for subtraction and '–' stands for division, then what will be the result of the following equation?
$7 \times 4 \div 10 \times 2 + 5 = ?$
(a) 7 (b) 0
(c) 11 (d) 15

10. If 'A' means '÷', 'B' means '+', 'C' means '×' and 'D' means '–', then
12 C 4 A 24 D 10 B 1 = ?
(a) $11\frac{1}{3}$ (b) 23
(c) – 7 (d) $16\frac{4}{5}$

EXPLANATORY ANSWERS

1. (c) : $15 \div 5 + 10 - 5 \times 3$

$3 + 10 - 15 = -2$

2. (d) : $20 + 40 \div 4 - 5 \times 6$

$20 + 10 - 30 = 0$

3. (c) : (a) $5 + 3 - 7 > 8 \div 4 + 1$

$1 > 3$

(b) $3 + 4 \times 2 = 9 \div 3 - 3$

$11 = 0$

(c) $5 \times 2 \div 2 < 10 - 4 + 8$

$5 < 14$

(d) $3 + 2 - 4 > 16 \times 2 \div 4$

$1 > 8$

4. (b) : (a) $4 + 6 \times 2 = 3 - 12 + 12$

$16 = 3$

(b) $10 \div 5 \times 5 = 9 - 3 + 4$

$10 = 10$

(c) $15 \times 2 - 5 = 12 \div 4 + 3$

$25 = 6$

(d) $13 \div 13 + 1 > 20 - 5 \times 2$

$2 > 10$

5. (d) : What is given is $a > b < c$

The equations are :

(a) $b = c \neq a$ which is wrong

(b) $b \neq a < c$ which is wrong

(c) $a < b > c$ which is wrong

(d) $b < a > c$ which is correct

Therefore, (d) is the answer.

6. (c) : The solved equations will be :

(a) $2 - 10 \times 4 \div 5 = 5 + 12 \div 6$

$2 - 8 = 5 + 2$

$-6 = 7$

which is wrong

(b) $27 \div 9 + 6 \neq 3 \times 6 - 9$

$3 + 6 \neq 18 - 9$

$9 \neq 9$

which is wrong

(c) $4 \div 2 \times 0 = 7 \div 1 \times 0$

$2 \times 0 = 7 \times 0$

$0 = 0$

which is correct

(d) $5 + 6 \div 3 - 2 = 8 \div 4 \times 3$

$5 = 6$

which is wrong

7. (d) : $25 \div 5 + 3 \times 6 - 8$

$5 + 18 - 8 = 15$

8. (c) : After interchanging the signs the equations are :

(a) $7 + 5 \times 3 = 22$ which is wrong

(b) $4 \times 9 + 1 = 37$ which is wrong

(c) $6 + 5 \times 8 = 46$ which is correct

(d) $2 \times 11 + 4 = 26$ which is wrong

9. (c) : $7 + 4 - 10 + 2 \times 5$

$7 + 4 - 10 + 10 = 11$

10. (c) : $12 \times 4 \div 24 - 10 + 1$

$2 - 10 + 1 = -7$

●●●

13 Missing Numbers

Playing with numbers and mathematical skills are needed to attempt these type of tests. The candidates have to work out the right combination of arithmetical symbols to arrive at the answer options which will take the place of the interrogation sign in the given questions.

EXERCISE

Directions: *In each question given below which one number can be placed at the sign of interrogation?*

1.

(*a*) 693 (*b*) 939
(*c*) 981 (*d*) 993

2.

(*a*) 68 (*b*) 100
(*c*) 72 (*d*) 81

3.

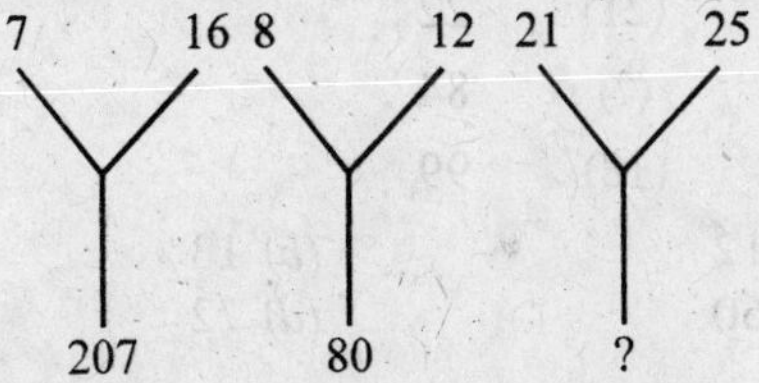

(*a*) 425 (*b*) 184
(*c*) 241 (*d*) 210

4.

(*a*) 35 (*b*) 37
(*c*) 45 (*d*) 48

5.

(*a*) 4 (*b*) 8
(*c*) 20 (*d*) 14

6.

14	9	4
12	7	2
10	5	0
16	11	?

(*a*) 9 (*b*) 6
(*c*) 3 (*d*) 7

7.

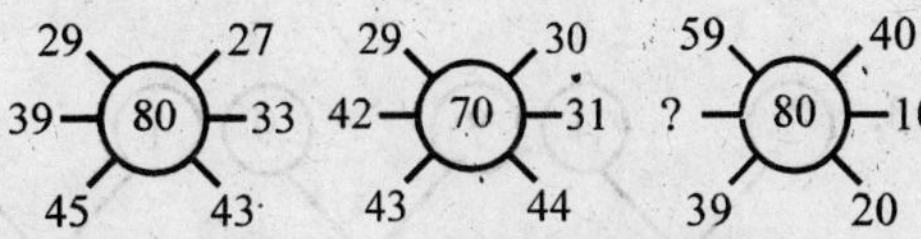

(*a*) 69 (*b*) 49
(*c*) 50 (*d*) 60

8.

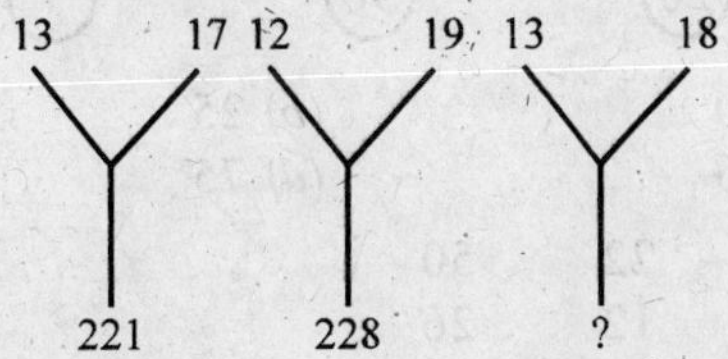

(*a*) 31 (*b*) 229
(*c*) 234 (*d*) 312

9.

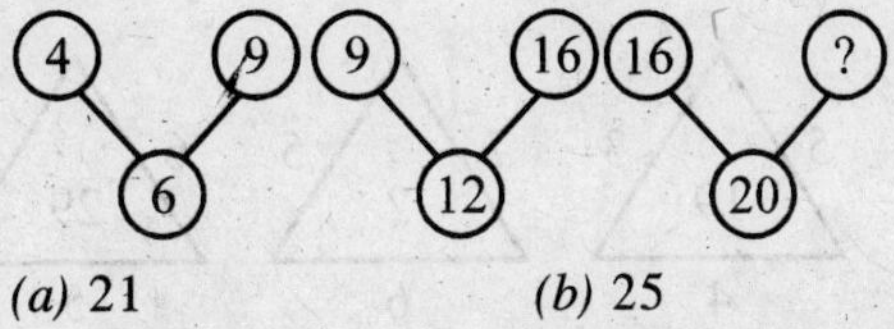

(*a*) 21 (*b*) 25
(*c*) 50 (*d*) 60

10. 51 (11) 61
64 (30) 32
35 (?) 43

(*a*) 25 (*b*) 27
(*c*) 32 (*d*) 37

11.

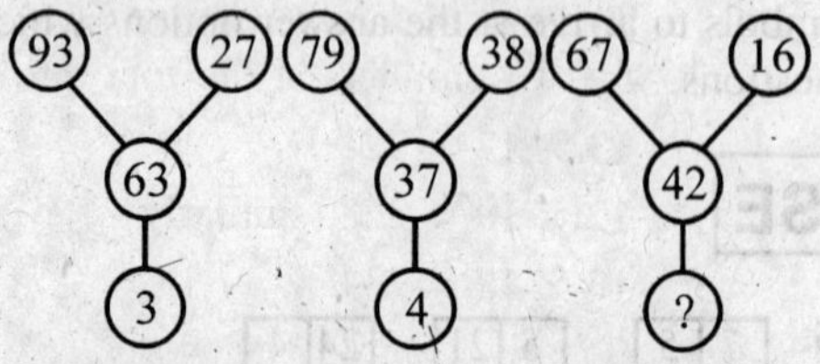

(*a*) 5 (*b*) 6
(*c*) 8 (*d*) 9

12.

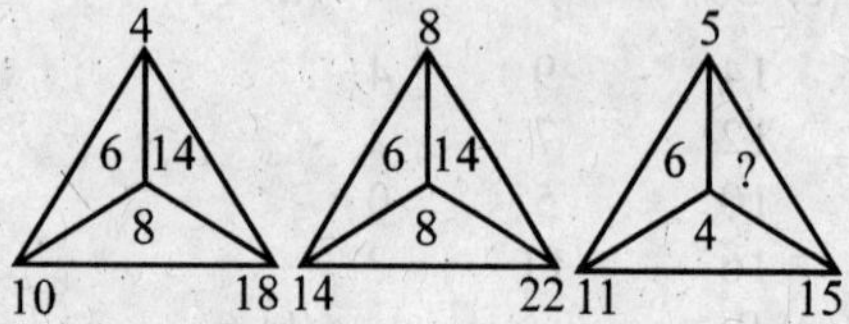

(*a*) 8 (*b*) 14
(*c*) 10 (*d*) 6

13.

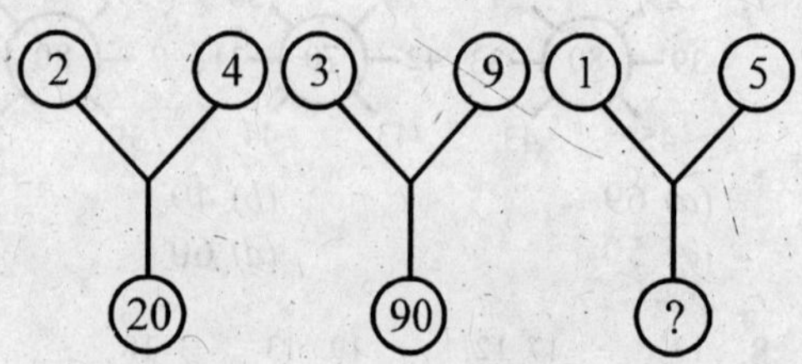

(*a*) 20 (*b*) 25
(*c*) 26 (*d*) 75

14. 27 22 50
13 12 26
9 2 ?

(*a*) 12 (*b*) 39
(*c*) 18 (*d*) 24

15.

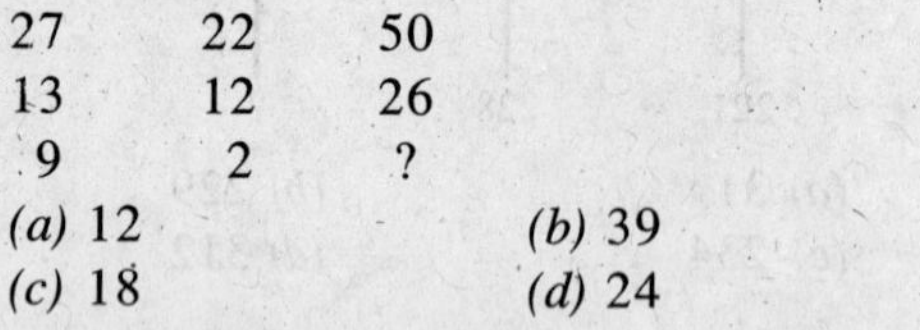

(*a*) 25 (*b*) 47
(*c*) 37 (*d*) 41

16.

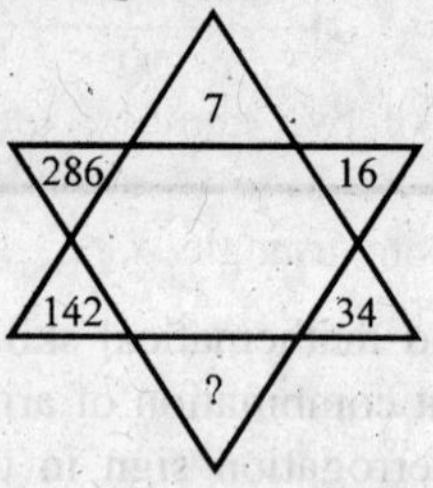

(*a*) 70 (*b*) 68
(*c*) 56 (*d*) 92

17.

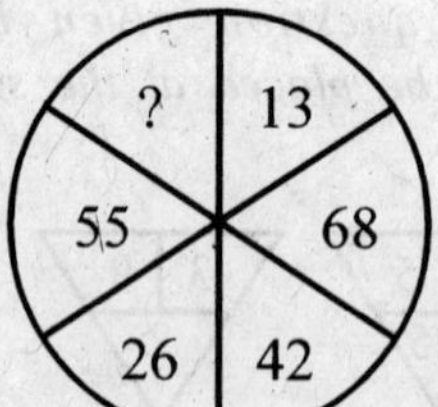

(*a*) 41 (*b*) 37
(*c*) 29 (*d*) 25

18.

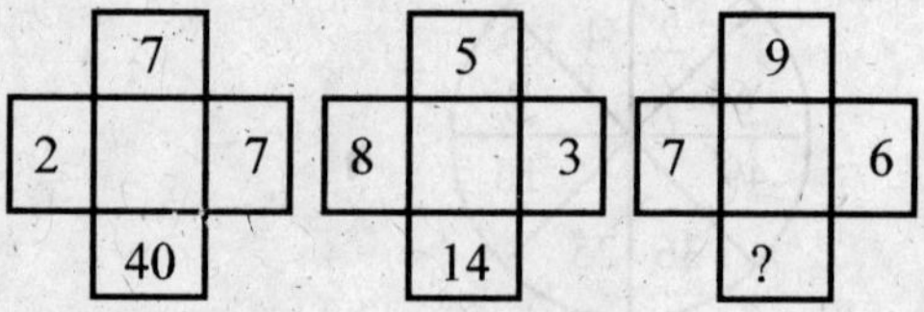

(*a*) 72 (*b*) 68
(*c*) 82 (*d*) 96

19. 42 (21) 22
78 (?) 84
162 (18) 99

(*a*) 12 (*b*) 13
(*c*) 60 (*d*) 72

20.

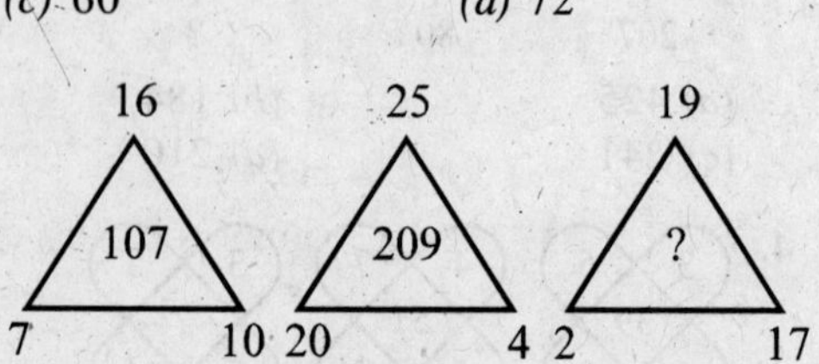

(*a*) 68
(*b*) 93
(*c*) 175
(*d*) 217

EXPLANATORY ANSWERS

1. (c) : The squares of two numbers on the top placed side by side gives the number inside the bottom triangle, *i.e.,*

6^2 and 3^2 = 369

2^2 and 5^2 = 425,

similarly

3^2 and 9^2 = 981.

2. (d) : Starting from number 4 the numbers are the squares of numbers in natural order

i.e., $2^2 = 4$, $3^2 = 9$, $4^2 = 16$ . . . . . $9^2 = 81$.

3. (b) : The number at the bottom is the difference of the squares of two numbers at the top, *i.e.,*

$16^2 - 7^2 = 256 - 49 = 207$

$12^2 - 8^2 = 144 - 64 = 80$, similarly

$25^2 - 21^2 = 625 - 441 = 184$.

4. (b) : The number in the centre is the sum of the products of diagonal numbers, *i.e.,*

$(3 \times 3) + (5 \times 6) = 39$

$(4 \times 4) + (7 \times 5) = 51$, similarly

$(3 \times 4) + (5 \times 5) = 37$.

5. (d) : Sum of two numbers on the top divided by 2 gives the third number, *i.e.,*

$(7 + 5) \div 2 = 6$

$(5 + 21) \div 2 = 13$, similarly

$(24 + 4) \div 2 = 14$.

6. (b) : The numbers in 2nd and 3rd columns are 5 less than the nunbers in 1st and 2nd columns respectively, *i.e.,*

$14 - 5 = 9$ and $9 - 5 = 4$

$12 - 5 = 7$ and $7 - 5 = 2$, . . . similarly

$16 - 5 = 11$ and $11 - 5 = 6$.

7. (a) : The sum of 3 numbers in each line in one figure is same, *i.e.,*

$29 + 80 + 43$ or $39 + 80 + 33$ or $45 + 80 + 27 = 152$

$29 + 70 + 44$ or $42 + 70 + 31$ or $43 + 70 + 30 = 143$,

similarly $59 + 80 + 20$ or $39 + 80 + 40 = 159$.

The missing number is :

$159 - (80 + 10) = 69$.

8. (c) : The number at the bottom is the product of two numbers at the top, *i.e.,*

$13 \times 17 = 221$

$12 \times 19 = 228$, similarly

$13 \times 18 = 234$.

9. (b) : Square of number at the bottom is equal to the product of two numbers at the top, *i.e.,*

$6^2 = 4 \times 9$, *i.e.,* 36

$12^2 = 9 \times 16$, *i.e.,* 144, similarly

$20^2 = 16 \times ?$, *i.e.,* 400. The missing number is $400 \div 16 = 25$.

10. (b) : The sum of the products of the digits of numbers in 1st and 3rd columns is the number in the 2nd column, *i.e.,*

$(5 \times 1) + (6 \times 1) = 11$

$(6 \times 4) + (3 \times 2) = 30$, similarly

$(3 \times 5) + (4 \times 3) = 27$.

11. (d) : The sum of numbers on right and centre subtracted from the number on the left gives the number at the bottom, *i.e.,*

$93 - (27 + 63) = 3$

$79 - (38 + 37) = 4$, similarly

$67 - (16 + 42) = 9$.

12. (c) : The number inside each triangle is the difference of the numbers at its base *i.e.*

$10 - 4 = 6$, $18 - 4 = 14$ and $18 - 10 = 8$

$14 - 8 = 6$, $22 - 8 = 14$ and $22 - 14 = 8$, similarly

$11 - 5 = 6$, $15 - 5 = 10$ and $15 - 11 = 4$.

13. (c) : The sum of squares of two numbers at the top gives the third number below, *i.e.,*

$2^2 + 4^2 = 20$

$3^2 + 9^2 = 90$, similarly

$1^2 + 5^2 = 26$.

14. (a) : The sum of numbers in 1st and 2nd column plus 1 is the number in the 3rd column, *i.e.*,
$27 + 22 + 1 = 50$
$13 + 12 + 1 = 26$, similarly
$9 + 2 + 1 = 12$.

15. (d) : The product of numbers on either side of the triangle plus the number at the base is the number inside the triangle, *i.e.*,
$(5 \times 3) + 4 = 19$
$(6 \times 4) + 5 = 29$, similarly
$(7 \times 5) + 6 = 41$.

16. (a) : Clockwise starting from number 7, the next number is obtained by doubling the number and adding 2, *i.e.*,
$(7 \times 2) + 2 = 16$
$(16 \times 2) + 2 = 34$ . . . , similarly
$(34 \times 2) + 2 = 70$
$(70 \times 2) + 2 = 142$
$(142 \times 2) + 2 = 286$.

17. (c) : The difference between the numbers in opposite sectors is 13, *i.e.*,
$26 - 13 = 13$
$68 - 55 = 13$, similarly
The missing number is $42 - 13 = 29$
($42 + 13 = 55$ is not given as option).

18. (b) : The number at the bottom is obtained by subtracting the sum of two numbers in the centre grid line from the square of the number at the top, *i.e.*,
$7^2 - (2 + 7) = 40$
$5^2 - (8 + 3) = 14$, similarly
$9^2 - (7 + 6) = 68$.

19. (b) : The number inside the brackets is obtained by multiplying the number on the left by 2 and then dividing the product by the sum of digits of number on the right, *i.e.*,
$(42 \times 2) \div (2 + 2) = 21$
$(162 \times 2) \div (9 + 9) = 18$, similarly
$(78 \times 2) \div (8 + 4) = 13$.

20. (a) : Subtracting the sum of squares of two numbers at the base from the square of number at the apex gives the number inside the triangle, *i.e.*,
$16^2 - (7^2 + 10^2) = 107$
$25^2 - (20^2 + 4^2) = 209$, similarly
$19^2 - (2^2 + 17^2) = 68$.

• • •

14 Alphabet Problems

Alphabet problems are fun to attempt. They are based on alphabetical series in natural as well as reverse order.

Natural Order

A B C D E F G H I J K L M N O P Q R S T U V W X Y Z

Reverse Order

Z Y X W V U T S R Q P O N M L K J I H G F E D C B A

Note : The series starts from A on reaching Z and from Z on reaching A. Of these A E I O U are vowels and the rest are consonants.

EXERCISE

1. Which letter should be ninth letter to the left of ninth letter from the right if the first half of the alphabet is reversed?

(a) I *(b)* D
(c) F *(d)* E

2. Starting from the fifth letter from the left, if twelve letters are written in reverse order, then which letter will be the seventh to the left of the fourteenth letter from the right?

(a) N *(b)* H
(c) L *(d)* O

3. What letter will come in the centre of sixth letter from the right and thirteenth letter from the left?

(a) Q *(b)* R
(c) P *(d)* S

4. If in the word "DISTURBANCE", the first letter is interchanged with the last letter, the second letter is interchanged with the tenth letter and so on, which letter would come after the letter "T" in the newly formed word?

(a) I *(b)* U
(c) N *(d)* S

5. If it is possible to make a meaningful word with the third, the fifth, the seventh and the tenth letters of the word PROJECTION. If no such word can be made, give 'O' as the answer. If more than one such word can be made, give 'M' as the answer.

(a) T *(b)* N
(c) O *(d)* M

6. A meaningful word is made if we take the first, fourth, fifth, seventh, tenth, eleventh and the twelfth letters of the word "FELICITATIONS". Which of the following will be the fifth letter of that word from the right end of that word?

(a) T *(b)* C
(c) N *(d)* I

7. On rearranging the jumbled spelling of the word SKARTINS, a language is obtained. What is the fifth letter from the right of the rearranged word?

(a) N *(b)* K
(c) R *(d)* S

8. If the 1st, 3rd, 5th, 7th, 10th and 13th letters of the word "ENTERTAINMENT" are used to make a meaningful word, then what two letters will come in the centre?

(a) A M *(b)* T T
(c) R E *(d)* N A

9. On rearranging the jumbled spelling of the word GRUBY a sport is obtained. What is the letter in the centre?

(*a*) R (*b*) B
(*c*) G (*d*) U

10. If the letters 'ERVSECI' can be rearranged to form a meaningful word what will be the fifth letter from the right?

(*a*) R (*b*) V
(*c*) E (*d*) None of these

11. From the word HASTEN how many independent meaningful English words can be made without changing the order of the letters and using each letter only once?

(*a*) 1 (*b*) 2
(*c*) 3 (*d*) 4

EXPLANATORY ANSWERS

1. (*d*) : MLKJIGHFEDCBANOPQRSTUVWXYZ

9th 9th

2. (*d*) : ABCDPONMLKJIHGFEQRSTUVWXYZ

7th 14th

3. (*a*) :

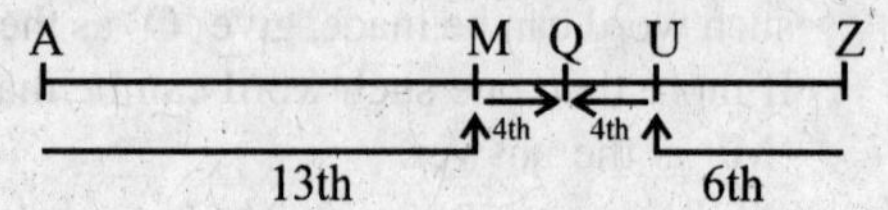

13th letter from left is 'M' and 6th letter from right is 'U'. The letter in the centre of 'M' and 'U' is 'Q'.

4. (*d*) : E C N A B R U T S I D

5. (*d*) : P R O J E C T I O N

The 3rd, 5th, 7th and 10th letters are OETN.

The words formed are TONE and NOTE.

6. (*b*) : F E L I C I T A T I O N S

The 1st, 4th, 5th, 7th, 10th, 11th and 12th lettes are FICTION.

The word is FICTION and 5th letter from right is 'C'.

7. (*d*) : The word is SANSKRIT and 5th letter from right is 'S'.

8. (*b*) : E N T E R T A I N M E N T

The 1st, 3rd, 5th 7th, 10th and 13th letters are ETRAMT.

The word formed is MATTER.

9. (*c*) : The sport is RUGBY. The letter in the centre is 'G'.

10. (*a*) : The word is SERVICE and fifth letter from right is 'R'.

11. (*b*) : The words formed are : HAS, TEN.

●●●

15

Logical Diagram

In these type of questions, a set of five different figures is given as options. Each figure represents a logical pattern of certain groups of related words wherein each word represents a class. One has to identify the most appropriate logical figure for the set of words given. Some of the relationships represented by these diagrams are given below. Understand the relationship patterns and then attempt the exercise following the explanation.

EXERCISE

Directions : *From the five logical Diagrams, select one which best illustrates the relationship among three given classes in the questions 1 to 10.*

(a)

(b)

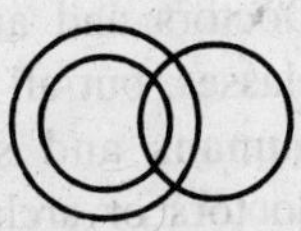

(c)

(d)

(e)

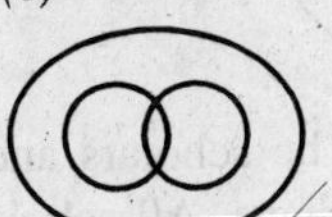

1. Birds, fruits, mangoes

2. Criminals, lawyers, bandits

3. Swimmers, bachelors, men

4. Smart, engineers, women

5. Vegetables, potatoes, brinjals

6. Grapes, sweet, fruit

7. Doctors, architects, humans

8. Scholars, people, Indians

9. Children, naughty, studious

10. Pens, pencils, stationery

Directions : *From the five logical diagrams select one which best illustrates the relationship among three given classes in questions 11 to 20.*

(a)

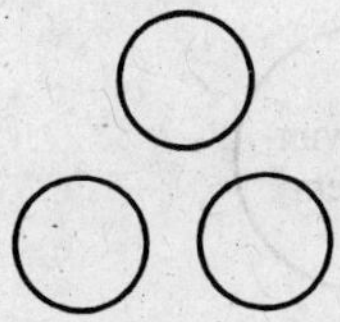

(b)

(c)

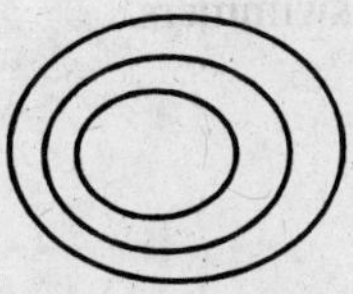

(d)

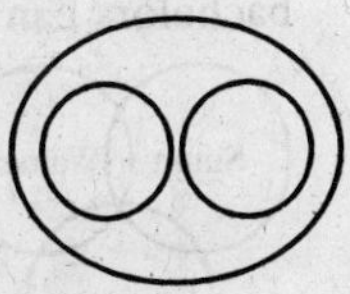

(e)

11. Ink, crayons, red

12. Canines, dogs, pups

13. Table, chair, stool

14. Ripe, mangoes, basket

15. Scholars, studious, illiterates

16. Cars, ships, means of conveyance

17. Age, number, thirteen

18. Country, state, continent

19. Father, parent, mother

20. Iron, metal, mercury

EXPLANATORY ANSWERS

1. *(a)* :

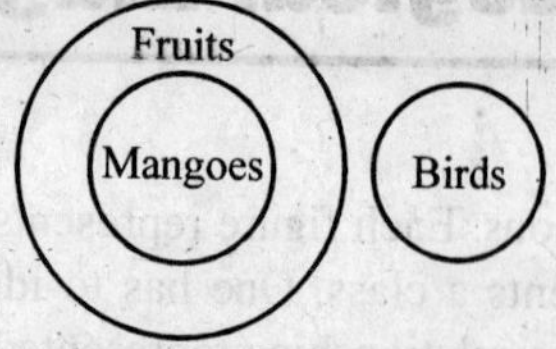

All mangoes are fruits, but neither fruits, nor mangoes can be birds.

2. *(a)* :

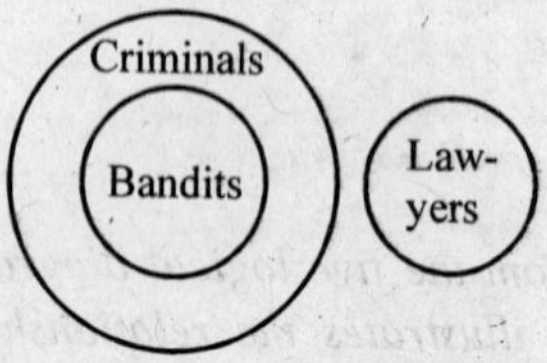

All bandits are criminal, but neither criminals nor bandits can be lawyers.

3. *(b)* :

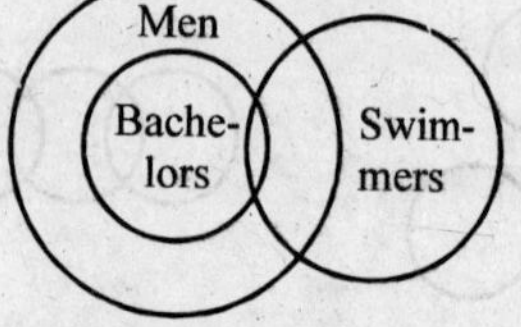

All bachelors are men and some men and bachelors can be swimmers.

4. *(c)* :

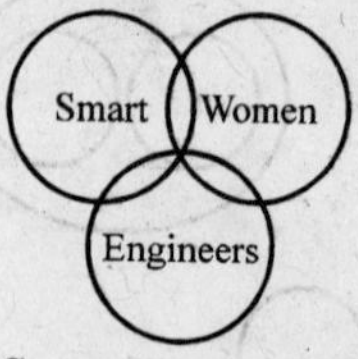

Some women can be smart and some women can be engineers and vice–versa. Some engineers can be women and some engineers can be smart and vice–versa.

5. *(d)* :

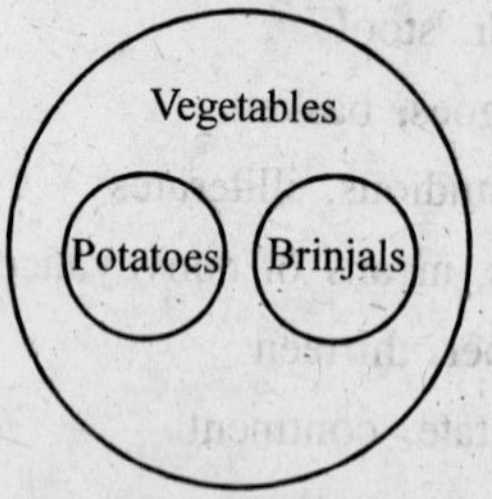

Potatoes and brinjals are vegetables but they have nothing in common. Some vegetables are potatoes and some are brinjals.

6. *(b)* :

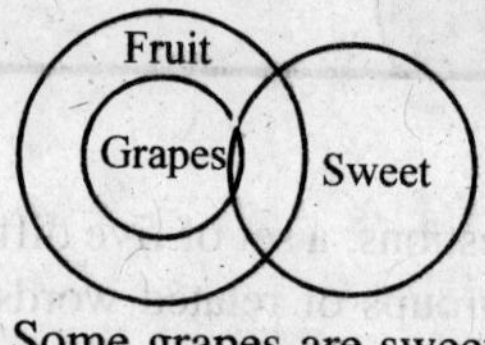

Some grapes are sweet and all grapes are fruit. But not all that is sweet is fruit.

7. *(d)* :

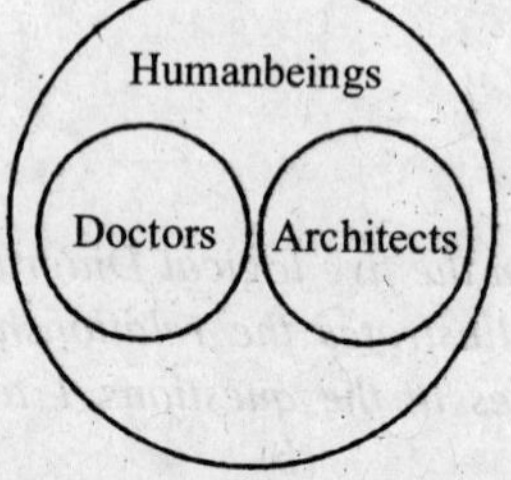

Doctors and architects are two separate classes, but all doctors and architects are humans and some humans are either doctors or architects.

8. *(e)* :

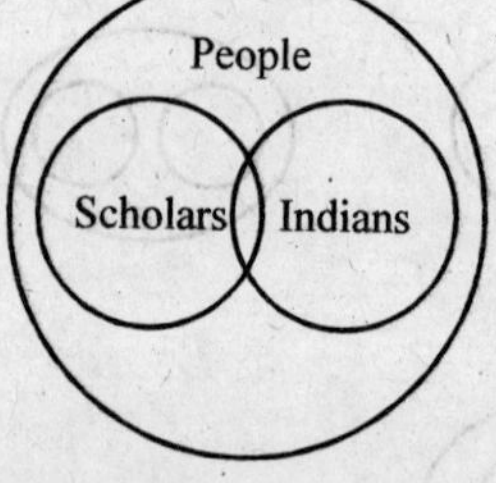

Some Indians can be scholars and some scholars can be Indians. All scholars and Indians are people.

9. *(c)* :

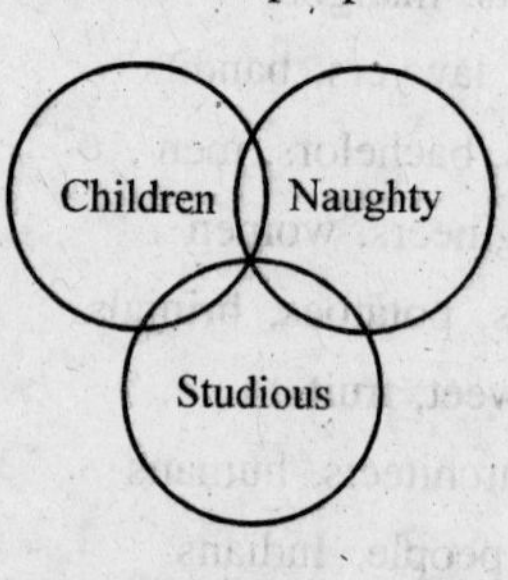

Some children can be naughty and some can be studious, some studious can be children and some naughty. Some naughty can be studious and some children.

10. *(d)* :

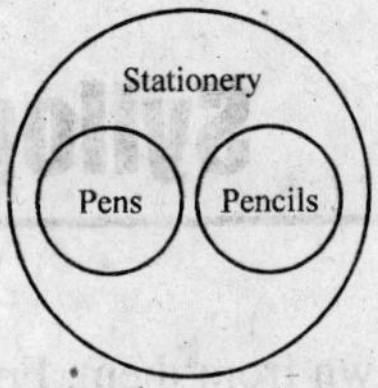

Pens and pencils both are items of stationery and some stationery is pens and pencils, but pens and pencils are two separate classes.

11. *(b)* :

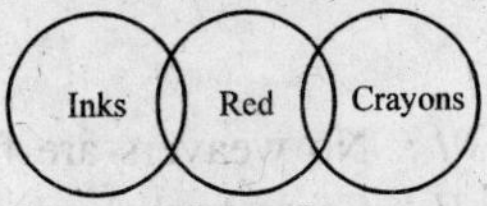

Some ink and some crayons can be red and some red units can be inks and crayons, but ink and crayon have nothing in common.

12. *(c)* :

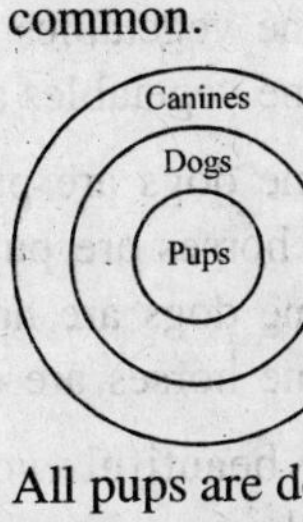

All pups are dogs and all dogs are canines. Some canines are dogs, of which some are pups.

13. *(a)* :

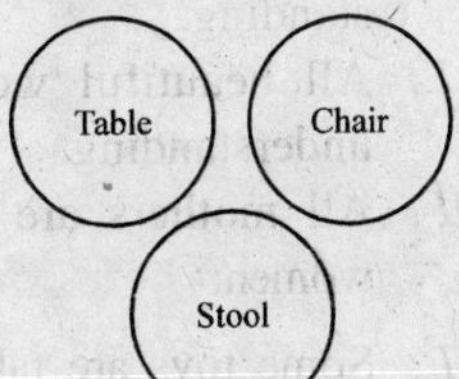

All three are different classes.

14. *(e)* :

Some mangoes are ripe and some ripe units are mangoes, but neither ripe units nor mangoes can be baskets.

15. *(e)* :

Some studious can be scholars and some scholars can be studious, but neither studious nor scholars can be illiterates.

16. *(d)* :

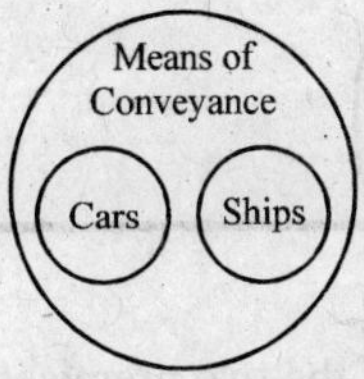

All cars and all ships are means of conveyance, but neither is contained in the other. Some means of conveyance are cars and some ships.

17. *(b)* :

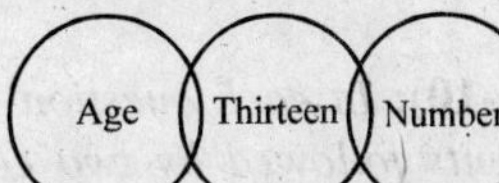

Some are aged thirteen and some numbers are thirteen. Some thirteen units are numbers and some ages. Age and number have nothing in common.

18. *(c)* :

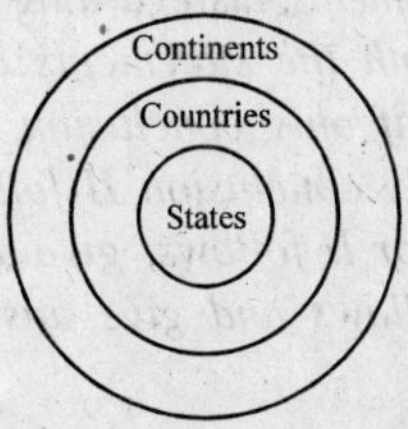

All continents contain countries within it and each country contains states within it.

19. *(d)* :

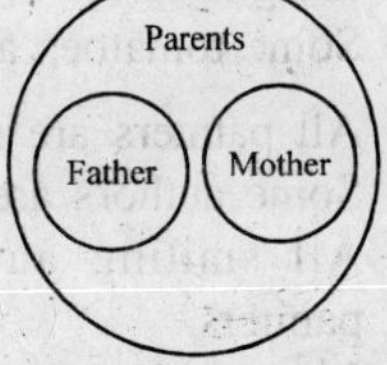

All fathers and mothers are parents, but they are two separate classes. Some of the parents are fathers and some are mothers.

20. *(d)* :

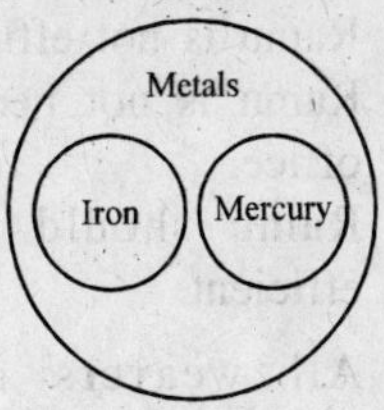

Iron and mercury are metals, but they have nothing in common. Some metals are iron and some mercury.

●●●

16 Syllogism

In this reasoning pattern, the two premises are followed by two conclusions drawn from them. Five options *(a)*, *(b)*, *(c)*, *(d)* and *(e)* are given as answers. Based on the two statements the candidate has to select the right option as answer.

EXERCISE

Directions (Qs. 1-10): *In each question below are given two statements followed by two conclusions numbered I and II. You have to take the two given statements to be true even if they seem to be at variance from commonly known facts and then decide which of the given conclusions logically follows from the two given statements, disregarding commonly known facts. Read both the statements and—*

Give answer (a) if only conclusion I follows; give answer (b) if only conclusion II follows; give answer (c) if either I or II follows; give answer (d) if neither I nor II follows and give answer (e) if both I and II follows.

1. *Statements* *I* : All tomatoes are red.
II : All grapes are tomatoes.
Conclusions *I* : All grapes are red.
II : Some tomatoes are grapes.

2. *Statements* *I* : All painters are smilling.
II : Some authors are painters.
Conclusions *I* : All smiling authors are painters.
II : Some authors are smiling.

3. *Statements* *I* : All peons in this office are efficient.
II : Ramu is not efficient.
Conclusions *I* : Ramu is not peon in this office.
II : Ramu should be more efficient.

4. *Statements* *I* : All weavers are hard working.
II : No hard working men are foolish.
Conclusions *I* : No weavers are foolish.
II : Some foolish are weavers.

5. *Statements* *I* : All fishes are cars.
II : All cars are vegetables.
Conclusions *I* : Some vegetables are cars.
II : Some vegetables are fishes.

6. *Statements* *I* : Some dogs are pups.
II : All horses are pups.
Conclusions *I* : Some dogs are horses.
II : Some horses are dogs.

7. *Statements* *I* : All beautiful women are mothers.
II : All mothers are understanding.
Conclusions *I* : All beautiful women are understanding.
II : All mothers are beautiful women.

8. *Statements* *I* : Some toys are tables.
II : No table is black.
Conclusions *I* : Some toys are black.
II : Some toys are not black.

9. *Statements* *I* : All rivers are mountains.
II : Some rivers are deserts.
Conclusions *I* : Some mountains are deserts.
II : Some deserts are not mountains.

10. *Statements* *I* : All men are horses.
II : All horses are elephants.
Conclusions *I* : All men are elephants.
II : All elephants are men.

Directions (Qs. 11-15): *In the following questions, select the set of conclusion which logically follows from the given statements.*

11. *Statements* *I :* All foxes are plates.
II : All plates are trees.
Conclusions I : All foxes are trees.
II : All trees are foxes.
III : Some trees are foxes.
IV : Some trees are plates.

(*a*) All conclusions are correct.
(*b*) Only conclusions I, III, and IV follow.
(*c*) Only conclusions II, III, and IV follow.
(*d*) Only conclusions I and IV follow.
(*e*) None of the above.

12. *Statements* *I :* Some cubes are squares.
II : All squares are circles.
Conclusions I : All cubes are circles.
II : Some circles are cubes.
III : Some circles are squares.
IV : All squares are cubes.

(*a*) Only conclusion I follows.
(*b*) Only conclusion I, II and III follow.
(*c*) All conclusions are correct.
(*d*) Only conclusions II and III follow.
(*e*) None of the above.

13. *Statements* *I :* All cups are goats.
II : All goats are tins.
Conclusions I : All goats are cups.
II : All tins are goats.
III : No cups are tins.
IV : No tins are cups.

(*a*) Only conclusions III and IV follow.
(*b*) Only conclusios I and II follow.
(*c*) Only conclusions I, II and III follow.
(*d*) All conclusions are correct.
(*e*) None of the above.

14. *Statements* *I :* All bombs are bags.
II : Some bags are jets.
Conclusions I : All bombs are jets.
II : All jets are bombs.
III : Some jets are bombs.
IV : Some bombs are jets.

(*a*) Only conclusion III follows.
(*b*) Only conclusions I and II follow.
(*c*) All conclusions are correct.
(*d*) Only conclusions III and IV follow.
(*e*) None of these.

15. *Statements* *I :* Some thorns are jackets.
II : Some jackets are boats.
Conclusions I : No thorns are boats.
II : All jackets are boats.
III : Some boats are thorns.
IV : No jackets are thorns.

(*a*) Either conclusion I or IV follows.
(*b*) Either conclusion I or II follows.
(*c*) Either conclusion I or III follows.
(*d*) No conclusion is correct.
(*e*) All conclusions are correct.

EXPLANATORY ANSWERS

1. (*e*) **:** When all tomatoes are red and all grapes are tomatoes, then all grapes are also red. When all grapes are tomatoes, then some tomatoes must be grapes. Therefore, both conclusions I and II are correct.

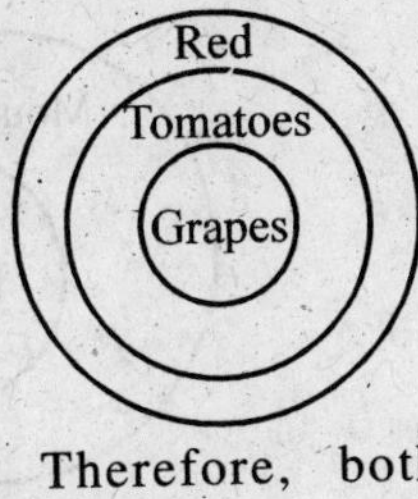

2. (*b*) **:** When all painters are smiling and some authors are painters, then some authors are smiling. Therefore, only conclusion II is correct.

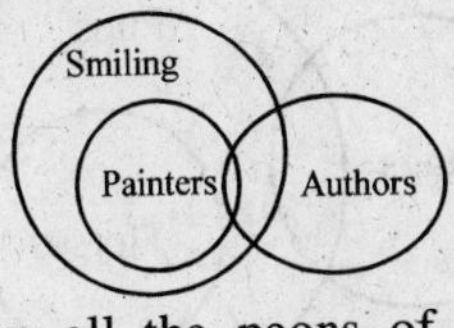

3. (*a*) **:** When all the peons of the office are efficient, then Ramu cannot be a peon in this office. Therefore, only conclusion I is correct.

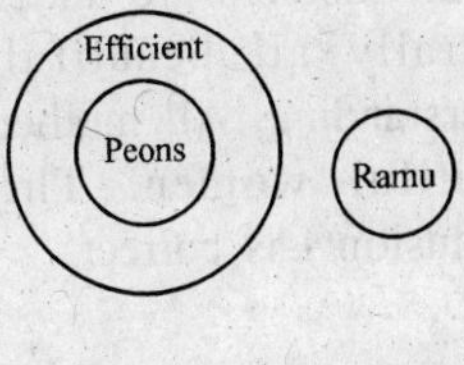

4. (a) : When all weavers are hardworking and no hardworking men are foolish, then no weavers are foolish. Therefore, only conclusion I is correct.

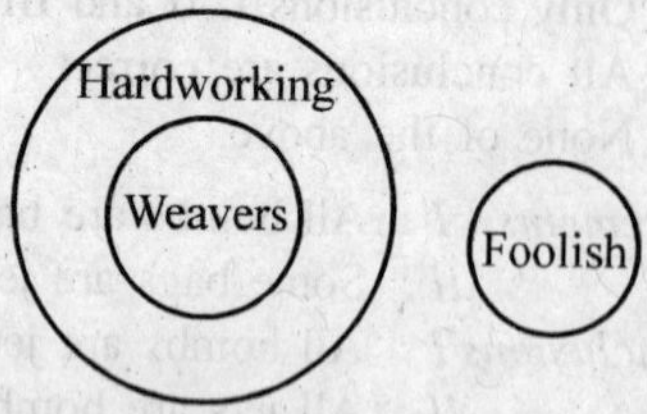

5. (e) : When all fishes are cars and all cars are vegetables, then all fishes will naturally be vegetables. This means that some vegetables are fishes. And when all cars are vegetables, then some vegetables will be cars naturally. Therefore, both the conclusions I and II are correct.

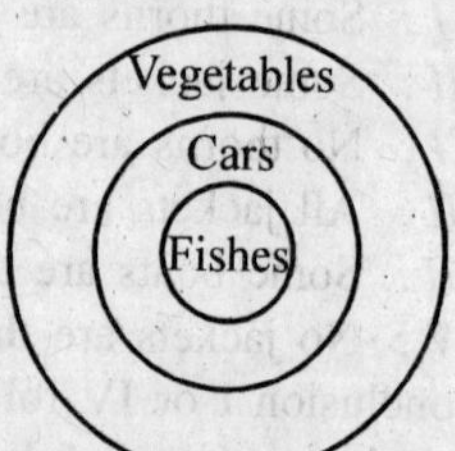

6. (d) : No relationship can be established between the two statements. Therefore, neither conclusion I nor conclusion II is correct.

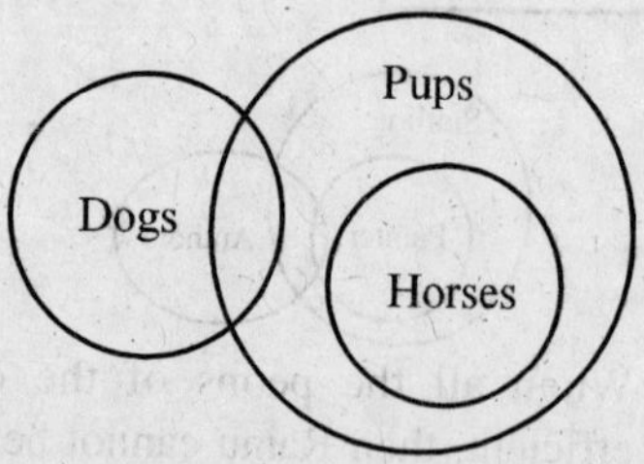

7. (a) : When all beautiful women are mothers and all mothers are understanding, then naturally all beautiful women are understanding. All mothers need not be beautiful women. Therefore, only conclusion I is correct.

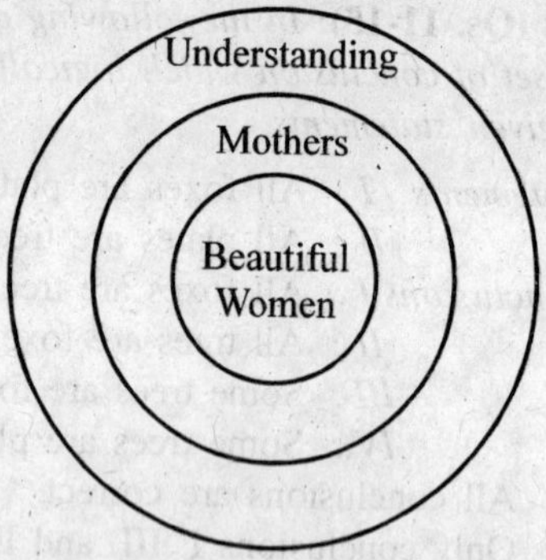

8. (c) : When some toys are tables and no table is black, then it is indicated that some toys can be black, as all toys are not tables. On the other hand, some toys may not be black. Therefore, there is a possibility that some toys may or may not be black. As such, either conclusion I or conclusion II can be correct.

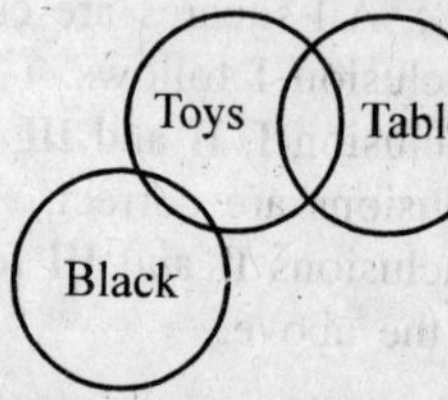

9. (e) : When all rivers are mountains and some rivers are deserts, then some deserts cannot be mountains and also, some mountains need not be deserts. Therefore, both conclusion I and conclusion II are correct.

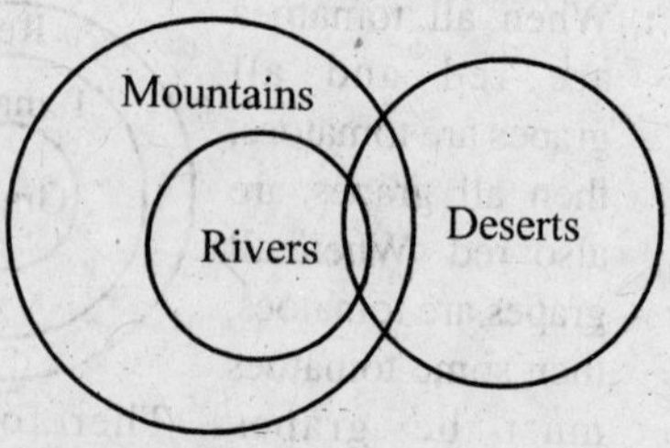

10. (a) : When all men are horses and all horses are elephants then, naturally all men are elephants, but all elephants need not be men. Therefore, only conclusion I is correct.

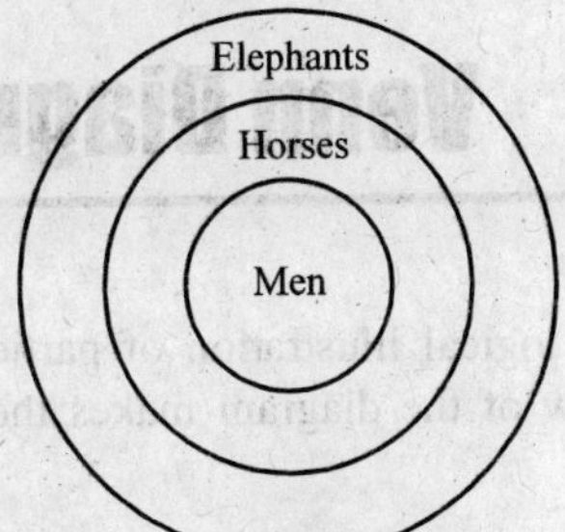

11. ***(b)*** **:**

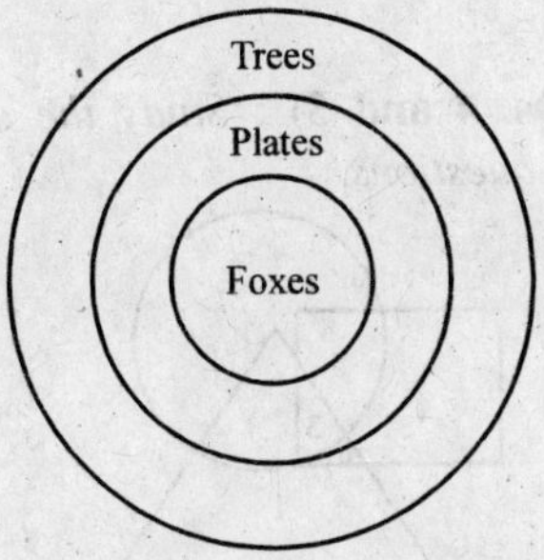

When all foxes are plates and all plates are trees, then naturally all foxes will be trees and some trees will then have to be foxes. And when all plates are trees then some trees will have to be plates. Therefore, only conclusions I, III and IV are correct.

12. ***(d)*** **:** When it is given that some cubes are squares and all squares are circles, then some cubes will naturally be circles, though all cubes cannot be circles. When some cubes are circles, then some circles will have to be cubes. And when all squares are circles, then some circles will have to be squares. As per given statement II, all squares are circles. Therefore all squares cannot be cubes. As such only conclu-sions II and III are correct.

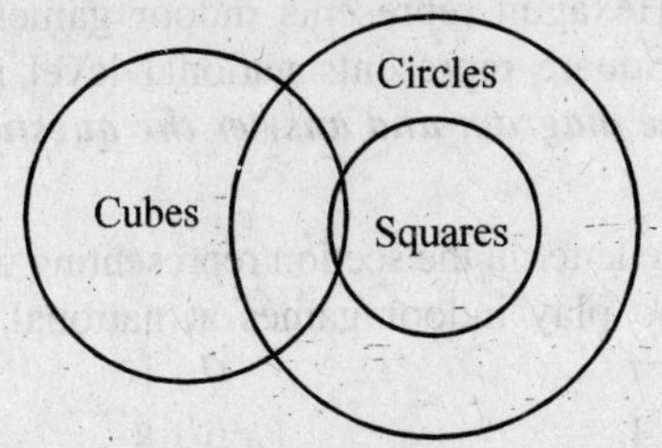

13. ***(e)*** **:** When all cups are goats, then only some goats can be cups. When all goats are tins, then only some tins can be goats. When all cups are goats and all goats are tins, then naturally all cups are tins and some tins must be cups. Therefore, all the conclusions are incorrect.

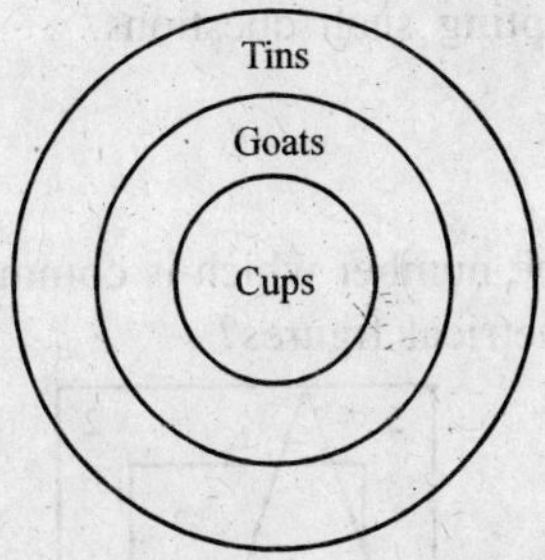

14. ***(e)*** **:** When all bombs are bags and some bags are jets then all bombs cannot be jets. 'Some bags' indicate that there is no chance of some bombs being jets, or some jets being bombs. Further all jets cannot be bombs. Therefore, all conclusions are incorrect.

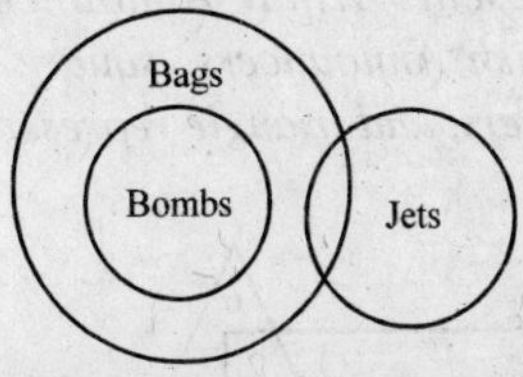

15. ***(d)*** **:** When some thorns are jackets and some jackets are boats, then some thorns may be boats but some boats cannot be thorns. As per Statement I, some thorns are jackets, some jackets need to be thorns. When Statement II conveys that some jackets are boats, then it is clear that all jackets cannot be boats. Therefore, no particular given conclusion can be drawn from the given statements.

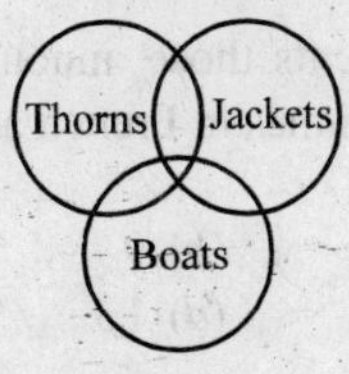

●●●

17 Venn Diagrams

In these type of questions, diagrammatic representation presents a logical illustration of particular class or statements based on which the questions are asked. A clear view of the diagram makes the concepts clear for attempting such questions.

EXERCISE

1. What is the number which is common to only two geometrical figures?

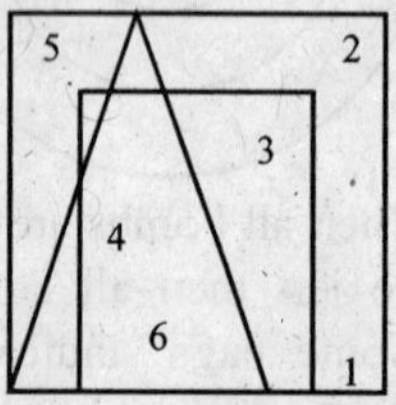

(*a*) 4 (*b*) 3
(*c*) 5 (*d*) 2

Directions (Qs. 2 and 3) : *In the following diagram, rectangle represents Hindi Announcers, circle represents English Announcers, square represents French Announcers, and triangle represents German Announcers.*

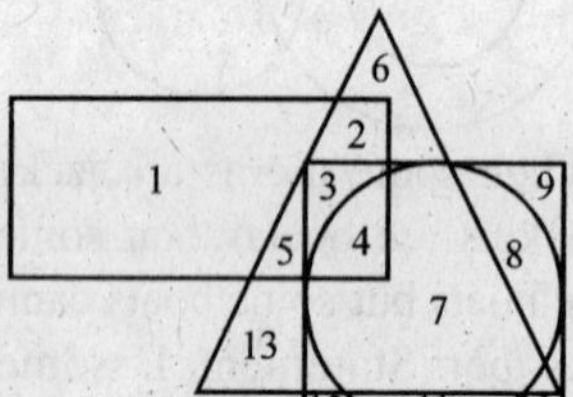

2. Which area represents those announcers who can present programmes in Hindi, French and German only?

(*a*) 1 (*b*) 2
(*c*) 3 (*d*) 4

3 Which area represents those announcers who can present programmes in French and English only?

(*a*) 7 (*b*) 9
(*c*) 11 (*d*) 13

Directions (Qs. 4 and 5) : *Study the diagram to answer these questions.*

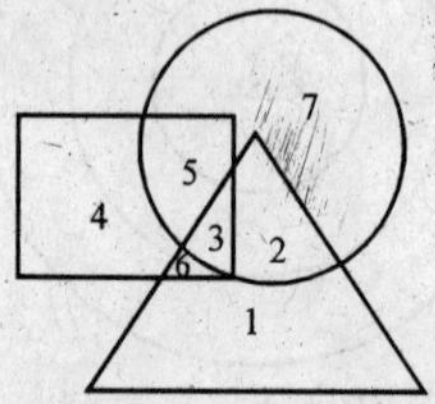

4. Which number is in all the geometrical figures?

(*a*) 5 (*b*) 6
(*c*) 2 (*d*) 3

5. Number 6 is in :

(*a*) Rectangle and triangle
(*b*) Circle and traingle
(*c*) Rectangle and circle
(*d*) Rectangle only

Directions (Qs. 6 to 9) : *In the following diagram*

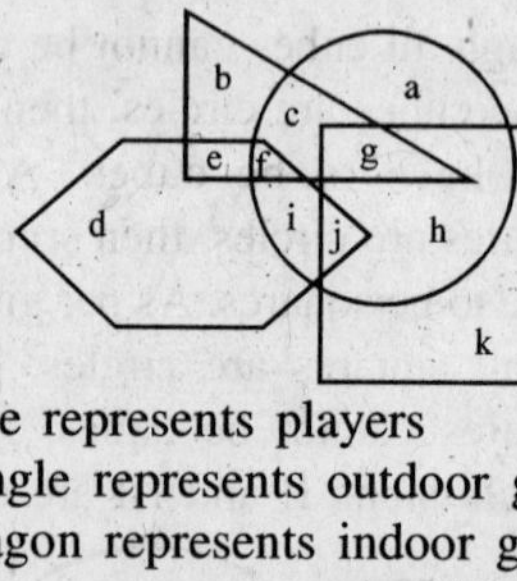

The Circle represents players
The Triangle represents outdoor games
The Hexagon represents indoor games and
The Square represents national level players

Study the diagram and answer the questions given below :

6. The letter in the section representing the players who play indoor games at national level is :

(*a*) f (*b*) i
(*c*) j (*d*) g

7. The letter representing the section of outdoor as well as indoor game players who do not play at the national level is :
(*a*) c (*b*) f
(*c*) e (*d*) i

8. The section representing national level players who do not play either outdoor or indoor games but still come under the category of players is :
(*a*) k (*b*) g
(*c*) c (*d*) h

9. Persons who play outdoor games but do not come under the category of players are represented in the section marked :
(*a*) b (*b*) c
(*c*) a (*d*) d

Direction : *Study the diagram given below.*

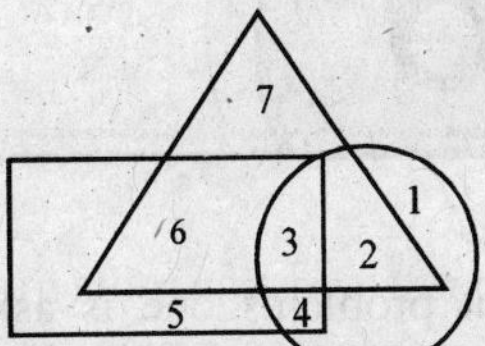

A college provides three different activities, students union represented by triangle, literary society represented by rectangle and social service league represented by circle.

10. Those who take part in both literary society and social service league but not in students union are represented by :
(*a*) 3 & 4 (*b*) 5 & 6
(*c*) 5 & 1 (*d*) 4

EXPLANATORY ANSWERS

1. **(*b*) :**

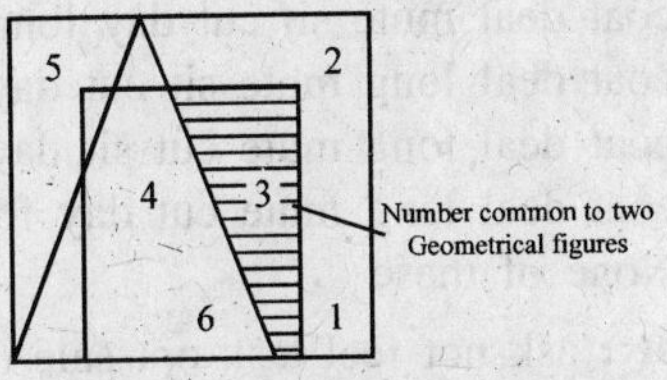

Note : Numbers 4 and 6 are common to all three geometrical figures.

2. **(*c*),** 3. **(*c*) :**

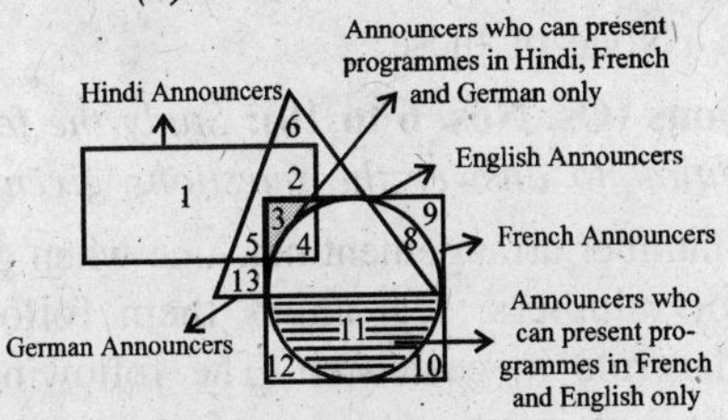

4. **(*d*),** 5. **(*a*) :**

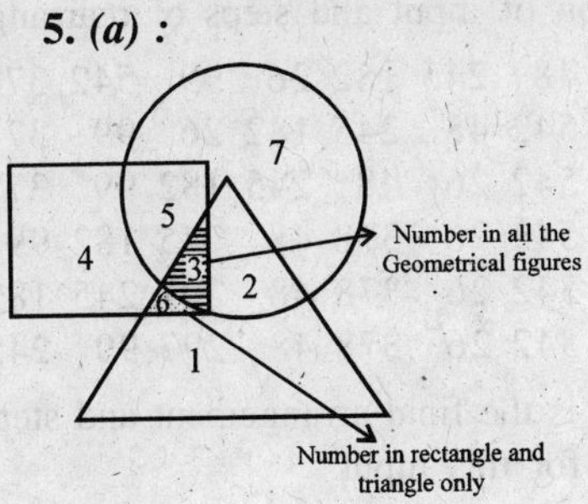

6. **(*c*),** 7. **(*b*),** 8. **(*d*),** 9. **(*a*) :**

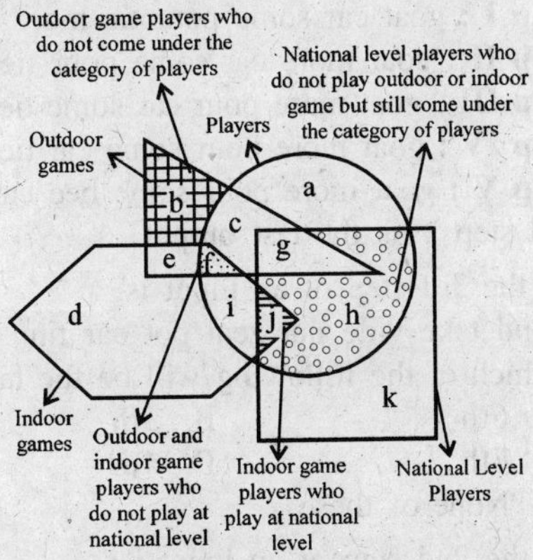

10. **(*d*)**

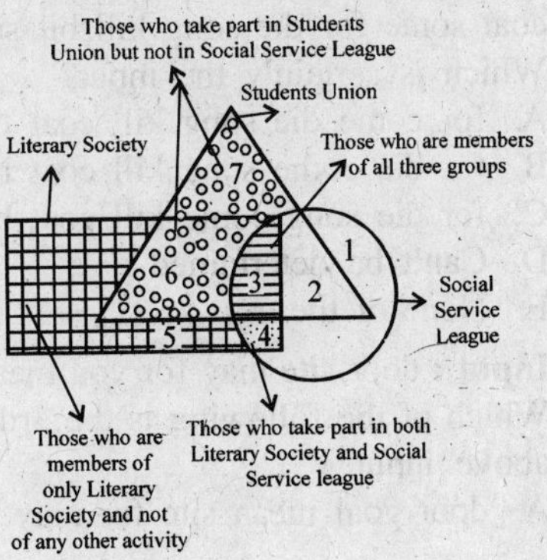

●●●

18 Input Interpretation

In input-output problems one is asked to imagine that there is some computer or a word-processing machine and it performs some operation on a given input. These operations are performed repeatedly as per a pre-fixed pattern and subsequently one has different output in different steps. One's primarily job is to deduce the rule followed by computer/machine in arranging numbers and words. One should analyze final arranged step while deducing rule applied.

EXERCISE

Directions (Qs. Nos. 1 to 5): *Study the following information carefully and answer the questions given below:*

When an input line of words is given to a word arrangement machine, it rearranges them following a particular rule in each step.

Input: car some pour tie more tin bee goat
Step I : goat car some pour tie more tin bee
Step II : goat more car some pour tie tin bee
Step III : goat more pour car some tie tin bee
Step IV : goat more pour some car tie tin bee
Step V : goat more pour some bee car tie tin
and step V is the last output.

1. If the 3rd step of an input is:
bend take vide nut zeal pot car tin.
Which of the following will be the last step?
A. 6th B. 5th
C. 7th D. 4th
E. None of these

2. If the 2nd step of an input is:
coat some for die song kill bit son.
Which is certainly the input?
A. for come die song kill coat bit son
B. for die come song kill coat bit son
C. for die song come kill coat bit son
D. Can't be determined
E. None of these

3. Input : door site may for you mean now goal
Which of the following is the 3rd step of the above input?
A. door goal mean site for may now you
B. door goal mean site may for you now
C. door site goal mean may for you now
D. Can't be determined
E. None of these

4. Input: mute deal sit cut coat day long for
Which of the following will be the 4th step?
A. coat deal mute sit cut day long for
B. coat deal long mute sit cut day for
C. coat deal long mute cut sit day for
D. coat deal long mute cut day for sit
E. None of these

5. Input : ask not feel task opt sale dark den
Which of the following will be the last step?
A. 5th B. 6th
C. 4th D. 7th
E. None of these

Directions (Qs. Nos. 6 to 10): *Study the following information to answer the questions given below:*

A number arrangement machine when given an input of numbers, rearranges them following a particular rule in each step. The following is an illustration of input and steps of rearrangement.

Input:	48	245	182	26	99	542	378	297
Step I	542	48	245	182	26	99	378	297
Step II	542	26	48	245	182	99	378	297
Step III	542	26	378	48	245	182	99	297
Step IV	542	26	378	48	297	245	182	99
Step V	542	26	378	48	297	99	245	182

This is the final arrangement and step V is the last step for this input.

6. What will be the fourth step for an input whose second step is given below?
Step II: 765 42 183 289 542 65 110 350
A. 765 42 542 350 183 289 65 110
B. 765 42 542 65 110 183 289 350
C. 765 42 542 65 183 289 110 350
D. Cannot be determined
E. None of these

7. What should be the third step of the following input?
Input: 239 123 58 361 495 37
A. 495 37 361 123 239 58
B. 495 37 58 361 123 239
C. 495 37 58 123 361 239
D. 495 37 361 239 123 58
E. None of these

8. How many steps will be required to get the final output from the following input?
Input: 39 88 162 450 386 72 29
A. Two B. Three
C. Four D. Six
E. None of these

9. What should be the last step of the following input?
Input: 158 279 348 28 326 236
A. 348 28 326 158 279 236
B. 348 28 326 236 158 279
C. 348 28 236 158 279 326
D. 348 28 158 326 236 279
E. None of these

10. If the first step of an input is "785 198 32 426 373 96 49", then which of the following steps will be "785 32 426 49 198 373 96"?
A. Third B. Fourth
C. Fifth D. Second
E. None of these

Directions (Qs. Nos. 11 to 15): *A word-number arrangement machine, when given an input as a set of words and numbers, rearranges them following a particular rule and generates stepwise outputs till the rearrangement is complete following that rule.*

Followings is an illustration of input and steps of rearrangement till the last step.

Input: pour ask 57 dear 39 fight 17 28
Step I : ask pour 57 dear 39 fight 17 28
Step II : ask 57 pour dear 39 fight 17 28
Step III : ask 57 dear pour 39 fight 17 28
Step IV : ask 57 dear 39 pour fight 17 28
Step V : ask 57 dear 39 fight pour 17 28
Step VI : ask 57 dear 39 fight 28 pour 17
and Step VI is the last output.

As per the rule followed in the above steps find out the answer to each of the following questions:

11. If step II of an input is "cut 97 38 end for 29 46 down", which of the following will be the last step?
A. Fifth B. Fourth
C. Sixth 4 D. Seventh
E. None of these

12. If the 4th step of an input is "ago 85 elite 79 exile fat 26 41", which of the following will definitely be the 2nd step of the input?
A. ago 85 79 elite fat 41 26 exile
B. ago 85 exile elite 41 26 fat 79
C. ago 85 26 exile 41 elite 79 fat
D. Cannot be determined
E. None of these

13. If the 1st step of an input is "car 17 vas tiger 92 87 like 52", which of the following will be the 4th step?
A. car 92 like 87 tiger 52 17 vas
B. car 92 like 87 17 vas tiger 52
C. car 92 like 87 tiger 17 vas 52
D. car 92 like 17 vas tiger 87 52
E. None of these

14. **Input:** zeal for 49 31 high 22 track 12
Which of the following will be the 3rd step?
A. for 49 high 31 track 22 zeal 12
B. for 49 high 31 zeal 22 track 12
C. for 49 high zeal 31 22 track 12
D. for 49 high 31 track zeal 22 12
E. None of these

15. **Input :** 19 feat 34 28 dog bag take 43
Which of the following steps would be "bag 43 dog 19 feat 34 28 take"?
A. Second
B. Fourth
C. First
D. Cannot be determined
E. None of these

Directions (Qs. Nos. 16 to 20): *A word-number arrangement machine, when given an input as a set of words and numbers, rearranges them following a particular rule and generates stepwise outputs till the rearrangement is complete following that rule.*

Followings is an illustration of input and steps of rearrangement till the last step.

Input: sine 88 71 cos theta 14 56 gamma delta 26

Step I: cos sine 71 theta 14 56 gamma delta 26 88

Step II: delta cos sine theta 14 56 gamma 26 88 71

Step III: gamma delta cos sine theta 14 26 88 71 56

Step IV: sine gamma delta cos theta 14 88 71 56 26

Step V: theta sine gamma delta cos 88 71 56 26 14

And Step V is the last Step of the arrangement of the above input as the intended arrangement is obtained.

As per the rules followed in the above steps, find out in each of the following questions the appropriate steps for the given input, Input for the questions

Input : for 52 all 96 25 jam road 15 hut 73 bus stop 38 46

(all numbers are in two digits)

16. Which word/number would be at the 6th position from the left in Step V?

A. 25 B. stop
C. jam D. all
E. road

17. Which of the following would be the Step III?

A. hut for bus all 25 jam road 15 stop 38 96 73 52 46
B. for us all 25 jam road 15 hut 38 stop 96 46 73 52
C. hut for bus all jam road 15 stop 38 96 73 52 46 25
D. for bus all 25 jam road 15 hut stop 38 46 96 73 52
E. None of the above

18. Which word/number would be at the 8th position from the right in Step IV?

A. 15 B. road
C. hut D. jam
E. stop

19. Which of the following would be Step VII?

A. stop road jam hut for bus all 15 96 73 52 46 38 25
B. road jam hut for bus all stop 15 25 38 46 52 73 96
C. stop road jam hut for bus all 96 73 52 46 38 25 15
D. jam hut for bus all 25 road stop 15 96 73 52 46 38
E. There will be no such step as the arrangement gets established at Step VI

20. Which step number would be the following output?
bus all for 52 25 jam road 15 hut stop 38 46 96 73

A. There will be no such step
B. III C. II
D. V E. VI

Directions (Qs 21 to 24.): *A word-number arrangement machine, when given an input as a set of words and numbers, rearranges them following a particular rule and generates stepwise outputs till the rearrangement is complete following that rule.*

Input : tall 48 13 rise alt 99 76 32 wise jar high 28 56 barn

Followings is an illustration of input and steps of rearrangement till the last step.

Input : tall 48 13 rise alt 99 76 32 wise jar high 28 56 barn

Step I: 13 tall 48 rise 99 76 32 wise jar high 28 56 barn alt

Step II: 28 13 tall 48 rise 99 76 32 wise jar high 56 alt barn

Step III: 32 28 13 tall 48 rise 99 76 wise jar 56 alt barn high

Step IV: 48 32 28 13 tall rise 99 76 wise 56 alt barn high jar

Step V: 56 48 32 28 13 tall 99 76 wise alt barn high jar rise

Step VI: 76 56 48 32 28 13 99 wise alt barn high jar rise tall

Step VII: 99 76 56 48 32 28 13 alt barn high jar rise tall wise

Step VII is the last step of the above input, as desired arrangement is obtained. As per the rules followed in the above steps, find out in each of the following questions the appropriate steps for the given input.

Input: 84 why sit 14 32 not best ink feet 51 27 vain 68 92 (All the numbers are two digit numbers)

21. Which step number is the following output?
32 27 14 84 why sit not 51 vain 92 68 feet best ink

A. Step V
B. Step VI
C. Step IV
D. Step III
E. There is no such step

22. Which word/number would be at 5th position from the right in Step V?

A. 14
B. 92
C. feet
D. best
E. why

23. How many elements (words or numbers) are there between 'feet' and '32' as they appear in the last step of the output?

A. One
B. Three
C. Four
D. Five
E. Seven

24. Which of the following represents the position of 'why' in the fourth step?

A. Eighth from the left
B. Fifth from the right
C. Sixth from the left
D. Fifth from the left
E. Seventh from the left

ANSWERS

1	2	3	4	5	6	7	8	9	10
B	D	E	C	A	C	D	E	A	B
11	**12**	**13**	**14**	**15**	**16**	**17**	**18**	**19**	**20**
A	D	B	C	E	A	D	B	C	A
21	**22**	**23**	**24**						
E	D	B	C						

EXPLANATORY ANSWERS

1.
Step III: bend take vide nut zeal pot car tin
! 4 ! 5 !

Step III : bend take vide nut zeal pot car tin
Step IV : bend take vide zeal nut pot car tin
Step V : bend take vide zeal car nut pot tin

2. Previous step can't be determined

3.
Input: door site may for you mean now goal
! ! 3 2 1

Input : door site may for you mean now goal
Step I : door goal site may for you mean now
Step II : door goal mean site may for you now
Step III : door goal mean site for may you now

4.
Input: mute deal sit cut coat day long for
! 2 4 1 3

Input: mute deal sit cut coat day long for
Step I: coat mute deal sit cut day long for
Step II: coat deal mute sit cut day long for
Step III: coat deal long mute sit cut day for
Step IV: coat deal long mute cut sit day for

5.
Input: ask not feel task opt sale dark den
! ! 2 4 ! 3 4 5

Input : ask not feel task opt sale dark den
Step I : dark ask not feel task opt sale den
Step II : dark feel ask not task opt sale den
Step III : dark feel sale ask not task opt den
Step IV : dark feel sale task ask not opt den
Step V : dark feel sale task den ask not opt

6.
Step II: <u>765</u> <u>42</u> 183 289 542 65 110 350
3 4

Step II : 765 42 183 289 542 65 110 350
Step III : 765 42 542 183 289 65 110 350
Step IV : 765 42 542 65 183 289 110 350

7.

Input: 239 123 58 361 495 37
3 1 2

Input: 239 123 58 361 495 37
Step I : 495 239 123 58 361 37
Step II : 495 37 239 123 58 361
Step III : 495 37 361 239 123 58

8.

Input: 39 88 162 450 386 72 29
! 4 1 3 5 2

Input: 39 88 162 450 386 72 29
Step I : 450 39 88 162 386 72 29
Step II : 450 29 39 88 162 386 72
Step III : 450 29 386 39 88 162 72
Step IV : 450 29 386 39 162 88 72
Step V : 450 29 386 39 162 72 88

10.

Step I : 785 198 32 426 373 96 49
1 2 3 4

Step I : 785 198 32 426 373 96 49
Step II : 785 32 198 426 373 96 49
Step III : 785 32 426 198 373 96 49
Step IV : 785 32 426 49 198 373 96

11.

Step II : cut 97 38 end for 29 46 down
! 5 ! ! 4 3

Step II : cut 97 38 end for 29 46 down
Step III : cut 97 down 38 end for 29 46
Step IV : cut 97 down 46 38 end for 29
Step V : cut 97 down 46 end 38 for 29

13.

Step I : car 17 vas tiger 92 87 like 52
2 4 3

Step I : car 17 vas tiger 92 87 like 52
Step II : car 92 17 vas tiger 87 like 52
Step III : car 92 like 17 vas tiger 87 52
Step IV : car 92 like 87 17 vas tiger 52

14.

Input: zeal for 49 31 high 22 track 12
1 2 3

Step I: for zeal 49 31 high 22 track 12
Step II: for 49 zeal 31 high 22 track 12
Step III: for 49 high zeal 31 22 track 12

15.

Input : 19 feat 34 28 dog bag take 43
3 1 2

Input : 19 feat 34 28 dog bag take 43
Step I : bag 19 feat 34 28 dog take 43
Step II : bag 43 19 feat 34 28 dog take
Step III : bag 43 dog 19 feat 34 28 take

Solution (16 to 20) :

Input : for 52 all 96 25 jam road 15 hut 73 bus stop 38 46
Step I : all for 52 25 jam road 15 hut 73 bus stop 38 46 96
Step II : bus all for 52 25 jam road 15 hut stop 38 46 96 73
Step III : for bus all 25 jam road 15 hut stop 38 46 96 73 52
Step IV : hut for bus all 25 jam road 15 stop 38 96 73 52 46
Step V : jam hut for bus all 25 road 15 stop 96 73 52 46 38
Step VI : road jam hut for bus all 15 stop 96 73 52 46 38 25
Step VII : stop road jam hut for bus all 96 73 52 46 38 25 15

Solution (21 to 24) :

Input : 84 why sit 14 32 not best ink feet 51 27 vain 68 92
Step I : 14 84 why sit 32 not best ink feet 51 27 vain 68 92 best
Step II : 27 14 84 why sit 32 not ink 51 vain 68 92 best feet
Step III : 32 27 14 84 why sit not 51 vain 68 92 best feet ink
Step IV : 51 32 27 14 84 why sit vain 68 92 best feet ink not
Step V : 68 51 32 27 14 84 why vain 92 best feet ink not sit
Step VI : 84 68 51 32 27 14 why 92 best feet ink not sit vain
Step VII : 92 84 68 51 32 27 14 best feet ink not sit vain why

●●●

English

1 Spelling Errors

The most common errors in English are of spellings of words. Even the most learned men are sometimes confused about the correct spellings of some words. One must keep and use a dictionary religiously. Never ignore and let pass a new word casually.

A number of question to test your knowledge of spellings are compiled here. Try to solve as many as you can.

Multiple Choice Questions

Directions: *Find the correctly spelt word out of the four options in each question.*

1. A. Accompalish B. Ackmplesh C. Acomplush D. Accomplish

2. A. Acommodation B. Acomodation C. Accomodation D. Accommodation

3. A. Astonished B. Astronished C. Astoneshed D. Asstonished

4. A. Benefeted B. Benefitted C. Benifited D. Benefited

5. A. Belligerent B. Beligirent C. Belligarant D. Belligerrent

6. A. Chancelery B. Chancellery C. Chancellary D. Chancelary

7. A. Discriminate B. Discremineta C. Discrimenate D. Discriminat

8. A. Damage B. Dammage C. Damaige D. Dammege

9. A. Efficiant B. Effecient C. Efficient D. Eficient

10. A. Extravagant B. Extreragent C. Extreregant D. Extravegent

11. A. Efflorascence B. Eflorescene C. Effllorescence D. Efflorescence

12. A. Equinimity B. Equanimmity C. Equannimity D. Equanimity

13. A. Farmament B. Farmement C. Fermament D. Fremament

14. A. Grieff B. Grief C. Grieef D. Grrief

15. A. Guarantee B. Garuntee C. Guaruntee D. Gaurantee

16. A. Hypocritical B. Hypocretical C. Hypocriticel D. Hypocirticel

17. A. Humurous B. Humorous C. Humoreus D. Humorrous

18. A. Itenerary B. Itinarery C. Itinarary D. Itinerary

19. A. Indipenseble B. Indispansible C. Indispensable D. Indipensable

20. A. Imprecticability B. Impracticebility
C. Impracticibility D. Impracticability

21. A. Incradulous B. Incredulous
C. Incridulous D. Incredalous

22. A. Juddicious B. Judiceous
C. Judicious D. Judiceus

23. A. Kleptomonia B. Kleptemonia
C. Kleptomania D. Klaptomania

24. A. Lackdaisical B. Lackadaisical
C. Lckadaisicle D. Lackadisical

25. A. Licentious B. Licontious
C. Licenttious D. Licientious

26. A. Meddicine B. Medicine
C. Medicene D. Medicinne

27. A. Meritricious B. Merefrecious
C. Meretricious D. Merritricious

28. A. Missunderstood B. Miesunderstood
C. Misunderstood D. Misunderstod

29. A. Occurad B. Occurred
C. Ocurred D. Occured

30. A. Osttentatious B. Ostentetious
C. Ostentatious D. Ostenttatious

31. A. Obnosious B. Obnoxeous
C. Obnoxious D. Obnoseous

32. A. Omenous B. Ominous
C. Ommineous D. Omineous

33. A. Pecification B. Pacification
C. Pecifacation D. Pecefication

34. A. Prograssive B. Progressive
C. Progresive D. Prograsive

35. A. Pasiveness B. Passiveness
C. Passeveniss D. Passivines

36. A. Polyendry B. Poliendry
C. Pollyendry D. Polyandry

37. A. Puerille B. Puerrile
C. Puerile D. Purrile

38. A. Pesanger B. Passenger
C. Pessenger D. Pasanger

39. A. Querrelsome B. Quarrelsame
C. Quarrelsome D. Querralsome

40. A. Rigourous B. Rigerous
C. Rigorous D. Regerous

41. A. Survellance B. Surveilance
C. Surveillance D. Survaillance

42. A. Schedule B. Schdule
C. Schedale D. Schedeule

43. A. Sepalchrle B. Sepalchral
C. Sepulchrle D. Sepulchral

44. A. Sympathetic B. Smypathetic
C. Sympothetic D. Sympethetic

45. A. Sincerely B. Sencerely
C. Sincerelly D. Sincerrely

46. A. Satellite B. Sattellite
C. Satelite D. Sattelite

47. A. Teracherous B. Treacherous
C. Treacheraus D. Treachereans

48. A. Uncivilized B. Uncevilized
C. Uncivillized D. Uncevelized

49. A. Vainglorious B. Vaniglorious
C. Vaniglerious D. Vaingloreus

50. A. Vulnarable B. Valnerable
C. Velnerable D. Vulnerable

ANSWERS

1	2	3	4	5	6	7	8	9	10
D	D	A	B	A	C	A	A	C	A
11	**12**	**13**	**14**	**15**	**16**	**17**	**18**	**19**	**20**
D	D	C	B	A	A	B	D	C	D
21	**22**	**23**	**24**	**25**	**26**	**27**	**28**	**29**	**30**
B	C	C	B	A	B	C	C	B	C
31	**32**	**33**	**34**	**35**	**36**	**37**	**38**	**39**	**40**
C	B	B	B	B	D	C	B	C	C
41	**42**	**43**	**44**	**45**	**46**	**47**	**48**	**49**	**50**
C	A	D	A	A	A	B	A	A	D

2 Spotting Errors

The most common errors in English are of spellings, grammar and usage of words. By regular practice, the errors can be easily spotted and minimised.

Common Errors with Nouns and Noun-Phrases

Incorrect	*Correct*
1. I have bought new *furnitures.*	I have bought new *furniture.*
2. The wages of sin *are* death.	The wages of sin *is* death.
3. She told these *news* to her mother.	She told her mother this *news.*
4. He took *troubles* to do his work.	He took *trouble* (or pains) over his work.
5. The *cattles* were grazing.	The *cattle* were grazing.
6. He showered *many abuses* on me.	He showered *much abuse* on me.
7. I spent the holidays with my *family members.*	I spent the holidays with my *family.*
8. There is no *place* in this compartment.	There is no *room* in this compartment.
9. Write this new *poetry* in your *copy.*	Write this new *poem* in your *note-book.*
10. He took *insult* at this.	He took *offence* at this.
11. Put your *sign* here.	Put your *signatures* here.
12. She is my *cousin sister.*	She is my *cousin.*
13. *Sunil's* my *neighbour's* house was burgled.	*Sunil* my *neighbour's* house was burgled.
14. I lost a *ten-rupees* note.	I lost *a ten-rupee* note.
15. Road closed for *repair.*	Road closed for *repairs.*
16. His house is out of *repairs.*	His house is out of *repair.*
17. What is the *reason* of an earthquake?	What is the *cause* of an earthquake?
18. This building is made of *stones.*	This building is made of *stone.*
19. I disapprove of *these kinds* of games.	I disapprove of *this kind* of games.
20. Veena's and Sheela's father is ill.	Veena and Sheela's father is ill.
21. His *son-in-laws* are doctors.	His *sons-in-law* are doctors.
22. *Alms* is given to the *poor.*	*Alms* are given to the poor.
23. He always keeps his words.	He always keeps his *word.*
24. I carried the *luggages.*	I carried the *luggage.*
25. *Two-third* of the work is left.	*Two-thirds* of the work is left.

Common Errors with Pronouns

Incorrect	Correct
1. Both did not go.	Neither went.
2. We all did not go.	None of us went.
3. Each of these boys play.	Each of these boys plays.
4. Whoever does best he will get a prize.	Whoever does best will get a prize.
5. One should not waste his time.	A man should not waste his time.
6. I and she are sisters.	She and I are sisters.
7. He is wiser than me.	He is wiser than I.
8. Between you and I, Anil is not to be trusted.	Between you and me, Anil is not to be trusted.
9. Nobody was there but I.	Nobody was there but me.
10. Who is there ? It is me.	Who is there ? It is I.
11. Only he and me can use this card.	Only he and I can use this card.
12. Let you and I go now.	Let you and me go now.
13. Everyone got one's pay.	Everyone got his pay.
14. Everyone is frightened when they see a tiger.	Everyone is frightened when he sees a tiger.
15. These two friends are fond of one another.	These two friends are fond of each other.
16. I did not like him coming at that hour.	I did not like his coming at that hour.
17. Who do you think I met?	Whom do you think I met?
18. You should avail this opportunity.	You should avail yourself this opportunity.
19. When you have read these books, please return the same to me.	When you have read the books, please return them to me.
20. They that are humble need fear no fall.	Those that are humble need fear no fall.

Common Errors with Adjectives

Incorrect	Correct
1. These all oranges are good.	All these oranges are good.
2. He held the book in the both hands.	He held the book in both hands.
3. Both men have not come.	Neither man has come.
4. That man should do some or other work.	That man should do some work or other.
5. He is elder than I.	He is older than I.
6. Shakespeare is greater than any other poets.	Shakespeare is greater than any other poet.
7. He is a coward man.	He is a cowardly man.
8. Many villagers cannot write his own name.	Many villagers cannot write their own name.
9. Each of us loves our home.	Each of us loves his home.
10. Much efforts bring their reward.	Much effort brings its reward.
11. He found hundred rupees.	He found a hundred rupees.
12. He had leave of four days.	He had four days leave.

Incorrect	Correct
13. This is a worth seeing sight.	This is a sight worth seeing.
14. He will spend his future life here.	He will spend the rest of his life here.
15. There is a best teacher in that class.	There is a very good teacher in that class.
16. Of the two plans this is the best.	Of the two plans this is the better.
17. He is becoming strong every day.	He is becoming stronger every day.
18. He is worst than I.	He is worse than I.
19. Jaipur is hot than Delhi.	Jaipur is hotter than Delhi.
20. In our library the number of books is less.	In our library the number of books is small.

Common Errors with Verbs

Incorrect	Correct
1. He asked had we taken our luggage.	He asked if we had taken our luggage.
2. She asked what are you doing.	She asked what we were doing.
3. Rama asked to Anil why he is angry.	Rama asked Anil why he was angry.
4. He does not care for his money.	He does not take care of his money.
5. He does not care for his work.	He takes no care over his work.
6. No one cared for him after his mother died.	No one took care of him after his mother died.
7. He got angry before I said a word.	He got angry before I had said a word.
8. I met a man who was my tutor 20 years ago.	I met a man who had been my tutor twenty years ago.
9. I had been for walking yesterday.	I went for a walk yesterday.
10. If I shall do this I shall be wrong.	If I do this I shall be wrong.
11. I have left trekking.	I have given up trekking.
12. I came to know as to how he did this.	I learnt how he did this.
13. I came to know why he was sad.	I found out why he was sad.
14. He knows to swim.	He knows how to swim.
15. The criminal's head was cut.	The criminal's head was cut off.
16. I said to him to go.	I told him to go.
17. I told the teacher to excuse me.	I asked the teacher to excuse me.
18. He is troubling me.	He is giving me trouble.
19. I have got a hurt on my leg.	I have hurt my leg.
20. She gave a speech.	She made a speech.

Common Errors in Subject-Verb Agreement

Incorrect	Correct
1. The owners of this factory *is* very rich.	The owners of this factory *are* very rich.
2. The pleasures of nature that one can experience at Shimla *is* beyond description.	The pleasures of nature that one can experience at Shimla *are* beyond description.

Incorrect	Correct
3. There *is* no street lights in our colony.	There *are* no street lights in our colony.
4. He and I *am* entrusted with the job.	He and I *are* entrusted with the job.
5. Rice and curry *are* his favourite dish.	Rice and curry *is* his favourite dish.
6. The honour and glory of our country *are* at stake.	The honour and glory of our country *is* at stake.
7. Time and tide *waits* for none.	Time and tide *wait* for none.
8. All the passengers with the driver *was* killed.	All the passengers, with the driver, *were* killed.
9. The teacher, with her students, *were* going out.	The teacher, with her students, *was* going out.
10. I as well as they *am* tired.	I as well as they *are* tired.
11. Not only the soldiers but their captain also *were* captured.	Not only the soldiers but their captain also *was* captured.
12. Neither you nor I *were* selected.	Neither you nor I *was* selected.
13. Either of these two applicants *are* fit for the job but neither want to accept it.	Either of these two applicants *is* fit for the job but neither wants to accept it.
14. One of these students are sure to stand first.	One of these students *is* sure to stand first.
15. Everyone of these workers want a raise.	Everyone of these workers wants a raise.
16. None of these letters has been answered so far.	None of these letters *have* been answered so far.
17. None of the girls were present at the party.	None of the girls *was* present at the party.
18. Many a battle were fought on Indian soil.	Many a battle *was* fought on Indian soil.
19. A lot of work remain to be done.	A lot of work *remains* to be done.
20. The majority of these girls likes music.	The majority of these girls *like* music.

Common Errors in the Use of Modals/Auxiliary Verbs

Incorrect	Correct
1. When I shall see him I shall tell him this.	When I *see* him, I shall tell him this.
2. If I should do wrong, he would punish me.	If I *did* wrong, he would punish me.
3. Until he will have confessed his fault, he will be kept in prison.	Until he *has* confessed his fault, he will be kept in prison.
4. She will obey me.	She *shall* obey me.
5. You would work hard.	You *should* work hard.
6. You shall find him in the garden.	You *will* find him in the garden.
7. He must have died of exposure, but we cannot be certain.	He *might* have died of exposure, but we cannot be certain.
8. You might not show disrespect to your elders.	You *must* not show disrespect to your elders.
9. You may take exercise in order to maintain good health.	You *must* take exercise in order to maintain good health.
10. He must be a crook for all we know.	He *may* be a crook for all we know.

Common Errors in the Use of Adverbs

Incorrect	*Correct*
1. He is very much angry.	He is *very* angry.
2. She was very good enough to help me.	She was *good enough* to help me.
3. She runs much fast.	She runs *very* fast.
4. She runs very faster than Seema.	She runs *much* faster than Seema.
5. It is bitter cold today.	It is *bitterly* cold today.
6. He is a much learned man.	He is a very learned man.
7. She is thinking very hardly.	She is thinking very hard.
8. To tell in brief the film was boring.	*In short* the film was boring.
9. He told the story in details.	He told the story *in detail.*
10. I did it anyhow.	I *managed to do* it somehow.
11. Aeroplanes reach Europe soon.	Aeroplanes reach Europe quickly.
12. Before long there were dinosaurs on the earth.	*Long ago,* there were dinosaurs on the earth.
13. This book is too interesting.	This book is *very* interesting.
14. He lives miserly.	He lives in *a miserly* way.
15. Just I had gone when she came.	I had just gone when she came.
16. He sings good.	He sings *well.*
17. He sings good than I.	He sings *better* than I.
18. Really speaking it is cold.	*As a matter of fact* it is cold.
19. He is enough tall to reach the ceiling.	He is *tall enough* to reach the ceiling.
20. He went directly to his college.	He went *direct* to his college.

Common Errors in the Use of Conjunctions

Incorrect	*Correct*
1. As he is fat so he runs slowly.	As he is fat *he* runs slowly.
2. If he is fat then he will run slowly.	If he is fat, he will run slowly.
3. Though he is fat still he runs fast.	Though he is fat, *he runs* fast.
4. *As* I pulled the trigger at the sametime he shook my arm.	As I pulled the trigger, he shook my arm.
5. No sooner I had spoken than he left.	No sooner *had* I spoken than he left.
6. Not only he will go, but also he will stay there.	Not only *will he* go, but he *will also* stay there.
7. Neither he comes nor he writes.	Neither *does he* come nor *does he* write.
8. Scarcely he entered the room than the telephone rang.	Scarcely *had* he entered the room *when the* telephone rang.
9. Hardly she had left the house than it began to rain.	Hardly *had she* left the house *when* it began to rain.
10. He is the fastest runner and he comes last.	He is the fastest runner *but* he comes last.
11. She is as innocent as if she looks.	She is as innocent as she looks.
12. Until he does not try he must be punished.	He must be punished unless he tries.
13. I want to know as to why you are late.	I want to know why you are late.

Incorrect	Correct
14. I am fond of Chinese food as for example sweet and sour prawns.	I am fond of Chinese food, for example, sweet and sour prawns.
15. He was angry therefore I ran away.	He was angry so I ran away.
16. I was trying to work, at that time he was disturbing me.	While I was trying to work, he was disturbing me.
17. Supposing if he is late, what will happen?	Supposing he is late (or if he is late) what will happen?
18. He asked me that why I was late.	He asked me why I was late.
19. Let us catch a taxi lest we should not get late.	Let us catch a taxi lest we should get late.
20. She dresses herself like the teacher does.	She dresses herself as the teacher does.
21. Wait while I come.	Wait *until* (or *till)* I come.
22. Until, there is corruption in India, there can be little progress.	*As long* as there is corruption in India there can be little progress.
23. I have never told a lie nor cheated anybody.	I have never told a lie *nor have I* cheated anybody.
24. Both Mohan as well as Arun are responsible for this action.	Both Mohan *and* Arun are responsible for this action.
25. Hindus and Muslims both are to blame for the riots.	*Both Hindus* and Muslims are to blame for the riots.

Common Errors in the Use of Prepositions

Incorrect	Correct
1. I will not listen him.	I will not listen *to* him.
2. Copy this word by word.	Copy this word *for* word.
3. He enquired from her where she lived.	He enquired *of* her where she lived.
4. Sign here with ink.	Sign here *in* ink.
5. Has she come in train or by foot?	Has she come *by* train or *on* foot?
6. She said this at his face.	She said this *to* his face.
7. Open the book on page one.	Open the book *at* page one.
8. I was invited for lunch.	I was *invited to* lunch.
9. I am ill since three months.	I have been *ill for* three months.
10. This paper is inferior than that.	This paper is inferior *to* that.
11. This resembles to that.	This *resembles* that.
12. My brother is superior than you in strength.	My brother is superior *to* you in strength.
13. He wrote me.	He wrote *to* me.
14. I shall explain them this.	I shall explain this *to* them.
15. Send this letter on my address.	Send this letter *to* my address.
16. He suggested me this.	He suggested this *to* me.
17. He goes *on his* work.	He goes *to his* work.
18. He *reached to* Nagpur.	He *reached* Nagpur.
19. He told *to me* to go.	He told *me* to go.
20. The term begins *from* July 1st.	The term begins *on* July 1st.

Miscellaneous Errors

Incorrect	*Correct*
1. Many *homes* are lying vacant.	Many *houses* are lying vacant.
2. It is cool in the *shadow* of the tree.	It is cool in the *shade* of the tree.
3. She *keeps* good health.	She *enjoys* good health.
4. My leg is *paining*.	*I am feeling pain* in my leg.
5. *See* this word in the dictionary.	*Look up* this word in the dictionary.
6. The train will arrive *just now*.	The train will arrive *shortly*.
7. They are *pulling* on well.	They are *getting* on well.
8. The river has *over flown* its bank.	The river has *over flown* its banks.
9. He was appointed *on* the post.	He was appointed *to* the post.
10. Last but not *the least,* we have to discuss the problem of over population.	Last but not *least,* we have to discuss the problem of over population.
11. *Cities* after *cities* fell.	*City* after *city* fell.
12. What is the use Munir going there?	What is the use of Munir going there?
13. He *did many mischief*.	He *made much mischief*.
14. It is exact five *in* my watch.	It is exact five *by* my watch.
15. I will dine with them on *next Sunday*.	I will dine with them *Sunday next*.
16. Misfortunes when faced bravely and *manly* become less troublesome.	Misfortunes when faced bravely and *manfully* become less troublesome.
17. I am *laid down* with fever.	I am *laid up* with fever.
18. He is habituated to smoking.	He is *addicted* to smoking.
19. *According to my opinion* he is right.	*In my opinion* (or according *to me)* he is right.
20. Could you please *open* this knot?	Could you please *untie* this knot?

Multiple Choice Questions

Directions: *In this section, each sentence has three parts, indicated by (A), (B) and (C). Read each sentence to find out whether there is an error. If you find an error in any one of the parts (A, B, C), indicate your response by marking the letter related to that part. If a sentence has no error, indicate this by marking '(D)' which stands for "No error". Errors may belong to grammar, usage or idiom. Ignore errors of punctuation, if any.*

1. (A) Beware of/(B) a fair-weather friend/(C) who is neither a friend in need nor a friend indeed/ (D) No error.

2. (A) Copernicus proved/(B) that Earth/(C) moves round the Sun./(D) No error.

3. (A) Seldom we have been treated/(B) in such a rude manner/(C) by the police personnel./(D) No error.

4. (A) Some men are born great,/(B) some achieve greatness/(C) and some had greatness thrust on them./(D) No error.

5. (A) The property/(B) was divided/(C) among the two brothers./(D) No error.

6. (A) I am quite certain/(B) that the lady is not only greedy/(C) but miserly./(D) No error.

7. (A) The aircraft overloaded/(B) there was something wrong of the battery/(C) and the engine was making a queer noise/(D) No error.

8. (A) A thorough inquiry of the misappropriation of funds/(B) is now imperative/(C) to bring the guilty to book/(D) No error.

9. (A) The brilliant success in the examination/ (B) as well as his record in sports/(C) deserves high praise/(D) No error.

10. (A) While travelling by a train/(B) on a cold winter night/(C) an argument rose between two passengers in our compartment/(D) No error.

11. (A) I cannot find/(B) where has he gone/(C) though I have tried may best/(D) No error.

12. (A) If I was/(B) the Prime Minister of India/(C) I would work wonders/(D) No error.

13. (A) Amit's severe bout of flu/(B) debilitated him so much/(C) that he was too tired to do for work for a week./(D) No error.

14. (A) This is the crux of the entire problem;/(B) everything centres on/(C) it being resolved./ (D) No error.

15. (A) One of the major aims of the Air Force/(B) was the complete demolition of all means of transportation/(C) by the bombing of rail lines and terminals./(D) No error.

16. (A) His strong voice cut over/(B) the hum of conversation/(C) like a knife through butter./ (D) No error.

17. (A) Even though they weren't expecting us/ (B) they managed to knock up/(C) a marvellous meal./(D) No error.

18. (A) The celebrated singer was/(B) surrounded by the usual crowd/(C) of lackeys and hanger-ons./(D) No error.

19. (A) If it weren't/(B) for you,/(C) I wouldn't be alive today./(D) No error.

20. (A) He looked like a lion/(B) baulked from/ (C) its prey./(D) No error.

21. (A) Widespread flooding/(B) is effecting/(C) large areas of the villages./(D) No error.

22. (A) She regards/(B) negotiating prices with customers/(C) as her special preserve./(D) No error.

23. (A) Often in political campaigns, a point is reached at which/(B) the candidates take out their gloves./(C) and start slugging with bare fists./(D) No error.

24. (A) If we really set to/(B) we can get the whole house/(C) cleaned in an afternoon./(D) No error.

25. (A) Pieces of rock plummeted/(B) down the mountainside/(C) in the ground below./(D) No error.

26. (A) Since the two parties each won/(B) the same number of seats,/(C) the minority party holds the balance of power./(D) No error.

27. (A) It's arrogant for you/(B) to assume you'll/ (C)win every time./(D) No error.

28. (A) We've paid for our travel and accommodation,/(B) so we need only to take/(C) some pocket-money with us./(D) No error.

29. (A) There's no evidence to show/(B) that information technology secrets are more/(C) vulnerable in India than Britain or the US./(D) No error.

30. (A) It is shameful that hunting/(B) is still considered sport/(C) by some unscrupulous people in the civilized world./(D) No error.

31. (A) The Prime Minister's good looks won him/ (B)the election but he has still to prove/(C) that he's not a just pretty face./(D) No error.

32. (A) The two books are the same/(B) except for the fact that this/(C) has an answer in the back./ (D) No error.

33. (A) He estimated his income tax bill/(B) by extrapolation over figures/(C) submitted in previous years./(D) No error.

34. (A) The modern office block/(B) sticks out like a sore thumb/(C) among the old buildings in the area./(D) No error.

35. (A) I will try to put over/(B) some feelers to gauge/(C) people's reactions to our proposal./ (D) No error.

36. (A) A major contribution of Mathura sculptors/ (B)of that period were the creation and popularization/(C) of the Buddha's image in human form./(D) No error.

37. (A) Amit has been deceiving Mona/(B) for many years but she/(C) has not still tumbled to it./(D) No error.

38. (A) Mahavira was an advocate of nonviolence and vegetarianism,/(B) who revived and reorganized the Jain doctrine/(C) and established rules for their monastic order. (D) No error.

39. (A) Microwaves are the principle carriers/(B) of television, telephone and data transmissions/(C)between stations on earth and between the earth and satellites./(D) No error.

40. (A) An unit is an abstract idea,/(B) defined either by reference to/(C) a randomly ch sen material standard or to a natural phenomenon./(D) No error.

41. (A) With the crisis deepening,/(B) the critics sense an opportunity/(C) about putting in place a more radical strategy./(D) No error.

42. (A) The salesman gave us/(B) a big spiel about why/(C) we should buy his product./(D) No error.

43. (A) I will need several weeks/(B) to invent the lie of the land before/(C) I can make any decision about the future of the business./(D) No error.

44. (A) You should be cautious/(B) and make a few discrete enquiries about/(C) the firm before you sign anything./(D) No error.

45. (A) Your husband doesn't/(B) believe that you are older/(C) than I./(D) No error.

46. (A) We are meeting today afternoon/(B) to discuss the matter/(C) and reach a compromise./(D) No error.

47. (A) Either Ram or/(B) you is responsible/(C) for this action./(D) No error.

48. (A) The student flatly denied/(B) that he had copied/(C) in the examination hall./(D) No error.

49. (A) By the time you arrive tomorrow/(B) I have finished/(C) my work./(D) No error.

50. (A) The speaker stressed repeatedly on/(B) the importance of improving/(C) the condition of the slums./(D) No error.

51. (A) The captain with the members of his team/(B) are returning/(C) after a fortnight./(D) No error.

52. (A) After returning from/(B) an all-India tour/(C) I had to describe about it/(D) No error.

53. (A) The teacher asked his students/(B) if they had gone through/(C) either of the three chapters included in the prescribed text./(D) No error.

54. (A) Although they are living in the country/(B) since they were married/(C) they are now moving to the town./(D) No error.

55. (A) Do you know/(B) how old were you/(C) when you came here?/(D) No error.

ANSWERS

1	2	3	4	5	6	7	8	9	10
D	B	A	C	C	C	B	A	D	C
11	**12**	**13**	**14**	**15**	**16**	**17**	**18**	**19**	**20**
B	A	C	C	B	A	A	C	C	C
21	**22**	**23**	**24**	**25**	**26**	**27**	**28**	**29**	**30**
C	A	A	A	C	A	A	B	D	B
31	**32**	**33**	**34**	**35**	**36**	**37**	**38**	**39**	**40**
C	C	C	D	A	B	C	C	A	A
41	**42**	**43**	**44**	**45**	**46**	**47**	**48**	**49**	**50**
C	D	D	D	C	A	B	D	B	A
51	**52**	**53**	**54**	**55**					
B	C	C	B	D					

3 Articles

Definite and Indefinite Articles

(i) 'A' and 'an' are Indefinite Articles.

(ii) 'The' is Definite Article.

(iii) 'A' and 'an' modify a noun in a general way.

(iv) 'The' particularises it. *e.g.*,

Mohan has **a pen.**

The pen which you gave me was expensive.

Vowel and Consonant Sounds

(i) 'A' is used before words starting with the sound of a consonant.

(ii) 'An' is used before a vowel sound (vowels a, e, i, o, u) *e.g.*,

a book, a cat, a useful thing, a European girl, a university,

but an FDR, an MA, an honest boy, an hour, an owl, an egg, an umbrella, etc.

Use of Articles 'A' and 'An'

A cat mews. (*i.e.*, every cat)

The cat of my neighbour mews day and night. (*i.e.*, a particular cat)

He gave me **an** egg. (Here 'an' means 'one')

Use of Article 'The'

1. 'The' is used before names of rivers, mountains, seas, oceans:

   The Himalayas, the Ganga, the Yamuna, the Bay of Bengal, the Indian Ocean, the Nile, the English Channel, *etc.*

2. Names of newspapers and magazines:

   The Times of India, the Tribune, The Sun, *etc.*

3. Names of the famous and holy books:
   The Guru Granth Sahib, The Gita, The Ramayana, *etc.*

4. Names of creations of nature:
   the sun, the earth, the moon, the sky, *etc.*

5. While using Adjectives as Nouns:
   The poor should be helped by **the rich.**

6. Sometimes with the Comparative Degree:
   The more you think, **the more** you worry.

7. With the Superlative Degree:
   She is **the most intelligent** girl in our school.

8. Before the imaginary lines and directions:
   The Latitude, The Equator, the east, the west, etc.

9. Before the names of musical instruments:
   the violin, the piano, the flute, etc.

10. While using a Proper Noun as a Common Noun:

    Mohan is **the Sachin** of our team.

Omission of Article 'The'

1. Before some Nouns used to convey general sense, articles are not used but are used to particularise them:
   Man is mortal.

2. Before Proper Nouns:
   Rakesh is an intelligent boy.

3. With Abstract Noun:
   Childhood is the prime time of one's life.
   The childhood of Sohan was full of sorrow.

4. With Material Nouns:
   Milk is an essential food.
   The milk of the cow is sweet.

5. Usually no article is used before names of diseases:
   Cancer is a fatal disease.
   However, when we talk about a disease figuratively, we use an article before its name, *e.g.* Corruption is a cancer.
6. Names of games and language:
   I like football.
   I can speak Punjabi, Hindi and English.
7. Gold is a precious metal.

NOTE: As you must have noted above, the definite article 'the' has been used where a noun is particularised.

Double Use of Article 'The'

Read the following sentences carefully to understand this :

1. The poet and novelist has been honoured.
   (The same person is the poet as well as novelist)
2. The poet and the novelist have been honoured.
   (The poet and the novelist are two different persons).
3. I have a black and white dog.
   (that is, one dog)
4. I have a black and a white dog.
   (that is, two dogs)

Multiple Choice Questions

Directions : *Fill in the blanks with suitable articles. Mark 'D' if no article required.*

1. Do you know .... boy in white?
A. a B. an
C. the D. No article

2. She is .... girl I am looking for.
A. a B. an
C. the D. No article

3. Have you read .... Mahabharat?
A. a B. an
C. the D. No article

4. ....rich are not always happy.
A. A B. An
C. The D. No article

5. Oranges are sold by .... dozen.
A. a B. an
C. the D. No article

6. Milk is sold by .... litre.
A. a B. an
C. the D. No article

7. .... Amazon is the longest river in the world.
A. A B. An
C. The D. No article

8. .... higher you climb, the colder it gets.
A. A B. An
C. The D. No article

9. She is .... untidy girl.
A. a B. an
C. the D. No article

10. I am .... M.A. is English.
A. a B. an
C. the D. No article

11. I have already spent .... few rupees I had.
A. a B. an
C. the D. No article

12. .... English are very hard-working.
A. A B. An
C. The D. No article

13. April is the fourth month of .... year.
A. a B. an
C. the D. No article

14. Rice is sold by .... kilogram
A. a B. an
C. the D. No article

15. She is .... best of the three girls.
A. a B. an
C. the D. No article

16. .... man in the car is a friend of mine.
A. A B. An
C. The D. No article

17. Brevity is .... soul of wit.
A. a B. an
C. the D. No article

18. .... thing of beauty is a joy for ever.
A. A B. An
C. The D. No article

19. .... little learning is a dangerous thing.
A. A B. An
C. The D. No article

20. .... best sauce for food is hunger.
A. A B. An
C. The D. No article

21. Birds of .... feather flock together.
A. a B. an
C. the D. No article

22. He makes .... living by begging.
A. a B. an
C. the D. No article

23. It is .... pity that he died so young.
A. a B. an
C. the D. No article

24. What .... nuisance it is?
A. a B. an
C. the D. No article

25. Delhi is .... London of India.
A. a B. an
C. the D. No article

26. Where is .... will, there is a way.
A. a B. an
C. the D. No article

27. Her father is .... physician and surgeon.
A. a B. an
C. the D. No article

28. This will benefit .... poor.
A. a B. an
C. the D. No article

29. ....bird in hand is better than two in a bush.
A. A B. An
C. The D. No article

30. As he is hard-working, he will win .... prize.
A. a B. an
C. the D. No article

31. .... water of this well is dirty.
A. A B. An
C. The D. No article

32. Only .... wearer knows where the shoe pinches.
A. a B. an
C. the D. No article

33. .... action will be taken against you.
A. A B. An
C. The D. No article

34. .... sun rises in the east.
A. A B. An
C. The D. No article

35. She was promoted to .... highest post.
A. a B. an
C. the D. No article

36. Did you see .... Taj Mahal?
A. a B. an
C. the D. No article

37. He is .... one-eyed man.
A. a B. an
C. the D. No article

38. This is .... useful book.
A. a B. an
C. the D. No article

39. Cloth is sold by .... metre.
A. a B. an
C. the D. No article

40. The sun sets in .... west.
A. a B. an
C. the D. No article

41. Amar bought......umbrella yesterday.
A. a B. an
C. the D. No article

42. Surinder is ...... honest boy.
A. a B. an
C. the D. No article

43. She wrote ...... book in French.
A. a B. an
C. the D. No article

44. ...... lion roars.
A. A B. An
C. The D. No article

45. ..... apple a day keeps the doctor away.
A. A B. An
C. The D. No article

46. John bought ...... car yesterday.
A. a B. an
C. the D. No article

47. His father is ..... engineer in the U.S.A.
A. a B. an
C. the D. No article

48. It is hard for ..... owl to fly during the day times.
A. a B. an
C. the D. No article

49. She had ..... rimmed hat.
A. a B. an
C. the D. No article

50. My uncle is ..... heart specialist.
A. a B. an
C. the D. No article

51. He looks as foolish as .... ass.
A. a B. an
C. the D. No article

52. Did you go to .... prison to visit him?
A. a B. an
C. the D. No article

53. I found .... one-rupee note in the market.
A. a B. an
C. the D. No article

54. It is a pleasure to meet such .... efficient man.
A. a B. an
C. the D. No article

55. The Sanyasi lived in a cave in .... Himalayas.
A. a B. an
C. the D. No article

56. There is .... union in our factory.
A. a B. an
C. the D. No article

57. He hit his wife on the head with .... umbrella.
A. a B. an
C. the D. No article

58. I caught him by .... collar.
A. a B. an
C. the D. No article

59. Child is .... father of man.
A. a B. an
C. the D. No article

60. He gazed at .... moon for two hours.
A. a B. an
C. the D. No article

ANSWERS

1	2	3	4	5	6	7	8	9	10
C	C	C	C	C	C	C	C	B	B
11	**12**	**13**	**14**	**15**	**16**	**17**	**18**	**19**	**20**
C	C	C	C	C	C	C	A	A	C
21	**22**	**23**	**24**	**25**	**26**	**27**	**28**	**29**	**30**
A	A	A	A	C	A	A	C	A	A
31	**32**	**33**	**34**	**35**	**36**	**37**	**38**	**39**	**40**
C	C	B	C	C	C	A	A	C	C
41	**42**	**43**	**44**	**45**	**46**	**47**	**48**	**49**	**50**
B	B	A	A	B	A	B	B	A	A
51	**52**	**53**	**54**	**55**	**56**	**57**	**58**	**59**	**60**
B	C	A	B	C	A	B	C	C	C

❑❑❑

4 Prepositions

A Preposition is a word that comes before a Pronoun or a Noun and expresses the relationship between Noun or Pronoun and some part of the remaining sentence.

(*a*) He is busy **with** his work.
(*b*) The boy jumped **into** the river.
(*c*) The birds are chirping **in** the trees.

In these sentences the words **with**, **into** and **in** show the relationship between the verbs **busy, jumped** and **chirping** with the nouns **work, river** and **trees** respectively.

Position of the Preposition

A. A Preposition usually precedes its object.
(*i*) He laughs **at** the poor.
(*ii*) He is angry **with** you.
(*iii*) She agrees **with** me.

B. In the case of Relative Pronouns it comes after the subject.
(*i*) This is the boy whom I was looking **for**.
(*ii*) That is the pen whose mention I was making **of**.

C. In the following cases, the Preposition comes after its object.
(*i*) Where is the boy you were complaining **against**?
(*ii*) What things are there you are looking **for**?
(*iii*) Who is there, you are waiting **for**?

Omission of the Prepositon

In many cases when the sentences contain Nouns of Time or Place, the Prepositions **from**, **in** and **for** are often omitted.

(*i*) He walked many kilometres.
(*ii*) He came to see me last year.
(*iii*) As I could not find my puppy anywhere, I looked here and there.

Prepositions are small words that show the relationship between one word and another. Prepositions in the following sentences show the position of the paper in relation to the desk, the book, hand and the door.

The paper is **on** the desk.
The paper is **under** the book.
The paper is **in** his hand.
The paper is **by** the door.

Common Prepositions

about	at	by
in	onto	toward
above	before	concerning
inside	out	under
across	behind	despite
into	over	until
after	below	down
like	since	up
against	beneath	during
near	through	upon
along	beside	except
of	throughout	with
amid	between	for
off	till	within
among	beyond	from
on	to	without

Multiple Choice Questions

Directions: *Select the most appropriate preposition from the given alternatives to fill in the blanks and make the sentence meaningfully complete.*

1. Don't try to be an advocate ..... these criminals.
A. for B. with
C. across D. in

2. The audience admired him ..... his sweet voice.
A. to B. on
C. for D. at

3. I want to check your bag ..... fake currency notes.
A. to B. for
C. upon D. on

4. The dew drops clung .... the blades of grass.
A. for B. on
C. to D. in

5. The thief was chased ..... by the police.
A. on B. after
C. into D. at

6. Please carry this bag ..... my room.
A. on B. for
C. to D. in

7. A lorry bumped ..... a car.
A. on B. over
C. into D. to

8. They were begging ..... food.
A. for B. on
C. to D. after

9. She always boasts ..... her wealth.
A. of B. for
C. on D. after

10. She banged ..... the door violently.
A. for B. to
C. on D. down

11. I applied ..... the post of a clerk.
A. for B. on
C. in D. to

12. I applied ..... the Principal for the post of a teacher.
A. to B. on
C. with D. for

13. I begged ..... him not to divulge the secret.
A. for B. of
C. with D. to

14. You had better borrow a pen ..... Rakesh.
A. over B. into
C. from D. by

15. I baked a cake ..... the guests.
A. to B. for
C. on D. of

16. She is confident ..... (her) success.
A. with B. on
C. of D. for

17. The doctor will cure you ..... malaria.
A. of B. with
C. for D. from

18. This law is common ..... all.
A. to B. upon
C. over D. at

19. She was condemned ..... her bad hand writing.
A. on B. for
C. into D. of

20. In summer there will be a great demand ..... desert cooler.
A. on B. with
C. for D. of

21. We shall wait ..... you.
A. on B. for
C. towards D. after

22. Tom displayed his injury ..... all his friends.
A. for B. upon
C. to D. at

23. She distributed the sweets ..... the two brothers.
A. among B. between
C. for D. in

24. Please distribute these apples ..... all.
A. among B. to
C. for D. at

25. It rarely happened that he defended ..... an innocent person.
A. against B. for
C. upon D. at

26. The parents were disappointed ..... the performance of their son.
A. on B. with
C. at D. of

27. Common salt dissolves ..... water.
A. for B. in
C. with D. by

28. This medicare is free ..... sugar.
A. on B. to
C. from D. of

29. The manager granted leave ..... the clerk.
A. to B. on
C. into D. for

30. The air was heavy ..... aroma of perfumes.
A. on B. with
C. into D. from

31. She had a quick glance ..... the magazine.
A. at B. from
C. into D. to

32. The climate of Kashmir is favourable ..... me.
A. with B. in
C. to D. for

33. They hate you ..... your poverty.
A. for B. on
C. in D. of

34. He is eligible ..... this post.
A. for B. to
C. with D. at

35. The smoke was emerging ..... down the foot of the hill.
A. on B. to
C. from D. at

36. The criminal managed to escape ..... the prison.
A. upon B. from
C. with D. of

37. You should educate your friends ..... the benefits of living in villages.
A. on B. towards
C. upon D. in

38. She made a lot of efforts ..... win the match.
A. for B. to
C. upon D. at

39. The new inspector will enquire ..... the murder case.
A. on B. for
C. into D. at

40. The retired soldiers were exempted ..... all taxes.
A. from B. to
C. on D. of

41. She was adept ..... journalism.
A. at B. on
C. with D. in

42. She is afraid ..... snakes.
A. on B. to
C. of D. with

43. I agree ..... your proposal.
A. for B. on
C. to D. with

44. The children were amazed ..... so big a python.
A. at B. on
C. in D. with

45. She was anxious ..... the final match.
A. about B. on
C. with D. for

46. He apologized ..... his being late.
A. towards B. for
C. on D. as

47. The children were amused ..... his jokes.
A. for B. to
C. at D. on

48. She is angry ..... you.
A. to B. with
C. on D. for

49. She is angry ..... your teasing remark.
A. at B. in
C. for D. with

50. A big patch of land was allocated ..... the refugees.
A. to B. for
C. in D. upon

ANSWERS

1	2	3	4	5	6	7	8	9	10
A	C	B	C	B	C	C	A	A	C
11	12	13	14	15	16	17	18	19	20
A	A	B	C	B	C	A	A	B	C
21	22	23	24	25	26	27	28	29	30
B	C	B	A	A	C	B	C	A	B
31	32	33	34	35	36	37	38	39	40
A	C	A	A	C	B	A	B	C	A
41	42	43	44	45	46	47	48	49	50
A	C	C	A	A	B	C	B	A	A

5 Synonyms & Antonyms

There are thousands of words in English language. No one can remember their meanings easily but with regular practice one can memorise most of them. A number of words with their Synonyms and Antonyms are compiled here. Try to learn as many as you can and answer the questions thereafter.

Words	Synonyms	Antonyms
Abandon	Cease, Forsake	Continue
Abhor	Hate, Loathe, Detest	Like, Love
Abiding	Enduring, Durable	Fleeting
Able	Proficient, Competent	Incompetent, Unfit
Ability	Skill, Power	Disability, Inability
Abortive	Fruitless, Futile	Fruitful, Successful
Abolish	Destroy, Undo	Restore, Revive
Abridge	Shorten, Curtail	Lengthen, Expand
Absolve	Forgive, Pardon, Excuse	Condemn
Accelerate	Hasten	Retard
Accord	Agreement, Harmony	Discord, Disagreement
Accumulate	Collect, Store, Amass	Distribute, Scatter
Adamant	Hard, Inflexible	Flexible
Adversity	Misfortune, Distress	Prosperity
Adept	Expert, Skilful	Inexpert, Unskillful
Aggravate	Heighten, Intensify	Quell, Suppress
Agile	Nimble	Clumsy, Undeft
Alert	Vigilant	Heedless
Allay	Calm, Soothe, Assuage	Arouse
Ameliorate	Improve, Advance, Amend	Worsen, Deteriorate
Ambiguous	Vague, Unclear	Clear
Amiable	Lovable, Agreeable	Disagreeable
Annihilate	Destroy	Create
Arduous	Hard, Strenuous	Easy

Words	*Synonyms*	*Antonyms*
Attacks	Assault	Defend
Audacity	Boldness	Cowardice
Auspicious	Favourable, Propitious, Lucky	Ominous, Inauspicious, Unlucky
Austere	Harsh, Severe, Rigorous	Easy-going
Authentic	True, Genuine	Spurious, False
Avarice	Greed	Generosity
Averse	Unwilling, Loath, Disinclined	Willing, Inclined
Aversion	Hostility, Hatred	Affinity, Liking
Base	Low, Mean, Ignoble	Noble, Exalted
Boisterous	Noisy, Stormy	Calm, Quiet
Brave	Courageous, Daring, Bold, Plucky	Cowardly, Dastardly, Timid
Brief	Short, Concise, Laconic	Lengthy, Diffuse
Bright	Vivid, Radiant	Dull, Dark
Brutal	Savage, Cruel	Humane, Kindly
Callous	Hard, Cruel, Indifferent	Soft, Tender, Concerned
Cautious	Careful, Wary	Rash, Reckless, Foolhardy
Censure (*n*)	Blame, Condemnation	Praise
Censure (*vb*)	Blame, Condemn	Praise, Commend
Circumscribed	Restricted, Confined, Limited	Unconfined, Unrestricted
Civil	Polite, Courteous, Gracious, Urbane	Rude, Uncivil, Impolite, Ungracious
Coerce	Compel, Force	Volunteer
Compassionate	Pitiful, Sympathetic, Merciful	Unsympathetic, Merciless, Cruel
Compress	Condense, Abbreviate	Expand, Lengthen
Conspicuous	Noticeable, Manifest	Inconspicuous
Constant	Steady, Steadfast, Uniform	Inconstant, Variable
Cordial	Friendly, Warm, Hearty	Cold, Unfriendly
Covert	Hidden, Secret	Overt, Open
Cruel	Savage, Ruthless, Vicious	Kind, Gentle, Benevolent
Cursory	Rapid, Superficial	Thorough, Exhaustive, Intensive
Credible	Believable, Probable, Plausible	Incredible, Unbelievable, Fantastic
Crafty	Cunning, Sly	Artless, Simple, Ingenuous
Costly	Expensive, Dear	Cheap, Inexpensive
Confidence	Trust, Reliance	Distrust, Doubt
Death	Decease, Demise	Existence, Life
Dearth	Scarcity, Lack, Want, Paucity, Shortage	Plenty, Abundance
Decay	Dissolution, Decline, Decomposition, Disintegration	Regeneration

Words	Synonyms	Antonyms
Deference	Respect, Reverence	Disrespect, Irreverence
Deficient	Lacking, Inadequate	Complete, Sufficient
Desolate	Lonely, Deserted	Crowded, Occupied
Destitute	Wanting, Needy	Rich, Affluent
Diligence	Industry, Perseverance	Idleness
Disgrace	Dishonour, Discredit	Honour, Credit
Dwindle	Decrease, Shrink	Grow, Increase
Earthly	Terrestrial, Mundane	Celestial, Heavenly, Unearthly
Eligible	Qualified, Suitable	Ineligible, Unsuitable
Emancipate	Liberate, Free	Enslave
Excited	Impassioned, Stimulated	Composed, Cool, Impassive
Extraordinary	Uncommon, Remarkable, Marvellous	Commonplace, Ordinary
Extravagant	Lavish, Prodigal, Wastrel, Spendthrift	Thrifty, Economical, Frugal
Fabricate	Construct, Make	Destroy
Fabulous	Fictitious, Mythical	Actual, Real
False	Untrue, Mendacious	True, Genuine
Famous	Well-known, Renowned	Obscure, Unknown
Fantastic	Fanciful, Imaginative, Visionary	Practical, Down to earth
Fearful	Nervous, Anxious, Afraid, Scared	Fearless, Dauntless
Felicity	Happiness	Sorrow
Gaiety	Joyousness, Hilarity	Mourning, Dullness
Garrulous	Talkative, Loquacious	Taciturn, Silent, Reserved
Generous	Liberal, Magnanimous	Stingy, Miserly
Gigantic	Huge, Colossal	Minute, Small
Graphic	Vivid, Pictorial, Meaningful	Vague
Guest	Visitor	Host
Guile	Fraud, Trickery	Artlessness, Ingenuousness
Gratitude	Gratefulness	Ingratitude, Ungratefulness
Gratuitous	Voluntary, Spontaneous, Unwarranted	Involuntary, Forced
Hamper	Hinder, Obstruct	Facilitate, Ease
Haughty	Arrogant, Proud	Humble, Modest
Hazardous	Dangerous, Perilous	Safe, Secure Protected
Headstrong	Obstinate, Stubborn	Weak-willed, Flexible

Words	Synonyms	Antonyms
Hope	Belief, Conviction, Expectation	Despair, Hopelessness
Improvident	Prodigal, Carelessness	Provident, Economical
Incessant	Unceasing, Continuous	Discontinuous
Indolent	Slothful, Lethargic	Active, Energetic
Joy	Delight, Pleasure	Sadness, Gloom
Jolly	Jovial, Merry	Gloomy, Sad
Judicious	Discreet, Prudent	Indiscreet, Injudicious
Knowledge	Enlightenment, Learning	Ignorance, Stupidity
Laborious	Industrious, Assiduous	Slothful, Lazy
Laxity	Slackness, Looseness	Firmness
Lenient	Mild, Forbearing	Strict, Stern
Lethal	Deadly, Fatal, Mortal	Life-giving, Vital, Vivifying
Liberal	Generous, Tolerant	Intolerant, Illiberal
Liberty	Freedom, Independence	Slavery, Bondage
Lively	Animated, Active	Dull, Listless
Loyal	Faithful, Devoted	Treacherous, Disloyal, Unfaithful
Lucky	Fortunate	Unlucky, Unfortunate
Lucrative	Profitable	Unprofitable
Magnanimous	Generous, Largehearted	Ungenerous, Stingy
Malady	Illness, Ailment	Health
Manifest	Noticeable, Obvious	Obscure, Puzzling
Meagre	Small	Plentiful, Large
Mean	Low, Abject	Noble, Exalted
Mendacious	False, Untruthful	Truthful
Misery	Sorrow, Distress	Happiness, Joy
Morbid	Sick, Diseased	Healthy
Mournful	Sorrowful, Sad	Joyful, Happy
Negligent	Careless, Heedless	Careful
Notorious	Infamous, Disreputable	Reputable
Obedient	Submissive, Compliant, Docile	Disobedient, Recalcitrant, Wayward
Obsolete	Antiquated, Out-of-Date	Current, Modern
Opportune	Timely, Seasonable	Inopportune
Opulence	Wealth, Riches	Penury, Poverty
Onerous	Heavy, Burdensome	Light, Easy
Palatable	Tasty, Delicious	Unpalatable
Pathetic	Touching	Joyous, Cheery
Persuade	Urge, Induce	Dissuade
Praise (*vb*)	Applaud, Eulogise	Condemn

Words	Synonyms	Antonyms
Praise (*n*)	Applause, Eulogy	Condemnation
Precarious	Risky, Uncertain	Safe, Certain
Pretence	Pretext, Excuse	Candour, Frankness
Propagate	Breed, Circulate	Terminate, Restrict
Quaint	Odd, Singular	Usual, Ordinary
Quell	Suppress, Subdue	Agitate, Arouse
Rare	Uncommon, Scarce	Common, Ordinary
Refined	Polished, Elegant	Crude, Coarse
Remote	Distant	Near, Close
Renown	Fame, Reputation	Infamy, Notoriety
Rigid	Stiff, Unyielding	Flexible, Yielding
Remorseful	Regretful, Repentant	Unrepentant
Rebellion	Revolt, Mutiny, Insurgency	Loyalty
Scared	Holy, Consecrated	Profane, Unholy
Sane	Sensible, Sound	Insane
Scold	Chide, Rebuke	Praise
Serious	Grave, Earnest	Frivolous
Shy	Bashful	Bold, Impudent
Simple	Plain, Artless	Complex, Cunning, Shrewd
Solitary	Single, Lonely, Secluded	Numerous, Multitude
Shallow	Superficial	Deep
Solace	Comfort, Relief	Discomfort, Grief
Spurious	Sham, False	Genuine, Authentic
Stagnant	Still, Motionless	Moving
Surplus	Excess	Deficit, Shortage
Tame	Gentle, Mild, Domesticated	Savage, Wild
Teacher	Instructor, Educator	Student, Pupil
Tedious	Wearisome, Monotonous	Agreeable, Lively
Temporal	Worldly, Secular	Spiritual
Temperate	Moderate	Immoderate, Intemperate
Tortuous	Winding, Circuitous	Straight, Direct
Tough	Hard, Strong	Tender, Soft, Flexible
Transient	Temporary, Fleeting	Lasting, Durable, Permanent
Trusworthy	Reliable	Unreliable, Untrustworthy
Tranquil	Calm	Agitated
Ugly	Unsightly, Repulsive	Beautiful, Attractive
Useful	Advantageous, Serviceable	Useless
Vehemence	Passion, Force	Apathy, Indifference

Words	Synonyms	Antonyms
Vindictive	Revengeful	Forgiving
Wholesome	Healthy	Unwholesome, Morbid, Unhealthy, Diseased
Wicked	Evil, Impious	Pious, Good
Wise	Sagacious, Erudite	Foolish, Stupid
Wrath	Anger, Fury, Rage	Love, Peace, Calm
Wreck	Ruin, Destroy	Create, Construct
Yield	Surrender, Submit	Resist, Revolt
Yielding	Submissive, Supple	Inflexible, Intractable
Yoke	Oppression, Bondage	Freedom
Zeal	Passion, Fervour	Apathy, Indifference
Zest	Relish, Enthusiasm	Distaste, Disrelish

Multiple Choice Questions

Directions (Qs. 1 to 50): *In the following questions choose the word which best expresses the MEANING of the given word.*

1. TEPID
   A. Hot B. Warm
   C. Cold D. Boiling
2. MAYHEM
   A. Jubilation B. Havoc
   C. Excitement D. Defeat
3. TIMID
   A. Fast B. Slow
   C. Medium D. Shy
4. CANTANKEROUS
   A. Quarrelsome B. Rash
   C. Disrespectful D. Noisy
5. PRECARIOUS
   A. Cautious B. Critical
   C. Perilous D. Brittle
6. TACITURNITY
   A. Dumbness B. Changeableness
   C. Hesitation D. Reserve
7. INEBRIATE
   A. Dreamy B. Stupefied
   C. Unsteady D. Drunken
8. HARBINGER
   A. Massenger B. Steward
   C. Forerunner D. Pilot
9. INTIMIDATE
   A. To hint B. Frighten
   C. Bluff D. Harass
10. IRONIC
    A. Inflexible
    B. Bitter
    C. Good-natured
    D. Disguisedly sarcastic
11. STRINGENT
    A. Tense B. Stringy
    C. Strict D. Causing to shrink
12. ECSTATIC
    A. Animated B. Bewildered
    C. Enraptured D. Wilful
13. COMMENSURATE
    A. Measurable B. Proportionate
    C. Beginning D. Appropriate
14. DESTITUTION
    A. Humility B. Moderation
    C. Poverty D. Beggary

15. ASCEND
A. Leap
B. Grow
C. Deviate
D. Mount

16. UNCOUTH
A. Ungraceful
B. Rough
C. Slovenly
D. Dirty

17. LYNCH
A. Hang
B. Madden
C. Killed
D. Shoot

18. LAUD
A. Lord
B. Eulogy
C. Praise
D. Extolled

19. CORRESPONDENCE
A. Agreements
B. Contracts
C. Documents
D. Letters

20. VENUE
A. Place
B. Agenda
C. Time
D. Duration

21. STERILE
A. Barren
B. Arid
C. Childless
D. Dry

22. SYNOPSIS
A. Index
B. Mixture
C. Summary
D. Puzzle

23. GERMANE
A. Responsible
B. Logical
C. Possible
D. Relevant

24. PONDER
A. Think
B. Evaluate
C. Anticipate
D. Increase

25. CANNY
A. Obstinate
B. Handsome
C. Clever
D. Stout

26. ABUNDANT
A. Ripe
B. Cheap
C. Plenty
D. Absent

27. CONSEQUENCES
A. Results
B. Conclusions
C. Difficulties
D. Applications

28. SHIVER
A. Shake
B. Rock
C. Tremble
D. Move

29. DILIGENT
A. Progressive
B. Brilliant
C. Inventive
D. Hard-working

30. DISTANT
A. Far
B. Removed
C. Reserved
D. Separate

31. FORAY
A. Excursion
B. Contest
C. Ranger
D. Intuition

32. FRUGALITY
A. Foolishness
B. Extremity
C. Enthusiasm
D. Economy

33. GARNISH
A. Paint
B. Garner
C. Adorn
D. Abuse

34. VIGOUR
A. Strength
B. Boldness
C. Warmth
D. Enthusiasm

35. CANDID
A. Apparent
B. Explicit
C. Frank
D. Bright

36. BRIEF
A. Limited
B. Small
C. Little
D. Short

37. GARRULITY
A. Credulity
B. Senility
C. Loquaciousness
D. Speciousness

38. FURORE
A. Excitement
B. Worry
C. Flux
D. Anteroom

39. NEUTRAL
A. Unbiased
B. Non-aligned
C. Undecided
D. Indifferent

40. LAMENT
A. Complain
B. Comment
C. Condone
D. Console

41. ADVERSITY
A. Failure
B. Helplessness
C. Misfortune
D. Crisis

42. TURN UP
A. Land up
B. Show up
C. Crop up
D. Come up

43. DEIFY
A. Flatter B. Challenge
C. Worship D. Face

44. ERROR
A. Misadventure B. Misgiving
C. Ambiguity D. Blunder

45. SHALLOW
A. Artificial B. Superficial
C. Foolish D. Worthless

46. MASSACRE
A. Murder B. Stab
C. Assassinate D. Slaughter

47. COMBAT
A. Conflict B. Quarrel
C. Feud D. Fight

48. VORACIOUS
A. Wild B. Hungry
C. Angry D. Quick

49. IMPROMPTU
A. Offhand B. Unimportant
C. Unreal D. Effective

50. RABBLE
A. Mob B. Noise
C. Roar D. Rubbish

Directions (Qs. 51 to 100): *In the following questions choose the word which is the exact OPPOSITE of the given words.*

51. STRINGENT
A. General B. Vehement
C. Lenient D. Magnanimous

52. FLIMSY
A. Frail B. Filthy
C. Firm D. Flippant

53. BUSY
A. Occupied B. Engrossed
C. Relaxed D. Engaged

54. ADAPTABLE
A. Adoptable B. Flexible
C. Yielding D. Rigid

55. LOVE
A. Villainy B. Hatred
C. Compulsion D. Force

56. BALANCE
A. Disbalance B. Misbalance
C. Debalance D. Imbalance

57. RELINQUISH
A. Abdicate B. Renounce
C. Possess D. Deny

58. MOUNTAIN
A. Plain B. Plateau
C. Precipice D. Valley

59. FICKLE
A. Courageous B. Sincere
C. Steadfast D. Humble

60. PERENNIAL
A. Frequent B. Regular
C. Lasting D. Rare

61. RARELY
A. Hardly B. Definitely
C. Frequently D. Periodically

62. STARTLED
A. Amused B. Relaxed
C. Endless D. Astonished

63. ADHERENT
A. Detractor B. Enemy
C. Alien D. Rival

64. QUIESCENT
A. Indifferent B. Troublesome
C. Weak D. Unconcerned

65. CONDENSE
A. Expand B. Distribute
C. Interpret D. Lengthen

66. BENIGN
A. Malevolent B. Soft
C. Friendly D. Unwise

67. OBSCURE
A. Implicit B. Obnoxious
C. Explicit D. Pedantic

68. HYPOCRITICAL
A. Gentle B. Sincere
C. Amiable D. Dependable

69. EVASIVE
A. Free B. Honest
C. Liberal D. Frank

70. INDUSTRIOUS
A. Indifferent B. Indolent
C. Casual D. Passive

71. EXTRICATE
A. Manifest B. Palpable
C. Release D. Entangle

72. LUCID
A. Glory B. Noisy
C. Obscure D. Distinct

73. INSIPID
A. Tasty B. Stupid
C. Discreet D. Feast

74. OBEYING
A. Ordering B. Following
C. Refusing D. Contradicting

75. VICTORIOUS
A. Defeated B. Annexed
C. Destroyed D. Vanquished

76. COMMISSIONED
A. Started B. Closed
C. Finished D. Terminated

77. VANITY
A. Pride B. Humility
C. Conceit D. Ostentious

78. ZENITH
A. Acme B. Top
C. Nadir D. Pinnacle

79. TANGIBLE
A. Ethereal B. Concrete
C. Actual D. Solid

80. REPRESS
A. Inhibit B. Liberate
C. Curb D. Quell

81. EPILOGUE
A. Dialogue B. Prelude
C. Post script D. Epigram

82. FRAUDULENT
A. Candid B. Direct
C. Forthright D. Genuine

83. LOQUACIOUS
A. Reticent B. Talkative
C. Garrulous D. Verbose

84. NIGGARDLY
A. Frugal B. Thrifty
C. Stingy D. Generous

85. PERTINENT
A. Irrational B. Irregular
C. Insistent D. Irrelevant

86. FAINT-HEARTED
A. Warm-hearted B. Full-blooded
C. Hot-blooded D. Stout-hearted

87. VIOLENT
A. Humble B. Harmless
C. Gentle D. Tame

88. STATIONARY
A. Active B. Mobile
C. Rapid D. Busy

89. HONORARY
A. Dishonourable B. Reputed
C. Paid D. Official

90. COMMON
A. Rare B. Small
C. Petty D. Poor

91. REPEL
A. Attend B. Concentrate
C. Continue D. Attract

92. ARTIFICIAL
A. Red B. Natural
C. Truthful D. Solid

93. CAPACIOUS
A. Limited B. Caring
C. Foolish D. Changeable

94. PROVOCATION
A. Vocation B. Pacification
C. Peace D. Destruction

95. METICULOUS
A. Mutual B. Shaggy
C. Meretricious D. Slovenly

96. ABLE
A. Disable B. Inable
C. Unable D. Enable

97. COMFORT
A. Uncomfort B. Miscomfort
C. Discomfort D. None of these

98. GAIN
A. Loose B. Fall
C. Lost D. Lose

99. SYNTHETIC
A. Affable B. Natural
C. Plastic D. Cosmetic

100. ACQUITTED
A. Freed B. Burdened
C. Convicted D. Entrusted

ANSWERS

1	2	3	4	5	6	7	8	9	10
B	B	D	A	B	D	D	C	B	D
11	**12**	**13**	**14**	**15**	**16**	**17**	**18**	**19**	**20**
C	C	B	C	D	A	C	C	D	A
21	**22**	**23**	**24**	**25**	**26**	**27**	**28**	**29**	**30**
A	C	D	A	C	C	A	C	D	A
31	**32**	**33**	**34**	**35**	**36**	**37**	**38**	**39**	**40**
A	D	C	A	C	D	C	A	A	A
41	**42**	**43**	**44**	**45**	**46**	**47**	**48**	**49**	**50**
C	B	C	D	B	D	D	B	A	A
51	**52**	**53**	**54**	**55**	**56**	**57**	**58**	**59**	**60**
C	C	C	D	B	D	C	D	C	D
61	**62**	**63**	**64**	**65**	**66**	**67**	**68**	**69**	**70**
D	B	B	A	C	A	C	B	B	B
71	**72**	**73**	**74**	**75**	**76**	**77**	**78**	**79**	**80**
D	C	A	A	A	D	B	C	A	B
81	**82**	**83**	**84**	**85**	**86**	**87**	**88**	**89**	**90**
B	D	B	D	D	D	C	B	C	A
91	**92**	**93**	**94**	**95**	**96**	**97**	**98**	**99**	**100**
D	B	A	B	D	C	C	D	B	C

□□□

6 One Word Substitutions

There are many words in English language which can be perfectly used for a number of words. These words help in expressing ideas in a short and correct manner for the right occasion. Such words not only enhance the vocabulary but also enable you to economise in the use of words to a great extent. Try to learn as many as you can.

Denoting Numbers

- A collection of poems — *anthology*
- A number of merchant ships protected by warships (in war-time) — *convoy*
- A number of stars grouped together — *constellation*
- A number of hired applauders, *i.e.* persons paid to clap — *claque*
- A number of people at church — *congregation*
- A number of people gathered together for some common purpose — *gathering, assembly, society*
- A group of people who get together to work for some cause of common interest — *coterie*
- A number of workmen, prisoners, thieves — *gang*
- A number of sheep — *flock*
- A number of geese — *gaggle*
- A number of leopards — *leap*
- A number of lions, monkeys — *pride, troop*
- A number of herrings, mackerel — *shoal*
- A number of fish taken in a net — *catch, haul*
- A number of whales, porpoises — *school, gam*
- A number of oxen or horses (two or more) harnessed together — *team*
- A number of ships, cars, buses — *fleet*

Denoting Places

- A place where bees are kept — *apiary*
- A place where birds are kept — *aviary*
- A place where fishes are kept — *aquarium*
- A dwelling-place of an animal underground — *burrow*
- A squirrel's home — *drey*
- A nest of a bird of prey — *eyrie, aerie*

- A place where spirituous liquors are produced *distillery*
- A place where clothes are washed and ironed *laundry*
- A place where Government records are kept *archives*
- A place where treasures of art, curiosities, etc. are preserved or exhibited *museum*
- A place where fruit trees are grown *orchard*

Pertaining to the Literary Sphere

- A work whose writer is unknown *anonymous*
- A record of one's life written by oneself *autobiography*
- The history of the life of a person *biography*
- The heading or short description of a newspaper article, chapter of a book etc. *caption*
- A humorous play, having a happy ending *comedy*
- A list of books in a library *catalogue, bibliography*
- A book in which the events of each day are recorded *diary*
- A books containing the words of a language with their definitions, in alphabetical order *dictionary*
- A book of names and addresses *directory*
- A short speech by a player at the end of a play *epilogue*
- A brief summary of a book *epitome*
- A book containing information on all branches of knowledge *encyclopedia*
- To remove the offensive portions of a book *expurgate*
- A speech delivered without earlier preparation *extempore*
- A noisy or vehement speech intended to excite passions *harangue*
- A written account, usually in book form of the interesting and memorable experiences of one's life *memoirs*
- A note to help the memory *memorandum*
- A declaration of plans and promises put forward by a candidate for election, political party or a sovereign *manifesto*
- A short speech by a player at the beginning of a play *prologue*
- Literary theft, or passing off an author's original work as one's own *plagiarism*
- Speaking aloud to oneself *soliloquy*
- A play with a sad or tragic end *tragedy*

Pertaining to Religion

- One who believes that man can have no knowledge of God but only of natural phenomena *agnostic*
- One who renounces his religious vows or forsakes his religious principles *apostate*
- One who does not believe in existence of God *atheist*
- One intolerantly devoted to a particular creed *bigot*
- To utter profane language against God or anything holy *blaspheme*
- A breaker of church images *iconoclast*
- Worship of images or idols *idiolatory*

- One who believes in God — *theist*
- One who believes in only one God — *monotheist*
- One who believes in many Gods — *polytheist*

Pertaining to Government

- To give up a throne or other office of dignity — *abdicate*
- Absence of government — *anarchy*
- Government by Sovereign of uncontrolled authority — *autocracy, despotism*
- Government by departments of states — *bureaucracy*
- Government of the people, for the people and by the people — *democracy*
- Government by the nobility — *aristocracy*
- The right of self-government — *autonomy*
- Government by a few — *oligarchy*
- Government by the wealthy — *plutocracy*
- Government by divine guidance — *theocracy*
- To decide a political question by the direct vote of the whole electorate — *referendum*
- Sweeping governmental change — *revolution*
- The science of government — *politics*

Pertaining to Professions

- One who attends to the diseases of the eye — *oculist*
- One who tests eyesight and sells spectacles — *optician*
- One who attends to the teeth — *dentist*
- One skilled in the care of hands and feet — *chiropodist*
- A physician who assists women at child-birth — *obstetrician*
- One who drives a motorcar — *chauffeur*
- One who makes or sells candles — *chandler*
- One who preserves the skins of animals and mounts them so as to resemble the living animals — *taxidermist*
- One who compiles a dictionary — *lexicographer*
- One who writes books — *author*
- One skilled in the treatment of diseases of animals — *veterinarian*
- A tradesman who manages funerals — *undertaker*
- One who draws up contracts and lends money on interest — *scrivener*
- One who lends money and keeps goods as security — *pawnbroker*
- A teacher who travels from place to place to give instruction. — *peripatetic*
- One who travels from place to place selling miscellaneous articles — *hawker, pedlar*
- One who collects postage stamps — *philatelist*
- One who lends money at exorbitant interest. — *usurer*
- One who takes care of a building — *janitor*
- One who sells sweets and pastries — *confectioner*
- One who works in a coalmine — *collier*
- One who flies an aeroplane — *pilot, aviator*

- One who studies rocks and soils — *geologist*
- One who shoes horses — *farrier*
- A professional rider in horses races — *jockey*
- One who deals in silks, cotton, woollen, and linen goods — *mercer*
- One who deals in wines — *vintner*
- One who deals in fish — *fishmonger*
- One who deals in iron and hardware — *ironmonger*
- One who sells fruits, vegetables, etc. from a barrow — *costermonger*
- One who sets type in a printing office — *compositor*

Pertaining to Medicine

- A substance which destroys or weakens germs — *antiseptic*
- Any medicine which produces insensibility — *anaesthetic*
- A medicine to counteract poison — *antidote*
- Want or poorness of blood — *anaemia*
- A medicine which alleviates pain — *anodyne*
- To cut off a person's body a part which is infected — *amputate*
- One who is recovering from illness — *convalescent*
- To be able to tell the nature of disease by its symptoms — *diagnose*
- A disease affecting many persons at the same place and time — *epidemic*
- A disease confined to a particular district or place — *endemic*
- To disinfect by smoke — *fumigate*
- Free or exempt from infection — *immune*
- A person who is sick — *invalid*
- A cure for all diseases — *panacea*
- A disease widely epidemic — *pandemic*
- Confinement to one place to avoid spread of infection — *quarantine*

Pertaining to Characteristics and Actions

- One who devotes his life to the welfare and interests of other people — *altruist*
- One who can use both hands with equal ease — *ambidexterous*
- One who fishes with a rod — *angler*
- One who kills secretly or by surprise — *assassin*
- A person who collects things belonging to ancient times — *antiquary*
- One who is always finding faults — *censorious*
- One living at the same time as another — *contemporary*
- One who sneers at the aims and beliefs of his fellowmen — *cynic*
- One who delights in speaking about oneself — *egotist*
- One who exalts his own opinion — *egoist*
- One who dies for a noble cause — *martyr*
- One who retires from society to live a solitary life — *recluse, hermit*
- One who maliciously sets fire to buildings — *incendiary*

- One who is banished from his home or his country *exile*
- One who takes refuge in a foreign country *refugee, alien*
- One who runs away from justice or the law *fugitive*
- One who walks in his sleep *somnambulist*
- One who looks on the bright side of things *optimist*
- One who looks on the dark side of things *pessimist*
- A hater of mankind *misanthropist*
- One who knows everything *omniscient*
- One who is all powerful *omnipotent*
- One who is present everywhere *omnipresent*
- One who devotes his service or wealth for the love of mankind *philanthropist*
- One new to anything *novice, tyro, neophyte*
- One who engages in any pursuit for the love of it, and not for gain *amateur*
- One who journeys to a holy place *pilgrim*
- A leader of the people who can sway his followers by his oratory *demagogue*
- One who has special skill in judging art, music, tastes, etc. *connoisseur*
- One whose reasoning is clever yet false *sophist*
- One who makes a display of his learning *pedant*
- One who is indifferent to pain or pleasure *stoic*
- One who loves his country and serves it devotedly *patriot*
- One devoted to the pleasures of eating and drinking *epicure*
- One who poses to be what he is not *hypocrite, impostor*
- One who foretells events *prophet*
- One who pretends to know a great deal about everything *mountebank, charlatan, quack*
- One versed in many languages *linguist*
- One who cannot pay one's debts *insolvent*
- One who takes over after another in office or employment *successor*
- One who has been before another in office or employment *predecessor*
- One who is opposed to intellectual progress *obscurant*
- One who abstains from alcoholic drinks *teetotaller*
- One who hides away on a ship to obtain a free passage *stowaway*
- One who spends very little *miser*
- One who spends too much *spendthrift*

Pertaining to War

- An unprovoked attack by an enemy *aggression*
- Shells, bombs, military stores *ammunition*
- A place where naval or military weapons are made or stored *ordnance*
- An agreement between belligerents to stop fighting *armistice*
- A general pardon of offenders *amnesty*
- To reduce to nothing *annihilate*
- Nations carrying on warfare *belligerents*

- To surround a place with the intention of capturing — *besiege*
- To camp in the open air without tents or covering — *bivouac*
- To seize for military use — *commandeer*
- A person who is forced by law to become a soldier — *conscript*
- An order prohibiting ships to leave the ports — *embargo*
- A number of firearms being discharged continuously — *fusillade*
- To make an examination or preliminary survey of enemy territory for military objectives — *reconnoitre*

Pertaining to Marriage and Children

- One who marries a second wife or husband while the legal spouse is alive — *bigamist*
- One vowed to a single or unmarried life — *celibate*
- One engaged to be married — *fiancé, fiancee*
- A child whose parents are dead — *orphan*
- A hater of marriage — *misogamist*
- One who has more than two wives at a time — *polygamist*

Pertaining to Death

- Dead and decaying flesh (esp. of animals) — *carrion*
- A monument set up for persons who are buried elsewhere — *cenotaph*
- To preserve a dead body from putrefaction — *embalm*
- Words inscribed on a tomb — *epitaph*
- An examination of dead body — *postmortem, autopsy*
- An account in the newspaper of the funeral of one deceased — *obituary*
- The property left to someone by a will — *legacy*
- Occurring after death — *posthumous*
- The act of killing a human being — *homicide*
- Murder of a new born child — *infanticide*
- Murder of a brother — *fratricide*
- Murder of a sister — *sororicide*
- Murder of a mother — *matricide*
- Murder of a father — *patricide*
- Murder of a parent — *parricide*
- Murder of a king — *regicide*

Pertaining to Sciences and Arts

- The study of all heavenly bodies and the earth in relation to them — *astronomy*
- The science of land management — *agronomics*
- The study of mankind — *anthropology*
- The study of physical life or living matter — *biology*
- The study of plants — *botany*
- The art of beautiful handwriting — *calligraphy*

- The science which deals with the varieties of human race *ethnology*
- The study of the origin and history of words *etymology*
- The study of coins *numismatics*
- The study of human face *physiognomy*
- The art of making fireworks *pyrotechnics*
- The study of birds *ornithology*
- The study of languages *philology*
- At home equally on land or in water *amphibious*
- The inside of a nut *kernel*
- The central or innermost part of fruit *core*
- The animals of a certain region *fauna*
- The plants and vegetation of a certain region *flora*
- Absence of rain for a long time *drought*
- To supply land with water by artificial means *irrigate*
- One who studies plant and animal life *naturalist*
- A cud-chewing animal, *e.g.* the cow *ruminant*
- A gnawing animal, *e.g.* the rat *rodent*
- A four-footed animal *quadruped*
- Animals which carry their young in a pouch, *e.g.* kangaroo *marsupials*
- Soil composed largely of decayed vegetable matter *humus*
- A preparation for killing insects *insecticide*
- A plant or animal growing on another *parasite*
- Living for many years *perennial*

Miscellaneous

- Loud enough to be heard *audible*
- Not distinct enough to be heard *inaudible*
- Fit for food *edible*
- Unfit for human consumption *inedible*
- Fit to be chosen or selected *eligible*
- Not having the qualities for being chosen *ineligible*
- Writing that is easy to read *legible*
- Writing that is difficult to decipher *illegible*
- Able to read *literate*
- Unable to read *illiterate*
- Born of married parents *legitimate*
- Born of unmarried parents *illegitimate*
- To send back a person to his own country *repatriate*
- To banish from one's country *expatriate*
- To move from one country to another *migrate*
- One who leaves his country to settle in another *emigrant*
- One who comes into a foreign country to settle there *immigrant*

- ❑ Incapable of being redeemed from evil, *i.e.* beyond correction — *incorrigible*
- ❑ That which cannot be rubbed out or blotted out — *ineffaceable, indelible*
- ❑ That which cannot be conquered — *invincible*
- ❑ Incapable of making errors — *infallible*
- ❑ That which cannot be avoided or prevented — *inevitable*
- ❑ Incapable of being burnt — *incombustible*
- ❑ That which easily catches fire — *inflammable, flammable*
- ❑ That which cannot be seen — *invisible*
- ❑ Living for ever — *immortal*
- ❑ Increase the gravity of an offence — *aggravate*
- ❑ Ordinary or commonplace remark — *platitude*
- ❑ That which cannot be satisfied — *insatiable*
- ❑ That which cannot be repaired — *irreparable*
- ❑ That which cannot be imitated — *inimitable*
- ❑ Persons (or efforts) that cannot be wearied — *indefatigable*
- ❑ One who eats too much — *glutton*
- ❑ To destroy completely — *annihilate*
- ❑ A statement open to more than one interpretation — *ambiguous*
- ❑ A round about way of speaking — *circumlocution*
- ❑ Cautious observation of events, etc. — *circumspection*
- ❑ That which cannot be hurt — *invulnerable*

Multiple Choice Questions

Directions: *Below are given some statements each of which is capable of being expressed by one word only. Each statement is followed by four such words of which only one is correct. Out of the given alternatives A, B, C and D choose the correct word which very closely fits each definition.*

1. A set of papers giving information about a person or event:

A. editorial B. agenda
C. dossier D. clippings

2. List and explanations of technical, difficult, etc. terms:

A. preface B. glossary
C. bibliography D. appendix

3. One who pays too much care to his clothes and personal appearance:

A. conscious B. dandy
C. cynosure D. leer

4. A child born after death of father:

A. effeminate B. immature
C. fatherless D. posthumous

5. A person who is hard to please:

A. insensible B. hypocrite
C. egoist D. fastidious

6. Complete failure in something attempted:

A. fiasco B. vain
C. falsies D. flop

7. A word which can be interpreted in any way:

A. confusing B. misnomer
C. ambiguous D. precise

8. A group of persons united by common interests:

A. society B. class
C. clique D. coterie

9. A person who is inexperienced and easily deceived:
A. fool B. immature
C. blackhorn D. greenhorn

10. Instruction by question and answer:
A. interrogatory B. catechism
C. bulletin D. alibi

11. Record of events by someone with first hand knowledge:
A. novice B. report
C. memoir D. itinerary

12. A mode of talk familiar to a particular group or profession:
A. jargon B. colloquial
C. slang D. abuses

13. Person who is crazy:
A. lackadaisical B. tarter
C. scrupulous D. loony

14. A person who readily believes others:
A. hasty B. immature
C. credulous D. credible

15. One who eats human flesh:
A. beast B. cannibal
C. maneater D. carnivorous

16. Intentional destruction of racial groups:
A. genocide B. homicide
C. fratricide D. communal riot

17. One with weakness of mind caused by old age:
A. dastard B. dotard
C. fop D. philanderer

18. Study of insects:
A. zoology B. philology
C. entomology D. etymology

19. A critical judge of any art particularly fine arts:
A. connoisseur B. veteran
C. philistine D. dilettante

20. One who introduces items of an entertainment:
A. consort B. compere
C. director D. introducer

21. A combination of business firms:
A. enterprise B. franchise
C. cartel D. autonomous

22. Freeing of suppressed emotions:
A. catastrophe B. catharsis
C. epilogue D. chagrin

23. One who believes in the power of fate:
A. optimist B. pessimist
C. fearful D. fatalist

24. The murder of brother:
A. genocide B. homicide
C. salvage D. fratricide

25. Additional to proper payment:
A. premium B. overtime
C. ex-gratia D. fringe

26. A person or thing used to tempt somebody into a position of danger:
A. decoy B. provocateur
C. jinx D. scapegoat

27. Custom of having more than one husband at the same time:
A. polygamy B. polyandry
C. bigamy D. sexagenary

28. A person of refined taste in food and drink:
A. emeritus B. epicure
C. glutton D. gourmand

29. A tombstone inscription:
A. epithet B. encomium
C. epistle D. epitaph

30. An office which has no work but high salary:
A. fortuitous B. gratuitous
C. sinecure D. ceremonial

31. One who is indifferent to pains and pleasure of life:
A. stoic B. metaphysical
C. pessimist D. sceptic

32. List of names of persons showing duties to be performed by each in turn:
A. notice B. bulletin
C. roster D. agenda

33. Long angry speech of criticism or accusation:
A. track record B. tirade
C. taut D. outburst

34. One who is in favour of never drinking alcoholic drinks:
A. idealist B. uxorious
C. teetotaller D. unalcoholic

35. Trying to win favour by flattery and charm:
A. smarmy B. shrewish
C. toady D. loquacious

36. A decision on which one cannot go back:
A. incorrigible B. irrevocable
C. rigid D. invulnerable

37. The science that studies the varieties of human race:
A. phrenology B. physiology
C. sociology D. ethnology

38. A person who hates women:
A. philogynist B. philatelist
C. misogamist D. misogynist

39. A group of people in a particular grade in an organisation:
A. colleague B. staff
C. echelon D. commission

40. Honourably discharged from service:
A. emeritus B. latitudinarian
C. infallible D. meritorious

41. One who does not believe in the existence of God:
A. atheist B. altruist
C. agnostic D. flippant

42. The large money paid for an early retirement:
A. goldmine B. golden handshake
C. gratuity D. lion's share

43. A hater of learning and knowledge:
A. misologist B. misogynist
C. philologist D. philanthropist

44. One who lives and acts for the welfare of others:
A. misanthrope B. credulous
C. altruist D. gregarious

45. Mental weariness for want of occupation:
A. desperate B. depression
C. fatigue D. ennui

46. That which makes it difficult to recognise the presence in real of somebody or something:
A. cover B. mask
C. make-up D. camouflage

47. To bear a hand in one's new business:
A. partnership B. interfere
C. assist D. join

48. One who renounces the world and practices self-discipline in order to attain salvation:
A. devotee B. ascetic
C. theist D. parsimonious

49. A place where gambling is practiced:
A. hotel B. motel
C. casino D. stadium

50. A sad song is a:
A. dirge B. elegy
C. ditty D. knell

ANSWERS

1	2	3	4	5	6	7	8	9	10
C	B	B	D	D	A	C	C	D	B
11	**12**	**13**	**14**	**15**	**16**	**17**	**18**	**19**	**20**
C	A	D	C	B	A	B	C	A	B
21	**22**	**23**	**24**	**25**	**26**	**27**	**28**	**29**	**30**
C	B	D	D	D	A	B	B	D	C
31	**32**	**33**	**34**	**35**	**36**	**37**	**38**	**39**	**40**
A	C	B	C	A	B	D	D	C	A
41	**42**	**43**	**44**	**45**	**46**	**47**	**48**	**49**	**50**
A	B	A	C	D	D	C	B	C	A

7 Idioms and Phrases

- An idiom is a group of words established by usage as having a meaning different from the individual words.
- A phrase is a small group of words standing together as an idiomatic expression.

Learn and practise as may as you can.

Idioms and Idiomatic Phrases

✦ **ABC** (basic principles)
She does not know the ABC of photography.

✦ **At one's beck and call** (ready to obey)
He had a dozen men at his beck and call.

✦ **At sixes and sevens** (in disorder)
The drawing room articles were lying at sixes and sevens on the floor.

✦ **A wet blanket** (a discouraging person)
Don't allow Rakesh to accompany you to the hunting trip because he is a wet blanket.

✦ **A big gun** (an important person)
Mr Smith is a big gun in our city.

✦ **At a stone's throw** (at a short distance from)
My school is at a stone's throw from my house.

✦ **A man of word** (a person who keeps his promise)
Mr Sharma is a man of word.

✦ **A man of a few words** (a remarkable person)
Gandhiji was a man of a few words.

✦ **At arm's length** (to keep away)
We should always keep bad boys at arm's length

✦ **A bolt from the blue** (a sudden and unexpected event)
The news of my friend's death came to me like a bolt from the blue.

✦ **A man of letters** (a scholar)
Radha Krishnan was a man of letters.

✦ **A hard nut to crack.** (a puzzling problem)
To get a win over American basket ball team is a hard nut to crack for India.

✦ **A yeoman's service** (service which is beneficial to the human beings)
He did yeoman's service through his life.

✦ **A snake in the grass** (a hidden foe)
Beware of him because he seems to be a snake in the grass.

✦ **Acid test** (hard test)
The election will be an acid test for the ruling party.

✦ **A wolf in sheep's clothing** (a hypocrite)
You should not keep company with him because he is a wolf in sheep's clothing.

✦ **At the eleventh hour** (at the last moment)
The war was about to start but fortunately at the eleventh hour a messenger came to the PM with a message of peace.

✦ **A great card** (an important person)
Mr Sood is a great card in the ministry of finance.

✦ **A fool of the first water** (one completely foolish)
Being a fool of the first water he could not solve even the simplest sum.

✦ **A bone of contention** (to be the cause of quarrel)
Kashmir is the bone of contention between India and Pakistan.

✦ **A green hand** (not very much experienced)
We shall pay a little to a green hand.

✦ **All in all** (completely)
Rajesh is all in all in this office.

✦ **A bed of roses** (a comfort)
Life is not a bed of roses.

✦ **An apple of discord** (to be the cause of)
Kashmir is an apple of discord between India and Pakistan.

✦ **A white elephant** (of no use)
This sort of glib talker always proves a white elephant in the end.

✦ **A red letter day** (An important day)
15th August is a red letter day for the Indians.

✦ **By hook or by crook** (by any means fair or foul)

✦ **Black sheep** (a traitor)
Later on Mr XYZ proved a black sheep.

✦ **By dint of** (by means of)
By dint of hard work, she earned a lot of money.

✦ **Break ones back** (to work hard to get something)
He broke his back to earn his livelihood.

✦ **Break the back of** (accomplish the hardest part of a certain job)
There is nothing to be worried about as we've already broken the back of the problem.

✦ **Beat about the bush** (to go on talking on some worthless topic)
Stop this beating about the bush, come to the main task.

✦ **Beyond one's means** (beyond one's budget)
He is living beyond his means, therefore, he is sure to get ruined.

✦ **Cut loose** (Keep away)
India should cut loose from bad politics.

✦ **Chips of the same block** (having the same taste)
They are the chips of the same block.

✦ **Cut-throat competition** (a stiff competition)
There is a cut-throat competition among the publishers in the market.

✦ **Come what may** (no matter what happens)
I'll do it come what may.

✦ **Drop someone a line** (send a letter, etc.)
Please drop me a line of your well-being.

✦ **Dull the edge of** (reduce the intensity of)
Take this pill and it will dull the edge of pain.

✦ **From hand to mouth** (without any saving)
The poor factory worker is living from hand to mouth.

✦ **Fair and square** (clean)
One must be fair and square in one's dealing.

✦ **Hard of hearing** (somewhat deaf)
She is a bit hard of hearing.

✦ **In the good books of** (be good in one's mind)
Jack is in the good books of his teachers.

✦ **In black and white** (in written)
Don't give him anything in black and white.

✦ **In cold blood** (mercilessly)
The old woman was murdered in cold blood.

✦ **In a crack** (all of a sudden or rapidly)
The thief left the place in a crack.

✦ **In full swing** (in full force)
The studies of the students are going on in full swing.

✦ **In the twinkling of an eye** (quickly)
The monkey ate up grams in the twinkling of an eye.

✦ **Keep the ball rolling** (to maintain the progress of some activity)
After the death of his father he had to take the charge of his office to keep the ball rolling.

✦ **Neck and neck** (even)
There is a neck and neck fight between the two boxers.

✦ **Once in a blue moon** (seldom)
She visits her brother once in a blue moon.

✦ **Slow and steady** (slowly but continually)
Slow and steady wins the race.

✦ **To cut a sorry figure** (present oneself in a bad way)
She cut a sorry figure on the stage.

✦ **To give a red carpet reception** (to give a warm welcome)
The PM was given a red carpet reception in America.

✦ **To dance one's tune** (to follow someone submissively)
He always dances to his brother's tune.

✦ **To turn a deaf ear to** (to disregard)
She turned a deaf ear to her parents' advice.

✦ **To call a spade a spade** (to speak the truth)
Gandhiji always called a spade a spade.

✦ **To bring to book** (to scold)
The naughty boy was brought to book by the teacher.

✦ **To cut short** (to reduce)
Smoking will cut short your life.
He wants to get money by hook or by crook.

✦ **To grease the palm of** (to bribe)
Rohit greased the palm of the clerk and got the file moved.

✦ **Through thick and thin.** (under all circumstances)
We'll stand by you through thick and thin.

✦ **To die by inches** (to die a painful death)
The old man died by inches.

✦ **To eat one's words** (to retract one's statement)
You'll have to eat your words because you have spoken without thinking.

✦ **To burn the midnight oil** (to work hard)
You'll have to burn the midnight oil if you want to get good marks.

✦ **To poke one's nose into** (to meddle with)
It is bad to poke your nose into others' affair.

✦ **To fall flat** (to have no effect)
His father's advice fell flat on him.

✦ **To make a clean breast of** (to confess)
He made a clean breast of his involvement in the bomb blast.

✦ **To get the better of** (overcome)
Anger got the better of him.

✦ **To break somebody's back** (to give too much work to him to do)
She broke his back by giving him so much hard work to do.

✦ **Throw cold water on** (to discourage)
She tried to throw cold water on his plan but he was well-determined.

✦ **The long and short of** (in brief)
The long and short of his lecture is that we should live like brothers.

✦ **To burn one's fingers** (to get oneself in trouble)
You have burnt your fingers by speaking against him.

✦ **To turn over a new leaf** (to change the course of life)
He has turned over a new leaf in his life.

✦ **To have one's own axe to grind** (to have vested interest)
He has his own axe to grind in this matter.

✦ **To take to one's heels** (to run away)
The thief took to his heels as soon as he saw the policeman.

✦ **To move heaven and earth** (to make too much effort)
The young man moved heaven and earth to find a job.

✦ **To be caught red handed** (to be caught at the time of committing a crime)
The clerk was caught red handed when he was accepting bribe from Mr ABC.

✦ **To receive with open arms** (to give a warm welcome)
The new president of the club was received with open arms by the members.

✦ **To be born with a silver spoon in one's mouth** (to be born in a rich family)
Mr. J. L. Nehru was born with a silver spoon in his mouth.

✦ **To come to light** (to be known)
A new disease has recently come to light.

✦ **To be the apple of one's eye** (be very dear)
He is the apple of his parent's eye.

✦ **To make fun of** (laugh at)
The children made fun of the waiter in the hotel.

✦ **To let the cat out of the bag** (to divulge secret)
It was Sohan who let the cat out of the bag by telling the real matter.

✦ **To open a new chapter** (to start some habit, etc.
By drinking, you've opened a new chapter in your life.

✦ **To make the flesh creep** (to terrify)
The story made my flesh creep.

✦ **To lose ground** (to retreat)
After fighting for some time the Pakistani army began to lose ground.

✦ **To bring to book** (to punish)
The student was brought to book by the teacher.

✦ **To show a clean pair of heels** (to run away)
The thief showed a clean pair of heels as soon as he saw the policeman approaching.

✦ **To gain ground** (to be established)
He gained ground in India in a few years.

✦ **To get wind of** (to get information)
I got wind of his secret plans.

✦ **Under a cloud** (be in trouble or in a state of disgrace or suspicion)
His company seemed to be under a cloud as it had no funds to pay the wages to the workers.

Verbal Phrases

✦ **Act upon** (to follow)
I acted upon my father's advice.

✦ **Act upto** (to perform within limits)
He acted upto his conscience.

✦ **Act beyond** (to perform crossing limits)
We should not act beyond our capacity.

✦ **Act for** (to perform in place of someone else)
The vice principal acted for the principal.

✦ **Back up** (to make a queue)
The vehicles began to back up.

✦ **Back down** (withdraw claim in the presence of opposition)
The leader backed down from his previous statement.

✦ **Back off** (draw back some plan or action)
They backed off from building a flyover.

✦ **Back out** (withdraw from a promise, etc.)
The government backed out of its promise.

✦ **Break down** (stop working) My car broke down on the highway.

✦ **Break into** (enter in certain premises by breaking the door, etc.)
Last night a thief broke into my neighbour's.

✦ **Break off** (stop all of a sudden)
She broke off and began to think over about her/his hand.

✦ **Break out** (spread)
Cholera has broken out in the town.

✦ **Break out of** (escape from)
A prisoner broke out of the prison last night.

✦ **Break up** (disperse)
The cloud of fog began to break up as the sun rose.

✦ **Break something up** (Cause something to break into small pieces)
She broke up the chocolate to distribute it among the girls.

✦ **Break with** (Cut off connection after quarrelling with someone)
He has broken with his brother.

✦ **Call on** (pay a visit to somebody)
I'll call on Mohan's today.

✦ **Call out** (to start)
The workers have called out a strike.

✦ **Call off** (to stop the strike etc.)
The workers have called off the strike.

✦ **Call at** (to visit someone's house)
I called at his house yesterday.

✦ **Call in** (send for)
Please call in the doctor.

✦ **Carry on** (continue)
Please carry on your work.

✦ **Carry something out** (perform a task)
Our company is carrying out a big deal with a foreign company.

✦ **Carry something over** (postpone)
The fancy dress competition had to be carried over till Monday)

✦ **Carry someone off** (kill somebody)
Cancer carried her off on the day of her 20th birthday.

✦ **Come of age** (get established)
As our company has come of age, so, there is no problem in selling our goods.

✦ **Come of** (belong to)
She comes of a royal family.

✦ **Come over** (surmount)
We at last came over all our problems.

✦ **Come off** (to take place)
The marriage of my brother comes off in the next month.

✦ **Come round** (agree)
At last he came round to my views.

✦ **Come under** (fall in the category of)
All these animals come under the same species.

✦ **Come down with** (suffer from)
She came down with whopping cough.

✦ **Come from** (be the nature of)
She came from London.

✦ **Come about** (happen)
The explosion came about when the worker struck the match to light a cigarette.

✦ **Cut off** (die)
The princess was cut off in the prime of her life.

✦ **Cut down** (reduce)
The prices of consumer goods should be cut down.

✦ **Cut someone out** (exclude someone)
His father cut him out of his will.

✦ **Fall in**
She fell in love with the prince.

✦ **Fall down** (fail)
The deal fell down for lack of transparency.

✦ **Fall out** (quarrel)
She fell out with his elder brother.

✦ **Fall through** (fail)
The project fell through for lack of funds.

✦ **Get away** (escape)
She got away with her life.

✦ **Get by** (to accomplish something with great difficulty)
She is not rich. She has just enough to get by.

✦ **Get on** (perform)
How are you getting on with your studies?

✦ **Get out** (become known)
The news got out that the PM was paying a visit to Russia.

✦ **Get over** (overcome)
At last I got over all obstacles.

✦ **Get up** (rise)
When do you get up in the morning?

✦ **Give up** (stop)
He gave up smoking.

✦ **Give out** (emit)
Garlic gives out a pungent smell.

✦ **Give in** (collapse)
The bridge gave in under the heavy load.

✦ **Give away** (distribute)
The Principal gave away the prizes.

✦ **Give out** (announce)
It was given out that the President of India would visit the place soon.

✦ **Go off** (explode)
The gun went off suddenly.

✦ **Go on** (continue)
She went on about how she flew the aeroplane.

✦ **Go through** (examine)
I'll go through this book later on.

✦ **Go up** (be built)
The construction of the house is going up.

✦ **Grind on** (continue for a long time in a tedious way)
The discussion over political issues ground on.

✦ **Grind something out** (produce something a tedious way)
She will grind some more short stories.

✦ **Look out** (be careful)
Look out! there is a snake.

✦ **Look down upon** (hate)
We should not look down upon the poor.

✦ **Look at** (watch)
Look at the blackboard.

✦ **Look after** (take care of)
We ought to look after our old parents.

✦ **Look into** (investigate)
The new police inspector will look into the matter.

✦ **Look up** (rise)
The prices of consumer goods are looking up.

✦ **Look back** (think of the past)
It made her feel disolate when she looked back on things of the past.

✦ **Make up** (to fulfil)
I'il make up my deficiency in Mathematics.

✦ **Make out** (understand)
I could not make out what she said.

✦ **Make up one' mind** (to resolve)
I have made up my mind to settle in the USA.

✦ **Make off** (leave hurriedly)
She made off without informing anybody.

✦ **Make something over** (transfer)
She should make her property over to her sons.

✦ **Make over** (hand over)
He made over the charge of the file to Mr Robert.

✦ **Pull back** (retreat)
The government has pulled back from its previous policy.

✦ **Pull something down** (demolish)
The authorities concerned pulled down a few building which were illegally built on government land.

✦ **Pull out** (pluck)
The child pulled out a few petals of the flower.

✦ **Pull through** (recover)
The patient will pull through.

✦ **Push on** (continue a journey)
It was getting darker but we pushed on.

✦ **Push at** (exert force)
He pushed at the bell, but it did not ring.

✦ **Push for** (demand persistently)
The workers have been pushing for the installation of new machines for five years.

✦ **Put out** (extinguish)
She put out the light.

✦ **Put on** (wear)
He put on an overcoat.

✦ **Put off** (postpone)
The plan had to be put off.

✦ **Put by** (spare something for future)
We must put by some money for future.

✦ **Put up with** (stay)
Your aunt is out of town for a couple of days, you may put up with us till she comes.

✦ **Put something down** (record something)
She put a new idea down on the paper.

✦ **Take after** (resemble)
He takes after his father.

✦ **Take off** (remove)
He took off his shoes.

✦ **Take something out** (obtain)
You may take out some money from Rohit if you want to purchase this car.

✦ **Take to** (fall into the habit of)
He took to gambling.

✦ **Turn something down** (reject something)
The judge turned down his appeal.

✦ **Turn on** (attack)
The thief turned on him with a knife.

Multiple Choice Questions

Directions: *Some idioms/phrases are given below with their probable meanings. Select the options with their correct meanings.*

1. **Carry out**
   A. To take from one place to another
   B. To continue
   C. To obey
   D. To make efforts

2. **In the same boat**
   A. A worn out choice
   B. Indifferent
   C. In identical circumstances
   D. Carry off

3. **In one's good book**
   A. A costly book
   B. A priceless treasure

C. In one's favour
D. An enchanting beauty

4. Keep a straight face
A. To do make up
B. To change clothes
C. Assume responsibility
D. To remain serious

5. To be above board
A. To have a good height
B. To be honest in any business deal
C. To have no debts
D. To try to be beautiful

6. On the face of it
A. To agree B. From an action
C. More than enough D. Apparently

7. Let the bygones be bygones
A. In one's favour B. To pretend
C. To forget the past D. Other choice

8. To split hairs
A. Major distinctions
B. Hair with two ends
C. To make minute distinction
D. Without distinction

9. Bread and butter
A. Both bread and butter
B. Something essential
C. Livelihood
D. Relevant things

10. To bell the cat
A. To catch a cat and tie a bell round its neck
B. To make an effort
C. To be quick
D. To face a risk

11. Hard and fast
A. Strict B. Solid
C. Fast moving D. Some hard surface

12. Part and parcel
A. The part of a parcel
B. An essential part
C. A missing parcel
D. Some part of a machine sent by parcel

13. Null and void
A. Something invalid
B. Something that can be avoided
C. Something that can be nullified
D. Something evil

14. To make clean breast of
A. To gain prominence
B. To praise oneself
C. To confess without reserve
D. To destroy before it blooms

15. Trump card
A. A powerful means of achieving an object
B. Resourcefulness
C. The best gamble to attain success
D. None of these

16. Tall talk
A. A discussion continued for a long time
B. A high sounding talk
C. A meaningful talk
D. A useless talk

17. Small talk
A. Gossip
B. A discussion carried on for a long time
C. A brief discussion
D. None of these

18. Throw out of gear
A. To replace B. Hinder, disturb
C. To decide D. Take up tune

19. To and fro
A. Back and forth B. Puzzled
C. Amazed D. Reprove

20. To bell the cat
A. To do an easy job
B. To be indifferent to
C. To undertake a difficult job
D. To clarify

21. To be under cloud
A. Puzzle
B. Enjoy the favour
C. Talk thoughtlessly
D. To be under suspicion

22. A labour of love
A. A tragic end
B. A funny thing
C. Not fruitful
D. Work done without payment

23. Follow suit
A. Follow an example B. Wear a new dress
C. Irrelevant D. A gay person

24. Foul play
A. Bad intentions
B. A play not well acted
C. A play not liked by the audience
D. None of these

25. To pick holes
A. To find some reason to quarrel
B. To destroy something
C. To criticise someone
D. To cut some part of an item

26. To smell a rat
A. To see signs of plague epidemic
B. To get bad smell of a dead rat
C. To suspect foul dealings
D. To be in a bad mood

27. To put a spoke in one's wheel
A. To encourage
B. Act without restraint
C. Risk something
D. To obstruct one's progress

28. To pull one's leg
A. To give up B. Take care of
C. To befool D. To know

29. To play with fire
A. Grasp the truth
B. To handle something dangerous
C. To ridicule
D. To flee away

30. To reckon with
A. Take up time
B. Make an inventory
C. To deal with
D. Submit to punishment

31. To run short
A. Talk until one is tired at
B. Apply to oneself
C. To get rid of
D. To have or be too little

32. A man of letters
A. A postman B. A learned man
C. A hypocrite D. An ignorant man

33. A maiden speech
A. A speech made in the parliament
B. A speech made before unmarried girls
C. A speech made by a political leader
D. A speech made for the first time

34. Order of the day
A. An order passed on a particular day
B. A current law
C. Something common or general
D. None of these

35. To end in smoke
A. To make completely understand
B. To ruin oneself
C. To excite great applause
D. None of these

36. To give vent to
A. To allow to flow forth
B. To prove a failure
C. To amass wealth
D. To evade

37. To eat humble pie
A. To apologise or confess
B. To order
C. To flatter
D. To get rid of

38. A black sheep
A. An unlucky person
B. A negro
C. An ugly person
D. None of these

39. To catch a tartar
A. To trap wanted criminal with great difficulty
B. To catch a dangerous person
C. To meet with disaster
D. To deal with a person who is more than one's watch

40. Sit on fence
A. To remain neutral
B. To show contempt
C. To enjoy the surroundings
D. To become fond of

41. Pay off old scores
A. To repay the debt
B. To have revenge
C. To invite
D. Secretly

42. Turn turtle
A. To cheat
B. To be lopsided
C. To frustrate
D. To dance to the tune

43. Wash one's hands of
A. To refuse B. To assist
C. To abuse D. To refuse to be

44. Under duress
A. Under compulsion
B. Willing
C. To elicit information
D. To demand

45. To turn the tables
A. To ruin someone
B. To turn the situation to one's own side
C. To reverse the situation
D. To move from one point to another

46. On the cards
A. Possibly B. Probably
C. Openly D. Likely

47. To leave someone in the lurch
A. To come to compromise with someone
B. Constant source of annoyance to someone
C. To put someone at ease
D. To desert someone in his difficulties

48. To play second fiddle
A. To be happy, cheerful and healthy
B. To reduce importance of one's senior
C. To support the role and view of another person
D. To do back seat driving

49. To yearn for
A. To weep for
B. To remember
C. To admire
D. To long for intensely

50. Call off
A. To finish B. To withdraw
C. To postpone D. To cry

ANSWERS

1	2	3	4	5	6	7	8	9	10
C	C	C	D	B	D	C	C	C	D
11	12	13	14	15	16	17	18	19	20
A	B	A	C	C	B	A	B	A	C
21	22	23	24	25	26	27	28	29	30
D	D	A	A	C	C	D	C	B	C
31	32	33	34	35	36	37	38	39	40
D	B	D	C	D	A	A	D	B	A
41	42	43	44	45	46	47	48	49	50
B	B	D	A	C	D	D	C	D	B

❑❑❑

8 Narration

Direct and Indirect Narration/Speech

The exact words spoken by the speaker are known as Direct Speech.

The words spoken by somebody and expressed by someone else with some modification are known as Indirect Speech.

(*a*) Ram says to me, "You do not help me."

(*b*) Ram tells me that I do not help him.

The sentence (*a*) shows the words spoken by Ram. So, it is a sentence of Direct Speech.

The sentence (*b*) shows the words spoken by Ram and expressed by someone else with certain modification. So, it is a sentence of Indirect Speech.

The following points should be noted while changing Direct Speech into Indirect speech:

1. The verb outside the inverted commas is called the Reporting Verb.
2. The verb or sentence inside the inverted commas is called the Reported Speech.
3. If the Reporting verb is in the Present or Future Tense, there is no change in the tense in the Reported Speech.
4. If the Reporting Verb is in the Past Tense, the Tense in the Reported Speech is changed.
5. The Reporting verb may be in any Tense, in it the Pronouns are changed as under:
   (*i*) First Person according to Subject
   (*ii*) Second Person according to Object
   (*iii*) Third Person, No change.
6. If the Reporting verb is in the Past Tense the Adverb will change as under in the Indirect Speech.

Direct	***Indirect***
now	then
here	there
after	before
today	that day
yesterday	the previous day
these	those
tomorrow	the next day
last week	the previous week
this	that

7. Adjectives/Determiners are changed as under:

Direct	***Indirect***
this	that
these	those

Rules for Change of Tense

Reporting Verb	Reporting Speech	Change of Tense
Present Tense	Any Tense	No change
Future Tense	Any Tense	No change
Past Tense	Present/Future Tense	Change into corresponding Past Tense
Past Tense	Past Indefinite Tense	Change into Past Perfect Tense
Past Tense	Past Continuous Tense	Change into Past Perfect Continuous Tense
Past Tense	Past Perfect/Perfect Continuous Tense	No change
Past Tense	Universal Truth	No change
Past Tense	Proverb	No change

Transformation of Speech Based on Special Rules

1. Rule Related to Interrogative Sentence

- If the answer of an interrogative sentence is possible in yes-no manner.

Illustration.

Dhoni said to Sachin, "Will you help me?"

Dhoni asked Sachin whether he would help him.

(**Note :** The answer of R.S. is possible in yes-no manner)

Rule of Transformation from Direct to Indirect speech

Step I : Change R.V. into ask.

Step II : In place of comma use 'if/whether'.

Step III : Change interrogative sentence into assertive sentence.

- If the answer of an interrogative sentence is not possible in yes-no manner.

Illustration:

Sachin said to Dhoni, "What do you want?"

Sachin asked Dhoni what he wanted.

(**Note :** Only in Step II, you have to avoid comma and inverted comma and rest will be same as mentioned above).

2. Rule related to Imperative Sentence

- Imperative sentence is a sentence which shows Order/Advice/Request

Illustration:

My teacher said to me, "Go there".

My teacher ordered me to go there.

Rule of Transformation from Direct to Indirect Speech

Step I : Change R.V. as per meaning/sense of R.S. into order/request/advise.

Step II : In place of comma, use 'to'.

Step III : Rest portion will be same.

3. Rule related to Optative Sentence

- Optative sentence is a sentence which expresses the feeling of bless/curse/pray/wish.

Illustration:

Mother said to me, "May you live long!"

Mother blessed me that I might live long.

Rule of Transformation from Direct to Indirect Speech

Step I : Change R.V. as per meaning/sense of R.S. into bless/curse/pray/wish.

Step II : In place of comma, use 'that'.

Step III : Change optative sentence into assertive sentence.

4. Rule related to Exclamatory Sentence

- Exclamatory sentence is a sentence which takes note of exclamatory (!) mark in that sentence showing inner feeling.

Illustration:

She said, "Alas! I am ruined".

She exclaimed with sorrow that she was ruined.

Rule of Transformation from Direct to Indirect Speech

Step I : Change R.V. as per meaning/sense of R.S. into exclaim/exclaims/exclaimed/will or shall exclaim + joy/sorrow/anger/surprise/applause/contempt.

Step II : Change comma into that.

Step III : Change note of exclamation (!) into full stop (.)

Step IV : Change exclamatory sentence into assertive sentence.

Universal, Historical truth, etc.

If the Reported Speech expresses a Universal or Historical or Habitual truth, its Tense will not change.

1. The teacher said to the students, "The sun rises in the east."

   The teacher told the students that the sun rises in the east.

2. My father said to me, "The First Battle of Panipat was fought in 1526."

   My father told me that the First Battle of Panipat was fought in 1526.

Multiple Choice Questions

Directions (Qs. 1 to 13): *Select the correct Indirect Speech for the following sentences:*

1. I said to him, "I shall help you."
A. I told him that I can help him.
B. I told him that I would help him.
C. I told him that I will help him.
D. I told him that I shall be helping him.

2. My Teacher said to me, "The earth revolves round the sun."
A. My teacher told me that the earth revolves round the sun.
B. My teacher told me that the earth revolve round the sun.
C. My teacher told me that the earth had been revolving round the sun.
D. My teacher told me that the earth has been revolving round the sun.

3. I said to my friend, "My father daily goes for a walk."
A. I told my friend that my father daily goes for a walk.
B. I told my friend that my father daily went for a walk.
C. I told my friend that my father has to go for a walk.
D. I told my friend that my father had gone for a walk.

4. He said to me, "May God bless you!"
A. He requested that God can bless me.
B. He prayed that God can bless me.
C. He prayed that God might bless me.
D. He prayed that God will bless me.

5. The patient said, "Thank you, doctor."
A. The patient thanked the doctor.
B. The patient requested the doctor with thanks.
C. The patient told the doctor thanks.
D. The patient suggested the doctor thanks.

6. Satish said, "No, I shall not talk to him."
A. Satish told that he should not talk to him.
B. Satish suggested that he would not have talked to him.
C. Satish exclaimed with sorrow that he would not talk with him.
D. Satish refused to talk to him.

7. The child said, "What a lovely place!"
A. The child exclaimed with sorrow that it was a lovely place.
B. The child thought that the place was lovely.
C. The child exclaimed with joy that the place was very lovely.
D. The child suggested that the place was lovely.

8. He said, "What a fool I have been!"
A. He told himself with sorrow that he was a fool.
B. He confessed with regret that he had been a great fool.
C. He said himself a fool.
D. He suggested that he could be a fool.

9. He said, "Alas! I am ruined."
A. He told me that he had been ruined.
B. He exclaimed with joy that he had been ruined.
C. He exclaimed with sorrow that he was ruined.
D. He told me that he should not be ruined.

10. The accused said, "I am not guilty."
A. The accused exclaimed with sorrow that I am not guilty.
B. The accused exclaimed with joy that he was not guilty.
C. The accused stated that he was not guilty.
D. The accused told me that he has not been guilty.

11. My teacher said, "The earth is round".
A. My teacher said that the earth was round.
B. My teacher says that the earth is round.
C. My teacher said that the earth is round.
D. My teacher ordered that the earth is round.

12. He said, "What a place it is!"
   A. He said that it was a very fine place.
   B. He said that is a very fine place.
   C. He said that the place is fine.
   D. He exclaimed with joy/surprise that it was a very fine place.

13. Ria said, "Shall I thread the needle?"
   A. Ria asked if she should thread the needle.
   B. Ria asked if she shall thread the needle.
   C. Ria ordered if she should thread the needle.
   D. Ria says that if she would thread the needle.

Directions (Qs. 14 to 33): *Pick out the correct alternative that completes the incomplete sentence which is changed into Indirect Narration.*

14. She said to me, "I shall see you as soon as I get time."
   She told me:
   A. that she will see me as soon as she will get time.
   B. that she would see me as soon as she would get time.
   C. she would see me whenever she got time.
   D. that she would see me whenever she gets time.

15. My secretary said to me, "Your plane will leave if you do not go at once."
   My secretary told me that:
   A. her plane would leave if she did not go at that time.
   B. her plane would leave if I do not go at once.
   C. my plane would leave if I did not go at that very time.
   D. my plane will leave if I did not go at that time.

16. My mother said to me, "Don't quarrel among yourselves".
   My mother:
   A. forbade me to quarrel among ourselves.
   B. asked me not to quarrel among ourselves.
   C. asked me that not to quarrel among ourselves.
   D. asked me to quarrel not among ourselves.

17. Her father said to her mother, "Excuse the daughter."
   Her father:
   A. requested her mother to excuse the daughter.
   B. asked her mother to excuse the daughter.
   C. asked her mother to have excused the daughter.
   D. asked her mother to have been excused.

18. He said to his friend, "Wait here till father comes."
   He requested his friend:
   A. to wait here till father had come.
   B. that to wait there till his friend came.
   C. to wait there till father came.
   D. to wait here until his friend came.

19. She said to her maid, "Run and catch the thief."
   She ordered her maid:
   A. ran and catch the thief.
   B. that to run and to catch the thief.
   C. ran and caught the thief.
   D. to run and catch the thief.

20. Anita said to Sunita, "What are you doing?"
   Anita asked Sunita:
   A. what she will be doing.
   B. that what she is doing.
   C. that what she was doing.
   D. what she was doing.

21. She said to me, "Are you meeting me today?"
   She enquired of me:
   A. whether I am meeting her that day.
   B. whether I was meeting her today.
   C. whether I was meeting her that day.
   D. I was meeting her that day.

22. Nitish said to me, "When did you buy this pen?"
   Nitish asked me:
   A. when I was to buy that pen.
   B. when I would buy that pen.
   C. when I had bought that pen.
   D. when I was buying that pen.

23. She said to me, "Are you going tc market?"
She enquired of me:
A. I am going to market.
B. I was going to market.
C. if I was going to market.
D. if I had been going to the market.

24. Damini said, "Why did not you change your clothes?"
Damini asked me:
A. why I had not changed my clothes.
B. why I did not change my clothes.
C. why I would not change my clothes.
D. why I have not been changing my clothes.

25. Umesh said to me, "Have you read that novel?"
Umesh asked me:
A. if he was reading that novel.
B. if he had read that novel.
C. if I had read that novel.
D. if I was reading that novel.

26. She said to me, "I shall forgive you."
She told me:
A. that she will forgive me.
B. that she was going to forgive me.
C. that she will not forgive me.
D. that she would forgive me.

27. I said to her, "It was very hot last night."
I told her:
A. that it had been very hot the previous night.
B. that it was very hot the previous night.
C. that it has been very hot the last night.
D. that it had been very hot this night.

28. She said to me, "I thank you for the help you have given."
She:
A. told me that she thanked me for the help I had given.
B. thanked me for the help I have given.
C. thanked to me for the help I have given.
D. thanked me for the help I had given.

29. Mohini said to me, "Trust in God."
Mohini advised me:
A. that I should trust in God.
B. should trust in God.
C. trusted in God.
D. to trust in God.

30. I said to him, "Let us go to school."
I told him:
A. we would go to school.
B. we shall go to school.
C. that we would go to school.
D. that we should go to school.

31. Rajni said, "May God bless you?"
Rajni:
A. exclaimed with wish that God might bless me.
B. expressed a wish that God might bless me.
C. asked God to bless me.
D. shouted with joy to bless me.

32. My mother said me, "Do not have so many friends."
My mother forbade me:
A. to have so many friends.
B. not to have so many friends.
C. to have been so many friends.
D. to possess so many friends.

33. Ram said, "Pay attention to me."
Ram asked:
A. pay attention to him.
B. paid attention to him.
C. having paid attention to him.
D. to pay attention to him.

Directions (Qs. 34 to 50): *In questions below, the sentences have been given in Direct/Indirect Speech. Out of the four alternatives suggested select the one which best expresses the given sentence in Indirect/Direct Speech.*

34. She said that her brother was getting married
A. She said, "Her brother is getting married."
B. She told, "My brother is getting married"
C. She said, "My brother is getting married".
D. She said, "My brother was married".

35. "Please don't go away", she said.
A. She said to please her and not go away.
B. She told me to go away.
C. She begged me not to go away.
D. She begged that I not go away.

36. "If you don't keep quiet I shall shoot you", he said to her in a calm voice.
A. He warned her to shoot if she didn't keep quiet calmly.
B. He said calmly that I shall shoot you if you don't be quiet.
C. He warned her calmly that he would shoot her if she didn't keep quiet.
D. Calmly he warned her that be quiet or else he will have to shoot her.

37. I told him that he was not working hard.
A. I said to him; "You are not working hard."
B. I told him, "You are not working hard."
C. I said, "You are not working hard."
D. I said to him, "He is not working hard."

38. She said that she would finish the work the next day.
A. She said, "I will finish the work the next day."
B. She said, "I will finish the work tomorrow."
C. She said, "You will finish the work tomorrow."
D. She said, "I finished the work."

39. She said to him, "Why don't you go today?"
A. She asked him why he did not go that day.
B. She said to him that why he don't go today.
C. She asked him not to go today.
D. She asked him why he did not go today.

40. "Are you alone, my son?" asked a soft voice close behind me.
A. A soft voice asked that what I was doing there alone.
B. A soft voice said to me are you alone son.
C. A soft voice from my back asked if I was alone.
D. A soft voice behind me asked if I was alone.

41. My cousin said, "My room-mate had snored throughout the night."
A. My cousin said that her room-mate snored throughout the night.
B. My cousin told me that her room-mate snored throughout the night.
C. My cousin complained to me that her room-mate is snoring throughout the night.
D. My cousin felt that her room-mate may be snoring throughout the night.

42. He asked Rama if he needed his help then.
A. He said to Rama, "Do you need my help?"
B. He told Rama, "Tell me if you need help."
C. He asked Rama, "Do I need your help?"
D. He said to Rama, "Do you need my help now?"

43. Nita ordered her servant to bring her a cup of tea.
A. Nita told her servant, "Bring a cup of tea."
B. Nita said, "Bring me a cup of tea."
C. Nita said to her servant, "Bring me a cup of tea."
D. Nita said to her servant, "Bring her that cup of tea."

44. He exclaimed with joy that India had won the Sahara Cup.
A. He said, "India has won the Sahara Cup."
B. He said, "India won the Sahara Cup."
C. He said, "How! India will win the Sahara Cup."
D. He said, "Hurrah! India has won the Sahara Cup."

45. The boy said, "Who dare call you a thief?"
A. The boy enquired who dared call him a thief.
B. The boy asked who called him a thief.
C. The boy told that who dared call him a thief.
D. The boy wondered who dared call a thief.

46. The little girl said to her mother, "Did the sun rise in the East?
A. The little girl said to her mother that the sun rose in the East.
B. The little girl asked her mother if the sun rose in the East.
C. The little girl said to her mother if the sun rises in the East.
D. The little girl asked her mother if the sun is in the East.

47. Dhruv said that he was sick and tired of working for that Company.

A. Dhruv said, "I am sick and tired of working for this Company."

B. Dhruv said, "He was tired of that Company."

C. Dhruv said to me, "I am sick and tired of working for this Company."

D. Dhruv said, "I will be tired of working for that Company."

48. He said to his father, "Please increase my pocket-money."

A. He told his father, please increase the pocket-money.

B. He pleaded his father to please increase my pocket-money.

C. He requested his father to increase his pocket-money.

D. He asked his father increase his pocket-money.

49. She said to her friend, "I know where is everyone."

A. She told that she knew where was everyone.

B. She told her friend that she knew where was everyone.

C. She told her friend she knew where is everyone

D. She told her friend that she knows where was everyone.

50. His father ordered him to go to his room and study.

A. His father said, "Go to your room and study."

B. His father said to him, "Go and study in your room."

C. His father shouted, "Go right now to your study room."

D. His father said firmly, "Go and study in your room."

ANSWERS

1	2	3	4	5	6	7	8	9	10
B	A	A	C	A	D	C	B	C	C
11	**12**	**13**	**14**	**15**	**16**	**17**	**18**	**19**	**20**
C	D	A	B	C	A	B	C	D	D
21	**22**	**23**	**24**	**25**	**26**	**27**	**28**	**29**	**30**
C	C	C	A	C	D	A	A	A	D
31	**32**	**33**	**34**	**35**	**36**	**37**	**38**	**39**	**40**
B	A	D	C	C	C	A	B	A	D
41	**42**	**43**	**44**	**45**	**46**	**47**	**48**	**49**	**50**
A	D	C	B	A	B	A	C	B	A

9 Voice

A sentence in active voice focuses on the person or thing doing the action. A sentence in passive voice focuses on the person or thing affected by the action.

e.g.,

The idol was built. (Active voice)
Someone built the idol. (Passive voice)

Transformation of Voice

- Voice and Tense are closely associated with each other.
- Tense plays an important role while transforming the voice.

On the basis of following points, voice can be transformed from active to passive voice.

The Present Indefinite Tense

Active voice: Subject + V_1 + Object
Passive voice: Subject + is, am, are + V_3 + by + Object

1. **Active voice:** He sings sweet songs.
   Passive voice: Sweet songs are sung by him.
2. **Active voice:** She does not cause any hindrance in my work.
   Passive voice: No hindrance in my work is caused by her.
3. **Active voice:** Do they love their country?
   Passive voice: Is their country loved by them?

The Present Continuous Tense

Active voice: Subject + is/am/are + V_1 + ing + Object.
Passive voice: Subject + is/am/are + being + V_3 + by + Object.

1. **Active voice:** She is cooking food.
   Passive voice: Food is being cooked by her.
2. **Active voice:** Rita is not knitting a sweater.
   Passive voice: A sweater is not being knitted by Rita.
3. **Active voice:** Is Meena baking a cake?
   Passive voice: Is a cake being baked by Meena?

The Present Perfect Tense

Active voice: Subject + has/have + V_3 + Object.
Passive voice: Subject + has/have + been + V_3 + by + Object.

1. **Active voice:** I have written an essay.
   Passive voice: An essay has been written by me.
2. **Active voice:** They have not whitewashed the fence.
   Passive voice: The fence has not been whitewashed by them.
3. **Active voice:** Have you cut the cake?
   Passive voice: Has the cake been cut by you?

The Past Indefinite Tense

Active voice: Subject + V_2 + Object
Passive voice: Subject + was/were + V_3 + by + Object

1. **Active voice:** He composed a new song.
   Passive voice: A new song was composed by him.
2. **Active voice:** He did not operate the computer.
   Passive voice: The computer was not operated by him.
3. **Active voice:** Did she catch a fish?
   Passive voice: Was a fish caught by her?

The Past Continuous Tense

Active voice: Subject + was/were + V_1 + ing + Object

Passive voice: Subject + was/were + being + V_3 + by + Object

1. **Active voice:** The farmers were ploughing the fields.

   Passive voice: The fields were being ploughed by the farmers.
2. **Active voice:** He was not administering the new drug to the patient.

   Passive voice: The new drug was not being administered to the patient by him.
3. **Active voice:** Was she sewing a dress?

   Passive voice: Was a dress being sewn by her?

The Past Perfect Tense

Active voice: Subject + had + V_3 + Object.

Passive voice: Subject + had + been + V_3 + by + Object

1. **Active voice:** He had issued me an import licence.

   Passive voice: I had been issued an import licence.
2. **Active voice:** We had not visited the Taj.

   Passive voice: The Taj had not been visited by us.
3. **Active voice:** Who had taught you English?

   Passive voice: By whom had you been taught English?

The Future Indefinite Tense

Active voice: Subject + will/shall + V_1 + Object.

Passive voice: Subject + will/shall + be + V_3 + by + Object.

1. **Active voice:** He will remove the dust from the shelf.

   Passive voice: The dust from the shelf will be removed by him.
2. **Active voice:** He will not open the main gate.

   Passive voice: The main gate will not be opened by him.
3. **Active voice:** Will you help us?

   Passive voice: Shall we be helped by you?

The Future Perfect Tense

Active voice: Subject + will/shall + have + V_3 + Object.

Passive voice: Subject + will/shall + have + been + V_3 + by + Object.

1. **Active voice:** They will have sold their house by then.

   Passive voice: Their house will have been sold by them by then.
2. **Active voice:** He will not have informed the police about it.

   Passive voice: The police will not have been informed about it by him.
3. **Active voice:** Will they have accepted the deal?

   Passive voice: Will the deal have been accepted by them?

Imperative Sentences

1. **Active voice:** Open the window.

   Passive voice: You are ordered to open the window.

   Or

   Let the window be opened.
2. **Active voice:** Please/kindly open the window.

   Passive voice: You are requested to open the window.
3. **Active voice:** Never make a noise.

   Passive voice: A noise should never be made.

Infinitives

1. **Active voice:** It is time to open the shop.

   Passive voice: It is time for the shop to be opened.
2. **Active voice:** He begged the officer to forgive him.

   Passive voice: He begged the officer to be forgiven.
3. **Active voice:** He has to break the door.

   Passive voice: The door has to be broken by him.

Prepositional Verb

1. **Active voice:** She laughed at the beggar.
   Passive voice: The beggar was laughed at by her.
2. **Active voice:** He listened to the news.
   Passive voice: The news was listened to by him.
3. **Active voice:** They called in the doctor.
   Passive voice: The doctor was called in by them.

Double Object

1. **Active voice:** He gave me a pen.
   Passive voice: A pen was given to me by him.

   Or

   I was given a pen by him.
2. **Active voice:** She told us a story.
   Passive voice: A story was told (to) us by her.

   Or

   We were told a story by her.

Use of Preposition other than 'by'

1. **Active voice:** The jug contains juice.
   Passive voice: Juice is contained in the jug.
2. **Active voice:** The audience thronged the hall.
   Passive voice: The hall was thronged with the audience.
3. **Active voice:** I know her.
   Passive voice: She is known to me.

Quasi Passive Verbs

1. **Active voice:** Quinine tastes bitter.
   Passive voice: Quinine is bitter when tasted.

   Or

   Quinine is bitter when it is tasted.
2. **Active voice:** Sugar is sweet (to taste).
   Passive voice: Sugar is sweet when tasted.

   Or

   Sugar is sweet when it is tasted.

Implied Sentences

1. **Active voice:** The driver drove the bus.
   Passive voice: The bus was driven.
2. **Active voice:** Someone read the news.
   Passive voice: The news was read.
3. **Active voice:** They say work is worship.
   Passive voice: It is said that work is worship.

Multiple Choice Questions

Directions (Qs. 1 to 20): *In the following questions, a sentence has been given in Active/Passive Voice. Out of the four alternatives suggested, select the one that Best Expresses the same sentence in Passive/Active Voice.*

1. Circumstances will oblige me to go.
A. I will oblige the circumstances and go.
B. I shall be obliged to go by the circumstances.
C. Under the circumstances, I should go.
D. I shall be obliged by the circumstances to go.

2. We waste much time on trifles.
A. Much time was wasted on trifles.
B. Much time will be wasted on trifles.
C. Much time is wasted by us on trifles.
D. Much time is wasted on trifles.

3. Mohan gave the beggar an old shirt.
A. An old shirt was given to Mohan by the beggar.
B. An old shirt was given to the beggar by Mohan
C. The begger was gave an old shirt by Mohan.
D. An old shirt was gave to the beggar by Mohan.

4. They have made him a king.
A. A king has been made by him.
B. He was made a king by them.
C. They have been made kings by him.
D. He has been made a king by them.

5. Who taught you English?
A. By whom English was taught to you?
B. By whom you were taught English?
C. By whom was English taught to you?
D. By whom are you taught English?

6. Was he knocking at the door?
A. Was the door being knocked at by him?
B. Was the door being knocked by him?
C. Was the door knocked by him?
D. Was the door knocking at him?

7. What was Rani doing?
A. What was done by Rani?
B. What was Rani being done?
C. What was being done by Rani?
D. What was being doing Rani?

8. Why were you wasting your time?
A. Why was your time being wasted?
B. Why was your time being wasted by you?
C. Why was your time wasted by you?
D. Why was your time wasted?

9. She has laid out a small garden.
A. A small garden has been laid by her.
B. A small garden has laid her.
C. A small garden being laid by her.
D. A small garden has been laid out by her.

10. She had already solved all the sums.
A. All the sums had already been solved by her.
B. All the sums have already been solved by her.
C. All the sums have been solved by her.
D. All the sums are solved by her.

11. He will have posted the letter.
A. The letter has been posted by him.
B. The letter will be posted by him.
C. The letter will have been posted by him.
D. The letter is posted by him.

12. They will have sold all the books by 4 P.M.
A. All the books will be sold by 4 P.M.
B. All the books will have been sold by 4 P.M.
C. All the books were being sold by 4 P.M.
D. All the books must be sold by 4 P.M.

13. Do you speak English?
A. Is English spoken by you?
B. Does English spoken by you?
C. Is English being spoken by you?
D. Does English being spoken by you?

14. Had they seen me before?
A. Had myself been seen by them before?
B. Had me being seen by them before?
C. Had I been seen by them before?
D. Had I being seen by them before?

15. May I take this pen?
A. May this pen will be taken by me?
B. May this pen shall be taken by me?
C. May this pen should be taken by me?
D. May this pen be taken by me?

16. Can we send it by air?
A. Can this be sent by air?
B. Can it be sent by air?
C. Can it go by air?
D. Can it be send by air?

17. Who wrote this book?
A. By whom was this book written?
B. By whom is this book written?
C. By whom was this book being written?
D. By whom is this book being written?

18. What did you buy?
A. What is bought by you?
B. What is being bought by you?
C. What was bought by you?
D. What was being bought by you?

19. Whom do you want?
A. Who is wanted by you?
B. Who is being wanted by you?
C. You are wanted by whom?
D. You are being wanted by whom?

20. When will you raise this question?
A. When this question will be raised by you?
B. When will this question be raised by you?
C. When this question is being raised by you?
D. When is this question being raised by you?

Directions (Qs. 21 to 35): *In each of the following questions, a sentence is given in Active Voice. Below it are given four alternatives suggesting the Passive Voice form of the above sentence. Choose the correct alternative.*

21. Who did this?
A. This was done by whom?
B. By whom was this done?
C. Who has done this?
D. By whom this was done?

22. One should keep ones promises.
A. Promises should be kept.
B. Ones promises should be kept by one.
C. Promises must be kept.
D. Ones promises one should keep.

23. Give the order.
A. Order given.
B. Order be given.
C. Let the order be given.
D. Order may be given by you.

24. You will have to do it.
A. It will be done by you.
B. It will have to be done by you.
C. It has to be done by you.
D. It would have to be done by you.

25. Keep to the left.
A. You are ordered to keep to the left.
B. You ought to keep to the left.
C. You are advised to keep to the left.
D. You must keep to the left.

26. They will arrange a party.
A. A party will have to be arranged by them.
B. A party they will have to arrange.
C. A party will be arranged by them.
D. A party by them will be arranged.

27. Someone has picked my pocket.
A. My pocket is picked.
B. My pocket has picked.
C. My pocket has been picked.
D. My pocket was picked.

28. He kept me waiting.
A. I kept waiting for him.
B. I kept waiting by him.
C. I was waiting for him.
D. I was kept waiting by him.

29. Why do you tell a lie?
A. Why is a lie told by you?
B. Why is told a lie by you?
C. Why is told by you a lie?
D. Why has a lie been told by you?

30. I have written a letter.
A. A letter is written by me.
B. A letter has been written by me.
C. A letter was written by me.
D. A letter had been written by me.

31. They will have helped you.
A. You will have helped by them.
B. You will have been helped by them.
C. You will be helped by them.
D. You will be helped by them.

32. Open the door.
A. Door may be opened.
B. Let the door be open.
C. Let the door be opened.
D. Door be opened.

33. I am reading a book.
A. A book is read by me.
B. A book is being read by me.
C. A book has been read by me.
D. A book in been read by me.

34. Why did your brother write such a letter?
A. Why your brother wrote such a letter?
B. Why was by brother written such a letter?
C. Why was such a letter written by your brother?
D. Why was written such a letter by your brother?

35. Did you run a great risk?
A. Was a great risk run by you?
B. Was run a great risk by you?
C. Was by you run a great risk?
D. Had you run a great risk?

Directions (Qs. 36 to 45): *In each of the following questions, a sentence is given in Passive Voice. Below it are given four alternatives suggesting the Active Voice form of the above sentence. Choose the correct alternative.*

36. He was made king.
A. He became king.
B. They made him king.
C. They had made him king.
D. He has been made king.

37. Good news is expected by us.
A. We are expecting good news.
B. We have been expecting good news.
C. We had expected good news.
D. We expect good news.

38. The child must be looked after.
A. The child you must look after.
B. You must look after the child.
C. You must look the child after.
D. You may look after the child.

39. What is wanted by you?
A. What you want?
B. What did you want?
C. What do you want?
D. What you do want?

40. Your father is known to me.
A. I am known to your father.
B. I know your father.
C. I have known your father.
D. I knew your father.

41. She may be told the story by you.
A. The story may be told by you to her.
B. You may tell the story to her.
C. You may tell her the story.
D. You may tell to her the story.

42. Duty ought to be done.
A. Let duty be done.
B. One ought to do one's duty.
C. One should do his duty.
D. Do you duty.

43. Is English spoken by you?
A. Did you speak English?
B. Do you speak English?
C. Have you spoken English?
D. Do you know how to speak English?

44. Gold coins are contained in this box.
A. This box contains gold coins.
B. This box has contained gold coins.
C. This box is containing gold coins.
D. This box has gold coins.

45. Character is revealed by manners.
A. Manners revealed character.
B. Manners reveal character.
C. Manners have revealed character.
D. Manners do reveal character.

ANSWERS

1	2	3	4	5	6	7	8	9	10
D	C	B	D	C	A	C	B	D	A
11	**12**	**13**	**14**	**15**	**16**	**17**	**18**	**19**	**20**
C	B	A	C	D	B	A	C	A	B
21	**22**	**23**	**24**	**25**	**26**	**27**	**28**	**29**	**30**
B	A	C	B	C	C	C	D	A	B
31	**32**	**33**	**34**	**35**	**36**	**37**	**38**	**39**	**40**
B	C	B	C	A	B	D	B	C	B
41	**42**	**43**	**44**	**45**					
C	B	B	A	B					

□□□

10 Sentence Completion

Filling the blanks is such an exercise that starts with the primary schools and continues at the highest level of competitive examinations. One must practise it regularly to score well.

Multiple Choice Questions

Directions: *Pick out the most effective word(s) from the given words to fill in the blanks and make the sentence meaningfully complete.*

1. One requires great .... to teach and handle little children who are restless.

A. patience B. attitude
C. determination D. knowledge

2. The researchers will .... some of the causes of increasing poverty in the state.

A. fund B. investigate
C. promote D. circulate

3. I usually perform .... when nobody is watching me.

A. alone B. good
C. better D. hard

4. It was .... to everyone that the minister had been drinking.

A. observed B. known
C. discovered D. realised

5. I would rather stay indoors .... the rain stops.

A. so B. waiting
C. until D. usually

6. The process should be completed as far as possible within a week, ... which the matter should be brought to notice of the officer concerned.

A. following B. failing
C. realizing D. referring

7. The officers are ..... to regular transfers.

A. free B. open
C. subject D. available

8. All letters received from Government should ..... be acknowledged.

A. suddenly
B. obviously
C. immediately
D. occasionally

9. Mumbai office ..... a meeting of senior officials to discuss the high incidence of frauds.

A. attended B. convened
C. reported D. registered

10. The note should be ..... to all the concerned departments for their consideration.

A. regulated B. requested
C. carried D. forwarded

11. Your present statement does not .... what you said last week.

A. accord to B. accord in
C. accord with D. accord for

12. I had a vague .... that the lady originally belonged to Scotland.
A. notion B. expression
C. imagination D. theory

13. The prisoner showed no .... for his crimes.
A. hatred B. obstinacy
C. remorse D. anger

14. It is inconceivable that in many schools children are subjected to physical .... in the name of discipline.
A. violation B. exercise
C. violence D. security

15. We have not yet fully realised the .... consequences of the war.
A. happy B. pleasing
C. grim D. exciting

16. Happiness consists in being .... what we have.
A. contented to B. contented with
C. contented for D. contented in

17. His rude behaviour is a .... his organization.
A. disgrace for
B. disgrace on
C. disgrace upon
D. disgrace to

18. No child is .... understanding. One has to wait and provide proper guidance.
A. dull to B. dull in
C. dull of D. dull for

19. I am fully .... the problems facing the industry.
A. alive with B. alive to
C. alive for D. alive on

20. The Romans were .... science.
A. bad in B. bad to
C. bad for D. bad at

21. Although I was .... of his plans, I encouraged him, because there was no one else who was willing to help.
A. sceptical B. remorseful
C. fearful D. excited

22. You have no business to .... pain on a weak and poor person.
A. inflict B. put
C. direct D. force

23. Her uncle died in a car accident. He was quite rich. She suddenly .... all her uncle's money.
A. succeeded B. caught
C. gave D. inherited

24. There was a major accident. The plane crashed. The pilot .... did not see the tower.
A. likely B. probably
C. scarcely D. hurriedly

25. The car we were travelling in .... a mile from home.
A. broke off B. broke down
C. broke into D. broke up

26. What are you .... in the kitchen cupboard?
A. looking in B. looking on
C. looking to D. looking for

27. I did not see the point of .... waiting for them, so I went home.
A. hanging around B. hang on
C. hang together D. hanging up

28. He lost confidence and .... of the deal at the last minute.
A. backed out B. backed on
C. backed down D. backed onto

29. To the dismay of all the students, the class monitor was ..... berated by the principal at a school assembly.
A. critically B. ignominiously
C. prudently D. fortuitously

30. All attempts to revive the fishing industry were ..... failure.
A. foredoomed to B. heading at
C. predicted for D. estimated to

31. There are ..... parked outside than yesterday.
A. fewer cars
B. few cars
C. less cars
D. a small number of cars

32. The minister had to ..... some awkward questions from reporters.
A. fend B. fend at
C. fend out D. fend off

33. The ..... of evidence was on the side of the plaintiff since all but one of the witnesses testified that his story was correct.
A. propensity B. force
C. preponderance D. brunt

34. Attention to detail is ..... of a fine craftsman.
A. hallmark B. stamp
C. seal of authority D. authenticity

35. Behaving in a .... and serious way, even in a .... situation, makes people respect you.
A. calm, difficult
B. steady, angry
C. flamboyant, tricky
D. cool astounding

36. Along with a sharp rise in ...., a recession would eventually result in more men, women, and children living in ....
A. crime, apathy
B. fatalities, poor
C. deaths, slums
D. unemployment, poverty

37. The government has .... to provide financial aid to the ones .... by severe floods in the city.
A. desired, troubled B. promised, havoc
C. failed, affected D. wanted, struck

38. An airplane with .... passengers on board made an unscheduled .... as the airport to which it was heading was covered with thick fog.
A. imitable, slip B. faulty, stop
C. variety, halt D. numerous, landing

39. Deemed universities .... huge fees, but have not been successful in providing .... education to our students.
A. collect, maintaining
B. pay, better
C. ask, good
D. charge, quality

40. If the banks desire to .... profit, they should get rid of .... measures.
A. lose, concentrate
B. increase, populist
C. earn, unhealthy
D. maximise, traditional

41. Leadership defines what the future should look like and ...... people with that vision.
A. aligns B. develops
C. trains D. encourages

42. We upset ourselves by responding in an ...... manner to someone else's actions.
A. unabashed B. irrational
C. arduous D. arguable

43. All the people involved in that issue feel a great ...... to his suggestion.
A. contradiction B. adherence
C. indifference D. repugnance

44. These elections will be remembered as much for its anti-incumbency mood as for its ...... mandate.
A. invincible B. rational
C. unprecedented D. deliberate

45. How do you expect us to stay in such a ...... building even if it can be hired on a nominal rent?
A. scruffy B. disperate
C. fragmented D. robust

46. ...... efforts from all concerned are required to raise the social and economic conditions of our countrymen.
A. Perpetual B. Dynamic
C. Massive D. Exploring

47. Many companies see technology as a ...... for a whole host of business problems.
A. consideration B. preference
C. linking D. panacea

48. Known as devout and serious person, she also has ...... sense of humour.
A. better B. plentiful
C. quick D. good

49. The matter would have become serious if ...... action had not been taken.
A. hasty B. fast
C. timely D. unusual

50. The ...... with which he is able to yield the paint brush is really remarkable.
A. ease B. practice
C. majesty D. sweep

51. You must ensure the correctness of the information before ....
A. drawing B. enabling
C. learning D. jumping

52. The rocket .... the target and did not cause any casualty.
A. sensed B. reached
C. missed D. exploded

53. It is desirable to take .... in any business if you want to make profit.
A. advice B. risk
C. loan D. recourse

54. They wasted all the money on purchase of some .... items.
A. excellent B. important
C. significant D. trivial

55. When he found the wallet his face glowed but soon it faded as the wallet was ....
A. empty B. vacant
C. recovered D. stolen

56. He has served the country by .... many significant positions.
A. appointing
B. creating
C. developing
D. holding

57. The frequent errors are a result of the student's ....
A. talent B. smartness
C. carelessness D. perception

58. The robbers eventually .... in breaking into the house.
A. succeeded B. decided
C. caught D. trained

59. I finally .... her to stay another day.
A. advised B. persuaded
C. suggested D. called

60. Most of the people who .... the book exhibition were teachers.
A. witnessed B. presented
C. conducted D. attended

ANSWERS

1	2	3	4	5	6	7	8	9	10
A	B	C	A	C	B	C	C	B	D
11	**12**	**13**	**14**	**15**	**16**	**17**	**18**	**19**	**20**
C	A	C	C	C	B	D	B	B	D
21	**22**	**23**	**24**	**25**	**26**	**27**	**28**	**29**	**30**
B	C	C	B	C	C	D	A	B	A
31	**32**	**33**	**34**	**35**	**36**	**37**	**38**	**39**	**40**
A	D	D	A	A	D	C	D	C	B
41	**42**	**43**	**44**	**45**	**46**	**47**	**48**	**49**	**50**
A	A	D	C	A	A	D	D	C	A
51	**52**	**53**	**54**	**55**	**56**	**57**	**58**	**59**	**60**
A	C	B	D	A	D	C	A	B	D

11 Sentence Improvement

One may use the same words in many ways but the best way is only one that makes the perfect usage of the words and conveys the proper meaning of the expression. Try it yourself in the following questions.

Multiple Choice Questions

Directions: *In these questions, a part of the sentence is bold. Below are given alternatives to the bold part at A, B and C which may improve the sentence. Choose the correct alternative. In case no improvement is needed, your answer is 'D'.*

1. Discreet salience **is extremely important** to create that 'irresistible-yet-unattainable' image for brands that want to take India seriously

A. was extremely important
B. is mainly important
C. was important extremely
D. No Improvement

2. This, over a designer outfit that he wanted for a friend's party and **that his sensitive** parents refused him.

A. which his sensitive
B. which his insensitive
C. that his insensitive
D. No Improvement

3. Goa was full of non-Goa property hunters **rushing about buying up the place** like tomorrow was an expired lease.

A. rushing in buying up the place
B. rushed about buying up the place
C. rushing about to buy up the place
D. No Improvement

4. Property hunting is a **tired and hungry** making business.

A. is a tiresome and hungry
B. is a tiring and hungry
C. is a tiring and waste
D. No Improvement

5. Cultural differences aside, **till luxury need speaks** in a manner that befits.

A. luxury still needs to speak
B. luxury still need to speak
C. luxury till need to speak
D. No Improvement

6. Indian food—the culinary avatar of the subcontinent's social history presented on a platter—**is without doubt the best food** in the world.

A. is undoubtedly the greatest food
B. is without doubt greatest food
C. is best food without doubt
D. No Improvement

7. It must retain the language of poetry. **It needed to create** stories, and not statements.
   A. It needed creating
   B. It needs creating
   C. It needs to create
   D. No Improvement
8. This year, Asia-Pacific has become the first region **to reach aggregate profiting** in biotech.
   A. to reach aggregated profitability
   B. to reach aggregate profitability
   C. to reach aggregate of profit
   D. No Improvement
9. India is deviating to embrace the West. If Western luxury brands deviate a little, **albeit selectively**, they will find rich Indian arms open far and wide.
   A. though selectively
   B. however selectively
   C. albeit selectedly
   D. No Improvement
10. China and India continued to attract attention and deals, motivated by the desire to increase access to these **largest and growing** drug markets and by the need to lower the costs of drug development.
   A. larger and growing
   B. large and growing
   C. larger and grown
   D. No Improvement
11. Luxury brands are **still above of the** clover curve here, with their elite (small) audiences.
   A. still ahead of the
   B. still in the
   C. still far of the
   D. No Improvement
12. Agencies **hence needed to be** sure of returns before investing, say admen.
   A. hence needs to be
   B. so needs to be
   C. hence need to be
   D. No Improvement
13. India is still a nascent market and that's the spirit everyone's **looking at it**.
   A. looking for it B. looking in it
   C. looking with it D. No Improvement
14. Questioning the state's move to allow women to serve liquor but not dance in bars **of the ground that** dancing aroused physical lust.
   A. on the grounds that
   B. of the grounds that
   C. over the grounds that
   D. No Improvement
15. For England the positives from their crushing series lose come in the shape of James Anderson and Kevin Pietersen, **both of which** have made significant strides up the rankings.
   A. both of which B. both of whom
   C. both of who D. No Improvement
16. International campaigns can work well for luxury here, **but context cannot be** ignored.
   A. so context cannot be
   B. but context cannot
   C. but context couldn't
   D. No Improvement
17. For one, the Indian luxury context, **while evolved rapidly**, still has its own meaning, and its own implications.
   A. while evolved rapid
   B. which evolving rapidly
   C. while evolving rapidly
   D. No Improvement
18. But too much of availability can compromise a luxury brand or **made it lose** its lustre.
   A. make her lose B. make him lose
   C. make it lose D. No Improvement
19. Still, it's under-the-upper **layers themselves who** are aspiring for slivers of luxury.
   A. layers themselves which
   B. layer itself who
   C. layers themself which
   D. No Improvement
20. It is like saying Hindi movies, with skimpily dressed dancers, would **effect public** order.
   A. effect your B. affect public
   C. affected public D. No Improvement

21. The court held that a few women being involved in prostitution was no **justice to deny other** bar girls the right to livelihood.
A. justification to declare other
B. justification to deny other
C. justice to let other
D. No Improvement

22. All-rounder cricketer has also made some progress **over the** player rankings.
A. above the B. at the
C. up the D. No Improvement

23. Former minister on Sunday **joined hands** with a suspended Lok Sabha member to float a new political outfit.
A. folded hands
B. walked hand in hand
C. shaked hands
D. No Improvement

24. Pakistan's former ministers will meet in London on Monday **to ask** a strategy to return home from exile.
A. to chalk out
B. to negotiate
C. to create
D. No Improvement

25. It's a family potboiler, medical thriller and political drama **all in one**—except that it's all too real and all too grim.
A. all 3 in one
B. all coupled into one
C. all rolled into one
D. No Improvement

26. India's efforts to get international support for its civil nuclear energy programme got **a go ahead on** Sunday as Germany indicated it would not come in the way of the India-US nuclear deal.
A. a life in B. a boost on
C. a boost at D. No Improvement

27. Is it time for old bungalows to **bite the dust**?
A. go down B. get down
C. come down D. No Improvement

28. The bungalows was an outward manifestation of a certain **way in life**, and with that era gone.
A. way for life B. way of life
C. way at life D. No Improvement

29. The builder Mittals will reportedly **raise their money**-raking high-rise behind it.
A. highten their money
B. rise their money
C. raise there money
D. No Improvement

30. The impatient present has usually demolished **more of the** past before we wake up to the irretrievable loss.
A. much of B. much of their
C. much of the D. No Improvement

31. Preservation is a romantic notion; demolition **quiet** more practical reasons.
A. has many, B. had many,
C. have many, D. No Improvement

32. You must get back to your **charming self** and impress the audience with your social skills.
A. own self B. main self
C. own uniqueness D. No Improvement

33. Stay focused on your goals and don't **get disturbed by** non-materialistic possessions.
A. get involved by
B. get betrayed by
C. get distracted by
D. No Improvement

34. You may appear more optimistic than your detractors **may want it to be.**
A. want you to be
B. wish yourself to be
C. seek you be
D. No Improvement

35. There are a number of mineral springs in the Czech territory, which **has been used** for medicinal purposes since the early 15th century.
A. have been used B. had been used
C. has being used D. No Improvement

36. The picturesque mountains **offers** excellent bungee jumping spots.
A. shows B. provides
C. offer D. No Improvement

37. Begin your **meal with** traditional faves like potato soup, beef soup with liver dumplings, or dill soup made from sour milk.
A. meals with B. meal in
C. meals of D. No Improvement

38. You can also **go to the** National Museum building and the famous Prague State Opera.
A. went to B. visit the
C. saw D. No Improvement

39. If they close the Gulf for a **length of time** to shipping, then certainly we could look at $150, probably higher.
A. larger amount of time
B. larger duration of time
C. larger amount of hours
D. No Improvement

40. **More of them** are owned by the state and even the privately-owned ones are open to the public.
A. Most of which B. Most of them
C. Most of all D. No Improvement

41. Constructed in the ninth century by the Prince Booivoj, the castle has transformed **oneself** from a wooden fortress surrounded by earthen bulwarks to the imposing form it has today.
A. himself B. herself
C. itself D. No Improvement

42. Apart from frequent art exhibitions, **their are also** permanent collections devoted to archaeology, anthropology, mineralogy, natural history and numismatics.
A. there is also B. there are also
C. their are also D. No Improvement

43. You can visit the Czech Museum of Fine Arts, **at a** permanent exhibition on Czech Kubism.
A. with a
B. for a
C. in a
D. No Improvement

44. Tensions **above** Iran come at a time of strong demand for energy.
A. under B. inside
C. over D. No Improvement

45. Because its shores line the narrow Straits of Hormuz, Iran **could quickly hit** both military and commercial shipping.
A. will quickly hit
B. shall quickly hit
C. will be quick hitting
D. No Improvement

46. For most people who exercise **at the** morning, there is no getting around the question: Eat and run? Or run and eat later?
A. in the
B. in
C. at the time of
D. No Improvement

47. Are ad agencies even attempting to peer into the keyhole of this indulgence sanctum to garner consumer insights **ahead of** the curve?
A. above
B. over
C. within
D. No Improvement

48. Too many people rush into the world of credit and don't stop to think about how **their actions could affect their** credit score and ability to qualify for credit in the future.
A. their actions may affect their
B. their actions might affect their
C. their actions will affect their
D. No Improvement

49. According to the report, **number of deal with** vaccines were energized by concerns around avian flu, SARS, and biodefence products, while looming patent expirations led to more deals in generics.
A. number of deals in
B. number of deal in
C. number of deals with
D. No Improvement

50. This is how the Bombay High Court responded to the state government's purported **moral stand which** dance bars were causing grave harm to society.

A. moral stand in

B. moral stand at

C. moral stand that D. No Improvement

51. If you have a high credit limit, use **at least a** third of it.

A. atleast a

B. at last a

C. utmost a

D. No Improvement

52. Fitness experts will say that **first eating provides** fuel for a proper workout.

A. eating in the beginning provides

B. first eat provides

C. eating first provides

D. No Improvement

53. One study that examined the claim directly in 1995 found that a group of people did **burned much calories from fat on days** when they exercised on an empty stomach than on days when they had a small breakfast first.

A. burn more calories from fat on days

B. burn more calorie from fat on days

C. burnt more calories from fat on days

D. No Improvement

54. Carefree children spent their afternoons **to run about barefoot**, their clothes dusty, and telltale twigs of the neighbour's mango tree in their hair.

A. running barefoot in the sun

B. run about barefoot in the sun

C. running about barefoot in the sun

D. No Improvement

55. A year ago, a 13-year-old girl attempted suicide because her mother **refuses to pay his** mobile bills.

A. refuses to pay her

B. refused to pay her

C. refused to pay his

D. No Improvement

ANSWERS

1	2	3	4	5	6	7	8	9	10
D	C	D	B	A	D	C	C	D	B
11	**12**	**13**	**14**	**15**	**16**	**17**	**18**	**19**	**20**
C	C	D	A	C	D	C	C	C	C
21	**22**	**23**	**24**	**25**	**26**	**27**	**28**	**29**	**30**
B	C	C	A	C	B	D	B	D	C
31	**32**	**33**	**34**	**35**	**36**	**37**	**38**	**39**	**40**
A	D	C	A	D	C	A	B	D	B
41	**42**	**43**	**44**	**45**	**46**	**47**	**48**	**49**	**50**
C	B	A	C	D	A	D	C	A	C
51	**52**	**53**	**54**	**55**					
C	C	A	C	B					

12 Reordering Words & Sentences

Different words form a sentence and convey their meaning only when arranged in a proper order. A Paragraph is formed from sentences, it will convey its true meaning and purpose only when the sentences are arranged in a proper manner. Try and practise it in this exercise.

Multiple Choice Questions

Directions (Qs. 1 to 20): *In the following questions, some parts of the sentence have been jumbled up. You are required to rearrange these parts which are labelled P, Q, R and S to produce the correct sentence. Choose the option with proper sequence.*

1. We are doing
P : to the people
Q : to give relief
R : all we can
S : but more funds are needed
The correct sequence should be
A. P Q R S B. R Q P S
C. Q P R S D. S P Q R

2. The man
P : when he was
Q : in the office last evening
R : could not finish
S : all his work
The correct sequence should be
A. P Q R S B. Q R S P
C. R Q P S D. R S P Q

3. The people decided
P : they were going
Q : how much
R : to spend
S : on the construction of the school building
The correct sequence should be
A. Q P R S B. P Q R S
C. P R Q S D. S Q P R

4. The man said that
P : those workers
Q : would be given a raise
R : who did not go on
S : strike last month
The correct sequence should be
A. P Q R S B. P R S Q
C. Q P R S D. R S P Q

5. I think
P : the members
Q : are basically in agreement
R : of the group
S : on the following points
The correct sequence should be
A. R Q P S B. S Q R P
C. P R Q S D. P Q S R

6. While it was true that
P : I had
Q : to invest in industry
R : some lands and houses
S : I did not have ready cash

The correct sequence should be

A. P Q R S B. P R S Q
C. S Q P R D. Q P R S

7. P : But for your help
Q : to finish this work
R : it would not have been possible
S : in time

The correct sequence should be

A. P R Q S B. S P Q R
C. R P Q S D. P Q R S

8. The boy
P : in the competition
Q : who was wearing spectacles
R : won many prizes
S : held in our college

The correct sequence should be

A. P Q R S B. R P S Q
C. Q R P S D. Q P S R

9. About 200 years ago,
P : in the south of India
Q : an old king
R : ruled over a kingdom
S : called Rajavarman

The correct sequence should be

A. Q S R P B. P Q R S
C. Q P S R D. Q S P R

10. P : his land
Q : a wooden plough
R : the Indian peasant still uses
S : to cultivate

The correct sequence should be

A. R Q P S B. Q P S R
C. S R Q P D. R Q S P

11. He was a man,
P : even if he had to starve
Q : who would not beg
R : borrow or steal
S : from anyone

The correct sequence should be

A. P Q R S B. P R Q S
C. Q R S P D. Q P R S

12. P : in the progress of
Q : universities play a crucial role
R : our civilization
S : in the present age

The correct sequence should be

A. S Q P R B. Q R S P
C. Q R P S D. S Q R P

13. P : far out into the sea
Q : for the next two weeks there were further explosions
R : which hurled
S : ashes and debris

The correct sequence should be

A. Q R P S B. R S P Q
C. Q R S P D. S R P Q

14. William Shakespeare,
P : in his lifetime
Q : the great English dramatist
R : wrote thirty-five plays
S : and several poems

The correct sequence should be

A. P Q R S B. R S P Q
C. Q S R P D. Q R S P

15. Whenever I am,
P : with an old friend of mine
Q : in New Delhi
R : to have dinner
S : I always try

The correct sequence should be

A. S Q P R B. Q S R P
C. R P S Q D. P R Q S

16. P : I don't know
Q : must have thought
R : what people sitting next to me
S : but I came away

The correct sequence should be

A. R S Q P B. R Q S P
C. P Q R S D. P R Q S

17. P : in estimating the size of the earth
Q : but they were hampered by the lack of instruments of precision
R : ancient astronomers
S : used methods which were theoretically valid

The correct sequence should be

A. R P Q S B. P R Q S
C. R S Q P D. R P S Q

18. P : It is a pity that
Q : by offering a handsome dowry
R : a number of parents think that
S : they will be able to ensure the happiness of their daughters

The correct sequence should be

A. S Q R P B. P R S Q
C. P S R Q D. P R Q S

19. The common man
P : in nurturing
Q : a more active role
R : communal harmony
S : should play

The correct sequence should be

A. P R S Q B. S Q P R
C. S Q R P D. P R Q S

20. The doctor
P : able to find out
Q : what has caused
R : the food poisoning
S : has not been

The correct sequence should be

A. S P R Q B. P R Q S
C. P R S Q D. S P Q R

Directions (Qs. 21 to 40): *A number of sentences are given below which when properly sequenced form a coherent paragraph. Each sentence is labelled as abcdef...... Choose the most logical order of sentences from among the given choices to construct a coherent paragraph:*

21. (a) Parts of northern region were pounded by heavy rains today,
(b) Vehicular traffic came to a near halt.
(c) As mid and high altitude areas of Himachal Pradesh were in grip of severe cold wave with snow lashing the tribal areas and mid ranges receiving showers.
(d) As the sky remained heavily overcast with dark clouds reducing the visibility considerably.
(e) A large number of tourists were forced to buy heavy woollens and stay indoors due to inclement weather.

A. ecabd B. adecb
C. edabc D. acbde

22. (a) The idea is that students should be able to find employment for themselves after the course.
(b) The Central Board of Secondary Education is planning a revamp of its vocational courses.
(c) For this it is necessary to tie up with the industry as well as mobilise schools for their support.
(d) While others will be made less academic and more in tune with the needs of the industry.
(e) A number of courses have been identified as 'deadwood' and will be done away with.

A. bedac B. abcde
C. acebd D. baced

23. (a) Clearly, age is not a deterrent in one's choice of learning.
(b) Perhaps, it was because of her childhood desire.
(c) When Rachna came to Delhi eight years back, she had not anticipated a career in the field of art.
(d) She has been successful in the various exhibitions that she has been part of in terms of business.
(e) She had got into expressing her thoughts with the help of a brush and colours only because her daughter refused to get initiated into it.
(f) She feels that her use of colour appeals to people.

A. aedcbf B. cdefba
C. cebadf D. acdebf

24. (a) The rehabilitation record has been dismal.
(b) It has been two years years since the earthquake rudely rattled the people of Gujarat.
(c) And since then, life has been a constant struggle.
(d) The quake set Gujarat's clock back by 10 years.
(e) Things changed forever.

A. bedca B. bcade
C. dbace D. edcba

25. (a) In fact, success in exams depended on rote learning from old notes.
(b) when he was studying civil engineering in a college in Gujarat.
(c) He was detained for lack of attendance.
(d) Lectures were soporific, classes rarely worth attending and 80 per cent attendance compulsory.
(e) The college became a trap he hated.
(f) His is a plight many engineers across India would identify with.
(g) He found the going tough.
A. abcdgef B. bgdacef
C. fabcdge D. abcdefg

26. (a) In a country that has close to 600 recognised engineering colleges, there are only seven IITs.
(b) Barring a few exeptions, the academic atmosphere in these is moribund.
(c) The very best students usually get there.
(d) many waste themselves in frustration.
(e) Most of those who get into engineering are good students.
(f) but about 1.25 lakh others and up in the remaining colleges.
A. aecfbd B. abecdf
C. abcdef D. acfbed

27. (a) Whatever the job market, common wisdom says that IIT graduates will find jobs where others have failed.
(b) The IIT brand name is a ticket to success.
(c) When recruiters go headhunting, the IITs are still top of their list.
(d) Its possessor is understood to have an excellent academic record and the will to succeed.
(e) In the job market, that counts.
A. bdeac B. abcde
C. abdce D. dbace

28. (a) It will pave the way ....
(b) signalling a new beginning in strategic ties......
(c) for a tangible Indian economic presence in Iran and Central Asia.
(d) Iran has offered India valuable road linkages to central Asia ......
(e) aimed at promoting peace and economic cooperation in the region.
A. dbeac B. debca
C. acebd D. abced

29. (a) A good college is essential for a successful career and admissions are based on marks.
(b) The marks-based system followed by all the boards in the country recognises only a small percentage of students as successful.
(c) The marks one scores in the crucial board exams dictate the path his life takes.
(d) Anyone scoring below a certain percentage is automatically branded a 'failure'.
(d) So if you cannot make it into the best college, your career is over even before it has started.
A. abcde B. bcdea
C. bdcae D. abdec

30. (a) The project has already started on an experimental basis in the west district.
(b) A website is soon going to be launched where application forms can be downloaded and submitted.
(c) Standing in a queue at a government office to submit application form will be a thing of the past.
(d) A unique code will be alloted while submitting the form which will help in finding the status of the application.
A. abcd B. dabc
C. cbda D. badc

31. (a) To curb bio-terrorism is a difficult task.
(b) To check these attacks and lessen their impact, we need an impartial team of sincere, strong and dedicated men.
(c) The media can play a strong role in stopping this unnecessary spread of panic.
(d) Since bio-terrorism is not visible or easily detectable, it can be used often.
(e) Men who honour the lives of their fellow countrymen before their own.

A. abcde B. dabce
C. adbec D. acbed

32. (a) He was dying.
(b) No one was ready to touch him as even shifting him from one place to another would lead to profuse bleeding.
(c) He was a five-day old infant, premature and bleeding profusely.
(d) Even if injected one small needle, blood would ooze out and continue to flow for an hour at a stretch.
(e) This small being had haematoma, a thick blood clot in his brain.

A. edbca B. cabde
C. eacdb D. cedba

33. (a) The day I don't treat a patient, I feel ....
(b) I have enough to eat, I crave for blessings now.
(c) But if a financially weak patient gives me only ₹ 50, I don't mind.
(d) Each month I do three to four operations free of cost.
(e) I have lost something in life.
(f) My consultation fee is ₹ 300.

A. fcdeab B. dfcbae
C. fcabde D. bdfcea

34. (a) When he was rushed to the nearby Primary Health Centre after his fall, the doctor referred him to a hospital.
(b) This worsened his injury.
(c) Had a little precaution been exercised after the accident, Tarun would have continued with his gymnastic classes.
(d) He was paralysed from waist downwards when he fell from the vaulting horse while doing gymnastics.
(e) However, the doctor forgot to tell Tarun's parents to take him on a stretcher as he had suffered spinal injuries.
(f) Tarun is wheelchair bound for two years.

A. fdeabc B. abcdef
C. fdcaeb D. fdbcae

35. (a) As the temperature rises, staying hydrated can become a greater challenge for people exercising both indoors and out.
(b) Several things can influence this process, including age, gender, physical conditioning. humidity and a lack of sufficient fluids.
(c) In hot weather, individuals can lose as much as two quarts of sweat per hour.
(d) As we age, we have a lower perceived level of thirst in response to fluid loss and early stages of dehydration.
(e) If not replenished, this can lead to dehydration, heat exhaustion and even heatstroke.

A. abcde B. dbcae
C. cbdea D. acebd

36. (a) The leopard was discovered in the servant quarters of a farmhouse.
(b) The injuries appeared to have been caused by the paws of the leopard, and were not teeth wounds.
(c) It took the wild life officials, Delhi Police and Delhi zoo vets eight hours to capture the leopard that had wandered into a factory in south Delhi.
(d) The leopard then jumped into the factory where the workers managed to lock it in a small generator room before calling in the police.
(e) Before its capture, the leopard attacked two women and a man in the farmhouse.

A. aebdc B. bdaec
C. eadbc D. adbec

37. (a) Police suspect a carpenter working at John's house as he has not reported for work since the day the boy went missing.
(b) John did not return home in the afternoon.
(c) John's mother had herself put the boy on the vehicle in the morning.
(d) John smiled at him and was last seen walking up to him.
(e) His parents called the school and were told John had not been to school at all and had been marked absent.
(f) He was about to enter the school when someone called out his name.

A. cfdbea B. debfca
C. bfdaec D. abcdef

38. (a) However, the mayhem over the last few months is deeply shocking.
(b) Yet I do not agree with the prophets of doom who see nothing but disaster ahead.
(c) When I came back to my motherland India after a stay in Switzerland, I felt I was trading a hotbed of intense religious and political violence for peace and quiet.
(d) I think our nation is searching for an identity.
(e) And a new vision of the future will emerge from this.

A. abcde B. cabde
C. cebad D. bedca

39. (a) An integrated and combined approach was required to reveal the mystery of the brain —its structure, composition and function.
(b) Since the early 80's, scientists were clear that the brain would be the final frontier to conquer.
(c) The initiative was flagged off and came to be known as the Human Brain Project.
(d) But that wasn't easy because understanding the brain involved completely integrating information from the level of the gene to the level of behaviour.
(e) To fulfill this requirement a group of American scientists from various disciplines decided to work together.

A. acbed B. bdaec
C. abdec D. badec

40. (a) A product is something that is made in a factory, a brand is something that is bought by a consumer.
(b) The trick therefore, lies in the brand positioning.
(c) For a consumer, the satisfaction of becoming associated with a name that is the 'best' and the 'leader' is far more important and at times makes him ignore the price factor.
(d) Brands come and go.
(e) Still there are those who manage to stay and develop an affinity with consumers.

A. aebcd B. debac
C. decab D. aecdb

ANSWERS

1	2	3	4	5	6	7	8	9	10
B	D	A	B	C	C	A	C	A	D
11	12	13	14	15	16	17	18	19	20
C	A	C	D	B	D	C	B	B	D
21	22	23	24	25	26	27	28	29	30
D	A	C	A	B	D	A	A	C	C
31	32	33	34	35	36	37	38	39	40
C	D	B	C	D	A	A	B	B	B

❑❑❑

13 Comprehension Passages

PASSAGES

Directions: *Read the following passages and answer the questions given below each.*

PASSAGE-1

In the Roman times, defected enemies were generally put to death as criminals for having offended the emperor of Rome. In the middle ages, however, the practice of ransoming of returning prisoners in exchange for money became common. Though some saw this custom as a step towards a most humane society, the primary reasons behind it were economic rather than humanitarian.

In those times, rulers had only a limited ability to raise taxes. They could neither force their subject to fight nor pay them to do so. The promise of material compensation in the form of goods and ransom was therefore the only way of inducing combatants to participate in a war. In the middle ages, the predominant incentive for the individual soldiers was the expectation of spoils. Although collecting ransom clearly brought financial gain, keeping a prisoner and arranging for his exchange had its cost. Consequently, procedures were devised to reduce transaction costs.

One such device was a rule asserting that the prisoner had to assess his own value. This compelled the prisoner to establish a value *without too much distortion;* indicating too low a value would increase, the captive's chances of being killed, while indicating too high a value would either ruin him financially or create a prohibitively expensive ransom that would also result in death.

1. It can be inferred from the passage that a medieval soldier

A. was less likely to kill captured members of opposing armies than was a soldier of the Roman Empire

B. was similar to a 20th century terrorist in that he operated on a basically independent level and was motivated solely by economic incentives

C. had few economic options and chose to fight because it was the only way to earn an adequate living

D. was motivated to spare prisoners' lives by humanitarian rather than economic ideals

2. Which of the following best describes the change in policy from executing prisoners in Roman times to ransoming prisoners in the middle ages?

A. The emperors of Rome demanded more respect than did medieval rulers and thus Roman subjects went to greater lengths to defend their nation

B. It was a reflection of the lesser degree of direct control medieval ruler had over subjects

C. It became a show of strength and honour warrior of the middles ages to be able to capture and return their enemies

D. Medieval soldiers were not as humanitarian as their ransoming practices might have indicated

3. The primary purpose of the passage is to
   A. discuss the economic basis of the medieval practice of exchanging prisoners for ransom
   B. examine the history of the treatment of prisoner of war
   C. emphasize the importance of a warrior's code of honour during the middle ages
   D. explore a way of reducing the cost of ransom

4. The author uses the phrase *"without too much distortion"* in order to
   A. indicate that prisoners would fairly assess their worth
   B. emphasize the important role medieval prisoners played in determining whether they should be ransomed
   C. explain how prisoners often paid more than an appropriate ransom in order to increase their chances for survival
   D. suggest that captors and captives often had understanding relationships

PASSAGE-2

The world dismisses curiosity by calling it idle or mere idle curiosity—even though curious persons are seldom idle. Parents do their best to extinguish curiosity in their children because it makes life difficult to be faced everyday with a string of unanswerable questions about what makes fire hot or why grass grows. Children whose curiosity survives parental discipline are invited to join our university. With the university, they go on asking their questions and trying to find the answers. In the eyes of a scholar, that is what a university is for. Some of the questions which the scholars ask, seem to the world to be scarcely worth asking, let alone answering. They asked questions too minute specialised for you and me to understand without years of explanation. If the world inquires of one of them why he wants to know the answer to a particular question he may say especially if he is a scientist, that the answer will in some obscure way make possible a new machine or weapon or gadget. He talks that way because he knows that the world understands and respects utility.

But to you who are now part of the university, he will say that he wants to know the answer simply because he does not know it, the way the mountain climber wants to climb a mountain, simply because it is there. Similarly a historian asked by an outsider why he studies history may come out with the argument that he has learnt to repeat on such occasions, something about knowledge of the past making it possible to understand the present and mould the future. But if you really want to know why a historian studies the past, the answer is much simpler, something happened and he would like to know what. All this does not mean that the answers which scholars find to their questions have no consequences. They may have enormous consequences but these seldom form the reason for asking the questions or pursuing the answers. It is true that scholars can be put to work answering questions for the sake of the consequences as thousands are working, now, for example, in search of a cure for cancer. But this is not the primary function of the scholars. For the consequences are usually subordinate to the satisfaction of curiosity.

1. According to the passage, the children make life difficult for their parents
   A. by their ceaseless curiosity
   B. by unceasing bombardment of questions
   C. by asking irrelevant questions
   D. by posing profound questions

2. The common people consider some of the questions that the scholars ask unimportant
   A. as they are too lazy and idle
   B. as they are too modest
   C. as it's beyond their comprehension
   D. as it is considered a waste of time

3. A historian really studies the past
   A. to comprehend the present and to reconstruct the future
   B. to explain the present and plan the future
   C. to understand the present and make fortune
   D. to understand the present and mould the future

4. Children whose curiosity survives parental discipline means
   A. children retaining their curiosity in spite of being discouraged by their parents
   B. children pursuing their mental curiosity
   C. children's curiosity subdued due to parents' intervention
   D. children being disciplined by their parents

5. According to the passage, parents do their best to discourage curiosity in their children
   A. because they have no time
   B. because they have no patience to answer them
   C. because they feel that their children ask stupid questions continuously
   D. because they are unable to answer all their questions

PASSAGE-3

The factor of geographical distribution is equally, possibly even more, significant that English is spoken as first or native language in at least four continents of the world, Russian in two, Chinese and the Indian languages in one. English is without question the closest approach to a world language today. It goes without saying that no two persons ever have an identical command of their common language. Certainly, they have not precisely the same vocabulary. There are at least minor differences in pronunciation, indeed the same individual will not pronounce his vowels and consonants in absolutely identical fashion everytime he utters them. Everyone possesses, in addition, certain individual traits of grammatical form and syntactical order, constituting that peculiar and personal quality of language which we term as style. All of this is implicit in the well-known phrase, 'Style is the man.' No men are identical, no two styles are the same. If this be true of but two persons, the potential of differences resident in a language spoken by more than 200 million truly staggers imagination.

1. The author argues that English is the closest approach to a world language because
   A. there are more native speakers of English than of any other language
   B. English has less number of mutually unintelligible dialects
   C. the geographical distribution of English covers a much greater area
   D. other languages are much too complex to be world languages

2. The fact that the same individual will not pronounce his vowels and consonants identically everytime shows that
   A. literary style varies from person to person
   B. mutual intelligibility is a myth
   C. vocabulary varies from individual to individual
   D. no two persons speak the same language exactly the same way

3. It is evident from the passage that style is
   A. a strange type of language
   B. a language where one does not have to be particular about correctness and grammar
   C. language used in a particular way by an individual
   D. a question of grammatical and syntactic correctness

4. According to some authorities
   A. more people speak Chinese dialect than English
   B. more people speak English as an auxiliary language than as a first language
   C. more people speak English in the UK than in England
   D. about one-fourth of the world's population speaks English

5. The overall implication of the passage is that
   A. to suppose that 230 million people speak English as a native language would certainly be an underestimate
   B. the 55 million inhabitants of the British Isles speak like the 30 million inhabitants of the dominions and colonies
   C. a little less than half the native English speakers in the world live in the US

D. about one-tenth of the total English-speaking world population lives in British dominions and colonies

PASSAGE-4

What is the future which awaits our children? The underlying assumption of the question, that Indian children have a common future, is itself dubious. It can legitimately be asked whether a student who is well-fed, attending a boarding school in the salubrious climate of the hills and learning to use computers has any future in common with a malnourished child who goes to a school with no blackboards, if indeed he does go to school. The latter may have no worthwhile future at all. And it might be worthwhile to analyse the significance of this marginalisation of more than 75 per cent of the children of this country.

The failure to provide an infrastructure for primary education in the villages of India more than 40 years after independence is in sharp contrast with the sophisticated institutions, for technical institutes of higher education are funded by the government, which essentially means that the money to support them comes from taxes. And, since indirect taxation forms a substantial part of the taxes collected by the government, the financial burden is borne by all the people. L.K. Jha put it graphically when he observed that 25 paise of every rupee spent on educating an IIT student comes from the pockets of men and women whose children may never enter a proper classroom.

1. The author is trying to highlight which of the following?
   A. Faulty system of direct taxes
   B. The greatness of L.K. Jha
   C. Need of sophisticated education for rural poor
   D. Need to have common future for Indian children

2. Which of the following pairs have been termed as 'sharp contrast' by the author?
   (*i*) Infrastructure for technical education
   (*ii*) Lack of infrastructure for rural primary schools
   (*iii*) 25 paise of every rupee earned by Government is spent on education
   (*iv*) The financial burden of higher technical education is borne by all people
   (*v*) 75% of children have limited opportunities
   A. (*ii*) and (*iv*) B. (*ii*) and (*iii*)
   C. (*iii*) and (*iv*) D. (*i*) and (*ii*)

3. Which of the following statements is not true?
   (*i*) The author welcomes Govt.'s initiative on primary education
   (*ii*) 75% of the children have a bright future
   (*iii*) 25% cost of educating a technocrat comes from poor people
   A. Only (*i*) B. Only (*ii*)
   C. Only (*iii*) D. Only (*i*) and (*ii*)

4. According to the author, who among the following does not have a hopeful and prosperous future?
   (*i*) All students from technical institutes
   (*ii*) All students financially supported by the Government
   A. Only (*i*) B. Only (*ii*)
   C. Both (*i*) and (*ii*) D. Neither (*i*) nor (*ii*)

5. What seems to be the likely answer of the author to the question posed by him in the first sentence of the passage?
   (*i*) There is no common future for the Indian children
   (*ii*) The future is worthwhile for majority of Indian children
   (*iii*) The majority may never enter a proper classroom
   A. Only (*i*) B. Only (*ii*)
   C. Only (*iii*) D. Both (*i*) and (*ii*)

6. What seems to be the purpose of the author in writing this passage?
   A. Setting goals for children of upper middle class
   B. Questioning the legitimacy of public schools
   C. Highlighting lack of infrastructural facilities for primary education
   D. Focusing on inequality in educational opportunities

PASSAGE-5

Cyber crime is the branded stigma defacing the culture and magnanimity of computer technology. It is upkeeping the flag with indomitable triumph against developing computer technology worldwide.

Modern age is striding with marching steps of technology revolution beating the past decade of ancestral belief with ultimate care. Computer invention has unfolded the mystery of quick access with the objective of minimum manpower and cutting the time consumption parameters.

As each coin has dual face of its portrait, likewise computer technology is sick of creeping virus. Synthetic man-made dilemma of site hackers activation is causing setback to the expanding anchor of revolutionary device with great loss of time, economy and data profile as suffered by consumers. A recent report from Internet security firm Websense estimates that 85.6 per cent of all the unwanted e-mails contained links to spam sites. The company's data suggests that the number of malicious sites grew 233 per cent in the last six months and saw 671 per cent growth in the number of malicious sites during the last year. In June alone, the total number of e-mails detected as containing viruses increased by 600 per cent compared to May.

Chat rooms, blogs and message-boards where the users post comments have been identified as the top targets of hackers and spammers due to the high traffic these attract. According to Websense, 95 per cent of user-generated comments to blogs, chat rooms and message-boards during the first half of the year were malicious.

It is advisable not to click on spurious links and stay away from keying in passwords at unknown sites as they are most likely to be spammed. Hackers can steal your passwords and log in to your account and access critical information like account numbers and contact details among other things.

1. The above passage is:

A. an advisory for the computer users.
B. an advisory for the Internet users.
C. a warning against possible threat to the Internet users.
D. related to chat rooms, blogs and message boards.

2. People who use chat rooms and blogs,

A. are safe and have no threats from spam.
B. are more prone to malicious e-mails.
C. create virus and hack the accounts of others.
D. are unsafe.

3. According to the writer, it is not safe to:

A. log on to spurious links.
B. access one's own account frequently.
C. have essential information stored in a computer.
D. include data-stealing code.

4. Hackers and spammers, according to the writer, are:

A. a new threat to the Internet users and the economy.
B. only pranksters and not serious threat to the system.
C. trained, professional technocrats who are an asset.
D. not expert professionals.

5. Which word in the passage is synonym of *weblog*?

A. blog B. password
C. site D. e-mail

6. Which agency has assessed the data record with spam sites?

A. Microsoft
B. Internet security from Google
C. Websense
D. Spammers

7. Which month dominates the e-mails detection data record?

A. May B. June
C. Last six months D. Last year

PASSAGE-6

Progress in life depends a good deal on crossing one threshold after another. Some time ago, a man watched his little nephew try to write his name. It was hard work, very hard work. The little boy had arrived at an effort threshold. Today he writes his name with comparative ease. No new threshold confronts him. This is the way with all of us. As soon as we cross one threshold, as soon as we conquer one difficulty, a new difficulty appears, or should appear. Some people make the mistake of steering clear of thresholds. Anything that requires genuine thinking and use of energy, they avoid. They prefer to stay in a rut where thresholds are not met. Probably, they have been at their job a number of years. Things are easy for them. They make no effort to seek out new obstacles to overcome. Real progress stops under such circumstances.

Some middle-aged and elderly people greatly enrich their lives by continuing to cross thresholds. One man went into an entirely new business when he was past middle life and made success of it, De Morgan didn't start to write novels until he was past sixty. Psychologists have discovered that man can continue to learn throughout his life. And it is undoubtedly better to try and fail than not to try at all. There one can be placed in the category of the Swiss mountaineer of whom it was said, *"He died climbing"*. When a new difficulty arises to obstruct your path, do not complain. Accept the challenge. Determine to cross this threshold as you have crossed numerous other thresholds in your past. In the words of a poet, do not rest but strive *to pass from dream to grander dream.*

1. What obstructs real progress in life?
A. Remaining at one and the same post
B. Avoiding the thinking and energy
C. Shunning every work
D. Stopping education

2. What does progress in life depend upon?
A. Good habits
B. Hardwork
C. Overcoming one difficulty after another
D. Spirit of service and cooperation

3. What does *'He died climbing'* signify?
A. He died when he was climbing the hill
B. He died before getting at the top
C. He strove hard till the last moment of life
D. He climbed the hill and then died

4. What does *'to pass from dream to grander dream'* mean?
A. Always having greater and greater aspiration in life
B. Seeing one good dream and then greater aspiration in life
C. Making plan after plan
D. Seeing one dream after the other

5. What did the man entering a new business past middle life do of his business?
A. He miserably failed in it
B. He achieved partial success
C. He dropped the business after some time
D. He achieved good success in it

6. How can you accomplish the most difficult tasks?
A. By mobilizing all possible resources
B. By avoiding all obstacles
C. By sticking to hardwork
D. By doing it bit by bit and persisting in the effort

7. What does De Morgan's life teach?
A. That it is futile to learn many things
B. That one is never old in case he has vigour
C. That it is never too late to learn
D. That creative writing can be made even late in life

8. How do middle-aged and elderly people add brilliance to their lives?
A. By overcoming difficulty one after another
B. By getting sycophants to surround them
C. By making fine speeches
D. By acquiring resourcefulness

9. What should we do when a new difficulty obstructs our path?
A. Run away from it
B. Be bold and face it
C. Manoeuvre to get it removed
D. Enlist other people's help to get it over

10. When did De Morgan start to write novels?
A. When he was sixty years old
B. When he was below sixty
C. When he studied psychology
D. None of these

PASSAGE-7

It is *heartening* to know that if one had not had any heart attack earlier and he stops smoking, his chances of having a heart attack *drop* to that of a non-smoker in about six months' time. Stopping of smoking is also the single most effective means of secondary prevention (recurrence of a heart attack) in heart patients.

Smoking leads to pain and stiffness in the legs while walking. No amount of drugs can help. The only remedy is to give up smoking. If women smoke during pregnancy, there is an increased risk of death of the baby in the womb or soon after birth. Even where the baby survives, there is likelihood of delayed physical and intellectual development of the baby till it reaches 11 years of age.

Still worse the fact about smoking is that passive smoking is equally dangerous. Passive smokers are those who do not smoke but being in the company of smokers have to inhale smoke exhaled by the smokers They are equally prone to heart diseases, lung cancer and bronchitis, for no fault of theirs. It is seen that the incidence of these diseases is greater among women whose husbands are *heavy* smokers As such, every non-smoker has a fundamental right to safeguard himself against the danger of passive smoking. "Your smoking is injurious to my health and I have a right to stop you from smoking" could be the slogan against passive smoking. It is a great threat to the health of the individual, the family and the society. In fact one has to choose between health and smoking including passive smoking. *One cannot have both.*

Another matter of *grave concern* about smoking is the long time interval between the start of smoking habit and the manifestation of deadly diseases like cancer, chronic bronchitis and heart attack. People are generally not aware of the link between smoking and the misery they have to undergo years later and younger people often fall victim to this menacing habit under the wrong impression that they are *immune* to its disastrous effects, not realising that they are *heading* towards catastrophe. The prolonged incubation period of many tobacco-related diseases has prevented recognition of the size of the threat and the *grim* picture of chronic and life-threatening diseases.

1. What is "passive smoking"?

A. Giving up the habit of smoking abruptly
B. Exhaling smoke by a non-smoker
C. Unintended intake of smoke exhaled by smokers
D. Smoking cigarettes which are harmless in nature

2. The effects of passive smoking are more and more prominently observed among

A. the children
B. the smokers
C. the wives of smokers
D. the non-smokers

3. Which of the following is a heartening thing, according to the author?

A. People who have had a heart attack stop smoking
B. It takes only six months for any person to quit smoking
C. The smoker carries the risk of heart attack for six months
D. None of these

4. Which of the following statements is/are false in the context of the passage?

(*i*) Passive smokers are not free from risk of heart diseases
(*ii*) Intake of certain medicines helps recover pain and stiffness in legs caused by smoking
(*iii*) Younger people are immune to the disastrous effects if their regular smoking is under control

A. (*i*) and (*ii*) only B. (*ii*) and (*iii*) only
C. (*ii*) only D. (*iii*) only

5. Which of the following is not mentioned in the passage as a likely result of smoking by women during pregnancy?

A. Death of baby before birth
B. Death of baby after birth
C. Survival of baby with some abnormality
D. Abnormal delay in the childbirth

6. Which of the following is considered by the author as a matter of "grave concern"?
   A. Inordinate delay in appearance of symptoms of hazards of smoking
   B. Long time required for giving up the habit of smoking
   C. Manifestation of deadly diseases like cancer, bronchitis, etc.
   D. Lack of awareness of people regarding the hazards of smoking

7. The youth feel that they are immune to the hazardous effects of smoking because
   A. these effects of smoking are not visible within a short time span
   B. they do not realise that they are heading towards disaster
   C. they feel a great thrill in acquiring the habit of smoking
   D. the link between smoking and its disastrous effects cannot be established

8. Which factor prevents people from realising the extent of threat of smoking hazards?
   A. Their lack of awareness of civic responsibilities
   B. Their firm belief that they are not immune to these hazards
   C. The less disastrous effects of tobacco-related diseases
   D. None of these

9. The last sentence of the third para *"One cannot have both"* means
   A. active smoking and passive smoking
   B. smoking and risk of heart diseases
   C. threat to the individual and also to the family
   D. None of these

Directions (Qs. 10 to 12): *Choose the word which is most nearly the **SAME** in meaning as the word given in bold capitals as used in the passage.*

10. HEADING
   A. crowning B. marching
   C. adorning D. title

11. HEAVY
   A. excessive B. bulky
   C. large D. thick

12. DROP
   A. roll B. escape
   C. remove D. reduce

Directions (Qs. 13 to 15): *Choose the word which is most nearly the **OPPOSITE** in meaning of the word given in bold capitals as used in the passage.*

13. GRIM
   A. dim B. dark
   C. presentable D. pleasant

14. IMMUNE
   A. free B. vulnerable
   C. powerful D. weak

15. HEARTENING
   A. cheerful B. miserable
   C. frightening D. dangerous

PASSAGE-8

The happy man is the man who lives objectively, who has free affections and wide interests, who secures his happiness through these interests and affections and through the fact that they, in turn, make him an object of interest and affection to many others. To be the recipient of affection is a potent cause of happiness, but the man who demands affection is not the man upon whom it is *bestowed.* The man who receives affection is, speaking broadly, the man who gives it. But it is useless to attempt to give it as a calculation, in the way in which one might lend money at interest, for a calculated affection is not genuine and is not felt to be so by the recipient.

What then can a man do who is unhappy because he is encased in self? So long as he continues to think about the causes of his unhappiness, he continues to be self-centred and therefore does not get outside the vicious circle, if he is to get outside it, it must be genuine interests, not by simulated interests adopted merely as a medicine. Although this difficulty is real, there is nevertheless much that he can do if he has rightly diagnosed his trouble. If, for example, his trouble is due to a sense of sin, conscious or unconscious, he can first persuade his conscious mind that he has no reason to feel sinful and then proceed, to plant his rational conviction in his unconscious mind, concerning himself meanwhile with some more or less neutral activity. If he succeeds in *dispelling* the sense of sin, it is possible that genuine objective interests will arise spontaneously. If his trouble is self-pity, he can deal with it in the same manner after first persuading himself that there is nothing extraordinarily unfortunate in his circumstances.

If fear is his trouble, let him practise exercises designed to give courage. Courage has been recognised from time immemorial as an important virtue, and a great part of training of boys and young men has been devoted to producing a type of character capable of fearlessness in battle. But moral courage and intellectual courage have been much less studied, they also, however, have their technique. Admit to yourself everyday at least one painful truth, you will find this quite useful. Teach yourself to feel that life still be worth living even if you were not, as of course you are, immeasurably superior to all your friends in virtue and in intelligence. Exercises of this sort prolonged through several years will at last enable you to admit facts *without flinching* and will, in so doing, free you from the empire of fear over a very large field.

1. Who according to the passage is the happy man?
   A who is encased in self
   B. who has free affection and wide interests
   C. who is free from worldly passions
   D. who has externally centre passions
2. According to the passage, calculated affection
   A. appears to be false and fabricated
   B. makes other pen-on to love you
   C. turns into permanent affection over a period of time
   D. leads to self-pity
3. Which of the following virtues, according to the passage, has been recognised for long as an important virtue?
   A. Patriotism B. Sacrifice
   C. Courage D. Self-consciousness
4. Which of the following, according to the passage, has not been studied much?
   A. Feeling of guilt and self-pity
   B. The state of mind of an unhappy man
   C. How to get absorbed in other interests
   D. Moral and intellectual courage
5. If a man is suffering from a sense of sin
   A. he should invite opinion of others
   B. he should admit his sin at once
   C. he should consciously realize that he has no reason to feel sinful
   D. he should develop a fearless character
6. What happens to a man who demands affection?
   A. His feelings are reciprocated by others
   B. He tends to take a calculated risk
   C. He becomes a victim of a viscious circle
   D. None of these
7. What should a man do who is suffering from the feeling of self-pity?
   A. He should control his passions and emotions
   B. He should persuade himself that everything is alright in his circumstances
   C. He should seek affection from others
   D. He should develop a feeling of fearlessness
8. How to get out of the viscious circle mentioned in the passage?
   A. By practicing skills of concentration
   B. By inculcating the habits of self-absorption
   C. Being true to others and one's internal circumstances
   D. None of these
9. Which of the following statements is not *true* in the context of the passage?
   A. Happy man has wide interests
   B. Courage has been recognized as an important virtue
   C. Unhappy man is encased in self

D. Issue of intellectual courage has been extensively studied

10. Which of the following words is ***SIMILAR*** in meaning of the word **'bestowed'** as used in the passage?

A. Conferred B. Accommodated
C. Trusted D. Withdrawn

11. Which of the following statements is *true* in the context of the passage?

A. All passions stem from unhappiness
B. The happy man lives in subjectively
C. Any virtue has a dark side also
D. One feels happy if one receives affection

12. Which of the following words is ***SIMILAR*** in meaning to the word **'flinching'** as used in the passage?

A. Wincing B. Convincing
C. Explaining D. Debating

13. What happens when you think about cause of your unhappiness?

A. You try to introspect and look critically at yourself
B. You realize that the life can be lived in different ways
C. You try to practice exercise designed to give courage
D. You remain a self-centred person

14. What according to the passage is the real cause of happiness?

A. Material rewards and incentives received
B. Critical analysis of the happy state of mind
C. Affection received from others
D. Calculated risks taken

15. Which of the following words is ***OPPOSITE*** in meaning of the word **'dispelling'** as used in the passage?

A. Giving B. Accumulating
C. Projecting D. Scattering

PASSAGE-9

Education, particularly higher education, is the obvious but crucially important instrument for nation building. As Confucious has said:

"If you are thinking of one year, plant rice. If you are thinking of a decade, plant trees. If you are thinking of a century, educate the people."

When we set about the task of higher education, we should be absolutely clear in our perception of the goals of education in the specific context of our nation's development. No *doubt,* one of the important aims of education would be to create the required range and nature of trained manpower assessed to be needed by different sectors of national growth. The entire educational apparatus must be geared progressively to fulfill the requirements of different phases of our growth in every sector—primary, secondary and *tertiary.* The aim must be to ensure that our country does not experience either *paucity,* or a *surfeit* of trained manpower in any specific segment of our economy. The requirements of our country, as a free, democratic, secular, socialist, nation, *aspiring* for rapid development, *entail* a specific recipe for our educational institutions. Today's educational institutions must therefore be developed accordingly and must regulate themselves to give the country the precise nature and quantum of trained manpower as projected by the requirements of our planned economy.

1. The author has quoted thoughts of Confucious to stress

A. importance of planting trees for human beings
B. the worthless efforts in planting rice
C. the benefits of investing in education
D. the need for assessing manpower requirement

2. Which statement cannot be made on the basis of the passage?

A. Higher education should keep in view the requirements of national economy
B. Higher education has not been employed for nation building
C. All levels of education have a role to play in nation's growth
D. In our country we need to have a specially planned educational system

3. The writer believes that
   A. there are no problems related to higher education
   B. investment in education is of long-range
   C. higher education should be used to assess manpower needs
   D. aims of higher education in India are absolutely clear
4. The author's expectations from higher education, are essentially
   A. unrealistic B. confusing
   C. critical D. vague
5. The writer indicates that
   A. higher education did not play any role in national growth
   B. primary education did not play any role in national growth
   C. our nation experiences paucity of trained manpower in many sectors
   D. today's higher education has no precise goals to achieve
6. Author has used the word 'apparatus' to indicate the
   A. scientific nature of education
   B. complicated organization demanded by education
   C. readily visible benefits of education
   D. entire equipment of education to perform particular function
7. Which of the following has not been conveyed by the passage?
   A. Education at any level can contribute in nation building
   B. Manpower needs in many areas can be fulfilled through higher education
   C. Rapid development of our nation is possible through higher education
   D. Present higher education does not ensure surfeit of trained manpower
8. This passage is likely to be addressed to
   A. politicians only
   B. scientists only
   C. students only
   D. cannot be said
9. Choose a suitable title to the passage:
   A. Manpower Planning in India
   B. Importance of Higher Education
   C. Demands of Higher Education
   D. Role of Higher Education in India

Directions (Qs.10 to 12): *Choose the word which is most nearly the **SAME** in meaning as the word given in bold capitals as used in the passage.*

10. DOUBT
   A. suspicion B. certain
   C. definite D. sure

11. TERTIARY
   A. last B. important
   C. third D. terminal

12. ASPIRING
   A. inquiring B. awaiting
   C. involving D. striving

Directions (Qs.13 to 15): *Choose the word which is most **OPPOSITE** in meaning as the word given in bold capitals as used in the passage.*

13. PAUCITY
   A. moderate B. enormity
   C. mediocrity D. littleness

14. SURFEIT
   A. abundance B. redundancy
   C. repletion D. lack

15. ENTAIL
   A. entitled B. ensure
   C. dismiss D. retain

PASSAGE-10

Books are a great treasurehouse of knowledge. They are the living examples of man's *march* on the path to higher and higher civilisation. The great men who died long ago, live in their books. We feel their very personality and existence when we read their books. We feel as if they were conversing with us.

Books not only store civilization but also carry it forward. All coming generations get the light of knowledge from the books written by their ancestors and try to improve upon that knowledge. Civilization cannot make much *headway* in a country where there are not many *great* books. We get through books the latest knowledge in the fields of arts, science, commerce, etc. This knowledge is helpful to us and *enables* us to achieve success in the field of our choice.

Books are never failing friends. They never *desert* us, not even when all fair-weather friends have deserted us. They dispel the dark clouds of gloom from our minds and increase our happiness if we are already happy. Through the ages, the scriptures and other great books have provided immeasurable *solace* to the wounded and strife-torn humanity.

There may be books prescribed for some course or profession, but then there are books for general study. The books of literature—poetry, drama, novel, short stories, etc., are generally highly thrilling and inspiring if they are written by a good author. There may be tragic, comical or humorous books. The question is that of an individual's choice.

To be a lover of books, though not to be bookworm, is a sign of good luck. A voracious reader gets much *more pleasure* from reading books than a miser gets in hoarding money. The knowledge embedded in books is valueless; so is pleasure obtained from reading them. A good book absorbs the whole spirit of man; the reader's pleasure is indescribable.

1. Which of the following, according to the passage, is not true about books?
   A. They are source of inspiration
   B. They are source of knowledge
   C. They are source of happiness
   D. They are means of livelihood

2. How do the books help in progress of civilization?
   A. Based on the earlier books new knowledge is obtained
   B. The books provide solution to many problems
   C. The books inspire the scientists
   D. Not mentioned in the passage

3. How do the books make people more happy?
   A. They help the reader to overcome the shadows of uncertainty
   B. They help bring in joy by amusing the reader through their content
   C. They help the reader to understand the darker side of life
   D. Not mentioned in the passage

4. Which of the following is the author's view about the knowledge and pleasure derived from books?
   (*i*) We get more of knowledge and less of pleasure
   (*ii*) We get more of pleasure and less of knowledge
   (*iii*) We get knowledge and pleasure in equal measure
   A. only (*i*) B. only (*ii*)
   C. either (*i*) or (*ii*) D. only (*iii*)

5. The high quality of books produced by a country indicates:
   A. it has a high rate of literacy
   B. it has a progressive civilization
   C. it is not an industrialised nation
   D. it has learned ancestors

6. Why are the books, according to the passage, called never-failing friends?
   A. Books do not betray individuals
   B. Books are inanimate
   C. Books always give companionship to the reader
   D. Books are available in the market anytime unlike others

7. How do the books help in bringing peace in the minds of people?
   A. Books provide information about the past civilization
   B. Books help people learn to take correct steps with the help of the recorded information
   C. Books act as a window to the minds of the great men
   D. Not mentioned in the passage

8. Which of the following has been described as a sign of good luck?
A. Being a miser
B. Having lot of money
C. Advancing the culture
D. A passion for books

Directions (Qs. 9 to 12): *Choose the word which is most nearly the **SAME** in meaning as the word given in bold capitals as used in the passage.*

9. SOLACE
A. peace B. tranquillity
C. calmness D. console

10. ENABLES
A. helps B. succeeds
C. promotes D. stops

11. HEADWAY
A. higher B. forge
C. movement D. improve

12. MARCH
A. move B. progress
C. pass D. register

Directions (Qs. 13 to 15): *Choose the word which is most **OPPOSITE** in meaning of the word given in bold capitals as used in the passage.*

13. GREAT
A. small B. thin
C. short D. ordinary

14. PLEASURE
A. displeasure B. pain
C. happiness D. hardship

15. DESERT
A. waterhole B. bitter
C. accompany D. propel

ANSWERS

PASSAGE-1

1	2	3	4
A	B	A	A

PASSAGE-2

1	2	3	4	5
A	C	D	A	D

PASSAGE-3

1	2	3	4	5
A	D	C	D	A

PASSAGE-4

1	2	3	4	5	6
D	A	D	A	A	D

PASSAGE-5

1	2	3	4	5	6	7
A	D	A	A	A	C	B

PASSAGE-6

1	2	3	4	5
A	C	C	A	D
6	**7**	**8**	**9**	**10**
D	B	A	B	D

PASSAGE-7

1	2	3	4	5
C	C	D	B	D
6	**7**	**8**	**9**	**10**
A	A	D	D	B
11	**12**	**13**	**14**	**15**
A	D	D	B	C

PASSAGE-8

1	2	3	4	5
B	A	C	D	C
6	**7**	**8**	**9**	**10**
D	B	D	D	A
11	**12**	**13**	**14**	**15**
D	D	D	C	B

PASSAGE-9

1	2	3	4	5
D	D	C	D	D
6	**7**	**8**	**9**	**10**
D	A	D	B	A
11	**12**	**13**	**14**	**15**
C	D	B	D	C

PASSAGE-10

1	2	3	4	5
D	A	D	D	B
6	**7**	**8**	**9**	**10**
A	D	D	D	A
11	**12**	**13**	**14**	**15**
D	B	D	D	C

□□□

14 Cloze Test

A cloze test is a procedure in which a person is asked to supply words that have been removed from a passage as a test of his ability to comprehend text. Practise it regularly to score well.

PASSAGES

Directions: *In each of the following passages some numbered blank spaces are given. For each numbered blank space four answer choices are given. Pick out the one which is the most appropriate for that blank space, keeping the trend of the passage in mind.*

Passage-1

Mankind's most ....(1).... treasure of thoughts is carefully preserved in the golden casket of books. The ....(2).... of books is as vast as the universe, for there is no corner of it which they have left ....(3).... . There is no ....(4).... of books on any topic, be it as simple as the composition of sodium nitrate or as ....(5).... as the mechanism of a spacecraft rocketing towards Mars. The ....(6).... of books is not only most easily available but is enlightened, dependable and lifelong. In times of distress they make us stoically ....(7).... of the object that causes uneasiness and we learn to ....(8).... with the sting of adversity.

Questions

1. A. costly B. important C. valuable D. vast

2. A. area B. scope C. storage D. kingdom

3. A. unexplored B. unseen C. untouched D. unapproached

4. A. lack B. dearth C. shortage D. insufficiency

5. A. extricate B. intricate C. intrinsic D. internecine

6. A. company B. assistance C. friendship D. companionship

7. A. defiant B. defendant C. defensible D. delusive

8. A. adapt B. adopt C. exist D. co-exist

Passage-2

Though the government has tried to ....(1).... Naxalism with all its might, much more needs to be done to totally root out the ....(2).... of Naxalism. The roots of Naxalism ....(3).... economic backwardness and social exploitation of the peasants and the weaker classes. Thus, the best way to ....(4).... Naxalism is to bring the naxals ....(5).... the mainstream. ....(6).... policies and schemes should be implemented effectively ....(7).... the Naxals economically stable. They should be ....(8).... to participate in democratic processes. The government has to ....(9).... the social upliftment of the Naxals. Use of force in ....(10).... Naxalism will yield little success.

Questions

1. A. crush B. handle
   C. tackle D. suppress
2. A. menace B. whole
   C. gamut D. stems
3. A. lies in B. are in
   C. abound in D. exist in
4. A. crash B. crush
   C. break D. defy
5. A. in B. on
   C. into D. within
6. A. Current B. Latest
   C. Occurring D. Existing
7. A. so that B. so as to make
   C. such that D. to make
8. A. insisted B. brought
   C. encouraged D. forced
9. A. assure B. insure
   C. guarantee D. ensure
10. A. countering B. defying
    C. banishing D. desecrating

Passage-3

We are living in very exciting ....(1).... . The ....(2).... change is dizzying and the impact this progress is having on our present and — more importantly — on our future is difficult to ....(3).... in its ...(4).... . This is the age of ....(5).... micro-processors, sophisticated software, new hardware technology and high bandwidth, high-speed networks. The PC gave us a new way to work, play and ....(6).... . In fact, it brought ....(7).... our desktops computing power, which until a few years ....(8).... had only been available to corporates. With the ....(9).... of the internet, the PC ....(10).... us the most convenient and flexible way to head on to the Net.

Questions

1. A. periods B. days
   C. phase D. times
2. A. phase B. pace
   C. sphere D. drastic
3. A. guess B. forecast
   C. comprehend D. approximate
4. A. whole B. entirety
   C. fruition D. fullness
5. A. strong B. changing
   C. powerful D. sonorous
6. A. convey B. communicate
   C. entertain D. enjoy
7. A. onto B. to
   C. on D. at
8. A. back B. earlier
   C. behind D. before
9. A. addendum B. adherence
   C. afoot D. advent
10. A. allowed B. privileged
    C. brought D. offered

Passage-4

What is required today in our country is ....(1).... of a new political culture based on full respect for human liberty, on pluralism and on a better social deal for all. The major ....(2).... facing us today is to carry out democratic transformation in all the ....(3)...., social, cultural, economic and political. The events of the 20th century ....(4).... one thing absolutely clear that human ....(5)...., everywhere, specially in countries whose political structures were ....(6).... to reflect the revolutionary aspirations of the people ....(7).... not only under stress and strain but are ....(8).... vast upheavals because of the ....(9).... of democracy. At the same time it has also to be understood that democracy cannot be ....(10).... into a static mould.

Questions

1. A. growing B. developing
   C. creating D. creation
2. A. development B. crisis
   C. challenge D. drawback
3. A. corners B. context
   C. realm D. spheres
4. A. have made B. has made
   C. had made D. made

5. A. travails B. traverse
C. traps D. transverse

6. A. supposed B. meant
C. caused D. forced

7. A. were B. was
C. are D. have been

8. A. developing B. evolving
C. experiencing D. faced with

9. A. denial B. rebuff
C. rebuttal D. absence

10. A. shaped B. flex
C. frozen D. caused

Passage-5

For centuries, women not only in India but all over the world ....(1).... treated as ....(2).... secondary position to men. ....(3).... human history men ....(4).... far greater power then women to name, classify, and order the worlds in which they both live. ....(5).... studies in various parts of the world point out to a wide ....(6).... in male and female roles ....(7).... cultures and demonstrate the possibility of change in these sex-determined roles. The 20th century in particular ....(8).... the cause of gender justice by internationalizing struggles for equality ....(9).... women and other oppressed people. Women's struggles against their ....(10).... were intertwined in ....(11).... degrees with ideologies and movements based on the values of freedom, self-determination, equality, democracy and justice.

Questions

1. A. has been B. have been
C. had been D. were

2. A. occupying B. taking
C. possessing D. serving

3. A. All through B. Throughout
C. Since D. From

4. A. have B. had
C. have had D. enjoy

5. A. Sociological B. Anthropological
C. General D. Practical

6. A. concord B. repulsion
C. disagreement D. variation

7. A. among B. across
C. between D. of

8. A. developed B. evolved
C. promoted D. entertained

9. A. for B. to
C. among D. by

10. A. subsidiary B. subsequent
C. subservience D. subordination

11. A. various B. varying
C changing D. differing

Passage-6

Visualisation is a strong ....(1).... to memory. Those persons who ......(2)..... a powerful memory cannot do so without taking the help of visualisation. Such persons have developed the skills to ....(3).... visualisation even in such ....(4).... tasks as remembering names and numbers. These persons have the names and numbers ....(5).... in their brain even after hearing those names and figures only once. On the other hand those who take the help of revising to memorise ....(6).... to forget it once they have ....(7).... the practice of revising ....(8).... the ones who have applied visualisation to memorise. Psychologists ....(9).... in visualisation a powerful tool for personality development. The more you visualise, the more you are ....(10).... your attitude and behaviour to the blue prints of your vision and ....(11).... more you are inching towards success.

Questions

1. A. way B. path
C. aid D. symptom

2. A. command B. master
C. rule D. enjoy

3. A. use B. apply
C. put D. place

4. A. trivial B. difficult
C. mundane D. unscrupulous

5. A. impress B. imprinted
C. impinge D. store

6. A. bent B. incline
C. prone d. tend

7. A. dropped B. left
C. gave up D. given up

8. A. unlike B. opposite
C. contrary D. not like

9. A. found B. have found
C. sees D. finds

10. A. shaping B. moulding
C. making D. attuning

11. A. actually B. factually
C. subsequently D. consequently

Passage-7

The development of an area depends on the resources ....(1).... in the area, the needs and ....(2).... of the people living there and the technological skill ....(3).... by them. Humans play an important and decisive role in the ....(4).... of development of an area. We choose the ....(5).... of resources which could be developed to our ....(6).... . The natural ....(7).... available in an area ....(8).... value as a resource only when people find a use for them. There are ....(9).... where large potential resources are available, but they ....(10).... developed for economic reasons. Lack of capital for investments, roads and railway lines, and other ....(11).... facilities may stand in the way of resource development.

Questions

1. A. present B. prevalent
C. available D. exist

2. A. inspirations B. aspirations
C. ambitions D. curiosity

3. A. handled B. practised
C. availed D. possessed

4. A. system B. design
C. pattern D. style

5. A. class B. group
C. variety D. types

6. A. good B. advantage
C. approach D. favour

7. A. secrets B. phenomenon
C. products D. endowments

8. A. get B. acquire
C. possess D. takes

9. A. instances B. events
C. circumstances D. happenings

10. A. have not yet been
B. haven't been
C. are not yet
D. yet have not been

11. A. common B. general
C. infrastructural D. structural

Passage-8

The Naxal problem in India is basically socio-economic in ....(1).... . The main reasons ....(2).... the Naxal movement in India are the ....(3).... of peasants and their weak social and economic position. ....(4).... of the peasants are landless labourers whose lands have been ....(5).... occupied by the landlords. Moreover, the landlords give ....(6).... wages to the peasants. Their ....(7).... suffering at the hands of the landlords thus encourage many peasants to take law ....(8).... their own hands. Due to their poor economic condition the peasants easily ....(9).... the trap of the naxal leaders who have their ....(10).... interests. Illiteracy, unemployment, police excesses, corruption and ....(11).... administration further ....(12).... this complex problem.

Questions

1. A. form B. shape
C. behaviour D. nature

2. A. for B. of
C. in D. behind

3. A. complaisance B. exploitation
C. domination D. exculpation

4. A. Many B. Much
C. Most D. All

5. A. imperiously B. imperatively
C. forcefully D. forcibly

6. A. improper B. small
C. inadequate D. insufficient

7. A. long B. brutal
C. pathetic D. great

8. A. in B. into
C. on D. by

9. A. fall into B. fall in
C. fell in D. fell into

10. A. selfish B. vested
C. vicious D. vindictive

11. A. failed B. improper
C. inefficient D. bureaucratic

12. A. heighten B. deepen
C. add D. worsen

Passage-9

No doubt various ....(1).... and Acts are there to eliminate the ....(2).... practice of child labour. But the ....(3).... is that, these are not being implemented in both letter and spirit, for which the ....(4).... of the problem remains as it was. Therefore a judicious, pragmatic, integrated and time-bound ....(5).... supplemented by ....(6).... follow-up action is essential to ....(7).... the problem that ....(8).... deep root in our Society. It is true that child labour can't be ....(9)... with a magic wand. If we ....(10).... time-bound goals and follow, of course, with the ....(11).... assistance of ILO and UNICEF, it is possible to eliminate the problem of child labour. With strong political will power and people's backing nothing is ....(12).... . Rather ....(13).... the bud we should let it blossom and spread its fragrance all around. ....(14).... lies the progress and prosperity of the society.

Questions

1. A. means B. methods
C. source D. provisions

2. A. unjust B. inhuman
C. mal D. illegal

3. A. anxiety B. abrasion
C. tragedy D. conclusion

4. A. magnitude B. depth
C. gravity D. soaring

5. A. approach B. analysis
C. survey D. scheme

6. A. continuous B. thorough
C. throughout D. regular

7. A. outroot B. uproot
C. downroot D. grassroot

8. A. have B. has
C. had D. has taken

9. A. wipe out B. wipe off
C. wipe up D. wiped

10. A. keep B. put
C. put up D. set

11. A. ongoing B. continuing
C. unending D. frequent

12. A. insurmountable B. intangible
C. inscrutable D. incorrigible

13. A. killing B. hurting
C. destroying D. nipping

14. A. Here B. There
C. Therein D. Herein

Passage-10

Every action we perform ....(1).... a result. And, naturally, we lay claim ....(2).... the results or fruits ....(3).... from that action in the ....(4).... that it is we who perform the action. This is .....(5).... ignorance because ....(6).... is it the Lord who ....(7).... the result of any action, it is by His will ....(8).... that even the action is accomplished. The will of the Lord ....(9).... whether we cooperate with His will or strive ....(10).... . If God wills that an action takes place, he arranges for the ....(11).... for it to happen. It is ....(12).... experience that sometimes despite our best efforts we ....(13).... achieve the results we desire, and at other times the seemingly most ....(14).... situations mysteriously get ....(15).... . ....(16).... way man chooses to act, both the act and the outcome of the cost are dependent ....(17).... on the will of the Lord.

Questions

1. A. produce B. produces
C. causes D. undergoes

2. A. on B. at
C. to D. for

3. A. occurring B. obtaining
C. deriving D. falling

4. A. belief B. hope
C. fantasy D. folly

5. A. sheen B. keen
C. sheer D. sheathe

6. A. alone B. only that
C. not only D. for only

7. A. declares B. decides
C. ordains D. ornate

8. A. completely B. entirely
C. only D. alone

9. A. prevails always
B. prevails everywhere
C. is prevalent
D. always prevails

10. A. alone B. always
C. constantly D. independently

11. A. wherewithal B. whereabouts
C. whatsoever D. wherefore

12. A. usual B. general
C. universal D. common

13. A. does not B. may not
C. do not D. might not

14. A. intractable B. intangible
C. internecine D. intricate

15. A. subsided B. resolved
C. solved D. converted

16. A. Whatever B. All the
C. All those D. Whichever

17. A. mainly B. actually
C. entirely D. generally

ANSWERS

PASSAGE-1

1	2	3	4	5	6
C	D	A	B	B	D
7	**8**				
A	D				

PASSAGE-2

1	2	3	4	5	6
C	A	A	B	C	D
7	**8**	**9**	**10**		
B	C	D	A		

PASSAGE-3

1	2	3	4	5	6
D	B	C	B	C	B
7	**8**	**9**	**10**		
A	D	D	D		

PASSAGE-4

1	2	3	4	5	6
D	C	D	A	A	B
7	**8**	**9**	**10**		
C	C	A	C		

PASSAGE-5

1	2	3	4	5	6
B	A	B	C	B	D
7	**8**	**9**	**10**	**11**	
B	C	D	D	B	

PASSAGE-6

1	2	3	4	5	6
C	A	B	C	B	D
7	**8**	**9**	**10**	**11**	
A	A	B	D	D	

PASSAGE-7

1	2	3	4	5	6
C	B	D	C	D	B
7	**8**	**9**	**10**	**11**	
D	B	A	A	C	

PASSAGE-8

1	2	3	4	5	6
D	A	B	C	D	C
7	**8**	**9**	**10**	**11**	**12**
A	B	A	B	C	D

PASSAGE-9

1	2	3	4	5	6
D	B	C	A	A	D
7	**8**	**9**	**10**	**11**	**12**
B	D	B	D	B	A
13	**14**				
D	C				

PASSAGE-10

1	2	3	4	5	6
B	C	B	A	C	C
7	**8**	**9**	**10**	**11**	**12**
C	D	D	D	A	D
13	**14**	**15**	**16**	**17**	
C	A	B	D	C	

□□□

ARITHMETICAL AND NUMERICAL ABILITY

NUMBER SYSTEM

1. There are four numbers A, B, C and D. Average of the first three i.e., A, B and C is 15 and that of B, C and D is 16. If the last number, i.e., D is 19, then the first number is—

A. 15 B. 16
C. 17 D. 18

2. Of the three numbers, the first is twice the second and thrice the third. If the average of three is 22, the three numbers are—

A. 12, 18, 36 B. 18, 12, 36
C. 36, 12, 18 D. 36, 18, 12

3. If a person is standing on the sixth number in the queue from both the ends, the total persons in the queue are—

A. 9 B. 11
C. 12 D. 13

4. A number 'x' when multiplied by 5 and added to three times its own gives 64, the number is—

A. 8 B. 12
C. 14 D. 18

5. A number which when multiplied by 11 is as much above 180 as it was originally below it. The number is—

A. 25 B. 30
C. 40 D. 45

6. The sum of a number and its reciprocal is thrice the difference of the number and its reciprocal. Find the number.

A. $\sqrt{2}$ B. $\sqrt{3}$
C. $\sqrt{5}$ D. $\sqrt{7}$

7. A boy was asked to find $\frac{7}{9}$ of a fraction. He made a mistake of dividing the fraction by $\frac{7}{9}$ and so got an answer which exceeded the correct answer by $\frac{8}{21}$. Find the correct answer.

A. $\frac{2}{3}$ B. $\frac{5}{7}$
C. $\frac{7}{12}$ D. $\frac{7}{15}$

8. There are 408 boys and 312 girls in a school, which are to be divided into equal sections of either boys or girls alone. Find the maximum number of boys or girls that can be placed in a section. Also find the total number of sections thus formed.

A. 10, 20 B. 24, 30
C. 24, 40 D. 30, 30

9. The sum of all possible two-digit number formed from three different one-digit natural numbers, when divided by the sum of the original three numbers is equal to—

A. 11 B. 18
C. 22 D. 36

10. There are four prime numbers written in ascending order. The product of the first three is 385 and that of the last three is 1001. The last number is—

A. 19 B. 17
C. 13 D. 11

11. If the number 357 ★ 25 ★ is divisible by both 3 and 5, then the missing digits in the unit's place and thousandth place respectively are—

A. 0, 4 B. 5, 4
C. 5, 6 D. 0, 6

12. The difference between two numbers is 1365. When the larger number is divided by the smaller one, the quotient is 6 and the remainder is 15. The smaller number is:

A. 360 B. 295
C. 270 D. 240

13. When a number is divided by 31, the remainder is 29. When the same number is divided by 16, what will be the remainder?

A. 15 B. 13
C. 11 D. Data inadequate

14. In dividing a number by 585, a student applied the method of short division. He divided the number successively by 5, 9 and 13 (factor of 585) and got the remainders 4, 8 and 12. If he had divided the number by 585, the remainder would have been:

A. 584 B. 292
C. 144 D. 24

15. When a number divided by 6 leaves a remainder 3. When the square of the same number is divided by 6, the remainder is:

A. 3 B. 2
C. 1 D. zero

ANSWERS

1	2	3	4	5	6	7	8	9	10
B	D	B	A	B	A	C	B	C	C
11	**12**	**13**	**14**	**15**					
C	C	D	A	A					

SOME SELECTED EXPLANATORY ANSWERS

1. $\frac{A+B+C}{3} = 15,$

or, $A + B + C = 15 \times 3 = 45$ ... (*i*)

$\frac{B+C+D}{3} = 16,$

or $B + C + D = 48$ ... (*ii*)

$D = 19$

$\therefore\ B + C + 19 = 48$

or, $B + C = 48 - 19 = 29$

But, $A + B + C = 45$

Putting the value of $B + C = 29$ in the above equation (*i*), we get $A + 29 = 45$

$\therefore A = 45 - 29 = 16.$

2. Let the third number $= x$

$\therefore$ First number $= 3x$

Second number $= \frac{3x}{2}$

$\therefore\ \frac{1}{3}\left[x+3x+\frac{3x}{2}\right] = 22 \Rightarrow \frac{11}{2}x = 66$

$\Rightarrow x = \frac{66\times 2}{11} = 12 =$ Third number,

$12 \times 3 = 36 =$ First number,

$\frac{12\times 3}{2} = 18 =$ Second number.

3. If the person is standing at sixth number in the queue from both sides, that means there are five persons ahead and five persons behind him. Hence, total number of persons in the queue is $5 + 1 + 5 = 11$.

4. $5 \times x + 3x = 64 \Rightarrow 8x = 64$

$\therefore\ x = \frac{64}{8} = 8.$

5. Let the number is x

$\therefore\ 180 - x = 11x - 180$

$\Rightarrow\ 180 + 180 = 11x + x$

$\Rightarrow\ 360 = 12x,$

$\Rightarrow\ x = \frac{360}{12} = 30.$

6. Let the no. $= x$ then its reciprocal $= \frac{1}{x}$

By the question, $\left(x+\frac{1}{x}\right) = 3\left(x-\frac{1}{x}\right)$

$$\Rightarrow \quad \frac{x^2+1}{x} = \frac{3(x^2-1)}{x}$$

$$\Rightarrow \quad x^2 + 1 = 3x^2 - 3$$

$$\Rightarrow \quad 3x^2 - x^2 = 3 + 1$$

$$\therefore \quad x = \sqrt{2}.$$

7. Let the required fraction = x

then, by the question $x \div \frac{7}{9} - x \times \frac{7}{9} = \frac{8}{21}$

$$\Rightarrow \quad x \times \frac{9}{7} - \frac{7x}{9} = \frac{8}{21}$$

$$\Rightarrow \quad \frac{32x}{63} = \frac{8}{21}$$

$$\Rightarrow \quad x = \frac{8}{21} \times \frac{63}{32} = \frac{3}{4}$$

Hence, the correct answer = $\frac{3}{4} \times \frac{7}{9} = \frac{7}{12}$.

8.

```
312) 408(1
     312
     ---
      96) 312 (3
          288
          ---
           24) 96 (4
               96
               --
                ×
```

$\therefore$ Maximum number of girls or boys that can be placed in a section = 24 and total number of such section = $\frac{408}{24} + \frac{312}{24}$

$= 17 + 13 = 30$

9. Let three different one digit natural numbers be x, y and z.

Then, sum of all possible two digits numbers

$= (10x + y) + (10y + x) + (10x + z)$

$\quad + (10z + x) + (10y + z) + (10z + y)$

$= 22x + 22y + 22z = 22\,(x + y + z)$

Hence, required number = 22.

10. Let four prime numbers be a, b, c and d respectively.

Now, $\frac{abc}{bcd} = \frac{385}{1001} \quad \Rightarrow \frac{c}{d} = \frac{5}{13}$

Hence, $a = 5$ and $d = 13$

11. 357 ★ 25 ★

For divisible by 5, the last digit must be either 0 or 5.

If last digit is 0, then other required digit will be 2 or 5 or 8

Hence, the numbers are (0, 2) or (0, 5) or (0, 8)

If last digit is 5, then other required digit will be 0 or 3 or 6 or 9

Hence, the numbers are (5, 0) or (5, 3) or (5, 6) or (5, 9)

So, correct option is (c).

12. Here, $(x + 1365) = 6x + 15$

$\Rightarrow 5x = 1350$

$\therefore \quad x = \frac{1350}{5} = 270$

Hence, the smaller number = 270.

13. The number = $31x + 29$.

Here, given data is inadequate.

14.

$$\begin{array}{r|l} 5 & a \\ \hline 9 & b-4 \\ \hline 13 & c-8 \\ \hline & 1-12 \end{array}$$

Now, $\quad c = 13 \times 1 + 12 = 25$

$\quad b = 9c + 8 = 9 \times 25 + 8 = 233$

$\quad a = 5b + 4 = 5 \times 233 + 4$

$\quad = 1165 + 4 = 1169$

$1169 = 585 \times 1 + 584$

Hence, required remainder = 584.

15. The number = $6x + 3$

Now, $(6x + 3)^2 = 36x^2 + 36x + 9$

$\quad = (36x^2 + 36x + 6) + 3$

$\quad = 6(6x^2 + 6x + 1) + 3$

Hence, required remainder = 3.

LCM AND HCF

1. The L.C.M. and H.C.F. of two numbers are 4284 and 32 respectively. If one of the numbers is 204, the other is
   A. 672 B. 576
   C. 676 D. 572
2. Two numbers are in the ratio of 8 : 15. If their H.C.F. is 4, the numbers are
   A. 32 and 60 B. 16 and 30
   C. 80 and 150 D. 64 and 120
3. The greatest number that will divide 366, 513 and 324 leaving the same remainder in each case is
   A. 21 B. 18
   C. 27 D. 42
4. The L.C.M. of two numbers is 45 times their H.C.F. If the sum of the L.C.M. and the H.C.F. of these two numbers is 1150 and one of the numbers is 125, then the other number is
   A. 256 B. 225
   C. 250 D. 255
5. The H.C.F. and the L.C.M. of two numbers are 50 and 250 respectively. On dividing one of these numbers by 2, 50 is obtained as quotient. The numbrs are
   A. 100, 125 B. 80, 100
   C. 125, 100 D. 200, 250
6. Three bells ring respectively at an interval of 15 seconds, 20 seconds and 24 seconds. If they ring continuously for 12 minutes then how many times, during this period, will they ring together?
   A. 2 times B. 6 times
   C. 5 times D. 3 times
7. If the sum of two numbers is 55 and the H.C.F. and L.C.M. of these numbers are 5 and 120 respectively. Find the sum of their reciprocals.
   A. $\frac{120}{11}$ B. $\frac{11}{120}$
   C. $\frac{601}{55}$ D. $\frac{55}{601}$
8. The LCM of two numbers is 48. The numbers are in the ratio of 2 : 3. The sum of the numbers is
   A. 64 B. 40
   C. 32 D. 28
9. Find the greatest number that will divide 43, 91 and 183 so as to leave the same remainder in each case.
   A. 13 B. 9
   C. 7 D. 4
10. The greatest possible length which can be used to measure exactly the length 7m, 3m 85cm, 12m 95 cm is
    A. 42 cm B. 35 cm
    C. 25 cm D. 15 cm
11. A, B and C start at the same time in the same direction to run around a circular park. A completes a round in 252 seconds, B in 308 seconds and C in 198 seconds, all starting at the same point. After what time will they meet again at the starting point?
    A. 46 minutes 12 seconds
    B. 45 minutes
    C. 42 minutes 36 seconds
    D. 26 minutes 18 seconds

12. Which of the following has most numbers of divisors?

A. 182 B. 176
C. 101 D. 99

13. Which is of the following is a co-primes?

A. (23, 92) B. (21, 35)
C. (18, 25) D. (16, 62)

14. Let N be the greatest number that will divide 1305, 4665 and 6905, leaving the same remainder in each case. Then find the sum of the digits in N.

A. 8 B. 6
C. 5 D. 4

15. The greatest number which one dividing 1657 and 2037 leaves remainder 6 and 5 respectively, is:

A. 305 B. 235
C. 127 D. 123

ANSWERS

1	2	3	4	5	6	7	8	9	10
A	A	A	B	A	B	B	B	D	B
11	**12**	**13**	**14**	**15**					
A	B	C	D	C					

SOME SELECTED EXPLANATORY ANSWERS

1. 1st number × 2nd number = LCM × HCF

$\therefore$ 204 × 2nd number = 4284 × 32

$\therefore$ 2nd number $= \dfrac{4284 \times 32}{204} = 672$

$\therefore$ 2nd number = 672

2. Let the numbers be $8x$ and $15x$

$8x = 2 \times 2 \times 2 \times x$

$15x = 3 \times 5 \times x$

$\therefore$ LCM of $8x$ and $15x = 2 \times 2 \times 2 \times x \times 3 \times 5$
$= 120x$

Now, 1st number × 2nd number = HCF × LCM

$\Rightarrow$ $8x \times 15x = 4 \times 120x$

$\Rightarrow$ $120x^2 = 4 \times 120x$

$\Rightarrow$ $x = 4$

$\therefore$ Numbers are 8 × 4 = 32 and 15 × 4 = 60

3. Difference between 366 and 513 = 513 − 366
= 147

and difference between 513 and 324
= 513 − 324 = 189

$\therefore$ HCF of 147 and 189

```
147) 189 (1
     147
     × 42) 147 (3
           126
           × 21) 42 (2
                 42
                 ×
```

$\therefore$ The required largest number is 21.

4. LCM of the two numbers = 45 × HCF

and LCM + HCF = 1150

$\Rightarrow$ 45 × HCF + HCF = 1150

$\Rightarrow$ HCF(45 + 1) = 1150

$\Rightarrow$ HCF $= \dfrac{1150}{46} = 25$

$\therefore$ LCM = 45 × 25 = 1125

$\because$ 1st number × 2nd number = LCM × HCF

$\therefore$ 125 × 2nd number = 1125 × 25

$\therefore$ 2nd number $= \dfrac{1125 \times 25}{125} = 225.$

5. According to the condition of the problem, 50 is obtained on dividing one of the numbers by 2

$\therefore$ One of the numbers = 50 × 2 = 100

Now, 1st number × 2nd number = LCM × HCF

$\therefore$ 100 × 2nd number = 250 × 50

$\therefore$ 2nd number $= \dfrac{250 \times 50}{100} = 125$

Hence, numbers are 100 and 125.

6. LCM of 15, 20 and 24

```
5 | 15, 20, 24
4 |  3,  4, 24
3 |  3,  1,  6
  |  1,  1,  2
```

LCM = 5 × 4 × 3 × 2 = 120

$\because$ 12 minutes = 12 × 60 = 720 seconds

$\therefore$ Number of times the bells will ring together during 12 minutes

$= \frac{720}{120} = 6$ times.

7. Let the number be x and y.

Then, $x + y = 55$;

$xy = \text{HCF} \times \text{LCM} = 5 \times 120$

$\therefore$ Sum of their reciprocals

$$= \frac{1}{x} + \frac{1}{y} = \frac{x+y}{xy} = \frac{55}{5 \times 120} = \frac{11}{120}$$

8. Let the two numbers be $2x$ and $3x$;

their LCM = $6x$

Now, $6x = 48$ $\therefore$ $x = 8$

Hence, the numbers are 2 × 8, 3 × 8 = 16, 24

Their sum = 16 + 24 = 40.

9.

```
2240) 3360 (1          1120) 5600 (5
      2240                   5600
      1120 ) 2240 (2           ×
             2240
               ×
```

Hence, N = HCF of 3360, 2240 and 5600 = 1120

Sum of digits in N = 1 + 1 + 2 + 0 = 4.

10. 7m = 700 cm;

3m 85 = 385 cm;

12m 95cm = 1295 cm

```
385) 700 (1
     385
     315) 385 (1
          315
           70) 315 (4
               280
                35 ) 70 (2
                     70
                      ×

35) 1295 (37
    105
     245
     245
      ×
```

Hence, required length = HCF of 700 cm, 385 cm, 1295 cm = 35 cm.

11.

2	252,	308,	198
2	126,	154,	99
3	63,	77,	99
3	21,	77,	33
7	7,	77,	11
11	1,	11,	11
	1,	1,	1

Hence, LCM = 2 × 2 × 3 × 3 × 7 × 11 = 2772

Hence, A, B, C will meet again at the starting point after 2772 sec. = 46 min 12 sec.

12. ***Numbers*** ***Their divisors***

182 → 1, 2, 7, 13, 14, 26, 91 and 182

176 → 1, 2, 4, 8, 16, 22, 44, 88 and 176

101 → 1 and 101

99 → 1, 3, 9, 11, 33 and 99

Therefore, 176 has the most number of divisors.

13. HCF of 23 and 92 = 23

HCF of 21 and 35 = 7

HCF of 18 and 25 = 1

HCF of 16 and 62 = 2

Hence, 18 and 25 are co-prime numbers.

14. N = HCF of (4665 – 1305), (6905 – 4665) and (6905 – 1305)

= HCF of 3360, 2240 and 5600 = 112

Sum of digit of 1 + 1 + 2 = 4.

15. Required number = HCF of (1657 – 6) and (2037 – 5) = HCF of 1651 and 2032 = 127.

```
1651) 2032 (1
      1651
       381) 1651 (4
            1524
             127) 381 (3
                  381
                   ×
```

AVERAGE

1. One-third of a certain journey was covered at the rate of 25 km per hour, one-fourth at the rate of 30 km per hour and the rest at the 50 km per hour. What is the average speed per hour for whole journey?

A. $33\frac{1}{3}$ kmph B. $44\frac{1}{4}$ kmph

C. $22\frac{1}{2}$ kmph D. 33 kmph

2. A batsman has a certain average of runs for 16 innings. In the 17th innings, he makes a score of 85 runs thereby increasing his average by 3. What is the average after the 17th inning?

A. 33 runs B. 34 runs

C. 37 runs D. 36 runs

3. The average of 6 observations is 12. A new seventh observation is included and the new average is decreased by 1. The seventh observation is

A. 1 B. 3

C. 5 D. 6

4. The average age of 30 students in a class is 12 years. The average age of a group of 5 of the students is 10 years and that of another group of 5 of them is 14 years. The average age of the remaining students is

A. 8 years B. 10 years

C. 12 years D. 14 years

5. Out of the three given numbers, the first number is twice the second and thrice the third. If the average of three numbers is 121, what is the difference between the first and third number?

A. 144 B. 77

C. 99 D. 132

6. If the average marks of three batches of 55, 60 and 45 students is 50, 55 and 60, then average marks of all the students is:

A. 55 B. 54

C. 54.68 D. 55.68

7. The average of 8 numbers is 20. The average of first two numbers is $15\frac{1}{2}$ and that of the next three is $21\frac{1}{3}$. If the sixth number is less than the seventh and eighth numbers by 4 and 7 respectively, then the eighth number is:

A. 27 B. 25

C. 22 D. 18

8. A pupil's marks were wrongly entered as 83 instead of 63. Due to that the average marks for the class got increased by half. What is the number of pupils in the class?

A. 73 B. 40

C. 40 D. 10

9. A cricketer whose bowling average is 12.4 runs per wicket takes 5 wickets for 26 runs and thereby decreases his average by 0.4. The number of wickets taken by him till the last match was:

A. 85 B. 80

C. 72 D. 64

10. The average weight of a class of 24 students is 35 kg. If the weight of the teacher is included, the average rises by 400 g. What is the weight of the teacher?

A. 55 kg B. 53 kg

C. 50 kg D. 45 kg

11. Nine men went to a hotel. Eight of them spent Rs. 3 for each over their meals and the ninth spent Rs. 2 more than the average expenditure of all the nine. What is the total money spent by them?

A. Rs. 29.25 B. Rs. 29.50
C. Rs. 29 D. Rs. 30

12. The average age of 24 students in a class is 10. If the teacher's age is included, the average increases by one. The age of the teacher is

A. 25 B. 30
C. 35 D. 40

13. The average of 5 consecutive even numbers A, B, C, D and E is 34. What is the product of B and D?

A. 1152 B. 1368
C. 1224 D. 1088

14. The average of 50 numbers is 30. If two numbers, 35 and 40 are discarded, then the average of the remaining numbers is nearly:

A. 29.68 B. 29.27
C. 28.78 D. 28.32

15. The average monthly salary of 20 employees of an organisation is Rs. 1500. If the manager's salary is added, then the average salary increases by Rs. 100. Find the manager's monthly salary?

A. Rs. 4800 B. Rs. 3600
C. Rs. 2400 D. Rs. 2000

ANSWERS

1	2	3	4	5	6	7	8	9	10
A	C	C	C	D	C	B	B	A	D
11	**12**	**13**	**14**	**15**					
A	C	A	A	B					

SOME SELECTED EXPLANATORY ANSWERS

1. Let the total distance covered during journey = 60 km

$\frac{1}{3}$ of the distance covered during journey

$$= 60 \times \frac{1}{3} = 20 \text{ km}$$

$\frac{1}{4}$ of the distance covered during journey

$$= \frac{1}{4} \times 60 = 15 \text{ km}$$

∴ The distance covered during the rest of journey = 60 – (20 + 15) = 25 km

Time taken to cover 20 km at 25 km/h

$$= \frac{20}{25} \text{ hours} = \frac{4}{5} \text{ hour}$$

Time taken to cover 15 km at 30 km/h

$$= \frac{15}{30} \text{ hours} = \frac{1}{2} \text{ hour}$$

Time taken to cover 25 km at 50 km/h

$$= \frac{25}{50} \text{ hours} = \frac{1}{2} \text{ hour}$$

$$\text{Total time taken} = \frac{4}{5} + \frac{1}{2} + \frac{1}{2}$$

$$= \frac{9}{5} \text{ hours}$$

$$\text{Hence average speed per hour} = 60 \div \frac{9}{5}$$

$$= \frac{60 \times 5}{9} = \frac{100}{3} \text{ km/h}$$

$$= 33\frac{1}{3} \text{ km/h}$$

2. Average increase in the score of 17 innings = 3 runs

Total increase in the score of 17 innings = 3 × 17 = 51 runs

∴ His average of 16 innings = 85 – 51 = 34 runs

Hence, average after the 17th innings
$= 34 + 3 = 37$ runs

3. Seventh observation $= (7 \times 11 - 6 \times 12) = 5$

4. Let, the required average age be x
Then, $5 \times 10 + 5 \times 14 + 20 \times x = 30 \times 12$
$\Rightarrow \quad 20x = 360 - 120$
$\Rightarrow \quad 20x = 240$
$\Rightarrow \quad x = 12$

5. Let the three numbers be x, $\frac{x}{2}$ and $\frac{x}{3}$ respectively,

Now, $\frac{1}{3}\left(x+\frac{x}{2}+\frac{x}{3}\right)=121$

$\Rightarrow \frac{11x}{6} = 121 \times 3$

$\therefore x = \frac{121 \times 3 \times 6}{11} = 198$

Hence, required difference $= x-\frac{x}{3} = \frac{2x}{3}$

$=\frac{2}{3} \times 198 = 132$

6. Required average Marks

$= \frac{55 \times 50+60 \times 55+45 \times 60}{55+60+45} = \frac{8750}{160} = 54.68$

7. Let the sixth, seventh and eighth numbers are x, $x + 4$ and $x + 7$.
Sum of last three numbers

$= 8 \times 20 - (2 \times \frac{31}{2}+3\times\frac{64}{3})$

$\Rightarrow x + x + 4 + x + 7 = 160 - 95$
$\Rightarrow 3x + 11 = 65$
$\Rightarrow 3x = 54 \qquad \therefore x = 18$
New eighth number $= x + 7 = 18 + 7 = 25$

8. Let the total number of pupils in the class be x; then,

$\frac{83-63}{x}=\frac{1}{2} \quad \Rightarrow \frac{20}{x}=\frac{1}{2} \qquad \therefore x = 40$

9. Let the number of wickets taken by him be x till the last match.

Then, $\frac{x \times 12.4+26}{x+5}=12$

$\Rightarrow 12.4x + 26 = 12x + 60$

$\Rightarrow 0.4x = 34 \quad \therefore \; x = \frac{340}{4}=85$

10. Let the weight of the teacher be x kgs, then

$\frac{24 \times 35+x}{25} = 35.4$

$\Rightarrow 840 + x = 885 \qquad \therefore \quad x = 45$ kgs

12. Age of the teacher $= (25 \times 11 - 24 \times 10)$ years
$= 35$ years

13. Let 5 consecutive even numbers A, B, C, D and E be x, $x + 2$, $x + 4$, $x + 6$ and $x + 8$ respectively.

Now, $\frac{x+x+2+x+4+x+6+x+8}{5} = 34$

$\Rightarrow 5x + 20 = 170$
$\Rightarrow 5x = 150 \qquad \therefore x = 30$
Then, $B = x + 2 = 30 + 2 = 32$;
$D = x + 6 = 30 + 6 = 36$
Hence, their product $= 32 \times 36 = 1152$

14. The average of remaining 48 numbers

$= \frac{50 \times 30-(35+40)}{48}=\frac{1500-75}{48}$

$= \frac{1425}{48} = 29.68$

15. Let manager's salary be Rs. x, then

$\frac{20 \times 1500+x}{21}=1600$

$\Rightarrow 30{,}000 + x = 33600$
$\therefore \; x =$ Rs. 3600

PROBLEMS BASED ON AGES

1. The ratio of ages of A and B is 3 : 11. After 3 years the ratio becomes 1 : 3. What are the ages of A and B?
A. 9 years, 33 years B. 10 years, 40 years
C. 9 years, 27 years D. None of these

2. Two years ago, the ratio of Ram's and Mohan's age was 3 : 2 and at present 7 : 5. What are their present ages?
A. 14 years, 10 years B. 15 years, 10 years
C. 13 years, 9 years D. None of these

3. The ages of Samir and Saurabh are in the ratio of 8 : 15 respectively. After 9 years the ratio of their ages will be 11 : 18. What is the difference between their ages in years?
A. 20 years B. 21 years
C. 22 years D. 24 years

4. The present age of father is 34 years more than that of his son. 12 years ago, father's age was 18 times the age of his son. The present age of son in years is:
A. 12 B. 14
C. 16 D. 18

5. A mother is 25 years older than her daughter. Five years ago, the age of the mother was 6 times the age of the daughter. What is the present age of mother?
A. 25 years B. 29 years
C. 32 years D. 35 years

6. The difference between the present ages of P and Q is 4 years. The ratio of their ages after 5 years will be 9 : 8. The present age of P is:
A. 24 years B. 30 years
C. 32 years D. None of these

7. Ten years ago, the age of Divya was half of the age of Namrata. If the ratio of present ages of both is 3 : 4, the sum of their present ages is:
A. 35 years B. 30 years
C. 25 years D. 18 years

8. The ratio between the present ages of A and B is 5 : 3 respectively. The ratio between A's age 4 years ago and B's age 4 years hence is 1 : 1. The ratio between A's age 4 years hence and B's age 4 years ago is:
A. 4 : 1 B. 3 : 1
C. 2 : 1 D. 1 : 3

9. Ram got married 8 years ago. His present age is $\frac{6}{5}$ times his age at the time of marriage. Ram's sister was 10 years younger to him at the time of his marriage. What is the present age of Ram's sister?
A. 40 years B. 38 years
C. 36 years D. 32 years

10. A father said to his son, "I was as old as you are at present at the time of your birth." If the father's age is 38 years now. Five years ago the age of son was:
A. 38 years B. 33 years
C. 19 years D. 14 years

ANSWERS

1	2	3	4	5	6	7	8	9	10
A	A	B	B	D	D	A	B	B	D

SOME SELECTED EXPLANATORY ANSWERS

1. Let the ages of A and B be $3x$ and $11x$ years; then

$\frac{3x+3}{11x+3} = \frac{1}{3}$ $\Rightarrow$ $9x + 9 = 11x + 3$

$\Rightarrow 2x = 6$ $\therefore$ $x = 3$

Hence, their present age, $3x = 3 \times 3 = 9$ years; $11x = 11 \times 3 = 33$ years

2. Let the present ages of Ram and Mohan are $7x$ and $5x$ years; then

$\frac{7x-2}{5x-2} = \frac{3}{2}$ $\Rightarrow$ $14x - 4 = 15x - 6$

$\therefore x = 2$

Hence, their present ages : $7 \times 2 = 14$ years and $5 \times 2 = 10$ years

3. Let the present ages of Samir and Saurabh are $8x$ and $15x$ years respectively; then

$\frac{8x+9}{15x+9} = \frac{11}{18}$ $\Rightarrow$ $144x + 162 = 165x + 99$

$\Rightarrow$ $21x = 63$ $\therefore$ $x = 3$

Hence, difference of their ages = $15x - 8x = 7x$ $= 7 \times 3 = 21$ years

4. Let the present ages of father and his son be $x + 34$ and x years respectively; then

$18(x - 12) = x + 34 - 12$

$\Rightarrow$ $18x - 216 = x + 22$

$\Rightarrow 17x = 238$ $\therefore$ $x = 14$

Hence, present age of his son = 14 years

5. Let the present ages of mother and her daughter are $(x + 25)$ and x years respectively; then

$6(x - 5) = x + 25 - 5$

$\Rightarrow$ $6x - 30 = x + 20$

$\Rightarrow$ $5x = 50$ $\therefore$ $x = 10$

Hence, the age of the mother = 10 + 25 = 35 years

6. Let the present ages of P and Q be $(x + 4)$ and x years;

then, $\frac{x+4+5}{x+5} = \frac{9}{8}$ $\Rightarrow$ $8x + 72$ $= 9x + 45$ $\therefore$ $x = 27$

Hence, present age of P = 27 + 4 = 31 years

7. Let the present ages of Divya and Namrata are $3x$ and $4x$ years respectively; then

$\frac{3x-10}{4x-10} = \frac{1}{2}$

$\Rightarrow$ $6x - 20 = 4x - 10$

$\Rightarrow$ $2x = 10$ $\therefore$ $x = 5$

Hence, sum of their ages = $3x + 4x = 7x$ $= 7 \times 5 = 35$ years

8. Let the present ages of A and B are $5x$ and $3x$ years respectively; then,

$\frac{5x-4}{3x+4} = 1$ $\Rightarrow$ $5x - 4 = 3x + 4$

$\Rightarrow 2x = 8$ $\therefore$ $x = 4$

Hence, their present ages are 20 years and 12 years.

So, required ratio = (20 + 4) : (12 − 4) = 24 : 8 = 3 : 1

9. Let the present age of Ram be x years; then

$\frac{x}{x-8} = \frac{6}{5}$ $\Rightarrow$ $5x = 6x - 48$

$\therefore$ $x = 48$

Hence, present age of Ram's sister = 48 − 10 = 38 years.

10. Let the age of father was x years at the time of his son's birth, then present age of father and his son will be $2x$ and x years,

Now, $2x = 38$ $\therefore$ $x = 19$ years

Hence, 5 years ago the age of son was 19 − 5 = 14 years

CHAIN RULE

1. A fort has provision for 50 days. After 15 days a reinforcement of 150 men arrives and the provision now lasts 25 days. How many men were there in the fort?
   A. 300 B. 225
   C. 275 D. 200
2. In a fort there is provisions for 40 days for 275 persons. If after 16 days 125 persons leave the fort for how many more days the provisions will last?
   A. 35 days B. 44 days
   C. 45 days D. 53 days
3. 60 men could complete a work in 250 days. They worked together for 200 days. After that the work had to be stopped for 10 days due to bad weather. How many more men should be engaged to complete the work in time?
   A. 20 B. 18
   C. 15 D. 10
4. A contractor undertook to complete a project in 90 days and employed 60 men on it. After 60 days, he found that $\frac{3}{4}$ of the work has already been completed. How many men can he discharge so that the project may completed exactly on time?
   A. 15 B. 20
   C. 30 D. 40
5. A flagstaff 17.5 m high casts a shadow of length 40.25 m. The height of the building, which casts a shadow of length 28.75m under similar condition will be:
   A. 21.25 m B. 17.5 m
   C. 12.5 m D. 10 m
6. If 5 men or 9 women can do a piece of work in 19 days, then 3 men and 6 women will do the same work in how many days?
   A. 21 B. 18
   C. 15 D. 12
7. A certain number of men can finish a piece of work in 100 days. If there were 10 men less, it will take 10 days more for the work to be finished. How many men were there originally?
   A. 110 B. 100
   C. 82 D. 75
8. Some persons can do a piece of work in 12 days. Two times the number of such persons will do half of that work in:
   A. 12 days B. 3 days
   C. 6 days D. 4 days
9. 2 men and 7 boys can do a piece of work in 14 days; 3 men and 8 boys can do the same in 11 days. Then 8 men and 6 boys can do three times of this work in
   A. 30 days B. 4 days
   C. 21 days D. 18 days
10. If 3 men or 6 boys, working 7 hours a day can do a piece of work in 10 days; how many days will it take to complete a piece of work twice as large with 6 men and 2 boys working together for 8 hours a day?
   A. 9 B. $8\frac{1}{2}$
   C. $7\frac{1}{2}$ D. $6\frac{1}{2}$

11. If 15 men can do a certain amount of work in 20 days working 8 hours a day, in how many days will 10 men do three times the work working 6 hours a day?

A. 120 days B. 70 days
C. 100 days D. None of these

12. 40 men consume 60 kgs of rice in 15 days, then in how many days will 30 men consume 12 kgs of rice?

A. 9 days B. $6\frac{1}{4}$ days
C. 4 days D. $3\frac{1}{4}$ days

13. 56 men can complete a piece of work in 24 days. In how many days can 42 men complete the same piece of work?

A. 48 B. 32
C. 20 D. 16

14. Running at the same constant rate, 6 identical machines can produce a total of 270 bottles per minute. At this rate, how many bottles could 10 such machines produce in 4 minutes?

A. 1400 B. 1600
C. 1800 D. 2000

15. 400 persons, working 9 hours a day complete $\frac{1}{4}th$ of the work in 10 days. The number of additional persons, working 8 hours a day, required to complete the remaining work in 20 days, is:

A. 275 B. 250
C. 675 D. 200

ANSWERS

1	2	3	4	5	6	7	8	9	10
B	B	C	B	C	C	A	B	C	C
11	**12**	**13**	**14**	**15**					
A	C	B	C	C					

SOME SELECTED EXPLANATORY ANSWERS

1. Days ↑ 35, 25; Men ↓ x, $x + 150$

$$\Rightarrow \frac{x+150}{x} = \frac{35}{25} \quad \Rightarrow 1 + \frac{150}{x} = \frac{35}{25}$$

$$\Rightarrow \frac{150}{x} = \frac{10}{25}$$

$$\therefore x = \frac{25}{10} \times 150 = 375$$

Required number of men = 375 – 150 = 225

2. Persons ↑ 275, 150; Days ↓ 24, x

$$\Rightarrow \frac{x}{24} = \frac{275}{150} \quad \therefore \quad x = \frac{275}{150} \times 24 = 44 \text{ days}$$

3. Days ↑ 50, 40; Men ↓ 60, x

$$\Rightarrow \frac{x}{60} = \frac{50}{40} \qquad \therefore \; x = \frac{50}{40} \times 60 = 75 \text{ men}$$

Hence, number of additional men = 75 – 60 = 15

4. Work ↓ $\frac{3}{4}$, $\frac{1}{4}$; Days ↑ 60, 30; Men ↓ 60, x

$$\Rightarrow \frac{x}{60} = \frac{60}{30} \times \frac{1/4}{3/4}$$

$$\therefore \quad x = \frac{60}{30} \times \frac{1}{3} \times 60 = 40 \text{ days}$$

Hence, number of men to be discharged = 60 – 40 = 20

5.

Shadow (m)	Object (m)
40.25	17.5
28.75 $\downarrow$	x $\downarrow$

$$\Rightarrow \frac{x}{17.5} = \frac{28.75}{40.25}$$

$$\therefore x = \frac{28.75 \times 17.5}{40.25} = 12.5 \text{ m}$$

6. 5 men $\equiv$ 9 women

$$\therefore 3 \text{ men} = \frac{9}{5} \times 3 = \frac{27}{5} \text{ women}$$

Hence, 3 men and 6 women $= \frac{27}{5} + 6$

$$= \frac{57}{5} \text{ women}$$

Women	Days
9	19
$\frac{57}{5}$ $\uparrow$	x $\downarrow$

$$\Rightarrow \frac{x}{19} = \frac{9 \times 5}{57}$$

$$\therefore \quad x = \frac{9 \times 5}{57} \times 19 = 15 \text{ days}$$

7.

Days	Men
100	x
110 $\uparrow$	$x - 10$ $\downarrow$

$$\Rightarrow \frac{x-10}{x} = \frac{100}{110} \quad \Rightarrow \quad 110x - 1100 = 100x$$

$$\Rightarrow 10x = 1100 \qquad \therefore x = 110$$

Hence, initially the number of men = 110

8.

Work	Persons	Days
1	x	12
$\frac{1}{2}$ $\downarrow$	$2x$ $\uparrow$	a $\downarrow$

$$\Rightarrow \frac{a}{12} = \frac{x}{2x} \times \frac{1}{2} \qquad \therefore \quad a = \frac{1}{4} \times 12 = 3 \text{ days}$$

9. Here, 14×2 men $+ 14 \times 7$ boys $\equiv 11 \times 3$ men $+ 11 \times 8$ boys

$\Rightarrow$ 28 men + 98 boys $\equiv$ 33 men + 88 boys

$\Rightarrow$ 5 men = 10 boys $\therefore$ 1 man = 2 boys

Then, 2 men and 7 boys $\equiv$ 4 boys + 7 boys = 11 boys

& also, 8 men and 6 boys $\equiv$ 16 boys + 6 boys = 22 boys

Work	Boys	Days
1	11	14
3 $\downarrow$	22 $\uparrow$	x $\downarrow$

$$\Rightarrow \frac{x}{14} = \frac{11}{22} \times \frac{3}{1}$$

$$\therefore \quad x = \frac{1}{2} \times 3 \times 14 = 21 \text{ days}$$

12.

Men	Rice (kgs)	Days
40	60	15
30 $\uparrow$	12 $\downarrow$	x $\downarrow$

$$\Rightarrow \frac{x}{15} = \frac{12}{60} \times \frac{40}{30}$$

$$\therefore \quad x = \frac{12}{60} \times \frac{40}{30} \times 15 = 4 \text{ days}$$

14.

Machines	Time (minutes)	Bottles
6	1	270
10 $\downarrow$	4 $\downarrow$	x $\downarrow$

$$\Rightarrow \frac{x}{270} = \frac{4}{1} \times \frac{10}{6}$$

$$\therefore \quad x = \frac{4 \times 10}{6} \times 270 = 1800 \text{ bottles}$$

15.

Work	Hours	Days	Persons
$\frac{1}{4}$	9	10	400
$\frac{3}{4}$ $\downarrow$	8 $\uparrow$	20 $\uparrow$	x $\downarrow$

$$\Rightarrow \frac{x}{400} = \frac{10}{20} \times \frac{9}{8} \times \frac{3/4}{1/4}$$

$$\therefore \quad x = \frac{1}{2} \times \frac{9}{8} \times 3 \times 400 = 675$$

Hence, number of additional persons $= 675 - 400 = 275$

TIME AND DISTANCE

1. Starting from a point at a speed of 4 km/hr a man reaches at a cerain place and returns back to the point from where he had started journey on bicycle at the speed of 16 km/hr. His average speed during the entire journey will be :

A. 6.4 km/h B. 8.4 km/h
C. 5.4 km/h D. 10 km/h

2. A motorist covers a certain distance at a average speed of 48 km/h in 45 minutes. What speed in km/h he must maintain to cover the same distance in 30 minutes?

A. 66 km/h B. 79 km/h
C. 80 km/h D. 72 km/h

3. A policeman saw a thief at a distance of 200 m. The policeman and the thief started running at the same time. If the policeman runs at a speed of $4\frac{1}{6}$ m per second and the thief at a speed of $3\frac{1}{3}$ m per second, after what time the policeman will catch the thief?

A. 12 min B. 10 min
C. 9 min D. 4 min

4. A monkey wants to climb up a glazed pole. He climbs 12 metres in 1 minute and then he slips back 3 metres in the next minute. If the pole is 63 metre high, how long does he take to climb at the top of the pole?

A. $11\frac{1}{4}$ min B. $12\frac{1}{2}$ min
C. $12\frac{3}{4}$ min D. $14\frac{3}{4}$ min

5. The distance between two stations A and B is 300 km. A train leaves the station A with a speed of 40 km/hr. At the same time another train departs from the station B with a speed of 50 km/hr. How much time will these two trains take to cross each other?

A. 3 hrs 40 min B. 3 hrs 20 min
C. 2 hrs 20 min D. 3 hrs 45 min

6. Nilesh goes to school from his village at the speed of 4 km/hr and returns from school to village at the speed of 2 km/hr. If he takes 6 hours in all, then what is the distance between the village and the school?

A. 8 km B. 6 km
C. 5 km D. 4 km

7. By increasing the speed of the bus by 10 km/hr the time of journey for 72 km is reduced by 36 minutes. What was the original speed of the bus?

A. 30 km/hr B. 35 km/hr
C. 40 km/hr D. 45 km/hr

8. A train covers a distance in 50 minutes, if it runs at a speed of 48 km/hr on an average. The speed at which the train must run to reduce the time of journey to 40 minutes will be:

A. 70 km/hr B. 60 km/hr
C. 55 km/hr D. 50 km/hr

9. A certain distance is covered by a vehicle at a certain speed. If half of this distance is covered by another vehicle in double the time, the ratio of the speeds of the two vehicles is:

A. 4 : 1 B. 1 : 4
C. 2 : 1 D. 1 : 2

10. A is faster than B. A and B each walk 24 km. The sum of their speeds is 7 km/hr and sum of times taken by them is 14 hours. What is the speed of A?

A. 7 km/hr B. 5 km/hr
C. 4 km/hr D. 3 km/hr

ANSWERS

1	2	3	4	5	6	7	8	9	10
A	D	D	C	B	A	A	B	A	C

SOME SELECTED EXPLANATORY ANSWERS

1. Average speed during the entire journey

$= \frac{2xy}{x+y} = \frac{2 \times 4 \times 16}{4+16} = \frac{8 \times 16}{20} = 6.4$ km/hr.

2. Let required speed be x km/hr; then

$x \times \frac{1}{2} = 48 \times \frac{3}{4}$ $\therefore$ $x = 48 \times \frac{3}{4} \times 2$

$= 72$ km/hr

3. Suppose the policeman will catch the thief after t seconds

then, $\left(\frac{25}{6} - \frac{10}{3}\right) t = 200 \Rightarrow \frac{5}{6} t = 200$

$\therefore$ $t = \frac{200 \times 6}{5} = 240$ sec = 4 min.

4. The monkey climbs 12 metres in 1 minute and then he slips back 3 metres in the next minute

$\therefore$ The monkey climbs in the first 2 minutes $= 12 - 3 = 9$ metres

$\therefore$ In the first 12 minutes the monkey climbs $= 9 \times 6 = 54$ metres

Remaining height of the pole to be covered by the monkey $= 63 - 54 = 9$ metre

$\therefore$ The monkey will climb the height of 9 metres in the 13th minute

$\because$ The monkey climbs 12 metres in 1 minute

$\therefore$ The monkey will climb 9 metres in $\frac{1}{12} \times 9$

$= \frac{3}{4}$ minute

$\therefore$ Time spent in climbing at the top of the pole $= \left(12 + \frac{3}{4}\right)$ minutes $= 12\frac{3}{4}$ minutes

5. The two trains are moving in the opposite directions

$\therefore$ Relative speed $= 40 + 50 = 90$ km/hr.

$\therefore$ Time taken to cross each other $= \frac{300}{90} = 3\frac{1}{3}$ hours or, 3 hours 20 minutes.

6. Let x km be the distance between village and the school; then

$\frac{x}{4} + \frac{x}{2} = 6 \Rightarrow \frac{3x}{4} = 6$

$\therefore$ $x = \frac{6 \times 4}{3} = 8$ km

8. Let x km/hr be the required speed of the train; then

$x \times \frac{40}{60} = 48 \times \frac{50}{60}$

$\therefore$ $x = \frac{48 \times 50}{40} = 60$ km/hr

9. Let x km/hr and t hr be the certain speed and certain time.

Then, ratio of their speeds $= \frac{x}{t} : \frac{x}{2 \times 2t} = 1 : \frac{1}{4}$ $= 4 : 1$

10. Let speeds of A and B are x_1 and x_2 km/hr and times taken by them are t_1 and t_2 hrs, then

$x_1 + x_2 = 7$ km/hr ...(i)

$t_1 + t_2 = 14$ hrs ...(ii)

Now, $\frac{24}{x_1} + \frac{24}{x_2} = 14 \Rightarrow \frac{24(x_1 + x_2)}{x_1 x_2} = 14$

$\therefore$ $x_1 x_2 = \frac{24 \times 7}{14} = 12$

Then, $x_1 - x_2 = \sqrt{(x_1 + x_2)^2 - 4x_1 x_2}$

$= \sqrt{(7)^2 - 4 \times 12} = 1$ ...(iii)

Solving *(i)* and *(iii)* we get $x_1 = 4$ km/hr

TIME AND WORK

1. A and B working together complete a work in 35 days. If A takes 60 days to complete it, how long would B alone take to complete it?
   A. 64 days B. 72 days
   C. 81 days D. 84 days

2. A few children working together can do a piece of work in 18 days. If the number of children employed on the work is made double, how long would they take to complete half of the work?
   A. $4\frac{1}{2}$ days B. $2\frac{1}{3}$ days
   C. $8\frac{3}{4}$ days D. $6\frac{1}{2}$ days

3. 10 men or 18 boys can do a piece of work in 15 days. In how many days would 25 men and 15 boys complete the same work working together?
   A. $5\frac{1}{2}$ days B. $4\frac{1}{2}$ days
   C. $6\frac{2}{3}$ days D. $2\frac{1}{3}$ days

4. A cistern is filled by a tap in $3\frac{1}{2}$ hours. Due to a leak in the bottom of the cistern, it takes half an hour longer to fill the cistern. If the cistern is full, how long will it take the leak to empty it?
   A. 28 hours B. 29 hours
   C. $31\frac{1}{3}$ hours D. 38 hours

5. A is twice as good a workman as B and thrice as good a workman as C. If C alone can do a piece of work in 24 days, how long would the three persons take to finish the work working together?
   A. $3\frac{3}{11}$ days B. $4\frac{4}{7}$ days
   C. $4\frac{4}{11}$ days D. $3\frac{4}{11}$ days

6. If 3 men and 5 women can do a piece of work in 8 days and 2 men and 7 boys can do the same work in 12 days. Find the number of boys, the work done by whom can equate the work done by 10 women.
   A. 19 boys B. 21 boys
   C. 23 boys D. 15 boys

7. 8 men alone can complete a piece of work in 12 days. 4 women alone can complete the same piece of work in 48 days and 10 children alone can complete the piece of work in 24 days. In how many days can 10 men, 4 women and 10 children together complete the piece of work?
   A. 6 B. 8
   C. 10 D. 15

8. A works twice as fast as B. If B can complete a piece of work independently in 12 days. Find in how many days A and B together can complete the work?
   A. 8 days B. 6 days
   C. 4 days D. 18 days

9. A contractor undertook to complete a project in 90 days and employed 60 men on it. After 60 days, he found that $\frac{3}{4}$ of the work has already been completed. How many men can he discharge so that the project may be completed exactly on time?

A. 15 B. 20
C. 30 D. 40

10. A can do a piece of work in 25 days and B can do it in 20 days. They work together for 5 days and then A goes away. In how many days will B finish the remaining work?

A. 33 days B. 20 days
C. 11 days D. 10 days

ANSWERS

1	2	3	4	5	6	7	8	9	10
D	A	B	A	C	B	A	C	B	C

SOME SELECTED EXPLANATORY ANSWERS

1. (A + B)'s 1 day's work = $\frac{1}{35}$

and also, A's 1 day's work = $\frac{1}{60}$

Hence, B's 1 day's work = $\frac{1}{35}-\frac{1}{60}=\frac{5}{420}=\frac{1}{84}$

So, B will do the whole work in 84 days.

3. 10 men $\equiv$ 18 boys

25 men $\equiv \frac{18}{10}\times 25 = 45$ boys

Hence, 25 men + 15 boys = 45 + 15 = 60 boys

Now, 18 boys can do a piece of work in 15 days.

Hence, 60 boys will do a piece of work in

$\frac{15\times 18}{60}=\frac{9}{2}$ days $= 4\frac{1}{2}$ days.

4. In 1 hour $\frac{2}{7}$ cistern is filled by the tap.

Hence, in $\frac{1}{2}$ hour $\frac{2}{14}=\frac{1}{7}$ cistern is filled by the tap.

So, $\frac{1}{7}$ cistern is emptied by the leakage in 4 hours.

So, 1 cistern will be emptied by the leakage in 28 hours.

6. Here, (3 men + 5 women) × 8

$\equiv$ (2 men + 7 boys) × 12

$\Rightarrow$ 40 women $\equiv$ 84 boys

$\therefore$ 10 women $\equiv \frac{84}{40}\times 10$ = 21 boys

Hence, work done by 10 women

= work done of 21 boys.

7. B's 1 day's work = $\frac{1}{4}-\frac{1}{12}=\frac{2}{12}=\frac{1}{6}$

Hence, B alone will complete the work in 6 days.

8. Ratio of efficiency of A and B = 2 : 1

Then, ratio of their time taking = 1 : 2

Hence, if B can complete the work in 12 days, then A in 6 days.

Now, (A + B)'s 1 day's work = $\frac{1}{6}+\frac{1}{12}=\frac{3}{12}=\frac{1}{4}$

So, A and B together can complete the work in 4 days.

9. After 60 days remaining work = $1-\frac{3}{4}=\frac{1}{4}$

In 60 days $\frac{3}{4}$ work has been done by 60 men

In 30 days $\frac{1}{4}$ work will be done by

$60\times\frac{4}{3}\times\frac{1}{4}\times\frac{60}{30}$ = 40 men.

Hence, required number of men = 60 – 40 = 20 (which are to be discharged).

BOATS AND STREAMS

1. A boat goes 6 km upstream and back to the starting point in 2 hours. If the current of the stream runs at the rate of 4 km/hr, find the speed of the boat in still water.
A. 6 km/hr B. 8 km/hr
C. 10 km/hr D. 12 km/hr

2. A boat covers 24 km upstream and 36 km downstream in 6 hours, while it covers 36 km upstream and 24 km downstream in 6½ horus. Find the speed of the current.
A. 2 km/hr B. 4 km/hr
C. 6 km/hr D. 8 km/hr

3. A man can row 5 km/hr in still water and the speed of the stream is 1.5 km/hr. He takes an hour when he travels upstream to a place and back again to the starting point. How far is the place from the starting point?
A. 2.275 km B. 3.5 km
C. 1.5 km D. None of these

4. The speed of a boat in still water is 6 km/hr and the speed of the stream is 1.5 km/hr. A man rows to a place at a distance of 22.5 km and comes back to the starting point. Find the total time taken by him.
A. 8 hours B. 10 hours
C. 12 hours D. 4 hours

5. A boat covers 20 km downstream and 6 km upstream in 3 hours, while it covers 30 km downstream and 12 km upstream in 5 hours. What is the speed of boat in still water?
A. 6 km/hr B. 8 km/hr
C. 10 km/hr D. 12 km/hr.

6. Samir can travel 12 miles downstream in a certain river in 6 hours less than it takes him to travel the same distance upstream. But when he could double his rowing rate for his 24-mile round trip, the downstream 12 miles would then take only one hour less than the upstream 12 miles. Find the speed of the current in miles/hour.
A. $2\frac{2}{3}$ B. $2\frac{1}{3}$
C. $1\frac{2}{3}$ D. $1\frac{1}{3}$

7. A boat takes 6 hours to travel from place M to N downstream and back from N to M upstream. If the speed of the boat in still water is 4 km/hr; what is the distance between two places?
A. 6 kms B. 8 kms
C. 12 kms D. Data inadequate

8. A man can row upstream at 8 km/hr and downstream at 13 km/hr. The speed of the stream is:
A. 2.5 km/hr B. 4.2 km/hr
C. 5 km/hr D. 10.5 km/hr

9. A man's speed with the current is 15 km/hr and the speed of the current is 2.5 km/hr. The man's speed against the current is:
A. 12.5 km/hr B. 10 km/hr
C. 9 km/hr D. 8.5 km/hr

10. A motorboat, whose speed is 15 km/hr in still water goes 30 km downstream and comes back in a total of 4 hours 30 minutes. What is the speed of the stream (in km/hr)?
A. 10 B. 6
C. 5 D. 4

ANSWERS

1	2	3	4	5	6	7	8	9	10
B	A	A	A	B	B	D	A	B	C

SOME SELECTED EXPLANATORY ANSWERS

1. Let the speed of a boat in still water = x km/hr; then

$$\frac{6}{x-4}+\frac{6}{x+4}=2 \Rightarrow \frac{2x}{x^2-16}=\frac{1}{3}$$

$\Rightarrow x^2 - 6x - 16 = 0$

$\Rightarrow (x - 8)(x + 2) = 0$

Hence, the speed of the boat = 8 km/hr.

2. Let x km/hr and y km/hr be the speeds of the boat in still water and the speed of the current respectively, then

$$\frac{24}{x-y}+\frac{36}{x+y}=6 \Rightarrow \frac{4}{x-y}+\frac{6}{x+y}=1 \quad ...(i)$$

And, $$\frac{36}{x-y}+\frac{24}{x+y}=\frac{13}{2} \quad ...(ii)$$

Solving these two equations, we get

$x + y = 12;\ x - y = 8$

Hence, $y = \frac{1}{2}(12-8) = 2$ km/hr.

3. Let required distance be x km, then

$$\frac{x}{5-1.5}+\frac{x}{5+1.5}=1 \Rightarrow \frac{x\times 2}{7}+\frac{x\times 2}{13}=1$$

$\Rightarrow\ 40x = 91 \qquad \therefore x = 91/40 = 2.275$ km

4. Required time period $= \frac{22.5}{6+1.5}+\frac{22.5}{6-1.5}$

$= \frac{45}{15}+\frac{45}{9} = 8$ hours.

5. Let x km/hr and y km/hr be the speed of boat in still water and speed of current respectively; then

$$\frac{20}{x+y}+\frac{6}{x-y}=3 \quad ...(i)$$

and also, $$\frac{30}{x+y}+\frac{12}{x-y}=5$$

$$\Rightarrow \frac{15}{x+y}+\frac{6}{x-y}=\frac{5}{2} \quad ...(ii)$$

Solving equations *(i)* & *(ii)*, we get $x + y = 10$ and $x - y = 6$

Since, $x = \frac{1}{2}(10 + 6) = 8$ km/hr.

6. Let x km/hr and y km/hr be the speed of rowing in still water and speed of the current respectively; then

$$\frac{12}{x-y}-\frac{12}{x+y}=6 \Rightarrow \frac{24y}{x^2-y^2}=6$$

$$\Rightarrow x^2 = y^2 + 4y \quad ...(i)$$

Again, $$\frac{12}{2x-y}-\frac{12}{2x+y}=1$$

$$\Rightarrow \frac{24y}{4x^2-y^2}=1 \Rightarrow x^2=\frac{y^2+24y}{4} \quad ...(ii)$$

From equations (i) and (ii), we get

$$y^2 + 4y = \frac{y^2+24y}{4} \Rightarrow 3y^2 = 8y$$

$$\therefore\ y=\frac{8}{3}=2\frac{1}{3} \text{ miles/hr.}$$

8. The speed of the stream $= \frac{1}{2}(13 - 8) = \frac{5}{2}$

$= 2.5$ km/hr.

9. The man's speed in still water

$= 15 - 2.5 = 12.5$ km/hr

Hence, the men's speed against the current

$= 12.5 - 2.5 = 10$ km/hr

10. Let speed of the stream be x km/hr, then

$$\frac{30}{15+x}+\frac{30}{15-x}=4\frac{1}{2} \Rightarrow \frac{30\times 30}{225-x^2}=\frac{9}{2}$$

$$\Rightarrow \frac{200}{225-x^2}=1 \qquad \Rightarrow x^2 = 225 - 200$$

$\Rightarrow x^2 = 25 \qquad \therefore\ x = 5$ km/hr.

ALLIGATION OR MIXTURE

1. A shopkeeper buys 26 kgs of milk @ Rs. 16 per kg. He also buys from another source an inferior quality of milk @ Rs. 10 per kg. How much quantity of the latter should he buy to mix it with the former so that he can sell the mixture @ Rs. 14 per kg without making any loss?

A. 13 kgs B. 12 kgs
C. 14 kgs D. 16 kgs

2. Two vessels A and B contain mixture of milk and water in the ratio 4 : 1 and 9 : 11 respectively. They are mixed in the ratio of 3 : 2. Find the ratio of milk : water in the resulting mixture.

A. 34 : 16 B. 33 : 17
C. 16 : 34 D. 17 : 33

3. A shopkeeper has 50 kgs of rice. He sells a part of it at 20% profit and the rest at 40% profit. If he gains 25% on the whole, find the quantity of each part.

A. 12.5 kgs and 37.5 kgs
B. 37.5 kgs and 12.5 kgs
C. 23.5 kgs and 21.5 kgs
D. 21.5 kgs and 23.5 kgs

4. A man bought a certain quantity of sugar for Rs. 8000. He sells one-fourth of it at 20% loss. At what per cent profit should he sell the remainder stock so as to make an overall profit of 20%?

A. 20% B. 30%
C. 35% D. 40%

5. Rs. 675 was divided among 75 boys and girls. Each boy gets Rs. 20 whereas a girl gets Rs. 5. Find the number of boys and girls.

A. 20, 55 B. 15, 60
C. 25, 50 D. 30, 45

6. A vessel contains mixture of liquids A and B in the ratio 3 : 2. When 20 litres of the mixture is taken out and replaced by 20 litres of liquid B, the ratio changes to 1 : 4. How many litres of liquid A was there initially present in the vessel?

A. 12 litres B. 18 litres
C. 24 litres D. 22 litres

7. A container is full of milk. One-third of milk is taken out of it and replaced by same quantity of water. Then again one-third of the mixture is taken out of it and replaced by the same quantity of water. The process is repeated 4 times. If 16 litres of milk is left in the container at the end of 4th operation, find the capacity of the container.

A. 76 litres B. 81 litres
C. 82 litres D. 85 litres

8. The cost of type-I rice is Rs. 15 per kg and type-II is Rs. 20 per kg. If both type I and type II are mixed in the ratio of 2 : 3, then find the price per kg of the mixed variety.

A. Rs. 19.50 B. Rs. 19
C. Rs. 18.50 D. Rs. 18

9. In what ratio must a grocer mix two varieties of tea worth Rs. 60 a kg and Rs. 65 a kg so that by selling the mixture at Rs. 68.20 a kg he may gain 10%?

A. 4 : 5 B. 3 : 5
C. 3 : 4 D. 3 : 2

10. A vessel contains 80 litres of milk. 16 litres of milk was taken out of the vessel and replaced by water. Then 16 litres of mixture was withdrawn and again replaced by water. The operation was repeated for third time. How much milk is now left in the vessel?

A. 96.40 litres B. 50.36 litres
C. 40.96 litres D. 32.76 litres

ANSWERS

1	2	3	4	5	6	7	8	9	10
A	B	B	B	A	B	B	D	D	C

SOME SELECTED EXPLANATORY ANSWERS

1. 16   10

14

4   2

or 2 : 1 $\dfrac{\text{Quantity of milk @ Rs.10 per kg}}{\text{Quantity of milk @ Rs. 16 per kg}} = \dfrac{1}{2}$

So, quantity of milk @ Rs. 10 per kg. $= \dfrac{26}{2}$

$= 13$ kgs.

2. Fraction is   *Milk*   *Water*

A : $\dfrac{4}{5}$ $\dfrac{1}{5}$

B : $\dfrac{9}{20}$ $\dfrac{11}{20}$

(3A + 2B) = A and B : $\left(\dfrac{12}{5}+\dfrac{9}{10}\right)$ $\left(\dfrac{3}{5}+\dfrac{11}{10}\right)$

$\dfrac{33}{10}$ $\dfrac{17}{10}$

So, Ratio of milk : water in the resulting mixture $= 33 : 17$.

3. 20%   40%

25%

15   5

or 3 : 1

Quantity sold at 20% profit $= \dfrac{3}{3+1} \times 50$

$= 37.5$ kgs.

Quantity sold at 40% profit $= (50 - 37.5)$

$= 12.5$ kgs.

4. Let the remainder stock be sold at x% profit.

-10 $+x$

+20

$(x-20)$ 30

$$\frac{x-20}{30} = \frac{1/4}{3/4}$$

or $x - 20 = 30 \times \dfrac{1}{3}$

or $x = 20 + 10$

$x = 30\%$ profit.

5. Average money per head (boy or girl)

$= \text{Rs.}\ \dfrac{675}{75} = \text{Rs.}\ 9$

(Boys) Rs. 20   (Girls) Rs. 5

(Average) Rs. 9

4   11

$$\text{Number of boys} = \frac{4}{4+11} \times 75 = 20$$

$$\text{Number of girls} = \frac{11}{4+11} \times 75 = 55.$$

6. % of liquid B initially present in the vessel

$$= \frac{2}{3+2} \times 100 = 40\%$$

% of liquid B finally present in the vessel

$$= \frac{4}{1+4} \times 100 = 80\%$$

The second solution is liquid B which is being mixed and it has 100% liquid B.

80% of liquid B present in the resultant mixture may be taken as average percentage. So, using rule of alligation on liquid B per cent, we can write,

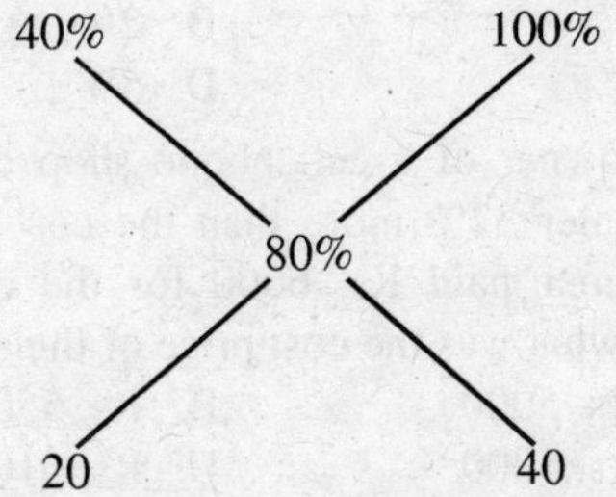

or 1 : 2

The ratio of liquid left in the vessel to liquid B being mixed = 1 : 2

Since the quantity of liquid B being mixed is 20 litres, the quantity of liquid left in the vessel is 10 litres.

Therefore, the total quantity of liquid initially present in the vessel

= 10 + 20 = 30 litres

$$\text{Quantity of liquid A} = \frac{3}{2+3} \times 30$$

= 18 litres.

7. Let capacity of the container be x litre; then

$$x(1 - 1/3)^4 = 16 \quad \Rightarrow \quad x\left(\frac{2}{3}\right)^4 = 16$$

$$\Rightarrow x \times \frac{16}{81} = 16 \qquad \therefore \; x = 81 \text{ litres}$$

8. Let the price per kg of mixed variety be Rs. x; then

By the rule of alligation,

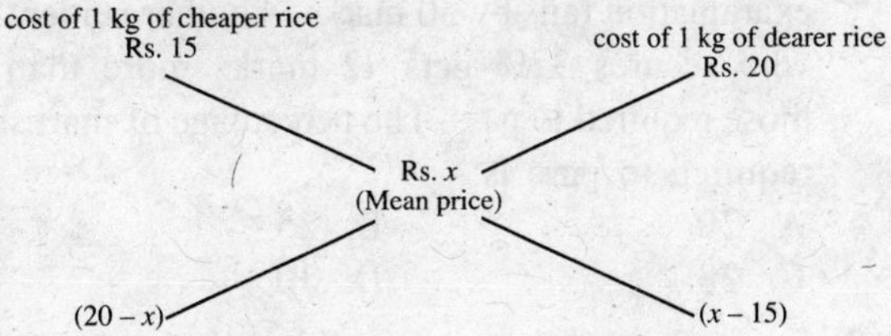

$$\text{Now, } \frac{20 - x}{x - 15} = \frac{2}{3} \quad \Rightarrow \quad 60 - 3x = 2x - 30$$

$$\Rightarrow 5x = 90 \qquad \therefore \; x = \text{Rs. } 18$$

9. S.P. of 1 kg mixture = Rs. 68.20,

Gain % = 10%

$$\text{Hence, C.P. of 1 kg mixture} = \frac{100}{110} \times \text{Rs. } 68.20$$

= Rs. 62

By the rule of alligation

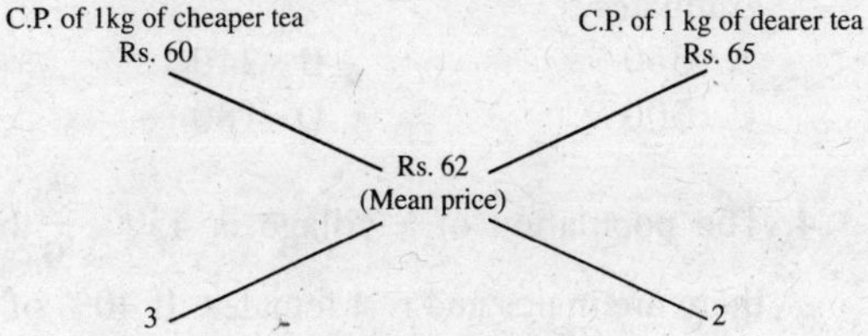

Hence, required ratio = 3 : 2

10. $$\text{Amount of milk left} = 80\left(1 - \frac{16}{80}\right)^3$$

$$= 80\left(\frac{4}{5}\right)^3$$

$$80 \times \frac{64}{125} = 40.96 \text{ litres.}$$

PERCENTAGE

1. A student who secures 20% marks in an examination fails by 30 marks. Another student who secures 32% gets 42 marks more than those required to pass. The percentage of marks required to pass is:

   A. 20 B. 25
   C. 28 D. 30

2. In a college election, a candidate secured 62% of the votes and is elected by a majority of 144 votes. The total number of votes polled is:

   A. 600 B. 800
   C. 925 D. 1200

3. In an organisation, 40% of the employees are matriculates, 50% of the remaining are graduates and the remaining 180 are postgraduates. How many employees are graduates?

   A. 360 B. 240
   C. 300 D. 180

4. The population of a village is 4500. $\frac{5}{9}$th of them are males and rest females. If 40% of the males are married, then the percentage of married female is :

   A. 35 B. 40
   C. 50 D. 60

5. A's income is 10% more than B's. How much per cent is B's income is less than A's?

   A. 10% B. 7%
   C. $9\frac{1}{11}$% D. $6\frac{1}{2}$%

6. If the price of a television set is increased by 25%, then by what percentage should the new price be reduced to bring the price back to original level?

   A. 15% B. 20%
   C. 25% D. 30%

7. In an election one of the two candidates gets 40% votes and loses by 100 votes. Total number of votes is :

   A. 500 B. 400
   C. 600 D. 1000

8. The gross income of a person is Rs. 20000. 10% of his income is exempted from income tax and his net income is Rs. 19100. The rate of income tax is :

   A. 3% B. 2%
   C. 4% D. 5%

9. The owner of a cell phone shop charges his customer 32% more than the cost price. If a customer paid Rs. 6600 for the cell phone, then what was the cost price of the cell phone?

   A. Rs. 5000 B. Rs. 5500
   C. Rs. 5800 D. Rs. 6100

10. If the cost of pins reduced by Rs. 4 per dozen, 12 more pins can be purchased for Rs. 48. The cost of pins per dozen after reduction is:

    A. Rs. 8 B. Rs. 12
    C. Rs. 16 D. Rs. 20

11. In an examination 80% of the students passed in Mathematics and 70% passed in English, while 10% students failed in both the subjects. If 360 students passed in both the subjects, find the total number of students who appeared in the examination.

    A. 400 B. 600
    C. 630 D. 640

12. Electric tax is increased by 20% and its consumption is decreased by 20%. The change in the expenditure is:

    A. 4% decrease B. 4% increase
    C. 5% decrease D. 5% increase

13. The selling price of certain commodity was reduced by 25%. As a result of it, the sales increased by 30%. What was the effect of it on cash collected by daily sales?

A. 2.5% decrease B. 2.5% increase
C. 5% decrease D. 5% increase

14. The wheat sold by a grocer contained 10% low quality wheat. What quantity of good quality wheat should be added to 150 kgs of wheat so that the percentage of low quality wheat becomes 5%?

A. 50 kgs B. 85 kgs
C. 135 kgs D. 150 kgs

15. Nilam spends 15% of her monthly income on household expenses. She spends 17% of the monthly income in travelling and 6% on medical expenses and saves the rest Rs. 15,500. What is her monthly income?

A. Rs. 20,000
B. Rs. 25,000
C. Rs. 30,000
D. Rs. 35,000

ANSWERS

1	2	3	4	5	6	7	8	9	10
B	A	D	C	C	B	A	D	A	B
11	**12**	**13**	**14**	**15**					
B	A	A	D	B					

SOME SELECTED EXPLANATORY ANSWERS

1. $20\% \text{ of } x + 30 = 32\% \text{ of } x - 42$

$\Rightarrow \quad 12\% \text{ of } x = 72$

$\Rightarrow \quad x = \frac{72 \times 100}{12} = 600$

Pass Mark $= 20\% \text{ of } 600 + 30 = 150$

Pass percentage $= \left(\frac{150}{600} \times 100\right)\% = 25\%$

2. $(62\% \text{ of } x - 38\% \text{ of } x) = 144$

$\Rightarrow 24\% \text{ of } x = 144 \quad \Rightarrow x = \frac{144 \times 100}{24} = 600$

3. Matriculates $= \frac{40}{100} x = \frac{2x}{5}$

Remaining $= \left(x - \frac{2x}{5}\right) = \frac{3x}{5}$

Graduates $= \frac{50}{100} \times \frac{3x}{5} = \frac{3x}{10}$

Remaining $= \frac{3x}{5} - \frac{3x}{10} = \frac{3x}{10}$

Now, $\frac{3x}{10} = 180$

$\therefore \ x = \frac{10 \times 180}{3} = 600$

$\therefore$ Graduates $= \frac{3 \times 600}{10} = 180$.

4. Males $= \left(\frac{5}{9} \times 4500\right) = 2500$

Females $= 2000$

$\therefore$ Married males $= \frac{40}{100} \times 2500 = 1000$

and married females $= 1000$

$\therefore$ Percentage of married females

$= \left(\frac{1000}{2000} \times 100\right)\% = 50\%$.

5. Required percentage $= \left[\frac{10}{(100+10)} \times 100\right]\%$

$= 9\frac{1}{11}\%$.

6. Required reduction $= \frac{25}{100+25} \times 100 = 20\%$.

7. Out of 100, difference in votes = (60 – 40) = 20

20% of x = 100

$\therefore x = \frac{100 \times 100}{20} = 500$.

8. Gross income = Rs. 20000

Income exempted from income tax = 10% of gross income

$\therefore$ Income on which income tax is chargeable = (100 – 10%) = 90% of gross income

$= 20000 \times \frac{90}{100} = \text{Rs. } 18000$

$\therefore$ Total income tax paid on

= Rs. 20000 – Rs. 19100

= Rs. 900

$\therefore$ Rate per cent of income tax $= \frac{900}{18000} \times 100$

$= 5\%$

9. Let cost price of the cell phone be Rs. x; then

$x + \frac{32}{100} \times x = 6600 \quad \Rightarrow \frac{132x}{100} = 6600$

$\therefore x = \frac{100 \times 6600}{132} = \text{Rs. } 5000.$

10. Let reduced price by Rs. x per dozen, then

$\frac{48}{x} - \frac{48}{x+4} = 1 \quad \Rightarrow \quad \frac{48 \times 4}{x^2 + 4x} = 1$

$\Rightarrow \quad x^2 + 4x - 192 = 0$

$\Rightarrow (x + 16)(x - 12) = 0$

$\therefore \quad x = \text{Rs. } 12.$

11. Here, percentage of students failed in Mathematics and English be 30% and 20% respectively.

Percentage of students failed either one or both subjects = 30 + 20 – 10 = 40%

Hence, percentage of pass students = 100 – 40 = 60%

Now, 60% = 360

$\therefore 100\% = \frac{360}{60} \times 100 = 600.$

12. Let initially electric tax is Rs. 100 and consumption = 100 units

Decrease in consumption

= 100 × 100 – 120 × 80 = Rs. 400

Hence, decrease percentage $= \frac{400 \times 100}{100 \times 100} = 4\%$.

13. Let the selling price of a commodity be Rs. 100 and number of sales = 100 units

Decrease in daily cash = 100 × 100 – 75 × 130 = Rs. 250

Hence, decrease percentage

$= \frac{250 \times 100}{100 \times 100} = 2.5\%.$

14. Let x kg of good wheat be added; then

$\frac{10}{100} \times 150 = \frac{5}{100}(150 + x)$

$\Rightarrow 150 + x = 300 \quad \therefore \quad x = 150$ kg.

15. Let her monthly income be Rs. x; then

$x - \left(\frac{15}{100} \times x + \frac{17}{100} \times x + \frac{6}{100} \times x\right) = 15{,}500$

$\Rightarrow x - \frac{38x}{100} = 15500 \quad \Rightarrow \frac{62x}{100} = 15500$

$\therefore x = \frac{15500 \times 100}{62} = \text{Rs. } 25000.$

PROFIT AND LOSS

1. Ashok bought 25 kg of rice at the rate of Rs. 6 per kg and 35 kg of rice at the rate of Rs. 7 per kg. He mixed the two and sold the mixture at the rate of Rs. 6.75 per kg. What was his gain or loss in the transaction?

A. Rs. 16 gain B. Rs. 16 loss
C. Rs. 10 gain D. None of these

2. Profit after selling a commodity for Rs. 425 is same as loss after selling it for Rs. 355. The cost of the commodity is :

A. Rs. 285 B. Rs. 390
C. Rs. 295 D. Rs. 400

3. Ram bought 4 dozen apples at Rs. 12 per dozen and 2 dozen at Rs. 16 per dozen. He sold all of them to earn 20%. At what price per dozen did he sell the apples?

A. Rs. 14.40 B. Rs. 16.00
C. Rs. 16.80 D. Rs. 16.20

4. At what price must Kantilal sell a mixture of 80 kg sugar at Rs. 6.75 per kg with 120 kg at Rs. 8 per kg to gain 20%?

A. Rs. 7.50 per kg B. Rs. 8.20 per kg
C. Rs. 8.35 per kg D. Rs. 9 per kg

5. A person bought an article and sold it at a loss of 10%. If he had bought it for 20% less and sold it for Rs. 55 more, he would have had a profit of 40%. The C.P. of the article is :

A. Rs. 200 B. Rs. 225
C. Rs. 250 D. None of these

6. A dealer sold a machine to a shopkeeper at 20% profit. The shopkeeper sold the machine to a customer so as to get 25% profit for himself. The difference between the selling price of the dealer and that of the shopkeeper was found to be Rs. 129. What is the initial price of the machine?

A. Rs. 410 B. Rs. 420
C. Rs. 430 D. Rs. 440

7. A man bought a horse and cart. If he sold the horse at 10% loss and the cart at 20% gain he would not loss anything. If he sold the horse at 5% loss and the cart at 5% gain he would lose Rs. 10 in the bargain. What did he pay for each?

A. Rs. 400, Rs. 200 B. Rs. 300, Rs. 300
C. Rs. 250, Rs. 350 D. Rs. 350, Rs. 250

8. The marked price of a radio is 20% more than its cost price. If a discount of 10% is given on the marked price, the gain percentage is:

A. 8 B. 10
C. 12 D. 15

9. A dishonest dealer sells his goods at the cost price and still earns a profit of 60% by underweight. What weight does he use for a kg?

A. 625 gms B. 750 gms
C. 800 gms D. 850 gms

10. A man sells two horses for Rs. 990 each. On one he gains 10% and the other he loses 10%. What is his total percentage of gain or loss in the transaction?

A. 1% gain B. 1% loss
C. 2% gain D. 2% loss

ANSWERS

1	2	3	4	5	6	7	8	9	10
C	B	B	D	C	C	A	A	A	B

SOME SELECTED EXPLANATORY ANSWERS

1. C.P. of 60 kg mixture = Rs. $(25 \times 6 + 35 \times 7)$ = Rs. 395

S.P. of 60 kg mixtire = Rs. (60×6.75) = Rs. 405

$\therefore$ Gain = Rs. $(405 - 395)$ = Rs. 10

2. Let C.P. = Rs. x

Then, $425 - x = x - 355 \Rightarrow 2x = 780$

$\therefore x =$ Rs. 390

3. C.P. of 6 dozen apples = Rs. $(12 \times 4 + 16 \times 2)$ = Rs. 80

$\therefore$ S.P. = Rs. $\left(\frac{120}{100} \times 80\right)$ = Rs. 96

$\therefore$ S.P. per dozen = Rs. $\left(\frac{96}{6}\right)$ = Rs. 16

4. C.P. of 1 kg sugar = $\frac{80 \times 6.75 + 120 \times 8}{200}$ = Rs. 7.50

$\therefore$ S.P. of 1 kg = Rs. $\left(\frac{120}{100} \times 7.50\right)$ = Rs. 9 per kg

5. Let C.P. = Rs. x,

then S.P. = $\frac{90}{100} \times x$ = Rs. $\frac{9x}{10}$

Now, when C.P. = Rs. $\frac{80x}{100}$ = Rs. $\frac{4x}{5}$;

then S.P. = $\frac{140}{100} \times \frac{4x}{5}$ = Rs. $\frac{28x}{25}$

But, $\frac{28x}{25} - \frac{9x}{10} = 55 \Rightarrow \frac{11x}{50} = 55$

$\therefore x =$ Rs. 250

6. Let the initial price = Rs. x; then C.P. for dealer

$= \frac{120}{100} \times x$ = Rs. $\frac{6x}{5}$

Again, C.P. for shopkeeper = $\frac{125}{100} \times \frac{6x}{5}$ = Rs. $\frac{3x}{2}$

Now, $\frac{3x}{2} - \frac{6x}{5} = 129 \Rightarrow \frac{3x}{10} = 129$

$\therefore x = \frac{10 \times 129}{3}$ = Rs. 430

7. Here, 10% C.P. of horse = 20% C.P. of cart;
Hence, C.P. of horse = $2 \times$ C.P. of cart;
Let C.P. of cart and horse be Rs. x and Rs. $2x$ respectively; then,

$\frac{5}{100} \times 2x - \frac{5}{100} \times x = 10 \Rightarrow \frac{1}{20}x = 10$

$\therefore x = 200$

Hence, C.P. of a cart = Rs. 200 and C.P. of a horse = 2×200 = Rs. 400

8. Let C.P. be Rs. 100; then marked price = Rs. 120

Since, S.P. = $\frac{90}{100} \times 120$ = Rs. 108

$\therefore$ Profit = $108 - 100$ = Rs. 8, Hence, gain = 8%.

9. Required weight = $\frac{100}{160} \times 1000$ = 625 gms.

10. Here, loss % = $\left(\frac{10}{10}\right)^2$ = 1%.

SIMPLE INTEREST

1. A lent a sum of Rs. 1250 to B at a certain rate of interest for 3 years and a sum of Rs. 1500 to C at the same rate of interest for 2 years. If he was paid total Rs. 258.75 as interest in both cases, find the rate of interest at which money was lent by him.

A. $4\frac{1}{6}\%$ B. $6\frac{1}{4}\%$

C. $2\frac{1}{7}\%$ D. $3\frac{5}{6}\%$

2. A invested Rs. 5000 at a certain rate of simple interest and Rs. 4000 for the same period at 1% higher rate of interest. If the interest in both cases is same, the former rate of interest is :

A. 3% B. 4%

C. 6% D. 5%

3. If a certain sum of money at simple interest amounts to Rs. 1900 in 3 years and to Rs. 2050 in 5 years, the rate per cent per annum is :

A. 4½% B. 3½%

C. 2½% D. 5¼%

4. A certain sum of money lent out on simple interest amounts to Rs. 1760 in 2 years and to Rs. 2000 in 5 years. Find the sum.

A. Rs. 1650 B. Rs. 1500

C. Rs. 1580 D. Rs. 1600

5. Out of the sum of Rs. 1550, a part was lent out at 5% p.a. simple interest and the remaining at 8% p.a. simple interest. If the total interest in both cases after 3 years is Rs. 300, the sum of money lent out at 8% p.a. simple interest was:

A. Rs. 760 B. Rs. 775

C. Rs. 750 D. Rs. 780

6. If simple interest on a certain sum of money for 4 years at 5% p.a. is same as the simple interest on Rs. 840 for 10 years at the rate of 4% p.a., the sum of money is:

A. Rs. 1780 B. Rs. 1660

C. Rs. 1680 D. Rs. 1620

7. What equal instalment of annual payment will discharge a debt which is due as Rs. 848 at the end of 4 years at 4% per annum simple interest?

A. Rs. 200 B. Rs. 212

C. Rs. 225 D. Rs. 250

8. Madhavi lent Rs. 5000 to Kamla for 5 years and Rs. 3000 to Vimla for 4 years. Find the rate of interest, if Madhavi gets an interest of Rs. 600 in the end.

A. 1.62% B. 2.5%

C. 3% D. 4%

9. A sum of money doubles itself in 7 years at simple interest. In how many years it will become four fold?

A. 10 years B. 14 years

C. 21 years D. 35 years

10. An amount doubles itself at the end of 8 years with a certain rate of simple interest. What will be the total simple interest on Rs. 8000 at that rate at the end of 4 years?

A. Rs. 2000 B. Rs. 4000

C. Rs. 6000 D. None of these

ANSWERS

1	2	3	4	5	6	7	8	9	10
D	B	A	D	C	C	A	A	C	B

SOME SELECTED EXPLANATORY ANSWERS

1. $\frac{1250 \times R \times 3}{100} + \frac{1500 \times R \times 2}{100} = 258.75$

$\Rightarrow 6750\ R = 25875$

$\therefore \quad R = \frac{25875}{6750} = \frac{23}{6} = 3\frac{5}{6}\%$

2. Here, $\frac{5000 \times R \times T}{100} = \frac{4000 \times (R+1) \times T}{100}$

$\Rightarrow 5R = 4R + 4 \quad \therefore \quad R = 4\%$

3. Simple interest for 2 years
= Rs. 2050 – Rs. 1900 = Rs. 150

$\therefore$ Simple interest for 1 year = Rs. $\frac{150}{2}$
= Rs. 75

Since simple interest for 3 years = Rs. 75 × 3
= Rs. 225

$\therefore$ Principal = Rs. 1900 – Rs. 225
= Rs. 1675

Hence, Rate = $\frac{75 \times 100}{1675 \times 1} = 4\frac{1}{2}\%$

4. Interest for 3 years = Rs. 2000 – Rs. 1760
= Rs. 240

$\therefore$ Interest for 1 year = Rs. $\frac{240}{3}$ = Rs. 80

And interest for 2 years = Rs. 80 × 2 = Rs. 160

$\therefore$ Principal = Rs. 1760 – Rs. 160 = Rs. 1600

5. Let Rs. x and Rs $(1550 - x)$ were lent out at 8% and 5% respectively; then

$\frac{x \times 8 \times 3}{100} + \frac{(1550 - x) \times 5 \times 3}{100} = 300$

$\Rightarrow 24x + 23250 - 15x = 30000$

$\Rightarrow 9x = 6750 \quad \therefore \quad x = \frac{6750}{9}$ = Rs. 750

6. Here, $\frac{P \times 5 \times 4}{100} = \frac{840 \times 4 \times 10}{100} \Rightarrow 5P = 8400$

$\therefore P = \frac{8400}{5}$ = Rs. 1680

7. Let equal instalment be Rs. x; then

$x + \frac{x \times 4 \times 3}{100} + x + \frac{x \times 4 \times 2}{100} + x + \frac{x \times 4 \times 1}{100} + x = 848$

$\Rightarrow 4x + \frac{24x}{100} = 848 \Rightarrow \frac{106x}{25} = 848$

$\therefore x = \frac{848 \times 25}{106}$ = Rs. 200

8. $\frac{5000 \times R \times 5}{100} + \frac{3000 \times R \times 4}{100} = 600$

$\Rightarrow \quad 250\ R + 120\ R = 600$

$\Rightarrow \quad 370R = 600$

$\therefore \quad R = \frac{600}{370} = 1.62\%$

9. Let principal be Rs. x; then amount = Rs. $2x$,
Hence, I = $2x - x$ = Rs. x.

$R = \frac{x \times 100}{x \times 7} = \frac{100}{7}\%$ p.a.

Now, amount = Rs. $4x$; then I = $4x - x$
= Rs. $3x$

Hence, T = $\frac{3x \times 100}{x \times \frac{100}{7}} = \frac{3 \times 100 \times 7}{100} = 21$ years

10. Let principal = Rs. x; then amount = Rs. $2x$;
I = $2x - x$ = Rs. x

$R = \frac{x \times 100}{x \times 8} = \frac{25}{2}\%$

Again, $I = \frac{8000 \times 25 \times 4}{100 \times 2}$ = Rs. 4000

COMPOUND INTEREST

1. The compound interest on a certain sum of money invested for 3 years at 5% per annum is Rs. 1891.50. What will be the simple interest on the same sum at the same rate for 2 years?
   A. Rs. 1700 B. Rs. 1200
   C. Rs. 1500 D. Rs. 2100

2. A sum of money lent out at a certain rate of simple interest amounts to Rs. 6600 in 2 years and to Rs. 6900 in 3 years. What will be the compound interest on the same sum of money if lent out at the same rate for 2 years?
   A. Rs. 605 B. Rs. 715
   C. Rs. 615 D. Rs. 595

3. A man deposits Rs. 1200 in a bank on the 1st day of each year. If the bank pays 5% per annum compound interest on deposited sum of money, what will be the amount to his credit on the 10th day of the second year?
   A. Rs. 2560 B. Rs. 2460
   C. Rs. 2370 D. Rs. 2860

4. If the difference between compound and simple interest on a certain sum of money for 3 years at 5% per annum is Rs. 244, the sum is :
   A. Rs. 40000 B. Rs. 25000
   C. Rs. 30000 D. Rs. 32000

5. A man purchased a sewing machine for Rs. 5000. If due to sustained use value of this sewing machine depreciates by 6% annually, find its value after 3 years.
   A. Rs. 3775.67 B. Rs. 4152.92
   C. Rs. 4250.25 D. Rs. 4356.25

6. Find the sum on which the difference between compound and simple interest for 3 years at 10% per annum will be Rs. 868.
   A. Rs. 29500 B. Rs. 27625
   C. Rs. 28500 D. Rs. 28000

7. Samir invested Rs. 15000 at the rate of interest 10% p.a. for 1 year. If the interest compound six months. What amount will Samir get at the end of the year?
   A. Rs. 16,500 B. Rs. 16525.50
   C. Rs. 16537.50 D. Rs. 18,150

8. The compound interest on a certain sum for 2 years at 10% per annum is Rs. 525. The simple interest on the same sum for double the time at half the rate per cent per annum is:
   A. Rs. 800 B. Rs. 600
   C. Rs. 500 D. Rs. 400

9. The least number of complete years in which a sum of money put at 20% compound interest will be more than doubled is:
   A. 6 B. 5
   C. 4 D. 3

10. On a sum of money, the simple interest for 2 years is Rs. 660, while the compound interest is Rs. 696.30, the rate of interest being the same in both cases. Find the rate of interest.
   A. Rs. 12% B. 11%
   C. 10% D. 9%

ANSWERS

1	2	3	4	5	6	7	8	9	10
B	C	B	D	B	D	C	C	C	B

SOME SELECTED EXPLANATORY ANSWERS

1. Here, $1891.50 = P\left[\left(1+\frac{5}{100}\right)^3 - 1\right]$

$\Rightarrow 1891.50 = P\left[\left(\frac{21}{20}\right)^3 - 1\right]$

$\Rightarrow 1891.50 = P\left(\frac{1261}{8000}\right)$

$\therefore P = \frac{1891.50 \times 8000}{1261} = \text{Rs. } 12000$

Now, $\text{S.I.} = \frac{12000 \times 5 \times 2}{100} = \text{Rs. } 1200$

2. Here, 1 year's S.I. = Rs. 6900 − Rs. 6600 = Rs. 300

∴ 2 year's S.I. = 300 × 2 = Rs. 600

∴ Principal = Rs. 6600 − Rs. 600 = Rs. 6000

Hence, $\text{Rate} = \frac{600 \times 100}{6000 \times 2} = 5\%$

$\therefore \text{C.I.} = 6000\left[\left(1+\frac{5}{100}\right)^2 - 1\right]$

$= 6000\left[\left(\frac{21}{20}\right)^2 - 1\right] = \frac{6000 \times 41}{400} = \text{Rs. } 615$

3. Required amount $= 1200\left(1+\frac{5}{100}\right) + 1200$

$= 1200 \times \frac{21}{20} + 1200 = 1260 + 1200 = \text{Rs. } 2460$

4. Here, $P\left[\left(1+\frac{5}{100}\right)^3 - 1\right] - \frac{P \times 5 \times 3}{100} = 244$

$\Rightarrow P \times \frac{1261}{8000} - \frac{3P}{20} = 244 \Rightarrow P \times \frac{61}{8000} = 244$

$\therefore P = \frac{244 \times 8000}{61} = \text{Rs. } 32000$

5. Here, value of the machine after 3 years

$= 5000\left(1-\frac{6}{100}\right)^3 = 5000 \times \frac{47}{50} \times \frac{47}{50} \times \frac{47}{50}$

= Rs. 4152.92.

6. Here, $P\left[\left(1+\frac{10}{100}\right)^3 - 1\right] - \frac{P \times 10 \times 3}{100} = 868$

$\Rightarrow P \times \frac{331}{1000} - \frac{3P}{10} = 868$

$\Rightarrow P \times \frac{31}{1000} = 868 \quad \therefore P = \frac{868 \times 1000}{31}$

= Rs. 28000

7. $A = 15000\left(1+\frac{5}{100}\right)^2 = 15000 \times \frac{441}{400}$

= Rs. 16537.50

8. Here, $P\left[\left(1+\frac{10}{100}\right)^2 - 1\right] = 525$

$\Rightarrow P\left[\frac{121}{100} - 1\right] = 525 \Rightarrow P \times \frac{21}{100} = 525$

$\therefore P = \frac{525 \times 100}{21} = \text{Rs. } 2500$

Hence, required S.I. $= \frac{2500 \times 5 \times 4}{100} = \text{Rs. } 500$

9. Here, $P\left(1+\frac{20}{100}\right)^n > 2P \Rightarrow \left(\frac{6}{5}\right)^n > 2$

Hence, if $n = 4$ then, $\left(\frac{6}{5}\right)^4 = \frac{1296}{625} > 2$

So, $n = 4$ years

10. Here, S.I. for 1 year = Rs. 330

Since, simple interest of Rs. 330 for 1 year = 696.30 − 660 = Rs. 36.30

Hence, required rate $= \frac{36.30 \times 100}{330 \times 1} = \frac{3630}{330}$

= 11%

AREA AND PERIMETER

1. If side of a square is reduced by 50%, its area will be reduced by

A. 50% B. 75%
C. 80% D. 60%

2. If each side of a square is doubled, its area will become

A. double
B. four times
C. three times
D. eight times

3. Three sides of a triangle are in the ratio of 17 : 15 : 8. If the perimeter of this triangle is 40 m, find its area

A. 50 sq. m. B. 49 sq. m.
C. 60 sq. m. D. 69 sq. m.

4. If the length of a rectangle is increased by 20% and width is decreased by 15%, then its area

A. decreases by 4% B. increases by 2%
C. decreases by 2% D. increases by 3%

5. If the length of a rectangle is increased by 20%, then by how much per cent its breadth must be decreased so as to keep its area unaltered?

A. 25% B. $8\frac{1}{3}\%$
C. $16\frac{2}{3}\%$ D. 20%

6. The ratio of length and breadth of a rectangular plot is 71 : 61 respectively. The area of the plot is 17324 m^2. What is perimeter of the plot?

A. 264 m B. 284 m
C. 528 m D. 614 m

7. If the length and breadth of a rectangular field are increased, the area increases by 50%. If the increase in length was 20%, by what percentage was the breadth increased?

A. 20% B. 25%
C. 30% D. 40%

8. The length and breadth of a varandah is 40 m and 15 m respectively. How many stone slabs of size 6 decimetre × 5 decimetre each are needed in flooring it:

A. 1000 B. 2000
C. 3000 D. 4000

9. The circumference of a circular plot is 396 m. What is the area of the circular plot?

A. 9,446 m^2 B. 9,856 m^2.
C. 12,474 m^2 D. 18,634 m^2

10. If the sides of an equilateral triangle are increased by 20%, 30% and 50% respectively to form a new triangle, the increase in the perimeter of the equilateral triangle is:

A. 25% B. $33\frac{1}{3}\%$
C. 50% D. 100%

ANSWERS

1	2	3	4	5	6	7	8	9	10
B	B	C	B	C	C	B	B	C	B

SOME SELECTED EXPLANATORY ANSWERS

1. Area of the square = x^2 sq. m.

Side of the new square = $x - 50\%$ of $x = \frac{x}{2}$ m

$\therefore$ Area of the new square = $\left(\frac{x}{2}\right)^2 = \frac{x^2}{4}$ sq. m.

$\therefore$ Reduction in area of the square = $x^2 - \frac{x^2}{4}$

$= \frac{3x^2}{4}$ sq. m.

$\therefore$ Percentage reduction = $\frac{3x^2/4}{x^2} \times 100 = 75\%$

2. Area of the square = x^2 sq. m

Now, area of the new square = $(2x)^2 = 4x^2$ sq. m

Hence, it is clear that if side of a square is doubled, its area becomes four times.

3. Suppose sides of the triangle are $17x$ m, $15x$ m and $8x$ metres

$\therefore$ Perimeter $= 17x + 15x + 8x = 40x$

Now, $40x = 40$

$\Rightarrow x = 1$ m

Therefore, the sides are $17 \times 1 = 17$ m, $15 \times 1 = 15$ m and $8 \times 1 = 8$ m

$\because (17)^2 = (15)^2 + (8)^2$,

i.e., it is a right angled triangle

$\therefore$ Area of the right angled triangle

$= \frac{1}{2} \times 8 \times 15 = 60$ sq.m.

4. Area of the rectangle = xy sq. metre

Area of the new rectangle = $\frac{120}{100}x \times \frac{85}{100}y$

$= 1.020\, xy$ sq. metre

$\therefore$ Increase in the area = $1.02\, xy - xy$

$= .02\, xy$ sq. m.

$\therefore$ Percentage increase = $\frac{.02xy}{xy} \times 100 = 2\%$

5. Area of the rectangle = xy

On reducing the breadth by A% and increasing the length by 20%

Length of the new rectangle = $\frac{120x}{100} x = 1.2x$

Breadth of the new rectangle = $y -$ A% of y

$= y\left(1 - \frac{A}{100}\right)$

$\therefore$ Area of the new rectangle = $1.2x \times y\left(1 - \frac{A}{100}\right)$

Now, $xy = 1.2\, xy\left(1 - \frac{A}{100}\right) \Rightarrow 1 = 1.2\frac{(100 - A)}{100}$

$\Rightarrow 1.2\text{ A} = 120 - 100$

$\therefore \text{A} = \frac{20}{1.2} = 16\frac{2}{3}\%$

6. Let length and breadth of a rectangle be $71x$ and $61x$ m; then

$71x \times 61x = 17324 \Rightarrow x^2 = \frac{17324}{71 \times 61} = 4$

$\therefore x = 2$

Hence, length = $71 \times 2 = 142$ m; breadth $= 61 \times 2 = 122$ m

Since, perimeter = $2(142 + 122) = 2 \times 264 = 528$ m

7. Here, $20 + x + \frac{20 \times x}{100} = 50 \Rightarrow x + \frac{x}{5} = 30$

$\Rightarrow \frac{6x}{5} = 30 \quad \therefore x = \frac{5 \times 30}{6} = 25$

Hence, breadth was increased by 25%

8. Required number of stone slabs = $\frac{40 \times 15}{\frac{6}{10} \times \frac{5}{10}}$

$= \frac{40 \times 15 \times 100}{6 \times 5} = 2000$

9. Radius of circular plot = $\frac{396 \times 7}{2 \times 22} = 63$ m

Area of the circular plot = $\frac{22}{7} \times 63 \times 63$

$= 12{,}474$ m^2

VOLUME AND SURFACE AREA

1. If a solid sphere of 3 cm radius is melted and recast into a right circular cone whose base radius is same as that of the sphere, the height of the cone will be

A. 8 cm B. 12 cm
C. 6 cm D. 5 cm

2. Diameter of a roller is 2.4 m and it is 1.68 m long. If it takes 1000 complete revolutions once over to level a field, the area of the field is

A. 12672 sq. m B. 12671 sq. m
C. 12762 sq. m D. 11768 sq. m

3. If each edge of a cube is increased by 10%, then by how much per cent will the surface area of this cube be increased?

A. 21% B. 18%
C. 15% D. 20%

4. Height and base radius of a solid cylinder are 14 m and 4 m respectively. It is melted and recast into a solid cone of the same base radius as that of the cylinder, what will be the height of the cone?

A. 21 m B. 42 m
C. 48 m D. 54 m

5. A room is in the form of a cube of side 10 m. How many bales of cotton can be kept in it if each bale covers 5 cu m space?

A. 100 B. 175
C. 200 D. 225

6. Three cubes having side 2 cm, 3 cm and 4 cm respectively are melted together to form a new cube. The side of the new cube will be

A. 3.526 cm B. 4.628 cm
C. 4.626 cm D. 4.528 cm

7. If base diameter of a cylinder is increased by 50%, then by how much per cent its height must be decreased so as to keep its volume unaltered?

A. 45.56% B. 55.56%
C. 50.16% D. 62.33%

8. The surface area of a cube is 600 sq. m. Its diagonal is

A. $10\sqrt{3}$ cm B. $5\sqrt{3}$ cm
C. $4\sqrt{2}$ cm D. $10\sqrt{2}$ cm

9. The base diameter of a conical tomb is 28 m and its slant height is 50 m. Find the cost of white washing its curved surface at the rate of 80 paise per sq. m?

A. Rs. 1860 B. Rs. 1760
C. Rs. 1950 D. Rs. 1875

10. The volume of a cuboid is 1120 cu cm and its height is 5 cm while the length and the breadth of the cuboid are in the ratio 8 : 7. The length of this cylinder exceeds the breadth by

A. 4 cm B. 2 cm
C. 7 cm D. 5 cm

ANSWERS

1	2	3	4	5	6	7	8	9	10
B	A	A	B	C	C	B	A	B	B

SOME SELECTED EXPLANATORY ANSWERS

1. Volume of the cone = Volume of the sphere

$\therefore \quad \frac{1}{3}\pi(3)^2 \times h = \frac{4}{3}\pi \times 3^3 \Rightarrow h = 12$ cm

Hence, height of the cone = 12 cm.

2. Surface area of the roller = $2\pi rh$

$= 2 \times \frac{22}{7} \times 1.2 \times 1.68 = 12.672$ sq. m

In one complete revolution, the roller covers 12.672 sq. m.

$\therefore$ It will cover in 1000 revolutions

$= 12.672 \times 1000 = 12672$ sq. m

Hence, area of the field = 12672 sq. m.

3. Percentage increase in the surface area of the cube $= \left(x + y + \frac{xy}{100}\right)\%$

$= \left(10 + 10 + \frac{10 \times 10}{100}\right)\% = 21\%.$

4. Here,

volume of the cone = Volume of the cylinder

$\Rightarrow \quad \frac{1}{3}\pi r^2 \times \text{height} = \pi r^2 \times 14$

$\therefore \quad$ Height $= 14 \times 3 = 42$ m

Thus, height of the cone = 42 m.

5. Volume of the cubical room $= (10)^3$

$= 1000$ cu m

Number of cotton bales which can be placed in the room

$= \frac{\text{Volume of the room}}{\text{Volume of each cotton bale}} = \frac{1000}{5} = 200.$

6. Volume of the new cube $= 2^3 + 3^3 + 4^3$

$= 8 + 27 + 64 = 99$cu cm

$\therefore$ Side of the new cube $= \sqrt[3]{99} = 4.626$ cm.

7. Change in the volume of the cylinder

$= \left(x + y + (-z) + \frac{xy + y(-z) + (-zx)}{100} + \frac{xy(-z)}{100^2}\right)\%$

Since volume of the cylinder remains unchanged.

$\therefore \quad$ Change $= 0\%$

Now, $\left(50 + 50 + (-z) + \frac{50 \times 50 - 50z - 50z}{100} + \frac{50 \times 50 \times (-z)}{100^2}\right) = 0$

$\therefore \quad 100 - z + 25 - z - .25z = 0$

$\Rightarrow 2.25z = 125 \Rightarrow z = \frac{125}{2.25} = 55.56$

$\therefore$ **Height of the cylinder should be decreased by 55.56%.**

8. Here, $\quad 6 \times (\text{side})^2 = 600$

$\Rightarrow \quad \text{side}^2 = 100$

$\Rightarrow \quad \text{side} = \sqrt{100} = 10$ cm

$\therefore$ Diagonal of the cube $= \sqrt{3} \times \text{side}$

$= \sqrt{3} \times 10$

$= 10\sqrt{3}$ cm.

9. Area of the curved surface of the cone

$= \frac{22}{7} \times \frac{28}{2} \times 50 = 2200$ sq. m.

$\therefore$ Cost of white washing at 80 paise per sq. m

$= 2200 \times \frac{80}{100} = $ Rs. 1760.

10. Suppose the length and the breadth of the cuboid are $8x$ cm and $7x$ cm

$\therefore$ Here, $\quad 8x \times 7x \times 5 = 1120$

$\Rightarrow x^2 = \frac{1120}{280} = 4 = (2)^2 \quad \Rightarrow \quad x = 2$

$\therefore$ Length of the cuboid $= 8 \times 2 = 16$ cm

Breadth of the cuboid $= 7 \times 2 = 14$ cm

Hence, it is clear that length of the cuboid exceeds the breadth by 2 cm.

ALGEBRIC OPERATION

1. If $x + \frac{1}{x} = 15$, then the value of $x^2 + \frac{1}{x^2}$ will be:

A. 228 B. 230
C. 323 D. 223

2. If $x = 12$ and $y = 4$, the value of $(x+y)^{x/y}$ will be:

A. 4096 B. 3896
C. 4196 D. 5086

3. If $x = 9$, $y = \sqrt{17}$, then the value of $\left(x^2 - y^2\right)^{-1/2}$ will be:

A. 2^{-4} B. 2^2
C. 3^{-3} D. 2^{-3}

4. What should be added to $\frac{x}{y}$ to get $\frac{y}{x}$?

A. $\frac{x^2 - y^2}{xy}$ B. $\frac{y^2 - x^2}{xy}$
C. $\frac{2xy}{x^2 - y^2}$ D. $\frac{y^2 - x^2}{2xy}$

5. If $x + y = 2z$, then the value of $\left(\frac{x}{x-z} + \frac{z}{y-z}\right)$ will be:

A. 1 B. 4
C. 3/2 D. 2

6. If $x + y + z = 0$, then the value of $\frac{(x+y)(y+z)(z+x)}{xyz}$ will be:

A. –3 B. –2
C. 0 D. –1

7. If $x + \frac{1}{x} = 3$, the value of $x^4 + \frac{1}{x^4}$ will be:

A. 49 B. 47
C. 37 D. 42

8. If $\left(x + \frac{1}{x}\right)^2 = 0$, then the value of $\left(x^2 + \frac{1}{x^2}\right)$ will be:

A. 1 B. –1
C. 2 D. –2

9. If $\left(a + \frac{2}{a}\right) = 3$, then the value of $\left(a - \frac{2}{a}\right)$ will be:

A. ± 4 B. ± 5
C. ± 2 D. ± 1

10. If $\sqrt{a} + \frac{1}{\sqrt{a}} = 4$, then the value of $a^2 + \frac{1}{a^2}$ will be:

A. 194 B. 199
C. 178 D. 192

ANSWERS

1	2	3	4	5	6	7	8	9	10
D	A	D	B	A	D	B	D	D	A

EXPLANATORY ANSWERS

1. $\because \quad x + \frac{1}{x} = 15$

$\Rightarrow \quad \left(x+\frac{1}{x}\right)^2 = (15)^2$

$\Rightarrow \quad x^2 + \frac{1}{x^2} + 2.x\frac{1}{x} = 225$

$\therefore \quad x^2 + \frac{1}{x^2} = 225 - 2$

$= 223.$

2. $(x+y)^{x/y} = (12+4)^{12/4}$

$= (16)^3 = 4096.$

$[\because x = 12, y = 4]$

3. $\left(x^2-y^2\right)^{-1/2} = (81-17)^{-1/2}$

$= (64)^{-1/2} = \frac{1}{\sqrt{64}} = \frac{1}{8} = 2^{-3}.$

4. Suppose A is added to $\frac{x}{y}$, then $\frac{x}{y} + A = \frac{y}{x}$

$\Rightarrow A = \frac{y}{x} - \frac{x}{y} = \frac{y^2-x^2}{xy}$

$\therefore$ when $\frac{y^2-x^2}{xy}$ is added to $\frac{x}{y}$, the sum so obtained will be $\frac{y}{x}$.

5. $\because \quad x + y = 2z$

$\Rightarrow \quad x - z = z - y = -(y - z)$

$\therefore \quad \frac{x}{x-z} + \frac{z}{y-z} = \frac{x}{-(y-z)} + \frac{z}{y-z} = \frac{z-x}{y-z} = 1.$

$[\because x - z = z - y]$

6. $\because \quad x + y + z = 0$

$\Rightarrow \quad x + y = -z$

$x + y + z = 0$

$\Rightarrow \quad y + z = -x$

and $\quad x + y + z = 0 \Rightarrow z + x = -y$

$\therefore \quad \frac{(x+y)(y+z)(z+x)}{xyz} = \frac{-z.-x.-y}{xyz} = -1.$

7. $\because \quad x + \frac{1}{x} = 3 \Rightarrow \left(x+\frac{1}{x}\right)^2 = (3)^2$

$\Rightarrow \quad x^2 + \frac{1}{x^2} + 2.x.\frac{1}{x} = 9$

$\Rightarrow \quad x^2 + \frac{1}{x^2} = 9 - 2 = 7$

$\because \quad x^2 + \frac{1}{x^2} = 7$

$\Rightarrow \quad \left(x^2+\frac{1}{x^2}\right)^2 = (7)^2$

$\Rightarrow x^4 + \frac{1}{x^4} + 2.x^2.\frac{1}{x^2} = 49$

$\therefore \quad x^4 + \frac{1}{x^4} = 49 - 2 = 47.$

8. $\left(x+\frac{1}{x}\right)^2 = 0$

$\Rightarrow \quad x^2 + \frac{1}{x^2} + 2x.\frac{1}{x} = 0 \Rightarrow x^2 + \frac{1}{x^2} = -2.$

9. $\because \quad \left(a-\frac{2}{a}\right)^2 = \left(a+\frac{2}{a}\right)^2 - 4.a.\frac{2}{a}$

$= (3)^2 - 8 = 9 - 8 = 1$

$\therefore \quad \left(a-\frac{2}{a}\right) = \sqrt{1} = \pm 1.$

10. $\because \quad \sqrt{a}+\frac{1}{\sqrt{a}} = 4 \Rightarrow \left(\sqrt{a}+\frac{1}{\sqrt{a}}\right)^2 = (4)^2$

$= a + \frac{1}{a} + 2.\sqrt{a}.\frac{1}{\sqrt{a}} = 16$

$\because \quad \left(a+\frac{1}{a}\right) = 14 \Rightarrow \left(a+\frac{1}{a}\right)^2 = (14)^2.$

$\Rightarrow \quad a^2 + \frac{1}{a^2} + 2.a.\frac{1}{a} = 196$

$\therefore \quad a^2 + \frac{1}{a^2} = 196 - 2 = 194.$

GENERAL AWARENESS

1. OUR INDIA

INDIA : AT A GLANCE

Population (2011)	:	1,21,08,54,977
Capital	:	New Delhi
Area	:	32,87,263 sq km
Geographic Location	:	Between 8º4' and 37º6' north latitudes
	:	Between 68º7' and 97º25' east longitudes
Coastline Length	:	7,516.6 km including the coastline of Lakshadweep, Andaman & Nicobar Islands.
Major Languages	:	22
National Anthem	:	Jana Gana Mana
National Currency	:	Rupee (₹)
National Animal	:	Tiger
National Aquatic Animal	:	Dolphin
National Bird	:	Peacock
National River	:	Ganga
Characteristics of Indian	:	Socialist, Secular, Democratic, Republic
Legislature	:	Bicameral Legislature at the Centre Uni/Bicameral Legislatures in States
Executive	:	President, Vice-President and Council of Ministers at the Centre Governor and Council of Ministers in States
Judiciary	:	Independent from Executive with Supreme Court at the apex of the hierarchy
Total Road Length	:	66.71 Lakh kms (March 2024)

India: States & Union Territories

States/Union Territories	Capital	Area in (Sq. Km.)	Language
Andhra Pradesh	Amravati	1,60,229	Telugu
Arunachal Pradesh	Itanagar	83,743	Nyishi, Miji, Wancho etc.
Assam	Dispur	78,438	Assamese
Bihar	Patna	94,163	Hindi, Maithili
Chhattisgarh	Raipur	136,034	Hindi
Goa	Panji	3,702	Marathi and Konkani
Gujarat	Gandhinagar	1,96,024	Gujarati
Haryana	Chandigarh	44,212	Hindi
Himachal Pradesh	Shimla	55,673	Hindi and Pahari
Jharkhand	Ranchi	79,714	Hindi, Santhali
Karnataka	Bengaluru	1,91,791	Kannada
Kerala	Thiruvananthapuram	38,863	Malayalam
Madhya Pradesh	Bhopal	308,000	Hindi
Maharashtra	Mumbai	307,713	Marathi
Manipur	Imphal	22,327	Manipuri
Meghalaya	Shillong	22,429	Khasi, Garo and English
Mizoram	Aizawl	21,081	Mizo and English
Nagaland	Kohima	16,579	Sema, English
Odisha	Bhubaneswar	155,707	Odia
Punjab	Chandigarh	50,362	Punjabi
Rajasthan	Jaipur	3,42,239	Hindi and Rajasthani
Sikkim	Gangtok	7,096	Bhutia, Nepali, Lepcha and Limbu
Tamil Nadu	Chennai	1,30,058	Tamil
Telangana	Hyderabad	1,14,840	Telugu
Tripura	Agartala	10,491	Bengali, Kakborak
Uttar Pradesh	Lucknow	2,40,928	Hindi and Urdu
Uttarakhand	Dehradun	53,484	Hindi
West Bengal	Kolkata	88,752	Bengali
Jammu & Kashmir	Srinagar (Summer) Jammu (Winter)	2,22,236*	Kashmiri, Urdu, Dogri
Andaman & Nicobar Island	Shri Vijaya Puram	8,249	Bengali, Hindi, Nicobarese, Tamil, Telugu, and Malayalam
Chandigarh	Chandigarh	114	Hindi, Punjabi
Dadra & Nagar Haveli and Daman and Diu	Daman	603	Gujarati and Hindi
Delhi	Delhi	1483	Hindi, Punjabi and Urdu
Lakshadweep	Kavaratti	32	Malayalam
Puducherry	Puducherry	492	Tamil, Telugu, Malayalam, English and French
Ladakh	Leh	—	Ladakhi

* *Including areas of Ladakh and illegally occupied by China and Pakistan.*

POPULATION

India's population according to the figures of 2011 Census, was 1,21,08,54,977 at the sunrise of March 01, 2011. India's population constitutes nearly 17.5 per cent of the total world population while her geographical area is only 2.42 per cent of the world area. With such a huge population to support on so small an area, the country finds herself in great difficulty in making any significant dent on its poverty and economic backwardness. India's national income, which is barely 2 per cent of the total global income, clearly shows the tremendous strain of population on her economy.

2011 Census Highlights

Population of India–Total Indian population is 17.7% of total world population	:	1,21,08,54,977 (Male: 62,32,70,258; Female: 58,75,84,719)
Decadal Growth (2001-2011)	:	17.7 per cent (Males: 17.1 per cent; Females: 18.3 per cent)
Hightest Decadal Growth (State-wise)	:	Meghalaya (27.9 per cent)
Lowest Decadal Growth (State-wise)	:	Nagaland (–0.6 per cent)
Most populous State	:	Uttar Pradesh
Density of population	:	382 persons per sq. km.
Most densly populated State	:	Bihar : 1106 per sq. km
Sex Ratio	:	943 females per 1000 males
Total Literacy Rate	:	73% (Males – 80.9%), (Females – 64.6%)
Highest Literacy (State-wise)	:	Kerala (94%)
Lowest Literacy (State-wise)	:	Bihar (61.8%)

OTHER DETAILS

(a) Population of India

1951	36,10,88,090	1961	43,92,34,771
1971	54,81,59,652	1981	68,33,29,097
1991	84,64,21,039	2001	102,87,37,436
2011	1,21,08,54,977		

(b) Density of Population (Persons per square kilometre)

1951	113	1961	138
1971	177	1981	216
1991	267	2001	324
2011	382		

(c) Annual Compound Rate of Growth

1941-1951	1.25 per cent	1951-1961	1.96 per cent
1961-1971	2.22 per cent	1971-1981	2.20 per cent
1981-1991	2.14 per cent	1991-2001	1.95 per cent
2001-2011	1.64 per cent		

India's Population At A Glance : 2011 (Final Data)

S.I. No.	State/UTs	Population	Sex Ratio	Density	Literacy Rate	(%) Decadel Growth Rate (2001-2011)
1.	Jammu & Kashmir	1,25,41,302	889	124	67.2	23.6
2.	Himachal Pradesh	68,64,602	972	123	82.8	12.9
3.	Punjab	2,77,43,338	895	551	75.8	13.9
4.	Chandigarh	10,55,450	818	9258	86.0	17.2
5.	Uttarakhand	1,00,86,292	963	189	78.8	18.8
6.	Haryana	2,53,51,462	879	573	75.6	19.9
7.	Delhi	1,67,87,941	868	11320	86.2	21.2
8.	Rajasthan	6,85,48,437	928	200	66.1	21.3
9.	Uttar Pradesh	19,98,12,341	912	829	66.7	20.2
10.	Bihar	10,40,99,452	918	1106	61.8	25.4
11.	Sikkim	6,10,577	890	86	81.4	12.9
12.	Arunachal Pradesh	13,83,727	938	17	65.4	26.0
13.	Nagaland	19,78,502	931	119	79.6	–0.6
14.	Manipur	28,55,794	985	128	79.2	24.50
15.	Mizoram	10,97,206	976	52	91.3	23.5
16.	Tripura	36,73,917	960	350	87.2	14.8
17.	Meghalaya	29,66,889	989	132	74.4	27.9
18.	Assam	3,12,05,576	958	398	72.2	17.1
19.	West Bengal	9,12,76,115	950	1028	76.3	13.8
20.	Jharkhand	3,29,88,134	949	414	66.4	22.4
21.	Odisha	4,19,74,218	979	270	72.9	14.0
22.	Chhattisgarh	2,55,45,198	991	189	70.3	22.6
23.	Madhya Pradesh	7,26,26,809	931	236	69.3	20.3
24.	Gujarat	6,04,39,692	919	308	78.0	19.3
25.	Daman & Diu	2,43,247	618	2191	87.1	53.8
26.	Dadra & Nagar Haveli	3,43,709	774	700	76.2	55.9
27.	Maharashtra	11,23,74,333	929	365	82.3	16.0
28.	Andhra Pradesh	4,93,86,799	993	308	67.0	11.0
29.	Karnataka	6,10,95,297	973	319	75.4	15.6
30.	Goa	14,58,545	973	394	88.7	8.2
31.	Lakshadweep	64,473	947	2149	91.8	6.3
32.	Kerala	3,34,06,061	1084	860	94.0	4.9
33.	Tamil Nadu	7,21,47,030	996	555	80.1	15.6
34.	Puducherry	12,47,953	1037	2546	85.8	28.1
35.	Andaman & Nicobar Island	3,80,581	876	46	86.6	6.9
36.	Telangana	3,51,93,978	988	307	66.4	13.58
	India	**1,21,08,54,977**	**943**	**382**	**73.0**	**17.7**

* * * * *

2. National Symbols

State Emblem: State Emblem of India is an adaptation from the Sarnath Lion Capital of Ashoka. It was adopted by the Government of India on January 26, 1950. In the adapted form, only three lions are visible, the fourth being hidden from the view. The wheel (Dharma Chakra) appears in relief in the centre of the abacus with a bull on the right and a horse on the left. The bell-shaped lotus has been omitted. The words ''Satyameva Jayate'' meaning ''Truth alone triumphs'' are inscribed below the Emblem in Devanagari script.

National Flag: The National Flag of India is a horizontal tricolour of deep saffron (Kesari), white and dark green in equal proportion. In the centre of the white band there is a wheel in navy blue colour. It has 24 spokes. The ratio of the length and the breadth of the flag is 3 : 2. Its design was adopted by the Constituent Assembly of India on July 22, 1947.

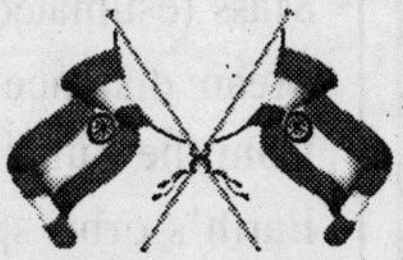

National Anthem: Rabindranath Tagore's song 'Jana-gana-mana' was adopted by the Constituent Assembly as the National Anthem of India on January 24, 1950.

Jana-gan-mana-adhinayaka jaya he,
Bharata-bhagya-vidhata
Punjab-Sindh-Gujarat-Maratha-Dravida-
Utkala-Banga
Vindhya-Himachala-Yamuna-Ganga Uchhala-
jaladhi-taranga.
Tava subha name jage, Tava subha asisa mange,
Gahe tava jaya gatha,
Jana-gana-mangala-dayak, jaya he Bharata
bhagya vidhata,
Jaya he, jaya he, jaya he, Jaya jaya jaya,
jaya he.

National Song: Bankim Chandra Chatterji's 'Vande Mataram' which was a source of inspiration to the people in their struggle for freedom, has been adopted as National Song. It has an equal status with the National Anthem.

Vande Mataram
Sujalam, suphalam, malayaja-shitalam,
Shasya shyamalam, Mataram
Shubhrajyotsna,pulkita yaminim,
Phulla kusumita drumadalashobhinim,
Subhasinim sumadhura—bhashinim,
Sukhadam, Varadam, Mataram.

National Bird and Animal of India: Peacock and Tiger; **National Aquatic Animal:** Dolphin; **National Flower:** Lotus; **National Calendar:** It was adopted on March 22, 1957. It has 365 days in the year and the first month of the year is Chaitra.

Months of the National Calendar

(1) Chaitra, (2) Vaishakha, (3) Jaishtha, (4) Ashadha, (5) Shravan, (6) Bhadra, (7) Ashvina, (8) Kartika, (9) Marga-Shirsha, (10) Pausha, (11) Magha, (12) Phalguna.

*****

3. THE UNIVERSE

The Solar System: Some Facts

Number of Planets: 8—Mercury, Venus, Earth, Mars, Jupiter, Saturn, Uranus and Neptune.

Largest most

Massive planet	Jupiter
Brightest planet	Venus
Brightest star	Sirius
Fastest orbiting planet	Mercury
Longest (Synodic) day	Mercury
Planet with largest moon	Jupiter
Greatest average density	Earth
Tallest mountain	Mars
Strongest magnetic fields	Jupiter
Most circular orbit	Venus
Shortest (synodic) day	Jupiter
Hottest planet	Venus
No moons	Mercury, Venus
Planet with moon with most eccentric orbit	Neptune
Lowest average density	Saturn
Greatest amount of liquid on the surface	Earth

The Earth: Facts and Data

Composition of the Earth: Aluminium (0.4%), Sulphur (2.7%), Silicon (13%), Oxygen (28%), Calcium (1.2%), Nickel (2.7%), Magnesium (17%), Iron (35%)

Surface area	:	510100500 sq km
Land Surface (29.1%)	:	148950800 sq km
Ocean Surface (70.9%)	:	361149700 sq km
Type of water	:	97% salt, 3% fresh
Total area of water	:	382672000 sq km
Equatorial diameter	:	12753 km
Equatorial Circumference	:	40066 km
Polar Circumference	:	39992 km
Polar diameter	:	12710 km
Equatorial radius	:	6376 km
Polar radius	:	6335 km
Mass (estimated weight)	:	594×10^{19} metric tons
Mean distance from the Sun	:	149407000 km
Earth's orbit speed (around sun)	:	107320 kmph
Period of Revolution (round the sun)	:	365 days 5 hrs 48 min. 45.51 seconds
Time of Rotation (on its axis)	:	23 hrs 56 min. 4.09 seconds
Inclination of the axis (to the plane of the eclipitc)	:	23°27'

Solar Statistics

Distance from the Earth	:	149.8 million km
Absolute Visual Magnitude	:	4.75
Diameter Core	:	13,84,000 km
Temperature	:	15000000 K
Photosphere Temperature	:	5770 K

Rotation as seen from the Earth (at the equator)	:	25.38 days
Rotation as seen from the Earth (near the poles)	:	33 days
Chemical Composition	:	Hydrogen 71% Helium 26.5% Other elements 2.5%
Age	:	About 4.5 billion years
Expected lifetime of a normal star	:	About 10 billion years

Oceans of the World

Pacific	16,62,41,000 sq km
Atlantic	8,65,57,000 sq km
Indian	7,34,27,000 sq km
Arctic	94,85,000 sq km

Longest Rivers

Name	*Country/ Continent*	*Length in Kilometres*
Nile	Africa	6650
Amazon	S. America	6437
Mississippi-Missouri	USA	6020
Yangtze-Kiang	China	5494
Ob-Irtysh	Russia	5410
Lena	Russia	4400
Hwang Ho	China	4344
Niger	Africa	4180
St. Lawrence	Canada (USA)	4023
Murray-Darling	Australia	3780
Volga	Russia	3690
Indus	Asia	2900
Danube	Europe	2850
Orinoco	S. America	2575

Major Riverside Cities

City	*River*	*Country*
Alexandria	Nile	Egypt
Amsterdam	Amsel	The Netherland
Ankara	Kizil	Turkiye
Baghdad	Tigris	Iraq
Bangkok	Menam	Thailand
Belgrade	Danube	Serbia
Berlin	Spree	Germany
Budapest	Danube	Hungary
Cairo	Nile	Egypt
Chittagong	Karnaphuli	Bangladesh
Karachi	Indus	Pakistan
Khartoum	Blue & White Nile	Sudan
Lahore	Ravi	Pakistan
Lisbon	Tagus	Portugal
Liverpool	Mersey	England
London	Thames	England
Moscow New	Moskva	Russia
Orleans	Mississipi	USA
New York	Hudson	USA
Paris	Seine	France
Yangon	Irawadi	Myanmar
Rome	Tiber	Italy

Major Gulfs of the World

Names	*Areas (Sq. Km.)*
Gulf of Mexico	15,44,000
Gulf of Hudson	12,33,000
Arabian Gulf	2,38,000
Gulf of St. Lawrence	2,37,000
Gulf of California	1,62,000
English Channel	89,900

Major Mountain Ranges of the World

Range	*Location*	*Length (km)*
Andes	South America	7,200
Himalayas-Karakoram-Hindukush	South Central Asia	5,000
Rockies	North America	4,800

Range	Location	Length (km)
Great Dividing Range	East Australia	3,600
Atlas	North West Africa	1,930
Western Ghats	Western India	1,610
Caucasus	Europe	1,200
Alaska	USA	1,130
Alps	Europe	1,050

Largest Deserts of the World

Subtropical

Sahara, North Africa	94,00,000 sq. km.
Kalahari, Southern Africa	9,00,000 sq. km.
Thar, India/Pakistan	2,00,000 sq. km.
Great Sandy, Australia	4,00,000 sq. km.

Cool Coastal

Atacama, Chile S.A.	1,40,000 sq. km

Cool Winter

Gobi, China	13,00,000 sq. km.
Colorado, Western USA (also called the painted desert)	3,37,000 sq. km.

Atmosphere

Composition of Gases in Atmosphere

Nitrogen	78.03%
Oxygen	20.99%
Argon	0.93%
Carbon dioxide	0.03%
Hydrogen	0.01%
Neon	0.0018%
Helium	0.0005%
Crypton	0.0001%
Xenon	0.000,005%
Ozone	0.000,0001%

World Important Local Winds

Chinoon: A warm day wind frequently experienced on the eastern side of the Rocky Mountains.

Fohn: A warm dry wind descending a mountain, as on the north side of the Alps.

Haboob: A sand storm or a dust storm in north and north-east Sudan near Khartoum.

Bagrrio: It is the tropical cyclone of the Philippine Island.

Loo: A hot wind which blows in summer season in Indian sub-continent.

Papasago: A cold northerly wind sometimes felt on the Mexico plateau.

Bora: It is the name given to the cold dry wind experienced particularly in winter along the eastern coast of the Atlantic Ocean and in northern Italy.

Black Toller: A hot dust wind which blows in the vast plain of North America.

Principal Mountain Peaks of the World

Mountains	Height in Metres	Range	Date of First Ascent
1. Mount Everest	8,848	Himalayas	May 29, 1953
2. K-2 (Godwin Austen)	8,611	Karakoram	July 31, 1954
3. Kanchenjunga	8,597	Himalayas	May 25, 1955
4. Lhotse	8,511	Himalayas	May 18, 1956
5. Makalu I	8,481	Himalayas	May 15, 1955
6. Dhaulagiri I	8,167	Himalayas	May 13, 1960
7. Mansalu I	8,156	Himalayas	May 9, 1956
8. Chollyo	8,153	Himalayas	Oct. 19, 1954
9. Nanga Parbat	8,124	Himalayas	July 3, 1953
10. Annapurna I	8,091	Himalayas	June 3, 1950

Mountains	Height in Metres	Range	Date of First Ascent
11. Gasherbrum I	8,068	Karakoram	July 5, 1958
12. Broad Peak I	8,047	Karakoram	June 9, 1957
13. Gasherbrum II	8,034	Karakoram	July 7, 1956
14. Shisha Pangma (Gosainthan)	8,014	Himalayas	May 2, 1964
15. Gasherbrum III	7,952	Karakoram	Aug. 11, 1975

Types of World Agriculture

Viticulture: The cultivation of the vine for production of grapes and wine.
Pisciculture: The breeding, rearing and transplantation of fish by artificial means.
Sericulture: The raising of silk worms for the production of raw silk.
Horticulture: To grow flower front, vegetables on small plots.
Apiculture: Bee keeping on a commercial scale for the sale of honey.
Floriculture: The cultivation of flowers or flowering plants.
Mariculture: Sea farming, or the cultivation of marine plants and animals for commercial purposes.
Olericulture: The cultivation of vegetables and kitchen herbs.

Famous Straits of the World

Strait	Between	Country
Malacca Strait	Andaman Sea and South China Sea	Indonesia
Palk Strait	Mannar and Bay of Bengal	India-Sri Lanka
Magellan Strait	Pacific and South Atlantic Ocean	Chile
Dover Strait	English Channel and North Sea	England-France
Berring Strait	Berring Sea and Chukasi Sea	Alaska-Russia
Sugaroo Strait	Japan Sea and Pacific Ocean	Japan
Sunda Strait	Java and Indian Ocean	Indonesia
Gibralter Strait	Mediterranean Sea and Atlantic Ocean	Spain
Harmuj Strait	Persia and Bay of Oman	Oman-Iran
Hudson Strait	Bay of Hudson and Atlantic Ocean	Canada

World's Famous Official Documents

White Paper: India; **Orange Book:** Netherlands; **Yellow Book:** France; **Green Book:** Italy and Iran; **White Book:** Portugal, China and Germany; **Grey Book:** Japan and Belgium.

Famous Newspapers of the World

Newspaper	Place of Publishing	Language
Daily News	New York (America)	English
Guardian	London (Britain)	English
Pravada	Moscow (Russia)	Russian
Al-Ahram	Cairo (Egypt)	Arabic
Merdeca	Jakarta (Indonesia)	Indonesian
Times	London (Britain)	English
People's Daily	Beijing (China)	Chinese
New Statesman	Britain	English
Daily Mirror	Britain	English
Hindu, Hindustan Times, Times of India, Tribune, Statesman, Indian Express, Economic Times	India	English
Hindustan, Nav Bharat Times, Rashtriya Sahara, Dainik Jagaran, Punjab Kesari	India	Hindi

Important Boundary Lines

Boundary Line	Countries
Hindenberg Line	Germany-Poland
Maginot Line	France and Germany
Mannerhein Line	Russia-Finland
Mc Mahon Line	India and China
Order Niesse Line	Germany-Poland
Radcliff Line	India-Pakistan
Seigfrid Line	Germany-France
Durand Line	Pakistan and Afghanistan
17th Parallel	The line which defined the boundary between North Vietnam and South Vietnam before the two were united.
38th Parallel	North Korea and South Korea
49th Parallel	U.S.A. and Canada

Areawise 10 Big and Small Countries

10 Big Countries

S. No.	Country	Area (sq. km)
1.	Russia (Europe-Asia)	17,098,242
2.	Canada (N. America)	99,84,670
3.	China (Asia)	95,96,961
4.	U.S.A. (N. America)	93,72,614
5.	Brazil (S. America)	85,14,877
6.	Australia (S. Pacific)	77,41,220
7.	India (Asia)	32,87,263
8.	Argentina (S. America)	27,80,400
9.	Kazakhstan (Europe-Asia)	27,24,900
10.	Algeria (Africa)	23,81,741

10 Small Countries

S. No.	Country	Area (Sq. km)
1.	Vatican City (Europe)	0.44
2.	Monaco (Europe)	1.95
3.	Nauru (Southern Pacific)	21.10
4.	Tuvalu	26.00
5.	San Marino (Europe)	61.00
6.	Liechtenstein (Europe)	160.00
7.	Marshall Island (Central Pacific)	181.00
8.	St. Kitts and Nevis (Eastern Caribbean)	261.00
9.	Maldives	298.00
10.	Malta	316.00

Populationwise 10 Big and Small Countries

10 Big Countries

S. No.	Country	Population (2021) (In Million)
1.	China (Asia)	1,397.898
2.	India (Asia)	1,339
3.	U.S.A. (North America)	334.998
4.	Indonesia (Asia)	275.122
5.	Pakistan (Asia)	238.181
6.	Nigeria (Africa)	219.464
7.	Brazil (South America)	213.445
8.	Bangladesh (Asia)	164.099
9.	Russia (Europe-Asia)	142.321
10.	Japan (Asia)	124.687

10 Small Countries

S. No.	Country	Population (2021)
1.	Vatican City (Europe)	1000
2.	Tuvalu (Southern Pacific)	11,448
3.	Palau (Western Pacific)	21,613
4.	San Marino (Europe)	34,467
5.	Monaco (Europe)	31,223
6.	Liechstein (Europe)	39,425
7.	St. Kitts and Nevis (Eastern Caribbean)	54,149
8.	Marshall Island (Central Pacific)	78,831
9.	Seychelles	96,387
10.	St. Vincent and The Grenadines	1,01,145

Signals/Signs and Meaning

Signal/Sign	*Meaning*
Red Triangle	Family Planning
Red Cross	Medical Help
Red Light	Danger, 'Stop' for the movement of vehicles
Green Light	Go
Olive Branch	Peace
White Pigeon or Dove	Peace
Black Strip on Arm	(i) Opposition (ii) Sorrow
Black Flag	Opposition
Red Flag	(i) Danger (ii) Revolution
White Flag	Treaty or Surrender
Yellow Flag	Vehicles with patients of contagious diseases
Two Bones across with a Skull	Danger of electricity
Half mast flown Flag	National mourning
Lotus	Sign of civilization and culture
Wheel (Chakra)	Sign of Progress
A blind folded woman with scale in hand	Sign of Justice
Reversed flown	National calamity flag

National Emblems of Important Countries

Country	*National Emblem*
America	Golden Rod
Australia	Kangaroo
Ireland	Shamrock
Italy	White Lily
Israel	Candelabrum
Iran	Rose
Canada	White Lily
Great Britain	Rose
Chile	Candor and Huemul
Germany	Corn Flower
Japan	Chrysanthemum
Zimbabwe	Zimbabwe Bird
Denmark	Beach
Turkiye	Crescent and Star
The Netherlands	Lion
New Zealand	Kiwi, Fern Southern Cross
Norway	Lion
Nepal	Kukri
Pakistan	Crescent
Poland	Eagle
France	Lily
Belgium	Lion
Bangladesh	Water Lily
Mongolia	The Soyombo
Russia	Double headed eagle
Lebanon	Cedar Tree
Sudan	Secretary Bird
Syria	Eagle
India	Lioned Capital

The Continents of the World

Name	*Area (In sq. km.)*	*Population (2021) (In million)*	*Per cent of the World's Population*
Asia (including the Middle East)	44,579,000	4,584	59.1
Africa	30,065,000	1,375	17.4
North America	24,256,000	373	4.78
South America	17,819,000	651	8.4
Antarctica	13,209,000	—	—
Europe	99,38,000	747	9.8
Australia (plus Oceania)	76,87,000	41.66	0.5

International Date Line

It roughly corresponds to 180°E or W meridian of longitude which falls on the opposite side of the Greenwich meridian and the date changes by one day (i.e. 24 hours), as this line is crossed. On crossing this line from east to west a day is added, and a day is subtracted on crossing it from west to east.

* * * * *

4. UNITED NATIONS

- **Origin:** UN Charter was signed by 50 members on June 26, 1945. It officially came into existence on October 24, 1945.
- **UN Charter:** The Charter is the Constitution of the UNO and contains its aims and objectives and rules and regulations for its functioning.
- **Aims and Objectives:** They are security, welfare and human rights.
- **Headquarters:** New York.
- **Flag:** The flag is light blue in colour, and emblazoned in white, in its centre is the UN symbol—a polar map of world embraced by twin olive branches open at the top.
- **Official Languages:** The official languages of the UN are: English, French, Chinese, Russian, Arabic and Spanish. However, working languages are English & French only.
- **Main Organs of the UN:** There are six main organs:

  1. General Assembly
  2. Security Council
  3. Economic and Social Council
  4. Trusteeship Council
  5. International Court of Justice, and
  6. Secretariat.

  1. **General Assembly:** It consists of representative of all members of the UN. Each member country has only one vote. It meets once a year and passes UN Budget.
  2. **Security Council:** It is the Executive body of the UN and is mainly responsible for maintaining international peace and security. It has 15 members, 5 of which (USA, UK, France, Russia and China) are permanent members. The 10 non-permanent members are elected by General Assembly for two-year term and are not eligible for immediate re-election.
  3. **Economic and Social Council:** It has 54 members elected by General Assembly.
  4. **Trusteeship Council:** It looks after interest of the people in areas not yet independent and leads them towards self-government.
  5. **International Court of Justice:** It has 15 judges, no two of whom may be nationals of the same state. They are elected by General Assembly and Security Council for a term of 9 years. The Court elects its President and Vice-President for a 3-year term.
  6. **Secretariat:** It is the Secretariat of the UN and is headed by the Secretary General.

Years Observed by United Nations

1967: International Tourism Year
1968: Human Rights Year
1970: International Education Year
1972: International Book Year
1973: Copernicus Year
1974: World Population Year
1975: International Women's Year
1979: International Year of the Child
1981: International Year of Disabled
1983: World Communication Year
1985: International Youth Year
1986: International Year of Peace
1987: International Year of Shelter for the Homeless

1990: International Literacy Year
1992: International Space Year
1993: International Year for World's Indigenous People
1994: International Year of Family
1995: International Year of Tolerance
1996: International Year for Eradication of Poverty
1998: Human Rights Year
1999: Year of Older Persons
2000: Year of the Culture of Peace
2001: International Year of Volunteer
2002: International Year of Eco-tourism
2003: International Year of Fresh Water
2004: International Rice Year
2005: International Year of Sports and Physical Education
2006: International Year of Deserts and Desertification
2008: International Year of Potato
2009: International Year of Astronomy
2010: International Year of Bio-diversity
2011: International Year of Forest
2012: International Year of Cooperatives
2013: International Year of Water Cooperation
2014: International Year of Family Farming
2015: International Year of Soils
2016: International Year of Pulses
2017: International Year of Sustainable Tourism for Development
2019: International Year of Indigenous Languages.
2020: International Year of Plant Health
2021: International Year of Peace and Trust
2022: International Year of Artisanal Fisheries and Aquaculture
2023: International Year of Millets
2024: International Year of Camelids
2025: International Year of Glaciers Preservation; International Year of Quantum Science and Technology; International Year of Cooperatives; International Year of Peace and Trust.

- **Present Membership:** At present 193 countries are members of the UN. South Sudan is the latest entrant to this world organisation.

Famous International Organisations, Headquarters and Year of Establishment

International Organisations	*Headquarters*	*Year of Establishment*
United Nations (U.N.)	New York	1945
International Monetary Fund (I.M.F.)	Washington D.C.	1945
World Health Organisation (W.H.O.)	Geneva	1948
Food & Agricultural Organisation (FAO)	Rome	1945
International Labour Organisation (ILO)	Geneva	1919
UNESCO	Paris	1946
International Court of Justice	The Hague	1945
Universal Postal Union (UPU)	Berne	1874
International Civil Aviation Organisation (ICAO)	Montreal	1947
UNIDO	Vienna	1966
International Atomic Energy Agency (IAEA)	Vienna	1957
International Finance Corporation (IFC)	Washington	1956
United Nations Development Programme (UNDP)	New York	1965
UNICEF	New York	1946
International Maritime Organisation (IMO)	London	1948
World Meteorological Organisation (WMO)	Geneva	1950
International Telecommunication Union (ITU)	Geneva	1865
Arab League	Cairo	1945
Commonwealth of Nations	London	1931
World Trade Organisation (WTO)	Geneva	1995

International Organisations	*Headquarters*	*Year of Establishment*
International Development Association (IDA)	Washington D.C.	1960
International Bank for Reconstruction and Development (IBRD)	Washington D.C.	1944
World Intellectual Property Organisation (WIPO)	Geneva	1967
Organisation of Islamic Conference (OIC)	Jeddah (Saudi Arabia)	1969
Red Cross	Geneva	1863
Interpol	Lyons	1923
Asian Development Bank (ADB)	Manila	1966
North Atlantic Treaty Organisation (NATO)	Brussels	1949
Association of South East Asian Nations (ASEAN)	Jakarta	1967
South Asian Association for Regional Cooperation (SAARC)	Kathmandu	1985
Asia-Pacific Economic Cooperation (APEC)	Singapore	1989
Organisation for Economic Cooperation and Development (OECD)	Paris	1961
Organisation of Petroleum Exporting Countries (OPEC)	Vienna	1960
Common Wealth of Independent States (CIS)	Minsk	1991
International Olympic Committee (IOC)	Lausanne	1894
European Union (EU)	Brussels	Changed form of EEC Established in 1958
Amnesty International (AI)	London	1961
Shanghai Cooperation Organisation (SCO)	Beijing	2002
BRICS Bank	Shanghai	2014

* * * * *

5. Indian Constitution & Polity

Indian Constitution is a comprehensive document and it is the lengthiest written Constitution in the World.

The Preamble of the Constitution: "We the people of India, having solemnly resolved to Constitute India into a Sovereign, Socialist, Secular Democratic Republic and to secure to all its citizen."

Justice: Social, economic and political.

Liberty: Of thought, expression, belief, faith and worship.

Equality: Of status and of opportunity, and to promote among them all.

Fraternity: Assuring the dignity of the individual and the unity and integrity of the nation. In our Constituent Assembly this twenty-sixth day of November, 1949, do hereby adopt, enact and give to ourselves this Constitution.

SCHEDULES TO THE CONSTITUTION

The Constitution of India originally contained only eight schedules. Presently there are 12 schedules in the constitution.

First Schedule: It consists the list of the States and Union territories. ***Second Schedule:*** This Schedule is related to salary and allowances of the President, Governors, Speaker, Supreme Court and High Court Judges etc. ***Third Schedule:*** Contains forms of oath and affirmation. ***Fourth Schedule:*** Contains allocation of seats to each State and Union territory in the Council of States. ***Fifth Schedule:*** Provides for administration and control of scheduled areas and scheduled tribes. ***Sixth Schedule:*** Provides for administration of Tribal Areas in Assam, Meghalaya and Mizoram. ***Seventh Schedule:*** Distribution of powers and functions between the centre and state governments under three lists. ***Eighth Schedule:*** The languages recognised by Parliament. ***Ninth Schedule:*** It contains laws passed by the Union or States which cannot be taken to courts. ***Tenth Schedule:*** Provisions as to disqualification on the ground of political defection. ***Eleventh Schedule:*** Provisions regarding powers, authority etc. of Panchayati Raj institutions. ***Twelfth Schedule:*** Provisions regarding powers, authority etc. of Municipalities etc.

Foreign Sources of Indian Constitution

Foreign Sources	*Subject*
Britain	Parliamentary system, collective responsibilities of Cabinet
America	Fundamental right, Citizenship, Independent Judiciary, Judicial review
Canada	Division of powers
Ireland	Directive principles
Germany	Emergency provisions
Russia	Fundamental duties
Australia	Concurrent list

THE SUPREME COURT

The Supreme Court of India consists of the Chief Justice and other Judges whose number is prescribed by the Parliament from time to time. In 1950 there was a Chief Justice and there were 7 Judges. But the number of Judges continued increasing as per the need. The Supreme Court, at present, consists of the Chief Justice and 33 Judges.

The Chief Justice and other Judges of the Supreme Court are appointed by the President of India. For appointing the Chief Justice of India, the other Judges of the Supreme or High Courts may be consulted. Usually, the senior-most Judge in the Supreme Court is appointed as the Chief Justice. For the appointment of other Judges of the Supreme Court, the Chief Justice has to be consulted. Usually, the Chief Justice himself consults a collegium of the four senior-most Judges, and all of them need to agree for any candidate to be recommended for the appointment of a judge.

A person can be appointed as a Judge of the Supreme Court only if he/she:

I. is a citizen of India;

II. must have been at least a Judge of a High Court or of two or more such Courts in succession for at least five years; or

III. must have been an advocate of a High Court or of two or more such Courts in succession for at least ten years; or

IV. is, in the opinion of the President, a distinguished jurist.

Judges of the Supreme Court hold office till they attain the age of 65 years. But they may be removed from office by an order of the President, passed after an address by each House of Parliament supported by a special majority on the ground of proved misbehaviour or incapacity.

The Jurisdiction and Powers of the Supreme Court

The Supreme Court of India is a powerful judiciary. The Constitution of India has defined its jurisdiction and powers in detail, it has Original. Appellate and Advisory Jurisdictions Besides these jurisdictions, it has a few other important functions.

(*i*) **Original Jurisdiction:** The Supreme Court alone has the authority to hear directly certain cases. These are:

(*a*) Disputes between the Union government and one or more State governments,

(*b*) Disputes between two or more States,

(*c*) Disputes between the Government of India and one or more States on the one side and one or more States on the other side.

(*ii*) **Appellate Jurisdiction:** The power of a superior or higher court to hear and decide appeals against the judgment of the lower court is called appellate jurisdiction. The Supreme Court is a court of appeal for constitutional, civil and criminal cases. It can hear appeals against the judgments of the High Courts. It also has the power to review its own judgment. It may in its own discretion grant special lease to appeal against any judgment or order delivered or passed by any court or tribunal within the territory of India.

Moreover, an Appeal may come to the Supreme Court in any criminal case, if the High Court certifies that the case is fit for appeal to the Supreme Court. The special appellate power has become a handy weapon in the hands of the Court to review the decisions pertaining to elections and Labour and Industrial Tribunals.

(*iii*) **Advisory Jurisdiction:** The Supreme Court has a special advisory jurisdiction in matters which may specifically be referred to it by the President of India. If at any time, it appears to the President that a question of law or fact has arisen or is likely to arise, which is of such public importance that it is urgent to obtain the opinion of the Supreme Court on it, he/she may refer it to the Supreme Court. The Supreme Court may, after such hearing as it thinks fit, report to the President its opinion thereon. The report or the opinion of the Supreme Court is of course, not binding on the President. Similarly, there is no compulsion for the Court to give its advice.

(*iv*) **Judicial Review:** The Supreme Court of India has the power to examine the validity of laws or executive orders. The Supreme Court has the powers to interpret the Constitution, and through this it has assumed the power of judicial review.

(*v*) **Guardian of the Constitution:** As the interpreter of the Constitution, the Supreme Court has the power to protect and defend the Constitution. If the Court finds that any law or executive order is against the Constitution, the same can be declared unconstitutional or invalid. Similarly the Supreme Court also acts as the custodian and protector of Fundamental Rights.

PARLIAMENT

Parliament is the national legislature of the Indian Union. It consists of two Houses known as the Council of States or the Rajya Sabha and the House of People or Lok Sabha. The President is an integal part of Parliament.

Rajya Sabha: The Rajya Sabha is the Upper House of the Parliament and it is constituted of representatives from the States or the Constituent units of the Indian Union. It is a permanent body, one third of its members retiring after every two years. Its maximum strength is 250. Out of these, twelve members are nominated by the President from well-known personalities in the realm of Science, Art, Literature and Social Service. Rest of 238 representatives of the States and Union Territories are elected.

Lok Sabha: The Lok Sabha whose life is five years, is the Lower House of Parliament and comprises of members directly elected by the people. The House of the people (Lok Sabha) at present consists of 543 members directly elected from the states and from Union Territories. By the 104th amendment of the Constitution the reservation for two members of Anglo Indian Community nominated by President have been abolished. The House of the People shall continue for five years (unless sooner dissolved) from the date of its meeting and no longer and the expiry of the said period of 5 years shall operate as dissolution of the House.

DIFFERENCE BETWEEN LOK SABHA AND RAJYA SABHA

- Members of Lok Sabha are directly elected by the eligible voters. Members of Rajya Sabha are elected by the elected members of State Legislative Assemblies in accordance with the system of proportional representation by means of single transferable vote.
- The normal life of every Lok Sabha is 5 years only while Rajya Sabha is a permanent body.
- Lok Sabha is the House to which the Council of Ministers is responsible under the Constitution. Money Bills can only be introduced in Lok Sabha. Also it is Lok Sabha, which grants the money for running the administration of the country.
- Rajya Sabha has special powers to declare that it is necessary and expedient in the national interest that Parliament may make laws with respect to a matter in the State List or to create by law one or more all-India services common to the Union and the States.

Parliamentary Committees: There are several Parliamentary Committees to assist the Parliament in its deliberations. These are appointed or elected by the respective Houses of Lok Sabha and Rajya Sabha on a motion made or are nominated by their presiding officers, i.e., the Speaker of Lok Sabha and the Chairman of Rajya Sabha respectively. Broadly, Parliamentary Committees are of two kinds–standing committees and ad-hoc committees. Among the Standing Committees, three are financial Committees:

(*i*) Public Account Committee;

(*ii*) Estimate Committee;

(*iii*) Public undertaking Committee.

Ad-hoc Committees are appointed as the need arises and cease to exist when the work is over.

Speaker of Lok Sabha: Speaker is elected by the Lok Sabha from among its members. The Speaker will have the final power to maintain order within the House of the People and to interpret its rules of procedure. Speaker decides whether a bill is a money bill or a non-money bill.

- There shall be a Speaker to preside over the house of the people. Speaker and Deputy-Speaker will be chosen among the members as soon as after the first sitting.
- They normally hold the office during the life of the house and may terminate earlier by the following ways:

(*a*) By ceasing to be a member of house

(*b*) By resignation addressed to Deputy-Speaker or vice-versa

(*c*) By removal from office by a resolution passed by a majority of all the then members of the House.

- He has the power to maintain order within the house, interpret its Rules of procedures, adjourn or suspend the House.
- The speaker shall preside over the joint sitting of the two houses of the parliament and when a money bill is transmitted from Lok Sabha to Rajya Sabha, the speaker shall endorse on the bill his certificate that it is a money bill.
- The deputy-speaker presides when the speaker is vacant or absent.
- The Speaker exercises a casting vote in case of tie.

Indian States and Union Territories: Allocation of Seats

S. No.	State/UTs	Seats of Lok Sabha	Seats of Rajya Sabha	Legislative Assembly	Legislative Council
1.	Andhra Pradesh	25	11	175	58
2.	Arunachal Pradesh	2	1	60	
3.	Assam	14	7	126	
4.	Bihar	40	16	243	75
5.	Chhattisgarh	11	5	90	
6.	Goa	2	1	40	
7.	Gujarat	26	11	182	
8.	Haryana	10	5	90	
9.	Himachal Pradesh	4	3	68	
10.	Jharkhand	14	6	81	
11.	Karnataka	28	12	224	75
12.	Kerala	20	9	140	
13.	Madhya Pradesh	29	11	230	
14.	Maharashtra	48	19	288	78
15.	Manipur	2	1	60	
16.	Meghalaya	2	1	60	
17.	Mizoram	1	1	40	
18.	Nagaland	1	1	60	
19.	Odisha	21	10	147	
20.	Punjab	13	7	117	
21.	Rajasthan	25	10	200	
22.	Sikkim	1	1	32	
23.	Tamil Nadu	39	18	234	
24.	Telangana	17	7	119	40
25.	Tripura	2	1	60	
26.	Uttar Pradesh	80	31	403	100
27.	Uttarakhand	5	3	70	
28.	West Bengal	42	16	294	

S. No.	State/UTs	Seats of Lok Sabha	Seats of Rajya Sabha	Legislative Assembly	Legislative Council
29.	Jammu & Kashmir	5	4	—	—
30.	Andaman & Nicobar Islands	1	—	—	—
31.	Chandigarh	1	—	—	—
32.	Dadra & Nagar Haveli and Daman & Diu	2	—	—	—
33.	Delhi	7	3	70	—
34.	Lakshadweep	1	—	—	—
35.	Puduchery	1	1	30	—
36.	Ladakh	1	—	—	—

Table of Precedence

1. President
2. Vice-President
3. Prime Minister
4. Governors of States within their respective states
5. Former Presidents

5A. Deputy Prime Minister

6. Chief Justice of India, Speaker of Lok Sabha
7. Cabinet Ministers of the Union, Chief Ministers of States within their respective States, Deputy Chairman NITI Aayog.
   Leaders of opposition in Rajya Sabha and Lok Sabha

7A. Holders of the Bharat Ratna Decoration

8. Ambassadors Extraordinary and Plenipotentiary and High Commissioners of Commonwealth Countries accredited to India
   Chief Ministers of States outside their respective States
9. Judges of the Supreme Court
10. Deputy Chairman Rajya Sabha, Deputy Chief Minister of States
    Deputy Speaker Lok Sabha, Members of the NITI Aayog, Minister of State of the Union and Other Minister in the Ministry of Defence.

PRESIDENT

The President is the Constitutional head of the Republic of India. He is more or less the titular head of the executive. Really speaking, he is the constitutional head but not the real executive. The real power is vested in the hands of the Council of Ministers.

Qualifications:

(*i*) Indian citizen,
(*ii*) age not less than 35 years,
(*iii*) should have qualification for election to Lok Sabha,
(*iv*) should not hold any office of profit,
(*v*) should not be a Member of Parliament or State Legislature.

Impeachment

- Impeachment is a quasi-judicial procedure in the parliament to remove the president from office due to the violation of the constitution. Either house may prefer this charge of violation of constitution before the other house. A house cannot prefer the charge unless
  - 14 days notice in writing signed by not less than ¼ of the total members of that house
  - the resolution should be passed by not less than 2/3 of the total membership of that house.
- The house may investigate or cause it to investigate and the president has the right to appear and to be represented before such investigation. As a result of such investigation, a resolution is passed by not less than 2/3 of the total membership of the house before which the charge has been preferred, such resolution shall has the effect of removing the president from the date on which the resolution is passed.

- A vacancy in the office of president may arise
  - On the expiry of his term
  - By death, resignation, impeachment or otherwise, *i.e.*, by setting aside of his election as president.
- If the vacancy is caused to the delay in the election of the president, the outgoing president must continue to hold the office and for all other occasions the vice-president shall act as the president. If the vice-president is not available, the chief justice will act as the president.

Powers of President

- Art. 53 says that the Executive Power of the Union shall be vested in the President. The executive power consists of—
  - Administrative Power
  - Diplomatic Power
  - Military Power
  - Legislative Power
  - Pardoning Power

VICE-PRESIDENT

The Vice-President acts as the ex-officio Chairman of the Council of States (Rajya Sabha). He is elected by an electoral college consisting of the members of both Houses of Parliament in accordance with the system of proportional representation by means of the single transferable vote. He must be a citizen of India, not less than 35 years of age, and should be eligible for election as a member of the Council of States. Disputes in connection with election of president or a vice-president are to be a dealt with in accordance with Article-71. Such disputes shall be decided by the Supreme Court.

COUNCIL OF MINISTERS

- India adopted the British pattern of parliamentary form of government with the President as the formal head of executive acting on the advice of ministers responsible to the popular house of the legislature.
- The constitution prescribes that there shall be a council of ministers with the Prime minister at the head to assist and advice the president. (Art. 74)
- The Prime Minister is selected by the President, the other ministers are appointed by the President on the advice of the Prime Minister (Art. 75) and the allocation of portfolios amongst them is also made by him.
- Ministers may be chosen from the members of either House and a minister has the right to speak in and take part in the proceedings of the other house though he has no right to vote in the House of which he is not a member.
- There is no bar to the appointment of a person from the outside the legislature as Minister. But he cannot continue as minister for more than 6 months unless he secures a seat in either house of the parliament.
- Art. 75(3) of the constitution says that the council of ministers shall be collectively responsible to the house of the people. So the ministry has to resign if it loses the confidence of the Lok Sabha.

CATEGORIES OF COUNCIL OF MINISTERS

- There are three categories of council of ministers. Cabinet Ministers, Ministers of State and Deputy Ministers.
- The cabinet meetings can be attended by all cabinet ministers, Minister of state and deputy minister attend only if invited.
- The constitution provides for the collective responsibility of the council of ministers to the house of people only. The ministry as body has to resign as soon as it loses the confidence of the Lok Sabha.

PRIME MINISTER

The Constitution lays down that there shall be a Council of Ministers headed by the Prime Minister to aid and advise the President in the exercise of his functions. The Prime Minister is the head of the Cabinet. Other Ministers are appointed by the President on his advice. He is the leader of the majority party in the Lok Sabha.

FUNDAMENTAL RIGHTS

Following fundamental rights are enjoyed by every Indian citizen, irrespective of caste, colour, creed and sex:

1. Right to Equality: No special privileges, no distinction on grounds of religion, caste, creed and sex.

2. Right to Freedom: The right to freedom of expression and speech, the right to choose one's own profession, the right to reside in any part of the Indian Union.

3. Right to Freedom to Religion: Except when it is in the interest of public order, morality, health or other conditions, everybody has the right to profess, practice and propagate his religion freely.

4. Cultural and Educational Rights: The Constitution provides that every community can run its own institutions to preserve its own culture and language.

5. Right against Exploitation: Traffic in human beings and forced labour and the employment of children under 14 years in factories or mines, are punishable offences.

6. Rights to Constitutional Remedies: When a citizen finds that any of his fundamental rights has been encroached upon, he can move the Supreme Court, which has been empowered to safeguard the fundamental rights of a citizen (Article 32).

Jurisdiction and Seat of High Courts

Name	*Year*	*Territorial Jurisdiction*	*Seat*
Allahabad	1866	Uttar Pradesh	Prayagraj (Bench at Lucknow)
Andhra Pradesh	2019	Andhra Pradesh	Amaravati
Bombay	1862	Maharashtra, Goa, Dadar and Nagar Haveli and Daman and Diu	Mumbai (Benches at Nagpur, Panaji and Aurangabad)
Calcutta	1862	West Bengal and Andaman & Nicobar	Kolkata (Circuit Benches at Shri Vijaya Puram and Jalpaiguri)
Chhattisgarh	2000	Chhattisgarh	Bilaspur
Delhi	1966	Delhi	Delhi
Gauhati	1948	Assam, Nagaland, Mizoram and Arunachal Pradesh	Guwahati (Benches at Kohima, Aizawl and Itanagar)
Gujarat	1960	Gujarat	Ahmedabad
Himachal Pradesh	1971	Himachal Pradesh	Shimla
Jammu & Kashmir and Ladakh	1928	Jammu & Kashmir, Ladakh	Srinagar and Jammu
Jharkhand	2000	Jharkhand	Ranchi
Karnataka	1884	Karnataka	Bengaluru (Circuit Benches at Dharwar and Gulbarga)
Kerala	1958	Kerala & Lakshadweep	Ernakulam
Madhya Pradesh	1956	Madhya Pradesh	Jabalpur (Benches at Gwalior and Indore)
Madras	1862	Tamil Nadu & Puducherry	Chennai (Bench at Madurai)
Orissa	1948	Odisha	Cuttack
Patna	1916	Bihar	Patna
Punjab and Haryana	1966	Punjab, Haryana and Chandigarh	Chandigarh
Rajasthan	1949	Rajasthan	Jodhpur (Bench at Jaipur)
Sikkim	1975	Sikkim	Gangtok

Name	Year	Territorial Jurisdiction	Seat
Uttarakhand	2000	Uttarakhand	Nainital
Tripura	2013	Tripura	Agartala
Meghalaya	2013	Meghalaya	Shillong
Manipur	2013	Manipur	Imphal
Telangana	2019	Telangana	Hyderabad

FUNDAMENTAL DUTIES

The fundamental duties for the Indian citizens have been incorporated in the Constitution through the Constitution (42nd) Amendment Act, 1976. These duties are: (*i*) to abide by the Constitution and respect its ideals and institutions, the National Flag and the National Anthem; (*ii*) to cherish and follow the noble deeds which inspired our national struggle for freedom; (*iii*) to uphold and protect the sovereignty, unity and integrity of India; (*iv*) to defend the country and render national service when called upon to do so; (*v*) to promote harmony and the spirit of common brotherhood amongst all the people transcending religious, regional or sectional diversities and to renounce practices derogatory to the dignity of women; (*vi*) to value and preserve the rich heritage of our composite culture; (*vii*) to protect and improve natural environment including forests, lakes, rivers and wildlife, and to have compassion for living creatures; (*viii*) to develop the scientific temper, humanism and the spirit of inquiry and reform; (*ix*) to safeguard public property and to abjure violence; (*x*) to strive towards excellence in all spheres of individual and collective activity so that the nation constantly rises to higher levels of endeavour and achievement. (*xi*) who is parent or guardian to provide opportunities for education to his child or, as the case may be, ward between age of six and fourteen years.

DIRECTIVE PRINCIPLES OF STATE POLICY

The Directive Principles of State Policy are contained in Article 36 to 51 in Part IV of the constitutions. Directive principles are not enforceable through courts. Main aim of Directive principles is to provide social and economic base of a genuine democracy.

Some Important Directive Principles:

- Provisions for adequate means of livelihood for all citizens (Art. 39).
- Right to work (Art. 41).
- Right to human condition of work and maternity relief (Art. 42).
- Right to a living wage and condition of work ensuring decent standard of life of worker (Art. 43).
- Common Civil Code (Art. 44).
- Prohibit consumption of liquor (Art. 47).
- Prevent slaughter of useful cattle (Art. 48).
- Organise Panchayati Raj (Art. 40).
- Separate the judiciary from the executive (Art. 50).
- Protect and maintain places of historic monuments (Art. 49).
- International peace (Art. 51).

Voting Age: The voting age in the election to the Lok Sabha and State Legislative Assemblies has been reduced from 21 to 18 years by the Constitution (61st) Amendment Act, 1989.

GOVERNOR

The Governor is appointed by the President and holds office during the pleasure of the President. Apart from the power to appoint the council of ministers, if the governor finds that the government of state cannot be carried on in accordance with the provisions of the constitution (Art. 356), he may send his report to the President who may assume to himself the functions of the government of the state. (This is popularly known as 'President's Rule').

THE ATTORNEY GENERAL OF INDIA

The Attorney General of India is the first law officer of the Government of India. Though he is not a member of cabinet he has the right to speak in the House of Parliament, but he has no right to vote. The Attorney General of India shall be appointed by the President and shall hold office during his pleasure.

His duty shall be to give advice on such legal matter from time to time as may be referred to him by the President.

COMPTROLLER & AUDITOR GENERAL OF INDIA (CAG)

The Comptroller and Auditor General of India is guardian of the public purse and it is his duty to see that not a *paisa* is spent out of consolidated fund of India or of a state without the authority of the appropriate legislature. He is appointed by President of India.

Status

- Appointed by the President.
- A person with long administrative experience & knowledge of accounts is appointed.
- Holds office for 6 yrs or till 65 yrs of age.
- The President can remove him only on the recommendation of the 2 houses of Parliament (as in case of judge of Supreme Court).

UNION PUBLIC SERVICE COMMISSION (U.P.S.C.)

This Commission is responsible for (i) recruitment to all civil services and posts, under the Union Government by written examinations, interviews and promotions, and (ii) advising the Government on all matters relating to methods of recruitment, principles to be followed in making promotions and transfers. Its Chairman is appointed by the President.

INTER-STATE COUNCILS

Article 263 provides for inter-state councils. The power of the President to set up Inter-State Councils not only for advising upon disputes but also for investigating and discussing subjects in which some or all of the states, or the Union and one or more of the states have common interest.

STAFF SELECTION COMMISSION

The Union Government has constituted the Staff Selection Commission for recruitment to non-technical Group C and some of Group B posts in the central departments and in subordinate offices. The administrative Reforms Commission had recommended the setting up of such a Commission.

ELECTION COMMISSIONER

- The Constitution provides for an independent election commission to ensure free and fair election to the Parliament, the State legislature and the offices of President and Vice-President.
- Consists of Chief Election Commissioner +2 Election Commissioners. They all enjoy equal powers.
- The Chief Election Commissioner is appointed by the President and the other Election Commissioners are appointed by the President after consultation with the Chief Election Commissioner. Article 324 also provides for the appointment of Regional Commissioners at the time of General Elections after consultation with the Election Commissioner.
- Election Commissioners are appointed for a term of 5 years.
- They are not eligible for re-appointment. Also, they cannot hold any office of profit after their retirement.
- The term of 5 years can by cut short by resignation or removal by President on recommendation of the Parliament (Same as that of Judge of the Supreme Court).

* * * * *

6. PLANNING IN INDIA

The need for planning was felt in India even before independence. A National Planning Committee was set up by the Indian National Congress as early as 1938. The Planning Commission was set up in 1950. It was an advisory body engaged in the task of meaningful national planning. The main objectives of India's Economic Planning are as follows : (*i*) securing an increase in National Income; (*ii*) achieving a planned rate of investment within a given period to bring the actual investment as a proportion of national income to a higher level; (*iii*) reducing inequality in the distribution of income and wealth; (*iv*) providing additional employment; (*v*) adopting measures to increase agricultural production, manufacturing capacity for producers and a favourable balance of payments.

Five Year Plans in India

Plans	Period	Investment (₹ Crore)	Objectives
First Plan	April 1, 1951–March 31, 1956	1,960	Priority to agriculture, electricity and irrigation.
Second Plan	April 1, 1956–March 31, 1961	4,672	Development of basic and heavy industries.
Third Plan	April 1, 1961–March 31, 1966	8,577	Long term development of India's economy.
Annual Plan	April 1, 1966–March 31, 1967	2,137	
Annual Plan	April 1, 1967–March 31, 1968	2,205	
Annual Plan	April 1, 1968–March 31, 1969	2,283	
Fourth Plan	April 1, 1969–March 31, 1974	15,779	Enlarge the income of rural population and supply of goods of mass consumption.
Fifth Plan	April 1, 1974–March 31, 1979	39,426	Attain increased self reliance and employment avenues.
Annual Plan	April 1, 1979–March 31, 1980	12,176	
Sixth Plan	April 1, 1980–March 31, 1985	1,09,292	Removal of unemployment
Seventh Plan	April 1, 1985–March 31, 1990	2,18,730	Food work and productivity were the basic priorities.
Eighth Plan	April, 1992–March 31, 1997	4,95,670	Raising employment
Ninth Plan	April 1, 1997–March 31, 2002	9,41,041	Agriculture and rural development
Tenth Plan	April 1, 2002–March 31, 2007	14,91,610	Growth rate 7.8 percent per annum.
Eleventh Plan	April 1, 2007–March 31, 2012	36,44,718	Literacy, Employment, Rural development & Transport development.
Twelfth Plan	April 1, 2012–March 31, 2017	43,30,000	Long term development of India's economy.

15-YEAR VISION PLAN

With the end of the Twelfth Plan in March 2017 the era of five year plans came to an end. NITI Aayog has come forward with a draft 15-year vision plan to catapult the country's economy to more than three times as compared to the present day. The new plan is set to replace the centralised five-year plans the country has been following for decades. The new plan is accompanied by shorter sub-plans—a seven-year strategy for 2017-24, and a three-year 'Action Agenda' from 2017-18 to 2019-20. No less than 300 specific action points covering a wide range of sectors have been drawn up as part of the 15-year vision. The 15-year vision document has a seven-year strategy document for 2017-24 as the 'National Development Agenda'. Separately, a three-year 'Action Agenda' from 2017-18 to 2019-20 is also under works to assess funding requirements. The three-year agenda is further divided into seven parts, with a number of specific action points for each part to boost economic growth. India's urban population is expected to increase by 22 crores by 2031. The plan is likely to lay emphasis on urban development, taking a note from China's elaborate long-term development agenda.

NITI AAYOG

The planning commission which has a legacy of 65 years has replaced by NITI Aayog. The utility and significance of the Planning Commission had been questioned for long. The replacement seems to be more relevant and responsive to the present economic needs and scenario in the country.

Evolution of NITI Aayog

The NITI Aayog was formed on January 1, 2015. In Sanskrit, the word "NITI" means morality, behaviour, guidance, etc. But, in the present context, it means policy and the NITI stand for National Institution for Transforming India. It is country's premier policy-making institution which is expected to bolster the economic growth of the country. It aims to construct a strong state that will help to create a dynamic and strong nation. This helps India to emerge as a major economy in the world. The NITI Aayog's creation has two hubs called "Team India Hub" and Knowledge and innovation Hub.

1. The Team India: It leads the participation of Indian states with the central government.
2. The Knowledge and innovation hub: it builds institution's think tank capabilities.

NITI Aayog is additionally creating itself as a State of the Art Resource Center, with the essential resources, knowledge, and skills that will empower it to act with speed, advance research and innovation, bestow crucial policy vision to the government and manage unforeseen issues. The reason for setting up the NITI Aayog is that the people had expectations for growth and development in the administration through their participation. This required institutional changes in administration and active strategy shifts that could seed and foster substantial scale change. The institution has completed four year of its life.

Members of NITI Aayog

The NITI Aayog comprises the following:

1. Prime Minister of India as the Chairperson
2. Governing Council comprising the Chief Ministers of all the States and Union territories with Legislatures and lieutenant governors of other Union territories.
3. Regional Councils will be formed to address specific issues and contingencies impacting more than one state or a region. These will be formed for a specified tenure.
4. Experts, specialists and practitioners with relevant domain knowledge as special invitees nominated by the Prime Minister
5. Full-time organizational framework (in addition to Prime Minister as the Chairperson) comprising
   - (*i*) *Vice-Chairperson*
   - (*ii*) *Members:* Three (3) Full-time
   - (*iii*) *Part-time members:* Maximum of two from leading universities research organizations and other relevant institutions in an ex-officio capacity. Part-time members will be on a rotational basis.
   - (*iv*) *Ex Officio members:* Maximum of four members of the Union Council of Ministers to be nominated by the Prime Minister.

(*v*) *Chief Executive Officer:* To be appointed by the Prime Minister for a fixed tenure, in the rank of Secretary to the Government of India.

FINANCE COMMISSION

Article 280 of the Constitution provides for the appointment of a finance commission every five year. President appoints chairman and members of this commission. Finance commission are to recommend to President the basis for the distribution of the net proceeds of taxes between the centre and the states and the principles which should govern the grants-in-aid to be given to the states out of the consolidated funds of India.

GOODS AND SERVICES TAX

At the stroke of midnight of June 30, 2017 as the world slept, India woke up to one of the biggest tax reforms since Independence. The New GST tax regime is expected to transform India into one single market. President shared the dais with the Prime Minister Narendra Modi, Speaker, Vice-President and Finance Minister for the launch of the GST. Also present were the country's corporate honchos. The new tax regime replaces 17 different Central and State taxes and 23 cesses, including service tax, value added tax, entry tax, excise duty among others. The GST is expected to remove the cascading effect of tax-on-tax and make it easier to do business in the country. After GST, goods will have uniform prices across the country.

NATIONAL DEVELOPMENT COUNCIL

The National Development Council, set-up in 1952, consists of representatives of the Central Government as well as the State governments. It is the supreme body insofar as planning is concerned and it determines policies, issues guidelines, reviews working of the plan and finally approves the plan. The Council consists of the Prime Minister (Chairman), all Union Cabinet Ministers, Chief Ministers of all States and Union Territories and the Vice Chairman and members of the NITI Aayog. For matters relating to Plans and planning, the Union Minister of Planning is responsible to the Parliament.

RESERVE BANK OF INDIA

- It is the Central Bank of the country.
- It was established on April 1, 1935 with a capital of ₹ 5 crore. This capital of ₹ 5 crore was divided into 5 lakh equity shares of ₹ 100 each. In the beginning, the ownership of almost all the share capital was with the non-government shareholders.
- It was nationalized on Jan 1, 1949 as govt. acquired the private shareholdings.
- **Governors:** Ist Governor - Sir Smith (1935-37)
  Ist Indian Governor - C.D. Deshmukh (1948-49)

Other Financial Institutions

- **Industrial Credit & Investment Corporation of India Bank (ICICI Bank) :** Established in 1955 as a public limited company to encourage and assist industrial units of the nation. It has been converted into a bank with effect from May 3, 2002.
- **Small Industries Development Bank of India (SIDBI) :** Established in 1990; promotes small scale sector.
- **National Bank of Agriculture & Rural Development (NABARD) :** Established on Nov 5, 1982; gives credit facilities to farmers.
- **Export-Import Bank of India (EXIM) :** Set-up on Jan 1, 1982; grants deferred credit to Indian exporters in order to operate in the International market.
- **Industrial Development Bank of India (IDBI) :** Established in 1964; to provide financial assistance to industrial enterprises.
- **Industrial Reconstruction Bank of India (IRBI) :** Set-up in 1971 with the objective of reviving and revitalizing sick industrial units in public and private sectors.

* * * * *

7. General Science

INVENTIONS AND DISCOVERIES

Important Inventions

Name of Invention	*Inventor*	*Nationality*	*Year*
Aeroplane	Orville & Wilbur Wright	U.S.A.	1903
Ball-Point Pen	John J. Loud	U.S.A.	1888
Barometer	Evangelista Torricelli	Italy	1644
Bicycle	Kirkpatrick Macmillan	Britain	1839-40
Bifocal Lens	Benjamin Franklin	U.S.A.	1780
Car (Petrol)	Karl Benz	Germany	1888
Celluloid	Alexander Parkes	Britain	1861
Cinema	Nicolas & Jean Lumiere	France	1895
Clock (mechanical)	I-Hsing & Liang Ling-Tsan	China	725
Diesel Engine	Rudolf Diesel	Germany	1895
Dynamo	Hypolite Pixii	France	1832
Electric Lamp	Thomas Alva Edison	U.S.A.	1879
Electric Motor (DC)	Zenobe Gramme	Belgium	1873
Electric Motor (AC)	Nikola Tesla	U.S.A.	1888
Electro-magnet	William Sturgeon	Britain	1824
Electronic Computer	Dr. Alan M. Turing	Britain	1943
Film (moving outlines)	Louis Prince	France	1885
Film (musical sound)	Dr. Le de Forest	U.S.A.	1923
Fountain Pen	Lewis E. Waterman	U.S.A.	1884
Gramophone	Thomas Alva Edison	U.S.A.	1878
Helicopter	Etienne Oehmichen	France	1924
Jet Engine	Sir Frank Whittle	Britain	1937
Laser	Charles H. Townes	U.S.A.	1960
Lift (Mechanical)	Elisha G. Otis	U.S.A.	1852
Locomotive	Richard Trevithick	Britain	1804
Machine Gun	James Puckle	Britain	1718
Microphone	Alexander Graham Bell	U.S.A.	1876
Microscope	Z. Janssen	Netherlands	1590
Motor Cycle	G. Daimler	Germany	1885
Photography (on film)	John Carbutt	U.S.A.	1888
Printing Press	Johann Gutenberg	Germany	c.1455
Razor (safety)	King C. Gillette	U.S.A.	1895
Refrigerator	James Harrison & Alexander Catlin	U.S.A.	1850

Name of Invention	Inventor	Nationality	Year
Safety Pin	Walter Hunt	U.S.A.	1849
Sewing machine	Barthelemy Thimmonnier	France	1829
Ship (steam)	J.C. Perier	France	1775
Ship (turbine)	Hon. Sir C. Parsons	Britain	1894
Skyscraper	W. Le Baron Jenny	U.S.A.	1882
Slide Rule	William Oughtred	Britain	1621
Steam Engine (condenser)	James Watt	Britain	1765
Steel Production	Henry Bessemer	Britain	1855
Steel (stainless)	Harry Brearley	Britain	1913
Submarine	David Bushnell	U.S.A.	1776
Tank	Sir Ernest Swinton	Britain	1914
Telegraph	M. Lammond	France	1787
Telegraph Code	Samuel F.B. Morse	U.S.A.	1837
Telephone (perfected)	Alexander Graham Bell	U.S.A.	1876
Television (mechanical)	John Logie Baird	Britain	1926
Television (electronic)	P.T. Farnsworth	U.S.A.	1927
Thermometer	Galileo Galilei	Italy	1593
Transformer	Michael Faraday	Britain	1831
Transistor	Bardeen, Shockley & Brattain	U.S.A.	1948
Washing Machine (elec.)	Hurley Machine Co.	U.S.A.	1907
Zip-Fastener	W.L. Judson	U.S.A.	1891

Important Discoveries

Discovery	Discoverer	Nationality	Year
Aluminium	Hans Christian Oerstedt	Denmark	1827
Atomic number	Henry Moseley	England	1913
Atomic structure of matter	John Dalton	England	1803
Chlorine	C.W. Scheele	Sweden	1774
Electromagnetic induction	Michael Faraday	England	1831
Electromagnetic waves	Heinrich Hertz	Germany	1886
Electromagnetism	Hans Christian Oersted	Denmark	1920
Electron	Sir Joseph Thomson	England	1897
General theory of relativity	Albert Einstein	Switzerland	1915
Hydrogen	Henry Cavendish	England	1766
Law of electric conduction	Georg Ohm	Germany	1827
Law of electromagnetism	Andre Ampere	France	1826
Law of falling bodies	Galileo	Italy	1590
Laws of gravitation & motion	Isaac Newton	England	1687
Laws of planetary motion	Johannes Kepler	Germany	1609-19
Magnesium	Sir Humphry Davy	England	1808
Neptune (Planet)	Johann Galle	Germany	1846
Neutron	James Chadwick	England	1932
Nickel	Axel Cronstedt	Sweden	1751
Nitrogen	Daniel Rutherford	England	1772

Discovery	*Discoverer*	*Nationality*	*Year*
Oxygen	Joseph Priestly C.W. Scheele	England, Sweden	1772
Ozone	Christian Schonbein	Germany	1839
Pluto (Planet)	Clyde Tombaugh	U.S.A	1930
Plutonium	G.T. Seaborg	U.S.A	1940
Proton	Ernest Rutherford	England	1919
Quantum Theory	Max Planck	Germany	1900
Radioactivity	Antoine Bacquerel	France	1896
Radium	Pierre & Marie Curie	France	1898
Silicon	Jons Berzelius	Sweden	1824
Special theory of relativity	Albert Einstein	Switzerland	1905
Sun as centre of solar system	Copernicus	Poland	1543
Uranium	Martin Klaproth	Germany	1789
Uranus (Planet)	William Herschel	England	1781
X-rays	Wilhelm Roentgen	Germany	1895

Geographical Explorations/Discoveries

Place	*Explorer/Discoverer*	*Nationality*	*Year*
America	Christopher Columbus	Italy	1492
Hawaii Islands (Sandwich Islands)	Captain James Cook	England	1778
Newfoundland	John Cabot	England	1497
New Zealand	Abel Janszoon Tasman	The Netherlands	1642
North Pole	Robert Peary	USA	1909
Sea Route to India (via Cape of Good Hope)	Vasco da Gama	Portugal	1498
South Pole	Roald Amundsen	Norway	1911

Scientific Instruments

Name of Instrument	*Used for*
Altimeter	measuring altitude
Ammeter	measuring strength of an electric current
Anemometer	measuring the velocity of wind
Audiometer	measuring level of hearing
Barometer	measuring atmospheric pressure
Callipers	measuring the internal and external diameters of tubes
Calorimeter	measuring quantity of heat
Compass	finding out direction
Dynamo	converting mechanical energy into electrical energy
Eudiometer	measuring volume changes during chemical reactions between gases
Galvanometer	detecting and determining the strength of small electric currents
Hydrometer	measuring specific gravity of a liquid
Hygrometer	measuring the humidity in the atmosphere
Lactometer	measuring the purity of milk
Manometer	measuring the gaseous pressure
Micrometer	measuring minute distances, angles, etc.

Name of Instrument	*Used for*
Microscope	seeing magnified view of very small objects
Periscope	with the help of this instrument an observer in a submarine can see what is going on the surface of the sea
Photometer	measuring intensity of light from distant stars
Pyrometer	measuring high temperatures
Radar	detecting and finding the presence and location of moving objects like aircraft, missile, etc.
Radiometer	measuring the emission of radiant energy
Rain Gauge	measuring the amount of rainfall
Seismograph	measuring and recording the intensity and origin of earthquake shocks
Sextant	measuring altitude and angular distances between two objects or heavenly bodies
Spectrometer	measuring the refractive indices
Spherometer	measuring the curvature of spherical objects/surface
Sphygmomanometer	measuring blood pressure
Stethoscope	ascertaining the condition of heart and lungs by listening to their function
Stroboscope	viewing objects that are moving rapidly with a periodic motion as if they were at rest
Tachometer	measuring the rate of revolution or angular speed of a revolving shaft
Telescope	viewing magnified images of distant objects
Theodolite	measuring the horizontal and vertical angles
Thermocouple	measuring the temperature inside furnaces and jet engines
Thermometer	measuring human body temperature
Thermostat	regulating constant temperature
Ultrasonoscope	measuring utrasonic sounds
Viscometer	measuring the viscosity of a fluid
Voltmeter	measuring potential difference between two points.

Diseases and the Parts of Body they Affect

Disease	*Part of body affected*
AIDS	Immune system of body
Arthritis	Inflammation of joints
Asthma	Lungs
Cataract	Eyes
Conjunctivitis	Eyes
Diabetes	Pancreas
Diphtheria	Throat
Glaucoma	Eyes
Eczema	Skin
Goitre	Front of the neck (due to enlargement of thyroid gland)
Gout	Joints of bone

Disease	*Part of body affected*
Jaundice	Liver
Meningitis	Brain or spinal cord
Pleurisy	Pleura (inflammation of)
Polio	motor neurons
Pneumonia	Lungs
Pyorrhoea	Sockets of teeth
Tuberculosis	Lungs
Typhoid	Intestine
Malaria	Spleen
Leukaemia	Blood
Rickets	Bones

* * * * *

8. SPACE RESEARCH

First in Space

First creator of rules regarding space research	— Isaac Newton
First artificial satellite launched in space	— Sputnik-1 (1957)
First living being sent in space	— Louika (a dog)
Firstever manned spacecraft	— Vostok-I
First man in space	— Yuri Gagarin, U.S.S.R. (1961)
First woman in space	— Valentina Tereshkova, U.S.S.R. (June 1963)
First man who moved in space out of the spacecraft	— Alexi Livonov, U.S.S.R. (June 1965)
First person to land on moon	— Neil Armstrong, America (21st July, 1969)
First fourwheeled carriage without human being on moon	— Leunokhev-I, U.S.S.R. (1970)
First space lab in orbit	— Skylab (America, 1973)
First space shuttle	— Columbia (America, 1981)
First Indian (man) in space	— Sq. led. Rakesh Sharma (13th April, 1984)
First Indian (Woman) in space	— Kalpana Chawla (19th Nov., 1997)
First American woman in space	— Sailyride (1983)
First spacecraft on Mars	— Pathfinder (6 July, 1997)
First woman who lead spacecraft	— Allin Collis (America)
First spacecraft without man	— Shenzoo, China (20th Nov. 1999)
First country in the world to succeed in an inter-planetary mission on mars in the maiden attempt	— India (MOM Spacecraft)

Indian Space Programme : At a Glance

Satellite	Date	Type	Launch Vehicle	Result
Aryabhatta	19-04-75	Scientific	Cosmos	successful
Bhaskara I	07-06-79	Geosurvey	Cosmos	successful
Rohini	10-08-79	Geosurvey	S.L.V.3	unsuccessful
Rohini D-1	18-07-80	Geosurvey	S.L.V.3	successful
Rohini	31-05-81	Scientific	S.L.V.3	successful
Apple	19-06-81	Communication	Ariane	successful
Bhaskara II	20-11-81	Geosurvey	Cosonos	successful
INSAT-1A	10-04-82	Multipurpose	Delta	unsuccessful
Rohini	17-04-83	Scientific	S.L.V.3	successful
INSAT-1B	30-08-83	Multipurpose	Space Shuttle	successful
SROSS I	24-03-87	Technical	ASLV-D1	unsuccessful
IRS-1A	17-03-88	Remote sensing	Vostok	successful
SROSS II	17-07-88	Technical	ASLV-D2	unsuccessful
INSAT-1C	21-07-88	Multipurpose	Ariane-4	unsuccessful

Satellite	Date	Type	Launch Vehicle	Result
INSAT-1D	12-06-90	Multipurpose	Delta	successful
IRS-1B	29-08-91	Remote sensing	Vostok	successful
IRS-1C	28-12-95	Remote sensing	PSLV-D3	successful
G-SAT-1	18-04-2001	Multipurpose	GSLV-D	successful
INSAT-3C	24-01-2002	Communication	Ariane-4	successful
INSAT-3E	28-09-2003	Communication	Ariane-5	successful
Cartosat-1 & HAMSAT	05-05-2005	Maping and Communication	PSLV-C6	successful
CARTOSAT-2	10-01-2007	Communication	PSLV-C7	successful
INSAT-4CR	02-09-2007	Communication	GSLV-Fo4	successful
Cartosat-2A	28-04-2008	Communication	PSLV-C9	successful
Chandrayaan-I	22-10-2008	Maping and Scientific	PSLV-C11	successful
RISAT-2 & ANUSAT	20-04-2009	Maping and Communication	PSLV-C12	successful
Oceansat-2	24-09-2009	Remote Sensing	PSLV-C14	successful
CARTOSAT-2B	12-07-2010	Communication	PSLV-C15	successful
RESOURCESAT-2	20-04-2011	Remote Sensing	PSLV-C16	successful
Megha-Tropiques	12-10-2011	Maping and Scientific	PSLV-C18	successful
RISAT-1	26-04-2012	Remote Sensing	PSLV-C19	successful
Spot-6	09-09-2012	Remote Sensing	PSLV-C21	successful
Saral	25-02-2013	Scientific	PSLV-C20	successful
MOM	5-11-2013	Mapping	PSLV-C25	successful
GSAT-14	05-01-2014	Communication	GSLV-D5	successful
Spot-7	30-06-2014	Remote Sensing	PSLV-C23	successful
GSAT-16	07-12-2014	Communication	Ariane-5	successful
Astrosat	28-09-2015	Mapping and Scientific	PSLV-C30	successful
GSAT-15	11-11-2015	Communication	Ariane-5	successful
TELEOS-1 & others	16-12-2015	Mapping and Scientific	PSLV-C29	successful
IRNSS-1E	20-01-2016	Mapping and Scientific	PSLV-C31	successful
IRNSS-1F	10-03-2016	Mapping and Scientific	PSLV-C32	successful
INSAT-3DR	08-09-2016	Meteorology	GSLV-F05	successful
SCATSAT-1 & others	26-09-2016	Multipurpose	PSLV-C35	successful
RESOURCESAT-2A	07-12-2016	Remote Sensing	PSLV-C36	successful
CARTOSAT-2 & 103 others	15-02-2017	Multipurpose	PSLV-C37	successful
GSAT-19	05-06-2017	Communication	GSLV MK-III-D1	successful
CARTOSAT-2E	23-06-2017	Earth observation Satellite	PSLV-C38	successful
GSAT-17	29-06-2017	Earth observation Satellite	Ariane-5 ECA	successful
INS-1C	10-01-2018	Technology Applications	PSLV-C40	successful
CARTOSAT-2F & 30 others	12-01-2018	Earth observation Satellite	PSLV-C40	successful
GSAT-6A	29-03-2018	Communications	GSLV-F08	successful
GSAT-7A	19-12-2018	Military Satellite	GSLV-MKII-F11	successful
GSAT-31	06-02-2019	Communication	Ariane-5 VCA	successful
Chandrayaan-II	22-07-2019	Mapping and Scientific	GSLV-MK-III	successful
RISAT 2BR1 & 9 others	11-12-2019	Mapping and Scientific	PSLV-C48	successful
GSAT-30	17-01-2020	Communication	Ariane-5	successful
EOS-01	07-11-2020	Earth observation	PSLV-C49	successful
CMS-01	17-12-2020	Communication	PSLV-XLC50	successful
EOS-04 and INS-2TD	14-02-2022	Earth observation	PSLV-C52	successful
DS-EO and others	30-06-2022	Earth observation	PSLV-C53	successful
36 Satellites of one web	23-10-2022	Earth observation	GSLV-Mark-3	successful
EOS-07	10-02-2023	Earth observation	SSLV-02	successful
TeLEOS-2 and LUMILITE-4	22-04-2023	Earth observation	PSLV-C55	successful
Chandrayaan-3	14-07-2023	Mapping and Scientific	LVM-3 M4	successful
Aditya-L1	02-09-2023	Solar observation	PSLV-C57	successful
XPoSAT	01-01-2024	Earth Observation	PSLV-C58	successful
INSAT-3DS	17-02-2024	Meteorological	GSLV-F14	successful
EOS-08	16-08-2024	Earth Observation	SSLV-D3	successful
Proba-3	05-12-2024	Earth Observation	PSLV-C59	successful
NVS-02	29-01-2025	Navigation	GSLV-F15	successful
NISAR	30-07-2025	Earth Observation	GSLV-F16	successful
Bluebird-6	24-12-2025	Communication	LVM3	successful

* * * * *

9. INDIAN HISTORY

Famous Sites of Indus Valley Civilization

Name of Site	Year of Excavation	River/ Sea coast	Discoverer
Harappa (Montgomery–Pakistan)	1921	Ravi River	Dayaram Sahney
Mohanjodaro (Larkana–Pakistan)	1922	Indus River	Rakhal Das Banerjee
Chanhudaro (Sindh–Pakistan)	1931	Indus River	N.G. Mazumdar
Alamgir pur (Meerut – U.P.)	1952-55	Hindan River	Yagyadatta Sharma
Ropar (Punjab)	1953	Sutlej River	Yagyadatta Sharma
Rangpur (Kathiabar–Gujarat)	1953	Bhabar River	Madho Swaroop Vatsa, Rang Nath Rao
Kotdigi (Sindh–Pakistan)	1953	Indus River	Fazal Ahmed Khan
Lothal (Ahmedabad–Gujarat)	1954	Bhogwa River	Rang Nath Rao
Kalibanga (Ganganagar–Rajasthan)	1961	Ghaggar	Brajwasi Lal
Surkotara (Kutch–Gujarat)	1967	Ghaggar River	Ravindra Singh Vishta
Banawali (Hissar–Haryana)	1973	Ghaggar River	Ravindra Singh Vishta
Balakote	1979	Arabian Sea	George F. Dales
Dhaulavira (Gujarat)	1963-68	—	J.P. Joshi
	1990-91	—	Dr. R.S. Vishta

Wellknown Quotations

"Swarajya is My Birthright"	— Bal Gangadhar Tilak
"Give me blood, I shall give you freedom"	— Netajee Subhash Chandra Bose
"Inqalab Zindabad"	— Bhagat Singh
"Saare Jahan Se Achcha, Hindustan Hamara"	— Dr. Mohammed Iqbal
"Dilli Chalo"	— Subhash Chandra Bose
"Sarfaroshi ki tamanna, Ab Hamare Dil Mein Hai."	— Ram Prasad Bismil
"I am socialist by nature".	— Jawahar Lal Nehru
"Go to Vedas"	— Swami Dayanand
"Aaram Haram Hai"	— Jawahar Lal Nehru
"Jai Jawan, Jai Kisan"	— Lal Bahadur Shastri
"Jai Jawan, Jai Kisan, Jai Vigyan"	— Atal Bihari Vajpayee
"Speak less, work more"	— Sanjay Gandhi
"Vijayee Vishwa Tiranga Pyara"	— Shyam Lal Gupta

"Quit India"	— Mahatma Gandhi
"Hindi, Hindu, Hindustan"	— Bhartendu Harishchandra
"Purna Swarajya"	— Jawahar Lal Nehru
"Every lathi blow inflicted on my body will prove a nail in British coffin"	— Lala Lajpat Rai
"Jai Hind"	— Subhash Chandra Bose
"Do or die"	— Mahatma Gandhi
"Who lives if India dies"	— Jawahar Lal Nehru
"Vande Mataram"	— Bankim Chandra Chatterjee
"Jana Gana Mana Adhinayaka Jai Hai"	—Rabindranath Tagore
"Hate sin, not the sinner."	— Mahatma Gandhi
"Service of the people is the service of God"	— Swami Vivekananda
"Truth and non-violence are my God."	— Mahatma Gandhi

Battles and Wars In India

War	*Year*	*Result*
Battle of Kalinga	(261 B.C.)	Ashoka defeated the king of Kalinga
Second battle of Tarain	(1192 A.D.)	Muhammad Gori defeated Prithviraj Chauhan
First battle of Panipat	(1526 A.D.)	Babar defeated Ibrahim Lodi
Battle of Khanwa	(1527 A.D.)	Babar defeated Rana Sanga
Battle of Chausa	(1539 A.D.)	Shershah Suri defeated Humayun and became ruler of Delhi
Second Battle of Panipat	(1556 A.D.)	Akbar defeated Hemu
Battle of Talikota	(1565 A.D.)	Allied forces of Bijapur, Bidar, Golkunda and Ahamadnagar defeated the King of Vijay Nagar
Battle of Haldighati	(1576 A.D.)	Some historian say that this battle was indecisive but some say that Rana Pratap was defeated by Akbar
Battle of Palasey	(1757 A.D.)	British forces defeated Nawab of Bengal Sirajudoulla
Battle of Wandiwash	(1760 A.D.)	British forces defeated the French
Third battle of Panipat	(1761 A.D.)	Maratha were defeated by Ahmad Shah Abadali
Battle of Buxar	(1764 A.D.)	British forces defeated the combined forces of Mir Quasim, Shah Alam Mughal empire and Awadh's Nawab
Third Anglo-Maratha War	(1792 A.D.)	Maratha were conclusively defeated
Fourth Anglo-Mysore War	(1799 A.D.)	Tipu Sultan died fighting the British forces
Second Anglo-Sikh War	(1848 A.D.)	British forces annexed Punjab from Sikh rulers
Indo-China War	(1962 A.D.)	China attacked India unilaterally and annexed some area
Indo-Pak War	(1965 A.D.)	Pakistan attacked India but had to suffer severe set-backs
Indo-Pak War	(1971 A.D.)	Pak declare war against India.

* * * * *

10. World Geography

Earth: The earth constitutes land, water and air. Land is made up of rocks and soil. It is distributed in continents and islands. The water found in oceans, seas, lakes, etc. occupies about 2/3 of the earth's surface. The earth is surrounded by a cover of air, called atmosphere, which extends up to several hundred kilometres above its surface.

Shape: In ancient times people believed that the earth was flat in shape. Greek philosopher Pythagoras (6th century BC) was the first person to declare that the earth was round. After careful measurement, the scientists have found that the earth is slightly oblate (flattened at poles) and not exactly round.

Motions: The earth has two motions: *(i) Rotation:* Earth makes a complete round on its axis once each 24 hours (more exactly 23 hours, 56 minutes and 4.09 seconds). It causes days and night on the earth. *(ii) Revolution:* The earth makes a complete round of the Sun in one year. This revolution of earth produces alternate seasons.

Some Facts: **(1)** Equal Day and Night — March 21 and September 23. **(2)** Longest Day — June 21. **(3)** Shortest Day — December 22. **(4)** The sunlight takes eight minutes in travelling from the Sun to the Earth. **(5)** Average speed of the earth in orbit ---- 66,600 miles (107,220 km) per hour. **(6)** Earth's equatorial diameter is about 7926 miles (12,756 km). **(7)** Water (oceans, seas, lakes and rivers) occupies nearly 75 per cent of the surface of the earth. **(8)** Earth's average distance from the Moon — 2,38,857 miles (3,84,400 km). **(9)** Earth's average distance from the Sun — 93 million miles (149.4 million km).

Greenwich Time: It is the local time of the Greenwich observatory in London on 0° meridian. Greenwich time is international standard time.

International Date Line: Half way round the earth from the Greenwich is International Date Line on 180° longitude. It runs down mid-Pacific. It is one day earlier on the east of this line than it is on the west of the line. When it is Monday east of the line, it is Tuesday west of the line.

Zones: On the basis of temperature and distribution of solar heat on the surface of the earth, the earth has been divided into five zones: (1) Torrid Zone, (2) North Temperate Zone, (3) South Temperate Zone, (4) Arctic Zone, and (5) Antarctic Zone.

Continents: Large land masses forming large geographical divisions are called continents. There are seven continents: (1) Asia (30.0%), (2) Africa (20.3%), (3) North America (16.3%), (4) South America (12.0%), (5) Antarctica (8.9%), (6) Europe (6.7%) and (7) Australia (5.2%).

Highest Mountain Peaks: (1) Everest (Asia-8848 metres), (2) Aconcagua (South America-6960 metres), (3) Mckinley (North America-6194 metres), (4) Kilimanjaro (Africa-5895 metres), (5) Elbrus (Europe-5642 metres), (6) Vinson Massif (Antarctica-5140 metres), (7) Kosciusko (Australia-2228 metres).

Largest Oceans: (1) Pacific Ocean (The largest, covers almost 1/3 of the earth's total area, and the deepest about 6.8 miles at Mariana Trench in western Pacific); (2) Atlantic Ocean, and (3) Indian Ocean. Other seas and gulfs are — the Mediterranean Sea, South China Sea, Bering Sea, Caribbean Sea, East China Sea, Sea of Japan, North Sea, Baltic Sea, Hudson Bay and Gulf of Mexico.

Longest Rivers: (1) Nile (6650 km-Africa), (2) Amazon (6570 km-South America), (3) Mississippi-Missouri (5970 km-North America), (4) Yangtze Kiang (5470 km-Asia), (5) Ob Irtysh (5150 km-Europe), (6) Congo (4666 km-Africa).

Great Deserts: (1) Sahara (94 lakh sq km-North Africa), (2) Libyan (11.65 lakh sq km-North Africa), (3) Australian (16 lakh sq km-Australia), (4) Gobi (13 lakh sq km-Mongolia), (5) Great Victoria (6,47,000 sq km-Australia), (6) Syrian (5,20,000 sq km Arabia), (7) Arabian (23,30,000 sq km Arabia).

Largest Islands: (1) Greenland (21,75,600 sq km) (2) New Guinea (7,77,000 sq km), (3) Borneo (7,25,545 sq km), (4) Malagasy (5,90,000 sq km), (5) Baffin Island (4,76,070 sq km).

Highest Waterfalls: (1) Angel (807 m-Venezuela), (2) Mongefossen (774 m-Norway), (3) Kukenaam (610 m-Venezuela), (4) Ribbon (491 m-USA), (5) King George VI (487 m-Guyana), (6) Upper Yosemite (435 m-USA).

Major Producers of Crops, Minerals and Industrial goods

Coal	China, USA, India, Australia, Indonesia, Russia
Cocoa	Cote d'Ivaire, Ghana, Indonesia, Nigeria
Coffee	Brazil, Vietnam, Columbia, Indonesia
Copper	Chile, Peru, China, USA
Cotton	China, India, USA, Pakistan, Brazil
Gold	China, Australia, Russia, USA, Canada
Grapes	China, Italy, USA, France, Spain
Iron ore	Australia, Brazil, China, India
Jute	India, Bangladesh, China
Manganese	South Africa, China, Australia
Petroleum	Russia, Saudi Arabia, USA, Iraq
Rice	China, India, Indonesia, Bangladesh
Rubber	Thailand, Indonesia, Malaysia, Vietnam, India
Silk	China, India, Uzbekistan, Thailand
Silver	Mexico, Peru, China, Chili
Steel	China, Japan, India, USA
Tea	China, India, Kenya, Sri Lanka
Wheat	China, India, USA, France, Russia
Diamond	Russia, Australia, Congo, Botswana
Tobacco	China, Brazil, India, USA, Indonesia

The Highest, Biggest and Longest in the World

Airport	*Largest*	King Fahd International Airport, Dammon (Saudi Arabia)
Animal	*Tallest*	Giraffe (Average height 6.09 m)
	Largest & Heaviest	Blue Whale (190 tonnes)
	Longest recorded	Boot lace Worm (55 m)
	Fastest	Cheetah (Approximately 100 km/hr)
Bay	*With maximum area*	Bay of Bengal (India: 217 million hc)
Building	*Tallest*	Burj Khalifa in Dubai (818 meter)
Canal	*Big ship (longest)*	Suez Canal (160 km) Busiest Kiel Canal (North Sea)
Church	*Largest*	Basilica of St. Peter (Vatican City Rome–Area 23000 sq. m.)
Continent	*biggest*	Asia (31,845,872 km^2)
	Smallest	Australia Mainland (Area 76,17,930 km^2)

Country	*Largest in Population (2023)*	China (over 140 crore)
	Largest in Area	Russia (17,098,242 sq. km)
	With largest electorate	India (over 90 crores)
	Smallest independent	State of Vatican City (0.44 km^2)
Delta	*Largest*	Sundarban's Ganga-Brahmaputra delta (1,05,000 sq. km)
Epic	*Longest*	Mahabharata
Film	*Most Oscars*	Ben Hur (11 Oscars—1959); Titanic (11 Oscars—1998); The Lord of Rings : The Return of the King (11 Oscars—2003).
Island	*Biggest*	Greenland (2,175,600 sq km)
Lake	*Largest*	Caspian Sea (Azerbaijan, Russia, Iran border: 37.18 lakh km^2)
	Deepest	Baikal (Siberia)
	Largest (fresh water)	Superior Lake (USA—Canada border: 82,350 km^2)
Mountain	*Highest peak*	Mt. Everest (8848 m; Nepal)
	Highest range	Himalayas, Asia (upto 4200 m)
	Greatest mountain range	Himalaya-Karakoram (96 out of 109 peaks over 7315 m are here)
Ocean	*Largest and Deepest*	The Pacific (Area: 166,240,000 km^2; Depth: 10,924 m)
Planet	*Biggest*	Jupiter (equatorial diameter 142984 km)
	Brightest, hottest and nearest to Earth	Venus
	Nearest to Sun	Mercury
Plateau	*Highest*	Tibetan Plateau (Central Asia: 4900 m)
Platform	*Longest (rail)*	Shree Siddharoodha Swamiji Railway Station Hubballi, Karnataka (India)
Religion	*Oldest*	Hinduism
Religion	*Largest*	Christianity
Rivers	*Longest*	(i) Nile (6650 km) (ii) Amazon (6437 km)
Sea	*Largest*	Philippine Sea (5,695,600 sq. km)
Star	*Brightest*	Sirius A (also called Dog Star)
Swimming course	*Longest recognised*	English Channel
Tunnel	*Longest (railway)*	Gotthard Base Rail Tunnel (Switzerland; 57.1 km)
	Largest (road)	Laerdal, Norway (24.51 km)
Wall	*Longest*	Great Wall of China
Waterfall	*Highest*	Salto-Angel (in Venezuela on a branch of river Carrao, 807 m.)

Capital & Currencies

Country	Capital	Currency
∗ Afghanistan	Kabul	Afghani
∗ Albania	Tirana	Lek
∗ Algeria	Algiers	Dinar
∗ Angola	Luanda	New Kwanza
∗ Argentina	Buenos Aires	Peso
∗ Armenia	Yeravan	Dram
∗ Australia	Canberra	Dollar
∗ Austria	Vienna	Euro
∗ Azerbaijan	Baku	Manat
∗ Bahrain	Manama	Dinar
∗ Bangladesh	Dhaka	Taka
∗ Barbados	Bridgetown	Dollar
∗ Belarus	Minsk	Ruble
∗ Belgium	Brussels	Euro
∗ Benin	Porto Novo	Franc (CFA)
∗ Bhutan	Thimphu	Ngultrum
∗ Bolivia	La paz	Boliviano
∗ Botswana	Gaborone	Pula
∗ Brazil	Brasilia	Real
∗ Bosnia Herzegovina	Sarajevo	Convertible Marka
∗ Bulgaria	Sofia	Lev
∗ Cambodia	Phnom-Penh	Riel
∗ Canada	Ottawa	Dollar
∗ Chile	Santiago	Peso
∗ China	Beijing	Yuan
∗ Colombia	Bogota	Peso
∗ Congo Republic	Brazzaville	Franc (CFA)
∗ Croatia	Zagreb	Kuna
∗ Cuba	Havana	Peso
∗ Cyprus	Nicosia	Euro
∗ Czech Republic	Prague	Koruna
∗ Denmark	Copenhagen	Krone
∗ Ecuador	Quito	Dollar
∗ Egypt	Cairo	Pound
∗ Estonia	Tallinn	Euro
∗ Ethiopia	Addis Ababa	Birr
∗ Fiji	Suva	Dollar
∗ Finland	Helsinki	Euro
∗ France	Paris	Euro
∗ Georgia	Tbilisi	Lari
∗ Germany	Berlin	Euro
∗ Ghana	Accra	Cedi
∗ Greece	Athens	Euro
∗ Guatemala	Guatemala City	Quetzal
∗ Guyana	George Town	Dollar
∗ Hungary	Budapest	Forint
∗ Iceland	Reykjavik	Krona
∗ India	New Delhi	Rupee
∗ Indonesia	Jakarta	Rupiah
∗ Iran	Teheran	Rial
∗ Iraq	Baghdad	Dinar
∗ Ireland	Dublin	Euro
∗ Israel	Jerusalem	Shekel
∗ Italy	Rome	Euro
∗ Jamaica	Kingston	Dollar
∗ Japan	Tokyo	Yen
∗ Jordan	Amman	Dinar
∗ Kazakhstan	Astana	Tenge
∗ Kenya	Nairobi	Shilling
∗ Korea (S)	Seoul	Won
∗ Korea (N)	Pyongyang	Won
∗ Kyrgyzstan	Bishkek	Som
∗ Kuwait	Kuwait City	Dinar
∗ Laos	Vientiane	Kip
∗ Latvia	Riga	Lat
∗ Lebanon	Beirut	Pound
∗ Liberia	Monrovia	Dollar
∗ Libya	Tripoli	Dinar
∗ Lithuania	Vilnius	Litas
∗ Luxembourg	Luxembourg	Euro
∗ Macedonia	Skopje	Dinar
∗ Malawi	Lilongwe	Kwacha
∗ Malaysia	Kuala Lumpur	Ringgit
∗ Maldives	Male	Rufiyaa
∗ Mali	Bamako	Franc (CFA)
∗ Mauritius	Port Louis	Rupee
∗ Mexico	Mexico City	Peso
∗ Moldavia	Chisinau	Leu
∗ Mongolia	Ulan Bator	Tugrik
∗ Morocco	Rabat	Dirham
∗ Mozambique	Maputo	Metical
∗ Myanmar	Nay Pyi Taw	Kyat
∗ Namibia	Winohoek	Dollar
∗ Nepal	Kathmandu	Rupee
∗ Netherlands	Amsterdam	Euro
∗ New Zealand	Wellington	Dollar
∗ Nigeria	Abuja	Naira
∗ Norway	Oslo	Krone
∗ Oman	Muscat	Rial
∗ Pakistan	Islamabad	Rupee

Country	Capital	Currency
✶ Panama	Panama City	Balboa
✶ Peru	Lima	Nuevo Sole
✶ Philippines	Manila	Peso
✶ Poland	Warsaw	Zloty
✶ Portugal	Lisbon	Euro
✶ Qatar	Doha	Riyal
✶ Romania	Bucharest	Leu
✶ Russia	Moscow	Ruble
✶ Saudi Arabia	Riyadh	Rial
✶ Senegal	Dakar	Franc (CFA)
✶ Slovakia	Bratislava	Euro
✶ Spain	Madrid	Euro
✶ Sri Lanka	Colombo	Rupee
✶ Sudan	Khartoum	Dinar
✶ Suriname	Paramaribo	Dollar
✶ Sweden	Stockholm	Krona
✶ Switzerland	Berne	Swiss Francs
✶ Syria	Damascus	Pound
✶ South Africa	Capetown (Legislative) Pretoria *(Administrative)*	Rand
✶ Tadzhikistan	Dushanbe	Somoni
✶ Taiwan	Taipei	Dollar
✶ Tanzania	Dodoma	Shilling
✶ Thailand	Bangkok	Baht
✶ Tunisia	Tunis	Dinar
✶ Turkiye	Ankara	Lira
✶ Turkmenistan	Ashgabat	Manat
✶ Uganda	Kampala	Shilling
✶ Ukraine	Kiev	Hryvna
✶ United Arab Emirates	Abu Dhabi	Dirham
✶ U.K.	London	Pound Sterling
✶ U.S.A.	Washington, D.C.	Dollar
✶ Uruguay	Montevideo	Peso
✶ Uzbekistan	Tashkent	Som
✶ Venezuela	Caracas	Bolivar Fuerte
✶ Vietnam	Hanoi	Dong
✶ Yemen	Sana'a	Rial
✶ Zimbabwe	Harare	Dollar
✶ Congo (Democratic Republic)	Kinshasa	Franc (CDF)
✶ Zambia	Lusaka	Kwacha

First in the World

First Chinese visitor to India	Fahien
First foreign invader of India	Alexander, the Great (Greek)
First person to climb Mt. Everest	Tenzing Norgay (India) and Edmund Hillary (New Zealand) (1953)
First atom bomb dropped at	Hiroshima (Japan)
First man in the space	Yuri Gagarin (former USSR)
First woman in the space	Valentina Tereshkova (former USSR)
First person to walk in the space	Alexei Leonov (former USSR)
First person to land on the moon	Neil Armstrong (USA)
First and the only woman to have climbed Mt. Everest twice	Santosh Yadav (Indian; May 12, 1992; May 10, 1993)
First person on Mt. Everest without oxygen	Phu Dorjee (Indian; May 9, 1984)
First person to climb Mt. Everest twice	Nawang Gombu
First President of the USA	George Washington
First woman Prime Minister	Sirimavo Bandaranaike (Sri Lanka)
First person to swim across English Channel	Mathew Webb
First woman to swim across English Channel	Gertrude Caroline Ederle
First woman to climb Mt. Everest	Junko Tabei (Japan)
First woman to climb Mt. Everest alone and without oxygen supplies	Alison Hargreaves (Britain: May 13, 1995)

First Aeroplane to fly around the world without refuelling	Voyager (Dec. 1986)
First test-tube Baby	Louise Brown (UK; 1978)
First all-talking Film	Jaz Singer (1927)
First Secretary-General of the UN	Trygve Lie (Norway: 1946-53)
First woman President of the UN General Assembly	Vijayalakshmi Pandit (India: 1953)
First woman to reach North Pole	Ann Bancroft (1986)
First person to reach North Pole	Robert Peary
First person to reach South Pole	Amundsen (1911)
First woman to command Spacecraft in space	Ellin Collins

Popular Names

Popular Name	*Real Name*
Badshah Khan	Abdul Ghaffar Khan
Bapu, Father of Nation	M.K. Gandhi
Bard of Avon	William Shakespeare
Chachaji *or* Panditji	Jawaharlal Nehru
Desert Fox	Gen. Rommel (Germany)
Desh Bandhu	C.R. Das
Father of English Poetry	Geoffrey Chaucer
Fuhrer	Adolf Hitler
Grand Old Man of India	Dadabhai Naoroji
Grand Old Man of Britain	W.E. Gladstone
Gurudev	Rabindra Nath Tagore
Guruji	M.S. Golwalkar
Grand Commoner	Pitt, the younger
Iron Man of India	Sardar Patel
Lady with the Lamp	Florence Nightingale
Lal, Bal, Pal	Lala Lajpat Rai, Bal Gangadhar Tilak, Bipin Chandra Pal
Li-Kwan	Pearl Buck
Little Corporal *or* Man of Destiny	Napoleon Bonaparte
Lokmanya	Bal Gangadhar Tilak
Lok Nayak	Jayaprakash Narain
Mahamana	Pt. Madan Mohan Malaviya
Maid of Orleans	Joan of Arc
Maiden Queen	Queen Elizabeth I
Man of Blood and Iron	Prince Bismark
Netaji	Subhash Chandra Bose
Nightingale of India	Sarojini Naidu
Priyadarshini	Indira Gandhi
Punjab Kesari	Lala Lajpat Rai
Wizard of the North	Walter Scott

Geographical Surnames

Geographical Surname	*Real Name*
Bengal's Sorrow	Damodar River
Blue Mountains	Nilgiri Hills
China's Sorrow	Hwang-Ho
City of Palaces	Kolkata
City of Skyscrapers *or* Empire City	New York
City of Dreaming Spires	Oxford
Cockpit of Europe	Belgium
Dark Continent	Africa
Emerald Isle	Ireland
Eternal City	Rome
Gateway of India	Mumbai
Gate of Tears	Strait of Bab-el-mandab
Gift of the Nile	Egypt
Granite City	Aberdeen (Scotland)
Hermit Kingdom	Korea
Holy Land	Jerusalem
Island of Pearls	Bahrain (Persian Gulf)
Island of Cloves	Zanzibar
Key to the Mediterranean	Gibraltar
Land of Five Rivers	Punjab
Land of Golden Pagoda	Myanmar (Burma)
Land of Kangaroo	Australia
Land of Maple Leaf/Lillies	Canada
Land of Midnight Sun	Norway
Land of Morning Calm	Korea
Land of the Rising Sun	Japan
Land of Thousand Lakes	Finland
Land of Thunderbolt	Bhutan
Land of the White Elephants	Thailand
Manchester of the Orient	Osaka (Japan)
Pearl of the Antilles *or* Sugar Bowl of the World	Cuba
Pink City	Jaipur
Playground of Europe	Switzerland
Queen of the Adriatic	Venice (Italy)
Roof of the World	Pamirs
Sick Man of Europe	Turkiye
Venice of the North	Stockholm (Sweden)
Windy City	Chicago
Whiteman's Grave	Guinea Coast of Africa
World's Loneliest Island	Tristan de Cunha

Countries'/Cities' Names—Old and New

Old Name	New Name
Abyssinia	Ethiopia
Basutoland	Lesotho
Bechuanaland	Botswana
British Honduras	Belize
Burma	Myanmar
Ceylon	Sri Lanka
Zaire	Congo
Constantinople	Istanbul
Dahomey	Benin
Dutch East Indies	Indonesia
East Pakistan	Bangladesh
Formosa	Taiwan
Gold Coast	Ghana
Leningrad	St. Petersburg
Leopoldville	Kinshasa
Mesopotamia	Iraq
North Rhodesia	Zambia
Nyasaland	Malawi
Peking	Beijing
Persia	Iran
Rangoon	Yangon
Salisbury	Harare
Siam	Thailand
South West Africa	Namibia
Southern Rhodesia	Zimbabwe
Turkey	Turkiye

IMPORTANT RESIDENCES

• **Buckingham Palace (London):** King/Queen of Britain • **10, Downing Street (London):** Prime Minister, Britain • **Elysee Palace (Paris):** President, France • **Rashtrapati Bhawan (New Delhi):** President, India • **White House (Washington):** President, USA • **Vatican (Rome):** Pope

Important towns situated on the River Banks

Town	River
Agra	Yamuna
Ahmedabad	Sabarmati
Ayodhya	Saryu
Baghdad	Tigris
Berlin	Spree
Cairo	Nile
Kolkata	Hooghly
Cuttack	Mahanadi
Delhi	Yamuna
Dibrugarh	Brahmaputra
Dublin	Liffey
Hardwar	Ganga
Hyderabad	Musi
Jabalpur	Narbada
Kanpur	Ganga
Karachi	Indus
Lahore	Ravi
Leh	Indus
London	Thames
Lucknow	Gomati
Nasik	Godavari
New York	Hudson
Paris	Seine
Patna	Ganga
Prayagraj	Confluence of the Ganga and the Yamuna
Rome	Tiber
Srinagar	Jhelum
Surat	Tapti
Sydney	Murray-Darling
Varanasi	Ganga
Vienna	Danube
Washington	Potamac
Yangon	Irawadi

Books and Authors

FOREIGN

Book	Author
Aesop's Fables	Aesop
Adventure of Robinson Crusoe	Daniel Defoe
Adventures of Sherlok Holmes	Arthur Conan Doyle
Alice in Wonderland	Lewis Carrol
Apple Cart	G.B. Shaw
Arabian Nights	Sir Richard Burton
As You Like It	William Shakespeare
A Tale of Two Cities	Charles Dickens
A Tale of Two Gardens	Octavio Paz
A Thousand Suns	Dominique Lapierre
August Coup	Mikhail S. Gorbachev
Ben Hur	Lewis Wallace
Candida	G.B. Shaw
Das Kapital	Karl Marx
David Copperfield	Charles Dickens
Divine Comedy	A. Dante
Doctor's Dilemma	G.B. Shaw
Famished Road	Ben Okri
Freedom From Fear	Aung San Suu Kyi
Gulistan Bostan	Sheikh Saadi
Gulliver's Travels	Jonathan Swift
Hamlet	William Shakespeare
Iliad	Homer
Inferno	A. Dante
In Memoriam	Lord Tennyson
Ivanhoe	Walter Scott
Julius Caesar	William Shakespeare
Lady Chatterley's Lover	D.H. Lawrence
Lajja	Taslima Nasreen
Les Miserable	Victor Hugo
Leviathan	Thomas Hobbes
Lolita	V. Nobokov
Lycidas	John Milton
Mein Kampf	Adolf Hitler
Merchant of Venice	William Shakespeare
Midnight's Children	Salman Rushdie

Book	Author
Moor's Last Sigh	Salman Rushdie
Mother	Maxim Gorky
Mother India	Katherine Mayo
Nana	Emile Zola
Ninteen Eighty Four	George Orwell
Odyssey	Homer
Origin of Species	Charles Darwin
Othello	William Shakespeare
Paradise Lost	John Milton
Paradise Regained	John Milton
Path to Power	Margaret Thatcher
Pickwick Papers	Charles Dickens
Pride and Prejudice	Jane Austen
Razor's Edge	Somerset Maugham
Republic	Plato
Romeo and Juliet	William Shakespeare
Round the World in Eighty Days	Jules Verne
Rubaiyat-i-Omar Khayyam	Edward Fitzgerald (Translator)
Shape of Things to Come	H.G. Wells
The Satanic Verses	Salman Rushdie
The Social Contract	Rousseau
The Tempest	William Shakespeare
Time Machine	H.G. Wells
Tom Sawyer	Mark Twain
Treasure Island	R.L. Stevenson
Twelfth Night	William Shakespeare
Uncle Tom's Cabin	H.B. Stowe
Unto This Last	John Ruskin
Utopia	Thomas More
Universe Around Us	James Jeans
Vicar of Wakefield	Oliver Goldsmith
War and Peace	Leo Tolstoy
Wealth of Nations	Adam Smith
Wonder That was India	A.L. Basham
Wuthering Heights	Emily Bronte

INDIAN

Book	Author
Abhigyan Shakuntalam	Kalidas
Ain-i-Akbari	Abul Fazal

Book	Author
Anand Math	Bankim Chandra Chatterjee

Book	Author
Arthashastra	Kautilya
A Suitable Boy	Vikram Seth
Bhagwat Gita	Ved Vyas
Chidambara	Sumitranandan Pant
Devdas	Sarat Chandra Chatterjee
Diwan-i-Ghalib	Mirza Ghalib
Discovery of India	Jawaharlal Nehru
Essays on Gita	Aurobindo Ghosh
Eternal India	Indira Gandhi
Faces of Everest	Major H.P.S. Ahluwalia
Ganadevata	Tarashankar Bandopadhyaya
Geet Govind	Jaya Dev
Geetanjali	R.N. Tagore
Glimpses of World History	Jawaharlal Nehru
Godaan	Prem Chand
Gul-e-Nagma	Firaq Gorakhpuri
Gunahon ka Devta	Dharmveer Bharti
Harsh Charita	Bana Bhatta
Hindu View of Life	S. Radhakrishnan
Idols	Sunil Gavaskar
India Divided	Dr. Rajendra Prasad
The Judgement	Kuldip Nayyar
Juhi ki Kali	Surya Kant Tripathi 'Nirala'
Justice of Peace ke Aansu	Janardan Prasad Singh
Chand ka Munh Terha Hai	Muktibodh
Kapalkundala	Bankim Chandra Chatterjee
Kadambari	Bana Bhatta
Kagaz Te Kanwas	Amrita Pritam
Kamayani	Jai Shankar Prasad
Kitni Nawon	S.H. Vatsyayan
Kumar Sambhav	Kalidas
Mahabharata	Ved Vyas

Book	Author
Malgudi Days	R.K. Narayan
Manvini Bhavai	Pannalal Patel
Mati Matal	Gopi Nath Mohanty
Meghdoot	Kalidas
Meri Ekyavan Kavitain	Atal Bihari Vajpayee
Meri Sansadiya Yatra	Atal Bihari Vajpayee
Mritunjaya	B.K. Bhattacharya
Mudrarakshasa	Vishakhadatta
My Experiments with Truth	M.K. Gandhi
My Own Boswell	M. Hidayatullah
My Presidential Years	R. Venkataraman
Nisheeth	Uma Shankar Joshi
'No, Sir'	P.G. Mavlankar
One Day Wonders	Sunil Gavaskar
Panchtantra	Vishnu Sharma
Passage to England	Nirad C. Chaudhuri
Prison Diary	Jaya Prakash Narayan
Raghuvansha	Kalidas
Rajtarangini	Kalhana
Ramayana	Balmiki
Ramcharit Manas	Tulsidas
Rukh Te Rishi	Harbhajan Singh
Satyarth Prakash	Swami Dayanand
Sur Sagar	Surdas
The Guide	R.K. Narayan
The Insider	P.V. Narasimharao
The Post Office — *Dak Ghar*	Rabindra Nath Tagore
The God of Small Things	Arundhati Roy
Urvashi	Ram Dhari Singh 'Dinkar'
Yama	Mahadevi Verma
My Country : My Life (Autobiography)	L.K. Advani
The Test of My Life	Yuvraj Singh
Twenty Years in a Decade	Shah Rukh Khan

IMPORTANT BOOKS WRITTEN IN JAIL

Book	Author
My Experiments with Truth	Mahatma Gandhi
Glimpses of World History	Jawaharlal Nehru
Discovery of India	
Gita Rahasya	Lokmanya Bal Gangadhar Tilak

Book	Author
Pilgrim's Progress	John Bunyan
Bible (in German language)	Martin Luther
Les Miserables	Victor Hugo
Long Walk to Freedom	Nelson Mandela

* * * * *

11. First in India

First in India

Nobel Prize for Literature (1913)	Rabindra Nath Tagore
Nobel Prize for Physics (1929)	C.V. Raman
Nobel Prize for Peace (1979)	Mother Teresa
Nobel Prize for Economics (1998)	Amartya Sen
Special Oscar award winner (1992)	Satyajit Ray
Governor-General of free India (Last also)	C. Rajagopalachari
Woman Governor of the State	Smt. Sarojini Naidu
Indian Commanders-in-Chief	General K.M. Cariappa
Woman Chief Minister of a State	Smt. Sucheta Kripalani
Woman President of United Nations General Assembly (1954)	Smt. Vijaylakshmi Pandit
President of International Court of Justice	Dr. Nagendra Singh
Woman to swim across the English Channel	Ms. Aarti Saha
Miss Universe	Miss Sushmita Sen
Miss World	Reita Faria
Indian to swim across the English Channel	Mihir Sen
Field Marshal	S.H.F.J. Manekshaw
Indian recipient of Victoria Cross	Khudadad Khan
Indian to conquer Mt. Everest	Sherpa Tenzing, May 29, 1953
Indian male cosmonaut (1984)	Rakesh Sharma
Indian female cosmonaut	Kalpana Chawla (19 Nov., 1997)
Woman to climb Mt. Everest	Miss Bachendri Pal, May 23, 1984
Woman to get Olympic Medal	Karnam Malleswari
Indian to address the UN General Assembly in Hindi	Atal Bihari Vajpayee
Newspaper	Bengal Gazette, Jan 27, 1780
Postage Stamp issued	In 1852
Telegraph line laid	In 1851, Kolkata; Diamond Harbour
Railways run	April 16, 1853; Bombay-Thana
Electric Train run	1925: Bombay-Kurla
Atomic Power Station	Tarapore (Maharashtra)
Passenger-cum-cargo ship made in India	Harshavardhan
Satellite	Aryabhatta (1975)
Rocket	Rohini (1967)
Atomic Reactor	Apsara (1956)
Climb Everest without oxygen	Phu Dorjee (1987)
First film (movie)	Raja Harishchandra (1913)
First film (talkie)	Alam Ara (1931)
Metro Railway	Kolkata Metro Railway

Test-tube baby, scientifically documented	Born on August 6, 1986 at K.E.M. Hospital, Mumbai
TV Centre	At Delhi
Indian to get an Oscar	Bhanu Athaiya
Woman pilot in IAF	Ms Harita Kaur Deol
Cellular Phone	Kolkata, August 1, 1995
Women president of Indian National Congress	Smt. Annie Besant
President of Indian National Congress	W.C. Banerjee (1885)
Indian who passed in I.C.S. Examination	Satendra Nath Tagore
Woman chief justice of High Court	Lila Saith (Himachal Pradesh)
Woman Foreign Secretary	Chokila Iyyar

First Important Officials of India

The Governor-General of free India	Lord Mountbatten
President	Dr. Rajendra Prasad
President (Female)	Pratibha Patil
Vice-President	Dr. S. Radhakrishnan
Prime Minister	Jawahar Lal Nehru
Prime Minister (Female)	Indira Gandhi
Deputy Prime Minister	Sardar Vallabhbhai Patel
Chief Justice	Harilal J. Kania
First Female Judge in Supreme Court	Smt. Meera Sahib Fatima Bibi
Speaker, Lok Sabha	Ganesh Vasudeo Mawlankar
Woman Speaker of Lok Sabha	Meira Kumar
Chief Election Commissioner	Sukumar Sen
Indian Commander-in-Chief	General K.M. Cariappa
Indian Chief of Army Staff	General Maharaj Rajendra Sinhji
Indian Chief of Air Staff	Air Marshal S. Mukherjee
Indian Chief of Naval Staff	Vice Admiral Ramdas Katari
Chief of Defence Staff (CDS)	General Bipin Rawat
Female Minister	Raj Kumari Amrit Kaur (Health Minister)
Female Governor	Sarojini Naidu (U.P.)
Female Chief Minister	Sucheta Kripalani (U.P. 1963)
Finance Commissioner	K.C. Niyogi
Leader of Opposition in Lok Sabha (Recognised)	Y.V. Chavan (Congress)
Leader of Opposition in Rajya Sabha (Recognised)	Kamalapati Tripathi (Congress)

Highest, Biggest, Largest & Longest in India

Award for Gallantry, Highest	Param Vir Chakra
Award, highest civilian	Bharat Ratna
Bank with largest number of branches	State Bank of India
River bridge, Longest	Bhupen Hazarika bridge Assam Lohit (Brahamputra) River
Cantilever Span Bridge, Largest	Howrah Bridge (Kolkata)
Cattle Fair, Largest	Sonepur Fair (Bihar)
City, Most Populous	Mumbai
Corridor, Longest	Ramanathaswamy Corridor, Tamil Nadu (1,220 mt.)
Desert, Largest	Thar (Rajasthan)
Dam, Longest	Hirakud Dam (Odisha)

Dam, Highest	Tehri Dam on Bhagirathi river in Uttarakhand (855 ft.)
Delta, Largest	Sunderban (12,872 Sq. km.)
Gateway, Highest	Buland Darwaja at Fatehpur Sikri (54 m.)
Lake, Largest (Fresh Water)	Wular Lake (Kashmir)
Literacy, Highest	Kerala
Museum, Largest	Indian Museum (Kolkata)
Mosque, Biggest	Jama Masjid (Delhi)
Peak, Highest	K-2 (8,611 mt.)
Railway Platform, Longest	Shree Siddharoodha Swamiji Railway Station Hubballi, Karnataka (1507 m)
Railway Bridge, Largest	Vembanad Bridge, Kerala (4.6 km)
River, Longest	The Ganga river (2,525 km.)
Rainfall, Highest (annual mean)	Mowsynram near Cherrapunji (Meghalaya)
Road, Longest	NH-44 (3,745 km)
Road-Rail Longest Bridge	Bogibeel bridge, Assam (4.94 km)
Rock-cut Temple, Largest	Kailash Temples, Ellora (Maharashtra)
State, maximum forest cover	Madhya Pradesh
State, Largest (area)	Rajasthan (3,42,239 sq. km.)
State, Most Populous	Uttar Pradesh (19,98,12,341)
State with Maximum density of population	Bihar (1106 persons per sq. km.)
Tunnel, Longest (Road)	Dr. Shyama Prasad Mukherjee Tunnel (J & K—9.28 kms)
Tunnel, Longest (Railway)	T-50 Tunnel (Khari-Sumber section) (12.77 kms) (J&K)
Waterfall, Highest	Kunchikal Waterfall, Karnataka (455 m.)
Zoo, Largest	Arignar Anna Zoological Park, Chennai, Tamil Nadu
Man-made Lake, Largest	Govind Sagar (Bhakra)

Indian Banks

- **Reserve Bank of India:** It was established in 1935 and nationalised in 1949. It is the Central Bank of the country and issues all currency notes except one rupee note. It acts as a banker to the Government and exercises control over other commercial banks in the country. Headquarters of Reserve Bank of India is in Mumbai.
- **The State Bank of India:** Largest commercial bank, alongwith its seven other associate banks was nationalised in 1955. On 1st April, 2017, the State Bank of India, which was India's largest bank, merged with five of its associate banks (State Bank of Bikaner & Jaipur, State Bank of Hyderabad, State Bank of Mysore, State Bank of Patiala and State Bank of Travancore), and with the Bharatiya Mahila Bank.
- **Nationalisation of Banks:** The Government of India on July 19, 1969, took over 14 biggest commercial banks incorporated in the country. On April 15, 1980, six more banks were nationalised. In March 1994, the Parliament passed the Banking Regulation (Amendment) Bill, 1994 which inter alia provided for establishment of private sector banks. Till March 2025 there were 12 public sector banks including SBI in India.

Insurance

- **Life Insurance Corporation of India:** The Life Insurance Corporation of India was founded in September 1, 1956 when the Parliament of India passed the Life Insurance of India Act that nationalised the private insurance industry in India.
- **General Insurance Corporation of India:** The entire general insurance business in India was nationalized by the Government of India (GOI) through the General Insurance Business (Nationalization) Act (GIBNA) of 1972. 55 Indian insurance companies and 52 other general insurance operations of other companies were nationalized.

✵✵✵✵✵

12. CULTURAL ACTIVITIES

AKADEMIES

There are three akademies for promotion of creative art.

1. **Lalit Kala Akademi, New Delhi:** Established in 1954, the Lalit Kala Akademi strives for the popularisation of Indian art within the country and in various countries of the world through exhibitions, publications, workshops and camps. Every three year it organises the Triennale India, an international exhibition. It publishes research papers on Indian arts. Besides organising seminars, it honours eminent artists. The Akademi has set up regional centres called Rashtriya Lalit Kala Kendras at Lucknow, Kolkata, Chennai and Bhubaneswar and a small office at Mumbai.

2. **Sangeet Natak Akademi, New Delhi:** The Sangeet Natak Akademi, set-up in 1953, aims at the promotion and development of dance, drama and music. It holds seminars and festivals, presents awards to the eminent artists and extends financial assistance to traditional teachers and scholarships to students. It also operates a scheme of exchange of troupes.

3. **Sahitya Akademi, New Delhi:** The Sahitya Akademi, established in 1954, has the main functions of development of Indian letters, setting up high literary standards, translation of literary works of one Indian language into other Indian languages, publication of books on history of literature and criticism, bibliographies and reference books. The Akademy has regional offices at Mumbai, Kolkata, Bengaluru and Chennai.

4. **National School of Drama:** It is one of the top theatre training institutes in the world and only one of its kind in India. It was set up in 1959 under Sangeet Natak Akademi but was later made autonomous organisation in 1975.

SCULPTURE

Archaeological Survey of India, set up in 1861, is responsible for preservation and maintenance of sculptures and historical monuments and manages a number of archaeological museums.

National Archives of India, established in 1891, it is the official custodian of all non-current records of permanent value of the Government of India and its predecessor bodies.

MUSEUMS

They are repositories of the cultural heritage and conserve and preserve historical technical and other materials against decay and transmit them to posterity as records of history.

MUSIC

Main Schools of Classical Music: There are two main schools of classical music, namely, the Hindustani and the Carnatic. The Hindustani school of classical music is in vogue in north-western India, eastern India and northern parts of the South India.

Musical Instruments: They are: Tabla, Mridangam, Pakhawaj, Chandai, Dholak, Veena, Sitar, Sarod, Gootuvadhyam, Sarangi, Flute, Nadaswaram, Shehnai, Shringi and Turahi.

DANCE

India has a very rich tradition of tribal, folk and classical dances.

Classical Dance

Dance	State	Famous Artists
Bharat Natyam	Tamil Nadu	Yamini Krishnamurthy, Rukmini Devi Arundale, Swapna Sundari, Sonal Mansingh, Vaijanti Mala, Mrinalini Sarabhai, Chandralekha, Indrani, Ram Gopal, Bal Saraswati
Kathakali	Kerala	Gopinath, K.K. Nayar, Kunju-Kurup, T.K. Chandu
Kuchipudi	Andhra Pradesh	Sapna Sundari, Raja Reddy, Shobha Nayar, Radha Reddy, Vedantam Satyanarayan, Vimpanti Chinna Satyam.
Kathak	North India	Birju Maharaj, Gopi Krishna, Shambhu Maharaj, Sitara Devi, Vishnu Sharma, Durga Lal, Shobhana Narayan
Odissi	Odisha	Kelucharan Mahapatra, Indrani Rehman, Madhavi Mudgal, Protima Bedi, Samyukta Panigrahi, Sonal Mansingh, Debudas
Manipuri	Manipur	Uday Shankar, Bipin Singh, Suryamukhi, Darohra Jhaveri

Famous Folk-Dance

State	Folk Dance
Andhra Pradesh	Dandari, Banjara
Asom	Bihu, Keli Gopal, Sataria
Bihar	Chhau, Magahi, Durga dance
W. Bengal	Kirtan, Kalatri, Asweabadh, Brita, Kalidance
Chhattisgarh	Saila, Karama, Bhagoria
Gujarat	Garba, Rasalila, Tippani, Dandia,
Haryana	Damyal, Lahoor
Himachal Pradesh	Dussehra dance, Hikat, Notio
Jammu & Kashmir	Dumhal
Jharkhand	Jhau, Ghumakudia, Jadur, Sarhul, Soharai, Karama, Vaima, Loojhari, Jat-Jatin, Vidayat
Karnataka	Yakshagan, Dolu Kunitha
Kerala	Mohini Attam, Padayuni
Madhya Pradesh	Lota Nritya, Jawara
Maharashtra	Tamasha, Dahi Handi, Gof, Deepak Dindi
Manipur	Dhol Cholam
Meghalaya	Nongakarem
Nagaland	Bamboo dance
Odisha	Chhau, Maya Shabari, Dalachai
Punjab	Gidda, Bhangra, Panihari
Rajasthan	Thumar, Kathaputali, Tera Tali
Tamil Nadu	Terukalathu, Kabalatam, Kargam, Pulivesham
Tripura	Hazagiri
Uttar Pradesh	Rasalila, Nautanki, Thali, Dhurang, Jhumela, Huraka, Bol.
Uttarakhand	Kajari, Karan
Goa	Dhode Modini

Musical Instruments and Artists

Musical Instrument	*Artists*
Flute	Hari Prasad Chaurasia, Panna Lal Ghosh, T.R. Mahalingam, N. Ramani, Vijaya Raghava Rao
Tabla	Allah Rakha, Gudai Maharaj, Latif Khan, Zakir Hussain
Violin	Lalgudi Jayaraman, L. Subramaniam, M.S. Gopal Krishnan, S. Subrahmaniam, V.G. Jog, N. Rajan
Shehnai	Bismilla Khan, Imrat Khan Ali Akbar
Sarod	Khan, Amjad Ali Khan, Alauddin Khan, Saren Rani, Brij Narayan
Sitar	Pandit Ravishankar, Vilayat Khan
Santur	Shiv Kumar Sharma
Rudraveena	Zia Mohiuddin Dagar
Pakhawaj	Govind Rao, Anokhe Lal, Kanthi Maharaj
Mridanga	Palghat R. Raghu, U.S. Burman
Harmonium	Purushottam Walawakar, M. Dhaulpuri
Guitar	Pt. Vishnu Mohan Bhatt, Brij Bhushan Kalra
Ghatam	T.H. Vinayakaram
Janjira	V. Nagarajan
Symphony	Jubin Mehta

Major Park & Wild Life Sanctuaries in India

India is rich in flora and fauna. However, due to increasing population and industrial and commercial activities, there has been acute pressure on forests. The Government has taken several steps to check the sharp fall in the number of these species. Among the measures are declaration of certain habitats as national parks and sanctuaries. 106 national parks and 573 sanctuaries have been established till March 2025, important ones being given below:

Assam: Kaziranga National Park (know for one-horn Rhinoceroses); Manas Sanctuary.

Jharkhand: Hazaribagh National Park; Betla Tiger Reserve Palamau.

Gujarat: Valvadar National Park, Bhavnagar; Marine National Park, Gir Forests.

Himachal Pradesh: Rohla National Park; Motichur Sanctuary.

Jammu & Kashmir: Dachigam Sanctuary.

Karnataka: Bandipur National Park; Bannargheta National Park, Bangalore; Nagorhole National Park, Coorg; Ranganthitto Bird Sanctuary.

Kerala: Eravikulam Rajmallay National Park, Idduki; Periyar Game Sanctuary.

Madhya Pradesh: Kanha National Park; Bandhavgarh National Park, Shahdol; Shivpuri National Park.

Maharashtra: Taloba National Park, Chandrapur; Panch National Park, Nagpur; Borivali National Park, Mumbai; Nawagaon National Park, Bandara; Melghat National Park.

Manipur: Keibul Lamjao National Park.

Odisha: Simlipal, Tiger Sanctuary.

Rajasthan: Sariska Sanctuary; Ghana Bird Sanctuary, Ranthambhor Sanctuary.

Sikkim: Khangchandzenda National Park, Gangtok.

Tamil Nadu: Vedanthangal Bird Sanctuary; Guindy National Park, Chennai; Mudumalai Sanctuary; Kalakad-Munden Thurai Reserve.

Uttar Pradesh: Chandraprabha Sanctuary; Dudhwa National Park, Lakhimpur.

West Bengal: Jaldapara Sanctuary; Sunderbans.

Uttarakhand: Corbett National Park; Nainital.

* * * * *

13. AWARDS

NATIONAL AWARDS

★ **Bharat Ratna:** This is India's highest civilian award. It is given for exceptional work on art, literature, science and recognition of public service of the highest order. Government servants are not eligible for it.

★ **Padma Vibhushan:** This award is given for exceptional and distinguished service in any field, including service rendered by Govt. servants.

★ **Padma Bhushan:** This award is given for distinguished service of a high order in any field, including service rendered by Govt. servants.

★ **Padma Shri:** This award is given for distinguished service in any field, including service rendered by Government servants.

GALLANTRY AWARDS

★ **Param Vir Chakra:** The highest award for bravery or some daring and pre-eminent act of valour or self-sacrifice in the presence of the enemy, whether on land, at sea or in the air.

★ **Mahavir Chakra:** It is the second highest decoration and is awarded for acts of conspicuous gallantry in the presence of the enemy, whether on land, at sea or in the air.

★ **Vir Chakra:** It is the third in order of awards given for acts of gallantry in the presence of enemy, whether on land, at sea or in the air.

★ **Ashok Chakra:** This medal is awarded for the most conspicuous bravery or some daring or pre-eminent act of valour or self-sacrifice on land, at sea or in the air but not in the presence of enemy.

★ **Vishishta Sewa Medal:** It is awarded to personnel of all the three Services in class I, II and III in recognition of distinguished service of the "most exceptional" and "exceptional" and a "high" order respectively. Prefixes *Parma* and *Ati* are added before first two categories of medals respectively.

★ **Jeewan Raksha Padak:** Awarded for meritorious acts or a series of acts of a human nature displayed in saving life from drowning, fire and rescue operations in mines etc.

National Sports Awards

★ **Major Dhyan Chand Khel Ratna Award:** The scheme was launched in the year 1991-92 with the objective of honouring sportspersons to enhance their general status and to give them greater dignity and place of honour in society. Under this scheme, an amount of ₹ 25 lakh is given as award for the most spectacular and outstanding performance by a sportsperson over a period of four years immediately preceding the year in which award is to be given.

★ **Dronacharya Award:** Dronacharya Award is an award presented by ministry of youth Affairs and Sports, Government of India for excellence in sports coaching. The Dronacharya (Lifetime) awardees gets ₹ 15 lakh and Dronacharya (Regular) awardees gets ₹ 10 lakh a bronze statuette of Dronacharya and scroll of honour. The award was instituted in 1985.

★ **Arjuna Award:** The Arjuna Awards are given by the ministry of youth Affairs and sports, government of India to recognize outstanding achievement in National sports. Instituted in 1961 the award carries a cash prize of 15,00,000 a bronze statue of Arjuna and a scroll.

★ **Arjuna Award (Lifetime):** Arjuna Award (Lifetime) is India's highest award for lifetime achievement in sports and games, given by the ministry of youth Affairs and sports, government of India. The award is initiated in 2002. The award carries a cash prize of ₹ 10,00,000 a plaque and a scroll of honour.

★ **Maulana Abul Kalam Azad Trophy:** This trophy was instituted in 1956-57. The top overall performing university in the inter-university tournaments is given the Maulana Abul Kalam Azad (MAKA) Trophy, which is a rolling trophy. A small replica of the MAKA Trophy is also awarded for retention by the university. In addition, the university also gets a cash prize of ₹ 15 lakh. The second and third best universities also receive cash awards amounting to ₹ 5 lakh and ₹ 3 lakh respectively.

Other Awards

★ **Jnanpith Award:** Awarded to outstanding authors of creative literature in any of the Indian languages recognised by the Constitution of India. It was sponsored by the Bharatiya Jnanpith a culturo-literary society founded in 1944 by Shanti Prasad Jain, an eminent industrialist.

★ **Sahitya Akademi Award:** It is awarded for outstanding literary works and comprises a cash prize of ₹ 1,00,000 in each of the 22 languages mentioned in the Eighth schedule of the Constitution and Rajasthani and English that it supports and a copper plaque.

★ **Saraswati Samman:** The award is given by K.K. Birla Foundation to an outstanding author for his literary work in any Indian language mentioned in the Eighth Schedule of the Constitution and published during the last 10 years.

★ **Dada Saheb Phalke Award:** The prestigious Dada Saheb Phalke Award is given to the persons for outstanding contribution to the growth and development of Indian cinema. First presented in 1969, the award was introduced by the government of India to commemorate Dadasaheb Phalke's contribution to Indian Cinema. Phalke, who is popularly known as and often regarded as a the Father of Indian Cinema was an Indian film-maker who directed India's first-length feature film, Raja Harishchandra. The first recipient of the award was actress Devika Rani, who was honoured at the 17th National film Awards.

★ **Indira Gandhi Award:** The award has been instituted for promoting national integration and understanding amongst the religious groups, communities and ethnic groups of India.

★ **Bhartendu Harishchandra Awards:** The Bhartendu Harishchandra Awards were instituted in 1983, by the Ministry of Information and Broadcasting for original Hindi writing on any subject in mass communications like journalism, publication, advertising, broadcasting films, etc.

INTERNATIONAL AWARDS

★ **Nobel Prizes:** The most prestigious award in the world is supported by the Nobel Foundation of US. This award was set up in 1900 under the will to Alfred Bernhard Nobel (1833-96). Alfred Nobel was an unmarried, Swedish scientist and chemical engineer who discovered Nitroglycerin ($C_3H_5N_3O_9$) and its use in the manufacture of dynamite in 1966. The interest accrued on the fortune left by him is divided annually among the persons who have made outstanding contribution in science, literature, peace and economics. Swedes found out about the prizes only after his death in 1896. When they read his will in which he had donated the annual income from his fortune to support the awards. In his will he ordered that 'the most worthy shall receive the prize, whether he is Scandinavian or not. This led to his criticism as being unpatriotic for not reserving the prizes only for Swedes.

Nobel Foundation's Prize Awarding Bodies

(*i*) The Royal Swedish Academy of Sciences, awards the Nobel prize in Physics and Chemistry.

(*ii*) The Nobel Assembly of Karolinska Chirugical Institute. Sweden, awards the Nobel Prize in Medicine and Physiology.

(*iii*) The Swedish Academy awards the Prize in Literature.

(*iv*) The Committee of the Norwegian Parliament awards the Prize for Peace.

(*v*) The Bank of Sweden awards the Nobel Prize in Economics.

★ **Ramon Magsaysay Award:** The Raman Magsaysay Award, named after a Philippines President, who died in an air crash in 1957, is given annually to Asian nationals or institutions who have made worthy contributions to public service, community leadership, journalism, literature and the creative arts and international understanding. It carries a gold medal, a certificate and US$ 50,000.

★ **Pulitzer Prize:** Instituted in 1970 and named after the US publisher Joseph Pulitzer (1847-1911). It is conferred annually in the United States for accomplishment in journalism, literature and music under the management to the Pulitzer Prize Board at Columbia University.

★ **Man Booker Prize:** Instituted in 1968, it is the highest literary award set up by the Booker Company and the British Publishers Association along the lines of the Pultizer Prize, of USA, worth £ 20,000 (1992). Since 2002, it has been known as the **'Man Booker Prize'**, reflecting the sponsorship by an investment company, the Man Group plc. The winner receives £ 50,000 and both the winner and the shorlisted authors are guaranteed a world wide readership plus a dramatic increase in book sales.

★ **Oscar Awards:** The annual Oscar presentation has been held since 1929. After three-quarters of a century of recognizing excellence in cinema achievement, the annual presentation of the Oscars has become the Academy of Motion Picture Arts and Sciences' most famous activity.

★ **Kalinga Award:** The award given for popularisation of science is an international award conferred annually by the United Nations Educational, Scientific and Cultural Organisation (UNESCO) to a person with a distinguished career of service in the interpretation of science and research to the public. The award was instituted in 1952 at the initiative of Mr Biju Patnaik the founder of the Kalinga Foundation Trust in Odisha.

★ **Grammy Award:** The Grammy Foundation was established in 1989 to cultivate an awareness, appreciation and advancement of the contribution of recorded music American culture from the and technical legends of the past to the still unimagined musical breakthroughs of the future generations of the music professionals. The Grammy Foundation works in partnership with its founder, the Recording Academy, to bring national attention to important issues such as the value and impact of music and arts education and the urgency of preserving our rich cultural legacy.

Highest Honours of Some Countries

Country	*Highest Honour*
India	Bharat Ratna
Pakistan	Nishan-e-Pakistan
Kuwait	Mubarak-Al-kabir Medal
Saudi Arabia	Shah Abdul Aziz Medal
Argentina	The Order of Sona Martin
Nicaragua	Augusto-Caesar Sandino Order
Vietnam	The order of the Golden Star
Hungary	The Order of Banner
Britain	Member of British Empire, Victoria Cross
Japan	Order of Moulovenice Sun
Denmark	Order of Diana Brog
France	Legend of Honour
America	Presidential Medal of Freedom
Germany	Pore Lee Merit Iron Cross
The Netherlands	Netherlands Lion

✸✸✸✸✸

COMPUTERS

Introduction

The term computer is derived from the Latin word compute, which means to calculate. A computer is an electronic machine, devised for performing calculations and controlling operations that can be expressed either in logical or numerical terms. In simple terms, a computer is an electronic device that performs diverse operations with the help of instructions to process the information in order to achieve the desired results. A Computer application extends to cover huge area including education, industries, government, medicine, scientific research etc.

A computer is one of the most influential forces available in modern times. Due to its memory, high speed and perfection, its application can be extended to almost infinite levels. Millions of complex calculations can be done in mere fraction of time. Difficult decisions can be made with accuracy for comparatively little cost. Computers are widely seen as instruments for future progress and as tools to achieve substantiality by way of improved access to information by means of video conferencing and e-mail. Indeed computers have left such on impression on modern civilization that we call this era as the information age.

Computer System

A computer system is a combination of various components. It performs the system functions such as input, processing, output, storage and control. A computer system consists of the following components: 1. Hardware; 2. Software

Hardware

The physical components of the computer, such as electrical, electronics and mechanical unit are known as the hardware of the computer. That is, the input units, output units and CPU are called hardware. Thus hardware is the equipment involved in the function of a computer. It consists of the components that can be physically handled.

Software

The computer performs operations like addition, subtraction, multiplication and division only when the user instructs it to do so. The user issues instructions and the CPU acts in accordance with the instructions. The sets of instructions, which control the sequence of operations, are known as programs, and collectively programs are called software. The software can be broadly classified into two types. They are: (a) System Software (b) Application Software.

Difference between Hardware & Software

Hardware

1. It is the physical unit of the computer
2. Hardware understands only machine language, lower level language or binary
3. It works with binary code, the presence or absence of Pulses as 1's or 0's.

Software

1. It is a collection of programs to bring the hardware system into operation
2. It is written by a well versed programmer and generally in higher level language which is readable by human being.
3. It is represented by the Higher Level Languages such as BASIC, COBOL, *etc.,*

System Software

System software consists of several Programs, which are directly responsible for controlling, integrating and managing the individual hardware components of a computer system. They provide basic functionality like file management, visual display and keyboard input which are used by application software. Some examples of system software are operating system, device drivers, language translators, system utilities.

Application Software

A computer program used to perform a specific task, rather than just managing a computer system. Some examples of application software are word processing, spread sheets, database management systems.

Two Types of Computer Systems

Analog Computers : The analog computers operate by measuring instead of counting. The analog computer works on the supply of continuous electrical signals. The display is also continuous. Its output is in the form of graphs.

Digital Computers : These computers work with quantities represented as digits. They operate on discrete quantities. In digital computer, both numeric and non-numeric information are represented as strings of digits. These computers use binary codes, 0's and 1's, to represent the information. The information is given to the computer in the form of discrete electrical signals.

Input/Output Devices

Input Devices : An input device is any machine that feeds data into a computer. For example, a keyboard is an input device. Input devices other than the keyboard are sometimes called alternate devices. Trackballs, mouse and light pens are all alternate input devices.

Output Devices : Output is anything that comes out of a computer. Output can be meaningful information or gibberish, and it can appear in a variety of forms - as binary numbers, as characters, as pictures, and as printed pages. Output devices include display screens, loudspeakers, printers, plotters, etc.

Computer Memory

There are two kinds of computer memory: primary and secondary. Primary memory is accessible directly by the processing unit. RAM is an example of primary memory. As soon as the computer is switched off the contents of the primary memory is lost. You can store and retrieve data much faster with primary memory compared to secondary memory. Secondary memory such as floppy disks, magnetic disk, etc., is located outside the computer. Primary memory is more expensive than secondary memory. Because of this the size of primary memory is less than that of secondary memory.

Types of Primary Memory

- Random Access Memory (RAM)
- Read Only Memory (ROM)
- Programmable Read Only Memory (PROM)
- Erasable Programmable Read Only Memory (EPROM)

Cache Memory

To decrease the mismatch in operating speed, a small memory chip is attached between CPU and Main memory whose access time is very close to the processing speed of CPU. It is called CACHE memory. CACHE memories are accessed much faster than conventional RAM. It is used to store programs or data currently being executed or temporary data frequently used by the CPU.

Types of Secondary Memory

- Magnetic Tape
- Magnetic Disk
- Floppy Disk
- Optical Disk–1. Compact Disk/ Read Only Memory (CD-ROM), 2. Erasable Optical Disk.

The memory is measured by the following units:

(*a*) **BIT (Binary digit):** It is the smallest possible unit of information. It can be either 0 or 1.

(*b*) **NIBBLE:** Four bits form one nibble.

(*c*) **BYTE:** It is a unit of information consisting of fixed number of bits. It is a combination of 8 bits.

(*d*) **CHARACTER:** It is represented by one byte. It can be a letter, digit, punctuation mark or special characters.

(*e*) **WORD:** The combination of 2 bytes or 4 bytes or 8 bytes is a word.

The data measurement is as follows:

8 bits - 1 byte

1024 bytes - 1 Kilo Byte (KB)

1024 KB - 1 Mega Byte (MB)

1024 MB - 1 Giga Byte (GB)

1024 GB - 1 Tera Byte (TB)

Word keyboard shortcuts

Action	*Key Stroke*
Open a file	Ctrl + O
New file	Ctrl + N
Close a file	Ctrl + W
Save As	F12
Save	Ctrl+S or Shift+F12
Print Preview	Ctrl + F2
Print	Ctrl + P
Show/Hide paragraph symbols	Ctrl + *
Spelling and grammar	F7
Help	F1
Find	Ctrl + F
Replace	Ctrl + H
Go To	Ctrl + G
Select all - entire document	Ctrl + A
Select from cursor to beginning of line	Shift + Home
Select from cursor to end of line	Shift + End
Go to beginning of line	Home
Go to end of line	End
Go to beginning of document	Ctrl + Home
Go to end of document	Ctrl + End
Cut	Ctrl + X
Copy	Ctrl + C
Paste	Ctrl + V
Undo	Ctrl + Z
Redo	Ctrl + Y
Format painter	Ctrl + Shift + C
Left alignment	Ctrl + L
Center alignment	Ctrl + E
Right alignment	Ctrl + R
Justified	Ctrl + J
Delete previous word	Ctrl + Backspace
Apply bulleted list	Ctrl + Shift + L
Indent	Ctrl + M
Page break	Ctrl + Enter
Font face	Ctrl + Shift + F
Font size	Ctrl + Shift + P
Bold	Ctrl + B
Italics	Ctrl + I
Underline	Ctrl + U
Double underline	Ctrl + Shift + D
Word underline	Ctrl + Shift + A
Change case	Shift + F3
Subscript	Ctrl + =
Superscript	Ctrl + Shift + =
Make web hyperlink	Ctrl + K
Go to next cell	Tab
Go to previous cell	Shift + Tab
Go to beginning of column	Alt + PageUp
Highlight to beginning of column	Alt + Shift + PageUp
Go to end of column	Alt + PageDown
Highlight to end of column	Alt + Shift + PageDown
Go to beginning of row	Alt + Home
Highlight to beginning of row	Alt+Shift+Home
Go to end of row	Alt + End
Highlight to end of row	Alt+Shift+End
Column break	Ctrl+Shift+Enter
Copyright ©	Alt + Ctrl + C
Date field	Alt + Shift + D
Go to footnotes	Alt + Ctrl + F
Show/Hide ¶	Ctrl + Shift + 8
Theasaurus	Shift + F7

Operating System

It is the first layer of software loaded into computer memory when it starts up. As the first software layer, all other software that gets loaded after it depends on it for various common core services. In simple words, the operating system organizes and controls the hardware. Examples of operating systems are Windows XP, UNIX, and Linux.

Programming Languages

Computers are machines. Unfortunately they cannot understand natural languages, such as Hindi, English, Tamil, etc. that human beings speak and understand. Therefore, to give instructions to computers, different languages have been developed. These languages are called computer languages. It is a general purpose language that is designed to combine business and scientific processing features and that can easily learned by novice programmers, yet contains advanced features for experienced programmers.

Computer languages are classified into three categories: 1. Low Level Language; 2. Machine language; 3. High level languages.

Compiler

A compiler is a kind of translator that translates a program into another program, known as target language. Usually, the term compiler is used for language translator of high-level language into machine language. The compiler replaces single high-level statement with a series of machine language instruction.

Interpreter

Unlike compilers, an interpreter translates a statement in a program and executes the statement immediately, before translating the next source language statement. Similar to compilers, every interpreted language such as BASIC and LISP has its own interpreters.

Computer Networks

A computer network, often simply referred to as a **network**, is a collection of computers and devices connected by communications channels that facilitates communications among users and allows users to share resources with other users.

Categories of Network

(*i*) **LAN :** LAN stands for Local Area Network. These networks evolved around the PC revolution. LANs enabled multiple users in a relatively small geographical area to exchange files and messages, as well as access shared resources such as file servers.

(*ii*) **WAN :** WAN stands for Wide Area Network. The interconnection of various LAN's through telephone network, which unites geographically distributed users, is achieved through WAN. In short when we log on to the internet, we become a part of a WAN.

(*iii*) **MAN :** MAN stands for Metropolitan Area Network. It is usually the interconnection between various LAN's in a particular geographical area like a metropolitan city like Bombay.

Internet

Internet is a communication network which bridges all the small computer networks worldwide as a whole. Internet is based upon Internet technology, in particular World Wide Web (WWW), to build Information System within organization or enterprise to accomplish standardization and automation. Fundamentally, it means network computing environments which let the users share the information through the Internet and Web browsers.

Characteristics of Intranet

The following are the important characteristics of the Intranet.

(*a*) It is an extended internet-private business networks located outside of the corporate firewall.

(*b*) It can be referred to an intranet that is partially accessible to authorized outsiders.

(*c*) It is a network that uses the internet to link businesses with others that share the common goals.

E-MAIL

E-mail is an electronic message sent from one computer to another. We can send or receive personal and business-related messages with attachments, such as pictures or formatted documents. We can even send songs and computer programs.

* * * * *

14. Sports

Important Cups & Trophies

International

Cup/Trophy	Sport	Cup/Trophy	Sport
American Cup	Yacht Racing	*Walker Cup*	Golf
Ashes	Cricket	*Westchester Cup*	Polo
Benson and Hedges	Cricket	*Wightman Cup*	Lawn Tennis
Canada Cup	Golf	*World Cup*	Cricket
Colombo Cup	Football	*World Cup*	Hockey
Corbitton Cup	Table Tennis (Women)	*Reliance Cup*	Cricket
Davis Cup	Lawn Tennis	*Rothman's Trophy*	Cricket
Derby	Horse Race	*William's Cup*	Basketball
Grand National	Horse Streple Chase Race	*European Champions Cup*	Football
Jules Rimet Trophy	World Soccer Cup	*Eisenhower Cup*	Golf
King's Cup	Air Races	*Essande Champions Cup*	Hockey
Merdeka Cup	Football	*Rene Frank Trophy*	Hockey
Ryder Cup	Golf	*Grand Prix*	Table Tennis
Swaythling Cup	Table Tennis (Men)	*Edgbaston Cup*	Lawn Tennis
Thomas Cup	Badminton	*Grand Prix*	Lawn Tennis
Uber Cup	Badminton (Women)	*World Cup*	Weightlifting
U. Thant Cup	Tennis		

National

Cup/Trophy	Sport	Cup/Trophy	Sport
Agarwal Cup	Badminton	*C.K. Naidu Trophy*	Cricket
Agha Khan Cup	Hockey	*Chakola Gold Trophy*	Football
All India Women's Guru Nanak Championship	Hockey	*Divan Cup*	Badminton
Bandodkar Trophy	Football	*Deodhar Trophy*	Cricket
Bangalore Blues Challenge Cup	Basketball	*Duleep Trophy*	Cricket
Barna-Bellack Cup	Table Tennis	*D.C.M. Cup*	Football
Beighton Cup	Hockey	*Durand Cup*	Football
Bombay Gold Cup	Hockey	*Dhyan Chand Trophy*	Hockey
Burdwan Trophy	Weightlifting	*Dr. B.C. Roy Trophy*	Football (Junior)
Charminar Trophy	Atheletics	*Ezra Cup*	Polo
Chadha Cup	Badminton	*F.A. Cup*	Football
		G.D. Birla Trophy	Cricket
		Ghulam Ahmed Trophy	Cricket
		Gurmeet Trophy	Hockey

- *Guru Nanak Cup* : Hockey
- *Gyanvati Devi Trophy* : Hockey
- *Holkar Trophy* : Bridge
- *Irani Trophy* : Cricket
- *I.F.A. Shield* : Football
- *Indira Gold Cup* : Hockey
- *Jawaharlal Challenge* : Air Racing
- *Jaswant Singh Trophy* : Best Services Sportsman
- *Kuppuswamy Naidu Trophy* : Hockey
- *Lady Rattan Tata Trophy* : Hockey
- *MCC Trophy* : Hockey
- *Moinuddaula Gold Cup* : Cricket
- *Murugappa Gold Cup* : Hockey
- *Modi Gold Cup* : Hockey
- *Narang Cup* : Badminton
- *Nehru Trophy* : Hockey
- *Nixan Gold Cup* : Football
- *Obaidullah Gold Cup* : Hockey
- *Prithi Singh Cup* : Polo
- *Rani Jhansi Trophy* : Cricket
- *Ranji Trophy* : Cricket
- *Rangaswami Cup* : Hockey
- *Ranjit Singh Gold Cup* : Hockey
- *Rajendra Prasad Cup* : Tennis
- *Ramanujan Trophy* : Table Tennis
- *Rene Frank Trophy* : Hockey
- *Radha Mohan Cup* : Polo
- *Raghbir Singh Memorial* : Football
- *Rohinton Baria Trophy* : Cricket
- *Rovers Cup* : Football
- *Sanjay Gold Cup* : Football
- *Santosh Trophy* : Football
- *Sir Ashutosh Mukherjee* : Football
- *Subroto Cup* : Football
- *Scindia Gold Cup* : Hockey
- *Sahni Trophy* : Hockey
- *Sheesh Mahal Trophy* : Cricket
- *Todd Memorial Trophy* : Football
- *Tommy Eman Gold Cup* : Hockey
- *Vittal Trophy* : Football
- *Vizzy Trophy* : Cricket
- *Vijay Merchant Trophy* : Cricket
- *Wellington Trophy* : Rowing
- *Wills Trophy* : Cricket

Sports Measurements

- *Badminton Courts:* 44 ft. by 20 ft. (doubles) 44 ft. by 17 ft. (singles)
- *Boxing Ring:* 12 ft. by 28 ft. Sq.
- *Cricket Pitch:* 22 yards (distance)
- *Derby Course:* 1½ miles. (2.4 km)
- *Football Field:*
  (a) Length : 100 – 120 yards.
  Breadth: 50 – 56 yards.
  (b) Rugby : 100 yards by 75 yards
- *Hockey Ground:* 100 yards by 55 to 60 yards
- *Lawn Tennis Court:* 78 ft. by 36 ft. (double), 78 ft. by 28 ft. (single)
- *Marathon Race:* 26 miles, 385 yards
- *Polo Ground:* 300 yards by 200 yards (if boarded)
- *Golf:* Hole 4½ inches in diameter.

Sports Terms

- **Badminton:** Mixed doubles; Deuce; Drop; Smash; Let; Foot work; Setting.
- **Base Ball:** Pitcher; Put out, Strike; Home; Bunt.
- **Billiards:** Cue; Jigger; Pot; Break; In Baulk; In Off; Cannons.
- **Boxing:** Upper cut; Round; Punch; Bout; Knock down; Hitting below the belt; Ring.
- **Bridge:** Finesse; Dummy; Revoke; Grand Slam; Little Slam; No Trump; Rubber.
- **Chess:** Bishop, Gambit; Checkmate; Stalemate.
- **Cricket:** L.B.W. *(leg before wicket)*; Creases, Popping-creases; Stumped; Bye; Leg-Bye; Googly; Hattrick; Maiden over; Drive; Bowling; Duck; Follow-on; No ball; Leg Break; Silly point; Cover point; Hit-wicket; Late-cut; Slip; Off-spinner.
- **Football:** Off Side; Block; Drop-kick; Penalty-kick (or *goal kick*); Corner-kick; Free-kick; Dribble; Thrown-in; Foul.
- **Golf:** Boggy; Foursome; Stymic; Tee; Put; Hole; Niblic; Caddie; Links; The green; Bunker.
- **Hockey:** Carried; Short Corner; Bully; Sticks; Off side; Roll in; Striking Circle; Under-cutting.
- **Horse racing:** Jockey; Punter.
- **Polo:** Bunker; Chukker; Mallet.
- **Tennis:** Back hand drive; Volley; Smash; Half-volley; Deuce; Service; Let; Grand Slam.

Name of Playing Compound of Different Games

Name of Compound	*Related Sports*	*Name of Compound*	*Related Sports*
Court	Lawn Tennis, Badminton, Netball, Hand ball, Volleyball, Squash, Kho-Kho, Kabaddi	Pool	Swimming
Diamond	Baseball	Alley	Bowling
Ring	Boxing, Skating, Wrestling, Circus, Riding display	Mat	Judo, Karate II
Course	Golf	Arena	Horse Riding
Board	Table Tennis	Vellodrum	Cycling
		Field	Polo, Football, Hockey
		Track	Athletics
		Pitch	Cricket, Rugby
		Rink	Ice Hockey

National Sports and Games of Some Countries

Australia	Cricket	Spain	Bull Fighting
Canada	Ice Hockey	USA	Baseball
England	Cricket and Rugby Football	China	Table Tennis
Russia	Chess	Malaysia	Badminton
Scotland	Rugby Football	Pakistan	Hockey

OLYMPIC GAMES

First of all these games were held by the Greeks in 776 B.C. on Mount Olympus in honour of the Greek God Zeus. In this way, the history of Olympic Games is about twenty eight hundred years old. These games continued to be held every four years until 394 A.D. When these games were stopped by a royal order of the emperor of Rome. The modern Olympic Games which started in Athens in 1896, are the result of the devotion and dedication of a French educator Baron Pierre de Coubertin and the first Olympic meet in the modern series was held in 1896 in Athens, the Capital of Greece. Since then, they are being held every four years except for breaks during world wars. The Olympic flag is white in colour with five coloured rings, each ring symbolic of a continent. Summer as well as winter Olympics are held in the same year.

COMMONWEALTH GAMES

The Commonwealth Games are held every four years, in the year in which Asian Games are held. All the Commonwealth Countries (former colonies of Britain) can take part in it. The first Commonwealth Games were held in 1930 at Hamilton (Canada).

ASIAN GAMES

After the Second World War, most of the Asian Countries gained independence. On the lines of Olympic Games, Asian Games were planned every four years. India hosted the first Asian Games in 1951.

CRICKET WORLD CUP

The first Cricket World Cup was organised in England in 1975. A separate women's Cricket World Cup has been held every 4 years since 1973. Australia is the winner of 2023 Cricket World Cup.

HOCKEY WORLD CUP

The first Hockey World Cup was organised in Barcelona (Spain) in 1971. Women's Hockey World Cup has been held since 1974.

FOOTBALL WORLD CUP

The Football World Cup is organised by FIFA (Federation of International Football Association). The World Cup is called 'Jules Rimet Cup' named after the name of FIFA President Jules Rimet. The first Football World Cup was organised in Uruguay in 1930.

Personalities Associated with Sports

- **Athletics:** Carl Lewis, Linford Christy, Ben Johnson, Calvin Smith, Edwin Moses, Sergei Bubka, Sebestian Coe, Rosa Mota, Harold Schmidt, Milkha Singh, P.T. Usha, Shiny Abraham, Jesse Owens, Jyotirmoy Sikdar.
- **Boxing:** Cassius Clay (Mohammad Ali), Joe Frazier, Mike Tyson, Larry Holmes, Frank Bruno, Henry Cooper, Archie Moore, Evander Holyfield, George Foreman.
- **Badminton:** Prakash Padukone, Syed Modi, Dinesh Khanna, Jamie Paulson, Nandu Natekar, Liem Swie King, Saina Nehwal, P.V. Sindhu.
- **Billiards:** Wilson Jones, Geet Sethi, Michael Ferreira, Pankaj Advani.
- **Chess:** Boris Spausky, Gary Kasparov, Anatoly Karpov, Victor Korchonoi, Vishwanathan Anand, Konern Humpy, Parveen Thipsay.
- **Cricket:** Sunil Gavaskar, Bishen Singh Bedi, Kapil Dev, Mohd. Azharuddin, Sachin Tendulkar, G.R. Vishwanath, Lala Amarnath, Ajit Wadekar, B.S. Chandrashekhar, E.A.S. Prasanna, S. Venkatraghvan, Don Bradman, Richard Hadlee, Gary Sobers, Ian Botham, Vivian Richards, Clive Llyod, Dilip Sardesai, Charles Griffith, Imran Khan, Mushtaq Mohammad, Geoff Boycott, Tony Greg, Wasim Akram, Richie Benaud, Michael Holding, Greg Chappell, Javed Miandad, Vijay Manjrekar, M.A.K. Pataudi, S.M.H. Kirmani, Bill Lawry, Clive Rice, Mark Taylor, Joel Garner, Arjuna Ranatunga, Arvinda De'Silva, Saurav Ganguly, Virat Kohli, M.S. Dhoni, Ajit Agarkar, Jacques Kallis, John Traicos, W.R. Hammond, Sanath Jaisurya.
- **Hockey:** Dhyan Chand, Ashok Kumar, Ajit Singh, Pargat Singh, Pritpal Singh, Zafar Iqbal, Shankar Laxman, Mervyn Fernandes, Mohammad Shahid, R. Charlesworth, Balbir Singh, Terry Walsh, Kishan Lal, Udlam Singh, Dhanraj Pillai.
- **Football:** Pele, Diego Maradona, Franz Beckenbour, Socrates, Raud Gullit, Garry Linekar, Emilo Butraguino, Coreca, P.C. Bannerji, Arunlal Ghosh, Chuni Goswami, Davor Suker, Ronaldo, Rivaldo, Deschamps.
- **Tennis (Lawn):** Bjorn Borg, Jimmy Connors, John Mcenroe, Ivan Lendl, Pete Sampras, Billie Jean Kings, Chris Evert Lloyd, Martina Navratilova, Steffi Graf, Stefan Edberg, Andre Agassi, Michael Chang, Boris Becker, Leander Paes, Vijay Amritraj, Anand Amritraj, Jaideep Mukherjee, Rod Laver, Roy Emerson, Naresh Kumar, Premjit Lall, Martina Hingis, Mary Pierce, Jana Novotna, Rozer Federer.
- **Golf:** Greg Norman, Jack Nikalus, Sandy Lyle, Seve Bellestros, Nick Faldo, Nick Price, Sher Ali, Jeeve Milkha Singh, S. Choudhary, R.K. Pitamber, Vikramjit Singh.
- **Gymnastics:** Nadia Comaneci, L. Latynina, V. Kaslavska, E. Szebo, W. Kim. Y. Ma, Y. Shrusunova, Daniela Silivas, A. Braglia, V. Chukarin, N. Andrianov, Sergi Kharkhov.
- **Swimming:** Arti Gupta, Arun Kumar Shaw, Baidyanath, Mihir Sen, Aarti Saha, Mark Spitz.
- **Wrestling:** Dara Singh, Bhim Sen, Mukhtiar Singh, Sudesh Kumar, Chandagi Ram.

Stadia in Various Cities of India

- **Delhi:** Ambedkar Stadium, Arun Jaitley Stadium, Jawaharlal Nehru Stadium, Indira Gandhi Indoor Stadium, Shivaji Stadium, National Stadium.
- **Mumbai:** Brabourne Stadium, Wankhede Stadium.
- **Kolkata:** Eden Gardens, Salt Lake Stadium, Ranjit Stadium, Subhas Sarovar.
- **Chennai:** Nehru Stadium, Chidambaram Stadium, Chepauk.
- **Cuttack:** Barabati Stadium.
- **Kanpur:** Green Park.
- **Jamshedpur:** Keenan Stadium.
- **Nagpur:** Vidarbha CA Ground
- **Jaipur:** Swai Mansingh Stadium
- **Gwalior:** Roop Singh Stadium
- **Vadodara:** Moti Bagh Stadium
- **Patna:** Moin-ul-Haq Stadium
- **Hyderabad:** Lal Bahadur Stadium
- **Patiala:** Yaduvindra Stadium.
- **Bengaluru:** Chinnaswami Stadium.
- **Siliguri:** Kanchenjunga Stadium.
- **Vishakhapatnam:** Indira Priyadarshini Stadium.

*****

15. NATIONAL/ INTERNATIONAL DAYS

JANUARY

Infant Protection Day	January 7
African National Congress Foundation Day	January 8
NRI Day (India)	January 9
World Laughter Day	January 10
National Youth Day (India)	January 12
Army Day (India)	January 15
Indian Tourism Day	January 25
Republic Day (India); International Customs Day	January 26
Martyrs' Day (India); World Leprosy Eradication Day	January 30

FEBRUARY

World Wetlands Day	February 2
World Marriage Day	Second Sunday of February
Valentine Day (World)	February 14
Mother Tongue Day (World)	February 21
National Science Day (India)	February 28

MARCH

International Women's Day;	March 8
World Disabled Day : World Consumer Rights Day	March 15
World Forestry Day; International Day for Elimination of Racial Discrimination	March 21
World Day for Water	March 22
World Meteorological Day	March 23
World TB Day	March 24

APRIL

National Maritime Day (India)	April 5
World Health Day	April 7
World Aviation and Cosmonautics Day	April 12
World Haemophilia Day	April 17
World Heritage Day,	April 18
Earth Day (World)	April 22
World Book and Copyright Day	April 23

MAY

Workers' Day (International Labour Day)	May 1
Press Freedom Day; World Asthma Day	May 3
World Red Cross Day	May 8
World Mother's Day (2nd Sunday of May)	May 8
World Thalassaemia Day	May 9
National Technology Day	May 11
International Nurses Day	May 12
International Day of the Family	May 15
World Telecommunication Day	May 17
Anti-Terrorism Day	May 21
Commonwealth Day	May 24
Anti-Tobacco Day	May 31

JUNE

International Day of Innocent Children Victims of Aggression	June 4
World Environment Day	June 5
Father's Day (3rd Sunday of June)	June 19
International Yoga Day	June 21
International Day Against Drug Abuse & Illicit Trafficking	June 26

JULY

Doctors' Day : July 1
American Independence Day : July 4
World Zoonosis Day : July 6
World Population Day : July 11

AUGUST

World Breast Feeding Week : August 1-7
International Friendship Day : August 3
Hiroshima Day : August 6
World Senior Citizen's Day : August 8
Quit India Day; Nagasaki Day : August 9
Indian Independence Day : August 15
International Day of the World's Indigenous People : August 18
Sadbhavna Divas (India) : August 20
National Sports Day (India) : August 29

SEPTEMBER

Teachers' Day : September 5
World (International) Literacy Day : September 8
Hindi Day (India) : September 14
All India Flag Day : September 15
World Ozone Day : September 16
Alzheimer's Day (World) : September 21
Day for Peace & Non-Violence (UN) : September 21
Rose Day (Welfare of Cancer Patients) World Heart Day : September 22
International Tiger Day : September 25
World Tourism Day : September 27

OCTOBER

International Day for the Elderly People : October 1
Gandhi Jayanti, International Day of Non-Violence : October 2
World Animal Day : October 2
World Vegetarian Day : October 2
World Habitat Day : October 3
World Animal Welfare Day : October 4
World Post Office Day : October 9
National Post Day (India) : October 10
World Allergy Awareness Day : October 11
UN International Day for Natural Disaster Reduction : October 13
World Standards Day : October 14
World Food Day : October 16
International Day for the Eradication of Poverty : October 17
UN Day : October 24
World Development Information Day : October 24
Infants Day : October 27
World Thrift Day : October 30
National Integration Day (India) : October 31

NOVEMBER

Legal Services Day : November 9
Children's Day (India) : November 14
Diabetes Day : November 14
National Epilepsy Day : November 17

DECEMBER

World AIDS Day : December 1
World Disabled Day : December 3
International Volunteer Development Day : December 5
Armed Forces Flag Day (India) : December 7
Human Rights Day (World) : December 10
National Energy Conservation Day : December 14
Farmer's Day : December 23

* * * * *

MULTIPLE CHOICE QUESTIONS

1. The part of the Sun, which is visible during eclipses only, is known as
A. photosphere
B. chromosphere
C. corona
D. all the parts are visible with naked eye

2. Sphygmomanometer is used for
A. measuring the brain pulse of a patient
B. measuring the systolic and diastolic blood pressures of man
C. measuring the amount of blood in a human body
D. measuring the haemoglobin count in a human body

3. The most abundant gas in air is
A. nitrogen B. hydrogen
C. oxygen D. ozone

4. The most commonly found acid in nature is
A. hydrochloric acid
B. sulphuric acid
C. lactic acid
D. acetic acid

5. This bomb is used to destroy living beings but would not damage the buildings and other property
A. napalm bomb
B. neutron bomb
C. hydrogen bomb
D. None of the above

6. Electrical energy is measured in terms of units which are also termed as
A. KW B. KWH
C. WH D. KVAR

7. In cold countries, the radiator water of cars is mixed with glycerol. This is done to
A. increase the specific heat of water
B. reduce the freezing point of water
C. improve the engine efficiency
D. glycerol is not added in radiator water

8. If the Richter scale shows a value of 7.2, then the seismograph indicates
A. an earthquake of low intensity
B. an earthquake of very high intensity
C. an earthquake of moderate intensity
D. either A or C

9. The theory of origin of species is based primarily on
A. the process of biological evolution
B. the process of natural selection
C. the evolution of life from the oceans
D. the evolution of man from apes

10. Common coal used in our households is
A. Anthracite B. Bituminous coal
C. Lignite D. All of the above

11. Some recent findings on moon, which point out towards the possibility of settlement of man on moon, include
A. nil atmospheric gases
B. ice reserves on the poles
C. micro-organisms
D. None of the above

12. Viagra is a medicine for
A. treatment of AIDS
B. treatment of female fertility
C. treatment of male impotency
D. treatment of Lukaemia

13. Rickets is a disease which is caused by the deficiency of
A. Vitamin A B. Riboflavin
C. Vitamin C D. Vitamin D

14. When a ship enters waters of the sea from a river, then its level
A. rises as the sea water is saline and hence bouyancy force is more

B. decreases as ocean is a large mass of water
C. remains the same as water is the same for the river and the sea
D. None of the above

15. The major constituent of pearl is
A. calcium carbonate
B. calcium oxide and ammonium chloride
C. organic mass
D. calcium carbonate and silica

16. A healthy person needs ..... calories per day.
A. 2200 B. 2400
C. 2500 D. 1800

17. The value of one (marine) Naut is
A. 1951 metre per hour
B. 1852 metre per hour
C. 2305 metre per hour
D. 1860 metre per hour

18. Acid and base combine to form
A. salt and nitrogen
B. nitrogen and oxygen
C. salt and water
D. acid and alkali

19. Cellulose could be obtained from
A. wood and cotton B. silk and cotton
C. paper and silk D. wood and silk

20. ELISA test is done for the detection of
A. cancer B. AIDS
C. diabetes D. None of the above

21. Triple Antigen, prevents
A. small pox, malaria, whooping cough
B. tetanus, diphtheria, small pox
C. whooping cough, tetanus, polio
D. diphtheria, tetanus, whooping cough

22. A freely falling body
A. would fall towards the surface of the earth
B. would have no weight
C. would have one half of its original weight
D. None of the above

23. If the motor neurons of the spinal cord of a child are damaged, then he would develop the following disease.
A. Rickets B. Polio
C. Diphtheria D. Jaundice

24. Which one of the following is not a part of the balanced diet?
A. Vitamins B. Carbohydrate
C. Proteins D. Alcohol

25. Which statement is not correct in connection with human physiology?
A. The length of the small intestine is 7 metres and its diameter is 2.5 cm.
B. There are 639 muscles in a human body
C. An infant breathes 45 times per minute whereas a six year old child breathes 25 times per minute
D. The weight of the adult human brain is nearly 700 gms

26. The bottles of beer are not kept in the deep freezer because
A. beer is an alcohol which could burst under conditions of low temperature
B. alcohol could damage the deep freezer due to its corrosive action if the bottles break accidently
C. water content in beer gets converted into ice which expends (after change of state from water to ice) and this could lead to bursting of beer bottles
D. the low temperature could degrade the beer and hence, it may not good remain for consumption

27. Rocket works on the basis of
A. principle of conservation of momentum
B. principle of relativity
C. principle of conservation of mass
D. principle of conservation of energy

28. Which one of the following groups is more closely related from the viewpoint of taxonomy?
A. silverfish, starfish, cuttlefish
B. earthworm, seahorse, hookworm
C. housefly, dragonfly, butterfly
D. None of the above

29. Red blood corpuscles are produced in
A. liver B. spleen
C. bone marrow D. kidneys

30. The disease for which the first oral drug has been developed for treatment.
A. Cancer B. Pneumonid
C. Small pox D. Plauge

31. E-comm is a short form of
A. Engineering Commercial
B. Electronic Commercial
C. Electronic Commerce
D. None of the above

32. High AC voltages are used for transmitting electric power because
A. at high voltages, current is low and hence, losses are low
B. the transmission of power is quicker
C. the high voltages a consume lesser materials for transmission
D. None of the above

33. There is a hole in the boat through which, water is seeping into the boat. Just before the boat capsizes
A. water level would decrease
B. water level would increase
C. water level would remain the same
D. None of the above

34. During which month, the rate of rotation of the earth on its axis is the fastest?
A. December
B. May
C. the rate of rotation is fixed
D. It is fastest when the earth is closest to the Sun.

35. The time taken by the Sun rays to reach the earth is
A. 9 minutes B. 10 minutes
C. 7 minutes D. 8 minutes

36. The outer planets are
A. Moon, Earth, Mercury, Venus
B. Jupiter, Saturn, Uranus, Earth, Mars
C. Jupiter, Uranus, Saturn, Neptune
D. None of the above

37. According to the astrophysicists
A. the universe is mobile and expanding
B. the universe is heading for a collision with another universe
C. the universe is stationary
D. the doomsday of universe is near due to the formation of many new black holes

38. Which is popular as the White City?
A. New York B. Belgrade
C. Bangalore D. Bab-el-mandab

39. The national currency of Haiti is
A. Rupiah B. Gourde
C. Quetzal D. Dong

40. Which one is not a news agency of India?
A. UNI
B. PTI
C. Hindustan Samachar
D. Reuters

41. The abundant element of the earth's atmosphere is:
A. Oxygen B. nitrogen
C. hydrogen D. CO_2

42. The first talking movie of India was ..... and the first silent movie of India was .....
A. Aan, Aawara
B. Raja Harish Chandra, Alamara
C. Alamara, Raja Harish Chandra
D. Purana Mandir, Raja Harish Chandra

43. Hair becomes grey because
A. rays of the Sun force it to become grey
B. the quantity of melanin is reduced in human body with growing age
C. there is a lack of vitamins in the body due to growing age
D. None of the above

44. Salaries of Supreme Court judges are drawn from:
A. Law Ministry Grants
B. Consolidated Fund of India
C. Home Ministry Grants
D. Parliamentary Grants

45. The term "Paper-gold" is associated with
A. deficit budgeting
B. loans from the World Bank
C. Special Drawing Rights (SDRs) from the IMF
D. None of the above

46. TRAI refers to
A. Terresteral Remote Sensing Authority of India
B. Telecommunication Research Authority of India
C. Transport Regulatory Authority of India
D. Telecom Regulatory Authority of India

47. NSDL is an organisation in India which
A. provides security to depositors
B. accepts deposits from recognised bodies

C. provides data security for on-line computer systems
D. None of the above

48. The enzyme pepsin converts
A. proteins into peptones
B. fats to amino acids
C. carbohydrates to sugars
D. proteins to amino acids

49. Who among the following is not a winner of the PVC?
A. Bana Singh
B. Nirmal Jeet Singh Sekhon
C. Somnath Sharma
D. Shanti Swaroop Rana

50. Which one of the following pairs is not correct?
A. Narmada – Betul district
B. Krishna – near Mahabaleshwar
C. Chambal – near Mhow
D. Godavari – Nashik district

51. The Japanese art of flower arrangement is known as
A. Bonsai
B. Ongami
C. Ikebota
D. None of the above

52. The meaning of the Latin word *Vive Rex* is
A. Long live the king!
B. Let the Nation Live
C. A middle course
D. Nothing wrong here

53. The permanent station of India in Antarctica is known as
A. *Vikalp*
B. Antarctica India Station
C. *Maitri*
D. *Dakshin Yamunotri*

54. A man dies due to electrocution because
A. electric current passes through his body to earth which leads to sudden contraction and expansion of muscles (including heart muscles) and this, alongwith development of heat in the body, leads to heart failure.
B. there is no resistance offered by the body
C. the body allows the current to flow through the blood which cannot circulate any longer
D. None of the above

55. "Blue Dwarfs" are
A. members of the Russian circus
B. warriors of Mongolia
C. young stars of the universe
D. naval officers in the high seas

56. What is a fly leaf?
A. thin paper sheet for making packaging material
B. a blank page at the beginning or end of a book
C. a marker in a book
D. a sheet of paper next to the main title of the book

57. Who is associated with the theory of inheritance of acquired characters?
A. Spencer
B. Mandeleev
C. Lamarck
D. All of the above

58. Ligaments and tendons in the body are made up of
A. skeletal tissue
B. muscular tissue
C. connective tissue
D. epithelial tissue

59. A cell membrane is
A. completely permeable
B. impermeable
C. semi-permeable
D. None of the above

60. The tenure of the non-permanent members of the UN Security Council is
A. one year
B. three years
C. two years
D. there is no fixed tenure

61. Why proper earthing is necessary?
A. It reduces the consumption of electricity
B. It allows the current to flow through the earth wire and into the earth, thus protecting the person
C. It allows the appliance to operate efficiently
D. None of the above

62. Which one of the following items has not been included in the minimum needs programme?
A. unemployment allowance
B. rural water supply
C. rural electrification
D. adult education

63. This is not the principle organ of digestion and absorption in the human body.
A. small intestine B. stomach
C. large intestine D. Both A and B

64. Which are the two stars which appear as morning stars in the Eastern sky and evening stars in the Western sky?
A. Jupiter and Mars
B. Mars and Venus
C. Saturn and Mercury
D. Mercury and Venus

65. Which planet rotates on its axis from East to West?
A. Mercury B. Jupiter
C. Earth D. Venus

66. The chemical compound present in the stone of human kidney is
A. calcium phosphate
B. calcium carbonate
C. silica
D. calcium oxalate

67. Which one of the following diseases would be caused by bacterial infection?
A. tetanus B. rabies
C. cancer D. malaria

68. India On-line Limited is
A. an advertising agency
B. a reservation office
C. an information service
D. an internet services provider

69. CTBT is related to
A. economic sanctions imposed by the USA on India
B. the codename of Pokharan-II blasts
C. the nuclear test ban treaty which India is being forced to adhere to
D. codename of Pakistani nuclear arsenal

70. The disagreement between Lok Sabha and Rajya Sabha is solved by:
A. setting up Joint Select Committee
B. dissolving Lok Sabha
C. setting up adjudication committee
D. calling a joint session

71. The national anthem was written by ..... and was translated into English by .....
A. Bankim Chandra Chatterji, Aurobindo Ghosh
B. Rabindra Nath Tagore, Aurobindo Ghosh
C. Bankim Chandra Chatterji, Rabindra Nath Tagore
D. the national anthem was originally written in English and was translated later

72. The tear in human body is a solution of :
A. Sodium hydroxide and sodium chloride
B. Calcium bicarbonate and sodium chloride
C. Magnesium bicarbonate and sodium hydroxide
D. Sodium bicarbonate and Magnesium chloride

73. The drug seroxat is
A. a new medicine for treating the lepers.
B. a new medicine developed by British scientists and is used for the treatment of shyness and social phobia
C. is anti-AIDS therapy developed by France
D. is an antacid developed in India under guidance of WHO

74. What is "Bermuda Triangle" sometimes referred to as the "Grakeyard of ships", located?
A. in the South Pacific ocean
B. in the North Atlantic ocean
C. in the Indian ocean
D. in the Arctic ocean

75. The theory propounded by Nobel laurate Professor Amartya Sen–is commonly known as
A. The Famine Economics
B. The Theory of Economic Divide
C. The Amartya Sen Shift
D. The Amartya Sen Divide

76. Which is known as the Electronics City of India?
A. Tumkoor B. Secunderabad
C. Bhopal D. None of the above

77. The main objective behind the creation of concept of *Navratnas* in the public sector was

A. to increase the control of the PSUs over economy
B. to boost local manufacturing and exports in the core sectors
C. to improve the functional autonomy
D. to improve their image and efficiency by giving them high status

78. The North American seaport on the Pacific side is
A. Baltimore B. Boston
C. New York D. Seattle

79. The old name of Harare was
A. Sam B. Rhodesia
C. Salisbury D. Batavia

80. The famous Prince of Wales Museum is located in
A. Mumbai B. Kolkata
C. Vadodara D. Bangalore

81. Who invented Atom Bomb (Uranium Fission)?
A. A W Haffmann
B. Otto Hahn
C. A Einstein
D. None of the above

82. The first ever woman to go into space was
A. Kalpana Chawla
B. Valentina Tereshkova
C. Mary Pierce
D. None of the above

83. The highest mountain peak in world is
A. Everest B. K-2
C. Kanchanjunga D. Makalu-I

84. The "Garden City" of England is
A. Portsmouth B. Manchester
C. Kent D. Warwickshire

85. *Habeas Corpus* is
A. an order of the International Court of Justice
B. a type of writ issued by a High Court or Supreme Court against illegal detention of a person.
C. the petition of a lawyer in the Supreme Court on behalf of his client for bail against the orders of any other court in India
D. None of the above

86. If impeachment motion is passed by the American Senate against the US President, he would have to
A. leave office and all his assets created by him during Presidency
B. leave office, lose his pensions, security cover and all those benefits that are accorded to a retired US President
C. jailed for five years and will not get any benefits.
D. retire honourably with all his benefits, compensations, assets and pensions remaining intact

87. Who appoints the non-permanent members of the UN Security Council?
A. the permanent members
B. the General Assembly
C. the International Court of Justice
D. None of the above

88. The Preamble of the Constitution was amended by:
A. 1st amendment B. 26th amendment
C. 42nd amendment D. 44th amendment

89. NNP is equal to
A. GNP + Depreciation
B. GNP – Depreciation
C. GNP + Exports
D. GNP – Exports

90. The official airline of Australia is
A. SIA B. Lufthansa
C. Modiluft D. None of the above

91. Which one of the following types of coal contains a higher percentage of carbon than the rest?
A. Bituminous Coal B. Lignite
C. Anthracite D. Peat

92. Ten Commandments were revealed by God to:
A. Abraham B. Moses
C. Jesus D. Peter

93. Kalinga in older days, is now known as:
A. Odisha B. Kohima
C. Karnataka D. Maharashtra

94. Bihu festival is celebrated in:
A. Gujarat B. Assam
C. Bihar D. West Bengal

95. Milk is an example of
A. gel B. emulsion
C. suspension D. mixture

96. The President can dissolve the Lok Sabha before expiry of its term, on the advice of:
A. Prime Minister
B. Speaker
C. Vice-President
D. Election Commissioner

97. In a landmark judgement, the Allahabad High Court ruled that
A. Capital Sentence is not to be imposed upon the rapists
B. pension is the fundamental right of the government employees
C. the Supreme Court should not be bothered for cases of financial compensation
D. None of the above

98. Tughlaq dynasty occupied Delhi throne after decline of:
A. Suri dynasty B. Slave dynasty
C. Lodhi dynasty D. Khilji dynasty

99. Governors of states are:
A. appointed by Chief Ministers
B. appointed by the President
C. elected by members of Legislative Assembly
D. elected by people

100. The partition of Bengal was carried out by:
A. Lord Curzon B. Lord Minto
C. Lord Canning D. Lord Ripon

101. The Air Force Day falls on
A. October 10 B. October 9
C. September 5 D. October 8

102. MAD stands for
A. Most Active Disease
B. Mica Aluminium Duo
C. Mutually Assured Death
D. Mutually Assured Destruction

103. "Disguised Unemployment" means
A. more persons employed for a job that only a few could accomplish
B. people without any technical jobs
C. woman without jobs in rural areas
D. employment of children in factories

104. In India, an active volcano is situated at
A. Lakshadweep
B. Chhotanagpur Plateau
C. Andaman and Nicobar
D. Malawa Plateau

105. The first country to establish trade relationships with India was
A. England B. France
C. The Netherlands D. Portugal

106. Which has the highest share of electrical power generation in India?
A. thermal power
B. nuclear power
C. hydro-power
D. naphtha-based and gas-based power

107. The great ocean liner, known to be the best and luxurious during her times, sank in the year
A. 1902 B. 1912
C. 1908 D. 1889

108. Who among the following is known as the Indian Napoleon?
A. Chandra Gupta Maurya
B. Bindusar
C. Samudra Gupta
D. Harshvardhana

109. Time gap between two sessions of Parliament cannot exceed:
A. 3 months B. 6 months
C. 1 year D. no fixed gap

110. In which state, Panchayati Raj was introduced for the first time?
A. Bihar
B. Punjab
C. Rajasthan
D. Andhra Pradesh

111. Which one is not a national duty?
A. Respect the Constitution
B. Respect the President
C. Defend the country
D. Protect natural environment

112. Treaty of Seringapatam was signed between:
A. Tipu Sultan and Nawab of Hyderabad
B. Tipu Sultan and English
C. Tipu Sultan & Rani of Jhansi
D. Tipu Sultan and French

113. NHRC stands for
A. National Hydro Research Committee
B. National Handicapped Rahabilitation Council
C. National Human Rights Commission
D. None of the above

114. "Water water everywhere but not a drop to drink" who stated these lines in a poem?
A. John Milton
B. Samuel Taylor Coleridge
C. Lord Byron
D. P.B. Shelley

115. Rabindranath Tagore gave up his knighthood after:
A. Jallianwala Bagh Tragedy
B. Introduction of separate electorates
C. Bengal faminine
D. Bengal Partition

116. Which country is known as the land of golden wool?
A. India B. Turkiye
C. Australia D. Myanmar

117. BIFR stands for
A. Bilateral and International Foreign Regulation
B. Board of Industrial Financial Resurrection
C. Board of Industrial and Financial Reconstruction
D. None of the above

118. Pinaca is a
A. drug for curing AIDS
B. multi-barrel rocket system
C. fighter aircraft developed by HAL
D. codename of the nuclear test operation carried out on May 11, 1998

119. Vice-President is ex-officio:
A. Member of Rajya Sabha
B. Chairman of Rajya Sabha
C. Member of Lok Sabha
D. Speaker of Lok Sabha

120. Vitamin C is not available in this food in sufficiently large quantities.
A. lemon B. tomato
C. cod liver oil D. fresh fruits

121. This book was not written in a jail
A. *Glimpses of World History* – J L Nehru
B. *The Bible* (German) – Martin Luther
C. *Les Miserables* – Victor Hugo
D. *Yama* – Mahadevi Verma

122. Who among the following can be removed from office through impeachment by Parliament?
A. Speaker of Lok Sabha
B. Prime Minister
C. President of India
D. Vice-President of India

123. The following is not the function of the liver.
A. to store excesssive sugar in the form of glycogen
B. the produce an antidote for neutralising poison
C. to manufacture red blood corpuscles
D. to purify the blood through bile

124. A fascist is a person whose views are extremely
A. left-winged B. rational
C. right-winged D. liberal

125. The famous mathematician and a professor of Astronomy designed this building in London
A. Westminister Abbey
B. St Paul's Cathedral
C. Stock Exchange
D. Tower of London

126. Which one of the following sounds cannot be heard by a human ear?
A. 30,000 vibrations per second
B. 10,000 vibrations per second
C. 1,000 vibrations per second
D. 300 vibrations per second

127. A weather balloon may not be inflated completely on the ground because
A. it cannot withstand the atmospheric pressure if inflated fully
B. if the balloon is inflated fully on ground, fuel consumption would be higher
C. the air inside the balloon expands as it rises and hence, the balloon could get burst
D. None of the above

128. Which one of the following vitamins is stored in the liver?
A. Vitamin C

B. Vitamin B_{12}
C. Vitamin A
D. Vitamin K and Vitamin A

129. All of the following are plant products except
A. silk B. cork
C. hemp D. linen

130. Which one of the following organs in the human body is known as "Adam's Apple"?
A. thyroid B. liver
C. thymus D. adrenal

131. Insecticides or medicines could be harmful
A. to the insects and weeds as they kill them instantaneously upon consumption
B. to the habitat as the environment could become polluted due to excessive usage of chemicals in our crop management processes
C. to the human beings and animals who consume the food adulterated by the insecticides and weedicides
D. to the transporters and movers of the crops who could inhale noxious fumes of insecticides and weedicides

132. Name the assassin of John Lennon
A. Art Buchwald
B. Lee Oswald
C. Mark David Chapman
D. None of the above

133. Which one of the following is not a sprinter?
A. Marion Jones
B. Florence Griffith Joyner
C. Ben Johnson
D. Susie O' Neill

134. Which of the following is called the "Gateway to the Pacific"?
A. Suez Canal
B. Bering Sea
C. Panama Canal
D. Gulf of Alaska

135. Which one of the following statements is true regarding the treaty on banning the landmines?
A. the USA does not want to sign the CTBT
B. the treaty was kept open for signatures in Ottawa in December, 1997.
C. India has already signed it
D. A and B are true

136. The General Assembly of the UNO has declined to reduce the budgetary contribution of this country as she has refused to pay her pending arrears.
A. the UK B. Iraq
C. Japan D. the USA

137. The famous Gandhian, who was also known as the "Frontier Gandhi," is
A. Liaqat Ali Khan
B. Yusuf Khan
C. Khan Abdul Ghaffar Khan
D. Abdul Wali Khan

138. Which one of the following is an alloy?
A. copper B. lanthanum
C. bronze D. uranium

139. World Environment Day is celebrated on
A. June 4 B. June 5
C. June 7 D. March 5

140. This country is the largest producer of cotton in the world.
A. India B. China
C. Egypt D. the USA

141. Which tax can be levied by Gram Panchayat?
A. Sales Tax B. Custom Duty
C. Tax on local fairs D. Land Revenue

142. The temples of Khajuraho were built by
A. Chalukyas B. Pallavas
C. Rashtrakutas D. Chandelas

143. National Remote Sensing Agency (NRSA) is located at:
A. Hyderabad
B. Bangalore
C. Thiruvananthapuram
D. Gadanki, near Tirupati

144. The clones for .... and .... have been developed.
A. man, cow B. crow, sheep
C. rat, cat D. sheep, rat

145. AWWA stands for
A. All Women Welfare Association
B. Army Wives Welfare Association
C. Airport Weather and Welfare Authority
D. None of the above

146. The popular book *The Gift of Time* by Jonathan Schell, deals with

A. the lewid affair of Bill Clinton and Monica Lewinsky
B. the elimination of nuclear weapons from the world
C. Indo-US relationships
D. the deteriorating environment in industrial America

147. How can a person move on a hard icy surface?
A. he should use roller skates
B. he should hop, sneeze, jump and step in the direction which is opposite to the direction of his required movement
C. he should hop, sneeze, jump and step in the direction in which the movement is required
D. he should skid on his knees and hands

148. Which states are deriving benefits from the Tungbhadra project?
A. Tamil Nadu, Karnataka, Kerala
B. Tamil Nadu only
C. Andhra Pradesh and Tamil Nadu
D. Tamil Nadu, Andhra Pradesh, Karnataka

149. Where did Mahatma Buddha's 'Mahaparinirvan' take place?
A. Lumbani B. Kushinagar
C. Bodh Gaya D. Kapilavastu

150. Pyroclastics are
A. non-toxic gases
B. lava flows
C. fragments of hot rock and spattering lava
D. pollutant chemicals from a leather factory

151. Which one of the following is not a sedimentary rock?
A. slate B. limestone
C. clay D. sandstone

152. Oketa is
A. used to define human-induced climatic changes
B. used to describe increasing drought periods of high magnitudes
C. a unit to describe the prevailing cloudiness
D. None of the above

153. The following state produces the maximum quantities (85 per cent) of raw silk in India
A. Kerala
B. Jammu and Kashmir
C. Karnataka
D. Tamil Nadu

154. Salal Hydro Electric Project is situated on the river
A. Beas B. Jhelum
C. Chenab D. Sutlej

155. Which is the largest island sea in the world?
A. Caribbean Sea B. Mediterranean Sea
C. Red Sea D. Beaufort Sea

156. What is the name of the bell used at the Lloyds in London?
A. The Great Bell B. The Charmer
C. The Tower Bell D. Lutine

157. What are "The Hagiographs?"
A. These are the poems written by Lord Byron
B. These are the holy writings of Jewish scriptures
C. These are the geographical lines representing same rainfall levels
D. None of the above

158. Which one of the following forms would provide the lowest protection?
A. Patent B. Trademark
C. Copyright D. Logo

159. Ladakh become a Union Territory in:
A. 2019 B. 2018
C. 2017 D. 2016

160. What does the 17th Parallel line separate?
A. South and North America
B. North and South Korea
C. South and North Yemen
D. South and North Vietnam

161. Operation Flood-II, the prestigious milk products revolution of India, was initiated on
A. October 1, 1979 B. October 2, 1979
C. January 26, 1979 D. October 2, 1978

162. After World War I, the peace treaty was signed in:
A. Geneva B. Versailles
C. Paris D. Venice

163. Potassium chloride is given to the patient for
A. curing his bleeding gums
B. reducing his cholestrol level
C. reducing his blood pressure
D. alleviating his arthiritis pain

164. What is notation?
A. It is another word for "Mutually Assured Destruction"
B. It is the Latin deformation of the phrase "to swim"
C. It is a term used to denote the growth of illeterate masses
D. None of the above

165. The hideout of Adolf Hitler in the mountains was
A. Stuttgart B. Heidelberg
C. Berchtesgaden D. Both A and C

166. Who stated, "Where wealth accumulates decay?"
A. J M Keynes B. Adam Smith
C. Frederic Engels D. Oliver Goldsmith

167. Who was the national leader who wrote History of India on the walls of the Andaman Cellular Jail?
A. Ambedkar B. Vir Savarkar
C. Nandlal Bose D. Jyotiba Phule

168. The USA does not possess the following space shuttle
A. Columbia B. Atlantis
C. Challenger D. Discovery

169. The term "White Elephant" is used to denote
A. very bright and white item
B. very costly and expensive item
C. an item or a head that is very costly to maintain
D. an item or a head that is a part of the national economic budget of a country

170. Kolar Gold Mines are in this state.
A. Karnataka B. Bihar
C. Odisha D. Madhya Pradesh

171. Which is the morning star?
A. Pluto
B. Venus
C. Neptune
D. None of the above

172. Which one of the following is not an alkali?
A. sodium hydroxide
B. calcium carbonate
C. magnesium hydroxide
D. sodium sulphate

173. Polar ice is melting due to greenhouse effect. This would lead to
A. more melting of the polar glaciers and hence, subsequent submerging of land areas of earth
B. increasing temperatures on polar caps
C. reduction in temperature of ocean waters and rise in temperature of the Arctic circle waters as well as those of the Antartic circle waters
D. no impact

174. *India 2020* is a book written by
A. Trilok Gurtu
B. Khushwant Singh
C. P Chidambaram
D. A P J Abdul Kalaam

175. The Panama Canal connects:
A. The Pacific and Atlantic Oceans
B. The Pacific and Arctic Oceans
C. The Atlantic and Arctic Oceans
D. The Atlantic and Indian Oceans

176. The following are single cell structures
A. Paramaecium B. Amoebia
C. Both A and B D. None of A or B

177. 'The Last Supper' was painted by:
A. Picasso B. Francis Bacon
C. Michaelangelo D. Raphael

178. The plants, which can resist high temperatures, are known as
A. thermophilic B. thermophobic
C. thermoduric D. Both A and B

179. Which one of the following vaccines is used for controlling tuberculosis among the cattle?
A. Cell Culture Vaccine
B. Goat Tissue Adapted Vaccine
C. Adjuvant Vaccine
D. BCG Vaccine

180. Which one of the following chemicals is carcinogenic if inhaled?
A. carbon dioxide
B. suspended particulate matter
C. lead oxide
D. sulphur dioxide

181. What is a "Tenurial System?"
A. It is a system that identifies the ownership of land and the relationship of the land owner with the actual cultivator

B. It identities the land size and the *modus-operandi* of its usage
C. It identifies the ownership of the land
D. None of the above

182. Pulses are deficient in
A. methionine B. lysine
C. leusine D. iso-leusine

183. Which types of roses are grown in India for industrial applications?
A. R Centripetala and Bushra Rose
B. R Damascena Var Bifera
C. Rosa Damascena
D. A, B and C

184. Why sprinkler irrigation is preferred over other methods of irrigation?
A. It is a cheap method and does not require canal-digging and canal maintenance
B. It uses water effectively and water resolves are optimally utilised
C. It does not require well-digging measures which are costly
D. It supplies water only to those fields where the same is required

185. The size of clay particles is
A. greater than 0.2 mm
B. 0.02 mm – 0.2 mm
C. 0.002 mm – 0.02 mm
D. less than 0.002 mm

186. Which one of the following plants is of great medicinal value?
A. Ranwolfia Serpentiana
B. Thea Sinesis
C. Coffea Robusta
D. Ficus Religiosa

187. Biological control agents of soil borne plant pathogens act by
A. rapidly repleting nutrients and thereby, causing starvation and death of the pathogen
B. secreting toxic metabolitics
C. direct parastism or predation on the pathogens
D. All of the above

188. Nearly 80 percent of sugarcane in India is planted during
A. July – December B. May – August
C. June – August D. December – Aprii

189. Soluble salt content of soil is determined by measuring its
A. pH Value
B. organic matter content
C. Sulphur content
D. electrical conductivity

190. Operation Flood is related to ..... whereas development of fisheries is related to .....
A. white revolution, black revolution
B. white revolution, blue revolution
C. green revolution, blue revolution
D. blue revolution, green revolution

191. An upper air wind system with very high velocities in certain parts of the atmosphere is called
A. Cyclone B. Anticyclone
C. Jet stream D. Tsunami

192. "Mixed Farming" refers to
A. farming by traditional and modern methods
B. agriculture and dairy farming clubbed together
C. farming without synthetic fertilisers but with traditional manure
D. farming with synthetic fertilisers and with traditional manure

193. The main constituent of *Gobar Gas* is
A. butane B. carbon monoxide
C. methane D. octane

194. Speed of sound waves is maximum in
A. solids B. liquids
C. gases D. vacuum

195. When a body gets positively charged, it actually
A. gains electrons
B. loses electrons
C. becomes a donor of ions
D. becomes a receptor of ions

196. Which type of nerves carries impulses from the sense organs in response to the stimulus?
A. sensory B. motor
C. secretory D. None of the above

197. Which gas does not pollute air (for human and animal consumption)?
A. carbon monoxide B. nitrogen dioxide
C. sulphur dioxide D. carbon dioxide

198. The human brain sends and receives signals as
A. electrical impulses
B. chemical impulses
C. motor movements
D. either A or B

199. "Foot and Mouth" disease attacks
A. cattle
B. pigs and cattle
C. sheep and pigs
D. cattle, sheep and pigs

200. While returning to earth, the spacecraft has a total communication blackout. The reason is
A. during the re-entry period, the density of the plasma generated by the intense functional heat is so high that the operational frequencies used for communication become much lesser than the plasma cut-off frequency, thus resulting in a total blackout
B. the electromagnetic waves present in the space above the earth temporarily over-power the communication system of the aircraft, thus completely crippling its operation and transmission
C. the force of gravity counters the radiowaves emitted by the aircraft
D. None of the above

201. The first winning stroke in Lawn Tennis gives the player:
A. 2 points B. 1 point
C. 10 points D. 15 points

202. Which of the following game is played for stipulated period of 70 minutes?
A. Hockey B. Football
C. Rugby D. Basketball

203. Who among the following was the Constitutional adviser to the Constituent Assembly of India?
A. Dr. B.R. Ambedkar B. Dr. B.N. Rao
C. K.M. Munshi D. M.C. Setalvad

204. Arjuna Award has been instituted for outstanding contribution in the field of
A. Social Service
B. Games and Sports
C. Literature
D. Art and Music

205. Murugappa Gold Cup is associated with:
A. Football B. Polo
C. Hockey D. Bridge

206. Jimmy Connors and Geoff Boycott are related with following games respectively:
A. Tennis, Football B. Tennis, Cricket
C. Chess, Cricket D. Football, Hockey

207. 'AVAHAN', the Indian segment of 'Bill and Melinda Gates Foundation', is engaged in the prevention of:
A. dengue B. polio
C. HIV/AIDS D. None of the above

208. The Constituent Assembly which framed the Constitution for Independent India was set up in:
A. 1945 B. 1946
C. 1947 D. 1949

209. The term 'Steeple Chase' is associated with which of the following games
A. Polo B. Tennis
C. Horse Racing D. Cricket

210. Who is known as Father of India's "White Revolution" and "Operation Flood"?
A. Dr. Verghese Kurien
B. J.B. Kripalani
C. Baba Amte
D. Har Gobind Khorana

211. The first Olympic games were revived by ..... in 1896 at Athens
A. Lord Welsley
B. Queen Elizabeth-I
C. Baron Piere de Cubertin
D. None of the above

212. The national game of the USA is
A. swimming B. baseball
C. athletics D. None of the above

213. Jules Rimmet Cup is associated with
A. hockey B. archery
C. football D. table tennis

214. The approximate weight of a cricket ball is
A. 5.25 Oz B. 6.30 Oz
C. 7.20 Oz D. 8.25 Oz

215. The number of players on each side in a basketball match is

A. 10 B. 6
C. 5 D. 8

216. The first woman in the history of US open Championship to have played 100 matches, is:

A. Martina Navaratilova
B. Chris Evert
C. Steffi Graf
D. Helena Sukova

217. Swaythling Cup is associated with

A. World Table Tennis Tournament (men)
B. World Table Tennis Tournament (university)
C. World Table Tennis tournament (women)
D. World Hockey Tournament (university)

218. Which one of the following is not a cricket - playing nation?

A. West Indies B. Zimbabwe
C. Kenya D. Columbia

219. The first recipient of Major Dhyan Chand Khel Ratna Award was:

A. Geet Sethi B. N Kunjurani Devi
C. V Anand D. P K Garg

220. The first Olympic Games were held at Olympia (Greece) in the year:

A. 300 BC B. 776 BC
C. 500 BC D. 394 AD

221. Which of the following is the National Game of Spain?

A. Bull fighting B. Baseball
C. Rugby D. Golf

222. 'Ashes' is the name of a series between ..... and ..... and it relates to .....

A. Pakistan, Australia, Hockey
B. India, England, Cricket
C. England, Australia, Cricket
D. New Zealand, Australia, Cricket

223. The term "Butterfly Stroke" is associated with

A. Kabaddi B. Wrestling
C. Polo D. Swimming

224. The Australian Open Tennis Women's Championship (2025) was won by

A. C. Martinez
B. Lindsay Davenport
C. Madison Keys
D. Monica Seles

225. 'Gambit' is a term normally associated with

A. Bridge B. Chess
C. Billiards D. Polo

226. 'Bunker' and 'Chukker' are the two terms associated with

A. Polo B. Rowing
C. Bungey Jumping D. Ice Hockey

227. A Lawn Tennis court measures

A. 78 feet by 28 feet B. 79 feet by 29 feet
C. 76 feet by 26 feet D. 70 feet by 24 feet

228. Vyas Samman is given for excellence in the field of:

A. Science B. Dance
C. Economics D. Literature

229. Which one of the following has been entrusted with the responsibility of training coaches in various disciplines of sports?

A. Tata Football Academy
B. Ministry of Human Resource Development
C. Netaji Subhash Institute of Sports
D. Lakshmibai National College of Physical Education

230. Name the city in which Golden Temple is located:

A. Ludhiana B. Chandigarh
C. Amritsar D. Delhi

231. Governor will act on the advice of Council of Ministers while

A. Dissolving the Legislative Assembly
B. Appointing the Chairman of the State Public Service Commission
C. Recommending for President's Rule in the State
D. Returning a bill for reconsideration

232. Who was the first deaf & dumb swimmer in the world to swim 30 km Gibralter strait?

A. Des Renford B. Mihir Sen
C. Arti Pradhan D. Taranath Shenoy

233. The height of the net in the centre of the tennis court is

A. 3 feet, 5 inches B. 3 feet, 2 inches
C. 2 feet, 8 inches D. 2 feet, 6 inches

234. 'Canon' is a sports term associated with the following game.
A. Billiards B. Volleyball
C. Shot-Put D. Table Tennis

235. The Himalayan Mountaineering Institute is located in
A. Leh B. Darjeeling
C. Kohima D. Dispur

236. The diameter of a golf hole is
A. 4.36 inches B. 4.50 inches
C. 5.63 inches D. 4.75 inches

237. The total distance of a Marathon Race is ..... miles and ..... yards.
A. 29, 388 B. 26, 380
C. 26, 385 D. 25, 372

238. The first woman, who won six gold medals in a single Olympics tournament, was
A. Evelyn Ashford
B. Florence Griffth Joyner
C. Kristin Otto
D. Susi Susanti

239. In which year on account of a decree issued by Roman Emperor the Olympic Games were ceased to be played?
A. 350 AD B. 394 AD
C. 300 BC D. 384 AD

240. Putney (UK) is a place most frequently associated with
A. swimming B. horse racing
C. boat rowing D. polo

241. The World Pole Vault Champion, from Ukraine, is
A. Sergei Bubka
B. Mikael Tillstrom
C. Todd Woodbridge
D. None of the above

242. The term 'Finesse' is normally associated with this game.
A. Chess B. Bridge
C. Snooker D. Rowing

243. The following trophy is not associated with cricket.
A. Ranji Trophy
B. Rohintan Baria Trophy
C. Ashes
D. Wimbledon Trophy

244. P.V. Sindhu is associated with which game?
A. Rowing B. Table Tennis
C. Badminton D. Boxing

245. When and where the first Asian Games were held?
A. 1955, Seoul B. 1951, New Delhi
C. 1954, Manila D. 1970, Bangkok

246. Music legend Bob Dylan became the first song-writer to win the Nobel Prize for Literature 2016. He belongs to which country?
A. France B. USA
C. Italy D. Britain

247. What is the measurement of a Golf Hole?
A. 3½ inch in diameter
B. 4½ inch in diameter
C. 7½ centimeter in diameter
D. 10 inch in diameter

248. The Supreme Court of India was set up by the
A. Regulating Act, 1773
B. Pitts India Act, 1784
C. Charter Act, 1813
D. Charter Act, 1833

249. K Sasikaran is well known as a
A. table tennis player
B. swimmer
C. chess player
D. football player

250. Which one of the following pairs is correctly matched?
A. Plimsoll Line : India and Afghanistan
B. Durand Line : India and Myanmar
C. Radcliff Line : India and Pakistan
D. Macmohan Line : India and Nepal

251. In which of the following years 'Nobel Prizes' were instituted?
A. 1910 B. 1905
C. 1901 D. 1911

252. The writer who refused the Nobel Prize for Literature was:
A. Winston Churchill B. Prem Chand
C. Jean Paul Sartre D. None of the above

253. Which country awards the Noble Prize?
A. USA B. India
C. Russia D. Sweden

254. In which of the following years Arjuna Awards were instituted
A. 1951 B. 1971
C. 1961 D. 1965

255. National Awards for Popularising Science was instituted in the year
A. 1981 B. 1985
C. 1987 D. 1988

256. The Government of which state has instituted the 'Tansen Samman'?
A. Madhya Pradesh
B. Uttar Pradesh
C. Gujarat
D. Maharashtra

257. Nobel Prizes are not given for which of the following fields?
A. Physics B. Music
C. Chemistry D. Peace

258. Who returned the award of 'Sir' given by the British government in protest against the "Jallianwala Bagh Massacre" on April 13, 1919?
A. Prem Chand
B. Thomas Roe
C. Rabindra Nath Tagore
D. Dada Bhai Nauroji

259. Nobel Prize is not awarded in the following disciplines
A. Chemistry and Physics
B. Literature and Peace
C. Economics and Medicine
D. Geography and Space Research

260. In which year Nehru Award for International Understanding instituted
A. 1965 B. 1969
C. 1974 D. 1964

261. Which of the following Indians was awarded Legion D award, the highest civilian awards of France
A. Jawahar Lal Nehru
B. Satyajit Ray
C. Mother Teresa
D. Shahrukh Khan

262. 'Pulitzer' prizes are awarded to Americans for excellence in
A. Films B. Journalism
C. Medicine D. Social Work

263. C.V. Raman received Nobel Prize in the year
A. 1934 B. 1931
C. 1932 D. 1930

264. Saraswati Samman is awarded by
A. Government of India
B. Sahitya Academy
C. K.K. Birla Foundation
D. Lalit Kala Akademi

265. On which day every year National Awards for Teachers are announced?
A. August 15 B. September 5
C. November 19 D. November 14

266. The National Award given to the distinguished sportsmen/women in India is known as
A. Dronacharya Award
B. Param Vir Chakra
C. Arjun Award
D. Nehru Award

267. The prestigious Ramon Magsaysay Award was instituted in the memory of Mr Ramon Magsaysay who was
A. the Secretary – General of UN
B. the Commander of NATO in Europe
C. the President of the Philippines
D. the President of Cambodia

268. The Kalinga Prize is awarded by UNESCO but it was founded by an Indian. His name is
A. Biju Patnaik B. Sharad Pawar
C. C V Raman D. Piloo Modi

269. Who was the first Indian to receive the World Food Prize
A. Dr. M.S. Swaminathan
B. Dr. Amrita Patel
C. Dr. Verghese Kurien
D. None of these

270. Jesse Owens Global award is given in the field of:
A. Literature B. Sports
C. Science D. Journalism

271. Nobel Alfred Bernhard after whom Nobel Prizes are given was:
A. Engineer B. Doctor
C. Chemist D. Pilot

272. Grammy Awards are given in the field of
A. painting B. architecture
C. music D. rock dance

273. The highest civilian award of India is
A. *Padma Vibhushan*
B. *Padma Shri*
C. *Bharat Ratna*
D. *Param Vir Chakra*

274. The highest military award of India is
A. Shaurya Chakra
B. Param Vishisht Sewa Medal
C. Param Vir Chakra
D. Kirti Chakra

275. The first ever B R Ambedkar National Award was given to
A. Baba Amte
B. T Shiv Shankar Pillai
C. International Red Cross
D. National Institute for Social Work and Social Sciences

276. 'Victory Medal' is awarded in:
A. UK B. USA
C. Russia D. France

277. Which one of the following is not a Shram Award
A. Shram Bhushan B. Shram Dev
C. Shram Devi D. Shram Vir

278. Dr Shanti Swaroop Bhatnagar Awards are given in any field of science by
A. Indian Council of Applied Economic Research
B. Defence Research and Development Organisation
C. National Institute for Social Work and Social Sciences
D. Tata Institute of Fundamental Research

279. Veda Samaj founded under the initiative of Kesab Chandra Sen in 1864 in Madras was renamed as the Brahmo Samaj of South India in 1871 by:
A. Sir R. Venkataratnam Naidu
B. K. Sreedharalu Naidu
C. Subbarayala Chetti
D. Rajagopala Naidu

280. First Miss World Competition was established by 'Miss World Incorporation' in the year
A. 1941 B. 1950
C. 1951 D. 1957

281. The size of an Olympic medal is ..... mm and thickness is ..... mm.
A. 50, 2.5 B. 60, 3.0
C. 60.5, 3.5 D. 55.2, 2.5

282. "Dhanwantari Award" is given in the field of
A. swimming B. Bharata Natyam
C. cinema D. medicine

283. Duncan Passage is situated betwee:
A. Minicoy and Amindiv
B. Minicoy and Maldives
C. South Andaman and Little Andaman
D. Little Andaman and Car Nicobar

284. Which is the second Highest Civilian award in India?
A. Padam Vibushan B. Padam Shri
C. Bharat Ratna D. Ashok Chakra

285. Gandhiji started the Dandi March for
A. Poorna Swaraj
B. Home-rule
C. Protest against the imposition of Salt Tax
D. Responsible Government

286. The second highest gallantry award in India is:
A. Padam Bhushan B. Vir Chakra
C. Mahavir Chakra D. Ashok Chakra

287. 'Mubarak-Al-Kabir' medal is the highest honour of
A. Kuwait B. Iran
C. Afghanistan D. Iraq

288. Bharatendu Harish Chandra awards are given annually for:
A. best local self administration
B. showing kindness and generosity of unusual kind
C. promoting original writing in Hindi
D. None of the above

289. Who replaced Planning Commission in 2015?
A. NITI Aayog B. NIYAM Aayog
C. NIYANTA Aayog D. PRITI Aayog

290. Who has been selected for the prestigious Jnanpith award for the year 2024?
A. Alok Puranik
B. Vinod Kumar Shukla
C. Mrinal Pandey
D. Vishwanath Tiwari

291. Neeraj Chopra is associated with which sports?
A. Weighlifting B. Boxing
C. Hockey D. Javelin Throw

292. Oscar award is related to
A. books
B. politics
C. European Community
D. films

293. USB stands for
A. Unique Serial Bus
B. Universal Serial Bus
C. Unary Serial Bus
D. Universal Secondary Bus

294. Out of the Gallantry awards — PVSM, AVSM and VSM — the most exceptional medal is
A. PVSM
B. AVSM
C. VSM
D. All have equal recognition status

295. *Jeewan Raksha Padak* is awarded for
A. bravery in the battle front
B. fine display of vocal music skills
C. saving the life of human beings
D. None of the above

296. Who is not eligible for Bharat Ratna?
A. A government official
B. A sportsperson
C. A film actress
D. A Prime Minister

297. Jamnalal Bajaj award is given in the field of
I. Social Work
II. Fine Arts
III. Application of Science and Technology
IV. Literature
A. I and II B. I, II and III
C. II and IV D. I and III

298. In which year Indira Gandhi Peace Prize was instituted?
A. 1985 B. 1984
C. 1986 D. 1987

299. Borlaug Award was instituted for recognising outstanding contribution in the field of:
A. Ecology B. Medicine
C. Agriculture D. Journalism

300. Except Dr. Nelson Mandela, who is the other non-Indian so far honoured with Bharat Ratna
A. Dr. Julius Nyerere
B. Helen Hint
C. Hideki Yuka
D. Khan Abdul Ghaffar Khan

301. The book "*The Insider*" is written by
A. Madhav Rao Scindia
B. Nana Patekar
C. Shobha De
D. P V Narasimha Rao

302. *India Wins Freedom* was written by
A. Dadabhai Nauroji
B. Ashfaqulla Khan
C. Sarojini Naidu
D. Maulana Abul Kalam Azad

303. *A Tale of Two Cities* is, in fact, the story of two famous cities. Those cities are
A. Paris and New York
B. London and New York
C. London and Paris
D. Stockholm and New York

304. *Ben Hur* was penned by
A. Lewis Wallace
B. Lord Byron
C. William Shakespeare
D. None of the above

305. *Panchatantra* was written by
A. R K Narayan B. R K Laxman
C. Vishnu Sharma D. None of the above

306. Arundhati Roy has been awarded the prestigious
A. Booker's Prize – 1997
B. Jnanpeeth Award – 1997
C. Sahitya Akademi Award – 1998
D. None of the above

307. Who wrote *Odyssey?*
A. George Orwell
B. Homer
C. Dom Moraes
D. None of the above

308. Which one of the following was not written by Shakespeare?
A. *As You Like It*
B. *Mcbeth*

C. *Hamlet*

D. *A Farewell to Arms*

309. Lewis Carol wrote a masterpiece. What is its name?

A. *Don Quixote*

B. *Alice in Wonderland*

C. *Adventures of Robinson Crusoe*

D. *Great Expectations*

310. The *Tamil Ramayana* is the work of

A. Tulsidas B. Jayangondar

C. Kambar D. Veda Vyas

311. In *Shrimad Bhagwat Geeta,* Lord Krishna teaches his disciple Arjuna to

A. rise to the occasion and fight with his near and dear ones

B. withdraw from the battlefield

C. do his duty and not to expect anything in return

D. attack the enemy in a planned and meticulous approach

312. Who wrote *Origin of Species?*

A. Charles Darwin

B. Alexander Flaming

C. G.B. Shaw

D. D.H. Lawrence

313. The poet and the well-known friend of Prithvi Raj Chauhan, who wrote *Prithvi Raj Raso,* was

A. Harisena B. Vishnu Datt

C. Chand Bardai D. None of the above

314. The first book was printed in India in the year 1561. Its name was

A. *The spiritual Compendium of the Christian Life*

B. *Aain-e-Akbari*

C. *Babur Nama*

D. *Ram Charit Manas*

315. The famous book *Runs and Ruins* was written by

A. Sir Donald Bradman

B. Sunil Gavaskar

C. Kapil Dev

D. Richard Hadlee

316. Adam Smith wrote the following famous book

A. The Wreck

B. Dr Zhivago

C. The Wealth of Nations

D. Tarzan of the Apes

317. H G Wells is known as a

A. poet

B. science-fiction writer

C. thriller-fiction writer

D. essay writer and critic

318. Tukaram wrote his devotional songs in this language

A. Urdu B. Gujarati

C. Hindi D. Marathi

319. Our ancient scholars and writers used this language for their social, religious and political books and works

A. Tamil

B. Sanskrit

C. Urdu

D. Hindi *(Devanagari)*

320. *Gora* is the hero of a book written by Rabindra Nath Tagore. What is the name of the book?

A. *Geetanjali* B. *Patanjali*

C. *Gora* D. *Twelfth Night*

321. Shylock is

A. the villain *in A Pound of Flesh* by William Shakespeare

B. an old Jew who is a famous hero of the Israeli nation

C. the hero of *Miranda,* written by William Shakespeare

D. the comic character of *Alice In the Wonderland* by Lewis Caroll

322. The following was a famous Hindi author and story-writer

A. Shobha De B. Aruna Asaf Ali

C. Mahadevi Verma D. Amrita Pritam

323. *Mudrarakshasa* was composed by

A. Vishakhadatta B. Bhavabhuti

C. Sivananda D. Jayadeva

324. *Razor's Edge* was written by

A. Toni Morrison

B. Saul Bellow

C. W Somerset Maugham

D. None of the above

325. *Sakharam Binder* is a famous play written by
A. Anil Barve B. Vijay Tendulkar
C. V S Naipaul D. Tasleema Nasreen

326. The major work of Sir Isaac Newton is
A. *Principia*
B. *Heritage*
C. *Human knowledge*
D. *I Dare*

327. The hero of *The Jungle Book,* written by Rudyard Kipling, is
A. the lion
B. Mowghuli
C. the father of Mowghuli
D. there is no hero

328. Who stated, "Peace hath her victories, no less renowned than war?"
A. Alfred Lord Tennyson
B. William Shakespeare
C. John Milton
D. None of the above

329. Macawber is a character who was created by
A. Thomas Hardy
B. P G Wodehouse
C. Charles Dickens
D. J W Von Goethe

330. *Pride and Prejudice* was written by
A. Anton Chekhov B. Maxim Gorky
C. Jane Austen D. Anthony West

331. *In the Afternoon Time* is the English translation of the autobiography of the famous poet, Harivansh Rai Bachchan. The autobiography was translated into English by
A. Vikram Seth
B. Dr Rupert Snell
C. William Faulkner
D. P D Tandon

332. Who is the author of the book *The Celestine Vision?*
A. Paul Hockins B. Salman Rushdie
C. Joseph Conrad D. James Redfield

333. The author of the famous book *Blue Mountain Revisited* is
A. Charles Kingsley B. Virginia Woolf
C. Arthur Koestler D. Peter Topkins

334. Homer was the great poet of the following language
A. Italian B. Greek
C. Arabic D. French

335. A factor which would strongly influence a business person to adopt a computer is its:
A. Accuracy
B. Reliability
C. Speed
D. All of these

336. *Godaan* was written by Munshi Prem Chand and it depicts
A. the methodology for taking adequate care of the cows
B. exploitation of simple rural folk by the rich landlords of rural India
C. the mutiny of 1857 in which, Indians refused to bite the *Kartoos* made with cow beef
D. None of the above

337. Manu wrote a book during ancient times in which, he divided the Aryan society into four distinct classes. What was the name of the book?
A. *Arthashastra* B. *Manusmriti*
C. *Moti Mahal* D. *My Truth*

338. R. Venkataraman wrote *My Presidential Years.* What was the main theme of the book?
A. It described the aristocratic procedures being followed in the *Rashtrapati Bhawan* during his tenure as President
B. It described the power equations and ploys in the centre and in the states during his term
C. It described how he felt caged while he was President due to a load of procedures and formalities
D. It explained the machinations of the political party which was in power during his tenure as President

339. The hero of the play cried in the end, "Et Tu, Brute!" and died. Which is the play and who is the author?
A. The Wealth of Nations — Adam Smith
B. Mein Kempf — Adolf Hitler
C. Julius Caesar — William Shakespeare
D. None of the above

340. Don Veto Corleone was the undisputed king of the underworld in this novel. This masterpiece was also converted into a film in which Al Pacino played the role of the Don. What is the name of the novel and that of the author?

A. *A Farewell to Arms* — E Hemingway
B. *The Godfather* — Mario Puzo
C. *From Here to Eternity* — James Jones
D. *Dialogue with Death* — Arthur Koestler

341. *Gypsy Camp Vanishes Into the Blue* was a famous blockbuster movie made by the erstwhile USSR. The original story was written by a famous author. His name is

A. Leo Tolstoy
B. Anton Chekhov
C. Maxim Gorky
D. Leon Uris

342. The total number of *Puranas* written during the Vedic age is

A. 22
B. 9
C. 18
D. 25

343. In computer network terminology. WAN stands for

A. World area network
B. Wide area network
C. Wide array net
D. Wireless area network

344. The first woman in the world to have climbed Mt. Everest twice is

A. Bachendri Pal
B. Molly Chacko
C. Santosh Yadav
D. Theresia Kiesl

345. According to *The Ramayana,* who received the last teaching lessons from the knowledgeable Ravana while he was on his death-bed?

A. Rama
B. Sugreeva
C. Laxmana
D. Both A and C

346. He was a German but he saved many a Jew from the cruel hands of the Nazis. A movie was made on this theme which won the coveted Oscar Prize. The book and the author are

A. *Operation Shylock* — Philip Roth
B. *Schindler's List* — Thomas Keneally
C. *The Rescue* — Joseph Conrad
D. *The Slave* — Isaac Bashevis Singer

347. He was the favourite assistant of Sherlock Holmes, the famous character created by Arthur Conan Doyle. His name is

A. Zhivago B. Watson
C. Hawkins D. Hector

348. He was a former member of British Parliament. He has written many hit fiction novels. One of his novels is

A. Shall We Tell the President?
B. The Rape of the Lock
C. Snow Country
D. Small Land

349. He wrote *Sharmili*, *Gaylord* and *Kati Patang*. His novels were written in Hindi and some of them have been converted into films also. His name is

A. Gita Mehta
B. B N Mullick
C. Nirad C Chaudhary
D. Gulshan Nanda

350. The oldest mountains in India according to geographical history are:

A. Satpuras B. Nilgiris
C. Vindhyas D. Aravallis

ANSWERS

1	2	3	4	5	6	7	8	9	10
C	B	A	D	B	B	B	B	B	A
11	**12**	**13**	**14**	**15**	**16**	**17**	**18**	**19**	**20**
B	C	D	A	A	C	B	C	A	B

21	22	23	24	25	26	27	28	29	30
D	B	B	D	D	C	A	C	C	C
31	32	33	34	35	36	37	38	39	40
C	A	A	C	D	C	A	B	B	D
41	42	43	44	45	46	47	48	49	50
B	C	B	B	C	D	A	A	D	A
51	52	53	54	55	56	57	58	59	60
D	A	C	A	C	B	C	A	C	C
61	62	63	64	65	66	67	68	69	70
B	A	C	B	D	D	A	C	C	D
71	72	73	74	75	76	77	78	79	80
B	B	B	B	C	D	C	D	C	A
81	82	83	84	85	86	87	88	89	90
B	B	A	C	B	B	B	C	B	D
91	92	93	94	95	96	97	98	99	100
C	B	A	B	B	A	B	D	B	A
101	102	103	104	105	106	107	108	109	110
D	D	A	C	D	A	B	C	B	C
111	112	113	114	115	116	117	118	119	120
B	B	C	B	A	C	C	B	B	C
121	122	123	124	125	126	127	128	129	130
D	C	D	C	B	A	C	C	A	A
131	132	133	134	135	136	137	138	139	140
C	C	D	C	D	D	C	C	B	B
141	142	143	144	145	146	147	148	149	150
C	D	A	D	B	B	B	D	B	C
151	152	153	154	155	156	157	158	159	160
A	C	C	C	B	D	B	A	A	D
161	162	163	164	165	166	167	168	169	170
B	B	C	B	C	D	B	C	C	A
171	172	173	174	175	176	177	178	179	180
B	D	A	D	A	C	C	C	D	C
181	182	183	184	185	186	187	188	189	190
A	A	D	B	D	A	D	D	D	B
191	192	193	194	195	196	197	198	199	200
C	B	C	A	B	A	D	B	D	A
201	202	203	204	205	206	207	208	209	210
D	A	B	B	C	B	C	B	C	A
211	212	213	214	215	216	217	218	219	220
C	B	C	A	C	B	A	D	C	B
221	222	223	224	225	226	227	228	229	230
A	C	D	C	B	A	A	D	C	C
231	232	233	234	235	236	237	238	239	240
A	D	B	A	B	B	C	C	B	C
241	242	243	244	245	246	247	248	249	250
A	B	D	C	B	B	B	A	C	C

251	252	253	254	255	256	257	258	259	260
C	C	D	C	C	A	B	C	D	D
261	262	263	264	265	266	267	268	269	270
B	B	D	C	B	C	C	A	C	B
271	272	273	274	275	276	277	278	279	280
C	C	C	C	D	B	B	C	B	C
281	282	283	284	285	286	287	288	289	290
B	D	C	A	C	C	A	C	A	B
291	292	293	294	295	296	297	298	299	300
D	D	B	A	C	A	D	C	C	D
301	302	303	304	305	306	307	308	309	310
D	D	C	A	C	A	B	D	B	C
311	312	313	314	315	316	317	318	319	320
C	A	C	A	B	C	B	D	B	C
321	322	323	324	325	326	327	328	329	330
A	C	A	C	B	A	B	C	C	C
331	332	333	334	335	336	337	338	339	340
B	D	D	B	D	B	B	C	C	B
341	342	343	344	345	346	347	348	349	350
C	C	B	C	C	B	B	A	D	D

* * * * *